The Black Book of Communism

The Black Book of
COMMUNISM

CRIMES, TERROR, REPRESSION

Stéphane Courtois
Nicolas Werth
Jean-Louis Panné
Andrzej Paczkowski
Karel Bartošek
Jean-Louis Margolin

Translated by Jonathan Murphy

and Mark Kramer

Consulting Editor Mark Kramer

Harvard University Press
Cambridge, Massachusetts
London, England 1999

Library of Congress Cataloging-in-Publication Data

Livre noir du communisme. English
  The black book of communism : crimes, terror, repression / Stéphane Courtois ... [et al.] ;
translated by Jonathan Murphy and Mark Kramer; consulting editor, Mark Kramer.
    p.   cm.
Includes bibliographical references and index.
ISBN 0-674-07608-7 (alk. paper)
1. Communism—History—20th century.   2. Political persecution.
3. Terrorism.   I. Courtois, Stéphane, 1947-   .   II. Kramer, Mark.
III. Title.
HX44.L59   1999
320.53′2—dc21   99-29759

Contents

Foreword: The Uses of Atrocity

Martin Malia

Communism has been the great story of the twentieth century. Bursting into history from the most unlikely corner of Europe amid the trauma of World War I, in the wake of the cataclysm of 1939–1945 it made a great leap westward to the middle of Germany and an even greater one eastward to the China Seas. With this feat, the apogee of its fortunes, it had come to rule a third of mankind and seemed poised to advance indefinitely. For seven decades it haunted world politics, polarizing opinion between those who saw it as the socialist end of history and those who considered it history's most total tyranny.

One might therefore expect that a priority of modern historians would be to explain why Communism's power grew for so long only to collapse like a house of cards. Yet surprisingly, more than eighty years after 1917, probing examination of the Big Questions raised by the Marxist-Leninist phenomenon has hardly begun. Can *The Black Book of Communism,* recently a sensation in France and much of Europe, provide the salutary shock that will make a difference?

Because a serious historiography was precluded in Soviet Russia by the regime's mandatory ideology, scholarly investigation of Communism has until recently fallen disproportionately to Westerners. And though these outside observers could not entirely escape the ideological magnetic field emanating from their subject, in the half-century after World War II they indeed accomplished an impressive amount.[1] Even so, a basic problem remains: the conceptual poverty of the Western empirical effort.

This poverty flows from the premise that Communism can be understood, in an aseptic and value-free mode, as the pure product of social process. Accordingly, researchers have endlessly insisted that the October Revolution was a workers' revolt and not a Party coup d'état, when it was obviously the latter riding piggyback on the former. Besides, the central issue in Communist history is not the Party's ephemeral worker "base"; it is what the intelligentsia victors of October later did with their permanent coup d'etat, and so far this has scarcely been explored.

More exactly, the matter has been obscured by two fantasies holding out the promise of a better Soviet socialism than the one the Bolsheviks actually built. The first is the "Bukharin alternative" to Stalin, a thesis that purports to offer a nonviolent, market road to socialism—that is, Marx's *integral* socialism, which necessitates the full suppression of private property, profit, and the market.[2] The second fantasy purports to find the impetus behind Stalin's "revolution from above" of 1929–1933 in a "cultural revolution" from below by Party activists and workers against the "bourgeois" specialists dear to Bukharin, a revolution ultimately leading to massive upward mobility from the factory bench.[3]

With such fables now consigned to what Trotsky called "the ash heap of history," perhaps a moral, rather than a social, approach to the Communist phenomenon can yield a truer understanding—for the much-investigated Soviet social process claimed victims on a scale that has never aroused a scholarly curiosity at all proportionate to the magnitude of the disaster. *The Black Book* offers us the first attempt to determine, overall, the actual magnitude of what occurred, by systematically detailing Leninism's "crimes, terror, and repression" from Russia in 1917 to Afghanistan in 1989.

This factual approach puts Communism in what is, after all, its basic human perspective. For it was in truth a "tragedy of planetary dimensions" (in the French publisher's characterization), with a grand total of victims variously estimated by contributors to the volume at between 85 million and 100 million. Either way, the Communist record offers the most colossal case of political carnage in history. And when this fact began to sink in with the French public, an apparently dry academic work became a publishing sensation, the focus of impassioned political and intellectual debate.

The shocking dimensions of the Communist tragedy, however, are hardly news to any serious student of twentieth-century history, at least when the different Leninist regimes are taken individually. The real news is that at this late date the truth should come as such a shock to the public at large. To be sure, each major episode of the tragedy—Stalin's Gulag, Mao Zedong's Great

Leap Forward and his Cultural Revolution, Pol Pot's Khmer Rouge—had its moment of notoriety. But these horrors soon faded away into "history"; nor did anyone trouble to add up the total and set it before the public. The surprising size of this total, then, partly explains the shock the volume provoked.

The full power of the shock, however, was delivered by the unavoidable comparison of this sum with that for Nazism, which at an estimated 25 million turns out to be distinctly less murderous than Communism. And the volume's editor, Stéphane Courtois, rather than let the figures speak for themselves, spelled out the comparison, thereby making the volume a firebrand. Arguing from the fact that some Nuremberg jurisprudence has been incorporated into French law (to accommodate such cases as that of Maurice Papon, a former minister of Giscard d'Estaing tried in 1997–98 for complicity in deporting Jews while a local official of Vichy), Courtois explicitly equated the "class genocide" of Communism with the "race genocide" of Nazism, and categorized both as "crimes against humanity." What is more, he raised the question of the "complicity" with Communist crime of the legions of Western apologists for Stalin, Mao, Ho Chi Minh, Fidel Castro, and indeed Pol Pot who, even when they "abandoned their idols of yesteryear, did so discreetly and in silence."

These issues have a special resonance in France. Since the 1930s, the left has been able to come to power only as a popular front of Socialists and Communists (whether under Léon Blum or François Mitterrand), a tandem in which the democratic partner was always compromised by its ally's allegiance to totalitarian Moscow. Conversely, since 1940 the right has been tainted by Vichy's links with Nazism (the subtext of the Papon affair). In such a historical context, "knowing the truth about the U.S.S.R." has never been an academic matter.

Furthermore, it happens that at the time the volume appeared the Socialist prime minister Lionel Jospin stood in need of Communist votes to assemble a parliamentary majority. Orators of the right, therefore, citing *The Black Book,* rose in the National Assembly to attack his government for harboring allies with an unrepented "criminal past." Jospin countered by recalling the Liberation coalition between Gaullists and Communists (which was fair game), only the better to conclude that he was "proud" to govern with them too (which was a gaffe, for at the Liberation the Gulag was not yet known). Nor was this just a hasty choice of words; in the eyes of the left that he leads, the Communists, despite their past errors, belong to the camp of democratic progress, whereas the right is open to suspicion of softness toward the National Front of the "fascist" Jean-Marie Le Pen (after all, the conservatives had once rallied to Vichy). The incident ended with the non-Gaullist right walking out of the chamber, while the Gaullists remained awkwardly in place. Thereupon the debate spread to television and the press.

Indeed, the debate divides the book's own authors. All are research scholars associated with the Centre d'Etude d'Histoire et de Sociologie du Communisme and its review, *Communisme*. Founded by the pioneer of academic Communist studies, the late Annie Kriegel, its mission is to exploit our new access to Soviet archives in conjunction with younger Russian historians. Equally to the point, these researchers are former Communists or close fellow-travelers; and it is over the assessment of their common past that they divide. Thus, once *The Black Book* raised the foreseeable political storm, Courtois's two key collaborators—Nicolas Werth for Russia, and Jean-Louis Margolin for China—publicly dissociated themselves from his bolder conclusions.

So let us begin with the debate, which is hardly specific to France. It breaks out wherever the question of the moral equivalence of our century's two totalitarianisms is raised, indeed whenever the very concept of "totalitarianism" is invoked. For Nazism's unique status as "absolute evil" is now so entrenched that any comparison with it easily appears suspect.

Of the several reasons for this assessment of Nazism, the most obvious is that the Western democracies fought World War II in a kind of global "popular front" against "fascism." Moreover, whereas the Nazis occupied most of Europe, the Communists during the Cold War menaced only from afar. Thus, although the stakes for democracy in the new conflict were as high as in its hot predecessor, the stress of waging it was significantly lower; and it ended with the last general secretary of the "evil empire," Mikhail Gorbachev, in the comradely embrace of the ultimate cold warrior, President Ronald Reagan. Communism's fall, therefore, brought with it no Nuremberg trial, and hence no de-Communization to solemnly put Leninism beyond the pale of civilization; and of course there still exist Communist regimes in international good standing.

Another reason for our dual perception is that defeat cut down Nazism in the prime of its iniquity, thereby eternally fixing its full horror in the world's memory. By contrast, Communism, at the peak of *its* iniquity, was rewarded with an epic victory—and thereby gained a half-century in which to lose its dynamism, to half-repent of Stalin, and even, in the case of some unsuccessful leaders (such as Czechoslovakia's Alexander Dubček in 1968), to attempt giving the system a "human face." As a result of these contrasting endings of the two totalitarianisms all Nazism's secrets were bared fifty years ago, whereas we are only beginning to explore Soviet archives, and those of East Asia and Cuba remain sealed.

The effect of this unequal access to information was magnified by more subjective considerations. Nazism seemed all the more monstrous to Westerners for having arisen in the heart of civilized Europe, in the homeland of Luther, Kant, Goethe, Beethoven, and indeed Marx. Communism, by contrast, appeared as less of a historical aberration in the Russian borderland of Europe—almost "Asia" after all—where, despite Tolstoy and Dostoevsky, civilization had never taken deep root.

The ultimate distinguishing characteristic of Nazism, of course, is the Holocaust, considered as the historically unique crime of seeking the extermination of an entire people, a crime for which the term "genocide" was coined around the time of Nuremberg. And therewith the Jewish people acquired the solemn obligation to keep the memory of its martyrs alive in the conscience of the world. Even so, general awareness of the Final Solution was slow to emerge, in fact coming only in the 1970s and 1980s—the very years when Communism was gradually mellowing. So between these contrasting circumstances, by the time of Communism's fall the liberal world had had fifty years to settle into a double standard regarding its two late adversaries.

Accordingly, Hitler and Nazism are now a constant presence in Western print and on Western television, whereas Stalin and Communism materialize only sporadically. The status of ex-Communist carries with it no stigma, even when unaccompanied by any expression of regret; past contact with Nazism, however, no matter how marginal or remote, confers an indelible stain. Thus Martin Heidegger and Paul de Man have been enduringly compromised and the substance of their thought tainted. By contrast, Louis Aragon, for years under Stalin the editor of the French Communist Party's literary magazine, in 1996 was published among the classics of the Pléiade; the press was lyrical in praise of his art, while virtually mute about his politics. (*The Black Book* reproduces a 1931 poem to the KGB's predecessor, the GPU.) Likewise, the Stalinist poet and Nobel laureate, Pablo Neruda, in the same year was sentimentalized, together with his cause, by an acclaimed film, *Il postino*—even though in 1939 as a Chilean diplomat in Spain he acted as a de facto agent of the Comintern, and in 1953 mourned Stalin with a fulsome ode. And this list of unparallel lives could be extended indefinitely.

Even more skewed is the situation in the East. No Gulag camps have been turned into museums to commemorate their inmates; all were bulldozed into the ground during Khrushchev's de-Stalinization. The only memorial to Stalin's victims is a modest stone brought to Moscow from the Arctic camp of Solovki and placed in Lubyanka Square (though well off to the side), where the KGB's former headquarters still stands. Nor are there any regular visitors to this lonely slab (one must cross a stream of traffic to reach it) and no more than an occasional wilted bouquet. By contrast, Lenin's statue still dominates most city centers, and his mummy reposes honorably in its Mausoleum.

Throughout the former Communist world, moreover, virtually none of its responsible officials has been put on trial or punished. Indeed, everywhere Communist parties, though usually under new names, compete in politics.

Thus, in Poland, Aleksander Kwasniewski, onetime member of General Jaruzelski's government, in 1996 won the presidency against the symbol of resistance to Communism, Lech Wałęsa (admittedly an inept campaigner). Gulya Horn, the prime minister of Hungary from 1994 to 1998, was a member of the country's last Communist government, and a member of the militia that helped suppress the 1956 revolt alongside the Soviet army. In neighboring Austria, by contrast, former president Kurt Waldheim was ostracized worldwide once his Nazi past was uncovered. Granted, card-carrying Western literati and latter-day Eastern *apparatchiki* never served as executioners for Stalin. Even so, does the present silence about their past mean that Communism was all *that* less bad than Nazism?

The debate around *The Black Book* can help frame an answer. On the one side, commentators in the liberal *Le Monde* argue that it is illegitimate to speak of a single Communist movement from Phnom Penh to Paris. Rather, the rampage of the Khmer Rouge is like the ethnic massacres of third-world Rwanda; or the "rural" Communism of Asia is radically different from the "urban" Communism of Europe; or Asian Communism is really only anticolonial nationalism. The subtext of such Eurocentric condescension is that conflating sociologically diverse movements is merely a stratagem to obtain a higher body count against Communism, and thus against all the left. In answer, commentators in the conservative *Le Figaro*, spurning reductionist sociology as a device to exculpate Communism, reply that Marxist-Leninist regimes are cast in the same ideological and organizational mold throughout the world. And this pertinent point also has its admonitory subtext: that socialists of whatever stripe cannot be trusted to resist their ever-present demons on the far left (those popular fronts were no accident after all).

Yet if we let the divided contributors to *The Black Book* arbitrate the dispute, we find no disagreement in this matter: the Leninist matrix indeed served for all the once "fraternal" parties. To be sure, the model was applied differently in different cultural settings. As Margolin points out, the chief agent of represssion in Russia was a specially created political police, the Cheka-GPU-NKVD-KGB, while in China it was the People's Liberation Army, and in Cambodia it was gun-toting adolescents from the countryside: thus popular ideological mobilization went deeper in Asia than in Russia. Still, everywhere the aim was to repress "enemies of the people"—"like noxious insects," as Lenin said early on, thus inaugurating Commmunism's "animalization" of its adversaries. Moreover, the line of inheritance from Stalin, to Mao, to Ho, to Kim Il Sung, to Pol Pot was quite clear, with each new leader receiving both material aid and ideological inspiration from his predecessor. And, to come full circle, Pol Pot first learned his Marxism in Paris in 1952 (when such philosophers as Jean-Paul Sartre and Maurice Merleau-Ponty were explaining how terror could be the midwife of "humanism").[4] So if the debate remains on the level of the quantitative atrocity, the double standard collapses, and Communism appears as the more criminal totalitarianism.

But if the debate is shifted to qualitative crime, this outcome is easily reversed. And here the decisive factor is, again, the Holocaust as the confirmation of Nazism's uniquely evil nature. Indeed, this standard has become so universal that other persecuted groups, from Armenians to the native peoples of both Americas, have appropriated (with varying degrees of plausibility) the term "genocide" to characterize their own experience. Not surprisingly, many of these implicit comparisons to the Holocaust have been rejected as illegitimate, even slanderous. And in fact one overexcited op-ed piece in *Le Monde,* from a respected researcher, denounced Courtois's introduction as antisemitic.

Yet there are other, less emotionally charged arguments for assigning a significant distinctiveness to Nazi terror. The criminal law everywhere distinguishes degrees of murder, according to the motivation, the cruelty of the means employed, and so on. Thus, Raymond Aron long ago, and François Furet recently, though both unequivocal about the evil of Communism, distinguished between extermination practiced to achieve a political objective, no matter how perverse, and extermination as an end in itself.[5] And in this perspective, Communism once again comes off as less evil than Nazism.

This plausible distinction, however, can easily be turned on its head. In particular, Eastern European dissidents have argued that mass murder in the name of a noble ideal is *more* perverse than it is in the name of a base one.[6] The Nazis, after all, never pretended to be virtuous. The Communists, by contrast, trumpeting their humanism, hoodwinked millions around the globe for decades, and so got away with murder on the ultimate scale. The Nazis, moreover, killed off their victims without ideological ceremony; the Communists, by contrast, usually compelled their prey to confess their "guilt" in signed depositions thereby acknowledging the Party line's political "correctness." Nazism, finally, was a unique case (Mussolini's Facism was not really competitive), and it developed no worldwide clientle. By contrast, Communism's universalism permitted it to metastasize worldwide.

A final position, forcefully expressed by Alain Besançon, is that murder is murder whatever the ideological motivation; and this is undeniably true for the equally dead victims of both Nazism and Communism.[7] Such absolute equivalence is also expressed in Hannah Arendt's *Origins of Totalitarianism:* both systems massacred their victims not for what they *did* (such as resisting the regime) but for who they *were,* whether Jews or kulaks. In this perspective, the distinction made by some, that the term petit-bourgeois "kulak" is more elastic and hence less lethal than biological "Jew," is invalidated: the social and the racial categories are equally psuedoscientific.

Yet none of these qualitative arguments can be "clinched"—unlike an empirically established victim count. And since there can be no consensus regarding degrees of political "evil," some researchers would claim that all value judgments merely express the ideological preferences of their authors.

Such "Positivist" social scientists, therefore, have averred that moral questions are irrelevant to understanding the past. An example is a recent volume devoted to political denunciation in modern Europe.[8] The introduction presents some fascinating facts: in 1939 the Gestapo employed 7,500 people in contrast to the NKVD's 366,000 (including Gulag personnel); and the Communist Party made denunciation an obligation, whereas the Nazi Party did not. But no conclusions are drawn from these contrasts. Instead we are told that under both regimes the population was given to denunciation as "an *everyday* practice," and for reasons of self-advancement more than for reasons of ideology. We are told further that denunciation was endemic in prerevolutionary rural Russia, and that it flourished under the French Jacobins and the English Puritans, the Spanish Inquisition and American McCarthyism. And in fact all the "witch crazes" enumerated in the introduction did have some traits in common.

The rub is, however, that this perspective reduces politics and ideology everywhere to anthropology. And with this accomplished, the editors blandly assure us that, contrary to Hannah Arendt, the "Nazi/Soviet similarities" are insufficient to make denunciation "a specifically 'totalitarian' phenomenon." What is more, the difference between Nazi/Communist systems and Western ones is "not qualitative but quantitative." By implication, therefore, singling out Communist and Nazi terror in order to equate them becomes Cold War slander—the ideological subtext, as it happens, of twenty-five years of "revisionist," social-reductionist Sovietology.

By the same token, this fact-for-fact's-sake approach suggests that there is nothing specifically Communist about Communist terror—and, it would seem, nothing particularly Nazi about Nazi terror either. So the bloody Soviet experiment is banalized in one great gray anthropological blur; and the Soviet Union is transmogrified into just another country in just another age, neither more nor less evil than any other regime going. But this is obviously nonsense. Hence we are back with the problem of moral judgment, which is inseparable from any real understanding of the past—indeed, inseparable from being human.

In the twentieth century, however, morality is not primarily a matter of eternal verities or transcendental imperatives. It is above all a matter of political allegiances. That is, it is a matter of left versus right, roughly defined as the priority of compassionate egalitarianism for the one, and as the primacy of prudential order for the other. Yet since neither principle can be applied absolutely without destroying society, the modern world lives in perpetual tension between the irresistible pressure for equality and the functional necessity of hierarchy.

It is this syndrome that gives the permanent qualitative advantage to Communism over Nazism in any evaluation of their quantitative atrocities. For the Communist project, in origin, claimed commitment to universalistic and egalitarian goals, whereas the Nazi project offered only unabashed national egoism. Small matter, then, that their practices were comparable; their moral auras were antithetical, and it is the latter feature that counts in Western, domestic politics. And so we arrive at the fulcrum of the debate: A moral man can have "no enemies to the left," a perspective in which undue insistence on Communist crime only "plays into the hands of the right"—if, indeed, any anticommunism is not simply a mask for antiliberalism.

In this spirit, *Le Monde*'s editorialist deemed *The Black Book* inopportune because equating Communism with Nazism removed the "last barriers to legitimating the extreme right," that is, Le Pen. It is true that Le Pen's party and similar hate-mongering, xenophobic movements elsewhere in Europe represent an alarming new phenomenon that properly concerns all liberal democrats. But it in no way follows that Communism's criminal past should be ignored or minimized. Such an argument is only a variant, in new historical circumstances, of Sartre's celebrated sophism that one should keep silent about Soviet camps "pour ne pas désespérer Billancout" (in order not to throw the auto workers of Billancout into despair). To which his onetime colleague, Albert Camus, long ago replied that the truth is the truth, and denying it mocks the causes both of humanity and of morality.[9]

In fact, the persistence of such sophistry is precisely why *The Black Book* is so opportune. What, therefore, do its provocative pages contain? Without pretension to originality, it presents a balance sheet of our current knowledge of Communism's human costs, archivally based where possible and elsewhere drawing on the best available secondary evidence, and with due allowance for the difficulties of quantification. Yet the very sobriety of this inventory is what gives the book its power; and indeed, as we are led from country to country and from horror to horror, the cumulative impact is overwhelming.

At the same time, the book quietly advances a number of important analytical points. The first is that Communist regimes did not just commit criminal acts (all states do so on occasion); they were criminal enterprises in their very essence: on principle, so to speak, they all ruled lawlessly, by violence, and without regard for human life. Werth's section on the Soviet Union is thus titled "A State against Its People" and takes us methodically through the successive cycles of terror, from Great October in 1917 to Stalin's death in 1953. By way of comparison, he notes that between 1825 and 1917 tsarism carried out 6,321 political executions (most of them during the revolution of 1905–1907), whereas in two months of official "Red Terror" in the fall of 1918 Bolshevism achieved some 15,000. And so on for a third of a century; for example, 6 million deaths during the collectivization famine of 1932–33, 720,000 executions during the Great Purge, 7 million people entering the Gulag (where huge numbers died) in the years 1934–1941, and 2,750,000 still there at Stalin's death. True, these aggregates represent different modes of state violence, not all of them immediately lethal; but all betoken terror as a routine means of government.

And the less familiar figures in Margolin's chapter on China's "Long March into Night" are even more staggering: at a minimum, 10 million "direct victims"; probably 20 million deaths out of the multitudes that passed through China's "hidden Gulag," the *laogai;* more than 20 million deaths from the "political famine" of the Great Leap Forward of 1959–1961, the largest famine in history. Finally, in Pol Pot's aping of Mao's Great Leap, around one Cambodian in seven perished, the highest proportion of the population in any Communist country.

The book's second point is that there never was a benign, initial phase of Communism before some mythical "wrong turn" threw it off track. From the start Lenin expected, indeed wanted, civil war to crush all "class enemies"; and this war, principally against the peasants, continued with only short pauses until 1953. So much for the fable of "good Lenin/bad Stalin." (And if anyone doubts that it is still necessary to make this case, the answer may be found, for example, in the maudlin article "Lenin" in the current edition of the *Encyclopaedia Britannica.*) Still another point is of a "technical" nature: the use of famine to break peasant resistance to regime economic "plans." And ever since Solzhenitsyn, such "pharaonic" methods have been contrasted with the technologically advanced Nazi gas chamber.

A more basic point is that Red terror cannot be explained as the prolongation of prerevolutionary political cultures. Communist repression did not originate from above, in traditional autocracies; nor was it simply an intensification of violent folk practices from below—whether the peasant anarchism of Russia, or the cyclical millenarian revolts of China, or the exacerbated nationalism of Cambodia, although all these traditions were exploited by the new regime. Nor does the source of Communist practices reside in the violence of the two world wars, important though this brutal conditioning was. Rather, in each case, mass violence against the population was a deliberate policy of the new revolutionary order; and its scope and inhumanity far exceeded anything in the national past.

A final point, insisted on by Courtois yet clear also in his colleagues' accounts, is that Communism's recourse to "permanent civil war" rested on the "scientific" Marxist belief in class struggle as the "violent midwife of history," in Marx's famous metaphor. Similarly, Courtois adds, Nazi violence was founded on a scientistic social Darwinism promising national regeneration through racial struggle.

This valid emphasis on ideology as the wellspring of Communist mass murder reaches its apogee in Margolin's depiction of escalating radicalism as the revolution moved East. Stalin, of course, had already begun the escalation by presenting himself as the "Lenin of today" and his first Five-Year Plan as a second October. Then, in 1953, four years after Mao came to power, his heirs ended mass terror: it had simply become too costly to their now superpuissant regime. To the Chinese comrades, however, Moscow's moderation amounted to "betrayal" of the world revolution just as it was taking off in Asia. Consequently, in 1959–1961 Mao was goaded to surpass his Soviet mentors by a "Great Leap Forward" beyond mere socialism, Moscow style, to full Communism as Marx had imagined it in the *Communist Manifesto* and the *Critique of the Gotha Program*. And in 1966–1976, by directing the anarchy of the Cultural Revolution against his own Party, he proceeded to outdo Stalin's Great Purge of *his* Party in 1937–1939. But the most demented spinoff of this whole tradition was Pol Pot's Khmer Rouge of 1975–1979; for this rampage against urban, "bourgeois" civilization expressed nothing less than an ambition to propel tiny Cambodia beyond Mao's "achievements" into the front rank of world revolution.

Yet the long-term inefficiency of such "progress" eventually led Mao's heirs, in their turn, to "betray" the Marxist-Leninist impetus by halting mass terror and turning halfway to the market. Thereby, after 1979, Deng Xiaoping ended worldwide the perverse Prometheanism launched in October 1917. Thus the Communist trajectory, as *The Black Book* traces it from Petrograd to the China Seas, inevitably suggests that ideology, not social process, fueled the movement's meteoric rise, and that ideology's practical failure produced its precipitate fall.

This transnational perspective goes far toward answering the great question posed by Communist history: namely, why did a doctrine premised on proletarian revolution in industrial societies come to power *only* in predominantly agrarian ones, by Marxist definition those least prepared for "socialism"? But socialist revolution for Marx was not just a matter of economic development; it was at bottom an eschatological "leap from the kingdom of necessity to the kingdom of freedom." Since such quasi-miraculous transformation has the strongest allure for those who have the greatest lag to overcome, it is hardly surprising that Marxism's line of march turned out to lead ever farther into the politically and economically backward East. Only by taking account of this paradoxical eastward escalation through increasingly extravagant "leaps" can we build a real historiography of the great twentieth-century story that was Communism.

And this brings us back to the vexed—and vexing—question raised by Stéphane Courtois in *The Black Book*: What of the moral equivalence of Communism with Nazism? After fifty years of debate, it is clear that no matter what the hard facts are, degrees of totalitarian evil will be measured as much in terms of present politics as in terms of past realities. So we will always encounter a double standard as long as there exist a left and a right—which will be a very long time indeed. No matter how thoroughly the Communist failure may come to be documented (and new research makes it look worse every day), we will always have reactions such as that of a Moscow correspondent for a major Western paper, who, after the fall, could still privately salute the Russian people with: "Thanks for having tried!"; and there will always be kindred spirits to dismiss *The Black Book*, a priori, as "right-wing anti-Communist rhetoric." For more mundane observers, however, it is at last becoming clear that our current qualitative judgments are scandalously out of line with the century's real balance sheet of political crime.

And this very absurdity perhaps brings us to a turning point. Ten years ago, the authors of *The Black Book* would have refused to believe what they now write. And exploration of the Soviet archives—and eventually those of East Asia—will continue to redress the balance. This comes at a time, moreover, when historical writing is turning increasingly to retrospective affirmative action, to fulfilling our "duty of remembrance" to all the oppressed of the past—indeed, when governments and churches formally apologize for their historic sins. Surely, then, the Party of humanity can spare a little compassion for the victims of the inhumanity so long meted out by so many of its own partisans.

Even so, such an effort at retrospective justice will always encounter one intractable obstacle. Any realistic accounting of Communist crime would effectively shut the door on Utopia; and too many good souls in this unjust world cannot abandon hope for an absolute end to inequality (and some less good souls will always offer them "rational" curative nostrums). And so, all comrade-questers after historical truth should gird their loins for a very Long March indeed before Communism is accorded its fair share of absolute evil.

The Black Book of Communism

Introduction: The Crimes of Communism

Stéphane Courtois

Life cannot withstand death, but memory is gaining in its struggle against nothingness.

Tzvetan Todorov, *Les abus de la mémoire*

It has been written that "history is the science of human misfortune."[1] Our bloodstained century of violence amply confirms this statement. In previous centuries few people and countries were spared from mass violence. The major European powers were involved in the African slave trade. The French Republic practiced colonization, which despite some good was tarnished by repugnant episodes that persisted until recently. The United States remains heavily influenced by a culture of violence deeply rooted in two major historical tragedies—the enslavement of black Africans and the extermination of Native Americans.

The fact remains that our century has outdone its predecessors in its bloodthirstiness. A quick glance at the past leads to one damning conclusion: ours is the century of human catastrophes—two world wars and Nazism, to say nothing of more localized tragedies, such as those in Armenia, Biafra, and Rwanda. The Ottoman Empire was undoubtedly involved in the genocide of the Armenians, and Germany in the genocide of the Jews and Gypsies. Italy under Mussolini slaughtered Ethiopians. The Czechs are reluctant to admit that their behavior toward the Sudeten Germans in 1945 and 1946 was by no means exemplary. Even Switzerland has recently been embroiled in a scandal over its role in administering gold stolen by the Nazis from exterminated Jews, although the country's behavior is not on the same level as genocide.

Communism has its place in this historical setting overflowing with trage-dies. Indeed, it occupies one of the most violent and most significant places of all. Communism, the defining characteristic of the "short twentieth century" that began in Sarajevo in 1914 and ended in Moscow in 1991, finds itself at center stage in the story. Communism predated fascism and Nazism, outlived both, and left its mark on four continents.

What exactly do we mean by the term "Communism"? We must make a distinction between the doctrine of communism and its practice. As a political philosophy, communism has existed for centuries, even millennia. Was it not Plato who in his *Republic* introduced the concept of an ideal city, in which people would not be corrupted by money and power and in which wisdom, reason, and justice would prevail? And consider the scholar and statesman Sir Thomas More, chancellor of England in 1530, author of *Utopia*, and victim of the executioner's ax by order of Henry VIII, who also described an ideal society. Utopian philosophy may have its place as a technique for evaluating society. It draws its sustenance from ideas, the lifeblood of the world's democracies. But the Communism that concerns us does not exist in the transcendent sphere of ideas. This Communism is altogether real; it has existed at key moments of history and in particular countries, brought to life by its famous leaders—Vladimir Ilich Lenin, Josif Stalin, Mao Zedong, Ho Chi Minh, Fidel Castro, and, in France, by Maurice Thorez, Jacques Duclos, and Georges Marchais.

Regardless of the role that theoretical communist doctrines may have played in the practice of real Communism before 1917—and we shall return to this later—it was flesh-and-blood Communism that imposed wholesale re-pression, culminating in a state-sponsored reign of terror. Is the ideology itself blameless? There will always be some nitpickers who maintain that actual Communism has nothing in common with theoretical communism. And of course it would be absurd to claim that doctrines expounded prior to Jesus Christ, during the Renaissance, or even in the nineteenth century were respon-sible for the events that took place in the twentieth century. Nonetheless, as Ignazio Silone has written, "Revolutions, like trees, are recognized by the fruit they bear." It was not without reason that the Russian Social Democrats, better known to history as the Bolsheviks, decided in November 1917 to call them-selves "Communists." They had a reason for erecting at the Kremlin a monu-ment to those whom they considered to be their predecessors, namely Sir Thomas More and Tommaso Campanella.

Having gone beyond individual crimes and small-scale ad-hoc massacres, the Communist regimes, in order to consolidate their grip on power, turned mass crime into a full-blown system of government. After varying periods, ranging from a few years in Eastern Europe to several decades in the U.S.S.R. and China, the terror faded, and the regimes settled into a routine of administering repressive measures on a daily basis, as well as censoring all means of communication, controlling borders, and expelling dissidents. However, the memory of the terror has continued to preserve the credibility, and thus the effectiveness, of the threat of repression. None of the Communist regimes currently in vogue in the West is an exception to this rule—not the China of the "Great Helmsman," nor the North Korea of Kim Il Sung, nor even the Vietnam of "good old Uncle Ho" or the Cuba of the flamboyant Fidel Castro, flanked by the hard-liner Che Guevara. Nor can we forget Ethiopia under Mengistu Haile Mariam, Angola under Agostinho Neto, or Afghanistan under Mohammed Najibullah.

Incredibly, the crimes of Communism have yet to receive a fair and just assessment from both historical and moral viewpoints. This book is one of the first attempts to study Communism with a focus on its criminal dimensions, in both the central regions of Communist rule and the farthest reaches of the globe. Some will say that most of these crimes were actions conducted in accordance with a system of law that was enforced by the regimes' official institutions, which were recognized internationally and whose heads of state continued to be welcomed with open arms. But was this not the case with Nazism as well? The crimes we shall expose are to be judged not by the standards of Communist regimes, but by the unwritten code of the natural laws of humanity.

The history of Communist regimes and parties, their policies, and their relations with their own national societies and with the international community are of course not purely synonymous with criminal behavior, let alone with terror and repression. In the U.S.S.R. and in the "people's democracies" after Stalin's death, as well as in China after Mao, terror became less pronounced, society began to recover something of its old normalcy, and "peaceful coexistence"—if only as "the pursuit of the class struggle by other means"—had become an international fact of life. Nevertheless, many archives and witnesses prove conclusively that terror has always been one of the basic ingredients of modern Communism. Let us abandon once and for all the idea that the execution of hostages by firing squads, the slaughter of rebellious workers, and the forced starvation of the peasantry were only short-term "accidents" peculiar to a specific country or era. Our approach will encompass all geographic areas and focus on crime as a defining characteristic of the Communist system throughout its existence.

Exactly what crimes are we going to examine? Communism has committed a multitude of crimes not only against individual human beings but also against world civilization and national cultures. Stalin demolished dozens of churches in Moscow; Nicolae Ceauşescu destroyed the historical heart of Bucharest to give free rein to his megalomania; Pol Pot dismantled the Phnom Penh cathedral stone by stone and allowed the jungle to take over the temples of Angkor Wat; and during Mao's Cultural Revolution, priceless treasures were smashed or burned by the Red Guards. Yet however terrible this destruction may ultimately prove for the nations in question and for humanity as a whole, how does it compare with the mass murder of human beings—of men, women, and children?

Thus we have delimited crimes against civilians as the essence of the phenomenon of terror. These crimes tend to fit a recognizable pattern even if the practices vary to some extent by regime. The pattern includes execution by various means, such as firing squads, hanging, drowning, battering, and, in certain cases, gassing, poisoning, or "car accidents"; destruction of the population by starvation, through man-made famine, the withholding of food, or both; deportation, through which death can occur in transit (either through physical exhaustion or through confinement in an enclosed space), at one's place of residence, or through forced labor (exhaustion, illness, hunger, cold). Periods described as times of "civil war" are more complex—it is not always easy to distinguish between events caused by fighting between rulers and rebels and events that can properly be described only as a massacre of the civilian population.

Nonetheless, we have to start somewhere. The following rough approximation, based on unofficial estimates, gives some sense of the scale and gravity of these crimes:

U.S.S.R.: 20 million deaths
China: 65 million deaths
Vietnam: 1 million deaths
North Korea: 2 million deaths
Cambodia: 2 million deaths
Eastern Europe: 1 million deaths
Latin America: 150,000 deaths
Africa: 1.7 million deaths
Afghanistan: 1.5 million deaths
The international Communist movement and Communist parties not in power: about 10,000 deaths

The total approaches 100 million people killed.

The immense number of deaths conceals some wide disparities according to context. Unquestionably, if we approach these figures in terms of relative weight, first place goes to Cambodia, where Pol Pot, in three and a half years, engaged in the most atrocious slaughter, through torture and widespread famine, of about one-fourth of the country's total population. However, China's experience under Mao is unprecedented in terms of the sheer number of people who lost their lives. As for the Soviet Union of Lenin and Stalin, the blood turns cold at its venture into planned, logical, and "politically correct" mass slaughter.

This bare-bones approach inevitably fails to do justice to the numerous issues involved. A thorough investigation requires a "qualitative" study based on a meaningful definition of the term "crime." Objective and legal criteria are also important. The legal ramifications of crimes committed by a specific country were first confronted in 1945 at the Nuremberg Tribunal, which was organized by the Allies to consider the atrocities committed by the Nazis. The nature of these crimes was defined by Article 6 of the Charter of the International Military Tribunal, which identified three major offenses: crimes against peace, war crimes, and crimes against humanity. An examination of all the crimes committed by the Leninist/Stalinist regime, and in the Communist world as a whole, reveals crimes that fit into each of these three categories.

Crimes against peace, defined by Article 6a, are concerned with the "planning, preparation, initiation, or waging of wars of aggression, or a war in violation of international treaties, agreements, or assurances, or participation in a common plan or conspiracy for the accomplishment of any of the foregoing." Unquestionably, Stalin committed such a crime by secretly negotiating two treaties with Hitler—those of 23 August and 28 September 1939 on the partition of Poland and on the annexation of the Baltic states, northern Bukovina, and Bessarabia to the U.S.S.R., respectively. By freeing Germany from the risk of waging war on two fronts, the treaty of 23 August 1939 led directly to the outbreak of World War II. Stalin perpetrated yet another crime against peace by attacking Finland on 30 November 1939. The unexpected incursion into South Korea by North Korea on 25 June 1950 and the massive intervention in that war by the Chinese army are of comparable magnitude. The methods of subversion long used by the Moscow-backed Communist parties likewise deserve categorization as crimes against peace, since they began wars; thus a Communist coup in Afghanistan led to a massive Soviet military intervention on 27 December 1979, unleashing a conflict that continues to this day.

War crimes are defined in Article 6b as "violations of the laws or customs of war. Such violations shall include, but not be limited to, murder, the ill-treatment or deportation of civilian residents of an occupied territory to slave labor camps or for any other purpose, the murder or ill-treatment of prisoners of war or persons on the seas, the killing of hostages, the plunder of public or private property, the wanton destruction of cities, towns, or villages, and any devastation not justified by military necessity." The laws and customs of war are written down in various conventions, particularly the Hague Convention of

1907, which states that in times of war "the inhabitants and the belligerents remain under the protection and the rule of the principles of the law of nations, as they result from the usages established among civilized peoples, from laws of humanity, and the dictates of the public conscience."

Stalin gave the go-ahead for large numbers of war crimes. The liquidation of almost all the Polish officers taken prisoner in 1939, with 4,500 men butchered at Katyń, is only one such episode, albeit the most spectacular. However, other crimes on a much larger scale are habitually overlooked, including the murder or death in the gulag of tens of thousands of German soldiers taken prisoner from 1943 to 1945. Nor should we forget the rape of countless German women by Red Army soldiers in occupied Germany, as well as the systematic plundering of all industrial equipment in the countries occupied by the Red Army. Also covered by Article 6b would be the organized resistance fighters who openly waged war against Communist rulers and who were executed by firing squads or deported after being taken prisoner—for example, the soldiers of the anti-Nazi Polish resistance organizations, members of various Ukrainian and Baltic armed partisan organizations, and Afghan resistance fighters.

The expression "crime against humanity" first appeared on 19 May 1915 in a joint French, British, and Russian declaration condemning Turkey's massacre of the Armenians as a "new crime by Turkey against humanity and civilization." The atrocities committed by the Nazis obliged the Nuremberg Tribunal to redefine the concept, as stated in Article 6c: "Murder, extermination, enslavement, deportation, and other inhumane acts committed against any civilian population before or during the war; or persecutions on political, racial, or religious grounds in execution of or in connection with any crime within the jurisdiction of the Tribunal, whether or not in violation of the domestic law of the country where perpetrated."

In his arguments at Nuremberg the French prosecutor general, François de Menthon, emphasized the ideological dimension of these crimes:

> I propose today to prove to you that all this organized and vast criminality springs from what I may be allowed to call a crime against the spirit, I mean a doctrine that, by denying all spiritual, rational, or moral values by which nations have tried for thousands of years to improve human conditions, aims to plunge humanity back into barbarism, no longer the natural and spontaneous barbarism of primitive nations, but into a diabolical barbarism, conscious of itself and using for its ends all material means put at the disposal of humanity by contemporary science. This sin against the spirit is the original sin of National Socialism from which all crimes spring.
>
> This monstrous doctrine is that of racism . . .
>
> Whether we consider a crime against peace or war crimes, we are

therefore not faced by an accidental or an occasional criminality that events could explain without justifying it. We are in fact faced by systematic criminality, which derives directly and of necessity from a monstrous doctrine put into practice with deliberate intent by the masters of Nazi Germany.

François de Menthon also noted that deportations were meant to provide additional labor for the German war machine, and the fact that the Nazis sought to exterminate their opponents was merely "a natural consequence of the National Socialist doctrine for which man has no intrinsic value unless he serves the German race." All statements made to the Nuremberg Tribunal stressed one of the chief characteristics of crimes against humanity—the fact that the power of the state is placed in the service of criminal policies and practice. However, the jurisdiction of the Nuremberg Tribunal was limited to crimes committed during World War II. Therefore, we must broaden the legal definition of war crimes to include situations that extend beyond that war. The new French criminal code, adopted on 23 July 1992, defines war crimes in the following way: "The deportation, enslavement, or mass-scale and systematic practice of summary executions, abduction of persons following their disappearance, torture, or inhuman acts inspired by *political, philosophical,* racial, or religious motives, and organized for the purpose of implementing a concerted effort against a civilian population group" (emphasis added).

All these definitions, especially the recent French definition, are relevant to any number of crimes committed by Lenin and above all by Stalin and subsequently by the leaders of all Communist countries, with the exception (we hope) of Cuba and the Nicaragua of the Sandinistas. Nevertheless, the main conclusions are inescapable—Communist regimes have acted "in the name of a state practicing a policy of ideological hegemony." Thus in the name of an ideological belief system were tens of millions of innocent victims systematically butchered, unless of course it is a crime to be middle-class, of noble birth, a kulak, a Ukrainian, or even a worker or a member of the Communist Party. Active intolerance was high on the Communists' agenda. It was Mikhail Tomsky, the leader of the Soviet trade unions, who in the 13 November 1927 issue of *Trud* (Labor) stated: "We allow other parties to exist. However, the fundamental principle that distinguishes us from the West is as follows: one party rules, and all the others are in jail!"[2]

The concept of a crime against humanity is a complex one and is directly relevant to the crimes under consideration here. One of the most specific is genocide. Following the genocide of the Jews by the Nazis, and in order to clarify Article 6c of the Nuremberg Tribunal, crimes against humanity were defined by the United Nations Convention on the Prevention and Punishment of Genocide of 9 December 1948 in the following way: "Genocide means any of the following acts committed with intent to destroy, in whole or in part, a national, ethnical, racial or religious group, as such: (a) killing members of the group; (b) causing serious bodily or mental harm to members of the group; (c) deliberately inflicting on the group conditions of life calculated to bring about its physical destruction in whole or in part; (d) imposing measures intended to prevent births within the group; (e) forcibly transferring children of the group to another group."

The new French criminal code defines genocide still more broadly: "The deed of executing a *concerted effort* that strives to destroy totally or partially a national, ethnic, racial or religious group, or a *group that has been determined on the basis of any other arbitrary criterion*" (emphasis added). This legal definition is not inconsistent with the philosophical approach of André Frossard, who believes that "it is a crime against humanity when someone is put to death purely by virtue of his or her birth."[3] And in his short but magnificent novel *Forever Flowing*, Vasily Grossman says of his hero, Ivan Grigorevich, who has returned from the camps, "he had remained exactly what he had been from his birth: a human being."[4] That, of course, was precisely why he was singled out in the first place. The French definition helps remind us that genocide comes in many shapes and sizes—it can be racial (as in the case of the Jews), but it can also target social groups. In *The Red Terror in Russia*, published in Berlin in 1924, the Russian historian and socialist Sergei Melgunov cited Martin Latsis, one of the first leaders of the Cheka (the Soviet political police), as giving the following order on 1 November 1918 to his henchmen: "We don't make war against any people in particular. We are exterminating the bourgeoisie as a class. In your investigations don't look for documents and pieces of evidence about what the defendant has done, whether in deed or in speaking or acting against Soviet authority. The first question you should ask him is what class he comes from, what are his roots, his education, his training, and his occupation."[5]

Lenin and his comrades initially found themselves embroiled in a merciless "class war," in which political and ideological adversaries, as well as the more recalcitrant members of the general public, were branded as enemies and marked for destruction. The Bolsheviks had decided to eliminate, by legal and physical means, any challenge or resistance, even if passive, to their absolute power. This strategy applied not only to groups with opposing political views, but also to such social groups as the nobility, the middle class, the intelligentsia, and the clergy, as well as professional groups such as military officers and the police. Sometimes the Bolsheviks subjected these people to genocide. The policy of "de-Cossackization" begun in 1920 corresponds largely to our definition of genocide: a population group firmly established in a particular territory, the Cossacks as such were exterminated, the men shot, the women, children, and the elderly deported, and the villages razed or handed over to new, non-Cossack occupants. Lenin compared the Cossacks to the Vendée during the French Revolution and gladly subjected them to a program of what Gracchus Babeuf, the "inventor" of modern Communism, characterized in 1795 as "populicide."[6]

The "dekulakization" of 1930–1932 repeated the policy of "de-Cossackization" but on a much grander scale. Its primary objective, in accordance with the official order issued for this operation (and the regime's propaganda), was "to exterminate the kulaks as a class." The kulaks who resisted collectivization were shot, and the others were deported with their wives, children, and elderly family members. Although not all kulaks were exterminated directly, sentences of forced labor in wilderness areas of Siberia or the far north left them with scant chance of survival. Several tens of thousands perished there; the exact number of victims remains unknown. As for the great famine in Ukraine in 1932–33, which resulted from the rural population's resistance to forced collectivization, 6 million died in a period of several months.

Here, the genocide of a "class" may well be tantamount to the genocide of a "race"—the deliberate starvation of a child of a Ukrainian kulak as a result of the famine caused by Stalin's regime "is equal to" the starvation of a Jewish child in the Warsaw ghetto as a result of the famine caused by the Nazi regime. Such arguments in no way detract from the unique nature of Auschwitz—the mobilization of leading-edge technological resources and their use in an "industrial process" involving the construction of an "extermination factory," the use of gas, and cremation. However, this argument highlights one particular feature of many Communist regimes—their systematic use of famine as a weapon. The regime aimed to control the total available food supply and, with immense ingenuity, to distribute food purely on the basis of "merits" and "demerits" earned by individuals. This policy was a recipe for creating famine on a massive scale. Remember that in the period after 1918, only Communist countries experienced such famines, which led to the deaths of hundreds of thousands, and in some cases millions, of people. And again in the 1980s, two African countries that claimed to be Marxist-Leninist, Ethiopia and Mozambique, were the only such countries to suffer these deadly famines.

A preliminary global accounting of the crimes committed by Communist regimes shows the following:

· The execution of tens of thousands of hostages and prisoners without trial, and the murder of hundreds of thousands or rebellious workers and peasants from 1918 to 1922
· The famine of 1922, which caused the deaths of 5 million people

- The extermination and deportation of the Don Cossacks in 1920
- The murder of tens of thousands in concentration camps from 1918 to 1930
- The liquidation of almost 690,000 people in the Great Purge of 1937–38
- The deportation of 2 million kulaks (and so-called kulaks) in 1930–1932
- The destruction of 4 million Ukrainians and 2 million others by means of an artificial and systematically perpetuated famine in 1932–33
- The deportation of hundreds of thousands of Poles, Ukrainians, Balts, Moldovans, and Bessarabians from 1939 to 1941, and again in 1944–45
- The deportation of the Volga Germans in 1941
- The wholesale deportation of the Crimean Tatars in 1943
- The wholesale deportation of the Chechens in 1944
- The wholesale deportation of the Ingush in 1944
- The deportation and extermination of the urban population in Cambodia from 1975 to 1978
- The slow destruction of the Tibetans by the Chinese since 1950

No list of the crimes committed in the name of Leninism and Stalinism would be complete without mentioning the virtually identical crimes committed by the regimes of Mao Zedong, Kim Il Sung, and Pol Pot.

A difficult epistemological question remains: Should the historian employ the primarily legal categories of "crime against humanity" and "genocide"? Are these concepts not unduly time specific—focusing on the condemnation of Nazism at Nuremberg—for use in historical research aimed at deriving relevant medium-term conclusions? On the other hand, are these concepts not somewhat tainted with questionable "values" that distort the objectivity of historical research?

First and foremost, the history of the twentieth century has shown us that the Nazis had no monopoly over the use of mass murder by states and party-states. The recent experiences in Bosnia and Rwanda indicate that this practice continues as one of the hallmarks of this century.

Second, although it might not be appropriate to revive historical methods of the nineteenth century, whereby historians performed research more for the purpose of passing judgment than for understanding the issue in question, the immense human tragedies directly caused by certain ideologies and political concepts make it impossible to ignore the humanist ideas implicit in our Judeo-Christian civilization and democratic traditions—for example, the idea of respect for human life. A number of renowned historians readily use the expression "crime against humanity" to describe Nazi crimes, including Jean-Perre Azema in his article "Auschwitz"[7] and Pierre Vidal-Naquet on the trial of Paul Touvier.[8] Therefore, it does not seem inappropriate to use such terms and concepts to characterize the crimes committed by Communist regimes.

In addition to the question of whether the Communists in power were directly responsible for these crimes, there is also the issue of complicity. Article 7(3.77) of the Canadian criminal code, amended in 1987, states that crimes against humanity include infractions of attempting, conspiring, counseling, aiding, and *providing encouragement for* de facto *complicity*.[9] This accords with the definition of crimes against humanity in Article 7(3.76) of the same code: "attempting or conspiring to commit, counseling any person to commit, aiding or abetting any person in the commission of, or *being an accessory after the fact* in relation to the act" (emphasis added). Incredibly, from the 1920s to the 1950s, when hundreds of thousands of people served in the ranks of the Communist International and local sections of the "world party of the revolution," Communists and fellow-travelers around the world warmly approved Lenin's and subsequently Stalin's policies. From the 1950s to the 1970s, hundreds of thousands of people sang the praises of the "Great Helmsman" of the Chinese Revolution and extolled the virtues of the Great Leap Forward and the Cultural Revolution. Much closer to our time, there was widespread rejoicing when Pol Pot came to power.[10] Many will say that they "didn't know." Undoubtedly, of course, it was not always easy to learn the facts or to discover the truth, for Communist regimes had mastered the art of censorship as their favorite technique for concealing their true activities. But quite often this ignorance was merely the result of ideologically motivated self-deception. Starting in the 1940s and 1950s, many facts about these atrocities had become public knowledge and undeniable. And although many of these apologists have cast aside their gods of yesterday, they have done so quietly and discreetly. What are we to make of a profoundly amoral doctrine that seeks to stamp out every last trace of civic-mindedness in men's souls, and damn the consequences?

In 1968 one of the pioneers in the study of Communist terror, Robert Conquest, wrote: "The fact that so many people 'swallowed' [the Great Terror] hook, line, and sinker was probably one of the reasons that the Terror succeeded so well. In particular, the trials would not be so significant had they not received the blessing of some 'independent' foreign commentators. These pundits should be held accountable as accomplices in the bloody politics of the purges or at least blamed for the fact that the political assassinations resumed when the first show trial, regarding Zinoviev in 1936, was given an ill-deserved stamp of approval."[11] If the moral and intellectual complicity of a number of non-Communists is judged by this criterion, what can be said of the complicity of the Communists? Louis Aragon, for one, has publicly expressed regret for having appealed in a 1931 poem for the creation of a Communist political police in France.[12]

Joseph Berger, a former Comintern official who was "purged" and then exiled to the camps, quotes a letter received from a former gulag deportee who remained a Party member even after her return:

My generation of Communists everywhere accepted the Stalinist form of leadership. We acquiesced in the crimes. That is true not only of Soviet Communists, but of Communists all over the world. We, especially the active and leading members of the Party, carry a stain on our consciences individually and collectively. The only way we can erase it is to make sure that nothing of the sort ever happens again. How was all this possible? Did we all go crazy, or have we now become traitors to Communism? The truth is that all of us, including the leaders directly under Stalin, saw these crimes as the opposite of what they were. We believed that they were important contributions to the victory of socialism. We thought everything that promoted the power politics of the Communist Party in the Soviet Union and in the world was good for socialism. We never suspected that conflict between Communist politics and Communist ethics was possible.[13]

Berger, however, tries to have it both ways. "On the other hand, I personally feel that there is a difference between criticizing people for having accepted Stalin's policy, which many Communists did not do, and blaming them for not having prevented his crimes. To suppose that this could have been done by any individual, no matter how important he might have been, is to misunderstand Stalin's byzantine tyranny."[14] Thus Berger has found an excuse for having been in the U.S.S.R. and for having been caught up in its infernal machine without any means of escape. But what self-deception kept Western European Communists, who had not been directly arrested by the People's Commissariat of Internal Affairs (NKVD, the secret police), blindly babbling away about the system and its leader? Why could they not hear the wake-up call at the very start? In his remarkable work on the Russian Revolution, *The Soviet Tragedy,* Martin Malia lifts a corner of the curtain when he speaks of "this paradox . . . that . . . [it] takes a great ideal to produce a great crime."[15] Annie Kriegel, another major student of Communism, insists that there is a cause-and-effect relationship between the two faces of Communism, as surely as day follows night.

Tzvetan Todorov offered the first response to this paradox:

A citizen of a Western democracy fondly imagines that totalitarianism lies utterly beyond the pale of normal human aspirations. And yet, totalitarianism could never have survived so long had it not been able to draw so many people into its fold. There is something else—it is a formidably efficient machine. Communist ideology offers an idealized model for society and exhorts us toward it. The desire to change the world in the name of an ideal is, after all, an essential characteristic of human identity . . . Furthermore, Communist society strips the individual of his responsibilities. It is always "somebody else" who makes the decisions. Remember, individual responsibility can feel like a crushing burden . . . The attraction of a totalitarian system, which has had a powerful allure for many, has its roots in a fear of freedom and responsibility. This explains the popularity of authoritarian regimes (which is Erich Fromm's thesis in *Escape from Freedom*). None of this is new; Boethius had the right idea long ago when he spoke of "voluntary servitude."[16]

The complicity of those who rushed into voluntary servitude has not always been as abstract and theoretical as it may seem. Simple acceptance and/or dissemination of propaganda designed to conceal the truth is invariably a symptom of active complicity. Although it may not always succeed, as is demonstrated by the tragedy in Rwanda, the glare of the spotlight is the only effective response to mass crimes that are committed in secret and kept hidden from prying eyes.

An analysis of terror and dictatorship—the defining characteristics of Communists in power—is no easy task. Jean Ellenstein has defined Stalinism as a combination of Greek tragedy and Oriental despotism. This definition is appealing, but it fails to account for the sheer modernity of the Communist experience, its totalitarian impact distinct from previously existing forms of dictatorship. A comparative synopsis may help to put it in context.

First, we should consider the possibility that responsibility for the crimes of Communism can be traced to a Russian penchant for oppression. However, the tsarist regime of terror against which the Bolsheviks fought pales in comparison with the horrors committed by the Bolsheviks when they took power. The tsar allowed political prisoners to face a meaningful justice system. The counsel for the defendant could represent his client up to the time of indictment and even beyond, and he could also appeal to national and international public opinion, an option unavailable under Communist regimes. Prisoners and convicts benefited from a set of rules governing the prisons, and the system of imprisonment and deportation was relatively lenient. Those who were deported could take their families, read and write as they pleased, go hunting and fishing, and talk about their "misfortune" with their companions. Lenin and Stalin had firsthand experience of this. Even the events described by Fyodor Dostoevsky in *Memoirs from the House of the Dead*, which had such a great impact when it was published, seem tame by comparison with the horrors of Communism. True, riots and insurrections were brutally crushed by the *ancien régime*. However, from 1825 to 1917 the total number of people sentenced to death in Russia for their political beliefs or activities was 6,360, of whom only 3,932 were executed. This number can be subdivided chronologically into 191 for the years 1825–1905 and 3,741 for 1906–1910. These figures were surpassed by the

Bolsheviks in March 1918, after they had been in power for only four months. It follows that tsarist repression was not in the same league as Communist dictatorship.

From the 1920s to the 1940s, Communism set a standard for terror to which fascist regimes could aspire. A glance at the figures for these regimes shows that a comparison may not be as straightforward as it would first appear. Italian Fascism, the first regime of its kind and the first that openly claimed to be "totalitarian," undoubtedly imprisoned and regularly mistreated its political opponents. Although incarceration seldom led to death, during the 1930s Italy had a few hundred political prisoners and several hundred *confinati*, placed under house arrest on the country's coastal islands. In addition, of course, there were tens of thousands of political exiles.

Before World War II, Nazi terror targeted several groups. Opponents of the Nazi regime, consisting mostly of Communists, Socialists, anarchists, and trade union activists, were incarcerated in prisons and invariably interned in concentration camps, where they were subjected to extreme brutality. All told, from 1933 to 1939 about 20,000 left-wing militants were killed after trial or without trial in the camps and prisons. These figures do not include the slaughter of other Nazis to settle old scores, as in "The Night of the Long Knives" in June 1934. Another category of victims doomed to die were Germans who did not meet the proper racial criteria of "tall blond Aryans," such as those who were old or mentally or physically defective. As a result of the war, Hitler forged ahead with a euthanasia program—70,000 Germans were gassed between the end of 1939 and the beginning of 1941, when churches began to demand that this program be stopped. The gassing methods devised for this euthanasia program were applied to the third group of victims, the Jews.

Before World War II, crackdowns against the Jews were widespread; persecution reached its peak during *Kristallnacht*, with several hundred deaths and 35,000 rounded up for internment in concentration camps. These figures apply only to the period before the invasion of the Soviet Union. Thereafter the full terror of the Nazis was unleashed, producing the following body count—15 million civilians killed in occupied countries, 6 million Jews, 3.3 million Soviet prisoners of war, 1.1 million deportees who died in the camps, and several hundred thousand Gypsies. We should add another 8 million who succumbed to the ravages of forced labor and 1.6 million surviving inmates of the concentration camps.

The Nazi terror captures the imagination for three reasons. First, it touched the lives of Europeans so closely. Second, because the Nazis were vanquished and their leaders prosecuted at Nuremberg, their crimes have been officially exposed and categorized as crimes. And finally, the revelation of the genocide carried out against the Jews outraged the conscience of humanity by its irrationality, racism, and unprecedented bloodthirstiness.

Our purpose here is not to devise some kind of macabre comparative system for crunching numbers, some kind of grand total that doubles the horror, some kind of hierarchy of cruelty. But the intransigent facts demonstrate that Communist regimes have victimized approximately 100 million people in contrast to the approximately 25 million victims of the Nazis. This clear record should provide at least some basis for assessing the similarity between the Nazi regime, which since 1945 has been considered the most viciously criminal regime of this century, and the Communist system, which as late as 1991 had preserved its international legitimacy unimpaired and which, even today, is still in power in certain countries and continues to protect its supporters the world over. And even though many Communist parties have belatedly acknowledged Stalinism's crimes, most have not abandoned Lenin's principles and scarcely question their own involvement in acts of terrorism.

The methods implemented by Lenin and perfected by Stalin and their henchmen bring to mind the methods used by the Nazis, but most often this is because the latter adopted the techniques developed by the former. Rudolf Hess, charged with organizing the camp at Auschwitz and later appointed its commandant, is a perfect example: "The Reich Security Head Office issued to the commandants a full collection of reports concerning the Russian concentration camps. These described in great detail the conditions in, and organization of, the Russian camps, as supplied by former prisoners who had managed to escape. Great emphasis was placed on the fact that the Russians, by their massive employment of forced labor, had destroyed whole peoples."[17] However, the fact that the techniques of mass violence and the intensity of their use originated with the Communists and that the Nazis were inspired by them does not imply, in our view, that one can postulate a cause-and-effect relationship between the Bolshevik revolution and the rise of Nazism.

From the end of the 1920s, the State Political Directorate (GPU, the new name for the Cheka) introduced a quota method—each region and district had to arrest, deport, or shoot a certain percentage of people who were members of several "enemy" social classes. These quotas were centrally defined under the supervision of the Party. The mania for planning and maintaining statistics was not confined to the economy: it was also an important weapon in the arsenal of terror. From 1920 on, with the victory of the Red Army over the White Army in the Crimea, statistical and sociological methods made an appearance, with victims selected according to precise criteria on the basis of a compulsory questionnaire. The same "sociological" methods were used by the Soviet Union to organize mass deportations and liquidations in the Baltic states and occupied Poland in 1939–1941. As with the Nazis, the transportation of deportees in cattle cars ushered in "aberrations." In 1943 and 1944, in the middle of the war, Stalin diverted thousands of trucks and hundreds of thousands of soldiers serving in the special NKVD troops from the front on a short-term basis in order to deport the various peoples living in the Caucasus. This genocidal impulse, which aims at "the total or partial destruction of a national, ethnic, racial, or religious group, or a group that has been determined on the basis of any other arbitrary criterion," was applied by Communist rulers against groups branded as enemies and to entire segments of society, and was pursued to its maximum by Pol Pot and his Khmer Rouge.

Efforts to draw parallels between Nazism and Communism on the basis of their respective extermination tactics may give offense to some people. However, we should recall how in *Forever Flowing* Vasily Grossman, whose mother was killed by the Nazis in the Berdychiv ghetto, who authored the first work on Treblinka, and who was one of the editors of the *Black Book* on the extermination of Soviet Jews, has one of his characters describe the famine in Ukraine: "writers kept writing . . . Stalin himself, too: the kulaks are parasites; they are burning grain; they are killing children. And it was openly proclaimed 'that the rage and wrath of the masses must be inflamed against them, they must be destroyed as a class, because they are accursed.'" He adds: "To massacre them, it was necessary to proclaim that kulaks are not human beings, just as the Germans proclaimed that Jews are not human beings. Thus did Lenin and Stalin say: kulaks are not human beings." In conclusion, Grossman says of the children of the kulaks: "That is exactly how the Nazis put the Jewish children into the Nazi gas chambers: 'You are not allowed to live, you are all Jews!'"[18]

Time and again the focus of the terror was less on targeted individuals than on groups of people. The purpose of the terror was to exterminate a group that had been designated as the enemy. Even though it might be only a small fraction of society, it had to be stamped out to satisfy this genocidal impulse. Thus, the techniques of segregation and exclusion employed in a "class-based totalitarianism" closely resemble the techniques of "race-based totalitarianism." The future Nazi society was to be built upon a "pure race," and the future Communist society was to be built upon a proletarian people purified of the dregs of the bourgeoisie. The restructuring of these two societies was envisioned in the same way, even if the crackdowns were different. Therefore, it would be foolish to pretend that Communism is a form of universalism. Communism may have a worldwide purpose, but like Nazism it deems a part of humanity unworthy of existence. The difference is that the Communist model is based on the class system, the Nazi model on race and territory. Thus the transgressions of Leninism, Stalinism, Maoism, and the Khmer Rouge pose a fresh challenge for humanity, and particularly for legal scholars and historians:

specifically, how do we describe a crime designed to exterminate not merely individuals or opposing groups but entire segments of society on a massive scale for their political and ideological beliefs? A whole new language is needed for this. Some authors in the English-speaking countries use the term "politicide." Or is the term "Communist crimes," suggested by Czech legal scholars, preferable?

How are we to assess Communism's crimes? What lessons are we to learn from them? Why has it been necessary to wait until the end of the twentieth century for this subject to show up on the academic radar screen? It is undoubtedly the case that the study of Stalinist and Communist terror, when compared to the study of Nazi crimes, has a great deal of catching-up to do (although such research is gaining popularity in Eastern Europe).

One cannot help noticing the strong contrast between the study of Nazi and Communist crimes. The victors of 1945 legitimately made Nazi crimes—and especially the genocide of the Jews—the central focus of their condemnation of Nazism. A number of researchers around the world have been working on these issues for decades. Thousands of books and dozens of films—most notably *Night and Fog, Shoah, Sophie's Choice,* and *Schindler's List*—have been devoted to the subject. Raul Hilberg, to name but one example, has centered his major work upon a detailed description of the methods used to put Jews to death in the Third Reich.[19]

Yet scholars have neglected the crimes committed by the Communists. While names such as Himmler and Eichmann are recognized around the world as bywords for twentieth-century barbarism, the names of Feliks Dzerzhinsky, Genrikh Yagoda, and Nikolai Ezhov languish in obscurity. As for Lenin, Mao, Ho Chi Minh, and even Stalin, they have always enjoyed a surprising reverence. A French government agency, the National Lottery, was crazy enough to use Stalin and Mao in one of its advertising campaigns. Would anyone even dare to come up with the idea of featuring Hitler or Goebbels in commercials?

The extraordinary attention paid to Hitler's crimes is entirely justified. It respects the wishes of the surviving witnesses, it satisfies the needs of researchers trying to understand these events, and it reflects the desire of moral and political authorities to strengthen democratic values. But the revelations concerning Communist crimes cause barely a stir. Why is there such an awkward silence from politicians? Why such a deafening silence from the academic world regarding the Communist catastrophe, which touched the lives of about one-third of humanity on four continents during a period spanning eighty years? Why is there such widespread reluctance to make such a crucial factor as crime—mass crime, systematic crime, and crime against humanity—a central factor in the analysis of Communism? Is this really something that is beyond human understanding? Or are we talking about a refusal to scrutinize the subject too closely for fear of learning the truth about it?

The reasons for this reticence are many and various. First, there is the dictators' understandable urge to erase their crimes and to justify the actions they cannot hide. Khrushchev's "Secret Speech" of 1956 was the first admission of Communist atrocities by a Communist leader. It was also the statement of a tyrant seeking to gloss over the crimes he himself committed when he headed the Ukrainian Communist Party at the height of the terror, crimes that he cleverly attributed to Stalin by claiming that he and his henchmen were merely obeying orders. To cover up the vast majority of Communist offenses, Khrushchev spoke only of victims who were Communists, although they were far fewer in number than the other kind. He defined these crimes with a euphemism, describing them in his conclusion as "abuses committed under Stalin" in order to justify the continuity of the system that retained the same principles, the same structure, and the same people.

In his inimitable fashion Khrushchev described the opposition he faced while preparing his "Secret Speech," especially from one of Stalin's confidants: "[Lazar] Kaganovich was such a yes-man that he would have cut his own father's throat if Stalin had winked and said it was in the interests of the cause—the Stalinist cause, that is . . . He was arguing against me out of a selfish fear for his own hide. He was motivated entirely by his eagerness to escape any responsibility for what had happened. If crimes had been committed, Kaganovich wanted to make sure his own tracks were covered."[20] The absolute denial of access to archives in Communist countries, the total control of the print and other media as well as of border crossings, the propaganda trumpeting the regime's "successes," and the entire apparatus for keeping information under lock and key were designed primarily to ensure that the awful truth would never see the light of day.

Not satisfied with the concealment of their misdeeds, the tyrants systematically attacked all who dared to expose their crimes. After World War II this became starkly clear on two occasions in France. From January to April 1949, the "trial" of Viktor Kravchenko—a former senior official who wrote *I Chose Freedom,* in which he described Stalin's dictatorship—was conducted in Paris in the pages of the Communist magazine *Les lettres françaises,* which was managed by Louis Aragon and which heaped abuse on Kravchenko. From November 1950 to January 1951, again in Paris, *Les lettres françaises* held another "trial"—of David Rousset, an intellectual and former Trotskyite who was deported to Germany by the Nazis and who in 1946 received the Renaudot Prize for his book *The World of Concentration Camps.* On 12 November 1949 Rousset urged all former Nazi camp deportees to form a commission of inquiry into the Soviet camp system and was savagely attacked by the Communist press, which denied the existence of such camps. Following Rousset's call, Margaret Buber-Neumann recounted her experience of being twice deported to concentration camps—once to a Nazi camp and once to a Soviet camp—in an article published on 25 February 1950 in *Figaro littéraire,* "An Inquiry on Soviet Camps: Who Is Worse, Satan or Beelzebub?"

Despite these efforts to enlighten humankind, the tyrants continued to wheel out heavy artillery to silence all those who stood in their way anywhere in the world. The Communist assassins set out to incapacitate, discredit, and intimidate their adversaries. Aleksandr Solzhenitsyn, Vladimir Bukovsky, Aleksandr Zinoviev, and Leonid Plyushch were expelled from their own country; Andrei Sakharov was exiled to Gorky; General Petro Hryhorenko was thrown into a psychiatric hospital; and Georgi Markov was assassinated with an umbrella that fired pellets filled with poison.

In the face of such incessant intimidation and cover-ups, the victims grew reluctant to speak out and were effectively prevented from reentering mainstream society, where their accusers and executioners were ever-present. Vasily Grossman eloquently describes their despair.[21] In contrast to the Jewish Holocaust, which the international Jewish community has actively commemorated, it has been impossible for victims of Communism and their legal advocates to keep the memory of the tragedy alive, and any requests for commemoration or demands for reparation are brushed aside.

When the tyrants could no longer hide the truth—the firing squads, the concentration camps, the man-made famine—they did their best to justify these atrocities by glossing them over. After admitting the use of terror, they justified it as a necessary aspect of revolution through the use of such catchphrases as "When you cut down a forest, the shavings get blown away" or "You can't make an omelet without breaking eggs." Vladimir Bukovsky retorted that he had seen the broken eggs, but no one he knew had ever tasted the omelet! Perhaps the single greatest evil was the perversion of language. As if by magic, the concentration-camp system was turned into a "reeducation system," and the tyrants became "educators" who transformed the people of the old society into "new people." The *zeks,* a term used for Soviet concentration camp prisoners, were forcibly "invited" to place their trust in a system that enslaved them. In China the concentration-camp prisoner is called a "student," and he is required to study the correct thoughts of the Party and to reform his own faulty thinking.

As is usually the case, a lie is not, strictly speaking, the opposite of the truth, and a lie will generally contain an element of truth. Perverted words are situated in a twisted vision that distorts the landscape; one is confronted with a myopic social and political philosophy. Attitudes twisted by Communist propaganda are easy to correct, but it is monumentally difficult to instruct false prophets in the ways of intellectual tolerance. The first impression is always the one that lingers. Like martial artists, the Communists, thanks to their incomparable propaganda strength grounded in the subversion of language, successfully turned the tables on the criticisms leveled against their terrorist tactics, continually uniting the ranks of their militants and sympathizers by renewing the Communist act of faith. Thus they held fast to their fundamental principle of ideological belief, as formulated by Tertullian for his own era: "I believe, because it is absurd."

Like common prostitutes, intellectuals found themselves inveigled into counterpropaganda operations. In 1928 Maksim Gorky accepted an invitation to go on an "excursion" to the Solovetski Islands, an experimental concentration camp that would "metastasize" (to use Solzhenitsyn's word) into the Gulag system. On his return Gorky wrote a book extolling the glories of the Solovetski camps and the Soviet government. A French writer, Henri Barbusse, recipient of the 1916 Prix Goncourt, did not hesitate to praise Stalin's regime for a fee. His 1928 book on "marvelous Georgia" made no mention of the massacre carried out there in 1921 by Stalin and his henchman Sergo Ordzhonikidze. It also ignored Lavrenti Beria, head of the NKVD, who was noteworthy for his Machiavellian sensibility and his sadism. In 1935 Barbusse brought out the first official biography of Stalin. More recently Maria Antonietta Macciochi spoke gushingly about Mao Zedong, and Alain Peyrefitte echoed the same sentiments to a lesser degree, while Danielle Mitterrand chimed in to praise the deeds of Fidel Castro. Cupidity, spinelessness, vanity, fascination with power, violence, and revolutionary fervor—whatever the motivation, totalitarian dictatorships have always found plenty of diehard supporters when they had need of them, and the same is true of Communist as of other dictatorships.

Confronted with this onslaught of Communist propaganda, the West has long labored under an extraordinary self-deception, simultaneously fueled by naïveté in the face of a particularly devious system, by the fear of Soviet power, and by the cynicism of politicians. There was self-deception at the meeting in Yalta, when President Franklin Delano Roosevelt ceded Eastern Europe to Stalin in return for a solemn undertaking that the latter would hold free elections at the earliest opportunity. Realism and resignation had a rendezvous with destiny in Moscow in December 1944, when General Charles de Gaulle abandoned hapless Poland to the devil in return for guarantees of social and political peace, duly assured by Maurice Thorez on his return to Paris.

This self-deception was a source of comfort and was given quasi-legitimacy by the widespread belief among Communists (and many leftists) in the West that while these countries were "building socialism," the Communist "Utopia," a breeding ground for social and political conflicts, would remain safely distant. Simone Weil epitomized this pro-Communist trendiness when she said, "revolutionary workers are only too thankful to have a state backing them—a state that gives an official character, legitimacy, and reality to their actions as only a state can, and that at the same time is sufficiently far away from them geographically to avoid seeming oppressive."[22] Communism was supposedly showing its true colors—it claimed to be an emissary of the Enlightenment, of a tradition of social and human emancipation, of a dream of "true equality," and of "happiness for all" as envisioned by Gracchus Babeuf. And paradoxically, it was this image of "enlightenment" that helped keep the true nature of its evil almost entirely concealed.

Whether intentional or not, when dealing with this ignorance of the criminal dimension of Communism, our contemporaries' indifference to their fellow humans can never be forgotten. It is not that these individuals are coldhearted. On the contrary, in certain situations they can draw on vast untapped reserves of brotherhood, friendship, affection, even love. However, as Tzvetan Todorov has pointed out, "remembrance of our own woes prevents us from perceiving the suffering of others."[23] And at the end of both world wars, no European or Asian nation was spared the endless grief and sorrow of licking its own wounds. France's own hesitancy to confront the history of the dark years of the Occupation is a compelling illustration in and of itself. The history, or rather nonhistory, of the Occupation continues to overshadow the French conscience. We encounter the same pattern, albeit to a lesser degree, with the history of the "Nazi" period in Germany, the "Fascist" period in Italy, the "Franco" era in Spain, the civil war in Greece, and so on. In this century of blood and iron, everyone has been too preoccupied with his own misfortunes to worry much about the misfortunes of others.

However, there are three more specific reasons for the cover-up of the criminal aspects of Communism. The first is the fascination with the whole notion of revolution itself. In today's world, breast-beating over the idea of "revolution," as dreamed about in the nineteenth and twentieth centuries, is far from over. The icons of revolution—the red flag, the International, and the raised fist—reemerge with each social movement and on a grand scale. Che Guevara is back in fashion. Openly revolutionary groups are active and enjoy every legal right to state their views, hurling abuse on even the mildest criticisms of crimes committed by their predecessors and only too eager to spout the eternal verities regarding the "achievements" of Lenin, Trotsky, or Mao. This revolutionary fervor is not embraced solely by revolutionaries. Many contributors to this book themselves used to believe in Communist propaganda.

The second reason is the participation of the Soviet Union in the victory over Nazism, which allowed the Communists to use fervent patriotism as a mask to conceal their latest plans to take power into their own hands. From June 1941, Communists in all occupied countries commenced an active and frequently armed resistance against Nazi or Italian occupation forces. Like resistance fighters everywhere, they paid the price for their efforts, with thousands being executed by firing squad, slaughtered, or deported. And they "played the martyr" in order to sanctify the Communist cause and to silence all criticism of it. In addition to this, during the Resistance many non-Communists became comrades-in-arms, forged bonds of solidarity, and shed their blood alongside their Communist fellows. As a result of this past these non-Communists may have been willing to turn a blind eye to certain things. In France, the Gaullist attitude was often influenced by this shared memory and was a factor behind the politics of General de Gaulle, who tried to play off the Soviet Union against the Americans.[24]

The Communists' participation in the war and in the victory over Nazism institutionalized the whole notion of antifascism as an article of faith for the left. The Communists, of course, portrayed themselves as the best representatives and defenders of this antifascism. For Communism, antifascism became a brilliantly effective label that could be used to silence one's opponents quickly. François Furet wrote some superb articles on the subject. The defeated Nazism was labeled the "Supreme Evil" by the Allies, and Communism thus automatically wound up on the side of Good. This was made crystal clear during the Nuremberg trials, where Soviet jurists were among the prosecutors. Thus a veil was drawn over embarrassing antidemocratic episodes, such as the German-Soviet pact of 1939 and the massacre at Katyń. Victory over the Nazis was supposed to demonstrate the superiority of the Communist system. In the Europe liberated by the British and the Americans (which was spared the sufferings of occupation) this was done for propaganda purposes to arouse a keen sense of gratitude to the Red Army and a sense of guilt for the sacrifices made by the peoples of the U.S.S.R. The Communists did not hesitate to play upon the sentiments of Europeans in spreading the Communist message.

By the same token, the ways in which Eastern Europe was "liberated" by the Red Army remain largely unknown in the West, where historians assimilate two very different kinds of "liberation," one leading to the restoration of democracies, the other paving the way for the advent of dictatorships. In Central and Eastern Europe, the Soviet system succeeded the Thousand Year Reich, and Witold Gombrowicz neatly captured the tragedy facing these peoples: "The end of the war did not bring liberation to the Poles. In the battlegrounds of Central Europe, it simply meant swapping one form of evil for another, Hitler's henchmen for Stalin's. While sycophants cheered and rejoiced at the 'emancipation of the Polish people from the feudal yoke,' the same lit cigarette was simply passed from hand to hand in Poland and continued to burn the skin of people."[25] Therein lay the fault line between two European folk memories. However, a number of publications have lifted the curtain to show

how the U.S.S.R. "liberated" the Poles, Germans, Czechs, and Slovaks from Nazism.[26]

The final reason for the gentle treatment of Communism is subtler and a little trickier to explain. After 1945 the Jewish genocide became a byword for modern barbarism, the epitome of twentieth-century mass terror. After initially disputing the unique nature of the persecution of the Jews by the Nazis, the Communists soon grasped the benefits involved in immortalizing the Holocaust as a way of rekindling antifascism on a more systematic basis. The specter of "the filthy beast whose stomach is fertile again"—to use Bertolt Brecht's famous phrase—was invoked incessantly and constantly. More recently, a single-minded focus on the Jewish genocide in an attempt to characterize the Holocaust as a unique atrocity has also prevented an assessment of other episodes of comparable magnitude in the Communist world. After all, it seems scarcely plausible that the victors who had helped bring about the destruction of a genocidal apparatus might themselves have put the very same methods into practice. When faced with this paradox, people generally preferred to bury their heads in the sand.

The first turning point in the official recognition of Communist crimes came on the evening of 24 February 1956, when First Secretary Nikita Khrushchev took the podium at the Twentieth Congress of the Communist Party of the Soviet Union, the CPSU. The proceedings were conducted behind closed doors; only delegates to the Congress were present. In absolute silence, stunned by what they were hearing, the delegates listened as the first secretary of the Party systematically dismantled the image of the "little father of the peoples," of the "genius Stalin," who for thirty years had been the hero of world Communism. This report, immortalized as Khrushchev's "Secret Speech," was one of the watersheds in the life of contemporary Communism. For the first time, a high-ranking Communist leader had officially acknowledged, albeit only as a tactical concession, that the regime that assumed power in 1917 had undergone a criminal "deviation."

Khrushchev's motivations for breaking one of the great taboos of the Soviet regime were numerous. Khrushchev's primary aim was to attribute the crimes of Communism only to Stalin, thus circumscribing the evil, and to eradicate it once and for all in an effort to salvage the Communist regime. A determination to carry out an attack on Stalin's clique, which stood in the way of Khrushchev's power and believed in the methods practiced by their former boss, entered equally into his decision. Beginning in June 1957, these men were systematically removed from office. However, for the first time since 1934, the act of "being put to death politically" was not followed by an *actual* death, and this telling detail itself illustrates that Khrushchev's motives were more complex. Having been the boss of Ukraine for years and, in this capacity, having carried out and covered up the slaughter of innocent civilians on a massive scale, he may have grown weary of all this bloodshed. In his memoirs, in which he was naturally concerned with portraying himself in a flattering light, Khrushchev recalled his feelings: "The Congress will end, and resolutions will be passed, all as a matter of form. But then what? The hundreds and thousands of people who were shot will stay on our consciences." As a result, he severely reprimanded his colleagues:

> What are we going to do about all those who were arrested and eliminated? . . . We now know that the people who suffered during the repressions were innocent. We have indisputable proof that, far from being enemies of the people, they were honest men and women, devoted to the Party, dedicated to the Revolution, and committed to the Leninist cause and to the building of Socialism and Communism in the Soviet Union . . . I still think it's impossible to cover everything up. Sooner or later people will be coming out of the prisons and the camps, and they'll return to the cities. They'll tell their relatives, friends, and comrades, and everyone back home what happened . . . we're obliged to speak candidly to the delegates about the conduct of the Party leadership during the years in question . . . How can we pretend not to know what happened? We know there was a reign of repression and arbitrary rule in the Party, and we must tell the Congress what we know . . . In the life of anyone who has committed a crime, there comes a moment when a confession will assure him leniency if not exculpation.[27]

Among some of the men who had had a hand in the crimes perpetrated under Stalin and who generally owed their promotions to the extermination of their predecessors in office, a certain kind of remorse took hold—a lukewarm remorse, a self-interested remorse, the remorse of a politician, but remorse nonetheless. It was necessary for someone to put a stop to the slaughter. Khrushchev had the courage to do this even if, in 1956, he sent Soviet tanks into Budapest.

In 1961, during the Twenty-second Congress of the CPSU, Khrushchev recalled not only the victims who were Communists but all of Stalin's victims and even proposed that a monument be erected in their memory. At this point Khrushchev may have overstepped the invisible boundary beyond which the very raison d'être of Communism was being challenged—namely, the absolute monopoly on power reserved for the Communist Party. The monument never saw the light of day. In 1962 the first secretary authorized the publication of *One Day in the Life of Ivan Denisovich*, by Aleksandr Solzhenitsyn. On 24

October 1964 Khrushchev was stripped of his powers, but his life was spared, and he died in obscurity in 1971.

There is a substantial degree of scholarly consensus regarding the importance of the "Secret Speech," which represented a fundamental break in Communism's twentieth-century trajectory. François Furet, on the verge of quitting the French Communist Party in 1954, wrote these words on the subject:

> Now all of a sudden the "Secret Speech" of February 1956 had single-handedly shattered the Communist idea then prevailing around the world. The voice that denounced Stalin's crimes did not come from the West but from Moscow, and from the "holy of holies" in Moscow, the Kremlin. It was not the voice of a Communist who had been ostracized but the voice of the leading Communist in the world, the head of the Communist Party of the Soviet Union. Thus, instead of being tainted by the suspicion that was invariably leveled at accusations made by ex-Communists, Khrushchev's remarks gained the luster that reflected glory upon its leader . . . The extraordinary power of the "Secret Speech" on the mind stemmed from the fact that it did not have any opponents.[28]

This event was especially paradoxical inasmuch as a number of contemporaries had long warned the Bolsheviks about the inherent dangers of this course of action. From 1917 to 1918 disgruntlement arose even within the socialist movement itself, including among believers in the "great light from the East," who were suddenly relentless in their criticism of the Bolsheviks. Essentially the dispute centered upon the methods used by Lenin: violence, crime, and terror. From the 1920s to the 1950s, while the dark side of Bolshevism was being exposed by a number of witnesses, victims, and skilled observers (as well as in countless articles and other publications), people had to bide their time until the Communist rulers would recognize this themselves. Alas, the significance of this undoubtedly important development was misinterpreted by the growing body of public opinion as a recognition of the errors of Communism. This was indeed a misinterpretation, since the "Secret Speech" tackled only the question of Communists as victims; but at least this was a step in the right direction. It was the first confirmation of the testimony by witnesses and of previous studies, and it corroborated long-standing suspicions that Communism was responsible for creating a colossal tragedy in Russia.

The leaders of many "fraternal parties" were initially unconvinced of the need to jump on Khrushchev's bandwagon. After some delay, a few leaders in other countries did follow Khrushchev's lead in exposing these atrocities. However, it was not until 1979 that the Chinese Communist Party divided Mao's policies between "great merits," which lasted until 1957, and "great errors," which came afterward. The Vietnamese contented themselves with oblique references to the genocide perpetrated by Pol Pot. As for Castro, the atrocities committed under him have been denied.

Before Khrushchev's speech, denunciation of crimes committed by Communists came only from their enemies or from Trotskyite dissidents or anarchists; and such denunciations had not been especially effective. The desire to bear witness was as strong among the survivors of Communist massacres as it had been among those who survived the Nazi slaughters. However, the survivors were few and far between, especially in France, where tangible experience of the Soviet concentration-camp system had directly affected only a few isolated groups, such as "In Spite of Ourselves," from Alsace-Lorraine.[29] Most of the time, however, the witness statements and the work carried out by independent commissions, such as David Rousset's International Commission on the Concentration Camp System and the Commission to Find the Truth about Stalin's Crimes, have been buried beneath an avalanche of Communist propaganda, aided and abetted by a silence born of cowardliness or indifference. This silence generally managed to win out over the sporadic moments of self-awareness resulting from the appearance of a new analytical work (such as Solzhenitsyn's *Gulag Archipelago*) or an irreproachable eyewitness account (such as Varlam Shalamov's *Kolyma Tales* and Pin Yathay's *Stay Alive, My Son*).[30] Regrettably, it was most tenacious in Western societies whenever the phenomenon of Communism came under the microscope. Until now they have refused to face the reality that the Communist system, albeit in varying degrees, possessed fundamentally criminal underpinnings. By refusing to acknowledge this, they were co-conspirators in "the lie," as perhaps best summed up by Friedrich Nietzsche: "Men believe in the truth of anything so long as they see that others strongly believe it is true."

Despite widespread reluctance to confront the issue, a number of observers have risen to the challenge. From the 1920s to the 1950s, for want of more reliable data (which were assiduously concealed by the Soviet regime) researchers were wholly reliant on information provided by defectors. Not only were these eyewitness accounts subject to the normal skepticism with which historians treat such testimony; they were also systematically discredited by sympathizers of the Communist system, who accused the defectors of being motivated by vengeance or of being the tools of anti-Communist powers. Who would have thought, in 1959, that a description of the Gulag could be provided by a high-ranking KGB defector, as in the book by Paul Barton?[31] And who would have thought of consulting Barton himself, an exile from Czechoslovakia whose real name was Jiří Veltruský, who was one of the organizers of the anti-Nazi insurrections in Prague in 1945 and who was forced to flee his country in 1948? Yet anyone who confronts the information held in recently opened classified archives will find that the accounts provided in 1959 were totally accurate.

In the 1960s and 1980s, Solzhenitsyn's *Gulag Archipelago* and later the "Red Wheel" cycle on the Russian Revolution produced a quantum shift in public opinion. Precisely because it was literature, and from a master craftsman, *The Gulag Archipelago* captured the true nature of an unspeakable system. However, even Solzhenitsyn had trouble piercing the veil. In 1975 one journalist from a major French daily compared Solzhenitsyn to Pierre Laval, Jacques Doriot, and Marcel Déat, "who welcomed the Nazis as liberators."[32] Nonetheless, his account was instrumental in exposing the system in much the same way that Shalamov brought Kolyma to life and Pin Yathay laid bare the atrocities in Cambodia. More recently still, Vladimir Bukovsky, one of the leading Soviet dissidents under Leonid Brezhnev, cried out in protest in *Reckoning with Moscow*, demanding the establishment of a new Nuremberg Tribunal to judge the criminal activities of the Communist regime. His book enjoyed considerable success in the West. At the same time, however, publications rehabilitating Stalin began to appear.[33]

At the end of the twentieth century, what motivation impels us to explore an issue so mired in tragedy, confusion, and controversy? Today, archives confirm these sporadic accounts of yesteryear, but they also allow us to go a step further. The internal archives maintained by the repressive apparatuses of the former Soviet Union, of the former "people's democracies," and of Cambodia bring to light the ghastly truth of the massive and systematic nature of the terror, which all too often resulted in full-scale crimes against humanity. The time has come to take a scholarly approach to this subject by documenting hard facts and by illuminating the political and ideological issues that obscure the matter at hand, the key issue that all these observers have raised: What is the true significance of crime in the Communist system?

From this perspective, what scholarly support can we count on? In the first place, our methods reflect our sense of duty to history. A good historian leaves no stone unturned. No other factors or considerations, be they political, ideological, or personal, should hinder the historian from engaging in the quest for knowledge, the unearthing and interpretation of facts, especially when these facts have been long and deliberately buried in the immense recesses of government archives and the conscience of the people. This history of Communist terror is one of the major chapters in the history of Europe and is directly linked to the two goals of the study of historical writing on totalitarianism. After all, we all know about the Hitlerian brand of totalitarianism; but we must not forget that there was also a Leninist and Stalinist version. It is no longer good enough to write partial histories that ignore the Communist brand of totalitarianism. It is untenable to draw a veil over the issue to ensure that the history of Communism is narrowed to its national, social, and cultural dimensions. The justice of this argument is amply confirmed by the fact that the phenomenon of totalitarianism was not limited to Europe and the Soviet period. The same applies to Maoist China, North Korea, and Pol Pot's Cambodia. Each national Communism has been linked by an umbilical cord to the Soviet womb, with its goal of expanding the worldwide movement. The history with which we are dealing is the history of a phenomenon that has spread throughout the world and that concerns all of humanity.

The second purpose of this book is to serve as a memorial. There is a moral obligation to honor the memory of the innocent and anonymous victims of a juggernaut that has systematically sought to erase even their memory. After the fall of the Berlin Wall and the collapse of Communism's center of power in Moscow, Europe, the continent that played host to the twentieth century's many tragedies, has set itself the task of reconstructing popular memory. This book is our contribution to that effort. The authors of this book carry that memory within themselves. Two of our contributors have a particular attachment to Central Europe, while the others are connected by firsthand experience with the theory and practice of revolution in 1968 or more recently.

This book, as both memorial and history, covers very diverse settings. It touches on countries in which Communism had almost no practical influence, either on society or on government power—Great Britain, Australia, Belgium, and others. Elsewhere Communism would show up as a powerful source of fear—in the United States after 1946—or as a strong movement (even if it never actually seized power there), as in France, Italy, Spain, Greece, and Portugal. In still other countries, where it had lost its decades-long grip on power, Communism is again reasserting itself—in Eastern Europe and Russia. Finally, its small flame is wavering in countries in which Communism still formally prevails—China, North Korea, Cuba, Laos, and Vietnam.

Others may have different perspectives on the issues of history and memory. In countries in which Communism had little influence or was merely dreaded, these issues will require a simple course of study and understanding. The countries that actually experienced the Communist system will have to address the issue of national reconciliation and decide whether the former Communist rulers are to be punished. In this connection, the reunified Germany may represent the most surprising and "miraculous" example—one need only think of the Yugoslav disaster by way of contrast. However, the former Czechoslovakia—now the Czech Republic and Slovakia—Poland, and Cambodia alike confront considerable trauma and suffering in their memory and history of Communism. In such places a modicum of amnesia, whether conscious or unconscious, may seem indispensable in helping to heal the spiritual, mental, emotional, personal, and collective wounds inflicted by a half-century or more of Communism. Where Communism still clings to power, the tyrants and their successors have either systematically covered up their actions, as in Cuba and China, or have continued to promote terror as a form of government, as in North Korea.

The responsibility for preserving history and memory undoubtedly has a moral dimension. Those whom we condemn may respond, "Who has given you the authority to say what is Good and what is Bad?"

According to the criteria proposed here, this issue was addressed well by the Catholic Church when Pope Pius XI condemned Nazism and Communism respectively in the encyclicals *Mit Brennender Sorge* of 14 March 1937 and *Divini redemptoris* of 19 March 1937. The latter proclaimed that God endowed humanity with certain rights, "the right to life, to bodily integrity, and to the necessary means of existence; the right to pursue one's ultimate goal in the path marked out for him by God; the right of association, and the right to possess and use property." Even though there is a certain hypocrisy in the church's pronouncement against the excessive enrichment of one class of people at the expense of others, the importance of the pope's appeal for the respect of human dignity is beyond question.

As early as 1931, Pius XI had proclaimed in the encyclical *Quadragesimo anno:* "Communism teaches and seeks two objectives: unrelenting class warfare and the complete eradication of private ownership. Not secretly or by hidden methods does it do this, but publicly, openly, and by employing any means possible, even the most violent. To achieve these objectives there is nothing it is afraid to do, nothing for which it has respect or reverence. When it comes to power, it is ferocious in its cruelty and inhumanity. The horrible slaughter and destruction through which it has laid waste to vast regions of Eastern Europe and Asia give evidence of this." Admittedly, these words originated from an institution that for several centuries had systematically justified the murder of non-Christians, spread the Inquisition, stifled freedom of thought, and supported dictatorial regimes such as those of General Francisco Franco and António Salazar.

However, even if the church was functioning in its capacity as a guardian of morality, how is a historian to respond when confronted by a "heroic" saga of Communist partisans or by a heartbreaking account from their victims? In his *Memoirs* François-René de Chateaubriand wrote: "When in the silence of abjection, no sound can be heard save that of the chains of the slave and the voice of the informer; when all tremble before the tyrant, and it is as dangerous to incur his favor as to merit his displeasure, the historian appears, entrusted with the vengeance of the people. Nero prospers in vain, for Tacitus has already been born within the Empire."[34] Far be it from us to advocate the cryptic concept of the "vengeance of the people." Chateaubriand no longer believed in this idea by the end of his life. However, at some modest level and almost despite himself, the historian can speak on behalf of those who have had their voices silenced as a result of terror. The historian is there to produce works of scholarship, and his first task is to establish the facts and data that will then become knowledge. Moreover, the historian's relationship to the history of Communism is an unusual one: Historians are obligated to chronicle the historiography of "the lie." And even if the opening of archives has provided them with access to essential materials, historians must guard against naïveté in the face of a number of complicated factors that are deviously calculated to stir up controversy. Nonetheless, this kind of historical knowledge cannot be seen in isolation from certain fundamental principles, such as respect for the rules of a representative democracy and, above all, respect for life and human dignity. This is the yardstick that historians use to "judge" the actors on the stage of history.

For these general reasons, no work of history or human memory can remain untouched by personal motives. Some of the contributors to this book were not always strangers to the fascinations of Communism. Sometimes they themselves took part (even if only on a modest scale) in the Communist system, either in the orthodox Leninist-Stalinist school or in its related or dissident varieties (Trotskyite, Maoist). And if they still remain closely wedded to the left—or, rather, precisely because they are still wedded to the left—it is necessary to take a closer look at the reasons for their self-deception. This mindset has led them down a certain intellectual pathway, characterized by the choice of topics they study, by their scholarly publications, and by the journals (such as *La nouvelle alternative* and *Communisme*) in which they publish. This book can do no more than provide an impetus for this particular type of reassessment. If these leftists pursue the task conscientiously, they will show that they too have a right to be heard on this issue, rather than leaving it to the increasingly influential extreme right wing. The crimes of Communism need to be judged from the standpoint of democratic values, not from the standpoint of ultranationalist or fascist philosophies.

This approach calls for cross-country analysis, including comparisons of China and the U.S.S.R., Cuba and Vietnam, and others. Alas, the documents currently available are decidedly mixed in quantity and quality; in some cases the archives have not yet been opened. However, we felt that we should carry on regardless, confining ourselves to facts that are crystal-clear and beyond question. We want this book to be a groundbreaking work that will lay a broad foundation for further study and thought by others.

This book contains many words but few pictures. The dearth of pictures is one of the more delicate issues involved in the cover-up of Communist crimes. In a media-saturated global society, the photographed or televised image has become the fount of "truth." Alas, we have only a handful of rare archival photographs of the Gulag and the *laogai*. There are no photographs of dekulakization or of the famine during the Great Leap Forward. The victorious powers at Nuremberg could at least photograph and film the thousands of bodies found at Bergen-Belsen. Those investigators also found photographs that had been taken by the tyrants themselves—for example, the picture of a Nazi shooting point blank at a woman with an infant in her arms. No such parallels existed in the darkness of the Communist world, where terror had been organized in strictest secrecy.

Readers may feel less than satisfied with the few photographic documents assembled here. They will need time to read, page after page, about the ordeal to which millions of people were subjected. They will have to make an effort to imagine the scale of the tragedy and to realize and appreciate how it will leave its mark on the history of the world for decades to come. Then readers must ask themselves the essential question, "Why?" Why did Lenin, Trotsky, Stalin, and others believe it necessary to exterminate all those whom they had branded as "enemies"? What made them imagine they could violate one of the basic tenets of civilization, "Thou shall not kill"? We will try, through this book, to answer that question.

A State against Its People: Violence, Repression, and Terror in the Soviet Union

Nicolas Werth

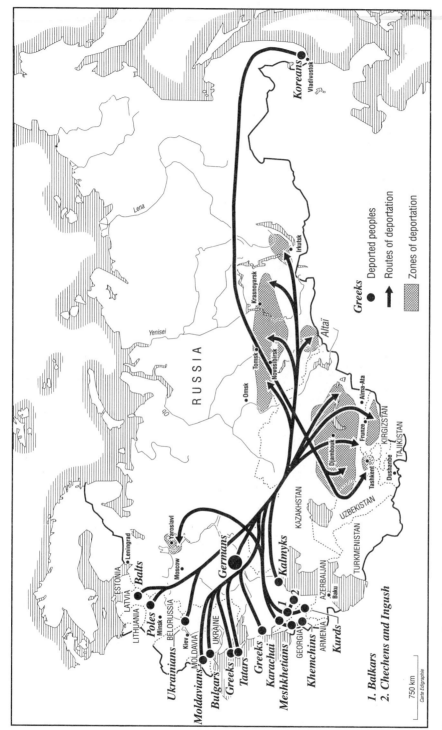

Deportation routes (based on a map in *L'histoire*, September 1994)

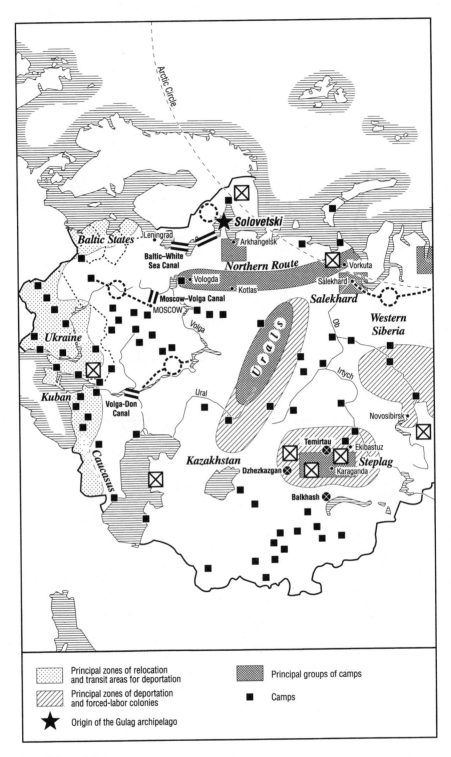

The Gulag archipelago

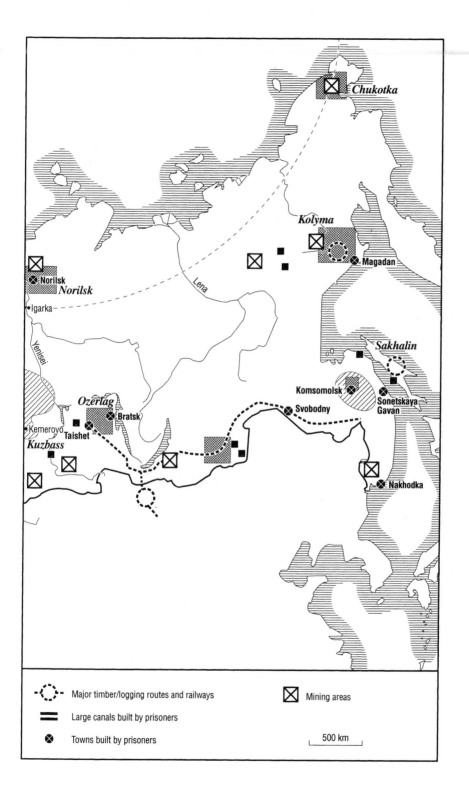

Chukotka

Kolyma

⊗ Magadan

Norilsk
⊗ Norilsk

• Igarka

Lena

Yenisei

Sakhalin

Komsomolsk ⊗
Sonetskaya
Gavan ⊗

Ozerlag
⊗ Bratsk
Svobodny

Kemerovo •
Taishet

Kuzbass

⊗ Nakhodka

---◯--- Major timber/logging routes and railways

══ Large canals built by prisoners

⊗ Towns built by prisoners

⊠ Mining areas

500 km

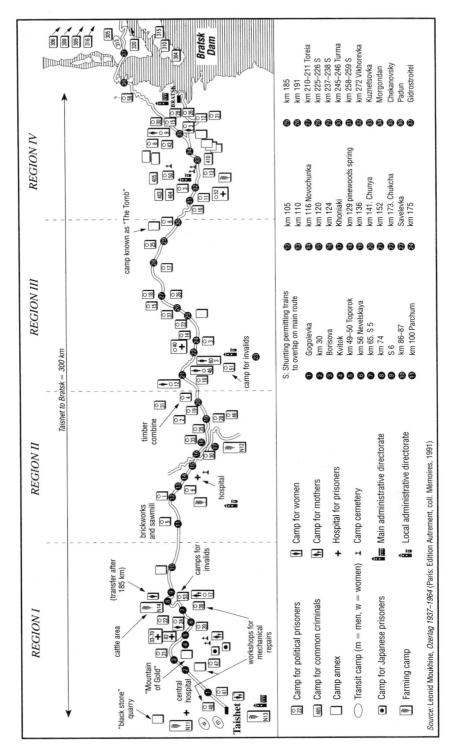

Source: Leonid Moukhine, *Ozerlag 1937–1964* (Paris: Edition Autrement, coll. Mémoires, 1991)

The Ozerlag archipelago

1 Paradoxes and Misunderstandings Surrounding the October Revolution

"With the fall of Communism, the necessity of demonstrating the 'historically inevitable' character of the Great Socialist October Revolution faded into the background, and 1917 could at last become a 'normal' historical event. Unfortunately, historians, like everyone else in our society, seem unwilling to break with the founding myth of Year Zero, of the year when it all seemed to begin—the happiness or misery of the Russian People."

These words, by a contemporary Russian historian, serve to illustrate an idea that has become a constant theme. More than eighty years after the event, the battle for control over the story of 1917 continues to rage.

For one historical school, which includes the proponents of what we might term the "liberal" version of events, the October Revolution was nothing more than a putsch imposed on a passive society. For these historians, October was the result of a clever conspiracy dreamed up by a handful of resourceful and cynical fanatics who had no real support anywhere else in the country. Today this is the preferred version of events for almost all Russian historians, as well as for the cultured elite and the leaders of post-Communist Russia. Deprived of all social and historical weight, the October Revolution of 1917 is reread as an accident that changed the course of history, diverting a prosperous, hard-working prerevolutionary Russia, well on its way to democracy, from its natural course. This view is defended quite loudly and fiercely, and as long as there exists a remarkable continuity in the power structure of post-Soviet Russia (nearly all of whose leaders are former Communist officials), there is a clear benefit to distancing present Russian society from the "monstrous Soviet parenthesis." All too clearly, it serves to liberate Russian society from any burden of guilt, and it marks a break with those obvious, public acts of contrition elicited by the painful rediscovery of Stalinism during the *perestroika* years. If it can be shown that the Bolshevik coup d'état of 1917 was nothing more than an accident, it follows that the Russian people were the collective innocent victims of these events.

Alternatively, Soviet historiography has attempted to demonstrate that the events of October 1917 were the logical, foreseeable, and inevitable culmination of a process of liberation undertaken by the masses, who consciously rallied to Bolshevism. In its various forms, this current of historiography has connected the story of 1917 to the issue of the legitimacy of the whole Soviet regime. If the Great Socialist October Revolution was the result of the inexorable march of history, and if it was an event that conveyed a message of emancipation to the entire world, then the Soviet political system and the state institutions that resulted from the revolution, despite the errors of the Stalinist period, were all necessarily legitimate. The fall of the Soviet regime naturally brought both a wholesale delegitimation of the October Revolution and the disappearance of the traditional Marxist view, which in its turn was consigned, in the famous Bolshevik formula, to "the dustbin of history." Nonetheless, like the memory of the Stalinist terror, the memory of the Marxist version of events lives on, perhaps even more vividly in the West than it does in the former U.S.S.R.

Rejecting both the liberal view and Marxist dogma, a third historiographic current has recently attempted to remove ideology from the history of the Russian Revolution altogether, in order to make clear, in the words of Marc Ferro, "why the uprising of October 1917 was simultaneously a mass movement and an event in which so few people actually took part." Among the many questions arising from the events of 1917, historians who refuse to accept the dominant oversimplified liberal view of events have identified some key problems. What role was played by the militarization of the economy and by the social unrest following from the entry of the Russian empire into World War I? Did a specific current of violence emerge that paved the way for political violence exercised against society in general? How did it come about that an essentially popular and plebeian movement, which was profoundly antiauthoritarian and antistate, brought to power the most dictatorial and most statist of political groups? Finally, what linkage can be established between the undeniable radicalization of Russian society throughout the year 1917 and the specific phenomenon of Bolshevism?

With the passage of time, and as a result of much recent stimulating and lively debate among historians, the October Revolution of 1917 now appears as the momentary convergence of two movements: on the one hand the carefully organized seizure of power by a party that differed radically in its practices, its ideology, and its organization from all other participants in the revolutionary process; and on the other a vast social revolution, which took many forms. The social revolution had many facets, including an immensely powerful and deep-rooted movement of rebellion among the peasantry, a rebellion whose origins stretched far back into Russian history and which was marked not simply by a hatred of the landowners, but also by profound distrust of both the city and the outside world in general—a distrust, in practice, of any form of state intervention.

The summer and autumn of 1917 thus appear as the culmination of the great cycle of revolts that began in 1902, and whose first real effects were felt from 1905 to 1907. The year 1917 was a decisive stage in the great agrarian revolution, a confrontation between the peasantry and the great landowners over the ownership of land, and, in the eyes of the peasants, the final longed-for realization of the "Black-Earth partition," or distribution of land according to the number of mouths to be fed in each family. But it was also an important stage in the confrontation between the peasantry and the state, in which the peasantry rejected all control by the city over the countryside. Seen from this point of view, 1917 was no more than a stage in the series of confrontations that continued in 1918–1922 and 1929–1933, and that ended in total defeat for the countryside as a result of enforced collectivization.

Throughout 1917, at the same time that the peasant revolution was gaining momentum, a process of fundamental decay was taking place in the army, which was made up of more than 10 million peasant soldiers mobilized to fight a war whose significance escaped them. Russian generals unanimously deplored the lack of patriotism among these peasant soldiers, whose civic horizons seldom extended beyond the boundaries of their own rural communities.

A third basic movement arose within the politically active industrial working class, highly concentrated in the big cities, which accounted for scarcely 3 percent of the working population. The urban milieu distilled all the social contradictions arising from a process of economic modernization that had lasted no more than a single generation. From this environment was born a movement aimed at the protection of the rights of workers, understood through a few key political slogans such as "workers' power" and "power to the soviets."

The fourth and final movement originated in the rapid emancipation of the diverse nations under imperial Russian rule. Many of these nations demanded first autonomy, then independence.

Each of these movements progressed at its own pace, according to its own internal dynamic; and each had its own specific aspirations, aspirations that clearly were not reducible to Bolshevik slogans or the political activities of that party. But each of these became a catalyst for the destruction of traditional institutions and the erosion of all forms of authority. For a brief but decisive instant in October 1917, the Bolshevik revolt—the action of a political minority acting in what was effectively a political vacuum—coincided with the aspirations of all these other movements, despite their disparate medium- and long-term objectives. For a short time the political coup d'état and social revolution coincided, or, more precisely, were telescoped together, before they moved apart again in the ensuing decades of dictatorship.

The social and national movements that exploded in the autumn of 1917 developed out of a particular conjunction of circumstances, including severe economic crisis, upheavals in social relations, the general failure of the apparatus of the state, and, perhaps most important, a total war that contributed to the general climate of brutality.

Far from reviving the tsarist regime and reinforcing the imperfect cohesion of society, World War I ruthlessly revealed the fragility of an autocracy already shaken by the revolution of 1905–06 and progressively weakened by political vacillation between insufficient concessions and reversions to stubborn conservatism. The war also underscored the weaknesses of an incomplete economic modernization dependent on regular inflows of foreign capital, specialists, and technology. Finally, the war reinforced the deep divide between urban Russia, the seat of power and industry, and rural Russia, the locus of largely independent and traditional communities.

Like all the other participants in the conflict, the tsarist government had counted on a quick war. Russia's lack of access to the sea and the economic blockade brutally revealed the extent of the country's dependence on foreign suppliers. The loss of its western provinces after the 1915 invasion by Austro-Hungarian forces deprived Russia of the products of Poland's highly developed industry. The domestic economy did not long withstand the test of war: a lack of spare parts plunged the transportation system into chaos as early as 1915. The almost complete conversion of Russian factories to the war effort squeezed production for domestic consumption, and within a few months shortages were common and inflation and poverty rampant. The situation deteriorated rapidly in the countryside: an abrupt end to agricultural loans and land reallocation, a large-scale mobilization of men into the army, the requisitioning of livestock and grain, the scarcity of manufactured goods, and the destruction of networks of exchange between town and country all brought the process of agrarian transformation, begun in 1906 by Prime Minister Pyotr Stolypin (assassinated in 1911), to a grinding halt. Three consecutive years of war strengthened the peasant belief that the state was an alien and hostile force. Daily privations in an army in which soldiers were treated more like serfs than like citizens exacerbated the tensions between officers and their men, while a series of defeats undercut the little prestige remaining to the imperial regime. The deep-seated tradition of violence in the Russian countryside, expressed in the immense uprisings of 1902–1906, grew ever stronger.

By the end of 1915 it was clear that the forces of law and order no longer existed. In the face of the regime's apparent passivity, committees and associations began to spring up everywhere, taking control of services no longer provided by the state, such as tending to the sick and bringing food to the cities and the army. The Russians in effect began to govern themselves; a great movement took shape whose depth and scope no one could have predicted. But in order to prevail, this movement would have needed encouragement and help from the seat of power, whose forces were concurrently dissolving.

Instead of attempting to build bridges between the government and the most advanced elements of civic society, Nicholas II clung to the image of himself as a populist monarch, the good paterfamilias of the state and the peasantry. He assumed personal command of the armies, a suicidal act for an autocracy staring national defeat in the face. Isolated in his private train at the Mogilev headquarters, from the autumn of 1915 onward, Nicholas II ceased to govern the country, surrendering that task to the Empress Alexandra, whose German origins made her very unpopular.

In fact the government had been losing its grip on power throughout 1916. The Duma, Russia's first nationally elected assembly, sat for only a few weeks a year, and governments and ministers, all equally unpopular and incompetent, came and went in quick succession. Rumors abounded that the Empress Alexandra's coterie, which included Rasputin, had conspired to open the country to enemy invasion. It became clear that the autocracy was incapable of winning the war, and by the end of 1916 the country was in effect ungovernable. In an atmosphere of political crisis, typified by the assassination of Rasputin on 31 December, strikes, which had been extremely rare at the outbreak of the war, became increasingly common. Unrest spread to the army, and the total chaos of the transport system broke the munitions distribution network. The days of February 1917 thus overtook an entirely discredited and weakened regime.

The fall of the tsarist regime, which came after just five days of workers' demonstrations and the mutiny of a few thousand men in the Petrograd garrison, revealed not only the weakness of the regime and the disarray of an army whose commanders did not even dare try to quell the popular uprising, but also the unpreparedness of the profoundly divided opposition, from the liberals of the Constitutional Democratic Party to the Social Democrats.

At no time did the political forces of the opposition shape or guide this spontaneous popular revolution, which began in the streets and ended in the plush suites of the Tauride Palace, the seat of the Duma. The liberals feared the mob; the socialists feared military reaction. Protracted negotiations between the liberals, who were concerned about the spread of the disturbances, and the socialists, who saw this "bourgeois" revolution as perhaps the first step on the long path to a socialist revolution, resulted in a vague idea of power-sharing. The liberal and socialist camps came to be represented in two distinct and incompatible institutions. The provisional government, concerned with the liberal objectives of social order and parliamentary democracy, strove to build a Russia that was modern, capitalist, and resolutely faithful to its French and British allies. Its archrival was the Petrograd Soviet, created by a handful of militant socialists in the great tradition of the St. Petersburg Soviet of 1905 to represent directly the revolutionary will of "the masses." But this soviet was itself a rapidly evolving phenomenon, at the mercy of its own expanding, decentralized structure and of the ever-changing public opinion it claimed to represent.

The three successive provisional governments that ruled Russia from 2 March to 25 October 1917 proved incapable of solving the problems inherited from the *ancien régime:* the economic crisis, the failing war effort, working-class unrest, and the agrarian problem. The new men in power—the liberals of the Constitutional Democratic Party, the majority in the first two governments, and the Mensheviks and Socialist Revolutionaries, the majority in the third—belonged to the cultivated urban elite, those advanced elements of civil society who were torn between a naive, blind trust in the "people" and a fear of the incomprehensible "dark masses" who engulfed them. For the most part, at least for the first few months of a revolution remarkable for its pacific nature, they gave free rein to the democratic impulse that had emerged with the fall of the old regime. Idealists like Prince Lvov, the head of the first two provisional governments, dreamed of making Russia "the freest country in the world." "The spirit of the Russian people," he wrote in one of his first manifestos, "has shown itself, of its own accord, to be a universally democratic spirit. It is a spirit that seeks not only to dissolve into universal democracy, but also to lead the way proudly down the path first marked out by the French revolution, toward Liberty, Equality, and Fraternity."

Guided by these beliefs, the provisional government extended democratic principles to as many as it could, bringing new freedoms and universal suffrage, outlawing all discrimination on grounds of class, race, or religion, recognizing the rights of both Poland and Finland to home rule, and promising autonomy to nationalist minorities. The government imagined that all these efforts would have far-reaching effects, causing an upsurge in patriotism, consolidating social cohesion, assuring military victory alongside the Allied forces, and solidly linking the new regime to other Western democracies. But out of a finicky solicitude for legality the government refused, in wartime conditions, to adopt measures that would have secured the future. It held firmly to remaining "provisional" and deliberately left unresolved the most pressing issues: the problem of the war and the problem of land. In the few months of its rule the provisional government proved no more capable than its predecessor of coping with the economic crisis, closely linked to the waging of the war; problems of supply, poverty, inflation, the breakdown of economic networks, the closing of businesses, and the massive upsurge in unemployment all exacerbated the climate of social tension.

In the face of the government's passivity, society continued to organize itself independently. Within a few weeks thousands of soviets, neighborhood and factory committees, armed groups of workers (the Red Guards), and committees of soldiers, peasants, Cossacks, and housewives sprang into existence. These were new forms of political expression in Russia, providing previously unknown forums for public opinion, claims for compensation, new initiatives, and debates. It was a veritable festival of liberty, which became more violent day by day, as the February revolution had unleashed resentment and social frustration long held in check. *Mitingovanie* ("the never-ending meeting") was the opposite of the democratic parliamentary process envisaged by the politicians of the new regime. The radicalization of social movements continued throughout 1917.

The workers' demands evolved from the economic—an eight-hour day, an end to fines and other onerous regulations, social insurance, wage increases—to political demands that implied a radical shift in social relations between workers and employers. Workers organized into factory committees whose chief objectives were control of the hiring process, the prevention of factory closings, and even control of the means of production. But to be viable, worker control required a completely new form of government, "soviet power," which alone was capable of radical measures, especially the seizure and nationalization of business, an aim that had been inconceivable in the spring of 1917.

The role of the peasant-soldiers—a mass of 10 million mobilized men—was decisive in the revolutions of 1917. The rapid dissolution of the Russian army, hastened by desertion and pacifism, propelled the collapse of state institutions. Basing their authority on the first decree issued by the provisional government—the famous "Order Number One," abolishing the worst of the disciplinary rules for soldiers in the imperial army—committees of soldiers pushed the limits of their power. They elected new officers and even took part in planning military strategies and tactics. This idea of "soldier power" paved the way for what General Aleksei Brusilov, commander in chief of the Russian army, termed a "Bolshevism of the trenches." In his description, "The soldiers didn't have the faintest idea of what Communism, the proletariat, or the constitution actually meant. They wanted peace, land, and the freedom to live without laws, without officers, and without landlords. Their Bolshevism was nothing more than a longing for an idealized sort of liberty—anarchy, in fact."

After the failure of the last Russian offensive in June 1917, the army began to fall apart; hundreds of officers, accused by the troops of being counterrevolutionaries, were arrested by the soldiers and massacred. The number of desertions soared—by August and September there were tens of thousands every day. The peasant-soldiers had one goal—to return home as quickly as possible, so as not to miss out on the distribution of land and livestock previously belonging to the landowners. From June to October 1917 more than 2 million soldiers, tired of the fighting and of the appalling deprivations they had lived through in their garrisons and trenches, deserted the rapidly disintegrating army. Inevitably their return increased the unrest pervading the countryside.

Until the summer of 1917, the agrarian trouble spots had been relatively localized, particularly in comparison with the agrarian revolts during the revolution of 1905–06. Once news of the tsar's abdication had spread, a peasant assembly met and drew up a petition containing their grievances and demands: the land should be given to whose who worked it, fallow land belonging to the landowners should be immediately redistributed, and all rents should be drastically reduced. Slowly the peasants became more and more organized, setting up agricultural committees on local and regional levels headed by leading members of the rural intelligentsia such as schoolteachers, agronomists, doctors, and Orthodox priests, all of whom sympathized with the aims of the Socialist Revolutionaries. From May and June onward, many agrarian committees simply seized agricultural material and livestock belonging to the landowners and appropriated woods, pastures, and fallow land. In this battle for land, the main victims clearly were the great land barons, but the kulaks (the better-off peasants, who had taken advantage of Stolypin's reforms to set up small holdings on their own and thus become free of obligations to the community) also suffered as a group. Even before the October Revolution the kulaks, who had been the soft targets of Bolshevik rhetoric—which caricatured them in slogans as "money-grubbing peasants," "the rural bourgeoisie," and "blood-sucking kulaks"—were no longer the important force they had been. In fact by this point many of them had been forced to return most of their livestock, machinery, and land to the community, which then redistributed it according to the ancestral egalitarian principle that counted the number of mouths to be fed.

During the summer the agrarian troubles became more and more violent, fueled by the return of hundreds of thousands of armed deserters. By the end of August, disillusioned by the broken promises of a government that seemed to be delaying agrarian reforms, the peasants mounted assaults on the manor houses, burning and sacking them in the hope of driving out the hated land-owners once and for all. In Ukraine and in the central provinces of Russia—Tambov, Penza, Voronezh, Saratov, Orel, Tula, and Ryazan—thousands of houses were burned and hundreds of landowners killed.

Faced with the expansion of this social revolution, the ruling elite and the political parties—with the notable exception of the Bolsheviks—all wavered between the desire to control the movement in some fashion and the temptation of a simple military putsch. After taking their places in the government in May, both the Mensheviks, who were popular in working-class areas, and the Social-ist Revolutionaries, who had a stronger base in the countryside than any other political group, proved unable to carry out the reforms they had always de-manded—particularly in the case of the Socialist Revolutionaries, land reform. For the most part, this failure stemmed from the fact that they were cooperating with a government concerned primarily with social order and law-abiding behavior. Once they had become the managers and leaders of an essentially bourgeois state, the moderate socialist parties left the more radical calls for reform to the Bolsheviks, without, however, reaping any great benefit from their participation in a government that was slowly losing its grip on the political realities in the country.

In the face of this growing anarchy, the captains of industry, the land-owners, the leaders of the army, and some of the more disillusioned liberals considered mounting a military coup, an idea proposed by General Lavr Kornilov. Most of them abandoned the idea, since a military putsch would inevitably have destroyed the civil power of the elected provisional government led by Aleksandr Kerensky. The failure of General Kornilov's putsch on 24–27 August did, however, lead to the final crisis of the provisional government. While the proponents of civil versus military dictatorships engaged in fruitless arguments, the central institutions of the state—the justice system, the civil service, the army—were disintegrating.

But it would be a mistake to describe the radicalization of the urban and rural populations as a process of "bolshevization." The shared slogans—"workers' power" and "power to the soviets"—had different meanings for the militant workers and the Bolshevik leaders. In the army, the "Bolshevism of the trenches" reflected above all a general aspiration for peace, shared by combatants from all the countries engaged in the bloodiest and most all-consuming war that the world had ever seen. The peasant revolution followed a more or less autonomous course, more sympathetic to the Socialist Revolu-tionary program, which favored the "Black-Earth partition" of land. The Bolshevik approach to the agrarian question was in fact antithetical to peasant wishes, favoring the nationalization of all land and its subsequent exploitation through enormous collective farms. In the countryside little was known about the Bolsheviks except for the confused reports brought home by deserters, whose message could be summed up in those two magic words "land" and "peace." Membership in the Bolshevik movement seems to have numbered no more than two thousand at the beginning of October 1917. But as a constellation of committees, soviets, and other small groups rushed to fill the wholesale institutional vacuum of that autumn, the environment was perfect for a small, well-organized group to exercise a disproportionate amount of power. And that is exactly what the Bolshevik Party did.

Since its founding in 1903, the party had remained outside the other currents of social democracy in both Russia and Europe, chiefly because of its will to break radically with the existing social and political order and because of its conception of itself as a highly structured, disciplined, elitist avant-garde of professional revolutionaries. The Bolsheviks were thus the complete opposite of the Menshevik and other European social-democratic parties, which allowed large memberships and widely differing points of view.

World War I further distilled Leninist Bolshevism. Rejecting collaboration with all other currents of social democracy, Lenin became increasingly isolated, justifying his theoretical position in essays like *Imperialism, the Highest Stage of Capitalism*. He began to argue that the revolution was destined to occur not in countries where capitalism was most advanced, but rather in countries like Russia that were considerably less developed economically, provided that the revolutionary movement was led by a disciplined avant-garde of revolutionaries who were prepared to go to extremes. That meant, in this case, creating a dictatorship of the proletariat and transforming "the imperialist war" into a civil war.

In a letter of 17 October 1917 to Aleksandr Shlyapnikov, Lenin wrote:

> The least bad thing that could happen in the short term would be the defeat of tsarism in the war . . . The essence of our work (which must be persistent, systematic, and perhaps extremely long-term) is to aim for the transformation of the war into a civil war. When that will happen is another question, as it is not yet clear. We must wait for the moment to ripen, and systematically force it to ripen . . . We can neither promise civil war nor decree it, but we must work toward that end for as long as we have to.

Throughout the war Lenin returned to the idea that the Bolsheviks had to be ready to encourage civil war by all possible means. "Anyone who believes in class war," he wrote in September 1916, "must recognize that civil war, in any class-based society, is the natural continuation, development, and result of class war."

After the February revolution (which occurred while most of the Bolsheviks were in exile or abroad), Lenin—unlike the vast majority of the leaders of his party—predicted the failure of the conciliatory policies pursued by the provisional government. In his four *Letters from Abroad*, penned in Zurich on 20–25 March 1917, of which the Bolshevik daily *Pravda* dared print only the first (so far were they from the political ideas held at the time by the leaders of the Petrograd Bolsheviks), he demanded an immediate rupture between the Petrograd Soviet and the provisional government, as well as active preparations for the subsequent "proletarian" stage of the revolution. As he saw it, the appearance of the soviets was the sign that the revolution had already passed through its "bourgeois phase." Revolutionary agents should now seize power by force and put a stop to the imperialist war, even if this meant the beginning of a civil war.

When he returned to Russia on 3 April 1917, Lenin continued to defend these extreme positions. In his famous *April Theses* he reiterated his implacable hostility to both a parliamentary republic and the democratic process. Met with blank incomprehension and outright hostility by most of the Bolshevik leaders in Petrograd, Lenin's ideas nevertheless began to take hold, particularly among the new recruits to the party, whom Stalin termed *praktiki,* "practitioners" (as opposed to the theoreticians). Within a few months plebeian elements, including peasant-soldiers, occupied a central place in the party and outnumbered the urban and intellectual elements. These militants, with their more humble origins, brought with them the violence of Russian peasant culture exacerbated by three years of war. With little background in politics, they sought to transform the original theoretical and intellectual Bolshevism unhindered by any of the limitations imposed by Marxist dogma. In particular, they had little interest in the question of whether a "bourgeois stage" was necessary in the transition to real socialism. Believing only in direct action and in force, they supported a strand of Bolshevism in which theoretical debates increasingly gave way to the far more pressing issue of the seizure of power.

Lenin was caught between two opposing forces: a plebeian mass increasingly impatient for action, made up of the sailors at the Kronstadt naval base near Petrograd, certain regiments in the capital, and the worker battalions of Red Guards in Vyborg; and a group of leaders haunted by fear that an overhasty insurrection would fail. Contrary to commonly held historical opinion, throughout 1917 the Bolshevik Party was profoundly divided, torn between the timidity of one group and the overenthusiasm of the other. At this stage the famous party discipline was more an act of faith than a concrete reality. In July 1917, as a result of troubles at the naval base and confrontations with the government forces, the Bolshevik Party was very nearly destroyed altogether. In the aftermath of the bloody demonstrations in Petrograd from 3 to 5 July, its leaders were arrested, and some, like Lenin himself, were forced into exile.

But the Bolshevik Party resurfaced at the end of August 1917, in a situation quite favorable for an armed seizure of power. The powerlessness of the government to resolve the great problems it faced had become clear, particularly in the wake of the decay of traditional institutions and authorities, the growth of social movements, and the failure of General Kornilov's attempted military coup.

Again Lenin's personal role, both as theorist and as strategist of the seizure of power, was decisive. In the weeks preceding the Bolshevik coup d'état of 25 October 1917, he personally prepared all the necessary stages for the military takeover. He was to be deterred neither by an unforeseen uprising of the masses nor by the "revolutionary legalism" of Bolsheviks such as Grigory Zinoviev and Lev Kamenev, who, made cautious by the bitter experience of the July days, preferred to have the support of a majority of social democrats and revolutionary socialists of all tendencies. From exile in Finland, Lenin sent a constant stream of articles and letters to the Central Committee of the Bolshevik Party, calling for the uprising to begin. "By making immediate offers of peace and giving land to the peasants, the Bolsheviks will establish a power base that no one will be able to overturn," he wrote. "There is no point in waiting for a formal majority for the Bolsheviks; revolutions do not wait for such things. History will never forgive us if we do not seize power immediately."

Lenin's urgency in the face of an increasingly revolutionary situation left most of the Bolshevik leaders skeptical and perplexed. It was surely enough, they believed, to stick behind the masses and incite them to spontaneous acts of violence, to encourage the disruptive influence of social movements, and to sit tight until the Second All-Russian Congress of Soviets, planned for 20 October. It was more than likely that the Bolsheviks would achieve a plurality at the assembly, since they would be overrepresented by the soviets from the great working-class areas and from the army. Lenin, however, greatly feared the power-sharing that might result if the transfer of power took place as a result of a vote at the Congress of Soviets. For months he had been clamoring for power to devolve to the Bolsheviks alone, and he wanted at all costs to ensure that the Bolsheviks seized power through a military insurrection, before the opening of the Second Congress. He knew that the other socialist parties would universally condemn such a move, and thus effectively force themselves into opposition, leaving all power in the hands of the Bolsheviks.

On 10 October, having returned secretly to Petrograd, Lenin gathered together twelve of the twenty-one members of the Central Committee of the Bolshevik Party. After ten hours of negotiations he persuaded a majority to vote in favor of the most important decision ever made by the party—to undertake an immediate armed uprising. The decision was approved by ten to two, the dissenters being Zinoviev and Kamenev, who wished to wait for the Second

Congress of Soviets. On 16 October, despite opposition from the moderate socialists, Trotsky therefore set up the Petrograd Revolutionary Military Committee (PRMC), a military organization theoretically under the control of the Petrograd Soviet but in fact run by the Bolsheviks. Its task was to organize the seizure of power through an armed insurrection—and thus to prevent a popular anarchist uprising that might have eclipsed the Bolshevik Party.

In accordance with Lenin's wishes, the number of direct participants in the Great Socialist October Revolution was extremely limited—a few thousand soldiers, the sailors from Kronstadt, Red Guards who had rallied to the cause of the PRMC, and a few hundred militant Bolsheviks from factory committees. Careful preparation and a lack of opposition allowed the whole operation to proceed smoothly and with very few casualties. Significantly, the seizure of power was accomplished in the name of the PRMC. Thus the Bolshevik leaders attributed all their power to a single event that no one outside the party's Central Committee could link to the Congress of Soviets.

Lenin's strategy worked. Faced with this *fait accompli*, the moderate socialists, after denouncing "an organized military action deliberately planned behind the back of the soviets," simply walked out of the Congress. Only the small group of left-wing Socialist Revolutionaries remained, and they joined the Bolsheviks in ratifying the coup, voting in a text drawn up by Lenin that gave "all power to the soviets." This purely formal resolution allowed the Bolsheviks to authenticate a fiction that was to deceive credulous generations for decades to come—that they governed in the name of the people in "the Soviet state." A few hours later, before breaking up, the Congress ratified a new Bolshevik government—the Soviet Council of People's Commissars (SNK), presided over by Lenin—and approved two decrees about peace and land.

Very soon misunderstandings and conflicts arose between the new regime and the social movements, which until then had acted independently to destroy the old political, social, and economic order. The first conflict of interest concerned the agrarian revolution. The Bolsheviks, who had always stood for the nationalization of all land, were now compelled by a combination of unfavorable circumstances to hijack the Socialist Revolutionary program and to approve the redistribution of land to the peasants. The "Decree on Land" stated that "all right of property regarding the land is hereby abolished without indemnity, and all land is hereby put at the disposal of local agrarian committees for redistribution." In practice it did little more than legitimate what had already taken place since the summer of 1917, namely the peasant confiscation of land from the landlords and the kulaks. Forced to go along with this autonomous peasant revolution because it had facilitated their own seizure of power, the Bolsheviks were to wait a decade before having their way. The enforced collectivization of the countryside, which was to be the bitterest confrontation between the Soviet regime and the peasantry, was the tragic resolution of the 1917 conflict.

The second conflict arose between the Bolshevik Party and all the spontaneous new social structures, such as factory committees, unions, socialist parties, neighborhood organizations, Red Guards, and above all soviets, which had helped destroy traditional institutions of power and were now fighting for the extension of their own mandates. In a few weeks these structures found themselves either subordinated to the Bolshevik Party or suppressed altogether. By a clever sleight-of-hand, "All power to the soviets," probably the single most popular slogan in the whole of Russia in October 1917, became a cloak hiding the power of the Bolshevik Party over the soviets. "Workers' control," another major demand of the workers, in whose interest the Bolsheviks claimed to be acting, was rapidly sidelined in favor of state control in the name of the workers over businesses and workforces. A mutual incomprehension was born between the workers, who were obsessed by unemployment, decline in real wages, and ever-present hunger, and a state whose only concern was economic efficiency. From as early as December 1917 the new regime was forced to confront mounting claims from workers and an increasing number of strikes. In a few weeks the Bolsheviks lost the greater part of the confidence that they had carefully cultivated in the labor force throughout the year.

The third misunderstanding developed between the Bolsheviks and the satellite nations of the former tsarist empire. The Bolshevik coup d'état had accelerated their desire for independence, and they thought that the new regime would support their cause. In recognizing the equality and sovereignty of the peoples of the old empire, as well as their right to self-determination and secession, the Bolsheviks seemed to have invited these peoples to break away from centralized Russian control. In a few months the Finns, Poles, Baltic nations, Ukrainians, Georgians, Armenians, and Azerbaijanis were claiming their independence. Overwhelmed, the Bolsheviks soon put their own economic needs before the rights of these nations, since Ukrainian wheat, the petroleum and minerals of the Caucasus, and all the other vital economic interests of the new state were perceived to be irreplaceable. In terms of the control it exercised over its territories, the new regime proved itself to be a more worthy inheritor of the empire than even the provisional government had been.

These conflicts and misunderstandings were never truly resolved, but continued to grow, spawning an ever increasing divide between the new Soviet regime and society as a whole. Faced with new obstacles and the seeming intransigence of the population, the Bolshevik regime turned to terror and violence to consolidate its hold on the institutions of power.

2 The Iron Fist of the Dictatorship of the Proletariat

The new Bolshevik power structure was quite complicated. Its public face, "the power of the soviets," was formally represented by the Central Executive Committee, while the lawmaking apparatus of government was the Soviet Council of People's Commissars (SNK), which struggled to achieve some degree of domestic and international legitimacy and recognition. The government also had its revolutionary organization in the form of the Petrograd Revolutionary Military Committee (PRMC), which had been so central in the actual seizure of power. Feliks Dzerzhinsky, who from the earliest days had played a decisive role in the PRMC, characterized it as "a light, flexible structure that could swing into action at a moment's notice, without any bureaucratic interference. There were no restrictions when the time came for the iron fist of the dictatorship of the proletariat to smite its foe."

How did this "iron fist of the dictatorship of the proletariat" (an expression later used to describe the Bolshevik secret police, the Cheka) work in practice? Its organization was simple and extremely effective. The PRMC was made up of some sixty officials, including forty-eight Bolsheviks, a few Socialist Revolutionaries of the far left, and a handful of anarchists; and it was officially under the direction of a chairman, the Socialist Revolutionary Aleksandr Lazimir, who was assisted in his operations by a group of four that included Aleksandr Antonov-Ovseenko and Dzerzhinsky. In fact during the fifty-three days of the PRMC's existence, more than 6,000 orders were drawn up, most of them scribbled on old bits of paper, and some twenty different people signed their name as chairman or secretary.

The same operational simplicity was to be found in the transmission of directives and the execution of orders: the PRMC acted through the intermediary of a network of nearly one thousand "commissars," who operated in many different fields—in military units, soviets, neighborhood committees, and administrations. Responsible only to the PRMC, these commissars often made decisions independently of the government or of the Bolshevik Central Committee. Beginning on 26 October (8 November),[1] while the Bolshevik leaders were off forming the government, a few obscure, anonymous commissars decided to "strengthen the dictatorship of the proletariat" by the following measures: forbidding counterrevolutionary tracts, closing all seven of the capital's principal newspapers (bourgeois and moderate socialist), taking control of radio and telegraph stations, and setting up a project for the requisitioning of apartments and privately owned cars. The closing of the newspapers was legalized by a government decree a few days later, and within another week, after some quite acrimonious discussions, it was approved by the Central Executive Committee of the Soviets.[2]

Unsure of their strength, and using the same tactic that had succeeded so well earlier, the Bolshevik leaders at first encouraged what they called the "revolutionary spontaneity of the masses." Replying to a delegation of representatives from rural soviets, who had come from the province of Pskov to inquire what measures should be taken to avoid anarchy, Dzerzhinsky explained that

> the task at hand is to break up the old order. We, the Bolsheviks, are not numerous enough to accomplish this task alone. We must allow the revolutionary spontaneity of the masses who are fighting for their emancipation to take its course. After that, we Bolsheviks will show the masses which road to follow. Through the PRMC it is the masses who speak, and who act against their class enemy, against the enemies of the people. We are here only to channel and direct the hate and the legitimate desire for revenge of the oppressed against their oppressors.

A few days earlier, at the 29 October (11 November) meeting of the PRMC, a few unidentified people had mentioned a need to combat the "enemies of the people" more vigorously. This formula would meet with great success in the months, years, and decades to follow. It was taken up again in the PRMC proclamation dated 13 November (26 November): "High-ranking functionaries in state administration, banks, the treasury, the railways, and the post and telegraph offices are all sabotaging the measures of the Bolshevik government. Henceforth such individuals are to be described as 'enemies of the people.' Their names will be printed in all newspapers, and lists of the enemies of the people will be put up in public places."[3] A few days after these lists were published, a new proclamation was issued: "All individuals suspected of sabotage, speculation, and opportunism are now liable to be arrested immediately as enemies of the people and transferred to the Kronstadt prisons."[4] In the space of a few days the PRMC had introduced two new notions that were to have lasting consequences: the idea of the "enemy of the people" and the idea of the "suspect."

On 28 November (11 December) the government institutionalized the notion of "enemy of the people." A decree signed by Lenin stipulated that "all leaders of the Constitutional Democratic Party, a party filled with enemies of the people, are hereby to be considered outlaws, and are to be arrested immediately and brought before a revolutionary court."[5] Such courts had just been set up in accordance with "Order Number One regarding the Courts," which effectively abolished all laws that "were in contradiction with the worker and peasant government, or with the political programs of the Social Democratic or Socialist Revolutionary parties." While waiting for the new penal code to be drawn up, judges were granted tremendous latitude to assess the validity of existing legislation "in accordance with revolutionary order and legality," a notion so vague that it encouraged all sorts of abuses. The courts of the old regime were immediately suppressed and replaced by people's courts and revolutionary courts to judge crimes and misdemeanors committed "against the proletarian state," "sabotage," "espionage," "abuse of one's position," and other "counterrevolutionary crimes." As Dmitry Kursky, the people's commissar of justice from 1918 to 1928, recognized, the revolutionary courts were not courts in the normal "bourgeois" sense of the term at all, but courts of the dictatorship of the proletariat, and weapons in the struggle against the counterrevolution, whose main concern was eradication rather than judgment.[6] Among the revolutionary courts was a "revolutionary press court," whose role was to judge all crimes committed by the press and to suspend any publication found to be "sowing discord in the minds of the people by deliberately publishing erroneous news."[7]

While these new and previously unheard-of categories ("suspects," "enemies of the people") were appearing and the new means of dealing with them emerging, the Petrograd Revolutionary Military Committee continued its own process of restructuring. In a city in which stocks of flour were so low that rations were less than half a pound of bread per day per adult, the question of the food supply was naturally of great importance.

On 4 (17) November a Food Commission was established, and its first proclamation stigmatized "the rich classes who profit from the misery of others," noting that "the time has come to requisition the surpluses of the rich, and all their goods as well." On 11 (24) November the Food Commission decided to send special detachments, made up of soldiers, sailors, workers, and Red Guards, to the provinces where cereals were produced "to procure food needed in Petrograd and at the front."[8] This measure, taken by one of the PRMC commissions, prefigured the forced requisitioning policy that was enforced for three years by detachments from the "food army," which was to be the essential factor in the conflicts between the new regime and the peasantry and was to provoke much violence and terror.

The Military Investigation Commission, established on 10 (23) November, was in charge of the arrest of "counterrevolutionary" officers (who were usually denounced by their own soldiers), members of "bourgeois" parties, and functionaries accused of "sabotage." In a very short time this commission was in charge of a diffuse array of issues. In the troubled climate of a starving city, where detachments of Red Guards and ad hoc militia groups were constantly requisitioning, commandeering, and pillaging in the name of the revolution, or on the strength of an uncertain mandate signed by some commissar, hundreds of individuals every day were brought before the commission for a wide variety of so-called crimes, including looting, "speculation," "hoarding products of the utmost necessity," "drunkenness," and "belonging to a hostile class."[9]

The Bolshevik appeals to the revolutionary spontaneity of the masses were in practice a difficult tool to use. Violence and the settling of old scores were widespread, as were armed robberies and the looting of shops, particularly of the underground stocks of the Winter Palace and of shops selling alcohol. As time passed the phenomenon became so widespread that at Dzerzhinsky's suggestion the PRMC established a commission to combat drunkenness and civil unrest. On 6 (19) December the commission declared a state of emergency in Petrograd and imposed a curfew to "put an end to the troubles and the unrest brought about by unsavory elements masquerading as revolutionaries."[10]

More than these sporadic troubles, what the revolutionary government feared was a widespread strike by state employees, which had started in the immediate aftermath of the coup d'état of 25 October (7 November). This threat was the pretext for the creation on 7 (20) December of the *V*serossiiskaya *Ch*rezvychainaya *K*omissiya po bor'be s kontr-revolyutsiei, spekulyatsiei i sabotazhem—the All-Russian Extraordinary Commission to Combat the Counterrevolution, Speculation, and Sabotage—which was to enter history under its initials as the *VChK*, abbreviated to the Cheka.

A few days after the creation of the Cheka, the government decided, not without hesitation, to disband the PRMC. As a provisional operating structure set up on the eve of the insurrection to direct operations on the ground, it had accomplished its task: it had facilitated the seizure of power and defended the new regime until it had time to create its own state apparatus. Henceforth, to avoid confusion about power structures and the danger of spreading responsibilities too widely, it was to transfer all its prerogatives to the legal government, the Council of People's Commissars.

At a moment judged to be so critical by their leaders, how could the Bolsheviks do without this "iron fist of the dictatorship of the proletariat"? At a meeting on 6 (19) December the government entrusted "Comrade Dzerzhinsky to establish a special commission to examine means to combat, with the most revolutionary energy possible, the general strike of state employees, and to investigate methods to combat sabotage." What Dzerzhinsky did gave rise to no discussion, as it seemed so clearly to be the correct response. A few days earlier, Lenin, always eager to draw parallels between the French Revolution and the Russian Revolution of 1917, had confided in his secretary Vladimir Bonch-Bruevich an urgent need to find "our own Fouquier-Tinville, to combat the counterrevolutionary rabble."[11] On 6 December Lenin's choice of a "solid proletarian Jacobin" resulted in the unanimous election of Dzerzhinsky, who in a few weeks, thanks to his energetic actions as part of the PRMC, had become the great specialist on questions of security. Besides, as Lenin explained to Bonch-Bruevich, "of all of us, it's Feliks who spent the most time behind bars of the tsarist prisons, and who had the most contact with the Okhrana [the tsarist political police]. He knows what he's doing!"

Before the government meeting of 7 (20) December Lenin sent a note to Dzerzhinsky:

> With reference to your report of today, would it not be possible to write a decree with a preamble such as the following: The bourgeoisie are still persistently committing the most abominable crimes and recruiting the very dregs of society to organize riots. The accomplices of the bourgeoisie, notably high-ranking functionaries and bank cadres, are also involved in sabotage and organizing strikes to undermine the measures the government is taking with a view to the socialist transformation of society. The bourgeoisie is even going so far as to sabotage the food supply, thus condemning millions to death by starvation. Exceptional measures will have to be taken to combat these saboteurs and counterrevolutionaries. Consequently, the Soviet Council of People's Commissars decrees that . . . .[12]

During the evening of 7 (20) December Dzerzhinsky presented his project to the SNK. He began his intervention with a speech on the dangers faced by the revolution "from within":

> To address this problem, the cruelest and most dangerous of all the problems we face, we must make use of determined comrades—solid, hard men without pity—who are ready to sacrifice everything for the

sake of the revolution. Do not imagine, comrades, that I am simply looking for a revolutionary form of justice. We have no concern about justice at this hour! We are at war, on the front where the enemy is advancing, and the fight is to the death. What I am proposing, what I am demanding, is the creation of a mechanism that, in a truly revolutionary and suitably Bolshevik fashion, will filter out the counterrevolutionaries once and for all!

Dzerzhinsky then launched into the core of his speech, transcribed as it appears in the minutes of the meeting:

> The task of the Commission is as follows: (1) to suppress and liquidate any act or attempted act of counterrevolutionary activity or sabotage, whatever its origin, anywhere on Russian soil; (2) to bring all saboteurs and counterrevolutionaries before a revolutionary court.
>
> The Commission will proceed by a preliminary inquiry, wherever this is indispensable to its task.
>
> The Commission will be divided into three sections: (1) Information; (2) Organization; (3) Operation.
>
> The Commission will attach particular importance to questions regarding the press, sabotage, the KDs [Constitutional Democrats], the right Socialist Revolutionaries, saboteurs, and strikers.
>
> The Commission is entitled to take the following repressive measures: to confiscate goods, expel people from their homes, remove ration cards, publish lists of enemies of the people, etc.
>
> Resolution: to approve this draft. To name the commission the All-Russian Extraordinary Commission to Combat the Counterrevolution, Speculation, and Sabotage.
>
> These resolutions are to be made public.[13]

This text, which discusses the founding of the Soviet secret police, undoubtedly raises a few questions. How, for example, is the difference between Dzerzhinsky's fiery-sounding speech and the relative modesty of the powers accorded the Cheka to be interpreted? The Bolsheviks were on the point of concluding an agreement with the left Socialist Revolutionaries (six of whose leaders had been admitted to the government on 12 December) to break their political isolation, at the crucial moment when they had to face the question of calling the Constituent Assembly, in which they still held only a minority. Accordingly they decided to keep a low profile, and contrary to the resolution adopted by the government on 7 (20) December, no decree announcing the creation of the Cheka and outlining its role was actually published.

As an "extraordinary commission," the Cheka was to prosper and act without the slightest basis in law. Dzerzhinsky, who like Lenin wanted nothing so much as a free hand, described it in the following astonishing fashion: "It is life itself that shows the Cheka the direction to follow." Life in this instance meant the "revolutionary terror of the masses," the street violence fervently encouraged by many of the Bolshevik leaders, who had momentarily forgotten their profound distrust of the spontaneous actions of the people.

When Trotsky, a people's commissar during the war, was addressing the delegates of the Central Executive Committee of the Soviets on 1 (14) December, he warned that "in less than a month, this terror is going to take extremely violent forms, just as it did during the great French Revolution. Not only prison awaits our enemies, but the guillotine, that remarkable invention of the French Revolution which has the capacity to make a man a whole head shorter."[14]

A few weeks later, speaking at a workers' assembly, Lenin again called for terror, describing it as revolutionary class justice:

> The Soviet regime has acted in the way that all revolutionary proletariats should act; it has made a clean break with bourgeois justice, which is an instrument of the oppressive classes . . . Soldiers and workers must understand that no one will help them unless they help themselves. If the masses do not rise up spontaneously, none of this will lead to anything . . . For as long as we fail to treat speculators the way they deserve—with a bullet in the head—we will not get anywhere at all.[15]

These calls for terror intensified the violence already unleashed in society by the Bolsheviks' rise to power. Since the autumn of 1917 thousands of the great agricultural properties had been attacked by brigades of angry peasants, and hundreds of the major landowners had been massacred. Violence had been omnipresent in Russia in the summer of 1917. The violence itself was nothing new, but the events of the year had allowed several different types of violence, already there in a latent state, to converge: an urban violence reacting against the brutality of capitalist relations at the heart of an industrial society; traditional peasant violence; and the modern violence of World War I, which had reintroduced extraordinary regression and brutality into human relations. The combination of these three forms of violence made for an explosive mix, whose effect was potentially devastating during the Russian Revolution, marked as it was by the failure of normal institutions of order and authority, by a rising sense of resentment and social frustrations accumulated over a long period, and by the political use of popular violence. Mutual suspicion had always been the norm between the townspeople and the peasants. For the peasants, more now than ever, the city was the seat of power and oppression; for the urban elite, and for professional revolutionaries who by a large majority were from the intelligentsia, the peasants were still, in Gorky's words, "a mass of half-savage people" whose "cruel instincts" and "animal individualism" ought to be brought to book by the "organized reason of the city." At the same time, politicians and intellectuals were all perfectly conscious that it was the peasant revolts that had shaken the provisional government, allowing the Bolsheviks, who were really a tiny minority in the country, to seize the initiative in the power vacuum that had resulted.

At the end of 1917 and the beginning of 1918, the new regime faced no serious opposition, and one month after the Bolshevik coup d'état it effectively controlled most of the north and the center of Russia as far as the mid-Volga, as well as some of the bigger cities, such as Baku in the Caucasus and Tashkent in Central Asia. Ukraine and Finland had seceded but were not demonstrating any warlike intentions. The only organized anti-Bolshevik military force was a small army of about 3,000 volunteers, the embryonic form of the future "White Army" that was being formed in southern Russia by General Mikhail Alekseev and General Kornilov. These tsarist generals were placing all their hopes in the Cossacks of the Don and the Kuban. The Cossacks were radically different from the other Russian peasants; their main privilege under the old regime had been to receive 30 hectares of land in exchange for military service up to the age of thirty-six. If they had no desire to acquire more land, they were zealous to keep the land they had already acquired. Desiring above all to retain their status and their independence, and worried by the Bolshevik proclamations that had proved so injurious to the kulaks, the Cossacks aligned themselves with the anti-Bolshevik forces in the spring of 1918.

"Civil war" may not be the most appropriate term to describe the first clashes of the winter of 1917 and the spring of 1918 in southern Russia, which involved a few thousand men from the army of volunteers and General Rudolf Sivers' Bolshevik troops, who numbered scarcely 6,000. What is immediately striking is the contrast between the relatively modest number of troops involved in these clashes and the extraordinary repressive violence exercised by the Bolsheviks, not simply against the soldiers they captured but also against civilians. Established in June 1919 by General Anton Denikin, commander in chief of the armed forces in the south of Russia, the Commission to Investigate Bolshevik Crimes tried to record, in the few months of its existence, the atrocities committed by the Bolsheviks in Ukraine, the Kuban, the Don region, and the Crimea. The statements gathered by this commission, which constitute the principal source of Sergei Melgunov's 1926 classic, *The Red Terror in Russia, 1918–1924,* demonstrate that innumerable atrocities were committed from January 1918 onward. In Taganrog units from Sivers' army had thrown fifty Junkers and "White" officers, their hands and feet bound, into a blast furnace. In Evpatoria several hundred officers and "bourgeois" were tied up, tortured, and thrown into the sea. Similar acts of violence occurred in most of the cities of the Crimea occupied by the Bolsheviks, including Sevastopol, Yalta, Alushta, and Simferopol. Similar atrocities are recorded from April and May 1918 in the big Cossack cities then in revolt. The extremely precise files of the Denikin commission record "corpses with the hands cut off, broken bones, heads ripped off, broken jaws, and genitals removed."[16]

As Melgunov notes, it is nonetheless difficult to distinguish the systematic practice of organized terror from what might otherwise be considered simply uncontrolled excesses. There is rarely mention of a local Cheka directing such massacres until August and September 1918; until that time the Cheka network was still quite sparse. These massacres, which targeted not only enemy combatants but also civilian "enemies of the people" (for instance, among the 240 people killed in Yalta at the beginning of March 1918, there were some 70 politicians, lawyers, journalists, and teachers, as well as 165 officers), were often carried out by "armed detachments," "Red Guards," and other, unspecified "Bolshevik elements." Exterminating the enemy of the people was simply the logical extension of a revolution that was both political and social. This conception of the world did not suddenly spring into being in the aftermath of October 1917, but the Bolshevik seizure of power, which was quite explicit on the issue, did play a role in its subsequent legitimation.

In March 1917 a young captain wrote a perceptive letter assessing the revolution and its effects on his regiment: "Between the soldiers and ourselves, the gap cannot be bridged. For them, we are, and will always remain, the *barini* [masters]. To their way of thinking, what has just taken place isn't a political revolution but a social movement, in which they are the winners and we are the losers. They say to us: 'You were the *barini* before, but now it's our turn!' They think that they will now have their revenge, after all those centuries of servitude."[17]

The Bolshevik leaders encouraged anything that might promote this aspiration to "social revenge" among the masses, seeing it as a moral legitimation of the terror, or what Lenin called "the just civil war." On 15 (28) December 1917 Dzerzhinsky published an appeal in *Izvestiya* (News) inviting all soviets to organize their own Chekas. The result was a swift flourishing of "commissions," "detachments," and other "extraordinary organizations" that the central authorities had great problems in controlling when they decided, a few months later, to end such "mass initiatives" and to organize a centralized, structured network of Chekas.[18]

Summing up the first six months of the Cheka's existence in July 1918, Dzerzhinsky wrote: "This was a period of improvisation and hesitation, during which our organization was not always up to the complexities of the situation."[19] Yet even by that date the Cheka's record as an instrument of repression was already enormous. And the organization, whose personnel had numbered no more than 100 in December 1917, had increased to 12,000 in a mere six months.

Its beginnings had been modest. On 11 (24) January 1918 Dzerzhinsky had sent a note to Lenin: "We find the present situation intolerable, despite the important services we have already rendered. We have no money whatever. We work night and day without bread, sugar, tea, butter, or cheese. Either take measures to authorize decent rations for us or give us the power to make our own requisitions from the bourgeoisie."[20] Dzerzhinsky had recruited approximately 100 men, for the most part old comrades-in-arms, mostly Poles and people from the Baltic states, nearly all of whom had also worked for the PRMC, and who became the future leaders of the GPU of the 1920s and the NKVD of the 1930s: Martin Latsis, Viacheslav Menzhinsky, Stanislav Messing, Grigory Moroz, Jan Peters, Meir Trilisser, Josif Unshlikht, and Genrikh Yagoda.

The first action of the Cheka was to break a strike by state employees in Petrograd. The method was swift and effective—all its leaders were arrested—and the justification simple: "Anyone who no longer wishes to work with the people has no place among them," declared Dzerzhinsky, who also arrested a number of the Menshevik and Socialist Revolutionary deputies elected to the Constituent Assembly. This arbitrary act was immediately condemned by Isaac Steinberg, the people's commissar of justice, who was himself a left Socialist Revolutionary and had been elected to the government a few days previously. This first clash between the Cheka and the judiciary raised the important issue of the legal position of the secret police.

"What is the point of a 'People's Commissariat for Justice'?" Steinberg asked Lenin. "It would be more honest to have a People's Commissariat for Social Extermination. People would understand more clearly."

"Excellent idea," Lenin countered. "That's exactly how I see it. Unfortunately, it wouldn't do to call it that!"[21]

Lenin arbitrated in the conflict between Steinberg, who argued for a strict subordination of the Cheka to the processes of justice, and Dzerzhinsky, who argued against what he called "the nitpicking legalism of the old school of the *ancien régime*." In Dzerzhinsky's view, the Cheka should be responsible for its acts only to the government itself.

The sixth (nineteenth) of January marked an important point in the consolidation of the Bolshevik dictatorship. Early in the morning the Constituent Assembly, which had been elected in November–December 1917 and in which the Bolsheviks were a minority (they had only 175 deputies out of 707 seats), was broken up by force, having met for a single day. This arbitrary act seemed to provoke no particular reaction anywhere in the country. A small demonstration against the dissolution of the assembly was broken up by troops, causing some twenty deaths, a high price to pay for a democratic parliamentary experiment that lasted only a few hours.[22]

In the days and weeks that followed the dissolution of the Constituent Assembly, the position of the Bolshevik government in Petrograd became increasingly uncomfortable, at the very moment when Trotsky, Kamenev, Adolf Yoffe, and Karl Radek were negotiating peace conditions with delegations from the Central Powers at Brest Litovsk. On 9 (22) January 1918 the government devoted all business to the question of its transfer to Moscow.[23]

What worried the Bolshevik leaders was not the German threat—the armistice had held good since 15 (28) December—but the possibility of a workers' uprising. Discontent was growing rapidly in working-class areas that just two months before had been solidly behind them. With demobilization and the consequent slump in large-scale orders from the military, businesses had laid off tens of thousands of workers, and increasing difficulties in supply had caused the daily bread ration to fall to a mere quarter of a pound. Unable to do anything to improve this situation, Lenin merely spoke out against "profiteers" and "speculators," whom he chose as scapegoats. "Every factory, every company must set up its own requisitioning detachments. Everyone must be mobilized in the search for bread, not simply volunteers, but absolutely everyone; anyone who fails to cooperate will have his ration card confiscated immediately" he wrote on 22 January (4 February) 1918.[24]

Trotsky's nomination, on his return from Brest Litovsk on 31 January 1918, to head the Extraordinary Commission for Food and Transport was a clear sign from the government of the decisive importance it was giving to the "hunt for food," which was the first stage in the "dictatorship of food." Lenin turned to this commission in mid-February with a draft decree that the members of the commission—who besides Trotsky included Aleksandr Tsyurupa, the people's commissar of food—rejected. According to the text prepared by Lenin, all peasants were to be required to hand over any surplus food in exchange for a receipt. Any defaulters who failed to hand in supplies within the required time were to be executed. "When we read this proposal we were at a loss for words," Tsyurupa recalled in his memoirs. "To carry out a project like this would have led to executions on a massive scale. Lenin's project was simply abandoned."[25]

The episode was nonetheless extremely revealing. Since the beginning of 1918, Lenin had found himself trapped in an impasse of his own making, and he was worried about the catastrophic supply situation of the big industrial centers, which were seen as isolated Bolshevik strongholds among the great mass of peasants. He was prepared to do anything to get the grain he needed without altering his policies. Conflict was inevitable here, between a peasantry determined to keep for itself the fruits of its labors and to reject any external interference, and the new regime, which was attempting to place its stamp on the situation, refused to understand how economic supply actually functioned, and desired more than anything to bring under control what it saw as growing social anarchy.

On 21 February 1918, in the face of a huge advance by the German army after the failure of the talks at Brest Litovsk, the government declared the socialist fatherland to be in danger. The call for resistance against the invaders was accompanied by a call for mass terror: "All enemy agents, speculators, hooligans, counterrevolutionary agitators, and German spies will be shot on sight."[26] This proclamation effectively installed martial law in all military zones. When peace was finally agreed at Brest Litovsk on 3 March 1918, it technically lost its legal force, and legally the death penalty was reestablished again only on 16 June 1918. Nevertheless, from February 1918 on the Cheka carried out numerous summary executions, even outside the military zones.

On 10 March 1918 the government left Petrograd for Moscow, the new capital. The Cheka headquarters were set up near the Kremlin, in Bolshaya Lubyanka Street, in a building that had previously belonged to an insurance company. Under a series of names (including the GPU, OGPU, NKVD, MVD, and KGB) the Cheka would occupy the building until the fall of the Soviet regime. From a mere 600 in March, the number of Cheka employees working at the central headquarters had risen to 2,000 in July 1918, excluding the special troops. At this same date the People's Commissariat of Internal Affairs, whose task was to direct the immense apparatus of local soviets throughout the country, had a staff of 400.

The Cheka launched its first major operation on the night of 11–12 April 1918, when more than 1,000 men from its special troop detachments stormed some twenty anarchist strongholds in Moscow. After several hours of hard fighting, 520 anarchists were arrested; 25 were summarily executed as "bandits," a term that from then on would designate workers on strike, deserters fleeing conscription, or peasants resisting the forced requisitioning of grain.[27]

After this first success, which was followed by other "pacification" operations in both Moscow and Petrograd, Dzerzhinsky wrote a letter to the Central Executive Committee on 29 April 1918 requesting a considerable increase in Cheka resources. "At this particular time," he wrote, "Cheka activity is almost bound to increase exponentially, in the face of the increase in counterrevolutionary activity on all sides."[28]

The "particular time" to which Dzerzhinsky was referring seemed indeed to be a decisive period for the installation of the political and economic dictatorship and the strengthening of repression against a population that appeared to regard the Bolsheviks with ever-increasing hostility. Since October 1917 the

Bolsheviks had done nothing to improve the everyday lot of the average Russian, nor had they safeguarded the fundamental liberties that had accrued throughout 1917. Formerly regarded as the only political force that would allow peasants to seize the land they had so long desired, the Bolsheviks were now perceived as Communists, who wanted to steal the fruits of the peasants' labors. Could these really be the same people, the peasants wondered, the Bolsheviks who had finally given them the land, and the Communists who seemed to be holding them for ransom, and wanted even the shirts from their backs?

The spring of 1918 was a crucial period, when everything was still up for grabs. The soviets had not yet been muzzled and transformed into simple tools of the state apparatus; they were still a forum for real political debate between Bolsheviks and moderate socialists. Opposition newspapers, though attacked almost daily, continued to exist. Political life flourished as different institutions competed for popular support. And during this period, which was marked by a deterioration in living conditions and the total breakdown of economic relations between the town and the country, Socialist Revolutionaries and Mensheviks scored undeniable political victories. In elections to the new soviets, despite a certain amount of intimidation and vote-rigging, they achieved outright victories in nineteen of the thirty main provincial seats where voting took place and the results were made public.[29]

The government responded by strengthening its dictatorship on both the political and the economic fronts. Networks of economic distribution had fallen apart as a result of the spectacular breakdown in communications, particularly in the railways, and all incentive for farmers seemed to have been lost, as the lack of manufacturing products provided no impetus for peasants to sell their goods. The fundamental problem was thus to assure the food supply to the army and to the cities, the seat of power and of the proletariat. The Bolsheviks had two choices: they could either attempt to resurrect some sort of market economy or use additional constraints. They chose the second option, convinced of the need to go ever further in the struggle to destroy the old order.

Speaking before the Central Executive Committee of the Soviets on 29 April 1918, Lenin went straight to the point: "The smallholders, the people who owned only a parcel of land, fought side by side with the proletariat when the time came to overthrow the capitalists and the major landowners. But now our paths have diverged. Smallholders have always been afraid of discipline and organization. The time has come for us to have no mercy, and to turn against them."[30] A few days later the people's commissar of food told the same assembly: "I say it quite openly; we are now at war, and it is only with guns that we will get the grain we need." Trotsky himself added: "Our only choice now is civil war. Civil war is the struggle for bread . . . Long live civil war!"[31]

A 1921 text by Karl Radek, one of the Bolshevik leaders, is revealing of

Bolshevik policies in the spring of 1918, several months before the outbreak of the armed conflict that for two years would find Reds and Whites at war:

> The peasants had just received the land from the state, they had just returned home from the front, they had kept their guns, and their attitude to the state could be summed up as "Who needs it?" They couldn't have cared less about it. If we had decided to come up with some sort of food tax, it wouldn't have worked, for none of the state apparatus remained. The old order had disappeared, and the peasants wouldn't have handed over anything without actually being forced. Our task at the beginning of 1918 was quite simple: we had to make the peasants understand two quite simple things: that the state had some claim on what they produced, and that it had the means to exercise those rights.[32]

In May and June 1918 the Bolshevik government took two decisive measures that inaugurated the period of civil war, which has come to be known as "War Communism." On 13 May 1918 a decree granted extraordinary powers to the People's Commissariat of Food, requiring it to requisition all foodstuffs and to establish what was in fact a "food army." By July nearly 12,000 people were involved in these "food detachments," which at their height in 1920 were to number more than 24,000 men, over half of whom were unemployed workers from Petrograd, attracted by the promise of a decent salary and a proportional share of the confiscated food. The second decisive measure was the decree of 11 June 1918, which established committees of poor peasants, ordering them to work in close collaboration with the food detachments and also to requisition, in exchange for a share of the profits, any agricultural surpluses that the better-off peasants might be keeping for themselves. These committees of poor peasants soon displaced the rural soviets, which the government judged to be untrustworthy, as they were contaminated with Socialist Revolutionary ideology. Given the tasks they were ordered to carry out—to seize by force the results of other people's labor—and the motivations that were used to spur them on (power, a feeling of frustration toward and envy of the rich, and the promise of a share in the spoils), one can imagine what these first representatives of Bolshevik power in the countryside were really like. As Andrea Graziosi acutely notes: "For these people, devotion to the cause—or rather to the new state—and an undeniable operational capacity went hand in hand with a rather faltering social and political conscience, an interest in self-advancement, and traditional modes of behavior, including brutality to their subordinates, alcoholism, and nepotism . . . What we have here is a good example of the manner in which the 'spirit' of the plebeian revolution penetrated the new regime."[33]

Despite a few initial successes, the organization of the Committees for the Poor took a long time to get off the ground. The very idea of using the poorest section of the peasantry reflected the deep mistrust the Bolsheviks felt toward peasant society. In accordance with a rather simplistic Marxist schema, they imagined it to be divided into warring classes, whereas in fact it presented a fairly solid front to the world, and particularly when faced with strangers from the city. When the question arose of handing over surpluses, the egalitarian and community-minded reflex found in all the villages took over, and instead of persecuting a few rich peasants, by far the greater part of the requisitions were simply redistributed in the same village, in accordance with people's needs. This policy alienated the large central mass of the peasantry, and discontent was soon widespread, with troubles breaking out in numerous regions. Confronted by the brutality of the food detachments, who were often reinforced by the army or by Cheka units, a real guerrilla force began to take shape from June 1918 onward. In July and August 110 peasant insurrections, described by the Bolsheviks as kulak rebellions—which in their terminology meant uprisings involving whole villages, with insurgents from all classes—broke out in the zones they controlled. All the trust that the Bolsheviks had gained by not opposing the seizure of land in 1917 evaporated in a matter of weeks, and for more than three years the policy of requisitioning food was to provoke thousands of riots and uprisings, which were to degenerate into real peasant wars that were quelled with terrible violence.

The political effects of the hardening of the dictatorship in the spring of 1918 included the complete shutdown of all non-Bolshevik newspapers, the forcible dissolution of all non-Bolshevik soviets, the arrest of opposition leaders, and the brutal repression of many strikes. In May and June 1918, 205 of the opposition socialist newspapers were finally closed down. The mostly Menshevik or Socialist Revolutionary soviets of Kaluga, Tver, Yaroslavl, Ryazan, Kostroma, Kazan, Saratov, Penza, Tambov, Voronezh, Orel, and Vologda were broken up by force.[34] Everywhere the scenario was almost identical: a few days after victory by the opposing party and the consequent formation of a new soviet, the Bolshevik detachment would call for an armed force, usually a detachment of the Cheka, which then proclaimed martial law and arrested the opposition leaders.

Dzerzhinsky, who had sent his principal collaborators into towns that had initially been won by the opposing parties, was an unabashed advocate of the use of force, as can be seen clearly from the directive he sent on 31 May 1918 to A. V. Eiduk, his plenipotentiary on a mission to Tver:

> The workers, under the influence of the Mensheviks, the Socialist Revolutionaries, and other counterrevolutionary bastards, have all gone on

strike, and demonstrated in favor of a government made up of all the different socialist parties. Put big posters up all over the town saying that the Cheka will execute on the spot any bandit, thief, speculator, or counterrevolutionary found to be conspiring against the soviet. Levy an extraordinary tax on all bourgeois residents of the town, and make a list of them, as that will be very useful if things start happening. You ask how to form the local Cheka: just round up all the most resolute people you can, who understand that there is nothing more effective than a bullet in the head to shut people up. Experience has shown me that you only need a small number of people like that to turn a whole situation around.[35]

The dissolution of the soviets held by the opposition, and the expulsion on 14 June 1918 of all Mensheviks and Socialist Revolutionaries from the All-Russian Central Executive Committee of Soviets, provoked protests and strikes in many working-class towns, where, to make matters worse, the food situation was still steadily deteriorating. In Kolpino, near Petrograd, the leader of a Cheka detachment ordered his troops to open fire on a hunger march organized by workers whose monthly ration of bread had fallen to two pounds. There were ten deaths. On the same day, in the Berezovsky factory, near Ekaterinburg, fifteen people were killed by a detachment of Red Guards at a meeting called to protest against Bolshevik commissars who were accused of confiscating the most impressive properties in the town and of keeping for themselves the 150-ruble tax they had levied on the bourgeoisie. The next day the local authorities declared a state of martial law, and fourteen people were immediately executed by the local Cheka, who refrained from mentioning this detail to headquarters in Moscow.[36]

In the latter half of May and in June 1918, numerous working-class demonstrations were put down bloodily in Sormovo, Yaroslavl, and Tula, as well as in the industrial cities of Uralsk, Nizhni-Tagil, Beloretsk, Zlatoust, and Ekaterinburg. The ever-increasing involvement of the local Chekas in these repressions is attested by the growing frequency in working-class environments of slogans directed against the "New Okhrana" (the tsarist secret police) who worked for what they termed the "commissarocracy."[37]

From 8 to 11 June 1918 Dzerzhinsky presided over the first All-Russian Conference of Chekas, attended by 100 delegates from forty-three local sections, which already employed more than 12,000 men. That figure would rise to 40,000 by the end of 1918, and to more than 280,000 by the beginning of 1921. Claiming to be above the soviets and, according to certain Bolsheviks, even above the Party, the conference declared its intention to "take full responsibility for the struggle against the counterrevolution throughout the republic, in its role as supreme enforcer of administrative power in Soviet Russia." The role that it proclaimed for itself at the end of the conference revealed the extent of the huge field of activity in which the political police was already operating, before the great wave of counterrevolutionary actions that would mark the summer. Modeled on the organization of the Lubyanka headquarters, each provincial Cheka was to establish the following departments and offices:

1. Information Department. Offices: Red Army, monarchists, cadets, right Socialist Revolutionaries and Mensheviks, anarchists, bourgeoisie and church people, unions and workers' committees, and foreigners. The appropriate offices were to draw up lists of suspects corresponding to all the above categories.
2. Department for the Struggle against the Counterrevolution. Offices: Red Army, monarchists, cadets, right Socialist Revolutionaries and Mensheviks, anarchists, unionists, national minorities, foreigners, alcoholism, pogroms and public order, and press affairs.
3. Department for the Struggle against Speculation and Abuses of Authority.
4. Department of Transport, Communication, and Ports.
5. Operational Department, including special Cheka units.[38]

Two days after the All-Russian Conference of Chekas, the government reinstated the death penalty, which had been abolished after the revolution of February 1917. Though formally reinstated by Kerensky in July 1917, it had been applied only at the front, in areas under military control. One of the first measures taken by the Second Congress of Soviets on 26 October (8 November) 1917 had been to abolish capital punishment, a decision that elicited a furious reaction from Lenin: "It's an error, an unforgivable weakness, a pacifist delusion!"[39] Lenin and Dzerzhinsky had been constantly trying to reinstate the penalty while knowing very well that in practice it could already be used whenever necessary, without any "nitpicking legalism," by organizations like the Cheka, which operated outside the law. The first legal death sentence was pronounced by a revolutionary court on 21 June 1918; Admiral A. Shchastnyi was the first "counterrevolutionary" to be shot "legally."

On 20 June V. Volodarsky, a Bolshevik leader in Petrograd, was shot down by a militant Socialist Revolutionary. This event occurred at a time of extreme tension in the old capital. In the preceding weeks, relations between Bolsheviks and workers had gone from bad to worse, and in May and June the Petrograd Cheka recorded seventy "incidents"—strikes, anti-Bolshevik meetings, demonstrations—led principally by metalworkers from labor strongholds, who had been the most ardent supporters of the Bolsheviks in the period leading up to the events of 1917. The authorities responded to strikes with lockouts at the large state-owned factories, a practice that became more and more widespread in the following months to break the workers' resistance. Volodarsky's assassination was followed by an unprecedented wave of arrests in the working-class areas of Petrograd. The Assembly of Workers' Representatives, a mainly Menshevik group that organized working-class opposition and was in fact a real opposition power to the Petrograd soviet, was dissolved. More than 800 leaders were arrested in two days. The workers' response to this huge wave of arrests was to call a general strike for 21 July 1918.[40]

From Moscow Lenin sent a letter to Grigori Zinoviev, president of the Petrograd Committee of the Bolshevik Party. The document is extremely revealing, both of Lenin's conception of terror and of an extraordinary political delusion. Lenin was in fact committing a huge political mistake when he claimed that the workers were protesting Volodarsky's death.

> Comrade Zinoviev! We have just learned that the workers of Petrograd wish to respond to Comrade Volodarsky's murder with mass terror, and that you (not you personally, but the members of the Party Committee in Petrograd) are trying to stop them: I want to protest most vehemently against this. We are compromising ourselves; we are calling for mass terror in the resolutions passed by the Soviet, but when the time comes for action, we obstruct the natural reactions of the masses. This cannot be! The terrorists will start to think we are being halfhearted. This is the hour of truth: It is of supreme importance that we encourage and make use of the energy of mass terror directed against the counterrevolutionaries, especially those of Petrograd, whose example is decisive. Regards. Lenin.[41]

3 The Red Terror

"The Bolsheviks are saying openly that their days are numbered," Karl Helfferich, the German ambassador to Moscow, told his government on 3 August 1918. "A veritable panic has overtaken Moscow . . . The craziest rumors imaginable are rife, about so-called 'traitors' who are supposed to be in hiding around the city."

The Bolsheviks certainly never felt as much under threat as they did in 1918. The territory they controlled amounted to little more than the traditional province of Muscovy, which now faced anti-Bolshevik opposition on three solidly established fronts: the first in the region of the Don, occupied by the Cossack troops of Ataman Krasnov and by General Denikin's White Army; the second in Ukraine, which was in the hands of the Germans and of the Rada, the national Ukrainian government; and a third front all along the Trans-Siberian Railway, where most of the big cities had fallen to the Czech Legion, whose offensive had been supported by the Socialist Revolutionary government in Samara.

In the regions that were more or less under Bolshevik control, nearly 140 major revolts and insurrections broke out in the summer of 1918; most involved peasant communities resisting the enforced commandeering of food supplies, which was being carried out with such brutality by the food army; protests against the limitations on trade and exchange; or protests against the new compulsory conscription for the Red Army.[1] Typically the angry peasants would flock en masse to the nearest town, besiege the soviet, and sometimes even attempt to set fire to it. The incidents usually degenerated into violence, and either local militias or, more and more often, detachments from the local Cheka opened fire on the protesters. In these confrontations, which became more frequent as time passed, the Bolshevik leaders saw a vast counterrevolutionary conspiracy directed against their regime by "kulaks disguised as White Guards."

"It is quite clear that preparations are being made for a White Guard uprising in Nizhni Novgorod," wrote Lenin in a telegram on 9 August 1918 to the president of the Executive Committee of the Nizhni Novgorod soviet, in response to a report about peasant protests against requisitioning. "Your first response must be to establish a dictatorial troika (i.e., you, Markin, and one other person) and introduce mass terror, shooting or deporting the hundreds of prostitutes who are causing all the soldiers to drink, all the ex-officers, etc. There is not a moment to lose; you must act resolutely, with massive reprisals. Immediate execution for anyone caught in possession of a firearm. Massive deportations of Mensheviks and other suspect elements."[2] The next day Lenin sent a similar telegram to the Central Executive Committee of the Penza soviet:

> Comrades! The kulak uprising in your five districts must be crushed without pity. The interests of the whole revolution demand such actions, for the final struggle with the kulaks has now begun. You must make an example of these people. (1) Hang (I mean hang publicly, so that people see it) at least 100 kulaks, rich bastards, and known bloodsuckers. (2) Publish their names. (3) Seize all their grain. (4) Single out the hostages per my instructions in yesterday's telegram. Do all this so that for miles around people see it all, understand it, tremble, and tell themselves that we are killing the bloodthirsty kulaks and that we will continue to do so. Reply saying you have received and carried out these instructions. Yours, Lenin.
>
> P.S. Find tougher people.[3]

In fact a close reading of Cheka reports on the revolts of the summer of 1918, reveals that the only uprisings planned in advance were those in Yaroslavl, Rybinsk, and Murom, which were organized by the Union for the Defense of the Fatherland, led by the Socialist Revolutionary Boris Savinkov; and that of workers in the arms factory of Evsk, at the instigation of Mensheviks and local Socialist Revolutionaries. All the other insurrections were a spontaneous, direct result of incidents involving local peasantry faced with requisitions or conscription. They were put down in a few days with great ferocity by trusted units from the Red Army or the Cheka. Only Yaroslavl, where Savinkov's detachments had ousted the local Bolsheviks from power, managed to hold out for a few weeks. After the town fell, Dzerzhinsky sent a "special investigative commission," which in five days, from 24 to 28 July 1918, executed 428 people.[4]

In August 1918, before the official beginning of the period of Red Terror on 3 September, the Bolshevik leaders, and in particular Lenin and Dzerzhinsky, sent a great number of telegrams to local Cheka and Party leaders, instructing them to take "prophylactic measures" to prevent any attempted insurrection. Among these measures, explained Dzerzhinsky, "the most effective are the taking of hostages among the bourgeoisie, on the basis of the lists that you have drawn up for exceptional taxes levied on the bourgeoisie . . . the arrest and the incarceration of all hostages and suspects in concentration camps."[5] On 8 August Lenin asked Tsyurupa, the people's commissar of food, to draw up a decree stipulating that "in all grain-producing areas, twenty-five designated hostages drawn from the best-off of the local inhabitants will answer with their lives for any failure in the requisitioning plan." As Tsyurupa turned a deaf ear to this, on the pretext that it was too difficult to organize the taking of hostages, Lenin sent him a second, more explicit note: "I am not suggesting that these hostages actually be taken, but that they are to be named explicitly in all the relevant areas. The purpose of this is that the rich, just as they are responsible for their own contribution, will also have to answer with their lives for the immediate realization of the requisitioning plan in their whole district."[6]

In addition to this new system for taking hostages, the Bolshevik leaders experimented in August 1918 with a tool of oppression that had made its first appearance in Russia during the war: the concentration camp. On 9 August Lenin sent a telegram to the Executive Committee of the province of Penza instructing them to intern "kulaks, priests, White Guards, and other doubtful elements in a concentration camp."[7]

A few days earlier both Dzerzhinsky and Trotsky had also called for the confinement of hostages in concentration camps. These concentration camps were simple internment camps in which, as a simple interim administrative measure and independently of any judicial process, "doubtful elements" were to be kept. As in every other country at this time, numerous camps for prisoners of war already existed in Russia.

First and foremost among the "doubtful elements" to be arrested were the leaders of opposition parties who were still at liberty. On 15 August 1918 Lenin and Dzerzhinsky jointly signed an order for the arrest of Yuri Martov, Fedor Dan, Aleksandr Potresov, and Mikhail Goldman, the principal leaders of the Menshevik Party, whose press had long been silenced and whose representatives had been hounded out of the soviets.[8]

For the Bolshevik leaders, distinctions among types of opponents no longer existed, because, as they explained, civil wars have their own laws. "Civil war has no written laws," wrote Martin Latsis, one of Dzerzhinsky's principal collaborators, in *Izvestiya* on 23 August 1918.

> Capitalist wars have a written constitution, but civil war has its own laws . . . One must not only destroy the active forces of the enemy, but also demonstrate that anyone who raises a hand in protest against class war will die by the sword. These are the laws that the bourgeoisie itself drew up in the civil wars to oppress the proletariat . . . We have yet to assimilate these rules sufficiently. Our own people are being killed by the hundreds of thousands, yet we carry out executions one by one after lengthy deliberations in commissions and courts. In a civil war, there should be no courts for the enemy. It is a fight to the death. If you don't kill, you will die. So kill, if you don't want to be killed![9]

Two assassination attempts on 30 August—one against M. S. Uritsky, the head of the Petrograd Cheka, the other against Lenin—seemed to confirm the Bolshevik leaders' theory that a real conspiracy was threatening their existence. In fact it now appears that there was no link between the two events. The first was carried out in the well-established tradition of populist revolutionary terror, by a young student who wanted to avenge the death of an officer friend killed a few days earlier by the Petrograd Cheka. The second incident was long attributed to Fanny Kaplan, a militant socialist with anarchist and Socialist Revolutionary leanings. She was arrested immediately and shot three days later without trial, but it now appears that there may have been a larger conspiracy against Lenin, which escaped detection at the time, in the Cheka itself.[10] The Bolshevik government immediately blamed both assassination attempts on "right Socialist Revolutionaries, the servants of French and English imperialism." The response was immediate: the next day, articles in the press and official declarations called for more terror. "Workers," said an article in *Pravda* (Truth) on 31 August, "the time has come for us to crush the bourgeoisie or be crushed by it. The corruption of the bourgeoisie must be cleansed from our towns immediately. Files will now be kept on all men concerned, and those who represent a danger to the revolutionary cause will be executed . . . The anthem of the working class will be a song of hatred and revenge!"

On the same day Dzerzhinsky and his assistant Jan Peters drafted an "Appeal to the Working Classes" in a similar vein: "The working classes must crush the hydra of the counterrevolution with massive terror! We must let the enemies of the working classes know that anyone caught in illegal possession of a firearm will be immediately executed, and that anyone who dares to spread the slightest rumor against the Soviet regime will be arrested immediately and sent to a concentration camp!" Printed in *Izvestiya* on 3 September, this appeal was followed the next day by the publication of instructions sent by N. Petrovsky, the people's commissar of internal affairs, to all the soviets.

Petrovsky complained that despite the "massive repressions" organized by enemies of the state against the working masses, the "Red Terror" was too slow in its effects:

> The time has come to put a stop to all this weakness and sentimentality. All the right Socialist Revolutionaries must be arrested immediately. A great number of hostages must be taken among the officers and the bourgeoisie. The slightest resistance must be greeted with widespread executions. Provincial Executive Committees must lead the way here. The Chekas and the other organized militia must seek out and arrest suspects and immediately execute all those found to be involved with counterrevolutionary practices . . . Leaders of the Executive Committees must immediately report any weakness or indecision on the part of the local soviets to the People's Commissariat of Internal Affairs. No weakness or indecision can be tolerated during this period of mass terror.[11]

This telegram, which marked the official start of full-scale Red Terror, gives the lie to Dzerzhinsky's and Peters' later claims that the Red Terror "was a general and spontaneous reaction of indignation by the masses to the attempted assassinations of 30 August 1918, and began without any initiative from the central organizations." The truth was that the Red Terror was the natural outlet for the almost abstract hatred that most of the Bolshevik leaders felt toward their "oppressors," whom they wished to liquidate not on an individual basis, but as a class. In his memoirs the Menshevik leader Rafael Abramovich recalled a revealing conversation that he had in August 1917 with Dzerzhinsky, the future leader of the Cheka:

> "Abramovich, do you remember Lasalle's speech about the essence of a Constitution?"
> "Of course."
> "He said that any Constitution is always determined by the relation between the social forces at work in a given country at the time in question. I wonder how this correlation between the political and the social might be changed?"
> "Well, by the various processes of change that are at work in the fields of politics and economics at any time, by the emergence of new forms of economic growth, the rise of different social classes, all those things that you know perfectly well already, Feliks . . ."
> "Yes, but couldn't one change things much more radically than that? By forcing certain classes into submission, or by exterminating them altogether?"[12]

This cold, calculating, and cynical cruelty, the logical result of an implacable class war pushed to its extreme, was shared by many Bolsheviks. Grigory Zinoviev, one of the main leaders, declared in September 1918: "To dispose of our enemies, we will have to create our own socialist terror. For this we will have to train 90 million of the 100 million Russians and have them all on our side. We have nothing to say to the other 10 million; we'll have to get rid of them."[13]

On 5 September the Soviet government legalized terror with the famous decree "On Red Terror": "At this moment it is absolutely vital that the Chekas be reinforced . . . to protect the Soviet Republic from its class enemies, who must all be locked up in concentration camps. Anyone found to have had any dealings with the White Guard organizations, plots, insurrections, or riots will be summarily executed, and the names of all these people, together with the reasons for their execution, will be announced publicly."[14] As Dzerzhinsky was later to acknowledge, "The texts of 3 and 5 September finally gave us a legal right that even Party comrades had been campaigning against until then—the right immediately to dispose of the counterrevolutionary rabble, without having to defer to anyone else's authority at all."

In an internal circular dated 17 September, Dzerzhinksy, invited all local Chekas to "accelerate procedures and terminate, that is, *liquidate*, any pending business."[15] In fact the "liquidations" had started as early as 31 August. On 3 September *Izvestiya* reported that in the previous few days more than 500 hostages had been executed by the local Cheka in Petrograd. According to Cheka sources, more than 800 people were executed in September in Petrograd alone. The actual figure must be considerably higher than that. An eyewitness relates the following details: "For Petrograd, even a conservative estimate must be 1,300 executions . . . The Bolsheviks didn't count, in their 'statistics,' the hundreds of officers and civilians who were executed on the orders of the local authorities in Kronstadt. In Kronstadt alone, in one night, more than 400 people were shot. Three massive trenches were dug in the middle of the courtyard, 400 people were lined up in front of them and executed one after the other."[16] In an interview given to the newspaper *Utro Moskvy* (Moscow morning) on 3 November 1918, Peters admitted that "those rather oversensitive [*sic*] Cheka members in Petrograd lost their heads and went a little too far. Before Uritsky's assassination, no one was executed at all—and believe me, despite anything that people might tell you, I am not as bloodthirsty as they say—but since then there have been too many killed, often quite indiscriminately. But then again, Moscow's only response to the attempt on Lenin's life was the execution of a few tsarist ministers."[17] According to *Izvestiya* again, a "mere" 29 hostages from the concentration camp were shot in Moscow on 3 and 4 September. Among the dead were two former ministers from the regime of Tsar Nicholas II, N. Khvostov (internal affairs) and I. Shcheglovitov (justice). Nonetheless, numerous eyewitness reports concur that hundreds of hostages were executed during the "September massacres" in the prisons of Moscow.

In these times of Red Terror, Dzerzhinsky founded a new newspaper, *Ezhenedelnik VChK* (Cheka weekly), which was openly intended to vaunt the merits of the secret police and to encourage "the just desire of the masses for revenge." For the six weeks of its existence (it was closed down by an order from the Central Committee after the raison d'être of the Cheka was called into question by a number of Bolshevik leaders), the paper candidly and unashamedly described the taking of hostages, their internment in concentration camps, and their execution. It thus constituted an official basic minimum of information of the Red Terror for September and October 1918. For instance, the newspaper reported that in the medium-sized city of Nizhni Novgorod the Cheka, who were particularly zealous under the leadership of Nikolai Bulganin (later the head of the Soviet state from 1954 to 1957), executed 141 hostages after 31 August, and once took more than 700 hostages in a mere three days. In Vyatka the Cheka for the Ural region reported the execution of 23 "ex-policemen," 154 "counterrevolutionaries," 8 "monarchists," 28 "members of the Constitutional Democratic party," 186 "officers," and 10 "Mensheviks and right Socialist Revolutionaries," all in the space of a week. The Ivanovo Voznesensk Cheka reported taking 181 hostages, executing 25 "counterrevolutionaries," and setting up a concentration camp with space for 1,000 people. The Cheka of the small town of Sebezhsk reported shooting "17 kulaks and one priest, who had celebrated a mass for the bloody tyrant Nicholas II"; the Tver Cheka reported 130 hostages and 39 executions; the Perm Cheka reported 50 executions. This macabre catalogue could be extended considerably; these are merely a few extracts from the six issues of the *Cheka Weekly*.[18]

Other provincial journals also reported thousands of arrests and executions in the autumn of 1918. To take but two examples, the single published issue of *Izvestiya Tsaritsynskoi Gubcheka* (News of the Tsaritsyn Province Cheka) reported the execution of 103 people for the week of 3–10 September. From 1 to 8 November 371 people appeared in the local Cheka court; 50 were condemned to death, the rest "to a concentration camp as a measure of hygiene, as hostages, until the complete liquidation of all counterrevolutionary insurrections." The only issue of *Izvestiya Penzenskoi Gubcheka* (News of the Penza Province Cheka) reported, without commentary, that "in response to the assassination of Comrade Egorov, a Petrograd worker on a mission in one of the detachments of the Food Army, 150 White Guards have been executed by the Cheka. In the future, other, more rigorous measures will be taken against anyone who raises a hand in protest against the iron fist of the proletariat."

The *svodki*, or confidential reports that the local Chekas sent to Moscow, which have only recently become public, also confirm the brutality of responses to the slightest incidents between the peasant community and the local authorities. These incidents almost invariably concerned a refusal to accept the requisitioning process or conscription, and they were systematically catalogued in the files as "counterrevolutionary kulak riots" and suppressed without mercy.

It is impossible to come up with an exact figure for the number of people who fell victim to this first great wave of the Red Terror. Latsis, who was one of the main leaders of the Cheka, claimed that in the second half of 1918 the Cheka executed 4,500 people, adding with some cynicism: "If the Cheka can be accused of anything, it isn't of being overzealous in its executions, but rather of failure in the need to apply the supreme punishment. An iron hand will always mean a smaller number of victims in the long term."[19] At the end of October 1918 the Menshevik leader Yuri Martov estimated the number of direct victims of the Cheka since the start of September to be "in excess of 10,000."[20]

Whatever the exact number of victims may have been that autumn—and the total reported in the official press alone suggests that at the very least it must be between 10,000 and 15,000—the Red Terror marked the definitive beginning of the Bolshevik practice of treating any form of real or potential opposition as an act of civil war, which, as Latsis put it, had "its own laws." When workers went on strike to protest the Bolshevik practice of rationing "according to social origin" and abuses of power by the local Cheka, as at the armaments factory at Motovilikha, the authorities declared the whole factory to be "in a state of insurrection." The Cheka did not negotiate with the strikers, but enforced a lockout and fired the workers. The leaders were arrested, and all the "Menshevik counterrevolutionaries," who were suspected of having incited the strike, were hunted down.[21] Such practices were normal in the summer of 1918. By autumn the local Chekas, now better organized and more motivated by calls from Moscow for bloodier repressions, went considerably further and executed more than 100 of the strikers without any trial.

The size of these numbers alone—between 10,000 and 15,000 summary executions in two months—marked a radical break with the practices of the tsarist regime. For the whole period 1825–1917 the number of death sentences passed by the tsarist courts (including courts-martial) "relating to political matters" came to only 6,321, with the highest figure of 1,310 recorded in 1906, the year of the reaction against the 1905 revolution. Moreover, not all death sentences were carried out; a good number were converted to forced labor.[22] In the space of a few weeks the Cheka alone had executed two to three times the total number of people condemned to death by the tsarist regime over ninety-two years.

The change of scale went well beyond the figures. The introduction of new categories such as "suspect," "enemy of the people," "hostage," "concentration camp," and "revolutionary court," and of previously unknown practices such as "prophylactic measures," summary execution without judicial process of hundreds and thousands of people, and arrest by a new kind of political police who were above the law, might all be said to have constituted a sort of Copernican revolution.

The change was so powerful that it took even some of the Bolshevik leaders by surprise, as can be judged from the arguments that broke out within the Party hierarchy from October to December 1918 regarding the role of the Cheka. On 25 October in the absence of Dzerzhinsky—who had been sent away incognito for a month to rebuild his mental and physical health in Switzerland—the Central Committee of the Bolshevik Party discussed a new status for the Cheka. Criticizing the "full powers given to an organization that seems to be acting above the soviets and above even the party itself," Nikolai Bukharin, Aleksandr Olminsky, who was one of the oldest members of the Party, and Petrovsky, the people's commissar of internal affairs, demanded that measures be taken to curb the "excessive zeal of an organization filled with criminals, sadists, and degenerate elements from the lumpenproletariat." A commission for political control was established. Lev Kamenev, who was part of it, went so far as to propose the abolition of the Cheka.[23]

But the diehard proponents of the Cheka soon regained the upper hand. Among their number, besides Dzerzhinsky, were the major names in the Party: Yakov Sverdlov, Stalin, Trotsky, and of course Lenin himself. He resolutely came to the defense of an institution "unjustly accused of excesses by a few unrealistic intellectuals . . . incapable of considering the problem of terror in a wider perspective."[24] On 19 December 1918, at Lenin's instigation, the Central Committee adopted a resolution forbidding the Bolshevik press to publish "defamatory articles about institutions, notably the Cheka, which goes about its business under particularly difficult circumstances." And that was the end of the debate. The "iron fist of the dictatorship of the proletariat" was thus accorded its infallibility. In Lenin's words, "A good Communist is also a good Chekist."

At the beginning of 1919 Dzerzhinsky received authorization from the Central Committee to establish the Cheka special departments, which thereafter were to be responsible for military security. On 16 March he was made people's commissar of internal affairs and set about a reorganization, under the aegis of the Cheka, of all militias, troops, detachments, and auxiliary units, which until then had been attached to different administrations. In May all these units—railway militias, food detachments, frontier guards, and Cheka battalions—were combined into a single body, the Troops for the Internal Defense of the Republic, which by 1921 numbered 200,000. These troops' various duties included policing the camps, stations, and other points of strategic importance; controlling requisitioning operations; and, most important, putting down peasant rebellions, riots by workers, and mutinies in the Red

Army. The Troops for the Internal Defense of the Republic represented a formidable force for control and oppression. It was a loyal army within the larger Red Army, which was constantly plagued by desertions and which never managed, despite a theoretical enrollment of between 3 million and 5 million, to muster a fighting force in excess of 500,000 well-equipped soldiers.[25]

One of the first decrees of the new people's commissar of internal affairs concerned the organization of the camps that had existed since the summer of 1918 without any legal basis or systematic organization. The decree of 15 April 1919 drew a distinction between "coercive work camps," where, in principle, all the prisoners had been condemned by a court, and "concentration camps," where people were held, often as hostages, as a result of administrative measures. That this distinction was somewhat artificial in practice is evidenced in the complementary instruction of 17 May 1919, which directed the creation of "at least one camp in each province, with room for a minimum of 300 people" and listed the sixteen categories of prisoners to be interned. The categories were as diverse as "hostages from the *haute bourgeoisie*"; "functionaries from the *ancien régime,* up to the rank of college assessor, procurator, and their assistants, mayors and assistant mayors of cities, including district capitals"; "people condemned, under the Soviet regime, for any crime of parasitism, prostitution, or procuring"; and "ordinary deserters (not repeat offenders) and soldiers who are prisoners in the civil war."[26]

The number of people imprisoned in work camps and concentration camps increased steadily from around 16,000 in May 1919 to more than 70,000 in September 1921.[27] These figures do not include several camps that had been established in regions that were in revolt against Soviet power. In Tambov Province, for example, in the summer of 1921 there were at least 50,000 "bandits" and "members of the families of bandits taken as hostages" in the seven concentration camps opened by the authorities as part of the measures to put down the peasant revolt.[28]

4   The Dirty War

The civil war in Russia has generally been analyzed as a conflict between the Red Bolsheviks and the White monarchists; but in fact the events that took place behind the lines of military confrontation are considerably more important. This was the interior front of the civil war. It was characterized above all by multifarious forms of repression carried out by each side—the Red repressions being much more general and systematic—against militant politicians of opposing parties or opposition groups, against workers striking for any grievance, against deserters fleeing either their units or the conscription process, or quite simply against citizens who happened to belong to a "suspect" or "hostile" social class, whose only crime often was simply to have been living in a town that fell to the enemy. The struggle on the interior front of the civil war included all acts of resistance carried out by millions of peasants, rebels, and deserters, and the group that both the Reds and the Whites called the Greens often played a decisive role in the advance or retreat of one or other side.

In 1919, for instance, massive peasant revolts against the Bolshevik powers in the mid-Volga region and in Ukraine allowed Admiral Kolchak and General Denikin to advance hundreds of miles behind Bolshevik lines. Similarly, several months later, the uprising of Siberian peasants who were incensed at the reestablishment of the ancient rights of the landowners precipitated the retreat of Kolchak's White Army before the advancing Reds.

Although large-scale military operations between the Whites and Reds lasted little more than a year, from the end of 1918 to the beginning of 1920, the greater part of what is normally termed the civil war was actually a dirty war, an attempt by all the different authorities, Red and White, civil and military, to stamp out all real or potential opponents in the zones that often changed hands several times. In regions held by the Bolsheviks it was the "class struggle" against the "aristocrats," the bourgeoisie, and socially undesirable elements, the hunt for all non-Bolshevik militants from opposing parties, and the putting down of workers' strikes, of mutinies in the less secure elements of the Red Army, and of peasant revolts. In the zones held by the Whites, it was open season on anyone suspected of having possible "Judeo-Bolshevik" sympathies.

The Bolsheviks certainly did not have a monopoly on terror. There was also a White Terror, whose worst moment was the terrible wave of pogroms carried out in Ukraine in the summer and autumn of 1919 by Simon Petlyura's detachments from Denikin's armies, which accounted for more than 150,000 victims. But as most historians of the Red Terror and White Terror have already pointed out, the two types of terror were not on the same plane. The Bolshevik policy of terror was more systematic, better organized, and targeted at whole social classes. Moreover, it had been thought out and put into practice before the outbreak of the civil war. The White Terror was never systematized in such a fashion. It was almost invariably the work of detachments that were out of control, taking measures not officially authorized by the military command that was attempting, without much success, to act as a government. If one discounts the pogroms, which Denikin himself condemned, the White Terror most often was a series of reprisals by the police acting as a sort of military counterespionage force. The Cheka and the Troops for the Internal Defense of the Republic were a structured and powerful instrument of repression of a completely different order, which had support at the highest level from the Bolshevik regime.

As in all civil wars, it is extremely difficult to derive a complete picture of all the forms of terror employed by the two warring parties. The Bolshevik Terror, with its clear methodology, its specificity, and its carefully chosen aims, easily predated the civil war, which developed into a full-scale conflict only at the end of the summer of 1918. The following list indicates in chronological order the evolution of different types of terror and its different targets from the early months of the regime:

· Non-Bolshevik political militants, from anarchists to monarchists.
· Workers fighting for the most basic rights, including bread, work, and a minimum of liberty and dignity.

- Peasants—often deserters—implicated in any of the innumerable peasant revolts or Red Army mutinies.
- Cossacks, who were deported en masse as a social and ethnic group supposedly hostile to the Soviet regime. "De-Cossackization" prefigured the massive deportations of the 1930s called "dekulakization" (another example of the deportation of ethnic groups) and underlines the fundamental continuity between the Leninist and Stalinist policies of political repression.
- "Socially undesirable elements" and other "enemies of the people," "suspects," and "hostages" liquidated "as a preventive measure," particularly when the Bolsheviks were enforcing the evacuation of villages or when they took back territory or towns that had been in the hands of the Whites.

The best-known repressions are those that concerned political militants from the various parties opposed to the Bolsheviks. Numerous statements were made by the main leaders of the opposition parties, who were often imprisoned and exiled, but whose lives were generally spared, unlike militant workers and peasants, who were shot without trial or massacred during punitive Cheka operations.

One of the first acts of terror was the attack launched on 11 April 1918 against the Moscow anarchists, dozens of whom were immediately executed. The struggle against the anarchists intensified over the following years, although a certain number did transfer their allegiance to the Bolshevik Party, even becoming high-ranking Cheka officials, such as Aleksandr Goldberg, Mikhail Brener, and Timofei Samsonov. The dilemma faced by most anarchists in their opposition to both the new Bolshevik dictatorship and the return of the old regime is well illustrated by the U-turns of the great peasant anarchist leader Nestor Makhno, who for a while allied himself with the Red Army in the struggle against the Whites, then turned against the Bolsheviks after the White threat had been eliminated. Thousands of anonymous militant anarchists were executed as bandits as part of the repression against the peasant army of Makhno and his partisans. It would appear that these peasants constituted the immense majority of anarchist victims, at least according to the figures presented by the Russian anarchists in exile in Berlin in 1922. These incomplete figures note 138 militant anarchists executed in the years 1919–1921, 281 sent into exile, and 608 still in prison as of 1 January 1922.[1]

The left Socialist Revolutionaries, who were allies of the Bolsheviks until the summer of 1918, were treated with relative leniency until February 1919. As late as December 1918 their most famous leader, Maria Spiridonova, presided over a party congress that was tolerated by the Bolsheviks. However, on

10 February 1919, after she condemned the terror that was being carried out on a daily basis by the Cheka, she was arrested with 210 other militants and sentenced by a revolutionary court to "detention in a sanatorium on account of her hysterical state." This action seems to be the first example under the Soviet regime of the sentencing of a political opponent to detention in a psychiatric hospital. Spiridonova managed to escape and continued secretly to lead the left Socialist Revolutionary Party, which by then had been banned by the Soviet government. According to Cheka sources, fifty-eight left Socialist Revolutionary organizations were disbanded in 1919, and another forty-five in 1920. In these two years 1,875 militants were imprisoned as hostages, in response to Dzerzhinsky's instructions. He had declared, on 18 March 1919: "Henceforth the Cheka is to make no distinction between White Guards of the Krasnov variety and White Guards from the socialist camp . . . The Socialist Revolutionaries and the Mensheviks arrested are to be considered as hostages, and their fate will depend on the subsequent behavior of the parties they belong to."[2]

To the Bolsheviks, the right Socialist Revolutionaries had always seemed the most dangerous political rivals. No one had forgotten that they had registered a large majority in the free and democratic elections of November and December 1917. After the dissolution of the Constituent Assembly, in which they held a clear majority of seats, the Socialist Revolutionaries had continued to serve in the soviets and on the Central Executive Committee of the Soviets, from which they were then expelled together with the Mensheviks in June 1918. Some Socialist Revolutionaries, together with Mensheviks and Constitutional Democrats, then established temporary and short-lived governments in Samara and Omsk, which were soon overturned by the White Admiral Kolchak. Caught between the Bolsheviks and the Whites, the Socialist Revolutionaries and the Mensheviks encountered considerable difficulties in defining a coherent set of policies with which to oppose the Bolshevik regime. The Bolsheviks, in turn, were extremely able politicians who used measures of appeasement, infiltration, and outright oppression to second-guess the more moderate socialist opposition.

After authorizing the reappearance of the Socialist Revolutionary newspaper *Delo naroda* (The people's cause) from 20 to 30 March, when Admiral Kolchak's offensive was at its height, the Cheka rounded up all the Socialist Revolutionaries and Mensheviks that it could on 31 March 1919, at a time when there was no legal restriction on membership of either of the two parties. More than 1,900 militants were arrested in Moscow, Tula, Smolensk, Voronezh, Penza, Samara, and Kostroma.[3] No one can say how many were summarily executed in the putting down of strikes and peasant revolts organized by Socialist Revolutionaries and Mensheviks. Very few statistics are available, and political: the elimination of special privileges for Communists, the release of political prisoners, free elections for soviets and factory committees, the end of conscription into the Red Army, freedom of association, freedom of expression, freedom of the press, and so forth.

What made these movements even more dangerous in the eyes of the Bolshevik authorities was their frequent success in rallying to their cause the military units stationed in the town in question. In Orel, Bryansk, Gomel, and Astrakhan mutinying soldiers joined forces with the strikers, shouting "Death to Jews! Down with the Bolshevik commissars!," taking over and looting parts of the city, which were retaken by Cheka detachments and troops faithful to the regime only after several days of fighting.[11] The repressions in response to such strikes and mutinies ranged from massive lockouts of whole factories and the confiscation of ration cards—the threat of hunger was one of the most useful weapons the Bolsheviks had—to the execution of strikers and rebel soldiers by the hundreds.

Among the most significant of the repressions were those in Tula and Astrakhan in March and April 1919. Dzerzhinsky came to Tula, the historical capital of the Russian army, on 3 April 1919 to put down a strike by workers in the munitions factories. In the winter of 1918–19 these factories had already been the scene of strikes and industrial action, and they were vital to the Red Army, turning out more than 80 percent of all the rifles made in Russia. Mensheviks and Socialist Revolutionaries were very much in the majority among the political activists in the highly skilled workforce there. The arrest, in early March 1919, of hundreds of socialist activists provoked a wave of protests that culminated on 27 March in a huge "March for Freedom and against Hunger," which brought together thousands of industrial and railway workers. On 4 April Dzerzhinsky had another 800 "leaders" arrested and forcibly emptied the factories, which had been occupied for several weeks by the strikers. All the workers were fired. Their resistance was broken by hunger; for several weeks their ration cards had not been honored. To receive replacement cards, giving the right to a half-pound of bread and the right to work again after the general lockout, workers had to sign a job application form stipulating, in particular, that any stoppage in the future would be considered an act of desertion and would thus be punishable by death. Production resumed on 10 April. The night before that, 26 "leaders" had been executed.[12]

The town of Astrakhan, near the mouth of the Volga, had major strategic importance in the spring of 1919, as it was the last Bolshevik stronghold preventing Admiral Kolchak's troops in the northwest from joining up with those of General Denikin in the southwest. This circumstance alone probably explains the extraordinary violence with which the workers' strike in the town was suppressed in March. Having begun for both economic reasons (the paltry

rations) and political reasons (the arrest of socialist activists), the strike intensified on 10 March when the 45th Infantry Regiment refused to open fire on
workers marching through the city. Joining forces with the strikers, the soldiers
stormed the Bolshevik Party headquarters and killed several members of the
staff. Sergei Kirov, the president of the regional Revolutionary Military Committee, immediately ordered "the merciless extermination of these White
Guard lice by any means possible." Troops who had remained faithful to the
regime and to the Cheka blocked all entrances to the town and methodically set
about retaking it. When the prisons were full, the soldiers and strikers were
loaded onto barges and then thrown by the hundreds into the Volga with stones
around their necks. From 12 to 14 March between 2,000 and 4,000 strikers were
shot or drowned. After 15 March the repressions were concentrated on the
bourgeoisie of the town, on the pretext that they had been behind this "White
Guard conspiracy" for which the workers and soldiers were merely cannon
fodder. For two days all the merchants' houses were systematically looted and
their owners arrested and shot. Estimates of the number of bourgeois victims
of the massacres in Astrakhan range from 600 to 1,000. In one week between
3,000 and 5,000 people were either shot or drowned. By contrast, the number
of Communists buried with great pomp and circumstance on 18 March—the
anniversary of the Paris Commune, as the authorities were at pains to point
out—was a mere 47. Long remembered as a small incident in the war between
the Whites and the Reds, the true scale of the killing in Astrakhan is now
known, thanks to recently published archival documents.[13] These documents
reveal that it was the largest massacre of workers by Bolsheviks before the
events at Kronstadt.

At the end of 1919 and the beginning of 1920 relations between the
Bolsheviks and the workers deteriorated even further, following the militarization of more than 2,000 businesses. As the principal architect of the militarization of the workplace, Trotsky laid out his ideas on the issue at the Ninth
Party Congress in March 1920. Trotsky explained that humans are naturally
lazy. Under capitalism, people were forced to search for work to survive. The
capitalist market acted as a stimulus to man, but under socialism "the utilization
of work resources replaces the market." It was thus the job of the state to direct,
assign, and place the workers, who were to obey the state as soldiers obey orders
in the army, because the state was working in the interests of the proletariat.
Such was the basis of the militarization of the workplace, which was vigorously
criticized by a minority of syndicalists, union leaders, and Bolshevik directors.
In practice this meant the outlawing of strikes, which were compared to desertion in times of war; an increase in the disciplinary powers of employers; the
total subordination of all unions and factory committees, whose role henceforth
was to be simply one of support for the producers' policies; a ban on workers'

leaving their posts; and punishments for absenteeism and lateness, both of which were exceedingly widespread because workers were often out searching for food.

The general discontent in the workplace brought about by militarization was compounded by the difficulties of everyday life. As was noted in a report submitted by the Cheka to the government on 16 December 1919:

> Of late the food crisis has gone from bad to worse, and the working masses are starving. They no longer have the physical strength necessary to continue working, and more and more often they are absent simply as a result of the combined effects of cold and hunger. In many of the metallurgical companies in Moscow, the workers are desperate and ready to take to take any measures necessary—strikes, riots, insurrections—unless some sort of solution to these problems is found immediately.[14]

At the beginning of 1920 the monthly salary for a worker in Petrograd was between 7,000 and 12,000 rubles. On the free market a pound of butter cost 5,000 rubles, a pound of meat cost 3,000, and a pint of milk 500. Each worker was also entitled to a certain number of products according to the category in which he was classed. In Petrograd at the end of 1919, a worker in heavy industry was entitled to a half-pound of bread a day, a pound of sugar a month, half a pound of fat, and four pounds of sour herring.

In theory citizens were divided into five categories of "stomach," from the workers in heavy industry and Red Army soldiers to the "sedentary"—a particularly harsh classification that included any intellectual—and were given rations accordingly. Because the "sedentary"—the intellectuals and aristocrats—were served last, they often received nothing at all, since often there was nothing left. The "workers" were divided into an array of categories that favored the sectors vital to the survival of the regime. In Petrograd in the winter of 1919–20 there were thirty-three categories of ration cards, which were never valid for more than one month. In the centralized food distribution system that the Bolsheviks had put in place, the food weapon played a major role in rewarding or punishing different categories of citizens. "The bread ration should be reduced for anyone who doesn't work in the transport sector, as it is now of such capital importance, and it should be increased for people who do work in this sector," wrote Lenin to Trotsky on 1 February 1920. "If it must be so, then let thousands die as a result, but the country must be saved."[15]

When this policy came into force, all those who had links with the country, and that meant a considerable number of people, tried desperately to go back to their villages as often as possible to bring back some food.

The militarization measures, designed to "restore order" in the factories,

had the opposite effect, and led to numerous stoppages, strikes, and riots, all of which were ruthlessly crushed. "The best place for strikers, those noxious yellow parasites," said *Pravda* on 12 February 1920, "is the concentration camp!" According to the records kept at the People's Commissariat of Labor, 77 percent of all large and medium-sized companies in Russia were affected by strikes in the first half of 1920. Significantly, the areas worst affected—metallurgy, the mines, and the transport sector—were also the areas in which militarization was most advanced. Reports from the secret Cheka department addressed to the Bolshevik leaders throw a harsh and revealing light on the repression used against factories and workers who resisted the militarization process. Once arrested, they were usually sentenced by revolutionary courts for crimes of "sabotage" and "desertion." At Simbirsk (formerly Ulyanovsk), to take but one example, twelve workers from the armaments factory were sent to camps in April 1920 for having "carried out acts of sabotage by striking in the Italian manner . . . spreading anti-Soviet propaganda, playing on the religious superstitions and the weak political convictions of the masses . . . and spreading erroneous information about Soviet policies regarding salaries."[16] Behind this obfuscatory language lay the likelihood that the accused had done little more than take breaks that were not authorized by their bosses, protested against having to work on Sundays, criticized the Communists, and complained about their own miserable salaries.

The top leaders of the Party, including Lenin, called for an example to be made of the strikers. On 29 January 1920, worried by the tense situation regarding workers in the Ural region, Lenin sent a telegram to Vladimir Smirnov, head of the Revolutionary Military Council of the Fifth Army: "P. has informed me that the railway workers are clearly involved in acts of sabotage . . . I am told that workers from Izhevsk are also involved in this. I am surprised that you are taking the matter so lightly, and are not immediately executing large numbers of strikers for the crime of sabotage."[17] Many strikes started up in 1920 as a direct result of militarization: in Ekaterinburg in March 1920, 80 workers were arrested and sent to camps; on the Ryazan–Ural Railway in April 1920, 100 railway workers were given the same punishment; on the Moscow–Kursk line in May 1920, 160 workers met the same fate, as did 152 workers in a metallurgy factory in Bryansk in June 1920. Many other strikes protesting militarization were suppressed in a similarly brutal fashion.[18]

One of the most remarkable strikes took place in the Tula arms factory, a crucial center of protest against the Bolshevik regime, which had already been severely punished for its actions in April 1919. On Sunday, 6 June 1920, a number of metallurgy workers refused to work the extra hours that the bosses demanded. Female workers then refused to work on that Sunday and on Sundays thereafter in general, explaining that Sunday was the only day they

could go out looking for food in the surrounding countryside. In response to a call from the factory bosses, a large detachment from the Cheka arrived to arrest the strikers. Martial law was decreed, and a troika made up of Party representatives and representatives of the Cheka was instructed to denounce a "counterrevolutionary conspiracy fomented by Polish spies and the Black Hundreds to weaken the combat strength of the Red Army."

While the strike spread and arrests of the "leaders" multiplied, a new development changed the usual course of developments; in hundreds, and then in thousands, female workers and simple housewives presented themselves to the Cheka asking to be arrested too. The movement spread, and the men demanded to be arrested en masse as well in order to make the idea of a Polish conspiracy appear even more ridiculous. In four days more than 10,000 people were detained in a huge open-air space guarded by the Cheka. Temporarily overwhelmed by the numbers, and at a loss about how to present the information to Moscow, the local Party organizations and the Cheka finally persuaded the central authorities that there was indeed an enormous conspiracy afoot. A Committee for the Liquidation of the Tula Conspiracy interrogated thousands of prisoners in the hope of finding a few guilty conspirators. To be set free, hired again, and given a new ration book, all the workers who had been arrested had to sign the following statement: "I, the undersigned, a filthy criminal dog, repent before the revolutionary court and the Red Army, confess my sins, and promise to work conscientiously in the future."

In contrast to other protest strikes, the Tula confrontation in the summer of 1920 was treated with comparative leniency: only 28 people were sentenced to camps, and 200 were sent into exile.[19] At a time when a highly skilled workforce was comparatively rare, the Bolsheviks could hardly do without the best armaments workers in the country. Terror, like food, had to take into account the importance of the sector in question and the higher interests of the regime.

However important the workers' front was strategically and symbolically, it was only one of the many internal fronts of the civil war. The struggle against the Greens, the peasants who were resisting requisitioning and conscription, was often far more important. Reports now available for the first time from the special departments of the Cheka and from the Troops for the Internal Defense of the Republic, whose task was to deal with deserters and to put down mutinies and peasant riots, reveal the full horror of the extraordinary violence of this "dirty war," which went on beyond the more obvious conflicts between the Reds and the Whites. It was in this crucial struggle between Bolshevik power and the peasantry that the policy of terror, based on an extremely pessimistic view of the masses, was really forged: "They are so ignorant,"

wrote Dzerzhinsky, "that they have no idea what is really in their own interest." The brute masses, it was felt, could be tamed only by force, by the "iron broom" that Trotsky mentioned in a characteristic image when describing the repressions he had used "to clean" Ukraine and "sweep away" the "bandit hordes" led by Nestor Makhno and other peasant chiefs.[20]

The peasant revolts had started in the summer of 1918. They became much more widespread in 1919 and 1920 and culminated in 1920–21, when they momentarily obliged the Bolshevik forces to retreat slightly.

There were two obvious reasons for these peasant revolts: the constant requisitioning of goods and the enforced conscription into the Red Army. In January 1919 the rather disorganized foraging for agricultural surpluses that had characterized the first operations of the summer of 1918 was replaced by a centralized and more carefully planned requisitioning system. Every province, district, canton *(volost)*, and village community had to hand over to the state a quota that was fixed in advance in accordance with estimates about the size of the harvest. In addition to grains, the quotas included some twenty-odd products such as potatoes, honey, eggs, butter, cooking oil, meat, cream, and milk. Each community was responsible for the collection itself. Only when the whole village had filled its quota did the authorities distribute receipts allowing people to buy manufactured goods, and even then only about 15 percent of the people's needs in that department were actually met. Payment for the agricultural harvest was more or less symbolic by this stage. By the end of 1920 the ruble had lost 96 percent of its previous value relative to the prewar gold-standard ruble. From 1918 to 1920 agricultural requisitioning increased threefold, and peasant revolts, though difficult to calculate exactly, seem to have increased at approximately the same rate.[21]

Opposition to conscription, after three years in the trenches in "the imperialist war," was the second most frequent reason for the peasant revolts, often led by the Greens. It also accounted for the groups of deserters hiding in the woods. It is now believed that in 1919 and 1920 there were more than 3 million deserters. In 1919 around 500,000 deserters were arrested by various departments of the Cheka and the special divisions created to combat desertion; in the following year the figure rose to between 700,000 and 800,000. Even so, somewhere between 1.5 and 2 million deserters, most of them peasants who knew the territory extremely well, managed to elude the authorities.[22]

Faced with the scale of the problem, the government took ever more repressive measures. Not only were thousands of deserters shot, but the families of deserters were often treated as hostages. After the summer of 1918 the hostage principle was applied in more and more ordinary situations. For example, a government decree of 15 February 1919 signed by Lenin encouraged local Chekas to take hostages from among the peasants in regions where the

railway lines had not yet been cleared of snow to a satisfactory standard: "And if the lines aren't swept properly, the hostages are to be shot."[23] On 12 May 1920 Lenin sent the following instructions to all the provincial commissions and detachments responsible for tracing deserters: "After the expiration of the seven-day deadline for deserters to turn themselves in, punishments must be increased for these incorrigible traitors to the cause of the people. Families and anyone found to be assisting them in any way whatsoever are to be considered as hostages and treated accordingly."[24] In practice this decree did nothing more than legally sanction what was already common practice. The tidal wave of desertions nonetheless rolled on. In 1920 and 1921, as in 1919, deserters accounted for most of the Green partisans, against whom, for three years (or in some regions four or even five), the Bolsheviks waged a relentless war of unimaginable cruelty.

Besides their resistance to requisitioning and conscription, the peasants generally rejected any intervention by what they considered to be a foreign power, in this case the Communists from the cities. As far as many of the peasants were concerned, the Communists responsible for the requisitioning were simply not the same people as the Bolsheviks who had encouraged the agricultural revolution in 1917. In the regions that were constantly changing hands between the Reds and the Whites, confusion and violence were at their height.

The reports from different departments of the Cheka responsible for suppressing the insurrections are an exceptionally good source of information, and allow us to see many different sides of this guerrilla war. They often draw a distinction between two types of peasant movement: the *bunt*, a spontaneous revolt and brief flare-up of violence with a relatively limited number of participants, typically between a few dozen to a hundred or so rebels; and the *vosstanie*, a large-scale insurrection involving thousands or even tens of thousands of peasants, organized into veritable armies capable of storming towns and cities, and held together by a coherent political program, usually with anarchist or Socialist Revolutionary tendencies. Excerpts from these reports give some idea of what went on:

> 30 April 1919. Tambov Province. At the beginning of April, in the Lebyadinsky district, a riot broke out among kulaks and deserters protesting the mobilization of men and horses and the requisitioning of grain. With cries of "Down with the Communists! Down with the Soviets!" the rebels stormed and burned several of the Executive Committees in the canton and killed seven Communists in a barbaric fashion, sawing them in half while they were still alive. Summoned by members of the requisitioning detachment, the 212th Battalion of the Cheka arrived and put down the kulak revolt. Sixty people were arrested, and

fifty were executed immediately; the village where the rebellion started was razed.

Voronezh Province, 11 June 1919, 16:15. Telegram. The situation is improving. The revolt in the Novokhopersk region is nearly over. Our planes bombed and set fire to the town of Tretyaki, one of the principal bandit strongholds. Mopping-up operations are continuing.

Yaroslavl Province, 23 June 1919. The uprising of the deserters in the Petropavlovskaya *volost* has been put down. The families of the deserters have been taken as hostages. When we started to shoot one person from each family, the Greens began to come out of the woods and surrender. Thirty-four deserters were shot as an example.[25]

Thousands of similar reports bear witness to the great violence of this war between the authorities and peasant guerrillas, often caused by desertion but described in the reports as kulak revolts or bandit uprisings.[26] The three excerpts above demonstrate the varieties of repression used most often by the authorities: the arrest and execution of hostages taken from the families of deserters or "bandits," and the bombing and burning of villages. These blind and disproportionate reprisals were based on the idea of the collective responsibility of the whole village community. The authorities generally laid down a deadline for the return of deserters, and once the deadline had expired, the deserters were considered to be "forest bandits" who were liable to be shot on sight. Moreover, it was made clear in the tracts of both the civil and the military authorities that "if the inhabitants of a village help the bandits in the forests in any way whatever, the whole village will be burned down."

Some of the more general Cheka reports give a clearer idea of the scale of this war in the countryside. In the period 15 October–30 November 1918, in twelve provinces of Russia alone, there were 44 *bunt* riots, in which 2,320 people were arrested, 620 were killed in the fighting, and 982 subsequently executed. During these disorders 480 Soviet functionaries were killed, as were 112 men from the food detachments, the Red Army, and the Cheka. In September 1919, for the ten Russian provinces for which reports are available, 48,735 deserters and 7,325 "bandits" were arrested, 1,826 were killed, 2,230 were executed, and there were 430 victims among the functionaries and the Soviet military. These very fragmentary reports do not include the much greater losses during the larger-scale peasant uprisings.

The uprisings can be grouped around several periods of greater intensity: March and April 1919 for the regions of the mid-Volga and Ukraine; February–August 1920 for the provinces of Samara, Ufa, Kazan, Tambov, and again Ukraine, which was retaken from the Whites by the Bolsheviks but whose heartlands were still controlled by the guerrilla peasants. From late 1920 through the first half of 1921 the peasant movement, very much on the defensive in Ukraine, the Don, and the Kuban, culminated in huge resistance in the central provinces of Tambov, Penza, Samara, Saratov, Simbirsk, and Tsaritsyn.[27] The only factor that diminished the intensity of the peasant war here was the arrival of one of the worst famines of the twentieth century.

It was in the rich provinces of Samara and Simbirsk, which in 1919 were required to provide more than one-fifth of the grain requisitions for the whole of Russia, that spontaneous peasant riots were transformed for the first time in March 1919 into a genuine insurrection. Dozens of towns were taken by the insurrectionist peasant army, which by then numbered more than 30,000 armed soldiers. The Bolshevik central powers lost all control of Samara for more than a month. The rebellion facilitated the advance toward the Volga of units from Admiral Kolchak's White Army, as the Bolsheviks were forced to send tens of thousands of men to deal with this extremely well-organized peasant army with a clear political program calling for free trade, free elections to the soviets, and an end to requisitioning and the "Bolshevik commissarocracy." Summing up the situation in April 1919, after the end of the uprising, the head of the Cheka in Samara noted that 4,240 of the rebels had been killed in the fighting, 625 had been subsequently shot, and 6,210 deserters and "bandits" had been arrested.

Just when the fire seemed to have been damped in Samara, it flared up again with unparalleled intensity in Ukraine. After the Germans and the Austro-Hungarians had left at the end of 1918, the Bolshevik government had decided to recapture Ukraine. The breadbasket of the old tsarist empire, Ukraine was now to feed the proletariat of Moscow and Petrograd. Requisitioning quotas were higher there than anywhere else in the Soviet empire. To meet them would have been to condemn thousands of villages, already badly damaged by the German and Austro-Hungarian occupations, to certain starvation. In addition, unlike the policy in Russia at the end of 1917 for the sharing of land among the peasant communities, the Bolshevik intention for Ukraine was a straightforward nationalization of all the great properties, which were the most modern in the old empire. This policy, which aimed to transform the great sugar- and grain-producing areas into huge collective farms with the peasants as nothing more than agricultural laborers, was bound to provoke resistance. The peasants had become militarized in the fight against the German and Austro-Hungarian occupying forces. By 1919 there existed real armies of tens of thousands of peasants, commanded by military chiefs and Ukrainian politicians such as Simon Petlyura, Nestor Makhno, Mykola Hryhoryiv, and Zeleny. The peasant armies were determined to implement their version of an agrarian revolution: land for the peasants, free trade, and free elections to the soviets, "without Muscovites or Jews." For many of the Ukrainian peasants, who had been born into a long tradition of antagonism between the countryside and the mostly Russian and Jewish towns, it was temptingly simple to make the equation Muscovites = Bolsheviks = Jews. They were all to be expelled from Ukraine.

These particularities of Ukraine explain the brutality and the length of the confrontations between the Bolsheviks and a large part of the Ukrainian peasantry. The presence of another party, the Whites, who were under assault at once by the Bolsheviks and by various peasant Ukrainian armies who opposed the return of the great landowners, rendered the political and military situation even more complex; some cities, such as Kyiv, were to change hands fourteen times in the space of two years.

The first great revolts against the Bolsheviks and their food-requisitioning detachments took place in April 1919. In that month alone, 93 peasant revolts took place in the provinces of Kyiv, Chernihiv, Poltava, and Odessa. For the first twenty days of July 1919 the Cheka's own statistics note 210 revolts, involving more than 100,000 armed combatants and several hundred thousand peasants. The peasant armies of Hryhoryiv, numbering more than 20,000, including several mutinying units from the Red Army, with 50 cannon and more than 700 heavy machine guns, took a whole series of towns in southern Ukraine in April and May 1919, including Cherkassy, Kherson, Nikolaev, and Odessa. They set up an independent interim government whose slogans stated their intentions quite clearly: "All power to the soviets of the Ukrainian people," "Ukraine for the Ukrainians, down with the Bolsheviks and the Jews," "Share out the land," "Free enterprise, free trade."[28] Zeleny's partisans, nearly 20,000 armed men, held the entire province of Kyiv except for a few big cities. Under the slogan "Long live Soviet power, down with the Bolsheviks and the Jews!" they organized dozens of bloody pogroms against the Jewish communities in the towns and villages of Kyiv and Chernihiv. The best known, thanks to numerous studies, are the actions of Nestor Makhno. At the head of a peasant army numbering tens of thousands, he espoused a simultaneously nationalist and social anarchist program that had been elaborated in several peasant congresses, including the Congress of Delegate Peasants, Workers, and Rebels of Gulyai-Pole, held in April 1919 in the midst of the Makhno uprising. The Makhnovists voiced their rejection of all interference by the state in peasant affairs and a desire for peasant self-government on the basis of freely elected soviets. Along with these basic demands came another series of claims, shared by other peasant movements, such as calls for the end of requisitioning, the elimination of taxes, freedom for socialist and anarchist parties, the redistribution of land, the end of the "Bolshevik commissarocracy," and the expulsion of the special troops and the Cheka.[29]

The hundreds of peasant uprisings in the spring and summer of 1919

spies and counterrevolutionaries in general." In Lander's words, "The Pyatigorsk Cheka decided straight out to execute 300 people in one day. They divided up the town into various boroughs and took a quota of people from each, and ordered the Party to draw up execution lists . . . This rather unsatisfactory method led to a great deal of private settling of old scores . . . In Kislovodsk, for lack of a better idea, it was decided to kill people who were in the hospital."[42]

One of the most effective means of de-Cossackization was the destruction of Cossack towns and the deportation of all survivors. The files of Sergo Ordzhonikidze, who was president of the Revolutionary Committee of the Northern Caucasus at the time, contain documents detailing one such operation in late October and early November 1920. On 23 October Ordzhonikidze ordered:

1. The town of Kalinovskaya to be burned
2. The inhabitants of Ermolovskaya, Romanovskaya, Samachinskaya, and Mikhailovskaya to be driven out of their homes, and the houses and land redistributed among the poor peasants, particularly among the Chechens, who have always shown great respect for Soviet power
3. All males aged eighteen to fifty from the above-mentioned towns to be gathered into convoys and deported under armed escort to the north, where they will be forced into heavy labor
4. Women, children, and old people to be driven from their homes, although they are to be allowed to resettle farther north
5. All the cattle and goods of the above-mentioned towns to be seized[43]

Three weeks later Ordzhonikidze received a report outlining how the operation had progressed:

Kalinovskaya: town razed and the whole population (4,220) deported or expelled
Ermolovskaya: emptied of all inhabitants (3,218)
Romanovskaya: 1,600 deported, 1,661 awaiting deportation
Samachinskaya: 1,018 deported, 1,900 awaiting deportation
Mikhailovskaya: 600 deported, 2,200 awaiting deportation

In addition, 154 carriages of foodstuffs have been sent to Grozny. In the three towns where the process of deportation is not yet complete, the first people to be deported were the families of Whites and Greens and anyone who participated in the last uprising. Among those still awaiting deportation are the known supporters of the Soviet regime and the families of Red Army soldiers, Soviet officials, and Communists. The delay is to be explained by the lack of railway carriages. On average, only one convoy per day can be devoted to these operations. To finish the operation as soon as possible, we urgently request 306 extra railway carriages.[44]

How did such "operations" come to an end? Unfortunately, there are no documents to provide an answer. It is clear that they continued for a considerable time, and that they almost always ended with deportations not to the great northern regions, as was to be the case for many years to come, but instead to the mines of Donetsk, which were closer. Given the state of the railways in 1920, the operation must have been fairly chaotic. Nonetheless, in their general shape and intention the de-Cossackization operations of 1920 prefigure the larger-scale dekulakization operations of ten years later. They share the same idea of collective responsibility, the same process of deportation in convoys, the same organizational problems, the same unpreparedness of the destinations for the arrival of prisoners, and the same principle of forcing deportees into heavy labor. The Cossack regions of the Don and the Kuban paid a heavy price for their opposition to the Bolsheviks. According to the most reliable estimates, between 300,000 and 500,000 people were killed or deported in 1919 and 1920, out of a population of no more than 3 million.

Among the atrocities whose scale is the most difficult to gauge are the massacres of prisoners and hostages who were taken simply on the basis of their "belonging to an enemy class" or being "socially undesirable." These massacres were part of the logic of the Red Terror in the second half of 1918, but on an even larger scale. The massacres on the basis of class were constantly justified with the claim that a new world was coming into being, and that everything was permitted to assist the difficult birth, as an editorial explained in the first issue of *Krasnyi mech* (The Red sword), the newspaper of the Kyiv Cheka:

> We reject the old systems of morality and "humanity" invented by the bourgeoisie to oppress and exploit the "lower classes." Our morality has no precedent, and our humanity is absolute because it rests on a new ideal. Our aim is to destroy all forms of oppression and violence. To us, everything is permitted, for we are the first to raise the sword not to oppress races and reduce them to slavery, but to liberate humanity from its shackles . . . Blood? Let blood flow like water! Let blood stain forever the black pirate's flag flown by the bourgeoisie, and let our flag be blood-red forever! For only through the death of the old world can we liberate ourselves forever from the return of those jackals![45]

Such murderous calls found many ready to respond, and the ranks of the Cheka were filled with social elements anxious for revenge, recruited as they

often were, as the Bolshevik leaders themselves acknowledged and even recommended, from the ranks of "the criminals and the socially degenerate." In a
letter of 22 March to Lenin, the Bolshevik leader Serafina Gopner described
the activities of the Ekaterinoslavl Cheka: "This organization is rotten to the
core: the canker of criminality, violence, and totally arbitrary decisions abounds,
and it is filled with common criminals and the dregs of society, men armed to
the teeth who simply execute anyone they don't like. They steal, loot, rape, and
throw anyone into prison, forge documents, practice extortion and blackmail,
and will let anyone go in exchange for huge sums of money."[46]

The files of the Central Committee, like those of Feliks Dzerzhinsky,
contain innumerable reports from Party leaders or inspectors from the secret
police detailing the "degenerate acts" of local Chekas "driven mad by blood
and violence." The absence of any juridical or moral norm often resulted in
complete autonomy for local Chekas. No longer answerable for their actions to
any higher authority, they became bloodthirsty and tyrannical regimes, uncontrolled and uncontrollable. Three extracts from dozens of almost identical
Cheka reports illustrate the slide into almost total anarchy.

First, a report from Smirnov, a Cheka training instructor in Syzran, in
Tambov Province, to Dzerzhinsky, on 22 March 1919:

> I have checked up on the events surrounding the kulak uprising in the
> Novo-Matryonskaya *volost*. The interrogations were carried out in a
> totally chaotic manner. Seventy-five people were tortured, but it is im-
> possible to make head or tail of any of the written reports . . . Five
> people were shot on 16 February, and thirteen the following day. The
> report on the death sentences and the executions is dated 28 February.
> When I asked the local Cheka leader to explain himself, he answered,
> "We didn't have time to write the reports at the time. What does it
> matter anyway, when we are trying to wipe out the bourgeoisie and the
> kulaks as a class?"[47]

Next, a report from the secretary of the regional organization of the
Bolshevik Party in Yaroslavl on 26 September 1919: "The Cheka are looting
and arresting everyone indiscriminately. Safe in the knowledge that they cannot
be punished, they have transformed the Cheka headquarters into a huge brothel
where they take all the bourgeois women. Drunkenness is rife. Cocaine is being
used quite widely among the supervisors."[48]

Finally, a report from N. Rosental, inspector of the leadership of special
departments, dated 16 October 1919:

> Atarbekov, chief of the special departments of the Eleventh Army, is
> now refusing to recognize the authority of headquarters. On 30 July,
> when Comrade [Andrei] Zakovsky, who was sent from Moscow to ex-

amine the work of special departments, came to see [Georgy] Atarbekov, the latter answered openly, "Tell Dzerzhinsky I am refusing his control." No administrative norm is being respected by these people, who for the most part are highly dubious, if not plainly criminal in their behavior. The Operations Department keeps almost no records whatever. For death sentences and the execution of such sentences, I found no individual judgments, just lists, for the most part incomplete, of people killed, with the mention "Shot at the behest of Comrade Atarbekov." As for the events of March, it is impossible to get any clear idea of who was shot or why . . . Orgies and drunkenness are daily occurrences. Almost all the personnel of the Cheka are heavy cocaine users. They say that this helps them deal with the sight of so much blood on a daily basis. Drunk with blood and violence, the Cheka is doing its duty, but it is made up of uncontrollable elements that will require close surveillance.[49]

The internal reports of the Party and the Cheka confirm the numerous statements collected in 1919 and 1920 by the enemies of the Bolsheviks, and particularly by the Commission of Special Inquiry into Bolshevik Crimes, established by General Denikin, whose archives, after being transferred from Prague to Moscow in 1945, were long inaccessible but are now open to public scrutiny. In 1926 the Russian Socialist Revolutionary historian Sergei Melgunov, in his book *The Red Terror in Russia*, had tried to catalogue the main massacres of prisoners, hostages, and civilians who were killed en masse by the Bolsheviks, usually on the basis of class. Though incomplete, the list of the principal episodes mentioned in that pioneering work is fully confirmed by a whole variety of documentary sources coming from the two different camps in question. Because of the organizational chaos that reigned in the Chekas, there are still gaps in this information regarding the exact number of people who died in the massacres, although we can be fairly certain of the number of massacres that took place. Using these various sources, one can attempt at least to list them in order of size.

The massacres of "suspects," "hostages," and other "enemies of the people" who were locked up as a preventive measure or for simple administrative reasons in prisons or concentration camps started in September 1918, in the first wave of Red Terror. Once the categories of "suspects," "hostages," and "enemies of the people" had been established, and the concentration camps were in place, the machinery of repression could simply swing into action. The trigger for this war, in which territory so often changed hands and each month brought some sort of turnaround in military fortunes, was usually nothing more than the taking of a village that until then had been occupied by the enemy.

The imposition of the "dictatorship of the proletariat" in cities that had been captured or retaken always went through the same stages: the dissolution of previously elected assemblies, a ban on all trade—which invariably meant immediate price rises for food, and subsequent shortages—the nationalization of all businesses, and the levying of a huge tax on the bourgeoisie—600 million rubles in Kharkiv in February 1919, 500 million in Odessa in April 1919. To ensure that this contribution was paid, hundreds of bourgeois would be taken as hostages and locked up in the concentration camps. In fact this contribution meant a sort of institutionalized pillaging, expropriation, and intimidation, the first step in the destruction of the "bourgeoisie as a social class."

"In accordance with the resolutions of the Workers' Soviet, 13 May has been declared the day of expropriation of the property of the bourgeoisie," announced the *Izvestiya* of the Council of Workers' Delegates of Odessa on 13 May 1919. "The property-owning classes will be required to fill in a questionnaire detailing foodstuffs, shoes, clothes, jewels, bicycles, bedding, sheets, silverware, crockery, and other articles indispensable to the working population . . . It is the duty of all to assist the expropriation commissions in this sacred task. Anyone failing to assist the expropriation commissions will be arrested immediately. Anyone resisting will be executed without further delay."

As Latsis, chief of the Cheka in Ukraine, acknowledged in a circular to local Chekas, the fruits of these expropriations went straight into the pockets of the Cheka or remained in the hands of the chiefs of the innumerable expropriation and requisitioning detachments or Red Guards.

The second stage of the expropriations was the confiscation of bourgeois apartments. In this "class war," humiliation of the enemy was extremely important. "We must treat them the way they deserve: the bourgeoisie respect only authority that punishes and kills," said the report of 26 April 1919 in the Odessa newspaper mentioned above. "If we execute a few dozen of these bloodsucking idiots, if we reduce them to the status of street sweepers and force their women to clean the Red Army barracks (and that would be an honor for them), they will understand that our power is here to stay, and that no one, neither the English nor the Hottentots, is going to come and help them."[50]

A recurring theme in numerous articles in Bolshevik newspapers in Odessa, Kyiv, Kharkiv, Ekaterinoslav, as well as in Perm, Ural, and Nizhni Novgorod, was the "humiliation" of bourgeois women, who were forced to clean toilets or the barracks of the Cheka or Red Guards. But this was merely the toned-down and politically presentable face of the much more brutal reality of rape, which according to innumerable statements took on gigantic proportions, particularly in the second reconquest of Ukraine and the Cossack regions of the Crimea in 1920.

The logical culmination of the "extermination of the bourgeoisie as a class," the execution of prisoners, suspects, and hostages imprisoned simply on the basis of their belonging to the "possessing classes," is recorded in many of the cities taken by the Bolsheviks. In Kharkiv there were between 2,000 and 3,000 executions in February–June 1919, and another 1,000–2,000 when the town was taken again in December of that year; in Rostov-on-Don, approximately 1,000 in January 1920; in Odessa, 2,200 in May–August 1919, then 1,500–3,000 between February 1920 and February 1921; in Kyiv, at least 3,000 in February–August 1919; in Ekaterinodar, at least 3,000 between August 1920 and February 1921; in Armavir, a small town in Kuban, between 2,000 and 3,000 in August–October 1920. The list could go on and on.

In fact many other executions took place elsewhere, but were not subject to close examination very soon afterward. Hence those that occurred in Ukraine or southern Russia are much better known than those of the Caucasus, Central Asia, and the Urals. The pace of executions was often stepped up as the enemy approached, or when the Bolsheviks were abandoning their position and "emptying" the prisons. In Kharkiv, in the days leading up to the arrival of the Whites, on 8 and 9 June 1919, hundreds of hostages were executed. In Kyiv more than 1,800 people were executed on 22–28 August, before the town was retaken by the Whites on 30 August. The same scenario played out at Ekaterinodar, where, in the face of the advancing Cossack troops, Atarbekov, head of the local Cheka, disposed of 1,600 bourgeois on 17–19 August, in a small provincial town whose population before the war numbered a mere 30,000 inhabitants.[51]

Documents from the inquiry commissions of the White Army, which sometimes arrived a few days or even a few hours after the executions, contain a mass of statements, testimonies, autopsy reports, and photographs of the massacres and information about the identity of the victims. Although those who were executed at the last minute, generally with a bullet in the back of the head, showed few traces of torture, this was not always the case for the bodies that were dug out of the mass graves. The use of the most dreadful types of torture is evident from autopsy reports, circumstantial evidence, and eyewitness reports. Detailed descriptions of the torture are to be found both in Sergei Melgunov's *Red Terror in Russia* and in the report by the Central Committee of the Socialist Revolutionary Party, *Cheka*, published in Berlin in 1922.[52]

It was in the Crimea, when the last units of Wrangel's White forces and the civilians who had fled before the Bolshevik advance were moving out, that these massacres were most intensive. From mid-November to the end of December 1920, more than 50,000 people were shot or hanged.[53] A large number of the executions happened immediately after the departure of Wrangel's troops. In Sevastopol several hundred dock workers were shot on 26 November for having assisted in the White evacuation. On 28 and 30 November the

Izvestiya of the Revolutionary Committee of Sevastopol published two lists of victims; the first contained 1,634 names, the second 1,202. In early December, when the first wave of executions had somewhat abated, the authorities began to draw up as complete a list as possible of the population of the main towns of the Crimea, where, they believed, tens or hundreds of thousands of bourgeois were hiding. On 6 December Lenin told an assembly in Moscow that 300,000 bourgeois were hiding out in the Crimea. He gave an assurance that in the very near future these "elements," which constituted "a reservoir of spies and secret agents ready to leap to the defense of capitalism," would all be "punished."[54]

The military cordon that was closing off the Perekop isthmus, the only escape route by land, was reinforced; and once the trap was laid, the authorities ordered all inhabitants to present themselves to the local Cheka to fill in a questionnaire containing some fifty questions about their social origins, past actions, income, and other matters, especially their whereabouts in November 1920 and their opinions about Poland, Wrangel, and the Bolsheviks. On the basis of these inquiries, the population was divided into three groups: those to be shot, those to be sent to concentration camps, and those to be saved. Statements from the few survivors, published in émigré newspapers the following year, describe Sevastopol, one of the towns that suffered most heavily under the repressions, as "the city of the hanged." "From Nakhimovsky, all one could see was the hanging bodies of officers, soldiers, and civilians arrested in the streets. The town was dead, and the only people left alive were hiding in lofts or basements. All the walls, shop fronts, and telegraph poles were covered with posters calling for 'Death to the traitors.' They were hanging people for fun."[55]

The last episode in the conflict between Whites and Reds was not to be the end of the terror. The military front of the civil war no longer existed, but the war to eradicate the enemy was to continue for another two years.

5 From Tambov to the Great Famine

At the end of 1920 the Bolshevik regime seemed poised to triumph. The remnants of the White armies had been defeated, the Cossacks had been beaten, and Makhno's detachments were in retreat. But although the war against the Whites was effectively over, the conflict between the new regime and large sections of the population was intensifying. The war against the peasants reached its height in the early months of 1921, when whole provinces were effectively beyond the control of the Bolsheviks. In the province of Tambov, one of the Volga provinces (which also included Samara, Saratov, Tsaritsyn, and Simbirsk) in western Siberia, the Bolsheviks held only the city of Tambov itself. The countryside was either in the hands of one of hundreds of groups of Greens or under the control of one of the peasant armies. Mutinies broke out daily in the local Red Army garrisons. Strikes, riots, and workers' protest movements multiplied in the few areas of the country where industry still functioned—Moscow, Petrograd, Ivanovo Voznesensk, and Tula. At the end of February 1921, sailors from the Kronstadt naval base near Petrograd mutinied. The situation was becoming explosive, and the country was becoming ungovernable. In the face of a huge wave of social unrest that threatened to sweep away the regime, the Bolshevik leaders were forced to retreat and take the only step that could momentarily calm the massive, dangerous, and widespread discontent: they promised an end to requisitioning, which was to be replaced by taxes in kind. In March 1921, against this backdrop of conflict between society and the regime, the New Economic Policy (NEP) came into being.

The dominant version of events has exaggerated for too long the extent to which March 1921 marked a break with the past. Hastily adopted on the last day of the Bolsheviks' Tenth Party Congress, the substitution of taxes in kind for requisitioning brought neither the end of the workers' strikes nor an abatement in terror. The archives that can now be consulted show that peace did not immediately result from this new regulation in the spring of 1921. In fact tensions remained extremely high until at least the summer of 1922 and in some regions until considerably later. Requisitioning detachments continued to scour the countryside, strikes were still put down brutally, and the last militant socialists were arrested. The "eradication of the bandits from the forests" was still pursued by any means possible, including large-scale executions of hostages and the bombing of villages with poison gas. In the final analysis, the rebellious countryside was beaten by the great famine of 1921–22: the areas that had suffered most heavily from requisitioning were the areas of rebellion and also the areas that suffered worst during the famine. As an "objective" ally of the regime, hunger was the most powerful weapon imaginable, and it also served as a pretext for the Bolsheviks to strike a heavy blow against both the Orthodox Church and the intelligentsia who had risen up against the regime.

Of all the revolts that had broken out since the introduction of requisitioning in the summer of 1918, the revolt of the peasants in Tambov was the largest, the most organized, and therefore the longest-lasting. Located less than 300 miles southeast of Moscow, Tambov Province had been one of the bastions of the Socialist Revolutionary Party since the turn of the century. From 1918 to 1920, despite heavy sanctions, the Party still had numerous militant activists. Tambov Province was also the largest wheat-producing area near Moscow, and since the autumn of 1918 more than 100 requisitioning detachments had been scouring this densely populated agricultural region. In 1919 a number of *bunty* (short-lived riots) had been put down as soon as they had flared up. In 1920 the requisitioning requirements were increased, from 18 million to 27 million *pudy*, while the peasants had considerably reduced the amount they sowed, knowing that anything they did not consume themselves would be immediately requisitioned.[1] To fill the quotas was thus to force the peasants into death by starvation. On 19 August 1920 routine incidents involving the food detachments abruptly degenerated in the town of Khitrovo. As the local authorities themselves acknowledged, "the detachments committed a series of abuses. They looted everything in their path, even pillows and kitchen utensils, shared out the booty, and beat up old men of seventy in full view of the public. The old men were being punished for the absence of their sons, who were deserters hiding in the woods. The peasants were also angry that the confiscated grain, which had been taken to the nearest station by the cartload, was being left to rot in the open air."[2]

From Khitrovo the revolt spread rapidly. By the end of August 1920 more than 14,000 men, mostly deserters, armed with rifles, pitchforks, and scythes, had chased out or massacred all representatives of the Soviet regime from the three districts of Tambov Province. In the space of a few weeks, this peasant revolt, which at first could not be distinguished from the hundreds of others that had broken out all over Russia and Ukraine over the previous two years, was transformed into a well-organized uprising under the inspirational leadership of a first-class warlord, Aleksandr Stepanovich Antonov.

A Socialist Revolutionary activist since 1906, Antonov had spent the years after 1908 as a political exile in Siberia, returning only in October 1917. Like many left Socialist Revolutionaries, he had rallied to the Bolshevik cause for a time, and had been the head of the local militia in Kirsanov, his native region. In August 1918 he had broken with the Bolsheviks and assumed leadership of one of the many bands of deserters that roamed the countryside, fighting in guerrilla style against the requisitioning detachments and attacking the few Soviet officials who dared go out into the remote villages. When the peasant revolt took hold in Kirsanov in August 1920, Antonov organized both a highly effective peasant militia and a remarkable information network that infiltrated even the Tambov Cheka. He also organized a propaganda service that distributed tracts and proclamations denouncing the "Bolshevik commissarocracy" and mobilized the peasants around key popular demands such as free trade, the end of requisitioning, free elections, the elimination of Bolshevik commissariats, and the disbanding of the Cheka.[3]

In parallel, the underground Socialist Revolutionary Party organization established the Union of Working Peasants, a clandestine network of militant peasants from the surrounding area. Despite serious tensions between Antonov and the leaders of the Union of Working Peasants, the peasant movement in the Tambov region basically had a military organization, an information network, and a political program that lent it strength and unity, things that no other peasant movement (with the possible exception of the Makhnovist movement) had possessed.

In October 1920 the Bolsheviks controlled no more than the city of Tambov and a few provincial urban centers. Deserters flocked by the thousands to join Antonov's peasant army, which at its peak numbered more than 50,000. On 19 October, realizing at last the gravity of the situation, Lenin wrote to Dzerzhinsky: "It is vital that this movement be crushed as swiftly as possible in the most exemplary fashion: we must be more energetic than this!"[4]

At the beginning of November the Bolsheviks in the area numbered no more than 5,000 Troops for the Internal Defense of the Republic. After the defeat of Wrangel in the Crimea, the number of troops deployed to Tambov Province quickly reached 100,000, including some detachments from the Red Army, who were nonetheless kept to a minimum when it came to suppressing popular revolts.

After 1 January the peasant revolts spread to several other regions, including the whole of the lower Volga (the provinces of Samara, Saratov, Tsaritsyn, and Astrakhan), as well as western Siberia. The situation became explosive as famine threatened these rich, fertile regions that had been overtaxed for several years. In Samara Province the commander of the Volga Military District reported on 12 February 1921 that "crowds of thousands of starving peasants are besieging the barns where the food detachments have stored the grain that has been requisitioned for urban areas and the army. The situation has deteriorated several times, and the army has been forced to open fire repeatedly on the enraged crowd." From Saratov the local Bolshevik leaders sent the following telegram to Moscow: "Banditry has overwhelmed the whole province. The peasants have seized all the stocks—3 million *pudy*—from the state grain stores. They are heavily armed, thanks to all the rifles from the deserters. Whole units of the Red Army have simply vanished."

At the same time, about 600 miles eastward, a new trouble spot was emerging. Having extracted all the resources that it could from the prosperous agricultural regions of southern Russia and Ukraine, the Bolshevik government in the autumn of 1919 had turned to western Siberia, where the quotas were fixed arbitrarily on the basis of wheat export figures dating from 1913. Evidently no attempt was made to consider the difference between the old harvest, which had been destined for export and had been paid for with gold-standard rubles, and the pitifully meager reserves that the peasants had set aside for requisitioning. As in other regions, the Siberian peasants responded with an uprising to protect the results of their labors and to assure their own survival. From January to March 1921 the Bolsheviks lost control of the provinces of Tyumen, Omsk, Chelyabinsk, and Ekaterinburg—a territory larger than France. The Trans-Siberian Railway, the only link between western Russia and Siberia, was also cut off. On 21 February a Russian peasant army seized the city of Tobolsk, which Red Army units did not manage to retake until 30 March.[5]

At the other end of the country, in both Petrograd, the old capital, and Moscow, the new one, the situation at the beginning of 1921 was almost as explosive. The economy had nearly stopped, and the transport system had ground to a halt. Most of the factories were closed or working at half-speed because of lack of fuel, and food supplies to the cities were in danger of ceasing altogether. All the workers were in the streets, in the surrounding villages scavenging for food, or standing around and talking in the freezing, half-empty factories, many of which had been stripped for items to exchange for food.

"Discontent is widespread," said a Cheka Information Department report on 16 January. "The workers are predicting the imminent demise of the regime. No one works any more because they are all too hungry. Strikes on a huge scale are bound to start any day now. The garrisons in Moscow are less and less trustworthy and could become uncontrollable at any moment. Preventive measures are required."[6]

On 21 January a government decree ordered a 30 percent reduction in bread rations for Moscow, Petrograd, Ivanovo Voznesensk, and Kronstadt. Coming at a time when the last White armies had been defeated and the government could no longer claim that the counterrevolutionaries were to blame, this measure was enough to light the powderkeg of rebellion. From the end of January to mid-March 1921, strikes, protest meetings, hunger marches, demonstrations, and factory sit-ins occurred daily, reaching their height in Moscow and Petrograd at the end of February and the beginning of March. In Moscow from 22 to 24 March there were serious confrontations between Cheka detachments and groups of demonstrators who were attempting to force their way into the barracks to join forces with the soldiers. Many of the workers were shot, and hundreds were arrested.[7]

In Petrograd the troubles became more widespread after 22 February, when workers from several of the main factories voted in a new "Plenipotentiary Workers' Assembly" that was strongly Menshevik and Socialist Revolutionary in character. In its first decree the assembly demanded the elimination of the Bolshevik dictatorship, free elections to the soviet, freedom of speech, assembly, and the press, and the release of all political prisoners. To achieve these ends the assembly called for a general strike. The military command failed to stop several regiments from holding meetings that passed motions of support for the strikers. On 24 February Cheka detachments opened fire on a workers' demonstration, killing twelve men. That same day, more than 1,000 workers and militant socialists were arrested.[8] Yet the ranks of the strikers continued to swell, with thousands of soldiers leaving their units to join forces with the workers. Four years after the February days that had overturned the tsarist regime, history seemed to be repeating itself as militant workers and mutinying soldiers joined forces. On 26 February at 9:00 P.M. Grigory Zinoviev, the head of the Bolshevik Party in Petrograd, sent a telegram to Lenin in panic: "The workers have joined up with the soldiers in the barracks . . . We are still waiting for the reinforcements we demanded from Novgorod. If they don't arrive in the next few hours, we are going to be overrun."

Two days later came the event that the Bolshevik leaders had been fearing above all else: a mutiny of the sailors aboard the two warships in the Kronstadt base near Petrograd. Zinoviev sent another telegram to Lenin on 28 February at 11:00 P.M.: "Kronstadt: the two main ships, the *Sevastopol* and the *Petropavlovsk*, have adopted Socialist Revolutionary and Black Hundred resolutions and given us an ultimatum to which we have twenty-four hours to respond. The situation among the workers is very unstable. All the main factories are on strike. We think that the Socialist Revolutionaries are going to step up protests."[9]

The demands that Zinoviev labeled "Socialist Revolutionary and Black Hundred" were the same things that the immense majority of citizens were demanding after three years of Bolshevik dictatorship: free and secret elections, freedom of speech, and freedom of the press—at least for "workers, peasants, anarchists, and left-wing socialist parties." They also demanded equal rations for all, the freeing of all political prisoners, the convocation of a special commission to reexamine the cases of those imprisoned in concentration camps, an end to requisitioning, the abolition of special Cheka detachments, and freedom for the peasants "to do whatever they want with their land, and to raise their own livestock, provided they do it using their own resources."[10]

At Kronstadt events were gathering momentum. On 1 March a huge meeting gathered together more than 15,000 people, a quarter of the entire civil and military population of the naval base. Mikhail Kalinin, president of the Central Executive Committee of the Soviets, arrived in person to try to defuse the situation; but he failed to make himself heard over the boos of the crowd. The following day the rebels, joined by at least 2,000 Bolsheviks from Kronstadt, formed a provisional revolutionary committee that attempted to link up with the strikers and soldiers from Petrograd.

The daily Cheka reports on the situation in Petrograd in the first week of March 1921 leave no doubt about the widespread popular support for the mutiny at Kronstadt: "The Kronstadt revolutionary committee clearly expects a general uprising in Petrograd any day now. They have made contact with the mutineers and with a number of the factories. Today, at a meeting in the Arsenal factory, workers voted for a resolution to join the general insurrection. A delegation of three people—including an anarchist, a Menshevik, and a Socialist Revolutionary—has been elected to keep in contact with Kronstadt."[11]

On 7 March the Petrograd Cheka received the order to "undertake decisive action against the workers." Within forty-eight hours more than 2,000 workers, all known socialist or anarchist sympathizers or activists, were arrested. Unlike the mutineers, the workers were unarmed and could put up little resistance to the Cheka detachments. Having thus broken the support for the insurrection, the Bolsheviks carefully prepared the assault on Kronstadt itself. The task of liquidating the rebellion was entrusted to General Mikhail Tukhachevsky. In opening fire on the crowd, the victor from the Polish campaign of 1920 used young recruits from the military school, who had no tradition of revolution, and special detachments from the Cheka. The operation began on 8 March. Ten days later Kronstadt fell after thousands of people had lost their lives. Several hundred rebels who had been taken prisoner were shot over the next few days. The records of the event, recently published for the first time, show that from April to June 1921, 2,103 were sentenced to death and 6,459 were sent to prison or to the camps.[12] Just before the fall of Kronstadt nearly 8,000 people managed to escape across the ice to Finland, where they were interned in transit camps in Terioki, Vyborg, and Ino. Deceived by the promise of an amnesty, a number of them returned to Russia in 1922, where they were immediately arrested and sent to camps on the Solovetski Islands and to Kholmogory, one of the worst concentration camps, near Arkhangelsk.[13] According to one anarchist source, of the 5,000 Kronstadt prisoners who were sent to Kholmogory, fewer than 1,500 were still alive in the spring of 1922.[14]

The Kholmogory camp, on the great river Dvina, was sadly famous for the swift manner in which it dispatched a great number of its prisoners. They were often loaded onto barges, stones were tied around their necks, their arms and legs were tied, and they were thrown overboard into the river. Mikhail Kedrov, one of the main leaders of the Cheka, had started these massive drownings in June 1920. Several eyewitness reports concur that a large number of the mutineers from Kronstadt, together with Cossacks and peasants from Tambov Province who had also been deported to Kholmogory, were drowned in the Dvina in this fashion in 1922. That same year, a special evacuation committee deported to Siberia some 2,514 civilians from Kronstadt, merely on the grounds that they had stayed in the town through the events.[15]

Once the Kronstadt rebellion had been crushed, the regime concentrated its energies on hunting down socialist activists, fighting strikes and "workers' complacency," quelling the peasant uprisings that continued despite the official ending of requisitioning, and taking measures to repress the church.

On 28 February 1921 Dzerzhinsky had ordered all the provincial Chekas "(1) to carry out immediate arrests of all anarchist, Menshevik, and Socialist Revolutionary intelligentsia, in particular the officials working in the People's Commissariats of Agriculture and Food; and (2) to arrest all Mensheviks, anarchists, and Socialist Revolutionaries working in factories and liable to call for strikes or demonstrations."[16]

Rather than marking the beginning of a relaxation in the repressive policies, the introduction of the NEP was accompanied by a resurgence in the repressions against the moderate socialist activists. The repressions were motivated not by the danger of their perceived opposition to the New Economic

Policy, but by the fact that they had been campaigning for it for so long, and might thus use it to justify their own approach to politics. "The only place for Mensheviks and Socialist Revolutionaries, whether they hide their allegiances or are open about them," wrote Lenin in 1921, "is prison."

A few months later, judging that the socialists were still making too much trouble, he wrote: "If the Mensheviks or Socialist Revolutionaries so much as peek out again, they must all be shot without pity." Between March and June 1921 more than 2,000 moderate socialist activists and sympathizers were again arrested. By now all the members of the Central Committee of the Menshevik Party were in prison; when threatened with expulsion to Siberia in January 1921 they began a hunger strike, and twelve of the leaders, including Fedor Dan and Boris Nikolaevsky, were expelled abroad and arrived in Berlin in February 1922.

One of the main priorities of the regime in the spring of 1921 was to revive industrial production, which had fallen to 10 percent of what it had been in 1913. Rather than relaxing the pressure on workers, the Bolsheviks maintained and even increased the militarization begun over the preceding years. The policies pursued in 1921 after the adoption of the NEP in the great industrial and mining region of the Donbass, which produced more than 80 percent of the country's coal and steel, seem particularly revealing of the sort of dictatorial methods used by the Bolsheviks to get the workers back to work. At the end of 1920 Georgy Pyatakov, one of the main leaders who was close to Trotsky, had been appointed head of the Central Directory of the Coal Industry. Within a year he increased coal production fivefold by means of a policy of unremitting exploitation and intimidation. Pyatokov imposed excruciating discipline on his 120,000 workers: any absenteeism was equated with an act of sabotage and punished with expulsion to a camp or even a death sentence. In 1921 18 miners were executed for "persistent parasitism." Work hours were increased, particularly on Sundays, and Pyatokov effectively blackmailed the workers into increasing productivity by threatening the confiscation of ration cards. These measures were taken at a time when the workers received between one-third and one-half of the bread ration they needed to survive; often at the end of the day they had to lend their boots to comrades who were taking over the next shift. The directory acknowledged that absenteeism among the workforce was due in part to epidemics, "permanent hunger," and "a total absence of clothes, trousers, and shoes." To reduce the number of mouths to feed when the threat of famine was at its height, Pyatokov on 24 June 1921 ordered the expulsion from the mining villages of everyone who did not work in the mines. Ration cards were confiscated from family members of miners. Rationing was also calculated strictly in accordance with the production of individual miners, thus introducing a rudimentary form of productivity-related pay.[17]

Such practices went directly against the ideas of equality of treatment that many workers, deceived by Bolshevik rhetoric, still cherished. In a remarkable way these measures prefigured those taken against the working classes in the 1930s. The working masses were nothing more than the *rabsila*—the work-force—which had to be exploited in the most effective manner possible. Doing so involved overturning legislation and the appeals of the unions, which were totally hamstrung and were ordered to support the directives of management at all costs. Militarization of the workforce seemed to be the most effective means of forcing the hungry, stubborn, and unproductive workers to cooperate. The similarities between this exploitation of the theoretically free workforce and the forced labor of the great penal colonies created in the early 1930s seem inescapable. Like so many other episodes in the formative years of Bolshevism, none of which can be explained through the context of the civil war, the events in the Donbass in 1921 prefigured a series of practices that were later to be found at the heart of Stalinism.

Among the other top-priority operations for the Bolshevik regime in the spring of 1921 was the "pacification" of all the regions that were in the hands of the peasants. On 27 April 1921 the Politburo appointed General Tukhachevsky to lead "operations to liquidate the Antonov elements in Tambov Province." With nearly 100,000 men at his disposal, including many special Cheka detachments, and equipped with airplanes and heavy artillery, Tukhachevsky waged war on the Antonov units with extraordinary violence. Together with Antonov-Ovseenko, president of the Plenipotentiary Commission of the Central Executive Committee established to constitute an occupying force in the region, he took hostages on an enormous scale, carried out executions, set up death camps where prisoners were gassed, and deported entire villages suspected of assisting or collaborating with the so-called bandits.[18]

Order No. 171, dated 11 June 1921 and signed by Antonov-Ovseenko and Tukhachevsky, shows clearly the sorts of methods used to "pacify" Tambov Province. The order stipulated:

1. Shoot on sight any citizens who refuse to give their names.
2. District and Regional Political Commissions are hereby authorized to pronounce sentence on any village where arms are being hidden, and to arrest hostages and shoot them if the whereabouts of the arms are not revealed.
3. Wherever arms are found, execute immediately the eldest son in the family.
4. Any family that has harbored a bandit is to be arrested and deported from the province, their possessions are to be seized, and the eldest son is to be executed immediately.
5. Any families sheltering other families who have harbored ban-

been threatening the region since at least 1919. The situation had deteriorated considerably throughout 1920. In their internal reports that summer the Cheka, the People's Commissariat of Agriculture, and the People's Commissariat of Food, fully aware of the gravity of the situation, drew up lists of districts and provinces judged to be starving or threatened by imminent famine. In January 1921 one report claimed that among the causes of the famine in Tambov was the "orgy" of requisitioning of 1920. It was quite obvious to the common people, as conversations reported by the political police made clear, that the "soviet regime is trying to starve out all the peasants who dare resist it." Though perfectly well informed of the inevitable consequences of the requisitioning policy, the government took no steps to combat these predicted effects. On 30 July 1921, while famine gripped a growing number of regions, Lenin and Molotov sent a telegram to all leaders of regional and provincial Party committees asking them to "bolster the mechanisms for food collection . . . step up the propaganda for the rural population, explaining the economic and political importance of the prompt paying of taxes . . . put at the disposal of the agencies for the collection of taxes in kind all the authority of the Party, and allow them to use all the disciplinary measures that the state itself would use."[28]

Faced with this attitude of the authorities, who seemed to be pursuing a policy of starving out the peasantry at all cost, the more enlightened intelligentsia began to react. In June 1921 the agronomists, economists, and university lecturers who belonged to the Moscow Agricultural Society established a Social Committee for the Fight against Famine. Among the first members were the eminent economists Nikolai Kondratyev and Sergei Prokopovich, who had been a minister of food in the provisional government; the journalist Ekaterina Kuskova, a close friend of Maksim Gorky; and various writers, doctors, and agronomists. In mid-July, with the help of Gorky, who was highly influential among Party leaders, a delegation from the committee obtained an audience with Lev Kamenev after Lenin had refused to see them. Following the interview Lenin, still distrusting what he described as the overly emotional reactions of certain other Bolshevik leaders, sent the following note to his colleagues in the Politburo: "This Kuskova woman must not cause any damage . . . We will use her name and her signature, and a carriage or two from the people who sympathize with her and her kind. Nothing more than that."[29]

Finally the committee members convinced some Party leaders of their usefulness. As internationally prominent scientists and writers, they were well known abroad, and many of them had taken an active part in aid for the victims of the famine of 1891. Moreover, they had numerous contacts with other intellectuals the world over, and seemed to be guarantors that the food would reach its intended destination, in the event that the appeal was successful. They were prepared to allow their names to be used, provided that some sort of official status was granted to the Committee for Aid to the Hungry.

On 21 July 1921 the Bolshevik government reluctantly legalized the committee, naming it the All-Russian Committee for Aid to the Starving. It was immediately given the emblem of the Red Cross and was permitted to collect food, medicine, and animal feed both in Russia and abroad and to share it out among the needy. It was allowed to use whatever means of transport necessary to distribute the food, to set up soup kitchens and local and regional committees, "to communicate freely with designated organizations abroad," and even "to discuss measures taken by local or central authorities that in its opinion are relevant to the question of the struggle against the famine."[30] At no other moment in the history of the Soviet regime was any other organization granted such privileges. The government's concessions were a measure of the scale of the catastrophe facing the country, four months after the official (and somewhat muted) introduction of the NEP.

One of the committee's first actions was to establish contact with the Patriarch Tikhon, head of the Orthodox Church, who immediately set up an All-Russian Ecclesiastical Committee for Aid to the Hungry. On 7 July 1921 the patriarch had a letter read out in all the churches: "Rotten meat would be gladly eaten by the starving population, but even that is now impossible to find. Cries and moans are all that one hears wherever one goes. People's minds turn even to thoughts of cannibalism . . . Lend a helping hand to your brothers and sisters! With the consent of your brethren, you may use church treasures that have no sacramental value, such as rings, chains, bracelets, decorations that adorn icons, and other items to help the hungry."

Having obtained the assistance of the church, the All-Russian Committee for Aid to the Starving contacted various international organizations, including the Red Cross, the Quakers, and the American Relief Association (ARA), presided over by Herbert Hoover; all responded positively. Even so, cooperation between the committee and the regime lasted only five weeks; on 27 August 1921 the committee was dissolved, six days after the government had signed an agreement with a representative of the ARA. For Lenin, now that the Americans were sending the first cargoes of food, the committee had served its purpose: "The name and the signature of Kuskova" had played the required role, and that was enough. In announcing this decision, Lenin wrote:

> I propose to dissolve the Committee immediately . . . Prokopovich is to be arrested for seditious behavior and kept in prison for three months . . . The other Committee members are to be exiled from Moscow immediately, sent to the chief cities of different regions, cut off if possible from all means of communication, including railways, and kept

under close surveillance. Tomorrow we will release a brief governmental communiqué saying that the Committee has been dissolved because it refused to work. Instruct all newspapers to begin insulting these people, and heap opprobrium upon them, accusing them of being closet White Guard supporters and bourgeois do-gooders who are much keener to travel abroad than to help at home. In general, make them look ridiculous and mock them at least once a week for the next two months.[31]

Following these instructions to the letter, the press unleashed a ferocious attack against the sixty famous intellectuals who had served on the committee. The titles alone of the articles demonstrate the eloquence of this campaign of defamation: "You shouldn't play with hunger" (*Pravda,* 30 August 1921); "Hunger Speculators" (*Kommunisticheskii trud,* 31 August 1921); "Committee for Aid . . . to the Counterrevolution" (*Izvestiya,* 30 August 1921). When someone tried to intercede in favor of the committee members who had been arrested and deported, Josif Unshlikht, one of Dzerzhinsky's assistants at the Cheka, declared: "You say the Committee has done nothing wrong. It's possible. But it has become a rallying point in society, and that we cannot allow. When you put a seed in water, it soon starts to sprout roots, and the Committee was beginning to spread its roots throughout society, undermining collectivity . . . we had no choice but to pull it up by the roots and to crush it."[32]

In place of the committee the government set up a Central Commission for Help for the Hungry, a slow-moving and bureaucratic organization made up of civil servants from various People's Commissariats, which was characterized by inefficiency and corruption. When the famine was at its worst in the summer of 1922 and nearly 30 million people were starving, the Central Commission was assuring an irregular supply to about 3 million people, whereas the Red Cross, the Quakers, and the ARA supplied about 11 million people per day. Despite the massive international relief effort, at least 5 million of the 29 million Russians affected died of hunger in 1921 and 1922.[33]

The last great famine that Russia had known, in 1891, had affected most of the same regions (mid-Russia, the lower Volga, and part of Kazakhstan) and had been responsible for the deaths of between 400,000 and 500,000 people. Both the state and society in general had fought extremely hard to save lives. A young lawyer called Vladimir Ilych Ulyanov was then living in Samara, the regional capital of one of the areas worst affected by the famine. He was the only member of the local intelligentsia who not only refused to participate in the aid for the hungry, but publicly opposed it. As one of his friends later recalled, "Vladimir Ilich Ulyanov had the courage to come out and say openly that famine would have numerous positive results, particularly in the appearance of a new industrial proletariat, which would take over from the bourgeoisie . . . Famine, he explained, in destroying the outdated peasant economy, would bring about the next stage more rapidly, and usher in socialism, the stage that necessarily followed capitalism. Famine would also destroy faith not only in the tsar, but in God too."[34]

Thirty years later, when the young lawyer had become the head of the Bolshevik government, his ideas remained unchanged: famine could and should "strike a mortal blow against the enemy." The enemy in question was the Orthodox Church. "Electricity will replace God. The peasants should pray to it; in any case they will feel its effects long before they feel any effect from on high," said Lenin in 1918 when discussing the electrification of Russia with Leonid Krasin. As soon as the Bolshevik regime had come to power, relations with the Orthodox Church had deteriorated. On 5 February 1918 the government had declared the separation of church and state and of the church and schools, proclaimed freedom of conscience and worship, and announced the nationalization of all church property. Patriarch Tikhon had vigorously protested this attack on the traditional role of the church in four pastoral letters to the faithful. The behavior of the Bolsheviks became more and more provocative. They ordered all church relics to be "valued," organized antireligious carnivals to coincide with traditional feast days, and demanded that the great monastery of the Trinity and St. Sergius near Moscow, where the relics of St. Sergius of Radonezh were kept, be turned into a museum of atheism. Numerous priests and bishops had already been arrested for protesting the intimidatory measures of the state when the Bolshevik leaders, on Lenin's orders, used the famine as a pretext to launch a large-scale campaign against the church.

On 26 February 1922 a government decree was published in the press ordering "the immediate confiscation from churches of all precious objects of gold or silver and of all precious stones that do not have a religious importance. These objects will be sent to the People's Commissariat of Finance and will then be transferred to the Central Committee for Help for the Hungry." The confiscations began in early March and were accompanied by many confrontations between the detachments responsible for impounding the church treasures and the church faithful. The most serious incidents took place on 15 March 1922 in Chuya, a small industrial town in Ivanovo Province, where troops opened fire on the crowd and killed a dozen of the faithful. Lenin used this massacre as a pretext to step up the antireligious campaign.

In a letter addressed to the Politburo on 19 March 1922, he explained, with characteristic cynicism, how the famine could be turned to the Bolsheviks' advantage and exploited to strike the enemy a mortal blow:

> Regarding the events at Chuya, which the Politburo will be discussing, I think a firm decision should be adopted immediately as part of the general campaign on this front . . . If we bear in mind what the newspa-

pers are saying about the attitude of the clergy toward the confiscation of church goods, and the subversive attitude that is being adopted by the Patriarch Tikhon, it becomes apparent that the Black Hundred clergy are putting into action a plan that has been developed to strike a decisive blow against us . . . I think our enemies are committing a monumental strategic error. In fact the present moment favors us far more than it does them. We are almost 99 percent sure that we can strike a mortal blow against them and consolidate the central position that we are going to need to occupy for several decades to come. With the help of all those starving people who are starting to eat each other, who are dying by the millions, and whose bodies litter the roadside all over the country, it is now and only now that we can—and therefore must—confiscate all church property with all the ruthless energy we can still muster. This is precisely the moment when the masses will support us most fervently, and rise up against the reactionary machinations of the petit-bourgeois and Black Hundred religious conspirators . . . we must therefore amass a treasure of hundreds of millions of gold rubles (think how rich some of those monasteries are!). Without treasure on that scale, no state projects, no economic projects, and no shoring up of our present position will be conceivable. No matter what the cost, we must have those hundreds of millions (or even billions) of rubles. This can be carried out only at the present moment. All evidence suggests that we could not do this at any other moment, because our only hope is the despair engendered in the masses by the famine, which will cause them to look at us in a favorable light or, at the very least, with indifference. I thus can affirm categorically that this is the moment to crush the Black Hundred clergy in the most decisive manner possible, and to act without any mercy at all, with the sort of brutality that they will remember for decades. I propose to implement our plan in the following manner: Only Comrade Kalinin will act openly. Whatever happens, Comrade Trotsky will not appear in the press or in public . . . One of the most intelligent and energetic members of the Central Executive Committee must be sent to Chuya, with oral instructions from one of the members of the Politburo. These instructions will stipulate that his mission in Chuya is to arrest a large number of members of the clergy, of bourgeoisie and petit-bourgeoisie, several dozen at least, who will all be accused of direct or indirect participation in violent resistance against the decree regarding the confiscation of church goods. Once back from this mission, the envoy will make a full report to the entire Politburo or to a meeting of two or three members. On the basis of this report, the Politburo, again orally, will issue precise instructions to the judicial authorities, to the effect that the trial of the Chuya rebels is to be expedited as rapidly as possible. The result of the trial is to be the execution, by public shooting, of a large number of the Chuya Black Hundreds as well as the shooting of as

many as possible from Moscow and other important religious centers . . . The more representatives from the reactionary clergy and the
recalcitrant bourgeoisie we shoot, the better it will be for us. We must
teach these people a lesson as quickly as possible, so that the thought of
protesting again doesn't occur to them for decades to come.[35]

As the weekly reports from the secret police indicate, the campaign to
confiscate church goods was at its height in March, April, and May 1922, when
it led to 1,414 incidents and the arrest of thousands of priests, nuns, and monks.
According to church records, 2,691 priests, 1,962 monks, and 3,447 nuns were
killed that year.[36] The government organized several large show-trials for members of the clergy in Moscow, Ivanovo, Chuya, Smolensk, and Petrograd. A
week after the incidents in Chuya, in accordance with Lenin's instructions, the
Politburo proposed a series of measures: "Arrest the synod and the patriarch,
not immediately, but between a fortnight and a month from now. Make public
the circumstances surrounding the business in Chuya. Bring to trial all the
priests and lay members of Chuya in one week's time. Shoot all the rebel
leaders."[37] In a note to the Politburo, Dzerzhinsky indicated that

> the patriarch and his followers . . . are openly resisting the confiscation
> of church goods . . . We already have enough evidence to arrest Tikhon
> and the more reactionary members of the synod. In the view of the
> GPU: (1) the time is right for the arrest of the patriarch and the synod;
> (2) permission should not be granted for the formation of a new synod;
> (3) all priests resisting the confiscation of church goods should be desig-
> nated enemies of the people and exiled to one of the Volga regions most
> affected by the famine.[38]

In Petrograd 77 priests were sent to camps; 4 were sentenced to death,
including the metropolitan of Petrograd, Benjamin, who had been elected in
1917 and enjoyed a wide popular following. Ironically, he was among those who
had spoken strongly in favor of the separation of church and state. In Moscow
148 priests and lay brethren were sent to the camps, and 6 received death
sentences that were immediately carried out. Patriarch Tikhon was placed
under close surveillance in the Donskoi monastery in Moscow.

On 6 June 1922, a few weeks after these legal travesties in Moscow, a large
public trial began, announced in the press since the end of February: thirty-
four Socialist Revolutionaries were accused of "counterrevolutionary and terrorist activities against the Soviet government," including most notably the
attempt to assassinate Lenin on 31 August 1918 and participation in the Tambov peasant revolt. In a scenario that was replayed over and over in the 1930s,
the accused included authentic political leaders, such as the twelve members of

the Central Committee of the Socialist Revolutionary Party, led by Avraham Gots and Dmitry Donskoi, and *agents provocateurs* instructed to testify against the others and to "confess their crimes." As Hélène Carrère d'Encausse has pointed out, this trial permitted the authorities to "test out the 'Russian doll' method of accusation, whereby one solid accusation—the fact that since 1918 the Socialist Revolutionaries had been opposed to Bolshevik rule—was cited to 'prove' that any opposition to the Bolsheviks' policies was, in the final analysis, an act of cooperation with the international bourgeoisie."[39]

At the conclusion of this parody of justice, after the authorities had orchestrated political demonstrations calling for the death penalty for the "terrorists," eleven of the accused leaders of the Socialist Revolutionary Party were condemned to death. Faced with protests from the international community, organized largely by exiled Russian socialists, and with the more serious threat of uprisings in the pro–Socialist Revolutionary countryside, the sentences were suspended on the condition that "the Socialist Revolutionary Party ends all conspiratorial, insurrectionary, and terrorist activities." In January 1924 the death sentences were reduced to five years' internment in the camps. Needless to say the prisoners were never set free, and were in fact executed in the 1930s, when international opinion and the danger of peasant uprisings no longer posed a threat to the Bolshevik leadership.

The trial of the Socialist Revolutionaries was one of the first opportunities to test the new penal code, which had come into force on 1 June 1922. Lenin had followed its elaboration quite closely. One of the code's functions was to permit the use of all necessary violence against political enemies even though the civil war was over and "expeditious elimination" could no longer be justified. The first drafts of the code, shown to Lenin on 15 May 1922, provoked the following reply to Kursky, the people's commissar of justice: "It is my view that the leeway for applying the death penalty should be considerably enlarged, and should include all the activities of Mensheviks, Socialist Revolutionaries, and others. Create a new punishment involving banishment abroad. And find some formulation that will link all these activities to the international bourgeoisie."[40] Two days later Lenin wrote again:

Comrade Kursky, I want you to add this draft of a complementary paragraph to the penal code . . . It is quite clear for the most part. We must openly—and not simply in narrow juridical terms—espouse a politically just principle that is the essence and motivation for terror, showing its necessity and its limits. The courts must not end the terror or suppress it in any way. To do so would be deception. They must give it a solid basis, and clearly legalize all its principles without any form of deception or deceit. It must be formulated as openly as possible: what we need to encourage is a revolutionary legal consciousness that will allow it to be applied wherever it is needed.[41]

In accordance with Lenin's instructions, the penal code defined counter-revolutionary activity as any action "aiming to attack or destabilize the power given to Soviet workers and peasants by the revolutionary proletariat," as well as "any action in favor of the international bourgeoisie that fails to recognize the validity of the Communist system and the fair distribution of property as a natural successor to the capitalist system, and any action that tries to reverse the situation by force, military intervention, economic blockade, espionage, illegal financing of the press, or other such means."

Anything that was classified as a counterrevolutionary action, including rebellion, rioting, sabotage, and espionage, was immediately punishable by death, as was participation in or support for any organization "that might provide support for the international bourgeoisie." Even "propaganda that might be of use to the international bourgeoisie" was considered a counter-revolutionary crime, punishable by incarceration for not less than three years or by lifelong exile.

Along with the legalization of political violence, discussed in early 1922, came nominal changes within the secret police. On 6 February 1922 the Cheka was abolished by decree, to be immediately replaced by the State Political Directorate Administration (Gosudastvennoe politicheskoe upravlenie; GPU), which was responsible to the People's Commissariat of Internal Affairs. Although the name had changed, the staff and the administrative structure remained the same, ensuring a high degree of continuity within the institution. The change in title emphasized that whereas the Cheka had been an extraordinary agency, which in principle was only transitory, the GPU was permanent. The state thus gained a ubiquitous mechanism for political repression and control. Lying behind the name change were the legalization and the institutionalization of terror as a means of resolving all conflict between the people and the state.

One of the new punishments instituted in the new penal code was lifelong banishment, with the understanding that any return to the U.S.S.R. would be greeted with immediate execution. It was put into practice from as early as 1922 as part of a long expulsion operation that affected nearly 200 well-known intellectuals suspected of opposing Bolshevism. Among them were many of the prominent figures who had participated in the Social Committee for the Fight against Famine, which had been dissolved on 27 July of that year.

In a long letter to Dzerzhinsky dated 20 May 1922, Lenin laid out a vast plan for the "banishment abroad of all writers and teachers who have assisted the counterrevolution . . . This operation must be planned with great care. A special commission must be set up. All members of the Politburo must spend two to three hours each week carefully examining books and newspapers . . . Information must be gathered systematically on the political past, the work, and the literary activity of teachers and writers."

Lenin led the way with an example:

As far as the journal *Ekonomist* is concerned, for example, it is clearly a center for White Guard activity. On the cover of the third issue (*N.B.:* as early as that!) all the collaborators are listed. I think they are all legitimate candidates for expulsion. They are all known counterrevolutionaries and accomplices of the Entente, and they make up a network of its servants, spies, and corrupters of youth. Things must be set in motion such that they are hunted down and imprisoned in a systematic and organized fashion and banished abroad.[42]

On 22 May the Politburo established a special commission, including notably Kamenev, Kursky, Unshlikht, and Vasily Mantsev (the last two being Dzerzhinksy's two assistants), to collect information on intellectuals to be arrested and expelled. The first two people expelled in this fashion were the two main leaders of the Social Committee for the Fight against Famine, Sergei Prokopovich and Ekaterina Kuskova. A first group of 160 well-known intellectuals, philosophers, writers, historians, and university professors, who were arrested on 16 and 17 August, were deported in September. Some of the names on the list were already famous internationally or would soon become so: Nikolai Berdyaev, Sergei Bulgakov, Semyon Frank, Nikolai Loski, Lev Karsavin, Fyodor Stepun, Sergei Trubetskoi, Aleksandr Isgoev, Mikhail Ossorgin, Aleksandr Kiesewetter. Each was forced to sign a document stating that he understood that if he ever returned to the U.S.S.R., he would immediately be shot. Each was allowed to take one winter coat and one summer coat, one suit and change of clothes, two shirts, two nightshirts, two pairs of socks, two sets of underwear, and twenty dollars in foreign currency.

Parallel to these expulsions, the secret police proceeded with its policy of gathering information about all second-tier intellectuals who were under suspicion and were destined either for administrative deportation to remote areas of the country, codified in law by a decree on 10 August 1922, or for the concentration camps. On 5 September Dzerzhinsky wrote to his assistant Unshlikht:

Comrade Unshlikht! Regarding the files kept on the intelligentsia, the system is not nearly sophisticated enough. Since [Yakov] Agronov left, we seem to have no one capable of organizing this properly. Zaraysky is still too young. It seems to me that if we are going to make any progress at all, Menzhinsky is going to have to take things in hand . . . It is essential to devise a clear plan that can be regularly completed and updated. The intelligentsia must be classed into groups and subgroups:

1. Writers
2. Journalicians and politicians
3. Economists: subgroups are very important here: (a) financiers, (b) workers in the energy sector, (c) transport specialists, (d) tradesmen, (e) people with experience in cooperatives, etc.
4. Technical specialists: here too subgroups are necessary: (a) engineers, (b) agronomists, (c) doctors, etc.
5. University lecturers and their assistants, etc.

Information on all such people must go to specific departments and be synthesized by the Main Department on the Intelligentsia. Every intellectual must have his own file . . . It must be clear in our minds that the objective of the department is not simply to expel or arrest individuals, but to contribute to general political matters and policies concerning intellectuals. They must be controlled, closely watched and divided up, and those who are ready to support the Soviet regime and demonstrate this by their actions and their words should be considered for promotion.[43]

A few days later Lenin sent a long memorandum to Stalin in which he returned over and over, in almost maniacal detail, to the question of a "definitive purging" of all socialists, intellectuals, and liberals in Russia:

Regarding the question of the expulsion of Mensheviks, populist socialists, cadets, etc., I would like to raise a few questions here. This issue came up in my absence and has not yet been dealt with fully. Has the decision been made yet to root out all the popular socialists? [Andrei] Pechekhonov, [Aleksandr] Myakotin, [A.G.] Gornfeld, [N.] Petrishchev, and the like? I think the time has come for them to be exiled. They are more dangerous than the Socialist Revolutionaries because they are more cunning. We could say the same of [Aleksandr] Potresov, [Aleksandr] Isgoev, and the rest of the staff at the journal *Ekonomist*, such as Ozerov and several others. The same applies to the Mensheviks such as [Vasily] Rozanov (a doctor, not to be trusted), Vigdorshik (Migulo or something like that), Lyubov Nikolaevna Radchenko and her young daughter (who seem to be two of the worst enemies of Bolshevism), and N. A. Rozhkov (he must be exiled, he really is incorrigible) . . . The Mantsev-Messing commission must draw up lists, and hundreds of these people should be expelled immediately. It is our duty to clean up Russia once and for all . . . All the authors at the House of Writers and Thinkers in Petrograd, too, must go. Kharkiv must be searched from top to bottom. We currently have absolutely no idea what is happening there; it might as well be in a foreign country. The city needs a radical cleansing as soon as possible, right after the trial of all the Socialist Revolutionaries. Do something about all those authors and writers in Petrograd (you can find all their addresses in *New Russian Thought,* no. 4, 1922, p. 37) and all the editors of small publishing houses too (their names and addresses are on page 29). This is all of supreme importance.[44]

6 From the Truce to the Great Turning Point

For slightly less than five years, from early 1923 until the end of 1927, there was a pause in the confrontation between society and the new regime. Lenin had died on 24 January 1924, already politically sidelined since his third stroke in March 1923, and the in-fighting surrounding his succession accounted for much of the political activity of the other Bolshevik leaders. Meanwhile society licked its wounds.

During this long truce the peasantry, who made up more than 85 percent of the population, tried to get agriculture moving again, to negotiate a price for their product, and to live, in the words of historian Michael Confino, "as though the peasant utopia actually worked." This "peasant utopia," which the Bolsheviks called *eserovshchina* (a term whose closest translation would be something like "Socialist Revolutionary mentality"), was based on four principles that had been at the heart of all the peasant programs for decades: first, the destruction of the traditional large estates, with the land distributed by household in accordance with the number of mouths to be fed; second, the freedom to dispose of the fruits of their labor however they wished, with all the benefits of free trade; third, peasant self-government, represented by a traditional village community; and finally, the Bolshevik state reduced to its simplest possible expression, one rural soviet for several villages, and a Communist Party cell for every hundred villages.

the main island of which was home to one of the largest Russian Orthodox monasteries. The GPU expelled the monks and established a chain of camps with the common name Special Camps of Solovetski (SLON). The first internees, from the Kholmogory and Pertaminsk camps, arrived in early July 1923. By the end of that year there were more than 4,000 prisoners, by 1927 there were 15,000, and by the end of 1928 there were nearly 38,000.

One of the peculiarities of the Solovetski camps was their relative autonomy. Apart from the director and a handful of support staff, all posts in the camps were filled by the prisoners themselves. Most of these were people who had collaborated with the secret police but had been sentenced for particularly serious abuses of their position. In the hands of such people, autonomy was bound to give rise to anarchy.

Under the NEP, the GPU administration recognized three categories of prisoners. The first included all those involved in politics, that is, people who were members of the old Menshevik, Socialist Revolutionary, or anarchist parties. In 1921 they had convinced Dzerzhinsky, who himself had spent nearly ten years as a political prisoner under the tsarist regime, that they deserved a less stringent fate. As a result they received a slightly larger food ration, known as the political ration, were allowed to keep more of their personal belongings, and were permitted to receive newspapers and journals. They lived in communities, and above all they were spared any forced labor. This privileged status was to last until the end of the decade.

The second group, numerically by far the largest, contained all the counterrevolutionaries: members of nonsocialist or new anarchist political parties, members of the clergy, veteran officers from the tsarist armies, civil servants from the old regime, Cossacks, participants in the Kronstadt and Tambov revolts, and anyone else who had been sentenced under Article 58 of the penal code.

The third category grouped together all common criminals sentenced by the GPU (bandits, counterfeiters) and former members of the Cheka who had been prosecuted for any number of offenses. The counterrevolutionaries, having been imprisoned with the common criminals who made all the laws in the camp, thus underwent endless privations and suffered starvation, the extreme cold of the winters, and the summer mosquitoes; one of the commonest tortures was to tie up prisoners naked in the woods, at the mercy of the mosquitoes, which were particularly voracious in these northern islands. The writer Varlam Shalamov, one of the most famous of the Solovetski prisoners, recalled that prisoners would deliberately ask to have their hands tied behind their backs, a procedure that was in fact enshrined in the regulations. "This was the only means of defense that the prisoners had against the laconic formula 'killed while attempting to escape.'"[10]

It was the Solovetski camps that, after the years of improvisation during the civil war, perfected the system of enforced labor that would see such a tremendous expansion after 1929. Until 1925 prisoners were kept occupied in a relatively unproductive manner inside the camps; but beginning in 1926 the camp administrators decided to set up production contracts with a number of state organizations. This arrangement meant the use of forced labor as a source of profit rather than as a tool for reeducation—the original ideology of the corrective work camps of 1919 and 1920. Reorganized under the name Directorate for Special Camps in the Northern Region (USLON), the Solovetski camps expanded in the surrounding area, initially on the shores of the White Sea. In 1926 and 1927 new camps were established near the mouth of the Pechora River, at Kem, and at other inhospitable nearby sites with densely wooded hinterlands. The prisoners carried out a precise program of production, chiefly involving the felling and cutting of timber. The exponential growth of the production programs soon required an even greater number of prisoners and eventually led, in June 1929, to a major restructuring of the detention system. Prisoners who were sentenced to more than three years were sent to work camps. This measure implied a veritable explosion in the work-camp system. As the experimental laboratory for forced labor, the "special camps" of the Solovetski archipelago were the testing ground for another archipelago that was coming into being, the immense Gulag archipelago.

The everyday activities of the GPU, including the sentencing of thousands of people to house arrest or to the camps, did not deter the secret police from involvement in specific operations of repression on a totally different scale. In the apparently calm years of the NEP, from 1923 to 1927, the peripheral republics of Russia—Transcaucasia and Central Asia—saw the bloodiest and most massive repressions. Most of these nations had fiercely resisted Russian expansionism in the nineteenth century and had only recently been reconquered by the Bolsheviks: Azerbaijan in April 1920, Armenia in December 1920, Georgia in February 1921, Dagestan at the end of 1921, and Turkestan, including Bukhara, in the autumn of 1920. They were still putting up strong resistance to the process of Sovietization. "We still control only the main cities, or rather the main city centers," wrote Jan Peters, the Cheka plenipotentiary envoy, in January 1923. From 1918 until the end of the 1920s, and in some regions until 1935–36, the greater part of Central Asia, with the exception of the towns, was still in the hands of the *basmachis*. The term *basmachis* ("brigands" in Uzbek) was applied by the Russians to all the partisans, both sedentary and nomadic, such as Uzbeks, Turkmenians, and Kirgiz, who were acting independently of one another in the various regions.

The main crucible of revolt was in the Fergana valley. After Bukhara fell to the Red Army in September 1920, the uprising spread to the western and southern regions of the old emirate of Bukhara and to the western region of the Turkmenian steppes. In early 1921 Red Army headquarters estimated the number of armed *basmachis* at about 30,000. The leadership of the movement was extremely heterogeneous, made up as it was of local chiefs from villages or tribes, traditional religious leaders, and Muslim nationalist leaders from abroad, such as Enver Pasha, the former Turkish minister of defense, who was killed in a battle with Cheka detachments in 1922.

The *basmachi* movement was a spontaneous uprising against the "infidel" and the "Russian oppressor," the old enemy who had returned in a new guise and who this time not only wanted land and cattle but also was attempting to profane the Muslim spiritual world. This essentially colonial war of "pacification," waged for more than ten years, required a large part of the Russian armed forces and the special troops of the secret police, one of whose principal sections became the Oriental Department. It is still impossible even to guess at the number of victims in this war.[11]

The second major sector of the GPU's Oriental Department was Transcaucasia. In the first half of the 1920s Dagestan, Georgia, and Chechnya were severely affected by the repressions. Dagestan resisted the Soviet invasion until 1921. Under the direction of Sheikh Uzun Hadji, the Muslim brotherhood of the Nakshbandis led a major rebellion among the people of the mountains, and the struggle against the Russian invaders took on the character of a holy war. It lasted for more than a year, and some regions were "pacified" only by heavy bombing and huge massacres of civilians, which persisted into 1924.[12]

After three years of independence under a Menshevik government, Georgia was occupied by the Red Army in February 1921, and it remained, in the words of Aleksandr Myasnikov, secretary of the Bolshevik Party Committee in Transcaucasia, "a distinctly arduous affair." The local Party was skeletal, having recruited scarcely 10,000 members over three years, and it faced opposition in the form of a highly educated and noble class of about 100,000 and a vigorous Menshevik resistance group (the Menshevik Party in 1920 had numbered some 60,000 local members). The terror in Georgia was carried out by the all-powerful Georgian Cheka, largely independent of Moscow and led by Lavrenti Beria, a twenty-five-year-old policeman who would soon rise rapidly in the Cheka. Despite this, at the end of 1922, the exiled Menshevik leaders managed to organize all the anti-Bolshevik parties into a secret committee for Georgian independence that prepared for an uprising. The revolt, which began in the small town of Chiatura, consisted mainly of peasants from the Gurev region and spread within a few days to five of the twenty-five Georgian regions. However, faced with the superior forces of a Russian army equipped with heavy artillery and air power, the insurrection was crushed within a week. Sergo

Ordzhonikidze, the first secretary of the Bolshevik Party Committee in Transcaucasia, and Lavrenti Beria used this uprising as the pretext to "finish off the Mensheviks and the Georgian nobility once and for all." According to recently published data, 12,578 people were shot between 29 August and 5 September 1924. Repressions were so widespread that even the Politburo reacted. The Party leadership sent a message to Ordzhonikidze instructing him not to execute a disproportionate number of people or to dispose of political enemies in such fashion without express authorization from the Central Committee. Nevertheless, summary executions continued for some months. Before a meeting of the Central Committee in Moscow in October 1924, Ordzhonikidze admitted that "perhaps we did go a little far, but we couldn't help ourselves."[13]

A year after the Georgian uprising had been crushed, the regime launched a massive "pacification" campaign in Chechnya, where people still went about their business as though Soviet power did not exist. From 27 August to 15 September 1925 more than 10,000 regular troops from the Red Army under the leadership of General Ierome Uborevich, backed by special units from the GPU, began an enormous operation to try to disarm the Chechen partisans who still held the countryside. Tens of thousands of arms were seized and nearly 1,000 "bandits" arrested. So fierce was the resistance that the GPU leader Unshlikht reported that "the troops were forced to resort to heavy artillery to bombard the rebel strongholds." At the end of this new "pacification" operation, carried out during what might be called the GPU's finest hour, Unshlikht concluded his report thus: "As was demonstrated by the experience of our struggle against the *basmachis* in Turkestan, and against the bandits in Ukraine, military repression is effective only when it is followed by an intensive process of Sovietization in the core of the country."[14]

After the death of Dzerzhinsky at the end of 1926, the GPU came under the leadership of Vyacheslav Rudolfovich Menzhinsky, who had been its founder's righthand man (and who was also of Polish extraction). By now the GPU was called upon more frequently by Stalin, who was preparing his political offensive against both Trotsky and Bukharin. In January 1927 the GPU received an order instructing it to accelerate the classification of "anti-Soviet and socially dangerous elements" in the countryside. In a single year the number of people thus classified rose from 30,000 to about 72,000. In September 1927 the GPU launched campaigns in several provinces to arrest kulaks and other "socially dangerous elements." With hindsight, these operations seem to have been preparatory operations for the great "dekulakization" programs of the winter of 1929–30.

In 1926 and 1927 the GPU showed itself also to be extremely active in the hunt for Communists of opposing tendencies, who were classified as either "Zinovievites" or "Trotskyites." The practice of classifying and following

Communists of different tendencies had first appeared in 1921. In September 1923 Dzerzhinsky had proposed "to tighten the ideological unity of the Party" by insisting that Communists agree to inform the secret police about the existence of splits or disagreements within the Party. The proposal had met with considerable hostility from several leaders, including Trotsky himself. Nonetheless, the practice of placing opponents under surveillance became increasingly widespread in the years that followed. The GPU was very closely involved with the purge of the Communist organization in Leningrad, carried out under Zinoviev in January and February 1927. Opponents were not simply expelled from the Party; several hundred were exiled to distant towns in the countryside, where their position was very precarious, since no one dared to offer them any work. In 1927 the hunt for Trotskyites—who numbered several thousand around the country—intensified considerably, and for a month it involved a number of units from the GPU. All opponents were classified, and hundreds of militant Trotskyites were arrested and then exiled as a simple administrative measure. In November 1927 all the main leaders of the so-called Left Opposition, including Trotsky, Zinoviev, Kamenev, Radek, and Rakovsky, were expelled from the Party and arrested. Anyone who failed to make a public confession was exiled. On 19 January 1928 *Pravda* announced the departure of Trotsky and a group of thirty Opposition leaders from Moscow to exile in Alma-Ata. A year later Trotsky was banned from the U.S.S.R. altogether. With the transformation of one of the main architects of the Bolshevik terror into a "counterrevolutionary," it was clear that a new era had dawned, and that a new Party strongman had emerged—Josif Stalin.

In early 1928, when the Trotskyite opposition had been eliminated, the Stalinist majority in the Politburo decided to end the truce with society, which seemed to be straying increasingly from the original path set by the Bolsheviks. The main enemy now, as ten years previously, was the peasantry, which was still perceived as a hostile, uncontrolled, and uncontrollable mass. This second stage of the war against the peasantry, as the historian Andrea Graziosi notes, "was markedly different from the first. The initiative was taken very much by the state this time, and all the peasantry could do was react, with ever decreasing strength, to the attacks carried out against it."[15]

Although the state of agriculture had improved since the catastrophic events of 1918–1922, the end of the decade saw the "peasant enemy" still weaker, and the state considerably stronger, than at the beginning. The authorities, for example, had considerably more information at their disposal about what actually went on in the villages. Thanks to its files on "socially dangerous elements," the GPU could carry out the first dekulakization raids, stamp out more and more "banditry," disarm the peasants, increase the proportion of villagers recruited as soldiers, and expand Soviet education. As the correspondence of Party leaders and the records of high-level discussions within the Party demonstrate, the Stalinist leadership, like its opponents Bukharin, Rykov, and Kamenev, was perfectly aware of what was at stake in this new assault on the peasantry. "There will be a peasant war, as in 1918–19," warned Bukharin. But Stalin was ready, since he knew that, whatever the cost, the regime would emerge the victor.[16]

The harvest crisis at the end of 1927 provided Stalin with the pretext he needed. November was marked by a spectacular decline in deliveries of agricultural products to the state collection centers, and by December this was beginning to take on catastrophic proportions. In January 1928 the facts had to be faced: despite a good harvest, the peasants had delivered only 4.8 million tons, down from 6.8 million the previous year. The new crisis had many causes, including the decline in the prices offered by the state, the cost and the scarcity of manufactured products, the disorganization of the collection agencies, the rumors of war, and, in general, the peasants' discontent with the regime. Nonetheless, Stalin was quick to label this a "kulak strike."

The Stalinist faction quickly used the reduced deliveries as a pretext to return to requisitioning and to the repressive measures used during the period of War Communism. Stalin visited Siberia in person. Other leaders, including Andrei Andreev, Anastas Mikoyan, Pavel Postyshev, and Stanislas Kossior, also left for the grain-producing centers in the Black Earth territories (fertile regions in southern Russia), Ukraine, and the Northern Caucasus. On 14 January 1928 the Politburo sent a circular to local authorities ordering them to "arrest speculators, kulaks, and anyone else interfering in the markets or in pricing policies." "Plenipotentiaries" (the term itself was a throwback to the requisitioning policies of 1918–1921) and detachments of militant Communists were sent into the countryside to remove local authorities judged to be too complacent toward the kulaks. They also sought out hidden grain surpluses, if necessary with the help of poor peasants, who were promised a quarter of all confiscated grain as compensation for their assistance.

To punish peasants who were unwilling to hand over their agricultural products at prices that were a mere third or even a quarter of the going market rate, the Soviet authorities doubled, tripled, or even quintupled the original amount to be collected. Article 107 of the penal code, which set a prison term of three years for anyone acting in a manner liable to increase prices, was also widely used. Taxes on the kulaks were increased tenfold in two years. The markets themselves were closed, a move that affected wealthier and poorer peasants alike. Within a few weeks all these measures clearly vitiated the uneasy truce existing between the regime and the peasantry since 1922–23. The requisitioning and repressive measures merely worsened the agricultural situation. In the short term, the use of force had allowed the authorities to obtain a harvest approximately the same size as that from the preceding year. In the long term, however, the consequences were similar to those during War Communism: peasants reacted by sowing considerably less the following year.[17]

The harvest crisis of the winter of 1927–28 played a crucial role in the events that followed. In particular, Stalin drew a whole series of conclusions from this crisis. He decided to to create "fortresses of socialism" in the countryside—giant *sovkhozy*, pilot farms run by the state, and *kolkhozy*, or collective farms—and to get rid of the kulaks once and for all by "liquidating them as a class."

In 1928 the regime also broke its truce with another social group, the *spetsy*, the "bourgeois specialists" left over from the intelligentsia of the *ancien régime*, who at the end of the 1920s still filled most of the managerial positions in industrial and government departments. At a meeting of the Central Committee in April 1928, it was announced that an industrial sabotage plan had been discovered in the Shakhty region, one of the mining areas of the Donbass, among the workers of the Donugol Company, which was known to employ "bourgeois specialists" and to have relations with finance companies in the West. A few weeks later, 53 of the accused, most of them engineers and middle-management workers, were tried in public in the first open political trial since that of the Socialist Revolutionaries in 1922; 11 were condemned to death, and 5 were executed. This show-trial, which was reported extensively in the press, serves as an illustration of the obsessive hunt for "saboteurs in the pay of foreign powers," a term used as a rallying call for activists and informers in the pay of the GPU. "Saboteurs" were blamed for all economic failures, and they became the excuse for using thousands of white-collar workers to build the new special offices of the GPU, known as the *sharashki*. Thousands of engineers and technicians who had been convicted of sabotage were punished by being sent to construction sites and high-profile civil engineering projects. In the months following the Shakhty trial the Economic Department of the GPU fabricated dozens of similar affairs, notably in Ukraine. In the Yugostal metallurgy complex in Dnepropetrovsk, 112 white-collar workers were arrested in May 1928.[18]

Not only white-collar industrial workers were targeted in the vast anti-specialist operations begun in 1928. Numerous university professors and students of "socially unacceptable" background were excluded from higher education in a series of purges of the universities designed to advance the careers of the new Red "proletarian" intelligentsia.

The new repressive measures and the economic difficulties of the later years of the NEP, which were marked by growing unemployment and upsurges in criminal activity, resulted in a huge increase in the number of criminal convictions: 578,000 in 1926, 709,000 in 1927, 909,000 in 1928, and 1,778,000 in 1929.[19] To curtail the rapid growth of the prison population, which in 1928 was supposed to be no higher than 150,000, the government made two important decisions. The first, a decree of 26 March 1928, was a proposal to replace all short-term prison sentences for minor offenses with corrective work, to be carried out without remuneration "in industry, on construction projects, or in forestry work." The second measure was a decree of 27 June 1929, which had enormous consequences. It recommended the transfer of all prisoners who were sentenced to more than three years to work camps whose aim was to be "the development of the natural resources of the northern and eastern regions of the country," an idea that had been in the air for a few years. The GPU was already involved in a vast enterprise of wood production for the export market, and had repeatedly asked for additional workers from the organizations at the Ministry of Internal Affairs responsible for incarcerations. The GPU's own prisoners in the special Solovetski camps, who numbered 38,000 in 1928, were not sufficient to meet the desired production targets.[20]

The drawing-up of the first Five-Year Plan highlighted questions about the division of the labor force and the exploitation of the inhospitable regions that were so rich in natural resources. In that respect the penal workforce, heretofore an untapped source of manpower, was considered a potentially extremely valuable asset—a major source of revenue, influence, and power. The leaders of the GPU, and in particular Menzhinsky and his aide Yagoda, both of whom had Stalin's backing, were well aware of the potential importance of the prisoners. In the summer of 1929 they put together an ambitious plan to colonize the Narym region, which covered 225,000 square miles of marshy pine forest in western Siberia. This plan was implemented in a decree of 27 June 1929. It was in this context that the idea of dekulakization began to take shape. The idea was to deport kulaks, defined as the better-off peasants, whom the official circles considered necessarily opposed to collectivization.[21]

Nonetheless, it took an entire year for Stalin and his followers to persuade other Party leaders to accept the policies of enforced collectivization, dekulakization, and accelerated industrialization—the three key aspects of a coherent program for the brutal transformation of the economy and society. The program called for the simultaneous dissolution of the traditional market economy, expropriation of all peasant land, and development of the natural resources of the inhospitable regions of the country using the forced labor of "kulaks" and other groups that were the targets of this "second revolution."

The "right-wing" opposition to these ideas, led notably by Rykov and Bukharin, thought that collectivization would result only in a new feudal exploitation of the peasantry, leading to civil war, increased terror, chaos, and new famines. This obstacle was finally eliminated in April 1929. Throughout the summer of 1929 the "rightists" were attacked in the Soviet press with unprecedented venom, accused of collaborating with capitalist elements and colluding with Trotskyites. Totally discredited, these opponents were forced to make public confessions at the Plenary Session of the Central Committee in November 1929.

During these episodes in the struggle between proponents and opponents of the NEP, the country sank further and further into economic crisis. The agricultural figures for 1928–29 were disastrous. Despite systematic recourse to a whole arsenal of coercive measures directed against the peasantry, including steep fines and prison sentences for anyone who refused to sell produce to the state, the amount gathered by the state in the winter of 1928–29 was considerably smaller than the preceding year, which understandably created a situation of extreme tension in the countryside. From January 1928 to December 1929—that is, even before enforced collectivization—the GPU recorded more than 1,300 riots and mass demonstrations in the countryside, which led to the arrest of tens of thousands of peasants. One other statistic is also a good indicator of the climate in the countryside at that time: in 1929 more than 3,200 Soviet civil servants were victims of terrorist attacks. In February ration cards appeared for the first time since the introduction of the NEP. Poverty again became widespread after the authorities closed down most small companies and peasant workshops, labeling them capitalist throwbacks.

In Stalin's view, the crisis in agriculture was the work of kulaks and other hostile forces who were attempting to undermine the Soviet regime. The stakes were set: the choice was to be made between rural capitalism and the *kolkhozy*. In June 1929 the government announced the beginning of a new phase, that of "mass collectivization." The targets of the first Five-Year Plan, ratified in April by the Sixteenth Party Congress, were retroactively rounded upward. The plan had originally foreseen the collectivization of around 5 million (or approximately 20 percent) of all farms before the end of the Five-Year Plan. In June it was announced that the objective was now 8 million farms for 1930 alone; by September the projected figure had risen to 13 million. Throughout the summer the authorities mobilized tens of thousands of Communists, trade unionists, members of the Communist youth organizations (the Komsomols), laborers, and students and sent them into rural villages together with local Party leaders and GPU officials. The pressure on the peasants intensified as local Party organizations strove to outdo each other to beat the collectivization records. On 31 October 1929 *Pravda* called for "total collectivization." A week later, on the twelfth anniversary of the Revolution, Stalin published his famous article "The Great Turning Point," which was based on the fundamentally erroneous idea that "the average peasant has welcomed the arrival of the *kolkhoz*." The NEP was definitively over.

7 Forced Collectivization and Dekulakization

Recent research in the newly accessible archives has confirmed that the forced collectivization of the countryside was in effect a war declared by the Soviet state on a nation of smallholders. More than 2 million peasants were deported (1.8 million in 1930–31 alone), 6 million died of hunger, and hundreds of thousands died as a direct result of deportation. Such figures, however, only hint at the size of this human tragedy. Far from being confined to the winter of 1929–30, the war dragged on until the mid-1930s and was at its peak in 1932 and 1933, which were marked by a terrible famine deliberately provoked by the authorities to break the resistance of the peasants. The violence used against the peasants allowed the authorities to experiment with methods that would later be used against other social groups. In that respect it marked a decisive step in the development of Stalinist terror.

In a report to a Central Committee plenum in November 1929, Vyacheslav Molotov declared: "The speed of collectivization is not really at issue in the plan . . . We still have November, December, January, February, and March, four and a half months in which, if the imperialists do not attack us head-on, we can make a decisive breakthrough in the economy and in collectivization." The committee endorsed the decision to speed up the pace of collectivization. A commission drew up a new timetable that was optimistically revised several times before being officially published on 5 January 1930. The Northern Caucasus and the lower and middle regions of the Volga were to be fully collectivized by the autumn of 1930, and the other grain-producing regions a year later.[1]

On 27 December 1929 Stalin demanded "the eradication of all kulak tendencies and the elimination of the kulaks as a class." A commission from the Politburo, presided over by Molotov, was charged with pursuing all measures needed to achieve this goal. The commission defined three categories of kulaks: those engaged in "counterrevolutionary activities" were to be arrested and transferred to GPU work camps or executed if they put up any sign of resistance. Their families were to be deported and all their property confiscated. Kulaks of the second category, who were defined as "showing less active opposition, but nonetheless archexploiters with an innate tendency to destabilize the regime," were to be arrested and deported with their families to distant regions of the country. Those in the third category, classified as loyal to the regime, were to be officially transferred to the peripheral regions of the districts in which they lived, "outside the collectivized zones, on land requiring improvement." The decree also stipulated that "the number of kulak farms to be liquidated within the next four months . . . should be between 3 percent and 5 percent of the total number of farms," a figure intended as a general guideline for the size of dekulakization operations.[2]

Coordinated in each district by a troika composed of the first secretary of the local Party Committee, the president of the local Soviet Executive Committee, and the chief of the local GPU, operations were carried out on the ground by special dekulakization commissions and brigades. The list of kulaks in the first category, which, according to the Politburo's guidelines, was to comprise some 60,000 heads of household, was to be drawn up by the secret police themselves. Lists of kulaks in the other two categories were made in situ at the recommendation of local village activists. Sergo Ordzhonkidze, one of Stalin's closest advisers, explained who these "activists" really were: "Because there are almost no Party activists in the villages, we generally install a young Communist in the village and force two or three poor peasants to join him, and it is this *aktiv* [activist cell] that personally carries out all the village business of collectivization and dekulakization."[3] Their instructions were quite clear: they were to collectivize as many farms as possible, and to arrest and label as a kulak anyone who put up resistance.

These practices naturally opened the way to all sorts of abuses and the settling of old scores, and difficult questions were raised regarding the categories of kulaks. In January and February 1930 the criteria established by the Party after considering innumerable reports from committees of economists and ideologues were scarcely applicable, since the ever-increasing taxes had impoverished all previously wealthy peasants. In the absence of external signs of wealth, the commissions had to resort to outdated and often incomplete tax returns kept by the rural soviet, information provided by the GPU, and denunciations by neighbors tempted by the possibility of gain. In practice, instead of the precise and detailed inventory that they were instructed to draw up before expropriating goods for the *kolkhoz*, the dekulakization brigades seemed to follow the motto "Eat, drink, and be merry, for it all belongs to us." According to a GPU report from Smolensk, "the brigades took from the wealthy peasants their winter clothes, their warm underclothes, and above all their shoes. They left the kulaks standing in their underwear and took everything, even old rubber socks, women's clothes, tea worth no more than fifty kopeks, water pitchers, and pokers . . . The brigades confiscated everything, even the pillows from under the heads of babies, and stew from the family pot, which they smeared on the icons they had smashed."[4] Dekulakized properties were often simply looted or sold at auction by the dekulakization brigades for absurd prices: wooden houses were bought for sixty kopeks, cows for fifteen.

In such conditions it is not surprising that in certain districts between 80 and 90 percent of those victimized by the dekulakization process were *serednyaki*, or middle-income peasants. The brigades had to meet the required quotas and, if possible, surpass them. Peasants were arrested and deported for having sold grain on the market or for having had an employee to help with harvest back in 1925 or 1926, for possessing two samovars, for having killed a pig in September 1929 "with the intention of consuming it themselves and thus keeping it from socialist appropriation." Peasants were arrested on the pretext that they had "taken part in commerce," when all they had done was sell something of their own making. One peasant was deported on the pretext that his uncle had been a tsarist officer; another was labeled a kulak on account of his "excessive visits to the church." But most often people were classed as kulaks simply on the grounds that they had resisted collectivization. At times confusion reigned in the dekulakization brigades to an almost comic extreme: in one city in Ukraine, for example, a *serednyak* who was a member of a dekulakization brigade was himself arrested by a member of another brigade that was operating on the other side of the town.

After a first phase that allowed some to settle old scores or quite simply to engage in looting, village communities began to harden their attitudes to both dekulakization and collectivization. The GPU recorded 402 revolts and mass peasant demonstrations against dekulakization and collectivization in January 1930, 1,048 in February, and 6,528 in March.[5]

This massive and quite unexpected resistance caused the government briefly to alter its plans. On 2 March 1930 all Soviet newspapers carried Stalin's famous article "Dizzy with Success," which condemned "the numerous abuses of the principle of voluntary collectivization" and blamed the excesses of collectivization and dekulakization on local bosses who were "drunk on success." The impact of the article was immediate: in March alone more than 5 million peasants left the *kolkhozy*. Trouble and unrest, linked to the often violent reappropriation of tools and cattle by their original owners, immediately flared up. Throughout March the central authorities received daily reports from the GPU of massive uprisings in western Ukraine, in the central Black Earth region, in the Northern Caucasus, and in Kazakhstan. The GPU counted more than 6,500 mass demonstrations during that critical month, more than 800 of which had to be put down by force. During these events more than 1,500 civil servants were killed, wounded, or badly beaten. The number of victims among the rebels is not known but must easily have totaled several thousand.[6]

By early April the authorities were forced into further concessions. Several circulars were sent to local authorities calling for a slowdown in collectivization, acknowledging that there was a genuine danger of "a veritable tidal wave of peasant wars" and of "the death of at least half of all local Soviet civil servants." That month the number of uprisings and peasant demonstrations began to decline, though it remained exceedingly high. The GPU reported 1,992 protests for April. The decrease became more apparent as the summer wore on. In June there were 886 revolts, 618 in July, and 256 in August. In all of 1930 nearly 2.5 million peasants took part in approximately 14,000 revolts, riots, and mass demonstrations against the regime. The regions most affected were the Black Earth region, the Northern Caucasus, and Ukraine, particularly the western parts, where whole districts, and notably the areas that bordered on Poland and Romania, temporarily slipped out of the control of the Soviet regime.[7]

One of the peculiarities of these movements was the key role played by women peasants, who were sometimes sent to the front lines in the hope that they would not suffer as severe a fate as the men who were captured.[8] Although the demonstrations by women often focused on the closure of churches or the collectivization of dairy farming, there were also bloody confrontations between GPU detachments and groups of peasants armed with axes and pitchforks. Hundreds of Soviet officials were attacked, and for a few hours or a few days the peasants would try to reclaim the administration of village affairs, demanding the return of confiscated tools and cattle, the dissolution of the *kolkhoz*, the reintroduction of free trade, the reopening of the churches, the restitution of all goods to the kulaks, the return of the peasants who had been deported, the abolition of Bolshevik power, and, in Ukraine at least, national independence.[9]

The peasants managed to postpone collectivization only through March and April. Their actions did not lead to the creation of a central movement of resistance, with leaders and regional organizations. Weapons, too, were in short supply, having been steadily seized by the authorities over the preceding decade. Even so, the revolts were difficult to put down.

The repressions were horrifying. By the end of March 1930, "mopping-up operations against counterrevolutionary elements" on the borders of western Ukraine led to the arrest of more than 15,000 people. In about forty days, from 1 February to 15 March, the Ukrainian GPU arrested 26,000 people, of whom 650 were immediately executed. According to the GPU's own records, 20,200 people received death sentences that year through the courts alone.[10]

While carrying out this repression of "counterrevolutionary elements," the GPU began to apply Yagoda's Directive No. 44/21, which called for the arrest of 60,000 kulaks of the first category. To judge by the daily reports that were sent to him, the operation was carried out exactly as planned. The first report, dated 6 February, noted 15,985 arrests; by 9 February the GPU noted that 25,245 kulaks had been "taken out of circulation." A secret report (*spetssvodka*) dated 15 February gave the following details: "The total number of liquidations, including both individuals taken out of circulation and larger-scale operations, has now reached 64,589. Of these, 52,166 are first category, arrested during preparatory operations, and 12,423 were arrested in larger-scale operations." In just a few days the target figure of 60,000 first-category kulaks had already been met.[11]

In reality the kulaks represented only one group of people "taken out of circulation." Local GPU agents everywhere had taken the opportunity to clear their district of "socially dangerous elements," among whom were "police officers from the old regime," "White officers," "priests," "nuns," "rural artisans," former "shopkeepers," "members of the rural intelligentsia," and "others." At the bottom of the report dated 15 February 1930, which detailed the categories of individuals arrested as part of the liquidation of kulaks of the first class, Yagoda wrote: "The regions of the northeast and of Leningrad have not understood the orders, or at least are pretending not to have understood them. They must be forced to understand. We are not trying to clear the territory of religious leaders, shopkeepers, and 'others.' If they write 'others,' that means they don't even know who it is they are arresting. There will be plenty of time to dispose of shopkeepers and religious leaders. What we are trying to do now is to strike at the heart of the problem by weeding out the kulaks and kulak counterrevolutionaries."[12] Even today it is impossible to say how many of the "kulaks of the first category" who were "liquidated" were actually executed, since there are no figures available.

Undoubtedly "kulaks of the first category" were a major part of the first groups of prisoners who were transferred to the labor camps. By the summer of 1930 the GPU had already established a vast network of such camps. The oldest group of prisons, on the Solovetski Islands, continued its expansion on the shores of the White Sea, from Karelia to Arkhangelsk. More than 40,000 prisoners built the Kem–Ukhta road, and thus facilitated most of the wood production that was exported from Arkhangelsk. The group of camps in the north, where nearly 40,000 other prisoners were detained, set about the construction of a 200-mile railway line between Ust, Sysolk, and Pinyug, and a road of the same length between Ust, Sysolk, and Ukhta. The 15,000 prisoners in the camps in the east were the sole source of labor for the Boguchachinsk Railway. The fourth group of camps, in Vichera, where some 20,000 prisoners were detained, provided the labor force for the construction of the great chemical plant of Berezniki in the Urals. Finally, the camps in Siberia, where 80,000 people were kept, provided the labor for the Tomsk–Eniseisk Railway and the Kuznetsk metallurgy complex.[13]

In a year and half, from the end of 1928 to the summer of 1930, forced labor in the GPU camps had more than tripled, from 40,000 to approximately 140,000. The successful use of forced labor encouraged the government to tackle more projects on a similar scale. In June 1930 the government decided to construct a canal more than 150 miles long, most of it through granite, linking the Baltic to the White Sea. In the absence of the necessary technology and machinery, it was calculated that a labor force of 125,000 would be required to carry out the task, using nothing but pickaxes, buckets, and wheelbarrows. Such a labor force was unprecedented; but in the summer of 1930, when dekulakization was at its height, the authorities had precisely that sort of spare labor capacity at their disposal.

In fact the number of people deported as kulaks was so great—more than 700,000 people by the end of 1930, more than 1.8 million by the end of 1931[14]—that the framework designed to cope with the process could not possibly keep up. Most of the kulaks in the second or third category were deported in improvised operations of almost total chaos, which often resulted in an unprecedented phenomenon of "abandonment in deportation." This provided no economic benefit for the authorities, although the plan had been to utilize this forced labor to its maximum capacity to develop the regions of the country that were inhospitable but rich in natural resources.[15]

Deportation of kulaks of the second category began in the first week of February 1930. According to a plan approved by the Politburo, 60,000 families were to be deported as part of a first phase that was to last until the end of April. The northern region was to receive 45,000 families, and the Urals 15,000. However, as early as 16 February, Stalin sent a telegram to Robert Eikhe, first secretary of the Party's regional committee in western Siberia: "It is inexcusable that Siberia and Kazakhstan are claiming not to be ready to receive deportees! It is imperative that Siberia receive 15,000 families between now and the end of April." In reply, Eikhe sent Moscow an estimate of the installation costs for the planned contingent of deportees, which he calculated to be 40 million rubles—a sum that he never, of course, received.[16]

The deportation operations were thus characterized by a complete lack of coordination between the place of departure and the destination. Peasants who had been arrested were thus sometimes kept for weeks in improvised prisons— barracks, administrative buildings, and railway stations—from which a great number managed to escape. The GPU had allocated 240 convoys of 53 carriages for the first phase. Each convoy, according to GPU regulations, consisted of 44 cattle trucks with 40 deportees apiece; 8 carriages to carry the tools, food, and personal belongings of the deportees (limited to 480 kilos per family), and 1 carriage to transport the guards. As the rather acerbic correspondence between the GPU and the People's Commissariat of Transport demonstrates, the formation of the convoys was invariably a painfully slow process. In the great depots, such as Vologda, Kotlas, Rostov, Sverdlovsk, and Omsk, convoys would remain for weeks, filled with their human cargo. These masses of women, children, and old men rarely passed unnoticed by the local population; many group letters, signed by the "Workers' and Employees' Collective of Vologda" or the "Railway Workers of Kotlas," were sent to Moscow complaining about "massacres of the innocent."[17]

Few detailed records were kept of the mortality rates for the convoys of 1930 and 1931, but the appalling conditions, the cold, the lack of food, and the rapid spread of disease must have cost a large number of lives.

When the railway convoys finally arrived at a station, the men were often separated from their families, kept provisionally in flimsy cabins, and then escorted to the new colonies, which, in accordance with official instructions, were "some way distant from any means of communication." The interminable journey thus sometimes continued for several hundred more kilometers, with or without the family, sometimes on convoys of sledges in the winter, in carts in the summer, or even on foot. From a practical point of view, the last stage in the journey of kulaks of the second category was often indistinguishable from the deportation of kulaks of the third category, who were being relocated to lands requiring improvement in the peripheral regions—regions that in Siberia or the Urals covered hundreds of thousands of square miles. As the authorities in the district of Tomsk, in western Siberia, reported on 7 March 1930,

> The first convoys of third-category kulaks arrived on foot, since we have no horses, sleighs, or harnesses . . . In general the horses that are assigned to the convoys are totally unsuited to journeys that are often of

more than 200 miles, for when the convoys are being made up, any of the good horses belonging to the deportees are quickly replaced with old nags . . . In view of the present situation, it is impossible to transport the two months' supplies that the kulaks are entitled to bring with them. It is also very hard to deal with the children and old men who usually make up some 50 percent of the contingent.[18]

In a similar report the Central Executive Committee of western Siberia demonstrated the impossibility of carrying out the instructions of the GPU regarding the deportation of 4,902 kulaks of the third category to two districts in the province of Novosibirsk: "The transportation, along 225 miles of road in appalling disrepair, of the 8,560 tons of grain and animal feed to which the deportees are theoretically entitled 'for their journey and their settling in,' would require the use of 28,909 horses and 7,227 horsemen (1 horseman for 4 horses)." The report concluded that "carrying out an operation of this scale would seriously compromise the spring sowing program, because the horses would be exhausted as a result, and would require several weeks of rest . . . It is thus of capital importance that the volume of provisions that the deportees are allowed to bring with them be decreased considerably."[19]

It was thus without provisions or tools, and often without any shelter, that the prisoners had to begin their new lives. One report from the province of Arkhangelsk in September 1930 admitted that of the planned 1,641 living quarters for the deportees, only 7 had been built. The deportees often "settled" on the bare earth, on the open steppes, or in the middle of the marshy pine forests. The fortunate ones who had been able to bring some tools with them could construct some sort of rudimentary shelter, often the traditional *zemlyanka*, a simple hole in the ground covered with branches. In some cases, when the deportees were to reside by the thousands near a large building or industrial complex that was under construction, they were lodged in primitive military camps, where they slept in three-tier bunk beds, with several hundred people per shack.

In all, 1,803,392 people were officially deported as part of the dekulakization program in 1930 and 1931. One might well wonder how many died of cold and hunger in the first few months of their "new life." The archives in Novosibirsk contain one startling document in the form of a report sent to Stalin in May 1933 by an instructor of the Party committee in Narym in western Siberia, concerning the fate met by two convoys of more than 6,000 people deported from Moscow and Leningrad. Although it concerns a later period and deals with a different category of deportee—not peasants but "outdated elements" thrown out of a new socialist town at the end of 1932—the document describes the fairly common phenomenon of "abandonment in deportation."

On 29 and 30 April 1933 two convoys of "outdated elements" were sent to us by train from Moscow and Leningrad. On their arrival in Tomsk they were transferred to barges and unloaded, on 18 May and 26 May, onto the island of Nazino, which is situated at the juncture of the Ob and Nazina rivers. The first convoy contained 5,070 people, and the second 1,044: 6,114 in all. The transport conditions were appalling: the little food that was available was inedible, and the deportees were cramped into nearly airtight spaces . . . The result was a daily mortality rate of 35–40 people. These living conditions, however, proved to be luxurious in comparison to what awaited the deportees on the island of Nazino (from which they were supposed to be sent on in groups to their final destination, the new sectors that are being colonized farther up the Nazina River). The island of Nazino is a totally uninhabited place, devoid of any settlements . . . There were no tools, no grain, and no food. That is how their new life began. The day after the arrival of the first convoy, on 19 May, snow began to fall again, and the wind picked up. Starving, emaciated from months of insufficient food, without shelter, and without tools, . . . they were trapped. They weren't even able to light fires to ward off the cold. More and more of them began to die . . . On the first day, 295 people were buried. It was only on the fourth or fifth day after the convoy's arrival on the island that the authorities sent a bit of flour by boat, really no more than a few pounds per person. Once they had received their meager ration, people ran to the edge of the water and tried to mix some of the flour with water in their hats, their trousers, or their jackets. Most of them just tried to eat it straight off, and some of them even choked to death. These tiny amounts of flour were the only food that the deportees received during the entire period of their stay on the island. The more resourceful among them tried to make some rudimentary sort of pancakes, but they had nothing to mix or cook them in . . . It was not long before the first cases of cannibalism occurred.

At the end of June the deportees began to be transported to the so-called village colonies. These places were nearly 150 miles farther up the river, deep in forests. They were not villages, but untamed wilderness. Some of the deportees somehow managed to build a primitive oven, so that they could bake bread. But for the rest there was little change from life as it had been on the island: the same feeling of purposelessness, the same fires, the same nakedness. The only difference was the bread ration, which came around every few days. The mortality rate was still appalling; for example, of the seventy-eight people who embarked from the island to the fifth colonial village, twelve were still alive when the boat arrived. Soon the authorities realized that these regions were simply not habitable, and the whole contingent was sent down the river once again. Escape attempts became more and more common.

> At the new location the surviving deportees were at last given some tools, and in the second half of July they began to build shelters that were half sunk into the ground . . . Cases of cannibalism were still being recorded. Slowly, however, life began to take a more normal course, and people began to work again, but they were so worn out from the events of the preceding months that even with rations of 1.5 to 2 pounds of bread a day they still fell ill and died, and ate moss, grass, leaves, etc. The result of all this was that of the 6,100 people sent from Tomsk (to whom another 500–700 were subsequently added from the surrounding regions), only 2,200 were still alive by 20 August.[20]

It is impossible to gauge how many similar cases of the abandonment of deportees there were, but some of the official figures give an indication of the losses. From February 1930 to December 1931 more than 1.8 million kulaks were deported; but on 1 January 1932, when the authorities carried out a general census, only 1,317,022 kulak deportees were recorded. Losses were thus close to half a million people, or nearly 30 percent of all deportees.[21] Undoubtedly, a not insignificant proportion of those had managed to escape.[22] In 1932 the fate of these "contingents" was for the first time made an object of systematic study by the GPU. After the summer of 1931 the GPU itself was responsible for all deportations of what were termed "specially displaced," from the initial deportation itself to the creation and management of the new village colonies. According to that initial study, there had been more than 210,000 escapes and approximately 90,000 deaths. In 1933, the year of the great famine, the authorities recorded the deaths of 151,601 of the 1,142,022 "specially displaced" who had been included in the census of 1 January 1933. The annual death rate was thus in the vicinity of 6.8 percent in 1932 and 13.3 percent in 1933. For 1930 and 1931 the data are incomplete but nonetheless eloquent: in 1931 the mortality rate was 1.3 percent per month among the deportees to Kazakhstan, and 0.8 percent per month for those to western Siberia. Infant mortality hovered around 8 percent and 12 percent per month and peaked at 15 percent per month for Magnitogorsk. From 1 June 1931 to June 1932 the mortality rate among the deportees in the region of Narym, in western Siberia, reached 11.7 percent for the year. On the whole, it is unlikely that the mortality rate for this period was lower than that of 1932, and was thus very likely in the same vicinity of 10 percent. One can thus estimate that approximately 300,000 deportees died during the process of deportation.[23]

For the central authorities, who were eager to make as much profit as possible from the labors of those they termed "special deportees," and after 1932 the labor of prisoners in "work colonies," the abandonment of deportees was a last resort, which could be blamed, as noted by N. Puzitsky, one of the GPU officials in charge of work-colony prisoners, on "the criminal negligence and political shortsightedness of local leaders, who haven't yet got used to the idea of colonization by ex-kulaks."[24]

In March 1931 a special commission was established to try to halt "the dreadful mess of the deportation of manpower." The commission was directly attached to the Politburo and presided over by V. Andreev, with Yagoda playing a key role. The first objective was the "rational and effective management of the work colonies." Preliminary inquiries by the commission had revealed that the productivity of the deported workforce was almost zero. Of the 300,000 workers in the colonies of the Urals, for example, in April 1931 a mere 8 percent were detailed to "wood chopping and other productive activities." All other able-bodied adults were "building their own living quarters . . . and generally just trying to survive." Another document calculated that the massive program of dekulakization had actually lost the state money. The average value of goods confiscated from kulaks in 1930 was 564 rubles per farm, a derisory sum (equivalent to fifteen months' wages for an average laborer). This figure demonstrates clearly how minimal the supposed riches of the kulaks actually were. The cost of deporting a kulak family, by contrast, was often more than 1,000 rubles.[25]

For the Andreev commission, rationalization of the management of "work colonies" entailed first and foremost an administrative reorganization of all the mechanisms dealing with the deportees. In the summer of 1931 the GPU had been given sole control of the administrative management of all population displacements, which previously had been under the control of the local authorities. A whole network of *komandatury* (commands) had been put into place; these became in effect a rival government administration that allowed the GPU to place huge areas under its control, where the specially displaced made up the greater part of the local population. The colonies were subject to extremely tight controls. Forced to reside in designated areas, workers were transferred by the administration either into state-run companies, into "agricultural or artisanal co-operative[s] of special status under the supervision of the local GPU commander," or into construction work, road-mending, or land-clearing. They were expected to produce 30–50 percent more than the free workers, and their pay (when they were paid at all) was cut by 15 percent or 25 percent. The rest was taken for the local GPU administration.

As documents from the Andreev commission confirm, the GPU was extremely proud that the resettlement cost of workers in the colonies was nine times less than that of camp prisoners. In June 1933 the 203,000 "specially displaced" in western Siberia, divided among 93 *komandatury*, were directed by a skeletal staff of 971.[26] It was the goal of the GPU to provide, in exchange for a commission (derived from a percentage of the wages earned plus an initial fixed sum), its own workforce for a number of industrial enterprises. These enterprises—such as Urallesprom (forestry), Uralugol, Vostugol (coal mining), Vostokstal (steel), Tsvetmetzoloto (nonferrous minerals), and Kuznetstroi (metallurgy)—exploited the various natural resources in the northern and eastern regions. In principle the companies were to provide living quarters for their workers, schools for the children, and a regular supply of food for all. In reality the managers usually treated these workers, whose status was comparable to that of prisoners, as a free source of labor. Workers in the colonies often received no salary, since whatever money they earned was generally less than the amount the administration kept for the construction of buildings, tools, obligatory contributions to unions, state loans, and other functions.

As the lowest category in the rationing hierarchy, these people were treated as pariahs, were often kept in conditions of near starvation, and were subject to all sorts of abuses and intimidatory practices. Among the most flagrant abuses cited in the reports were totally unrealistic work targets, nonpayment of wages, beatings, and confinement in unheated prison cells in the dead of winter. Women prisoners were traded with GPU officers in exchange for food or were sent as maids "for all services" to the local chiefs. The following remark by the director of one of the forestry companies in the Urals was quoted and often criticized in GPU reports of the summer of 1933, and summed up very well the attitude of many such directors toward their highly expendable human resources: "If we wanted to, we could liquidate all of you. If we were to do so, the GPU would promptly send us another hundred thousand just like you."

Gradually the use of forced labor began to take on a more rational character, if only because of the need for higher industrial productivity. During 1932 the idea of colonizing the most inhospitable regions with deportees was abandoned, and increasing numbers were sent to civil engineering projects and to industrial and mining areas. In certain sectors the proportion of deportees working and even living alongside free workers was extremely high, and in some places deportees were in the majority. In the Kuzbass mines at the end of 1933, more than 41,000 forced laborers accounted for 47 percent of the miners. In Magnitogorsk the 42,462 deportees recorded in the census of September 1932 constituted two-thirds of the local population.[27] Living in specially designated areas between one and four miles from the construction site, they worked in teams alongside free workers, and inevitably the differences between them gradually eroded. By force of circumstance—that is, through economic necessity—those who had suffered from dekulakization and were promoted to the status of forced laborers were slowly reintegrated into a society in which all levels of society were marked by a general fear of repression, and no one knew which class would be the next to suffer exclusion.

8 The Great Famine

T he great famine of 1932–33 has always been recognized as one of the darkest periods in Soviet history. According to the irrefutable evidence that is now available, more than 6 million people died as a result of it.[1] However, the catastrophe was not simply another in the series of famines that Russia had suffered at irregular intervals under the tsars. It was a direct result of the new system that Nikolai Bukharin, the Bolshevik leader who opposed Stalin on this issue, termed the "military and feudal exploitation" of the peasantry. Famine was a tragic illustration of the formidable social regression that accompanied the assault on the countryside through forced collectivization at the end of the 1920s.

Unlike the famine of 1921–22, which the Soviet authorities acknowledged and even sought to redress with help from the international community, the famine of 1932–33 was always denied by the regime. The few voices abroad that attempted to draw attention to the tragedy were silenced by Soviet propaganda. The Soviet authorities were assisted by statements such as that made by Edouard Herriot, the French senator and leader of the Radical Party, who traveled through Ukraine in 1933. Upon his return he told the world that Ukraine was full of "admirably irrigated and cultivated fields and collective farms" resulting in "magnificent harvests." He concluded: "I have crossed the whole of Ukraine, and I can assure you that the entire country is like a garden in full bloom."[2] Such blindness was the result of a marvelous show put on for foreign guests by the GPU, with an itinerary that included nothing but *kolkhozy* and model children's gardens. The blindness was perhaps also reinforced by political considerations, notably the desire of French leaders not to jeopardize the meeting of minds with the Soviet Union regarding Germany, which had become a threat with Adolf Hitler's rise to power.

Nonetheless a number of high-ranking politicians in Germany and Italy had remarkably precise information about the scale of the catastrophe facing the Soviet Union. Reports from Italian diplomats posted in Kharkiv, Odessa, and Novorossiisk, recently discovered and published by the Italian historian Andrea Graziosi, show that Mussolini read such texts extremely carefully and was fully aware of the situation but did not use it in his anti-Communist propaganda.[3] On the contrary, the summer of 1933 was marked by the signing of an important Italian-Soviet trade agreement and a pact of friendship and nonaggression. Denied, or sacrificed on the altar of "reasons of state," the truth about the great famine, long known only through small-circulation pamphlets published by Ukrainian émigré organizations, was not widely comprehended until the latter half of the 1980s, following the publication of a series of works by Western historians and by a number of researchers in the former Soviet Union.

To come to grips with the famine of 1932–33, it is vital to understand the context of the relations existing between the Soviet state and the peasantry as a result of the forced collectivization of the countryside. In the newly collectivized areas, the role of the *kolkhoz* was a strategic one. Part of its role was to ensure the delivery of a fixed supply of agricultural products to the state by taking an ever-larger share of the collective harvest. Every autumn the government collection campaign became a sort of trial of strength between the state and the peasants, who desperately tried to keep back enough of the harvest to supply their own needs. Quite simply, the requisitioning was a threat to the peasants' survival. The more fertile a region, the bigger a share the state demanded. In 1930 the state took 30 percent of the agricultural production of Ukraine, 38 percent in the rich plains of the Kuban in the Northern Caucasus, 33 percent of the harvest in Kazakhstan. In 1931, when the harvest was considerably smaller, the percentages for the same areas were 41.5, 47, and 39.5 percent, respectively. Removing produce on such a scale created total chaos in the cycle of production. Under the NEP, peasants sold between 15 and 20 percent of their total production, keeping 12–15 percent back for sowing, 25–39 percent for their cattle, and the rest for their own consumption. Conflict was inevitable between the peasants, who had decided to use every possible means to keep a part of the harvest, and the local authorities, who were obliged to carry out at all costs a plan that looked ever more unrealistic, particularly so in

1932, when the government collection target was 32 percent higher than it had been the previous year.[4]

The collection campaign in 1932 got off to a very slow start. As soon as the threshing began, the collective farmers tried to hide or steal part of the harvest every night. A movement of passive resistance took shape, strengthened by the tacit agreement of almost all concerned, including collective farm workers, brigadiers, accountants, farm managers (many of whom had themselves been peasant workers until their recent promotion), and even local secretaries of the Party. To collect the grain they wanted, the central authorities had to send out new shock troops, recruited in the towns from among the Communists and Komsomols.

The following report, from an instructor of the Central Executive Committee to his superiors regarding his mission in a grain-producing region in the lower Volga, gives an idea of the warlike climate in the countryside at this time:

> The arrests and searches are being carried out by almost anyone: by members of the rural soviet, anyone sent from the towns, the shock troops, and any Komsomol that has the time and energy. This year, 12 percent of all the farmers have been tried already, and that doesn't include the deported kulaks, peasants who were fined, etc. According to the calculations of the previous district procurator, over the course of the last year 15 percent of the whole adult population has been the victim of some sort of repression or other. If one adds the fact that over the last month about 800 farmers have been thrown out of the *kolkhozy*, you get an idea of the scale of this government repression . . . If we discount the cases in which large-scale repressions are really justified, we must admit that the effectiveness of repressive measures is bound to diminish whenever they pass a certain threshold, since it becomes literally impossible to carry them out . . . The prisons are all full to bursting point. Balachevo prison contains more than five times as many people as it was originally designed to hold, and there are 610 people crammed into the tiny district prison in Elan. Over the last month, Balachevo prison has sent 78 prisoners back to Elan, and 48 of them were less than ten years old. Twenty-one were immediately released. To show how insane this method is—I mean coercion, the only method they use—I will say a few words about the individual peasants here, who are just trying to be good farmers.
>
> One example of how the peasants are being victimized: In Mortsy one peasant, who had actually fulfilled his quota, came to see Comrade Fomichev, the president of the District Executive Committee, and asked to be deported to the north, because, as he explained, "No one can live under these conditions." I know of another similar instance in which sixteen peasants from the rural soviet of Aleksandrov all signed a peti-

tion also asking to be deported out of their region . . . In short, violence seems to be the only way of thinking now, and we always "attack" everything. We "start the onslaught" on the harvest, on the loans, etc. Everything is an assault; we "attack" the night from nine or ten in the evening till dawn. Everyone gets attacked: the shock troops call in everyone who has not met his obligations and "convince" him, using all the means you can imagine. They assault everyone on their list, and so it goes, night after night.[5]

Among the whole range of repressive laws, one famous decree, promulgated on 7 August 1932, played a decisive role when the war between the peasantry and the regime was at its height. It provided for the execution or sentencing to ten years in a camp for "any theft or damage of socialist property." It came to be known among the people as "the ear law," for people condemned under it had often done nothing more than take a few ears of corn or rye from the fields of the *kolkhoz*. From August 1932 to December 1933 more than 125,000 people were sentenced under this terrible law, and 5,400 received death sentences.[6]

Despite these draconian measures, the amount collected was still insufficient. In mid-October 1932 the government collection plan for the main grain-producing areas of the country had achieved only 15–20 percent of its target. On 22 October the Politburo sent two extraordinary commissions to Ukraine and the Northern Caucasus, one led by Vyacheslav Molotov, the other by Lazar Kaganovich, in an attempt to speed up the collection process.[7] On 2 November Kaganovich's commission, which included Genrikh Yagoda, arrived in Rostov-on-Don. They immediately called a meeting of all the Party district secretaries for the Northern Caucasus region, who adopted the following resolution: "Following the particularly shameful failure of the grain collection plan, all local Party organizations are to be obliged to break up the sabotage networks of kulaks and counterrevolutionaries, and to crush the resistance of the rural Communists and *kolkhoz* presidents who have taken the lead in this sabotage." For certain districts that had been blacklisted (according to the official terminology), the following measures were adopted: the immediate removal of all products from shops, a total ban on trade, the immediate repayment of all loans, sudden extraordinary taxes, and the swift arrest of all "saboteurs," "foreign elements," and "counterrevolutionaries" with the help of the GPU. Where sabotage was suspected, the population was deported on a massive scale.

In November 1932, the first month of the fight against sabotage, 5,000 rural Communists who were judged to have been "criminally complacent" regarding sabotage of the collection campaign and 15,000 collective farm workers were arrested in the region of the Northern Caucasus, which was highly strategic from the standpoint of agricultural production. In December the massive deportation of whole villages began, including the Cossack *stanitsy* that had already suffered similar measures in 1920.[8] The number of special work colonizers deported began to climb rapidly again. Records from the gulags note the arrival of 71,236 deportees in 1932; the following year the number of new "specially displaced" soared to 268,091.[9]

In Ukraine the Molotov commission took similar measures. The commission blacklisted all districts in which the required collection targets had not been met, with the same consequences described above: a purge of local Party administrations, the massive arrest not simply of workers on the collective farms, but also of managers suspected of "minimizing production." Soon the same measures were being applied in other grain-producing regions as well.

Could these repressive measures employed by the state have won the war against the peasants? Definitely not, according to one lucid report from the Italian consul in Novorossiisk:

> The Soviet state is powerful, and armed to the teeth, but it cannot fight this sort of battle. There is no enemy against which to take up a battle formation on the steppes. The enemy is everywhere and must be fought on innumerable fronts in tiny operations: here a field needs hoeing, there a few hundredweight of corn are stashed; a tractor is broken here, another sabotaged there; a third has gone astray . . . A depot has been raided, the books have been cooked, the directors of *kolkhozy*, through incompetence or dishonesty, never tell the truth about the harvest . . . and so on, infinitely, everywhere in this enormous country . . . The enemy is in every house, in village after village. One might as well try to carry water in a sieve.[10]

To defeat the enemy, only one solution was possible: he would have to be starved out.

The first reports on the risk of a "critical food situation" for the winter of 1932–33 reached Moscow in the summer of 1932. In August Molotov reported to the Politburo that there was "a real risk of famine even in areas where the harvest has been exceptionally good." But his intention was still to carry out the projected collection plan, regardless of the cost. That same month, Pyotr Isaev, the president of the Council of People's Commissars of Kazakhstan, informed Stalin of the scale of the famine in that republic, where collectivization and enforced settlement programs had totally destabilized the traditional nomadic economy. Even hard-line Stalinists such as Stanislas Kossior, first secretary of the Communist Party of Ukraine, and Mikhail Khataevich, first Party secretary in the region of Dnepropetrovsk, asked Stalin to revise the collection plan downward. "If only so that in the future production can increase in accordance with the needs of the proletarian state," wrote Khataevich to Molotov in November 1932, "we must take into consideration the minimum needs of the collective farmers, or there will be no one left to sow next year's harvest."

"Your position is profoundly mistaken, and not at all Bolshevik," Molotov replied. "We Bolsheviks cannot afford to put the needs of the state—needs that have been carefully defined by Party resolutions—in second place, let alone discount them as priorities at all."[11] A few days later the Politburo sent local authorities a letter ordering new raids on all collective farms that had not met the required targets; this time they were to be emptied of all the grain they contained—including the reserves kept back for sowing the next year's harvest.

Forced by threats and sometimes torture to hand over all their meager reserves, and lacking the means or even the possibility of buying any food, millions of peasants from these rich agricultural regions had no option but to leave for the cities. On 27 December, however, in an attempt to curtail the rural exodus, "liquidate social parasitism," and combat "kulak infiltration of the towns," the government introduced new identity papers and obligatory registration for all citizens. In the face of the peasants' flight for survival, on 22 January 1933 it effectively decreed the death of millions who were starving. An order signed by Molotov and Stalin instructed local authorities and above all the GPU to ban "by all means necessary the large-scale departure of peasants from Ukraine and the Northern Caucasus for the towns. Once these counter-revolutionary elements have been arrested, they are to be escorted back to their original place of residence." The circular explained the situation as follows: "The Central Committee and the government are in possession of definite proof that this massive exodus of the peasants has been organized by the enemies of the Soviet regime, by counterrevolutionaries, and by Polish agents as a propaganda coup against the process of collectivization in particular and the Soviet government in general."[12]

In all regions affected by the famine, the sale of railway tickets was immediately suspended, and special barricades were set up by the GPU to prevent peasants from leaving their district. At the beginning of March 1933 a report from the secret police noted that in one month 219,460 people had been intercepted as part of the operation to limit the exodus of starving peasants to the cities, that 186,588 had been escorted back to their place of origin, and that others had been arrested and sentenced. No mention was made of the fate of the people expelled from the towns.

On that point the following testimony from the Italian consul in Kharkiv, one of the regions worst affected by the famine, is more revealing:

> A week ago, a special service was set up to try to protect children who have been abandoned. Along with the peasants who flock to the towns because there is no hope of survival in the countryside, there are also

children who are simply brought here and abandoned by their parents, who then return to their village to die. Their hope is that someone in the town will be able to look after their children . . . So for a week now, the town has been patrolled by *dvorniki*, attendants in white uniforms, who collect the children and take them to the nearest police station . . . Around midnight they are all transported in trucks to the freight station at Severodonetsk. That's where all the children who are found in stations and on trains, the peasant families, the old people, and all the peasants who have been picked up during the day are gathered together . . . A medical team does a sort of selection process . . . Anyone who is not yet swollen up and still has a chance of survival is directed to the Kholodnaya Gora buildings, where a constant population of about 8,000 lies dying on straw beds in the big hangars. Most of them are children. People who are already starting to swell up are moved out in goods trains and abandoned about forty miles out of town so that they can die out of sight. When they arrive at the destination, huge ditches are dug, and the dead are carried out of the wagons.[13]

In the countryside the death rate was at its highest in the summer of 1933. As though hunger were not enough, typhus was soon common, and in towns with populations of several thousand there were sometimes fewer than two dozen survivors. Cases of cannibalism are recorded both in GPU reports and in Italian diplomatic bulletins from Kharkiv: "Every night the bodies of more than 250 people who have died from hunger or typhus are collected. Many of these bodies have had the liver removed, through a large slit in the abdomen. The police finally picked up some of these mysterious 'amputators' who confessed that they were using the meat as a filling for the meat pies that they were selling in the market."[14]

In April 1933 the writer Mikhail Sholokhov, who was passing through the city of Kuban, wrote two letters to Stalin detailing the manner in which the local authorities had tortured all the workers on the collective farm to force them to hand over all their remaining supplies. He demanded that the first secretary send some sort of food aid. Here are excerpts from his letter of 4 April.

> The Vechenski district, along with many other districts in the Northern Caucasus, failed to fulfill its grain quota this year not on account of some "kulak sabotage," but because of bad leadership at the local Party headquarters . . .
>
> Last December the Party regional committee, with a view to accelerating the government's collection campaign, sent the plenipotentiary Ovchinnikov. He took the following measures: (1) he requisitioned all available grain, including the advance given by the *kolkhoz* leaders to all the collective farmers for sowing this year's harvest; and (2) he divided

by family the entire quota that was due to the state from the collective farmers. The immediate result of these measures was that when the requisitioning began, the peasants hid and buried the grain. The grand total found came to 5,930 hundredweight . . . And here are some of the methods that were used to recover these 593 tons, some of which had been buried since 1918:

The "cold" method: the worker is stripped bare and left out in the cold, stark naked in a hangar. Sometimes whole brigades of collective workers are treated in this fashion.

The "hot" method: the feet and the bottom of the skirt of female workers are doused with gasoline and then set alight. The flames are put out, and the process is repeated . . .

In the Napolovski *kolkhoz* a certain Plotkin, plenipotentiary for the district committee, forced the collective workers to stretch out on stoves heated till they were white hot; then he cooled them off by leaving them naked in a hangar . . .

In the Lebyazhenski *kolkhoz* the workers were all lined up against a wall and an execution was simulated.

I could give a multitude of similar examples. These are not "abuses" of the system; this is the present system for collecting grain.

If it seems to you that this letter is worthy of the attention of the Central Committee, then please send us some real Communists, who could unmask the people here who have struck a mortal blow against the collective farming system. You are our only hope.[15]

In his reply on 6 May, Stalin made no attempt to feign compassion:

Dear Comrade Sholokhov,

I have received both of your letters and have granted the things that you request. I have sent Comrade Shkiryatov to sort out the matters to which you referred. I would ask you to assist him. But, Comrade, that is not all I wish to say. Your two letters paint a picture that is far from objective, and I would like to say a few words about that.

I have already thanked you for these letters, which pick up on one of the minor inconveniences of our system, in which, while we try to do good and to disarm our enemies, some of our Party officials attack our friends, and sometimes can be quite sadistic about this. But do not allow these remarks to fool you into thinking that I agree with everything you say. You see one aspect of things and describe it quite forcefully, but it is still only one aspect of things. To avoid being mistaken in politics—and your letters, in this instance, are not literature, they are pure politics—one must see another aspect of reality too. And the other aspect in this instance is that the workers in your district—not just in your district, but in many districts—went on strike, carried out acts of sabotage, and were prepared to leave workers from the Red Army without bread! The fact that this sabotage was silent and appeared to be quite peaceful (there was no bloodshed) changes nothing—these people deliberately tried to undermine the Soviet state. It is a fight to the death, Comrade Sholokhov!

Of course this cannot justify all the abuses carried out by our staff. The guilty few will be forced to answer for their actions. But it is as clear as day that our respected workers are far from being the innocent lambs that one might imagine from reading your letters.

I hope you stay well, and I offer a warm handshake. Yours, J. Stalin[16]

In 1933, while these millions were dying of hunger, the Soviet government continued to export grain, shipping 18 million hundredweight of grain abroad "in the interests of industrialization."

Using the demographic archives and the censuses of 1937 and 1939, which were kept secret until very recently, it is possible to evaluate the scale of the famine in 1933. Geographically, the hunger zone covered the whole of Ukraine, part of the Black Earth territories, the fertile plains of the Don, the Kuban, and the Northern Caucasus, and much of Kazakhstan. Nearly 40 million people were affected by famine or scarcity. In the regions worst affected, such as the rural zones surrounding Kharkiv, the mortality rate from January to June 1933 was ten times higher than normal: 100,000 deaths in June 1933 as opposed to 9,000 deaths in June 1932. Many deaths went unrecorded. The mortality rates were higher in the countryside than in the cities, but the cities were scarcely spared: Kharkiv lost 120,000 inhabitants in a year, Krasnodar 40,000, and Stavropol 20,000.

Outside the immediate hunger zone, demographic losses attributable to the scarcity of food were far from negligible. In the rural zones around Moscow, mortality rates climbed by 50 percent from January to June 1933; in the town of Ivanovo, for instance, which had been a center for hunger riots in 1932, mortality rose by 35 percent in the first half of the year. In total, for the year 1933 and for the whole of the country, there were 6 million more deaths than usual. As the immense majority of those deaths can be attributed directly to hunger, the death toll for the whole tragedy must therefore be nearly 6 million. The peasants of Ukraine suffered worst of all, with 4 million lives lost. There were a million deaths in Kazakhstan, most of them among the nomadic tribes who had been deprived of their cattle by collectivization and forced to settle in one place. The Northern Caucasus and the Black Earth region accounted for a million more.[17]

Five years before the Great Terror that was to strike the intelligentsia, industrial administrators, and the Party itself, the Great Famine of 1932–33 appeared as the decisive episode in the creation of a system of repression that was to consume class after class and social group after social group. Through the violence, torture, and killing of entire populations, the great famine was a huge step backward both politically and socially. Tyrants and local despots proliferated, ready to take any step necessary to force peasants to abandon their goods and their last provisions, and barbarism took over. Extortion became an everyday practice, children were abandoned, cannibalism reappeared, epidemics and banditry were rampant, new death camps were set up, and peasants were forced to face a new form of slavery, the iron rule of the Party-state. As Sergo Ordzhonikidze lucidly remarked to Sergei Kirov in January 1934, "Our members who saw the situation of 1932–33 and who stood up to it are now tempered like steel. I think that with people like that, we can build a state such as history has never seen."

Should one see this famine as "a genocide of the Ukrainian people," as a number of Ukrainian historians and researchers do today?[18] It is undeniable that the Ukrainian peasantry were the principal victims in the famine of 1932–33, and that this "assault" was preceded in 1929 by several offensives against the Ukrainian intelligentsia, who were accused of "nationalist deviations," and then against some of the Ukrainian Communists after 1932. It is equally undeniable that, as Andrei Sakharov noted, Stalin suffered from "Ukrainophobia." But proportionally the famine was just as severe in the Cossack territories of the Kuban and the Don and in Kazakhstan. In this last republic, from 1930 onward, the enforced collectivization and settling of the indigenous nomadic peoples had disastrous consequences, with 80 percent of all livestock killed in two years. Dispossessed of their goods and reduced to a state of famine, 2 million Kazakhs emigrated; nearly half a million went to Central Asia, and approximately 1.5 million went to China.

In many regions, including Ukraine, the Cossack areas, and certain districts of the Black Earth territories, the famine was the last episode in the confrontation between the Bolshevik state and the peasantry that had begun in 1918–1922. There is a remarkable coincidence between the areas that mounted stiff resistance to requisitioning in 1918–1921 and to collectivization in 1929–30, and the zones that were worst affected by the famine. Of the 14,000 riots and peasant revolts recorded by the GPU in 1930, more than 85 percent took place in regions "punished" by the famine of 1932–33. The richest and most dynamic agricultural regions, which had the most to offer the state and the most to lose in the extortionate system of enforced collectivization, were precisely the regions worst affected by the great famine of 1932–33.

9 Socially Foreign Elements and Cycles of Repression

Although the peasantry as a whole paid the heaviest price in the Stalinist transformation of society, other social groups, classified as "socially alien elements" in the "new socialist society," were also stigmatized, deprived of their civil rights, thrown out of their jobs and their homes, pushed further down the social scale, and sent into exile. "Bourgeois specialists," "aristocrats," members of the clergy and of the liberal professions, entrepreneurs, shopkeepers, and craftsmen were all victims of the anticapitalist revolution that was launched in the early 1930s. Other townspeople who simply failed to fit into the category of "proletarian worker and builder of socialism" also suffered various repressive measures.

The infamous Shakhty trial clearly marked the end of the truce that had begun in 1921 between the regime and the "specialists." Coming as it did just before the launching of the first Five-Year Plan, the political lesson of the trial was clear: skepticism, indecision, and indifference regarding the aims of the Party would automatically be labeled "sabotage." To doubt was to betray. *Spetseedstvo*—harassment of the specialist—was deeply rooted in the Bolshevik mentality, and the political signal given by the Shakhty trial was received loud and clear at a grass-roots level. The *spetsy* were to become the scapegoats for economic failure and for the frustrations engendered by the sharp decline in living standards. By the end of 1928, thousands of managers and bourgeois engineers had been fired and deprived of both ration cards and the right to medical attention; sometimes they were even driven out of their homes. In 1929 thousands of civil servants in the State Planning Administration (Gosplan), the Supreme National Council for the Economy, and the People's Commissariats of Finance, Commerce, and Agriculture were purged because of their "right-wing deviations," "sabotage," or "membership in a socially alien class." It was notable that 80 percent of the more senior civil servants at the People's Commissariat of Finance had served under the old regime.[1]

The purge of certain sectors of the administration intensified after the summer of 1930, when Stalin decided to dispose of all "right-wingers" such as Aleksei Rykov, claiming that they were secretly conspiring with "specialist saboteurs." In August and September 1930 the GPU stepped up its campaign and arrested all well-known specialists working for Gosplan, the State Bank, and the People's Commissariats of Finance, Commerce, and Agriculture. Those arrested included Professor Nikolai Kondratyev, the inventor of the famous "Kondratyev cycle," former deputy minister in charge of food supplies for the provisional government of 1917, and then the director of an Institute for Economic Studies at the Finance Ministry. Others arrested included Professors Nikolai Makarov and Aleksandr Chayanov, who occupied important posts in the Agriculture Ministry; Professor Andrei Sadyrin, a member of the board of directors at the State Bank; and Professor Vladimir Groman, one of the best-known economic statisticians at Gosplan.[2]

In all these cases Stalin personally instructed the GPU, since he was careful to follow all matters pertaining to the "bourgeois specialists." The GPU prepared dossiers demonstrating the existence of a network of anti-Soviet organizations, linked together by a "Peasant Workers' Party," supposedly headed by Kondratyev, and an "Industrial Party" headed by Aleksandr Ramzin. The investigators extracted a number of confessions from some of those arrested. Many admitted their connection with "right-wingers" such as Rykov, Bukharin, and Sergei Syrtsov; many others confirmed their participation in totally fictitious plots to eliminate Stalin and overthrow the Soviet regime with the assistance of émigré anti-Soviet and secret service organizations abroad. Pursuing the matter further, the GPU extracted confessions from two instructors at the military academy concerning preparations for a plot to be led by the chief of the General Staff of the Red Army, Mikhail Tukhachevsky. In a letter to Sergo Ordzhonikidze, Stalin made it clear that he could not risk arresting Tukhachevsky himself but was content with the destruction of smaller targets, other "specialist saboteurs."[3] Thus the techniques for fabricating evidence to implicate as "terrorists" any who opposed the Stalinist party line were already perfectly honed by 1930. For the time being, however, Stalin was content to use relatively moderate tactics designed to discourage the little opposition that remained, and to frighten into submission those who were as yet undecided.

On 22 September 1930 *Pravda* published the "confessions" of forty-eight civil servants from the People's Commissariats of Finance and Commerce, all of whom took responsibility for "the difficulties currently being experienced in the supply of food, and for the sudden disappearance of silver coins." A few days previously, in a letter addressed to Molotov, Stalin had given strict instructions: "It is imperative to: (1) carry out a radical purge of the whole of the People's Commissariat of Finance and the State Bank, regardless of any objections from doubtful Communists like Pyatakov and [Aleksandr] Bryukhanov; (2) shoot at least twenty or thirty of the saboteurs who have managed to infiltrate these organizations . . . (3) step up GPU operations all over the country to try to recover all the silver coins that are still in circulation." On 25 September 1930 all forty-eight civil servants were executed.[4]

In the months that followed there were several identical show-trials. Some were held *in camera*, including the trials of specialists from the Supreme Council of the National Economy and from the "Peasant Workers' Party." Others were held in public, such as the trial of specialists from the "Industrial Party," eight of whom "confessed" to having established a vast network of 2,000 specialists dedicated to organizing economic subversion at the instigation of foreign embassies. All these trials fed the myth of sabotage, which, like the myth of the conspiracy, was soon at the center of Stalinist ideology.

In four years, from 1928 to 1931, 138,000 civil servants were removed from office, and 23,000 of these were classed as "enemies of Soviet power" and stripped of their civil rights.[5] The specialist witch-hunt became even more widespread in industry, where the great pressure to increase productivity led to an increase in the number of accidents, a considerable decline in quality of production, and more frequent breakdowns. Between January 1930 and June 1931, 48 percent of all engineers in the Donbass region were dismissed or arrested, and 4,500 "specialist saboteurs" were "unmasked" in the first half of 1931 in the transport sector alone. The hunt for these specialists, new and totally unattainable industrial targets set by the authorities, and growing indiscipline in the workplace caused considerable long-term damage to Soviet industry.

Realizing the scale of the problem, Party leaders were forced to adopt a series of corrective measures. On 10 July 1931 the Politburo took steps to try to limit the number of victims among the *spetsy*. The Politburo immediately released several thousand engineers and technicians, "above all those working in metallurgy and the coal industry," ended the entry restrictions to higher education for the children of "specialists," and banned the GPU from arresting "specialists" without prior permission from the relevant ministry. The mere fact that these measures were announced demonstrates how widespread discrimination and oppression had become. After the Shakhty trial, tens of thousands of engineers, agronomists, technicians, and administrators had been victims of this form of terror.[6]

Among the other social categories proscribed in the "new socialist society," members of the clergy fared especially badly. The years 1929 and 1930 were marked by a second great offensive by the Soviet state against the church, following up on the attacks of 1918–1922. At the end of the 1920s, a number of prelates opposed the pledge of allegiance to the Soviet regime announced by Metropolitan Sergei, who had succeeded Tikhon as head of the church. Even so, the Orthodox Church remained an important force in Soviet society. Of the 54,692 churches that had been active in 1914, around 39,000 were still holding services at the beginning of 1929.[7] Emelyan Yaroslavsky, president of the "League of the Militant Godless," founded in 1925, admitted that fewer than 10 million people, out of a total population of 130 million, had actually broken with religion.

The antireligious offensive of 1929–30 occurred in two stages. The first began in the spring and summer of 1929 and was marked by a reintroduction and reinforcement of the antireligious legislation of 1918–1922. On 8 April 1929 an important decree was promulgated to increase the local authorities' control over parish life, imposing new restrictions on the activity of religious societies. Henceforth any activity "going beyond the limits of the simple satisfaction of religious aspirations" fell under the law. Notably, section 10 of the much-feared Article 58 of the penal code stipulated that "any use of the religious prejudices of the masses . . . for destabilizing the state" was punishable "by anything from a minimum three-year sentence up to and including the death penalty." On 26 August 1929 the government instituted the new five-day work week—five days of work, and one day of rest—which made it impossible to observe Sunday as a day of rest. This measure was deliberately introduced "to facilitate the struggle to eliminate religion."[8]

These decrees were no more than a prelude to a second, much larger phase of the antireligious campaign. In October 1929 the seizure of all church bells was ordered because "the sound of bells disturbs the right to peace of the vast majority of atheists in the towns and the countryside." Anyone closely associated with the church was treated like a kulak and forced to pay special taxes. The taxes paid by religious leaders increased tenfold from 1928 to 1930, and the leaders were stripped of their civil rights, which meant that they lost their ration cards and their right to medical care. Many were arrested, exiled, or deported. According to the incomplete records, more than 13,000 priests were "dekulakized" in 1930. In many villages and towns, collectivization began symbolically with the closure of the church, and dekulakization began with the removal of the local religious leaders. Significantly, nearly 14 percent of riots and peasant uprisings in 1930 were sparked by the closure of a church or the removal of its bells.[9] The antireligious campaign reached its height in the winter of 1929–30; by 1 March 1930, 6,715 churches had been closed or destroyed. In the aftermath of Stalin's famous article "Dizzy with Success" on 2 March 1930, a resolution from the Central Committee cynically condemned "inadmissible deviations in the struggle against religious prejudices, particularly the administrative closure of churches without the consent of the local inhabitants." This formal condemnation had no effect on the fate of people deported on religious grounds.

Over the next few years these great offensives against the church were replaced by daily administrative harassment of priests and religious organizations. Freely interpreting the sixty-eight articles of the government decree of 8 April 1929, and going considerably beyond their mandate when it came to the closure of churches, local authorities continued their guerrilla war with a series of justifications: "unsanitary condition or extreme age" of the buildings in question, "unpaid insurance," and nonpayment of taxes or other of the innumerable contributions imposed on the members of religious communities. Stripped of their civil rights and their right to teach, and without the possibility of taking up other paid employment—a status that left them arbitrarily classified as "parasitic elements living on unearned wages"—a number of priests had no option but to become peripatetic and to lead a secret life on the edges of society. Hence, despite Metropolitan Sergei's pledge of allegiance to the Soviet regime, schisms developed within the church, particularly in the provinces of Voronezh and Tambov.

The followers of Aleksei Bui, a bishop of Voronezh who had been arrested in 1929 for his unflagging hostility to any compromise between the church and the regime, set up their own autonomous church, the "True Orthodox Church," which had its own clergy of wandering priests who had been expelled from the church headed by the patriarch. This "Desert Church" had no buildings of its own; the faithful would meet to pray in any number of places, such as private homes, hermitages, or even caves.[10] These "True Orthodox Christians," as they called themselves, were persecuted with particular severity; several thousand of them were arrested and deported as "specially displaced" or simply sent to camps. The Orthodox Church itself, in the face of this constant pressure from the authorities, saw a clear decline in the numbers of its followers, even if, as the census of 1937 was to demonstrate, 70 percent of adults continued to think of themselves as having religious beliefs. On 1 April 1936 only 15,835 Orthodox churches remained in service in the U.S.S.R. (28 percent of the prerevolutionary total), 4,830 mosques (32 percent of the prerevolutionary figure), and a few dozen Catholic and Protestant churches. The number of registered priests was a mere 17,857, in contrast to 112,629 in 1914 and 70,000 in 1928. The clergy, in the official terminology, had become "the debris of a dying class."[11]

The kulaks, *spetsy*, and members of the clergy were not the only victims of the terror of the early 1930s. In January 1930 the authorities launched a vast campaign to "evict all entrepreneurs." The operation was aimed in particular at shopkeepers, craftsmen, and members of the liberal professions—all of the nearly 1.5 million people who had worked in the minuscule private sector under the NEP. These small entrepreneurs, whose average working capital did not exceed 1,000 rubles, and 98 percent of whom did not have a single employee, were rapidly evicted by a tenfold increase in their taxes and the confiscation of their goods. As "socially undesirable elements," "socially unnecessary," or "alien elements," they were stripped of their rights in the same way as the disparate collection of "aristocrats" and "members of the possessing classes and of the apparatus of the old tsarist state." A decree of 12 December 1930 noted more than 30 different categories of *lishentsy*, citizens who had been deprived of their civil rights, including "ex-landowners," "ex-shopkeepers," "ex-nobles," "ex-policemen," "ex-tsarist civil servants," "ex-kulaks," "ex- employees or owners of private companies," "ex-White officers," ex-priests, ex-monks, ex-nuns, and "ex-members of political parties." The discrimination carried out against the *lishentsy*, who in 1932 together with their families totaled some 7 million people, entailed the elimination of their voting rights and their rights to housing, health care, and ration cards. In 1933 and 1934 the measures became even stricter with the inception of "passportization" to clear the towns of "socially undesirable elements."[12]

By destroying social structures and traditional rural ways of life, the forced collectivization of the countryside and the accelerated program of industrialization spurred the migration of an enormous number of peasants to the towns. Peasant Russia became filled with vagabonds, the *Rusbrodyashchaya*. From late 1928 until late 1932, Soviet cities were flooded by an influx of peasants—12 million by official estimates—fleeing collectivization and dekulakization. The regions surrounding Moscow and Leningrad alone were swollen by more than 3.5 million migrants. Among these were a number of enterprising peasants who had preferred to flee their villages, even at the price of being classified as kulaks, rather than enter a *kolkhoz*. In 1930–31 the huge public works programs absorbed these peasants without too many difficulties. But in 1932 the authorities began to worry about the massive and uncontrolled movements of a vagabond population that threatened to destabilize the urban areas. Their presence also threatened to jeopardize the rationing system that had been carefully structured since 1929; the claimants for ration cards increased from 26 million in 1929 to nearly 40 million in late 1932. Migrants often forced the authorities to transform factories into huge refugee camps. Gradually the migrants were considered responsible for an increasing range of negative phenomena, such as absenteeism, lapses in discipline at work, hooliganism, poor quality of work, alcoholism, and criminality, all of which had a long-term destabilizing effect on industrial production.[13]

To combat this *stikhia*—a blanket term used to describe natural disasters, anarchy, or any sort of disorder—the authorities enacted a series of repressive measures in October 1932, ranging from harsh new employment laws to purges of "socially foreign elements." The law of 15 November 1932 severely punished absenteeism at work by immediate dismissal, confiscation of cards, and even eviction. Its affirmed intention was to unmask "pseudoworkers." The decree of 4 December 1932, which gave employers responsibility for issuing ration cards, aimed chiefly at the removal of all "dead souls" and "parasites" who were wrongfully included on some of the less tightly controlled municipal rationing lists.

The keystone of the new legislation was the introduction of the internal passport on 27 December 1932. The "passportization" of the population addressed several carefully defined objectives, as the preamble to the decree explained: it was intended "to eliminate all social parasitism," to prevent "infiltration" by kulaks into city centers and markets, to limit the rural exodus, and to safeguard the social purity of the towns. All adult townspeople over age sixteen who had not yet been deprived of their rights, such as railway workers, permanent workers on construction sites, and agricultural workers on state farms, automatically received a passport from the police. The passport was valid only after it received an official stamp *(propiska)* showing the legal residence of the citizen in question. The status of the individual depended on his or her *propiska* and could determine whether an individual received a ration card, a social security card, or the right to a home. All towns were categorized as either "open" or "closed." The closed cities—initially Moscow, Leningrad, Kyiv, Odessa, Minsk, Kharkiv, Rostov-on-Don, and Vladivostok—were those that had been awarded a privileged status and were better supplied. Right of residence in a closed city was obtainable only through family ties, marriage, or a specific job that officially entitled the worker to a *propiska*. In the open cities, a *propiska* was much easier to obtain.

The passportization operations lasted a whole year, and by the end of 1933, 27 million passports had been issued. The first effect was to allow the authorities to purge the cities of undesirable elements. Begun in Moscow on 5 January 1933, within the first week passportization "discovered" 3,450 "ex-

White Guards, ex-kulaks, and other criminal elements." Nearly 385,000 people were refused passports in the closed cities and forced to vacate their homes within ten days. Moreover, they were prohibited from residing in any other city, even an open one. The chief of the passport department of the NKVD noted in his report of 13 August 1934 that "to that figure should be added all those who preferred to leave the towns of their own accord when passportization was first announced, knowing that they would in any case be refused a passport. In Magnitogorsk for example, nearly 35,000 immediately left the town . . . In Moscow, during the first two months of the operation, the population fell by 60,000. In Leningrad, in a single month, 54,000 people vanished back into the countryside." Some 420,000 people were expelled from the open cities.[14]

Police raids and spot-checks for papers resulted in the exile of hundreds of thousands of people. In December 1933 Genrikh Yagoda ordered his men to "clean up" the railway stations and the markets in the closed cities every week. In the first eight months of 1934 more than 630,000 people in the closed cities were stopped for violations of the passport laws. Of these, 65,661 were imprisoned and then usually deported as socially undesirable elements with the status of "special displaced." Some 3,596 were tried in court, and 175,627 were sent into exile without any status; the others escaped with a fine.[15]

The most spectacular operations took place in 1933. From 28 June to 3 July, 5,470 Gypsies from Moscow were arrested and deported to Siberian "work villages";[16] from 8 to 12 July, 4,750 "socially undesirable elements" were arrested and deported from Kyiv; in April, June, and July, three waves of police activity in Moscow and Leningrad resulted in the deportation of 18,000 people.[17] The first of those contingents was sent to the island of Nazino, with the results described earlier. More than two-thirds of the deportees died within a month.

A Party instructor in Narym, in the report quoted earlier, commented on the identity of "socially undesirable elements" who had been deported as the result of a simple police raid:

> There are many such examples of totally unjustified deportations. Unfortunately, all these people, many of whom were Party members or workers, are now dead. They were precisely the people who were least adapted to the situation. For example, Vladimir Novozhilov from Moscow was a driver in the steamroller factory in Moscow who had been decorated three times and was married with a child. He tried to go to the cinema with his wife, and while she was getting ready he went out without his papers to buy cigarettes. He was then stopped by the police in the street and picked up. Another example was [K.] Vinogradova, a collective farm worker. She was going to visit her brother, the chief of police in the eighth sector in Moscow, when she got picked up by the

police after getting off the train at the wrong station. She was deported. Or Nikolai Vasilievich Voikin, who had been a member of the Komsomol since 1929, and was a worker in the Serpukhov Red Textile factory, having been decorated three times. He was on his way to a soccer game one Sunday and had forgotten his papers. He was arrested and deported. Or I. M. Matveev, a builder on the construction site of the new No. 9 bakery. He had a seasonal worker's passport, valid until December 1933, and was picked up with that passport. He reported that no one had even wanted to look at his papers.[18]

In 1933 the purge in the towns was accompanied by numerous similar operations in industry and government. In the railways, a strategic sector ruled by Andreev and then by Kaganovich, 8 percent of all personnel (nearly 20,000 people) were removed in the spring of 1933. The following extract from a report by the chief of the Transport Department of the GPU on "The Elimination of Anti-Soviet and Counterrevolutionary Elements from the Railways" describes how such operations were normally carried out:

> The purge operations carried out by the Transport Department of the GPU of the Eighth Region had the following results: In the penultimate purge operation, 700 people were arrested and tried. The numbers were as follows: there were 325 parcel pilferers, 221 smalltime hooligans and criminals, 27 bandits, and 127 counterrevolutionaries. Some 73 of the people pilfering parcels were clearly part of an organized network and were consequently executed. In the last purge operation, around 200 people were arrested. For the most part these were kulaks. More than 300 suspect employees have also been dismissed by the administration. This means that in the last four months, the total number of people who have been expelled from the network for one reason or another is 1,270. The purge continues.[19]

In the spring of 1934 the government took a series of repressive measures aimed at curbing the number of young vagabonds and juvenile delinquents, the products of dekulakization, the famine, and the general breakdown in social relations whose influence was beginning to be felt more and more in the cities. On 7 April 1935 the Politburo promulgated a decree aimed at "bringing to justice, and punishing with the full force of the law, any adolescent older than twelve years who is convicted of burglary, acts of violence, grievous bodily harm, mutilation, or murder." A few days later the government sent out secret instructions to the courts confirming that the penal sanctions regarding adolescents "did indeed include society's last line of defense"—the death penalty. The previous portions of the penal code that forbade the sentencing of minors to death were thereby abrogated.[20] The NKVD was also instructed to reorganize the detention centers for underage criminals, which until then had been run under the auspices of the Legal Department of the People's Commissariat of Preliminary Investigations, and to set up a network of "work colonies" for minors instead. However, in the face of growing juvenile delinquency and homelessness, the measures had little discernible effect. A report on "The Elimination of Underage Vagabondage during the Period from 1 July 1935 to 1 October 1937" concluded:

> Despite the reorganization of the services, the situation has barely improved . . . After February 1937 there was a large influx of vagabonds from the country and the rural areas, particularly from the areas affected by the poor harvest of 1936 . . . The large-scale departure of children from the countryside because of temporary material difficulties affecting their families can be explained not only by the bad organization of the "poor funds" in the *kolkhozy,* but also by the criminal practices of many *kolkhoz* directors, who, in an attempt to get rid of young beggars and vagabonds, give them a "certificate of vagabondage and mendicancy" and send them off to the railway station for the nearest town . . . The problem is compounded by the railway administration and the transport police, who, instead of arresting these underage vagabonds and sending them to the special NKVD centers built for that purpose, simply put them all on special trains "to clean up their sector" and pack them off to the big cities.[21]

A few figures provide an idea of the magnitude of the problem. In 1936 alone more than 125,000 underage vagabonds passed through the special NKVD centers. From 1935 to 1939 more than 155,000 minors were sent to the NKVD work colonies, and 92,000 children aged twelve to sixteen appeared in court from 1936 to 1939. On 1 April 1939 it was calculated that more than 10,000 children were incarcerated in the gulags.[22]

In the first half of the 1930s, the repression carried out by the Party and state against society varied in its intensity. Moments of violent confrontation, with terrorist measures and massive purges, alternated with moments of quiet, when a certain equilibrium was found and a brake was put on the chaos.

The spring of 1933 marked the apogee of the first great cycle of terror launched in 1929 with the dekulakization program. The authorities were confronted by several previously unknown problems. How, for example, could a harvest be assured the following year in areas that had been almost emptied by famine? "Unless we take into consideration the basic needs of these collective farmers," warned a high-ranking regional Party official in the autumn of 1932, "there will be no one left to sow, let alone reap, the harvest."

Similarly, what was to be done with the hundreds of thousands who then filled the prisons, but whose labor the camp system was not yet ready to exploit? "What possible effect can these super-repressive laws have on the population," wondered another local Party official in March 1933, "when they know that at the judiciary's suggestion, hundreds of collective farmers, who last month were condemned to two years' imprisonment for sabotaging the harvest, have already been released?"

In the summer of 1933 the authorities came up with answers revelatory of the two diverse directions that social policy was to take in the years leading up to the Great Terror in the autumn of 1936. The first question, how to ensure a reasonable harvest in areas ravaged by famine, was answered with cold logic: large numbers of the urban population were rounded up and sent out to the fields in an extremely militarized fashion. On 20 July 1933 the Italian consul in Kharkiv described this phenomenon: "The enforced conscription of people from the city is assuming enormous proportions. This week alone, at least 20,000 people are being sent out to the countryside every day . . . The day before yesterday, the market was surrounded, and every able-bodied person—men, women, young boys and girls—was rounded up, escorted to the railway station by the GPU, and sent off to the fields."[23]

The large-scale arrival of city-dwellers in the starving countryside created its own tensions. On several occasions peasants set fire to the living quarters reserved for the "conscripts," who had been warned by the authorities not to venture out into the villages, which were "filled with cannibals." Despite this hostility the harvest for 1932–33, collected in October, was respectable. That development was attributable to several factors, including exceptionally good weather, the mobilization of every available spare worker, and the will to survive of those who were trapped in their own villages.

The second question, how to deal with the tremendous increase in the prison population, was also answered in a pragmatic manner—with the release of several hundred thousand people. A confidential circular from the Central Committee on 8 May 1933 acknowledged the necessity of "regulating arrests . . . presently made by just about anyone," "curbing the overcrowding of prisons," and "reducing the population of the prisons, over the next two months, from 800,000 to 400,000, not including the camps."[24] The operation in fact took over a year and finally resulted in the release of 320,000 prisoners.

The year 1934 was marked by a certain relaxation of political repression. The number of convictions handed down by the GPU declined from 240,000 in 1932 to 79,000 in 1933.[25] The secret police were reorganized. As a result of a government decree on 10 July 1934, the GPU became a department of the new People's Commissariat of Internal Affairs, whose authority extended throughout the U.S.S.R. Henceforth it had the same name as the People's Commissariat of Internal Affairs itself—Narodnyi komissariat vnutrennikh del, or NKVD—and it lost some of its previous judicial powers. In the new scheme of things, after initial questioning all files had to be sent "to the relevant judicial departments." Moreover, the police no longer had the power to pass death sentences on prisoners without first consulting the central political authorities. An appeals procedure was also set up, and all death sentences were now to be approved by a special commission of the Politburo.

These changes, proudly depicted as measures to "reinforce the legal mechanism of socialism," had very limited effects in practice. The new legal regulations to control the number of arrests had almost no impact, since Andrei Vyshinsky, the procurator general, gave a free hand to all the repressive organizations. Moreover, as early as September 1934 the Politburo broke its own rules regarding the need to confirm all death sentences, authorizing local leaders in a number of different areas to pass death sentences without first consulting Moscow. The calm was therefore short-lived.

After Sergei Kirov, a member of the Politburo and first secretary of the Party organization in Leningrad, was shot on 1 December 1934 by Leonid Nikolaev, a young Communist who had managed to find his way into the Leningrad Party headquarters with a gun, a new cycle of terror began.

For several decades it was widely believed that Stalin had played an important role in the assassination of Kirov, who was his chief political rival. This belief stemmed from the "revelations" made by Nikita Khrushchev in the secret report he presented on the night of 24–25 February 1956 to the Soviet delegates at the Twentieth Party Congress. The theory has recently been called into question, particularly in the work of Alla Kirilina, who draws on previously unavailable archival sources.[26] In any case it is indisputable that Stalin used the assassination for his own political ends to crystallize the idea of conspiracy, which was always a central motif in Stalinist rhetoric. It allowed him to maintain the atmosphere of crisis and tension by "proving" the existence of a huge conspiracy against the country, its leaders, and socialism itself. It even became a convenient explanation for the failures of the system: when everything went badly and life was no longer "happy and merry," in Stalin's famous expression, then it was "all the fault of Kirov's assassins."

A few hours after the assassination was announced, Stalin drafted the decree that came to be known as the "Law of 1 December." This extraordinary measure, authorized by the Politburo two days later, ordered that the period of questioning for suspected terrorists be reduced to ten days, allowed suspects to be tried without legal representation, and permitted executions to be carried out immediately. The law marked a radical break with the relaxation of terror only a few months earlier, and it became the ideal instrument for the launching of the Great Terror.[27]

In the following weeks a number of Stalin's opponents within the Party were accused of terrorist activities. The press announced that the "odious crime" had been the work of a secret terrorist group directed from its "Center in Leningrad," and that it included, besides Nikolaev himself, thirteen former Zinovievites. All members of the group were tried *in camera* on 28 and 29 December, condemned to death, and immediately executed. On 9 January 1935 the infamous trial of the "Leningrad Zinovievite Counterrevolutionary Center" began, and 77 people, including many famous Party militants who had opposed Stalin at some point, received prison sentences. The unmasking of the "Leningrad Center" led to the subsequent discovery of a "Moscow Center," whose 19 supposed members included Zinoviev and Kamenev themselves. Members of the "Moscow Center" were accused of "ideological complicity" with Kirov's assassins and went to trial on 16 January 1935. Zinoviev and Kamenev admitted that their "previous activity in opposing the Party line, when looked at objectively, could not fail to have acted as a catalyst and provoked the worst instincts of these criminals." This extraordinary public admission of "ideological complicity," coming after so many disavowals and public denials, led to five- and ten-year sentences respectively. From December 1934 to February 1935, 6,500 people were sentenced under the new procedures to combat terrorism.[28]

The day after Zinoviev and Kamenev were convicted, the Central Committee sent a secret circular to all Party organizations, titled "Lessons to Be Drawn from the Cowardly Murder of Comrade Kirov." The text affirmed the existence of a plot that had been led by "two Zinovievite cells . . . which were fronts for White Guard organizations" and reminded all members of the permanent struggle against "anti-Party groups" such as Trotskyites, Democratic Centralists, and right- and left-wing splinter groups. Anyone who had previously opposed Stalin on any matter became a suspect. The hunt for enemies intensified, and in January 1935, 988 former Zinoviev supporters were exiled from Leningrad to Siberia and Yakutsk. The Central Committee ordered all local Party organizations to draw up lists of Communists who had been banned in 1926–1928 for belonging to the "Trotskyite and Zinoviev-Trotskyite bloc," and arrests were later carried out solely on the basis of these lists. In May 1935 Stalin sent out another letter to all Party organizations ordering careful checks to be carried out on the Party membership card of every Communist.

The official version of Kirov's assassination, which claimed that it had been carried out by someone who had entered Smolny using a fake Party membership card, served to demonstrate the "immense political importance" of the campaign to check all membership cards. The operation went on for more than six months and was carried out with the full assistance of the secret police. The NKVD supplied all the files required on "suspicious Communists," and the Party organizations in turn informed the NKVD about people barred from the Party as a result of the campaign. The whole operation resulted in the exclusion of 9 percent of Party members, or approximately 250,000 people.[29] At a Central Committee meeting in late December 1935 Nikolai Ezhov, the head of the Main Department in charge of the operation, produced incomplete data suggesting that 15,218 of the "enemies" who had been expelled from the Party had also been arrested during the campaign. Nevertheless Ezhov believed that the purge had not been a great success because it had taken three times longer than originally planned, on account of the "ill will and sabotage" of several "bureaucratic elements who were still working in the directorate." Although one of the Party's main concerns had been to root out Trotskyites and Zinovievites, only 3 percent of those who had been excluded actually belonged to either of those categories. Local Party leaders had often been reluctant "to contact the NKVD and hand over lists of people to be exiled immediately by means of an administrative decision." In short, in Ezhov's opinion, the card-check campaign had revealed the extent to which local Party offices were inclined to present a united front of passive resistance against the authorities.[30] This was an important lesson that Stalin would always remember.

The wave of terror that struck immediately after the assassination of Kirov did not affect just the previous opponents of Stalin within the Party. On the pretext that "White Guard terrorist elements have penetrated the country from the West," the Politburo on 27 December 1934 ordered the deportation of 2,000 "anti-Soviet" families from the frontier districts of Ukraine. On 15 March 1935 similar measures were taken to deport "all doubtful elements from the frontier districts of the Leningrad region and the autonomous republic of Karelia . . . to Kazakhstan and western Siberia." The principal victims were nearly 10,000 Finns, the first of many ethnic groups to suffer deportations that would reach their peak during World War II. In the spring of 1936 a second mass deportation of 15,000 families took place, involving nearly 50,000 people, most of them Poles and Germans from Ukraine, who were deported to the Karaganda region in Kazakhstan and settled there on the collective farms.[31]

The cycle of repression intensified over the next two years, with the NKVD handing down 267,000 sentences in 1935 and 274,000 in 1936. At the same time a few measures were taken to appease the population. The category of *lishentsy* was abolished, sentences of less than five years of imprisonment for collective farm workers were annulled, 37,000 people who had been sentenced under the law of 27 August 1932 were released early, the civil rights of the "specially displaced" were reinstated, and discriminatory practices were ended that had forbidden the children of deportees from gaining access to higher education. Such measures often had contradictory results. Deported kulaks, for example, who had their civil rights reinstated five years after their deportation, were ultimately forbidden to leave the area in which they had been resettled. As soon as their rights had been returned, they had begun to go back to their villages, which had resulted in a multitude of insoluble problems: Were they to be allowed to join the collective farms? Where were they to live now that their houses and goods had been confiscated? The logic of repression allowed for only slight pauses in the process: there was no going back.

Tension between society and the regime increased still further when the government decided to endorse the Stakhanovite movement, named after Andrei Stakhanov, who, thanks to an extraordinary process of teamwork and reorganization, had managed to increase coal production fourteenfold. A huge productivity campaign began, and two months later, in November 1935, a "Conference of Avant-Garde Workers" was held in Moscow. Stalin himself emphasized the "profoundly revolutionary nature of a movement that has managed to free itself of the habitual conservatism of engineers, technicians, and managers." In fact, given the nature of Soviet industry at the time, the introduction of Stakhanovite days, weeks, and even decades had a profoundly negative effect on production: equipment wore out more quickly, accidents in the workplace soared, and increases in production were almost inevitably followed by a period of decline. Returning to the *spetseedstvo* theme of the late 1920s, the authorities again took to blaming economic difficulties on so-called saboteurs who had infiltrated the management, especially the engineers and specialists. Once again any doubt expressed about the Stakhanovites, any break in the rhythm of production, or any technical breakdown came to be regarded as counterrevolutionary action. In the first six months of 1936 more than 14,000 managers in industry were arrested for sabotage. Stalin used the Stakhanovite campaign to unleash a new wave of terror, to be remembered forever as the Great Terror.

10 The Great Terror (1936–1938)

Much has been written about the Great Terror, which was also known in the Soviet Union as the *Ezhovshchina*, "The Reign of Ezhov." It is undoubtedly true to say that when Nikolai Ezhov was in charge of the NKVD (from September 1936 to November 1938), the effects of repression were felt at every level of Soviet society, from the Politburo all the way down to simple citizens arrested in the street. For decades the tragedy of the Great Terror was passed over in silence. The West saw only the three spectacular public trials in Moscow in August 1936, January 1937, and March 1938, when Lenin's most illustrious companions (among them Zinoviev, Kamenev, Nikolai Krestinsky, Rykov, Pyatokov, Radek, and Bukharin) admitted to organizing terrorist centers with Trotskyite and Zinovievite or right-wing Trotskyite tendencies, plotting to overthrow the Soviet government or to assassinate its leaders, plotting to reinstate capitalism, carrying out acts of sabotage, undermining the military might of the U.S.S.R., and conniving to break up the Soviet Union and help foreign powers by facilitating the independence of Ukraine, Belarus, Georgia, Armenia, and the Soviet Far East . . .

As huge, stage-managed events, the trials in Moscow were also a highly effective tactic to deflect the attention of fascinated foreign observers from events that were going on elsewhere, especially the massive repressions against all social categories. For these observers, who had already kept silent about

komandatury revealed situations that were intolerable in the eyes of the authorities. In the region of Arkhangelsk, for example, of the 89,700 colonizers who had been assigned residency there, a mere 37,000 remained.

The obsession with the ideas of the kulak saboteur who had managed to infiltrate a business and of the kulak bandit who roamed the streets goes some way toward explaining how this "category" became the centerpiece in the great repressive operation that Stalin concocted in early July 1937.

On 2 July 1937 the Politburo sent local authorities a telegram ordering that "all kulaks and criminals must be immediately arrested . . . and after trial before a troika [a commission consisting of the regional Party first secretary, the procurator, and the regional NKVD chief] the most hostile are to be shot, and the less active but still hostile elements deported . . . It is the Central Committee's wish that the composition of the *troiki* be presented to it within five days, together with the numbers of those shot and deported."

In the following weeks the central authorities received "indicative figures" sent in by the local authorities, on the basis of which Ezhov prepared Operational Order No. 00447, dated 30 July 1937, which he submitted to the Politburo for ratification the same day. During this particular operation 259,450 people were arrested and 72,950 shot.[7] These numbers were inexact, since many regions had not yet sent their calculations to the central authorities. As in the days of the dekulakization operations, all regions received quotas for each of the two categories: those to be shot and those to be deported.

It is notable that the victims of this operation belonged to a mysterious sociopolitical group that was much larger than the categories initially enumerated. Besides the "ex-kulaks" and the "criminal elements," those to be found now included "socially dangerous elements," "members of anti–Soviet parties," "former tsarist civil servants," and "White Guards." These designations were applied quite freely to any suspect, regardless of whether he was a Party member, a member of the intelligentsia, or an ordinary worker. The relevant offices of the GPU and the NKVD had had many years to draw up the necessary lists of suspects, and plenty of time to keep them up to date.

The operational order of 30 July 1937 also gave local leaders the right to ask Moscow for further lists of suspects to be eliminated. The families of people condemned to the camps or to death could also be arrested to swell the quotas.

By the end of August the Politburo was assailed with numerous requests for the quotas to be raised. From 28 August to 15 December 1937 it ratified various proposals for increases so that an additional 22,500 individuals were executed and another 16,800 were condemned to camps. On 31 January 1938, at the instigation of the NKVD, a further increase of 57,200 was accepted, 48,000 of whom were to be executed. All operations were to have been finished on 15 March 1938, but once again the local authorities, who had been purged several times in the preceding years and whose new staff were eager to show their zeal, demanded another increase in the numbers. From 1 February to 29 August 1938 the Politburo ratified the requests, thus sanctioning the elimination of a further 90,000 suspects.

In this fashion, an operation that was originally planned for four months went on for over a year, and affected at least 200,000 more people than those originally planned for in the quotas.[8] Any individual suspected of the wrong social origins was a potential victim. People living in the frontier zones were also particularly vulnerable, as was anyone who had any contacts outside the country, no matter how far removed. Such people, including anyone who owned a radio transmitter, collected stamps, or spoke Esperanto, stood a very good chance of being accused of espionage. From 6 August to 21 December 1937, at least ten operations similar to the one begun by Operational Order No. 00447 were launched by the Politburo and the NKVD to liquidate groups of suspected spies or "subversives" nationality by nationality: Germans, Poles, Japanese, Romanians, Finns, Lithuanians, Latvians, Greeks, and Turks. Over a fifteen-month period, from August 1937 to November 1938, several hundred thousand people were arrested in these antiespionage operations.

Among the operations about which some information is available (although it is still fragmentary; the ex-KGB and Russian Presidential archives, where the most sensitive documents are kept, are still secret and closed to researchers) are the following:

- The operation to "liquidate the German contingent working in all offices linked to National Defense" on 20 July 1937
- The operation to "liquidate all terrorist activity, subversion, and espionage by the network of Japanese repatriated from Kharbin," launched on 19 September 1937
- The operation to "liquidate the right-wing military and Japanese Cossack organization," launched on 4 August 1937, in which more than 19,000 people died from September to December 1937
- The operation to "repress the families of enemies of the people," set in motion by NKVD Order No. 00486 on 15 August 1937

This very incomplete list of one small part of the operations decreed by the Politburo and carried out by the NKVD suffices to underscore the centralized nature of the mass repressions of 1937 and 1938. These actions, like all the actions decided by the center but implemented by local authorities—including dekulakization, the purging of the towns, and the hunt for specialists—were often carried out with tragic excesses in the local communities. After the Great Terror, a single commission was sent to make inquiries in Turkmenistan about excesses committed under the *Ezhovshchina*. In this small republic of 1.3 million inhabitants (0.7 percent of the Soviet population), 13,259 had been sentenced by the NKVD *troiki* in the period August 1937–September 1938 as part of the operation to "liquidate ex-kulaks, criminals, and other anti-Soviet elements." Of these, 4,037 had been shot. The quotas fixed by Moscow had been respectively 6,227 (the total number of sentences) and 3,225 (the total number of executions).[9] One can easily imagine that similar excesses were common in all other regions of the country. They were a natural result of the quota scheme. Planned orders from the center and bureaucratic reflexes, which had been well assimilated and drummed into civil servants for many years, naturally spurred local officials to try to anticipate and surpass the desires of superiors further up the hierarchy and the directives that arrived from Moscow.

Another series of documents also highlights the centralized nature of the mass slaughter ordered by Stalin and ratified by the Politburo. These are the lists of people to be sentenced that were drawn up by the Commission for Judicial Affairs of the Politburo. The sentences for people who were summoned before the military collegium of the Supreme Court, the military courts, or the Special Board of the NKVD were all predetermined by the Commission for Judicial Affairs of the Politburo. This commission, of which Ezhov himself was a member, submitted at least 383 lists to be signed by Stalin and the Politburo. These lists contained some 44,000 names of Party leaders or members, as well as the names of prominent figures from industry and the army. At least 39,000 of them were condemned to death. Stalin's own signature appears at the bottom of 362 lists, with Molotov's signature on 373, Kliment Voroshilov's on 195, Kaganovich's on 191, Andrei Zhdanov's on 177, and Mikoyan's on 62.[10]

All these leaders arrived in person to carry out purges of local Party organizations after the summer of 1937. Kaganovich was sent to purge the Donbass regions of Chelyabinsk, Yaroslavl, Ivanovo, and Smolensk; Zhdanov, after purging his own region of Leningrad, went to Orenburg, Bashkiria, and Tatarstan; Andreev went to the Northern Caucasus, Uzbekistan, and Tajikistan; Mikoyan went to Armenia; and Khrushchev went to Ukraine.

While most instructions about mass repressions, like all other resolutions adopted by the Politburo, were ratified by Stalin as a matter of course, it now appears, in the light of archival material that has recently become available, that Stalin was also the author and initiator of most of the repressive measures. For example, when on 27 August 1937 at 5:00 P.M. the Secretariat of the Central Committee received a communication from Mikhail Koroshenko, first secretary of the regional Party committee in western Siberia, regarding the proceedings of a trial of some agronomists who had been accused of sabotage, Stalin himself sent a telegram back ten minutes later, saying: "I advise the sentencing to death of all saboteurs in Andreev's district, and the public proclamation of their execution in the local papers."[11]

All documents that are now available (protocols from the Politburo, Stalin's diary, and the list of visitors he received at the Kremlin) demonstrate that Stalin meticulously controlled and directed Ezhov's every move. He corrected instructions to the NKVD, masterminded all the big public trials, and even wrote the scripts for them. During preparations for the trial of Marshal Tukhachevsky and other Red Army leaders for their participation in a "military conspiracy," Stalin saw Ezhov every day.[12] At each stage of *Ezhovshchina*, Stalin retained political control of events. It was he who decided the nomination of Ezhov to the post of people's commissar of internal affairs, sending the famous telegram from Sochi to the Politburo on 25 September 1936: "It is absolutely necessary and extremely urgent that Comrade Ezhov be nominated to the post of People's Commissar of Internal Affairs. Yagoda is plainly not up to the task of unmasking the Trotskyite and Zinovievite coalition. The GPU is now four years behind in this business." It was also Stalin who decided to put a stop to the "excesses of the NKVD." On 17 November 1938 a decree from the Central Committee put a (provisional) stop to the organization of "large-scale arrest and deportation procedures." One week later, Ezhov was dismissed from the post of People's Commissar and replaced by Beria. The Great Terror thus ended as it had begun, on Stalin's orders.

In seeking to tally the number and categories of the victims of the *Ezhovshchina*, we now have at our disposal a few extremely confidential documents drawn up for Nikita Khrushchev and the main leaders of the Party during de-Stalinization. Foremost among these is a long study of "repressions carried out during the era of the personality cult," conducted by a commission established at the Twenty-second Congress of the Soviet Communist Party and led by Nikolai Shvernik.[13] Researchers can thus compare these figures with other sources of statistics about the Gulag Administration, the People's Commissariat of Justice, and legal records that are now also available.[14]

It appears that during 1937 and 1938, 1,575,000 people were arrested by the NKVD; of these, 1,345,000 (85.4 percent) received some sort of sentence and 681,692 (51 percent of those who were sentenced) were executed.

People arrested were sentenced in different ways. Cases involving white-collar workers, politicians, military leaders, economists, and members of the intelligentsia—the highest-profile category—were judged by military tribunals and the Special Board of the NKVD. Given the scale of these operations, the government in late August 1937 set up *troiki* at regional levels made up of the local procurator, the chief of the local police, and the head of the local branch of the NKVD. These *troiki* meted out an extremely perfunctory form of justice, since their main aim was to comply with resolutions and quotas sent out in advance by the central offices. Often they did little more than pick up suspects who had been under surveillance for some time, "reactivating" old lists. The trial was as simple as possible: the *troiki* would often see hundreds of files in a single day, as is evident from the recent publication of the *Leningrad List of Martyrs*, a directory showing month by month the names of inhabitants of the city who were condemned to death as a result of Article 58 of the penal code, beginning in August 1937. The usual interval between the arrest and the death sentence was a few weeks. The sentence, against which there was no appeal, was then carried out in a few days. The probability of being arrested merely to fill a quota for a specific operation depended on a series of coincidences in all the large-scale repressive operations carried out around that time, including the liquidation of the kulaks launched on 30 July 1937, the operation to liquidate criminal elements begun on 12 September 1937, and the "repression of families of enemies of the people." If the list of names on file was not long enough, the local authorities would use any means necessary to find the extra names to "comply with the established norms." To give but one example, in order to fill the category of "saboteurs," the NKVD in Turkmenia used the pretext of an industrial fire to arrest everyone who was on the site and forced them all to name their "accomplices."[15] Communist cadres were only a tiny share of the 681,692 people executed. Programmed from on high and arbitrarily inventing categories of political enemies, the terror, by its very nature, generated side effects that were always highly indicative of the culture of violence endemic at the lowest levels of the hierarchy.

These figures are far from exhaustive. They do not include any of the deportations carried out during these years, such as those from the Soviet Far East between May and October 1937, when 172,000 Koreans were moved to Kazakhstan and Uzbekistan. Nor do they include the number of people who died from torture during imprisonment or on the way to the camps (an unknown number), or the number of prisoners who died in the camps during these years (approximately 25,000 in 1937, more than 90,000 in 1938).[16] Even when rounded down in relation to extrapolating from the eyewitness reports of survivors, the figures are still a shocking reminder of the size of these mass killings, carried out by the hundreds of thousands against a whole society.

It is now possible to analyze further the categories of victims of these mass slaughters. We now have some statistics, to be discussed at length in the next chapter, on the number of prisoners in the gulags at the end of the 1930s. This information covers all groups of prisoners, not simply those arrested during the Great Terror, without specifying the categories of victims condemned to the camps during the *Ezhovshchina*. Nevertheless, some patterns are discernible, notably a sharp increase in the number of victims who had had some form of higher education (over 70 percent in 1936–1939), confirming that the terror at the end of the decade was aimed particularly at the educated elite, whether they were Party members or not.

Because the purge of Party cadres was the first event of the Stalin era to be publicly denounced (at the Twentieth Party Congress), it is one of the best-known aspects of the Great Terror. In his "Secret Speech" at the Congress, Khrushchev covered this phenomenon at some length. It had affected five members of the Politburo who were faithful Stalinists (Postyshev, Jan Rudzutak, Eikhe, Kossior, Anatoly Chubar), 98 of the 139 members of the Central Committee, and 1,108 of the 1,996 delegates to the Seventeenth Party Congress in 1934. It had equally affected the leaders of the Komsomol: 72 of the 93 members of the Central Committee were arrested, as well as 319 of the 385 regional secretaries and 2,210 of the 2,750 district secretaries. Generally speaking, the local and regional headquarters of the Party and the Komsomol were entirely restaffed. All were suspected of sabotaging the decisions handed down by Moscow and of opposing central control of local affairs. In Leningrad, where the Party had been led by Zinoviev and where Kirov had been assassinated, Zhdanov and Zakovsky (the chief of the regional NKVD) arrested more than 90 percent of the Party cadres. These numbers represent only a tiny share of the people from Leningrad who were victims of repression from 1936 to 1939.[17] To ensure that the purges were carried out with maximum efficiency, representatives from the central authorities together with troops from the NKVD were sent out in the provinces on a mission described in *Pravda* as an attempt "to smoke out and destroy the bugs' nests of the Trotskyite-fascists."

Some regions seemed to suffer more than others, especially Ukraine. In 1938 alone, after the nomination of Khrushchev as head of the Ukrainian Communist Party, more than 106,000 people were arrested in Ukraine, and the majority of these were executed. Of the 200 members of the Central Committee of the Ukrainian Communist Party, 3 survived. The same scenario was repeated in all local and regional Party headquarters, where dozens of public trials were organized for previous Communist leaders.

Unlike the trials *in camera* or the secret sessions of the *troiki,* in which the fate of the accused was dispatched in a few minutes, the public trials of leaders were strongly populist in nature and fulfilled an important propaganda role. As Stalin said in a speech of 3 March 1937, the intention was to denounce these local leaders, "those new lords, who are so smug and filled with overconfidence . . . and who through their inhuman attitudes inevitably create suffering and discontent, and end up encouraging the formation of an army of Trotskyites." It was thought that this would strengthen the alliance between "the ordinary people, the simple militants who believed in justice," and the Leader himself. Imitating the great trials in Moscow, but this time on a local and district scale, these public trials were generally reported in detail in the relevant local press and became the extraordinary focus of ideological, popular, and populist mobilization. Because of the manner in which these public trials unmasked conspiracies, the central preoccupation with Communist ideology, and the carnival atmosphere that reigned when those who had been rich and powerful were cast down and the poor people exalted, the trials, in Annie Kriegel's words, became "a formidable mechanism for social cleansing."

The repression directed at local Party leaders was, of course, only the tip of the iceberg. One example is a detailed report from the regional department of the NKVD in Orenburg "on operational measures for the liquidation of clandestine groups of Trotskyites and Bukharinites, as well as other counter-revolutionary groups, carried out from 1 April to 18 September 1937" (that is, before Zhdanov visited the province to accelerate the purge).[18] In this province the following Party members were arrested:

> 420 "Trotskyites," all of whom were politicians or economists of the
> first rank
> 120 "right-wingers," all of whom were local leaders of some importance

These 540 Party cadres represented 45 percent of the local officials. After Zhdanov's mission to Oranienburg, 598 more cadres were arrested and executed. Before the autumn of 1937 almost all Party leaders in the province and every economist of note were eliminated. They were replaced by a new generation, who were rapidly promoted to the front line, the generation of Brezhnev, Kosygin, Dmitry Ustinov, and Gromyko—in short, the generation that was to make up the Politburo of the 1970s.

In addition to the thousands of Party cadres who were arrested, there were a number of ordinary Party members and ex-Communists, who were particularly vulnerable. These simple citizens, who had been in the NKVD's files for years, in fact made up the greater part of the victims who suffered in the Great Terror. To return to the Orenburg NKVD report:

> Slightly more than 2,000 members of a right-wing military Japanese Cossack organization [of whom approximately 1,500 were executed]
> More than 1,500 officers and tsarist civil servants exiled to Oranienburg from Leningrad in 1935 [these were "socially alien elements" exiled to various regions after the assassination of Kirov]
> 250 people arrested as part of the Polish affair
> 95 people arrested . . . as part of the affair concerning elements originating from Kharbin

3,290 people arrested as part of the operation to liquidate all ex-kulaks

1,399 people arrested during the operation to liquidate all criminal elements

If one also includes the 30-odd people from the Komsomol and 50 cadets from the local military training academy, it becomes apparent that the NKVD arrested more than 7,500 people in this province in five months. Again, this was before the intensification of the repression under Andrei Zhdanov. As spectacular as this proportion might appear, the arrest of 90 percent of the local *nomenklatura* represented only a negligible proportion of the victims of the repression, most of whom fell into other categories specifically defined by the Politburo and approved by Stalin himself.

Certain categories of officials were particularly singled out: for example, diplomats and all the personnel at the People's Commissariat of Foreign Affairs, who naturally were accused of espionage; or factory directors and personnel from the ministries for economic affairs, who were often suspected of sabotage. Among high-ranking diplomats arrested and, for the most part, executed were Krestinsky, Grigory Sokolnikov, Aleksandr Bogomolov, Konstantin Yurenev, Nikolai Ostrovsky, and Antonov-Ovseenko, who were posted respectively in Berlin, London, Beijing, Tokyo, Bucharest, and Madrid.[19]

Whole ministries fell victim to the repressions. In the relatively obscure People's Commissariat of Machine Tools, an entire directorate was replaced; and all but two of the managers of factories dependent on this ministry were arrested, together with almost all engineers and technicians. The same was true for several other industrial sectors, notably aeronautical industry, naval construction, metallurgy, and transport, for which only fragmentary information is available. After the end of the Great Terror, at the Seventeenth Congress in March 1939, Kaganovich noted that "in 1937 and 1938 the leading personnel in all heavy industry was entirely replaced, and thousands of new men were appointed to the posts of those who had been unmasked as saboteurs. In some branches of industry, there had been several layers of saboteurs and spies . . . Now we have in their place cadres who will accept any task assigned to them by Comrade Stalin."

Among the party cadres hit hardest by the *Ezhovshchina* were the leaders of foreign Communist parties and leaders of the Communist International, who were staying in Moscow at the Hotel Lux.[20] German Communist Party leaders who were arrested included Heinz Neumann, Hermann Remmel, Fritz Schulte, and Hermann Schubert, all of whom had been members of the Politburo; Leo Flieg, a secretary of the Central Committee; Heinrich Susskind and Werner Hirsch, the editors of the newspaper *Rote Fahne*; and Hugo Eberlein,

who had been the German Party delegate at the founding conference of the
Communist International. In February 1940, several months after the signing
of the German-Soviet pact, 570 German Communists who had been locked up
in Moscow prisons were handed over to the Gestapo on the frontier bridge at
Brest Litovsk.

The purges were equally savage in the Hungarian Workers' (Communist)
Party. Béla Kun, the instigator of the Hungarian revolution in 1919, was
arrested and executed, together with twelve other people's commissars from
the ephemeral Communist government in Budapest who had taken refuge in
Moscow. Nearly 200 Italian Communists were also arrested (including Paolo
Robotti, the brother-in-law of Palmiro Togliatti, the Italian Communist Party
leader), as well as approximately 100 Yugoslav Communists (including Milan
Gorkić, the Party secretary general; Vladimir Čopić, secretary and director of
the Organization of the International Brigades; and three-quarters of the members of the Central Committee).

The vast majority of the victims of the Great Terror were anonymous.
The following is an excerpt from an "ordinary" file of 1938, dossier no. 24260:[21]

1. Name: Sidorov
2. First name: Vasily Klementovich
3. Place and date of birth: Sechevo, Moscow region, 1893
4. Address: Sechevo, Kolomenskii district, Moscow region
5. Profession: co-operative employee
6. Union membership: co-operative employees' union
7. Possessions at time of arrest (detailed description): 1 wooden
   house, 8 meters by 8, covered in sheet metal, with partially covered courtyard 20 meters by 7; 1 cow, 4 sheep, 2 pigs, chickens
8. Property in 1929: identical, plus 1 horse
9. Property in 1917: 1 wooden house, 8 meters by 8, 1 partially
   covered courtyard 30 meters by 20, 2 barns, 2 hangars, 2
   horses, 2 cows, 7 sheep
10. Social situation at moment of arrest: employed
11. Service in tsarist army: 1915–16 foot-soldier, second class, 6th
    Infantry Regiment of Turkestan
12. Military service in the White Army: none
13. Military service in the Red Army: none
14. Social origin: I consider myself the son of an ordinary peasant
15. Political history: no party memberships
16. Nationality and citizenship: Russian, U.S.S.R. citizen
17. Communist Party membership: no
18. Education: basic
19. Present military situation: reservist
20. Criminal record: no

21. State of health: hernia
22. Family situation: married. Wife: Anastasia Fedorovna, 43
    years old, *kolkhoz* worker; daughter: Nina, 24 years old

Arrested 13 February 1938 on the orders of the leaders of the district NKVD.

An excerpt from the interrogation protocol:

Question: Explain your social origins, your social situation, and your situation before 1917.

Reply: I come originally from a family of small merchants. Until about 1904 my father had a little shop in Moscow, on Zolotorozhskaya Street, where, according to what he told me, he did business but had no employees. After 1904 he was forced to close the shop, for he couldn't compete with the bigger shops. He came back to the country, to Sechevo, and rented six hectares of arable land and two hectares of meadow. He had one employee, a man called Goryachev, who worked with him for many years, until 1916. After 1917 we kept the farm, but we lost the horses. I worked with my father until 1925; then, after he died, my brother and I shared out the land between us.

I don't think I am guilty of anything at all.

An excerpt from the charges drawn up:

Sidorov, hostile to the Soviet regime in general and to the Party in particular, was given to systematically spreading anti-Soviet propaganda, saying, "Stalin and his gang won't give up power. Stalin has killed a whole mass of people, but he doesn't want to go. The Bolsheviks will hold on to power and go on arresting honest people, and you can't even talk about that, or you'll end up in a camp for 25 years."

The accused pleaded not guilty but was unmasked by several witnesses. The affair has been passed on to the troika for judgment.

Signed: S. Salakayev, Second Lieutenant in the Kolomenskaya district police.

Agreed: Galkin, Lieutenant in the State Security, Chief of the State Security detachment in the Kolomenskaya district.

An excerpt from the protocol of the troika's decision, 16 July 1938:

V. K. Sidorov affair. Ex-shopkeeper, previously kept a shop with his father. Accused of spreading counterrevolutionary ideas among *kolkhoz* workers, characterized by defeatist statements together with threats against Communists, criticism of Party policies and of the government.

Verdict: SHOOT Sidorov Vassily Klementovich; confiscate all his goods.

Sentence carried out on 3 August 1938.
Posthumously rehabilitated on 24 January 1989.

The heaviest price of all was paid by the Polish Communist Party. The situation of Polish Communists was somewhat unusual, in that their Party emerged out of the Social Democratic Party of the Kingdoms of Poland and Lithuania, which in 1906 was admitted, on an autonomous basis, to the Social Democratic Workers' Party in Russia. The links between the Russian Party and the Polish Party had always been very close. Many Social Democratic Poles—Dzerzhinsky, Menzhinsky, Unshlikht (all of whom had been directors of the GPU), and Radek, to name but a few—had gone on to make a career in the Bolshevik Party.

In 1937–38 the Polish Communist Party was completely liquidated. The twelve Polish members of the Central Committee living in Russia were executed, as were all Polish representatives of the various offices of the Communist International. On 28 November 1937 Stalin signed a document proposing a "purge" of the Polish Communist Party. Generally, after a party had been purged Stalin chose new personnel to lead it from one of the rival factions of the liquidated group. In the case of the Polish Communist Party, all the factions were equally accused of "following the orders of counterrevolutionary Polish secret services." On 16 August 1938 the Executive Committee of the International voted for the dissolution of the Polish Communist Party. As Dmitry Manuilsky explained, "Polish fascist agents have infiltrated the party and taken up all the key positions."

On the grounds that they had been "caught out" and found "lacking in vigilance," Soviet officials in the Communist International were naturally the next victims of the purges. Almost all the Soviet cadres in the International (including Wilhelm Knorin, a member of the Central Executive Committee; V. A. Mirov-Abramov, chief of the Department of Foreign Ties; and Gevork Alikhanov, the head of the Department of Cadres), a total of several hundred people, were removed. The only survivors of the International purge were a few leaders such as Manuilsky and Otto Kuusinen, who were completely in Stalin's power.

The military was another sector hit hard in 1937 and 1938, as carefully kept records testify.[22] On 11 June 1937 the press announced that a military court sitting *in camera* had condemned Marshal Tukhachevsky to death for treason and espionage. Tukhachevsky was deputy commissar of defense and the principal architect of the modernization of the Red Army. Recurring differences had led to his growing opposition to Stalin and Voroshilov after the Polish campaign of 1920. Also condemned were seven army generals: Jonas Yakir, the military commander of the Kyiv region; Uborevich, commander of the Belarus region; and Robert Eideman, Avgust Kork, Vitvot Putna, Fred Feldman, and Vitaly Primakov. Over the next ten days 980 high-ranking officers were arrested, including twenty-one army corps generals and thirty-seven division generals. The "military conspiracy" affair, implicating Tukhachevski and his accomplices, had been several months in the planning. The accused were arrested in May 1937. Subject to brutal interrogation led by Ezhov himself (when Tukhachevsky was rehabilitated twenty years later, it was revealed that several pages of the deposition were stained with blood), all were forced into confessions before judgment was passed. Stalin personally supervised the whole affair. Around 15 May he had received via the Soviet ambassador in Prague falsified files compiled by the Nazi secret services containing fake letters that had supposedly passed between Tukhachevsky and members of the German high command. In fact the German secret service had been manipulated by the NKVD.

In two years the purge of the Red Army eliminated:

3 out of 5 marshals (Tukhachevsky, Aleksandr Egorov, and Vasili Blücher, the last two executed in February and October 1937, respectively)
13 out of 15 army generals
8 out of 9 admirals
50 out of 57 army corps generals
154 out of 186 division generals
16 out of 16 army commissars
25 out of 28 army corps commissars

From May 1937 to September 1938, 35,020 officers were arrested or expelled from the army. It is still unclear how many were executed. Around 11,000 (including Generals Konstantin Rokossovsky and Aleksandr Gorbatov) were recalled in 1939–1941. But a new wave of purges began after September 1938, so that according to the most serious estimates, the total number of arrests in the army during the Great Terror was about 30,000 cadres out of a possible 178,000.[23] Though proportionally less significant than has generally been believed, the purge of the Red Army, notably at the higher levels, had serious effects on the Russo-Finnish conflict of 1939–40 and the initial phase of the war with Germany, when it constituted one of the heaviest handicaps for Soviet military effectiveness.

Stalin took the menace of Nazi Germany much less seriously than did other Bolshevik leaders, especially Bukharin and Maksim Litvinov, who was people's commissar of foreign affairs until April 1939. Stalin did not hesitate to sacrifice the majority of the best officers in the Red Army and replace them with entirely untried substitutes. Stalin wished his army to be staffed with those who had no memory of the controversial episodes in which he had participated as military chief in the civil war, and who would not be tempted to argue, as Field Marshal Tukhachevsky might have, with the military and political decisions that Stalin took at the end of the 1930s, especially the rapprochement with Nazi Germany.

The intelligentsia were another social group who fell victim to the Great Terror, and about whom relatively abundant information is available.[24] A recognized social group since the mid-nineteenth century, most of the Russian intelligentsia had been a center of resistance against tyranny and intellectual constraint. This fact had accounted for their victimization in the previous purges of 1922 and 1928–1931. Now, in March and April 1937, a virulent press campaign railed against "deviationism" in economics, history, and literature. All branches of learning and creativity were targeted, and political and doctrinal pretexts often served to cover personal ambition or rivalry. In the field of history, for example, all the followers of Mikhail Pokrovsky, who had died in 1932, were arrested. Teachers and professors were especially vulnerable, since their lectures were readily accessible to zealous informers. Universities, institutes, and academicians were all decimated, notably in Belorussia (where 87 of the 105 academics were arrested as "Polish spies") and in Ukraine. In the latter republic a first purge of "bourgeois nationalists" had taken place in 1933, when several thousand Ukrainian intellectuals were arrested for "having transformed the Ukrainian Academy of Sciences, the Shevchenko Institute, the Agricultural Academy, the Ukrainian Marxist-Leninist Institute, and the People's Commissariats of Education, Agriculture, and Justice into havens for bourgeois nationalists and counterrevolutionaries" (a speech by Pavel Postyshev, 22 June 1933). The Great Purge of 1937–38 thus finished off an operation that had actually begun four years earlier.

All scholarly fields with the slightest connection to politics, ideology, economics, or defense were also affected. The main figures in the aeronautics industry, notably Andrei Tupolev (the renowned aeronautical engineer) and Sergei Korolev (one of the founders of the first Soviet space program), were arrested and sent to NKVD research centers similar to the those described by Solzhenitsyn in *First Circle*. Of the twenty-nine astronomers at the great Pulkovo observatory, twenty-seven were arrested. Nearly all the statisticians from the national economic headquarters were arrested after completing the January 1937 census, which was annulled for "gross violations of elementary procedures of the science of statistics, and for contravening governmental orders." Arrests were made of numerous linguists opposed to the theories of the Marxist linguist Nikolai Marr, who was officially supported by Stalin; and of several hundred biologists who opposed the charlatanism of the "official" biologist Trofim Lysenko. Other victims included Professor Solomon Levit, the director of the medical genetics institute; Nikolai Tulaikov, the director of the Institute of Cereals; the botanist A. Yanata; and the academician Nikolai Vavilov, president of the Lenin Academy of Agricultural Science, who was arrested on 6 August 1940 and died in prison on 26 January 1943.

Accused of defending hostile and foreign points of view and of straying beyond the boundaries of Socialist Realism, writers, publishers, theater directors, and journalists all paid a heavy price during the *Ezhovshchina*. Approximately 2,000 members of the writers' union were arrested, deported to camps, or executed. Among the most famous victims were Isaac Babel, author of *The Red Cavalry* and *Odessa Tales,* who was shot on 27 January 1940; the writers Boris Pilnyak, Yury Olesha, Panteleimon Romanov; and the poets Nikolai Klyuev, Nikolai Zabolotsky, Osip Mandelstam (who died in a Siberian transit camp on 26 December 1938), Gurgen Maari, and Titsian Tabidze. Many musicians were also arrested, including the composer Andrei Zhelyaev and the conductor E. Mikoladze, as were famous figures from the theater, such as the great director Vsevolod Meyerhold, whose theater was closed early in 1938 on the ground that it was "foreign to Soviet art." Having refused to make a public act of contrition, Meyerhold was arrested in June 1939, tortured, and executed on 2 February 1940.

During these years the authorities sought the "complete liquidation" (to use their own expression) of the last remaining members of the clergy. The census of January 1937 revealed that approximately 70 percent of the population, despite the pressures placed on them, still replied in the affirmative when asked "Are you a believer?" Hence Soviet leaders embarked on a third and decisive offensive against the church. In April 1937 Malenkov sent a note to Stalin suggesting that legislation concerning religious organizations was outdated, and he proposed the abrogation of the decree of 8 April 1929. "This decree," he noted, "gave a legal basis for the most active sections of the churches and cults to create a whole organized network of individuals hostile to the Soviet regime." He concluded: "The time has come to finish once and for all with all clerical organizations and ecclesiastical hierarchies."[25] Thousands of priests and nearly all the bishops were sent to camps, and this time the vast majority were executed. Of the 20,000 churches and mosques that were still active in 1936, fewer than 1,000 were still open for services at the beginning of 1941. In early 1941 the number of officially registered clerics of all religions had fallen to 5,665 (more than half of whom came from the Baltic territories,

Poland, Moldavia, and western Ukraine, all of which had been incorporated in 1939–1941), from over 24,000 in 1936.[26]

From this information it is possible to conclude that the Great Terror was a political operation initiated and led by people at the highest levels in the party under the supreme direction of Stalin.

Moreover, the Great Terror achieved two of its main objectives. The first was to establish a civil and military bureaucracy made up of young cadres brought up in the strict Stalinist spirit of the 1930s. These were officials who, as Kaganovich said at the Seventeenth Party Congress, "would accept without question any task assigned to them by Comrade Stalin." Before the late 1930s, various government administrations were a heterogeneous mixture of "bourgeois specialists" trained under the old regime and Bolshevik cadres, many of whom had been trained on the job during the civil war and were quite incompetent. Each institution had tried to preserve some sort of professionalism and administrative logic, as well as a degree of autonomy from the ideological voluntarism and orders that came from the center. This was particularly demonstrated in the campaign to verify all Party identity cards in 1935, when local Communist leaders had put up passive resistance. It was also obvious in the refusal of statisticians to "brighten up" the figures from the January 1937 census and bring them into line with Stalin's wishes. Stalin realized that a significant proportion of the cadres, whether Communist or not, were not prepared to follow blindly orders that came from the center. His goal was to replace these officials with people more obedient to his wishes.

The second objective of the Great Terror was to complete the elimination of "socially dangerous elements," a group whose members continued to grow. As the penal code indicated, any individual "who had committed an act hostile or dangerous to society, or who had relations with a criminal milieu or a criminal record" was liable to be classed as a socially dangerous element. Hence, anyone whose social group contained the prefix "ex-" was socially dangerous: ex-kulaks, ex-criminals, ex-tsarist civil servants, ex-members of the Menshevik Party, ex–Socialist Revolutionaries, and so on. All these categories had to be eliminated during the Great Terror because, as Stalin stated at the plenum of the Central Committee in February–March 1937, "the nearer we come to socialism, the more the remnants of the moribund social classes fight back."

In this speech Stalin had emphasized the idea that the U.S.S.R.—the only country that had built socialism—was surrounded by hostile enemy powers. According to Stalin, the countries bordering the U.S.S.R.—Finland, the Baltic states, Poland, Romania, Turkey, Japan, and others, assisted by France and Great Britain—were sending "armies of spies and subversives" on a mission to sabotage the socialist project. As a unique and sacred state, the U.S.S.R. had inviolable frontiers that were the front lines in a struggle against an ever-present enemy. In this context, the hunt for spies (that is, anyone who had simply made contact with the outside world, no matter how tenuous it might have been) took on great importance. The elimination of potential and mythical "fifth columnists" was at the heart of the Great Terror.

The huge categories of victims listed above—cadres and specialists, socially dangerous and alien elements, and spies—all demonstrate the logic of the massive killings of the Great Terror, which was responsible for nearly 700,000 deaths in two years.

Moscow, 1936. Stalin is surrounded (from left to right) by N. Khrushchev, who distinguished himself in the repressions in Ukraine; A. Yadanov, an ideological official who launched the postwar campaign against "cosmopolitanism"; L. Kaganovich, the railway commissar; K. Voroshilov, commissar of defense; V. Molotov, Stalin's chief assistant, who died in 1986; M. Kalinin; and Marshal M. Tukhachevski, who was liquidated in 1937. Second row: G. Malenkov (2nd from left), N. Bulganin (5th), and Elena Stassova (8th), who endorsed Stalin's politics inside the Comintern. © Arch. russes de photographies, Krasnogorsk

Feliks Dzershinsky, founder of the Cheka and head of the GPU (secret police) until he died in 1926, leaving a permanent mark on the regime. © D. R.

L. Beria voting, in an imitation of democracy. As the successor to V. Menzhinsky, G. Yagoda, and N. Ezhov, Beria controlled the secret police and the forces of repression until he was arrested in June 1953 by his rivals Khrushchev, Malenkov, and Molotov. © Lapi-Viollet

When the Bolsheviks started the civil war they unleashed a wave of violence on a scale the world had rarely seen. Here in Orsha in 1918 a Polish officer is hanged and impaled by soldiers of the newly created Red Army. © L'illustration/Sygma

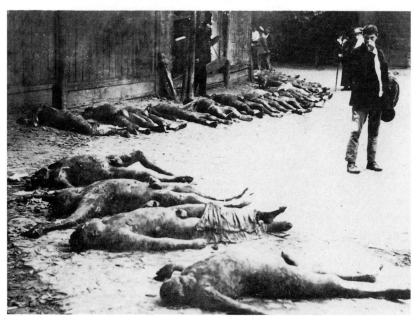

Kyiv, 1918. After the retreat of the Red Army, the bodies of victims of the Cheka were exhumed at 5 Sadovaya Street, where the "instrument of Bolshevik terror" (as the Cheka described itself) maintained one of its facilities. © Musée d'histoire contemporaine-BDIC

A terrible famine devastated the Volga region as a result of the civil war and Bolshevik policies in the countryside. In 1921 and 1922 the famine led to the death of around 5 million people; the first victims were almost invariably children. © Musée d'histoire contemporaine-BDIC

Lenin was forced to accept aid from abroad, and trains filled with munitions came in from the Red Cross, the Nansen Committee, and the American Relief Administration. Russian intellectuals who helped arrange the aid were subsequently arrested and sentenced to death on Lenin's orders. When F. Nansen himself intervened, they were banished from Russia instead. © Musée d'histoire contemporaine-BDIC

1930–31. Peasants resisting collectivization confronted the Red Guards who came to seize the harvest, and then took refuge in the forests. GPU troops often set fire to the trees to force the peasants to emerge. © D. R.

The construction site of the BBK, or Belomorkanal, the canal between the White Sea and the Baltic. This pharaonic project resulted in the deaths of tens of thousands of prisoners in 1932–33. The canal was opened amid great pomp by Stalin and his acolytes but proved to be useless. © Coll. Tomasz Kizny/Vu

To collectivize the land in a "great assault on the peasantry," Stalin used starvation as a weapon, particularly against the Ukrainians. This policy resulted in the death of roughly 6 million people, including 4 million in Ukraine. Here in Kharkiv in 1933, the peasants became indifferent to the daily phenomenon of death. Cannibalism was so widespread that the government printed posters that said: "Eating your children is an act of barbarism." © D. R.

The Belomorkanal orchestra. Construction of the canal, an absurd enterprise, was intended to be part of the "reeducation" of the detainees. © D. R.

The backs of propaganda photographs were often used by detainees to draw attention to their plight and to portray life and death in the Soviet camps. This drawing by Evrosina Kernevskaya portrays arrival in a "reeducation work camp" in Siberia in April 1943. © Dessin de Kersnovskaïa

A purge session of the Party. Initially used as a means of ideological control over militant Party workers, the *chistka* (purge) became a ritual that could lead to the denunciation of anyone. Self-criticism sessions resulted more and more often in arrests a few days or weeks later. © Roger-Viollet

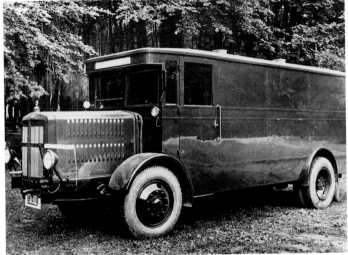

"Innocent Russia writhed in pain / Beneath the bloody boots / and the dark wheels of the Black Marias," wrote the poet Anna Akhmatova in her well-known "Requiem." Her own son was imprisoned and killed. These trucks, known to Muscovites as "black crows," took prisoners from the Lubyanka to Lefortovo and Butyrka prisons. The trucks were sometimes disguised as bakers' delivery vans. © Roger-Viollet

The Lubyanka, Moscow, about 1925. In the basement of the GPU headquarters were special rooms in which enemies of the regime were executed with a bullet in the neck. The building came to symbolize the arbitrary cruelty of the regime. © D. R.

The Shakhty trial in Donbass in 1928 inaugurated a new category of enemies of the regime: the "specialists," who were accused of sabotage when Stalin launched the first Five-Year Plan. The intention was to impose Stalin's principles of the "second revolution" on cadres in industry. Standing, right: procurator N. Krylenko, who was himself liquidated in 1938. © Roger-Viollet

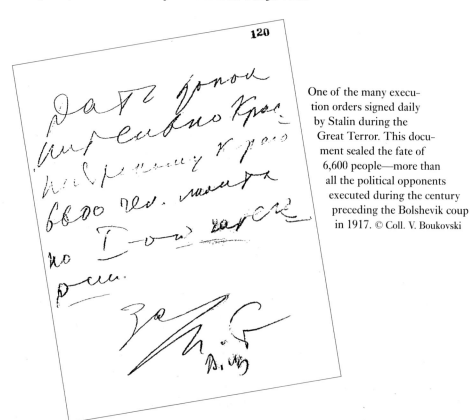

One of the many execution orders signed daily by Stalin during the Great Terror. This document sealed the fate of 6,600 people—more than all the political opponents executed during the century preceding the Bolshevik coup in 1917. © Coll. V. Boukovski

Walk, Estonia, 1919. When the Bolsheviks attempted to seize power, they executed hostages taken from the ranks of the elite. When they withdrew, they left behind hundreds of dead. The extermination of political adversaries and of entire social groups was considered necessary for victory in the civil war. These massacres prefigured the large-scale deportations of Estonians, Latvians, and Lituanians in 1940–41 and 1944–45. © D. R.

Germany, Pentecost 1927. A national meeting of the Rote Front (Red Front), a paramilitary organization generally considered to have been an embryonic Red Army. The Red Front had its origins in the culture of civil war celebrated by Louis Aragon: "Proletariat, know your strength/ Know your strength and unleash it/ . . . Open fire on those on those know-it-all Social Democrats / Open fire, open fire / . . . Open fire, I tell you / Under the guidance of the Communist Party . . ." (from *Le front rouge*, 1931). © D. R.

Spain, 1937. Hoping to exploit the Spanish civil war to his advantage, Stalin sent a number of emissaries and agents. The NKVD (the successor to the GPU) was instructed to liquidate anyone who obstructed its international strategy, including anarchists, Trotskyites, and militants from the Marxist Workers' Unification Party. The leader of that party, Andreu Nin, was kidnapped in June 1937 and tortured before being killed by agents working under Ernő Gerő, the future leader of the Hungarian Communist Party. Meanwhile an international campaign was carried out in the Communist press, accusing the antifascists of being agents working for Franco. © D. R.

On 20 August 1940, Ramon Mercader, an agent from the Special Tasks Department of the NKVD, attacked Leon Trotsky (right) with an ice pick. Trotsky died the next day. Stalin had personally ordered the chief of the department, Pavel Sudoplatov (left, in a picture from 1942), to eliminate Trotsky, who at the time was the head of the Fourth International. © D. R. *(left)*, © Roger Viollet

Katyn, Russia, April 1943. The Germans discovered here the bodies of 4,500 Polish officers buried in mass graves. A Red Cross commission concluded that they had been killed by Soviet troops in the spring of 1940, when around 25,000 people disappeared. Katyn came to be a symbol of mass murder and official lies. Until 1989 the Communist government in Poland and Communists throughout the world attributed the massacre to the Germans. © D. R.

Vynnytsa, Ukraine, June 1943. Here trenches dating from 1937–38 were opened and hundreds of bodies exhumed. The authorities had built a park and a summer theater on the site. Similar trenches were discovered in Zhytomyr, Kamenets-Podolski, and other areas. Such macabre discoveries continue even today. In 1997, 1,100 bodies were exhumed in St. Petersburg, and another 9,000 were found in a mass grave in the forests of Karelia. © D. R.

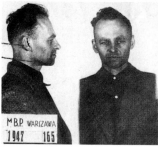

The Jewish cemetery, Warsaw. A monument erected in secret in 1987 to the memory of Viktor Alter and Henryk Erlich. Leaders of the Jewish Socialist Workers' Party, they were first sentenced for supposedly having ties with the Nazi Party. They were sentenced to death a second time and kept in solitary confinement. Erlich hanged himself in his cell on 15 May 1942; Alter was shot on 17 February 1943, a few days after the victory at Stalingrad. © D. R.

Witold Pilecki, a Polish resistance fighter, deliberately had himself captured by German forces (above) so that he could set up a resistance network in Auschwitz. He subsequently escaped and continued to fight the Nazis. He was arrested in May 1947 by the Communist secret police (below), tortured, sentenced to death, and executed. He was rehabilitated in 1990. © D. R.

A monument erected in Warsaw in 1996 in homage to Jewish and Catholic Poles who were deported to the far north, Siberia, Kazakhstan, and other distant regions in 1939–1941 and 1944–45. © A. Tabor

East Berlin, 17 June 1953. Protesting wage cuts, workers went on strike on 16 June and demonstrated in the streets. Soviet tanks then took up position (here on the Leipzigerstrasse). Sixteen demonstrators were killed, hundreds were wounded, and thousands of people received long prison sentences. The East German uprising was the first great crack to appear in a "people's democracy." © D. R.

Budapest, October 1956. The first antitotalitarian revolution mobilized the entire population against the secret police and the Communist Party. The resistance fighters managed to delay Soviet intervention. © Archive Photos

Budapest, November 1956. Soviet tanks took to the streets; the population resisted with guns. The Hungarian Workers' (Communist) Party, the country's only party, was reestablished in power at the cost of about 3,000 lives. More than 25,000 people were imprisoned. Tens of thousands of Hungarians fled into exile. © D. R.

Poznań, Poland, 28 June 1956. Workers in a railway factory went on strike, and demonstrations followed, with shouts of "bread and liberty." Dozens died in the ensuing repressions. Demonstrators here are waving a blood-stained Polish flag in front of the Fiat factory. © U. S. I. S./Archives T. Etiévé

Gdańsk, December 1970. Striking workers in the Baltic ports demonstrated against sharp increases in food prices. Hundreds of demonstrators were killed and wounded. One of the victims was carried on a door (below) and immortalized in a ballad: "A boy from Grabowek / A boy from Chylonia / Today the police opened fire / and Janek Wisniewski fell." The song was revived in August 1980, when the free Solidarity trade union was born. © D. R.

Nikolai Petkov, a democrat who fought in the resistance against the fascists, was deputy prime minister in the coalition government after the liberation of Bulgaria. Having resigned in protest against the terror, he was arrested and condemned to death after a show-trial on 16 August 1947. He was hanged on 23 September. © D. R.

In the State Court in Prague, Milada Horaková (second from left) was condemned to death on 8 June 1950 with three other defendants. They were hanged on 27 June 1950. © D. R.

Prague, August 1968. During the Soviet invasion the inhabitants of the city were quick to draw a comparison with the Nazi invasion of 1938. Here they greet the Soviet troops with mock Nazi salutes. © D. R.

- 600,000 registered deaths among the deportees, refugees, and "specially displaced."
- Approximately 2,200,000 deported, forcibly moved, or exiled as "specially displaced people."
- A cumulative figure of 7 million people who entered the camps and Gulag colonies from 1934 to 1941 (information for the years 1930–1933 remains imprecise).

On 1 January 1940 some 1,670,000 prisoners were being held in the 53 groups of corrective work camps and the 425 corrective work colonies. One year later the figure had risen to 1,930,000. In addition, prisons held 200,000 people awaiting trial or a transfer to camp. Finally, the NKVD *komandatury* were in charge of approximately 1.2 million "specially displaced people."[9] Even if these figures are heavily rounded down to bring them into line with estimates made by previous historians and eyewitnesses, which often confused the numbers of those entering the gulags with the numbers already present at a certain date, the data still give a good idea of the scale of the repressive measures against the Soviet people in the 1930s.

From the end of 1939 to the summer of 1941 the camps, colonies, and special Gulag settlements saw the arrival of yet another wave of prisoners. This was partly the result of the Sovietization of the new territories, and partly the result of the unprecedented criminalization of various sorts of behavior, notably in the workplace.

On 24 August 1939 the world was stunned to learn that a mutual pact of nonaggression had been signed the previous day between Stalin's U.S.S.R. and Hitler's Germany. The announcement of the pact sent shock waves through much of the world, where public opinion was totally unprepared for what appeared to be a *volte-face* in international relations. At the time, few people had realized what could link two regimes that apparently professed such opposed ideologies.

On 21 August 1939 the Soviet government adjourned negotiations with the Franco-British mission that had arrived in Moscow on 11 August. The mission had hoped to conclude a pact that would reciprocally engage all three of the parties in the event of a hostile action by Germany against any one of them. Since early that year, Soviet diplomats, led by Vyacheslav Molotov, had progressively distanced themselves from the idea of an agreement with France and Britain, which Moscow suspected were prepared to sign another Munich treaty to sacrifice Poland, leaving the Germans a free hand in the east. While negotiations between the Soviet Union on the one hand, and the French and

British on the other, became bogged down in insoluble problems, especially the question of permission for Soviet troops to cross Polish territory, contacts between Soviet and German representatives at various levels took a new turn. On 14 August von Ribbentrop, the German foreign minister, offered to come to Moscow to conclude a momentous political agreement with the Soviet Union. The following day, Stalin accepted the offer.

On 19 August, after a series of negotiations begun in late 1938, the German and Soviet delegations signed a commercial treaty that looked extremely promising for the U.S.S.R. That same evening, the Soviet Union accepted von Ribbentrop's offer to visit Moscow to sign the pact of nonaggression already worked out in Moscow and sent ahead to Berlin. The German minister, who had been given extraordinary powers for the occasion, arrived in Moscow on the afternoon of 23 August. The nonaggression treaty was signed during the night and made public the following day. Meant to last for ten years, it was to come into effect immediately. The most important part of the agreement, outlining spheres of influence and annexations in Eastern Europe, obviously remained secret. The Soviet Union denied the existence of the secret protocol until 1989. According to the secret agreement, Lithuania fell under German control, and Estonia, Latvia, Finland, and Bessarabia would be given to Soviet control. The maintenance of some sort of sovereign Polish state was left unresolved, but it was clear that after German and Soviet military intervention in Poland, the U.S.S.R. was to recover the Ukrainian and Belorussian territories it had lost under the Riga treaty in 1920, together with part of the "historically and ethnically Polish" territories in the provinces of Lublin and Warsaw.

Eight days after the signing of the pact, Nazi troops marched into Poland. One week later, after all Polish resistance had been crushed, and at the insistence of the Germans, the Soviet government proclaimed its intention to occupy the territories to which it was entitled under the secret protocol of 23 August. On 17 September the Red Army entered Poland, on the pretext that it was coming to the aid of its "Ukrainian and Belorussian blood brothers," who were in danger because of "the disintegration of the Polish state." Soviet intervention met with little resistance, since the Polish army had been almost completely destroyed. The Soviet Union took 230,000 prisoners of war, including 15,000 officers.[10]

The idea of installing some sort of Polish puppet government was rapidly abandoned, and negotiations were opened on the fixing of the border between Germany and the U.S.S.R. On 22 September it was drawn along the Vistula in Warsaw, but after von Ribbentrop's visit to Moscow on 28 September it was pushed farther east, to the Bug. In exchange for this concession, Germany agreed to include Lithuania in the sphere of Soviet control. The partitioning of Poland allowed the U.S.S.R. to annex vast territories of 180,000 square kilometers, with a population of 12 million Belorussians, Ukrainians, and Poles. On 1 and 2 November, after a farcical referendum, these territories were attached to the Soviet republics of Ukraine and Belorussia.

By this time the NKVD "cleansing" of the regions was already under way. The first targets were the Poles, who were arrested and deported en masse as "hostile elements." Those most at risk were landowners, industrialists, shop-keepers, civil servants, policemen, and "military colonists" *(osadnicy wojskowe)* who had received a parcel of land from the Polish government in recognition of their service in the Soviet-Polish war of 1920. According to records kept in the Special Colonies Department of the Gulag, 381,000 Polish civilians from the territories taken over by the U.S.S.R. in September 1939 were deported between February 1940 and June 1941 as "specially displaced people" to Sibe-ria, the Arkhangelsk region, Kazakhstan, and other far-flung corners of the U.S.S.R.[11] The figures given by Polish historians are much higher, arguing for approximately 1 million deportees.[12] There are no precise figures for the arrest and deportation of civilians carried out between September 1939 and January 1940.

For later periods, archival documents contain evidence for three great waves of arrests and deportations, on 9 and 10 February, 12 and 13 April, and 28 and 29 June 1940.[13] The return trip for the convoys between the Polish border and Siberia, Kazakhstan, or the Arctic regions took two months. As for the Polish prisoners of war, only 82,000 out of 230,000 were still alive in the summer of 1941. Losses among the Polish deportees were also extremely high. In August 1941, after reaching an agreement with the Polish government-in-exile, the Soviet government granted an amnesty to all Poles who had been deported since November 1939, but to only 243,100 of the 381,000 "specially displaced." In total more than 388,000 Polish prisoners of war, interned refu-gees, and deported civilians benefited from this amnesty. Several hundred thousand had died in the previous two years. A great number had been executed on the pretext that they were "unrepentant and determined enemies of Soviet power."

Among the latter were the 25,700 officers and Polish civilians whom Beria, in a top-secret letter to Stalin on 5 March 1940, had proposed to shoot.

> A large number of ex-officers from the Polish army, ex-officials from the Polish police and information departments, members of nationalist counterrevolutionary parties, members of opposition counterrevolu-tionary organizations that have rightly been unmasked, renegades, and many others, all sworn enemies of the Soviet system, are at present being detained in prisoner-of-war camps run by the NKVD in the

U.S.S.R. and in the prisons situated in the western regions of Ukraine and Belorussia.

The army officers and policemen who are being held prisoner are still attempting to pursue their counterrevolutionary activities and are fomenting anti-Soviet actions. They are all eagerly awaiting their liberation so that once more they may enter actively into the struggle against the Soviet regime.

NKVD organizations in the western regions of Ukraine and in Belorussia have uncovered a number of rebel counterrevolutionary organizations. The Polish ex-army officers and policemen have all been playing an active role at the head of these organizations.

Among the renegades and those who have violated state borders are numerous people who have been identified as belonging to counterrevolutionary espionage and resistance movements.

14,736 ex-officers, officials, landowners, policemen, prison guards, border settlers *(osadniki)*, and information agents (more than 97 percent of whom are Polish) are at present being detained in prisoner of war camps. Neither private soldiers nor noncommissioned officers are included in this number. Among them are:

295 generals, colonels, and lieutenant colonels
2,080 commanders and captains
6,049 lieutenants, second lieutenants, and officers in training
1,030 officers and police NCOs, border guards, and gendarmes
5,138 policemen, gendarmes, prison guards, and information
    officers
144 officials, landowners, priests, and border settlers

In addition to the above, 18,632 men are detained in prisons in the western regions of Ukraine and Belorussia (10,685 of whom are Polish). They include:

1,207 ex-officers
5,141 ex–information officers, police, and gendarmes
347 spies and saboteurs
465 ex-landowners, factory managers, and officials
5,345 members of various counterrevolutionary resistance move-
    ments and diverse other elements
6,127 renegades

Insofar as all the above individuals are sworn and incorrigible enemies of the Soviet regime, the U.S.S.R. NKVD believes it necessary to:

1. Order the U.S.S.R. NKVD to pass judgment before special courts on:
   a. the 14,700 ex-officers, officials, landowners, police officers, information officers, gendarmes, special border guards, and prison guards detained in prisoner-of-war camps
   b. the 11,000 members of the diverse counterrevolutionary espionage and sabotage organizations, ex-landowners, factory managers, ex-officers of the Polish army, officials, and renegades who have been arrested and are being held in the prisons in the western regions of Ukraine and Belorussia, so that THE SUPREME PENALTY BE APPLIED, DEATH BY FIRING SQUAD.
2. Order that individual files be studied in the absence of the accused, and without particular charges being lodged. The conclusions of the inquiries and the final sentence should be presented as follows:
   a. a certificate produced by the Directorate for Prisoner of War Affairs of the NKVD of the U.S.S.R. for all individuals detained in prisoner-of-war camps
   b. a certificate produced by the Ukrainian branch of the NKVD and the Belorussian NKVD for all other people arrested.
3. Files should be examined and sentences passed by a tribunal made up of three people—Comrades [Vsevolod] Merkulov, [Bogdan] Kobulov, and [Ivan L.] Bashtakov.

Some of the mass graves containing the bodies of those executed were discovered by the Germans in April 1943 in the Katyń forest. Several huge graves were found to contain the remains of 4,000 Polish officers. The Soviet authorities tried to blame this massacre on the Germans; only in 1992, on the occasion of a visit by Boris Yeltsin to Warsaw, did the Russian government acknowledge the Soviet Politburo's sole responsibility for the massacre of the Polish officers in 1940.

As soon as the Polish territories were annexed, the Soviet government summoned the heads of the Estonian, Latvian, and Lithuanian governments to Moscow and imposed "mutual assistance treaties" on them, according to which they "invited" the U.S.S.R. to set up military bases on their territory. Immediately, 25,000 Soviet soldiers marched into Estonia, 30,000 into Latvia, and 20,000 into Lithuania. These troops far outnumbered the standing armies in each of the theoretically independent countries. The entry of Soviet troops in October 1939 marked the real end of the independence of the Baltic states. On 11 October Beria gave the order to "stamp out anti-Soviet and antisocialist elements" in these countries. The Soviet military police then began arresting officers, civil servants, and intellectuals considered untrustworthy.

In June 1940, shortly after the successful German offensive in France, the Soviet government acted on the clauses contained in the secret protocol of 23 August 1939. On 14 June, on the pretext that there had been "acts of provocation carried out against the Soviet garrisons," it sent an ultimatum to the Baltic leaders, ordering them to form "governments prepared to guarantee the honest application of a treaty of mutual assistance, and to take steps to punish all opponents of such a treaty." In the days that followed, several hundred thousand more Soviet troops marched into the Baltic states. Stalin sent representatives to the capital cities: Vyshinsky to Riga, Zhdanov to Tallinn, and Vladimir Dekanozov, the chief of the secret police and deputy minister of foreign affairs in the U.S.S.R., to Kaunas. Their mission was to carry out the Sovietization of the three republics. Parliaments and all local institutions were dissolved and most of the members arrested. Only the Communist Party was authorized to present candidates for the elections on 14 and 15 July 1940.

In the weeks following the farcical elections, the NKVD, under the leadership of General Ivan Serov, arrested between 15,000 and 20,000 "hostile elements." In Latvia alone, 1,480 people were summarily executed at the beginning of July. The newly "elected" parliaments requested that their countries be admitted into the U.S.S.R., a request that was granted in early August by the Supreme Soviet, which then proclaimed the birth of three new Soviet Socialist Republics. While *Pravda* wrote that "the sun of the great Stalinist constitution will henceforth be shining its gratifying rays on new territories and new peoples," what was actually beginning for the Baltic states was a long period of arrests, deportations, and executions.

Soviet archives also contain the details of a large deportation operation carried out under the orders of General Serov during the night of 13–14 May, when "socially hostile" elements from the Baltic region, Moldavia, Belorussia, and western Ukraine were rounded up. The operation had been planned a few weeks previously, and on 16 May 1941 Beria wrote to Stalin regarding the latest project to "clean up regions recently integrated into the U.S.S.R. and remove all criminal, socially alien, and anti-Soviet elements." In total, 85,716 people were deported in June 1941, including 25,711 from the Baltic states. Vsevolod Merkulov, the second in command at the NKVD, in a report dated 17 July 1941, tabulated the results of the operation in the Baltics. During the night of 13–14 June, 11,038 members of "bourgeois nationalist" families, 3,240 members of the families of former policemen, 7,124 members of families of landowners, industrialists, and civil servants, 1,649 members of the families of former officers, and 2,907 "others" were deported. The document makes clear

created the autonomous Volga German Republic. Numbering around 370,000, the Volga Germans accounted for only a quarter of the population of German immigrants located throughout Russia (chiefly in the regions of Saratov, Stalingrad, Voronezh, Moscow, and Leningrad), Ukraine (where there were 390,000), the Northern Caucasus (chiefly in the regions of Krasnodar, Ordzhonikidze, and Stavropol), and even in the Crimea and Georgia. On 28 August 1941 the Presidium of the Supreme Soviet issued a decree stipulating that all Germans in the autonomous Volga Republic, the Saratov region, and Stalingrad were to be deported to Kazakhstan and Siberia. The decree portrayed this move as a humanitarian measure.

At a time when the Red Army was retreating on all fronts and losing tens of thousands every day as soldiers were killed or taken prisoner, Beria diverted more than 14,000 men from the NKVD for this operation, which was led by the people's commissar of internal affairs, General Ivan Serov, who had already shown his efficiency in this sort of exercise during the ethnic cleansing of the Baltic states. Even if one takes account of the extraordinary circumstances and the unforeseen defeat of the Red Army, the cruelty with which the operation was carried out is astounding. From 3 to 5 September 1941, 446,480 Germans were deported in 230 convoys, which on average contained 50 trucks. This meant that there were nearly 2,000 people per convoy, or 40 per truck. Traveling at only a few kilometers per hour, these convoys took between four and eight weeks to reach their destinations in Omsk, Novosibirsk, Barnaul in southern Siberia, and the Krasnoyarsk region of eastern Siberia. As in the case of the previous deportations from the Baltic states, the displaced persons, according to the official instructions, had "a certain time to gather enough food for a minimum period of one month."

The following are excerpts from the decree of 28 August 1941.

According to reliable information received by the military authorities, the German population living in the Volga region is harboring tens of thousands of saboteurs and spies who, at the first hint of a signal from Germany, will immediately organize disruptive activities in the regions they inhabit. The Soviet authorities had not previously been aware of the presence or the numbers of these saboteurs and spies. The German population of the Volga is nurturing in its bosom enemies of the people and of Soviet power . . .

If acts of sabotage are indeed carried out on Germany's orders by German saboteurs and spies in the autonomous Volga Republic or in neighboring areas, then blood will flow, and the Soviet government, as is only appropriate in times of war, will be obliged to take punitive measures against the German population of the Volga. To avoid this eventuality and to save much bloodletting, the Presidium of the Supreme

Soviet of the U.S.S.R. has approved a decision to transfer the whole German population of the Volga district elsewhere, providing them with land and help from the state so that they can resettle in other regions.

Districts where abundant land is available have been put aside to this end in Novosibirsk and Omsk, Altai, Kazakhstan, and other areas contiguous with these territories.

While the main deportation was under way, secondary operations were carried out as military fortunes rose and fell. On 29 August 1941 Molotov, Malenkov, and Zhdanov proposed to Stalin that they should cleanse the city and region of Leningrad of the 96,000 people of German and Finnish origin living there. The following day, German troops reached the Neva, cutting the railway line that linked Leningrad with the rest of the country. The risk of encirclement became more and more serious by the day, and the relevant authorities had taken no measures to evacuate the civilian population of the city or to prepare any foodstocks in the event of a siege. Nonetheless, on that same day, 30 August, Beria sent out a circular ordering the deportation of 132,000 people from the Leningrad region: 96,000 by train and 36,000 by river. As it turned out, the NKVD had time to arrest and deport only 11,000 Soviet citizens of German origin before the arrival of German army units forced a suspension of the deportations.

Over the next several weeks similar operations were begun in the Moscow region, where 9,640 Germans were deported on 15 September; in Tula, where 2,700 were deported on 21 September; in Gorky (formerly Nizhni Novgorod), where 3,162 were deported on 14 September; in Rostov, where 38,288 were deported between 10 and 20 September; in Zaporizhzhia (31,320 between 25 September and 10 October); in Krasnodar (38,136 on 15 September); and in Ordzhonikidze (77,570 on 20 September). In October 1941 there was a further deportation of 100,000 Germans living in Georgia, Armenia, Azerbaijan, the Northern Caucasus, and the Crimea. As of 25 December 1941, 894,600 Germans had been deported, most of them to Kazakhstan and Siberia. If the Germans deported in 1942 are taken into account, in all roughly 1,209,430 were deported in less than a year—very close to the 1,427,000 Germans reported in the 1939 census.

More than 82 percent of the German population in Soviet territory were thus deported, at a moment when all police and military forces should have been concentrating on the armed struggle against the invading enemy rather than the deportation of hundreds of thousands of innocent Soviet citizens. In fact the proportion of Soviet citizens of German origin who were deported was even higher than these figures suggest, if one also includes the tens of thousands of soldiers and officers of German origin who were expelled from Red

Army units and sent off in disciplinary battalions of the "work army" to Vorkuta, Kotlas, Kemerovo, and Chelyabinsk. In this last city alone, more than 25,000 Germans were soon working in the metallurgy plant. Working conditions and the chances of survival were little better in the work camps than they were in the gulags.

Because information about the convoys is so piecemeal, it is impossible today to calculate how many of these Germans died in the transfer to the new settlements. It is also unclear how many convoys actually reached their destination in the chaos engulfing Russia in the autumn of 1941. At the end of November, according to the plan, 29,600 German deportees were to arrive in the region of Karaganda. But on 1 January 1942 only 8,304 had actually arrived. The intention was for 130,998 individuals to settle in the area, but in fact no more than 116,612 made it. What happened to the others? Did they die en route, or were they transferred elsewhere? The Altai region was slated to receive 11,000 deportees, but actually received 94,799. Worse still are the NKVD reports on the arrival of the deportees, which leave no doubt that the regions were totally unprepared for them.

In the prevailing environment of secrecy, local authorities were informed only at the last minute about the arrival of tens of thousands of deportees. No living quarters were ready, so the deportees were kept in stables, barracks, or outside, exposed to the elements, even though winter was coming on fast. Nonetheless, over the preceding ten years the authorities had acquired considerable experience in such matters, and the "economic implantation" of the new arrivals was carried out far more efficiently than the arrival of the kulaks back in the early 1930s, when they had often been abandoned in the forests. After a few months most of the deportees were living as "specially displaced," which is to say that they were living under extremely harsh conditions. They lived under the control of NKVD *komandatury* on collective farms, experimental farms, or industrial complexes, where food was poor and work was hard.[1]

The deportation of the Germans was followed by a second great wave of deportations, from November 1943 to June 1944, when six peoples—the Chechens, the Ingush, the Crimean Tatars, the Karachai, the Balkars, and the Kalmyks—were deported to Siberia, Kazakhstan, Uzbekistan, and Kirgizstan on the pretext that they had "collaborated massively with the Nazi occupier." This main wave of deportations was followed by other operations from July to December 1944, which were intended to cleanse the Crimea and the Caucasus of several other nationalities judged to be untrustworthy: the Greeks, the Bulgars, the Armenians from the Crimea, the Meskhetian Turks, the Kurds, and the Khemshins of the Caucasus.[2]

Recently available archival documents have shed no new light on the supposed collaboration of the mountain peoples of the Caucasus, the Kalmyks, or the Crimean Tatars with the Nazis. Some facts point to a small number of collaborators in the Crimea, in Kalmykia, in the Karachai lands, and in Kabardino-Balkaria, but no evidence exists of general policies of collaboration in these regions. It was after the loss by the Red Army at Rostov-on-Don in July 1942, and during the German occupation of the Caucasus from the summer of 1942 to the spring of 1943, that the most controversial collaborationist episodes took place. In the power vacuum between the Soviet army's departure and the arrival of the Germans, local leaders set up "National Committees" in Mikoyan-Shakhar, in the autonomous region of Karachaevo-Cherkess; in Nalchik, in the autonomous republic of Kabardino-Balkaria; and in Elista, in the autonomous republic of Kalmykia. The German army recognized the authority of these local committees, which for a few months enjoyed religious, economic, and political autonomy. Once this experiment in the Caucasus had reinforced the "Muslim Myth" (the notion that Islamic regions of the U.S.S.R. could be exploited) in Berlin, the Crimean Tatars were also permitted to set up their own "Central Muslim Committee," based in Simferopol.

Nevertheless, because the Nazis feared that there might be a resurgence of the Pan-Turkic movement, which had been crushed by the Red Army in the mid-1920s, they never gave the Crimean Tatars the autonomy the Kalmyks, Karachai, and Balkars enjoyed for a few months. In exchange for the small measure of autonomy they were accorded, these local authorities contributed a few troops to break the resistance of the nearly negligible forces that had remained loyal to the Soviet regime. In all, these units amounted to no more than a few thousand men: six Tatar battalions in the Crimea, and one body of Kalmyk cavalry.

The autonomous republic of Chechnya-Ingushetia was only partially occupied by Nazi detachments for approximately ten weeks, from early September to mid-November 1942. There was not the slightest evidence of collaboration. The Chechens, however, had always been a rebellious people. The Soviet authorities had launched several punitive expeditions in 1925 to confiscate some of the arms held by the population, and again in 1930–1932 to try to break the resistance of the Chechens and Ingush against collectivization. In March and April 1930, and again in April and May 1932, in a struggle against the "bandits," the special troops of the NKVD had called in artillery and air support. This provoked a strong groundswell of resistance to centralized power and a desire for independence among people who had always struggled against the influence of Moscow.

The five big deportation movements between November 1943 and May 1944 were carried out in accordance with the usual methods, but unlike the earlier deportations of the kulaks, the operations were marked by "remarkable organizational efficiency" (in Beria's words). The logistical preparation was carefully organized for several weeks and was overseen personally by Beria and his assistants Ivan Serov and Bogdan Kobulov, all of whom traveled in their special armored train. The operation involved a huge number of convoys: 46 convoys of 60 trucks for the deportation of 93,139 Kalmyks on 27–30 December 1943, and 194 convoys of 64 trucks for the deportation on 23–28 February 1944 of 521,247 Chechens and Ingush. For these exceptional operations when the war was at its height, the NKVD used 119,000 troops.

The operations, which were planned down to the last minute, began with the arrest of "potentially dangerous elements," between 1 and 2 percent of the population, most of whom were women, children, and old people. The vast majority of adult men were fighting under the Russian flag. If one is to believe the reports sent to Moscow, the operations were carried out extremely swiftly. The Crimean Tatars had been rounded up on 18–20 May 1944. On the evening of the first day, Kobulov and Serov, who were in charge of the operation, sent a telegram to Beria: "At 8:00 P.M. today, 90,000 people were moved to the station. Seventeen convoys have already taken 48,400 people to their destination. Twenty-five convoys are being loaded up. The operation is running extremely smoothly. It continues." On 19 May, Beria informed Stalin that on the second day 165,515 people had been assembled in the stations, and that 136,412 of these had been loaded into convoys. On 20 May, Serov and Kobulov sent Beria a telegram announcing that the operation had finished at 4:30 that afternoon, with a total of 173,287 people in transit. The last four convoys carrying the 6,727 who remained were to leave that evening.[3]

From the reports of the NKVD bureaucracy it would appear that these deportation operations, affecting hundreds of thousands of people, were a pure formality, each operation more "successful," "effective," or "economical" than the last. After the deportation of the Chechens, Ingush, and Balkars, Solomon Milstein, a civil servant in the NKVD, drew up a long report on the "savings of trucks, planks, buckets, and shovels during these last deportations in comparison with earlier ones."

> Experience gained from transporting Karachai and Kalmyks has made it possible for us to take certain measures that have allowed us to pare back what is needed for convoys and hence ultimately to diminish the number of journeys that need to be made. We now put 45 people into each cattle truck as opposed to the previous 40. By placing the people together with their possessions, we also cut down on the number of trucks required, thus saving 37,548 meters of planks, 11,834 buckets, and 3,400 stoves.[4]

What dreadful reality lay beyond this bureaucratic dream of an NKVD operation carried out with terrifying efficiency? The experiences of some of the survivors were collected at the end of the 1970s. One recalled: "The journey to the destination of Zerabulak, in the Samarkand region, took twenty-four days. From there we were taken to the Pravda *kolkhoz,* where our job was to repair horse carts . . . We worked hard, and we were always hungry. Many of us could barely stand. They had deported thirty families from our village. There were one or two survivors from five families. Everyone else died of hunger or disease." Another survivor recounted that

> in the tightly shut wagons, people died like flies because of hunger and lack of oxygen, and no one gave us anything to eat or drink. In the villages through which we passed, the people had all been turned against us, and they had been told that we were all traitors, so there was a constant rain of stones against the sides and doors of the wagons. When they did open the doors in the middle of the steppes in Kazakhstan, we were given military rations to eat but nothing to drink, and we were told to throw all the dead out beside the railway line without burying them. We then set off again.[5]

Once they had arrived at their destinations in Kazakhstan, Kirgizstan, Uzbekistan, or Siberia, the deportees were assigned to *kolkhozy* or to local industry. Problems with housing, work, and survival were their everyday lot, as is clear from the local NKVD reports that were sent to Moscow and kept in the extensive files of the "special peoples" section of the Gulag. One report from Kirgizstan in September 1944 mentions that of the 31,000 families recently deported there, only 5,000 had been housed. And "housed" itself seems to have been quite a flexible term. The text reveals that in the district of Kameninsky the local authorities had housed 900 families in eighteen apartments in one *sovkhoz* (state farm); in other words, there were 50 families in each apartment. These families, many of whom had a large number of children, must have taken turns sleeping in the apartment, and the rest of the time were forced to sleep outside as the harsh winter approached.

In a letter to Mikoyan in November 1944, more than a year after the deportation of the Kalmyks, Beria himself acknowledged that "they had been placed in exceptionally difficult living conditions with extremely poor sanitation. Many of them had no underwear, no shoes, and very few clothes." Two years later two NKVD leaders reported that "30 percent of the Kalmyks who are fit to work are unable to work because they have no shoes. The fact that they are totally unadapted to the severe climate and to the unusual conditions, and that they have no knowledge of the local language, also implies another whole series of difficulties."[6] Uprooted from their homes, hungry, and working on collective farms so poorly managed that they could barely manage to feed themselves, or in factories for which they had received no training, many deportees were very poor workers. "The situation of the Kalmyks deported to Siberia is tragic," D. P. Pyurveev, the former president of the Autonomous Republic of Kalmykia, wrote to Stalin.

> They have lost all their cattle. They arrived in Siberia having nothing at all . . . They are very poorly adapted to the new living conditions in the region to which they have been sent . . . The Kalmyks working on the collective farms receive almost nothing at all, since even the original workers on the farms cannot feed themselves. Those who have been sent to factories instead are finding it extremely hard to adjust to this new existence, and also to the fact that they are unable to buy a normal food ration because they are not paid properly.[7]

Condemned to spending their lives standing in front of machinery, the Kalmyks, who were a nomadic agricultural people, often saw all of their tiny salary taken away in fines.

A few figures give an idea of the scale of death among the deportees. In January 1946 the Administration for Special Resettlements calculated that there were 70,360 Kalmyks remaining of the 92,000 who had been deported two years previously. On 1 July 1944, 35,750 Tatar families representing 151,424 people had arrived in Uzbekistan; six months later there were 818 more families but 16,000 fewer people. Of the 608,749 people deported from the Caucasus, 146,892, or nearly 1 in 4, had died by 1 October 1948, and a mere 28,120 had been born in the meantime. Of the 228,392 people deported from the Crimea, 44,887 had died after four years, and there had been only 6,564 births.[8] The extremely high mortality rate becomes even more apparent when one also takes into account the fact that between 40 percent and 50 percent of the deportees were under sixteen years of age. "Death from natural causes" was thus only a tiny part of these statistics. The children who did survive had little future: of the 89,000 children deported to Kazakhstan, fewer than 12,000 had been given places in schools four years later. Moreover, official instructions insisted that all school lessons for children of "specially displaced peoples" were to be carried out exclusively in Russian.

These were not the only official deportations carried out during the war. On 29 May 1944, a few days after the end of the operation to deport the Tatars from the Crimea, Beria wrote to Stalin: "The NKVD also thinks it reasonable to expel from the Crimea all the Bulgars, Greeks, and Armenians." The Bulgars were accused of "having actively assisted the Germans in making bread and other foodstuffs for the German army" and of "having collaborated with the German military authorities in searching for soldiers from the Red Army and for partisans." The Greeks were accused of "having set up small industries after the arrival of the invading forces; the German authorities also helped the Greeks do business, organize transport etc." The Armenians, in their turn, were accused of having set up a collaborationist center in Simferopol called the Dromedar, presided over by E. Dro, the Armenian army general. Their purposes supposedly were "not only religious and political, but also to develop small industries and private businesses." In Beria's opinion, the organization "had collected funds both for the military needs of the Germans and with a view to setting up an Armenian legion."[9]

Four days later, on 2 June 1944, Stalin signed a decree from the State Committee for Defense ordering that "the expulsion of the Crimean Tatars should be accompanied by the expulsion of 37,000 Bulgars, Greeks, and Armenians, accomplices of the Germans." As had been the case for the other contingents of deportees, the decree arbitrarily fixed the quotas for each "welcome region": 7,000 for the Gurev region, in Kazakhstan; 10,000 for Sverdlovsk Province; 10,000 for Molotov Province, in the Urals; 6,000 for Kemerovo Province; and 4,000 for Bashkiria. As was always the claim, "the operation was successfully carried out" on 27 and 28 June 1944. Over those two days, 41,854 people were deported, that is, "111 percent of the planned number," as the report emphasized.

Once the Crimea had been purged of Germans, Tatars, Bulgars, Greeks, and Armenians, the NKVD decided to cleanse the Caucasus regions. Based on the same underlying preoccupation with the cleansing of national boundaries, these large-scale operations were in many ways the natural continuation of the antiespionage operations of 1937–38 in a more systematic form. On 21 July 1944 a new decree from the State Committee for Defense signed by Stalin ordered the deportation of 86,000 Meskhetian Turks, Kurds, and Khemshins from the border regions of Georgia. Given the mountainous nature of the territory and the nomadic lifestyles of many of these peoples, who until recently had been part of the Ottoman Empire and had always passed freely between the Soviet and Turkish lands, the preparations for the deportations were particularly long. The operation lasted from 15 to 25 November 1944 and was carried out by 14,000 special troops from the NKVD. Nine hundred Studebaker trucks, provided by the Americans as part of the lend-lease arrangement that supplied large quantities of munitions for the Allies in the anti-German war effort, were diverted to help carry out the deportations.[10]

In a report to Stalin on 28 November, Beria claimed to have transferred 91,095 people in ten days "under particularly difficult conditions." In Beria's opinion, all of these were Turkish spies, even though more than 49 percent were under sixteen. "The majority of the population of this region have family ties with the inhabitants of the border districts of Turkey. They are for the most part smugglers, show a strong inclination to emigrate, and provide many recruits for the Turkish intelligence services and for the gangs of bandits that operate all along the border." According to the statistics from the "people movements" section of the Gulag, nearly 94,955 people were deported to Kazakhstan and Kirgizstan. Between November 1944 and July 1948, 19,540 Meskhetians, Kurds, and Khemshins, approximately 21 percent of all the people moved, died as a result of deportation. This mortality rate of 20–25 percent in four years was almost identical for all such peoples punished by the regime.[11]

The deportation of hundreds of thousands of people on ethnic criteria during the war increased the number of "specially displaced" from approximately 1.2 million to more than 2.5 million. The victims of dekulakization operations before the war had made up the greater part of the "specially displaced," but their number fell from approximately 936,000 at the outbreak of war to 622,000 in May 1945. In fact tens of thousands of adult males formerly classed as kulaks, with the exception of heads of families, were conscripted into the army during the war. Their wives and children then recovered their previous status as free citizens and were no longer classed as "specially displaced." But with conditions as they were during the war, the newly freed were in practice rarely able to leave their designated residences, particularly because all their goods and even their houses had been confiscated.[12]

Conditions for survival in the gulags were most difficult in the years 1941–1944. Famine, epidemics, overcrowding, and inhuman exploitation were added to the continual suffering of the *zeks*, who were also subject to unusually harsh conditions at work and were constantly monitored by an army of informers whose task was to expose the "counterrevolutionary organizations of prisoners." Summary executions occurred every day.

The rapid German advance in the first months of the war forced the NKVD to evacuate several prisons, labor colonies, and camps that would otherwise have fallen into enemy hands. Between July and December 1941, 210 colonies, 135 prisons, and 27 camps, containing nearly 750,000 prisoners, were transferred to the east. Summarizing "gulag activity in the Great Patriotic War," the Gulag chief, Ivan Nasedkin, claimed that "on the whole, the evacuation of the camps was quite well organized." He went on to add, however, that "because of the shortage of transport, most of the prisoners were evacuated on foot, over distances that sometimes exceeded 600 miles."[13] One can well imagine the condition in which the prisoners arrived at their destinations. When there was not enough time for a camp to be evacuated, as was often the case in the opening weeks of the war, the prisoners were simply executed. This was particularly the case in western Ukraine, where at the end of June 1941 the NKVD massacred 10,000 prisoners in Lviv, 1,200 in the prison at Lutsk, 1,500 in Stanisłwow, and 500 in Dubno. When the Germans arrived, they discovered dozens of mass graves in the regions of Lviv, Zhytomyr, and Vynnytsa. Using these "Judeo-Bolshevik atrocities" as a pretext, the Nazi *Sonderkommandos* in their turn immediately massacred tens of thousands of Jews.

All administration reports from the gulags for the years 1941–1944 emphasize the horrendous deterioration of living conditions in the camps during the war.[14] In the overcrowded camps, the living space of each prisoner fell from 1.5 square meters to 0.7; prisoners must have taken turns sleeping on boards, since beds were then a luxury reserved for workers with special status. Average daily caloric intake fell by 65 percent from prewar levels. Famine became widespread, and in 1942 typhus and cholera began to appear in the camps. According to official figures, nearly 19,000 prisoners died of these diseases each year. In 1941 there were nearly 101,000 deaths in the labor camps alone, not including the forced-labor colonies. Thus the annual death rate was approaching 8 percent. In 1942 the Gulag Administration registered 249,000 deaths (a death rate of 18 percent), and in 1943, 167,000 deaths (a death rate of 17 percent).[15] If one also includes the executions of prisoners and deaths in the prisons and in the forced-labor colonies, one can roughly calculate that there were some 600,000 deaths in the gulags in 1941–43 alone. The survivors were also in a pitiful state. According to the administration's own figures, only 19 percent of all prisoners by the end of 1942 were capable of heavy physical labor, 17 percent were capable of medium physical labor, and 64 percent were able to perform "light work"—which meant that they were sick.

Here are excerpts from a report, dated 2 November 1941, from the assistant chief of the Operational Department of the Gulag Administration on the situation in the Siblag camps.

According to information received from the operational department of the Novosibirsk NKVD, there has been a sharp increase in mortality among the prisoners in the Akhlursk, Kuznetsk, and Novosibirsk departments of Siblag . . .

The causes of this increase, as well as of the huge rise in the number of recorded instances of disease, is undoubtedly widespread undernourishment resulting from the constant lack of food and the harsh working conditions, which place great strain on the heart.

The lack of medical attention given to prisoners, the difficulty of the work they carry out, the long working day, and the lack of sufficient nourishment all contribute to the sharp increase in the death rate . . .

Numerous deaths from malnutrition, undernourishment, and widespread epidemics have also been recorded among the prisoners sent from different sorting centers to the camps. On 8 October 1941 more than 30 percent of the 539 prisoners sent from the Novosibirsk sorting center in the Marinskoe division were extremely underweight and covered with lice. Six corpses also arrived with the prisoners.[16] On the night of 8–9 October another five died. In another convoy that arrived from the same sorting center in the Marinskoe division on 20 September, all the prisoners were covered in lice, and a considerable portion of them had no underwear . . .

Recently, in the Siblag camps, there were numerous acts of sabotage by the medical staff made up of prisoners. One assistant from the Azher camp, in the department of Taiginsk, sentenced under section 10 of Article 58,[17] organized a group of prisoners to sabotage production.[18] Members of the group were caught sending sick workers to the hardest physical labor sites, rather than curing them, in the hope that this would slow down camp production and prevent the targets from being met.

Assistant Chief of the Operational Department of the Gulag Administration, Captain of the Security Forces, Kogenman.

These "severe health problems encountered by prisoners," to use the Gulag euphemism, did not prevent the authorities from exerting even greater pressure on the prisoners, often until they dropped. "From 1941 to 1944," the chief of the Gulag wrote in his report, "the average worth of a day's work rose from 9.5 to 21 rubles." Hundreds of thousands of prisoners were drafted into the armaments factories to replace the manpower that had been conscripted into the army. The Gulag's role in the war economy came to be extremely prominent. According to estimates by the penal administration, prisoner manpower was responsible for nearly a quarter of all production in certain key sectors of the armaments industry, notably in metallurgy and mining.[19]

Despite the "solid patriotic attitude" of the prisoners, 95 percent of whom "were strongly committed to the socialist cause," the oppression, notably against political prisoners, was as intense as ever. As a result of a decree issued by the Central Committee on 22 June 1941, not a single "58" (a prisoner sentenced as a result of Article 58 of the penal code) was to be released before the end of the war, even if he had served his time. Prisoners sentenced for political crimes (such as belonging to a counterrevolutionary party or to a right-wing or Trotskyite organization) or for espionage, treason, or terrorism were isolated in heavily guarded special camps in areas where the climate was most severe, such as the Kolyma region and the Arctic. In such camps the annual death rate regularly reached 30 percent. After a decree of 22 April 1943, specially reinforced punishment camps were opened up, which in effect became death camps, since the prisoners were exploited in a manner that made survival extremely unlikely. A twelve-hour working day under poisonous conditions in the gold, coal, lead, and radium mines, most of which were situated in the Kolyma and Vorkuta regions, was tantamount to a death sentence.[20]

From July 1941 to July 1944 special courts in the camps sentenced 148,000 prisoners to new punishments and executed 10,858 of these: 208 were executed for espionage, 4,307 for subversive and terrorist activities, and 6,016 for having organized an uprising or riot in the camps. According to NKVD figures, 603 "prisoner organizations" in the gulags were eliminated during the war.[21] Although it is possible that these figures were meant to show the continued vigilance of the system despite considerable restructuring—many of the special troops who had guarded the camps had been assigned to other tasks, notably to deportation activities—there is no doubt that during the war the camps faced their first mass escapes and their first large-scale revolts.

In fact the population of the camps changed considerably during the war. Following the decree of 12 July 1941 more than 577,000 prisoners who, as the authorities themselves acknowledged, had been sentenced for "insignificant crimes such as unjustified absenteeism at work or petty theft" were set free and immediately integrated into the Red Army. During the war more than 1,068,000 prisoners went directly from the gulags to the front, if one includes those who served out their sentences in full.[22] The weakest prisoners and those least adapted to the harsh conditions that prevailed in the camps were among the approximately 600,000 who died in the gulags in 1941–1943. While the camps and colonies were being emptied of so many who had been sentenced for minor offenses, the toughest and most recalcitrant stayed behind and survived, whether they were political prisoners or common criminals. The share of those sentenced to long terms of imprisonment (eight years or more) as a result of Article 58 increased from 27 to 43 percent of all prisoners. This change in the complexion of the prison population was to become all the more marked in 1944 and 1945, when the gulags grew immensely, increasing their population by more than 45 percent between January 1944 and January 1945.

The U.S.S.R. in 1945 is best remembered as a country devastated but triumphant. As François Furet once wrote: "In 1945, as a great glorious state, the U.S.S.R. joined tremendous material might to a messianic new vision of man." No one remembers, or at least no one seems willing to recall, the other—well hidden—side of the story. As the Gulag archives demonstrate, the year of victory was also the apogee of the Soviet concentration-camp system. When peace was made with the rest of the world, the struggles within continued unabated; there was no let-up in state control over a society bruised from four years of war. On the contrary, 1945 was a year when regions were reoccupied by the Soviet Union as the Red Army advanced west, and when millions of Soviet citizens who had managed to escape the system were also finally forced to submit.

The territories annexed in 1939–40—the Baltic states, western Belorussia,

Moldavia, and western Ukraine—which had been free of Soviet control during most of the war, were forced to undergo a second process of Sovietization. Nationalist opposition movements had sprung up in protest against the Soviet Union, beginning a cycle of armed struggle, persecution, and repression. Resistance to annexation was particularly fierce in western Ukraine and the Baltic states.

The first occupation of western Ukraine, from September 1939 to June 1941, had brought about the formation of a fairly powerful armed resistance movement, the OUN, or Organization of Ukrainian Nationalists. Members of this organization subsequently enlisted as special troops in SS units to fight Communists and Jews. In July 1944, when the Red Army arrived, the OUN set up a Supreme Council for the Liberation of Ukraine. Roman Shukhovich, the head of the OUN, became commander of the UPA, the Ukrainian insurgent army. According to Ukrainian sources, the UPA had more than 20,000 members by the autumn of 1944. On 31 March 1944, Beria signed an order stipulating that all family members of soldiers in the OUN and UPA were to be arrested and deported to the region of Krasnoyarsk. From February to October 1944, 100,300 civilians (mainly women, children, and old people) were deported under Beria's order. As for the 37,000 soldiers who were taken prisoner during this time, all were sent to the gulags. In November 1944, after the death of Monsignor Andrei Shcheptytsky, metropolitan of the Uniate Church of Ukraine, the Soviet authorities forced that religious body to merge with the Orthodox Church.

To root out all opposition to Sovietization, NKVD agents targeted the schools. After leafing through the schoolbooks of children who had attended school when western Ukraine had still been a part of "bourgeois" Poland, they drew up lists of people to be arrested as a preventive measure. At the top of these lists were the names of the most able pupils, whom they judged to be "potentially hostile to the Soviet system." According to a report by Kobulov, one of Beria's assistants, more than 100,000 "deserters" and "collaborators" were arrested between September 1944 and March 1945 in western Belorussia, another region considered "full of elements hostile to the Soviet regime." The few statistics available for Lithuania in the period 1 January–15 March 1945 note 2,257 ethnic-cleansing operations.

These operations were also notable for the death of more than 6,000 "bandits" and for the arrest of more than 75,000 "bandits, deserters, and members of nationalist groups." In 1945 more than 38,000 "members of the families of socially alien elements, bandits, and nationalists" were deported from Lithuania. In 1944–1946 the proportion of people from these regions imprisoned in the gulags increased 140 percent for Ukrainians and 420 percent for people from the Baltic states. By the end of 1946, Ukrainians became 23 percent and Baltic nationals 6 percent of the population in the camps, and thus were more highly represented than the rest of the Soviet population.

The growth of the gulags in 1945 can also be explained by the transfer of thousands of prisoners from "control and filtration camps." These were camps that had been set up after 1941 in parallel to the Gulag labor camps. They were intended to contain Soviet prisoners of war who had been set free or had managed to escape from enemy prisoner-of-war camps; all were suspected of being potential spies or at least of having been contaminated by their stay outside the Soviet system. The camps imprisoned men of draft age from territories formerly occupied by the enemy, as well as the senior officials *(starosti)* and any others who had occupied a position of authority—no matter how minor—during the occupation. From January 1942 to October 1944 more than 421,000 people, according to official figures, passed through the control and filtration camps.[23]

After the advance of the Red Army in the west and the retaking of territories that had been under the control of the Germans for two to three years, the liberation of Soviet prisoners of war and those held in labor camps and the repatriation of both military and civilian Soviet citizens became an urgent matter. In October 1944 the Soviet government established a Repatriation Affairs Department, headed by General Filip Golikov. In an interview published in the press on 11 November 1944, the general stressed that "the Soviet regime is most concerned about the fate of its children who were dragged into Nazi slavery. They will be respectfully received back home like honest children of the fatherland. The Soviet government believes that even Soviet citizens who under the threat of Nazi terror committed acts that went against the interests of the U.S.S.R. will not be held responsible for those actions, provided that these people are prepared to carry out their normal duties as Soviet citizens upon their return." This declaration, which was widely circulated, managed to deceive the Allies. How else can one explain the zeal with which they carried out the clauses of the Yalta agreement concerning the repatriation of all Soviet citizens "present outside the borders of the home country"? While the agreement stipulated quite clearly that only people who had worn German uniforms or actively collaborated with the enemy would be forcibly repatriated, any Soviet citizen found outside the national boundaries was, in practice, handed over to NKVD agents in charge of their return.

Three days after the cessation of hostilities, on 11 May 1945, the Soviet government ordered the creation of 100 new control and filtration camps, each containing space for 10,000 people. Repatriated Soviet prisoners of war were under the jurisdiction of SMERSH (Death to Spies), the counterespionage organization, while civilians were filtered on an ad-hoc basis through the

NKVD. Between May 1945 and February 1946 more than 4.2 million Soviet citizens were repatriated, including 1,545,000 surviving prisoners of war out of the 5 million captured by the Germans and 2,655,000 civilians, work deportees, or people who had fled to the West when the fighting had broken out. After their obligatory stay in the filtration and control camps, 57.8 percent of those repatriated, mostly women and children, were allowed to return to their homes; 19.1 percent were drafted back into the army, often into disciplinary battalions; 14.5 percent were sent, generally for at least two years, into "reconstruction battalions"; and 8.6 percent, or about 360,000 people, were either sentenced to between ten and twenty years in the gulags, most of them for "treason against the fatherland," or sent to an NKVD *komandatura* with the status of "specially displaced person."[24]

A singular fate was reserved for the *Vlasovtsy*, the Soviet soldiers who had fought under the Soviet general Andrei Vlasov. Vlasov was the commander of the Second Army who had been taken prisoner by the Germans in July 1942. On the basis of his anti-Stalinist convictions, General Vlasov agreed to collaborate with the Nazis to free his country from the tyranny of the Bolsheviks. With the support of the German authorities, Vlasov formed a Russian National Committee and trained two divisions of an "Army for the Liberation of Russia." After the defeat of Nazi Germany, the Allies handed over General Vlasov and his officers to the Soviet Union, and they were promptly executed. The soldiers from Vlasov's army, following an amnesty decree of November 1945, were deported for six years to Siberia, Kazakhstan, and the far north. In early 1946, 148,079 *Vlasovtsy*, most of them noncommissioned officers, were accused of treason and sent to the gulags.[25]

The "special resettlements," the gulags, the forced-labor colonies, the control and filtration camps, and the Soviet prisons had never held as many prisoners as they did in the year of victory: a grand total of nearly 5.5 million people. This figure was eclipsed by the festivities of victory and the "Stalingrad effect." The end of World War II began a new period in Soviet history, destined to last nearly a decade, when the Soviet model was to elicit a fascination shared by tens of millions of citizens from countries the world over. The fact that the U.S.S.R. had paid the heaviest human toll for its victory over Nazism—a toll greatly magnified by Stalin's own mistakes and misjudgments—served to mask the character of the Stalinist dictatorship and cleared the regime of all suspicions formerly aroused in the era of the Moscow trials and the Nazi-Soviet pact.

13 Apogee and Crisis in the Gulag System

The last years of Stalinism were marked neither by a new Great Terror nor by more public show-trials. But the heavy and oppressive climate continued in postwar Russia, and the criminalization of different types of social behavior reached its height. The hope that the regime might relax its grip after the long and murderous war proved vain. "The people have suffered too much, and it is inconceivable that the past should repeat itself," wrote Ilya Ehrenburg in his memoirs on 9 May 1945; but he immediately added: "Yet I am filled with perplexity and anguish." This foreboding was all too prophetic.

"The population is torn between despair in the face of an extremely difficult material situation, and the hope that something is going to change." So read several inspection reports sent to Moscow in September and October 1945 by instructors from the Soviet Central Committee who were touring different provinces. The reports claimed that many parts of the country were still in chaos. Production was delayed by an immense and spontaneous migration of workers who had been sent east during the evacuations of 1941 and 1942. A wave of strikes of unprecedented size were rocking the metallurgy industry in the Urals. Famine and terrible living conditions were becoming the norm. The country had 25 million people without homes, and bread rations were less than one pound per day for manual laborers. At the end of October 1945 the situation was so bad in Novosibirsk that the heads of the regional

Party committee went so far as to suggest that the workers not participate in the parade to mark the occasion of the October Revolution, because so many of the population lacked clothes and shoes. In the face of such misery, rumors spread quickly, particularly concerning the imminent abandonment of collective farming practices, since it had been demonstrated yet again that the *kolkhozy* were incapable of feeding the peasants and providing them with a few *pudy* of wheat in exchange for a whole season's work.[1]

It was on the agricultural front that the situation was most perilous. The countryside was devastated by war and a severe drought; and with both machinery and manpower in critically short supply, the harvest of the autumn of 1946 was catastrophic. Once again the government was forced to continue rationing, despite Stalin's promise in a speech on 9 February 1946 that rationing would end. Refusing to look into the reasons for this agricultural disaster, and blaming the failure on the greed of a few private farmers, the government decided to "eliminate all violations of the status of the *kolkhozy*" and to go after "hostile and foreign elements sabotaging the collection process, thieves, and anyone caught pilfering the harvest." On 19 September 1946 a Commission for Kolkhoz Affairs was established, chaired by Andrei Andreev; its task was to confiscate all the land that had been "illegally appropriated" by *kolkhoz* workers during the war. In two years the administration managed to recover nearly 10 million hectares that peasants had whittled away, trying to gather more land in an attempt to survive.

On 25 October 1946 a government decree titled "The Defense of State Cereals" ordered the Ministry of Justice to dispatch all cases of theft within ten days, and to apply once again the full force of the law of 7 August 1932, which by then had fallen into disuse. In November and December 1946 sentences were handed down against more than 53,300 people, most of them collective farm workers, who were sent to the camps for the theft of grain or bread. Thousands of *kolkhoz* chiefs were arrested for "sabotaging the countryside collection campaign." Initially collections typically met 33 percent of their targets, but in these two months the share rose to 77 percent.[2] This increase came at a price: Behind the euphemism "delay in the collection in the countryside" lurked the bitter realities of another famine.

The famine of the autumn and winter of 1946–47 struck the regions most severely affected by the drought of the summer of 1946, that is, the provinces of Kursk, Tambov, Voronezh, Orel, and Rostov. There were at least 500,000 victims. As in 1932, the famine of 1946–47 was passed over in total silence. The refusal to lower the obligatory collection targets when the harvest in some areas reached scarcely 250 kilos per hectare meant that shortage evolved into famine. The starving workers often had no choice but to steal a few reserves simply to survive. In one year, recorded thefts rose by 44 percent.[3]

On 5 June 1947 two decrees issued by the government the previous day were published, both of which were very close to the spirit and letter of the famous law of 7 August 1932. These stipulated that any "attack on state or *kolkhoz* property" was punishable by a camp sentence of between five and twenty-five years, depending on whether it was an individual or collective crime, and whether it was a first or repeat offense. Anyone who knew of preparations for a theft, or was a witness and failed to inform the police, received a sentence of one to three years. A confidential circular reminded courts that petty thefts in the workplace, which until then had carried a maximum penalty of the loss of civil rights for one year, henceforth fell within the remit of these new laws of 4 June 1947.

In the second half of that year more than 380,000 people, including 21,000 under age sixteen, were sentenced as a result of this new, draconian law. For the theft of no more than a few kilos of rye, one could be sentenced to eight to ten years in the camps. An example is the following verdict of the People's Court in the Suzdal district, in Vladimir Province, dated 10 October 1947: "While on duty guarding the *kolkhoz* horses at night, N. A. and B. S., two minors of fifteen and sixteen, were caught in the act of stealing three cucumbers from the *kolkhoz* vegetable patch . . . N. A. and B. S. have thus been sentenced to eight years custody in an ordinary labor colony."[4] Over a period of six years, as a result of the decrees of 4 June, 1.3 million people were sentenced, 75 percent to more than five years. In 1951 they accounted for 53 percent of all common criminals in the gulags, and nearly 40 percent of all prisoners.[5] At the end of the 1940s, strict enforcement of the decrees of 4 June considerably increased the average length of sentences passed by ordinary courts; the share of sentences exceeding five years rose from 2 percent in 1940 to 29 percent in 1949. At this high point of Stalinism, "ordinary" repressive punishments, of the sort meted out by people's courts, took the place of the extrajudicial NKVD terror that had been more the norm in the 1930s.[6]

Among people sentenced for theft were numerous women, war widows, and mothers with young children who had been reduced to begging and stealing to survive. At the end of 1948 the gulags contained more than 500,000 prisoners (twice as many as in 1945). Some 22,815 children under age four were kept in the "infant houses" located in the women's camps. By early 1953 this figure rose to more than 35,000.[7] To prevent the gulags from turning into vast nurseries, the government was forced to decree a partial amnesty in April 1949, so that nearly 84,200 mothers and children were set free. Even so, the permanent influx of hundreds of thousands of people charged with petty thefts meant that until 1953 there was still a relatively high number of women in the gulags, who generally accounted for 25–30 percent of all prisoners.

In 1947 and 1948 the armory of repressive laws was augmented by several more decrees that were quite revealing of the climate at the time: a decree forbidding marriages between Soviet citizens and foreigners on 15 February 1947 and another decree on "penalties for divulging state secrets or losing documents containing state secrets" on 9 June 1947. The best known is the decree of 21 February 1948, according to which "all spies, Trotskyites, saboteurs, right-wingers, Mensheviks, Socialist Revolutionaries, anarchists, nationalists, Whites, and other anti-Soviet groups, on completion of their camp sentences, will be exiled to the Kolyma regions, the provinces of Novosibirsk and Krasnoyarsk . . . and to certain distant regions of Kazakhstan." In reality, prison administrations preferred to keep these "anti-Soviet elements" (mostly the Article 58 political prisoners sentenced in 1937 and 1938) under close guard, and arbitrarily extended their sentences by another ten years.

On the same day, 21 February 1948, the Presidium of the Supreme Soviet adopted another decree ordering the deportation from the Ukrainian S.S.R. of "all individuals refusing to comply with the minimum number of work days in the *kolkhozy* and living like parasites." On 2 June the measure was extended to the rest of the country. The dilapidated collective farms were in no position to guarantee the slightest remuneration to workers, and so numerous workers regularly had failed to comply with the minimum number of work days imposed by the administration. Millions were thus suddenly under threat from this new law. Understanding that the strict application of this new decree on "parasitism" would disrupt production even further, local authorities were generally lax in applying the law. Nonetheless, in 1948 alone more than 38,000 "parasites" were deported and assigned a residence in an NKVD *komandatura*. These repressive measures totally eclipsed the symbolic (and short-lived) abolition of the death penalty on 26 May 1947. On 12 January 1950 capital punishment was reinstated to permit the execution of the accused in the "Leningrad Affair" of that year.[8]

In the 1930s the "right to return" of deportees and the "specially displaced" had led to some contradictory and incoherent government policies. At the end of the 1940s the question was resolved in a fairly radical manner: it was decided that all people who had been deported in 1941–1945 had in fact been deported "in perpetuity." The problem posed by the fate of the children of deportees who had reached the age of majority thus disappeared immediately. They and their children, too, were always to remain "specially displaced."

In the period 1948–1953 the number of "specially displaced" continued to grow, from 2,342,000 in early 1948 to 2,753,000 in January 1953. This increase was the result of several new waves of deportation. On 22 and 23 May 1948 the NKVD launched a huge roundup named "Operation Spring" in Lithuania, a nation still resisting enforced collectivization. Within forty-eight hours 36,932 men, women, and children were arrested and deported in thirty-two convoys. All were categorized as "bandits, nationalists, and family members of these two categories." After a journey lasting between four and five weeks, they were divided up among the various *komandatury* in eastern Siberia and set to work in the harsh conditions of the different logging centers. One NKVD note observed that

> the Lithuanian families sent as a workforce to the Igara forestry center (in the Krasnoyarsk territory) are presently living in conditions that are quite inappropriate for the local climate: the roofs leak, there is no glass in the windows, no furniture, and no beds. The deportees sleep on the floor, on beds of moss or straw. This overcrowding, and the constant breaking of the sanitary regulations, have led to cases of typhus and dysentery, which are sometimes fatal, among the specially displaced.

In 1948 alone nearly 50,000 Lithuanians were deported as "specially displaced," and 30,000 were sent to the gulags. In addition, according to figures from the Ministry of Internal Affairs, 21,259 Lithuanians were killed in "pacification operations" in that republic. At the end of 1948, despite ever-more-vigorous pressure from the authorities, less than 4 percent of the land had undergone collectivization in the Baltic states.[9]

Early in 1949 the Soviet government decided to accelerate the process of Sovietization in the Baltic countries and to "eradicate banditry and nationalism once and for all" in these newly annexed republics. On 12 January the Council of Ministers issued a decree "on the expulsion and deportation from the Lithuanian, Latvian, and Estonian S.S.R.s of all kulaks and their families, the families of bandits and nationalists whose present situation is illegal, the families of bandits killed in armed confrontations, any bandits arrested or freed who are still carrying out hostile operations, and the families of any bandit's accomplices." From March to May 1949 nearly 95,000 people were deported from the Baltic republics to Siberia. According to the report addressed to Stalin by Sergei Kruglov on 18 May 1949, these "elements who are hostile and dangerous to the Soviet regime" included 27,084 under the age of sixteen, 1,785 young children who had no family left, 146 disabled people, and 2,850 infirm elderly.[10] In September 1951 a new series of sweeps resulted in the deportation of another 17,000 so-called Baltic kulaks. For the years 1940–1953 the number of deportees from the Baltic is estimated at 200,000, including about 120,000 Lithuanians, 50,000 Latvians, and just over 30,000 Estonians.[11] To these figures one should add the number of people from the Baltic imprisoned in the gulags—a total of 75,000 in 1953, including 44,000 in special camps that were reserved for hard-line political prisoners. In the special camps, 20 percent of the inmates were of Baltic origin. In total, 10 percent of the entire adult Baltic population was either deported or in a camp.

The Moldavians, another nationality occupied by the U.S.S.R., also strongly resisted Sovietization and collectivization. At the end of 1949 the authorities carried out a huge deportation sweep among "socially alien and hostile elements." The operation was overseen by the first secretary of the Communist Party in Moldavia, Leonid Ilych Brezhnev, later to become general secretary of the Communist Party of the U.S.S.R. A report from Kruglov to Stalin dated 17 February 1950 revealed that 94,792 Moldavians had been deported "in perpetuity" as "specially displaced." If the same death rate during transport applied to the Moldavian operation as in other deportations, this would mean that approximately 120,000 people, nearly 7 percent of the population, were taken from Moldavia. In June 1949, 57,680 Greeks, Armenians, and Turks from the shores of the Black Sea were deported to Kazakhstan and Altai.[12]

Throughout the second half of the 1940s the OUN and UPA partisans captured in Ukraine accounted for a large share of the "specially displaced." From July 1944 to December 1949 the Soviet authorities made seven appeals to the insurgents to give up their weapons, promising amnesty, but with no tangible results. In 1945–1947 the countryside of western Ukraine was still largely in the hands of the rebels, who were supported by a peasantry hostile to any form of collectivization. The rebel forces operated on the borders of Poland and Czechoslovakia, fleeing over the border when pursued. One can gain some idea of the size of the rebel movement in the agreement that the Soviet government signed with Poland and Czechoslovakia to coordinate the struggle against the Ukrainian gangs. As a result of the agreement, the Polish government moved the whole of its Ukrainian population to the northwest of Poland to deprive the rebellion in Ukraine of its base.[13]

The famine of 1946–47 forced tens of thousands of peasants from eastern Ukraine to flee to the less affected west, and it also swelled the number of rebels. To judge from the last amnesty proposal, signed by the Ukrainian minister of internal affairs on 30 December 1949, the rebel gangs were not made up solely of peasants. The text also mentions, among the various categories of bandits, "young people who have fled the factories, the Donetsk mines, and the industrial schools." Western Ukraine was finally "pacified" at the end of 1950, after forced collectivization of the land, the displacement of whole villages, and the arrest and deportation of more than 300,000 people. According to statistics from the Ministry of Internal Affairs, nearly 172,000 members of the OUN and the UPA were deported as "specially displaced" to Kazakhstan and Siberia in 1944–1952, often together with their families.[14]

Deportation operations for what the Ministry of Internal Affairs described as "diverse contingents" continued right up until Stalin's death. In 1951 and 1952, as a result of various small-scale operations, the following were deported: 11,685 Mingrelians and 4,707 Iranians from Georgia, 4,365 Jehovah's Witnesses, 4,431 "kulaks" from western Belorussia, 1,445 "kulaks" from western Ukraine, 1,415 "kulaks" from the Pskov region, 995 people from the sect that called itself "True Orthodox Christians," 2,795 *basmachis* from Tajikistan, and 591 "vagabonds." These deportees received slightly lesser sentences of between ten and twenty years.

As the recently opened Gulag archives demonstrate, the early 1950s were the most intense period of operation; never had so many people been detained in the camps, forced-labor colonies, and penal settlements. This was also a period of unprecedented crisis in the system.

In the first months of 1953 the gulags contained 2,750,000 prisoners, who were grouped into three categories:

· Those incarcerated in the approximately 500 labor colonies, found in all regions, containing between 1,000 and 3,000 prisoners on average, most of whom were common criminals serving sentences of less than five years
· Those incarcerated in some 60 large penal complexes, or labor camps, which were mainly in the northern and eastern regions of the country, each holding tens of thousands of prisoners, common criminals, and political prisoners all serving sentences of more than ten years
· Those imprisoned in the approximately 15 special-regime camps, which had been established following secret instructions from the Ministry of Internal Affairs on 7 February 1948 to house only political prisoners considered particularly dangerous, totaling approximately 200,000 people[15]

This huge concentration-camp universe thus contained 2,750,000 prisoners; another 2,750,000 "specially displaced people" were controlled by a different part of the Gulag Administration. These numbers made for serious problems in administration and control, as well as in economic profitability. In 1951 General Kruglov, the minister of internal affairs, was worried about the constant decline in productivity among penal workers. He began a vast inspection campaign to assess the state of the gulags. When the commissions reported back, they revealed an extremely tense situation.

First of all, in the special-regime camps where "political" prisoners (Ukrainian and Baltic "nationalists" from defeated guerrilla organizations, "foreign elements" from newly incorporated regions, real or supposed "collaborators," and other "traitors to the fatherland") had been arriving since 1945, the detainees were far more determined than the "enemies of the people" of the 1930s, who had been former Party cadres convinced that their imprisonment had been the result of a terrible misunderstanding. These new people, by contrast, condemned to twenty or twenty-five years with no hope of an early release, felt they had nothing left to lose. Moreover, their isolation in the

special-regime camps had removed them from the influence of common criminals. As Aleksandr Solzhenitsyn pointed out, the one thing that prevented an
atmosphere of solidarity from developing among prisoners was precisely the
presence of common criminals. Once this obstacle had been removed, the
special camps quickly became hotbeds of resistance and revolt against the
Soviet regime. Ukrainian and Baltic prisoners were particularly active in re-
volting against the system. Strikes, hunger strikes, mass escapes, and riots all
became increasingly common. Research so far reveals sixteen large-scale riots
and revolts in 1950–1952, each involving hundreds of prisoners.[16]

The Kruglov inspections of 1951 also revealed that the system was deteriorating in ordinary camps, where "a general laxity in discipline" was to be
discerned. In 1951 a million work days were lost to protests and strikes by
prisoners. There was also a rising crime rate in the camps, an increasing number
of violent confrontations between prisoners and guards, and a decline in the
productivity of the penal workforce. According to the authorities, the situation
was largely the result of conflicts between rival gangs of prisoners, with one
group that refused to work and despised the other groups that did work,
labeling them collaborators. In-fighting among factions and fights among prisoners had a corrosive effect on discipline and generally created disorder. Deaths
from stabbing were more common than deaths from hunger or disease. A
conference of gulag commanders held in Moscow in January 1952 acknowledged that "the authorities, who until now have been able to gain a certain
advantage from the hostilities between various groups of prisoners, [are] beginning to lose their grip on the situation . . . In some places, certain factions
are even beginning to run the camp along their own lines." To break up groups
and factions, it was decided that prisoners should be moved between camps
more frequently, and that at the biggest penitentiaries, which often held between 40,000 and 60,000 people, there should be a permanent reorganization
into separate sections.[17]

In addition to noting the considerable problems generated by the different
factions, many inspection reports from 1951 and 1952 acknowledged a need
both for a complete reorganization of the prisons and their systems of production, and for a considerable scaling down of the entire operation.

In January 1952 Colonel Nikolai Zverev, the commander of the concentration camps in Norilsk, where 69,000 prisoners were kept, sent a report to
General Ivan Dolgikh, the commander in chief of the gulags, with the following
recommendations:

1. Isolate the factions. "But," Zverev noted, "given the great number of
   prisoners who belong to one or other of the rival factions, we would be
   lucky if we could even simply isolate the leaders."
2. Abandon the huge production zones, where tens of thousands of pris-

oners belonging to one faction or another are currently working without supervision.

3. Establish smaller production units to ensure better surveillance of the prisoners.

4. Increase the number of guards. "But," Zverev added, "it is currently impossible to organize the guards in the desired fashion, since almost double the number of guards is required."

5. Separate free workers from prisoners at all production sites. "But the technical links between the different companies that make up the Norilsk complex, and the requirement that production be continuous, coupled with the serious housing shortage, all mean that it is currently impossible to segregate the prisoners and the free workers in a satisfactory manner . . . Generally speaking, the problem of productivity and of uninterrupted production could be resolved only by the early release of 15,000 prisoners, who in any case would be forced to remain at the same site."[18]

Zverev's last proposal was far from incongruous, given the climate of opinion at the time. In January 1951 Kruglov had asked Beria for the early release of 6,000 prisoners, who were then to be sent as free workers to an enormous construction site for the hydroelectric power station in Stalingrad, where 25,000 prisoners were then toiling away in what was perceived to be an extremely ineffectual manner. The practice of early release, particularly for prisoners who had some qualifications, was fairly frequent in the early 1950s. It also called into question the economic value of an outdated system of concentration camps.

Faced with this huge increase in prisoners who were far less docile than those in the past, and with a whole series of logistical and surveillance problems (Gulag personnel now numbered approximately 208,000), the enormous administrative machine found it more and more difficult to produce its *tufta*—the false accounts of its success. To resolve this enduring problem, the authorities had a choice of two solutions: either to exploit all manpower to the maximum, without regard for human losses, or to ensure the Gulag's survival by treating the manpower with greater consideration. Until 1948 the first solution was preferred; but at the end of the 1940s it dawned on Party leaders that with the country bled dry by the war and manpower scarce in every sector of the economy, it was far more logical to use the prisoner workforce in a more economical fashion. To try to stimulate production, bonuses and salaries were introduced, and food rations were increased for prisoners who met their quotas. As a result, the death rate fell immediately by 2–3 percent. But the reforms quickly came up against the harsh realities of life in the concentration camps.

By the beginning of the 1950s, the production infrastructure in general was more than twenty years old and had had no benefit of any recent investment. The huge penitentiaries, which held tens of thousands of prisoners and which had been built to use the extensive workforce in the big projects of the time, were extremely difficult to reorganize, despite the numerous attempts from 1949 to 1952 to break them up into smaller production units. The tiny salaries given to prisoners, generally a few hundred rubles per year (fifteen to twenty times less than the pay of a free worker), were an inadequate stimulus to increased productivity. More and more prisoners were downing tools, refusing to work, and forming organized groups that required ever-closer surveillance. Regardless of whether they were better paid or guarded more closely, all prisoners, both those who cooperated with the authorities and those who preferred to show solidarity with the other strikers, began to cost more and more in economic terms.

All the information available from the inspection reports of 1951 and 1952 points in the same direction: The gulags had become a much harder mechanism to control. All the large-scale Stalinist projects that were being built with largely penal manpower, including the hydroelectric power stations in Kuibyshev and Stalingrad, the Turkmenistan canal, and the Volga–Don canal, fell considerably behind schedule. To speed up work, the authorities were forced to bring in a large number of additional free workers, and to grant early release to a number of prisoners in an attempt to motivate the others.[19]

The Gulag crisis sheds new light on the amnesty of 1.2 million prisoners decreed by Beria scarcely three weeks after Stalin's death, on 27 March 1953. Certainly, political reasons alone could not have motivated Stalin's potential successors to unite in proclaiming a partial amnesty. All were aware of the immense difficulty of managing the overcrowded and unprofitable gulags. Yet at the very moment when all the penal authorities were asking for a reduction in the number of prisoners, Stalin, who was suffering increasingly from paranoia in his old age, was preparing a second Great Terror. Such contradictions abounded in the last, most troubled period of the Stalinist regime.

14 The Last Conspiracy

On 13 January 1953, *Pravda* announced the purported discovery of a plot by a "terrorist group of doctors" consisting of first nine and then fifteen famous physicians, more than half of whom were Jewish. They were accused of having abused their high positions in the Kremlin to shorten the lives of Andrei Zhdanov (a member of the Politburo who had died in 1948) and Aleksandr Shcherbakov (who had died in 1950) and of having attempted to assassinate several Soviet military officers at the behest of American intelligence services and a Jewish charitable organization, the American Joint Distribution Committee. While the woman who denounced the plot, Dr. Lydia Timashuk, was solemnly awarded the Order of Lenin, the accused were interrogated and forced to "confess." As in 1936–1938, thousands of meetings were held to call for the punishment of the guilty and to demand further inquiries and a return to old-fashioned Bolshevik vigilance. In the weeks following the announced discovery of the "Doctors' Plot," a huge press campaign reestablished the climate that had prevailed during the Great Terror, with demands that "criminal negligence within the Party ranks be definitively stamped out, and all saboteurs punished." The idea of a huge conspiracy among intellectuals, Jews, soldiers, industrial managers, senior Party officials, and leading representatives from the non-Russian republics began to take hold, recalling the worst years of the *Ezhovshchina*.

Documents relating to this affair, which are now available for the first time, confirm that the Doctors' Plot was a decisive moment in the history of postwar Stalinism.[1] It marked both the peak of the "anticosmopolitan" (that is, antisemitic) campaign that had begun in 1949 (and whose first stirrings can be traced back to 1946–47) and the beginning of a new general purge, a new Great Terror that was halted only by Stalin's death, a few weeks after the story of the conspiracy broke. A third factor of some importance was the power struggle among factions in the Ministry of Internal Affairs and the Ministry of State Security, which had been separated in 1946 and subjected to constant reorganizations ever since.[2] Splits within the secret police were a reflection of struggles at the very top of the hierarchy, where Stalin's potential heirs were constantly jockeying for position. One final troubling aspect of the affair was that eight years after public revelation of the horrors of the Nazi death camps, it allowed the deep-seated tsarist antisemitism, which the Bolsheviks had previously eschewed, to resurface, thus demonstrating the confusion of the last years of Stalinism.

The complexities of this affair, or rather of these several converging affairs, are not our concern here; it is enough to recall the major outlines of the plot. In 1942 the Soviet government, with a view to putting pressure on American Jews to force the U.S. government to open a second front against Germany as soon as possible, set up a Soviet Jewish Anti-Fascist Committee, chaired by Solomon Mikhoels, the director of the famous Yiddish theater in Moscow. Hundreds of Jewish intellectuals were soon active in the movement, including the novelist Ilya Ehrenburg, the poets Samuel Marchak and Peretz Markish, the pianist Emil Guilels, the writer Vasily Grossman, and the physicist Pyotr Kapitza, the father of the Soviet nuclear bomb. The committee soon outgrew its original purpose as an official propaganda machine and became instead a genuine center for Jewish solidarity, and also a representative body for Soviet Jewry. In February 1944 the leaders of the committee—Mikhoels, Isaac Fefer, and Grigory Epstein—sent Stalin a letter proposing the creation of an autonomous Jewish republic in the Crimea to replace the largely unsuccessful national Jewish state of Birobidzhan established in the 1930s. During the previous decade fewer than 40,000 Jews had moved to this distant, forgotten region of deserts and marshes in extreme eastern Siberia, on the borders of China.[3]

The committee also dedicated itself to collecting statements about Nazi massacres of Jews and any "abnormal events concerning Jews," a euphemism for any antisemitic behavior noted in the population. There were a considerable number of such "events." Antisemitic traditions were still strong in Ukraine and in certain western regions of Russia, notably in the ancient "pale of settlements" of the Russian empire, where Jews had been authorized to live by the tsarist authorities. The first defeats of the Red Army revealed how wide-spread antisemitism actually was among the population. NKVD reports about attitudes of the population revealed that many people had responded positively to Nazi propaganda claiming that the Germans were fighting only Communists and Jews. In regions that had been occupied by the Germans, and particularly in Ukraine, the open massacre of Jews met with little resistance from the local population. The Germans recruited more than 80,000 troops in Ukraine, and some of these definitely participated in the massacre of Jews. To counter Nazi propaganda and to mobilize the whole of the country around the theme of the struggle for survival of the whole Soviet people, Bolshevik ideology was initially quite resistant to the specific nature of the Holocaust. It was against this backdrop that first anti-Zionism and then official antisemitism began to flour-ish. Antisemitism was particularly virulent in the Agitprop (Agitation and Propaganda) Department of the Central Committee. As early as August 1942 that body sent out an internal memorandum regarding "the dominant role played by Jews in artistic, literary, and journalistic milieus."

The activism of the Jewish Anti-Fascist Committee was soon a cause of concern to the authorities. In early 1945 the Jewish poet Peretz Markish was forbidden to publish. The appearance of the *Black Book* about Nazi atrocities against Jews was canceled on the pretext that "the central argument of the whole book is the idea that the Germans made war on the U.S.S.R. only as an attempt to wipe out the Jews." On 12 October 1946, Viktor Abakumov, the minister of state security, sent a note to the Central Committee about "the nationalist tendencies of the Jewish Anti-Fascist Committee."[4] Because Stalin sought to follow a foreign policy favorable to the establishment of the state of Israel, he did not react immediately. Only after the U.S.S.R. had voted at the United Nations to partition Palestine, on 29 November 1947, was Abakumov given a free hand to liquidate the committee.

On 19 December 1947 several of the committee's members were arrested. On 13 January 1948 Solomon Mikhoels was found murdered in Minsk; accord-ing to the official version of events, he had been in an auto accident. On 21 November 1948 the Jewish Anti-Fascist Committee was broken up on the pretext that it had become a "center for anti-Soviet propaganda," and its various publications, including the notable Yiddish journal *Einikait*, were banned.[5] In the following weeks the remaining members of the committee were arrested, and in February 1949 the vast "anticosmopolitan" campaign began in the press. Jewish theater critics were denounced for their inability to under-stand the Russian national character: "What vision can a [Abram] Gurvich or a [Josif] Yuzovsky possibly have of the national character of Russian So-viet men?" asked *Pravda* on 2 February 1949. Hundreds of Jewish intellectuals were arrested, notably in Moscow and Leningrad, in the first few months of 1949.

A revealing document from this period, a decree from the Judicial Collegium of the Leningrad Court, dated 7 July 1949 and recently published in *Neva* magazine, condemned Achille Grigorevich Leniton, Ilya Zeilkovich Serman, and Rulf Alexandrovna Zevina to ten years in the camps for several alleged crimes, most significantly for "having criticized in an anti-Soviet manner the resolution of the Central Committee regarding the magazines *Zvezda* and *Leningrad* . . . for interpreting Marx's opinions on international affairs in a counterrevolutionary manner, for praising cosmopolitan writers . . . and for spreading lies about Soviet government policy regarding the question of nationality." After an appeal the sentence was increased to twenty-five years by the Judicial Collegium of the Supreme Court, which justified its verdict as follows: "The sentence passed by the Leningrad Court failed to take account of the gravity of the offenses committed . . . The accused had been involved in counterrevolutionary activities, using nationalist prejudices to proclaim the superiority of one nation over the other nations of the Soviet Union."[6]

Thereafter Jews were systematically removed from all positions of authority in the arts and the media, in journalism and publishing, and in medicine and many other professions. Arrests became more and more common, striking all sorts of milieus. A group of "engineer saboteurs" in the metallurgy complex in Stalino, almost all of whom were Jewish, were sentenced to death and executed on 12 August 1952. Paulina Zhemchuzhina, Molotov's Jewish wife, who was a top manager in the textile industry, was arrested on 21 January 1949 for "losing documents containing state secrets" and was sent to a camp for five years. The wife of Stalin's personal secretary Aleksandr Poskrebyshev, who was also Jewish, was accused of espionage and shot in July 1952.[7] Both Molotov and Poskrebyshev continued to serve Stalin as though nothing had happened.

Despite this widespread antisemitism, preparations for the trial of the Jewish Anti-Fascist Committee dragged on for a long time. The trial did not begin, *in camera*, until May 1952, more than two and a half years after the arrest of the accused. The incomplete documentary evidence now available suggests two possible reasons for the exceptionally long period of preparation. One is that Stalin was then orchestrating in great secrecy the "Leningrad Affair," an important case that together with the Jewish Anti-Fascist Committee matter was to form one of the cornerstones of the great final purge. The other is that Stalin was concurrently involved in completely reorganizing the security services. Abakumov's arrest in July 1951 proved to be the central episode in this reorganization. This action was directed against the powerful Lavrenti Beria, the longtime head of the secret police and a member of the Politburo. Thus the Jewish Anti-Fascist Committee affair was at the heart of a power struggle, and was also to form a keystone in the series of arguments that were to result in the Doctors' Plot and lead to a second Great Terror.

Of all these purported activities, the Leningrad Affair, which led to the secret executions of the main leaders of the Soviet Communist Party's second-most-important branch organization, is still by far the most mysterious. Stalin had always been suspicious of the city. On 15 February 1949 the Politburo adopted a resolution "on the anti-Party activities of [Nikolai] Kuznetsov, [M. I.] Rodionov, and [Pyotr] Popkov," three high-ranking Party officials. The three were immediately forced to resign, as were Ivan Voznesensky, the president of Gosplan, the state planning department, and most of the members of Leningrad's Party apparatus. In August–September 1949 all these officials were arrested and accused of having attempted to establish an "anti-Party" group with the help of American intelligence services. Abakumov then launched a witch-hunt for anyone who had once been a member of the Party in Leningrad but had since moved to another city or republic. Hundreds of Communists in Leningrad were arrested, and about 2,000 were hounded out of the Party and deprived of their jobs. The repression had some strange twists, striking the city itself as a historical entity. In August 1949 the authorities decided to close the Museum of the Defense of Leningrad, which was a reminder of the heroism of the city during the siege of the Great Patriotic War. A few months later Mikhail Suslov, a high-ranking CPSU official responsible for ideological affairs, was instructed by the Central Committee to form a commission for the liquidation of the museum. This commission functioned until the end of February 1953.[8]

The accused in the Leningrad Affair—Kuznetsov, Rodionov, Popkov, Voznesensky, Ya. F. Kapustin, and P. G. Lazutin—were judged *in camera* on 30 September 1950 and executed the following day, one hour after the verdict was announced. The entire business was shrouded in secrecy; nobody was informed of it, not even the daughter of one of the principal suspects, who was the daughter-in-law of Anastas Mikoyan, the Soviet trade minister and a member of the CPSU Politburo. In October 1950 other travesties of justice condemned to death dozens of Party leaders who had belonged to the Leningrad organization: K. Soloviev, first secretary of the Crimean regional committee; Aleksei Badaev, second secretary of the Leningrad regional committee; Verbitsky, second secretary of the Murmansk regional committee; M. V. Basov, first deputy chairman of the Russian Council of Ministers; and many others.[9]

It is not yet clear whether this purge of the Leningrad Party organization was a simple settling of scores between factions of the Party apparatus or another link in a whole chain of affairs, stretching from the liquidation of the

Jewish Anti-Fascist Committee to the Doctors' Plot, and including the arrest of Abakumov and the Mingrelian nationalist plot. This second hypothesis is perhaps the more probable. The Leningrad Affair was without doubt a significant stage in the preparation of a great purge, for which the public signal was given on 13 January 1953. In quite significant fashion, the crimes of which the fallen Leningrad leaders were accused were strongly reminiscent of the dark years of 1936–1938. At the first plenary meeting of Leningrad Party cadres in October 1949, Andrei Andrianov, the new first secretary, announced to the startled audience that the previous leaders had been found to have published Trotskyite and Zinovievite literature: "In documents published by these people, they were surreptitiously passing on the opinions of some of the worst enemies of the people, Zinoviev, Kamenev, Trotsky, and others." Beyond the grotesqueness of the accusation, the message was clear for Party cadres. A new 1937 was indeed beginning.[10]

After the execution of the principal suspects in the Leningrad Affair in October 1950, there was much maneuvering and countermaneuvering within the security services and the Ministry of Internal Affairs. Having become suspicious of Beria himself, Stalin invented a fictitious Mingrelian nationalist plot whose aim was supposedly to join Mingrelia, the region in Georgia where Beria got his start, to Turkey. Beria was thus forced to lead a purge within the Georgian Communist Party.[11] In October 1951 Stalin dealt Beria another blow by having a group of elderly Jewish cadres in the security forces and the judiciary arrested, including Lt. Colonel Naum Eitingon, who under Beria's orders had organized Trotsky's assassination; General Leonid Raikhman, who had taken part in setting up the Moscow trials; Colonel Lev Shvartzman, the torturer of Babel and Meyerhold; and Lev Sheinin, the examining magistrate who had been Vyshinsky's righthand man during the Moscow show-trials of 1936–1938. All were accused of organizing a huge Jewish nationalist plot, led by Abakumov, the minister of state security and Beria's principal assistant.

Abakumov had been secretly arrested a few months earlier, on 12 July 1951. He was first accused of having deliberately killed Jacob Etinger, a well-known Jewish doctor who had been arrested in November 1950 and had died in custody shortly afterward. It was claimed that by "eliminating" Etinger, who in his long career had looked after Sergei Kirov, Sergo Ordzhonikidze, Marshal Tukhachevsky, Palmiro Togliatti, Tito, and Georgi Dimitrov, Abakumov had ensured that "a criminal group of nationalist Jews who had infiltrated the highest levels of the Ministry of State Security would not be unmasked." A few months later it was claimed that Abakumov himself was the brains behind the whole nationalist Jewish plot. Abakumov's arrest in July 1951 thus constituted a vital link in the formulation of a vast "Judeo-Zionist plot," and provided the transition between the still-secret liquidation of the Jewish Anti-Fascist

Committee and the Doctors' Plot, which was to be the public signal for the beginning of a new purge. One can therefore conclude that it was during the summer of 1951, and not at the end of 1952, that the scenario began to take shape.[12]

The secret trial of the members of the Jewish Anti-Fascist Committee lasted from 11 to 15 July 1952. Thirteen of the accused were sentenced to death and executed on 12 August 1952 along with ten other "engineer saboteurs," all Jewish, from the Stalin automobile factory. In all, the Jewish Anti-Fascist Committee affair led to 125 sentences, including 25 death sentences, which were carried out immediately, and 100 camp sentences of between ten and twenty-five years.[13]

By September 1952 the scenario for the Judeo-Zionist conspiracy was ready, but it was not put into action until after the Nineteenth Party Congress, in October (thirteen and a half years after the Eighteenth Congress). As soon as the Congress adjourned, most of the Jewish doctors who were to be accused in the Doctors' Plot were arrested, imprisoned, and tortured. These arrests, which were kept secret for some time, coincided with the trial of Rudolf Slánský, the former general secretary of the Czechoslovak Communist Party, and of thirteen other Czechoslovak Communist leaders, which began in Prague on 22 November 1952. Eleven of them were condemned to death and hanged. One of the peculiarities of that travesty, which was organized in its entirety by Soviet advisers from the secret police, was its openly antisemitic character. Eleven of the fourteen accused were Jewish, and the charge was that they had set up a "Trotskyite-Titoist-Zionist terrorist group." Preparations for the trials included a witch-hunt for Jews in all the Eastern European Communist parties.

The day after the execution of eleven of the accused in the Slánský trial, Stalin forced the Presidium of the CPSU Central Committee to vote for a resolution titled "On the Present Situation at the Ministry of State Security," which ordered a "tightening of discipline within the state security organs." The ministry itself was brought under the spotlight: supposedly it had been too lax, shown a lack of vigilance, and allowed "saboteur doctors" to operate with impunity. A further step had thus been taken. Stalin's intention, clearly, was to use the Doctors' Plot against both the Security Ministry and Beria himself. And Beria, who was himself a specialist in such affairs, must have been well aware of the implications of what he could see. ·

What exactly happened in the weeks leading up to Stalin's death is still largely unknown. Preparations for the interrogation and trial of the doctors who had been arrested continued behind the scenes as an official campaign gathered momentum for a "reinforcement of Bolshevik vigilance," a "struggle against all forms of complacency," and exemplary punishments for the "cosmopolitan assassins." Each day more arrests widened the scope of the "conspiracy."

On 19 February 1953 Ivan Maisky, a deputy minister of foreign affairs and one of Molotov's chief aides, who had previously been Soviet ambassador in London, was arrested. After relentless interrogation he "confessed" that he had been recruited as a British spy by Winston Churchill, together with Aleksandra Kollontai, a grand figure in the history of Bolshevism, who had been one of the leaders of the Workers' Opposition in 1921 and who until the end of World War II had been the Soviet ambassador in Stockholm.[14]

Despite the sensational progress that was made in "uncovering" the conspiracy from its beginning on 13 January to Stalin's death on 5 March, it is noteworthy that unlike during the years 1936–1938, none of the other leaders of the regime came forward in public and openly endorsed the investigation of the affair. According to testimony from Nikolai Bulganin in 1970, Stalin was the main inspiration and orchestrator of the Doctors' Plot, and only four of the other top leaders actually knew what was going on: Georgy Malenkov, Mikhail Suslov, Martemyam Ryumin, and Sergei Ignatiev. Accordingly, everyone else must have felt under threat. Bulganin also claimed that the trial of the Jewish doctors was to have opened in mid-March, and was to have been concluded with the massive deportation of Soviet Jews to Birobidzhan.[15] Given the current state of knowledge and the continued lack of access to the Russian Presidential Archive, where the most secret and sensitive files are kept, it is impossible to know with certainty whether plans were really afoot for a large-scale deportation of Jews in early 1953. One thing alone is certain: Stalin's death finally put an end to the list of the millions of victims who suffered under his dictatorship.

15 The Exit from Stalinism

Stalin's death, coming in the middle of the Soviet Union's seven decades of existence, marked a decisive stage. Although it was not the end of the system, it was at least the end of an era. As François Furet wrote, the death of the Supreme Leader revealed "the paradox of a system that was supposedly part of the laws of social development, but in which everything actually depended on one man, so much so that when he died, it seemed that the system had lost something essential to its continued existence." One of the major components of this "something essential" was the high level of inhuman repression by the state against the people in a number of different forms.

For Stalin's main collaborators, including Malenkov, Molotov, Voroshilov, Mikoyan, Kaganovich, Khrushchev, Bulganin, and Beria, the political problem posed by Stalin's death was extremely complex. They had at once to assure the continuity of the system, divide up responsibilities, and find some sort of equilibrium between individual dominance—however attenuated—by any one of their number and collective rule, which would take account of all their ambitions and skills. They also promptly had to introduce a number of major changes, about which there was considerable agreement.

The difficulty of combining these diverse objectives accounts for the extremely slow and tortuous process that started with Stalin's death and culminated in the elimination of the threat posed by Beria, who was arrested on 26 June 1953.

The shorthand reports that are now available of the plenary sessions of the Central Committee on 5 March 1953 (the day of Stalin's death) and again from 2 to 7 July 1953 (after the elimination of Beria) help explain why the Soviet leaders began this "exit from Stalinism" that Nikita Khrushchev was to transform into "de-Stalinization."[1] The process would have its high points at the Twentieth Congress of the Soviet Communist Party in February 1956 and the Twenty-second Congress in October 1961.

One impetus for the move away from Stalinism was quite simply a defense mechanism, an instinct for survival. During the last few months of Stalin's reign, almost all the top leaders had become aware of how vulnerable they actually were. No one had been safe—not Voroshilov, who had been accused of being an agent for foreign intelligence services; nor Molotov and Mikoyan, who had been removed from the Presidium of the Central Committee, nor Beria, who had been under threat from intrigues at the heart of the security services orchestrated by Stalin himself. Further down the hierarchy, the bureaucratic elites that had been regrouping since the war also feared and ultimately rejected the terrorist aspects of the regime. The omnipotence of the secret police was the last obstacle to their enjoying a stable career. What had to be dismantled, as Martin Malia has phrased it, was "the mechanism set up by Stalin for his own private use" to ensure that no single figure would be able to advance further than his colleagues and political rivals. Rather than differences of opinion about the reforms that had to be undertaken, what really mobilized Stalin's heirs to turn against Beria was the fear of seeing another dictator come to power. Beria appeared to be the most powerful figure because he had the whole state security apparatus and the Ministry of Internal Affairs at his disposal. The lesson was quite obvious to all concerned: the apparatus of repression should never again "escape the control of the Party" and be allowed to become the weapon of a single individual and thus threaten the political oligarchy.

The second and more profound reason for the change was the realization shared by all the main leaders, from Khrushchev to Malenkov, that economic and social reform was now of prime necessity. The exclusively repressive management of the economy, based on the authoritarian control of almost all agricultural production, the criminalization of various forms of behavior, and the atrophying Gulag system, had resulted in a serious economic crisis and social stagnation that rendered impossible any increase in labor productivity. The economic model put into place in the 1930s against the will of the vast majority of the people had brought the results described above and was now perceived to be outdated.

The third reason for change was the struggle for power itself, which led to a constant raising of the stakes among the politicians. It was Nikita Khrushchev, who for reasons that will not be detailed here (suffice it to say that he was able to confront his own Stalinist past, seemed to feel genuine remorse, was a skillful politician and a great populist with a real belief in a better future, and had the will to return to what he considered to be a legitimately socialist position), went further than his colleagues in aiming for a slow and gradual process of de-Stalinization, not only in the political arena but also in the day-to-day lives of the people.

What were the principal steps of this movement in dismantling the repressive machinery? In the space of a few years the Soviet Union changed from a country with an extremely high level of legal and extralegal repression into an authoritarian police state, where for more than a generation the memory of the terror was one of the most effective guarantees of post-Stalinist order.

Less than two weeks after Stalin's death, the gulag system was completely reorganized and brought under the authority of the Ministry of Justice. Its economic infrastructure was immediately transferred to the relevant industrial ministries. Even more spectacular than these administrative changes, which demonstrated clearly that the Ministry of Internal Affairs was losing its place as the most powerful ministry, was the announcement, in *Pravda* on 28 March 1953, of a large amnesty. By virtue of a decree promulgated by the Presidium of the Supreme Soviet of the U.S.S.R. the previous day and signed by its president, Voroshilov, the following were granted amnesty:

> Anyone sentenced to less than five years
> Anyone sentenced for lying, economic crimes, and abuses of power
> Pregnant women and mothers with children under age ten, minors, men over fifty-five, and women over fifty

In addition, the amnesty provided for the halving of all other sentences except those handed out for counterrevolutionary activities, grand theft, banditry, and premeditated murder.

In a few weeks about 1.2 million prisoners—nearly half the population of the camps and penal colonies—were released from the gulags. Many of them were small-time criminals sentenced for petty theft; still more were simple citizens who had been convicted under one of the innumerable repressive laws that governed every sphere of activity, from "leaving the workplace" to "breaking the law regarding internal passports." This partial amnesty, which notably excluded political prisoners and special deportees, reflected in its very ambiguity the still ill-defined changes that were afoot. The spring of 1953, a time of tortuous reasoning, was also a time of intense power struggles when even

Lavrenti Beria, the first deputy chairman of the Council of Ministers and minister of internal affairs, seemed to be turning into a great reformer.

What considerations dictated such a large amnesty? According to Amy Knight, the biographer of Beria, the amnesty of 27 March 1953, which was adopted at the behest of the minister of internal affairs himself, was part of a series of political measures indicating a new, liberal direction in the thinking of Beria, who, like the others, was involved in the power struggle after Stalin's death and was thus also caught up in the spiral of rising political stakes. To justify the amnesty, Beria had sent a note to the Presidium of the Central Committee on 24 March in which he explained that of the 2,526,402 prisoners in the gulags, only 221,435 were "particularly dangerous criminals," and that most of those were kept in special camps. In an astonishing admission, he noted that an overwhelming share of prisoners posed no threat to the state. A large amnesty was therefore desirable to free up a penal system that was both over-crowded and intrinsically unwieldy.[2]

The issue of the increasing difficulty of managing the gulags was regularly raised in the early 1950s. The crisis in the camps, which was widely acknowl-edged before Stalin's death, puts the amnesty of 27 March in a new light. Economic as well as political reasons induced the potential successors of Stalin to proclaim a large but partial amnesty. They were aware that the gulags were overcrowded and totally inefficient.

Here, as elsewhere, no radical measures could be taken so long as Stalin was still alive. As the historian Moshe Lewin once noted so aptly, everything was "mummified" in the last years of the dictatorship.

Even after Stalin's death, of course, not everything was possible. The principal victims of the system's arbitrary nature—the political prisoners con-demned for counterrevolutionary activities—failed to benefit from the amnesty. The exclusion of political prisoners from the amnesty sparked a number of riots and revolts among prisoners in the special gulag camps and in the Rechlag and Steplag.[3]

On 4 April it was announced in *Pravda* that the conspirators of the Doctors' Plot had themselves been the victims of a miscarriage of justice, and that their confessions had been extracted "by illegitimate means of interroga-tion," which everyone understood to mean torture. The importance of this acknowledgment was amplified further by a resolution adopted by the Central Committee a few days later "on legal violations by the state security forces." It emerged clearly that the Doctors' Plot had not been an isolated incident, and that for some years the security forces had been abusing their powers and had been involved in illegal activities. The Party claimed that it was now rejecting these methods and clamping down on the excessive powers of the police. The hope engendered by these statements immediately elicited an enormous response, and the courts were swamped by hundreds of thousands of demands for rehabilitation. Prisoners, particularly those in the special camps, were exasperated by the limited and selective nature of the amnesty of 27 March. They were well aware of the turmoil among the guards and the systemwide crisis, and they simply turned on the guards and commanders, refusing to work or to obey orders. On 14 May 1953 more than 14,000 prisoners from different sections of the Norilsk penitentiary organized a strike and formed committees composed of delegates elected from various national groups, in which Ukrainians and people from the Baltic states played key roles. The main demands of the prisoners were a reduction of the working day to nine hours, the elimination of labels on their clothes, an end to restrictions on communication with their families, the removal of all informers, and an extension of the amnesty to include political prisoners.

The official announcement on 10 July 1953 of the arrest of Beria, who was accused of being an English spy and an avowed enemy of the people, confirmed the prisoners' impression that something had indeed changed in Moscow and made them even more forceful in their demands. The strike became increasingly widespread; on 14 July more than 12,000 prisoners from the Vorkuta prison complex also went on strike. One sure sign that things had changed was that the authorities began to negotiate with the prisoners, repeatedly postponing an attack.

Unrest was endemic in the special camps from the summer of 1953 until the Twentieth Party Congress in February 1956. The largest and most sustained revolt broke out in May 1954, in the third section of the Steplag prison complex in Kengir, near Karaganda in Kazakhstan. It went on for forty days and was put down only after special troops from the Internal Affairs Ministry had surrounded the camp with tanks. About 400 prisoners were arrested and resentenced, and the six surviving members of the commission that had led the resistance were executed.

Another sign that things had genuinely changed with the death of Stalin was the fact that some of the demands made by the striking prisoners in 1953 and 1954 were actually met; the working day was indeed reduced to nine hours, and other significant improvements in the quality of life for prisoners were introduced.

In 1954–55 the government took a series of measures that significantly altered the enormous power of the state security forces, which had been totally reorganized in the aftermath of Beria's arrest. The *troiki*—the special courts that judged all cases handled by the secret police—were abolished altogether. The secret police were reorganized into an autonomous entity, renamed the Komitet Gosudarstvennoi Bezopasnosti (the Committee for State Security, or KGB), purged of one-fifth of all personnel who had worked there before

Stalin's death, and placed under the authority of General Ivan Serov, whose achievements included oversight of the deportation of various ethnic groups during the war. An associate of Nikita Khrushchev, Serov embodied many of the ambiguities of a transitional period in which previous leaders were still in positions of authority. The government decreed more partial amnesties, the most important of which, in September 1955, freed everyone who had been sentenced in 1945 for "collaborating with the enemy," as well as the remaining German prisoners of war. Finally, several measures benefited the "specially displaced," who were henceforth allowed to move around more freely, and no longer required to register quite so regularly at the local *komandatury*. Following high-level German-Soviet negotiations, German deportees, who represented 40 percent of those held in special colonies (more than 1,000,000 out of approximately 2,750,000), were the first to benefit in September 1955 from the easing of restrictions. However, the wording of the new laws made it clear that the lifting of judicial restrictions and the changes in professional status and residency requirements would not lead to "the return of confiscated goods or a right to return to the place from which the 'specially displaced' had originated."[4]

These restrictions were a significant part of the partial and gradual process that came to be known as de-Stalinization. Carried out under the direction of a Stalinist, Nikita Khrushchev (who, like all the other leaders of his generation, had played a major role in the worst acts of repression, such as dekulakization, purges, deportations, and executions), de-Stalinization could afford to condemn only certain excesses of the "cult of personality." In his "Secret Speech" to the Soviet delegates at the Twentieth Party Congress on 24 February 1956, Khrushchev was extremely selective in his condemnation of Stalinism and did not call into question any of the major decisions taken by the Party since 1917. This selectivity was also apparent in the chronology of the Stalinist "deviation." Because this deviation supposedly began in 1934, it excluded the crimes of collectivization and the famine of 1932–33. The selectivity was also apparent in the choice of victims, who were all Communists and had generally followed the Stalinist line; they were never ordinary citizens. By restricting the list of victims of oppression to Communists who had suffered at Stalin's hand, and by focusing solely on historical episodes that happened after the assassination of Kirov, the Secret Speech evaded the central question of the collective responsibility of the Party toward society since 1917.

The Secret Speech was followed by a series of concrete measures to complete the limited steps that had already been taken. In March and April 1956 decrees were issued in regard to "specially displaced" persons from ethnic groups that had been punished for supposedly collaborating with Nazi Germany and deported in 1943–1945. These people, according to the decrees, were "no longer to be subject to administrative surveillance by the Internal Affairs Ministry." There was, however, no restoration of their confiscated goods, nor were they allowed to return home. These half-measures were met with considerable anger; many deportees refused to sign statements requiring them to abandon all claims for compensation, the restoration of their goods, and the right to return home. Faced with a remarkable shift in the political climate and the popular mood, the Soviet government made new concessions. On 9 January 1957 the government once again recognized the republics and autonomous regions of the deported peoples, which had been abolished in the immediate aftermath of the war. Only the autonomous republic of the Tatars in the Crimea was not reinstated.

For more than three decades the Crimean Tatars struggled for their right to return home. From 1957 on, the Karachai, Kalmyks, Balkars, Chechens, and Ingush slowly began to return by the tens of thousands. Nothing was made easy for them by the authorities. Numerous disputes broke out between deportees trying to move back into their former homes and the Russian colonists who had been brought there from neighboring regions in 1945. Having no *propiski*— licenses from the local police granting the right to live in a given place—the returning deportees were again forced to live in shantytowns, encampments, and other temporary housing, under the permanent threat of arrest for failing to comply with passport laws (an offense that brought two years' imprisonment). In July 1958 the Chechen capital, Grozny, was the scene of bloody confrontations between Russians and Chechens. An uneasy peace was established only after the authorities freed up funds to build accommodations for the former deportees.[5]

Officially, the category of "specially displaced" existed until January 1960. The last deportees to be freed from this pariah status were Ukrainians and people from the Baltic states. Faced with the prospect of more administrative obstacles to their return, more than half of the Ukrainians and Baltic peoples settled in the places to which they had been deported.

In 1954–55 90,000 "counterrevolutionaries" were released from the gulags; in 1956–57, after the Twentieth Congress, nearly 310,000 were freed. On 1 January 1959 only 11,000 political prisoners remained in the camps.[6] To expedite the release of prisoners, more than 200 special review commissions were sent into the camps, and several amnesties were decreed. Liberation, however, was not synonymous with rehabilitation. In 1956 and 1957 fewer than 60,000 people received any sort of pardon. The vast majority had to wait for years, and sometimes decades, before obtaining a certificate of rehabilitation. Nevertheless, the year 1956 remained engraved in popular memory as the year of the return, admirably described by Vasily Grossman in his novel *All Things Pass*. This great return, which took place in almost total silence as far as official pronouncements were concerned, together with the realization that for millions no return would ever be possible, threw many people into deep confusion and began a vast social and moral trauma, a tragic confrontation in a divided society. As Lidia Chukovskaya wrote, "two Russias looked each other in the eye: the one who had imprisoned, and the one who had been imprisoned." Faced with such a situation, the initial response of the authorities was not to accede to the demands of any individual or group regarding the prosecution of officials who had broken socialist law or used any illegal methods of investigation during the "cult of personality." The only means of appeal were the Party control commissions. The political authorities sent instructions to the courts regarding pardons, making it clear that the first priorities were Party members and soldiers. There were no purges.

After the release of political prisoners, the post-Stalin gulags saw the number of inmates dwindle, before stabilizing in the late 1950s and early 1960s at around 900,000 prisoners: a core of 300,000 common criminals and repeat offenders serving long sentences and 600,000 petty criminals who had been sentenced in accordance with laws requiring prison terms quite out of proportion to the offense committed. The pioneering role played by the gulags in colonization and in exploitation of the natural and mineral wealth of the far north and east began to fade, and the huge Stalinist prisons were slowly broken up into smaller units. The geography of the gulags changed, too. Most camps were again established in the European part of the U.S.S.R. Confinement in the post-Stalin era took on the more conventional purpose that it has in other societies, although it retained features that distinguished it from the normal legal system. Various groups were sporadically added to the common criminals in accordance with whatever crackdown was in force at the time—on alcoholism, vandalism, "parasitism"—and a few (several hundred each year) were sentenced under Articles 70 and 190 of the new penal code, adopted in 1960.

These commutations and amnesties were completed by some major changes in penal legislation. Among the first reforms was the law of 25 April 1956, which abolished the 1940 law forbidding workers to leave the workplace. This first step in the decriminalization of the labor laws was followed by several other partial measures, which were systematized with the adoption of new "Foundations of Penal Law" on 25 December 1958. The new laws did away with several key terms from earlier penal codes, including "enemy of the people" and "counterrevolutionary crimes." The age of legal responsibility was raised from fourteen to sixteen; the use of violence and torture to extract confessions was outlawed; people accused of crimes were to be present at all stages of the inquiry and were entitled to a lawyer who was aware of the details of the case; and, with few exceptions, all trials were to be public. The penal code of 1960 did, however, retain several articles allowing for the punishment of any form of political or ideological deviancy. Under Article 70, anyone "caught spreading anti-Soviet propaganda . . . in the form of mendacious assertions denigrating the state" could be given a sentence of six months to seven years in the camps, followed by exile for two to five years. Article 190 required a sentence of three years in the camps or in community-service work for any failure to denounce anti-Soviet behavior. During the 1960s and 1970s these two articles were widely used to punish political or ideological "deviancy." Ninety percent of the several hundred people sentenced each year for "anti-Sovietism" were found guilty under these two articles.

During the political thaw, when the quality of life was clearly rising although memories of the oppression remained strong, active forms of debate or dissent remained rare. KGB reports noted 1,300 "opponents" in 1961, 2,500 in 1962, 4,500 in 1964, and 1,300 in 1965.[7] In the 1960s and 1970s three categories of citizens were the object of particularly close surveillance by the KGB: religious minorities (such as Catholics, Baptists, members of the Pentecostal Church, and Seventh-Day Adventists); national minorities who had been hardest hit by the Stalinist repressions (notably people from the Baltic states, Tatars from the Crimea, ethnic Germans, and Ukrainians from western Ukraine, where anti-Soviet resistance had been particularly strong); and the creative intelligentsia belonging to the dissident movement that grew up in the 1960s.[8]

After a last anticlerical campaign, launched in 1957, which limited itself to closing several churches that had reopened since the war, the confrontation between the Orthodox Church and the state subsided into uneasy cohabitation. The attention of the KGB's special services was directed more toward religious minorities, who were often suspected of receiving assistance and support from abroad. A few numbers demonstrate that this was indeed a marginal concern: from 1973 to 1975, 116 Baptists were arrested; in 1984, 200 Baptists were either in prison or serving a sentence in a camp, and the average sentence was only one year.

In western Ukraine, one of the regions most resistant to Sovietization, a dozen or so nationalist groups in the OUN tradition were broken up in Ternopil, Zaporizhzhia, Ivano-Frankivsk, and Lviv between 1961 and 1973. Sentences passed on the members of these groups generally amounted to five to ten years in prison. In Lithuania, another region that had been brutally brought to heel in the 1940s, local sources reveal that there were comparatively few arrests in the 1960s and 1970s. The murder of three Catholic priests under suspicious circumstances in 1981, in which it was almost certain that the KGB was involved, was, however, felt to be an act of intolerable provocation.

Until the breakup of the U.S.S.R., the Crimean Tatars, who had been deported in 1944 and whose autonomous republic was never reinstated, remained a burdensome legacy of the Stalinist era. At the end of the 1950s the Crimean Tatars, most of whom had been settled in Central Asia, began a campaign (yet another sign that times really had changed) petitioning for their collective rehabilitation and for authorization to return to their homeland. In 1966 a petition of 130,000 signatures was delivered by a Tatar delegation to the Twenty-third Party Congress. In September 1967 a decree from the Presidium of the Supreme Soviet annulled the charge of "collective treason." Three months later a new decree authorized the Tatars to settle in a location of their choice, provided they respected the passport laws, which required a legal document to work in any given place. Between 1967 and 1978 fewer than 15,000 people—about 2 percent of the Tatar population—managed to comply with the passport law and return home. The Crimean Tatar movement was assisted by General Petro Grigorenko, who was arrested in May 1967 and sent to a psychiatric hospital, a form of imprisonment used for several dozen people each year in the 1970s.

Most historians date the beginning of the dissident movement from the first big public trial of political prisoners in the post-Stalin era. In February 1966 two writers, Andrei Sinyavsky and Yuri Daniel, were given sentences of seven and five years respectively in a prison camp. On 5 December 1965, shortly after the arrest of the writers, a demonstration of about fifty people supporting them took place in Pushkin Square in Moscow. The dissidents, who in the 1960s numbered a few hundred intellectuals, and who at the height of the movement a decade later numbered between 1,000 and 2,000, began a radically different means of protest. Instead of arguing against the legality of the regime, they demanded a strict respect for Soviet laws, for the constitution, and for international agreements signed by the U.S.S.R. Dissident action followed the same line. They refused to be treated as an underground group, they were quite open about their structure and movements, and they made great use of publicity to advertise their actions by cooperating as often as possible with the international media.

In the disproportionate struggle between a few hundred dissidents and the might of the Soviet state, the weight of international opinion was extremely important, particularly following the publication in the West in 1973 of Aleksandr Solzhenitsyn's *Gulag Archipelago* (which was quickly followed by his expulsion from the Soviet Union). In the space of a few years, because of the actions of a tiny minority, the issue of human rights in the U.S.S.R. became a major international concern and the central subject of the Conference on Security and Cooperation in Europe, which culminated in the Helsinki Accords of 1975. The final document produced by the conference, which was signed by the U.S.S.R., strengthened the position of the dissidents. They organized committees to ensure that the Helsinki agreement was upheld in the cities in which they lived (Moscow, Leningrad, Kyiv, Vilnius, and so on) and to forward any information about human-rights violations. This information-gathering had already started under more difficult conditions in 1968, with the appearance every few months of an underground bulletin called the *Chronicle of Current Events*, which listed any violations of liberty or human rights. In this new context, human-rights violations in the U.S.S.R. swiftly came under international scrutiny, and the secret police in particular were held in check. As opponents of the regime became recognized figures, their arrest could no longer pass unnoticed, and information about their fate could spread rapidly abroad. Significantly, patterns of police behavior were soon linked to the state of détente; arrests were more numerous in 1968–1972 and in 1979–1982 than in 1973–1976. It is still impossible to calculate the number of people arrested for political reasons in the years 1960–1985. Dissident sources listed hundreds of arrests in the worst years; in 1970 the *Chronicle of Current Events* reported 106 sentences, including 21 forcible incarcerations in psychiatric hospitals "as a security measure." In 1971 the figures in the *Chronicle* were 85 and 24, respectively. In 1979–1981, years of international confrontation, almost 500 people were arrested on similar charges.

The phenomenon of dissidence was an expression of radical opposition reflecting a totally different conception of politics, one that counterposed individuality to collectivity. But in a country in which the government had always been opposed to freedom of speech, and particularly to the free expression of opinions contrary to its own, such a phenomenon was unlikely to have a huge effect on society in general. The real change was elsewhere, in the many different spheres of cultural and social autonomy that developed in the 1960s and 1970s, and even more so in the 1980s, with the gradual realization by one part of the political elite that changes as radical as those of the 1950s were once again of prime importance.

Conclusion

The preceding chapters do not pretend to offer any new revelations about the use of state violence in the U.S.S.R., or about the forms of oppression exercised by the government during the first half of the Soviet regime's existence. Such things have been explored for some time now by historians who did not have to wait for the opening of the archives to see the development or scale of the terror. On the other hand, the opening of the archives does allow an account of the terror's chronological development and of its scale and various forms. Accordingly, the outline presented in the preceding pages constitutes a first step in compiling an inventory of questions that must be asked about the use of violence, its constant recurrence, and its meaning in different contexts.

As such, this research is part of a larger movement that has been under way for a decade now both in the West and in Russia. Since the first partial opening of the archives, historians have been trying to reconcile one brand of historiography, born in unusual circumstances, with the newly available data. For several years now, a number of historians, particularly in Russia, have been publishing material that has formed the basis of many other studies and university courses. Some fields of investigation have been better covered than others, particularly the concentration camps, the confrontation between the government and the peasantry, and decision making at high levels of government. Historians such as V. N. Zemskov and N. Bugai have tried to calculate the number of deportations that took place in the Stalinist era. V. P. Danilov in Russia and A. Graziosi in Italy have highlighted the continuity in the clashes between the peasantry and the new regime. Looking at the archives of the Central Committee, O. Khlevnyuk has shed important light on the functioning of the Kremlin "First Circle."

Using such research as a basis for my own, I have attempted to demonstrate how, in the years following 1917, cycles of violence became the norm in the U.S.S.R. These cycles of violence lie at the heart of the social history of the Soviet Union, a history that is still waiting to be written. Building upon earlier efforts to explore the most tragic aspects of this history, I have drawn upon sources that most clearly expose the different forms of violence and repression, the practices involved, and the groups victimized. These sources also reveal the contradictions and inconsistencies, such as the extreme violence of the Leninist discourse regarding Menshevik opponents, who were "all to be shot" but who were usually imprisoned instead; the extraordinary violence of the requisitioning detachments, which at the end of 1922 were still terrorizing the countryside at a time when the NEP had technically already been in place for more than a year; and the contradictory alternation in the 1930s between spectacular waves of mass arrests and huge amnesties to "empty the prisons." The multiplicity of cases yields an inventory of the forms of violence and oppression used, broadening the scope of the investigation into the practices, the scale, and the meaning of mass terror.

The persistence of such practices until Stalin's death and their determining influence in the social history of the U.S.S.R. seem to justify the relegation of political history to second place, at least in the early stages of such an investigation. In this reconstruction I have tried to synthesize long-acknowledged facts with recently released documentary evidence, which constantly raises new questions. Many of these documents are reports from the grass-roots level, such as the correspondence of civil servants relating to the famine, local Cheka reports on the strikes at Tula, and administrative reports on the state of prisoners in the concentration camps—all of which reveal the concrete reality of that extremely violent world.

Before addressing the major questions at the heart of this study, it is necessary to recall the different cycles of violence and repression.

The first cycle, from the end of 1917 to the end of 1922, began with Lenin's seizure of power, which he saw as a necessary part of civil war. After a brief phase in which spontaneous social violence was channeled into more official structures, which then acted as catalysts in breaking up the old order, a deliberate offensive against the peasantry took shape in the spring of 1918. This offensive, even more than the military confrontations between the Reds and the Whites, was to provide the model for several decades of terror. It destroyed people's faith in the machinery of politics. What is striking is the constant refusal to negotiate despite the high stakes involved, the regime's tenuous hold on power, and its frequent deviations from proclaimed goals, particularly evident in the repressive measures taken against the working classes—the group one would have imagined to be the natural ally of the Bolsheviks. In this respect the Kronstadt revolt was a clear sign of things to come. The first cycle did not end with the defeat of the Whites or with the NEP, but was prolonged by the very people it created. It came to an end only with the famine of 1922, which broke the last peasant resistance.

What can one make of the short pause, from 1923 to 1927, between the two cycles of violence? There were some indications that once the civil war was over and the manpower of the secret police was scaled back, a truce of sorts would be established with the peasantry, and a reform of the legal system could be carried out. Despite these palliatives, the secret police not only remained in existence but also preserved their main functions and continued their control, eavesdropping, and surveillance operations. The pause was notable for its brevity.

Whereas the first cycle of repressions was marked by direct and generalized confrontation, the second began with an offensive by the Stalinist group against the peasantry in the context of political in-fighting at the top. The second cycle of violence was perceived as a new beginning by all parties concerned. Politicians again used methods that had been tried and tested over previous years. Violence had become such an everyday occurrence, so much a way of life, that the new terror went on for another quarter of a century. The second war against the peasantry was decisive in institutionalizing terror as a means of government. This was manifested in several different ways. Collectivization made use of preexisting social tensions, reawakening the archaic violence that was lurking beneath the surface in society; it began the system of mass deportations; and it became the proving ground for up-and-coming politicians. Furthermore, by setting up a predatory system that disrupted the cycle of production—in Bukharin's words, "the military and feudal exploitation of the peasantry"—a new form of slavery was invented. This opened the way for the most extreme experiments of Stalinism and the famine of 1933, which in the grand total of deaths under Stalin accounts for the highest number. After that limit had been reached—when there were no peasants left to sow the next harvest, and the prisons were full—another brief, two-year truce was established, and for the first time there was an amnesty. But such rare moments of relaxation did little more than generate new tensions. For example, the children of deported kulaks had their civil rights restored, but they were not permitted to return home.

After the war against the peasants, the terror began to manifest differently during the 1930s and 1940s, changing in intensity and form. The time of the Great Terror, from late 1936 to 1938, brought more than 85 percent of all the death sentences handed down during the entire Stalinist period. During these years the social origins of the victims were often extremely mixed. Although many cadres were arrested and executed, the terror claimed victims from all social backgrounds, many of whom were chosen arbitrarily when quotas had to be filled. This blind and barbarous repression, when the terror was at its height, seems to indicate that some obstacles were simply insurmountable, and that liquidation was the only course the state could find to impose its will.

Another way of investigating the sequence of repressions is to look at the social groups that were affected. Insofar as different areas of social interaction became increasingly subject to legislation throughout the decades, several discrete offensives can be discerned. The last one in particular was aimed at the ordinary people of the country, with the increase in legislation in 1938 focused almost exclusively on the working classes.

After 1940, in the context of the Sovietization of the new territories that had been annexed and the "Great Patriotic War," a series of repressions resumed. This time there were new groups of victims—the "nationalists" and "enemy peoples" who subsequently underwent systematic deportation. The early stages of this new wave were already visible in 1936 and 1937, notably in the deportation of Koreans, when the frontiers were being tightened.

The annexation of eastern Poland and then of the Baltic states in 1939–1941 led to the elimination of the "nationalist bourgeoisie" and to the deportation of specific minority groups, for example the Poles from eastern Galicia. This last practice intensified during the war despite the more pressing need to defend a country facing possible annihilation. The successive deportation of whole groups—such as Germans, Chechens, Tatars, Kalmyks—also revealed the expertise that had been developed in these operations in the 1930s. The practices, however, were not confined to the war years. They continued in other forms throughout the 1940s as part of the long process of pacification and Sovietization in the newly annexed regions of the Soviet empire. At the same time the influx of huge nationalist contingents into the Soviet gulags had an important influence on the structure and composition of the concentration camp world. Representatives of the "punished peoples" and nationalist resistance fighters soon outnumbered the Soviet prisoners.

In parallel to that growth, the years immediately following the war saw yet another hardening of government policy toward various forms of civil behavior, resulting in a steady increase in the gulag population. The same period marked the numerical apogee of that population and the beginning of the crisis of the gulags, which were outdated, paralyzed by multiple internal tensions, and beset by ever-greater problems of economic inefficiency.

The last years of the Stalinist period, still largely shrouded in uncertainty, show a series of relapses: a resurgence of latent antisemitism; a return of the idea of the conspiracy, rivalry, and in-fighting among ill-defined factions; and the elitist and clique-ridden nature of the secret police and the regional Party organizations. Historians are led to wonder whether plans were being laid for a last campaign, a new Great Terror, whose principal victims might have been the Soviet Jews.

This brief overview of the first thirty-five years of Soviet history underscores the continuity of extreme violence as a means of political control of the society.

The classic question, often raised in this context, concerns the continuity between the first Leninist cycle and the second Stalinist cycle: to what extent did the former prefigure the latter? The historical configuration in both cases is really quite incomparable. The "Red Terror" grew out of the widespread confrontations of the autumn of 1918. The extreme nature of the repressions was in part a reaction to the radical character of the times. But the restarting of the war against the peasantry, which was at the root of the second wave of terror, occurred during what was basically a time of peace, and was part of a long-lasting offensive against the majority of society. Besides these important differences in context, the use of terror as a key instrument in the Leninist political project had been foreseen before the outbreak of the civil war, and was intended to be of limited duration. From that point of view, the short truce ushered in by the NEP and the complex debates among Bolshevik leaders about possible ways forward seem to indicate the possibility of normalized relations between the Bolsheviks and society and the abandonment of terror as a means of government. In practice, however, during this period the rural world lived in retreat, and the relationship between the government and society was characterized largely by mutual ignorance.

The war against the peasants is the nexus linking these two cycles of violence. The practices that emerged in 1918–1922 continued. In both periods, requisitioning campaigns were used, social tensions within the peasantry were encouraged, and archaic forms of brutality became commonplace. Both executioners and victims had the conviction that they were reliving a previous scenario.

Even if the Stalinist era represents a specific social context in the use of terror as a means of government and social management, questions remain about links with other periods in Soviet history. In that respect the policy of deportation, for example, might have an important antecedent in the de-Cossackization operations of 1919–20. At the moment when Cossack territories were being seized, the government began a deportation operation that affected the entire indigenous population. That operation followed one that had targeted the better-off Cossacks, ending in "large-scale physical extermination" thanks to the overzealousness of local agents. These events could be said to foreshadow the practices of a decade later, albeit on a totally different scale. Both involved the stigmatization of an entire social group, an overreaction at the local level, and an attempt at eradication through deportation. In all of these aspects there are troubling similarities to the practices of dekulakization.

If one examines in a wider sense the phenomenon of exclusion and isolation of enemy groups, and the consequent creation of a camp system during the civil war, one is forced to acknowledge that there are indeed important differences between the two cycles of repression. The camps that were developed and used during the civil war in the 1920s bore little resemblance to those of the 1930s. The great reforms of 1929 not only led to the abandonment of normal systems of detention, but also laid the foundation for a new system characterized above all by the idea of forced labor. The appearance and development of the gulag system point to the existence of a grand plan for the exclusion of a certain segment of the population, and the use of that segment in a project to transform the economy and society as a whole. Several elements point clearly to the existence of such a grand design, and have been the object of important studies. First, there is the extent to which the terror was a well-planned and well-orchestrated phenomenon. The use of quotas stretched from dekulakization to the Great Terror, a fact that can be interpreted as being part of such a plan. The archives confirm an obsession with numbers and statistics that permeated administrative organs from top to bottom. Regular, perfectly balanced statistics evince an obsessive preoccupation with the mathematical dimensions of the repression process. While such figures can never be entirely trusted, they do allow historians to reconstruct periods of intensity in the phenomenon. The chronology of the various waves of oppression is better understood today, and supports the theory of an ordered series of operations.

To a significant degree, however, reconstruction of the entire series of repressive procedures, of the chain of command, and of the methods of implementation counteracts the theory of a well-conceived, long-term plan. Looking at the planning of repressions, one can see that chance played a huge role and that cracks appeared at all stages of the operations. The deportation of the kulaks is a case in point. They were often deported with no destination in mind, and their "abandonment in deportation" is a clear indicator of the prevailing chaos. Likewise, the "campaigns of emptying" the camps suggest a lack of planning. In the transmission and execution of orders, troops often went too far too soon and were guilty of "excessive zeal" or "deviation from the path" at a grass-roots level.

The role of the gulags is also extremely complex and seems to become more so as research progresses. In contrast to the vision of a Stalinist order in which gulags were the hidden but entirely representative face of the regime, documents now available suggest contradictory interpretations. The successive arrival of repressed groups often promoted disorganization rather than efficiency in the system. Despite an extremely elaborate system of classification of the detainees, boundaries between different categories were fragile and often illusory. Moreover, the question of the system's economic profitability remains unanswered.

To contend with these contradictions, improvisations, and illogicalities, several hypotheses have been put forward to explain the frequent recourse to mass repression and the way in which violence and terror seemed to create their own logic.

Historians have stressed the role played by improvisation and the general lack of focus in directing "the Great Moment" of modernization and the unleashing of the Stalinist cycles of repression. Often the authorities would step up the intensity of terror so that they could persuade themselve that they were in control of volatile situations. They were quickly caught up in an extreme spiral of violence that almost immediately became self-perpetuating. The scale of this phenomenon escaped contemporary historians and is only now beginning to be understood. The process of repression itself, seemingly the only possible response to the conflicts and obstacles confronted by the authorities, generated uncontrollable movements that fueled the terror.

The central place of terror in the political and social history of the U.S.S.R. poses increasingly complex questions today. Current research seems to negate many of the conclusions previously drawn by Sovietologists. While historians still seek a general and definitive explanation of the whole phenomenon, it is extremely resistant to understanding. More progress is being made in understanding the mechanisms and dynamics of the violence itself.

Many gray areas remain, particularly regarding the everyday behavior of people reacting to the violence. If one wishes to find out who the executioners actually were, then it is the whole of society that must be questioned—all those who took part in the events, not just the victims.

World Revolution, Civil War, and Terror

Stéphane Courtois, Jean-Louis Panné, and Rémi Kauffer

16 The Comintern in Action

Stéphane Courtois and Jean-Louis Panné

From early on, Lenin was determined to foment socialist revolution throughout Europe and the rest of the world. This goal was partly the logical fulfillment of the *Communist Manifesto* of 1848, with its famous slogan "Workers of the world, unite!" In 1917 the spread of Bolshevism initially seemed to be an urgent matter, since the revolution in Russia, it was thought, would be endangered without revolutions in more advanced countries. In this respect Lenin looked above all to Germany, with its enormous, well-organized proletariat and its formidable industrial capacity. What had first been simply a need of the moment was transformed into a full-fledged political project: world socialist revolution.

At first the progress of events seemed to prove the Soviet leader right. The breakup of the German and Austro-Hungarian empires following their defeat in World War I brought about a series of political upheavals in Europe, many of which had a strongly revolutionary character. Even though the Bolsheviks could not take any immediate action themselves, and had to rely solely on their propaganda to give them influence abroad, revolution seemed to be breaking out spontaneously in the wake of the German and Austro-Hungarian defeat.

The Revolution in Europe

Germany was the first country to feel the effects of revolutionary upheaval. Even before its surrender, it faced a general mutiny of its naval fleet. The defeat of the Reich and the emergence of a republic led by Social Democrats resulted in some fairly violent reactions in the army and the police force, as well as among ultranationalist and revolutionary groups that admired the actions of the Bolsheviks in Russia.

In Berlin in December 1918 Rosa Luxemburg and Karl Liebknecht published the program of the Spartakus group, breaking away from the Independent Social Democratic party a few days later to set up the German Communist Party (KPD) through a merger with a few other groups. In early January 1919 the Spartakists, led by Liebknecht—who was more of a radical revolutionary than Luxemburg and, like Lenin, opposed the idea of a Constituent Assembly—tried to start an insurrection in Berlin.[1] The revolt was quickly crushed by the military on orders of the Social Democratic government. The two leaders of the revolt were arrested and shot on 15 January. This pattern recurred in Bavaria, where on 13 April 1919 Eugen Leviné, a KPD leader, assumed leadership of a Republican Council, which nationalized the banks and started to form a Red Army. The Munich Commune was crushed by the military on 30 April, and Leviné was arrested on 13 May, court-martialed, condemned to death, and shot on 5 June.

The most famous example of these revolutionary movements was in Hungary. In defeat, Hungary had found the forced loss of Transylvania, decreed by the victors of the war, a hard pill to swallow.[2] It became the first genuine instance of the Bolsheviks' exporting their revolution. Beginning in early 1918 the Bolshevik Party collected all non-Russian Communist sympathizers into a group called the Federation of Foreign Communist Groups. As a result, there existed a Hungarian group in Moscow made up, for the most part, of former prisoners of war. In October 1918 this group sent some 20 members back to Hungary. On 4 November the Hungarian Workers' (Communist) Party (HCP) was established in Budapest under the leadership of Béla Kun. Kun had been a prisoner of war and had quickly rallied to the Bolshevik revolution, becoming president of the Federation of Foreign Communist Groups in April 1918. He arrived in Hungary in November, accompanied by 80 activists, and was immediately elected Party leader. It has been estimated that in late 1918 and early 1919 another 250 to 300 "agitators" and revolutionaries arrived in Hungary. With financial support provided by the Bolsheviks, the Hungarian Communists set about spreading propaganda, and their influence soon began to grow.

The official newspaper of the Social Democrats, the *Népszava* (The voice of the people), which was firmly opposed to the Bolsheviks, was attacked on

18 February 1919 by a group of soldiers and unemployed workers who had been mobilized by the Communists. Their aim was either to take control of the printing press or to destroy it. The police intervened, and in the ensuing conflict 8 people died and 100 were injured. The same night, Béla Kun and his collaborators were arrested. At the police headquarters many of the prisoners were beaten by the police in revenge for their colleagues who had died in the attempt to break up the attack on the *Népszava*. Hungary's president, Mihály Károlyi, sent his secretary to inquire after the health of the Communist leader, who was subsequently granted extremely liberal custodial restrictions and allowed to pursue his activities, and was soon able to reverse the setback despite his detention. On 21 March, while still in prison, he achieved a major success by bringing about the merger of the HCP and the Social Democratic Party. At the same time, President Károlyi's resignation opened the way for the establishment of a "republic of soviets," the freeing of all imprisoned Communists, and the organization on the Bolshevik model of a Revolutionary Council of State modeled on the Soviet People's Commissars. This republic lasted 133 days, from 21 March until 1 August 1919.

At their first meeting the commissars decided to establish revolutionary courts with judges chosen from among the people. Lenin, whom Béla Kun had hailed as the leader of the world proletariat, was in regular contact by telegram with Budapest after 22 March (218 messages were exchanged), and he advised shooting the Social Democrats and "petits-bourgeois." In his message to the Hungarian workers on 27 May 1919, he justified this recourse to terror: "The dictatorship of the proletariat requires the use of swift, implacable, and resolute violence to crush the resistance of exploiters, capitalists, great landowners, and their minions. Anyone who does not understand this is not a revolutionary." Soon the commissars of commerce, Mátyás Rákosi, and of economic affairs, Eugen Varga, and the head of the new courts had alienated all businessmen, industrial employees, and lawyers. One proclamation posted on the walls summed up the mood of the moment: "In the proletarian state, only the workers are allowed to live!" Work became obligatory, and all businesses employing more than twenty workers were immediately nationalized, followed by businesses employing more than ten, and soon the rest as well.

The army and the police force were dissolved, and a new army was created, composed exclusively of revolutionary volunteers. Soon a Terror Group of the Revolutionary Council of the Government was formed and quickly became known as "Lenin's Boys." The Terror Group murdered about ten people, including a young naval ensign, Ladislas Dobsa; a former first secretary of state and his son, who was the chief of the railways; and three police officers. "Lenin's Boys" answered to a retired sailor named József Czerny, who recruited them from among the most radical Communists, particularly former prisoners of war who had taken part in the Russian Revolution. Czerny was politically closer to Tibor Szamuely, the most radical of the Communist leaders, than he was to Béla Kun, who at one point proposed dissolving "Lenin's Boys." In response Szamuely gathered together his troops and marched on the House of Soviets. Kun received the support of the Social Democrat József Haubrich, joint people's commissar of war. Finally negotiations began, and Czerny's men agreed to join forces with the People's Commissariat of the Interior or to enlist in the army, which in fact most of them did.

With some twenty of "Lenin's Boys," Szamuely then went to Szolnok, the first city to be taken by the Hungarian Red Army, where he executed several locals accused of collaborating with the Romanians, who were considered national enemies because of their takeover of Transylvania and political enemies because of their regime's opposition to the Bolsheviks. One Jewish schoolboy who tried to plead for his father's life was killed for calling Szamuely a "wild beast." The chief of the Red Army tried in vain to put a brake on Szamuely's appetite for terror. Szamuely had requisitioned a train, and was traveling around the country hanging any peasants opposed to collectivization measures. Accused of having killed more than 150 people, his assistant József Kerekes admitted to having shot 5 and having hanged 13 others with his own hands. Although the exact number of people killed has never been established, Arthur Koestler claimed that there were perhaps slightly fewer than 500, but went on to note: "I have no doubt that Communism in Hungary would have followed the same path as its Russian model, and soon degenerated into a totalitarian police state. But that certitude, which came only much later, does nothing to dim the glorious days of hope of the early days of the revolution."[3] Historians attribute some 80 of the 129 recorded deaths to "Lenin's Boys," but it is likely that the real number was at least several hundred.

Faced with mounting opposition and a worsening of the threat posed by the Romanian troops, the revolutionary government drew upon popular antisemitism. One poster denounced Jews who refused to fight at the front: "Exterminate them, if they won't give their lives to the sacred cause of the dictatorship of the proletariat!" Béla Kun ordered the arrest of 5,000 Polish Jews who had come looking for food; he then confiscated their goods and had them expelled. The HCP radicals demanded that Szamuely take charge of the situation, and called for a "Red St. Bartholomew's Day Massacre," thinking for whatever reason that this was the only means of halting the decline of the Republic of Councils. Czerny tried to reorganize "Lenin's Boys," and in mid-July an appeal appeared in *Népszava:* "All previous members of the Terror Group, who were demobilized when the group was broken up, are requested to turn up at József Czerny's office to reenlist." The following day an official denial was published: "Notice is hereby given that no reestablishment of the 'Lenin's Boys' group can possibly be envisaged. Such great atrocities against the honor of the proletariat were committed by the group as to preclude any future role played by them in the service of the Republic of Councils."

The last weeks of the Budapest Commune were chaotic. Béla Kun faced an attempted coup against his leadership, possibly led by Szamuely. On 1 August 1919 he left Budapest under the protection of the Italian military. In the summer of 1920 he took refuge in the U.S.S.R. and was immediately named a political commissar of the Red Army on the southern front. There he distinguished himself by executing officers from Wrangel's army who had agreed to surrender if their lives would be spared. Szamuely attempted to flee to Austria but was arrested on 2 August and committed suicide soon afterward.[4]

The Comintern and Civil War

At the very moment when Béla Kun and his companions were attempting to set up a second Soviet state, Lenin decided to establish an international organization whose aim was to spread the revolution throughout the world. The Communist International—also known as Comintern or the Third International—was created in Moscow in March 1919 and immediately began to compete fiercely with the International of Socialist Workers (the Second International, which had been established in 1889). The Comintern Congress of 1919 had no real organizational capacity, and in practice did little more than answer the urgent need for Communist propaganda to capture the attention of the spontaneous revolutionary movements that were then shaking Europe. The real foundation of the Comintern should instead be dated from its Second Congress, in the summer of 1920, when twenty-one conditions of admission were laid down that had to be met by all socialists who wished to be associated with the organization. Thereafter, as the "headquarters of world revolution," the organization was extremely centralized and totally controlled by the Bolshevik Party, which lent it prestige, experience, and real political power in financial, military, and diplomatic terms.

From the outset Lenin regarded the Comintern as one of several instruments for international subversion—others included the Red Army, diplomacy, and espionage—and its political agenda closely followed the Bolsheviks' key idea that the time had come to stop talking and to take up armed struggle. The manifesto adopted at the Second Congress proudly announced: "The Communist International is the international party for insurrection and proletarian dictatorship." Consequently, the third of the twenty-one conditions stipulated that "in almost all the countries of Europe and America, the class struggle is moving into the period of civil war. Under such conditions Communists can no longer trust bourgeois law. It is the duty to set up everywhere, in parallel to the legal organization, an underground movement capable of decisive action in the service of the revolution at the moment of truth." These euphemisms were transparent: The "moment of truth" was the moment of revolutionary insurrection, and "decisive action" was participation in civil war. The policy was applied to all countries regardless of political regime, including democracies, republics, and constitutional monarchies.

The twelfth condition outlined the organizational necessities occasioned by the preparations for civil war: "At the present moment of hard-fought civil war, the Communist Party will be able to fulfill its role only if it is organized in a totally centralized fashion, if its iron discipline is as rigorous as that of any army, and if its central organization has sweeping powers, is allowed to exert uncontested authority, and enjoys the unanimous confidence of its members." The thirteenth condition also prescribed the action to be taken in the event of dissent among the militants: "Communist parties . . . must proceed with periodic purges of their organizations to eliminate all members who are petits-bourgeois or have ulterior motives."

At the Third Congress, which took place in Moscow in June 1921 with the participation of many recently established Communist parties, the directions were made even clearer. The "Thesis on Tactics" indicated that "the Communist Party must educate large sections of the proletariat, with both words and deeds, and inculcate the idea that any economic or political struggle, when the circumstances are favorable, can be transformed into civil war, in the course of which it is the duty of the proletariat to seize power." In addition, the "Theses on the Structure, Methods, and Action of Communist Parties" elaborated at length on "openly revolutionary uprisings" and "the organization of combat" that it was the duty of each Communist Party to foment. The theses made it clear that preparatory work was indispensable as long as "it is momentarily impossible to form a regular Red Army."

The step from theory to practice was taken in March 1921 in Germany, where the Comintern envisaged large-scale revolutionary action under the leadership of Béla Kun, who in the meantime had been elected a member of the Comintern Presidium. Launched at the moment when the Bolsheviks were putting down the Kronstadt rebellion, the "March Action" in Saxony was a genuine attempt at insurrection that met with failure despite the violent means involved, including an attempt to dynamite the express train from Halle to Leipzig. This failure immediately resulted in the first purge of the Comintern's internal ranks. Paul Levi, one of the founders and the president of the KPD, was sidelined because of his criticism of what he termed "adventurism." Already under the influence of the Bolshevik model, the Communist parties, which from an institutional point of view were merely the national sections of the International, rapidly became more and more subordinate, before surrendering completely to the Comintern. This subordination was both political and organizational, as the Comintern came to make all major decisions for these parties and ultimately decided all questions of policy. The "insurrectionist tendency" owed much to Grigory Zinoviev but was criticized by Lenin himself. Although Lenin was fundamentally in agreement with Paul Levi, he handed control of the KPD over to Levi's opponents in order to strengthen his own control over the Comintern.

In January 1923 French and Belgian troops occupied the Ruhr to exact the reparations from Germany that had been mandated by the Treaty of Versailles. This move brought about a rapprochement between nationalists and Communists over their common opposition to "French imperialism." In concrete terms the military occupation prompted a movement of passive resistance by the population, a movement that was backed by the government. The already unstable economic situation deteriorated rapidly, the value of the currency plunged, and by August one dollar was worth 13 million marks. Strikes, demonstrations, and riots were widespread, and on 13 August, with revolution in the air, the government of Wilhelm Cuno fell.

In Moscow the Comintern leaders thought that a new October Revolution was still possible. Once the differences among Trotsky, Zinoviev, and Stalin over who would take the lead in a new revolution were settled, the Comintern set about the serious business of armed insurrection. Emissaries (August Guralsky and Mátyás Rákosi) were sent to Germany, accompanied by civil war specialists such as General Aleksander Sklobewski, alias Gorev. The plan was to rely on a government of workers made up of left-wing Social Democrats and Communists and to use it to procure arms for the masses. In Saxony, Rákosi planned to blow up a railway bridge that linked the province to Czechoslovakia in order to provoke Czechoslovak involvement and thus sow further confusion.

The actions were to start on the anniversary of the Bolshevik Revolution. Excitement mounted in Moscow, where it was believed that victory was certain. The Red Army was mobilized on the western frontier, ready to come to the aid of the insurrection. In mid-October, Communist leaders joined the governments of Saxony and Thuringia with orders to reinforce the several hundred proletarian militias, made up of 25 percent Social Democratic workers and 50 percent Communists. But on 13 October the government of Gustav Stresemann declared a state of emergency in Saxony, taking direct control of the province, with the Reichswehr ready to intervene. Despite this turn of events, Moscow called the workers to arms, and Heinrich Brandler, having just returned from Moscow, called for a general strike at a workers' conference in Chemnitz on 21 October. This move failed when the Social Democrats refused to follow the Communist lead. The Communists then canceled the strike, but because of faulty communications this message never arrived in Hamburg, where on the morning of 23 October Communist Combat Groups of 200–300 attacked the various police stations. Despite the element of surprise, they failed to attain their objectives. The police counterattacked together with the Reichswehr, and after thirty-one hours of fighting, the Hamburg Communists were totally isolated and forced to surrender. The hoped-for "second October" failed to materialize. Nevertheless, the "M–Apparat" (Military Apparatus) remained an important part of the KPD until the 1930s, and has been described in detail by one of its leaders, Jan Valtin, whose real name was Richard Krebs.[5]

The next scene for an attempted insurrection was the Republic of Estonia. This was the second attack by Communists against the small country. On 27 October 1917 a Council of Soviets had seized power in Tallinn, dissolved the assembly, and annulled election results that had been unfavorable to the Communists. However, the Communists retreated en masse before the German Expeditionary Force. On 24 February 1918, just before the arrival of the Germans, the Estonians proclaimed independence. The German occupation lasted until November 1918. Following the defeat of the kaiser the German troops were forced to retreat, and the Communists again took the initiative. On 18 November a Communist government for Estonia was set up in Petrograd, and two divisions of the Red Army invaded. The aim of this offensive was clearly explained in the newspaper *Severnaya Kommuna* (The Northern Commune): "It is our duty to build a bridge connecting the Russian Soviets to the proletariat of Germany and Austria . . . Our victory will link the revolutionary forces of Western Europe to those of Russia. It will lend irresistible force to the universal social revolution."[6] In January 1919 the Soviet troops were stopped by an Estonian counterattack within twenty miles of the capital. Thus this second offensive also failed. On 2 February 1920 the Russian Communists recognized Estonian independence with the Tartu peace accord. By this time the Bolsheviks had already carried out a number of massacres in the areas they had taken over. On 14 January 1920, the day before their retreat, they killed 250 people in Tartu and more than 1,000 in the Rakvere district. When Wesenburg was liberated on 17 January, three mass graves were discovered, containing 86 bodies. In Tartu hostages were shot on 26 December 1919 after their arms and legs had been broken and in some cases their eyes cut out. On 14 January the Bolsheviks had time to kill only 20 people, including Archbishop Plato, of the 200 they were holding prisoner in Tartu. Because the victims had been clubbed to death with axes and rifle butts—one officer was found with his insignia nailed to his body—they were extremely difficult to identify.

Despite this defeat, the Soviet Union had not given up hope of establishing a satellite state on its borders. In April 1924, during secret negotiations in Moscow with Zinoviev, the Estonian Communists prepared for an armed uprising. They created combat teams structured in companies, and by the autumn had organized more than 1,000 men. They then set about demoralizing the army. The initial plan was to start the uprising and then to reinforce it with a general strike. The Estonian Communist Party, which had nearly 3,000 members and had suffered severe repression, tried to seize power in Tallinn on 1 December 1924, seeking to proclaim a Soviet Republic that would immediately demand affiliation with the Russian Soviet Republic, thus justifying the arrival of the Red Army. The coup failed within a single day. "The working masses . . . did not actively assist the insurgents in the struggle against the counterrevolutionaries. Most of the working classes of Revel [Tallinn] remained disinterested spectators." Jan Anvelt, who had directed operations, fled to the U.S.S.R., where he worked as a functionary in the Comintern for many years before dying in one of the purges.[7]

After Estonia the action moved to Bulgaria. In 1923 the country faced grave difficulties. Aleksandr Stamboliski, the leader of the coalition formed by the Communists and his own Agrarian Party, was assassinated in June and replaced as head of the government by Aleksandr Tsankov, who had the support of both the police and the army. In September the Communists launched an insurrection that lasted a week before being harshly repressed. After April 1924 they changed tactics, using assassinations and direct action. On 8 February 1925 an attack on the Godech police station led to four deaths. On 11 February in Sofia the parliamentary deputy Nikolas Milev, who was the head of the journal *Slovet* and president of the Union of Bulgarian Journalists, was assassinated. On 24 March a manifesto of the Bulgarian Communist Party (BKP) prematurely announced the inevitable fall of Tsankov, revealing the link between the terrorist actions and the Communists' political objectives. In early April an attack on King Alexander I very nearly succeeded, and on 15 April General Kosta Georgiev, one of his advisers, was killed.

What followed was one of the most devastating episodes of these years of political violence in Bulgaria. On 17 April, at Georgiev's funeral in the Cathedral of the Seven Saints in Sofia, a terrible explosion caused the dome to fall in. Among the 140 dead were 14 generals, 16 commanding officers, and 3 parliamentary deputies. According to Viktor Serge, the attack was organized by the military section of the Communist Party. The presumed perpetrators of the attack, Kosta Yankov and Ivan Minkov, two of the leaders of the organization, were later shot in a gunfight while resisting arrest.

This terrorist act was exploited to justify fierce reprisals, with 3,000 Communists arrested and 3 hanged publicly. Some members of the Comintern later claimed that the head of the Bulgarian Communists, Georgi Dimitrov, who led the Party in secret from Vienna, was responsible for this action. In December 1948, at the Fifth Congress of the Bulgarian Communist Party, Dimitrov accepted responsibility on behalf of both himself and the military organization. According to other sources, the man behind the dynamiting of the cathedral was Meir Trilisser, head of the Foreign Section of the Cheka and later deputy head of the GPU, who was decorated in 1927 with the Order of the Red Flag for services rendered.[8] In the 1930s Trilisser was one of the ten secretaries of the Comintern assured permanent control of the organization by the NKVD.

After this series of failures in Europe the Comintern, at Stalin's instigation, turned its attention to China. In a state of anarchy, torn apart by internal wars and social conflicts, but at the same time experiencing a huge wave of nationalism, China seemed ripe for an "anti-imperialist revolution." One sign of the times was that in the autumn of 1925 the Chinese students at the Communist University of the Workers of the East (KUTV), which had been established in April 1921, were reorganized into the new Sun Yat-sen University.

Duly influenced by leaders from the Comintern and the Soviet government, the Chinese Communist Party, which was not yet under the leadership of Mao Zedong, was pushed in 1925–26 into a close alliance with the Nationalist Party, the Kuomintang, led by the young Chiang Kai-shek. The tactic chosen by the Communist Party was to place all hope in the Kuomintang, using it as a sort of Trojan horse to smuggle in the revolution. The Comintern emissary, Mikhail Borodin, arrived as an adviser to the Kuomintang. In 1925 the left wing of the Nationalist Party, which favored collaboration with the Soviet Union, took control of the party. The Communists then stepped up their propaganda, encouraging social unrest and increasing their influence until they gained control over the Kuomintang's Second Congress. But an obstacle soon appeared in the person of Chiang Kai-shek, who was worried by the continuing expansion of Communist influence. He feared, quite correctly, that the Communists were attempting to sideline him. Seizing the initiative, he proclaimed martial law on 12 March 1926, arresting all Communists in the Kuomintang and the Soviet military advisers (although they were released a few days later), silencing the leader of the party's left wing, and imposing an eight-point plan whose purpose was to limit the prerogatives and activities of Communists in the party. Chiang thus became the undisputed leader of the Nationalist army. Borodin accepted the new situation.

On 7 July 1926 Chiang Kai-shek, with considerable military backup from the Soviets, launched a Nationalist attack on the north of the country, which was still under the control of the warlords. On 29 July he proclaimed martial law in Canton. The countryside in Hunan and Hubei was undergoing an agrarian revolution whose dynamics called into question the alliance between the Communists and the Nationalists. In the great industrial metropolis of Shanghai, the unions began a general strike as the army approached. The Communists, who included Zhou Enlai, called for an insurrection, counting on the immediate entry of the army into the town. But no such event took place. The uprising of 22–24 February 1927 failed, and the strikers were ferociously punished by General Li Baozhang.

On 21 March a new, larger general strike took place, and the uprising swept away the authorities in power. One division of the Nationalist army, whose general had been convinced to take part, entered Shanghai and was soon joined by Chiang Kai-shek, who was determined to take control of the situation. His success was made easier by the fact that Stalin, deceived by the "anti-imperialist" dimension of the policies of Chiang and his armies, gave the order to make peace with the Kuomintang and to stand beside them. On 12 April 1927 Chiang repeated in Canton the operation that he had carried out in Shanghai, ordering the Communists to be hunted down and beaten up.

But Stalin changed course at the worst possible moment. In August, to avoid losing face with his critics in the opposition, he sent two personal emissaries, Vissarion Lominadze and Heinz Neumann, to relaunch the insurrectional movement after breaking the alliance with the Kuomintang.[9] Despite the failure of the "autumn harvest revolt" orchestrated by his two envoys, they continued trying to foment revolution in Canton "to be able to bring news of victory to their chief" (as Boris Suvarin put it) at the Fifteenth Bolshevik Party Congress. This maneuver indicated the extent of the Bolsheviks' disdain for human life, including now even the lives of their supporters. The senselessness of the Canton Commune attests to that disregard for loss of life as much as the terrorist actions in Bulgaria had a few years earlier.

In Canton several thousand insurgents were caught in a confrontation for forty-eight hours with troops that outnumbered them by five or six to one. The commune had been badly prepared; insufficiently armed, it also pursued policies not favored by the Cantonese workers. On the night of 10 December 1927 loyal Communist troops took up positions in the assembly areas that were usually used by the Red Guards. As in Hamburg, the rebels initially benefited from the element of surprise, but the advantage was soon lost. The proclamation of a "soviet republic," on the morning of 12 December evoked no response from the local population. The Nationalist forces counterattacked in the afternoon, and the following day the red flag that had flown over the police headquarters was removed by the victorious troops. The reprisals were savage, and thousands died.

The Comintern should have drawn lessons from this experience, but it was not in a position to study the major underlying questions. Once again the use of violence was justified against all targets, in terms that demonstrated clearly how much the culture of civil war had taken root among the Communist cadres. *The Armed Uprising,* published by the Comintern in 1931 and soon translated into several languages, offers the following terrifying bit of self-criticism, with its transparent conclusions: "We should have got rid of the counterrevolutionaries more carefully. In all the time that Canton was in the hands of the revolutionaries, *we killed only 100 people.* The prisoners were killed only after a normal trial before the commission for the fight against the reactionaries. In combat, in the middle of a revolution, *this procedure was too lenient.*"[10] This lesson would be remembered.

Following this disaster the Communists withdrew from the towns and regrouped in the distant countryside. After 1931 they established free zones protected by the Red Army in Hunan and Kiangsi. It was thus very early on that the idea took root among the Communists in China that the revolution was above all a military affair. This belief institutionalized the political function of the military, which naturally resulted in ideas like Mao's famous formula, "Power comes out of the barrel of a gun." What followed demonstrated all too clearly that this was indeed the essence of the Communist vision of how power was to be seized and kept.

Despite the Chinese disaster and the European failures of the early 1920s, the Comintern was convinced that it was on the right track. All Communist parties, including the legally constituted ones in democratic republics, possessed a secret military wing that made occasional public appearances. The model most often followed was that of the KPD in Germany, which was controlled by Soviet military cadres and which possessed a large M–Apparat, whose task was to liquidate opponents (particularly those who belonged to the right wing) and informers who might have infiltrated the Party, but which also played a larger paramilitary role thanks to the famous Rote Front (Red Front), which had several thousand members. There was nothing unusual about political violence in the Weimar Republic, but the Communists did not concentrate their attention only on extreme right-wing movements such as the newly formed Nazi Party. They also broke up socialist meetings held by people they termed "sociotraitors" or "sociofascists."[11] Nor did they hesitate to attack the police, whom they saw as the representatives of a reactionary or even fascist state. The events of 1933 and what followed of course demonstrated that the real fascist enemy was the National Socialist Party, and that it would have been more sensible to form an alliance against the Nazis with the other socialist parties who sought to defend "bourgeois democracy." But the Communists altogether rejected the idea of democracy.

In France, where the political climate was much calmer, the French Communist Party (PCF) also had its own armed section. It was led by Albert Treint, one of the Party secretaries, who had served as a captain during the war and thus had military experience. Their first public appearance was on 11 January 1924, at a Communist meeting where a group of anarchists were objecting vociferously: Treint gave the order, and ten men armed with revolvers rose up and opened fire on the anarchists from point-blank range, killing two of them outright and wounding several others. Because of lack of proof, none of the assassins was ever prosecuted. A year later, on 25 April 1925, a few weeks before the municipal elections, the PCF security services were involved in another violent incident at an electoral meeting of a right-wing organization called the Patriotic Youth Group, in the rue Damrémont in Paris. Some of the militants were armed and did not hesitate to make use of their weapons. Three of the Patriotic Youth Group were killed instantly; another died a few days later. Jean Taittinger, the leader of the Patriotic Youth Group, was arrested, and the police made several raids on the houses of the Communist militants.

Nevertheless, the Party continued to act in the same vein. In 1926 Jacques Duclos, who as a newly elected parliamentary deputy enjoyed full parliamentary immunity, was placed in charge of the Anti-Fascist Defense Groups, consisting of former servicemen from World War I, and the Young Anti-Fascist Guards, recruited from among the Communist Youth groups. These paramilitary groups, closely modeled on the German Rote Front, paraded in uniform on 11 November 1926. At the same time Duclos was in charge of antimilitarist propaganda, publishing a review called *Le combattant rouge*, which taught the art of civil war, describing and analyzing historic street combats and the like.

The Armed Uprising, which described various insurrections since 1920, was republished in France in early 1934.[12] The political misfortunes of the French Popular Front in the summer and autumn of 1934 caused the book to wane in popularity, but that decline had little effect on the fundamental role of violence in Communist practice. The justification of violence, the day-to-day practice of class hatred, and the theory of civil war and terror were used again in 1936 in Spain, where the Comintern sent a number of its cadres who distinguished themselves in the Communist repressions.

The selection and training of cadres to join future armed uprisings occurred in close liaison with the Soviet secret services, and with one service in particular, the GRU (Glavnoe razvedyvatel'noe upravlenie, or Main Intelligence Directorate). Created by Trotsky as the Fourth Bureau of the Red Army, the GRU never abandoned this educational role even when circumstances changed and it was scaled down considerably. Even in the early 1970s some of the young cadres in the French Communist Party underwent training in the U.S.S.R. (learning how to shoot, strip, and assemble various firearms, make bombs and radio transmitters, and use sabotage techniques) with the Spetsnaz, the special Soviet troops who were used to train the security forces. The GRU also had a number of military advisers who could be sent to friendly parties whenever necessary. Manfred Stern for instance, the Austro-Hungarian who was lent to the KPD M-Apparat for the Hamburg uprising in 1923, was subsequently also sent to China and Manchuria before becoming better known as "General Kleber" in the International Brigades in Spain.

Many of these underground military organizations were run by unsavory characters. The members were often simply the local bandits, who occasionally formed gangs in their own right. The "Red Guards" or "Red squadrons" of the Chinese Communist Party in the second half of the 1920s provide one of the most striking examples. Their sphere of activity was Shanghai, which was then the epicenter of Party operations. Led by Gu Shunzhang, a former gangster affiliated with the secret Green Band society, the more powerful of the two Shanghai mafia families, they were in daily conflict with their Nationalist opponents, particularly with the Blue Shirts, who modeled themselves on the Fascists. These two adversaries engaged in a series of conflicts in which terror was traded for terror, ambushes were a daily occurrence, and revenge killings were commonplace. All these activities had the full support of the Soviet consul in Shanghai, who had his own military specialists such as V. Gorbatyuk, as well as manpower at his disposal.

In 1928 Gu Shunzhang's men liquidated two suspects who had been freed by the police: He Jiaxing and He Jihua were riddled with bullets while they slept. Outside, other conspirators set off some fireworks to cover the sound of the gunfire. Similarly efficacious methods were adopted to settle differences of opinion within the Party itself. Sometimes a simple accusation was considered sufficient evidence. On 17 January 1931, furious at having been outmaneuvered by Pavel Mif, the Comintern delegate, and by the other leaders acting under orders from Moscow, He Mengxiong and some twenty comrades from the workers' faction met at the Oriental Hotel in Shanghai. As soon as they began their discussion, armed policemen and agents of the Diaocha Tongzhi (the central investigative bureau of the Kuomintang) burst into the room and arrested everyone. The Nationalists had received an anonymous tip-off about the meeting.

After the defection of Gu Shunzhang in April 1931, his immediate return to the fold of the Green Band (he had earlier switched sides to the Blue Shirts), and his submission to the Kuomintang, a special committee of five Communist cadres—Kang Sheng, Guang Huian, Pan Hannian, Chen Yun, and Ke Qingshi—took charge of operations in Shanghai. In 1934, the year when the urban apparatus of the CCP almost fell apart for good, Ding Mocun and Li Shiqun, the last two leaders of armed groups of Communists in the city, fell into the hands of the Kuomintang. They went on to work for the Japanese before coming to a sorry end: Ding Mocun was shot by the Nationalists for treason in 1947, and Li Shiqun was poisoned by a Japanese officer. Kang Sheng became the head of Mao's secret police from 1949 until his death in 1975, and was thus one of the main butchers of the people of China under the Communist regime.[13]

Sometimes members of foreign Communist groups were used in covert police operations inside the U.S.S.R. This seems to have been the case in the Kutepov affair. In 1924 General Aleksandr Kutepov was called to Paris by Grand Duke Nicholas to become the head of the General Military Union (ROVS). In 1928 the GPU decided to break up this organization. The general disappeared on 26 January, and rumors began to fly, some of them undoubtedly started by the Soviet Union itself. After two independent inquiries it became clear who was responsible for the kidnapping. The first inquiry was conducted by Vladimir Burtsev, who was famous for having unmasked Evno Azev, the Okhrana (tsarist secret police) agent who had infiltrated the Socialist Revolutionary organization; the other was led by Jean Delage, a journalist at the *Echo de Paris.* Delage proved that the general had been taken to Houlgate and put on a Soviet ship, the *Spartak,* which left Le Havre on 19 February. The general was never seen alive again. On 22 September 1965 Soviet general N. Shimanov claimed responsibility for the operation in the Soviet army's main newspaper, *Red Star,* and revealed the name of the perpetrator of the incident: "Sergei Puzitsky . . . not only took part in the capture of the bandit Savinkov . . . but also led the operation to arrest General Kutepov and other White Guard chiefs in exemplary fashion."[14] Today the circumstances of the kidnapping are better known. The general's émigré organization had been infiltrated by the GPU. In 1929 a former minister from the White government of Admiral Kolchak, Sergei Nikolaevich Tretyakov, had secretly switched to the Soviet side and was handing on information under the code name Ivanov No. UJ\1. Thanks to the detailed information he passed to his contact Vechinkin, Moscow knew almost all there was to know about the general's movements. A commando group posing as policemen seized Kutepov's car on the street, while a Frenchman, Charles Honel, who was a mechanic in a garage in the suburbs of Paris, asked Kutepov to follow him. Honel's brother Maurice, who was also involved in the operation because of his contacts with the Soviet secret services, would be elected a Communist member of Parlement in 1936. Kutepov refused to cooperate, and he was stabbed to death and his body buried in the basement of Honel's garage.[15]

Kutepov's successor, General E. K. Miller, had as his second in command Nikolai Skoblin, who was in fact a Soviet agent. With his wife, the singer Nadya Plevitskaya, Skoblin organized the abduction of General Miller. On 22 September 1937 Miller disappeared, and on 23 September the Soviet ship *Maria Ulyanovna* left Le Havre. Subsequently General Skoblin also disappeared, and suspicions focused increasingly on the ship. General Miller was of course on board, but the French government decided not to detain the ship. Once in Moscow Miller was interrogated and tortured.[16]

Dictatorship, Criminalization of Opponents, and Repression within the Comintern

At Moscow's instigation, the Comintern installed an armed group within each Communist Party to prepare for revolution and civil war against the reigning powers. It also introduced its brethren to the same police tactics and terror that were used in the U.S.S.R. At the Tenth Congress of the Bolshevik Party, which took place from 8 to 16 March 1921, the same time as the Kronstadt rebellion, the bases for a dictatorial regime for the Party itself were laid down. During preparations for the congress no fewer than eighteen different platforms were proposed and discussed. These debates were the last vestiges of the democracy that had struggled to establish itself in Russia. It was only within the Party that this supposed freedom of speech prevailed, and even there it was short-lived. Lenin set the tone on the second day: "We do not need opposition, comrades; this is not the moment for that. Be here, or in Kronstadt with a rifle: but do not join the opposition. Do not hold it against me, this is just the way it is. It is time to end opposition. In my opinion, the Congress should vote for an end to all opposition, and pull a veil over it; we have had enough of it already."[17] His targets were the people who, without constituting a group in the normal sense of the word, and without publishing anything, nonetheless united around two opposition platforms. The first was known as the Workers' Opposition and included Aleksandr Shlyapnikov, Aleksandra Kollontai, and Yuri Lutovinov. Members of the second group were known as Democratic Centralists and included Timofei Sapronov and Gavriil Myasnikov.

The congress was nearly over when Lenin presented two resolutions, the first concerning Party unity and the second "unionist and anarchist deviation within the Party," which was in effect an attack on the Workers' Opposition. The first text demanded the immediate dissolution of all groups centered upon a particular platform and their expulsion from the Party. One unpublished article of this resolution, which remained secret until October 1923, gave the Central Committee the power of enforcement. Feliks Dzerzhinsky's police thus had a new field of operations: any opposition group within the Party itself became subject to surveillance, and if necessary was punished by expulsion from the Party, which for true militants was a form of political death.

Even though their call for the end of freedom of speech contradicted Party statutes, both motions were carried. Radek gave an almost prescient justification for the first one: "I am sure that it could be used against us, and yet I am voting for it . . . In times of danger, the Central Committee must take severe measures that it considers necessary against even the best comrades . . . Even the Central Committee itself might make mistakes, but that is preferable to the general chaos we are witnessing at the moment." This choice, which was the result of a particular set of circumstances but was entirely in keeping with the Bolsheviks' most profound instincts, was an extremely important one for the future of the Soviet Party, and accordingly for the Comintern as well.

The Tenth Party Congress also reorganized the Party Control Committee, whose role it defined as "the consolidation of unity and authority within the Party." From that time on, the commission assembled personal dossiers on all Party activists. These dossiers could be used if necessary as the basis for accusations, giving details of attitudes toward the political police, participation in opposition groups, and so on. As soon as the congress ended, harassment and intimidation of members of the Workers' Opposition began. Later Shlyapnikov explained that "the struggle was not carried out on ideological grounds, but was more a simple question of removing the people in question from their posts, moving them from one district to another, or even excluding them from the Party."

A new series of checks began in August and went on for several months. Nearly one-fourth of all Party activists were thrown out. Periodic recourse to the *chistka* (purge) became an integral component of Party life. Aino Kuusinen described this cyclical practice:

> *Chistka* meetings took the following form: the name of the accused was read out, and he was ordered to take the stand. Then members of the Purification Committee would ask questions. Some managed to explain themselves with relative ease; others had to undergo this severe test for some time. If anyone had personal enemies, that could give a decisive turn to events: in any case, expulsion from the Party could be pronounced only by the Control Commission. If the accused was not found guilty of anything that would have led to expulsion from the Party, the procedure was closed without a vote's being cast. But if the opposite was the case, no one ever intervened in favor of the accused. The President simply asked, "Kto protiv?" [Who is opposed?] and because no one dared to object, the case was deemed to have been decided unanimously.[18]

The effects of the Tenth Congress were felt quickly: in February 1922 Gavriil Myasnikov was suspended for one year for having defended freedom of the press against Lenin's orders. Finding no support within the Party, the Workers' Opposition appealed to the Comintern ("Declaration of the 22").

Stalin, Dzerzhinsky, and Zinoviev then called for the expulsion of Aleksandr Shlyapnikov, Aleksandra Kollontai, and G. Medvedev, but this expulsion was rejected by the Eleventh Congress. Ever more in thrall to Soviet power, the Comintern was soon forced to adopt the same internal regime as the Bolshevik Party. This was the logical consequence of the preceding events and in itself quite unsurprising.

In 1923 Dzerzhinsky demanded an official resolution from the Politburo that would oblige all Party members to denounce to the GPU any opposition activity they encountered. Dzerzhinsky's proposal led to a new crisis within the Bolshevik Party. On 8 October Trotsky sent a letter to the Central Committee, followed on 15 October by the "Declaration of the 46." The ensuing debate centered on the "new direction" of the Russian Party and was hotly contested in all sections of the Comintern.[19]

Simultaneously, at the end of 1923, it was decreed that all Comintern sections should undergo a process of "Bolshevization," reorganizing their structures more tightly and reinforcing their allegiance to Moscow. Resistance to these measures led to a considerable increase in the power of the International's "holy missionaries," against a background of debates concerning the evolution of power in Soviet Russia.

Boris Suvarin (sometimes spelled Souvarine), one of the leaders of the French Communist Party, took a stand against the new line, denouncing the low tactics being used by Kamenev, Zinoviev, and Stalin against their opponent Trotsky. On 12 June 1924 Suvarin was summoned to the Thirteenth Congress of the Communist Party in the Soviet Union and asked to explain himself. The meeting became acrimonious, in the manner of meetings where full confessions were expected. A commission was hastily put together to examine the "Suvarin case," and he was suspended from the Party. The reaction of the other French Party leaders was a clear indication of the prevailing mood. On 19 July an anonymous author wrote in *L'humanité:* "In our Party [the PCF], which the revolutionary battle has not yet completely purified of its social-democratic remnants, individual personalities still play too big a role . . . Only after petit-bourgeois individualism has been destroyed once and for all will the anonymous iron cohorts of the French Bolsheviks take shape. If we wish to be worthy of the Communist International to which we belong and to follow in the steps of the glorious Russian Party, we must mercilessly punish all those in our ranks who fail to comply with our rules!" This line was to govern the PCF for many decades. The unionist Pierre Monatte summed up the change in a single word: the "corporalization" (turning everyone into little corporals) of the Communist Party.

During the Fifth Congress of the Comintern in the summer of 1924, Zinoviev threatened to "break the bones" of his opponents, demonstrating clearly the sort of behavior that was becoming the norm in Communist circles. Unfortunately, it was to rebound on him: it was his bones that were broken by Stalin when he was removed from the post of Comintern President in 1925. Zinoviev was replaced by Bukharin, who soon suffered the same fate. On 11 July 1928, just before the Sixth Congress of the Comintern (17 July–1 September), Kamenev had a secret meeting with Bukharin at which he took notes. Bukharin explained that he was a victim of the police regime, that his phone was being tapped, and that he was being followed by the GPU. His fear was quite real as he said, "He'll strangle us . . . we can't bring division into the Party, because he'd strangle us." The "he" in question was Stalin.

The first person whom Stalin tried to "strangle" was Leon Trotsky. The onslaught against Trotskyism, launched in 1927, was an extension of the earlier campaign against Trotsky himself. Hints of this had come during a Bolshevik Party conference in October 1926, when Yuri Larin, writing in *Pravda,* had demanded that "either the Opposition must be expelled and legally destroyed, or we must solve the problem with guns in the streets, as we did with the left Socialist Revolutionaries in July 1918 in Moscow." The Left Opposition, as it was officially called, was isolated and getting weaker all the time. The GPU initiated a campaign of intimidation against it, claiming that the group had a secret press, directed by a former officer from Wrangel's army (who in fact was a GPU agent), where Opposition documents were being printed. On the tenth anniversary of October 1917, the Opposition decided to disseminate its own agenda. Brutal police tactics prevented this from happening, and on 14 November 1927 both Trotsky and Zinoviev were expelled from the Bolshevik Party. The next step was to exile the best-known opposition activists to far-flung regions of the Soviet Union. Christian Rakovsky, the former Soviet ambassador to France, was exiled to Astrakhan, on the Volga, then to Barnaul, in Siberia. Viktor Serge was sent to Oranienburg in the Urals, in 1933. Others were expelled from the Soviet Union altogether. Trotsky was first taken by force to Alma-Ata, in Kazakhstan; a year later he was expelled to Turkey and thus avoided the prison sentence that awaited most of his followers. These followers were becoming more and more numerous, and like the activists of what had been the Workers' Opposition and the Democratic Centralist Group they were being arrested and sent to special prisons known as "political detention centers."

From this time on, foreign Communists who either were members of the Comintern abroad or were living in Russia were arrested and interned in the same fashion as activists in the Russian Party. It was claimed that they should be treated as Russians since any foreign Communist who stayed in Russia for any length of time was required to join the Bolshevik Party and thus was subject to its discipline. One well-known case was that of the Yugoslav Communist Ante Ciliga, a member of the Yugoslav Politburo who was sent to Moscow in 1926 as a Yugoslav Communist Party (YCP) member of the Comintern. He made contact with Trotsky's opposition group and increasingly distanced himself from the Comintern, where there was never any real debate about ideas, and whose leaders never hesitated to use intimidatory methods to counter opposition of any kind. Ciliga termed this the "servility system" of the international Communist movement. In February 1929, at a General Assembly of Yugoslav Communists in Moscow, a resolution was adopted condemning the policies of the YCP. This resolution was tantamount to a condemnation from the Comintern itself. An illegal group—according to the rules that were then in place—was then organized by those who opposed the Soviets' official line. A commission began an inquiry into Ciliga, who was suspended for one year. Ciliga refused to abandon his "illegal" activities and settled in Leningrad. On 1 May 1930 he returned to Moscow to meet with other members of his Russo-Yugoslav group, which had become extremely critical of the way industrialization was being carried out and sought to form a new party. On 21 May he and his companions were arrested and sent to the "political detention center" in Verkhne-Uralsk on the basis of Article 59 of the penal code. For more than three years he demanded the right to leave Russia, constantly writing letters of protest and conducting a series of hunger strikes while being moved from prison to prison. During one moment of freedom he attempted suicide. The GPU attempted to persuade him to give up his Italian citizenship. After a further exile in Siberia, he was finally expelled on 3 December 1935, and that in itself was an exceptional event.[20]

Thanks to Ciliga, we have a good idea of what life was like in the political detention centers. "Comrades would send us newspapers that appeared in the prisons. What a range of opinion, what freedom of thought there was in those articles! What passion and openness in the discussion of questions that were not simply abstract and theoretical, but were also the burning issues of the day! And our freedom did not stop there either. During our daily walk, we would pass through a series of rooms, and the inmates would gather in the corners and conduct proper meetings, with a president, a secretary, and speakers who took the floor in turns." He also described the physical conditions:

> Our diet was that of the traditional *muzhik* [peasant]: bread and soup day and night, all year long . . . For lunch there was a soup made from bad fish or rotten meat. For dinner we had the same soup without the fish or meat . . . The daily bread ration was 700 grams, the monthly sugar ration was one kilo, and we also had a tobacco ration, some cigarettes, tea, and soap. The diet was monotonous, and there was never

enough food. We constantly had to fight against reductions in our rations: I could not begin to describe how we fought for our right to the tiniest little scraps. But if we compare how we lived to the regimes in force in the normal prisons, where hundreds of thousands of detainees were all crammed in together, and certainly to the gulags, where millions of people were crushed, our regime was privileged by comparison.[21]

Such privileges of course were all relative. In Verkhne-Uralsk the prisoners went on hunger strike three times, in April and then again in the summer of 1931, and again in December 1933, to fight for their rights and above all to protest the lengthening of their sentences. After 1934 the special treatment of such political prisoners was largely ended, although it remained in place in Verkhne-Uralsk until 1937, and conditions rapidly worsened. Some detainees died after being beaten, others were shot, and others simply disappeared altogether, as Vladimir Smirnov did in Suzdal in 1933.

The criminalization of real or imaginary opponents within the various Communist Parties was soon extended to high-ranking members. José Bullejos, the leader of the Spanish Communist Party, and several of his colleagues were called to Moscow in the autumn of 1932 and their policies severely criticized. When they refused to submit to the dictates of the Comintern, they were expelled from the Party en masse on 1 November and found themselves under house arrest in the Hotel Lux, where the members of the Comintern were based. The Frenchman Jacques Duclos, the former Comintern delegate in Spain, brought them the news of their expulsion and explained to them that any attempt to resist would be met with "the full force of Soviet law."[22] Bullejos and his companions had an extremely difficult time trying to leave the U.S.S.R.; it took two months of tense negotiations before their passports were returned to them.

The same year saw the epilogue to an extraordinary series of events concerning the French Communist Party. Early in 1931 the Comintern had sent a representative and several instructors to the PCF with orders to bring the situation there under control. In July the head of the Comintern, Dmitry Manuilsky, came secretly to Paris and revealed to an amazed local Politburo that a group in their midst was attempting to sow disorder in the Party ranks. In fact the mission itself was an attempt to sow discord in the Party and hence to weaken the grip of French Party leaders and increase their dependence on Moscow. Among the heads of this mythical group was Pierre Celor, one of the main leaders of the Party since 1928, who was called to Moscow on the pretext that he was to be elected to the post of PCF representative at the Comintern. As soon as he arrived he was treated as an *agent provocateur* and a social outcast.

Having no money, Celor managed to get through the winter thanks to the ration card of his wife, who had accompanied him to Moscow and who still had a post in the Comintern. On 8 March 1932 he was called to a meeting with several secret-police investigators, who during a twelve-hour interrogation tried to make him admit that he was a "police agent who had infiltrated the Party." Celor refused to admit any such thing, and after several more months of harassment he returned to France on 8 October 1932, only to be publicly denounced as a police spy.

In 1931 French Communist Louis Aragon wrote the following poem, titled "Prelude to the Cherry Season":

> I sing the GPU which is taking shape
> In the France of today
> I sing the GPU we need in France
> I sing the GPUs of nowhere and everywhere
> I call for the GPU to prepare the end of the world
> Call for the GPU to prepare the end of the world
> To defend the betrayed
> To defend those always betrayed
> Ask for a GPU, you whom they bend and whom they kill
> Ask for a GPU
> You need the GPU
> Long live the GPU the dialectical figure of heroism
> Real heroes not imbecile idiot pilots
> Who people think are heroes just because they
> Fly in the face of the earth
> Long live the GPU, true image of materialist splendor
> Long live the GPU; down with Chiappe and the *Marseillaise*
> Long live the GPU; down with the pope and the bugs
> Long live the GPU; down with money and banks
> Long live the GPU; down with the cheating East
> Long live the GPU; down with the family
> Long live the GPU; down with infernal laws
> Long live the GPU; down with socialist assassins like
> Caballero Boncour MacDonald Zoergibel
> Long live the GPU; down with the enemies of the proletariat
> LONG LIVE THE GPU.[23]

In 1932 cadre sections on the model of the Bolshevik Party were established in many Communist Parties. These sections were dependent on the Central Section of the Comintern cadres. Their task was to keep complete records on all Party activists and to gather biographical and autobiographical questionnaires on all the leaders. More than 5,000 such dossiers from the French Party alone were sent to Moscow before the war. The biographical questionnaire contained more than seventy questions and was divided into five broad sections: origins and current social situation, role in the Party, education and intellectual activities, participation in social life, and any legal records that might be relevant. This material was catalogued in Moscow, where the records were kept by Anton Krajewski, Moisei Chernomordik, and Gevork Alikhanov, the successive heads of the Comintern cadre section, which was also linked to the foreign section of the NKVD. In 1935 Meir Trilisser, one of the NKVD's highest-ranking agents, was appointed secretary of the Central Executive Committee of the Comintern and placed in charge of the cadre section. Under the pseudonym Mikhail Moskvin he collected information and denunciations and decided who was to be disgraced, which was the first step on the way to liquidation.[24] It was the job of all cadre sections to draw up blacklists of enemies of the U.S.S.R. and of Communism.

In rapid order, various sections of the Comintern began to recruit intelligence agents for the U.S.S.R. In some cases the people who agreed to undertake this illegal and clandestine work were genuinely unaware that they were working for the Soviet secret services, including the GRU, the Foreign Section (Inostrannyi otdel'; INO) of the Cheka-GPU, and the NKVD. Relations among these organizations were formidably complicated. Moreover, they fought among themselves to recruit new agents, often attempting to entice agents from rival services. Elizaveta Poretskaya gives many examples of such practices in her memoirs.[25]

In 1932, when the cadres began to be controlled by emissaries from the Comintern, the PCF itself started keeping records on all people it considered suspect or dangerous. The official function of the cadre sections was to recruit the best activists; another function was to compile lists of people who had been found wanting in some way. From 1932 to June 1939 the PCF drew up twelve documents with titles such as "Blacklist of provocateurs, traitors, and police informers thrown out of French revolutionary organizations" and "Blacklist of provocateurs, thieves, crooks, Trotskyites, and traitors thrown out of workers' organizations in France." To justify such lists, which by the start of World War II contained more than 1,000 names, the PCF used a simple political argument: "The struggle of the bourgeoisie against the working classes and revolutionary organizations in our country is becoming ever more intense."

Activists were required to submit information about the appearance of suspects (List no. 10, from August 1938, specified "size and build, hair, eyebrows, forehead, nose, mouth, chin, shape of face, complexion, distinguishing marks") and "any information that might help locate" them, such as their address and place of work. All activists were thus required to some extent to behave like Cheka members.

Some suspects undoubtedly were genuine crooks; others were simply opposed to the Party line, irrespective of whether they belonged to the Party. The first targets in the 1930s were the Trotskyites and the followers of Jacques Doriot in Saint-Denis. The French Communists simply repeated the arguments of their Soviet counterparts: the Trotskyites had become "a gang of criminals and unscrupulous saboteurs, subversive agents, and assassins following the orders of foreign espionage services."[26]

The war, the banning of the PCF because of its support for the German-Soviet pact, and the German occupation induced the Party to intensify its secret-police activities. All PCF members who refused to accept the German-Soviet pact were denounced, including those who joined the resistance. Among these were Adrien Langumier, an editor at Jean Luchaire's *Temps nouveaux*; and René Nicod, a former Communist deputy from Oyonnax, whose ties with his former comrades remained close. Jules Fourier was another Communist whom the Party police tried unsuccessfully to liquidate: Fourier, after voting in favor of full powers for Pétain, set up a resistance network in 1941 and was subsequently deported to Buchenwald and Mauthausen.

Other targets included those who in 1941 participated in the French Workers' and Peasants' Party (POPF); one of its leaders, Marcel Gitton, a former PCF Party secretary, was shot in September by militant Communists. The PCF declared this group "traitors to the Party and to France." Sometimes their accusatory statements were followed by the note "punished accordingly." There were also cases of militants such as Georges Déziré, who were suspected of treason and assassinated, only to be rehabilitated after the war.

In the midst of the persecution of Jews, the Communist Party used strange methods to denounce its enemies: "C . . . Renée, also known as Tania, or Thérèse, of the 14th *arrondissement*, Bessarabian Jew"; "De B . . . Foreign Jew, a rebel who insults the CP and the U.S.S.R." Immigrant Manpower (the MOI), an organization that grouped all foreign militant Communists, had used similar language: "R. Jew (not his real name). Works with a group of enemy Jews." The hatred for Trotskyites also remained strong: "D . . . Yvonne. 1, Place du Général Beuret, Paris 8 . . . A Trotskyite, has had liaisons with the POUM. Insults the U.S.S.R." It is quite probable that in the course of arrests such lists fell into the hands of the Vichy police or the Gestapo. What then happened to the people on the lists?

In 1945 the PCF released another series of blacklists of political enemies, some of whom had already survived several assassination attempts. The institutionalization of the blacklist quite obviously echoes the lists of potential criminals drawn up by Soviet security services such as the Cheka, the GPU, and the NKVD. It was a universal practice among Communists, which began in the early days of the civil war in Russia. In Poland, at the moment the war ended, such lists contained forty-eight categories of people to be watched.

In-fighting among the various services was ended by a simple change that united the Comintern and the secret services under the control of the head of the CPSU, making them directly accountable to Stalin himself for their actions. In 1932 Mikhail Ryutin, who had been zealous and relentless in carrying out repression against his own friends, suddenly found himself in opposition to Stalin. He drew up a statement saying that "Stalin today has the infallible status of a pope at the Comintern. He controls, by direct and indirect means, all the leading cadres of the Comintern, not simply in Moscow but everywhere, and this is the decisive argument that confirms his invincibility in political questions."[27] By the end of the 1920s the Comintern, which was also financially dependent on the Soviet state, had lost all semblance of independence. It was not long before this material dependence, which went hand in hand with political dependence, accompanied an even more sinister dependence on the secret police.

The inevitable result of the ever-increasing police pressure on Comintern members was fear and mistrust. As soon as the threat of denunciation became widespread, a general lack of confidence became apparent in all quarters. Denunciation came in two forms: either a voluntary declaration, or a statement taken from people as a result of mental or physical torture. Sometimes fear was enough. And there were other militants who were proud to denounce their colleagues. The case of the French Communist André Marty is characteristic of the paranoia that was so widespread at the time, and the senseless rush to appear to be the most vigilant Communist of them all. In a letter marked "strictly confidential" addressed to the General Secretary of the Comintern, Georgi Dimitrov, and dated 23 June 1927, he wrote a lengthy denunciation of Eugen Fried, the representative of the International in France, pretending to be amazed that Fried had not yet been arrested by the French police, and expressing extreme suspicion of this fact.[28]

The phenomena of terror and the public trials inevitably met with different responses abroad. In Paris Boris Suvarin made the following remarks in *Le Figaro littéraire* on 1 July 1937:

> It is a great exaggeration to claim that the Moscow trials are an exclusively Russian phenomenon. While there are of course national characteristics involved, one can also discern many other more general truths.
>
> First, one should abandon the idea that what can be understood by Russians cannot possibly be understood by the French. In fact the admissions that have been made are as puzzling to the people of Russia as

they are to the people of France. Those who, out of some fanatical sense of devotion to the Bolshevik cause, find it all quite natural are probably more numerous abroad than they are in Russia . . .

In the early years of the Russian Revolution, it was easy to put everything down to the idea of the "Slavic soul"; yet the events that were reputed to be exclusively Slavic phenomena have subsequently been witnessed in Italy and Germany. When the beast in man is unleashed, the same consequences are visible everywhere, irrespective of whether the man in question is Latin, German, or Slav, however different he may appear on the surface.

And in any case, in France and everywhere else there are millions of people who are in Stalin's pocket. The editors of *L'humanité* are identical with the men at *Pravda* when it comes to flattery and sycophancy, and they don't have the excuse that a totalitarian dictator is breathing down their necks. When an academician like [Vladimir] Komarov demeans himself in Red Square yet again by asking for more blood, one must bear in mind that if he had not done so, he would have been effectively committing suicide. And with that in mind, what are we to make of men like Romain Rolland, [Paul] Langevin, and [André] Malraux, who admire and actively support the so-called Soviet regime with its "culture" and "justice," and who aren't forced to do so by hunger or torture?

In the same vein as the Marty letter is one sent to "Comrade L. P. Beria" (the people's commissar of internal affairs in the U.S.S.R.) by the Bulgarian Stella Blagoeva, an obscure employee in the cadre section of the Executive Committee of the Comintern:

> The Executive Committee of the Communist International possesses information drawn up by a series of comrades, all militants in friendly parties, that we feel should be addressed to you so that you may check the information and accordingly take any steps necessary . . . One of the secretaries of the Central Committee of the Hungarian Communist Party, [Frigyes] Karikás, has taken part in conversations that seem to indicate insufficient devotion to the Party of Lenin and Stalin . . . Comrades have also been asking a very serious question: How is it that in 1932 the Hungarian court condemned him to only three years in prison, whereas during the dictatorship of the proletariat in Hungary Karikás carried out death sentences pronounced by the revolutionary tribunal . . . There are many indications from comrades from Germany, Austria, Lithuania, Poland, and elsewhere that political emigration is becoming a dirty business . . . This problem must be addressed in a determined fashion.[29]

Arkady Vaksberg notes that the Comintern archives also contain dozens (perhaps even hundreds) of denunciations, a phenomenon that attests to the moral decay that took hold within the Comintern and among officials of the Soviet Communist Party. This decay was quite apparent during the great trials of members of the Bolshevik "old guard," who had lent their support to the establishment of power on the basis of "the absolute lie."

The Great Terror Strikes the Comintern

The assassination of Sergei Kirov on 1 December 1934 provided Stalin with an excellent pretext for moving from severe repression to real terror both in the Russian Communist Party and in the Comintern.[30] Until then, terror had been used as a weapon only against the general population. After Kirov's murder, it was used mercilessly against the very people who wielded power in the Party itself.

The first victims were the members of the Russian Opposition who were already in prison. From the end of 1935 on, anyone whose sentence had expired was automatically reimprisoned. Several thousand militant Trotskyites were grouped together in the Vorkuta region. There were some 500 in the mine, 1,000 in the Ukhto-Pechora camp, and several thousand in the Pechora region. On 27 October 1936, 1,000 prisoners (including women and children) began a hunger strike that lasted thirty-two days. They demanded separation from the common criminals and the right to live with their families. The first death among the prisoners came after four weeks. Several others met the same fate before the authorities agreed to their demands. The following autumn, 1,200 prisoners (about half of whom were Trotskyites) were grouped together near an old brickworks. At the end of March the camp administration posted a list of 25 prisoners, who received a kilo of bread and orders to prepare to leave. A few minutes later, shots were heard. The worst possible scenario soon proved to be true when the other prisoners saw the convoy escort return to the camp. Two days later there was a new list and a similar fusillade, and so it continued until the end of May. The guards generally disposed of the bodies by pouring gasoline over them and setting them on fire. The NKVD announced on the radio the names of those shot, claiming that they had been killed "for counter-revolutionary agitation, sabotage, banditry, refusing to work, and attempting to escape." Even women were not spared. The wife of any activist who was executed was also condemned to capital punishment, as were any children over age twelve."[31]

Approximately 200 Trotskyites in Magadan, the capital of Kolyma, also went on hunger strike in the hope of being granted the status of political prisoners. Their declaration denounced the "gangster executioners" and "Stalin's fascism, even worse than Hitler's." On 11 October 1937 they were condemned to death, and 74 of them were executed on 26–27 October and 4 November. Such executions continued throughout 1937 and 1938.[32]

Wherever orthodox Communists were to be found, they were given orders to combat the Trotskyite minority in their midst. After the war in Spain the operation took a new turn, with the completely spurious revelation of links between Trotskyism and Nazism, made even as Stalin was preparing to sign a pact with Hitler.

Soon the Great Terror launched by Stalin reached the Central Committee of the Comintern. A 1965 survey of the liquidation of Comintern workers was Branko Lazich's evocatively titled "Martyrology of the Comintern."[33] Boris Suvarin ended his "Commentaries on the Martyrology," which followed Lazitch's article, with a remark concerning the humble collaborators at the Comintern, the anonymous victims of the Great Purge. It is a useful comment to bear in mind when looking at this particular chapter of the history of Soviet Communism: "Those who died in the massacres at the Comintern were *no more than the tiniest fraction of an enormous massacre, that of millions of workers and peasants* who were sacrificed without rhyme or reason by a monstrous tyranny hidden by a proletarian label."

Officials in both the central and the national offices were affected by the mechanisms of repression in the same way that ordinary citizens were. The Great Purge of 1936–37 claimed not only opponents of the regime but also officials in the Comintern apparatus and similar organizations: the Communist Youth International (KIM), the Red Trade Union International (Profintern), Red Aid (MOPR), the International Leninist School, the Communist University of Western National Minorities (KUMNZ), and other organizations. Wanda Pampuch-Bronska, the daughter of one of Lenin's old companions, reported under a pseudonym that in 1936 the KUMNZ was broken up, and its entire staff and almost all its students arrested.[34]

The historian Mikhail Panteleev, reviewing the records of the various Comintern sections, has so far found 133 victims out of a total staff of 492 (that is, 27 percent).[35] Between 1 January and 17 September 1937, 256 people were fired by the Secretariat Commission of the Executive Committee, made up of Mikhail Moskvin (Meir Trilisser), Wilhelm Florin, and Jan Anvelt; and by the Special Control Commission, created in May 1937 and consisting of Georgi Dimitrov, Moskvin, and Dmitry Manuilsky. In general, arrest soon followed dismissal: Elena Walter, who was fired from Dimitrov's secretariat on 16 October 1938, was arrested two days later, although Jan Borowski (Ludwig Komorovsky) was fired from the Central Executive Committee of the Comintern on 17 July and not arrested until 7 October. In 1937, 88 Comintern employees were arrested, and another 19 the following year. Others were arrested at their desks, including Anton Krajewski (Władysław Stein), who was then the press attaché in charge of propaganda and was imprisoned on 27 May 1937. Many were arrested immediately following missions abroad.

All sections of the Comintern, from the Secretariat itself to its various representatives in the Communist Parties, were affected in some manner. In 1937 and 1938 forty-one people were arrested at the Secretariat of the Executive Committee. In the Department for International Relations (the OMS), thirty-four were arrested. Moskvin himself fell victim on 23 November 1938 and was condemned to death on 1 February 1940. Jan Anvelt died while being tortured, and A. Munch-Peterson, a Dane, died in a prison hospital as a result of chronic tuberculosis. Fifty officials, including nine women, were shot. A Swiss national, Lydia Dübi, who was in charge of the underground Comintern network in Paris, was called to Moscow in early August 1937. No sooner had she arrived than she was arrested, together with her colleagues Karl Brichman and Erwin Wolf, and accused of having belonged to an "anti-Soviet Trotskyite organization" and of having spied for Germany, France, Japan, and Switzerland. She was condemned to death by the Military Collegium of the Supreme Court of the U.S.S.R. on 3 November and was shot a few days later. Her Swiss nationality afforded her no protection, and her family was brutally informed of the outcome with no explanation. The principle of familial responsibility, which was used against the general population, was also brought to bear on members of the Comintern. L. Jankowska, a Pole, was condemned to eight years in prison for being a "member of the family of a traitor to the fatherland," a status she acquired when her husband, Stanisław Skulski (Mertens), was arrested in August 1937 and shot on 21 September.

Osip Pyatnitsky (Tarchis) had been second in command to Manuilsky at the Comintern and had been in charge of the finances of foreign Communist Parties and secret liaisons with the Comintern worldwide. In 1934 he was appointed head of the political and administrative section of the Central Committee of the CPSU. On 24 June 1937 he intervened in a plenary session of the Central Committee to protest the intensification of repressions and the granting of special powers to the head of the NKVD, Nikolai Ezhov. Stalin was furious; he broke up the session and exerted great pressure to bring Pyatnitsky into line. All in vain: when the session opened the next day, Ezhov accused Pyatnitsky of being a former agent of the tsarist police, and had him arrested on 7 July. Ezhov then forced Boris Müller (Melnikov) to testify against Pyatnitsky, and after Müller himself was executed on 29 July 1938, the Military Collegium of the Supreme Court passed sentence on Pyatnitsky, who refused to plead guilty to the fabricated charge that he was a spy for Japan. He was condemned to death and shot on the night of 29–30 July.

Many of the staff at the Comintern who were executed were accused of belonging to "the anti-Comintern organization led by Pyatnitsky, [Wilhelm Hugo] Knorin, and Béla Kun." Others were simply labeled Trotskyites or counterrevolutionaries. Béla Kun, the former head of the Hungarian Commune, who had taken a stand against Manuilsky, was in turn accused by Manuilsky (probably on Stalin's orders), who twisted his words until they amounted to a direct attack on Stalin. Kun protested his innocence and reiterated his attack against Manuilsky and Moskvin, who he claimed were responsible for the poor reputation of the CPSU abroad and the general inefficiency of the Comintern. No one among those present, including Palmiro Togliatti, Otto Kuusinen, Wilhelm Pieck, Klement Gottwald, and Arvo Tuominen, came to his defense. When the meeting ended, Georgi Dimitrov tabled a motion requesting that the "Kun affair" be examined by a special commission. Kun was arrested as soon as he left the room and was executed in the basement of the Lubyanka building at an unknown date.[36]

According to Mikhail Panteleev, the ultimate aim of these purges was the eradication of all resistance to Stalinism.[37] The main targets of the repression were those who had been Opposition sympathizers or who had had any relationship with known Trotskyites. Other victims included German militants belonging to the faction led by Heinz Neumann, who was himself liquidated in 1937, and other former militants from the Democratic Centralist Group. At the time, according to Yakov Matusov, joint chief of the First Department of the secret Political Section of the Main Directorate for State Security (Glavnoe upravlenie gosudarstvennoi bezopasnosti; GUGB), then part of the NKVD, all high-ranking leaders in the state apparatus, unbeknownst to them, had dossiers containing evidence that could be used against them at any moment. Kliment Voroshilov, Andrei Vyshinsky, Lazar Kaganovich, Mikhail Kalinin, and Nikita Khrushchev all had such files. It is thus more than probable that similar files were kept on the activities of Comintern leaders.

The highest-ranking non-Russian Comintern leaders also actively participated in the repression. One symptomatic case was that of Palmiro Togliatti, one of the secretaries of the Comintern, who, after Stalin's death, was hailed as one of the people who had been openly opposed to terrorist methods. Togliatti himself accused Hermann Schubert, an official in the Red Aid, and prevented him from giving an account of his actions. Schubert was arrested shortly afterward and shot. The Petermanns, a German couple who were Communists and had arrived in the U.S.S.R. after 1933, were accused by Togliatti at a meeting of being Nazi agents, on the grounds that they had kept in touch with their family in Germany. They were arrested a few weeks later. Togliatti was present when everyone turned on Béla Kun, and he signed the order that sent him to his death. He was also present at the liquidation of a

Polish Communist in 1938. On that occasion he endorsed the Moscow trials, and saying: "Death to the cowards, spies, and fascist agents! Long live the Party of Lenin and Stalin, the vigilant guardian of the victories of the October Revolution, and the sure guarantor of the triumph of the revolution throughout the world! Long live the heir of Feliks Dzerzhinsky, Nikolai Ezhov!"[38]

Terror within the Communist Parties

Once the Central Bureau of the Comintern had been purged, Stalin set about attacking the other sections. The German section was the first to suffer. In addition to the descendants of the Volga Germans, the German community in Soviet Russia included militants from the German Communist Party (KPD) and antifascist refugees and workers who had left the Weimar Republic to help build socialism in the Soviet Union. But none of these people were exempt when the arrests began in 1933. In all, two-thirds of the antifascists in exile in the U.S.S.R. were affected by the repression.

The fate of militant German Communists is well documented thanks to the existence of lists of cadres, *Kaderlisten,* which were drawn up under the KPD leaders Wilhelm Pieck, Wilhelm Florin, and Herbert Wehner and used to punish or expel Communists and victims of repression. The earliest list dates from 3 September 1936, the last from 21 June 1938. A document from the late 1950s, drawn up by the control commission of the SED (the Socialist Unity Party, the name taken by the German Communist Party when it regrouped after World War II), lists some 1,136 people. Arrests reached their peak in 1937, when 619 people were arrested, and continued until 1941, when 21 were arrested. The fate of 666 of these people is unknown, although it is almost certain that they died in prison. At least 82 were executed, 197 died in prison camps, and 132 were handed over to the Nazis. Approximately 150 survived their long sentences and eventually managed to leave the U.S.S.R. One of the ideological reasons invoked to justify the arrest of these militants was that they had failed to stop Adolf Hitler's rise to power, as though Moscow itself had played no role in the Nazi seizure of power.[39]

The most tragic episode of all, the occasion on which Stalin displayed the full extent of his cynicism, was the handing over to Hitler of the German antifascists. This took place in 1937, when the Soviet authorities began expelling Germans from the U.S.S.R. On 16 February ten were condemned and then handed over by the Soviet special services. The names of some of them are well known: Emil Larisch, a technician who had been living in the U.S.S.R. since 1921; Arthur Thilo, an engineer who had arrived in 1931; Wilhelm Pfeiffer, a Communist from Hamburg; and Kurt Nixdorf, a university employee at the Marx-Engels Institute. All had been arrested in 1936 on charges of spying or "fascist activities," and the German ambassador, Werner von der Schulenberg, tried to intervene on their behalf with Maksim Litvinov, the Soviet minister of foreign affairs. Arthur Thilo managed to get to the British consulate in Warsaw, but many were not so lucky. Pfeiffer tried to get himself expelled to England, knowing that if he returned to Germany he would be arrested immediately. Eighteen months later, on 18 August 1938, he was taken to the Polish border and was never heard from again. Otto Walther, a lithographer from Leningrad who had lived in Russia since 1908, arrived in Berlin on 4 March 1937 and subsequently killed himself by throwing himself out a window of the house in which he was living.

At the end of May 1937, von der Schulenberg sent two new lists of Germans who had been arrested, and whose expulsion he considered desirable. Among the 67 names were several antifascists, including Kurt Nixdorf. In the autumn of 1937 negotiations took a new turn, and the Soviet Union agreed to speed up expulsions in response to German demands, since only 30 had actually been expelled so far. In November and December 1937 another 148 Germans were expelled, and in 1938 the number rose to 445. Generally the people to be expelled (including several members of the Schutzbund, the paramilitary arm of the Austrian Social Democratic Party) were escorted to the frontier with Poland, Lithuania, or Finland, where they were immediately registered and classified by the German authorities. In some cases, including that of the Austrian Communist Paul Meisel, victims were taken in May 1938 to the Austrian frontier via Poland and were then handed over to the Gestapo. Meisel, who was Jewish, subsequently died in Auschwitz.

This understanding between Nazi Germany and Soviet Russia prefigured the Nazi-Soviet pact of 1939, when, according to Jorge Semprum, "the truly convergent nature of all totalitarian systems was revealed." After the pact was signed, the expulsions increased dramatically. Once Poland was crushed by Hitler and Stalin, the two powers had a common border, so the victims could pass directly from a Soviet prison to a German one. From 1939 to 1941, as a result of an agreement signed on 27 November 1939, between 200 and 300 German Communists were handed over to the Gestapo as a measure of the goodwill of the Soviet authorities toward their new allies. Approximately 350 people were expelled between November 1939 and May 1941, including 85 Austrians. One of these was Franz Koritschoner, a founding member of the Austrian Communist Party, who had become an official in the Red Trade Union International. After being deported to the far north, he was handed over to the Gestapo in Lublin, transferred to Vienna, tortured, and executed in Auschwitz on 7 June 1941.

The Soviet authorities refused to take Jewish origins into account in their decisions to expel people. Hans Walter David, for example, a KPD member who was a composer and a conductor, as well as being Jewish, was handed over to the Gestapo and gassed in 1942 in the Majdanek camp. There were many other cases, some recounted in the memoirs of Alexander Weissberg, a physicist who survived to tell his story. Margaret Buber-Neumann, the companion of Hans Neumann, who had been pushed out of the KPD leadership and had emigrated to the U.S.S.R., also wrote of the extraordinary complicity that existed between the Nazis and the Soviet Union. After being arrested in 1937 and deported to Karaganda, in Siberia, she was handed over to the Gestapo along with many other unfortunates and interned in Ravensbrück.[40]

Weissberg recalled his transfer to the Germans:

> On 31 December 1939, we were awakened at six in the morning . . . After we had dressed and shaved we had to spend a few hours in a waiting room. One Jewish Communist from Hungary called Bloch had fled to Germany after the fall of the Commune in 1919. He had lived there with false papers and managed to continue working secretly as a Party activist. Later he emigrated with the same false papers. He had been arrested, and despite his protests was to be handed over to the German Gestapo . . . Just before midnight some buses arrived, and we were taken to the station . . . During the night of 31 December 1939–1 January 1940, the train started moving. It was carrying seventy beaten men back home . . . The train continued on through the devastated Polish countryside toward Brest Litovsk. On the Bug River bridge the other European totalitarian regime was waiting, in the form of the German Gestapo.[41]

Weissberg managed to escape the Nazi prisons, joined the Polish rebels, and fought alongside them. At the end of the war he crossed into Sweden and then went to England.

Margaret Buber-Neumann described the later stages of the same transfer:

> Three people refused to cross the bridge: a Hungarian Jew named Bloch, a Communist worker who had already been sentenced by the Nazis, and a German teacher whose name I cannot remember. They were dragged across the bridge by force. The SS disposed of the Jew immediately. We were then put on a train and taken to Lublin . . . In Lublin we were handed over to the Gestapo. There it became apparent that not only were we being handed over to the Gestapo, but that the NKVD had also sent all our records and documents to the SS. In my dossier, for instance, it was noted that I was the wife of Neumann and that he was one of the Germans most hated in Nazi Germany.[42]

Buber-Neumann remained in Ravensbrück until its liberation in April 1945.

At the same time that the German Communists were suffering, the cadres in the Palestinian Communist Party (PCP), many of whom had emigrated from

Poland, were also caught up in the terror. Joseph Berger, secretary of the PCP from 1929 to 1931, was arrested on 27 February 1935 and was liberated only after the Twentieth Soviet Party Congress in 1956. His survival was exceptional. Other militants were executed, and many more died in camps. Wolf Averbuch, the director of a tractor factory in Rostov-on-Don, was arrested in 1936 and executed in 1941. The systematic liquidation of members of the PCP and of socialist Zionist groups who had come to the U.S.S.R. is related to the more general Soviet policy toward the Jewish minority after the establishment of Birobidzhan as a Jewish autonomous region, all of whose leaders were arrested. Professor Iosif Liberberg, the president of the Executive Committee of Birobidzhan, was denounced as an "enemy of the people," and all the other cadres of state institutions in the autonomous region were also purged. Samuel Augursky was accused of belonging to a fictitious Judeo-Fascist Center. The entire Jewish section of the Russian Party (the Evreiskaya sektsiya) was taken apart. The goal of destroying all Jewish institutions was implemented even as the Soviet state was seeking support from Jewish notables abroad.[43]

The Polish Communists figure second only to Russians themselves in terms of the number who suffered in the purges. Unlike its counterparts elsewhere, the Polish Communist Party (KPP) had been dissolved following a vote by the Central Executive Committee of the Comintern on 16 August 1938. Stalin had always been suspicious of the KPP, which he felt was filled with deviationists. Many Polish Communists had been part of Lenin's entourage before 1917 and had enjoyed special protection in the U.S.S.R. as a result. In 1923 the KPP had taken a stand in support of Trotsky, and after Lenin's death it had voted in favor of the pro-Trotsky Opposition. The influence of Rosa Luxemburg on the KPP was also criticized. At the Fifth Congress of the Comintern in June–July 1924, Stalin sidelined the people who had been the Party leaders—Adolf Warsky, Henryk Walecki, and Wera Kostrzewa—in what was clearly the first step toward total control of the KPP by the Comintern. The KPP was then denounced as a hotbed of Trotskyism. But even this declaration does little to explain the radical purge that then struck the Party, many members of which were Jewish. There also followed the Polish Military Organization (POW) affair in 1933 (discussed in Chapter 19). Other factors should also be borne in mind, such as the fact that the Comintern had a policy of systematically weakening the Polish state to increase its dependence on both the U.S.S.R. and Germany. The theory that the most important element behind the liquidation of the KPP was the need to prepare for the signing of the German-Soviet agreements deserves to be taken seriously. How Stalin went about it is also quite revealing. He made sure (with the assistance of the Comintern) that each of the victims was brought back to Moscow, and that as few as possible escaped. The only ones who survived were those who were imprisoned in Poland, such as Władysław Gomułka.

In February 1938 the official Comintern bulletin that came out twice a week, *La correspondance internationale,* launched an attack, signed by J. Swiecicki, on the KPP. During the purge that began in June 1937, when General Secretary Julian Lenski was called to Moscow and immediately disappeared, twelve members of the Central Committee, many leaders slightly lower in the hierarchy, and several hundred militants, including Poles who had enlisted in the International Brigades, were liquidated. The political leaders of the Dombrowski Brigade, Kazimierz Cichowski and Gustav Reicher, were arrested upon their return to Moscow. Stalin did not permit a new Polish Communist Party to be formed until 1942, under the name Polish Workers' Party (PPR), so that a new government could be formed to rival the official government-in-exile that had been set up in London.

The Yugoslav Communists also suffered badly under the Stalinist terror. After being banned in 1921, the Yugoslav Communist Party had been forced to regroup abroad, in Vienna from 1921 to 1936, and in Paris from 1936 to 1939; but after 1925 its main center was Moscow. A small core of Yugoslav émigrés first formed among the students at the Communist University of Western National Minorities (KUMNZ), the Sverdlov Communist University, and the International Leninist School. This group was considerably strengthened by a second wave of émigrés after King Alexander took power as dictator in 1929. In the 1930s the 200 to 300 Yugoslav Communists residing in the U.S.S.R. had a fairly high profile in the international organizations, particularly in the Comintern and the International Youth Organization. They were thus usually members of the CPSU.

They began to acquire a bad reputation because of the numerous factional struggles to take control of the YCP. Intervention by the Comintern became more and more frequent and constraining. In mid-1925 the first *chistka* (purge) took place at the KUMNZ, where the Yugoslav students were favoring the Opposition and opposing the rector, Maria J. Frukina. A few students were disgraced and expelled, and four of them (Ante Ciliga, V. Dedić, A. Dragić, and G. Eberling) were arrested and banished to Siberia. Another sixteen militants were expelled in another purge in 1932.

In the aftermath of the Kirov assassination, control over political émigrés was reinforced, and in the autumn of 1936 all YCP militants were investigated before the terror began. Although little is known about the fate of the anonymous workers, we do know that eight secretaries of the YCP's Central Committee, fifteen other members of the Central Committee, and twenty-one secretaries from regional or local bodies were arrested and disappeared. Sima Markević, one of the secretaries, who had been forced to flee to the U.S.S.R. and had worked at the Academy of Sciences, was arrested in July 1939, sentenced to ten years of hard labor, and forbidden any contact with the outside world. He died in prison. Others were executed immediately, including the Vujović brothers, Radomir (a member of the YCP Central Committee) and Gregor (a member of the Central Youth Committee). Another brother, Voja, who had been the head of the Communist Youth International and a Trotsky sympathizer, also disappeared. Milan Gorkić, a secretary of the Central Committee of the Yugoslav Communist Party from 1932 to 1937, was accused of having established "an anti-Soviet organization within the International, and of having directed a terrorist group within the Comintern, which was led by Knorin and Pyatnitsky."

In the mid-1960s the YCP rehabilitated about 100 victims of the repression, but no systematic investigation was ever undertaken. Such an inquiry would of course also have raised the question of the number of victims of the repression of supporters of the U.S.S.R. in Yugoslavia after the 1948 schism. And it would have demonstrated quite convincingly that the ascension of Tito (Josip Broz) to the leadership of the Party in 1938 took place as a result of a particularly bloody purge. The fact that Tito rose up against Stalin in 1948 takes nothing away from his responsibility for the purges of the 1930s.

The Hunt for Trotskyites

Having thinned the ranks of foreign Communists living in the U.S.S.R., Stalin turned his attention to dissidents living abroad. Thus the NKVD gained an opportunity to demonstrate its power worldwide.

One of the most spectacular cases was that of Ignaz Reiss, whose real name was Nathan Poretsky. As a young Jewish revolutionary in Central Europe who had emerged from the Great War, Reiss was among many who were eagerly recruited by the Comintern.[44] A professional agitator, he worked in the international underground network and carried out his work with such efficiency that he was decorated with the Order of the Red Flag in 1928. After 1935 he was "retrieved" by the NKVD, which took control of all foreign networks and put him in charge of espionage in Germany. The first of the great Moscow trials came as a terrible shock to Reiss, who then decided to break with Stalin. All too familiar with the house rules, he prepared his defection with extreme care. On 17 July 1937 he sent an open letter to the CPSU Central Committee in which he explained his position and attacked Stalin and Stalinism by name, calling it "that admixture of the worst types of opportunism, unprincipled, bloody, and deceptive, which is threatening to poison the whole world and to kill off what remains of the Workers' Movement." Reiss also explained his move into the Trotskyite camp, and in doing so unknowingly signed his own death warrant. The NKVD immediately contacted its network in France and found Reiss in Switzerland, where an ambush was laid for him. In Lausanne on the night of 4 September he was riddled with bullets by two French Communists while a female NKVD agent attempted to kill his wife and child with a box of poisoned chocolates. Despite a long police search in both France and Switzerland, the killers and their accomplices were never found. Trotsky immediately suspected Jacques Duclos, one of the PCF secretaries, and he told his own secretary, Jan Van Heijenoort, to send the following telegram to the head of the French government: "Chautemps Head of Government France / regarding Ignaz Reiss assassination affair / my files stolen among other crimes / suggest at least interrogating Jacques Duclos Vice President Chamber of Deputies ex-GPU agent."[45]

Duclos had been vice president of the Chamber of Deputies since 1936. Nothing was done to follow up on this telegram.

The assassination of Reiss was quite spectacular, but it was part of a much wider movement to liquidate Trotskyites wherever possible. It is hardly surprising that Trotskyites were massacred in the U.S.S.R. along with all the others who died in the purges. What is more surprising is the lengths to which the secret services went to destroy their opponents abroad, as well as the different Trotskyite groups that had sprung up in so many countries. The main method used was the patient covert infiltration of all such groups.

In July 1937 Rudolf Klement, the leader of the International Secretariat of the Trotskyite Opposition, disappeared. On 26 August a headless, legless body was fished out of the Seine and was soon identified as the body of Klement. Trotsky's own son, Lev Sedov, died in Paris shortly after a medical operation, but the suspicious circumstances surrounding his death led his family to believe it was an assassination organized by the Soviet secret services, although this is denied in the memoirs of Pavel Sudoplatov.[46] But undoubtedly Lev Sedov was being closely watched by the NKVD. In fact one of his close friends, Mark Zborowski, was an agent who had infiltrated the Trotskyite movement.

Sudoplatov did admit, however, that in March 1939 he had been personally ordered by Beria and Stalin to assassinate Trotsky. Stalin told him: "We must do away with Trotsky this year, before the outbreak of the war that is inevitably coming." He added, "You will be answerable to no one but Beria for this, and you are to take full charge of the mission."[47] The manhunt was launched, and after Paris, Brussels, and the United States the leader of the Fourth International was found in Mexico. With the help of the Mexican Communist Party, Sudoplatov's men prepared a first attempt on Trotsky's life on 24 May, which he miraculously escaped. The infiltration by Ramón Mercader under an assumed name finally provided Sudoplatov with the means to eliminate Trotsky. Mercader gained the confidence of one of the female members of Trotsky's group and managed to get into contact with him. Rather warily, Trotsky agreed to meet him to go over an article Mercader had supposedly written in Trotsky's defense. Mercader then stabbed Trotsky in the head with an ice pick. Mortally wounded, Trotsky cried out for help, and his wife and bodyguards threw themselves on Mercader. Trotsky died the next day.

The connections among the various Communist parties, the Comintern sections, and the NKVD had been denounced by Trotsky, who knew very well that the Comintern was dominated by the GPU and the NKVD. In a letter of 27 May 1940 to the procurator general of Mexico, three days after the first attempt on his life, he wrote that "the traditions and methods of GPU organization are by now well established outside the Soviet Union. The GPU needs a legal or semilegal cover for its activities, and an environment favorable for the recruiting of new agents, and it finds the necessary environment and conditions in the so-called Communist parties."[48] In his last text, regarding the assassination attempt of 24 May, he visited in detail the incident that had nearly taken his life. For him, the GPU (Trotsky always used that 1922 abbreviation from the days when he had been associated with it) was "Stalin's main weapon for wielding power" and was "the instrument of totalitarianism in the U.S.S.R.," from which "a spirit of servitude and cynicism has spread throughout the Comintern and poisoned the workers' movement to the core." He described at some length how this had influenced matters: "As organizations, the GPU and the Comintern are not identical, but they are indissolubly linked. The one is subordinate to the other, and it is not the Comintern that gives orders to the GPU but quite the contrary: the GPU completely dominates the Comintern."[49]

This analysis, backed up a wealth of examples, was the result of Trotsky's twofold experience as one of the leaders of the nascent Soviet state, and also as a man on the run from the NKVD killers who trailed him around the world, and whose names today are in no doubt. They were the successive directors of the Special Tasks Department established in December 1936 by Nikolai Ezhov: Sergei Spiegelglass (who failed), Pavel Sudoplatov (who died in 1996), and Naum Eitingon (who died in 1981), who finally succeeded thanks to many accomplices.[50]

Most of the details about Trotsky's assassination in Mexico on 20 August 1940 are known thanks to successive inquiries carried out on the spot and again later by Julian Gorkin.[51] In any case the man who ordered the killing was never in any doubt, and the people directly responsible were also known. All of this was later confirmed by Pavel Sudoplatov. Jaime Ramón Mercader del Rio was the son of Caridad Mercader, a Communist who had been working for the services for a long time and who became the mistress of Naum Eitingon. Mercader had approached Trotsky using the name Jacques Mornard, who did in fact exist, and who died in Belgium in 1967. Mornard had fought in Spain, and it was probably there that his passport was borrowed by the Soviet services. Mercader also used the name Jacson, with another false passport, which had belonged to a Canadian who had fought in the International Brigades and had died at the front. Ramón Mercader died in 1978 in Havana, where Fidel Castro had invited him to work as an adviser to the Ministry of the Interior. He had been decorated with the Order of Lenin for his crime, and he was buried quietly in Moscow.

Although Stalin was now rid of his most important adversary, the hunt for Trotskyites continued. The French example is revealing of militant Communists' reflexive response to small Trotskyite organizations. During the occupation of France, some Trotskyites may well have been denounced by Communists to the French and German police.

In the prisons and camps of Vichy, Trotskyites were systematically separated from the rest. In Nontron, in the Dordogne, Gérard Bloch was ostracized by the Communist collective led by Michel Bloch, the son of the writer Jean-Richard Bloch. Later incarcerated in the Elysée prison, Gérard Bloch was warned by a Catholic teacher that the Communist collective of the prison had decided to execute him by strangling him in the night.[52]

In this context of blind hatred, the disappearance of four Trotskyites, including Pietro Tresso, the founder of the Italian Communist party, from the FTP (Francs-Tireurs et Partisans) "Wodli" *maquis* in Haute-Loire is of greater significance. The FTP was a Stalinist organization through which the Communist-dominated National Front operated. Having escaped from the prison in Puy-en-Velay with their Communist colleagues on 1 October 1943, five Trotskyite militants were "captured" by the Communist *maquis*. One of them, Albert Demazière, somehow managed to break away from his companions, and he was the only one to survive: Tresso, Pierre Salini, Jean Reboul, and Abraham Sadek were executed at the end of October, after a farcical trial.[53] Witnesses and the people involved (who are still alive) reported that the militants had been plotting to poison the water supply in the camp, an almost atavistic explanation that smacks of antisemitism against Trotsky (similar accusations were made against his own son Sergei in the U.S.S.R.) and against at least one of the prisoners, Abraham Sadek. The Communist movement showed that it, too, was capable of the crudest antisemitism. Before the four Trotskyites were killed, they were photographed, probably so that they could be identified back at PCF headquarters, and forced to write a summary of their lives.

Even inside the concentration camps, the Communists attempted to annihilate their closest rivals by taking advantage of the hierarchies that existed there. Marcel Beaufrère, leader of the Breton regional section of the Internationalist Workers' Party, was arrested in October 1943 and deported to Buchenwald in January 1944. The interblock chief (who was himself a Communist) suspected him of being a Trotskyite. Ten days after Beaufrère's arrival, a friend informed him that the Communist cell in Block 39—his block—had condemned him to death and was sending him as a guinea pig to be injected with typhus. Beaufrère was saved at the last minute through the intervention of German militants.[54] The Communists often used the concentration-camp system to get rid of their political enemies, deliberately sending them to the hardest sections, even though they themselves were victims of the same Gestapo officers and the same SS divisions. Marcel Hic and Roland Filiâtre, who were deported to Buchenwald, were sent to the terrible camp Dora "with the assent of KPD cadres who had high administrative functions in the camp," according to Rodolphe Prager.[55] Hic died there; Filiâtre survived another attempt on his life in 1948.

Other liquidations of militant Trotskyites took place during the liberation. Mathieu Buchholz, a young Paris worker from the "Class War" group, disappeared on 11 September 1944. In May 1947 his group claimed that this had been the work of Stalinists.

The Trotskyite movement had a sizable impact in Greece. A secretary from the Greek Communist party (the KKE), Pandelis Poliopolos, who was shot by the Italians, had joined the movement before the war. During the war the Trotskyites rallied to the cause of the National Liberation Front (EAM), founded in June 1941 by the Communists. Ares Velouchiotes, the leader of the People's Army for National Liberation (ELAS), ordered some twenty Trotskyite leaders to be killed. After the liberation the persecution of Trotskyites continued, and many were tortured to reveal the names of their colleagues. In 1946, in a report to the Central Committee of the Communist Party, Vasilis Bartziotas noted that 600 Trotskyites had been executed by OPLA (Organization for the Protection of the Popular Struggle), a figure that probably also includes anarchists and other dissident socialists.[56] The Archeo-Marxists, militants who had broken with the KKE in 1924, were also persecuted and assassinated.[57]

It was no different for Albanian Communists. After unification in 1941, differences emerged among the left-wing groups that rallied around Anastaste

Lula, primarily between the Trotskyites and leaders of the orthodox parties (Enver Hoxha, Mehmet Shehu) who were being advised by the Yugoslavs. Lula was summarily executed in 1943. After several attempts on his life, Sadik Premtaj, another popular Trotskyite leader, managed to reach France, but in May 1951 he fell victim to another assassination attempt by Djemal Chami, a former member of the International Brigades and an Albanian agent in Paris.

In China an embryonic movement had taken shape in 1928 under the leadership of Chen Duxiu, one of the founders and earliest leaders of the Chinese Communist Party. In 1935 it still had only a few hundred members. In the war against Japan some of them managed to infiltrate the Eighth Army of the People's Liberation Army (PLA), the armed force of the Communist Party. Mao Zedong had them executed and liquidated their battalions. At the end of the civil war they were systematically hunted down and killed. The fate of many of them is still unknown.

For a while the situation in Indochina was quite different. Trotskyites from the Tranh Dau (The Struggle) and Communists put up a common front from 1933 onward. The influence of Trotskyites was strongest in the south of the peninsula. In 1937 a directive from Jacques Duclos forbade the Indochinese Communist Party to cooperate with the Tranh Dau militants. In the months following the conflict with the Japanese, another Trotskyite branch—the International Communist League—gained an ascendancy that troubled the Communist leaders. In September 1945, when the British troops arrived, the International Communist League shattered the peaceful welcome that the Viet Minh (the Democratic Front for Independence) had reserved for them. On 14 September the Viet Minh launched a huge operation against the Trotskyite cadres. Most of them were executed shortly after their capture. Having fought against the Anglo-French troops in the paddy fields, they were crushed by the Viet Minh troops. In the second part of the operation the Viet Minh turned against the Tranh Dau. Imprisoned in Ben Suc, they too were executed as the French troops approached. Ta Tu Thau, the leader of the movement, was executed in February 1946. Ho Chi Minh himself wrote that all Trotskyites were "traitors and spies of the lowest sort."[58]

In Czechoslovakia, the fate of Zavis Kalandra is typical of the fate of all his companions. In 1936 Kalandra had been thrown out of the Czechoslovak Communist Party for writing a leaflet denouncing the Moscow trials. He later fought in the resistance, and was deported by the Germans to Oranienburg. Arrested in November 1949, he was accused of plotting against the republic and tortured. His trial began in June 1950; he made a "full confession" and was sentenced to death on 8 June. In *Combat* on 14 June, André Breton asked Paul Eluard to intervene in his favor; both had known him since before the war.

Eluard replied: "I am too busy worrying about innocent people who are protesting their innocence to worry about guilty people who have admitted their guilt."[59] Kalandra was executed on 27 June with three of his companions.

Foreign Antifascist and Revolutionary Victims of the Terror in the U.S.S.R.

The Communist terror targeted more than the Comintern, Trotskyites, and other dissidents. In the 1930s there were still many foreigners living in the U.S.S.R. who were not Communists but who had been attracted by the Soviet dream. Many of them paid the highest price for the passion they had felt for Soviet Russia.

In the early 1930s the Soviet Union launched a propaganda campaign in the Karelia region, making much of the possibilities offered by the frontier regions between Russia and Finland and of the golden opportunity presented there to "build socialism." Some 12,000 people left Finland to live in Karelia and were joined there by another 5,000 Finns from the United States. Most of the latter were members of the American Association of Finnish Workers and were experiencing tremendous hardship because of the stock-market crash of 1929. Amtorg agents (Amtorg was the Soviet advertising agency) promised them work, good salaries, housing, and a free trip from New York to Leningrad. They were told to bring all their possessions with them.

What Aino Kuusinen termed "the rush for Utopia" soon turned into a nightmare. As soon as the Finns arrived, their machinery, tools, and savings were confiscated. They were forced to hand over their passports and effectively found themselves prisoners in an underdeveloped region where there was nothing but forest and conditions were extremely harsh.[60] According to Arvo Tuominen, who led the Finnish Communist Party and held a key position in the Presidium of the Comintern Executive Committee until 1939 before being condemned to death and then having his sentence commuted to ten years' imprisonment, at least 20,000 Finns were detained in concentration camps.[61]

Forced to live in Kirovakan after World War II, Aino Kuusinen also witnessed the arrival of the Armenians, another set of victims of clever propaganda who came to live in the Soviet Republic of Armenia. In response to Stalin's appeal to all Russians living abroad to return home to rebuild the country, many Armenians, most of whom had been living in exile in Turkey, mobilized to promote the Armenian Republic, which they envisaged as the land of their forefathers. In September 1947 several thousand of them gathered in Marseille, and 3,500 boarded the ship *Rossiya*, which carried them to the U.S.S.R. As soon as the ship had entered Soviet territorial waters in the Black Sea, the attitude of the authorities changed markedly. Many understood immediately that they had walked into a terrible trap. In 1948 another 200 Armenians arrived from the United States. Deceived by the festivities, they met the same fate: their passports were confiscated as soon as they arrived. In May 1956 several hundred Armenians in France demonstrated when Christian Pineau, the minister of foreign affairs, was to visit Erevan. Only 60 families managed to leave the U.S.S.R. during these repressions.[62] Almost all left as soon as they could.

The terror affected not only those who had returned to the U.S.S.R. by choice, but also those who had already suffered under other dictatorial regimes. According to Article 29 of the 1936 Soviet constitution, "The U.S.S.R. grants asylum to all foreign citizens persecuted for defending the interests or rights of workers, for their scholarly work, or for their struggle to achieve national liberation." In his novel *Life and Fate*, Vasily Grossman describes a confrontation between an SS soldier and an ex-militant Bolshevik. In a long monologue the SS soldier sums up the fate of thousands of men, women, and children who came to seek refuge in the U.S.S.R.: "Who is in the camps in peacetime, when there are no more prisoners of war? The enemies of the party, and the enemies of the people. They are people whom you know very well, because they're in your camps too. And if your prisoners came into our SS camps in peacetime, we wouldn't let them out again because your prisoners are our prisoners too."[63]

Whether they came from abroad solely because of Soviet propaganda, because they sought refuge or security that they could not expect in their countries of origin, or because of their political beliefs, all immigrants were treated as potential spies. At least such was the excuse for condemning the majority of them.

One of the first waves of immigration was that of Italian anti-Fascists in the mid-1920s. A number of them, believing that they had at last found the true home of socialism and the country of their dreams, were cruelly deceived and suffered egregiously under the terror. Italian Communists and sympathizers numbered around 600 in the U.S.S.R. in the mid-1930s—about 250 émigré political cadres and another 350 undergoing training in the political schools. Because many of the students left the U.S.S.R. after their schooling, and another 100 activists left to fight in Spain in 1936–37, the Great Terror affected only those who remained. Around 200 Italians were arrested, mostly for espionage, and about 40 were shot, 25 of whom have been identified. The remainder were sent to the gulags, to the Kolyma gold mines or to Kazakhstan. Romolo Caccavale has published a moving study tracing the movements and tragic destiny of several dozen of these activists.[64]

A typical case is that of Nazareno Scarioli, an anti-Fascist who had fled Italy in 1925. From there he reached Berlin and finally Moscow. Welcomed by the Italian section of the Red Cross, he worked in an agricultural colony near Moscow for one year before being transferred to a second colony in Yalta, where some twenty other Italian anarchists were working under the direction of Tito Scarselli. In 1933 the colony was dissolved, and Scarioli returned to Moscow, where he found a job in a biscuit factory. He played an active role in the Italian community there.

Then came the years of the Great Purge. Fear and terror divided the Italian community, and everyone began to suspect his own comrades. The Italian Communist leader Paolo Robotti announced to the Italian club the arrest of thirty-six "enemies of the people" who worked in a ball-bearing factory. Robotti forced each person present to approve the arrest of the workers whom he knew personally. When the time came to vote, Scarioli refused to raise his hand, and he was arrested the following night. After being tortured at the Lubyanka building, he signed a confession. He was then deported to the Kolyma region and forced to work in a gold mine. Many other Italians shared the same fate, and many died, including the sculptor Arnaldo Silva; an engineer called L. Cerquetti; the Communist leader Aldo Gorelli, whose sister had married Egidio Sulotto, the future Communist politician; Vicenzo Baccala, the former secretary of the Rome committee of the Italian Communist Party; a Tuscan, Otello Gaggi, who worked as a porter in Moscow; Luigi Calligaris, a laborer in Moscow; Carlo Costa, a Venetian unionist working in Odessa; and Edmundo Peluso, who had been a friend of Lenin's in Zurich. In 1950 Scarioli, who then weighed 36 kilos, left Kolyma but was forced to continue working in Siberia. In 1954 he was granted amnesty and subsequently received a full pardon. He then waited another six years for a visa to return to Italy.

The refugees were not limited to members of the Italian Communist Party or to Communist sympathizers. Some were anarchists who had been persecuted at home and decided to move to the Soviet Union. The most famous of such cases is that of Francesco Ghezzi, a militant unionist and freedom fighter, who arrived in Russia in June 1921 to represent the Italian Trade Union at the Red Trade Union International. In 1922 he traveled to Germany, where he was arrested; the Italian government had charged him with terrorism and demanded his extradition. A vigorous campaign by his supporters in Italy saved him from the Italian prisons, but he was forced to return to the U.S.S.R. In the autumn of 1924 Ghezzi, who was linked closely to Pierre Pascal and Nikolai Lazarevich, had his first run-in with the GPU. In 1929 he was arrested again, sentenced to three years in prison, and interned in Suzdal under what were criminal conditions, considering that he was suffering from tuberculosis. His friends organized a support campaign in France and Switzerland, and Romain Rolland, among others, signed a petition in his favor. The Soviet authorities then spread the rumor that Ghezzi was a secret Fascist agent. When he was freed in 1931 he returned to work in a factory. He was arrested again in 1937, but this time his friends abroad could find out nothing about his whereabouts. He was reported dead in Vorkuta in late August 1941.[65]

In Linz on 11 February 1934, when the leaders of the Austrian Schutzbund decided to resist all attacks from the Heimwehren (the Patriotic Guard), who were trying to ban the Socialist Party, they could hardly have imagined the fate that awaited them.

The Heimwehren attack in Linz forced the Social Democrats to begin a general strike in Vienna, which was followed by an uprising. But Engelbert Dollfuss was victorious after four days of hard fighting, and the militant socialists who escaped prison sentences or internment either went into hiding or fled to Czechoslovakia, while others went on to fight later in Spain. Some of them, attracted by intensive propaganda against the Social Democratic leadership, fled to the Soviet Union. On 23 April 1934, 300 people arrived in Moscow, and smaller convoys continued arriving right up until December. The German embassy calculated that there were 807 Schutzbund immigrants in the U.S.S.R.[66] If one includes their families, about 1,400 people had sought refuge in the U.S.S.R.

The first convoy to arrive in Moscow was greeted by the leaders of the Austrian Communist Party (KPO), and the combatants paraded through the streets. They were taken in hand by the Central Council of Trade Unions. One hundred twenty children whose fathers had fallen on the barricades or been condemned to death were gathered together and sent off to the Crimea for a while, before all being housed in Children's Home No. 6 in Moscow, which was specially built for them.[67]

After a few weeks' rest, the Austrian workers were sent out to factories in Moscow, Kharkiv, Leningrad, Gorky, and Rostov. They quickly became disenchanted by the terrible working conditions. Austrian Communist leaders were forced to intervene. The Soviet authorities tried to pressure them into taking Soviet citizenship, and by 1938, 300 of them had done so. But significant numbers also contacted the Austrian embassy in the hope of being repatriated. Seventy-three succeeded in returning to Austria in 1936. According to the Austrian embassy, 400 had made the return journey before the spring of 1938 (after the Anschluss of March 1938, all Austrians became German subjects). Another 160 traveled to Spain to fight in the war there.

But many did not have a chance to leave the U.S.S.R.; 278 Austrians were arrested between late 1934 and 1938.[68] In 1939 Karlo Stajner met a Viennese named Fritz Koppensteiner in Norilsk but lost touch with him.[69] Some were executed, notably Gustl Deutch, a former leader from the Floridsdorf quarter and a former commander of the "Karl Marx" Regiment, whose brochure, *February Combat in Floridsdorf,* the Soviet Union had published in 1934.

Even Children's Home No. 6 was not spared. In the autumn of 1936 arrests began among the parents of those housed there, and the children were then taken into NKVD custody and sent away to orphanages. The mother of Wolfgang Leonhard disappeared after her arrest in October 1936. In the summer of 1937 he received a postcard from the Komi republic, informing him that she had been sentenced to five years in a forced-labor camp for "Trotskyite counterrevolutionary activities."[70]

On 10 February 1963 the socialist journal *Arbeiter Zeitung* told the story of the Sladek family. In mid-September 1934 Frau Sladek and her two sons went to Kharkiv to join her husband, Josef Sladek, a *Schutzbunder* who had worked on the railways in Semmering and then fled to the U.S.S.R. In 1937 the NKVD began its arrests among the Austrian community in Kharkiv, later than it had in Moscow and Leningrad. Josef Sladek's turn came on 15 February 1938. In 1941, before the German attack, Frau Sladek asked permission to leave the country and went to the German embassy. On 26 July the NKVD also arrested her son Alfred, age sixteen, and Victor, age eight, who was sent to an NKVD orphanage. NKVD functionaries, seeking to extract a confession from Alfred at all costs, beat him and told his mother that he had been shot. Evacuated because of the German advance, the mother and son then met by chance in the Ivdel camp, in the Urals. Frau Sladek had been sentenced to five years for espionage; Alfred had been sentenced to ten years for espionage and anti-Soviet agitation. Transferred to the Sarma camp, they found Josef Sladek, who had been sentenced in Kharkiv to five years of prison. They were then separated again. Set free in 1946, Frau Sladek was assigned residency in Solikamsk, in the Urals, where she was joined by her husband one year later. By now Josef was suffering from tuberculosis and a weak heart and was unable to work. He died a beggar on 31 May 1948. In 1951 Alfred was freed and rejoined his mother. In 1954, after many more hardships, they managed to reach Austria and returned to Semmering. The last time they had seen Victor was seven years earlier. They never heard from him again.

In 1917 there were 2,600 Yugoslavs living in Russia, and by 1924 the number had risen to 3,750. Their numbers were swelled by industrial workers and specialists from America and Canada who had come with all their belongings to try to "build socialism." They lived in colonies all over the country, from Leninsk to Magnitogorsk and Saratov. Between 50 and 100 of them helped build the Moscow subway. As with the other nationalities, Yugoslav emigration was limited. Božidar Maslarić claimed in 1952 that their fate was one of the worst, adding that "the vast majority were arrested in 1937 and 1938, and their fate remains unknown."[71] His view is supported by the fact that several hundred émigrés disappeared without a trace. Even now no definite information is available about the fate of the Yugoslavs who worked in the U.S.S.R., in particular concerning those who worked on the subway, protested against their working conditions, and were subsequently taken away, never to be seen again.

In mid-September 1939 the division of Poland between Nazi Germany and the Soviet Union, which had been secretly decided on 23 August 1939, came into force. The two invaders coordinated their action to control the population, and the Gestapo and the NKVD worked together. Out of a Jewish community of 3.3 million, 2 million fell into the German zone of occupation. After the persecutions, massacres, and burning of synagogues came the establishment of the ghettoes, first in Łódź on 30 April 1940, and then in Warsaw in October, before it was closed on 15 November.

Many Polish Jews had fled east before the advancing German army. In the winter of 1939–40 the Germans were not overly worried about people fleeing over the border, but many of those who did try their luck met an unexpected obstacle: "The Soviet Guards in the 'classless society' in their long fur coats, with their bayonets at the ready, often greeted with police dogs and bursts of automatic gunfire the nomads who had set out for the promised land."[72] From December 1939 to March 1940 the Jews found themselves trapped in a no-man's-land about a mile wide, on the west bank of the Bug, and were forced to camp out under the stars. Most of them then turned around and returned to the German zone.

L. C., "I.D. no. 15015," a former soldier in the Polish army of General Ladislav Anders, later summed up the situation as follows:

> The territory was a sector of about 600–700 meters, where about 800 people had been stranded for several weeks. Ninety percent of them were Jews who had escaped from the Germans. We were ill and constantly damp from the incessant autumn rain, and we huddled together for warmth. The "humanitarian" Soviet border guards wouldn't give us even a mouthful of bread or hot water. They didn't even let through the peasants from the surrounding countryside, who were willing to help us stay alive. Many of us died there as a result . . . I can confirm that the people who went back home to the German side were right to do so, because the NKVD was no better than the Gestapo from any point of view. The only difference was that the Gestapo killed you more quickly, while the NKVD killed and tortured in a horribly long and slow way, so that anyone who survived all of this came out a broken man and was an invalid for the rest of his life.[73]

Symbolically, Israel Joshua Singer had his hero die in this no-man's-land, after he had become an "enemy of the people" and had been forced to flee from the U.S.S.R.[74]

In March 1940 several hundred thousand refugees—some historians put the figure at around 600,000—were forcibly given Soviet passports. The Soviet-German pact included the exchange of refugees. With their families broken apart and with poverty and NKVD oppression becoming ever more unbearable, some decided to try to return to the German part of prewar Poland. Jules Margoline, who had wound up in Lviv, in western Ukraine, reported that in the spring of 1940 "the Jews preferred the German ghetto to Soviet equality."[75] It seemed to them a much better idea to try to flee the zone of occupation to reach a neutral country than to attempt flight through the Soviet Union itself.

Early in 1940 deportations affecting Polish citizens began (see Chapter 19 for details), continuing into June. Poles of all denominations were taken by train to the far north and to Kazakhstan. Margoline's own convoy took ten days to reach Murmansk. One of the great observers of life in the concentration camps, he wrote:

> The main difference between the Soviet camps and detention camps in the rest of the world is not their huge, unimaginable size or the murderous conditions found there, but something else altogether. It's the need to tell an endless series of lies to save your own life, to lie every day, to wear a mask for years and never say what you really think. In Soviet Russia, free citizens have to do the same thing. Dissembling and lies become the only means of defense. Public meetings, business meetings, encounters on the street, conversations, even posters on the wall all get wrapped up in an official language that doesn't contain a single word of truth. People in the West can't possibly understand what it is really like to lose the right to say what you think for years on end, and the way you have to repress the tiniest "illegal" thought you might have and stay silent as the tomb. That sort of pressure breaks something inside people.[76]

A 1992 article revealed the fate of two Polish socialists.[77] Viktor Alter (born in 1890), a municipal magistrate in Warsaw, was a member of the Socialist Workers' International and had also been the president of the Federation of Jewish Unions. Henryk Erlich was a member of the Communal Council of Warsaw and the editor of a Jewish daily called *Folkstaytung*. Both were also members of the Bund, the Jewish Socialist Workers' Party. In 1939 they took refuge in the Soviet zone. Alter was arrested on 26 September in Kowel, Erlich on 4 October in Brest Litovsk. Transferred to Lubyanka, Alter was sentenced to death on 20 July 1940 for anti-Soviet activities (it was claimed that he had been in league with the Polish police and been in charge of illegal Bund action). The sentence imposed by the Military Collegium of the Supreme Court of the U.S.S.R. was commuted to ten years in camp. On 2 August 1940 Erlich was sentenced to death by a court-martial of the NKVD forces in Saratov, but his sentence, too, was reduced to ten years in camp. Freed in September 1941 after the Sikorsky-Maisky agreement, Alter and Erlich were summoned to meet Beria, who proposed that they establish a Jewish anti-Nazi committee, which they agreed to do. They were sent to Kuibyshev and were arrested again on 4 December, accused of having collaborated with the Nazis. Beria ordered that they be given solitary confinement, and thereafter they were known as prisoners 41 (Alter) and 42 (Erlich), their identity not to be revealed to anyone. On 23 December 1941, now considered to be Soviet citizens, they were again condemned to death under section 1 of Article 58, which punished treason. Over the following weeks they sent a series of requests to the authorities, probably unaware that they had again been sentenced to death. Henryk Erlich hanged himself from the bars of his cell on 15 May 1942. Until the archives were opened, it was believed that he had been executed.

Viktor Alter had also threatened to commit suicide. Beria ordered a closer watch to be kept on him, and he was executed on 17 February 1943. The sentence, passed on 23 December 1941, had been personally approved by Stalin. Significantly, the execution took place shortly after the victory in Stalingrad. The Soviet authorities added a further calumny to the execution, claiming that Alter and Erlich had been spreading propaganda in favor of the signing of a peace treaty with Nazi Germany.

In the winter of 1945–46 the physician Jacques Pat, secretary of the Jewish Workers' Committee of the United States, went to Poland to begin an inquiry into Nazi crimes. On his return he published two articles in the *Jewish Daily Forward* on the fate of Jews who had fled to the U.S.S.R. By his calculations, and on the basis of hundreds of interviews, 400,000 Polish Jews had died in deportation, in the camps, and in forced-labor colonies. At the end of the war 150,000 chose to take back Polish citizenship so that they could leave the U.S.S.R. "The 150,000 Jews who are today crossing the Soviet-Polish border are no longer interested in talking about the Soviet Union, the Socialist fatherland, dictatorship, or democracy. For them such discussions are over, and their last word is this gesture of flight."[78]

The Forced Return of Soviet Prisoners

If having any contact with people from abroad, or simply being a foreigner, made one suspect in the eyes of the regime, then having been kept prisoner for four years during the war outside one's national territory was also enough to make a Russian soldier a traitor as far as the Soviet authorities were concerned. Under Decree No. 270 in 1942, which modified Article 193 of the penal code, any soldier captured by the enemy *ipso facto* became a traitor. The circumstances under which the capture had taken place and the subsequent conditions of captivity were of little importance. In the case of the Russians, the conditions had often been atrocious, as Hitler considered that all Slavs were subhuman and hence were to be disposed of en masse. Of the 5.7 million Russian prisoners of war, 3.3 million died of hunger and the poor conditions.

It was thus very early on that Stalin, in response to the Allies' preoccupation with the idea that there were Russian soldiers in the Wehrmacht, decided to obtain permission to repatriate all Russians who found themselves in the Western zone. This permission was quickly granted. From the end of 1944 to January 1945 more than 332,000 Russian prisoners (including 1,179 from San Francisco) were transferred the Soviet Union, often against their will. This transaction seemed to pose no crisis of conscience among British and American diplomats, who were fairly cynical about the whole affair, since, like Anthony Eden, they were aware that this was a question that had to be settled by the use of force.

At the Yalta conference (5–12 February 1945) the three Allied powers—Soviet, British, and American—drew up secret agreements that covered soldiers as well as displaced civilians. Churchill and Eden accepted the idea that it was up to Stalin to decide the fate of prisoners who had fought in the Russian Liberation Army commanded by General Andrei Vlasov, as though he had offered some sort of guarantee that they would be well treated.

Stalin knew very well that some of the Soviet soldiers had been taken prisoner principally because of the disorganization of the Red Army, for which he had been mainly to blame, and thanks to the widespread military incompetence of the generals, of which he himself was one. We can also be sure that many of the soldiers simply had no desire to fight for a regime that they hated, and, in Lenin's expression, they had probably "voted with their feet."

Once the Yalta accords had been signed, convoys left Britain weekly for the U.S.S.R. From May to July 1945 more than 1.3 million people who had been living in the Western occupied zones, and who were considered Russian by the British, including people from the Baltics, which had been annexed in 1940, and Ukrainians, were repatriated. By the end of August more than 2 million of these "Russians" had been handed over. Sometimes they were kept in terrible conditions. Individual and collective suicides involving whole families were frequent, as was mutilation. Often, when the prisoners were handed over to the Soviet authorities, they tried to put up passive resistance, but the Anglo-Americans did not hesitate to use force to satisfy Moscow's requirements. When the prisoners arrived in the U.S.S.R., they were placed under police control. The day the ship *Almanzora* arrived in Odessa, on 18 April, summary executions took place. This was also the case when the *Empire Pride* arrived in port in the Black Sea.

The West feared that the Soviet Union might hold French, British, or

American prisoners as hostages and use them as a sort of currency in ex-change—an attitude very indicative of their view of the Soviet *diktats* demand-ing the repatriation of all Russians, even those who had fled the revolution after 1917. This conscious policy of the Western allies did not in fact facilitate the return of their own citizens, but it did allow the Soviet Union to send out a veritable army of officials to hunt down people attempting to resist these laws. The officials themselves often acted with supreme disregard for local laws.

In the French zone of occupation, the *Bulletin* of the military administra-tion in Germany affirmed that on 1 October 1945, 101,000 "displaced persons" had been sent back to the Soviet Union. Even in France itself, the authorities accepted the creation of seventy transit camps that were somehow exempt from French law. One of these, Beauregard, was in the Paris suburbs. France had no control over what happened in such camps, which were operated by the NKVD with impunity on French soil. These operations, which started as early as September 1944 with the help of Communist propaganda, had been carefully planned by the Soviet Union. The Beauregard camp was not closed until November 1947 by the French security forces, after a scandal concerning the abduction of children of divorced parents who were feuding. The closure came at the behest of Roger Wybot, who noted that "this camp, according to the information I have in my possession, was less a transit camp than a sort of sequestration center."[79] Protests against such policies were few, and took place too late to be of any use. One did appear in the summer of 1947, in the Socialist review *Masses:*

> One can easily imagine Genghis Khan, at the height of his powers, closing his frontiers to prevent his slaves from running away. But it is hard to imagine that he would be granted the right to extradite them from abroad . . . This is a true sign of our postwar moral decay . . . What moral or political code can possibly be used to oblige people to go and live in a country where they will live and work as slaves? What gratitude does the world expect from Stalin for turning a deaf ear to the cries of all the Russian citizens who have taken their own lives rather than return home?

The editors of *Masses* went on to denounce the recent expulsions:

> Spurred on by the criminal indifference of the masses regarding viola-tions of the right to asylum, the British military authorities in Italy have just been accessories to a heinous crime: on 8 May, 175 Russians were taken from Camp 7 in Ruccione, and another 10 people from Camp 6 (where whole families are being kept), allegedly to be sent to Scotland. When these 185 people were somewhat distant from the camp, all ob-jects that could possibly have been of assistance to them, had they

wanted to take their own lives, were removed from their possession, and they were informed that their real destination was not in fact Scotland, but Russia. Despite the precautions, some of them still managed to kill themselves. That same day another 80 people, all of Caucasian origin, were taken from the camp in Pisa. All were taken to the Russian zone in Austria, in railway carriages guarded by British troops. Some of them tried to escape and were shot by the guards.[80]

The repatriated prisoners were interned in special camps called "filtration and control camps" (established in late 1941), which were scarcely different from the forced-labor camps, and which became officially a part of the Gulag Administration in January 1946. In 1945, 214,000 prisoners passed through them.[81] These prisoners, sent into the Gulag at its height, generally received six-year sentences, in accordance with section 1(b) of Article 58. Among them were the former members of the Russian Liberation Army, who had participated in the liberation of Prague, where they had fought against the SS.

Enemy Prisoners

The Soviet Union had not ratified the 1929 Geneva Convention on prisoners of war. Theoretically, all prisoners were protected by the convention even if their country was not a signatory, but the Soviet government took little account of this. In victory, it still kept between 3 million and 4 million German prisoners. Among them were soldiers freed by the Western forces who had come back to the Soviet zone and been deported farther east to the U.S.S.R.

In March 1947 Vyacheslav Molotov declared that a million Germans had been repatriated (1,003,974 was the exact number) and that there were still 890,532 interned in various camps. The figures provoked some controversy. In March 1950 the Soviet Union declared that the repatriation process was complete, but humanitarian organizations claimed that at least 300,000 prisoners of war and 100,000 expatriate civilians remained in the U.S.S.R. On 8 May 1950 Luxembourg protested the ending of repatriation operations, in part because at least 2,000 Luxembourg nationals were still trapped in the Soviet Union. Was the holding back of information the cover for a more sinister fate? This seems quite likely, given the atrocious conditions in the camps.

One estimate made by a special commission (the Maschke commission) claimed that nearly 1 million German prisoners of war died in Soviet camps. A typical case involved the 100,000 German prisoners taken by the Red Army at Stalingrad, of whom only 6,000 survived. In addition to the Germans, there were still around 60,000 Italian survivors in February 1947 (the figure of 80,000 has also often been put forward in this context). The Italian government claimed that only 12,513 of those soldiers had returned to Italy at that date. Romanian and Hungarian soldiers found themselves in the same position after the war. In March 1954, 100 volunteers from the Spanish "Azul" division were finally liberated. This survey would not be complete without mention of the 900,000 Japanese soldiers taken prisoner in Manchuria.

The Unwilling

There was a saying in the camps that summed up the diverse national origins of their inhabitants: "If a country isn't represented in the gulags, it doesn't really exist." France also had prisoners in the gulags, and French diplomacy was remarkably slow in coming to their aid.

The French departments of Moselle, Bas-Rhin, and Haut-Rhin were treated in a special way when they came under Nazi occupation: Alsace-Lorraine was annexed, Germanized, and even Nazified. In 1942 the Germans decided forcibly to conscript those born in 1920–1924. Many young people from Alsace and Moselle did their utmost to avoid service. By the end of the war, twenty-one age groups had been mobilized in Alsace, and another fourteen in Moselle, or 130,000 people in all. Many of these soldiers, who were known in France as the Malgré-nous, or "In Spite of Ourselves," were sent to the eastern front, where 22,000 of them died. When the Soviet authorities found out about this unusual situation from the Free French, they began to appeal to French soldiers to desert, promising them that they would be reenlisted in a regular French army. Whatever the circumstances were, 23,000 people from Alsace-Lorraine were taken prisoner; at least this was the number of files handed over to the French government in 1995. Many of these were kept in Camp 188, in Tambov, guarded by the Ministry of Internal Affairs (Ministerstvo vnutrennikh del, or MVD—formerly the NKVD) in terrible conditions: they were undernourished (receiving only 600 grams of black bread a day), forced to work in the forests, and lived in primitive, half-buried huts, with no medical care. People who escaped from this death camp estimated that at least 10,000 of their companions died there in 1944 and 1945. Pierre Rigoulot gives the figure of 10,000 deaths in different camps, including those who died in transit.[82] After lengthy negotiations, 1,500 prisoners were freed in the summer of 1944 and were repatriated to Algiers. Although Tambov was the camp where the greatest number of people from Alsace-Lorraine were interned, there were certainly others that housed French prisoners, a sort of specialized subarchipelago.

Civil War and War of National Liberation

Although the signing of the German-Soviet pact in September 1939 had brought about the collapse of a considerable number of Communist parties, whose members were unable to accept Stalin's abandonment of an antifascist policy, the German attack on the Soviet Union on 22 June 1941 immediately reactivated the antifascist response. The very next day the Comintern sent out a message by radio and telegram that the time had come for a temporary halt to the socialist revolution, and that all energy should be channeled into the struggle against fascism and the war for national liberation. The message also demanded that all Communist parties in occupied countries rise up immediately. The war was thus an opportunity to try out a new form of action: the armed struggle and the sabotage of Hitler's war machine, which promised valuable practice in guerrilla tactics. Paramilitary organizations were thus strengthened to form the core of armed Communist groups. Where geography and circumstances were favorable, they formed guerrilla forces of considerable efficacy, particularly in Greece and Yugoslavia after 1942, and in Albania and northern Italy after 1943. In the most successful situations, this guerrilla action gave Communists the opportunity to seize power, with recourse to civil war if necessary.

Yugoslavia furnished the clearest example of this new direction. In the spring of 1941 Hitler was forced to come to the aid of his Italian ally, Benito Mussolini, whose forces were being held in check in Greece by a small but determined army. In April Germany also had to intervene in Yugoslavia, where the government that supported the Nazis had been overthrown in a pro-British coup. In both of these countries, small but experienced Communist parties had existed in secret for many years, since being banned by the dictatorial regimes of Milan Stojadinović and Joannes Metaxas.

After the armistice, Yugoslavia was divided up among the Italians, Bulgarians, and Germans. The right-wing extremist Ustasha group in Croatia, led by Ante Pavelić, tried to establish an independent state, but it amounted to little more than an apartheid regime that subordinated the Serbs and carried out massacres of Jews and Gypsies. The Ustasha sought to eliminate all its opposition, driving numerous Croats to join the resistance.

After the surrender of the Yugoslav army on 18 April 1941, the first to form a resistance movement were the royalist officers around Colonel Draža Mihailović, who was soon appointed commander in chief of the Yugoslav resistance, and then minister of war for the royal government-in-exile in London. Mihailović created a largely Serb army in Serbia, the Chetniks. Only after the German invasion of the U.S.S.R., on 22 June 1941, did the Yugoslav Communists rally to the idea of national liberation to "free the country from the yoke of fascism and start the socialist revolution."[83] But whereas Moscow wanted to support the royalist government for as long as possible so as not to alienate the U.S.S.R.'s British allies, Tito felt confident enough to follow his own line, and he refused to pledge allegiance to the royalist government-in-exile. Recruiting soldiers regardless of their ethnic background—Tito himself was a Croat—the Communist partisan leader began to establish guerrilla bases in Bosnia in 1942. The two movements were soon opposed on key issues. Faced with a Communist threat, Mihailović chose to appease the Germans and even to form an alliance with the Italians. The situation became a veritable imbroglio, mixing war for national liberation and civil war, political and ethnic rivalries, all within the larger context of occupation by foreign troops. Both sides committed numerous massacres and atrocities as each tried to exterminate its rivals and to impose its own power on the population.

Historians estimate that there were slightly more than 1 million deaths, out of a total population of just 16 million. Executions, the shooting of prisoners and the wounded, and vicious cycles of revenge dragged on endlessly in a culture that had a long tradition of violent opposition between clans. There was, however, a difference between the massacres carried out by the Chetniks and those carried out by the Communists. The Chetniks, who hated any form of centralized authority—many groups were actually outside the control of Mihailović—carried out their massacres far more often on an ethnic rather than a political basis. The objectives of the Communists were much more clearly military and political. Milovan Djilas, one of Tito's assistants, said many years later:

> We were quite put out by the excuses the peasants gave for rallying to the Chetniks: they claimed to be afraid that their houses would be burned and that they would suffer other reprisals. This question came up in a meeting with Tito, and he offered the following argument: If we can make the peasants understand that if they join with the invader [note the interesting slippage here from Chetnik (royalist Yugoslav resistance fighter) to "invader"], we will burn down their houses, too, they might change their minds . . . After some hesitation, Tito made up his mind, and said: "All right, we can burn down the odd house or village now and then." Tito later issued orders to this effect, which looked all the more resolute simply because he was taking a firm stand.[84]

Following Italy's surrender in September 1943, Churchill's decision to help Tito rather than Mihailović, and Tito's formation of the Yugoslav National Anti-Fascist Council for Liberation (AVNOJ) in December 1943, the Communists had a clear political advantage over their rivals. By the end of 1944 and early 1945 the Communist partisans had taken over nearly the whole of Yugoslavia. As the German surrender approached, Pavelić and his army, his aides, and their families—in all, tens of thousands of people—set off for the Austrian frontier. Slovenian White Guards and Chetniks from Montenegro joined them in Bleiburg, where they all surrendered to British troops, who handed them over to Tito.

Soldiers and policemen of all types found themselves forced to walk to their deaths, hundreds of miles across the country. The Slovenian prisoners were taken back to Slovenia near Kočevje, where as many as 30,000 were killed.[85] In defeat, the Chetniks were unable to avoid the vengeance of the partisans, who never took prisoners. Milovan Djilas described the end of many of the Serb soldiers without going into any of the macabre details of the last period of the campaign: "Draža Mihailović's troops were completely annihilated at about the same time as the Slovenians. The small groups of Chetniks who managed to get back to Montenegro after they had been defeated brought the full story of the horror they had seen. No one has ever spoken of that again, not even people who make much of their revolutionary spirit, as though it was all a terrible nightmare."[86] Once captured, Draža Mihailović was tried, sentenced to death, and shot on 17 July 1946. At his "trial," all offers to bear witness for him by various officers from the Allied missions who had been sent to his aid and who had fought the Germans by his side were turned down.[87] After the war, Stalin once shared his philosophy with Milovan Djilas: "Anyone who occupies a territory always imposes his own social system on it."

When the war ended, the Greek Communists were in a situation roughly similar to that of the Yugoslavs. On 2 November 1940, a few days after the Italian invasion of Greece, Nikos Zachariadis, the secretary of the Greek Communist Party (KKE), who had been in prison since 1936, sent out a call to arms: "The Greek nation is now engaged in a war for its national liberation from the fascism of Mussolini . . . Everyone must take his place, and everyone must fight."[88] But on 7 December a manifesto from the underground Central Committee called into question this decision, and the KKE returned to the official line recommended by the Comintern, that of revolutionary defeatism. On 22 June 1941 came the spectacular U-turn: the KKE ordered its militants to organize "the struggle to defend the Soviet Union and the overthrow of the foreign fascist yoke."

The experience with clandestine activity had been crucial for the Communists. On 16 July 1941, like their counterparts in other countries, the Greek Communists formed a National Workers' Front for Liberation (Ergatiko Ethniko Apelevtheriko Metopo, EEAM), an umbrella organization for three unions. On 27 September they established the EAM (Ethniko Apelevtheriko Metopo), the Party's political arm. On 10 February 1942 they announced the creation of the People's Army for National Liberation (Ellinikos Laikos Apelevtherotikos), or ELAS. By May 1942 the first ELAS partisans were operating under the leadership of Ares Velouchiotes (Thanassis Klaras), an experienced militant who had signed a recantation in exchange for his freedom. From this point on, ELAS numbers continued to grow.

The ELAS was not the only military resistance movement. The National Greek Democratic Union, (Ethnikos Demokratikos Ellinikos Syndesmos), or EDES, had been created by soldiers and republican civilians in September 1941. Another group of resistance fighters was formed by a retired colonel, Napoleon Zervas. A third organization, the National Social Liberation Movement (Ethniki Kai Koiniki Apelevtherosis), or EKKA, came into being in October 1942 under Colonel Dimitri Psarros. All these organizations were constantly trying to recruit from one another.

But the success and strength of the ELAS made the Communists hopeful of imposing their leadership on all the armed resistance groups. They attacked the EDES partisans several times, as well as the EKKA, who were forced to suspend operations to regroup. In late 1942 Major G. Kostopoulos (a renegade from the EAM) and Colonel Stefanos Sárafis formed a resistance unit in the heart of a zone that had been captured by the EAM in western Thessaly, at the foot of the Pindus Mountains. The ELAS surrounded them and massacred all those who did not escape or who refused to enroll in their ranks. Taken prisoner, Sárafis finally agreed to assume leadership of the ELAS units.

The presence of British officers who had come to help the Greek resistance was a cause of concern to the ELAS chiefs, who feared that the British would attempt to reinstate the monarchy. But there was a difference in viewpoint between the military branch, directed by Ares Velouchiotes, and the KKE itself. The latter, led by Giorgis Siantos, wished to follow the official line as laid down by Moscow, advocating a general antifascist coalition. The actions of the British were momentarily beneficial because in July 1943 their military mission convinced the three main protagonists to sign a pact. At that time the ELAS had some 18,000 men, the EDES 5,000, and the EKKA about 1,000.

The Italian surrender on 8 September 1943 immediately modified the situation. A fratricidal war began when the Germans launched a violent offensive against the EDES. The guerrillas, forced to retreat, confronted several large ELAS battalions, which threatened to annihilate the EDES. The KKE leadership decided to abandon the EDES, hoping thus to check British policy. After four days of fighting, the partisans led by Zervas escaped encirclement.

This civil war within the main war was of great advantage to the Germans as they swept down upon the resistance units one by one.[89] The Allies thus took the initiative to end the civil war. Fighting between the ELAS and the EDES stopped in February 1944, and an agreement was signed in Plaka. The agreement was short-lived; a few weeks later the ELAS attacked Colonel Psarros' EKKA troops. He was defeated after five days and taken prisoner. His officers were massacred; Psarros himself was beheaded.

The Communists' actions demoralized the resistance and discredited the EAM. In several regions, hatred for the EAM was so strong that a number of resistance fighters joined the security battalions set up by the Germans. The civil war did not end until the ELAS agreed to collaborate with the Greek government-in-exile in Cairo. In September 1944 six members of the EAM-ELAS became members of the government of national unity presided over by Georges Papandreou. On 2 September, as the Germans began to evacuate Greece, the ELAS sent its troops to conquer the Peloponnese, which had always eluded its control thanks to the security battalions. All captured towns and villages were "punished." In Meligala, 1,400 men, women, and children were massacred along with some 50 officers and noncommissioned officers from the security battalions.

Nothing now seemed to stand in the way of EAM-ELAS hegemony. But when Athens was liberated on 12 October it escaped the guerrillas' control because of the presence of British troops in Piraeus. The KKE leadership hesitated to undertake a trial of strength, unsure of whether it wanted a place in a coalition government. When the ELAS refused a government demand to demobilize, Iannis Zegvos, the Communist agriculture minister, demanded that all government units be disbanded too. On 4 December, ELAS patrols entered Athens, where they clashed with government forces. By the following day, almost the entire capital had fallen under the control of the 20,000-strong ELAS forces; but the British stood firm, awaiting reinforcements. On 18 December the ELAS again attacked the EDES in Epirus and at the same time launched a bloody antiroyalist operation.

The offensive was contained, and in talks held in Varkiza the Communists resigned themselves to a peace accord under which they agreed to disarm. The accord was something of a sham, however, since large numbers of weapons and munitions remained carefully hidden. Ares Velouchiotes, one of the principal warlords, rejected the Varkiza conditions, rejoined the partisans with about one hundred men, and then crossed into Albania in the hope of continuing the armed struggle from there. Later, asked about the reasons for the defeat of the EAM-ELAS, Velouchiotes replied frankly: "We didn't kill enough people. The English were taking a major interest in that crossroads called Greece. If we had killed all their friends, they wouldn't have been able to land. Everyone described me as a killer—that's the way we were. Revolutions succeed only when rivers run red with blood, and blood has to be spilled if what you are aiming for is the perfectability of the human race."[90] Velouchiotes died in combat in June 1945 in Thessaly, a few days after he was thrown out of the KKE. The defeat of the EAM-ELAS unleashed a wave of hatred against the Communists and their allies. Groups of militants were assassinated by paramilitary groups, and many others were imprisoned. Most of the leaders were deported to the islands.

Nikos Zachariadis, the secretary general of the KKE, had returned in May 1945 from Germany, where he had been deported to Dachau. His first declarations clearly announced KKE policy: "Either the EAM struggle for national liberation is finally rewarded with the establishment of a people's democracy in Greece, or we return to a similar but even more severe regime than the last fascist monarchist dictatorship." Greece, exhausted by the war, seemed to have little chance of enjoying peace at last. In October the Seventh Party Congress ratified Zachariadis' proposal. The first stage was to obtain the departure of the British troops. In January 1946 the U.S.S.R. demonstrated its interest in Greece by claiming at a United Nations Security Council meeting that the British presence constituted a danger to the country. On 12 February 1946, when defeat for the Communists in the coming elections seemed inevitable—they were calling on their voters to abstain—the KKE organized an uprising, with the help of the Yugoslav Communists.

In December 1945 the members of the KKE Central Committee had met with various Bulgarian and Yugoslav officers. The Greek Communists were assured that they could use Albania, Bulgaria, and Yugoslavia as bases. For more than three years their troops did so, retreating with their wounded into these countries and using them to regroup and build up supplies and munitions. These preparations took place a few months after the creation of the Communist Information Bureau (Cominform), the Moscow-dominated grouping of world Communist parties. It seems that the Greek Communist uprising was perfectly coordinated with the Soviet Union's new policies. On 30 March 1946 the KKE declared that a third civil war was under way. The first attacks by the Democratic Army (AD), which had been established on 28 October 1946 and was led by General Markos Vafiadis, followed the usual pattern: police stations were attacked, their occupants killed, and leading local figures executed. The KKE openly continued such actions throughout 1946.

In the first months of 1947 General Vafiadis intensified his campaign, attacking dozens of villages and executing hundreds of peasants. The ranks of the AD were swollen by enforced recruitment.[91] Villages that refused to cooperate suffered severe reprisals. One village in Macedonia was hit particularly hard: forty-eight houses were burned down, and twelve men, six women, and two babies were killed. After March 1947 municipal leaders were systematically eliminated, as were priests. By March the number of refugees reached 400,000. The policy of terror was met with counterterror, and militant left-wing Communists were killed in turn by right-wing extremists.

In June 1947, after a tour of Belgrade, Prague, and Moscow, Zachariadis announced the imminent formation of a "free" government. The Greek Communists seemed to believe that they could follow the same path taken by Tito a few years earlier. The government was officially created in December. The Yugoslavs provided nearly 10,000 volunteers recruited from their own army.[92] Numerous reports from the UN Special Commission on the Balkans have established the great importance of this assistance to the Democratic Army. The break between Tito and Stalin in 1948 had direct consequences for the Greek Communists. Although Tito continued his aid until the autumn, he also began a retreat that ended with closure of the border. In the summer of 1948, while the Greek government forces were engaged in a massive offensive, the Albanian leader Enver Hoxha also closed his country's border. The Greek Communists became increasingly isolated, and dissent within the Party grew. The fighting continued until August 1949. Many of the combatants fled to Bulgaria and thence to other parts of Eastern Europe, settling particularly in Romania and the U.S.S.R. Tashkent, the capital of Uzbekistan, received thousands of refugees, including 7,500 Communists. After this defeat, the KKE in exile suffered a number of purges, and as late as 1955 the conflicts between the pro- and anti-Zachariadis factions was still extremely fierce, so much so that at one point the Soviet army was forced to intervene, resulting in hundreds of casualties.[93]

During the civil war of 1946–1948, Greek Communists kept records on all the children aged three to fourteen in all the areas they controlled. In March 1948 these children were gathered together in the border regions, and several thousand were taken into Albania, Bulgaria, and Yugoslavia. The villagers tried to protect their children by hiding them in the woods. The Red Cross, despite the enormous obstacles placed in their path, managed to count 28,296. In the summer of 1948, when the Tito-Cominform rupture became apparent, 11,600 of the children in Yugoslavia were moved to Czechoslovakia, Hungary, Romania, and Poland, despite many protests from the Greek government. On 17 November 1948, the Third UN General Assembly passed a resolution roundly condemning the removal of the Greek children. In November 1949 the General Assembly again demanded their return. These and all subsequent UN resolutions remained unanswered. The neighboring Communist regimes claimed that the children were being kept under conditions superior to those they would be experiencing at home, and that the deportation had been a humanitarian act.[94]

In reality the enforced deportation of the children was carried out in appalling conditions. Starvation and epidemics were extremely common, and many of the children simply died. Kept together in "children's villages," they were subjected to courses in politics in addition to their normal education. At age thirteen they were forced into manual labor, carrying out arduous tasks such as land reclamation in the marshy Hartchag region of Hungary. The intention of the Communist leaders was to form a new generation of devoted militants, but their efforts ended in failure. One Greek called Constantinides died on the Hungarian side fighting the Soviet Union in 1956. Others managed to flee to West Germany.

From 1950 to 1952 only 684 children were permitted to return to Greece.

By 1963, around 4,000 children (some of them born in Communist countries) had been repatriated. In Poland, the Greek community numbered several thousand in the early 1980s. Some of them were members of Solidarity, and were imprisoned after the introduction of martial law in December 1981. In 1989, when democratization was well under way, several thousand Greeks still living in Poland began to return home.

The warm welcome extended to the defeated Greek Communists in the U.S.S.R. contrasted strangely with Stalin's annihilation of the Greek community that had lived in Russia for centuries. In 1917 the number of Greeks in the Soviet state was between 500,000 and 700,000, concentrated for the most part around the Caucasus and the Black Sea. By 1939 the number had fallen to 410,000, mainly because of "unnatural" deaths, not emigration; and there were a mere 177,000 remaining by 1960. After December 1937 the 285,000 Greeks living in the major towns were deported to the regions of Arkhangelsk, the Komi republic, and northeastern Siberia. Others were allowed to return to Greece. During this period A. Haitas, a former secretary of the KKE, and the educator J. Jordinis died in purges. In 1944, 10,000 Greeks from the Crimea, the remnants of what had been a flourishing Greek community there, were deported to Kirgizstan and Uzbekistan, on the pretext that they had adopted a pro-German stance during the war. On 30 June 1949, in a single night, 30,000 Greeks from Georgia were deported to Kazakhstan. In April 1950 the entire Greek population of Batumi suffered a similar fate.

In other countries in Western Europe, Communist attempts to seize power after liberation from Nazi rule were rapidly snuffed out by the presence of Anglo-American forces and by Stalin's directive at the end of 1944 urging Communists to cache their arms and wait for a better time to seize power. This line was confirmed by a report of a meeting in the Kremlin on 19 November 1944 between Stalin and Maurice Thorez, the secretary general of the French Communist Party, before he returned to France after spending the war in the U.S.S.R.[95]

After the war, and at least until Stalin's death in 1953, the violent methods and terror that had become the norm inside the Comintern continued in the international Communist movement. In Eastern Europe the repression of real or supposed dissidents by means of rigged show-trials was especially intense (see Chapter 20 for details). The pretext for this terror was the confrontation between Tito and Stalin in 1948. Having challenged Stalin's omnipotence, Tito was transformed into a new Trotsky. Stalin tried to have him assassinated, but Tito was extremely wary and had his own highly effective state security apparatus. Unable to eliminate Tito himself, Communist parties around the world launched a series of symbolic political murders and excluded all "Titoists" from their ranks, treating them as scapegoats at every opportunity. One of the first expiatory victims was the secretary general of the Norwegian Communist Party, Peder Furubotn, a former Comintern official who had worked in Moscow, and who had already eluded one such purge by escaping to Norway in 1938. At a Party meeting on 20 October 1949, a Soviet agent named Strand Johansen accused Furubotn of Titoism. Confident that he would be given a fair hearing within the Party, Furubotn called a meeting of the Central Committee on 25 October, where he announced his immediate resignation and that of his team, provided that a new election for the Central Committee took place immediately and that the accusations against him were examined by an international panel of experts. Furubotn had thus temporarily outmaneuvered his opponents. But to general amazement, Johansen and several armed men burst into the Central Committee the following day and expelled Furubotn's supporters at gunpoint. They then organized a meeting where Furubotn's expulsion from the Party was agreed. Furubotn himself had anticipated these Soviet-style tactics and had barricaded himself in his house with a few armed colleagues. Most of the military forces of the Norwegian Communist Party died in the ensuing gunfight. Johansen himself was manipulated by the Soviet Union to such an extent over the next several years that he eventually went mad.[96]

The last act in this period of terror inside the international Communist movement took place in 1957. Imre Nagy, the Hungarian Communist who for a while had led the 1956 revolt in Budapest (see Chapter 20), had taken refuge in the Yugoslav embassy, fearing for his life. After some tortuous maneuvering, Soviet KGB officers took him into custody and then transferred him for trial to the new Hungarian government of János Kádár. Unwilling to take sole responsibility for what was clearly going to be a legalized murder, the Hungarian Workers' Party used the first World Conference of Communist Parties, held in Moscow in November 1957, to have all the Communist leaders present vote for Nagy's death. Included among them were the Frenchman Maurice Thorez and the Italian Palmiro Togliatti. Only the Polish leader, Władysław Gomułka, refused to endorse the move. Nagy was condemned to death and hanged on 16 June 1958.[97]

17 The Shadow of the NKVD in Spain

Stéphane Courtois and Jean-Louis Panné

On 17 July 1936 the Spanish military in Morocco, under the leadership of General Francisco Franco, rose up against the Republican government. The next day the mutiny spread throughout the peninsula. On 19 July it was checked in many cities, including Madrid, Barcelona, Valencia, and Bilbao, thanks to a general strike and the mass mobilization of the working classes. Months earlier, on 16 February 1936, the Popular Front's margin of victory in the Spanish elections had been extremely narrow, 4,700,000 votes (267 deputies), compared to 3,997,000 (132 deputies) for the right and 449,000 for the center. The Socialists had won 89 seats, the Republican left 84, the Republican Union 37, and the Spanish Communist Party (PCE) 16. The Marxist Workers' Unification Party (POUM), born in 1935 from the fusion of Joaquín Maurin's workers' and peasants' bloc and the Communist left of Andreu Nin, won a single seat. One of the main forces in Spain was not represented at all. The anarchists of the National Confederation of Labor (CNT) and the Federation of Iberian Anarchists (FAI)—which had 1,577,547 members, compared to the 1,444,474 members of the Socialist Party and the General Workers' Union— had, in accordance with their principles, not put forward any candidates for the election.[1] The Popular Front would have been unable to win without the votes of the anarchists' supporters. Support for the Communist Party was actually much less than the figure of 16 elected members suggests. They claimed to have 40,000 members, but in reality fewer than 10,000 sympathizers were present in the many fragmented organizations that did not depend directly on the Communist Party.

The left was thus extremely divided, and the right was powerful and concentrated in the Falange faction. The cities were seething with political demonstrations and strikes, and unrest spread to the countryside, where peasants began to take over land. The army was strong, the government was divided, there was a multitude of plots afoot, and political violence was constantly escalating. All these factors indicated that a civil war was brewing, and this was indeed the outcome desired by many.

The Communist Line

To increase their political clout, the Communists had proposed joining with the Socialists. This tactic at first succeeded only with the two parties' youth organizations. On 1 April 1936 the Unified Socialist Youth group was formed. This event, however, was followed on 26 June by one of much greater importance—the creation of the Unified Socialist Party of Catalonia.

The Comintern had not been particularly interested in Spain, and began to pay attention to the country only after the fall of the monarchy in 1931 and the workers' uprising in Asturias in 1934. The Soviet Union had been equally uninterested, and the two countries did not sign a pact of mutual recognition until August 1936, after the civil war had broken out. A month earlier the Soviet government had signed a noninterventionist pact adopted by France and England in July, in the hope of preventing the war from escalating internationally.[2] The Soviet ambassador, Marsel Israelovich Rosenberg, took up office on 27 August.

In the government of Francisco Largo Caballero, formed in September 1936, the Communist Party had only two ministers: Jesús Hernández at the Education Ministry, and Vincente Uribe at the Ministry of Agriculture. But the Soviet Union very quickly acquired much greater influence in the government. Thanks to the sympathy of several other members of the government (including Juan Alvarez del Vayo and Juan Negrín), Marsel Rosenberg became a sort of deputy prime minister and even took part in meetings of the Council of Ministers. He had several considerable advantages, since the U.S.S.R. was eager to arm the Republicans.

Soviet intervention in an area so far outside the U.S.S.R.'s normal sphere of influence became a matter of special importance. It came at a key moment, when Spain was weakened by a powerful social movement and a civil war. In 1936–1939 the country became a sort of laboratory where the Soviet authorities not only applied new political strategies and tactics but also tried out techniques that would be used during and after World War II. Their aims were manifold, but their primary goal was to ensure that the Spanish Communist Party (by now run entirely by the Comintern and the NKVD) seized power and established a state that would become another Soviet satellite. To achieve their goal, they used traditional Soviet methods, such as establishing an omnipresent police force and liquidating all non-Communist forces.

In 1936 the Italian Communist Palmiro Togliatti (known then as Mario Ercoli), who was a member of the Comintern directorate, defined the specific features of the Spanish civil war, which he characterized as "a war of national revolution." In his view, the nationalist, popular, and antifascist nature of the Spanish revolution presented the Communists with a new agenda: "The people of Spain are solving the problems of the bourgeois democratic revolution in a new fashion." He quickly identified the Republican and Socialist leaders as enemies of this new conception of revolution, calling them "elements who hide behind anarchist principles and weaken the unity and cohesiveness of the Popular Front with premature projects for forced 'collectivization.'" He established Communist hegemony as a clear objective, to be realized by "a common front of Socialist and Communist parties, the creation of a single Communist Youth Organization, the creation of a single Proletarian Party in Catalonia [the PSUC], and the transformation of the Communist Party itself into a large-scale party of the masses."[3] In June 1937 Dolores Ibarruri—a Spanish Communist better known by the name "La Pasionaria," who became famous because of her calls for resistance—proposed a new objective: "a democratic parliamentary republic of a *new sort*."[4]

Immediately after the Franquista *pronunciamento*, Stalin again demonstrated his relative indifference to the whole Spanish situation. Jef Last, who accompanied André Gide to Moscow in the summer of 1936, recalled: "We were quite indignant at finding such a total lack of interest in the events there. At no meeting did this subject ever arise, and whenever we attempted to engage officials privately in conversation on the topic, they scrupulously avoided airing their own opinion."[5] Two months later, given the turn of events, Stalin realized that he could take advantage of the situation for both diplomatic and propaganda purposes. By cooperating with the noninterventionist pact, the Soviet Union might gain greater international recognition and might even be able to break up the Franco-British bloc. At the same time, of course, the Soviet Union was secretly supplying the Republicans with guns and lending military aid, hoping to exploit the Popular Front government in France, which seemed ready to collaborate with the Soviet secret services in organizing further help for the Republican forces in Spain. Acting on Léon Blum's instructions, Gaston Cusin, the deputy head of the Cabinet at the Finance Ministry, met with Soviet officials and emissaries who had established their headquarters in Paris to organize the shipment of arms and the recruiting of volunteers for Spain. Although the Soviet Union initially intended to avoid an overt role, the Comintern mobilized all its sections for the cause of Republican Spain, using the conflict as a tremendous vehicle for antifascist propaganda, with particularly good results for the Communist movement.

In Spain itself, the main Communist tactic was to occupy more and more positions in the Republican government so as to direct policy in accordance with the interests of the Soviet Union. Julian Gorkin, one of the POUM leaders, was probably among the first to suggest that there was a link between Soviet policies in Republican Spain and the ideals of a people's democracy, in an essay titled *España, primer ensayo de democracia popular.*[6] By contrast, the Spanish historian Antonio Elorza believes that Communist policies in Spain came mostly from "a monolithic rather than a pluralist conception of political relations in the Popular Front and from the role of the Party, which naturally tried to turn the alliance into a platform for its own hegemony." Elorza emphasizes the invariant pattern of Soviet policy, which encouraged the Spanish Communist Party to exert itself against all antifascists, "not simply enemy fascist groups, but also any internal opposition." He adds: "As such, the project was a direct precursor of the strategy for taking power in all so-called people's democracies."[7]

Moscow predicted success in the elections of September 1937, when the option of voting a straight ticket would allow the Spanish Communist Party to profit from the national plebiscite. The goal, inspired and closely followed by Stalin himself, was the establishment of "a democratic republic of a new type," to be accompanied by the elimination of all ministers hostile to Communist policies. But the Communists failed, mostly because of opposition from their allies, and because of the worrying turn of events with the failure of the offensive in Teruel on 15 December 1937.

"Advisers" and Agents

As soon as Stalin had decided that Spain presented important opportunities for the Soviet Union and that intervention was therefore necessary, Moscow sent a large contingent of advisers and other personnel to that country. First and foremost among these were the 2,044 military advisers (according to one Soviet source), including the future marshals Ivan Konev and Georgy Zhukov, as well as General Vladimir Gorev, the military attaché in Madrid. Between 700 and 800 would stay permanently. Moscow also mobilized its Comintern workers and other emissaries of various sorts, in both official and unofficial capacities. Those who stayed included the Argentinian Vittorio Codovilla, who played a considerable role in the Spanish Communist Party from the early 1930s on, eventually becoming its leader; the Hungarian Ernő Gerő (known as "Pedro"), who was to become a high-ranking Communist in Hungary after the war; the Italian Vittorio Vidali (suspected of taking part in the assassination of the Cuban Communist student leader Julio Antonio Mella in 1929), who went on to become the chief political commissar of the Communist 5th Regiment; the Bulgarian Stepan Minev (Stepanov), who had worked in Stalin's Secretariat from 1927 to 1929; and the Italian Palmiro Togliatti, who arrived in 1937 as a Comintern representative. Others came on inspection tours, including the French Communist Jacques Duclos.

At the same time the Soviet Union sent a large number of officers from its special services: Vladimir Antonov-Ovseenko (who had taken part in the assault on the Winter Palace in Petrograd in 1917), who arrived in Barcelona on 1 October 1936;[8] Aleksandr Orlov (whose real name was L. Feldbin), an NKVD leader in Spain; the Pole Artur Staszewski, a former Red Army officer who at the time was a commercial attaché; General Ian Berzin, chief of the intelligence services of the Red Army; and Mikhail Koltsov, the editor of *Pravda* and a secret spokesman for Stalin, who established himself in the Ministry of War. From 1936 on, Leonid Eitingon, the deputy head of the NKVD station in Spain, was in charge of terrorist operations in Barcelona. His colleague Pavel Sudoplatov arrived in Barcelona in 1938.[9]

In short, as soon as Stalin decided to intervene in Spain, he sent in a genuine army that could act decisively in several different domains. A formal decision was probably made on the night of 14 September 1936 in Moscow at a special meeting at the Lubyanka convened by Genrikh Yagoda, the head of the NKVD. There, plans for action in Spain were coordinated to achieve two main objectives: to combat the Franquistas and the German and Italian agents and, at the same time, to remove the threat posed by enemies of the U.S.S.R. and Communism in the Republican camp. Intervention was to be as covert as possible so that the position of the Soviet government would not be compromised. If General Walter Krivitsky, the chief of the NKVD's external forces in Western Europe, is to be believed, only 40 of the approximately 3,000 Soviet agents in Spain saw active service; the rest were advisers, politicians, or gatherers of intelligence.

The first concentrated Soviet effort was in Catalonia. In September 1936 the General Commissariat for Public Order in Catalonia, which had already been infiltrated by Communists, created the Grupo de Información (Information Group) inside the Catalan Secret Services (SSI), led by Mariano Gómez Emperador. This official service, which soon employed some fifty people, was in fact a camouflaged NKVD cell. At the same time the Unified Socialist Party of Catalonia—a name chosen by the Communists—formed a Servicio Extranjero (Foreign Service) in room 340 of the Hotel Colón in the Plaza de

Catalunya. The latter's task was to control all foreign Communists arriving in Barcelona to fight in Spain. The Servicio Extranjero was tightly controlled by the NKVD and a front for its covert operations.

Both services were under the local control of Alfredo Hertz, an NKVD commander who worked under the direct authority of Orlov and Gerő. Hertz was a German Communist whose true identity has never been established. He had started out in the Cuerpo de Investigación y Vigilancia (Corps of Investigation and Vigilance), where he had been in charge of passport control, including all entry and exit visas to and from Spain. He was also extremely skilled in his use of the Assault Troops, the elite police division. With his information network in place inside the General Commissariat of Public Order, Hertz filtered information from all other Communist parties—blacklists of other antifascist groups, denunciations of Communists who had criticized the Party, biographical information supplied by the cadre sections of the different branches of the Party—and sent it on to the State Department, which was controlled by the Communist Victorio Sala. Hertz set up his own service, the Servicio Alfredo Hertz, which had a legal front but was in fact a private political police force made up of foreign Communists and Spanish nationals. Under his leadership, a list was drawn up of all foreign residents in Catalonia (later this was done for the rest of Spain), with a separate list of wayward people to be eliminated. From September to December 1936 the persecution of opponents was not systematic, but gradually the NKVD drew up real plans to purge all political opponents among the Republicans. The first targets were the Social Democrats, followed by the anarchosyndicalists, the Trotskyites, and then the more rebellious of the Communists. Many of these so-called enemies had called into question the value of the pro-U.S.S.R. alignment. As was always the case on such occasions, there were personal vendettas and feuds to be settled too.[10]

The most banal as well as the most sophisticated police methods imaginable were employed by these double or even triple agents. The first police task was the "colonization" of the Republican administration, the army, and the police. The gradual takeover of key posts and the formation of Communist cells were made possible by the fact that the Soviet Union was one of the few countries supplying weapons to the Republican forces, and could demand political favors in return. In contrast to Hitler's and Mussolini's extension of aid to Franco's nationalist forces, the Soviet Union refused to grant the Republicans any credit; it demanded that all arms be paid for in advance in gold from the Bank of Spain. The gold was taken back to the U.S.S.R. by Communist agents. Each delivery of arms thus presented one more opportunity to blackmail the government.

Julian Gorkin, the POUM militant, provides a striking example of this mixture of war and politics. Early in 1937, Largo Caballero, the head of the

Spanish government, with the support of President Manuel Azaña, had authorized Luis Araquistain, the Spanish ambassador in Paris, to begin secret negotiations with Dino Grandi, the Italian ambassador in London, and Hjalmar Schacht, Hitler's financier, under the authority of Léon Blum and Anthony Eden. The aim was to bring an end to the war. To thwart these plans, Juan Alvarez del Vayo, the minister of foreign affairs, who was favorably disposed toward the Spanish Communists, informed Communist leaders about the negotiations. The Communists, together with the Soviet secret service, decided to push Largo Caballero out of office, thus eliminating the possibility of a negotiated settlement of the conflict, which would have compelled all the Italian and German forces to retreat.[11]

"After the Lies, Bullets in the Neck"

The notion of "lies" and "bullets in the neck" was how Viktor Serge, the Russo-Belgian writer set free by the U.S.S.R. in April 1936, explained Communist policy to Julian Gorkin when they met in 1937. The Communists in Spain faced two serious obstacles: the huge anarchosyndicalist CNT, which was outside Communist influence; and the POUM, which was fundamentally opposed to Communist policies. The POUM was an easy target for Communist exploitation because of its marginal position in Spanish politics. It was also reputed to be politically close to Trotsky. In 1935 Andreu Nin and Julian Gorkin had tried to convince the Catalan authorities that Trotsky, who had been chased out of France, should be allowed to settle in Barcelona. In the context of the hunt for Trotskyites taking place in the Soviet Union, it is hardly surprising that the Comintern Secretariat, meeting on 21 February 1936 (five days after the electoral victory of the Spanish Popular Front), gave the Spanish Communist Party permission to begin "an energetic struggle against the Trotskyite counterrevolutionary sect."[12] In addition, the POUM had spoken out in the summer of 1936 in defense of the victims of the first show-trials in Moscow.

On 13 December 1936 the Communists managed to eject Andreu Nin from the General Catalan Council. They demanded his removal on the grounds that he had insulted the U.S.S.R., and they threatened to disrupt the delivery of arms if they did not get their way. On 16 December *Pravda* began an international campaign against everyone who opposed Soviet policy: "In Catalonia the elimination of Trotskyites and anarchosyndicalists has begun. It will be carried out with the same energy and dedication as in the U.S.S.R."

To the Communist mind, political deviation was the equivalent of treason, and everywhere it was met with the same punishment. Calumny and lies were spread about the POUM, whose front-line troops were accused of having abandoned their positions, even when Communist troops had refused to support them.[13] *L'humanité*, the French Communist Party daily, was especially vicious in its attacks, reprinting a series of articles by Mikhail Koltsov, a close friend of Louis Aragon and Elsa Triolet. The central theme of the campaign was repeated endlessly: the POUM was an accomplice of Franco, in league with the fascist cause. The Communists took the precaution of infiltrating POUM ranks with agents whose task was to gather information and draw up blacklists, so that they could identify the relevant militants when they were arrested. One particularly well-known case is that of Lev Narvich, who after contacting Nin was unmasked and executed by a POUM self-defense squad. The executions came after the disappearance of Nin himself and the arrest of other leaders.

May 1937 and the Liquidation of the POUM

On 3 May 1937, assault troops led by the Communists mounted an attack on the Barcelona central telephone exchange, which was in the hands of the CNT and the Socialist trade union, Unión General de Trabajadores (UGT). The operation was led by Rodríguez Salas, the chief of police and a member of the PSUC. The Communists had prepared for the attack by increasing the level of propaganda and harassment and closing down both the POUM radio station and *La batalla*, the POUM's official newspaper. On 6 May, 5,000 police agents headed by leading Communists arrived in Barcelona. The ensuing violent confrontations between Communist and non-Communist forces left nearly 500 dead and another 1,000 wounded.

Taking advantage of the confusion, the Communists seized every opportunity to liquidate their political opponents. Camillo Berneri, the Italian anarchist philosopher, and his companion Francesco Barbieri were abducted and killed by a squad of twelve men; their bodies were found riddled with bullets the following day. Only days before, Berneri had prophetically written in his journal, *Guerra di classe:* "Today we fight Burgos, tomorrow we must fight Moscow for our freedom." Alfredo Martínez, the secretary of the Free Youth of Catalonia movement; Hans Freund, the militant Trotskyite; and Erwin Wolf, a former secretary of Trotsky, met the same fate.

Kurt Landau, an Austrian and an opposition Communist, had been a militant in Germany, Austria, and France before moving to Barcelona and joining the POUM. He was arrested on 23 September and then disappeared. His wife, Katia, who was herself imprisoned, wrote about these purges: "The Party houses, including 'La Pedrera' and 'Paseo de García,' and the 'Karl Marx' and 'Voroshilov' barracks, were just death traps. Witnesses last saw the men from the radio station alive in La Pedrera. Young anarchists were taken to the barracks to be tortured in the most vile manner, mutilated, and killed. Their bodies were later found by accident." She quotes one article from the anarchosyndicalist paper *Solidaridad obrera:* "It was determined that before dying they had been tortured in a grisly manner, as was evident from the presence of serious contusions and bruises on the stomach, which seemed swollen and deformed . . . It was clear that one of the bodies had been hung by the feet, and the head and neck were terribly bruised. The head of another of these unfortunates had obviously been beaten with the butt of a rifle."

Many militants such as Guido Picelli simply disappeared for good, without a trace. George Orwell, who had enlisted as a volunteer in the POUM, lived through these days and was forced to go into hiding and to flee. His account of May 1937 in Barcelona survives in an appendix in *Homage to Catalonia.*

Assassinations planned by the Communist police squads were not confined to Barcelona. In Tortosa on 6 May, twenty CNT militants who had been arrested by government forces from Valencia were spirited out of their cells in the basement of the town hall and slaughtered. Fifteen more freedom fighters were coldly executed the following day in Tarragon.

Although the Communists were unable to kill off all their opponents, they did manage to deprive them of political power. José Díaz, the secretary general of the Spanish Communist Party, had declared in May that "the POUM should be removed from the political life of the country." Largo Caballero, the head of the government, refused to give in to Communist demands that the POUM be dissolved. On 15 May, after the events in Barcelona, he was forced to resign. His successor, Juan Negrín, was a "moderate" Socialist in thrall to the Communists. Thus the final obstacle to the Communist political takeover was removed. Not only did Negrín align himself with the Communists—writing to the London *Times* correspondent Herbert L. Matthews that the POUM "was controlled by elements who rejected anything that might constitute a single, supreme direction in the struggle, or any sort of common discipline"—but he also approved the use of terror as a method of political control.[14] Julian Gorkin witnessed the radical change: "A few days after Juan Negrín's government had been formed, Orlov was already acting as though Spain was some sort of Communist satellite. He turned up at the headquarters of the security offices and asked for Colonel Antonio Ortega, whom he now considered to be one of his subordinates, and demanded warrants for the arrest of members of the POUM Executive Committee."[15]

On 16 June 1937 Negrin officially banned the POUM and had the entire Executive Committee arrested. This decision allowed Communist agents to act with a semblance of legality. At 1:00 P.M. on 16 June, Andreu Nin was arrested by the police. None of his companions ever saw him again, living or dead.

Police officers from Madrid, under orders from the Communists, took over the newspaper *La batalla* and the various POUM buildings. Two hundred militants, including Julian Gorkin, Jordi Arquer, Juan Andrade, and Pedro

Bonet, were imprisoned. Later, to justify the liquidation of the POUM, the Communists fabricated charges of treason, claiming that POUM members had been spying for Franco. On 22 June a special tribunal was established and the propaganda campaign launched. Conveniently, police investigations turned up documents relating to espionage. "Max Rieger" (the name was either a collective pseudonym or a pseudonym for a journalist working under specific orders) gathered together all these forgeries and published them under the title *Espionage in Spain*, which came out simultaneously in several languages.

Under Orlov's orders and protected by Vidali, Ricardo Burillo, and Gerő, Nin was tortured. However, he neither admitted anything that could be used to prove the validity of the accusations made against his party nor signed any declaration. The Communists were thus compelled to liquidate him and to use his disappearance to discredit him, claiming that he had gone over to the Francoist side. Again, assassination and propaganda went hand in hand. The opening of the Moscow archives confirmed what Nin's friends and supporters had supposed all along.[16]

After the activity against the POUM on 16 and 17 June, a systematic manhunt against all "traitors"—Trotskyites and others—began. The Communists used information gathered by the police to carry out these operations. They set up illegal prisons, called *cekas*, hispanicizing the name of the first Russian secret police agency, the Cheka. The names of these places are now known: the central *ceka* in Barcelona was at 24 Avenida Puerta del Angel, with other branches in the Hotel Colón in the Plaza de Catalunya, the former Atocha convent in Madrid, Santa Ursula in Valencia, and Alcalá de Henares. Several private houses were also requisitioned and served as centers for detention, interrogation, and execution.

In early 1938 some 200 antifascists and anti-Stalinists were held in the Santa Ursula *ceka*, which soon came to be known as the Dachau of Republican Spain. "When the Stalinists decided to open a *ceka*," one victim recalled,

> there was a small cemetery being cleaned out nearby. The Chekists had a diabolical idea: they would leave the cemetery's tombs open, with the skeletons and the decomposing bodies in full view. That's where they locked up the most difficult cases. They had some particularly brutal methods of torture. Many prisoners were hung up by their feet, upside down, for whole days. Others they locked in tiny cupboards with just a tiny air hole near the face to breathe through . . . One of the worst methods was known as "the drawer"; prisoners were forced to squat in tiny square boxes for several days. Some were kept there unable to move for eight to ten days.

To do this sort of work, Soviet agents used depraved individuals who felt that their actions had already been approved by "La Pasionaria" (Dolores Ibarruri). She had once said at a meeting in Valencia: "It is better to kill one hundred innocents than to let one guilty person go."[17]

The use of torture was systematic.[18] One common technique was to force the prisoner to drink soapy water, a powerful emetic. Some techniques were typically Soviet, such as sleep deprivation or enclosure in a tiny space known as a cupboard cell, where the prisoner could not sit or stand, was unable to move his limbs, could scarcely breathe, and was constantly blinded by an electric light. Aleksandr Solzhenitsyn describes one such cell at length in *The Gulag Archipelago*, in his account of his arrival at Lubyanka.

Summary executions were also common practice:

> Lieutenant Astorga Vayo, a member of the Military Investigation Serv-ice and the NKVD, came up with an excellent means of preventing escape: as the prisoners were lined up in rows of five, they would shoot four prisoners for every one who was missing, and they also threatened to shoot the rows both in front and behind. Some of his comrades objected to this practice, but Vayo, though relieved of his functions, was promoted and became the head of one of the main concentration camps in Catalonia, Onells de Nagaya, in Lérida Province.[19]

Opinions vary on the total number executed. Katia Landau gives a figure of 15,000 prisoners, including 1,000 POUM members, in both official and unofficial prisons.[20] Yves Lévy, who carried out an inquiry at the time, men-tioned "approximately 10,000 civil and military revolutionaries in prison," including members of the POUM, the CNT, and the FAI. Some died as a result of their treatment, including Bob Smilie, a correspondent for the Independent Labour Party (a radical socialist group that had split from the British Labour Party in 1932) who was closely aligned with the POUM; and Manuel Maurin, the brother of Joaquín Maurin, who had been imprisoned by the Franquistas but whose life had been spared in the *cárcel modelo* (model prison) in Barcelona. According to Julian Gorkin, some 62 people in Santa Clara had been sentenced to death by the end of 1937.

Once the POUM had been crushed and the Socialists outmaneuvered or sidelined, there remained the anarchists. In the months following the Republi-can riposte to the military *pronunciamento*, agrarian collectives had proliferated under the anarchists' influence, particularly in Aragon. A few weeks after the events of May 1937, villages and towns in Aragon were besieged by the Assault Troops. The Congress of Collectives was taken over, and on 11 August a decree was published ordering the dissolution of the Aragon Council. Its president, Joaquín Ascaso, was arrested and charged with theft. He was replaced by a governor-general named José Ignacio Mantecón, a member of the Republican left who was a Communist mole.[21] This was a direct attack on the CNT, designed to undermine its foundations.

The Eleventh Division, under the command of the Communist Enrique Lister, who had already carried out numerous operations in Castile (such as executions and violence against peasant collectives), broke up the collectives with the help of the Twenty-seventh Division (known as the "Karl Marx" Division of the PSUC) and the Thirtieth Division. Hundreds of freedom fighters were arrested and eliminated from municipal councils and replaced by Communists. The land that had been turned into collectives was returned to its original owners. The operation was timed to coincide with a large-scale operation against Zaragoza, to make it look as if the actions were justified by the preparations for the offensive. Despite the massacre of hundreds, the peasants formed yet more collectives. In Castile, operations against the peasants were led by the famous Communist general Valentín González, who was known as "El Campesino" (The Peasant). According to César M. Lorenzo, González surpassed even Lister in his cruelty.[22] Once again hundreds of peasants were massacred and villages burned, but this time the CNT reacted with military force and halted El Campesino's campaign.

The NKVD at Work

In Spain in 1937, the NKVD, under the name Grupo de Información, had become a sort of annex of the Ministry of Internal Affairs. Communist agents also controlled the leadership of the security department, and during the spring and summer of 1937 the Servicio Alfredo Hertz saw its most intense period of activity. Hertz himself was described by Julian Gorkin as "one of the great masters of interrogation and execution." Hubert von Ranke, who had been employed by Ernő Gerő since 1930, worked alongside Hertz.[23] He had been a political commissar in the Thälmann battalion in the International Brigades before being made head of security for German-speaking foreigners. That was probably how he came to arrest Erwin Wolf, who was subsequently released but disappeared for good shortly afterward.

Arrested by two members of the Grupo de Información on 11 September 1937, Katia Landau later wrote about von Ranke's methods: "One of the worst GPU agents, Moritz Bressler, alias von Ranke, reduced all accusations to the minimum. He and his wife, Seppl Kapalanz, once arrested a comrade on the suspicion that he had knowledge of the whereabouts of Kurt Landau. 'If you don't give us his address,' they said, 'you'll never get out of prison. He's an enemy of Stalin and of the Popular Front. And as soon as we find out where he lives, we're going to kill him.'"[24]

On the night of 9–10 April 1937 a young Russian émigré named Marc Rein, who had been a volunteer in extreme left-wing movements in Norway and Germany, disappeared from his hotel room in Barcelona. A few days later his friends noticed his absence and raised the alarm. Marc Rein was the son of Rafael Abramovich, the exiled Russian leader of the Second International. That fact, together with the determination of his friends and family to discover his fate, caused a great stir abroad and much soul-searching in Republican Spain. The Spanish government was forced to assign one of its own agents to launch an inquiry, which found the Servicio Alfredo Hertz responsible for the disappearance. The conflict between the NKVD police and the government became so bitter that on 9 July 1937 the secretary of state at the Ministry of Internal Affairs provoked a confrontation between one of his own intelligence agents (SSI 29) and Hertz and Gómez Emperador. The next day SSI 29 was himself arrested by the Servicio Hertz. However, the secret service that employed him was powerful enough to get him released the following day. SSI 29, whose real name was P. Laurencic, was found in 1938 and arrested by the Franquistas, sent before a miliary tribunal, and executed as an NKVD agent.

Although the Rein affair remains unresolved to this day, it did have the effect of ending the activities of Alfredo Hertz and Gómez Emperador in July 1937. Their secret services were disbanded and restructured under the new leadership of Victorio Sala. On 15 August, Indalecio Prieto, the minister of defense and a Socialist, established the Servicio de Investigación Militar (SIM) as an umbrella for all political surveillance and counterespionage organizations. The SIM soon had 6,000 agents in its service. Numerous "technicians" from the Servicio Hertz simply went straight into the organization. In 1939 Prieto admitted that the SIM, which in principle was a counterespionage agency, had basically been created by the Soviet NKVD, and that in no time at all, despite the precautions taken, it was controlled by the Communists and used for their own purposes.[25] Under pressure from the Soviet Union and the Communists, Prieto was removed from the government on 5 April 1938.

Julián Gorkin described the activities of the SIM:

> They arrested everyone according to their own whims or some policy of NKVD reprisals. Suspects were then thrown into prison, and charges were drawn up . . . The SIM kept files for months and months, on the pretext that it always needed more information. The SIM was also the scourge of all the magistrates and lawyers, because if a judge was convinced of the prisoner's innocence, the SIM would simply override his decision.[26]

The Swiss Communist Rudolf Frei, a retired mechanic who had taken courses at the International Leninist School in Moscow in 1931–32, was in charge of organizing the transfer of volunteers from Basel to Spain. At his own request he was transferred to Spain in late 1937 and was put in charge of the control service of the SIM, where he was to keep an eye specifically on the Swiss volunteers.[27]

After the summer of 1938, many of the antifascists who had been kept in the prisons controlled by the Communists were taken to the front and forced, along with the Franquista prisoners, to carry out heavy work such as terracing, often under very harsh conditions, without food or medical care, and under the permanent threat of Communist attacks. Karl Bräuning, a member of a dissident German Communist group, managed to escape and six months later, in December 1939, told some friends about his experience:

> What we lived through in July was horrible and cruel. Dostoevsky's *House of the Dead* is nothing in comparison . . . And we were so hungry that we were often delirious. I'm half the man I used to be, just skin and bones. We were ill all the time and had no strength left at all. There's no difference between men and animals when you get down to that stage, it's just pure barbarism. Fascism still has a lot to learn from those bandits; it's culture and luxury in comparison. It must have been written in our files that we were literally to be worked to death by legal means, because that's exactly what they tried to do.[28]

A "Moscow Show-Trial" in Barcelona

Despite the restructuring, infiltration, and camouflage operations, the NKVD encountered obstacles. Because of the savage repression against it, the POUM received support from various revolutionary groups. These groups formed in France a Cartel for the Defense of Revolutionary Prisoners in Republican Spain. Thus overt public action was opposed to covert Soviet maneuvering. Three delegations were sent to Spain to investigate. The third, led by John MacGovern of the Independent Labour Party and by Félicien Challaye in November 1937, was allowed to visit the prisons in Barcelona, notably the model prison where 500 antifascists were kept, and to collect their testimony on what they had suffered. MacGovern and Challaye managed to arrange for a dozen prisoners to be freed. They also tried to get access to the secret NKVD prison in Junta Square, but, despite the support of Manuel de Irujo, the minister of justice, they were forbidden to enter. MacGovern concluded: "The mask has been dropped. We have raised the veil and shown who holds the real power. The ministers wanted to help, but they really couldn't."[29]

From 11 to 22 October 1938, members of the POUM Executive Committee—Gorkin, Andrade, Pascal Gironella, José Rovira, Arquer, Bonet, Jean Reboul, and José Escuder—were brought before a special court in a scenario highly reminiscent of the Moscow show-trials. One of the aims of the trial was to lend credibility to Moscow's claim that Trotskyites were endangering the Party on all fronts. However, Spanish militants roundly rejected the accusation. André Gide, Georges Duhamel, Roger Martin du Gard, François Mauriac, and Paul Rivet sent telegrams to Juan Negrin demanding that the accused be given a fair trial. Because the charges were based on confessions extracted by force, some considerable confusion followed. The Communist press vigorously demanded death sentences, but none was handed down.[30] Even so, the POUM militants were convicted on 2 November and sentenced to fifteen years in prison (the only exceptions were Jordi Arquer, who received eleven years; and David Rey, who was acquitted). They were found guilty of having "falsely claimed in the newspaper *La batalla* that the government of the Republic obeys orders from Moscow and systematically hunts down all those who refuse to obey such orders"—a statement that itself seemed more like a confession.

When the defeat of the Republic was complete in March 1939, the last chief of the SIM tried to hand these prisoners over to the Franquista forces so that they might be shot, counting on the enemies of the Republic to finish the sinister task that the NKVD agents had begun. Luckily, all the members of the POUM Executive Committee managed to escape.

Inside the International Brigades

The rallying cry to the cause of the Republican struggle had echoed around the world. Numerous volunteers came to Spain to fight the nationalists, and they enlisted in the militias or in fighting groups sponsored by organizations to which they were sympathetic. But the International Brigades were created at Moscow's instigation and constituted a genuine Communist army, even though not all their troops were Communists.[31] A distinction should also be made between the real combatants at the front and the men who formally belonged to the Brigades but were absent from the field of battle. The history of the Brigades is not simply the story of heroic battles fought on the front line.

The Brigades grew exponentially throughout the autumn and winter of 1936 as tens of thousands of volunteers flocked in from all around the world. The Communists did not accept all newcomers instantly, since they needed to prevent infiltration by double agents, Nazis, and Franquistas. While the Great Terror was at its height in Russia, the orthodoxy of the volunteers in Spain was also tested. The task of rooting out *agents provocateurs*—of unmasking any dissident, critical, or undisciplined elements—fell to the cadre services of the various Communist parties. Surveillance and control of volunteers also took place outside Spain. For example, the Zurich police seized from the German Communist Alfred Adolf a list of the names of "undesirable" volunteers, which he had intended to send to Soviet agents in Spain. In the autumn of 1937 a document of the Executive Committee of the Comintern noted that the Brigades should be cleansed of all politically questionable volunteers and that "the selection of volunteers should be carefully controlled to prevent intelligence agents, fascist spies, and Trotskyites from slipping into the Brigades."[32] A personal file for each Brigade member, including political details, was sent to the Comintern headquarters in Moscow and regularly updated. The archives have yielded up tens of thousands of such files.

André Marty, a member of the French Communist Party Politburo and a secretary in the Comintern, who had arrived in Spain in August 1936 as a Comintern delegate to the Republican government, became the official chief of the Albacete base, where the International Brigades were organized. Along with the Brigades, the Communists created a new Fifth Regiment, under the control of Enrique Lister, who had been trained at the Frunze Military Academy in the U.S.S.R. in 1932. The SIM was also present in Albacete.

The scale of violent repressions within the Brigades is still a subject of controversy. Some commentators persist in denying that Marty bore any responsibility, despite overwhelming evidence to the contrary. Others claim that the executions in question were justified by the circumstances. El Campesino explained as follows: "Of course he had no choice but to get rid of some of the dangerous elements. That he executed some people is quite incontrovertible; but they were all deserters, or had killed someone, or were traitors in some way."[33] The testimony of Gustav Regler, an assistant commissar in the 12th Brigade, confirms that executions occurred. During a battle near El Escorial, two anarchist volunteers had shown signs of weakness; Regler had them arrested and proposed to send them to a sanatorium. He said as much to Marty, who sent the two anarchists straight to Alcalá de Henares. Much later Regler learned that this in fact was not a sanatorium, but a center where Soviet NKVD squads executed people.[34] A note signed in Marty's own hand, found in the Moscow archives, explained to the Central Executive Committee of the Spanish Communist Party: "I am also not at all happy that spies and fascists whom I sent to Valencia to be liquidated are being sent back to me here at Albacete. You know very well that the International Brigades cannot do this themselves here at Albacete."[35] One can well imagine that it would have been difficult to execute "spies and fascists" in the middle of a military base. Whoever these "spies and fascists" were, he preferred that the dirty work be done elsewhere by other people, out of his sight.

A recent film has recounted the execution in November 1937 of Erich Frommelt, a member of the Thälmann battalion of the 12th Brigade, who was condemned to death on charges of desertion at 11:15 P.M. on one day and executed the next day at 4:45 P.M.[36] Officially, Frommelt was listed as having died in the battle of Teruel. Such dissembling naturally raises questions about who the "deserters" really were. Roger Codou, another member of the International Brigades, consulted their prison files and noted numerous references to "death by hydrocution," which in his view was simply a euphemism for execution. There were two special prisons for members of the International Brigades: one in the Horta district of Barcelona, where there were 265 prisoners in 1937; and the other in Castellón de la Plana. It is difficult to calculate the number of Brigade members who were liquidated. According to Julian Gorkin, André Marty was personally responsible for approximately 500 executions of "undisciplined members or those who were simply suspected of having 'oppositional' tendencies."[37]

Robert Martin, from Glasgow, also testified to the frequency of arrests in Albacete. When he himself was arrested, he was placed in a cell with seventy other Brigade members who had seen combat, some of whom were wounded. The extremely harsh conditions spurred some prisoners to start a hunger strike. After being told that they would be set free, they were taken to Barcelona in small groups. Martin and his group were taken to the Falcon Hotel, which had been the headquarters of the POUM before being transformed into a prison, and then to Corsiga Street, where they were photographed and their fingerprints taken. After a miraculous escape, Martin managed to cross into France and heard nothing more about the fate of his companions.[38]

According to the Social Democrat Max Reventlow, the Republican forces had at least 650 prisoners with them during the Republican retreat after the nationalist breakthrough to the Mediterranean. Once the prisoners arrived in Catalonia, they were transferred to the prisons of Horta and Castellón, both of which were under the command of the Croatian F. I. Ćopić. Sixteen of them were shot as soon as they arrived. In these prisons, a special commission pronounced death sentences, with no possibility of appeal. After an escape by 50 prisoners, another 50 were shot. The practice of torture was common. One German lieutenant, Hans Rudolph, was tortured for six days, his arms and legs broken and his fingernails ripped out. He was executed on 14 June 1938, along with 6 other prisoners, with a bullet in the neck. Ćopić himself was later accused of espionage but was saved by the intervention of Luigi Longo, André Marty, and his brother, Colonel Vladimir Ćopić.[39]

After killing an SS guard, the German Communist Deputy Hans Beimler escaped from Dachau. Upon reaching Spain he helped establish the Thälmann battalion. He was killed on 1 December 1936 in Palacete. Gustav Regler claimed that Beimler fell victim to a bullet from the nationalists. Antonia Stern, Beimler's companion, who was stripped of her rights and expelled from Spain, disputed this version of events. She claimed that Beimler had spoken out against the first Moscow show-trial and had been in contact with the former directors of the KPD, Arkady Maslow and Ruth Fischer, who led an opposition group in Paris. On the basis of a report from the Secret Intelligence Service, a special department of the Catalan Police Department that dealt with informers in the Communist ranks, Pierre Broué also believes that Beimler was assassinated.[40]

Stalin and his agents cynically exploited the idealism that had brought so many to Spain to fight for the Republican cause, then abandoned the country and the Brigades to their fate. By then he was preparing his rapprochement with Hitler.

Exile and Death in the "Fatherland of the Proletariat"

After the Republican defeat, a committee presided over by Togliatti was formed in Paris in March 1939 to select Spaniards worthy of emigrating to the "fatherland of the proletariat." El Campesino wrote about the conditions of his departure for the U.S.S.R.[41] On 14 May 1939 he sailed from Le Havre on the *Siberia* with 350 other people, including members of the Politburo and Central Committee of the Spanish Communist Party, Communist deputies, the commanders of the Fifth Regiment, and some 30 Brigade chiefs. El Campesino was present when Togliatti's committee was established under the aegis of the NKVD. Its function was to monitor the 3,961 Spanish refugees, who were immediately divided into eighteen groups and sent to different towns. In exile, most of the leaders spied and informed on their compatriots, such as the former secretary of the Spanish Communist Party Committee in Jaén, who had half the Spanish contingent in Kharkiv arrested; and Jorge Cortina, who had many injured people deported to Siberia. Accused of being a Trotskyite, El Campesino was thrown out of the Frunze Military Academy and in March 1942 was working on the subway system in Moscow. He was later deported to Uzbekistan and then to Siberia. In 1948 he managed to escape to Iran.

José Díaz, the former secretary general of the Spanish Communist Party, died on 19 March 1942 after falling from his window on the fourth floor of a building in Tbilisi, at a moment when none of his family were present. El Campesino and his compatriots believed that this death was in fact an assassination. Just before his death, Díaz had been writing a book about his experiences and seemed quite disillusioned by what he had seen. He had also written a letter to the authorities, protesting the conditions in which children were being kept in the Tbilisi colony.

During the civil war, thousands of Spanish children aged five to twelve had been sent to the U.S.S.R.[42] Their living conditions changed dramatically after the Republican defeat. In 1939 their teachers were accused of Trotskyism, and, according to El Campesino, 60 percent of them were arrested and imprisoned in the Lubyanka; the rest were sent to work in factories. One young woman was tortured for more than twenty months before being executed. The fate of the children was particularly harsh because all the colonies were directed by Soviet officials. The Kaluga colony was particularly severe under the strong authority of Juan Modesto, a general who had learned his trade in the Fifth Regiment, and of Enrique Lister.[43] In 1941, according to Jesús Hernández, roughly 50 percent of the children there had developed tuberculosis, and 750 of them (15 percent) died before the exodus of 1941. The adolescents ended up in the Urals and in central Siberia, particularly in Kokand, where they formed criminal gangs, while the women fell into prostitution. Many of them committed suicide. According to Hernández, 2,000 of the 5,000 children died.[44] In 1947, on the tenth anniversary of their arrival in the U.S.S.R., a ceremony took place at the Stanislavsky Theater in Moscow involving 2,000 young Spanish people. In September 1956, 534 of them returned to Spain. In all, only 1,500 were ever permitted to return.

Other Spaniards came to know both life and death in the Soviet Union. Among these were the non-Communist sailors and pilots who came voluntarily to the Soviet Union to train. El Campesino tells the story of a group of 218 pilots who arrived in 1938 for what was supposed to be a six- to seven-month training period in Kirovabad. At the end of 1939 Colonel Martínez Cartón, a member of the Spanish Communist Party Politburo and an NKVD agent, gave the pilots a choice between remaining in the U.S.S.R. or departing from the country. Those who chose to leave were sent to work in factories. On 1 September 1939 they were all arrested, and charges were drawn up against them. Some were tortured, others were killed in the Lubyanka; most received camp sentences of ten to fifteen years. Of the group that went to Pechoralev, there were no survivors at all. Out of the original group of 218, there were 6 survivors.

In 1947 some refugees managed to leave the U.S.S.R. Those who stayed were forced to sign a document saying that they would not try to leave again. In April 1948 José Ester (Mauthausen political deportee no. 64553) and José Domenech (Neuengamme political deportee no. 40202) held a press conference in Paris on behalf of the Spanish Federation of Deportees and Political Internees to reveal the details they had gathered concerning deportees of Camp 99 in Karaganda, Kazakhstan, northwest of Lake Balkhash. Ester and Domenech supplied the names of 59 deportees, including 24 pilots and 33 sailors. In a broadside dated 1 March 1948, the two former deportees explained their actions as follows: "It is a binding duty for us, and an imperative for anyone who has known famine, cold, and desolation under a regime like that of the SS or the Gestapo, and it is a civic duty for everyone for whom the words Freedom and Human Rights have any sense at all, to stand up and demand out of solidarity the freedom of these men, who are facing the threat of certain death."

After World War II, the Communists and their special services continued to liquidate their opponents. Joan Farré Gasso, a former POUM leader from Lérida, took part in the French resistance during the war. He was arrested and imprisoned in Moissac by the Vichy regime, but was freed again at the end of the war, when he tried to rejoin his wife in a small village in French Catalonia. On the way to Montauban he was stopped by the Communist *maquis*, or *guerrilleros españoles*, who executed him on the spot.[45] This assassination prolonged the civil war in Spain in its most sinister aspect: the liquidation of thousands of the bravest and most determined antifascists. The Spanish example shows the impossibility of separating the legal and criminal enterprises of the Communists in their pursuit of their political objectives. Although it may be true that political and social violence was the norm in interwar Spain, and that the civil war allowed this violence to erupt on a massive scale, it is still the case that the Soviet Union brought into the equation the might of a party-state born out of war and violence. Moscow's intervention was intended solely to promote Soviet interests while pretending it was essential for the struggle against fascism.

It is clear that the real goal of Stalin and his henchmen was to take control of the destiny of the Republic. To that end, the liquidation of left-wing opposition to the Communists—Socialists, anarchosyndicalists, POUMists, and Trotskyites—was no less important than the military defeat of Franco.

18 Communism and Terrorism

Rémi Kauffer

In the 1920s and 1930s the international Communist movement concentrated on the preparation of armed insurrections, all of which ultimately failed. As a result, the movement largely abandoned this type of action. In the 1940s it profited instead from wars of liberation from the Nazis or from Japanese expansionism, and in the 1950s and 1960s it focused on the process of decolonization, creating groups of organized insurgents that were slowly transformed into regular Red Armies. In Yugoslavia, China, North Korea, Vietnam, and Cambodia this tactic worked, allowing the Communist Party to seize power. However, the failure of guerrilla movements in South America—where they were opposed by special troops trained by the Americans—was an incentive for the Communists to resume the "terrorist" methods that until then they had used relatively infrequently, the most memorable exception being the Sofia Cathedral explosion in 1924. The distinction between terrorism pure and simple and preparations for an armed uprising may sometimes appear slightly academic, since the same people are usually involved. Moreover, the one course of action does not preclude the other. Many national liberation movements have combined terrorism and guerrilla warfare in their actions, as was the case with the Front de Libération Nationale (FLN) and the Armée de Libération Nationale in Algeria.

The Algerian case is an interesting one in that the supporters of French

Algeria saw the nationalist uprising as a plot drawn up in Moscow, and found more confirmation of this idea in the fact that at the time of the battle of Algiers (1956–57) the Algerian Communist Party had provided Yacef Saadi, the FLN chief for the capital, with a number of its best explosives specialists. Can one conclude from this that the nationalist movement was in thrall to the Communists? In many respects, this was clearly not the case. The Algerian Communist Party and the FLN were constantly at loggerheads. In the international arena, the FLN benefited from the open political support of the U.S.S.R., but apart from a few extremely limited operations by its special services, Moscow was careful not to implicate itself directly in the conflict with France. In fact the main arms suppliers to the FLN were Nasser's Egypt, Tito's Yugoslavia, and Czechoslovakia, which acted on behalf of the Eastern Bloc. In addition, a number of FLN cadres had been trained in underground techniques by the Czechs in Prague. But the Soviet Union deliberately remained in the background. Did the Soviet Union already have an intuition that the future state of Algeria would be politically close to Moscow but at the same time careful to retain its independence? The fact is that the Soviet special services never had oversight of the holy of holies of the new regime, the Military Security, in contrast to the Cuban Dirección General de Inteligencia (DGI).

Another example of Soviet prudence regarding extremely controversial nationalist movements is the Irish case. As an offspring of the IRA (the Irish Republican Army, formed in Dublin after the failure of the 1916 Easter uprising), "Republicanism" was a way of thinking quite specific to Northern Ireland. Apart from social issues, after 1921 the IRA's nationalist program (the reunification of Ireland through the wresting of the six northern counties from the British crown) was at the center of all its actions. In contrast, the pro-Soviet figures who in 1933 formed the Communist Party of Ireland distanced themselves further and further from purely nationalist preoccupations to highlight the importance of the class struggle.

The IRA needed arms to fight the British. Between the wars, it repeatedly tried to get them from the U.S.S.R., but Moscow politely refused. Undoubtedly it did not seem particularly judicious to arm pro-independence forces at the risk of open conflict with Great Britain. The fact that several hundred IRA members joined the International Brigades and fought in Spain did little to change Moscow's position. In 1939–40, when the IRA was starting a new bombing campaign in Britain, its most secret team was a small group of militant nationalists who were less likely to arouse suspicion by virtue of being Protestant. The core of this group consisted of Communists, notably Betty Sinclair. Throughout Europe, groups of saboteurs such as the Ernst Wollweber network were ready to attack not only German ships but also French and British vessels. Moscow intended to use the IRA to sabotage British ships, thinking that using the underground organization would mask the Soviet origins of the sabotage. But the project came to nothing. Moscow retained a certain suspicion of the Irish, who would ally themselves with anyone simply to procure arms for their own ends, but who refused categorically to pay any political price by compromising their own political agenda. In the early 1970s the IRA again took up arms (and more usually its speciality, explosives) against the British following a revolt of the Catholic ghettoes in Northern Ireland. Contrary to a widely held belief, neither the bombs nor the explosives came from the Soviet Union either directly or indirectly. In fact the IRA's main support, both historically and today, has come from the Irish-American community in the United States.

The "hand of Moscow" was thus not omnipresent. But it played an active role in supporting certain Middle Eastern terrorist groups. Starting from the idea that the Palestinian organizations represented a national liberation movement comparable to the Algerian FLN, the Soviet Union was quick to come out in favor of Yasser Arafat's Palestine Liberation Organization (PLO) and its main component, El Fatah. But the KGB also kept its eye on another Palestinian nationalist group, the Popular Front for the Liberation of Palestine (PFLP), led by Doctor George Habash. Claiming to be a radical Marxist group, this highly structured movement had no qualms about carrying out terrorist attacks and spectacular hijackings. Its first attack was the hijacking of an El Al aircraft in July 1968, followed by an attack on the Athens airport in December. These actions culminated in 1970, just before the troops of King Hussein crushed the Palestinians in Jordan, with the blowing up of three aircraft—a TWA Boeing, a Swissair DC-8, and a BOAC Viscount VC-10—at Zarka, in Jordan, where they had been rerouted and the passengers taken prisoner.

One of the PFLP cadres, Nayef Hawatmeh, who was worried by what he perceived as overly violent terrorism, formed a breakaway group in 1970–71 called the Democratic and Popular Front for the Liberation of Palestine (DPFLP). After a period of continued terrorism, the DPFLP renounced violence in the name of the international proletariat and the working masses and aligned itself along ever more orthodox Communist lines, thus becoming in principle the main Soviet ally on Palestinian questions. Yet this was not really the case, for at the same time the KGB was stepping up its support for the PFLP. Habash himself was soon sidelined by his own assistant and director of operations, Wadi Haddad, a retired dental surgeon who had trained at the American University in Beirut.

Dr. Haddad was a man of considerable experience. In the opinion of Pierre Marion, the former head of the DGSE, the French special services, Haddad is the real inventor of modern terrorism: "It is he who dreamed up its structures, he who trained its main practitioners; it is he who perfected recruitment and training methods, he who refined tactics and techniques."[1] In late

1973 and early 1974 he broke from the PFLP to set up his own organization, the PFLP-EOC (PFLP External Operations Command), which was entirely dedicated to international terrorism, while Habash's organization carried out other activities, including guerrilla operations against the Israeli army and cooperative projects in the Palestinian refugee camps.

The Soviet KGB decided to support Haddad's terrorist group, as is evident from a straightforward message of 23 April 1974, with the filing designation of 1071-1/05. This message from the KGB was addressed to Leonid Brezhnev, the general secretary of the Soviet Communist Party:

> Since 1968 the Committee for State Security has been in secret contact with Wadi Haddad, a member of the Politburo of the PFLP and the head of External Operations for the PFLP.
>
> When he met the KGB chief for the Lebanon region last April, Wadi Haddad revealed in confidence the PFLP program for subversive activities and terrorism, the main points of which are listed below.

There followed a list of terrorist targets in Israel and planned subversive actions against Israeli territory, attacks against diamond companies and Israeli diplomats, and sabotage of oil refineries and supertankers in Saudi Arabia, the Persian Gulf, and even Hong Kong. The KGB report continued:

> W. Haddad asks us to help his organization obtain certain special materials that are indispensable for subversive actions of this type. While he cooperates with us and asks us for help, W. Haddad is well aware that in principle we disapprove of terror, and he asks nothing of us with regard to PFLP activities. The nature of our relationship with W. Haddad allows us to a certain extent to control the activities of the External Operations Command of the PFLP, to exert on it an influence beneficial to the Soviet Union, and to use the forces of this organization to carry out active operations in the appropriate manner when they are in our interest.

Beyond the double-talk, the conclusion was obvious: principles count for nothing so long as one can strike at the enemy without getting caught. Passed on to Suslov, Nikolai Podgorny, Kosygin, and Gromyko, the document was approved on 26 April 1974.[2]

Haddad's most gifted pupil was a young Venezuelan, Ilyich Ramirez-Sanchez, better known by the name Carlos. The two of them worked with the survivors of an Asian terrorist group, the Japanese Red Army (JRA), whose history is instructive. Created at the end of the 1960s, when student radicalism in Japan was at its height and Maoism was in the air, the JRA quickly made contact with North Korean agents (the Korean community is quite large throughout the Japanese archipelago). The Korean agents passed instructions to their cadres and brought the arms the JRA was lacking, but they were unable to prevent a split in the group in the early 1970s, which resulted in a bloody conflict between the dissenting and orthodox factions. Accordingly, some of the cadres simply defected to North Korea, taking refuge in Pyongyang, where they remain as businessmen and intermediaries with the West. The other faction decided to internationalize its affairs even further, and joined up with Wadi Haddad. As a result of this alliance, three members of the JRA acted on behalf of the PFLP in killing twenty-eight people at Tel Aviv's Lod airport in May 1972.

The fact that the PFLP-EOC had worked hand in hand with the Swiss Nazi banker François Genoud, as was revealed by Pierre Péan in *L'extrémiste* (where Genoud admitted this openly), was clearly no problem for the KGB.[3] Neither were the subsequent spectacular terrorist activities of Carlos, first for the PFLP-EOC and later for the KGB itself, through his connections with about fifteen secret services in Arab and Eastern bloc countries. A partial inventory follows.

Ilyich Ramirez-Sanchez, the son of a Venezuelan lawyer who was a great admirer of Lenin (he had named his three sons Vladimir, Ilyich, and Ulyanov), when brought to trial in France in 1997, told Judge Jean-Louis Bruguière that he had first met a member of the PFLP in 1969. The man in question was Rifaat Abul Aoun, and the meeting took place in Moscow, where the bored young student who later came to be known as Carlos was studying physics, chemistry, and Marxism-Leninism. Carlos felt disappointed by the lack of activity in the Latin American Communist parties, and was ready for action of a more violent and radical nature. The PFLP-EOC offered him the opportunity for such action not long after his arrival in Jordan. After a period of training he became an operational agent in early 1971, passing easily through Europe because of his wealthy upbringing and his consequently urbane manner. Surface appearances aside, he soon carried out a series of spectacular and bloody terrorist acts.

On 27 June 1975 Carlos killed two policemen in Paris and grievously injured a third. In December he led an attack on the OPEC offices in Vienna, killing three people before fleeing to Algiers. With the other members of his team, who were Germans from a radical left-wing group calling themselves the Revolutionary Cells (led by Johannes Weinrich), he moved about in Libya, Yemen, Iraq, and Yugoslavia. He was also often in East Germany, where the Ministerium für Staatssicherheit (Ministry for State Security), or Stasi, watched him very closely, wary of a man capable of such audacious acts.

"Separat" was the code name of Carlos' organization within the Stasi. In 1980 a top-secret file was sent to Erich Mielke, the head of the Stasi. It was called quite simply "Project for Stasi action regarding treatment and control

of Carlos' group." According to Bernard Violet, the author of a highly informative biography of Carlos, "Weinrich and Pascale Kopp [Carlos' assistant and
companion] were not really Stasi agents. They never carried out a mission for
the Stasi, and they were not actually on the payroll for passing information back
to the Germans. But they were very important go-betweens linking the East
German special services and the members of the group." After naming Carlos'
successive East German contacts—Colonel Harry Dahl, Hörst Franz, Günther
Jäckel, and Helmut Voigt—Violet adds: "Carlos was fully aware of the contacts
that these two [Weinrich and Kopp] had with the [East] German secret services."

   Carlos' ties to the Stasi did not stop him from striking up an alliance with
the Romanians, or from imposing on the Hungarian state security forces by
treating Budapest as a base. His group, which renamed itself the Organization
for Armed Struggle for Arab Liberation, carried out ever-bloodier attacks.
Colonel Voigt of the Stasi blamed the "Separat" group for the attack on the
Maison de France in West Berlin on 25 August 1983, in which two people died.
That attack was blamed at the time on another terrorist group linked to the
Eastern bloc and based in Beirut, called the Secret Army for the Liberation of
Armenia.

   It might seem amazing that the Stasi showed such indulgence toward an
agent who never seemed to do them any favors. This decision was apparently
taken at the very top of the Stasi hierarchy. One unproved psychological
explanation is that Erich Mielke, who was the head of various KPD combat
groups before the war and was charged with the murder of two policemen in
Berlin, saw a lot of himself in the Venezuelan terrorist and in the other members of the Baader Meinhof gang, the most prominent terrorist group in West
Germany. But there must be a more objective link between the Stasi and these
international terrorist groups. Neither Mielke nor anyone else in the Stasi
seems to be much of a romantic revolutionary in spirit. If Carlos and his group
had links with at least fifteen different secret services in Arab and Eastern bloc
countries, we can be sure that it was not a matter of chance.

The indulgence with which Communist countries treated Middle Eastern extremists was not reserved for Carlos alone. Abu Nidal and his Fatah Revolutionary Council, who were violently opposed to Yasser Arafat and the PLO,
working first for the Iraqis and then for the Syrians, also benefited from such
support, but to a lesser degree, since they were judged to be less controllable.
Nevertheless, their leader, when extremely ill, could still travel in secret to the
other side of the Iron Curtain for medical help.

   Another example of direct intervention by Eastern bloc countries in modern international terrorism is their manipulation of the German RAF (Rote

Armee Fraktion), better known in the West as the Baader Meinhof gang. Born out of student protest, this small organization of about fifty agents and about one thousand supporters launched itself into terrorism in the 1970s, mainly attacking American interests in Germany. After 1977 and the assassination of the West German "patron of patrons" Hans Martin Schleyer, followed by the death in prison of the group's two leaders, Ulrike Meinhof and Andreas Baader, it found more support on the other side of the Berlin Wall, so much so that its own identity gradually faded and the group became more or less a secret arm of the Stasi itself. After German reunification, the last group members who had escaped prison continued to live in the former East Germany.

The manipulation of guerrilla and terrorist groups is seldom easy; it requires delicacy and great political skill. Perhaps for that reason the KGB, through one of its most brilliant agents, Oleg Maksimovich Nechiporenko, and with the help of the North Koreans, chose in 1969–70 to form a revolutionary movement that was entirely under its own control. The Movimiento de Acción Revolucionaria (MAR) was finally destroyed by the Mexican police in 1971.[4] Quite clearly the objective of this bold initiative was to avoid the threats, lack of discipline, and double-dealing that were rife in other Castroist and Maoist organizations. Some of these groups did manage to escape from their mentors. The Spanish FRAP—the Revolutionary Anti-Fascist Patriotic Front—flirted for a while in the early 1970s with the Chinese and Albanians in the vain hope of obtaining arms, and then transformed itself into GRAPO—the Anti-Fascist Resistance Group of October First. In contrast, Abimaël Guzmán's Peruvian Sendero Luminoso (Shining Path) army, which claims allegiance to hard-line Maoist doctrines and the prolonged popular war, always hated Deng Xiaoping and still has little to do with the new Chinese leadership. In December 1983 it even went so far as to attack the Chinese embassy in Lima.

In a few rare cases—for the risks are too great in the modern period—Communist countries carried out terrorist attacks themselves through their own secret services. This happened, for example, in 1987, when a team of two North Korean agents, one an experienced cadre called Kim Seung-il, and the other a young woman called Kim Hyuon-hee, who had trained for three years at the military academy in Keumsung, failed to rejoin their flight during a stopover in Abu Dhabi, leaving a bomb in a radio on the Korean Airlines plane that was heading for Bangkok. Some 115 people died in the subsequent blast. When arrested, Kim Seung-il committed suicide, while Kim Hyuon-hee made a full confession and went on to write a book about her experiences. It is still too soon to determine how much of the book is fabrication. However true it is, it remains the case that by 1997 the only Communist country systematically committed to the practice of terrorism was North Korea.

The Other Europe:
Victim of Communism

Andrzej Paczkowski and Karel Bartošek

19 Poland, the "Enemy Nation"

Andrzej Paczkowski

Soviet Repression of the Polish People

Poland was one of the nations that suffered the most under Soviet rule. This was the case even though Feliks Dzerzhinsky, the man who masterminded the early Soviet terror, was himself Polish, as were many others who worked in the various repressive organizations that characterized Soviet rule, including the Cheka, the OGPU, and the NKVD. There are several reasons for Poland's special status as an "enemy nation." Some are specific to the Soviet regime; others can be put down to the traditional hostility between Russians and Poles. Thus, the origins of this conflict were rooted both in the distant past and in the mistrust that various leaders—and in particular Stalin—felt toward Poland and its nationals. Between 1772 and 1795 Poland had been partitioned three times, and each time the tsarist empire had taken the lion's share. The Poles had risen up against Russia in 1830 and 1863, but both rebellions had been violently suppressed. Thereafter patriotism and resistance against foreign occupation—whether Russian or Prussian—had been centered in the nobility and the Catholic clergy. World War I and the collapse of the three empires—German, Russian, and Austro-Hungarian—that had oppressed Poland for more than a century offered a historic opportunity for Poland's rebirth as an independent nation. But the drive for independence, led by an army of volunteers under Józef Piłsudski, immediately came into conflict with the revolutionary aims of Moscow, for which control of Warsaw was vital to extending the revolution to Germany.

In the summer of 1920, Lenin launched a Red Army offensive against Warsaw. This audacious move was thwarted by nationwide Polish resistance, and in 1921 the Soviet Union was forced to sign the Treaty of Riga, which was favorable to Poland. Stalin, whose own carelessness had contributed to the defeat of the Red Army, never forgot this affront or forgave those who criticized him on this occasion: Trotsky, who was the head of the Red Army; and Marshal Tukhachevsky, who was the commander of the troops. The events of 1921 provided the framework for the ill will felt by Soviet leaders, and by Stalin in particular, toward Poland, the Poles, and those who had fought so hard for independence—the nobility, the army, and the church.

The Poles, regardless of whether they were Soviet citizens, suffered every aspect of Stalinist terror: the hunt for spies, dekulakization, anticlericalism, national and ethnic "cleansing," the Great Purge, the purges of border regions and of the Red Army itself, "pacification" operations to help the Polish Communists into power, and all the forms that terror took, including forced labor, the execution of prisoners of war, and mass deportations of groups of people labeled as "socially dangerous elements."

The Polish Military Organization (POW) Affair and the "Polish Operation" of the NKVD (1931–1938)

By 1924 the repatriation of Poles under the Treaty of Riga was coming to an end, although there were still between 1.1 and 1.2 million in the U.S.S.R. The vast majority of these lived in either Ukraine or Belorussia. At least 80 percent were peasants who had resided there since the Polish colonization of the region in the seventeenth and eighteenth centuries. There were also sizable Polish communities in the large cities such as Kyiv and Minsk. Another 200,000 Poles lived in Russia itself, principally in Moscow and Leningrad, as well as in the Caucasus and Siberia. Among these were several thousand exiled Communists and about an equal number who had taken part in the revolution and civil war. The rest were economic refugees who moved there earlier in the century.

Tension persisted between the two countries, despite the signing of the peace treaty and the establishment of diplomatic relations. Given the scale of the Polish-Soviet conflict in 1920 and the strength of the belief that the "fortress of the proletariat" was being assaulted by imperialists, it is hardly surprising that so many Poles in the U.S.S.R. found themselves accused of spying. In 1924–1929 several hundred were shot, although only a handful had actually been involved in espionage. During the Soviet campaign against religion, several hundred Catholics were persecuted and dozens were shot or disappeared. Although this repression seems insignificant in comparison with the scale of the repression against the Russian Orthodox Church, it resulted in the disappearance of a church that had formed the foundation of social, cultural, and spiritual life for hundreds of thousands of Polish peasants.

These peasants were among the victims of collectivization. According to official classifications in use at the time, 20 percent of them were designated as kulaks and a slightly larger share as "subkulaks." In Ukraine, Polish resistance was fierce and had to be broken by force. According to approximate figures at the time, the population of the regions inhabited by Poles fell by around 25 percent in 1933 alone. In Belorussia the collectivization of Polish farms was less brutal.

Aside from the repression of "Polish spies," the logic of the repressions was clear—they were part of the "class struggle" (that is, collectivization and the campaign against religion) as it was then conceived. But along with collectivization, another form of repression was launched: between 15 August and 15 September 1933 the authorities arrested about twenty Polish Communists, most of whom were émigrés, including one member of the Politburo of the Polish Communist Party, the KPP. Subsequent waves of arrests followed. All these people were accused of belonging to a "POW [Polish Military Organization] espionage and sabotage operation."

The Polish Military Organization, or POW, had been formed in 1915 by Józef Piłsudski as an underground organization whose activities were directed against Austro-Hungary and Germany, and in 1918–1920 it had carried out reconnaissance missions in the areas where the civil war was raging, principally in Ukraine. It definitively ceased operations in 1921. Most of its members were leftists; many belonged to the Polish Socialist Party; several had broken with the Socialists to establish the Communist Party. In 1933 the POW quite simply no longer existed. Nevertheless, several Poles (including the well-known avant-garde poet Witold Wandurski) were arrested, falsely charged with belonging to the organization, condemned to death, and shot. Others died in prison. Those who survived in prison were later shot during the Great Purge.

For several years the POW affair fed internal conflicts in the KPP: it was as bad to be accused of being a POW agitator as it was to be labeled a Trotskyite. More important, the OGPU (and later the Main Directorate for State Security of the NKVD) began to compile detailed files and records of Poles working in the Soviet administration, the Comintern, and the security services. These were complemented by lists of Poles living in Ukraine and Belorussia in the two so-called autonomous Polish regions. The first, in Ukraine, called the "Julian Marchlewski" (after one of the founders of the KPP who had died in 1925), had been established in 1925; the second, in Belorussia, had been created in 1932 and bore the name of Feliks Dzerzhinsky. These regions, with their own local governments, newspapers, theater, schools, and publishing houses, were "Soviet Polish" enclaves in the U.S.S.R.

September 1935 saw a new wave of arrests in Minsk, Kyiv, and Moscow, officially aimed at putting an end once and for all to the supposed POW network. Liquidation of the autonomous Polish regions began at the same time. During the time of the Great Purge in 1936–1938, arrests of NKVD officials of Polish origin began, reaching to the very top of the security hierarchy before spreading ever more widely at the base. During a plenary session of the Central Committee of the Soviet Communist Party in June 1937, Nikolai Ezhov affirmed that the POW "had infiltrated the Soviet counterespionage and intelligence services" and that the NKVD "had broken and liquidated the largest Polish espionage operation." Hundreds of Poles, many of them KPP leaders, had already been interned, and the false accusations against them were "substantiated" by confessions extracted under torture.

In the summer of 1937 the NKVD embarked on new repressions against national minorities, beginning with the Germans and moving on to the Poles. On 11 August Ezhov signed Operational Order No. 00485:

I order that:

1. On 20 August 1937 a vast operation is to begin, with the aim of completely eradicating all local POW organizations. Particular attention is to be paid to the cadres responsible for subversion, espionage, and rebellion in industry, communications, *sovkhozy*, and *kolkhozy*. This operation is to be carried out within three months—that is, it is to be completed on or before 20 November 1937.

2. Arrests are to be made of:
   a. the most active members of the POWs (see enclosed list) found during the investigation who have remained unidentified until now
   b. all Polish prisoners of war who are still in the U.S.S.R.
   c. all Polish refugees, regardless of the date of their arrival in the U.S.S.R.
   d. all political immigrants and political prisoners who have been exchanged with Poland
   e. former members of the Polish Socialist Party and all other anti-Soviet parties
   f. local anti-Soviet elements and the most active nationalists in the Polish regions

3. The arrest operation is to be divided into two phases: first, all relevant personnel in the NKVD, the Red Army, the weapons factories, the military departments of all other enterprises, the railway, road, shipping, and aviation industries, the energy sector, industry in general, and refineries and gas works; second, all those who work in industries where national security is not at such a premium, such as the *sovkhozy* and *kolkhozy*, and in government administration.

4. All investigations are to be carried out simultaneously. During the investigations, considerable pressure must be brought to bear on all organizers and leaders of subversive groups to force them to divulge all their collaborators and reveal the true extent of their networks. This information must be acted on immediately, so that all spies, harmful elements, and subversive groups can be arrested on the basis of this information. To carry out such investigations, a special task force is to be established.

5. Classify all people arrested during the investigation in one of two categories:

   a. Those in the first category, people belonging to Polish espionage networks, groups of saboteurs, subversive agents, and Polish insurrectionists, must be shot.

   b. Those in the second category, people less active than the first, are to receive prison or camp sentences of five to ten years.

A decision by the NKVD and the Soviet Council of People's Commissars on 15 November 1938 formally ended the "Polish Operation," although it was in fact prolonged by a purge of NKVD agents who had taken part in its earlier stages. The repressions wiped out many Polish Communist leaders (46 full members and 24 nonvoting, or candidate, members of the Central Committee of the Polish Workers' Party were shot) as well as ordinary citizens—workers and, above all, peasants. According to an NKVD report of 10 July 1938, the number of prisoners of Polish origin was 134,519, 53 percent of whom came from Ukraine or from Belorussia. Between 40 and 50 percent (that is, between 54,000 and 67,000) were shot.[1] The survivors were sent to camps or deported to Kazakhstan.

The Poles account for some 10 percent of the total number of victims of the Great Purge, and for around 40 percent of the victims of purges against national minorities. These figures are, if anything, understated, since thousands of Poles were deported from Ukraine and Belorussia for reasons unconnected with the "Polish Operation." It was not only the Polish Communist suites and offices at the Hotel Lux that were emptied, but whole Polish villages and *kolkhozy* as well.

Katyń, Prisons, and Deportations (1939–1941)

A secret protocol to the nonaggression pact signed by the U.S.S.R. and Germany on 23 August 1939 partitioned Poland into "spheres of interest." The order to attack Poland was given on 14 September 1939, and three days later the Red Army invaded the country with orders to "liberate" the parts described as "western Belorussia" and "western Ukraine" from what was termed "the Polish fascist occupation" and to incorporate these territories into the U.S.S.R. Annexation proceeded quickly, accompanied by measures to repress and intimidate the population. On 29 November the Presidium of the Supreme Soviet of the U.S.S.R. extended Soviet citizenship to all residents in the new territories. Vilnius and its surroundings were ceded to Lithuania, then in its last few months of independence. The Soviet system of repression and internal control was extended to these new regions. The regime rightly foresaw that a considerable local resistance movement would take shape; almost immediately, some detachments from the Polish army who had avoided capture set about organizing resistance. In response the NKVD sent troops into the Polish regions and began to establish its own units, replete with a large staff and border guards. The new authorities had to solve the problem of what to do with the prisoners of war, as well as to determine how society in general would respond to the new system.

Moscow's main preoccupation was the Polish army, which had consisted of 240,000 to 250,000 troops, including 10,000 officers. The Soviet authorities made some important decisions immediately after the attack on Poland was launched: On 19 September Lavrenti Beria set up within the NKVD a new Directorate for Prisoners of War (Glavnoe upravlenie po delam voenno-plennykh), or GUVP, under Order No. 0308, as well as a network of prison camps. In early October 25,000 Polish prisoners of war were sent to mend roads, and 12,000 were put at the disposal of the People's Commissariat of Heavy Industry to be used as forced labor. A still unknown number were dispersed in small groups throughout the huge gulag system. At the same time officers' camps were established in Starobielsk and in Kozielsk, and a special camp for policemen, prison guards, and frontier guards in Ostaszków. Soon Beria formed another special group to begin prosecutions inside the camps. At the end of February 1940, 6,192 policemen and 8,376 officers had been interned.

Moscow was undecided regarding their fate. Many expected that some of them, beginning with those in the camp at Ostaszków, would be charged with offenses under section 13 of Article 58 of the penal code, aimed at people who "had resisted the international workers' movement." It did not take much imagination to see that this could be applied to any Polish police officer or prison guard. The punishment was usually five to eight years in the camps, and in some cases deportation to Siberia (and in particular to Kamchatka).

A decision was finally made in late February 1940, perhaps because of a sudden turn in the secret war with Finland. If one is to judge from documents that are now public, this decision was unexpected. On 5 March, at Beria's instigation, the Politburo decided to "apply the supreme penalty" to prisoners in Kozielsk, Starobielsk, and Ostaszków, as well as to another 11,000 Poles imprisoned in western Ukraine and Belorussia (see the extract in Chapter 11).

This verdict was approved by a special tribunal, the troika of Ivan L. Bashtakov, Bogdan Z. Kobulov, and Vsevolod N. Merkulov. Beria's memorandum was approved by Stalin, Voroshilov, Molotov, and Mikoyan, all of whom prominently signed it. The clerk noted that Kalinin and Kaganovich, who were absent, also supported the proposal.

Technical preparations went on for a month. Over the next six weeks, from 3 April to 13 May, all the prisoners were taken out of the camps in small groups. A total of 4,404 people were taken from Kozielsk camp to Katyń, where they were shot with a bullet in the neck and buried in a mass grave. The 3,896 Starobielsk prisoners were shot in the NKVD headquarters in Kharkiv, and their bodies buried in an outlying region of the city, Pyatishatki. The 6,287 from Ostaszków were executed in the NKVD headquarters in Kalinin (formerly Tver) and buried in the Mednoe district of the city. In all, 14,587 people were liquidated. On 9 June 1940 an assistant to the head of the NKVD, Vasily V. Chernyshev, filed a report saying that the camps were now empty and awaiting new prisoners.

Stanisław Swianiewicz, who escaped the Katyń massacre at the last minute, when, at Moscow's orders, he was suddenly separated from the group of captured Polish officers and transferred to a prison in Smolensk, gave the following account:

> Below the ceiling [of the railway car] I could look through a hole in the wall and see what was happening outside . . . In front of us there was a grassy square . . . The place was cordoned off by large numbers of NKVD troops, their bayonets fixed at the ready.
>
> This was different from what we had already been through. Even at the front, after we had been taken prisoner, our captors had never fixed bayonets . . . An ordinary-looking bus arrived in the square. It was much smaller than the ones usually found in cities in the West. The windows had been chalked up so you couldn't see inside. Its capacity was probably about thirty people. The entrance was at the back.
>
> We wondered why we couldn't see through the windows. The bus backed up until it was nearly touching the railway car, so that the prisoners could get straight in, without having to get down. The NKVD were watching closely on both sides, bayonets at the ready . . . Every half-hour the bus would take away another load. Therefore, the place where the prisoners were being taken wasn't far away . . .
>
> The NKVD colonel, a very tall man who had taken me out of the car, was standing in the middle of the square with his hands deep in his pockets. It was obvious that he was in charge of the whole operation. But what was the point? I must say that looking out at that fine spring day, it never crossed my mind that these people were all being taken away to be executed.[2]

The 11,000 prisoners mentioned by Beria were only a tiny portion of all the Polish prisoners. Of the other categories of prisoners, the largest was the *bezhentsy*, people arrested after they had fled the German occupation of western Poland. More than 145,000 *bezhentsy* passed through the various prisons; some were sent on to other prisons, and others were allowed to leave. Another category was the *perebezhchiki*, Poles arrested while trying to flee into Lithuania, Romania, or Hungary. Some of them were freed after a few weeks, but around 10,000 were sentenced by the OSO (Osoboe Soveshchanie, the special NKVD board) to anywhere from three to eight years, and they ended up in the gulags, especially in the Dallag but also in Kolyma. Some of them were shot in accordance with Beria's order of 5 March 1940. The third category consisted of militants from the resistance networks, officers who had not been mobilized in 1939, high-ranking officials in the state apparatus or local governments, and various sorts of *pomeshchiki* (landowners)—in sum, all those deemed *sotsialno opasnyi*, or "socially dangerous elements." Most of the 7,305 who were shot (out of a total of 11,000 prisoners) under the directive of 5 March came from the last category. The place of their burial is still unknown; all that is known is that 3,405 were shot in Ukraine and 3,880 in Belorussia.

The total number of people imprisoned in territories incorporated into the U.S.S.R. (including Lithuania in 1940) has not yet been established definitively, but as of 10 June 1941 there were 39,600 prisoners in western Ukraine and Belorussia, of whom roughly 12,300 had already been sentenced. Their number had doubled since March 1940. The proportion of common criminals versus political prisoners is also unknown.

After the German attack on the Soviet Union, most of the prisoners met a terrible fate. In the prisons of western Ukraine alone, around 6,000 people were executed, although it is highly unlikely that they had received death sentences for any crime. In the NKVD reports these mass killings were regarded as simply "a decrease in the number of people belonging to the first category."[3] In one instance several hundred prisoners were killed for attempting to flee a convoy. In another case the convoy commander took personal responsibility for shooting 714 prisoners (500 of whom had not appeared before any court), killing several of them himself.

Mass deportation was another tactic used in the new territories of the U.S.S.R. Though consisting chiefly of four separate large-scale operations, the deportation of families or small groups began as early as November 1939. The real number of people involved is not known. The same can be said about the numbers of those deported from Bessarabia and the eastern regions of Belorussia and Ukraine in the latter half of 1940. Until recently the only figures available were those provided by the Polish resistance or those issued by the Polish embassy in 1941. Today the NKVD archives make it clear that these numbers are actually a bare minimum and will almost certainly have to be revised upward.

The first wave of deportations began on 10 February 1940, as a result of a decision by the Soviet Council of People's Commissars on 5 December 1939. The preparations, particularly the reconnaissance on the ground and the compilation of lists, took two months. The organizers of the deportation had many technical obstacles to surmount, including a dearth of railway tracks of the correct gauge for Soviet trains. The entire operation was directed in person by Vsevolod Merkulov, one of Beria's assistants, an unusual measure that underscores the importance of the operation for the Soviet Union. The deportation of February 1940 took its greatest toll on the peasantry, the inhabitants of villages, forestry workers, and the settlers who had moved into these regions as part of a political strategy to "Polonize" the area. According to NKVD statistics, some 140,000 were deported, 82 percent of whom were Polish. The operation also included Ukrainians and Belorussians. The convoys left for northern Russia, the Komi republic, and western Siberia.

Even before Soviet leaders approved the execution of the prisoners, the SNK ordered a new wave of deportations on 2 March 1940. This time the families of prisoners were deported (even as their husbands or fathers were being executed) as well as "socially dangerous elements." The NKVD figures show that approximately 60,000 people were deported, almost entirely to Kazakhstan, enduring terrible conditions of famine and cold. A good deal is now known about this operation from survivors' testimony. One such survivor, Lucyna Dziurzyńska-Suchon, recalled:

> I can still remember one of the worst times in our life. For a few days we had had nothing to eat at all, literally nothing. It was winter, and the cabin was covered in snow. We could still get out thanks to a tunnel that someone had dug on the outside . . . Mother could still get out to work. She was just as hungry as we were. We just lay there, huddling together in the straw to try to keep warm. We kept seeing tiny lights dancing before our eyes, and we were too weak to stand. It was really cold in the cabin . . . We just slept, we just slept the whole time. My brother would wake from time to time and cry out that he was hungry. That was all he could say, except "Mother, I'm dying." Mother cried a lot. She went to ask for help from our friends in one of the neighboring cabins. It was no use. We just had to pray to "Our Father" all the time. It probably was a miracle that saved us. A friend came from another cabin with a handful of wheat.

The third operation, also a result of the March SNK decree, took place during the night of 28–29 June 1940 and affected all those who before September 1939 had not lived in the territories annexed by the Soviet Union, and had not returned home across the Soviet-German demarcation line in Poland. (People who had fled after the partition and had been found in the other zone still had the right to return home. Thus 60,000 people, including 1,500 Jews, returned to the German sector from the Soviet zone.) Of the 80,000 Poles who were deported as part of this operation, 84 percent were Jews, who, if they managed to escape the massacre carried out by the Einsatzgruppen (Task Forces, a euphemism for Nazi death squads) in the summer of 1941, were sent to the gulags.

The fourth and final operation began on 21 May 1941, following a decision by the Central Committee of the Soviet Communist Party (CPSU) and the Soviet Council of People's Commissars on 14 May. Its aim was to cleanse the border regions and the Baltic regions of "undesirable elements." The deportees belonged to the category of *silposelentsy*, people who had been sentenced to twenty years or more of forced exile in the designated regions (particularly in Kazakhstan). This wave of deportations affected 86,000 people in the border regions, not counting Estonia, Latvia, and Lithuania.

Using the NKVD's own figures, we arrive at a total of between 330,000 and 340,000 people deported. If we include the other available figures, the number of victims of these repressions rises to between 400,000 and 500,000. Some groups wound up in distant parts of the U.S.S.R., notably the more than 100,000 young men who were forced to work in Soviet industry (above all in the mining districts of Donetsk, the Urals, and western Siberia), and the 150,000 men who were mobilized into the *stroibatal'ony*, the construction battalions of the Red Army.

During the two years of Soviet rule in the eastern half of Poland, approximately 1 million people (10 percent of the population) were directly affected by Soviet repression in one form or other: execution, prison, the camps, deportation, or forced labor. No fewer than 30,000 people were shot, and another 90,000 to 100,000 (8–10 percent of the deportees) died in the camps or en route in railway convoys.

The NKVD against the Armia Krajowa (Homeland Army)

During the night of 4–5 January 1944, the first Red Army tanks crossed the Polish-Soviet border established in 1921. In reality this border was recognized neither by Moscow nor by the Western powers, and following the revelation of the Katyń massacres, the Soviet Union had broken all diplomatic links with the legal Polish government-in-exile in London on the pretext that the Poles had demanded an international inquiry by the Red Cross, a demand that by chance coincided with a similar request by the German authorities. The Polish resistance assumed that as the front approached, the Homeland Army, or Armia

accord that affected Poland. The democratic forces had already declared their willingness to negotiate directly with the Soviet Union. The verdict of the trial was reached the same day that the United States, the U.S.S.R., and Great Britain consented to the agreement among various Polish parties for the formation of a coalition government, in which the Communists and their satellite parties held a huge majority. The sentences at the trial were relatively light—the longest was ten years in prison—but three of the accused never returned to Poland. Leopold Okulicki, the general commander of the AK, died in prison in December 1946.

The System of Repression, 1944–1989

The extent of political repression in Poland and the various forms it took reflected the evolution of the political system. To paraphrase a popular saying, "Tell me the exact system of repression, and I'll tell you the phase of Communism to which it corresponds."

Two major problems affect a description and analysis of the repressive system. First, because various aspects of repression were extremely secret, many of the documents are still classified. Second, looking at the past only from the point of view of repression risks a somewhat deformed assessment of the Communist system, since even in the most repressive periods the system did have other functions. Nonetheless, the centrality of repression is of fundamental importance in any evaluation of the regime and its ideological roots. During the forty-five years of the Communist Party's monopoly on power in Poland, five phases of repression are discernible. The one thing they all had in common was their dependence on the existence of a secret police force accountable to the policymaking unit of the Party and a few of its leaders.

The Conquest of the State, or Mass Terror (1944–1947)

On the domestic level, the foundations of the Communist state in Poland were established by the presence of the Red Army. In matters of foreign policy, Stalin's oversight was decisive. The role of the Soviet security system was not limited to fighting enemies of the new regime. The NKVD/KGB, with a few minor but important modifications, became the model of choice for the Polish Communists who were trained at the NKVD officers' school in Kuibyshev. In addition, a core of several hundred advisers (or *sovetniki*, with General Serov at their head as chief adviser) was set up, forming the central structure of the Polish Security Service. Because the security chiefs at the Lubyanka had access to any information they wanted through a network of Soviet experts, Moscow did not have to establish its own full-fledged intelligence network in Poland.

Because of the political and ideological interests common to the Polish Communists and the Soviet state, the Polish Security Service became an integral part of the Soviet machine. This commonality of interest was even more apparent where the Polish military counterespionage system was concerned.

In Poland the Communists had been a marginal group, with no chance of being elected to power in a democratic process. They were all the more unpopular because the majority of Poles were traditionally wary of, or even overtly hostile to, the U.S.S.R. and Russia in particular, especially after the recent bitter experience of "liberation" by the Red Army. In the early years of the postwar period, the main opposition to Sovietization came from resistance movements, underground political groups, and legal parties, among which the only important one was the Polish Peasant Party, the PSL. The first task that the new Communist-led government set for itself was breaking the resistance of the Polish people so that a Soviet-style system could be consolidated. It is significant that the first representative of the Committee of National Liberation (created in Moscow on 21 July 1944) to make an appearance in public was the minister of public security, Stanisław Radkiewicz. A full year passed before the Polish security apparatus (known after 1945 as the Ministry of Public Security, or MBP) was able to take over the consolidation of power launched by the Red Army and the NKVD. By the second half of 1945 the MBP had developed an operational structure that employed more than 20,000 officials (not including its police), as well as a military organization known as the Internal Security Corps (KBW) of around 30,000 heavily armed soldiers. The war against the resistance, which was quite intense until 1947 and continued until the early 1950s, was both bloody and brutal. Polish historians disapprove of the use of the term "civil war" in this context, given the large numbers of Soviet military and NKVD troops deployed in the country.

The security apparatus employed a wide range of methods, from infiltration and provocation to the pacification of entire regions. It had an absolute material advantage over the partisans—more and better communications and weapons, as well as the option to call in KBW troops, an asset that the regime never hesitated to exploit. According to the Third Department, which was responsible for combatting the anti-Communist resistance, 1,486 people died in the conflicts in 1947, while the Communist losses were a mere 136.[7] Large-scale pacification operations were led not only by the KBW but also by specially assigned units of the regular army. Around 8,700 opponents of the government were killed in 1945–1948. Most of these operations were led by the Commission for State Security, presided over by the ministers of security and defense. Mass deportations also occurred whenever they were deemed necessary. That was precisely how the problem posed by the Ukrainian resistance in southeastern Poland was resolved: from April to July 1947, all Ukrainians in Poland (around

140,000 people) were deported as part of Operation Wisła (Vistula) and resettled in what had been the German territories in the west and north of the country.

The records of the Security Service show that many of these operations were planned with great care. Examples include the massive fraud perpetrated during the referendum of June 1946, the "preparations" for the elections of January 1947 (that is, the enormous propaganda machine that was put into action), the thousands of arrests, particularly during the election campaign, the systematic recourse to fraud, and the development of a network of collaborators—some 17,500 as of 1 January 1946. However, it is clear that the most characteristic tactic was the use of brute force, even though the precise number of prisoners is still not known. In 1947 approximately 32,800 people were arrested by the Third Department (many of whom were ordinary criminals). The Fourth Department, whose task was to safeguard industry, arrested 4,500 people that same year. In the weeks preceding the elections, between 50,000 and 60,000 militants from the PSL (the Peasant Party) were arrested by the various departments of the MBP, the military police, the KBW, and the army. There are many known cases of murder, some definitely carried out by local branches of the Communist Party.

Interrogations were often extremely brutal. Beatings and torture were common, and the detention conditions were inhuman.

Kazimierz Moczarski, an anti-Nazi resistance fighter arrested in 1945, was imprisoned for 225 days in the same cell as SS general Jürgen Stroop, who had been in charge of the annihilation of the Warsaw ghetto in 1943. After Moczarski was freed he wrote a memoir of this confrontation.[8] The following account records his treatment during his imprisonment.

Kazimierz Moczarski
Prisoner sentenced to life imprisonment
Article 2 of decree of 31 August 1944

Sztum Central Prison
23 February 1955

Tribunal of the Supreme Penal Chamber
Ref. III K 161/52

Following the request for a retrial and reconsideration of previous events drawn up by my lawyers, I declare the following:

During the investigation carried out by an officer of the former Ministry of Public Security from 9 January 1949 to 6 June 1951, I underwent forty-nine different types of torture and beatings, among which I single out in particular:

1. Blows from a hard-rubber truncheon on particularly sensitive parts of the body (bridge of nose, chin, salivary glands, protruding parts like shoulder blades).
2. Blows from a whip covered with sticky rubber to the external parts of my bare feet, particularly my toes, an extremely painful method.
3. Blows from a hard-rubber truncheon on my heels (in a series of ten blows, on each heel, several times a day).
4. Hair torn out on my temples and neck ("plucking the goose"), beard, chest, perineum, and sexual organs.
5. Cigarette burns on my lips and eyelids.
6. Burning of the fingers of both hands.
7. Sleep deprivation: For seven to nine days prisoners are forced to stand upright in a dark cell and are kept awake with blows to the face . . . This method, which the officers called "the beach," or *Zakopane*, brings on a state of near madness. Prisoners experience severe mental problems, and see visions like those experienced by people taking mescaline or peyote.

I should add that for six years and three months I was deprived of a walk. For two years and ten months I never had a bath. For about four and a half years I was kept in total isolation with no possibility of contacting the outside world (no news of my family, no letters, books, newspapers, etc.).

The tortures and agony I describe above were carried out by, among others, Lt. Colonel Józef Dusza, Commandant Jerzy Kaskiewicz, and Captain Eugeniusz Chimczak to terrorize me and to extract confessions that were not true, but that were considered necessary to confirm the charges and accusations that had been leveled against me.

They were acting under the orders of Colonel [Józef] Rozański, Colonel [Anatol] Fejgin, and the deputy minister. General [Roman] Romkowski told me on 30 November 1948, in the presence of Colonel Rozański, that I was to undergo an investigation that would be "sheer hell." This is in effect what happened.[9]

In many cases the authorities were not content with a summary condemnation, and instead staged open trials, during which a hand-picked "public" would humiliate the accused prisoners and demonstrate "the hatred of the people" toward them. The dates of some trials were fixed to coincide with various elections so that the propaganda effect was maximized. This was the case for the trial of the largest underground group, Wolność i Niezawisłość (WIN; Liberty and Independence). The accused had to wait from November 1945 until January 1947 before finally coming to trial one week before the elections. Another common procedure was the condemnation of anti-German resistance fighters as collaborators. The Communists' reasoning here was quite simply that anyone who was not with them was against them. Consequently, the AK, the main anti-German resistance unit, was considered to be an ally of Hitler because it had not actually fought alongside the Red Army. To lend credence to these charges, Gestapo functionaries were brought forward to bear false witness and justify the accusations.

One of the most scandalous miscarriages of justice was that of Witold Piłecki. Born in 1901, Piłecki participated in the defense of Vilnius against the Bolsheviks in 1920. A landowner and an officer in the reserves, he organized cavalry squads that were incorporated into the army in 1939. After the defeat of Poland he set up one of the first underground resistance movements, the Secret Polish Army (founded on 10 November 1939). In 1940, at his own initiative and with the authorization of his superior officers in the AK, he allowed himself to be caught in a raid and taken to Auschwitz (he was prisoner no. 4859) to form a resistance network. In April 1943 he escaped to carry on his resistance activities, particularly in the Niepodległość (Independence) network, and subsequently took part in the Warsaw uprising. After the city's surrender, he was sent to the officers' camp *(Oflag)* in Murnau. When he was freed, he joined the second corps of General Ladislav Anders' army. In the autumn of 1945 he returned to Poland to rejoin the underground movement, organizing a small and highly efficient network to gather intelligence about the Bolshevization of the country and send it back to General Anders. He was arrested on 5 May 1947, tortured, and given three death sentences on 15 March 1948. The principal charge was "espionage for a foreign power," in this case the Polish army in the West. He was executed on 25 May 1948 and rehabilitated in 1990.

The Party leaders themselves decided the sentences in the major trials. The Party also kept a close watch on all appointments to key posts in the Security Service.

All organized and coordinated resistance was broken in the autumn of 1947. After the flight of several leaders of the PSL and the arrest of the fourth leader of the WIN, the resistance network ceased to exist as a nationwide movement. The political situation began to stabilize: exhausted after years of war, society gave up all hope of assistance from the Western powers. The need to adapt to the new reality was paramount, however shameful and unwanted that reality might be. The Communist coup in Czechoslovakia in February 1948 reinforced Moscow's grip on Central and Eastern Europe. The Polish Communist Party prepared to fuse with its main ally, the Socialist Party. With economic improvements and progress in reconstruction, Polish settlement in previously German territories caught the interest of the public. Such factors enabled the Communist Party to proceed to the following stage: the Sovietization of Poland and the domination of the whole of society. Quite logically the MBP began to reduce its personnel, and the number of its agents and secret collaborators (some 45,000 at the time) began to fall.

The Conquest of Society, or Generalized Terror (1948–1956)

In the aftermath of the Prague coup and Yugoslavia's demotion to pariah status in the international Communist movement, the Eastern-bloc countries went through similar transformations, including the absorption of socialist parties by Communist parties, the formation (*de facto* or *de jure*) of a one-party system, total centralization of economic planning, accelerated industrialization programs along the lines of the Stalinist five-year plans, the beginnings of collectivization in agriculture, and an intensification of activity against the church. Mass terror became commonplace.

From 1945 through 1947, thousands of people who had never taken any part in opposition activity fell victim to pacification campaigns and preventive measures, even though the machinery of repression was directed, in principle, against the concrete enemies of the regime and active militants such as the Polish Workers' Party (PPR). After 1948, the Security Service used terror to subjugate the whole of society, including segments that were more or less favorably disposed toward the regime. In this period of generalized terror, anyone, including Communist Party leaders and high-ranking state officials, could suddenly fall under close scrutiny by the Security Service or become yet another of its victims. Although some functionaries in the MBP had called for "intensification of revolutionary vigilance" as early as 1947, it was only in 1948 that this slogan became the key to the actions of the Security Service, echoing the Stalinist call for "intensification of the class struggle."

The point of departure was the conflict with Tito, which, for Central and Eastern Europe, played a role similar to that of the fight against the Trotskyites in the U.S.S.R. In Poland the issue arose in early September 1948 with the "critique of right-wing nationalist deviation" directed against the general secretary of the PPR, Władysław Gomułka. The first arrests in mid-October did not affect his immediate entourage, but everyone familiar with the Moscow trials of the 1930s knew very well that once the base was attacked, it was not long before the very top fell victim, too.

In a generalized system of repression, the Communists suffered less than the rest of the population, but their experiences were far from negligible. In Poland a relatively small number of victims were involved. In seeking to uncover "an espionage and subversion network" the Security Service turned its attention to the army, concentrating on career officers who had enlisted before the war. In this instance, joint action by the MBP and the military Main

Intelligence Directorate (GZI) led to the arrest of hundreds of officers, followed by many trials and twenty executions. The disappearance from the public stage of Gomułka, who was arrested with several hundred officials from all levels of the Party, was a clear signal: the time had come for the total submission of the Party apparatus, including the Security Service itself. Several high-ranking officials from the Security Service also found themselves in prison. Because Gomułka was never actually put on trial,[10] the Sovietization of Poland was not marked by any one main show-trial, such as that of László Rajk in Budapest or of Rudolf Slánský in Prague.

Only a small part of the Security Service, which had grown spectacularly since 1949 and employed some 34,000 people by 1952, was involved in the affair concerning the "provocation within the workers' movement." The agents in question all belonged to Department 10, which employed about 100 people altogether. A Security Commission headed by Bolesław Bierut (who had succeeded Gomułka in 1948) was established by the Politburo to handle many of the most important investigations of the organizational problems of the MBP and GZI, and to formulate general directives.

The omnipresence of the "Bezpieka" (the name by which the Security Service was popularly known) in all domains of social and political life was one of the main features of the era. In the summer of 1949, when a network of 74,000 informers was no longer sufficient for the Security Service's needs, small units called Protection Squads (Referat Ochrony, or RO) were established in all industrial enterprises. Within a few years there were 600 such cells. Inside the MBP, particular attention was given to several departments of the Economic Protection Section. From 1951 through 1953 the majority of people arrested (around 5,000 to 6,000 each year) were victims of this service, which had the largest network of informers (26,000 people) at its disposal. Any breakdown or disruption in industry was automatically considered to be the result of sabotage or subversion. In some cases, dozens of workers from a single company were imprisoned. To help protect state institutions, the Security Service was asked to give assessments of candidates doing polytechnic studies. In 1952, some 1,500 people were prevented from carrying out their studies as a result of the service's conclusions.

The "protection and organization of agricultural cooperatives" (that is, collectivization) and the controls and decrees on wheat and meat quotas constitute a separate chapter. In this last case, the most active institution was not the security apparatus but the police and the Special Commission for the Fight against Economic Abuses and Sabotage, established in 1945. This name, which recalled that of the Cheka, struck terror into people's hearts. Thousands of peasants in fifteen regions were imprisoned for failing to deliver their quotas. The security forces and the police carried out the arrests according to a specific political plan: the better-off peasants (kulaks) were arrested first, even if they had delivered their quota. They were held for several weeks without trial before being sentenced, and their wheat, livestock, and other property were confiscated. The Extraordinary Commission also preyed upon the urban population. Most sentences were for speculation, black marketeering, or, in 1952–1954, hooliganism. The commission's rulings became more and more repressive. In 1945–1948 it sent 10,900 people to forced-labor camps; in 1949–1952 the figure reached 46,700. The total for the years up to 1954 was 84,200. These verdicts were not for political crimes, but the nature of the measures, affecting the rural population and so-called speculators, stemmed from the same repressive system.

The main objective of the security apparatus was the pursuit of underground militants. The targets included former PSL militants, soldiers who had returned from the West, and officials, political cadres, and officers from before the war. In early 1949, registers of suspect elements were standardized into several categories. By January 1953 the Security Service had files on 5.2 million individuals, one-third of the adult population. Despite the elimination of illegal organizations, the number of political trials continued to rise. The number of prisoners rose as a result of the various "preventive measures." Thus in October 1950, as a result of "Operation K," 5,000 people were arrested in one night. In 1952 more than 21,000 people were arrested. According to official figures, in the second half of 1952 there were 49,500 political prisoners. There was even a special prison for juvenile political delinquents, of whom there were 2,500 in 1953.

After the liquidation of the opposition, the Catholic Church was the principal independent institution that remained. It was watched much more closely after 1948, and was the object of constant attacks. In 1950 the imprisonment of bishops began. In September 1953 Bishop Czesław Kaczmarek was tried and received a prison sentence of twelve years, and Stefan Cardinal Wyszyński, the primate of Poland, was also interned. In all, more than 100 priests were sent to prison. Jehovah's Witnesses, who were considered to be American spies, were a particular target. In 1951 more than 2,000 of them were imprisoned.

This was a period when everyone seemed to be going to prison: members of the Politburo, prewar officials (including the former prime minister), generals, commanders of the AK, bishops, partisans who had fought the Germans and then turned their weapons against the Communists, peasants who refused to join the *kolkhozy*, miners in a pit where a fire had broken out, young people arrested for breaking the glass on a poster or for writing graffiti on the walls. Any potential opponent of the system was removed from society, and all freedom of action was prohibited. One of the main functions of the system of generalized terror was the diffusion throughout society of a feeling of permanent fear and atomization.

A political prisoner named Andrzej Staszek described conditions in Wronki prison shortly before 1950:

> Tuberculosis was the worst illness in postwar Poland . . . We were seven in a cell. It was small, barely eight square meters, and we had hardly any room to move. One day an eighth prisoner arrived, and we could see immediately that there was something seriously wrong with him. He didn't have a bowl or a blanket and he looked seriously ill. It soon became clear that this man was suffering from advanced stages of tuberculosis. His body was covered with tubercular sores. When I saw how frightened my companions were, I started to feel really scared too . . . We tried to keep as far away as possible from him. But you can imagine how absurd the situation was, when in a cell of eight square meters seven men are trying to keep an eighth away. The situation got worse when they brought the next meal. He didn't have a bowl, and no one was going to bring him one. I looked at the others, but no one would meet anyone else's eye or look at him.
>
> I couldn't take this any more, so I gave him my plate. I told him to eat first, and that I would eat afterward. He turned his dead and apathetic face to me (he seemed quite indifferent to everything), and I heard him say, "The thing is, I'm dying . . . I have only a few days left." "You eat, eat to my health," I told him, as the others looked on horrified. Then they began to try to avoid me as well as him. When he finished, I washed off the plate with what little water there was, and I began to eat.[11]

The system began to change slightly at the end of 1953. The network of informers was dismantled, conditions in the prisons began to improve, some of the prisoners were released for health reasons, fewer people were put on trial, and sentences became lighter. Beatings and torture became less frequent. Officers who had particularly bad reputations were dismissed, Department 10 was broken up, and staffing levels at the Security Service were cut. When on 28 September 1954 Radio Free Europe began transmitting a series of reports by Józef Światło, the former deputy head of Department 10 who had "chosen liberty" (defected) in December 1953, it was like a bomb going off. In a few weeks the MBP was restructured and superseded by the Ministry of Internal Affairs (MSW) along with a separate Committee for Public Security (KBP). The minister and three of the five deputy ministers of the MBP were forced to resign. In December 1953 Gomułka was set free and the head of the Investigations Department, Józef Rozański, imprisoned instead. The Special Commission for the Fight against Economic Abuses and Sabotage was disbanded. In January 1955 the Central Committee denounced "faults and errors," putting all the blame for these on the Security Service, which had supposedly "put itself above the Party." Some of the MBP executioners were arrested, and the numbers employed by the Security Service were again cut.

In fact, however, most of these changes were a sham. In 1955 there were still around 30,000 political prisoners, and the latter half of that year saw the trial of former minister Włodzimierz Lechowicz, who had been arrested in 1948 by the special Światło group.[12] Marian Spychalski, who had been a member of the Politburo until 1949, was arrested in 1950 and remained in prison without trial until April 1956. A real abatement in political repression came only after the Twentieth Soviet Party Congress in 1956 and the death of Bierut at nearly the same time. An amnesty was then proclaimed, although 1,500 political prisoners remained behind bars. Some of those who had been sentenced were rehabilitated. Both the procurator general and the minister of justice were replaced, and the former deputy minister for security and the head of the former Department 10 were arrested. Control of the prisons, which until then had been run by the Internal Affairs Ministry, was handed over to the Justice Ministry. As a result of much in-fighting, the security organs began to lose their sense of direction, and some of the more secret collaborators began to withdraw their services. The strategy, however, did not change: the Security Service was still interested in exactly the same people, and the prisons had been only half emptied. Thousands of investigations were still carried out, and even after reductions the network of informers numbered 34,000. The system of generalized terror simply functioned on a slightly smaller scale. It had obtained its objectives: the most active opponents of the regime had died by the thousands, and society had understood the lesson, now knowing the fate that awaited "defenders of people's democracy."

Real Socialism, or Selective Repression (1956–1981)

The cataclysm of "iron socialism" was of relatively short duration in Poland, and with the coming of the thaw, the strategy of the Security Service began to change slightly. The control exercised by the security organs over the population was more discreet. At the same time, the security forces stepped up their surveillance of legal and underground opposition movements, the Catholic Church, and intellectual circles.

Politicians expected the security apparatus to be ready to disperse street demonstrations at a moment's notice, a new role that began during the second great revolt of workers in the Eastern bloc, in Poznań in June 1956. The security forces, the police, and the KBW had all been caught by surprise by the strike, both in practical terms and from an ideological point of view, and the strike had been followed by a demonstration involving tens of thousands of protestors who had attacked a number of public buildings. In one sense, the

Poznań revolt was the last chapter in the civil war of 1945–1947, and was the only occasion when the demonstrators were the first to open fire. The Party reacted brutally: the prime minister declared that "any hand raised against the people's regime will be cut off." The army moved in with tanks. Around seventy people died, hundreds were arrested, and dozens of demonstrators were brought before the courts; but the sentences issued during this period of thaw, which set in during October 1956, were relatively light.

Shortly after the Eighth Plenum of the Central Committee of the Polish United Workers' Party (PZPR, as the Communist Party had been renamed), held on 19–21 October 1956, the KBP was dissolved and the Security Service integrated into the MSW. The number of personnel in the security apparatus fell by 40 percent, leaving 9,000, and 60 percent of all informers were dismissed. The so-called Protection Squads inside industry were suppressed, and half of the investigations then under way were abandoned. The last Soviet advisers returned to Moscow and were replaced by an official KGB mission. The organization of the security apparatus was reviewed again, and many of the cadres, who were for the most part of Jewish origin, were dismissed to make way for younger people. The whole repressive apparatus was radically scaled back. However, the Party leadership, including Gomułka, who had returned to power in October 1956, opposed the trial of these officials. As a result, only a few discreet trials were ever held. The general concern among PZPR leaders was not to disturb a mechanism that might be called on again.

As early as February 1957, at the first general meeting of the MSW, Minister Jerzy Wicha affirmed that the notion of an "intensification of the class struggle" (as Stalin had proposed) was quite wrong, but he also managed to claim that the struggle was becoming more and more radical.[13] From this moment until the end of the system, the Security Service and other organizations, including the PZPR, the army, and the propaganda machine, constantly acted in this contradictory manner.

Twenty years of silent, calm, and well-organized work, occasionally punctuated by strikes and revolts, formed the basis for the system of repression. This consisted of a control system with a large number of informers as well as eavesdropping techniques and the monitoring of correspondence, all of which was slowly perfected over the years. In the 1970s the new Security Service (Służba bezpieczeństwa; SB) paid particularly close attention to economic targets, but its main interests, unlike those of the previous security services, were the use of new technology and the profitability of various enterprises. Breakdowns no longer led to the arrest of workers, but to discreet pressure from the Party organization for the removal of inefficient managers. The MSW had one means of persuasion that had been irrelevant in the Stalinist years but that now became extremely valuable: the authority to deliver a passport (which was good for only one trip). Because many people would quite willingly cooperate so that they would be granted a passport, the MSW could pick up all sorts of intelligence about what was happening inside institutions, businesses, and universities. Slowly but systematically, the SB rebuilt its network, particularly in areas that were considered sensitive. In the struggle against the church the MSW established a new, specialized department in June 1962 that soon had several hundred employees. In the first half of the 1960s, there were numerous attacks by the police on congregations who gathered to defend chapels or crosses that had been erected without the permission of the authorities. Although court sentences were relatively light, hundreds of people were beaten, and many more were fined.

In 1967, after the Six-Day War between the Israelis and Arabs, the struggle against "Zionism" became the new order of the day. This particular rallying cry had a triple political, social, and international function, and the government needed a new means of motivating nationalist fervor. A number of PZPR officials began purveying antisemitic ideas to sideline the old guard and improve their own career prospects. The antisemitic campaign also served to discredit the student protest movements of March 1968. A special service employing dozens of officials was created. The MSW passed on information to local Party organizations to attack various individuals. The Security Service, in Poland as well as in the U.S.S.R., was the great inspiration for "Antisemitism without Jews," promoted by both the Party and the state. (This phrase was commonly used to describe the Communist regime's promotion of antisemitism even though Poland's once-huge community of Jews had been reduced to a trivial number by the Holocaust.)

The SB's comprehensive penetration of public groups undermined many attempts to form illegal organizations. The members of such organizations, who in many cases were very young, henceforth constituted the majority of political prisoners. Most organizations had only a few dozen members. Intellectuals were watched extremely closely. If necessary the security forces could, with the express permission of the authorities, identify people who collaborated with Radio Free Europe or the international press. Isolated arrests on such grounds took place throughout the 1960s. The most important case was that of Melchior Wankowicz, an elderly writer who had a large following. The SB watched Communist heretics most closely of all. Cases in which Trotskyites or Maoists were incarcerated met with relative indifference, but one exception was the case of Jacek Kuroń and Karol Modzielewski. In 1970 forty-eight people from the illegal political group known as Ruch (Movement) were arrested. The leaders were sentenced to seven or eight years in prison—and this in a period of relative leniency.

The use of violent repression had never ceased. Just a year after Gomułka's return to power, when young people came out in protest against the closure of the weekly *Po prostu* (Simply), which in 1956 had played a considerable role in the pressure for change. Dozens of people were beaten, and ten received sentences. The strikes and demonstrations in March 1968 were extremely widespread. The protests were broken up with tremendous brutality; 2,700 people were arrested, and 1,000 went before courts of various types. Dozens received prison sentences of several years, and hundreds were forcibly enlisted in the army for "retraining."

Demonstrations by workers had different effects. Those that took place in December 1970 took a dramatic turn in the towns on the Baltic coast. Despite the presence of special police units, the authorities called in the army as they had done in Poznań fourteen years earlier. According to official statistics, forty-five people were killed. Thousands of people were beaten by the police, often inside the police stations. Workers had to pass through what was known as "the road to health," which consisted of two rows of policemen hitting them with truncheons. But in keeping with the times, there were no prosecutions by the authorities after the events of December, and all detainees were released after Gomułka stepped down that month. In industry, the ringleaders of the strikes suffered various types of intimidation.

During the relatively brief strikes that erupted in several towns in 1976, the authorities forbade the use of arms by special police units, but this measure was not sufficient to prevent several killings. Roughly 1,000 people were arrested, several hundred were fined, and a few dozen received prison sentences.

The trials that followed were the occasion for renewed contact among the families of the accused workers, young people, and dissident intellectuals, and they sparked a large human-rights movement among the intelligentsia. They also resulted in the establishment—for the first time since the PSL had been disbanded in 1947—of organized opposition groups, notably the Workers' Defense Committee (KOR) and the Movement for the Defense of Human and Civil Rights (ROPCIO). Faced with this new situation, the authorities were forced to make a tactical choice. For several reasons, chief among them the regime's growing financial dependence on the West and the threat that a domestic crackdown would provoke international reprisals, the government decided instead to employ tactical harassment: keeping people under close watch for forty-eight hours (a measure authorized by the penal code), firing people from their jobs, using psychological pressure, confiscating copying equipment, and rejecting passport applications. The SB rapidly developed a large network of agents. In 1979 the Special Department for Defense of the Economy was reactivated in response to fears that the influence of the opposition would spread to industry.

This development had almost no lasting effect, and in mid-1980 a new wave of strikes began. Hard-liners were still in charge at the top of the Party, but no one would take responsibility and make the decision to crush the strikes by force. In any case, as was pointed out at a PZPR Politburo meeting on 28 August 1980, the troops that would be required were neither numerous enough nor at all willing to confront the hundreds of thousands of strikers who were occupying hundreds of factories. On this occasion, the strikers, unlike in 1956, 1970, and 1976, followed the advice of Jacek Kuroń, who had counseled: "Don't just break up the Party committees; organize your own."

The government used the same tactics with Lech Wałęsa's Solidarity trade union as it had in previous years. The intention was to weaken the union by provoking divisions within it and gradually bringing it under the control of the PZPR, as had been done in the 1940s with the Front for National Unity. In October 1980 the MSW and the army made preparations to impose martial law (*stan wojenny*, or "a state of war"). The MSW systematically infiltrated Solidarity (by the following summer there were more than 2,400 informers in Warsaw alone) and tried a series of small-scale confrontations to gauge the reaction of the union, arresting its members for forty-eight hours without charge and using force to evacuate public buildings that were occupied. By February 1981 the lists of people to be arrested were ready, and the prisons had been prepared for their arrival, but the PZPR leadership decided to continue with just harassment and provocation techniques, as in Bydgoszcz in March 1981, when plainclothes police attacked unionists. The Polish Security Service, which initially had been rather passive, received reinforcements, and after the strikes of 1980 the Stasi, the East German secret police, set up an operational group in Warsaw.[14] This in itself was quite an event, although the collaboration of Eastern-bloc security services against the democratic opposition, coordinated by the KGB, had already been in place for a few years.

This situation continued until early December 1981, when, to test the power of Solidarity, the antiterrorist unit of the police broke up a strike at the fire department in Warsaw. Ten days later, in the early hours of 13 December, martial law was declared in Poland.

"A State of War," an Attempt at Generalized Repression

What followed was a large-scale police and military operation that had been prepared with astonishing precision. More than 70,000 soldiers and 30,000 police, armed with 1,750 tanks, 1,900 armored personnel carriers, and 9,000 trucks and cars, along with several helicopter squadrons and transport aircraft, went into action. Forces were concentrated in the main cities and industrial centers. Their task was to break the strikes and to paralyze the normal life of the country in a way that would cow the population and preclude any response by Solidarity. Telephone lines were cut (resulting in numerous deaths, as people were unable to phone for ambulances), and the borders and gasoline stations were closed. Passes were required to move from one locality to another. A strict curfew and comprehensive censorship were enforced. After ten days the strikes and the demonstrations came to an end, proving the effectiveness of the plan. Fourteen were killed, and several hundred were injured. About 4,000 strikers were arrested, and the first trials, which began at Christmas, resulted in prison sentences of three to five years (with some as long as ten years). All the accused were judged by special military courts, which were responsible for halting and punishing "any infraction of martial law." Throughout this time the Soviet, East German, and Czechoslovak armies were also on a war footing, ready to step in if the strikes and demonstrations turned into a full-scale insurrection that the Polish army could not quell.

The second part of the repression consisted of the internment of all opposition and Solidarity militants, which began just before midnight on the night of 12–13 December. In a few days, by means of this simple administrative decision, more than 5,000 people were locked up in forty-nine isolation centers located outside the main cities. The primary objectives were to paralyze the union and to replace the leaders with SB collaborators. The strategy of internment, which lasted for twelve months, was a seemingly less rigorous form of imprisonment and relatively easy to apply, since it dispensed with the need for magistrates or trials. In principle the SB did not use "forbidden methods" (torture) on people who were interned, imprisoned, or sentenced, contenting itself instead with "persuasion techniques" backed up by force. The SB also intensified the recruitment of collaborators and efforts to persuade militants to emigrate, often blackmailing their families.

General Wojciech Jaruzelski, who had taken over as PZPR first secretary on 18 October 1981 (he retained his earlier posts as prime minister and defense minister), had to cope with ultra-hard-liners in the Party, among them Party cadres in industry, army officers, and retired MSW officials. These individuals had formed self-defense groups (although no one had attacked them), arming themselves with heavy guns. They demanded that those interned be brought to trial and given stiffer sentences, including the death penalty. The hard-liners wanted generalized terror; they regarded generalized repression (with no death sentences) as unacceptably lenient. Despite an aggressive propaganda campaign against Solidarity, the Party leaders decided against using the methods demanded by the hard-liners. Rather than crush social resistance by Stalinist methods, they decided to "reduce tensions." Despite this policy, the authorities forcefully suppressed Solidarity's demonstrations on 1 and 3 May 1982 (marking the anniversary of the 1791 constitution and hence a traditional festival) and on 31 August 1982 (the anniversary of the Gdansk agreement of 1980).

Thousands of people were arrested, hundreds were brought to trial, and six people were killed. In these public trials, some of the leaders of the Solidarity underground were sentenced to up to five years' imprisonment. After the internment centers were closed in December 1982 and martial law was formally lifted on 22 July 1983, there were still perhaps as many as 1,000 political prisoners incarcerated for underground union activity, underground printing, the dissemination of forbidden literature and books, or sometimes just for taking up a collection for prisoners. The authorities also dismissed many people from their jobs. Thousands of strikers suffered in that fashion in December 1981, and journalists in particular were singled out for "verification procedures"—in all, more than a thousand of them lost their jobs.

With the exception of the first few weeks after 13 December 1981, Poland did not again experience a period of repression comparable to that of 1949–1956. The security apparatus did use a number of new methods, known in the language of the secret services as "disinformation and disorientation," which had already been practiced in the 1970s when the Ministry of Internal Affairs set up the autonomous Group D of the Fourth Department, with many local branches. Until 1981 this new department concentrated its attention on the church and similar organizations. After martial law was proclaimed, it broadened its activities to include Solidarity and carried out a series of attacks against the union's properties. Group D also burned union buildings, set fire to cars, beat up Solidarity militants, sent death threats, and distributed false tracts and fake underground newspapers. In a few cases, victims were abducted and left by the side of the road after being given huge doses of barbiturates or other drugs. Several people died in beatings, including a schoolboy called Grzegorz Przemyk, who was killed in a police station in 1983.

One of the best-known actions of this type, carried out by officers from Group D, was the murder of Father Jerzy Popiełuszko on 19 October 1984. According to the official version of events, the murderers were acting on their own, without the knowledge of their superiors. This claim seems highly implausible, given that the security system was very tightly controlled and all important actions required a ministerial green light. In this case the MSW did eventually prosecute and punish the culprits, but there were several other cases of murders of priests and people linked to Solidarity that went unpunished. If one is to judge by the reaction of the population, this sort of activity did not achieve its main objective, which was to spread fear in selected circles. Instead, opponents of the regime seem to have become more and more resolute.

The period following the violent confrontations of the first days of martial law and the full-scale repression of the demonstrations in 1982–83 was marked by more limited repression. Underground militants were aware that they were rarely risking more than a few years in prison and that there were regular amnesties of political prisoners. By this stage of its evolution, the system was far from its Stalinist origins.

From Cease-Fire to Capitulation, or the Government in Disarray (1986–1989)

That was the situation at the end of 1986, when under the influence of *perestroika* and *glasnost* in the Soviet Union and the stagnation of the Polish economy, General Jaruzelski's team tried to pick out opposition groups with which it could arrive at a compromise. This effort was preceded by a considerable abatement of repression. On 11 September 1986 the minister of internal affairs, General Czesław Kiszczak, announced the liberation of the remaining 225 political prisoners. To maintain a minimum punitive standard, it was decided that any participation in a forbidden organization or an underground publication was to be punished by a fine or by detention under house arrest or in a minimum-security facility. These repressions were thus similar to those of 1976–1980, with one important difference: now the government was confronted not by hundreds, but by tens of thousands of militants. In early 1988, after a first wave of strikes, repressions increased again, but on 26 August a communiqué announced the opening of negotiations with Solidarity.

Although security-force personnel were frustrated with these developments, most behaved with discipline. However, it is likely that some of them attempted to prevent an agreement from being reached. In January 1989 two priests who worked for the pastoral section of Solidarity at a local level were murdered. It is still unclear whether this was simply a criminal act or the work of Group D.

After the elections of 4 June 1989 and the installation of the government of Tadeusz Mazowiecki, control of the "ministries of force" (Internal Affairs and Defense) remained in the hands of their previous chiefs. On 6 April 1990 the SB was dissolved and replaced by the Bureau for State Protection, the UOP.

In Poland the Communist system could never truly claim any legitimacy or legal basis, since it respected neither international law nor its own constitution. As a criminal entity from its birth in 1944–1956, the system was always ready to resort to brute force (including military force) on a grand scale.

Select Bibliography

The preceding chapter is based largely on my archival work for the Commission for Constitutional Responsibility, which has given me access to many files that are still secret, particularly for the years 1980–1982. The following selection lists the most complete works published since the recent opening of the relevant Soviet archives.

Bedyński, Krystian. *Służba więzienna jako organ bezpieczeństwa publicznego, 1944–1956* (The prison system as an organ of public security, 1944–1956). Warsaw: BGW, 1988.

Chmielarz, Andrzej, and Andrzej K. Kunert, eds. *Proces szesnastu: Dokumenty NKWD* (The trial of sixteen: Documents of the NKVD). Warsaw: Oficyna Wydawnicza Rytm, 1995.

Ciesielski, Stanisław, Grzegorz Hryciuk, and Aleksander Srebakowski. *Masowe deportacje radzieckie w okresie II wojny światowej* (Mass Soviet deportations during World War II). Wrocław: Instytut Historyczny Uniwersytetu Wrocławskiego, 1994. See especially the chapter on Polish deportations, pp. 26–82.

Dudek, Antoni, and Tomasz Marszałkowski. *Walki uliczne w PRL, 1956–1989* (Street battles in Poland, 1956–1959). Kraków: Wydawn. Krakowske, 1992.

Eisler, Jerzy. *Marzec 1968: Geneza, przebieg, konsekwencje* (March 1968: Origin, development, consequences). Warsaw: Wydawn. Naukowe, 1991.

Golimont, Andrzej. *Generałowie bezpieki* (Generals of the security apparatus). Warsaw: BGW, 1992.

Gross, Jan T. *Revolution from Abroad: The Soviet Conquest of Poland's Western Ukraine and Western Belorussia.* Princeton: Princeton University Press, 1988.

Iwanow, Mikołaj. *Polacy w Związku Radzieckim w latach 1921–1939* (Poles in the Soviet Union, 1921–1939). Warsaw: Wydawn. Uniwersytetu Wrocławskiego, 1990.

Jarosz, Dariusz, and Tadeusz Wolsza, eds. *Komisja Specjalna do Walki z Nadużyciami i Szkodnictwem Gospodarczym, 1945–1954: Wybór dokumentów* (Special Commission for the Fight against Economic Abuses and Sabotage, 1945–1954: Selected documents). Warsaw: Karta, 1995.

Komorowski, Krzysztof, ed. *Armia Krajowa: Rozwój organizacyjny* (Homeland Army: Organizational development). Warsaw: Wydawn. Bellona, 1996.

Machcewicz, Paweł. *Polski rok 1956* (Poland's year 1956). Warsaw: Oficyna Wydawn. Mówią Wieki, 1993.

Maciszewski, Jarema, ed. *Tragedia Komunistycznej Partii Polski* (The tragedy of the Polish Communist Party). Warsaw: Książka i Wiedza, 1989.

Marat, Stanisław, and Jacek Snopkiewicz. *Ludzie bezpieki: Dokumenty czasu bezprawia* (The security forces: Documentation of a period of lawlessness). Warsaw: Polska oficyna wyd., 1990.

Materski, Wojciech, and Andrzej Paczkowski, eds. *NKWD o Polsce i Polakach: Rekonesans archiwalny* (The NKVD on Poland and the Poles: An archival investigation). Warsaw: Instytut Studiów Politycznych PAN, 1996.

Materski, Wojciech, et al., eds. *Katyń: Dokumenty zbrodni* (Katyń: Documents of a crime). Warsaw: Wydawn. "TRIO," 1995.

Michel, P., and G. Mink. *Mort d'un prêtre. L'affaire Popiełuszko, analyse d'une logique normalisatrice.* Paris: Fayard, 1985.

Nalepa, Edward Jan. *Pacyfikacja zbuntowanego miasta: Wojsko Polskie w czerwcu 1956 r. w Poznaniu w swietle dokumentów wojskowych* (Pacification of a rebel town: The Polish army in Poznań in June 1956 in light of military documents). Warsaw: Wydawn. Bellona, 1992.

Noskova, A. F., ed. *NKVD i polskoe podpole 1944–1945 (po "osobym papkam" J. V. Stalina* (The NKVD and the Polish underground, 1944–1945, based on the "special files" of J. V. Stalin). New ed. Moscow: Institut balkanistiki i slavyanovedeniya, 1994.

Otwinowska, Barbara, and Jan Zaryn, eds. *Polacy wobec przemocy 1944–1956* (Poles in the face of violence, 1944–1956). Warsaw: Editions Spotkania, 1996.

Paczkowski, Andrzej, ed. *Aparat bezpieczeństwa w latach 1944–1956: Taktyka, strategia, metody* (The security apparatus, 1944–1956: Tactics, strategy, methods). 2 vols. Warsaw: Instytut Studiów Politycznych Polskiej Akademii Nauk, 1994, 1996.

Poksiński, Jerzy. *TUN: Tatar—Utnik—Nowicki.* Warsaw: Wydawn. Bellona, 1992.

Popiński, Krzysztof, Aleksander Kokurin, and Aleksander Gurjanow. *Drogi śmierci: Ewakuacja więzień sowieckich z Krezów Wschodnich II Rzeczypospolitej w czerwcu i lipcu 1941* (Paths of death: The evacuation of Soviet prisoners from eastern Poland under the Second Republic in June and July 1941). Warsaw: Karta, 1995.

"Ręka Jeżowa." *Karta* (Warsaw), no 11, special issue (1993).

Sariusz-Skapska, Isabella. *Polscy świadkowie Gulagu: Literatura lagrowa, 1939–1989* (Polish witnesses of the Gulag: Literature from the camps, 1939–1989). Kraków: Universitas, 1995.

Siedlecki, Julian. *Losy Polaków w ZSRR w latach 1939–1986* (The fate of Poles in the U.S.S.R., 1939–1986). London: Gryf, 1987.

Suchorowska, Danuta. *Wielka edukacja: Wspomnienia więźniów politycznych PRL, 1945–1956* (A great education: Memoirs of political prisoners in Poland, 1945–1956). Warsaw: Agencja Omnipress, 1990.

Szwagrzyk, Krzysztof. *Golgota we Wrocławiu* (The Golgotha of Wrocław). Wrocław: Komisja Badania Zbrodni Przeciwko Narodowi Polskiemu, 1995.

Topol, Andrzej, ed. *Obozy pracy przymusowej na Górnym Śląsku* (Forced-labor camps in Upper Silesia). Katowice: Wydawn. Uniwersytetu Śląskiego, 1994.

Turlejska, Maria. *Te pokolenia żałobami czarne: Skazani na śmierce i ich sędziowie 1944–1954* (These generations black with mourning: Those condemned to death and their judges, 1944–1954). London: "Aneks," 1989.

Walichnowski, Tadeusz, ed. *Ochrona bezpieczeństwa państwa i porządku publicznego w Polsce, 1944–1988* (Defense of state security and public order in Poland, 1944–1988). Warsaw: ASW, 1989.

Zaron Piotr. *Obozy jeńców polskich w ZSRR w latach 1939–1941* (Camps of Polish prisoners in the U.S.S.R., 1939–1941). London: Unicorn Publishing Studio, 1994.

20 Central and Southeastern Europe

Karel Bartošek

"Imported" Terror?

In Central Europe, one must always think of terror in relation to the war, which was its most extreme expression in the first half of this century. World War II, which began in this region, far surpassed General Ludendorff's "total war." What Miguel Abensour described as the "democratization of death" thereafter affected tens of millions of people as total annihilation became an integral part of the idea of war. Nazi barbarism struck the entire population, particularly with the extermination of the Jews. The figures themselves are eloquent: in Poland, military losses accounted for 320,000 dead, while civilian losses were 5.5 million; in Hungary, there were 140,000 military losses and more than 300,000 civilian deaths; in Czechoslovakia, civilian losses were 80–90 percent of the total.

But the great terror of the war did not come to an end with the German defeat. With the arrival of the Red Army, the fighting arm of the Communist regime, populations underwent "national cleansing," which had a quite specific character in this region. Political commissars and counterintelligence units in this army, under SMERSH and the NKVD, were deeply involved in such operations. The repression was especially severe in the countries that had sent troops to fight against the Soviet Union—Hungary, Romania, and Slovakia— where the NKVD deported hundreds of thousands to the Soviet gulags. Their exact number is still being calculated.

According to new studies in Hungary and Russia published since the opening of the archives—studies that are quite conservative regarding the exact figures—hundreds of thousands of people were deported: soldiers and civilians, children as young as thirteen, and old men of eighty. Approximately 40,000 were taken to the Transcarpathian region of Ukraine, which had belonged to Czechoslovakia but was occupied by Hungary in 1939 in accordance with the 1938 Munich agreement and then annexed by the Soviet Union in 1944. From Hungary, which had a population of about 9 million in 1944, more than 600,000 people were deported (the Soviet figure of 526,604 is based on the number of people who arrived at the camps; it does not take into account those who died in transit camps in Romania). There were camps in Braşov, Timişoara, Sighet Marmaţiel, Moldavia, Bessarabia, and Sambor; around 75 percent of all deportees passed through these. Among the deportees were Jews who had been engaged in the work battalions of the Hungarian army. Two-thirds of these prisoners were sent to forced-labor camps and one-third to prison camps, where the mortality rate, as a result of epidemics, was twice as high. Current estimates suggest that around 200,000 of these deportees from Hungary—including people belonging to the German minority, Russians who had arrived after 1920, and French and Poles who were living in Hungary—never returned.[1]

Some of these purges were carried out by "popular" or "extraordinary" courts. At the end of the war, and in the first months of the postwar period, violent extrajudicial action was common, including executions, assassinations, torture, and the taking of hostages. This was facilitated by the absence of, or the failure to respect, international conventions regarding prisoners of war or the civilian population. Bulgaria, which had a population of 7 million at the time, was particularly noteworthy in this respect. Immediately after 9 September 1944, when the Popular Patriotic Front seized power and the Red Army marched into the country, a police force and a security department controlled by the Communist Party moved into action. On 6 October "people's tribunals" were established by decree. By March 1945 they had issued 10,897 sentences in 131 trials and condemned 2,138 people to death, including the regents, the brother of King Boris III, high-ranking officers, policemen, judges, industrialists, and journalists. According to specialists, a savage purge accounted for the death or disappearance of another 30,000 to 40,000 people, mainly the local nobility, mayors, teachers, Orthodox priests, and shopkeepers. In 1989, thanks to witnesses who were no longer afraid to talk, previously unknown mass graves were uncovered. Yet Bulgaria had never sent troops to fight the Soviet Union and had saved most of its Jews from genocide. To get an idea of the scale of Communist repression in the country, one can compare the number of victims from the period of monarchic rule in 1923–1944, often thought of as dictatorial:

according to an investigation by the new parliament in 1945, 5,632 people were assassinated, executed, or died in prison or as a result of a prison sentence during that period.[2] From 1941 to 1944, the years of antifascist resistance and its repression, only 357 people—not even all resistance fighters—were condemned to death and lost their lives.

Purges under the influence of the Red Army brought about a generalized fear in the societies concerned. The purges affected not only those who had actively supported the Nazis or the local fascists, but also many others who were innocent or had simply refused to take sides.

In a Bulgarian documentary made after the fall of the Communist regime in the early 1990s, one woman recounted an episode in the autumn of 1944:

> The day after my father was first arrested, another policeman arrived around midday and instructed my mother to go to Police Station No. 10 at five o'clock that afternoon. My mother, a beautiful and kind woman, got dressed and left. We, her three children, all waited for her at home. She came back at half past one in the morning, white as a sheet, with her clothes tattered and torn. As soon as she came in, she went to the stove, opened the door, took off all her clothes, and burned them. Then she took a bath, and only then took us in her arms. We went to bed. The next day she made her first suicide attempt, and there were three more after that, and she tried to poison herself twice. She's still alive, I look after her, but she's quite severely mentally ill. I have never found out what they actually did to her.[3]

At this time, after the "liberation by the Red Army," which, according to the official propaganda, established international relations of a "new type," many people tried to change their affiliations, and denunciations flew thick and fast. Name changes were common; Rosenzweigs often quickly became Rozańskis, and Breitenfelds became Bares.

The terror in Central and Southeastern Europe did not stop with this. The armed struggle against the new authorities continued in Poland, prolonging the war, and also affected Slovakia in 1947, when the Bandera units fleeing from Ukraine arrived. At the same time, armed groups of former members of the fascist Iron Guard, calling themselves the "Black Shawls," roamed the Carpathian Mountains. Central Europe was still prey to virulent antisemitism. The last pogroms or attempted pogroms in European history took place in 1946 in Poland, Hungary, and Czechoslovakia.

An aggressive anti-German nationalism took hold in Central Europe. Although this was understandable in light of the Nazi German occupation, it hindered the evolution of democratic behavior. Violence was common on a day-to-day level, particularly in the deportation of millions of people belonging to German minorities who had been in some regions since as long ago as the thirteenth century. More than 6.3 million Germans were forced to leave their homes in the territories of Silesia and Pomerania, which had been given to Poland; roughly 3 million were thrown out of Czechoslovakia, 200,000 from Hungary, and more than 100,000 from Yugoslavia. These impersonal figures represent millions of individual dramas. While many of the men were soldiers in prisoner-of-war camps, women, children, and old people were forced out of their houses, apartments, businesses, workshops, and farms. This massive transfer, which took place with official backing from the Allies in the summer of 1945, had been preceded in some countries by unofficial outbreaks of violence. Czech nationalists had been particularly ruthless, and in the hunt for Germans had killed several thousand civilians.

Thus there were elements of terror present in Central Europe before the installation of the Communist regimes, and violence was an integral part of the recent experience and mentality of the countries concerned. Societies were often powerless to resist the new wave of barbarism that was about to descend upon them.

The Communist parties were instrumental in the new violence. Their leaders and disciples were often faithful followers of the Bolshevik doctrine, "enriched" in the Soviet Union under the leadership of Stalin. As we have seen in previous chapters, the goal of all their actions was quite clear: to ensure by any means necessary that the Communist Party had a monopoly on power, and that the Party played the same leading role that it did in the Soviet Union. There was never any attempt at power-sharing, political pluralism, or parliamentary democracy, even if the parliamentary system was formally retained. The doctrine in place at the time presented the Soviet Union as the glorious victor in the struggle against Nazi Germany and its allies, and the principal force and universal guide toward worldwide revolution. Naturally, local Communist forces were expected to coordinate and subordinate their activities to the center of world Communism, in Moscow, and its chief, Stalin.

The Communist monopoly on power was assured almost at the moment of liberation in two countries: in Yugoslavia, where the Communists were led by Josip Broz, better known as Tito; and in Albania, where Enver Hoxha had risen to the leadership of the Communist Party. These two leaders had dominated their respective national resistance movements against the Nazi or Italian invaders, and despite pressure from outside, and even from the Soviet Union, they accepted power-sharing for only very limited periods.

Rarely in the course of history had the arrival of a new regime been preceded by a bloodbath on the scale of the one seen in Yugoslavia, where out of a population of 15.5 million, 1 million people died. A series of ethnic, religious, ideological, and civil wars tore the country apart, and many of the victims were women, children, and old people. This was a truly fratricidal war, and the genocide and purges ensured that at the moment of liberation, Tito and the Communist Party had hardly any political rivals left. They swiftly set about eliminating them all the same. Events took a similar turn in neighboring Albania, with the help of the Yugoslav Communists.

In other countries in Central and Southeastern Europe, with the exception of Czechoslovakia, the prewar Communist parties had been marginal forces, with only a few thousand members. In Bulgaria, for instance, the Party had been an important force from 1919 to 1923 and had then been forced underground (although it did play an important role in the resistance). Throughout the region, Party leaders were convinced that the moment was right and that they had the support of the Red Army. They quickly emerged as an important political force and joined the new governments. Almost everywhere Communists took charge of the ministries in charge of repression (the internal affairs and justice ministries) and of those that might be used in a similar manner, such as the defense ministries. In 1944–45 Communist parties held the Ministry of Internal Affairs in Czechoslovakia, Bulgaria, Hungary, and Romania; the Ministry of Justice in Bulgaria and Romania; and the Ministry of Defense in Czechoslovakia and Bulgaria. The ministers of defense in both Czechoslovakia and Bulgaria, Generals Ludvík Svoboda and Damian Velchev, were crypto-Communists. Communists were also in charge of the state security or secret police (the Durzhavna Sigurnost in Bulgaria, and the Államvédelmi Osztály, or AVO—later the Államvédelmi Hatóság, or AVH—in Hungary) and of the intelligence services in the armed forces. In Romania the Special Service, which was the precursor of the infamous Securitate, was controlled by Emil Bodnăraş, a former army officer who, according to Cristina Boico, had been a Soviet agent in the 1930s.[4] Everywhere the Communists strengthened their grip on the apparatus of terror. The need for absolute control of the AVO was stressed by Mátyás Rákosi, the secretary general of the Hungarian Workers' (Communist) Party: "This is the only institution of which we must keep total control, categorically refusing to share it with any other parties in the coalition, regardless of the proportion of our respective forces."[5]

The Political Trials of Non-Communist Allies

Occasional speeches given by certain Communist leaders regarding the "national road to Socialism" without the Soviet-style "dictatorship of the proletariat" often acted as a cover for the real strategies followed by Communist parties in Central and Southeastern Europe. This strategy was identical with the Bolshevik practices used in Russia in 1917, and repression followed the tried and tested Soviet pattern. In the same manner that the Bolsheviks had eliminated their initial allies such as the Socialist Revolutionaries, the Central and East European Communist parties eliminated their coalition partners. Analysts have discussed the "process of Sovietization" in these countries, and the strategic plan laid out in Moscow. It was Stalin himself who ordered the rejection of the Marshall Plan in the summer of 1947, and who instigated the creation of the Communist Information Bureau (the Cominform) in September 1947 to increase his control of the parties in power.

There were, of course, many differences in the trajectory of events in these various countries. But everywhere it was the aim of the Communist parties to eliminate their actual or potential adversaries and to crush all political, ideological, and spiritual competitors. Marxist-Leninist doctrine demanded that the rivals be wiped out for good, and all means to that end were considered legitimate, including death sentences, execution, long prison sentences, and forced exile in the West. The last of these options was a less cruel procedure, but it was very effective at breaking down resistance, and its importance has been generally underestimated in the analysis of the history of these countries. After all, the right of abode and the right to a home are fundamental human rights. In addition, in 1944–45 tens of thousands of Hungarians, Slovaks, Poles, and other nationals fled their countries in fear of the Red Army.

The first tool used in the panoply of repression was the political trial of non-Communist leaders, many of whom had been resistance fighters and had suffered in the prisons and camps of the Nazis or fascists. Under the direct control of the Red Army, the trials began first in the countries that had been allies of Nazi Germany, notably Hungary, Romania, and Bulgaria. In the inter-Allied commissions that were created in 1944 and existed until 1947, the Soviet military was a dominant force and often forcibly imposed its own point of view. In Hungary the Smallholders' Party, which had been the great victor in the 1945 elections, gaining 57 percent of the vote, became the target not only of considerable political wrangling but also of large-scale police operations. In January 1947 the Ministry of Internal Affairs, under the control of the Communist László Rajk, who had fought in the International Brigades in Spain and been a leader of the resistance toward the end of the war, announced the discovery of a plot against the state involving the Hungarian "Community" group, which had been set up in secret during the war to fight the Nazi invaders. The police arrested a minister and several deputies from the Smallholders' Party; the alleged ringleader, György Donáth, was sentenced to death and executed; the others received long prison sentences.

In February 1947 Béla Kovacs, the secretary general of the Smallholders, was arrested by the Soviet authorities for "plotting against the security of the Red Army." He was detained in the Soviet Union until 1956. The number of victims rose rapidly, for in Hungary, as everywhere else, the Communist secret police believed that every plot must include a large number of people.

The result of all this was that two years after the end of the war what had been the most important party in Hungary was "decapitated and decimated."[6] Like Béla Kovacs, its main representatives—Ferenc Nagy, the president of its council; Zoltán Tildy, his predecessor; Béla Varga, president of the National Assembly; József Kövago, the mayor of Budapest—and dozens of deputies and other party members were all either in prison or in exile. Between late 1947 and early 1949, both the Independence Party and the People's Democratic Party were dissolved. In what was known as the "salami tactics" later recommended by Mátyás Rákosi, the secretary general of the Hungarian Workers' Party, who had returned from Moscow with the Red Army, opponents, such as the Smallholders' Party, were eliminated in successive slices. The belief was that a few slices at a time would never result in violent indigestion.

In February 1948 the persecution of the Social Democrats in Hungary continued with the arrest of Justus Kelemen, under secretary of state to the minister of industry. Persecution of the Social Democrats (excluding Poland) probably began in Bulgaria, where in June 1946 their leader Krastiu Pastukhov was sentenced to five years in prison. By the summer of 1946 fifteen members of the Central Committee for Independent Social Democracy, led by Kosta Lulchev, found themselves in prison. Lulchev and other leaders were arrested in 1948 and sentenced in November to fifteen years in prison. This form of repression struck hard at all those opposed to the forced unification of Social Democratic and Communist parties, such as Constantin Titel Petrescu and Anton Dimitriu, the president and secretary general of the Independent Social Democratic Party in Romania, who were arrested in May 1948.

Many of these prisoners were detained under an extremely harsh regime in the political prison at Sighet Marmațiel, on the northwestern border of Romania. In May 1950 police trucks brought more than 200 well-known leading figures to Sighet, including several people who had served in the government after 1945. Most of them were quite old, notably the leader of the National Peasant Party, Iuliu Maniu, who was seventy-three, and the head of the Brătianu family (instrumental in the founding of modern Romania), who was eighty-two. The prison was filled with politicians, generals, journalists, priests, Greek and Catholic bishops, and others. In the space of five years, fifty-two of these prisoners died.

The alliance with the Social Democrats thus revealed itself to be purely tactical; pluralism of workers' movements never really had a place under Communist regimes. In the Soviet-occupied zone of Germany, which later became East Germany, 5,000 Social Democrats, of whom 400 died in prison, were sentenced by Soviet and East German courts between 1945 and 1950. The last great trial of Social Democrats in this period took place in Prague in 1954.

In Bulgaria, in the run-up to the elections of 27 October 1946, twenty-four Agrarian Union Party activists were killed. Nikolai Petkov, the party's leader, was arrested on 5 June 1947 while attending a session at the National Assembly with twenty-four other deputies. A republican Francophile, he had spent seven years of exile in France after his brother, a deputy for the Agrarian Union Party, was assassinated in 1924. In 1940 Petkov had been interned for a few months in a camp in Gonda Voda and then placed under house arrest. At that time he made preparations to set up a Patriotic Front, which included in its ranks many Communist resistance fighters. He became deputy prime minister in the interim government of Bulgaria at the end of the war, but resigned in protest against the terrorist violence carried out by the minority Communists during the period of cleansing. After Petkov became the head of the opposition, his earlier alliance with the Communists counted for nothing. He was brought up on spurious charges of conspiring in an armed plot against the government, tried on 5 August, and condemned to death on 16 August.

After the summary statement of the prosecution requesting the death sentence, Petkov had the right to make a last statement. He calmly took a paper out of his pocket and read out the following:

> Respected Judges, being of calm conscience and fully aware of my responsibility to the Bulgarian justice system, to Bulgarian society in general, and to the political organization of which I am a member and for which I am ready to lay down my life, I believe it is my duty to make the following declaration.
>
> I have never participated, nor ever had the intention of participating, in any illegal activity directed against the popular government of 9 September 1944, of which, together with the rest of the Agrarian Union, I was an architect.
>
> I have been a member of the Bulgarian Agrarian Union since 1923. The fundamental principles of its ideology are peace, order, legality, and popular power. Its only weapons are the ballot box and the written and spoken word. The Agrarian Union of Bulgaria has never had any recourse to secret or conspiratorial organizations, and has never taken part in any coup d'état, although it has often been the victim of such actions.

Petkov then went on to describe the events of 9 June 1923 and 19 May 1934, "the beginnings of fascism in Bulgaria," and the events surrounding his resignation from the government.

> If, as my accusers have suggested, I really was greedy for power and mindful only of my career, today I would be deputy chairman of the Council of Ministers of Bulgaria. From the moment I went over to the opposition, and from the moment of my arrest, I have not ceased to work toward an understanding between the Agrarian Union and the Communist Workers' Party, which I consider to be a historical necessity.

I have never been part of any reactionary force either within the country or abroad.

Respected judges, for more than two years now, since 25 June 1945 to give the exact date, I have been the victim of the cruelest and most merciless campaign ever directed against a politician in Bulgaria. No part of my private or public life has been spared. I have been burned in effigy three times in Sofia alone and about ten times elsewhere. I have read my own obituary notice at the entrance to the cemetery in Sofia on these occasions, and I never complained. I will also face with courage anything else that awaits me, for such is the ineluctable nature of the sad reality that is Bulgarian politics today.

As a modest worker in public life, I don't have the right to complain, particularly when two people universally recognized as great men of state, Dimitri Petkov and Petko Petkov, were assassinated like traitors in the streets of Sofia. [Petkov's father, Dimitri, then chairman of the National Council, had been shot twice in the back on 11 March 1907. Petko, his brother, a deputy, had been shot repeatedly in the chest on 14 June 1924 and died immediately.]

Respected judges, I allow myself to believe that in reaching a verdict you will leave aside political concerns that have no place in a court of law, and look only at the facts that have been established. I am sure, or at least I hope, that in following your conscience as judges you will acquit me of the charges laid against me.

On 16 August, after hearing the sentence that condemned him to death by hanging "in the name of the people of Bulgaria," Nikolai Petkov cried out loudly: "No! Not in the name of the people of Bulgaria! I am being sent to my death by your foreign masters from the Kremlin and elsewhere. The people of Bulgaria, crushed by this bloody tyranny that passes for justice, will never believe your lies!"[7]

Petkov was hanged on 23 September. Among the Communist leaders and State Security (Durzhavna Sigurnost) workers who arranged his arrest and trial was a certain Traicho Kostov, who was himself hanged two years later.

In the two other former Nazi client states, political trials were also used first against the leaders of the powerful agrarian parties, who had contributed to breaking the alliance with Germany and thus provoked the arrival of the Red Army. In Romania in October 1947 Iuliu Maniu and Ion Mihalache were sentenced to life imprisonment on the basis of police evidence after a lengthy trial, together with seventeen other key officials from the National Peasant Party. The trial paved the way for the massive prosecution of non-Communist politicians. Maniu died in prison in 1952. Even before the elections of 18 November 1946, several politicians, including the liberal Vintila Brătianu, were convicted by a military court on charges of running a terrorist organization.

Concerning the political trials of previous allies, Czechoslovakia perhaps offers the purest and most cynical examples. It ended the war on the side of the victors, and its restoration in 1945 swiftly enabled people to forget the earlier alliance of the Slovaks with Germany, which had effectively been ended by the Slovak national uprising against the Nazi occupiers in late August 1944. In November 1945, as a result of the accord signed with the Allies, the Red Army was forced to retreat, as were the Americans, who had occupied the province of Western Bohemia. The Czechoslovak Communist Party won the elections in May 1946, but it was in the minority in Slovakia, where the Democratic Party gathered 62 percent of the vote. The politicians who had been sharing power with the Communists since the liberation had already proved their attachment to freedom and democracy by taking part in the resistance inside and outside the country, as well as in Slovakia.

The opening of the Czechoslovak and Soviet archives has brought to light the perverse behavior of the followers of the Bolsheviks. In December 1929 their leader, Klement Gottwald, had made the following claims in a speech to the parliament in response to accusations that the Czechoslovak Communist Party was following orders from Moscow: "We are the party of the Czecho-slovakian proletariat, and naturally our supreme revolutionary headquarters is in Moscow. And you know very well why we go to Moscow: we go there to learn from the Russian Bolsheviks how to wring your necks. You all know that the Bolshevik Russians are past masters in that art!"[8]

After the elections of May 1946 this determined "wringer of necks," whose trajectory from autodidact worker to leader of the Czechoslovak Communist Party was akin to that of the Frenchman Maurice Thorez, became the chairman of the Council. He then became the director of all the repressions, first behind the scenes and then in public.

The first target of political maneuvering and harassment by the State Security (Státní bezpečnost; StB) organization was the Slovak Democratic Party. The other non-Communist Czech parties, many of which were fueled by anti-Slovak nationalism, mounted little opposition to these tactics. In September 1947 the Communist-controlled police announced the "discovery" of a plot against the state in Slovakia. As a result of the ensuing crisis the Democratic Party lost its majority in the Slovak government, and two of its three general secretaries were arrested.

The process of repression was accelerated considerably with the Prague coup in February 1948, which opened wide the door for a Communist Party monopoly of power. During the crisis in February, which was provoked by the resignation of a majority of the non-Communist ministers, many people found themselves in prison, including the Slovak Ján Ursíny, the president of the Democratic Party, who had been deputy prime minister in the Gottwald government until he was forced to resign in the autumn of 1947; and Prokop Drtina, the justice minister. Both men had been in the resistance during the occupation.

The leaders of the Slovak Democratic Party were the first to be tried publicly, in April and May 1948. Twenty-five people were sentenced, one for thirty years. By then the general aims of judicial and police repression seem to have been already established: enemies inside the army and the security services were sought out, as were Democratic-Liberal and Social Democratic Party leaders, all of whom had been allies until February 1948; some of them had even been strongly in favor of close cooperation with the Communists.

The cases of Heliodor Pika and Josef Podsednik are typical of the fate of political prisoners at this time.

General Heliodor Pika, a great patriot and democrat, had played an important role in the resistance. Favorably disposed toward cooperation with the Soviet Union, he was promoted to the leadership of the Czechoslovakian military delegation in the U.S.S.R. in the spring of 1941, well before 22 June and the German attack. His actions and policies favoring amicable collaboration with Moscow had been well known since the 1930s, as well as his conflicts with the Soviet state. The latter stemmed from his attempts to free the more than 10,000 Czech citizens who were in Soviet camps and prisons, mostly for "illegal crossing of U.S.S.R. borders" in 1938–39, when they had attempted to join the Czechoslovak army that was forming inside the U.S.S.R. His patriotism and his services to the "national and democratic revolution" were incontestable even after 1945, when he was working as first assistant to the Czechoslovak army's chief of staff.

Since late 1945, Pika's activities had been closely monitored by the military intelligence services, led by Bedřich Reičin, a Communist with close ties to the Soviet intelligence services. In February 1948 General Pika was dismissed from the army; in May he was arrested and accused of sabotaging the Czechoslovak war effort in the U.S.S.R. by working as a British agent. He was sentenced to death on 28 January 1949 by a special court established in mid-1948 for purposes of political repression. He was hanged on the morning of 21 June 1949 in the courtyard of the prison in Plzeň. Bedřich Reičin told his colleagues that the Soviet Union had demanded the general's liquidation because he had known too much about the Soviet intelligence services. Such knowledge undoubtedly also explains why Reicin himself was hanged three years later.

In February 1948 Josef Podsednik was the mayor of Brno, the capital of Moravia. He had attained the post in the democratic elections of 1946 as a candidate for the National Socialist Party (a party created in the early years of the century that had nothing in common with Hitler's version of "National Socialism"). As a man who favored the democratic and humanitarian ideal of

Tomáš Masaryk, the first president of the republic, Podsednik was a representative figure for a great number of Czech Socialists, who numbered more than 60,000 as of 31 December 1947. He was also a sincere believer in cooperation with the Communists. After February 1948 the mayor of Brno decided to emigrate, but then abandoned the idea in order to concentrate on helping former party members who were being persecuted. Arrested on 3 September 1948, he was sentenced by the State Court in March 1949 to eighteen years in prison for illegal activities, attempting to overthrow the regime by violent means, liaison with reactionary foreign powers, and so on. Nineteen other party members who were condemned at the same time received sentences totaling seventy-four years in prison. All the witnesses in this trial were themselves political prisoners awaiting trial. Other groups, including thirty-two activists from southern Moravia, were later sentenced as part of the "Podsednik affair" to a total of sixty-two years' imprisonment.

The Podsednik trial was a public one. Years later, Podsednik, who was released in 1963 after serving fifteen years of his sentence, noted: "A few dozen of the Czechoslovak Communist Party leaders came to the trial, which was the first big political trial to be heard in the State Court, and they included Otto Šling [who was later to receive the death sentence in the Slánský trial], who laughed at the moment the sentence was read out."

The elimination of Democratic and Socialist allies in Czechoslovakia culminated in the trial of Milada Horáková, which took place in Prague from 31 May to 8 June 1950. Thirteen people—the leaders of the Socialist Party, the Social Democratic Party, and the People's Party, as well as one Trotskyite—were sentenced. Four, including Horáková, received the death penalty; another four received life imprisonment; and five were given sentences of between 15 and 28 years (totaling 110 years). The report prepared by the official Commission of Inquiry during the Prague Spring in 1968 shows that 300 other political trials were linked to the Milada Horáková trial, and that more than 7,000 former members of the Socialist Party alone were sentenced. Many of the larger trials took place from May through July of 1950 in several provincial towns to demonstrate the national dimension of the supposed conspiracy. In thirty-five trials there were 639 sentences handed out, including 10 death sentences, 48 sentences of life imprisonment, and a total of 7,850 years in prison.

The Milada Horáková trial was a milestone in several respects. According to the distinguished Czech historian Karel Kaplan, it was the country's first real show-trial, and the first trial prepared directly by Soviet "advisers," the heads of the Soviet special services, who had come to help orchestrate the terror. It was a carefully prepared spectacle in which all the participants, from witnesses to judges, knew their lines beforehand, and the whole show served as an enormous propaganda coup for the authorities.

The trial also marked an important stage in the history of repression in Europe in general, and not simply in the history of Communism: a woman was hanged, a woman who had fought bravely in the resistance in the earliest days of the occupation of Czechoslovakia in March 1939, and who had then been imprisoned for nearly five years by the Nazis. A female victim, in short, who was also a democrat, who had never intended to put up any sort of armed resistance to the Communist dictatorship.

The affair raises many questions. Why did the West not protest more vociferously against this crime? Why did no one respond to Albert Einstein's protests or collect signatures for a petition? Why did the others who had fought in the resistance against the Nazis in the rest of Europe fail to respond, and why did they not try to save one of their own from the gallows?

The following account of a Communist intellectual party game in Paris at about this time sheds some light on the mentality then prevailing.

"Psychodramas" weren't much talked about at the end of 1951. I turned up with Claire toward midnight on New Year's Eve, coming from one family party at my relatives' to this other family party at Pierre Courtade's house. [He was a Communist journalist and writer.] Everyone was very happy. In fact, everyone was quite drunk. "You're the one we were waiting for," said all my friends. They explained the game to me. Jean Duvignaud [an art historian and sociologist] said that every epoch invents its own literary genre or form: the Greeks had had tragedy, the Renaissance the sonnet, the classical age the five-act play in verse with the three unities, etc. The socialist age had invented its own form: the Moscow show-trial. These partygoers, who were all slightly the worse for drink, had decided to play at being on trial. All they needed was an accused, and as I had come last I was the obvious choice. Roger Vailland [a Communist writer] was the prosecutor, Courtade was the defense lawyer. I had to take my place in the dock. I resisted rather feebly, and then decided to go along with it. The charges were very serious, as I had broken ten different articles of the Code, and was accused of sabotaging the ideological effort, collaborating with the cultural enemy, plotting with international spies, philosophical high treason, etc. When I wanted to *argue* during the examination, the procurator, lawyer, witnesses, etc. all got quite angry. My lawyer's address to the court was terrible, and he pleaded that there were attenuating circumstances, but that I should be relieved of the burden of life as soon as possible. Thanks to the alcohol, the clowning around soon became quite nightmarish, and what was supposed to be a parody really began to hurt. When the sentence was passed (I got the death sentence, of course), two women there, including my wife, really began to get quite upset. Everyone was shouting and crying, looking in the cupboards for indigestion tablets, putting cold compresses on heads, etc. We all—judge, lawyer, and accused—attended to these people and tried to calm them down. I think I was the only one who wasn't drunk; but I wasn't the only one to feel ashamed.

No doubt about it, looking back on it now we were all quite mad. There must be a point past which madness diminishes your responsibility. But before you get to that point, madness doesn't relieve you of the burden of your responsibility. You *choose* madness to escape the noose that is closing around your neck, which you don't dare slip.

Our insanity was the consequence of the insanity of the moment. We were rationalizing and internalizing a sort of general dementia.[9]

The Destruction of Civil Society

To understand what made such show-trials possible, we have to think very carefully about the meaning of "civil society." Civil society evolves with capitalism and the formation of the modern state. As the counterpart to the power of the state, it is also an independent force. It depends first of all on a system of needs, in which private economic activity plays a primary role. Civil society supposes an individual who has many needs, and it depends on the values of these individuals, their consciences, actions, and their sense of freedom. Individuals are both selfish and citizens interested in public affairs and the community. Lubomir Sochor, a philosopher and political thinker, defines civil society as "the ensemble of suprafamilial, nonstate institutions that organize the members of society into coordinated groups and allow them to express their opinions and particular interests. Of course, the prerequisite is that these institutions and organisms are autonomous and are not merely transformed into offshoots of the state apparatus, or simple 'transmission belts' for state power."[10] Among the organizations of civil society that constitute a means of social control over the state are groups such as corporations and associations, churches, unions, municipalities and local government bodies, regional self-government groups, and political parties, as well as general public opinion.

The constant strategy of Communist repression, whose central aim was always the establishment of absolute power and the elimination of political rivals and anyone else who had any sort of real power in society, was to attack systematically all the organisms of civil society. Because the aim was a monopoly on power and truth, the necessary targets were all other forces with political or spiritual power. Hence the systematic targeting of unionists and political activists, priests, journalists, writers, and the like.

There was also a sort of international criterion that operated in the choice of victim. Governments that were totally subordinate to the Soviet Union decreed that the many rich links existing between civil society and the outside world should all be severed. Social democrats, Catholics, Trotskyites, Protestants, and others were all targeted not simply because of their domestic activities, but also because by their very nature they had strong, useful, and quite traditional links with the outside world. The interests and aims of the global strategy of the U.S.S.R. demanded that all these links be cut.

In the new "people's democracies," civil society was on the whole quite weak. Before the war, its development had been halted by authoritarian or semiauthoritarian regimes or by a rather backward level of economic and social life. War, fascism, and the different policies of the occupying forces were all factors in its relative weakness. When the liberation finally came, the behavior of the Soviet Union and the bloody purges that followed were a further impediment to the development of civil society.

Soviet intervention in the occupied zone of East Germany goes a long way toward explaining the relatively mild nature of judicial and police repressions there, and the absence of show-trials in the German Democratic Republic during the period up to 1949. Elsewhere, repression and show-trials invariably accompanied the founding of the new regimes. But in East Germany at that moment there was no need for recourse to such means, since the new government's aims had already been attained by policies pursued earlier. According to studies conducted since the fall of the Berlin Wall in 1989, the occupying Soviet forces interned 122,000 people in their zone in 1945–1950, 43,000 of whom died in detention and 736 of whom were executed. By its own estimates, the SED (Socialist Unity Party) adopted repressive measures against 40,000 to 60,000 people.[11]

Czechoslovakia is an exception of a different type, because of the violent repression of civil society after February 1948. Of all the countries in Central and Southeastern Europe, it was the only one with a history of parliamentary democracy in the interwar years, although there had been a limited experiment in Romania as well. Czechoslovakia, at the time, was also one of the ten most industrialized countries in the world. At the moment of liberation, it had by far the most structured and developed civil society in Central and Southeastern Europe, and it had quickly tried to reorganize itself in 1945. By 1946 more than 2.5 million citizens, or nearly half the adult population, belonged to one or another of the four main Czech political parties in Bohemia, Silesia, and Moravia. Two million Czechs and Slovaks were members of unions. Hundreds of thousands of people belonged to numerous organizations and associations. One organization alone, the Sokol (Falcon) Club, a politicized sporting association that had existed since the previous century and had been an important factor in nationalist affirmation, counted more than 700,000 members in 1948. The first Sokol members were arrested in the summer of 1948 at the *slet*, the annual sporting assembly festival. The first political trials of the members began in September. Two years later, with several thousand of its leaders arrested, the organization had been almost completely destroyed. The segments in the villages were simply integrated into the state apparatus. Like so many other organizations in civil society, such as the Boy Scouts and various Catholic and Protestant organizations, the Sokol was reduced to nothing by persecutions and repression, purges, the occupation or expropriation of property, and the confiscation of goods—all activities in which the secret police, under the cover of the "action committees" created in February 1948, excelled.

For the Communist governments, the churches were the greatest obstacle to annihilation or control of the mechanisms of civil society. The Catholic Church, with its organization directed from the Vatican, represented a rival international faith to the one with its headquarters in Moscow. Moscow's well-defined strategy was to force the Roman Catholic and Uniate churches to break their links with the Vatican and to keep the resulting "national" churches in its own power. This much can certainly be understood from consultations that took place between Soviet leaders and the Information Bureaus of the different Communist Parties in June 1948, as reported by Rudolf Slánský, the secretary general of the Czechoslovak Communist Party.

To reduce the influence of the churches on society, bring them under the bureaucratic control of the state, and transform them into instruments of policy, the Communists combined repression, attempts at corruption, and even infiltration of the church hierarchy. The opening of the archives, in Czechoslovakia for instance, has revealed that numerous priests and even a few bishops actively collaborated with the secret police. Were they perhaps trying to avoid a worse fate?

The first antireligious repressions—if one excludes the victims of the purges, such as the Bulgarian priests mentioned above—probably took place in Albania. Gaspar Thaci, the archbishop of Shkodër, died under house arrest at the hands of the secret police. Vinçent Predushi, archbishop of Durrës, who was sentenced to thirty years of hard labor, died in February 1949, probably as a result of torture. In February 1948 five clergymen, including Bishops Gjergj Volaz and Fran Gjini of the apostolic delegation, were condemned to death and shot. More than a hundred priests, nuns, and seminarians were executed or died in custody. At least one Muslim also died as part of this wave of persecution, a lawyer by the name of Mustafa Pipa, who was executed for coming to the defense of the Franciscans. Years later, in 1967, Enver Hoxha was to declare that Albania had become the first officially atheist state in the world. The official newspaper *Nendori* (November) proudly announced that same year that all mosques and churches, 2,169 in total, including 327 Catholic sanctuaries, had been destroyed or closed.

In Hungary violent confrontations between the government and the

Catholic Church began in the summer of 1948, with the nationalization of numerous religious schools.[12] Five priests were sentenced in July, and more in August. Jószef Cardinal Mindszenty, the indomitable primate of Hungary, was arrested on 26 December 1948 and sentenced to life imprisonment on 5 February 1949. He was accused of plotting with various accomplices against the state and of espionage for foreign imperial powers, including the United States. A year later the government occupied most convents and monasteries, expelling the majority of the twelve thousand monks and nuns. In June 1951 Monsignor József Grősz, the archbishop of Kalocsa, leader of the episcopate and a close friend of Mindszenty, met the same fate as the primate. Persecution of the churches and religious orders in Hungary did not affect only Catholics. The Lutheran and Calvinist churches were considerably less numerous but were also affected and also lost pastors and bishops, including an eminent Calvinist, Bishop László Ravasz.

In Czechoslovakia as in Hungary, the government tried to create a dissenting faction within the Catholic Church that was ready to collaborate with the government. When this tactic met with only partial success, the scale of repressions increased. In June 1949 Josef Beran, the archbishop of Prague, who had been imprisoned by the Nazis in 1942 in camps in Terezin and Dachau, was placed under house arrest and later interned. In September 1949 several dozen vicars who were protesting the new law concerning churches were arrested. On 31 March 1950 a trial of several high-ranking church officials began in Prague; they were accused of spying for the Vatican and other foreign powers, organizing arms caches, and preparing a coup d'état. The Redemptorist Ján Mastiliak, the rector of the theological institute, received a life sentence, and others received a total of 132 years of prison. On the night of 13–14 April 1950 a massive operation against the convents was carried out, which had been prepared with military precision by the Ministry of Interior. Almost all the nuns and priests were removed and interned. At the same time the police placed all bishops under house arrest and forbade them to communicate with the outside world.

In the summer of 1950 in eastern Slovakia the regime ordered the liquidation of the Greek Catholic Uniate Church and ordered it to fuse with the Orthodox Church, a procedure that had been used in Soviet Ukraine in 1946. Dissenting priests were interned or thrown out of their parishes. The archpriest of Soviet Ruthenia, József Csati, was convicted in a trial that was clearly rigged, and then deported to a camp in Vorkuta, in Siberia, where he was imprisoned until 1956.

Repression against the churches was conceived and controlled by Czechoslovak Communist Party leaders. In September 1950 the leadership approved a series of trials of Catholics, which opened in Prague on 27 November 1950. Nine people connected to the bishops, headed by Stanislav Zela, the vicar-general of Olomouc, in central Moravia, were given heavy sentences. On 15 January 1951, this time in Bratislava, the capital of Slovakia, a trial of three bishops, including the bishop of the Greek Catholic Church, was finally concluded. In these two trials, all those accused of being "agents of the Vatican in Czechoslovakia" were sentenced to terms ranging from ten years to life imprisonment. This tactic was used for the last time later that year in trials of more people connected to the bishops. But the repressions did not end there. The bishop of Litoměřice, in Central Bohemia, Štěpán Trochta, a resistance fighter who had been arrested in May 1942 and detained in concentration camps in Terezin, Dachau, and Mauthausen, was sentenced to twenty-five years in prison in July 1954.

The people who conceived and carried out these repressions sought not only to remove those at the top of the hierarchy, but to strike at all Christian intellectuals in general. Ružena Vacková, who had fought in the resistance and was a professor of art history at Charles University, was also a great supporter of the cause of political prisoners. She was arrested in June 1952 and imprisoned until 1967. The Catholic intelligentsia was quite severely affected by this and another trial in 1952. The second took place in July in Brno, the capital of Moravia, and was probably the largest political trial of "men of letters" in the history of twentieth-century Europe.

One of those tried in Brno was Bedřich Fučik, a Czech Catholic intellectual who had little time for the church hierarchy. Arrested in the spring of 1951, he was tortured throughout his interrogation. One day, after giving the usual evasive answers to his torturers for seven hours—"nothing," "I don't know," "none," and so forth—he finally cracked and began to "confess." "Leave me alone, I beg you," he told them. "I can't stand it any more. It's the anniversary of my mother's death today." For a whole week before the trial, he was coached in the answers he was to give the court. He weighed 48 kilos (he had weighed 61 kilos before his arrest) and was in a very bad physical state. Fučik was sentenced to prison for fifteen years but was amnestied and released in 1960. The following is an excerpt from several interviews he gave to Karel Bartošek, recorded in Prague between 1978 and 1982.

B.: Did you have the feeling, when you were in court, that you were like an actor in a play?

F.: Absolutely. I knew that from the very beginning.

B.: Why did you agree to go along with it? How could you, as a Catholic intellectual, accept this highly staged Stalinist comedy?

F.: This was the worst thing that one takes away from prison, the thing that haunts you the most. The hunger, the cold, the black hole they keep you in, the terrifying headaches at the time when I seemed to be losing my sight, all those things, you can forget them, even if they always stay with you, hidden away in your brain somewhere. But the one thing I'll never forget, the most horrible thing that will never leave me, is the way that suddenly there are two people inside you, two different men. The first one, me, the person I had always been, and me, the second one, the new one who says to the old one, "you're a criminal, you did such and such . . ." The first one fights back, and an argument follows between these two people, its like a total doubling of the personality, the one relentlessly humiliating the other. "You're lying! It's not true!" and the other saying "Yeah, okay, it's true, I did do it, I signed, etc."

B.: You're not the only one who made such a confession, of course. Many people did. You were men, strong-willed individuals, all with your own unique physical and mental characteristics, yet you all acted in a similar or even identical manner: you all went along with the game, and learned the parts you had been assigned. I've talked a lot about the causes of these "confessions" with Communists, and the way such men were beaten and broken at the end of it all. But you are a man with a different vision of the world. What happened inside you? Why did you collaborate with the government?

F.: I couldn't protect myself, physically or mentally, against their relentless brainwashing any longer. I gave in. I've already told you about the moment that something cracked inside me. [At this point he became more and more agitated, and was almost shouting.] After that, I simply wasn't myself any longer . . . I consider the state of nonbeing to be the greatest humiliation, the lowest thing that one can experience, it's like a destruction of being itself. And they make you do it to yourself.

Repression of the churches followed a similar pattern in the Balkans. In Romania, the liquidation of the Greek-Catholic Uniate Church, which was second only to the Orthodox Church in the number of its followers, became more intense in the autumn of 1948. The Orthodox Church stood by in silence, and its hierarchy generally supported the regime—a fact that did not prevent the government from closing many of its churches and imprisoning a number of its leaders. In October all the Uniate bishops were arrested. The Greek-Catholic Church was officially banned on 1 December 1948. At that time its faithful numbered 1,573,000 (out of a population of 15 million people), and it had 2,498 buildings and 1,733 priests. The authorities confiscated all its goods, closed the cathedrals and churches, and in some cases even burned its libraries. More than 1,400 priests (about 600 in November 1948 alone) and some 5,000 followers were sent to prison, where approximately 200 were murdered.

In May 1948, with the arrest of ninety-two priests, it was the turn of the Roman Catholic Church, which had 1,250,000 followers in Romania, to undergo repression. The government closed all the Catholic schools and nationalized the religious charities and medical centers. In June 1949 several Roman Catholic bishops were arrested, and the following month all monastic orders were banned. Repressions culminated in September 1951 with a large trial in Bucharest in which several bishops and eminent lay figures were convicted of "espionage."

One of the Greek-Catholic bishops, who had been ordained secretly and who served fifteen years in prison followed by a period of hard labor, had the following to say:

> For years on end we endured torture, blows, hunger, cold, the confiscation of our goods, and endless mockery and ridicule in the name of the Church. We would kiss our handcuffs, our chains, and the iron bars of our cells as though they were sacred objects, and we loved our prison clothes as if they were sacred vestments. We had chosen our cross to bear, and we kept it, despite the constant offers of freedom, money, and the easy life if we renounced our faith. Our bishops, priests, and faithful were sentenced in total to more than fifteen thousand years in prison, and they served well over one thousand. Six bishops were imprisoned for refusing to renounce their allegiance to Rome. And despite the blood of all these victims, our Church today has as many bishops as it had at the time when Stalin and the Orthodox Patriarch Justinian triumphantly proclaimed its death.[13]

Ordinary People and the Concentration Camp System

The history of dictatorships is complex, and the history of Communism no less so. Its birth in Central and Southeastern Europe was at times marked by massive popular support, linked to the crushing of the Nazi menace as well as to the unquestionable skill with which the Communist leaders nurtured people's illusions and fanaticism. The Left Bloc, for instance, which was established in Hungary at the initiative of the minority Communist Party after the elections of November 1945, organized a demonstration by more than 400,000 people in Budapest in March 1946.

The newly installed Communist regimes favored the promotion of hundreds of thousands of people from socially disadvantaged backgrounds. In highly industrialized Czechoslovakia, where the workers made up some 60 percent of the population in the Czech lands and 50 percent in Slovakia, between 200,000 and 250,000 workers took the places of people who had been removed in purges or who came to fill various departments. The vast majority of them, of course, joined the Czechoslovak Communist Party. Millions of peasants and agricultural workers in Central and Southeastern Europe undeniably did benefit immediately from the agrarian reforms and the redistribution of previously privately owned land (including land that had belonged to the Catholic Church) and of the confiscated property of the expelled Germans.

This happiness of the few, built on the misery of others, was often short-lived, for Bolshevik doctrine mandated the liquidation of all private property. In pursuit of the "intensification of class war" and "the offensive struggle of the masses," in 1945 all the new regimes implemented a broad program of nationalization of properties previously owned by "Germans, traitors, and collaborators." Once the Communists' monopoly of power was assured, it was the turn of the small landowners, shopkeepers, and artisans to have their property seized. The owners of small workshops and modest shops, who had never exploited anyone other than perhaps themselves or members of their families, had good reason to be unhappy. The peasants' turn came in 1949–50, when they were forced into collectivization. The workers in large industrial centers also suffered from new measures that affected their freedoms and their standard of living, often wiping out the gains they had made in the past.

As discontent grew, social tension increased. To express discontent, the workers soon tired of vocal or written demands and began to organize strikes and demonstrations in the streets. In the summer of 1948, a few months after "victorious February," a strike supported by demonstrations began in fifteen Czech and Moravian cities and in three Slovak cities. The strikes began again in late 1951 in all the industrial regions, with protest meetings in the factories and demonstrations of between 10,000 and 30,000 people in the streets of Brno. Then, in early June 1953, to protest against a draconian currency reform, strikes and work stoppages were declared in about ten of the major factories, often accompanied by demonstrations, which in Plzeň became a rebellion. In 1953, 472 strikers and protesters were arrested, and the Communist Party leadership immediately demanded that a list of all participants in the strikes be drawn up, so that they could be "isolated and placed in work camps."

Peasants also revolted from time to time. One of the participants in the Romanian peasant revolt of July 1950 recalled how they all met outside the Communist Party headquarters, unarmed and peaceable, only to be fired upon by a Communist militant.

> After that we forced our way into the building, and we threw the portraits of Stalin and Gheorghiu Dej on the floor and stomped on them . . . Reinforcements arrived quite soon, first of all the village gendarmes . . . Luckily, a young girl named Maria Stoian had cut the wires at the telephone exchange and rung the bells. But the Bolsheviks shot at

us as much as they could . . . In midmorning, about ten o'clock I think, the Securitate arrived with machine guns and all sorts of heavy weapons. Women and children fell to their knees. "Don't shoot us or our children! You've all got children too, and relatives! We're dying of hunger, and we've come here to beg for our wheat not to be taken away!" Lt. Major Stănescu Martin gave the order to open fire.

The author of this statement was arrested, tortured, and sent away into forced labor until 1953.[14]

Under these regimes, which systematically denied freedom and fundamental human rights, any expression of discontent was treated as political and "antistate." The leaders used persecution to plunge society into what Karel Kaplan described as the "psychology of fear," which they viewed as a "stabilizing factor" for the regime.

In the years 1949–1954 millions of people were affected by repression— not only those in prison, but also members of their families. The repression took multiple forms. There were mass deportations from Budapest, Sofia, Prague, and Bucharest to the provinces. In the summer of 1951 they included 14,000 Jews from Budapest, who had survived the wartime massacres and formed the largest Jewish community in Europe. Also affected were the families of émigrés, students who were thrown out of their universities, and hundreds of thousands named on the lists of those judged to be "politically suspect" or "hostile." Such lists were first instigated by the security forces in 1949 and continued to grow longer and longer.

The immense sea of suffering was constantly augmented. After the elimination of figures from political parties and civil society, repression turned to ordinary people. In factories, "troublemakers" were treated as "saboteurs" and were punished with "class justice." The same fate awaited those in the villages who had enjoyed authority because of their knowledge or wisdom, and who simply failed to believe that collectivization was the best or fairest agricultural method. Millions of people then began to see that the promises made earlier, to encourage them to follow Communist ideas, had often been no more than tactical lies. Some dared to voice their discontent.

In-depth studies of the social dimension of these repressions and of the persecution of ordinary people are still rare. We do have quite reliable statistics for the Czech provinces and for Slovakia, where the archives are now open. In most of the other countries we are forced to make do with the investigations of journalists and with eyewitness reports, which luckily have been quite numerous since 1989.

In Czechoslovakia, as early as mid-1950, people described as workers made up 39.1 percent of all those imprisoned for crimes against the state. Office workers, who were often victims of purges in the administration, were second, with 28 percent. The proportion of peasants was slightly lower. In 1951–52 nearly half of all the people arrested by State Security were workers.

The "Report on the Activity of the Courts and the Magistrates" for 1950 presents statistics for people sentenced for "minor crimes against the Republic" (such as inciting people to rebel, spreading false reports, and small-scale sabotage), adjudicated in the Czech provinces by local courts. Of these, 41.2 percent were workers, and 17.7 percent were peasants. In Slovakia the figures were 33.9 percent and 32.6 percent, respectively. Although the share of workers and peasants brought to trial in the main state courts was somewhat smaller, the social category of workers, including agricultural workers, accounted for 28.8 percent of those sentenced (this figure also includes the peasantry), 18.5 percent of those sentenced to death, and 17.6 percent of those sentenced to life imprisonment.

The same pattern was common in other countries, although the peasants were sometimes the main victims of repression. This influx of ordinary people into the prisons was tied to the expansion of the camps and the creation of a concentration-camp *system*, which was perhaps the most remarkable feature of the barbarism of the Communist regimes. The prisons were never large enough to receive a mass of prisoners, and governments again followed the lead of the Soviet Union and created their own gulag archipelago.

Both Bolshevism and Nazism enriched the history of repression in the twentieth century by establishing camp systems in times of peace. As Annette Wieviorka pointed out in a special issue on camps in the journal *Vingtième siècle* in 1997, before the invention of the Gulag and the Lagers (the gulags came first), prison camps had been a wartime means of repression and exclusion. During World War II the concentration-camp system arose in continental Europe, and camps, Lagers, and gulags were to be found from the Urals to the foothills of the Pyrenees. But their history did not end with the defeat of Germany and its allies.

During the war the fascist and dictatorial regimes allied with Germany had incorporated the camp into the culture of their countries. In Bulgaria the conservative government had established an internment camp on the small island of Saint Anastasia in the Black Sea, near Burgas, and then built the camps of Gonda Voda and Belo Pole, where political opponents were interned. In 1941–1944 the populists in power in Slovakia had built fifteen "penitential work establishments" near civil-engineering projects that lacked manpower, and sent there "asocial elements," which generally meant Romany Gypsies. In Romania camps had been created for political prisoners by the dictatorial regime of Marshal Ion Antonescu, most notably the Tîrgiu Jiu camp, in the territory between the Dniester and the Bug, which was used for racial repression.

Thus, when the war ended there were already well-established camps that could serve as transit points for the new deportees (as in the case of Hungary) or as internment camps for people suspected of having collaborated with the Nazis. This was the new function of Buchenwald and Sachsenhausen, infamous concentration camps under the Nazis that lay in the Soviet-occupied zone of East Germany.

After 1945 new types of camps sprang up, to which governments sent their political adversaries. The camps may have been established first in Bulgaria, where a 1945 decree allowed the police to establish camps to educate people through work, known as labor-educational communes (*trudovo-vuzpi-tatchni obshchezhitiya*, or TVO). Hundreds of people, including dozens of anarchists, were sent to the Kutsian camp, near the mining center in Pernik, which at the time was already known as "the kiss of death," and to Bobov Dol and Bogdanov Dol, known to its inmates as "the camp of shadows." After receiving detailed information about these sites in March 1949, French anarchists denounced them publicly as "Bolshevik concentration camps."[15]

The "Gulag archipelago" came to Central and Southeastern Europe in 1949–50. Unlike the case of the Nazi camps, there is no mass of studies and eyewitness testimony to provide a picture of these camps. Nevertheless, we must attempt at least a sketch, both to deepen our understanding of the nature of the Communist regimes and to do justice to the memory of the victims who lost their lives in this part of Europe.

An analysis of the Soviet system leads to the conclusion that the main purpose of the camps was economic. Obviously, the system was meant to isolate and punish certain segments of society. But the geographic distribution of the camps makes it clear that they were situated primarily where the authorities most needed disciplined, plentiful, and cheap manpower. These modern slaves may not have built pyramids, but they did build canals, dams, factories, and buildings in honor of the new pharaohs. They also worked in coal, anthracite, and uranium mines. Could it be that the choice of prisoners and the extent and rhythm of repression were all influenced by the needs of the construction sites and the mines?

In Hungary and Poland the camps were systematically located near mining areas. In Romania the vast majority of the camps were set up along the route of the Danube–Black Sea canal and in the delta of the Danube. The biggest and most important group of camps was known as the Poarta Alba, where names like Cernavodă, Medgidia, Valea Neagra, and Basarabi were engraved in people's memories, together with places in the Danube delta (Periprava, Chilia Veche, Stoenesti, Tataru). The Danube–Black Sea canal soon became known as "the canal of death." This was indeed a terrible place, where thousands of peasants who had opposed collectivization were sent, along with other "suspect individuals." In Bulgaria, detainees in the Kutsian camp worked an open-cast mineral mine, in Bukhovo they worked in a uranium mine, and in Belene they shored up the banks of the Danube. In Czechoslovakia, the camps were grouped mainly around the uranium mines in the Jáchymov region, in Western Bohemia, and in the coalfields of Ostrava, in Northern Moravia.

Why were such places known as "labor camps"? Could the leaders possibly have been unaware that "Arbeit macht frei" had been the inscription above the gates of Nazi death camps? Living conditions in these camps, particularly in the period 1949–1953, were extremely hard, and the daily tasks usually resulted in the total exhaustion of inmates.

One former inmate of a labor camp recalled conditions there in a 1988 interview for a program called "The Other Europe."

After the war Imre Nyeste, a Hungarian resistance fighter in charge of a youth organization, had refused to join the Communist Party. After his trial he was sentenced to a labor camp, where he stayed until 1956. Inmates there broke stones for twelve hours a day in winter and sixteen hours a day in summer. But worst of all for him was the hunger.

> The difference between the Communist secret police and the Nazis—I am one of the happy few who have experience of both—isn't a question of their respective levels of brutality and cruelty. The torture chamber in a Nazi jail is the same as one in a Communist jail. The difference is elsewhere. If the Nazis arrested you as a political dissident, in general what they wanted to know was what your activities were, who your friends were, what your intentions were, etc. The Communists never bothered with all that. They already knew when they arrested you what sort of confession you were going to sign. But you yourself did not. I had no idea that I was going to become an "American spy"![16]

The exact number of prisons and camps is now more or less clear, but determining the number of inmates is more difficult. For Albania, a map drawn up by Odile Daniel locates nineteen camps and prisons. A map of the Bulgarian gulag prepared in 1990 shows eighty-six localities. Around 187,000 people were imprisoned in Bulgaria in the period 1944–1962, according to a list compiled in 1989 by the association of former political prisoners. That figure includes not only those sentenced but also those sent to camps without trial and those kept for weeks on end in police stations—often a means used to force peasants to join agricultural cooperatives. According to other estimates, approximately 12,000 people were in camps between 1944 and 1953, and 5,000 between 1956 and 1962.

In Hungary several hundred thousand people were prosecuted in 1948–1953, and, according to different estimates, between 700,000 and 800,000 were convicted. Most cases were trials for "crimes against state property." Here, as in other countries, administrative internments carried out by the secret police should also be included in the figures. In the German Democratic Republic before the Berlin Wall had been erected, new political prisoners (other than those mentioned in the previous section) seem to have been quite rare.

In Romania, estimates for the number of people incarcerated throughout the Communist period vary between 300,000 and 1 million. The second figure probably includes not only political prisoners but also common criminals (although for crimes like "parasitism" it is extremely hard to tell the two apart). The British historian Dennis Deletant estimates that approximately 180,000 people were detained in camps in Romania in the early 1950s. In Czechoslovakia, the number of political prisoners for the years 1948–1954 has now been established at 200,000. For a population of 12.6 million inhabitants, there were 422 camps and prisons. The figure for those imprisoned includes not only those brought to trial and sentenced, but also those sent to prison without trial or interned in camps on the whim of local authorities.

The penal world differed only slightly from country to country, since all were modeled quite closely on the Soviet system, whose emissaries often came to inspect such establishments. However, Czechoslovakia, Bulgaria, and Romania added some new elements to the Soviet system.

Czechoslovakia brought bureaucratic perfectionism. Some analysts believe that the weight of the Austro-Hungarian imperial bureaucracy left an imprint on the behavior here. The Czechoslovak government provided itself with ample legislation to legitimate its actions, including Law 247 of 25 October 1948, which ratified the forced-labor camps (*tábory nucené práce,* or TNP) for people aged eighteen to sixty. Their purpose was to educate prisoners for a period ranging from three months to two years, which could be shortened or lengthened at will. The law was aimed at delinquents and at the work-shy, but also at those whose "lifestyle needed improvement." Administrative penal Law 88 of 12 July 1950 authorized sending to the TNP anyone who, for example, failed to respect "the protection of agriculture and forestry" or who "demonstrated an attitude hostile toward the people's democratic order of the Republic or its construction." As was pointed out in the National Assembly, these measures necessitated "effective repression of all class enemies."[17]

Under these laws, sentencing to the camps was decided by a commission of three members, created first by a national regional committee and after 1950 by a national district committee or, alternatively, by a special penal commission from the committees headed by the chief of the local branch of the security forces. In all provinces, most of those sent to the TNP were ordinary people, and, as studies carried out since 1989 have confirmed, most of them were workers.

In 1950 the Communist bureaucracy came up with another means of repression, using the army: the technical support battalion (*pomocný technický prapor*, or PTP). Those inducted into these battalions were often significantly older than those doing military service, and they were forced to work extremely hard in the mines, living in conditions similar to those of the labor camps.

Romania was also quite innovative. The Securitate, the Romanian secret police, used all the classic methods of torture during their interrogations: beatings, blows to the soles of the feet, hanging people upside down, and so forth. But in the prison built in the 1930s in Pitești, about 110 kilometers from Bucharest, the cruelty far surpassed those usual methods. The philosopher Virgil Ierunca recalls: "The most vile tortures imaginable were practiced in Pitești. Prisoners' whole bodies were burned with cigarettes: their buttocks would begin to rot, and their skin fell off as though they suffered from leprosy. Others were forced to swallow spoonfuls of excrement, and when they threw it back up, they were forced to eat their own vomit."[18]

These tactics were part of a program of "reeducation." Romania was probably the first country in Europe to introduce the methods of brainwashing used by the Communists in Asia. Indeed, these tactics may well have been perfected there before they were used on a massive scale in Asia. The evil goal of the enterprise was to induce prisoners to torture one another. The idea was conceived in the prison in Pitești. The experiment began in early December 1949 and lasted approximately three years. It resulted from an agreement between the Communist Alexandru Nikolski, one of the chiefs of the Romanian secret police, and Eugen Turcanu, a prisoner who had been arrested in 1948 because of his role as a student organizer for the fascist Iron Guard in 1940–41. After arriving in prison, Turcanu became the head of a movement called the Organization of Prisoners with Communist Beliefs, or OPCB. The goal of the organization was the reeducation of political prisoners, combining study of the texts of Communist dogma with mental and physical torture. The hard core of reeducators consisted of fifteen hand-picked detainees, who first had to make contact with other prisoners and win their confidence.

According to Virgil Ierunca, reeducation occurred in four phases. The first phase was known as "exterior unmasking." The prisoner had to prove his loyalty by admitting what he had hidden when the case had been brought against him and, in particular, admit his links with his friends on the outside. The second phase was "interior unmasking," when he was forced to denounce the people who had helped him inside the prison. The third phase was "public moral unmasking," when the accused was ordered to curse all the things that he held sacred, including his friends and family, his wife or girlfriend, and his God if he was a believer. In the fourth phase, candidates for joining the OPCB had to "reeducate" their own best friend, torturing him with their own hands and thus becoming executioners themselves. "Torture was the key to success.

It implacably punctuated all confessions, between sentences. You couldn't escape the torture. You might perhaps be able to shorten it, if you admitted the worst horrors. Some students were tortured for two months; others, who were more cooperative, got away with a week."[19]

Eugen Turcanu devised especially diabolical measures to force seminarians to renounce their faith. Some had their heads repeatedly plunged into a bucket of urine and fecal matter while the guards intoned a parody of the baptismal rite. One victim who had been systematically tortured in this fashion developed an automatic response that went on for about two months: every morning, to the great delight of his reeducators, he would plunge his own head into the bucket.

Turcanu also forced the seminarians to take part in black masses that he orchestrated himself, particularly during holy week and on Good Friday. Some of the reeducators played the part of choirboys; others masqueraded as priests. Turcanu's liturgy was extremely pornographic, and he rephrased the original in a demonic fashion. The Virgin Mary was called "the Great Whore," and Jesus "that cunt who died on the cross." One seminarian undergoing reeducation and playing the role of a priest had to undress completely and was then wrapped in a robe stained with excrement. Around his neck was hung a phallus made of bread and soap and powdered with DDT. In 1950 on the Saturday before Easter the students who were undergoing reeducation were forced to pass before the priest, kiss the phallus, and say, "He is risen."[20]

In 1952 the Romanian authorities tried to extend the Piteşti experiment, particularly in the work camps on the Danube—Black Sea canal. When Western radio stations got wind of the operation, the Communist leaders decided to end the "reeducation" program. In a trial in 1954, Turcanu and six accomplices were condemned to death, but no one else in the police hierarchy was ever held accountable.

The Lovech camp in Bulgaria offers a third and final example of the new elements added by Central and Southeastern Europe to the history of Communist repression. This camp was established in 1959, six years after Stalin's death and three years after Khrushchev's speech at the Twentieth Party Congress condemning the Stalinist camps. It was a time when many of the camps for political prisoners were being closed, even in the Soviet Union. The Lovech camp was not particularly large—its capacity was about 1,000 prisoners—but the killings carried out there by the executioners were truly atrocious. People were tortured and finished off in the most primitive fashion imaginable: they were simply clubbed to death.

The government opened the Lovech camp after closing the camp at Belene—a camp unforgettable to the Bulgarians, since the bodies of prisoners who died there were fed to the pigs. Officially, the camp was created to deal with repeat offenders and hardened criminals. But according to eyewitness reports made in 1990, most of the inmates were in fact sent there without trial: "You're wearing jeans, you've got long hair, you listen to American music, you speak the language of a country that is hostile to us, you've been talking to tourists . . . off to camp with you!" Accordingly, the majority of people in the camp were very young.

In the preface to a book of statements from victims, their families, and former members of the repressive apparatus, Tzvetan Todorov summed up life in Lovech as follows:

> During morning roll call, the chief of police (i.e., the head of the State Security forces in the camp) would choose his victims. He would take a little mirror out of his pocket and shove it in their faces, saying, "Here, take a last look at your face!" The victims were then given a sack, in which they would be brought back to the camp that evening: they had to carry it themselves, like Christ carrying his own cross up to Golgotha. They left for the site, which in fact was a quarry. There they were beaten to death by the brigadiers and tied up in the sack with some wire. That night their comrades would have to bring them back to the camp in a handcart, and the bodies were then stacked up behind the toilets until there were twenty of them, when a truck would arrive and take them away. Those who didn't make their daily quota were singled out during the evening roll call; the police chief would draw a circle in the sand with his baton, and the designated people who were pushed into the circle were beaten repeatedly.[21]

The exact number of deaths in this camp has not yet been established. The camp was closed by the authorities in 1962. Although the regime inside the camp began to improve a little in 1961, and although the actual number of deaths was only a few hundred, the name Lovech will always remain an important symbol of barbarism in formerly Communist countries.

This mass terror cannot be explained as "natural for those times," or as part of the Cold War that began in 1947 and reached its height with the Korean war of 1950–1953. The opponents of Communist power inside these countries, despite their huge majority, demonstrated almost no interest in violent or armed struggle (Poland is a notable exception, and there were also armed groups in Bulgaria and Romania). Their opposition was often spontaneous, unorganized, and quite democratic. Some of the politicians who had not immediately emigrated believed that the repression would be short-lived. Armed resistance was rare, and when it did occur it was usually a case of the secret services settling grudges, or of underworld killings being passed off as political murders, rather than a result of genuine political opposition.

Thus there is no way to explain the violence of the repression by pointing to violence in society or the scale of opposition. The "class struggle" was highly orchestrated, and opposition networks were sometimes deliberately established by *agents provocateurs* from the secret police. Occasionally those agents were in turn killed by the secret services.

People still try to explain away the history of Communism with reference to the "spirit of the moment" or the "context of the time." But such attempts are part of a specifically ideological approach to history and a revisionism that does not correspond to the facts as they have now come to light. Scholars and others should pay closer attention to the social dimensions of the repression, and concentrate more on the persecution of ordinary people.

The Trials of Communist Leaders

The persecution of fellow Communists is one of the most important episodes in the history of repression in Central and Southeastern Europe in the first half of the twentieth century. Neither the international Communist movement nor any of its local branches ever ceased to denounce "bourgeois justice and legality" and fascist and Nazi repression. Undoubtedly, there were thousands of militant Communists who died as victims of Nazi and fascist repression during World War II.

But the persecution of Communists did not stop with the progressive installation of "people's democracies," when the "dictatorship of the proletariat" took over from the "dictatorship of the bourgeoisie."

In Hungary in 1945 the secret police imprisoned Pál Demeny, József Skólnik, and a number of their friends. All considered themselves to be Communists, and it was under that label that they had led underground resistance groups, to which they had often recruited young people and workers. In the industrial centers, membership in their groups was higher than that of Communist groups who had sworn allegiance to Moscow, and who considered competitors like Demeny to be Trotskyites or "deviationists." When the moment of liberation finally arrived, Demeny met the same fate that befell those he had fought against, and he was imprisoned until 1957. In Romania the fate of Ştefan Foriş, general secretary of the Romanian Communist Party in the mid-1930s, was even more tragic. He was accused of being a police agent, kept under surveillance until 1944, and killed in 1946 with a blow from an iron bar. His mother, who had looked everywhere for him, was found drowned in a river in Transylvania with stones tied around her neck. Ceauşescu denounced the political assassination of Foriş and his friends in 1968.

The examples of Demeny, Foriş, and others demonstrate quite clearly that for the people in charge, there were "good" Communists, who were in the Party and faithful to Moscow, and "bad" Communists, who refused to join what they saw as a Party with no independence. The principle varied over time in certain countries, but the dialectic of Communist persecution became considerably more complicated after 1948, when it moved inside the Party itself.

In late June 1948 the Cominform, which had been established in September 1947 and included all the Communist parties then in power except Albania, together with the two most powerful Communist parties in Western Europe—the French and Italian—roundly condemned Tito's Yugoslavia and called for his overthrow. In the months that followed, "deviationism" (opposition to the reigning powers in Moscow) began to take shape as a new phenomenon in the Communist movement. The desire to be autonomous and independent of the center, which previously had been discernible only in small groups, now became the province of an entire state. One small Balkan state, in which the Communist Party's monopoly on power had already been tried and tested, challenged the entire Communist empire. The increasingly tense situation offered new perspectives on the repression of Communists. Communists themselves, as well as citizens of Communist states, could now be accused of being allies or agents of hostile foreign Communist powers.

There were two important aspects of this historical novelty in the persecution of Communists—events in Yugoslavia and the repression of Titoists—and little attention has been paid to the former until now. After what the newspapers described as the Tito-Stalin split, Yugoslavia went through an economic crisis worse, according to some, than the one experienced during the war. Links to the outside world were repeatedly cut, and with Soviet tanks deployed near the border the country was under serious threat. In 1948–49 the prospect of a Soviet invasion and a new war was not a happy one in a country already devastated by war and its aftermath.

The government in Belgrade reacted to the accusation of "Yugoslav treason" and threats of force by isolating those who were faithful to Moscow, whom it termed *informbirovtsi* (Cominformers), as well as anyone who approved the Cominform resolution of June 1948. This isolation was not merely a process of internment that would have prevented contact with the outside world. Tito's government was still deeply imbued with Bolshevik ideas and came up with the solution one might expect: it opened more prison camps. Yugoslavia has many islands, and in an allusion perhaps to the first Bolshevik camp set up in the Solovetski archipelago, the main camp was called Goli Otok, or "Naked Island." This was no ordinary camp; it used reeducation methods similar to those practiced in Pitești in Romania. For instance, there was a practice known as the "walk of dishonor" or "jack-rabbit," which forced newcomers to run a gauntlet of prisoners, who, partly to improve their standing with the authorities, would beat them, insult them, and throw stones as they passed. There were also rituals of criticism, self-accusation, and confession.

Torture was the daily bread of the internees. Among the methods was one known simply as "the bucket," which forced a prisoner's head into a receptacle filled with excrement. Another, called "the bunker," forced prisoners to stay in a tiny space for long periods. The most widespread method used by reeducators—reminiscent of work done in Nazi camps—was stone-breaking on the rocky islands of the Adriatic. To complete the humiliation, the stones were thrown back into the sea at the end of the day.

The persecution of Communists in Yugoslavia that began in 1948–49 was probably one of the most massive persecution movements that Europe had yet witnessed, including those of the Soviet Union from the 1920s to the 1940s, Germany in the 1930s, and the repression of Communists during the Nazi occupation. What happened in Yugoslavia was a truly immense phenomenon considering the number of inhabitants and the number of Communists. According to official sources that were long kept secret, the purges affected 16,371 people, 5,037 of whom were brought to trial, and three-quarters of whom were sent to Goli Otok and Grgur. Independent analysis by Vladimir Dedijer suggests that between 31,000 and 32,000 people went through the Goli Otok camp alone. But even the most recent research has been unable to come up with a figure for the number of prisoners who died as victims of executions, exhaustion, hunger, epidemics, or even suicide—a solution chosen by many Communists to escape their cruel situation.

The other aspect of the persecution of Communists is better known: the repression of Titoists in the other "people's democracies." This usually took the form of show-trials aimed at affecting public opinion in the countries concerned, as well as serving an international function. The progress of these trials proved that Moscow's suspicions were well founded: the principal enemy was within the Communist Party itself. Vigilance and mistrust, it followed, must therefore become a way of life for true Communists.

In early 1948 the Romanian Communist Party opened the case of Lucrețiu Pătrășcanu, an intellectual and renowned Marxist theorist who had been a founding member of the Party in 1921 at the age of twenty-one and minister of justice since 1944. Some aspects of his case foreshadowed the campaign against Tito. Dismissed from office in February 1948 and imprisoned, Pătrășcanu was condemned to death in April 1954, one year after the death of Stalin, and executed on 16 April. The mystery of this late execution has not yet been cleared up. One theory is that Gheorghe Gheorghiu-Dej, the general secretary of the Romanian Communist Party, feared Pătrășcanu's rehabilitation, viewing him as a potential rival. This idea is only partly plausible, however, inasmuch as the two had been in conflict since the war.

In 1949 the first trials of Communist leaders in countries bordering Yugoslavia took place. The first were in Albania, where the leadership had close ties to the Yugoslav Communists. The designated victim, Koci Xoxe, had been a chief of the armed Communist resistance before being made minister of internal affairs and general secretary of the Party after the war. Xoxe was devoted to Tito's cause. After a political campaign within the Party in the autumn of 1948 attacking the "pro-Yugoslav Trotskyite faction led by Xoxe and Kristo," all allies of the Yugoslav Communists were arrested in March 1949. Xoxe was brought to trial in Tirana with four other leaders—Pandi Kristo, Vasco Koleci, Nuri Huta, and Vango Mitrojorgji. He was sentenced to death on 10 June and executed the next day. His four companions received heavy sentences, and it was not long before other pro-Yugoslav Communists in the Albanian Party also fell victim to the purge.

A second show-trial in the anti-Tito series took place in September 1949 in Budapest. The accused was László Rajk, who had fought in the International Brigades in Spain. Rajk had been one of the heads of the resistance and as a minister of internal affairs had carried out severe repressions of non-Communist democrats before being made minister of foreign affairs. After his arrest in May 1949, Rajk was tortured and blackmailed by his previous colleagues, who told him that he would not be killed if he helped the Party. He was ordered to confess in court and to reel off a string of accusations against Tito and the Yugoslavs as "enemies of people's democracy." The verdict of the Hungarian court was reached on 24 September, with no right to appeal: László Rajk, Tibor Szönyi, and András Szalai were condemned to death, and the Yugoslav Lazar Brankov and the Social Democrat Pál Justus were given life sentences. Rajk was executed on 16 October. In a subsequent trial a military court condemned four high-ranking officers to death.

In the repressions following the Rajk trial, 94 people in Hungary were arrested, sentenced, and interned; 15 were executed; 11 others died in prison; and 50 of the accused received prison sentences of more than ten years. The total number of deaths in this affair was about 60, including a number of suicides among prisoners, their relatives, and judges and police officers caught up in the affair.

Animosities within the leadership, and the zeal of the general secretary of the Party, Mátyás Rákosi, and the chiefs of the secret police, influenced the choice of victims and their leader, László Rajk. These and other factors, however, should not obscure the essential fact that many of the main decisions were made in Moscow by, among others, the heads of the security forces and intelligence services responsible for Central and Western Europe. This had been the case since the earliest waves of repression. Soviet leaders were preoccupied with discovering a huge international anti-Soviet conspiracy. The Rajk trial played a key role, particularly through its main witness, the American Noel Field, who was secretly a Communist and helped the Soviet Union, as has recently been proved in the archives.[22]

This attempt to find an international conspiracy in Titoism was also evident in the trial of Traicho Kostov, in Sofia. Kostov was an experienced Comintern official who had been condemned to death by the previous regime. He had fought in the resistance during the war, had been made vice president of the National Council after the war, and was considered the heir apparent to Georgi Dimitrov. Dimitrov was a previous general secretary of the Comintern and had been head of the Bulgarian Communist Party since 1946, but in 1949 his health began to deteriorate steadily. He was treated in the Soviet Union beginning in March of that year but died on 2 July.

From late 1948, the "Muscovites" at the head of the Bulgarian Communist Party (that is, the leaders who had spent the war in Moscow, people of the same mold as Rákosi in Hungary and Gottwald in Czechoslovakia) had been criticizing the faults and failures of Kostov, above all his "incorrect relationship with the U.S.S.R." concerning economic questions, despite his "self-criticism." With the consent of Dimitrov, who had condemned Kostov in violent terms in a letter dispatched on 10 May from a Soviet sanatorium, Kostov was arrested in June 1949 with several other collaborators.

The trial of Traicho Kostov and the nine accused with him opened in Sofia on 7 December 1949. A verdict was reached one week later, and Kostov was sentenced to death as an agent of the Bulgarian police of the old regime, as a Titoist traitor, and as an agent of Western imperialism. Four other leaders—Ivan Stefanov, Nikolai Pavlov, Nikolai Nechev, and Ivan Tutev—were given life sentences; three more received fifteen years, one received twelve years, and another received eight years. Two days later, after Kostov's appeal for clemency was rejected, he was hanged.

The Sofia trial has a unique place in the history of the trials of Communist leaders under Communist regimes. While giving his evidence Kostov contradicted statements that had been forced from him under torture and claimed his innocence. He was immediately silenced but was able to make a last plea that he was a friend of the Soviet Union. He was prevented from finishing, but his outburst made those who staged subsequent show-trials extremely careful in their preparations.

The Kostov affair did not end in Bulgaria with the execution of the principal victim. In August 1950 the trial of twelve of his collaborators, chosen from leading economic officials, took place. Another trial of two more "members of Kostov's band of conspirators" took place in April 1951, which in turn was followed by a third trial of two members of the Central Committee of the Bulgarian Communist Party. There were also several related trials of army officers and members of the security forces.

In Czechoslovakia, the leaders had been warned in June 1949 that a number of conspirators were plotting within the Communist Party. To flush them out—and to find in particular the "Czech Rajk"—a special group was set up in Prague, consisting of leaders from the Central Committee, the secret police, and the Control Commission of the Czechoslovak Communist Party. The first Communist leaders, initially of the third order, were arrested in 1949. But during this first wave of trials the regime could mount only one anti-Tito trial. It took place from 30 August to 2 September 1952 in Bratislava, the capital of Slovakia. Sixteen people, including ten Yugoslavs, were brought to trial. Their leader was Stefan Kević, the vice-consul of Yugoslavia in Bratislava. Two Slovaks were condemned to death in the trial, and one of them, Rudolf Lančanič, was executed.

In late 1949 the police began to close in on the "Czech Rajk," reinforced by the assistance of experienced agents from the Soviet KGB. The Soviet advisers made no secret of their aims. One of them, Mikhail Likhachev, irritated by the lack of zeal of a Slovak security leader, exclaimed, "Stalin sent me to set up the trials, and I don't have any time to waste. I haven't come here to discuss things with people, I have come to Czechoslovakia to cut off heads [*svolchit golovy*]. I'll kill 150 people with my own hands before I get into trouble!"[23]

The historical reconstruction of this repression has been carried out meticulously because historians in 1968 had access to secret Party and police archives and after November 1989 were able to pursue the question even further.

The Pavlík couple—Gejza and Charlotte—were arrested in May 1949 as part of the preparations for the Rajk trial in Hungary. The trial of Gejza Pavlík began in June 1950. In June 1949 the Hungarian Party leader Mátyás Rákosi gave a list to the Czechoslovak Communist leader Klement Gottwald in Prague of about sixty Czechoslovak leaders whose names had come up in the course of the Rajk investigation. As a result of the Rajk case, and under pressure from the Soviet and Hungarian security forces, Prague became more and more obsessed with Communists who had been exiled to the West during the war, and in particular with those who had served in the International Brigades. That autumn the Czechoslovak Communist Party set up a special section of the state security forces to unmask enemies inside the Party. They did not hesitate to use former members of the Gestapo, the "specialists" of the Communist movement. After the arrest of Evžen Löbl, the deputy minister of foreign trade, in November 1949, repression against the Communists intensified. It reached the highest-ranking cadres and intensified further in 1950, affecting even regional Party leaders.

In January and February 1951 a great wave of arrests swept through a section of the power structure. Among fifty arrests of high-ranking Party and state officials was the detention of a group of "Francophone Communists" and others accused, like Karel Šváb, of having contact in one manner or another with foreign parties.

The hunt for the "Czech Rajk" took more than two years, and during that time a variety of people were accused of being at the head of such a plot. It was only in the summer of 1951 that Stalin, with the consent of Klement Gottwald, decided that the man in question must be Rudolf Slánský, the general secretary of the Czechoslovak Communist Party, whose righthand man was Bedřich Geminder, another key figure in the Comintern. Geminder's name was found next to that of Slánský almost everywhere, from the correspondence between Stalin and Gottwald to the interrogations of Communists imprisoned in the lead-up to Slánský's arrest. If worse came to worst, thought the Soviet advisers, they could pin most charges on Geminder instead. The state security forces arrested both men on 24 November 1951. In subsequent months two other leaders joined them behind bars: Rudolf Margolius, deputy minister of foreign trade, on 12 January 1952; and Slánský's assistant, Josef Frank, on 23 May 1952.

Soviet advisers and their local assistants took turns torturing and breaking the accused in preparation for the show-trial. On 20 November 1952 the trial of "the conspiracy against the state with Rudolf Slánský at its head" finally began. The verdict was pronounced one week later. Eleven of the accused were sentenced to death, and three received life imprisonment. On the morning of 3 December 1953, between 3:00 and 5:45 A.M., the eleven were hanged at Pankrac prison in Prague.

Aside from the trials of Bolshevik leaders in Moscow in the 1930s, the Slánský trial was the most spectacular and the most talked-about judicial proceeding in the history of Communism. Among the condemned were a number of eminent figures on the international Communist scene who had made Prague the Communist Geneva during the Cold War. The Czech capital had played a crucial role, particularly in relations with the French and Italian Communist Parties.

Rudolf Slánský, who had been general secretary of the Czechoslovak Communist Party since 1945, was a faithful servant of Moscow and the president of the "Group of Five," a special body established to follow the repressions day by day. Among its functions was the approval of dozens of death sentences.

Bedřich Geminder and Josef Frank were deputy general secretaries. Geminder had held a high position in the Comintern and had returned specially from Moscow to Prague to lead the International Department of the Czechoslovak Communist Party. Frank had been a prisoner in a Nazi concentration camp from 1939 to 1945 and had supervised economic affairs and the financial aid sent to Western Communist Parties. As deputy minister of foreign trade, Rudolf Margolius had maintained relations with various businesses and commercial enterprises that were under the control of the Party. Otto Fischl, the deputy minister of finance, also had in-depth knowledge of the financial affairs of the Czechoslovak Communist Party. Ludvík Frejka had participated during the war in the Czech resistance based in London, and since 1948, when Gottwald had become president of the republic, Frejka had been head of the Economic Department in the Treasury.

Among those sentenced who had links with the Soviet special services, either directly or through the Communist International, were Bedřich Reicin, the head of military intelligence and deputy minister of defense since 1948; Karel Šváb, who had been a prisoner in a Nazi concentration camp and was head of personnel in the Czechoslovak Communist Party, a function that had brought him an appointment as deputy minister of state security; André Simone, a journalist who before the war had worked in Germany and France; and Artur London, who had assisted the Soviet NKVD during the war in Spain, fought in the resistance in France, been deported, helped the Communist intelligence services after 1945 in Switzerland and France, and been made deputy minister of foreign affairs in Prague early in 1949.

Two other figures from the Foreign Affairs Ministry were among those sentenced. The first was a Slovak, Vladimír Clementis, who had been a Communist lawyer before the war and been exiled to France. From abroad, he had been critical of the German-Soviet pact, a stance that resulted in his expulsion from the Party, although the decision was reversed in 1945. He had been minister of foreign affairs since the spring of 1948. The other was Vavro Hajdů, a deputy minister, who was also a Slovak. The third Slovak involved in the trial, Evžen Löbl, who had spent the war in London, was deputy minister of foreign trade when he was arrested.

Otto Šling had also participated in the Czech resistance in London after fighting in the International Brigades in Spain. After the war he had become the regional secretary of the Communist Party in Brno, the capital of Moravia.

The three who received life sentences—Vavro Hajdů, Artur London, and Evžen Löbl—saw their Jewish origins produced as evidence in court. This was also the case for all those condemned to death, with the exceptions of Clementis, Frank, and Šváb.

Although the Slánský trial became a symbol of repression in the "people's democracies," most of the victims of the repression were not Communists. In 1948–1954 Communists in Czechoslovakia accounted for 0.1 percent of all people sentenced, 5 percent of those condemned to death, and 1 percent of all deaths, including death sentences, suicides provoked by persecution, and deaths in prison or in the camps as a direct consequence of imprisonment (accidents in the mines or shootings by guards during attempted escapes, termed "acts of rebellion").

The Slánský trial was carefully prepared by Soviet advisers who were acting on orders from the highest authorities in Moscow. It was part of the second wave of the great political trials of Communist leaders in the "people's democracies" after 1949.

In Czechoslovakia the Slánský trial was followed by others in 1953 and 1954, despite the deaths of both Stalin and Gottwald in March 1953. The culmination came in 1954. The first great trial in the series took place in Prague from 26 to 28 January. Marie Švermová, a founding member of the Czechoslovak Communist Party and a member of its leadership from 1929 to 1950, was sentenced to life imprisonment; six other high-ranking Party members who had been accused of the same crimes were given sentences totaling 113 years. In a second trial, from 23 to 25 February, seven members of the "Great Trotskyite Council," all Czechoslovak Communist Party activists, received sentences totaling 103 years. A third trial took place in Bratislava on 21–24 April, in which previous leaders of the Slovak Communist Party were accused of "bourgeois nationalist" tendencies. Gustáv Husák, who had been a leader in the resistance, was sentenced to life; the four other accused received 63 years in total. In six more trials in 1954 the accused were high-ranking army officers, economic officials (eleven of whom were collectively sentenced to 204 years in prison), and Social Democrats. As had been the custom for several years in all important trials, the political secretary of the Czechoslovak Communist Party approved the charges and the sentences, and the Party leadership then drew up a report on the progress of the trial.

The trials of 1953 and 1954 were not the big show-trials of previous years. The last political trial for the period 1948–1954, which took place on 5 November 1954, was that of Edward Outrat, an economist.

Osvald Závodský, the last Communist to be executed in this wave of repressions, had fought in the International Brigades, had served in the resistance and then been deported during the war, and by 1948 had become chief of State Security. The court sentenced him to death in December 1953, and the government refused to commute the sentence. He clearly knew too much about the Soviet special services. He was hanged in Prague on 19 March 1954.

Various questions arise here. How did this repression of such high-ranking Communists come about? Was there a logic in the choice of victims? The opening of the archives has confirmed many ideas put forward before 1989: the trials were all fabrications, confessions were systematically extracted by force, and operations were directed from Moscow against a frenzied ideological backdrop that was initially anti-Titoist but soon acquired an anti-Zionist and anti-American character. Several facts have supplemented our knowledge of events. But this opening of the archives also allows us to formulate some hypotheses about the second wave of repression against Communists, launched by an immediate need to stamp out the Yugoslav heresy.

Richly documented studies have confirmed the obvious causes. Intervention by Moscow was clearly the determining factor. The trials of Communists were directly related to the international situation at the time; after Tito's revolt the Stalinist regime had to impose total control upon the Communist movement and to accelerate the process of making the Communist states satellites of the Soviet Union. The repression was also linked to the social, economic, and political problems of each country. The condemned Communist leaders served as scapegoats; their faults were used to explain away the failures of the government and to channel the people's anger. The omnipresent terror sowed and nurtured fear among the leaders; it was a means of obtaining absolute obedience and total submission to Party orders and to the needs of the "peace camp," which were defined by Soviet leaders.

Dissension within the leadership was also a major factor in the choice of victims. Hatreds and reciprocal jealousies, so frequent in any basically colonial society, likewise played a role. Moscow acted as a central manipulator, pulling the strings and frightening its servants; it had long had detailed information on all those jealousies and hatreds.

Each of the two waves of repression sweeping over the Communist leaders had a model victim. In one case repression was concentrated on those who had fought as volunteers in the civil war in Spain, had served in the resistance abroad or in Yugoslavia, or had spent time in France or England. In the other case, in Hungary, Bulgaria, and Slovakia, the victims were chiefly those who had fought in the resistance inside the country.

But we should go further and ask why the Slánský trial in particular was so important, and why it effectively became a worldwide spectacle. What underlying interests of Stalinist power surfaced here? Why was it accorded such publicity? Why were the sentences so brutal? Why was the violence so spectacular at a moment when the Soviet Union seemed to have such a tight grip on the "people's democracies"? Much more is constantly being discovered about such questions, particularly concerning the sort of control that Moscow exercised, the letters it sent and the meetings it organized, and above all the exact role of the Soviet advisers *in situ*.

Let us formulate an initial hypothesis for the logic behind this repression: the Soviet bloc was preparing for war in Europe. "American imperialism" had become the principal enemy, and Soviet leaders believed—or wished to make people think they believed—that an American attack on them was being prepared. The Slánský trial, its development, its carefully organized echoes, and its violently anti-American ideology (the pervasive antisemitism was secondary), were all a part of Soviet preparations for war. The terror was aimed not only at the Communist ranks but also at the enemy. Stalin had already used it in the Soviet Union during the great purges of the 1930s and in the lead-up to the war. Did he believe that he could use the tactic again?

Those who have worked in the archives agree that around 1951–52, when the war in Korea was still under way, the Soviet Union was making intense preparations for a war in Europe, and might even have been preparing for a full-scale invasion and occupation of Western Europe. At a meeting of political and military officials in 1951, Stalin referred to the likelihood of war in 1953. Militarization of the economy was everywhere at its maximum.

Czechoslovakia would have played a major role in any such contingencies. The country had had a highly developed armaments industry since the days of the Austro-Hungarian monarchy. In the 1930s Czechoslovakia was one of the world's major exporters of arms. After 1949 it also began to supply weapons to the Soviet Union. Soviet advisers oversaw a militarization of the Czechoslovak economy, an intensification of propaganda about the imminence of war, an unprecedented increase in the defense budget—over five years, spending on the military increased by 700 percent—the ravaging of civil society, and the comprehensive pillaging of Czechoslovakia's uranium mines.

The military historian Jindřich Madrý, who has worked in archives opened since 1989, recently concluded that "until May 1953, Czechoslovakia's armaments industry had been geared up to the maximum for what was regarded as an 'inevitable war.' "[24] The projected 1953 budget for the Ministry of Defense was ten times greater than that of 1948. In line with Soviet demands, the Czechoslovak economy was to evolve on a war footing. On 1 January 1953 the army numbered 292,788 men, twice its size in 1949. In April the president of the republic lengthened the term of military service to three years. Financial and material reserves were stockpiled in preparation for war. It is against this backdrop that one should place the monetary reform of June 1953, which stripped away savings. According to some indications, the situation changed in June 1953, when "inevitable war" no longer seemed the preferred strategy of Moscow's new leadership.

If we view the repression of Communist leaders from this perspective, we can more clearly understand the logic behind the choice of victims. "Big Brother" was well aware who his loyal comrades were, and he had an idea of who his enemies were in the West. This "pedagogy of corpses" seemed to be the height of Machiavellian policy. What better way was there to convince one's enemies of one's vigor and determination (and even at times to give the illusion of being weak) so as to plunge them into complete disarray? What better way was there to convince one's loyal allies, who knew all one's secrets, of the gravity of the situation and the necessity of iron discipline as well as the necessity of sacrifice in the coming conflict?

The answer was to sacrifice the most loyal, to choose victims who would ensure that the decision had the widest possible repercussions both internationally and in the Soviet Union, to use the cheapest lies and worst calumnies as weapons. If those tried had been the likes of Antonín Zapotocký or Antonín Novotný, who were hardly known in Moscow or elsewhere, the effect of the spectacle would have been greatly diminished. Can anyone seriously believe today that Thorez, Togliatti, Khrushchev, and Gottwald believed that Rudolf Slánský, Bedřich Geminder, and their companions really were American agents? The effort of trying to believe it wore everyone down, and wearing people down was the name of the game.

If what Annie Kriegel has called "that infernal pedagogy" was to be echoed around the world, the victims had to be well-known figures in the antifascist movements in Spain, France, England, and the U.S.S.R. They were well-known for having been deported or otherwise persecuted by the Nazis. The members of the Soviet security organs knew very well what sort of service had been rendered to them by these people and how loyal to Moscow they really were. Among the Communists who were sacrificed, many were themselves responsible for the earlier persecution or assassination of other non-Communists, and many had collaborated very closely with Soviet organizations.

The trials continued in 1953 and 1954, until the moment when the Soviet Union decided to opt for a new policy of "peaceful coexistence."

A second hypothesis, which it seems important to advance here, concerns the widespread antisemitism in the repression of the Communists. Analyses of the trials regularly mention "the struggle against Zionism and the Zionists," and there is no doubt that this aspect was linked to changes in Soviet policy regarding Israel and the Arab world. The new state of Israel, to whose birth Czechoslovakia in particular had greatly contributed (supplying arms to the Haganah), became the Great Enemy, and Soviet policy realigned itself behind the Arab struggle for national liberation.

Nicolas Werth (see Part I) has already pointed out the antisemitic elements in the repressions in the Soviet Union after December 1947 and in the preparation for the "great final purge" of the 1950s. In Central Europe, antisemitism was quite apparent in the Rajk trial, when the judge stressed the Jewish origins of the names of four of the accused, including Rajk. This antisemitism reached its height in the Slánský trial, which stressed the Jewish origins of eleven of the accused and their alleged links with international Zionism.

To appreciate the extent of this latent antisemitism, one need only read one of the reports from a Moscow adviser already cited above, Comrade Likhachev, who had asked for information about the subversive activities of certain Slovak leaders. According to a statement by his Slovak interlocutor, Likhachev declared: "I don't care where this information comes from. I don't even care if it's true or not. I'm ready to believe it, and let me do the rest. Why worry about these Jewish shits anyway?"[25]

There is another, unknown side to this intractable antisemitism. It would appear that Stalin and his followers wanted to settle scores with all the Jews in the International, definitively eliminating them. These Jewish Communists did not practice their religion; they seem to have identified with the nation to which they belonged or with the international Communist community. We have no sources to indicate how they thought their identity had been affected by the Holocaust. But, of course, many of their relatives had died in Nazi death camps.

After the war there were still many Jewish Communists occupying key posts in parties and organizations in Central Europe. In a comprehensive survey of Hungarian Communism, Miklós Molnar writes: "At the very top of the hierarchy, almost without exception, the leaders were of Jewish origin, as they were in a slightly lower proportion in the Central Committee, the secret police, the press and publishing houses, and the theater and cinema . . . Although a policy was in place to promote young workers to positions of influence, the fact remains that for the most part power was wielded by the Jewish petite bourgeoisie."[26] In January 1953 Gábor Peter, the chief of the Hungarian secret police and an old friend of Rajk, found himself in prison as a Zionist conspirator. An official speech by Rákosi, who was himself a Jewish Communist, stigmatized "Peter and his gang" and turned him into a scapegoat.

In Romania, the fate of Jewish Comintern worker Ana Pauker was settled in 1952. She had been a member of the ruling "troika," together with Gheorghiu-Dej, the Party leader, and Vasile Luca. According to a statement that cannot be confirmed from other sources, at a meeting with Gheorghiu-Dej in 1951 Stalin expressed surprise that agents of Titoism and Zionism had not yet been arrested in Romania, and demanded immediate action. As a result Vasile Luca, the minister of finance, was dismissed in May 1952 along with Teohari Gheorghescu, the minister of interior, and sentenced to death. Luca's sentence was later commuted to life imprisonment, and he died in prison. Ana Pauker, the minister of foreign affairs, was sacked in early July, arrested in February 1953, and freed in 1954, returning to family life. The antisemitic repression moved on to smaller targets.

Events that took place around this time in Moscow, such as the complete reorganization of the security services and the arrest of the chief of the secret police, Viktor Abakumov, in July 1951, permit yet a third hypothesis: infighting within the Soviet security services may have been decisive in the choice of victims who collaborated with the services and in the sentences they were given. Karel Kaplan has recently pointed out that "it remains an open question whether the liquidation of a group of people who cooperated with the Soviet security services and their replacement by others (Karol Bacílek, A. Keppert, and others) originated in the conflicts and changes in the central security apparatus in Moscow."[27]

The validity of this last hypothesis cannot be established until after

lengthy work in the principal Moscow archives. There is no doubt that at the
end of Stalin's reign, differences existed among his potential successors, including Khrushchev, Malenkov, and Beria, who were in charge of different
parts of the security apparatus. We already have a reasonable idea of the sort
of rivalry that existed between military intelligence and the NKVD, which were
in open competition in the "people's democracies."[28]

The Prague archives reveal a lack of resolution on the part of the Soviet
security services. In the spring of 1950, Moscow began to replace the advisers
it had sent to Prague the previous autumn, who had failed to produce the
desired results. In a meeting in the Kremlin on 23 July 1951 attended by
Gottwald (who had been invited by Alexej Čepička, the minister of national
defense), Stalin criticized these advisers for their irresponsible work. He subsequently wrote a letter to Gottwald, which was brought from Moscow by
Čepička, about the respective fates of Slánský and Geminder:

> Regarding your positive appreciation of the work of Comrade
> [Vladimir] Boyarsky [the main Soviet adviser] and your desire to keep
> him in the post of adviser to the minister of national security for the
> Republic of Czechoslovakia, we are of a quite different opinion. The
> experience of Boyarsky's work in the Czech Republic has shown that he
> lacks the necessary qualities and qualifications to carry out his task as
> adviser in a satisfactory fashion. This is why we have decided to recall
> him from Czechoslovakia. If you feel you really need an adviser for State
> Security (and it is your decision) we will attempt to find a more reliable
> replacement who has more experience.[29]

Under these conditions, the position of the heads of State Security was
extremely precarious: the chief of the Czechoslovak officers responsible for
training noted in a memorandum to one of his advisers that "one never leaves
the security services early, unless it is in a box." Jindřich Veselý, chief of State
Security, made an unsuccessful suicide attempt in 1950; a second attempt, in
1964, was successful. Before he died he wrote a long explanation of the motives
for his action, which can be consulted in the archives of the Central Committee
of the Czechoslovak Communist Party and appears to be totally sincere. He
knew perfectly well that Stalin regularly liquidated the heads of his security
services and wished to avoid his own liquidation.

A fourth hypothesis might also be advanced to explain the logic of the
choice of victims among Communist leaders. There was clearly a need for a
large show-trial in the Soviet Union, to crown the series of political trials in
other countries and to punish the supposed culprits in a huge international plot
in the center, in Moscow itself. The new elements brought to light by Nicolas

Werth earlier in this book are strong arguments for this interpretation of the repression exercised against Communists in Central and Southeastern Europe.

From "Post-Terror" to Post-Communism

Before examining the period extending from 1955 to 1989, which the historian Miklós Molnar has called the "post-terror," we should take note of a few facts that may shed light on the evolution of the repression and its logic.

Let us note first that the mass terror and repression implemented in the Communist regimes were in violation of fundamental liberties and human rights. These had been acknowledged in international conventions, particularly in the Universal Declaration of Human Rights, which was passed in the United Nations General Assembly in December 1948 despite the abstention of the U.S.S.R. and five "people's democracies." Repression violated the constitutions of all the countries in which it was implemented, and it was the leaders of the Communist parties in these countries who were behind these unconstitutional actions. In Czechoslovakia, for instance, the "leading role of the Communist Party" did not become a part of the constitution until 1960, when Czechoslovakia became the second Communist country to adopt a socialist constitution. No legislation ever allowed the widespread use of torture during questioning and detention, and no law ever gave power to the secret police to resort to the massive fabrication of evidence. It is worth remembering in this context that the commentaries accompanying the first reassessments of Communist trials criticized the police for "placing themselves above the Party" but not for placing themselves "above the law." Clearly, the aim was to diminish or eliminate any responsibility by the political leaders for the functioning of the police system.

The specific nature of Communist dictatorship should also be borne in mind. This was not one state that covered one-sixth of the globe, but several states and an international movement. Communist dictatorships were intimately linked with one another and with their center, Moscow. Thanks to the opening of the archives we know that after 1944, repression in these countries was inspired and directed by a very powerful international Communist apparatus within the Communist International itself, which was integrated into the central Soviet apparatus. On 12 June 1943, after the dissolution of the Comintern announced on 9 June, the International Information Department of the Central Committee of the Soviet Communist Party (Cominform) was created, with Aleksandr Shcherbakov at its head, assisted by Georgi Dimitrov and Dmitry Manuilsky. This department gave constant instructions to foreign Communist parties. Dimitrov, who was the real chief from the very beginning, was officially instated as head in late December 1943 by a decision of the Soviet

Politburo. The department sent out its directives through the foreign offices of Communist Parties in the U.S.S.R. (only Yugoslavia and Albania had no such offices), by radio or mail, and later on by "consultations" in Moscow. Władysław Gomułka received such a directive from Dimitrov on 10 May 1945. He was reproached for using insufficiently severe measures in Poland, and told that "one can never have too many concentration camps." The concentration-camp system was thus already envisaged for political enemies at the end of the war.[30]

The spread of the Bolshevik experiment to states not integrated into the Soviet Union was not without risks. Nationalist sentiment persisted and was often expressed, despite attempts from Moscow to homogenize the different regimes in the Eastern bloc. After the events in Yugoslavia in 1948–49, in Hungary in 1953–1956, and in Poland in 1956, the diversification of Communist regimes became still more pronounced with the break between the Soviet Union and China in the 1960s and its repercussions in the European satellite states, particularly in Albania and Romania.

Finally, it should be noted that Communists who had formerly held power were able to confront their past as oppressors; and this is one of the major differences between Nazism and Communism. Nazism never had a Khrushchev, nor men like Imre Nagy, Alexander Dubček, or Mikhail Gorbachev. In the 1950s the rehabilitation of victims became a major factor in the power struggles to succeed the great leaders who had died, such as Stalin and Gottwald in 1953 or Bierut in Poland in 1956, or those who had been removed as General Secretary, like Rákosi in Hungary in 1956. Rehabilitation did not involve simply denouncing obvious injustices; it also implied searching out the culprits. The importance of rehabilitation in the struggles at the top of the parties lasted into the 1960s, particularly in Czechoslovakia. The phenomenon also touched many of the real believers in Communism, above all the intelligentsia, for whom the Communist ideal had a moral dimension and who felt betrayed by the revelation of the crimes of the regime. From 1953 to the 1960s, the history of repression is also a history of amnesties, even if they were often only partial.

So in 1955–56, the massive, grinding machine was still functioning, but it was becoming rusty. Officials in the secret police, the consummate actors in the repressions of 1949–1953, had been fired, and sometimes arrested and sentenced, however leniently. Political leaders were also obliged to resign, sometimes to be replaced by former prisoners, like Gomułka in Poland and Kádár in Hungary. On the whole, repressions seemed to be easing considerably.

But the founding period of many of the Communist regimes had left many open wounds. Mass terror did not completely disappear as a method of repression in the 1950s and 1960s. It surely can be said to have continued with the various Soviet military interventions in Eastern Europe. Driving a tank through the street was one highly effective means of sowing terror and panic in the population.

Soviet tanks intervened for the first time in East Germany on 17 June 1953 to crush spontaneous uprisings by workers in East Berlin and other cities, sparked by government measures that created difficult conditions in the workplace. According to the most recent studies, at least 51 people died in the riots and ensuing repression: 2 were crushed by tanks, 7 were sentenced to death by Soviet courts and 3 by German courts, 23 died of wounds received during the clashes, and 6 members of the security forces lost their lives. By 30 June, 6,171 people had been arrested, and another 7,000 were arrested subsequently.[31]

After the Twentieth Congress of the Soviet Communist Party, Soviet leaders ordered two more spectacular military interventions, in Hungary in 1956 and in Czechoslovakia in 1968. In both cases the use of force was intended to crush a popular antitotalitarian revolt.

In Hungary the Soviet army was already in place, and its units went into action twice: at 2:00 A.M. on 24 October in Budapest, before retreating on 30 October; and on the night of 3–4 November. The worst of this fighting ended on 6 November, with a few pockets of resistance in the suburbs holding out until 14 November, as did the insurgents in the Mecsek Mountains. Confrontations with the army continued in December, linked to demonstrations in the streets. In Salgótarján on 8 December, 131 people were killed in crossfire between Soviet and Hungarian units.

Thus for a few weeks violent death was part of everyday life for the Hungarians. Nearly 3,000 people died in the fighting, two-thirds of them in Budapest; and nearly 15,000 people were wounded. Thanks to the opening of the archives, historians have also been able to establish the number of victims on the side of the oppressors: between 23 October and 12 December, the secret police (the AVH), the Soviet and Hungarian armies, and the Hungarian Ministry of Internal Affairs recorded the loss of 350 lives; 37 people from the AVH, the police, and the army were executed without trial, some shot, some lynched. Thus, according to a number of historians, "the honor of the revolution was sullied."[32]

The repression that followed the crushing of the Hungarian revolution, in which the Soviet military police played an important role until early 1957, affected more than 100,000 people. Tens of thousands were interned in camps that were officially created on 12 December; 35,000 people were prosecuted and around 25,000 jailed. Several thousand Hungarians were deported to the U.S.S.R., 229 rebels were condemned to death and executed, and 200,000 people emigrated.

Repression followed the tried and tested pattern. Extraordinary courts were set up in the form of People's Tribunals and Special Chambers of Military

Courts. The trial of Imre Nagy took place in the People's Tribunal in Budapest. Nagy was a Communist of long standing who had emigrated to Moscow during the war. Removed from power in 1948, he became prime minister in 1953, and had been ousted again in 1955 before taking the lead role in the revolutionary government. The trial of Nagy and those accused with him ended in June 1958. Two of the defendants were absent. Géza Losonczy, a Communist journalist and former resistance fighter who had been imprisoned from 1951 to 1954, and had been a minister in the Nagy government, died in custody on 21 December 1957, almost certainly with the help of his questioners. József Szilagyi, another Communist of long standing, who had fought in the resistance and been imprisoned during the war, and had risen to become head of Nagy's cabinet in 1956, was condemned to death on 22 April 1958 and executed two days later. According to documents now available, Szilagyi resisted with tremendous courage, repeatedly telling his accusers that in comparison with the Communist prisons, the prisons of Miklós Horthy's interwar regime had been like mere hospitals.

The Imre Nagy trial opened on 9 June 1958; the verdict was reached on 15 June. The death sentence passed on three of the accused was carried out the following day. Besides Imre Nagy, the others who received death sentences were General Pál Maleter, who had been a resistance fighter during the war, a Communist since 1945, and minister of defense in the revolutionary government in 1956; and Miklós Gimes, a Communist journalist who had founded an underground newspaper after the failure of the revolution. Five others received sentences ranging from five years to life.

The Imre Nagy trial, one of the last great political trials in the Eastern bloc, confirmed that it was impossible for the Communist regime, propped up by Soviet military intervention, not to resort to this supreme form of repression. But the days of the big show-trials were over: Nagy's trial took place *in camera*, in a specially converted chamber of the police headquarters at the central prison in Budapest. In 1958 Nagy and his companions, who refused to recognize the legitimacy of Soviet intervention and the seizure of power by János Kádár, and who stood as symbols of the popular revolt, could not possibly remain alive.

New research underscores the cruelty of these repressions and refers to this period as one of terror; but it also reveals the ambivalent nature of the period and its differences from the years 1947–1953. In 1959, when the first trials of the rebels took place, a partial amnesty had already been declared. In 1960 the exceptional measures that had been decreed began to be phased out, and the internment camps were closed. In 1962 there was a purge of officers in the secret police who had fabricated evidence in the Rákosi period; Rajk and 190 other victims were also definitively rehabilitated. In 1963 a general amnesty was declared, but it did not apply to the rebels who had been condemned as "murderers." Violent repression came to an end. Nevertheless the rehabilitation of Imre Nagy and his followers did not occur until 1989, and even in 1988, police in Budapest beat up demonstrators who were commemorating the thirtieth anniversary of his death.

Two external factors influenced this evolution. The first was obviously the criticism of Stalin's reign inside the Soviet Union and the sidelining of various Stalinist leaders. The second was the thaw in international relations that accompanied the idea of peaceful coexistence between East and West. The effects of these changes were not felt in Hungary alone.

After the execution of the eleven accused in the Slánský trial in Czechoslovakia in December 1952, the bodies were cremated and the ashes simply scattered on the frozen roads and fields around Prague. Six years later, incineration no longer seemed the answer for Communist authorities. Alajos Dornbach, the civil-rights lawyer who demanded a reopening of the Nagy case in 1988, provided the following information about the successive disposals of the bodies.[33]

Once Imre Nagy and his companions were executed, they were first buried under a thick layer of concrete inside the prison on Kozma Street, where the trial had taken place. But burying bodies in a place unknown to the families became a source of anxiety. In the summer of 1961 they were exhumed and buried in extreme secrecy, at night, in the main communal cemetery in Budapest, near the place where Géza Losonczy and József Szilagyi, two others who had died as a result of the trial, had been laid to rest. The coffins were passed over the wall, and the cemetery employees knew nothing about the burial of these three corpses, who were given false names. For thirty years the families searched in vain for the burial place. On the basis of fragmentary information they began to erect gravestones in Lot 301 in the communal cemetery; but the police threatened them when they came to visit and knocked down the stones on several occasions, trampling them with horses.

In March 1989 the bodies were finally exhumed again. An autopsy performed on Géza Losonczy revealed several broken ribs, some of which had preceded death by three to six months, and some of which were much more recent. The government then ordered a few young officers to conduct an inquiry into the location of the graves. Sándor Rajnai, who had been in charge of the Nagy trial and was the Hungarian ambassador to Moscow in 1988–89, was among those who refused to help this commission.

Twelve years after the events in Hungary, Soviet tanks rolled into Czechoslovakia to spread mass terror there. The military intervention of 1968 was quite different from that of 1956, although the aim was identical: to crush a popular revolt against "Soviet socialism." The passage of time had brought a new international situation and a specific moment in world Communism. Most of the assault troops came from the Soviet Union, but four other Warsaw Pact countries also participated: Bulgaria, Hungary, Poland, and East Germany all sent troops. There was another fundamental difference: Soviet troops were not already stationed in Czechoslovakia as they had been in Hungary in 1956, when Hungary was basically an occupied country. In Czechoslovakia, the Soviet Union feared a massive armed resistance movement leading to a localized or even a European war.

For this reason, a huge number of troops were deployed. The operation began during the night of 20–21 August, under the code name "Danube." It had been minutely prepared since 8 April, when Marshal Andrei Grechko, the Soviet minister of defense, had signed Order GOU/1/87654, mobilizing Soviet troops in East Germany, Poland, and Hungary. Most of these were tank regiments, and tanks now became the symbol of oppression, as they did in Tiananmen Square in Beijing in 1989. More than 165,000 men and 4,600 tanks were sent in the first wave; five days later Czechoslovakia was occupied by twenty-seven divisions, with 6,300 tanks, 800 aircraft, 2,000 artillery pieces, and approximately 400,000 soldiers. To appreciate the scale of the terror here, it should be borne in mind that in 1940 Hitler invaded France with approximately 2,500 tanks and that in 1941 the Germans used 3,580 tanks in the attack on the Soviet Union. At the time, Czechoslovakia had a population of approximately 14.3 million, a small fraction of the population of France in 1940.

But no war occurred, and resistance to the invasion was quite peaceful. The invaders killed 90 people, mostly in Prague; around 300 Czechs and Slovaks were seriously injured; and another 500 sustained minor injuries. The number of victims among the invading forces (as a result of incompetent handling of weapons, execution of deserters, or the usual road accidents) is not yet known. All we know with certainty is that one Bulgarian was shot by Czechoslovak civilians. The Soviet authorities arrested and deported several Czechoslovak leaders, but within a few days the Soviet Politburo had to set them free and open negotiations with them. The political scenario that had been envisaged after the intervention was a failure, insofar as the occupying forces failed to set up a collaborationist "workers' and peasants' government" as they had planned.

Repression linked to this military intervention did not stop in 1968. Several people acquired—and retain—the status of symbolic victims by becoming "human torches," setting themselves on fire in public to protest the occupation. The first to choose this fate was Jan Palach, a twenty-year-old student who set himself alight at 2:30 P.M. on 16 January 1969 in the center of Prague; his death three days later was followed by huge demonstrations. In February Jan Zajíc, another student, followed suit. A third human torch, a forty-year-old Communist called Evžen Plocek, sacrificed himself in early April in Jihlava, in Moravia.

Repression reverted to an old pattern in Czechoslovakia, carried out for the most part by internal security forces, the army, and the regular police force. The pressure exerted by the Soviet occupying army was immense. More fuel was added to the fire by spontaneous demonstrations by more than half a million people during the night of 28–29 March 1969. Czechs and Slovaks went out onto the streets in sixty-nine cities to cheer the victory of their national ice-hockey team over the Soviet Union in the world championships; and twenty-one of the thirty-six Soviet garrisons came under attack. Alexander Dubček, who was still the secretary general of the Czechoslovak Communist Party (until 17 April), was told that if the situation failed to improve, he risked meeting the same fate as Imre Nagy.

The repressive potential of the "normalized" Czechoslovak forces—the special units in the army and police, and the People's Militia at factories—was put to the test on the first anniversary of the invasion, but these forces had been carefully prepared. There were numerous confrontations with the demonstrators, most of whom were quite young. The fighting was intense, especially in Prague, where two young men died on 20 August. Tanks and armored cars were seen on the streets of all the main cities. Military historians consider this episode the biggest combat operation by the Czechoslovak army in the postwar period. Three more demonstrators lost their lives on 21 August, and dozens more were seriously wounded. Thousands of people were arrested and beaten by the police. By the end of 1969, 1,526 demonstrators had been sentenced under a decree from the Presidium of the Federal Assembly, which had the force of law and had been signed by the chairman of that legislative body, President Dubček himself.[34]

In 1969 a few more people who had been involved in the 1968 revolt were imprisoned, including a group from the Revolutionary Youth Movement (Hnutí revolučního mládeže), which had been active in preparing the demonstrations to mark the anniversary of the events of 1968, and which had been infiltrated by the secret police. Despite strong pressure from hard-liners, the government did not give an automatic green light to the trials of the reform-minded Communist leaders of 1968. Analysts have often pointed out that the new leadership was perhaps rather wary of the process, fearing it would backfire. Gustáv Husák, the new first secretary of the Czechoslovak Communist Party, chosen as Dubček's replacement by the Soviet leadership, knew the pattern all too well. He himself had been sentenced to life imprisonment back in 1954 in a trial of "Slovak bourgeois nationalists," and had spent nine years behind bars. Nonetheless, mass repressions were approved by Moscow and carried out in a cruel and insidious fashion, as part of a subtle strategy to inspire fear. Hundreds of thousands of people could no longer take part in public life and were forbidden to work in their professions, and their children were prevented from entering secondary or higher education, effectively being held hostage. When "normalization" began, the regime lashed out at the elements in society that had begun to regroup in 1968, and roughly seventy organizations were banned or forcibly merged with other governmental organizations. Censorship was also rigorously enforced. Tens of thousands of Czechs and Slovaks joined those who had gone into exile after February 1948. During the forty years of Communist rule, around 400,000 people, most of whom were well-qualified and highly trained, chose exile from their homeland. After 1969, many of them were sentenced in absentia.

Political trials reappeared after the crushing of the Prague Spring. The trial of the sixteen members of the HRM took place in March 1971; the leader, Petr Uhl, received a four-year sentence. Nine other trials followed in the summer of 1972. Most of the accused were "second-rank" protagonists in 1968, charged with illegal activity following the occupation. Of the 46 accused, two-thirds of whom were ex-Communists, thirty-two received prison sentences totaling ninety-six years; and sixteen others; after being detained for several months, received suspended sentences of twenty-one years. The longest sentence imposed was one for five and a half years in prison, which was mild in comparison to the atrocities of the founding years of the regime. Some of those sentenced in this particular wave of repression—Petr Uhl, Jaroslav Sabata, Rudolf Battek—were imprisoned again when their sentences expired and spent nine years behind bars in the 1970s and 1980s. At that time, Czechoslovakia had one of the worst records for political persecution in Europe.

The great revolts of 1956 and 1968 and their crushing by the Soviet Union reveal another important aspect of the logic of repression: events in one country had repercussions elsewhere, particularly when military engagement was involved. As a result of the Hungarian revolution in 1956, the post-Stalinist leadership of the Czechoslovak Communist Party was prepared to send units from the Czechoslovak army into Hungary. At the same time, it stepped up domestic repression, sent a number of political prisoners who had recently been freed back to prison, and prosecuted the Czechs and Slovaks who were in sympathy with the Hungarian revolt. Of the 1,163 who were taken into custody, mostly for verbal expressions of solidarity, 53.5 percent were workers. Sentences, however, were rarely for more than a year in prison. Repression at that time was much more severe in Albania, where on 25 November 1956 the Hoxha regime announced the sentencing and execution of three "Titoist" leaders: Liri Gega, a member of the Central Committee of the Albanian Communist Party (who was pregnant at the time); General Dale Ndreu; and Petro Buli. In Romania, Gheorghiu-Dej, who was beginning to play the Chinese card in his relations with the U.S.S.R., provided clemency to persecuted nationalists even as he instigated a large trial of high-ranking industrialists involved in international trade, many of whom were Jewish Communists.

In 1968 many of the Communist regimes, including the U.S.S.R., feared contagion from the ideas of the Prague Spring and stepped up their repression both before and after the military intervention in Czechoslovakia. The fate of Alfredo Foscolo is a good indicator of the spirit of the times. Born of a Bulgarian mother and a French father who had taught in Bulgaria until 1949, Foscolo often spent his holidays in Bulgaria. In 1966, while studying law and Oriental languages in Paris, he typed 500 copies of a tract in France and brought them to his friends in Sofia. The tract demanded free elections, freedom of the press, and freedom of movement, autonomy for workers, the abolition of the Warsaw Pact, and the rehabilitation of the victims of repression. That same year he had a daughter with Raïna Aracheva, a Bulgarian. Frédy and Raïna then asked for official authorization to marry, which was slow in coming. Then came the events of 1968. Alfredo Foscolo described what followed:

> In early 1968 I was drafted for military service. In July the Bulgarian embassy informed me that I would receive authorization to get married if I went to Sofia. I had a fourteen-day furlough, and I rushed down there. But when I got there I met with another refusal. This was August 1968, and on 21 August the Soviets marched into Prague; a week later, still empty-handed, I got onto the Orient Express to return to Paris. But it took me several years to get home. I was arrested at the border by agents from the Durzhavna Sigurnost. I effectively disappeared for two weeks while I was kept in the State Security headquarters. During that time Captain [A.] Nedkov told me that I had a simple choice: either I admitted that I was an imperialist agent, or no one would ever hear of me again. I accepted, in the hope that the truth might come out in a trial.
>
> The trial began on 6 January 1969. Two friends, as well as Raïna, were beside me in the witness box. When the prosecutor demanded the death sentence for me, my lawyer answered that it was in fact what I deserved, but that he was pleading for clemency all the same. The whole trial was a farce, played out purely for the purposes of propaganda. I was sentenced to twenty-seven years in prison, including fifteen years of solitary confinement for espionage. My friends got ten and twelve years, and Raïna, who hadn't known anything about the tracts, got one year. Another friend, who was a political refugee in Paris, was sentenced to death in absentia.
>
> After a month on death row in the central prison in Sofia (7th division), I was transferred to the prison in Stara Zagora, where most of the 200 to 300 political prisoners in Bulgaria were kept. I learned a lot there about the prison history of Bulgaria over the first twenty-five years

of Communism, and quickly saw that what I had been through was nothing in comparison to what thousands of Bulgarians had lived through. I also witnessed a revolt on 8 October 1969, which led to the deaths of a number of prisoners. At the same time, a new request for authorization to marry, made during our detention, was rejected.

Quite unexpectedly, I was freed on 30 April 1971 and sent back to France. Our arrest in 1968 and the big trial that followed against the backdrop of the Czechoslovak affair had all clearly been intended to implicate "imperialist forces" in the freedom movement in the Eastern bloc. But by 1971, with negotiations over the Helsinki agreement under way, the world had changed again, and my presence in Bulgarian jails was no longer desirable. Unfortunately, my two Bulgarian friends did not benefit from that new clemency.

When I got back to Paris, I tried a variety of schemes to enable Raïna and my daughter to join me there. Finally, on 31 December 1973, I went to Sofia in secret, under a false name, with two other false passports. Thanks to those documents and a lot of luck, we managed to slip across the Bulgarian-Turkish border on the night of 1–2 January 1974. Two days later we were in Paris.[35]

In the period 1955–1989 repression followed a fairly predictable pattern: a powerful police presence constantly harassed the opposition, whether opposition took the form of spontaneous social movements such as strikes or street protests, or was deliberately structured, with well-formulated demands and a well-organized network. In the second half of the 1970s the apparatus of repression developed an ever-larger network of informers to infiltrate and destroy opposition movements that had benefited from the 1975 Helsinki agreement. That this form of control was needed in ever-increasing amounts was undoubtedly a sign of the decline of the system. In Czechoslovakia, for instance, in 1954–1958 there had been roughly 132,000 officially recruited secret informers. By the end of the 1980s the number had risen to 200,000.

The logic of repression in the post-terror period was also marked by specific national characteristics and by the trajectory of internal power struggles in the countries concerned. Regimes acted differently depending on their confidence in their legitimacy or the success or failure of political and economic projects. On 13 August 1961, at the initiative of the SED leadership and with approval from the Soviet leadership, the Berlin Wall was erected, a clear sign that the East German regime was panicking about its own future.

In Romania, the Communist leadership had clearly expressed its independence by refusing to participate in the military intervention in Czechoslovakia. Nonetheless this brand of "national Communism" revealed itself to be the most repressive (with the possible exception of Albania), particularly in the

1980s. Repression was inherent in the Communist system, even without guidance from Moscow.

In the late 1970s Nicolae Ceauşescu, who styled himself "the Great Leader" (Conducător) in the manner of Hitler, Mussolini, and Stalin, was facing a tremendous economic and social crisis in Romania, and a large protest movement began to emerge. The movement was inspired by the struggles for democratic rights occurring in other countries, but in Romania the movement was strengthened by the participation of workers. The great strike of 35,000 miners in the Jiu valley in August 1977; the demonstrations and strikes of the summer of 1980 in which factories were occupied in Bucharest, Galaţi, Tîrgovişte, and the mining regions; the uprising in the Motru valley in the autumn of 1981; and other manifestations of discontent all provoked severe and massive repression: arrests, forced evacuations, house arrests, beatings, summary firings from jobs, incarceration in psychiatric hospitals, trials, and assassinations. Repression won in the short term, but opposition inevitably resurfaced. Demonstrations and strikes broke out again in 1987 and culminated in 1988 in a popular uprising in Braşov, Romania's second-largest city. Confrontations with the forces of law and order were extremely violent and bloody, resulting in deaths and hundreds of arrests.

The suffering of some of Romania's political prisoners seemed eternal. One example was the case of Gheorghiu Calciu Dumitreasa, known as Father Calciu. Born in 1927, he was arrested while a medical student and was imprisoned in Piteşti (see above). His captivity lasted until 1964. When he came out of prison, he decided to become a priest. He became involved with the founders of the Free Union of Romanian Workers (SLOMR). Arrested again, he was sentenced *in camera* on 10 May 1979 to ten years for "passing on information and endangering state security." In prison he went on five separate hunger strikes. Another example was Ion Puiu, a leader of the National Peasant Party who received a twenty-year sentence in 1947 and was released in 1964. In 1987 he was again imprisoned for his involvement in opposition movements.

In 1987 a French journal listed some cases of current Romanian political prisoners:[36]

· Francise Barabas, a forty-year-old mechanic in a textile factory, had been sentenced to six years in prison. A Hungarian from Transylvania, with his brother and fiancée he had distributed some tracts in Hungarian that read "Down with the shoemaker [Ceauşescu's first trade]! Down with the murderer!"
· Ion Bugan, an electrician born in 1936, had been sentenced to ten years for driving around Bucharest in March 1983 with a sticker on his car that read: "Executioners, we don't want you any more."

· Ion Guseila, an engineer, had been sentenced to four years in prison in late 1985 for distributing tracts that demanded a new head of state.
· Gheorghiu Nastasescu, a fifty-six-year-old construction worker, had been sentenced to nine years for spreading antigovernment propaganda. He had already spent four years in prison for antisocialist propaganda. In the autumn of 1983 he had dropped fliers off some scaffolding in Bucharest urging people to show their discontent.
· Victor Totu, Gheorghiu Pavel, and Florin Vlascianu, all workers born in 1955, had been sentenced to seven or eight years. On 22 August 1983, on the eve of the national holiday, they had been caught writing anti-Ceaușescu graffiti comparing his regime to that of the Nazis.
· Dimitru Iuga had been forty when he was sentenced to ten years in 1983. He had held several meetings trying to organize young people to demonstrate against Ceaușescu. They were determined to act peacefully. Seven of them were sentenced to five years, and were freed—although Iuga was not—in an amnesty in 1984.
· Nicolae Litoiu at age twenty-seven had been sentenced in 1981 to fifteen years for "plotting against state security." In the summer of 1981 he had thrown a firecracker onto one of the Party's stands at Ploiești, and had also dropped fliers from the top of the Omnia store in Ploiești. His brother-in-law had been sentenced to eight years for having known in advance of these events and not having acted.
· Attila Kun, a doctor, had been sentenced to three years in January 1987 for refusing to deliver a death certificate for a political prisoner who had died under torture.
· I. Borbely, a fifty-year-old philosophy professor, had been sentenced to eight years in 1982 for publishing an underground newspaper in Hungarian.

Variations in the degree of repression were always linked to changes in the international political situation, to relations between Eastern and Western Europe, and to changes in Soviet policy. From Brezhnev to Gorbachev the world changed dramatically, as did the ideology of repression. After the 1960s people were very rarely persecuted as "Titoists" or "Zionists." In most countries the focus shifted to "ideological subversion" or "illegal relations with foreign countries," particularly, of course, with the West.

"Milder" repressions then became more common in several countries. Involuntary exile, especially in East Germany and Czechoslovakia, and "psychiatric treatment" on the Soviet model often replaced imprisonment. As violence within the regimes drew wider comment in the West, some victims began telling their stories to mass-circulation newspapers. Increased media coverage forced many regimes, even the Romanians, to reflect more on their actions.

But if the suffering was less intense, the repressions were no less real. The slave-labor camps disappeared, except in Albania and Bulgaria (where they were used in the 1980s as internment camps for Turks). But political trials continued, marking out the evolution of all these countries except Hungary. As before 1956, trials were aimed chiefly at people who wished to improve civil society, at opposition figures who were to be liquidated, at independent unions, and at those who had helped the churches to survive in the shadows. Communist leaders were also placed on trial. Examples include Paul Merker in East Germany, who was sentenced to eight years' imprisonment in March 1955 and freed the following year; Rudolf Barak, the Czechoslovak minister of interior, who received a six-year sentence in April 1962; and Milovan Djilas, a vocal Yugoslav dissident who was first imprisoned in 1956–1961 and again in 1962–1966. When Albania broke with the U.S.S.R. and aligned itself with China, pro-Soviet officials, such as Liri Beleshova, a member of the Politburo, and Koço Tashko, the president of the Control Commission of the Albanian Communist Party, were punished severely. Similarly, Rear Admiral Temo Sejko was executed in May 1961 along with several other officers. In 1975, after Albania had broken with China, Enver Hoxha liquidated Beqir Balluku, the minister of defense, and Petrit Dume, the chief of staff.

In the many political trials of the period, death sentences were rare, except for genuine cases of espionage, and were rarely carried out. This was true for the Bulgarian Dimitar Penchev, who in 1961 was sentenced to death, together with an accomplice, for attempting to resurrect the Agrarian Union Party of Nikolai Petkov. His sentence was commuted to twenty years, and he was freed in the autumn of 1964 as part of a general amnesty. He was then forced to work as a laborer, but he had not seen the last of prison. He was jailed again from 1967 to 1974 for illegally attempting to cross the border, an escapade that led to the death of one of his friends. In 1985, suspected of terrorist offenses, Penchev spent two months in the prison camp on Belene Island, before ending up under house arrest in a small mining village called Bobov Dol.

The number of deaths and victims of repression was clearly lower in the period of post-terror than it was in the period up to 1956. Apart from those mentioned above who were killed in Hungary in 1956 and in 1968–69 in Czechoslovakia, only a few hundred died. Many of them, about two hundred in all, were shot trying to cross the border between East Germany and the Berlin Wall. One of the last political prisoners during this period, the Czechoslovak dissident Pavel Wonka, died in prison from insufficient medical attention on 26 April 1988.

Calculations of the victims are piecemeal and difficult to make. Among the deaths one must include assassinations by the secret police that were sometimes passed off as car accidents, as was the case for two Romanian engineers who led a strike in the Jiu valley in 1977 and who were killed a few weeks after the strike had been broken.

Future research on the period after 1956 will perhaps result in a typology of victims and a profile of the typical prisoner. We know that many of the victims of this period were not always in prison, as was the case for those killed during military intervention or while desperately trying to cross a border. It would also be wrong to concentrate too specifically on high-profile victims such as the Czech playwright Václav Havel, the Hungarian philosopher István Bibo, the Romanian writer Paul Goma, or other members of the intelligentsia, while overlooking tens of millions of ordinary people in the countries concerned. Indeed, cynics might suggest that in fact no one of the stature of Babel or Mandelstam was executed between 1956 and 1989. There was, of course, the assassination of the Bulgarian writer Georgi Markov in London in September 1978, executed with the poison-tipped umbrella of a Bulgarian secret agent. There may have been other young victims, whose talent was never allowed to flourish. But everywhere, particularly in Romania, most of the victims who were imprisoned and killed were simply the people in the streets; and history should never forget the names of ordinary people.

It is well known that Communist dictatorships feared artists and creative people, and anyone who could express himself with originality. In early 1977 the Communist leaders in Czechoslovakia panicked when they were faced with 260 signatures on the opposition manifesto known as Charter 77. But Communist regimes were considerably more frightened when tens of thousands of people took to the streets.

By the end of the 1980s, people were suddenly no longer afraid of mass terror. And thus there finally came a general assault on all government power.

The Complex Management of the Past

Is it possible to forget, or to make people forget, the suffering brought on by a system and its jackbooted agents, when the suffering lasted for decades? Can one be generous and indulgent toward those who have been defeated, when they are executioners or torturers? When one wishes to set up democracy and the rule of law, what can be done with previous leaders and their assistants, particularly when they were so numerous and the state apparatus was so vast?

The new democracies in Central and Southeastern Europe have sought answers to these questions. The cleansing of the Communist apparatus was the order of the day, even if this meant dredging up extremely unpleasant memories. Not surprisingly, the new leaders, who include many former Communists, are divided in their views about how extensive this cleansing should be and the methods it should involve. There have been calls for radical measures—for the banning of Communist parties as criminal organizations, and for trials of all former leaders who are still alive. On the other hand, there is an overwhelming desire to avoid a purge reminiscent of old Communist practices. For the Polish prime minister Tadeusz Mazowiecki or for the president of the Czech and Slovak republics, Václav Havel, denouncing the crimes of the previous regime and removing its agents from positions of authority could not mean a return to the methods of the previous regime. These anti-Communist democrats did not want to govern in an atmosphere of fear. György Dalos, a Hungarian writer and a longtime opponent of the authoritarian regime, wrote in 1990 that "purification and cleansing, even if one hides behind terms like 'spring cleaning,' can still create a deep-seated feeling of insecurity among those who worked under the old regime, whom we still need very much . . . It would be very serious if fear gave rise to a new 'loyalty,' which frankly would have very little to do with the idea of democracy itself."[37]

In the first days after freedom had been restored, victims of the Communist regimes, concretely identified, living or dead, silent or vocal, were at the center of investigations of responsibility. Victims of all different types were in the spotlight, from people who had been unjustly executed or imprisoned to people whose livelihoods had been taken away, to people who had been humiliated on a daily basis by their submission to the lies of the Party. Post-Communist society had to face up to what Václav Havel termed this "monstrous heritage," and to face as well the grave issues of crime and punishment. In seeing the victim as the main witness to suffering, societies necessarily appealed to their new political officials, to provide a framework that would either exploit or calm the resentment produced by this suffering. There were some who exploited the situation for personal gain, and those who wanted to prevent the rise of blind vengeance, those who simply watched, and those who were conscious of human frailty and sought the true causes of the evil, while proposing democratic measures. A "silent majority" had existed in all the Communist regimes; and ironically, those who had remained most passive, becoming semi-collaborators, ended up calling most loudly for brutal revenge on the oppressors.

It is hardly surprising that after so many years of amputated memories, the interpretation of the recent past was so impassioned. Naturally, there was an explosion in publishing after the abolition of censorship, as a multiplicity of viewpoints began to emerge. The journalistic, highly media-focused approach, with its constant hunt for sensationalism, led to oversimplification, a black-and-white view in which history was reduced to victims versus executioners, until suddenly it seemed possible to believe that a whole nation had been resistance fighters against a regime imposed from abroad. In the process, words lost their finer meanings. The term "genocide" was bandied about: the Communists had perpetrated genocide on the Romanians, the Czechs, and others; the Czechs had tried to launch genocide against the Slovaks. In Romania, people began talking about a "Red holocaust"; and in Bulgaria the formula "innumerable Auschwitzes lacking only crematoria" became the standard way of referring to the gulags.

These approaches to the recent past have already been the object of dispassionate studies, which demonstrate clearly how strongly the effects of World War II persist in post-Communist societies. The extreme case is that of the former Yugoslavia, where the recent war was, in part, an extension of the conflicts generated fifty years before, and where memories were flagrantly manipulated to fuel the conflict. The shadows of the war have not dissipated, particularly among the former allies of Nazi Germany. If Marshal Pétain had been Romanian or Slovak, many would have claimed him as a victim of Communism, as was the case with the Romanian dictator Antonescu and the Slovak president Monsignor Jozef Tiso, both of whom were sentenced to death and executed after the war for the atrocities committed within their countries.

The history of Communist regimes is now extremely politicized, especially when parties and movements seek to rediscover their ancestors and traditions. The Pole Andrzej Paczkowski, one of the authors of this book, speaks unhesitatingly about a "civil war" in Poland over the search for origins, although happily this war is merely one of words. The past is manipulated and used as a tool as ancient myths and legends are reborn and new ones appear. The myth of the number of victims is one that commands special attention. According to the French historian Robert Frank, the figure becomes a key symbol, a mathematical truth; it lends authority to discourses about death, and it transforms mass deaths into a kind of sacrament. Hence the special need for prudence among those researching new national or social mythologies.

The Hungarian György Litván, director of the Institute for the History of the Hungarian Revolution of 1956, has suggested that a politically aware interpretation of extreme points in history facilitates in-depth analysis of the political evolution of a country. He claims that a country's relation to the recent past can tell us much more about the democratic roots of certain types of discourse than it can about economic problems or other changes that might be under way at the time.

All memories are "created" to some extent, and the official version of events is no exception. Panels of legislators and decisionmakers select the traditions that will underlie new constitutions, choose the figures whose heads will appear on stamps and banknotes, determine the national holidays to be celebrated, the medals to be handed out, the events to be commemorated, and the names to be given to streets, squares, and public places—and, of course, draw up the curriculum to be taught in schools. The heroes and victims of the Communist period cannot be forgotten. Nevertheless, many post-Communist regimes have decided to put the Communist period in their history in brackets. This is hardly new in the twentieth century, as the Italian historian Maria Ferretti, who specializes in Russian memory, has pointed out: Benedetto Croce proposed a similar approach in order to bury the ghost of Italian fascism.[38] Bracketing, however, is always an illusion, and whole decades cannot simply be buried and forgotten. These decades have molded the outlook of the vast majority of the citizens in each country, and they have also determined the course of social and economic development. Dispassionate analyses attempt to propose explanations of behavior, including the absence (or inadequacy) of historical self-criticism among individuals, groups, and whole peoples; the desire to avoid any reflection about collective responsibility (in the form of tacit support for the regime); or the presence of a "martyred people" mentality that excuses an entire nation for everything. (Alexandra Laignel-Lavastine has studied the idea of "collective martyrology" in Romania, which is accompanied by an "innocence complex" that causes everything to be seen as someone else's fault.)

Control over the past in post-Communist states is a topic sufficiently complex to merit a book-length study in its own right. Most notable at this point are the differences among the countries concerned. In Romania in particular, men from the old Communist regime kept power until the legislative and presidential elections of November 1996, and a similar situation existed for some time in Bulgaria as well. But even in those two countries, considerable documentation about repression under the Communists is now available. Yet although citizens in all the countries have in their own possession considerable documentation pertaining to the years of Communist rule, and although victim testimonies are now commonplace, in-depth histories based on a close scrutiny of archival sources are still lacking, except perhaps in the Czech Republic, Poland, and Hungary.

It should also be pointed out that no Communist Party has yet been banned. These parties have changed their names except in the Czech Republic, where a referendum inside the Party resulted in a decision to keep the name unchanged. Almost everywhere, the most compromised leaders have been thrown out and the leadership entirely replaced.

Few trials of people responsible for the repressions have taken place. The most spectacular one occurred in Romania, where a pseudotrial ended in the execution of Nicolae Ceauşescu and his wife on 25 December 1989, after which the dictator's body was shown on national television. In Bulgaria, Todor

Zhivkov, the former general secretary of the Party, was tried in April 1991 but allowed to go free. Paradoxically he most visibly failed to live up to one of the mottoes of the Bulgarian Party elite: "We took power with bloodshed, we won't give it up without bloodshed." In Albania, some of the Communist leaders were sentenced for "abuse of public goods and infringing the equality of citizens"; one such person was the wife of Enver Hoxha, who received an eleven-year prison sentence. In Czechoslovakia, Miroslav Štěpán, a member of the Party Presidium and first secretary of the Prague municipal Party committee, was sentenced to two years in prison in 1991 for violence carried out against a crowd of demonstrators on 17 November 1989. Several trials have been brought against the former leaders of East Germany. The most recent was the trial of the last Communist leader, Egon Krenz, in August 1997. He was sentenced to six and a half years in prison and freed pending an appeal. As of 1999 charges were still being pressed against General Wojciech Jaruzelski for the deaths of strikers in Gdańsk in December 1970, when as defense minister he relayed the orders to open fire. (Jaruzelski was granted a pardon by the Polish parliament in 1996 on separate charges brought against him for his role in imposing martial law in December 1981.) Similarly, an effort is still under way in Prague to try a few of the Czechoslovak Communist leaders who "invited" in the occupying forces in 1968.

Post-Communist justice has also involved several trials of officials from the various security services directly implicated in crimes. One of the most interesting was the trial in Poland of Adam Humer and eleven other officers from the UB (Urząd Bezpieczeństwa, the Security Bureau) for crimes committed during the repression of the opposition in the late 1940s and early 1950s. Humer was a colonel at the time, and the deputy head of the Investigations Department of the Ministry of Public Security until 1954. These crimes are generally described as crimes against humanity. At the end of the trial, which lasted two and a half years, Humer was sentenced on 8 March 1996 to nine years' imprisonment. In Hungary, those who shot at civilians on 8 December 1956 in Salgótarján, an industrial town northeast of Budapest, were convicted in January 1995 of crimes against humanity. But the verdict reached in January 1997 by the Hungarian Supreme Court decreed that after 4 November 1956, because of the illegal intervention of Soviet forces, a state of war existed between Hungary and the U.S.S.R., and therefore these crimes had to be considered war crimes instead.

Of all the countries of the former Soviet bloc, the Czech Republic has developed perhaps the most original approach to the management of the country's Communist past. It is the only country to have adopted laws mandating the return of goods confiscated by the authorities after 25 February 1948, and decreeing the mass rehabilitation of all those unjustly convicted. In 1994, for example, regional and district courts rehabilitated approximately 220,000 people. Until 1998, when Poland adopted a law requiring the screening of all judicial and police officials, the Czech Republic was alone in having passed a law on "lustration," limiting access to public office. The law requires verification of and open access to any senior official's past as it appears in the police records of the old regime. It is also the only country that has a special administrative body, the Bureau for Documentation and Inquiry into the Crimes of Communism, to pursue members of the old regime. As an integral part of the Investigations Bureau of the Police of the Czech Republic, this body has full powers to gather information and file charges for any Communist crime committed from 1948 to 1989. The Bureau for Documentation has a staff of about 90. It intervenes with legal opinions in judicial procedures; it has to make the case for each crime, assemble the necessary evidence, and then submit the case to the department for public prosecutions. Of the 98 people investigated in 1997, 20 cases were deemed valid, 5 were actually taken to court, and a single person—a former investigator in the State Security organs—was sentenced to five years in prison. All cases are to be concluded by 29 December 1999.

The current director of the Bureau of Documentation, Václav Benda, a mathematician by training and an important figure in the opposition during the 1970s and 1980s, himself spent four years in prison. Today he is a Christian Democratic senator, and in a recent interview he made clear his position regarding Communist crimes and crimes against humanity:

> The waiver of the statute of limitations for crimes against humanity does exist in our legislation, but we are not sure what Communist crimes it can be applied to. We can't automatically define all the crimes of Communism as crimes against humanity. Besides, our international position on the elimination of the statute of limitations was taken by Czechoslovakia in 1974, and legal opinions differ as to whether we can consider that crimes committed before that date fall within the remit of the waiver of the statute of limitations.[39]

Pavel Rychetský, who was deputy prime minister of the federal government in 1991 and 1992, is now a Social Democratic senator and chairman of the Legislative Commission of the Czech Senate. In June 1997 he told us:

> In the Czech Republic, everyone believes that we do need trials, not simply to punish the old men, but to bring everything that happened out into the open, as a sort of catharsis. In fact most of the information is out in the open already, and it's hard to believe we will find out anything that is worse than the things we already know. Genocide, as a crime against humanity, is of course without a statute of limitations. But none of the Communist crimes in Czechoslovakia fell under that category,

and we will never be able to prove that any actions corresponding to a really close definition of genocide were ever carried out. By contrast, in the Soviet Union there were certainly crimes of genocide committed against ethnic groups or specific segments of the population, such as the Cossacks and the Chechens. But those crimes can't really be punished either, because they were not explicitly against any law that was in force at that time.

These examples, of which many more could be found, lead inexorably to the conclusion that numerous crimes have gone unpunished, because of the statute of limitations, lack of witnesses, or lack of proof. After the fall of Communism, justice has once again become independent of executive power, and it has ensured that the principles of so-called civilized countries are respected, including both the principle of the statute of limitations and the idea that no law can have retroactive effects. However, some countries have amended their legislation to allow the prosecution of certain crimes. In Poland, the law of 4 April 1991 replaced the law of April 1984 on the Principal Commission for Research into the Crimes of Hitler and the Institute for National Memory. The new law places Communism in the same category as fascism and introduces the concept of Stalinist crimes, which it defines as "any attacks on individuals or groups of people committed by the Communist authorities or inspired or tolerated by them during the period preceding 31 December 1956."[40] Such crimes are not subject to a statute of limitations. In 1995, the articles in the penal code regarding the statute of limitations were modified, allowing the most serious crimes committed against civil liberties before 31 December 1989 to be prosecuted within a thirty-year period starting on 1 January 1990. In the Czech Republic, the law regarding the "illegitimacy of the Communist regime and resistance to it," adopted in 1993, extended the statute of limitations for crimes committed between 1948 and 1989 that could be described as "political."

Dealing with the past is an extremely complex business. But I would like to finish this section on a personal note. In my opinion, the punishment of the guilty was not carried out promptly enough or in an appropriate manner. Despite the efforts of many, myself included, Czechoslovakia, for instance, has failed to introduce any new categories of crime such as "national indignity," which could be punishable by "national degradation" and the removal of rights, as was done in France in the aftermath of World War II. On the other hand, the Germans' opening of the Stasi archives to any interested citizen seems a brave and good decision. It increases a sense of responsibility, inviting everyone to take charge of his or her own "trial": your husband was an informer, and now you know . . . what are you going to do?

Whatever happens, the wounds will take some time to heal.

IV

Communism in Asia: Between Reeducation and Massacre

Jean-Louis Margolin and Pierre Rigoulot

Introduction

Two features distinguish Communism in Asia from Communism in Europe. First, with the exception of North Korea, most of the regimes established themselves through their own efforts and built independent political systems with a strongly nationalist character. (Laos is a partial exception in this regard, because of its dependence on Vietnam.)

Second, at the time this book was written all these regimes were still in power, even to a certain extent in Cambodia. Therefore, the only essential archives then open were those dealing with the Pol Pot period in Cambodia (the Comintern archives in Moscow do not cover any of the regimes still in place.)[1] Even so, our knowledge of these regimes and their past has increased considerably. It is now relatively easy to do field research in China, Vietnam, Laos, and Cambodia, and some interesting sources are now available there: official media (including translations of Chinese radio transmissions available from various Western sources), the regional press, memoirs by former leaders of the regimes, written testimonies of refugees who fled abroad, and oral records gathered inside the countries. For internal political reasons, Cambodians are now encouraged to decry the Pol Pot period, and the Chinese to denounce the horrors of the Cultural Revolution. However, this selective opening of materials has had some bizarre effects. For example, we still have no access to any debates that may have taken place among Party leaders; we still have no idea how or why Chairman Mao's designated successor, Marshal Lin Biao, died in 1971; and Mao's intentions during the Cultural Revolution remain quite mysterious. Little is known about the purges of the 1950s in China and in Vietnam, and perhaps even less about the Great Leap Forward. Almost nothing is known about events in the vast death camps located in western China. As a rule, more is known about the fate of Communist cadres and intellectuals who suffered in the repressions than about the fate of normal citizens, who account for the great majority of the victims. North Korea, one of the last bastions of hard-line Communism, is still solidly closed to the outside world, and until very recently almost no one ever managed to leave the country.

For all these reasons, the account that follows is inevitably somewhat approximate, and some of the figures are rather speculative. But the ends and means of Communism in the Far East are very much evident.

Main units of the *laogai* penal network (based on a map in Jean-Luc Domenach, *Chine: L'archipel oublié*, Paris: Fayard, 1992)

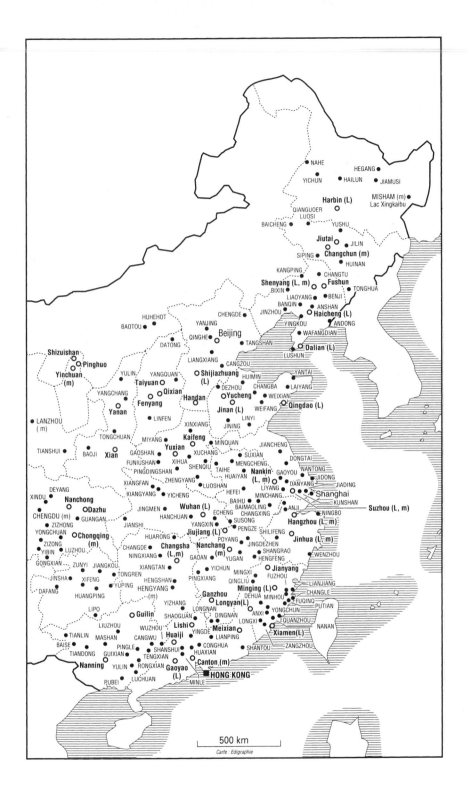

NAHE
HEGANG
YICHUN   HAILUN   JIAMUSI

Harbin (L)   MISHAM (m)
Lac Xingkaibu
QIANGUOER
LUOSI
BAICHENG   YUSHU
Jiutai   JILIN
SIPING   **Changchun (m)**
HUINAN
KANGPING   CHANGTU
Shenyang (L, m)   **Fushun**
BIXIN   TONGHUA
LIAOYANG   BENJI
HUHEHOT   BANQIN   ANSHAN
JINZHOU   **Haicheng (L)**
CHENGDE   YINGKOU   ANDONG
BAOTOU   YANJING   WAFANGDIAN
QINGHE   **Beijing**   **Dalian (L)**
DATONG   TANGSHAN   LUSHUN
Shizuishan   LIANGXIANG
Pinghuo   YULIN   CANGZOU   YANTAI
Yinchuan   YANGQUAN   **Shijiazhuang**   HUIMIN
(m)   **Taiyuan**   **(L)**   DEZHOU   LAIYANG
YANGCHANG   **Qixian**   CHANGBA   WEIXIAN
Fenyang   **Handan**   **Yucheng**   **Qingdao (L)**
Yanan   LINFEN   **Jinan (L)**   WEIFANG
LANZHOU   XINXIANG   LINYI
(m)   TONGCHUAN   MIYANG   JINING
TIANSHUI   BAOJI   **Xian**   **Kaifeng**   MINQUAN
GAOSHAN   **Yuxian**   SUXIAN   JIANCHENG
FUNIUSHAN   XIHUA   XUCHANG   MENGCHENG   DONGTAI
DEYANG   PINGDINGSHAN   SHENQIU   TAIHE   GAOYOU   NANTONG
XINDU   XIANGYANG   ZHENGYANG   HUAIYAN   **Nankin**   JIDONG   JIADING
Nanchong   XIANGFAN   YICHENG   LUOSHAN   **(L, m)**   DANYANG   KUNSHAN
Dazhu   JINGMEN   HEFEI   LIYANG   **Shanghai**
CHENGDU (m)   GUANGAN   **Wuhan (L)**   BAIHU   MINCHANG   ANJI   **Suzhou (L, m)**
ZIZHONG   JIANSHI   HANCHUAN   BAIMAOLING   CHANGXING   NINGBO
YONGCHUAN   HUARONG   ECHENG   SUSONG   **Hangzhou (L, m)**
Chongqing   CHANGDE   **Jiujiang (L)**   YANGXIN   PENGZE   SHILIFENG   **Jinhua (L, m)**
ZIGONG   **(m)**   **Changsha**   **Nanchang**   POYANG   JINGDEZHEN
YIBIN   LUZHOU   NINGXIANG   **(L,m)**   **(m)**   YUGAN   SHANGRAO   WENZHOU
GONGXIAN   ZUNYI   JIANGKOU   XIANGTAN   GAOAN   HENGFENG
JINSHA   XIFENG   YUPING   TONGREN   PINGXIANG   YICHUN   MINGXI   **Jianyang**
DAFANG   HUANGPING   HENGSHAN   QINGLIU   FUZHOU
HENGYANG   **Ganzhou**   DEHUA   **Minging (L)**   LIANJIANG
LIPO   **(m)**   YIZHANG   **Longyan(L)**   MINHOU   CHANGLE
Guilin   SHAOGUAN   LONGNAN   ANXI   YONGCHUN   FUQINQ
TIANLIN   LIUZHOU   DINGNAN   LONGXI   QUANZHOU   PUTIAN
BAISE   WUZHOU   **Lishi**   YINGDE   **Meixian**   **Xiamen(L)**   NANAN
MASHAN   **Huaiji**   LIANPING   ZANGZHOU
TIANDONG   PINGLE   CANGWU   SHANSHUI   CONGHUA   SHANTOU
GUIXIAN   TENGXIAN   HUAXIAN
Nanning   YULIN   RONGXIAN   **Gaoyao**   **Canton (m)**
PUBEI   LUCHUAN   **(L)**   **HONG KONG**
MINLE

500 km
Carte : Edigraphie

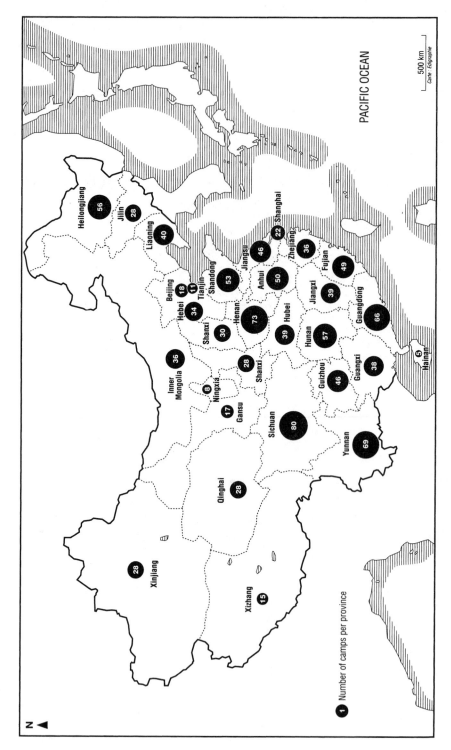

Forced-labor camps in the People's Republic of China

1 Number of camps per province

PACIFIC OCEAN

500 km
Carte : Edigraphie

21 China: A Long March into Night

Jean-Louis Margolin

> After our armed enemies have been crushed, there will still be our
> unarmed enemies, who will try to fight us to the death. We must never
> underestimate their strength. Unless we think of the problem in pre-
> cisely those terms, we will commit the gravest of errors.

Thus Mao Zedong adjured the Central Committee of the Seventh Congress of
the Chinese Communist Party in March 1949.[1]

Was repression in Communist China simply a replication of the practices
of the Soviet Big Brother? After all, until the early 1980s Stalin's portrait was
still to be seen everywhere in Beijing.[2] In some respects the answer is no. In
China, murderous purges in the Party itself were very rare, and the secret police
were relatively discreet, although the influence of their leader, Kang Sheng,
and of the Yan'an *maquis* was constantly in the background from the 1940s until
his death in 1975.[3] But in other respects the answer is assuredly yes. Even if
one excludes the civil war, the regime must be held accountable for a huge
number of deaths. Although the estimates are quite speculative, it is clear that
there were between 6 million and 10 million deaths as a direct result of the
Communist actions, including hundreds of thousands of Tibetans. In addition,

This chapter is dedicated to Jean Pasqualini (d. 9 October 1997), who revealed the horrors
of the Chinese concentration camps to the world.

tens of millions of "counterrevolutionaries" passed long periods of their lives inside the prison system, with perhaps 20 million dying there. To that total should be added the staggering number of deaths during the ill-named Great Leap Forward—estimates range from 20 million to 43 million dead for the years 1959–1961—all victims of a famine caused by the misguided projects of a single man, Mao Zedong, and his criminal obstinacy in refusing to admit his mistake and to allow measures to be taken to rectify the disastrous effects. The answer again is yes if one looks at the scale of the genocide in Tibet; some 10 to 20 percent of the inhabitants of the "rooftop of the world" died as a result of Chinese occupation. The genuine surprise of Deng Xiaoping as he observed that the massacre in Tiananmen Square in June 1989, where perhaps 1,000 died, was totally insignificant in comparison to the scale of events in China in the comparatively recent past, clearly amounts to an admission of guilt. One can hardly argue that these massacres were the sad consequences of an extremely bloody civil war, since the war was not in fact particularly violent and the regime was firmly entrenched by 1950. Nor can one argue that this was the continuation of a generally bloodstained history. If one discounts the Japanese occupation, which was not followed by famine or other disasters, one has to go back to the third quarter of the nineteenth century to find slaughters on anything resembling a comparable scale. And at that time there was nothing to compare to the generality or the systematic and carefully planned character of the Maoist atrocities, despite the dramatic nature of events in China at the time.

An analysis of Chinese Communism is doubly important. Since 1949, the Beijing regime has governed nearly two-thirds of all people who lived under the red flag. When the Soviet Union finally broke up in 1991 and Eastern Europe abandoned Communism, the figure rose to nine-tenths. It is therefore quite clear that whatever happens to "real socialism" now depends on the development of Communism in China. Beijing has been a sort of second Rome for Marxism-Leninism, openly so since the Sino-Soviet break of 1960, but in actuality since the birth of the free zone of Yan'an in 1935–1947 after the Long March. Korean, Japanese, and even Vietnamese Communists would retreat to China to consolidate their strength. Although Kim Il Sung's regime predates the triumph of the Chinese Communist Party, and owes its existence to Soviet occupation, it also owes its survival during the Korean war to the intervention of more than 1 million armed Chinese "volunteers." Repressions in North Korea were based quite closely on the Stalinist model, but what the master of Pyongyang took from Maoism, which after Yan'an became synonymous with Chinese Communism, was the idea not of the Party line but of the mass line—the intense effort to classify and mobilize the entire population—and its logical consequence, an insistence on permanent education as a means of social control. Kim paraphrased Mao when he noted that "the mass line is to mount an active defense of the interests of the working masses, to educate and reeducate them so that they rally to the cause of the Party, to count on their strength, and to mobilize them for revolutionary tasks."[4]

Even more apparent is China's influence on Asian Communist regimes established after 1949. The memoirs of the Vietnamese leader Hoang Van Hoan, who went over to Beijing, reveal that from 1950 until the Geneva accord of 1954 numerous Chinese advisers trained troops and administrators for the Viet Minh, and that from 1965 to 1970 some 30,000 soldiers from Beijing helped North Vietnamese troops in their fight against the South.[5] General Vo Nguyen Giap, the victor at Dien Bien Phu, indirectly acknowledged the Chinese contribution in 1964: "After 1950, in the wake of the Chinese victory, our army and our people learned some precious lessons from the Chinese People's Liberation Army. We educated ourselves according to the military thought of Mao Zedong. That was the important factor that allowed our army to mature and that led to our successive victories."[6] The Vietnamese Communist Party, which at the time was known as the Workers' Party, inscribed in its statutes in 1951 that "The Workers' Party recognizes the theories of Marx, Engels, Lenin, and Stalin and the thought of Mao Zedong, adapted to the realities of the Vietnamese revolution, as the theoretical foundation of its thought and as the magnetic needle that points the way in all its activities."[7] The "mass line" and the idea of reeducation were placed at the center of the Vietnamese political system. The *cheng feng* ("the reform of work style"), which had been invented in Yan'an, was transcribed into Vietnamese as *chinh huan* and became the justification for the ferocious purges of the mid-1950s.[8] In 1975–1979 Cambodia under the Khmer Rouge also received powerful support from Beijing and tried to carry out what Mao himself had failed to accomplish, taking up in particular the idea of the Great Leap Forward. All these regimes, like that of Mao, were strongly colored by their military origins (though less so in North Korea, even if Kim often boasted of his alleged exploits as a guerrilla fighter against the Japanese), which inevitably resulted in a permanent militarization of society. This occurred the least in China, which had no front line. It is notable that the central role played by the secret police in the Soviet system was in China always played by the army, which sometimes carried out repressive measures on its own.

A Tradition of Violence?

During his lifetime, Mao Zedong was so powerful that he was often known as the Red Emperor. In light of what is now known about his unpredictable character, his ferocious egotism, the vindictive murders he committed, and the life of debauchery that he led right up to the end, it is all too easy to compare him to one of the despots of the Middle Kingdom (ancient China).[9] Yet the violence that he erected into a whole system far exceeds any national tradition of violence that we might find in China.

As in most other countries, there had been periods of great bloodletting in China, which usually occurred against a backdrop of religious tension or an irreconcilable ideological clash. What separates the two great Chinese traditions of Confucianism and Taoism is less the theoretical differences than the conflict between the focus by Confucius on society and on rationality and the emphasis by Lao Tsu, the great promoter of Taoism, on the individual and intuitive and irrational aspects of behavior. Chinese generally incorporate some mixture of these two traditions. Sometimes in moments of crisis Taoists will gain the upper hand among the disinherited and the lost, launching a massive assault on the bastions of Confucianism—the educated and the state. Over the centuries there have been numerous uprisings inspired by apocalyptic, messianic sects, including the Yellow Turbans of 184, the Maitreyist revolt of Faqing in 515, the Manichean rebellion of Fang La in 1120, the White Lotus in 1351, and the Eight Trigrams of 1813.[10] The message of these movements was often quite similar, synthesizing Taoism and popular Buddhism, and often using the figure of Maitreya, the Buddha of the future whose imminent, luminous, and redemptive coming is to be accomplished in a universal cataclysm of the old world. The faithful, the chosen few, must help bring about the realization of the prophecy for salvation to occur. All contingent links must be broken, even with one's own family. According to the chronicle of the Wei dynasty in 515, "Fathers, sons, and brothers did not know one another."[11]

In China most morality is based on respect for familial obligations. Once these are broken, anything can happen. The replacement family that the sect becomes annihilates the idea of the individual. The rest of humanity is condemned to hell in the hereafter and to violent death in this world. Sometimes, as in 402, officials were cut into pieces, and if their wives and children refused to eat them, they were dismembered themselves. In 1120 massacres evidently involved millions of people. All values can be inverted: according to a proclamation of 1130, "The killing of people is the carrying out of the *dharma* [Buddhist law]." Killing becomes an act of compassion, delivering the spirit. Theft serves the purposes of equality, suicide is an enviable happiness; the worse a death is, the greater its reward will be. According to a text from the nineteenth century, "Death by slow slicing will ensure one's entry [into heaven] in a crimson robe."[12] From certain points of view it is difficult not to draw a comparison here between this millenarian cruelty and the Asian revolutions of this century. This does not help explain a number of the latter's characteristics, but it does help explain why they sometimes triumphed, and why the violence that accompanied them could initially appear quite ordinary and normal.

Social safeguards were nonetheless extremely powerful, a fact that explains why society was only rarely troubled. European visitors in the Middle Ages and the Enlightenment were always struck by the tremendous peace that reigned in the old empire. Confucianism, the official doctrine taught in the countryside, made benevolence the cardinal virtue of the sovereign and modeled the state on the family. Without any risk of anachronism, one can speak here of humanist principles that have valorized human life from time immemorial. Looking at the work of thinkers who have been the cardinal points of reference for nearly twenty-one centuries of imperial rule, we can single out the Chinese philosopher Mo Ti (ca. 479–381 B.C.), who condemned wars of aggression thus: "If a simple homicide is to be considered a crime, but the multiple homicide that is an attack on another country is to be considered a good action, can we possibly call that a reasonable distinction between good and evil?"[13] In his famous treatise *The Art of War*, Sun Tzu (writing around 500 B.C.) noted that "war is like fire; people who do not lay down their arms will die by their arms." One should fight for economic reasons, as swiftly and efficiently as possible: "No long war ever profited any country: 100 victories in 100 battles is simply ridiculous. Anyone who excels in defeating his enemies triumphs before his enemy's threats become real." Saving one's strength is essential, but neither should one allow oneself to annihilate the enemy entirely: "Capturing the enemy is far better than destroying him: do not encourage murder." That is perhaps less of a moral tenet than an opportunistic consideration: massacres and atrocities provoke hatred and lend the enemy the energy of despair, possibly allowing him to turn the situation around in his favor. In any case, for the victor, "The best policy is to capture the state intact: it should be destroyed only if no other options are available."[14]

Such is the typical reasoning of the great Chinese tradition, as illustrated above all by Confucianism: ethical principles are derived not from some transcendental vision, but from a pragmatic vision of social harmony. This is surely one of the reasons for their effectiveness. A different "pragmatic" approach, developed by lawmakers who were contemporaries of Confucius and Sun Tzu, implied that the state must affirm its omnipotence by terrorizing society. The fundamental failure of this approach was immediately apparent, even in its hour of glory during the short Qin dynasty, in the third century B.C. Despite enormous variations from one reign to the next, such arbitrary rule became more and more uncommon, particularly after the Northern Song dynasty (960–1127). The most common punishment for errant officials became the long walk into exile, which did not exclude the possibility of pardon and return. The Tang dynasty in 654 drew up an extremely humane penal code, which took into account both the intentions of individuals and any repentance they might show and abolished the idea of familial responsibility in case of rebellion. The procedures leading to capital punishment became very long and complex, some of the more horrible punishments were abolished altogether, and an appeals procedure was also established.[15]

State violence was thus quite limited and controlled. Chinese historians have always been appalled by the behavior of the first emperor, Qin Shi (221–210 B.C.), who buried alive 460 administrators and men of letters, burned all the classical literature (and made anyone who mentioned it subject to capital punishment), condemned to death or deported at least 20,000 nobles, and killed as many as several hundred thousand people during the construction of the Great Wall. This emperor was explicitly taken as a model by Mao. With the arrival of the Han dynasty (206 B.C.–220 A.D.), Confucianism returned to the fore, and the empires never again saw such severe tyranny or such bloody massacres. The law was strict, and justice was harsh, but apart from the (regrettably frequent) times of rebellion and the invasions from abroad, human life was safer there than it was in most other states in the ancient world or in medieval and modern Europe.

Admittedly, even under the peaceful Song dynasty in the twelfth century some 300 offenses were punishable by death, but in principle every sentence had to be checked and countersigned by the emperor himself. Wars often dragged on until hundreds of thousands had lost their lives, and the death count inevitably rose during the ensuing epidemics, famines, disruption of the transport system, and floodings of the Yellow River. The Taiping revolt and its repression were responsible for between 20 million and 100 million deaths, causing the population of China to fall from 410 million in 1850 to 350 million in 1873.[16] But only a small fraction of those dead, probably about 1 million, can be considered to have been intentionally killed in connection with the revolt.[17] In any case this was an exceptionally troubled period, marked by immense rebellions, repeated attacks by Western imperialists, and the growing despair of a population living in abject poverty. It was in this context that the two, three, or four generations who preceded the Communist revolutionaries grew up. It made them accustomed to a level of violence and social disintegration unprecedented in China's history.

Even in the first half of this century there was no warning, in scale or in kind, of what Maoism would unleash. True, the relatively undramatic revolution of 1911 was followed by a growing number of deaths in the sixteen years before the partial stabilization imposed by the Kuomintang regime. In Nanjing, a hotbed of revolution, the dictator Yuan Shih-kai ordered several thousand people executed from July 1913 to July 1914.[18] In June 1925 the police in Guangzhou killed fifty-two people taking part in a workers' demonstration. In

May 1926 in Beijing, forty-seven students were killed in a peaceful anti-Japanese demonstration. In April and May 1927 in Shanghai, and then in other big cities in the east, thousands of Communists were executed by a coalition uniting the head of the new regime, Chiang Kai-shek, and the local secret societies. In *The Human Condition* André Malraux recalled the atrocious nature of some of the executions, which took place in a locomotive boiler. Although the first episodes of the civil war between nationalists and Communists do not appear to have involved any massacres greater than those in the Long March of 1934–35, the Japanese did commit thousands of atrocities in the huge part of China that they occupied from 1937 to 1945.

More murderous than many of these events were the famines of 1900, 1920–21, and 1928–1930 that struck the north and northwest of the country, the areas most vulnerable to drought. The second of these caused the death of 500,000 people, and the third between 2 million and 3 million.[19] But although the second was made worse by the disruption of the transport system as a result of the civil war, one can hardly say this was an intentional effect that should be described as a massacre. The same cannot be said about Henan, where in 1942–43 between 2 million and 3 million people, or 5 percent of the population, died of hunger, and many cases of cannibalism were recorded. Even though the harvest had been disastrous, the central government in Chongqing refused to reduce the tax levy. In effect, the government seized from a great number of peasants all the goods they produced. The proximity of the front was another factor. The peasants were drafted to help with military operations, such as the digging of a 500-kilometer antitank trench, which in practice proved useless.[20] This was a foretaste of other great errors of judgment such as the Great Leap Forward, even if in this case the war might be seen to have provided an excuse. The resentment felt by the peasants was enormous.

The most numerous and, taken as a whole, the most murderous atrocities occurred quietly and left few traces. These often involved the poor fighting the poor, far from the main centers, in the great ocean of China's villages. Innumerable brigands roamed at large, sometimes in organized gangs, pillaging, looting, racketeering, and kidnaping. They killed anyone who resisted or whose ransom was not delivered in time. When they were captured, the whole village would join in their execution. For the peasants, the soldiers were sometimes worse than the bandits they were supposed to be fighting. In 1932 a petition from Fujian demanded that all the forces of law and order be withdrawn, "so that we will have only the bandits to fight."[21] In the same province in 1931, angry peasants annihilated the majority of a band of 2,500 soldiers who had pillaged and raped the local populace. In 1926 a group of peasants to the west of Hunan, under the cover of the secret society of the Red Lances, apparently killed 50,000 "soldier-bandits" serving a local warlord. When the Japanese began their offensive in the same region in 1944, the locals, remembering the earlier murderous troops, hunted them down and buried some alive.[22] And yet the Chinese soldiers were no different from their executioners. They were simply peasants, the unlucky and terrified victims of conscriptions that, according to the American General Wedemeyer, had hit the villages like a flood or a famine and had taken an even greater number of victims.

Numerous other revolts, generally less violent, focused on various government exactions: taxes on land, opium, alcohol, and livestock; forced conscription; government loans; unfair judgments. The worst violence often involved peasants against peasants. There were savage wars between villages. Clans and secret societies ravaged the countryside and, by honoring the cult of murdered ancestors who demanded to be avenged, created inextinguishable hatreds. In September 1928, for example, the Little Swords in Jiangsu Province massacred 200 Big Swords and burned six villages. Violent hostility between the Black Flag and Red Flag villages of the eastern part of Guangdong Province dated from the late nineteenth century. In Puning County, in the same region, the Lin clan hunted down and killed anyone bearing the patronymic Ho, including lepers, who were often burned alive, and numerous Christians. Such struggles were neither political nor social; they were simply jockeyings for position by local gangs. The adversaries were often immigrants, or simply people who lived on the other side of the river.[23]

A Revolution Inseparable from Terror (1927–1946)

When in January 1928 the inhabitants of a Red Flag village saw a group approach brandishing a scarlet flag, they rallied enthusiastically to one of the first Chinese "soviets," that of Hai-Lu-Feng, directed by P'eng P'ai. The Communists tailored their speeches to take account of local hatreds and used the coherence of their message to win the locals over to their own ends while allowing the new partisans to give full vent to their cruelest impulses. These few months in 1927–28 adumbrated the worst excesses of the Cultural Revolution and the Khmer Rouge forty and fifty years later. The movement had been prepared since 1922 by intense activity in Communist Party–led peasant unions, which had produced a strong polarization between "poor peasants" and "landowners," with the latter being constantly denounced. Although neither traditional conflicts nor social realities had accorded much importance to this division, the canceling of debts and the abolition of tenant farming ensured wide support for the new soviets. P'eng P'ai took advantage of it to establish a regime of "democratic terror": the whole people were invited to public trials of "counterrevolutionaries," who almost invariably were condemned to death. Everyone participated in the executions, shouting out "kill,

kill" to the Red Guards whose task it was to cut victims into pieces. Sometimes the pieces were cooked and eaten, or force-fed to members of the victim's family who were still alive and looking on. Everyone was then invited to a banquet, where the liver and heart of the former landowner were shared out, and to meetings where a speaker would address rows of severed heads freshly skewered on stakes. This fascination for vengeful cannibalism, which later became common under the Pol Pot regime, echoes a very ancient East Asian archetype that appears often at cataclysmic moments of Chinese history. At a time of foreign invasions in 613, Emperor Yang of the Souei dynasty avenged himself on one rebel by pursuing even his most distant relations: "Those who were punished most severely were broken apart, and their heads were displayed on stakes, or they were dismembered and shot full of arrows. The emperor then ordered all the state dignitaries to eat the flesh of the victims piece by piece."[24] The great writer Lu Xun, who was an admirer of Communism before it became imbued with nationalism and antiwestern sentiments, wrote that "Chinese people are cannibals." Less popular than these bloody orgies were the actions of the Red Guards in 1927 in the temples and against the Taoist monks. The faithful painted the idols red in an attempt to save them, and P'eng P'ai himself began to benefit from the first signs of deification. Fifty thousand people, including many peasants, fled the region during the four months of the soviet's reign.[25]

P'eng P'ai, who was shot in 1931, was the first real promoter of rural militarized Communism. His ideas were picked up by a previously marginal Communist cadre, Mao Zedong (himself of peasant origin), and theorized in his 1927 *Report on the Peasant Movement in the Hunan*. This peasant Communism represented an alternative to the Communism of the urban workers' movement, which at the time had been weakened as a result of repressions carried out by Chiang Kai-shek's Kuomintang. It quickly gathered momentum and resulted in the establishment in 1928 of the first Red Bases in the Jinggang Mountains, between Hunan and Jiangxi. It was in the eastern part of that province that on 7 November 1931, the anniversary of the October Revolution, the consolidation and extension of the main base led to the proclamation of a Chinese Republic of Soviets, with Mao presiding over the Council of People's Commissars. Until its final triumph in 1949, Chinese Communism was to go through many incarnations and terrible setbacks, but the main model was established here: concentrating the energy of the revolution on the construction of a state, and focusing the efforts of that state, which was to be warlike by nature, on forming a strong army to crush the enemy, which was the central government of Nanjing, presided over by Chiang Kai-shek. There is nothing surprising in the fact that the military and repressive apparatus was present from the very beginning. We are a long way here from Russian Bolshevism, and even further from pure Marxism. Bolshevism was an intermediary means, linked to a strategy for seizing power and reenforcing a national revolutionary state, through which the founders of the Chinese Communist Party, and in particular their major thinker, Li Dazhao, came to Communism in 1918 and 1919.[26] Wherever Chinese Communism triumphed, it was the socialism of the barracks, of courts-martial, and of firing squads that took power. P'eng P'ai was simply the first to provide this model.

The originality of Chinese Communist repressive practices is attested by one surprising fact: the Stalinist Great Terror of 1936–1938 was predated by the terror carried out by the Chinese soviets, which according to some estimates claimed 186,000 victims, excluding the war dead, in Jiangxi in 1927–1931.[27] Most of these people had offered some sort of resistance to the radical agrarian reforms, which had been imposed almost immediately, or to the heavy taxation and the mobilization of young people that were justified as a military necessity. In the areas where Communism was especially radical (in 1931 Mao was criticized and temporarily removed from the leadership because of his terrorist excesses, which had alienated the population) or where local cadres had been marginalized (as happened around the soviet "capital," Ruijin), the Nanjing forces encountered only weak resistance. Resistance was more vigorous, and sometimes even victorious, in bases that were established later, which tended to be more autonomous and whose leaders had learned the painful lessons of the politics of terror.[28] The same tensions were felt at the North Shaanxi base, centered in Yan'an, although by then the Communist Party had learned to deal with them through more selective and less bloody repressions. Fiscal pressure on the peasants was acute: 35 percent of the harvest was taken in 1941, four times as much as in the zones held by the Kuomintang. Villagers went so far as to call openly for Mao's death. Repressions were severe, but there were also concessions: the Party began secretly to grow and export opium, which until 1945 accounted for 26–40 percent of all public revenues.[29]

As so often under Communist regimes, the repression of Party activists left more traces, since these people knew how to express themselves and since their networks often survived. Some scores were settled decades later, and the cadres who suffered most were invariably those who had the closest links with the population. Their enemies, most of whom worked for the central apparatus, would often accuse them of being overly concerned with local issues, which undoubtedly did lead to some moderation in their views, and perhaps even led them to question the orders they had been given. This conflict, however, masks another: local activists often came from the wealthier segments of the peasantry and from the families of landowners (who furnished the literate core of the Party) who had rallied to Communism as a radical form of nationalism. On the other hand, the militants from the center and the soldiers from the regular army were recruited mainly from the lower strata and the marginalized segments of society, including bandits, beggars, mendicant monks, mercenaries, and, among the women, prostitutes. From as early as 1926 Mao had intended members of these groups to play a major part in the revolution: "These people can fight with great courage, and, led in the right manner, they will become a genuine revolutionary force."[30] He was still trying to identify with them in 1965, when he presented himself to Edgar Snow, an American journalist, as "an aged monk, walking along with an umbrella full of holes, under the stars."[31] The remainder of the population, with the exception of a minority of resolute opponents (many of whom were also members of the elite), was startlingly passive and unemotional, according to Communist leaders. This assessment included the "poor and semipoor peasantry," which constituted the class base of the Communist Party in the countryside. Once the people from the center had become cadres, they owed their entire social status to the Party and were often hungry for revenge. With the support of the Center[32] they tended to choose the most radical solutions, such as the elimination of local cadres wherever this seemed appropriate or necessary. After 1946 this became a very common response to the bloodier aspects of agrarian reform.[33]

The first recorded purge, in 1930–31, ravaged the Donggu base in northern Jiangxi. There the tensions described above were exacerbated by the AB (Anti-Bolshevik) Corps, a highly active secret police force linked to the right wing of the Kuomintang, which sowed suspicion of treachery among Communist Party members. These suspicions arose because the local Communist Party had found many recruits among the secret societies. Even the head of the Three Dots society enlisted in the Party in 1927, in what at the time was considered a major coup for the Communists. Initially, numerous local cadres were executed. Then the purge spread to the Red Army itself, resulting in the liquidation of around 2,000 soldiers. A number of cadres escaped and attempted to stir up a revolt against Mao, the "Emperor of the Party." They were invited to take part in negotiations, arrested, and killed. The Second Army, one unit of which was in revolt, was entirely disarmed and its officers executed. Persecution decimated civil and military cadres for more than a year, claiming thousands of victims. Of the nineteen highest-ranking local cadres, who included the founders of the base, twelve were executed as "counterrevolutionaries," five were killed by the Kuomintang, one died of illness, and the last one gave up the revolution altogether and emigrated.[34]

In the early days of Mao's presence in Yan'an, the elimination of the base's founder, the legendary guerrilla fighter Liu Zhidan, seemed to fit the same pattern, revealing a central apparatus without scruples but with considerable Machiavellian reasoning. The man responsible seems to have been the Moscow-allied Bolshevik Wang Ming, who had not yet been sidelined inside the leadership and who evidently wanted to control Liu's troops. Liu confidently accepted his arrest and under torture refused to admit anything. His main supporters were then buried alive. Zhou Enlai, one of Wang Ming's adversaries, set him free, but because Liu insisted on retaining autonomy in command, he was labeled an "unrepentant right-winger." Sent to the front, he was soon killed, possibly with a bullet in the back.[35]

The most famous purge of the period before 1949 began with an attack on the most brilliant Communist intellectuals of Yan'an in June 1942. As he did again fifteen years later on a nationwide scale, Mao first authorized a two-month period of free criticism. Then suddenly all militants were "invited" to "struggle" at thousands of meetings against Ding Ling, who had denounced the sham of official equality between men and women, and against Wang Shiwei, who had advocated freedom of expression and creativity for artists. Ding cracked and made a full public apology and attacked Wang, who refused to give way. Wang was thrown out of the Communist Party, put in prison, and executed during the provisional evacuation of Yan'an in 1947. The dogma of the submission of intellectuals to politicians, promulgated by the Party president in February 1942 in his *Remarks on Art and Literature,* soon had the force of law. *Cheng feng* sessions proliferated until people began to submit.

A Comintern representative in Yan'an commented on Maoist methods there:

> Party discipline is based on stupidly rigid forms of criticism and self-criticism. The president of each cell decides who is to be criticized and for what reason. In general it is a Communist who is attacked each time. The accused has only one right: to repent his "errors." If he considers himself to be innocent or appears insufficiently repentant, the attacks are renewed. It is a real psychological training . . . I understood one tragic reality. The cruel method of psychological coercion that Mao calls moral purification has created a stifling atmosphere inside the Party in Yan'an. A not negligible number of Party activists in the region have committed suicide, have fled, or have become psychotic. The *cheng feng* method is a response to the principle that "everyone should know the intimate thoughts of everyone else." This is the vile and shameful directive that governs every meeting. All that is personal and intimate is to be displayed shamelessly for public scrutiny. Under the protocol of criticism and self-criticism, the thoughts and aspirations and actions of everyone are on full view.[36]

In early July 1943 the purge revived and expanded. The leader of this "Campaign of Salvation," aimed at protecting people from their own hidden doubts and insufficiencies, was Politburo member Kang Sheng, whom Mao had appointed in June 1942 to head a new General Studies Commission, which was to supervise "Rectification." This "black shadow," who dressed in black leather, rode a black horse, and was invariably accompanied by a savage black dog, had been trained by the NKVD in Russia and organized the first "mass campaign" in Communist China: criticisms and public self-criticisms, selective arrests leading to confessions that in turn led to more arrests, public humiliations, beatings, and the elevation of the thoughts of Chairman Mao to the status of inviolable faith, the only sure point of reference. During one meeting Kang Sheng gestured at the entire audience and declared: "You are all agents of the Kuomintang . . . the process of your reeducation will go on for a long time."[37] Arrest, torture, and death became more and more common, claiming at least sixty members of the Center (some of whom took their own lives), until the Party leadership itself became concerned, despite Mao's assertion that "spies are as numerous as the hairs on a head."[38] After 15 August "illegal methods" of repression were banned, and on 9 October, Mao, in the sort of about-turn that was to become his trademark, proclaimed: "We should not kill anyone; many should never have been arrested at all."[39] The campaign was then definitively stopped. In December Kang Sheng was himself forced to perform an act of self-criticism and to admit that only 10 percent of all those arrested had been guilty and that the dead should be rehabilitated. His career stagnated from then until the Cultural Revolution in May 1966. Mao himself, appearing before an assembly of high-ranking cadres in April 1944, was forced to apologize and to bow three times in homage to the innocent victims before he was applauded. Once again his spontaneous extremism had met with stiff resistance. But the memory of the terror of 1943 remained indelible among those who had lived through it. What Mao lost in popularity, he gained in fear.[40]

Repression became ever more sophisticated. While war against both the Japanese and the Kuomintang saw an increasing number of terrorist massacres claiming thousands of victims,[41] the assassination of carefully targeted individuals became more and more common. As is common practice among gangs and secret societies, the targets were often renegades. According to one guerrilla chief, "We killed a great number of traitors, so that the people had no choice but to continue on the path to revolution."[42] The prison system expanded, with the result that executions became less common than before. In 1932 the Chinese soviets in Jiangxi had established corrective labor camps, which ironically had been anticipated by a Kuomintang law. Beginning in 1939, prisoners with long-term sentences were assigned to labor and production centers by a new type of court set up to handle these cases. There were three reasons for this: the authorities did not wish to disaffect the population with punishments that seemed too harsh, they wanted to make use of the large, captive workforce, and they wanted to convert new faithful to the cause by a clever process of reeducation. Even Japanese prisoners of war could thus be integrated into the

People's Liberation Army (PLA), the heir to the Chinese Red Army, and used to fight Chiang Kai-shek.[43]

Agrarian Reform and Urban Purges (1946–1957)

By the time the Communists seized power in China in 1949, violence and massacres were already everyday events, and governance often consisted in settling scores with one's neighbors. The actions taken to establish a new state were thus a sort of riposte to other very real acts of violence (one of the victims of P'eng P'ai, a local magistrate, had ordered the execution of almost 100 peasants) and were recognized as such by many rural communities. For this reason the period has been glorified both in official post-Maoist history (until the Antiright movement of 1957, the Helmsman was perceived to have steered a steady course) and in the memory of many eyewitnesses and those who were or were perceived to be the direct beneficiaries of the suffering of their fellow countrymen. The Communists themselves, including Communist intellectuals, were not affected too badly by the purges. Yet what resulted was in fact the bloodiest wave of repressions yet launched by the Chinese Communists, affecting the entire country. In its breadth of application, generality, length, and planned and centralized nature, the repression marked a new departure for the sort of violence seen in China. There were brief moments of respite, but almost every year saw the launching of a new "mass campaign." The Yan'an "Rectification" of 1943 may have been a sort of dress rehearsal on a local scale. Where certain social strata were concerned, the massacres took on a genocidal aspect previously unknown in China, at least on a national scale. Even the Mongols in the thirteenth century had ravaged only the northern parts of the empire. Some of the atrocities occurred in the context of a brutal three-year civil war; one example is the massacre of 500 mostly Catholic inhabitants of the Manchurian town of Siwanze after its capture. In addition, once the Communists had gained a considerable advantage in 1948, they abandoned their previous practice of freeing prisoners for propaganda reasons. Henceforth people were locked up by the hundreds of thousands, and the prisons quickly became overcrowded. These prisoners became the first occupants of the new labor camps, called the *laodong gaizao*, or *laogai* for short, which combined a drive for reeducation with a concern for the war effort.[44] But during the period of hostilities the worst atrocities were committed behind the lines, outside any military context.

The Countryside: Modernization and Social Engineering

Unlike the Russian Revolution of 1917, the Chinese Revolution of 1949 began in the countryside and spread to the cities. It is therefore logical that the urban purges were preceded by the movement for agrarian reform. As we have already seen, the Communists had extensive experience with this policy. But to maintain a unified anti-Japanese front with the central Kuomintang government, after 1937 they were forced to be silent about this fundamental aspect of their program. Only in 1946, after the Japanese defeat, did they relaunch agrarian reform as part of the civil war that was to carry them into power. Teams of thousands of professional agitators, most of whom came from outside the regions in which they worked so that they could avoid any feeling of solidarity with local inhabitants, clans, and secret societies, traveled from village to village, especially in the zones that had been liberated by the PLA. As the movement progressed, they spread across the south and west of the country, not including Tibet for the moment.

The agrarian revolution, which was to engulf hundreds of thousands of Chinese villages one by one, was neither the result of manipulation from on high nor a response by the Communist Party to the "will of the masses."[45] The masses had many reasons to be discontented and to desire change. One of the most salient was the inequality to be found among peasants. For example, in the village of Long Bow (Shanxi), where William Hinton followed the revolution, 7 percent of the peasants owned 31 percent of the cultivable land and 33 percent of the draft animals.[46] A national inquiry in 1945 attributed approximately 26 percent of all land to 3 percent of the population.[47] Inequality in the distribution of property was compounded by the effects of usury (3–5 percent per month, upward of 100 percent per year), which was controlled by a very small group of people in the richest rural areas.

Were these areas the richest, or simply the least poor? Although there were properties of several hundred hectares in the southern coastal regions, most properties there measured no more than two to three hectares. In Long Bow, which had 1,200 inhabitants, the richest property measured scarcely ten hectares. Furthermore, the defining limits among the different peasant groups were often vague; most rural people fell into an intermediate category between those who had no land at all and the landowners whose main source of income was not their own labor. In comparison with the extreme social contrasts found in Europe before 1945 and still visible in much of South America even today, rural Chinese society was in fact relatively egalitarian. Conflict between the rich and poor was far from being the principal cause of the conflict. As in 1927 in Hai-Lu-Feng, the Communists, including Mao himself, began to play at social engineering by trying artificially to polarize carefully defined rural groups and then decreeing that this polarization was the major cause of peasant discontent. These groups were determined in a highly arbitrary fashion, often in accordance with quotas fixed by the Party: 10–20 percent "privileged" per village, depending on political vicissitudes and the location of the zone. The path toward salvation was then easy to find.

The agitators began by dividing the peasantry into four groups—poor, semipoor, average, and rich. Anyone outside these categories was decreed a landowner and thus became a marked man. Sometimes, in the absence of clear distinguishing factors and because it pleased the poorest villagers, the rich peasants were added to the list of landowners. Although the destiny of small rural landowners was henceforth mapped out quite clearly, the path toward it was somewhat tortuous, though usually politically effective. It was simply a matter of ensuring the participation of the "great masses" so that they would fear the consequences of the failure of Communism; and if it was possible to give them the illusion that they had some sort of free will, too, then the government happily cooperated with their decisions. There is no doubt that it was an illusion, for everywhere, almost simultaneously, the process and the results were identical, despite the enormous variation in conditions from region to region. It is now known exactly what sort of effort was required of the activists to give the illusion that the peasant revolution was a spontaneous movement, and how they constantly had to refrain from using their basic mechanism, which of course was terror, to achieve their ends most effectively. During the war, many young people preferred to flee to the zones held by the Japanese rather than enroll in the PLA. The peasants, who generally formed an apathetic mass, were ideologically quite distant from the ideals of the Communist Party and were often so in thrall to the landowners that they continued secretly to work on the landowners' farms even after the government had reduced their size as a prologue to agrarian reform. Among themselves, the agitators classed peasants according to their political position as activists, ordinary peasants, reactionaries, or supporters of the landowners. They then attempted to transfer these categories onto actual social groups; the result was a sort of Frankenstein sociology that allowed old grudges and private quarrels, such as the desire to get rid of a troublesome husband, to resurface.[48] The classification could be revised at will; to complete the redistribution of land, the authorities in Long Bow swiftly changed the number of peasants who fell into the poor category from 95 to 28 (out of 240).[49] Among the Communist cadres, civilians were generally classed as "workers," and soldiers as "poor peasants" or "medium peasants," despite their actual origins among the more privileged social classes.[50]

The key element in agrarian reform was the "bitterness meeting." Landowners were called before an assembly of the entire village, where for good measure they were often labeled "traitors." (The Communists systematically associated all landowners with those who really had collaborated with the Japanese invaders and, except in 1946, quickly "forgot" that poor peasants had often collaborated too.) Whether out of fear of these people who so recently had been powerful or out of a sense of injustice, things often began very slowly,

and the militants were forced to hurry things along a bit by physically beating
and humiliating the accused. At that point the opportunists or those who bore
a grudge against the accused would begin the denunciations and accusations,
and the temperature would begin to rise. Given the tradition of peasant violence, the outcome was usually a death sentence for the landowner (accompanied by confiscation of all goods and possessions) and immediate execution
with the active participation of the peasants. The cadres often attempted, not
always successfully, to bring the prisoner before the local magistrate to have the
sentence confirmed. This Grand Guignol theater in which everyone knew his
role by heart prefigured the "struggle meetings" and self-criticism sessions that
were to become the everyday lot of all Chinese people right up to Mao's death
in 1976. From these early days the traditional Chinese propensity for ritual and
conformism, which any cynical government could use and abuse at will, was
immediately apparent.

There is no precise tally of the number of victims, but because there
was necessarily at least one per village, 1 million seems to be the absolute
minimum, and many authors agree on a figure of between 2 million and
5 million dead.[51] In addition, between 4 million and 6 million Chinese "kulaks"
were sent to the new *laogai*, and almost double that number were placed under
observation for varying lengths of time by the local authorities, which meant
constant surveillance, ever harder work, and persecutions in the case of any
"mass campaign."[52] If we extrapolated from the number killed in Long Bow—
15—we would arrive at the top end of the estimates. But the reform process
started early there, and after 1948 some of the excesses of the previous period
were banned. Long Bow had been hit extremely hard, with a massacre of the
whole family of the president of the local Catholic association (and the closure
of the church), beatings, confiscation of the goods of poor peasants who had
shown solidarity with the rich, and a search for any "feudal origins" in the last
three generations (which meant that almost no one was safe from some sort of
reclassification). People were tortured to death in attempts to force them to
reveal the whereabouts of alleged treasure. Interrogations were systematically
accompanied by torture with red-hot irons. The families of people who were
executed were tortured and the tombs of their ancestors robbed and destroyed.
One cadre, who was a former bandit and a renegade Catholic, forced a four-
teen-year-old girl to marry his son and declared to the world at large: "My
word is law, and anyone I condemn to death dies."[53] On the other side of China,
in Yunnan, the father of He Liyi, a police officer in the previous government,
was classified as a landowner on those grounds alone. As an official, he was
sentenced to hard labor. In 1951, in the middle of the agricultural reforms, he
was paraded from town to town as a "class enemy" before being sentenced to
death and executed, without ever being accused of any particular act. His eldest

son, a soldier who had been officially congratulated for having rallied soldiers from the Kuomintang to the PLA cause, was nonetheless classified as a reactionary and placed under observation.[54] All of these acts appear to have been popular among most of the peasants, who were then allowed to share the expropriated land. Some, however, for a variety of reasons (often related to the experience of their families), perceived themselves as having been affected by these arbitrary executions. Their desire for revenge was sometimes expressed indirectly, during the Cultural Revolution, as a sort of ultraradicalism against the existing establishment.[55] Thus the massacre of scapegoats did not unite peasants behind Party "justice" in the manner intended.

The real aims of this vast movement were primarily political, secondarily economic, and only lastly social. Although 40 percent of the land was redistributed, the small number of rural rich and the extreme population density in most of the countryside meant that the economic situation of most peasants improved only marginally. After the reform movement, the average plot measured 0.8 hectare.[56] Other countries in the region—Japan, Taiwan, and South Korea—where the distribution of land was even more inequitable carried out equally radical agrarian reforms in the same period with considerably greater success. As far as we know, there was not a single death associated with those reforms, and people were compensated more or less satisfactorily for their losses. The terrible violence in China seems to have been a result not of the reforms themselves, but of the power struggle carried out by the Chinese Communists, in which a minority of activists were chosen as militants and cadres, a "blood pact" with the mass of villagers implicated them in the executions, and the Communist Party demonstrated to the world that it was capable of the worst atrocities. All these things also allowed the Communists to develop an intimate knowledge of the way in which villages functioned, knowledge that was to be extremely helpful when the Party sought to dispose of industrial capital in the service of collectivization.

The Cities: "The Salami Tactic" and Expropriations

Although the massacres were supposed to be a spontaneous movement from below, Mao Zedong thought it a good idea, during the phase of radicalization that followed the entry of the Chinese troops into the Korean conflict in November 1950, to sanction them personally and publicly, remarking: "We surely must kill all those reactionary elements who deserve to be killed."[57] But what was new at the time was not the agrarian reform, which, at least in northern China, was drawing to an end. (In southern China, which was "liberated" later, and particularly in areas filled with civil unrest, such as Guangdong, the movement was still far from finished in early 1952.)[58] It was rather the spread of the violent purges to the cities, through a series of carefully targeted "mass movements" that aimed to bring into submission, either simultaneously or one at a time, entire groups—intellectuals, the bourgeoisie, small bosses, non-Communist militants, and overly independent Communist cadres—who threatened the totalitarian control of the Chinese Communist Party. This approach was remarkably similar to what had occurred a few years earlier, when the "people's democracies" of Eastern Europe were being established through so-called "salami tactics." This was the period when Soviet influence was most pronounced, both in the economy and in repressive political measures. At the same time, and despite some extremely powerful alliances that were struck at this time between two previously opposing groups—class enemies and brigands—who were united by being labeled "enemies of the people's government," criminals and marginalized elements were treated extremely severely, and there were crackdowns on prostitution, gambling, and opium dealing. According to the Communist Party's own figures, 2 million bandits were liquidated between 1949 and 1952, and as many again were locked up in prison.[59]

The system of control, most of which was in place before victory was achieved, soon had considerable means at its disposal. At the end of 1950 it had a militia 5.5 million strong. By 1953 it had added another 3.8 million activists, as well as 75,000 informers charged with coordinating the activists and ensuring their zeal. In the towns a perfect traditional system of mutual control *(baojia)* had been restored by the Kuomintang, in which groups of fifteen to twenty families were watched over by neighborhood committees, who were in turn subordinate to street or district committees.[60] Nothing was supposed to escape their vigilance. Any nocturnal visit or stranger who came for more than a day had to be recorded by the residents' committee. Such visitors had to have a *hukou*, a certificate stating that they had registered in the town; the requirement had been established to prevent a rural exodus. Accordingly, everyone became a police informer to some extent. The police themselves, who at first served the same function they had under the old regime, as part of the justice and prison systems (roles that made them natural targets for future movements once their transitory usefulness was past), quickly burgeoned in number: when Shanghai was taken in May 1949 there were 103 police stations; by the end of the year there were 146. The troops in the security services (the secret police) numbered 1.2 million. Even the smallest brigades opened improvised prisons, and the harshness of conditions in the official prisons reached unprecedented levels: up to 300 in cells of 100 square meters, and 18,000 in Shanghai's central prison; starvation-level rations and overwork; inhuman discipline and a constant threat of physical violence (for instance, people were beaten with rifle butts to make them keep their heads high, which was obligatory when marching). The mortality rate, which until 1952 was certainly in excess of 5 percent per year—the average for 1949–1978 in the *laogai*—reached 50 percent during a six-month period in Guangxi, and was more than 300 per day in one mine in Shanxi. The most varied and sadistic tortures were quite common, such as hanging by the wrists or the thumbs. One Chinese priest died after being interrogated continuously for 102 hours. The most brutish people were allowed to operate with impunity. One camp commander assassinated or buried alive 1,320 people in one year, in addition to carrying out numerous rapes. Revolts, which were quite numerous at that time (detainees had not yet been ground into submission, and there were many soldiers among them), often degenerated into veritable massacres. Several thousand of the 20,000 prisoners who worked in the oilfields in Yanchang were executed. In November 1949, 1,000 of the 5,000 who mutinied in a forest work camp were buried alive.[61]

The campaign to eliminate "counterrevolutionary elements" was launched in July 1950, followed in 1951 by the "Three Anti" (antiwaste, anticorruption, antibureaucracy) and "Five Anti" movements (against bribery, fraud, tax evasion, lying, and revealing state secrets, all aimed at the bourgeoisie) and the campaign to "reform thought," which was directed at Westernized intellectuals. Members of the last group were forced to undergo regular periods of "reeducation" and to prove to the local labor collective *(danwei)* that they had made progress. The temporal conjunction of these movements reveals their essential intent: to demonstrate to the urban elite that no one was safe. The definition of "counterrevolutionary" in particular was so vague and so wide that any past or current position that diverged even slightly from the Party line was enough to bring condemnation. The result was that local Party secretaries had almost all the repressive power they could want. With encouragement from the Center and with help from the security forces, they could use and abuse their power at will. Alain Roux's term "Red Terror" applies, especially to the year 1951.[62]

The few official figures available are appalling. There were 3,000 arrests in one night in Shanghai (and 38,000 in four months), 220 death sentences and public executions in a single day in Beijing, 30,000 interrogations over nine months in Beijing, 89,000 arrests and 23,000 death sentences in ten months in Guangzhou. More than 450,000 small businesses were investigated, including 100,000 in Shanghai alone; at least one-third of the bosses and numerous managers were found guilty of some sort of fraud, usually tax evasion, and punished with varying degrees of severity. Around 300,000 of them received prison sentences.[63] Foreign residents were also targeted: 13,800 "spies" were arrested in 1950, including many priests; one Italian bishop was condemned to life imprisonment. As a direct result of this persecution, the number of Catholic missionaries fell from 5,500 in 1950 to a few dozen in 1955, after which the Chinese faithful began to feel the full force of repression without any awkward witnesses from abroad. There were at least 20,000 arrests in 1955; the number of Christians of all denominations who were arrested over the next two decades ran into the hundreds of thousands.[64] Former political and military cadres from the Kuomintang, who had been granted amnesty in 1949 in an attempt to slow their massive exodus to Taiwan and Hong Kong, were decimated more than two years later, with the press sternly noting that "even the extreme kindness of the people toward such reactionaries has its limits." Penal legislation continued to facilitate oppression, punishing past as well as current "counterrevolutionaries" through retroactive legislation. Judgment could also be passed "by analogy" to a similar crime if the accused had not committed any specific act that fell within the remit of a particular law. Penalties were extremely severe: eight years in prison was a minimum for ordinary crimes; the norm was nearer twenty years.

It is still difficult to venture with precision beyond the few official figures. But Mao himself spoke of the liquidation of 800,000 counterrevolutionaries. Executions in the cities almost certainly reached 1 million, that is, one-third of the probable number of liquidations in the countryside. But since at least five times as many people lived in the country as lived in the city, we can assume that the repressions were harsher in urban areas. The picture becomes even darker if one includes the 2.5 million people who were imprisoned in reeducation camps, a figure that represents approximately 4.1 percent of the urban population, as opposed to 1.2 percent for the countryside.[65] Then there are the numerous suicides of people harried by the authorities. On some days in Guangzhou as many as fifty people committed suicide. Chow Chingwen estimates the total number of suicides at around 700,000.[66] Urban purges closely resembled those of the agrarian reforms, differing substantially from the essentially secret purges in the U.S.S.R. carried out by the police. In China the local Party committee had a firm grip on the police. The committee's primary aim was to ensure that as large a segment of the population as possible took part in the repressions, while being careful to ensure that full control of the proceedings remained with the Party.

Workers, within the framework of the street committees, attacked the "lairs" of "capitalist tigers," forcing them to open their accounts to public scrutiny, to be criticized and to criticize themselves, and to accept state control over their affairs. If they repented completely, they were then invited to participate in investigative groups and to denounce their colleagues. If they were at all uncooperative, the whole cycle began again. The situation was very similar for intellectuals: they had to attend "submission and rebirth" meetings at their workplace, confess their errors, and show that they had definitively abandoned "liberalism" and "Westernism," understood the evils of "American cultural imperialism," and had killed the "old man" inside them with all his doubts and independent thoughts. During this period, which could range from two months to a year, all other activities were banned. Their accusers had all the time they needed, and there was no means of escape except suicide, a traditional Chinese solution chosen by those who wished to escape repeated humiliations and the ignominy of the obligatory denunciations by colleagues or who simply could take no more. The same phenomena recurred during the Cultural Revolution on an even larger scale, often accompanied by physical violence. For the moment, the entire population and all the activities of the towns passed under the absolute control of the Party. Heads of industry were subjected to ever-increasing restrictions. Beginning in 1951 they were forced to make all their accounts public and were subjected to crippling taxes. In December 1953 they were forced to hand over their entire capital to the state. In 1954, by which time rationing was ubiquitous, they had to affiliate themselves with public supply companies. In October 1955 they were again forced to submit to general scrutiny, and they held out for no more than two weeks. In January 1956 they were "offered" collectivization in exchange for a modest pension for life and sometimes a place as technical director in what had been their own company. The Cultural Revolution later reneged even on these promises. One person from Shanghai who refused to cooperate was brought to trial on various charges by his workers, was ruined in two months and then sent to a labor camp. Many of the heads of small and medium-sized companies, which were systematically plundered, took their own lives. The heads of larger companies tended to fare better, since their knowledge of and contacts with the extensive network of Chinese who lived abroad were recognized as being useful: even then it was realized that competition with Taiwan was of great importance.[67]

The repressive machinery rolled on and on. The campaigns of 1950 and 1951 were declared to be over in 1952 or 1953, and with good reason: the repressions had been so widespread that there were few opponents left. Nevertheless, repression continued. In 1955 the Party began a new campaign to eliminate "hidden counterrevolutionaries," known as *sufan*, targeting the intelligentsia in particular, including any former Party members and sympathizers who had shown a modicum of independence. One example was the brilliant Marxist writer Hu Feng, who was a disciple of the revered Lu Xun, and who in July 1954 had denounced the "five daggers" used by the Central Committee to attack writers and particularly the idea that all creativity should submit to the Party line. In December an enormous campaign was launched against him. Prominent intellectuals took turns denouncing him, and the masses rushed in for the kill. Hu found himself totally isolated and made a public act of contrition in January 1955, but this act was not accepted. He was arrested in July along with 130 "accomplices" and spent ten years in a camp. He was arrested again in 1966 and moved around within the penitentiary system until his complete rehabilitation in 1980.[68] In the accompanying purge, Party members were affected on a large scale for the first time: the *People's Daily* announced that 10 percent of Party members were hidden traitors, a figure that seems to have been used as a guideline for arrest quotas.[69] In estimating the number of victims of the *sufan* campaign, one source gives 81,000 arrests (which seems rather modest), while another gives 770,000 deaths. There is at present no way of determining the truth.

The well-known Hundred Flowers Campaign of May and June 1957 was also part of the mass repressions and the cycle of successive campaigns. In this case the crushing of the "poisonous weeds" destroyed the optimism generated during the few weeks of liberalization proclaimed and then withdrawn by Mao. The brief liberalization had two objectives. First, as in all rectification movements, Mao initially encouraged people to speak freely about their grievances, then crushed those who had revealed "evil thoughts."[70] Second, in the face of the harsh criticism, he sought to reunite the Party around radical positions he had adopted in the aftermath of the Twentieth Soviet Communist Party Congress, which had emphasized the need for the legal regulation of repressive practices in order to increase juridical control over activities of the security service and over the execution of sentences, thus calling into question Mao's own position.[71] Communist intellectuals, frightened by the Yan'an experience, for the most part prudently stayed quiet. But hundreds of thousands of people who were more naive, and particularly those who had taken part in the events of 1949 or who were members of "democratic parties" that the Communist Party had allowed to survive, were caught in the trap of their own outspokenness once the brutal Antirightist operation began. There were in general few executions, but between 400,000 and 700,000 cadres, including at least 10 percent of all Chinese intellectuals, technicians, and engineers, were given the invidious label "right-winger" and sentenced to twenty years of "repentance" in prisons or camps in remote regions. Those who did not succumb to age, the famines of 1959–1961, or despair when a decade later the Red Guards rampaged through the country with new persecutions still had to wait until 1978 for the first rehabilitations. In addition, millions of cadres and students, including 100,000 in Henan alone, were moved to the countryside, either provisionally or definitively.[72] Sending them to the countryside was a punishment, but it was also preparation for the Great Leap Forward, which would focus mainly on the rural areas.

During the Antirightist "struggle," penal detention was generally preceded by social exclusion. No one wanted to know "right-wingers"; no one would even offer them hot water. They still had to go to work, but there they had to make confession after confession and to attend an endless succession of "criticism and education" meetings. Because housing was generally based on employment, their neighbors and colleagues, and even their children, gave them no respite, hurling sarcastic taunts and insults, forbidding them to walk on the left side of the road, and chanting a children's song that ended with the line "The people will fight right-wingers to the death."[73] The wisest course of action was silent acceptance, lest one make things worse.[74] It is easy to understand why suicides were so common. After the innumerable inquiries and criticism sessions, and after the purge that affected 5 percent of the members of every labor unit (7 percent in the universities, which were singled out for particular attention during the Hundred Flowers campaign), Party officials were placed at the head of the main cultural institutions.[75] The brilliant intellectual and cultural flourishing that China had witnessed in the first half of the century simply died. The Red Guards tried to kill off even its memory.[76]

This was the moment when Maoist society reached its maturity. Even the later upsets of the Cultural Revolution did not destabilize it for more than a moment. No page would be turned thereafter until the first great reforms of Deng Xiaoping. Its basis can be summed up in the words of the Helmsman: "Never forget the class struggle!" And in practice everything did rest upon the labeling and classification of people, first sketched out in rural areas at the time of agrarian reform and in the towns during the mass movements of 1951, but completed only in 1955. The labor collective had a role to play in the process, but in every case it was the police who had the final say. As before, the social groupings were quite fantastical, with diabolical consequences for tens of millions of people. In 1948 an official in Long Bow stated that "the way one makes one's living determines the way one thinks."[77] According to the Maoist logic, the reverse was also true. Social groups, which were divided up in a fairly arbitrary fashion, were mixed with political groups, resulting in a binary division between "red" categories, such as workers, poor peasants, medium peasants, party cadres, PLA soldiers, and "martyrs of the revolution"; and "black" categories, such as landowners, rich peasants, counterrevolutionaries, "evil elements," and right-wingers. Between these two groups were some "neutral" categories, such as intellectuals and capitalists; but these, together with the marginalized in society, especially Party leaders who had "chosen the capitalist way," were progressively shifted toward the "black" category. During the Cultural Revolution, intellectuals were officially placed in the "stinking ninth [black] category." The labels stuck no matter what one did later. Even after an official rehabilitation, a right-winger would remain a target for mass campaigns and would never have the right to return to the city. The infernal logic of the system was such that there were always enemies to hunt down and kill. If the stock of enemies ran low, it could be increased by an expansion of incriminating traits or by a search for people who had fallen back into old ways. Any Communist cadre could thus become a right-winger.

These classifications had less in common with Marxist classes than they did with Indian castes, even though traditionally China had known no such system. To some extent they took into account the social system that had existed before 1949, but not the enormous changes that had come about in the meantime. They also addressed another perceived problem. Traditionally the father's name had been passed on automatically to his children (while women by contrast retained their maiden names). This hereditary system threatened to cause ossification in a purportedly revolutionary society and posed an insurmountable obstacle to those who were not "well born." Discrimination against these "blacks" and their children was quite systematic, not only for entry into universities and into normal life (as stipulated in a directive of July 1957) but also for entry into political life. It was very difficult for them to obtain permission to marry a "red" partner, and society tended to ostracize them, since as a general rule people were afraid that they might have problems with the authorities if they associated with such people. It was during the Cultural Revolution that labeling attained its height and its worst effects, even for the regime itself.

The Greatest Famine in History (1959–1961)

For many years one myth was common in the West: that although China was far from being a model democracy, at least Mao had managed to give a bowl of rice to every Chinese. Unfortunately, nothing could be further from the truth. The modest amount of food available per person probably did not increase significantly from the beginning to the end of his reign, despite demands made on the peasantry on a scale rarely seen in history. Mao and the system that he created were directly responsible for what was, and, one hopes, will forever remain, the most murderous famine of all time, anywhere in the world.

Undoubtedly it was not Mao's intention to kill so many of his compatriots. But the least one can say is that he seemed little concerned about the death of millions from hunger. Indeed, his main concern in those dark years seems to have been to deny a reality for which he could have been held responsible. It is always difficult to apportion blame in such situations, to know whether to attack the plan itself or its application. It is, however, indisputable that the Party leadership, and especially Mao himself, displayed economic incompetence, wholesale ignorance, and ivory-tower utopianism. The collectivization of 1955–56 had been more or less accepted by most peasants: it grouped them around their own villages, and it allowed them to pull out of the collective—70,000 farms did so in Guangdong in 1956–57, and many of the bigger collectives were broken up.[78] The apparent success of reform and the good harvest of 1957 pushed Mao to propose—and to impose on the more reluctant farmers—the goals of the Great Leap Forward (first announced in December 1957 and refined in May 1958) and the means of achieving it—the People's Commune (announced in August 1958).

Within a very short time ("Three years of hard work and suffering, and a thousand years of prosperity," said one slogan at the time), the Great Leap Forward caused nationwide disruption of the peasant way of life. Peasants were to form themselves into huge groups of thousands or even tens of thousands of families, with everything to become communal, including food. Agricultural production was to be developed on a massive scale through pharaonic irrigation projects and new farming methods. Finally, the difference between agricultural and industrial work was to be abolished as industrial units, in particular small furnaces, were created everywhere. The goal was quite similar to the Khrushchev ideal of the "agrotown." The aim was to ensure the self-sufficiency of local communities and to accelerate industrial takeoff by creating new rural industries and using the large agricultural surpluses that the communes were to make for the state and the industry it controlled. In this happy dream that was to bring real Communism within reach, the accumulation of capital and a rapid rise in the standard of living were to go hand in hand. All that had to be done was to achieve the simple objectives set by the Party.

For months everything seemed to be going perfectly. People worked night and day under red flags blowing in the wind. Local leaders announced the breaking of one record after another as people produced larger quantities "more quickly, better, and more economically." As a result, the goals were continually raised even higher: 375 million tons of grain for 1958, almost double the 195 million tons of the preceding year. In December it was announced that the goal had been met and the results verified by the staff of the Central Statistics Bureau, who had been sent out to the countryside after expressing doubts. The original plan had been to surpass Great Britain in fifteen years; now it appeared certain that it would be done in two. As production quotas continued to rise, it was decided to move more people into industrial production. In Henan, a province intended to serve as a model, 200,000 workers were generously moved to other, more needy regions where results had been poorer.[79] "Socialist emulation" was pushed ever further: all private land and free trade was abolished along with the right to leave the collective, and there was a massive campaign to collect metal tools to transform everything into steel. At the same time, any wood, including doors, was collected to fuel the new furnaces. As compensation, all communal food reserves were eaten at memorable banquets. "Eating meat was considered revolutionary," according to one witness in Shanxi.[80] This was no problem because the next harvest was bound to be enormous. "The human will is the master of all things," the press in Henan had already proclaimed, at the provincial hydraulic conference in October 1957.[81]

But soon the leaders who still emerged from the Forbidden City from time to time (which Mao seldom did) were forced to face facts. They had fallen into their own trap, believing in the power of their own optimism and thinking that after the Long March, success would naturally follow because they felt themselves omnipotent and were used to commanding the workers and the economy like soldiers in a battle. It was easier for cadres to doctor the figures or to put intolerable pressure on administrators to deliver them than it was to admit that the sacrosanct objectives had not been reached. Under Mao, a move to the left (since voluntarism, dogmatism, and violence were left-wing virtues) was always less dangerous than right-wing mediocrity. In 1958–59, the bigger a lie was, the faster its author was promoted. The headlong race was under way, the barometers of success were soaring, and all potential critics were in prison or working on the irrigation projects.

The reasons for the catastrophe were fairly technical. Some agricultural methods advocated by the Soviet academic Trofim Lysenko, who rejected genetics, won great favor in China under the auspices of Mao. They were imposed on the peasants, and the results were disastrous. Mao had proclaimed his belief that "in company grain grows fast; seeds are happiest when growing together"—attempting to impose class solidarity on nature.[82] Accordingly, seeds were sown at five to ten times the normal density, with the result that millions of young plants died. The intensity of the farming methods dried out the soil or caused the salt to rise. Wheat and maize never grow well together in the same fields, and the replacement of the traditional barley crop with wheat in the high, cold fields of Tibet was simply catastrophic. Other mistakes were made in the nationwide campaign. The extermination of the sparrows that ate the grain resulted in a massive increase in the number of parasites. A large amount of hydraulic equipment that had been hurriedly and carelessly built was found to be useless or even dangerous because of the increased erosion and the risk of flooding at the first high tide. Moreover, the cost of its construction in terms of human life had been enormous: more than 10,000 out of 60,000 workers had died on one site in Henan. Risking everything on one large cereal crop (as on steel in industry, where the slogan was "Big is beautiful") ruined all the smaller associated agricultural activities, including the raising of livestock that was often vital for balance in the ecosystem. In Fujian, for instance, the highly profitable tea plantations were all resown as rice fields.

From an economic point of view, the reallocation of resources was disastrous. Although the accumulation of capital reached a record level (43.4 percent of the gross domestic product in 1959) it was used to build ill-conceived or badly finished irrigation projects and to develop industry inside the towns.[83] Although one famous Maoist slogan proclaimed that "China walks on two feet," all the blood from agriculture was pumped into industry. The incompetent allocation of capital was a decisive factor in the no less aberrant allocation of manpower: state industry took on 21 million new workers in 1958, which represented an 85 percent rise in a single sector in one year. In 1957–1960 the share of the population working outside agriculture increased from 15 percent to 20 percent, and all these people had to be fed by the state. Meanwhile, workers in the countryside were being exhausted by everything except agriculture. They were being drafted into large engineering projects, small steelworks whose output for the most part was worthless, the destruction of traditional villages, and the construction of new towns. After the marvelous harvest of 1958, it was decided that cereal production could be cut by 13 percent.[84] This combination of "economic delirium and political lies" resulted in the harvests of 1960, which many of the peasants were too weak to gather.[85] Henan, the first province to be declared "100 percent hydraulic," since the construction of dikes and irrigation work there was technically finished, was also one of the regions hardest hit by the famine; estimates of the deaths there vary from 2 million to 8 million.[86] The state quota had reached its height, going from 48 million tons of cereal in 1957 (17 percent of all production), to 67 million in 1959 (28 percent), to 51 million in 1960. The trap closed around those who had lied, or rather, around their administrators. In the supposedly model district of Fengyang (Anhui), 199,000 tons of grain were announced for 1959, a considerable increase over the 178,000 tons of the previous year; but real production was a mere 54,000 tons, as opposed to 89,000 in 1958. Despite the shortfall, the state took a very real part of this phantom harvest, claiming 29,000 tons. The following year, almost everyone had to eat clear rice soup, and the somewhat surreal slogan for the year 1959 in the *People's Daily* was: "Live frugally in a year of plenty." The national press began to sing the praises of a daily nap, and medical professors came out to explain the particular physiology of the Chinese, for whom fat and proteins were an unnecessary luxury.[87]

There was perhaps still time to change direction and alter things for the better. Steps were taken in that direction in December 1958. But the inception of a serious split with the U.S.S.R., and above all the attack in July 1959 by the well-respected Marshal Peng Dehuai on the Communist Party Politburo and Mao's strategy, gave Mao purely tactical political reasons to refuse to acknowledge that the country was facing any difficulties and thus to acknowledge any blame. The overly lucid minister of defense was thus replaced by Lin Biao, who showed himself to be a servile creature of the Helmsman. Peng was sidelined but not actually arrested at the time. In 1967 he was thrown out of the Party and sentenced to life in prison, dying in 1974. Mao's hatred was long-lasting. To turn the situation to his advantage, he tried in 1959 to reinforce the Great Leap Forward by calling for people's communes to be extended into the cities (a strategy never actually implemented). China then experienced its great famine, but Mao would survive. As Lin Biao was to say later, it is geniuses who make history.

Mao Zedong and the Chinese Communists took power in 1949. In 1958 they launched the Great Leap Forward to accelerate the process of industrialization. Its chief effect, however, was an immense famine. While Mao and Peng Chen were posing for these propaganda photographs, an estimated 30 million Chinese were dying of hunger.
© Eastfoto

Mao launched the Great Proletarian Cultural Revolution in 1966 to bring the country firmly under his control once more, but he succeeded mainly in starting a civil war. Red Guards spread destruction and humiliation around the country, lynching and murdering countless people. Here a historian named Chien Po-tsan is handed over to the mob. © D. R.

Those branded "enemies of the people" by gangs of fanatics were mistreated, beaten, and in many cases killed. Here a rich peasant is shot for having "exploited the peasantry."
© Archive Photos

Beijing, 1973. The display of portraits of Lenin and Stalin (Mao described the latter as the "great friend of the Chinese people") demonstrates that the founders of the U.S.S.R., despite the Sino-Soviet conflict, were still the essential points of reference for the Chinese Communist regime. © Archive Photos

The theatricality of Communism. From high on the ramparts of the Forbidden City, the leaders of the Chinese Communist Party survey the massed ranks of their subjects in Tiananmen Square. The distance between the leaders and the militarized assembly is characteristic of the regime. © Keystone

An agitprop scene with Red
Guards in Tiananmen Square.
Many of them suffered harsh
reprisals once Mao believed
that he had attained his objectives. Years later, many finally
spoke about the realities of
the Cultural Revolution and
joined the struggle for the
"fifth modernization" (i.e.,
democracy) after Mao's death.
© Eastfoto

In the spring of 1989 a new generation of Beijing students took
over Tiananmen Square. Their
principal demand was for democracy, symbolized here by a statue
placed in front of the giant portrait of Mao. © Catherine
Henriette/AFP

After several weeks the government used force against the student movement, which had great popular support. On the night of 4–5 June, tanks broke up the student camp. One thousand students died.
© Koichi Imaeda / Magnum Photos

Chinese dissidents refused to abandon the struggle. One example is the former Red Guard Wei Jingsheng (seated, right). Initially sentenced to 15 years in prison for "counterrevolutionary crimes," he was sentenced again in December 1995 to another 14-year term. In November 1997, after nearly 19 years in prison, he was released and exiled to the United States.
© Xinhua News Agency / AFP

China's own gulag system, the *laogai,* is a vast network of prison-factories based exclusively on penal labor. Many products made there are destined for export. Harry Wu was imprisoned in one for 19 years for criticizing the Soviet invasion of Hungary. He managed to gather considerable documentation about his experience. The two photographs here were taken in secret.

© D. R.

In a major offensive against South Vietnam in the spring of 1968, the Viet Minh army took the town of Hué. When South Vietnamese forces recaptured the town, they found several mass graves. © Gamma

A Communist reeducation camp in North Vietnam. The aim of reeducation is very specific: detainees are to approve of the system that has imprisoned them and to adopt the ideology of their oppressors. © Henri Bureau/Sygma

Terror as a means of education: the execution of a "counterrevolutionary" provides the opportunity to reinforce a political and social system. © Coll. Doan Van Toai

The victory of the Communist regime in Vietnam in 1975 led to a mass exodus of locals who felt their lives to be at risk. "Boat people" fled in small, rickety craft, preferring to risk their lives at sea, where pirate attacks were common, than to remain under the new dictatorship. © K. Gangler/ Sygma

Cambodia, April 1975. The victorious Khmer Rouge entering Phnom Penh. In a short time, young soldiers, mostly aged fifteen and sixteen, became the instruments of Pol Pot, "Big Brother Number One," emptying the capital of all its inhabitants. © A. Borrel/Sipa Press

After the fall of Pol Pot's regime, the new pro–Vietnamese government opened a "museum of genocide" in which the skulls of thousands of unidentified victims of the Khmer Rouge were displayed. © Spengler/Sygma

The Tuol Sleng prison, a former school, was one of the worst centers for torture and execution. Each prisoner—every man, woman, and child—was photographed before being cruelly executed. © Photo Reza/Sygma

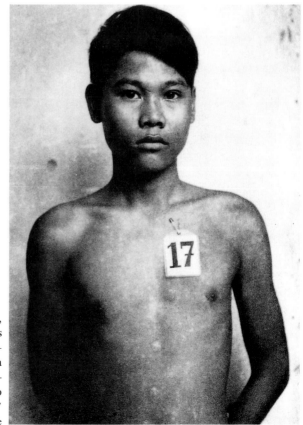

The photographer said: "As a rule, I took the photographs as soon as the prisoners arrived, after a number had been pinned on them with a safety pin. If they arrived bare-chested, the number was pinned to their skin." © Photo Archive Group/ Tuol Sleng, Musée du génocide

Pol Pot, his comrades, and his family, 1986. In July 1997 Pol Pot was dragged before a pseudotribunal by his own lieutenants and judged in a trial in which other political concerns were clearly paramount. He died of a heart attack in April 1998. © Archive Photos

Behind the minefields, the Khmer Rouge still have a number of active units in Cambodia. Cambodia has the highest proportion of victims of landmines in the world. Most victims are children and adolescents. © Lovinny/Gamma

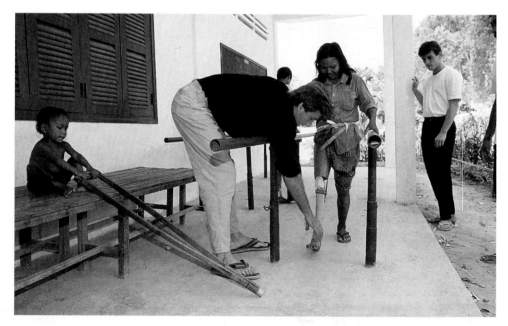

When the Batista regime fell in Cuba, Castro was only one of the rebels involved, and hopes for change were high among Cubans. Castro's rapid seizure of power brought considerable opposition among other factions. Left to right: Pedro Luis Boitel, a prisoner who died on hunger strike in 1972; Humberto Sori Marin, who was shot after attempting to organize an armed struggle agains his former comrade-in-arms, Castro; and the poet Jorge Valls, who was sentenced to 20 years in prison and only recently freed. © D. R., © Luc Adrian *(right)*

General Ochoa, the former commander of the Cuban force in Angola, was accused by Castro of plotting against him. On the grounds that Ochoa had been trafficking in drugs (as the special services of the regime had done for years), Castro had him condemned to death and executed. © F. Carrie/Gamma

Castro effectively muzzled society through the use of Committees for Defense of the Revolution (CDRs) established throughout the country. They were essentially designed to keep watch over families. The other major element in the Cuban repressive apparatus is the popular tribunal, usually held in CDR headquarters. © L'illustration/Sygma

Long before the boat people fled Vietnam, tens of thousands of *balseros* were leaving Cuba on makeshift rafts like the one pictured here. Thousands died at sea. © Viviane Rivière/Sipa Press

Fidel Castro with Eden Pastora Gomez, known as Comandante Zero, the most prestigious Sandinista guerrilla chief in the struggle against Somoza. Pastora became a vociferous opponent of the Sandinista regime in Managua when it attempted to turn the country into a Soviet-style republic. He started a new guerrilla war, which lasted until 1986 (right). © D. R.

In Peru the Shining Path, a Maoist terrorist group, does not hesitate to massacre peasants who refuse to cooperate. Seventy-two people lost their lives in the village of Mazamari in this particular attack. Pictured is the head of one victim. © Monica San Martin/Gamma

Ethiopia, 14 September 1979. The Soviet prime minister, Aleksei Kosygin, on a visit to Addis Ababa for the fifth anniversary of Mengistu Haile Mariam's seizure of power. His dictatorial regime was run along Soviet lines. The Workers' Party of Ethiopia expressed a desire to be "the inheritors of the great October Revolution." © Lefort/Gamma

In the mid-1980s drought hit Ethiopia, causing widespread famine. Mengistu used the weapon of hunger to force large segments of the population to move out of areas where guerrillas were operating. Ethiopians thus became hostages in a "political reorganization of the territory." © C. Steele-Perkins/Magnum Photos

Supported by the Soviet Union after 1974, the Popular Movement for the Liberation of Angola also received help from Cuba in 1975. Tens of thousands of "volunteers" came to fight the non-Marxist movements, rivals of the MPLA, before beginning a withdrawal in January 1989. © P. Aventurier/Gamma

On 27 December 1979, Soviet troops entered Afghanistan in response to appeals from the local Communist leaders, who were losing control. An extremely bloody war ensued. In the face of widespread resistance, the Soviet troops carried out a "scorched-earth" policy, destroying towns and villages. Children were often the first victims of antipersonnel mines (above). Over ten years, Soviet military operations claimed 1–1.5 million lives, of which 90 percent were civilians. © L. Van der Stockt/Gamma

Martwa Droga, the Road of Death. In 1949 Stalin began a railway link north of the Arctic Circle between Sakhelard and Igarka. "Onward to Communism" proclaims the banner above. After Stalin's death, the project was abandoned. The "locomotive of history," which once pulled Trotsky's train before pulling so many boxcars of deportees, now lies a rusting wreck in the forest. © Tomasz Kizny/Vu

The resulting famine affected the whole country. In Beijing, playing fields and recreation areas were transformed into allotments, and 2 million chickens were to be found on people's balconies in the capital.[88] No province was spared, despite the immense size of the country and the wide variety of climates and cultures. That fact alone shows the ridiculousness of the official explanation, which blamed the famine on some of the worst climatic conditions of the century. In fact 1954 and 1980 saw far greater climatic disturbances. In 1960, only 8 of the 120 Chinese weather stations noted a drought of any consequence, and only a third mentioned drought as a problem at all.[89] The 1960 harvest of 143 million tons of grain was 26 percent lower than that of 1957, which was almost the same as that of 1958. The harvest had fallen to its level in 1950, while the population had grown by 100 million during the decade.[90] The towns, which were generally privileged in terms of allocations of food stocks, partly because of the proximity of the government, were not hit as hard. In 1961, at the darkest moment, their inhabitants on average received 181 kilos of grain, whereas peasants received 153; the peasants' ration had fallen by 23 percent, that of the townspeople by 8 percent. Mao, in the tradition of Chinese leaders, but in contradiction to the legend that he encouraged to grow up around him, showed here how little he really cared for what he thought of as the clumsy and primitive peasants.

There were considerable variations among regions. The most fragile regions, in the north and northwest, the only ones that had really suffered famine over the last century, were the hardest hit. By contrast, in Heilongjiang, in the far north, which was relatively untouched and largely virgin territory, the population climbed from 14 million to 20 million as the region became a haven for the hungry. As in earlier European famines, regions that specialized in commercial agricultural products (such as oil seed, sugarcane, sugar beet, and above all cotton) saw production fall dramatically, sometimes by as much as two-thirds. Since the hungry no longer had the means to buy their products, hunger struck here with particular severity. The price of rice on the free market (or on the black market) rose fifteen- or even thirtyfold. Maoist dogma exacerbated the disaster: because people's communes had a duty to be self-sufficient, the transfer of goods between provinces had been drastically reduced. There was also a lack of coal as hungry miners left to find food or to cultivate allotments wherever they could. The situation was compounded by the general apathy and dissolution brought on by hunger. In industrialized provinces such as Liaoning the effects were cumulative: agricultural production in 1960 fell to half of 1958 levels, and whereas an average of 1.66 million tons of foodstuffs had arrived in that region each year during the 1950s, after 1958 transfers for the whole country fell to a mere 1.5 million tons.

The fact that the famine was primarily a political phenomenon is demonstrated by the high death rates in provinces where the leaders were Maoist radicals, provinces that in previous years had actually been net exporters of grain, like Sichuan, Henan, and Anhui. This last province, in north-central China, was the worst affected of all. In 1960 the death rate soared to 68 percent from its normal level at around 15 percent, while the birth rate fell to 11 percent from its previous average of 30 percent. As a result the population fell by around 2 million people (6 percent of the total) in a single year.[91] Like Mao himself, Party activists in Henan were convinced that all the difficulties arose from the peasants' concealment of private stocks of grain. According to the secretary of the Xinyang district (10 million inhabitants), where the first people's commune in the country had been established, "The problem is not that food is lacking. There are sufficient quantities of grain, but 90 percent of the inhabitants are suffering from ideological difficulties."[92] In the autumn of 1959 the class war was momentarily forgotten, and a military-style offensive was launched against the peasants, using methods very similar to those used by anti-Japanese guerrilla groups. At least 10,000 peasants were imprisoned, and many died of hunger behind bars. The order was given to smash all privately owned cutlery that had not yet been turned to steel to prevent people from being able to feed themselves by pilfering the food supply of the commune. Even fires were banned, despite the approach of winter. The excesses of repression were terrifying. Thousands of detainees were systematically tortured, and children were killed and even boiled and used as fertilizer—at the very moment when a nationwide campaign was telling people to "learn the Henan way." In Anhui, where the stated intention was to keep the red flag flying even if 99 percent of the population died, cadres returned to the traditional practices of live burials and torture with red-hot irons.[93] Funerals were prohibited lest their number frighten survivors even more and lest they turn into protest marches. Taking in the numerous abandoned children was also banned, on the ground that "The more we take in, the more will be abandoned."[94] Desperate villagers who tried to force their way into the towns were greeted with machine-gun fire. More than 800 people died in this manner in the Fenyang district, and 12 percent of the rural population, or 28,000 people, were punished in some manner. This campaign took on the proportions of a veritable war against the peasantry. In the words of Jean-Luc Domenach, "The intrusion of Utopia into politics coincided very closely with that of police terror in society."[95] Deaths from hunger reached over 50 percent in certain villages, and in some cases the only survivors were cadres who abused their position. In Henan and elsewhere there were many cases of cannibalism (63 were recorded officially): children were sometimes eaten in accordance with a communal decision.[96]

In 1968 Wei Jingsheng, an eighteen-year-old Red Guard pursued by the authorities like millions of others, took refuge with his family in a village in Anhui, where he heard many stories about the Great Leap Forward:[97]

As soon as I arrived here, I often heard peasants talking about the Great Leap Forward as though it was some sort of apocalypse that they had by some miracle escaped. Quite fascinated, I questioned them in detail about the subject so that soon I too was convinced that the "three years of natural catastrophes" had not been as natural as all that, and had rather been the result of a series of political blunders. The peasants said, for example, that in 1959–60, during the "Communist Wind" [one of the official names for the Great Leap Forward] their hunger had been so great that they had not even been strong enough to harvest the rice crop when it was ready, and that it would otherwise have been a relatively good year for them. Many of them died of hunger watching the grains of rice fall into the fields, blown off by the wind. In some villages there was literally no one left to take in the harvest. One time I was with a relative who lived a small distance away from our village. On the way to his home, we went past a deserted village. All the houses had lost their roofs. Only the mud walls remained.

Thinking it was a village that had been abandoned during the Great Leap Forward, when all the villages were being reorganized and relocated, I asked why the walls hadn't been knocked down to make room for more fields. My relative replied: "But these houses all belong to people, and you can't knock them down without their permission." I stared at the walls and couldn't believe that they were actually inhabited. "Of course they were inhabited! But everyone here died during the 'Communist Wind,' and no one has ever come back. The land was then shared out among the neighboring villages. But because it seemed possible that some of them might come back, the living quarters were never shared out. Still, that was so long ago, I don't think anyone will come back now."

We walked along beside the village. The rays of the sun shone on the jade-green weeds that had sprung up between the earth walls, accentuating the contrast with the rice fields all around, and adding to the desolation of the landscape. Before my eyes, among the weeds, rose up one of the scenes I had been told about, one of the banquets at which the families had swapped children in order to eat them. I could see the worried faces of the families as they chewed the flesh of other people's children. The children who were chasing butterflies in a nearby field seemed to be the reincarnation of the children devoured by their parents. I felt sorry for the children, but not as sorry as I felt for their parents. What had made them swallow that human flesh, amidst the tears and grief of other parents—flesh that they would never have imagined tasting, even in their worst nightmares? In that moment I understood what a butcher he had been, the man "whose like humanity has not seen in several centuries, and China not in several thousand years":[98] Mao Zedong. Mao Zedong and his henchmen, with their criminal political system, had driven parents mad with hunger and led them to hand their own children over to others, and to receive the flesh of others to appease their own hunger. Mao Zedong, to wash away the crime that he had committed in assassinating democracy [an allusion to the Hundred Flowers trap], had launched the Great Leap Forward, and obliged thousands and thousands of peasants dazed by hunger to kill one another with hoes, and to save their own lives thanks to the flesh and blood of their childhood companions. They were not the real killers; the real killers were Mao Zedong and his companions. At last I understood where Peng Dehuai had found the strength to attack the Central Committee of the Party led by Mao, and at last I understood why the peasants loathed Communism so much, and why they had never allowed anyone to attack the policies of Liu Shaoqi, "three freedoms and one guarantee." For the good and simple reason that they had no intention of ever having to eat their own flesh and blood again, or of killing their companions to eat them in a moment of instinctual madness. That reason was far more important than any ideological consideration.

At the moment that Yuri Gagarin was being launched into space, a country possessing more than 30,000 miles of railway lines and an extensive radio and telephone network was being ravaged by a subsistence crisis of the sort that had plagued premodern Europe, but on a scale that in the eighteenth century would have affected the population of the entire world. Literally countless millions were trying to boil grass and bark to make soup, stripping leaves off trees in the towns, wandering the roads of the country desperate for anything to eat trying vainly to attack food convoys, and sometimes desperately banding together into gangs (as in the Xinyang and Lan Kao districts in Henan).[99] They were sent nothing to eat, but on occasion the local cadres who were supposedly responsible for the famine were shot. There were armed raids on houses all over the country in a search for ground maize.[100] An enormous increase in disease and infections increased the death rate further, while the birth rate fell to almost zero as women were unable to conceive because of malnutrition. Prisoners in the *laogai* were not the last to die of hunger, although their situation was no less precarious than that of the neighboring peasants who came to the camps to beg for something to eat. In August 1960, after one year of famine, three-quarters of Jean Pasqualini's work brigade were dead or dying, and the survivors were reduced to searching through horse manure for undigested grains of wheat and eating the worms they found in cowpats.[101] People in the camps were used as guinea pigs in hunger experiments. In one case flour was mixed with 30 percent paper paste in bread to study the effects on digestion, while in another study marsh plankton were mixed with rice water. The first experiment caused atrocious constipation throughout the camp, which caused many deaths. The second also caused much illness, and many who were already weakened ended up dying.

For the entire country, the death rate rose from 11 percent in 1957 to 15 percent in 1959 and 1961, peaking at 29 percent in 1960. Birth rates fell from 33 percent in 1957 to 18 percent in 1961. Excluding the deficit in births, which was perhaps as many as 33 million (although some births were merely delayed), loss of life linked to the famine in the years 1959–1961 was somewhere between 20 million and 43 million people.[102] The lower end of the range is the official figure used by the Chinese government since 1988. This was quite possibly the worst famine not just in the history of China but in the history of the world. The second worst had occurred in northern China in 1877–78 and had taken between 9 million and 13 million lives. The one that had struck the U.S.S.R. in a similar political and economic context in 1932–1934 had caused around 6 million deaths, a smaller proportion of the total population than in China during the Great Leap Forward.[103] Under normal conditions, mortality in the countryside was between 30 percent and 60 percent higher than in the cities. In 1960 it doubled, climbing from 14 percent to 29 percent. Peasants managed to delay the effects of the famine slightly by consuming their own livestock, which amounted to using up their productive capital. In 1957–1961, 48 percent of pigs and 30 percent of all dairy animals were slaughtered.[104] The surface area given over to nonfood crops such as cotton, which was the country's main industry at the time, diminished by more than one-third in 1959–1962, and this fall in production inevitably hit the manufacturing sector. Although after 1959 peasant markets were reopened to stimulate production, the prices demanded were so high and the quantities available so low that few of the starving could find enough to survive. In 1961, for example, the price of pork was fourteen times higher in the markets than in the state shops. The price of feed went up less than that of grain in the pastoral northwest, which was chronically deficient in grain. In Gansu people were still dying of hunger in 1962, and the grain ration was equivalent to only half the official limit for conditions of "semi-starvation."

Whether through unawareness of or, more likely, indifference to the several million lives that had to be sacrificed to build Communism, the state responded (if such a word can be used here) to the crisis with measures that under the circumstances were quite simply criminal. Net grain exports, principally to the U.S.S.R., rose from 2.7 million tons in 1958 to 4.2 million in 1959, and in 1960 fell only to the 1958 level. In 1961, 5.8 million tons were actually imported, up from 66,000 in 1960, but this was still too little to feed the starving.[105] Aid from the United States was refused for political reasons. The rest of the world, which could have responded easily, remained ignorant of the scale of the catastrophe. Aid to the needy in the countryside totaled less than

450 million yuan per annum, or 0.8 yuan per person, at a time when one kilo of rice on the free market was worth 2 to 4 yuan. Chinese Communism boasted that it could move mountains and tame nature, but it left these faithful to die.

From August 1959 until 1961, the Party acted as though it was powerless to help, simply standing by and watching events unfold. Criticizing the Great Leap Forward, behind which Mao had thrown all his weight, was a dangerous business. But the situation became so bad that Liu Shaoqi, the number two leader in the regime, finally put the Chairman on the defensive and imposed a partial return to the easier form of collectivization that had been the policy before the invention of the people's communes. People were again allowed to own a small amount of land, peasant markets were reopened, small private workshops were opened, and labor teams were subdivided into labor brigades, which were equivalent to the size of the earlier village teams. As a result of these measures the country quickly emerged from the famine.[106] But it did not emerge as fast from poverty. Agricultural production, which had grown steadily from 1952 to 1958, had lost its way, and the effects were felt for two decades. Confidence would return only "when the belly was full" (as Mao said would occur in the people's communes). Overall agricultural production doubled between 1952 and 1978, but during this time the population rose from 574 million to 959 million, and most of the per-capita increase in production had taken place in the 1950s. In most places production did not reach 1957 levels until at least 1965 (and as late as 1968–69 in Henan).[107] Overall, agricultural productivity was severely affected; the Great Leap Forward's astonishing waste of resources caused it to fall by about one-quarter. Not until 1983 did productivity again reach 1952 levels.[108] Eyewitness reports from the days of the Cultural Revolution all concur that China was still a traditional village society of great poverty, functioning as a subsistence economy where luxuries were extremely rare (cooking oil, for instance, was like gold dust).[109] The Great Leap Forward made the people extremely suspicious of the regime's propaganda. It is hardly surprising that the peasants responded most enthusiastically to Deng Xiaoping's economic reforms, and were the driving force behind the reintroduction of a market economy twenty years after the launch of the people's communes.

The disasters of 1959–1961, the regime's great secret, which many foreign visitors also managed to deny, were never recognized for what they really were. Liu went out on a limb in January 1962 when he claimed at a conference of cadres that 70 percent of the famine had been due to human error.[110] It was impossible to say any more than that without directly incriminating Mao. Even after his death, in the Chinese Communist Party's televised final verdict on his life in 1981, there was no criticism of the Great Leap Forward.

The *Laogai:* The Hidden Gulag

Chinese Communism has many skeletons in the closet, and it is amazing how long they have escaped the world's attention. The immense concentration-camp system is no exception. There were nearly 1,000 large-scale camps as well as innumerable detention centers (see the maps at the beginning of the chapter), but in many histories of the People's Republic, even in some of the more detailed and recent works, they receive no mention. The repressive apparatus hid itself extremely well. Because punishment by prison or forced labor smacked too much of the old regime, people were sent instead for "reform" or "reeducation" through labor. The main internment camps were disguised as large public enterprises, so one had to know, for instance, that the "Jingzhou Industrial Dye Works," which was the name on the door, was actually Prison No. 3 of Hubei Province, or that the "Yingde Tea Plantation" was Labor Reeducation Center No. 7 of Guangdong Province.[111] Even the families of prisoners wrote only to an anonymous post office box. Throughout the Mao era, visits were forbidden during the whole instruction process, which generally lasted for more than a year. Particularly during the Cultural Revolution, relatives were not always notified about the incarceration or even the death of prisoners, or were informed only much later. The children of Liu Shaoqi, the former president of the Republic, who was held in a secret prison, did not learn about his death in November 1969 until August 1972; only then were they allowed to visit their mother, who like her husband had been locked up since August 1967.[112] If prisoners ever went out into the world, they were under strict orders to remain invisible. Accustomed to hanging their heads and staying silent in their cells, they received strange new orders at the station: "Behave normally in the train. It is forbidden, I repeat, forbidden to bow your head. If anyone has to go to the latrine, signal to the guard, the fist with the thumb sticking out. Smoking and talking will be allowed. No funny stuff. The guards have orders to shoot."[113]

For many years statements from former prisoners were extremely rare. One reason was that under Mao it was extremely difficult for anyone who had entered the penal system to emerge from it. Another was that prisoners who were freed had to swear that they would not talk about their experiences; otherwise they would be reimprisoned. So it was foreigners, who formed only a tiny fraction of the number of those imprisoned, who provided most of the stories that still account for most of the available information. Because the foreign prisoners were protected by their governments, they generally came out alive. Some were explicitly charged with the mission to bear witness to the outside world of the suffering of the army of people trapped in those forgotten prisons. Such was the case of Jean Pasqualini, whose Chinese name was Bao Ruo-wang. One of his fellow prisoners told him why he and his companions were looking after him so carefully: "All these people, and none of them will ever make it out, myself included. Lifetime contract. You are the only one who is different, Bao. You might get out the big door someday. It could happen to a foreigner, but not to us. You will be the only one who can tell about it afterward if you do. That's why we wanted to keep you alive . . . Don't worry, as long as you're here, you'll live. I can promise you that. And if you get transferred to other camps, there will be other people who think like us. You're precious cargo, old man!"[114]

The Biggest Penal System of All Time

The *laogai* was a sort of nonplace, a black hole where the light of Maoism blinded tens of millions of people. As a rough indication, Harry Wu calculates that up to the mid-1980s some 50 million people passed through the system.[115] Many died there. According to estimates by Jean-Luc Domenach, there were roughly 10 million detainees each year, which equals 1–2 percent of the overall population. Given that the mortality rate was around 5 percent, some 20 million Chinese must have died during imprisonment, including approximately 4 million in 1959–1962 during the famine caused by the Great Leap Forward (although a return to normal rations took place only in 1964).[116] Along with Jean Pasqualini's extraordinary revelations, two recent studies (those of Wu and Domenach) now yield a better general picture of the least-known of the century's three great concentration-camp systems.

The scale of the system was enormous, as were the variety of prisoners and the system's durability (the first great wave of liberations began only in 1978). In 1955, 80 percent of inmates were technically political prisoners, although many common criminals had been reclassified as political offenders and their sentences correspondingly lengthened. By the beginning of the following decade the share of political prisoners had fallen to 50 percent, and by 1971 to one-third—perhaps indications of popular discontent with the regime, and of the rise of criminality in a situation of political instability.[117] Internment took a variety of forms.[118] There were preventive centers, prisons (including special establishments for former leaders), the official *laogai*, and more moderate deportation centers, known as *laojiao* and *jiuye*. Detention centers, numbering some 2,500 and located in various cities, were stepping-stones on the way to the penal archipelago. Here detainees waited while the cases against them were drawn up—a process that sometimes took ten years. Sentences of less than two years were also served in these centers. The approximately 1,000 prisons proper contained only 13 percent of detainees and generally were run directly by the central authorities. In these heavily guarded, high-security centers people with the stiffest sentences were detained. They included those sentenced to death with the sentence suspended for two years, which was usually converted to life imprisonment "for sincere reform of character" at the end of the two years. These prisons also housed the more sensitive cases, including high-ranking cadres, foreigners, priests, dissidents, and spies. Living conditions were extremely variable, and in some cases were almost luxurious: in Beijing Prison No. 1, a model prison where foreign visitors were taken on tours, people ate as much as they wanted and slept on a tatami rather than on wooden slats.[119] But harsh discipline, the severity of the industrial labor performed there, and the constant ideological battering often led prisoners to request transfer to the "open air" of the labor camps.

The majority of detainees ended up in these huge camps, which were scattered all over the country. The biggest and the most populated were situated in the semidesert zones of northern Manchuria, Inner Mongolia, Tibet, Xinjiang, and above all Qinghai, which was a genuine penal province—the Chinese equivalent of the Russian Kolyma, with a climate that was scorching in the summer and freezing in the winter.[120] Camp No. 2 there was perhaps the largest in China, holding at least 50,000 deportees.[121] The camps in the distant western and northeastern regions were reputed to be extremely harsh, but on the whole working conditions were worse in the prison factories in the urban zones than at these huge state penal farms. Because detainees were in principle under the authority of the provincial or municipal administration (Shanghai had a network of camps spread over several different regions), they tended to come from the same general area, so that, for example, there were no Tibetan detainees in eastern China. Unlike Soviet camps, Chinese camps were integrated into the local or regional economic framework and only occasionally were part of national projects such as the "friendship railway" to Soviet Kirgiziya (Kirgizstan), whose construction was halted for more than thirty years on account of the Sino-Soviet split.

The inmates of the camps were divided into three categories. Under Mao the biggest group, which stayed the longest, consisted of people who had been sentenced specifically to the *laogai*, which can be translated as "reform through labor."[122] These medium- or long-term prisoners were organized in a military fashion into squadrons, battalions, companies, and so on. They had lost their civil rights, received no payment for their labor, and were rarely allowed to receive visitors. In the same camps, or occasionally in special establishments, was a second category, those who were there for "reeducation through labor," or *laojiao*. This was a form of administrative detention invented in August 1957 in the heat of the Antirightist campaign, and to some extent it formalized the extrajudicial incarceration activities of the security forces. Victims were not actually sentenced, so there was no fixed term for their detention, and they had not been formally stripped of their civil rights, although it was impossible, for example, to vote in the camps. They received a small wage, most of which was held back to pay for their food and lodging. Most of the crimes of which they were accused were slight, and their stay in the *laojiao* was rarely longer than a few years, but they were given to understand that much depended on their attitude. The discipline and the detention and working conditions in the *laojiao* were very similar to those found in the *laogai*, and both were in practice run by the state security organs.

Slightly more privileged were the "forced job-placement personnel" of the *jiuye*, who were sometimes known as "free workers" although they had no right to leave their place of work, which was usually a camp, except perhaps twice a year. They were treated better and paid slightly more than the *laojiao* prisoners, and they could bring their families to the camps or even get married there. They lived, however, in semiprison conditions. These were a sort of decompression chamber for the camps, where people who had been freed were often kept for the rest of their lives. Until the 1960s, 95 percent of all prisoners in the *laogai* were kept in the *jiuye* once their sentences had been served. At the beginning of the 1980s that figure was still 50 percent, plus between 20 percent and 30 percent of former *laojiao* prisoners.[123] Cut off from their original milieus, having lost their jobs and their right to reside in a city, generally divorced because wives were constantly incited by the authorities to leave "criminal" husbands, and condemned to being suspects for the rest of their lives because they had "sinned" once, they had nowhere left to go, and thus were forced to resign themselves to their condition. Because they had nothing left to hope for, even the *laogai* prisoners felt sorry for them:

> The free workers we began running across were a sorry lot. They looked as if they belonged in prison. They were lazy, unskilled, and dirty. Evidently they had concluded that nothing was worth the effort any more, and in a way they were right. They were constantly hungry and subject to the orders of guards and warders, and they were locked up at night just like the rest of us. The only difference between our condition and theirs was the home visit privilege. Nothing else counted. True, they now received salaries, but they had to spend them on food and clothing, which were no longer gifts of the government. These free workers just didn't give a damn.[124]

Under Mao, any sentence was thus effectively a life sentence.

The Search for the "New Man"

Imprisonment with no possibility of returning to society was a fundamental contradiction of the much-vaunted aim of the penal system: the reform of the detainee and his transformation into a "new man." As Jean-Luc Domenach has pointed out, the system constantly claimed that "detention is not a punishment, but an opportunity for the criminal to reform his habits."[125] One internal document from the security services made clear the process that faced new detainees: "One can submit to the law only if one has first acknowledged the error of one's ways. Acceptance and submissiveness are the first two lessons that prisoners must be taught, and they must keep these lessons in mind throughout their stay." Once prisoners had broken with their past, they could begin to accept "correct ideas": "It is imperative that the four basic educational principles be instilled to set the criminal's political ideas back on the right path: Marxism-Leninism, faith in Maoism and socialism, the Communist Party, and the democratic dictatorship of the people."[126] As a consequence, penitentiaries were above all places to teach these "bad students" who had been unruly or slow to learn; for such at least was the thinking of the Party. "Welcome to our new schoolmates!" read one banner that Pasqualini came across in a labor camp.[127] And there certainly were studies involved. During the training period, there were at least two hours of study each day, after dinner in the cells. But when the progress of some prisoners was unsatisfactory or when there were political campaigns, study could last a whole day, a week, or even a month. In many cases "nonstop study" lasting from two weeks to three months served as a sort of introduction to the penal system.[128] Classes followed an extremely rigid pattern, during which it was forbidden to walk around, to get up (or even to change one's sitting posture), to talk, or, of course, to fall asleep, which was a permanent temptation after a hard day's work. Pasqualini, who was brought up a Catholic, was surprised to discover meditation, confession, and repentance reinvented as Marxist-Leninist practices, with the only difference being the relentlessly public nature of the acts. The goal was no longer to rebuild a bridge between man and God, but to dissolve the individual into a mass submissive to the Party. To vary things a little, the sessions that centered upon confessions (which were extremely detailed) alternated with reading and commentary on the *People's Daily* or discussion of an event chosen for their edification. During the Cultural Revolution, the works of Chairman Mao were read instead; everyone was obliged to carry around a copy of the volume of his thoughts.

In all cases the aim was the same: the destruction of individual personality. The cell chief, who was himself a prisoner, and who usually had been a Party member, had a key role to play here: "He would constantly start the ball rolling in group discussions or tell stories with moral principles for our instruction. All the other things we might have talked about—family, food, sports, pastimes, or sex of course—were totally forbidden. 'Facing the government, we must study together and watch each other'; that was the motto, and it was written up everywhere in the prison." Confession was a good idea, as was admitting that one had done wrong because one was bad: "Whatever category we fit into, all of us have committed our crimes because we had very bad thoughts," the cell chief would say.[129] And if that was the way it was, then the explanation had to be that everyone was contaminated by capitalist, imperialist, or reactionary ideas. In the final analysis, in a society in which nothing escaped politics, all crimes were political.

The solution, then, was quite simple: change people's ideas. Because in China ritual was inseparable from the heart, Marshal Lin Biao promoted a model that encouraged people to want to become another revolutionary in a blue boilersuit, or a hero like the soldier Lei Feng, who was proud to be a tiny cog in the great machine in the service of the Cause, and who had been lucky enough to die while on a mission in the early 1960s. "The prisoner," Lin Biao declared, "quickly learns to talk in noncommittal slogans. The danger of this, of course, is that he might end up thinking in slogans. Most do. Generally it takes the realities of camp life to pull him out of it."[130]

Jean Pasqualini recalls an episode exemplary of the schizophrenic universe created by the system of confession:

> On a cold, windy night at study time, I left the cell to go out and take a leak. When the cold northwesterly wind caught me, I felt less inclined to walk the 200 yards over to the latrine. I went over to a storage building and pissed against the wall. After all, I reasoned, no one would see me in the dark.
>
> I was wrong. I had barely finished when I received a very sharp and swift kick in the ass. When I turned around I could make out only a silhouette, but the voice belonged to a warder.
>
> "Don't you know the sanitation rules?" he demanded. "Who are you anyway?"
>
> I gave my name, and what happened next was a lesson I would never forget . . .
>
> "I admit that I am wrong, warder, but what I am doing is only a violation of prison regulations, whereas you have broken the law. Government members are not allowed to lay hands on prisoners. Physical violence is forbidden."
>
> There was a pause while the silhouette considered, and I expected the worst.

"What you say is right, Bao," he said with measured calm. "I admit that I have made a mistake—and I will bring up this subject at our [the warders'] next self-criticism session. Would you be ready to return to your cell and write me a thorough confession?"

I was surprised by his reaction. I was touched, too; for here was a warder admitting his mistake before a prisoner. An unheard-of thing! What else could I do but blurt out, "Yes, warder, I certainly will."

. . . I sat in my place and began preparing my confession. At the weekly examination of conscience a few days later, I read it aloud for the entire cell to hear.

"What I did may appear on the surface to be not too serious," I added after I had finished reading, "but on further examination it demonstrates a disregard for the teachings of the government and a resistance to reform. By pissing I was displaying my anger in an underhanded manner. It was a cowardly act. It was like spitting in the face of the government when I though no one was looking. I can only ask that the government punish me as severely as possible."

The confession was sent to Warder Yang, and I waited. I was bracing myself for another bout of solitary. Two nights later Yang came to the cell with his verdict.

"A few days ago," he said, "one of you thought he was above the law and committed a big mistake . . . We'll let him go this time, but don't think this means that you can always weasel out of trouble by just writing an apology."[131]

The so-called brainwashing described by a number of Western observers was precisely that. There was nothing subtle about it; it was simply the rather brutish imposition of a heavy-handed ideology with a simplistic answer for everything. The essential point was to ensure that prisoners had no chance of individual expression. The means were multiple. The most original were systematic underfeeding which weakened resistance, and permanent saturation with the message of orthodoxy. These techniques were used in a context in which there was no free time (study, work, and obligatory exercises filled the long days) or personal space (the cells were overcrowded, the lights were kept on all night, and very few personal belongings were permitted), and no opportunity to express one's own ideas: all the obligatory contributions to discussions were carefully recorded and kept in the file of the person who had made them. Pasqualini paid dearly for one remark in 1959, in which he showed a slight lack of enthusiasm for the Chinese intervention in Tibet. Another original feature of the system was the delegation of most of the ideological work to the prisoners, demonstrating the effectiveness of the system. The prisoners searched each other, evaluated their companions' performance at work and controlled the amount of food they ate, discussed the extent of "reform" undergone by those who were to be set free; above all, criticized their cell companions to push them to complete self-criticism in order to demonstrate their own progress.[132]

Pasqualini recalls the use of food as a weapon:

What power food can have—it is the only important thing, the greatest joy, and the most powerful motivating force in the entire prison system. I had the bad luck to go to Grass Mist Lane [one of the biggest detention centers in Beijing] only a month after rationing had been introduced as a formal part of the interrogation process. No greater weapon exists for inducing cooperation. The distressingly thin and watery corn gruel, the hard little loaves of *wo'tou* [a Chinese equivalent of bread, eaten more than rice in northern China], and the sliver of vegetable became the center of our lives and the focus of our deepest attentions. As rationing continued and we grew thinner, we learned to eat each morsel with infinite attention, making it last as long as possible. Rumors and desperate fantasies circulated about how well prisoners ate in the camps. These rumors, I later learned, were often planted by the interrogators to encourage confessions. After a year of this diet I was prepared to admit virtually anything to get more food.

The starvation was painstakingly studied—enough to keep us alive, but never enough to let us forget our hunger. During my fifteen months in the interrogation center, I ate rice only once and never ate meat. Six months after my arrest, my stomach was entirely sunken in, and I began to have the characteristic bruised joints from simple body contact with the communal bed. The skin on my ass hung loose like the teats of an old woman. Vision became unclear, and I lost my power of concentration. I reached a sort of record point for vitamin deficiency when I was finally able to snap off my toenails without using the clipper. My skin rubbed off in a dusty film. My hair began falling out . . .

"Life here didn't used to be so bad," Loo told me. "We used to have a meal of rice every 15 days, steamed white bread at the end of every month, and some meat on big holidays, like the New Year, 1 May, and 1 October. It was alright."

What changed it all was that some people's delegation came to inspect the prison during the Hundred Flowers period [in fact during the Antirightist movement that followed]. They were horrified to see prisoners eating enough. It was intolerable, they concluded, that these counterrevolutionaries, the scum of society and the enemies of the people, should have a standard of living higher than that of many peasants. From November 1957 on there was no more rice or meat or wheat flour for prisoners on festive occasions.

Food obsessed us so completely that we were insane, in a way. We were ready for anything. It was the perfect climate for interrogations. Every one of us began begging to be sent to the camps. No one ever left the Grass Mist Lane without specifically requesting it in writing. There was even a form for it. "Please give me the authorization to show repentance for my sins by working in the camps."

Later, no matter how bad the conditions became in the camps, every warder could truthfully tell us that we were there only because we had asked for it.[133]

The more traditional methods of persuasion were also used on prisoners. The incentive offered was the promise of better treatment for people who admitted their crimes, behaved well, made an active contribution to the retraining of their companions, and denounced their accomplices or rebellious companions. Denunciation was an essential test of genuine reform. In the words of one of the official formulas, "the denunciation of others is a very good method of repentance." Inside the investigation bureau was a banner that proclaimed: "Leniency to those who confess; severity to those who resist; redemption to those who obtain merits; rewards to those who gain big merits."[134] Many of those who had received long sentences showed themselves to be zealous propagandists in the hope of getting their sentences shortened. The problem—and Pasqualini gives several examples—was that they never got anything in return: either their good conduct was never enough to prevent a heavy sentence, or, worse still—as sentences were usually announced only orally and people were often not present at their own trial—the reduction in the sentence brought it down to the length that had always been foreseen anyway. One old detainee explained the system as follows: "Communists don't feel obliged to keep promises they make to their enemies. As a means to an end, they feel free to use any scheme or ruse that happens to serve them, and that includes threats and promises . . . And remember another thing—Communists don't have any respect for turncoats either."[135]

Coercive measures were more common. Sentences were lengthened for anyone who failed to confess, who refused to denounce his comrades ("withholding information from the government is a punishable offense"),[136] who spoke in what was judged to be a heretical fashion, or who appealed his sentence and thereby demonstrated that he refused to accept the will of the masses. Thus it was relatively easy to have one's sentence changed from five years to life. Prisoners could also drastically affect the lives of their fellow prisoners. The "career" of the cell chief depended on the others, so he would always attack those who resisted the most and was generally supported by the others in these attacks. In addition to this process of weeding out, there was the "test" or "struggle." There was nothing spontaneous about this; the victim had been chosen by the prison authorities, and the time and the place were also determined in advance. The atmosphere recalled that of the peasant pogroms during the agrarian reform, although here death was only rarely a consequence. Pasqualini recalls:

> Our victim was a middle-aged prisoner charged with having made a false confession. He was an obstinate counterrevolutionary, a cadre shouted to us through a cardboard megaphone . . . Every time he raised his head to say anything—truth or falsehood, that wasn't our concern—we drowned him with roaring cries of "Liar! Scum!" or even "Son of a bitch!" and the like . . . The struggle continued for about three more hours like this, and with every minute that passed we grew colder and meaner. I almost think we would have been capable of tearing him to pieces to get what we wanted. Later, when I had the time to reflect, I realized that of course we had been struggling ourselves at the same time, mentally preparing to accept the government's position with passionate assent, whatever the merits of the man we were facing.[137]

Under such conditions the vast majority of prisoners were eventually beaten into submission. In this process the role of the Chinese approach to identity was at most secondary. Many French prisoners of war held by the Viet Minh, who on the whole were treated better than the Chinese prisoners but went through a similar process of reeducation, reacted in the same way.[138] The effectiveness of the reeducation process derived from a combination of two powerful means of psychological persuasion. One was radical infantilization, in which the Party and the administration became father and mother, reteaching the prisoner how to talk and walk (head down, at double speed, with the guard shouting out instructions) and controlling his appetite and hygiene, all in a relation of absolute dependence. The other was the fusion of the prisoners into a single unit, in which every gesture and every word were significant. This group became a replacement family even as contact with the real family became almost impossible. Wives were forced to divorce their husbands and children to disown their parents.

We may well wonder how deep the personal reform really went. Speaking in slogans and reacting like an automaton were forms of self-abasement and could lead to "psychic suicide,"[139] but they were also means of self-protection and survival. The idea that people could maintain a sort of private space by somehow splitting their personality is perhaps naive. But people who ended up no longer hating Big Brother were often reasoning strategically rather than through conviction. Pasqualini notes that in 1961 his reeducation seemed to be complete and he sincerely believed everything that the guards told him. But he adds: "I also knew well that it was very much in my interest to keep my behavior as close as possible to the letter of the law." Pasqualini provides another example in the response to an ultra-Maoist cell chief: To prove his ardor and devotion to the regime, he claimed that prisoners should be allowed to work even after the temperature fell below the legal limit of five degrees above zero Fahrenheit and that they should be allowed to get up earlier to do more work. The guard interrupted this speech, judging it to be "totally unorthodox"—and the other prisoners were mightily relieved.[140] Like so many Chinese, they did have some belief in the system, but what they really wanted was to avoid trouble at all costs.

Once a Criminal Always a Criminal

There was no room in this system for the idea that an accusation might have been false or that anyone on trial might be acquitted. In China, people were not arrested because they were guilty; they were guilty because they had been arrested. All arrests were carried out by the police, which were part of the "people's government" led by the Communist Party and controlled by Mao Zedong. To question the reason for one's arrest was tantamount to opposing Chairman Mao, thus revealing that one really was a counterrevolutionary. By the same line of reasoning, any prison guard who was being disobeyed could simply shout "What! Do you dare to disobey the people's government?" Acceptance of one's crimes and total submissiveness were the only options possible. Self-castigation was the rule in the cells: "You are a counterrevolutionary. All of us are. Otherwise we would not be here."[141] According to the delirious logic of the system, the accused had to provide the motives for his arrest himself. "Tell us why you are here" was usually the first question the instructor asked a new prisoner. He also had to draw up the charges he would face, including a recommendation for sentencing. Prisoners were also required to present successive confessions (as soon as a serious problem arose, they had to start again from the beginning), which sometimes took months and sometimes ran to hundreds of pages, detailing whole decades of people's lives. The interrogations themselves went on for long periods, some for as long as 3,000 hours.[142] As people said, the Party had plenty of time. The interrogators often used sleep deprivation (which was reinforced by the fact that many interrogations took place at night), the threat of extreme punishment—even execution—or a terrifying visit to a torture chamber, later claimed to be a "museum."[143]

Nien Cheng, a former inmate of a Shanghai prison, recalls:

> The day after I returned from the prison hospital, the guard on duty handed me a pen and a bottle of ink. She said, "Get on with writing your confession! The interrogator is waiting for it."
>
> I picked up the roll of paper the interrogator had given me and saw that instead of the blank sheets I was given in the winter of 1966 when I was told to write my autobiography, page one had a special quotation of Mao. It was enclosed in a red-lined square under the heading "Supreme

Directive," and it said, "They are allowed only to be docile and obedient. They are not allowed to speak or to act out of turn." At the bottom of the sheet, where the prisoner usually signed his name, was written, "signature of criminal."

My immediate reaction was anger at the insulting word "criminal," and determination not to sign my name after it. However, after several minutes of consideration, I devised a scheme to exploit the situation . . .

Under the printed quotation of Mao, I drew another square over which I also wrote "Supreme Directive." Within the square, I wrote another of Mao's quotations: it did not appear in the Little Red Book, but I remembered it from his essay "On the Internal Contradictions of the People." The quotation said, "Where there is counterrevolution, we shall certainly suppress it. When we make a mistake, we shall certainly correct it" . . .

I handed the paper to the guard on duty. That very afternoon, I was called for interrogation.

Except for the soldier, the same men were in the room. A dark scowl was on each face, which I had anticipated when I decided to contest their right to assume I was a criminal when I was not. I did not wait for a signal from the interrogator, but bowed to Mao's portrait immediately. The quotation the interrogator chose for me to read was, "We must exercise the full power of dictatorship to suppress the running dogs of the imperialists and those who represent the interests of the landlords and the Kuomintang reactionary clique. They have only the right to be docile and obedient. They do not have the right to speak or to act out of turn."

The paper I had written was in front of the interrogator. After I sat down, he banged the table while glaring at me. Then he banged the table again and shouted, "What have you done here?" He pointed at the paper. "Do you think we are playing a game with you?"

I remained silent.

"Your attitude is not serious," the old worker said.

"If you do not change your attitude, you will never get out of this place," the young worker said.

Before I could say anything, the interrogator threw my account on the floor, scattering the pages, and stood up. He said, "Go back to your cell and write it again!"

A guard appeared at the doorway and shouted, "Come out!"[144]

Physical violence as such was quite rare, at least between the mid-1950s and the Cultural Revolution. Anything that resembled torture, such as blows or even insults, was strictly forbidden, and the prisoners knew this; if they could prove that they had been maltreated, they had some small hope of redress. Thus the only real violence was extremely subtle, consisting either in a "struggle session," in which other prisoners were permitted to inflict blows on the victim; or in confinement in unheated, badly ventilated cells so small that it was impossible to stretch out, where prisoners were permanently hand-cuffed or chained, often with their hands behind their backs, so that hygiene and eating were almost impossible. Prisoners in these cells usually died if the punishment lasted more than eight days. Permanent manacling in too-tight handcuffs was one of the commonest forms of quasi-torture, causing rapid swelling of the hands, intolerable pain, and often irreversible scarring.

> To put those special handcuffs tightly on the wrists of a prisoner was a form of torture commonly used in Maoist China's prison system. Sometimes additional chains were put around the ankles of the prison-ers. At other times a prisoner might be manacled and then have his handcuffs tied to a bar on the window so that he could not move away from the window to eat, drink, or go to the toilet. The purpose was to degrade a man in order to destroy his morale . . . Since the People's Government claimed to have abolished all forms of torture, the officials simply called such methods "punishment" or "persuasion."[145]

The official purpose of these measures was to obtain a confession, which itself carried the force of proof, and denunciations, which showed the pris-oner's sincerity, as well as proving that the police accusation was well founded. The rule was that three denunciations validated the arrest, and so the chain extended endlessly. With few exceptions, the tactics used by the police were the same as those used by police everywhere: highlighting contradictions, pretend-ing that all is known already, and comparing one confession with other confes-sions or denunciations. Denunciations, whether they were extracted by force or were spontaneous (the streets of most cities had a special "denunciation box") were in general so numerous that it was extremely difficult to hide anything of any significance about one's past. It was the act of reading the letters in which he had been denounced that finally broke Pasqualini's resis-tance: "It was a frightening revelation. On those hundreds of pages were handwritten denunciations from colleagues, friends, and various people I had encountered only once or twice . . .—how many people whom I had trusted without a second thought had betrayed me!"[146] Nien Cheng, who was freed in 1973 without having made any confession (this was quite unusual, and a result partly of extraordinary strength of character and partly of changes in police practice after the Cultural Revolution), was surrounded for years afterward by relatives, friends, students, and servants all of whom had reported her to the security forces. Some of them even admitted as much, claiming that they had had no choice in the matter.[147]

When the case was finally ready, the "true story" of the prisoner's guilt was staged as a coproduction between the prisoner and the judge and involved "the semantic subversion of the real facts."[148] The "crime" had to have had some real impact (it was more useful if both the judge and the prisoner believed this to some extent, and it helped a lot if others were implicated, too), but it was totally recast in a paranoid fashion, as the constant expression of some radical and desperate political opposition. So the simple act of mentioning in a letter abroad that grain rations had fallen slightly in Shanghai during the Great Leap Forward became the official proof that one was a spy, despite the fact that the figures had already been published in the official press and were well known to all the foreigners in town.[149]

The usual outcome was abdication of the personality, as Pasqualini attests:

> It doesn't take a prisoner long to lose his self-confidence. Over the years Mao's police have perfected their interrogation methods to such a fine point that I would defy any man, Chinese or not, to hold out against them. Their aim is not so much to make you invent nonexistent crimes, but to make you accept your ordinary life, as you led it, as rotten and sinful and worthy of punishment, since it did not accord with the police's conception of how life should be led. The basis of their success is despair, the prisoner's perception that he is utterly and hopelessly and forever at the mercy of his jailers. He has no defense, since his arrest is absolute and unquestionable proof of his guilt. (During my years of prison, I knew of one man who was in fact arrested by mistake—right name but wrong man. After a few months he had confessed all the crimes of the other. When the mistake was discovered, the prison authorities had a terrible time persuading him to go home. He felt himself too guilty for that.) The prisoner has no trial, only a well-rehearsed ceremony that lasts perhaps half an hour; no consultation with lawyers; no appeal in the Western sense.[150]

Once the sentence had been passed, the prisoner was sent off to a labor camp, such as a state farm, a mine, or a factory. Although studies at these camps continued (though in a less intense manner), and although prisoners were occasionally subjected to "struggle sessions" to remind them of their place, the essential thing was to work. There was nothing hypothetical about the final word in the term "reform through labor." People were graded according to their capacity to keep going for twelve hours a day on two meals as meager as those in the detention centers. The incentive now was to get the food ration of a "high-performance worker," which meant that one ate considerably more than the normal workers. Results were averaged out for the whole cell or room, to encourage teamwork and to see who could work sixteen or eighteen hours a day for the good of the team. In the late 1950s, this was known as "doing a Sputnik." There were no days off other than the big national holidays, when the prisoners had to put up with interminable political speeches. They had hardly enough clothing. In the 1950s, people simply wore what they had been wearing at the moment of their arrest. Winter jackets were provided only in the camps of northern Manchuria, the Chinese equivalent of Siberia, and the rules were that prisoners received one new undergarment per year.[151]

The average food ration was between 12 and 15 kilos of grain each month, although any detainee accused of not pulling his weight could be put on iron rations of 9 kilos per month. This ration was lower than that in French prisons in the early nineteenth century, lower than that in the Soviet camps, and about the same as that in the Vietnamese camps of 1975–1977.[152] The vitamin and protein deficiencies were quite frightening: the prisoners were fed almost no meat, nor did they receive any sugar or oil. They had very few vegetables and little fruit, so many resorted to stealing food, a crime for which the punishments were particularly severe. People also tried to feed themselves as much as they could, searching out edible plants and little animals, with dried rat being particularly sought after. Medical care was minimal except where highly contagious diseases were concerned, and those who were too weak, too old, or too desperate were sent to true death camps, where rations were so low that life was quickly extinguished.[153] The only advantages of the labor camps over the detention centers were that discipline was slightly less harsh and that hardened prisoners were slightly more willing to bend the rules once the guards had turned their backs, though never going so far as to revert to linguistic or behavioral habits from their previous lives. However, life was bearable, and there was a modicum of solidarity among the prisoners.

The further detainees advanced in the *laogai* system, the dimmer the original idea of reeducation became. The trajectory followed by individuals was similar to that of the country itself: after the "perfection" phase in the *laogai* (from about 1954 to 1965), during which millions of zealous "students" disciplined themselves with very little outside intervention and sometimes became faithful Communists inside the prison, the system began to unravel slightly and to lose its way. This coincided with the arrival in the camp system of more and more common criminals, many of them extremely young, as part of the general demoralization that seemed to follow the Cultural Revolution. Slowly the system began to lose the grip that it held on society, while inside the camps a number of gangs began to form among the detainees. Obedience and respect for authority were no longer automatic; they had to be gained either through concessions or by recourse to violence—and this violence was no longer simply a one-way process. The real victim was the idea that people's thoughts could be reformed though suppression of the will. But a certain amount of contradiction had been inscribed inside the project from the very beginning. On the one hand there was the imperative to raise people above themselves, to force them to improve and purify themselves so that they could rejoin the proletarian mass that was marching toward the radiant future. On the other hand, there was the sinister reality of a life to be passed in captivity, regardless of what was achieved there, or, in the rare case of a real liberation, social ostracism, because there was no way to wash away the crime that had landed one in prison. In short, a discourse about the perfectibility of man failed to mask the absolute rigidity of a society ruled by fate, whether that fate involved a momentary error or, more often, having been born into the wrong family. The same inhuman and insupportable contradiction would produce both the societal implosion known as the Cultural Revolution and its unresolved failure.

We leave the *laogai* with an account of a summary execution:

In the middle of them all was the barber, tied up in chains and fetters. A rope around his neck and cinched at the waist kept his head bowed. His hands were tied behind his back. The guards shoved him directly in front of us. He stood there silently, like a trussed penitent, as the steam wisped up around his feet. Yen had prepared a speech.

"I have something awful to speak about. I'm not happy to do it and it's nothing to be proud of. But it's my duty and it should be a lesson for you. This rotten egg here was jailed on a morals charge—homosexual relations with a boy. He received only seven years for this offense. Later, when working in the paper mill, his behavior was constantly bad and he stole repeatedly. His sentence was doubled. Now we have established that while here he seduced a young prisoner nineteen years old—a mentally retarded prisoner. If this happened in society, he would be severely punished. But by doing what he did here, he not only sinned morally, but he also dirtied the reputation of the prison and the great policy of reform through labor. Therefore, in consideration of his re-peated offenses, the representative of the Supreme People's Court will now read you his sentence."

The man in the blue uniform strode forward and read out the somber document, a recapitulation of the offenses that ended with the decision of the People's Court: death with immediate execution of sentence.

Everything happened so suddenly then that I did not even have the time to be shocked or frightened. Before the man in the blue uniform had even finished pronouncing the last word, the barber was dead. The guard standing behind him pulled out a huge pistol and blew his head open. A shower of blood and brains flew out and splattered those of us in the front rows. I looked away from the hideous twitching figure on the ground and vomited. Yen came up to speak again.

"Let this serve as a warning to you. I have been authorized to tell you that no more leniency will be shown in this camp. From now on, all moral offenses will be punished in the same way. Now go back to your cells and discuss this."[154]

The Cultural Revolution: Anarchic Totalitarianism (1966–1976)

By comparison with the terrifying but almost unknown horrors of the agrarian revolution and the Great Leap Forward, the effect of the "Great Proletarian Cultural Revolution" seems almost modest. Estimates vary greatly for the number of dead: most authors cite figures between 400,000 and 1 million, although Domenach calculates between 1 million and 3 million.[155] The Cultural Revolution's effects, past and present, on the world's imagination and memory stem not only from the extreme radicalism of its discourse and actions but also from its visibility; largely an urban phenomenon, it occurred in the age of television, for which it presented superb images of deftly organized political ceremonies filled with a touching fervor. Furthermore, unlike earlier movements, the Cultural Revolution was officially condemned in China itself almost as soon as it was over, when it became quite acceptable to complain about the excesses of the Red Guards, particularly if the excesses involved older cadres and Communist leaders. Less welcome were complaints about the massacres carried out by the PLA during the return to order.

The Cultural Revolution was full of paradoxes. First, it was a moment when extremism seemed almost certain to carry the day, and when the revolutionary process seemed solidly institutionalized, having swept through all the centers of power in a year. But at the same time it was a movement that was extremely limited in scope, hardly spreading beyond the urban areas and having a significant impact only on schoolchildren. At that time the countryside was still recovering from the Great Leap Forward, tension with the U.S.S.R. was at its peak, and the "Cultural Revolution Group" (CRG) decided that the peasantry, the army, and scientific research (which for the most part centered upon nuclear weapons) should remain unaffected.[156] The CRG's theory was that the country would have to step back slightly so that it could spring forward better: in the long run no sector of society or the state could escape the revolutionary process. But rural people clung tightly to the small freedoms they had been granted by Liu Shaoqi, and especially to their small private plots of land. There was no intention of destroying either defense or the economy: the recent experience of the Great Leap Forward inspired prudence on the latter score. The main aim instead was to seize the initiative in the intellectual and artistic "superstructure" of society and to take control of the state. This last objective was never fully realized. Although the rules were sometimes broken, there are no reports of major confrontations or massacres in the villages, where the vast majority of the population still lived; some 64 percent of incidents classed as rural took place in the outlying areas of major urban areas.[157] However, in the final stages of the emergence from the revolution there are reports of numerous executions of individuals who had taken the wrong side in the conflict and of Red Guards who had fled to the countryside. The major difference between these events and the purges of the 1950s was that in this case there was never a clear aim to eliminate a whole section of the population. Even intellectuals, who were particularly affected at the outset, were not for long the prime targets of persecutions. Moreover, the persecutors often came from within their own ranks. The most murderous episodes were generally the result of police brutality or of relatively spontaneous violence on a local scale, and not the result of a general strategy. On the rare occasions when the central government did issue edicts ordering military operations that resulted in massacres, these were essentially reactive measures to a situation that was perceived to have got out of hand. In general, such situations bore a closer resemblance to the events of 1989 than they did to the agrarian revolution. The Cultural Revolution, in many ways, was the first sign that Chinese Communism had reached an impasse and was running out of steam.

By way of contrast, a second paradox explains the presence of the Cultural Revolution in this account: the Red Guard movement was a "repressive rebellion,"[158] and the manner in which it was put down was even more repressive. A degree of terror had been present in Chinese Communism since the end of the 1920s. In 1966–67 the most radical groups, whose primary goal was to attack state institutions, still had a foot in government and had several friends there, including Mao himself, who was constantly invoked whenever a tactical decision was to be taken. In the great Chinese tradition, these radical groups used the government's authority even in rebellion itself, and they never refused to outdo one another in repression. Criticizing the government for its softness toward the class enemy, they established their own heavily armed squads of "investigators," their own police of morals, their own "tribunals," and their own prisons. Throughout the Cultural Revolution, "one finds again and again the struggle of low against high, but the 'low' were mobilized, drilled, and terrorized by a government and an elite that dared not identify itself as such." The government's reinvention of itself under another name, in a form that allowed it to criticize and even punish itself, was representative of the "definitive formula of Maoism, which, after a lengthy quest, ended up combining rebellion and authority into the permanent principle of an alternative form of politics that was above both the state and society."[159] This was not, of course, a real alternative, for it was founded on illusion; hence the enormous frustration among those who really tried to create a revolution. "Changing everything so that it all remained the same," in the classic formula from *The Leopard,* ultimately meant that the people questioned not just the revolution but also the whole center of power. This was a movement among a minority, but it had important consequences, leading, for example, to the Democracy Wall of 1979. Its most daring theorist, Wei Jingsheng, highlights the ultimately fatal contradictions in a movement that emerged from legitimate discontent:

> This explosion of anger quickly turned into a personality cult centered upon a tyrant and was channeled into the struggle to impose tyranny on the people . . . This led to an absurd and paradoxical situation in which a people rose up against its own government in order to defend it. The people came out in opposition to the hierarchical system that was causing them so much suffering, while brandishing banners in support of the founders of the system. They demanded democratic rights while denigrating democracy and allowed themselves to be guided, in their struggle to impose their rights, by the ideas of a despot.[160]

The Cultural Revolution gave birth to an abundant literature of great interest and quality, and there are many eyewitness reports available from both the victims and their persecutors. As a result it is much better known than any previous episode in Chinese history. It really was more of a revolution (abortive, incomplete, a PLA-like imitation of the others but a revolution nonetheless) than simply another mass campaign. There was much more to it than repression, terror, and crime, and it was an extremely protean movement, varying greatly in its effects from one place to another. Only the repressive aspects will concern us here. These can be divided into three quite distinct categories: violence against intellectuals and political cadres, mostly in 1966–67; a series of confrontations among factions of the Red Guards in 1967–68; and the brutal repressions carried out by the army to restore order in 1968. In 1969, at the Ninth Chinese Communist Party Congress, some of the changes from 1966 were institutionalized in a rather halfhearted way, while inside the palace there began a struggle for the succession to Mao Zedong, who by then was quite weakened by illness. There were numerous tremors: Lin Biao, the official successor, was eliminated in September 1971; Deng Xiaoping was restored as Deputy Prime Minister in 1973, and large numbers of cadres who had been eliminated as "revisionists" were reintegrated into the power structure; in 1974 there was a major "leftist" offensive within the Party; in 1976, between the death of the moderate prime minister Zhou Enlai in January and that of Mao Zedong himself in September, the "Shanghai Four," led by Mao's wife, Jiang Qing, tried to seize power; by October the Four were no more than a "Gang" and were all in prison. The country was then led for two years by Hua Guofeng, who officially declared the Cultural Revolution to be at an end. Repressions in the years following the crushing of the Red Guards were harsh but very similar to those of the 1950s.

Prominent Figures in the Revolution

The Cultural Revolution was the convergence of one man and an entire generation. That man of course was Mao Zedong. Having been at the heart of government during the disaster of the Great Leap Forward, he had suffered a loss of prestige and been forced to hand over power for two years in 1962 to the President of the Republic, Liu Shaoqi. Reduced to the (admittedly prestigious) position of Party chairman, he began to rely more and more on his eloquence, since he had few rivals as a public speaker. A seasoned old campaigner, he was aware of the dangers of being simultaneously worshipped as a figurehead and effectively marginalized in that position, so he began to look for more effective ways of imposing his choices. The Party was kept well in hand by Liu and his assistant, the secretary general Deng Xiaoping, and was protected from any outside influence. The government, which as in all Communist countries was under the control of the Communist Party, was run effectively by Zhou Enlai, an intelligent opportunist and a moderate in thought if not in deed; in fact he was a relatively neutral figure in the confrontation between the two factions. Mao was aware that he had lost the support of many cadres and intellectuals in the purges of 1957, and the support of the rural masses in the famine of 1959–1961. But in a country like Communist China, a passive majority that is divided and afraid counts for much less than an active minority that is in the right place. Since 1959 the PLA had been led by Lin Biao, one of Mao's devoted supporters. Lin gradually transformed the PLA into an alternative center of power that after 1962 played a major role in the Movement for Socialist Education, an antirightist purge promoting military qualities such as puritanism, discipline, and devotion to the cause. After 1964 at least one-third of all new political cadres came up through PLA ranks, and they cooperated closely with a small group of intellectuals and failed artists who gathered around Jiang Qing and her program for the total destruction of all art and literature that failed to follow the Party line. Military training became obligatory for all students, and after 1964 armed militia groups were established or reorganized in all factories, districts, and rural areas. The army itself was never a candidate for power, as it was effectively controlled by the Party; and the mediocre Lin Biao, who was widely rumored to be a heroin addict, had no deeply held political convictions.[161] The army above all was Mao's life insurance policy, or, as he said himself, his own Great Wall.[162]

The other strategic lever on which Mao believed he would always be able to count was the younger generation, or more exactly the part of it that was in secondary education, higher education, and the professional training institutes, including in particular the military academies, which were the only part of the PLA authorized to train Red Guard units.[163] These had the immense advantage of being concentrated in the cities, and particularly in the major cities, where the struggles for power would inevitably take place. One-quarter of all the inhabitants of Shanghai attended one or another such school.[164] People who in 1966 were between ages fourteen and twenty-two would be Mao's most enthusiastic tools, for they were both fanatically dogmatic and enormously frustrated. Belonging to the first generation educated entirely after the 1949 revolution, they were both too young and too urban to know anything of the horrors of the Great Leap Forward;[165] Liu and his henchmen would come to regret not having criticized it officially. Spoiled by the regime, persuaded that they were for Mao the clean white page on which the great epic of Chinese Communism was to be written, assured by Mao that "the world belongs to you; the future of China is yours," they had quickly learned, in the words of one Red Guard song, that "the Party is our father and our mother."[166] Faced with any conflict about paternity, their choice was clear: they were to renounce their parents. Pasqualini recounts the story of the visit of one child, "a mean little brat of around ten or eleven," to see his father in the *laogai* in 1962:

> "I didn't want to come here," he brayed loudly, "but my mother made me. You are a counterrevolutionary and a disgrace to the family. You have caused grave losses to the government. It serves you right that you are in prison. All I can say is that you had better reform yourself well, or you will get what you deserve." Even the guards were shocked by this tirade. The prisoner returned to the cell in tears—itself forbidden— muttering, "If I had known that this would happen I would have strangled him the day he was born." Tien [the guard] let the incident pass without even a reproach.[167]

The child would have been fifteen years old in 1966, just the right age to join the Red Guards. The youngest were often the most violent, and the most zealous to humiliate their victims.

At the same time, these youngsters also felt frustrated. They had had no opportunity for heroism, whereas the generation of their parents was always telling them about its revolutionary or wartime experiences: the Long March, the first red bases, the anti-Japanese guerrilla operations of 1936–1938. Once again, to paraphrase Marx, history was to repeat itself, but this time as farce. Deprived of most of their literary heritage and of freedom of discussion by the hyperprudent teachers who had escaped the "Rectification" repression of 1957, they used the little knowledge they had—bits of Mao with a pinch of Lenin added—to question, in the name of the revolution, the gray mess that it had become as a result of its institutionalization. Many of them, who came from "black" categories and had been subjected to obstacles such as class-based selection procedures and quotas, had little real hope of ever achieving a job or situation in life that reflected their worth or their ambitions. The elite scholarly institutions in which "blacks" were often in the majority were also often the most revolutionary, and the Cultural Revolution Group's decree of 1 October 1966 officially opening the Red Guard to the "ill born" was an essential step in the launching of the process.[168]

The authorizations, on 16 November and 15 December, for the formation of Red Guard groups in the factories and the villages decisively extended the movement. The same period brought the repeal of much of the negative political legislation enacted to control workers at the beginning of the Cultural Revolution. Seizing the moment, those who had been rehabilitated sought the abolition of the label "right-wing" and the destruction of the secret files in which everyone's opinions and "errors" were kept. Two types of workers joined forces with the students: "backward elements" and others who had been discriminated against politically (although in practice everything had become political) regardless of their age; and seasonal workers, generally quite young, who were paid by the day and thus had no job security or union membership, and who wanted wage increases and permanent contracts.[169] The latter group in fact accounted for the majority of workers in the new large factories. There were also many young cadres who saw an unexpected opportunity to advance their careers, managers who had been punished in some manner in the past and who were eager for some sort of revenge, and the usual opportunists.[170] The resulting coalition was a mixed bag of malcontents who, filled with bitterness and a desire to better themselves socially, were ready to launch an assault on all institutions—schools, factories, and offices. But in the final analysis they were always in the minority, accounting for only 20 percent of city dwellers and for an even smaller minority countrywide. Thus they could succeed only when the state was paralyzed by contradictory orders from the Center and when the PLA was hampered by its own regulations. Ultimately it was always Mao himself who alternately spurred and checked the pace of revolution, although he, too, was often unsure what to do; power struggles and rapidly changing local situations left him constantly seeking a conciliation between rebellion and his own hold on power. When these "rebels"—whose only unity consisted in the name—finally did seize power (or rather, had it handed to them), the contradictions within their ranks and their own selfish ambitions immediately took over, giving rise to terrible struggles, often armed ones, among groups that had been able to define themselves only as being *against* something.[171]

The Red Guards' Hour of Glory

The persecutions carried out in 1966 by the students and schoolchildren who made up the majority of the "rebel revolutionaries" typify the entire Cultural

Revolution. There were relatively few deaths, and no new tactics were used. Though carried out with the enthusiasm and sadism of youth, otherwise they were very similar to the purges launched against intellectuals in the 1950s. We might well wonder if they were even spontaneous. It would surely be absurd to believe that Mao and his henchmen pulled the strings in every Red Guard unit, but, for instance, the jealousy of Mao's wife, Jiang Qing, toward Wang Guangmei, the wife of President Liu Shaoqi, is clearly discernible behind the misfortune that befell Liu.[172] He was forced to carry out an act of self-criticism and, when Mao believed he was sufficiently isolated, was thrown into prison, where he died under torture. On the other hand, Zhou Enlai, who was also severely criticized, escaped humiliation. The really sensational aspect of the movement was the use of Red Guards to settle scores at the top, showing the definitive end to the Party solidarity that predated even the Long March. This was augmented by purges of young Communist cadres, 60 percent of whom were removed from their posts, although many, like Deng Xiaoping, were reintegrated a few years later, even before Mao's death in 1976. Even in these cases violence was far from extreme. Unlike in Stalin's U.S.S.R. in the 1930s, many of the high-ranking leaders and cadres survived the bad treatment they received. One little-known minister of mining was beaten to death by Red Guards, but there were no high-level judicial executions. Liu died insane in 1969. Peng Dehuai had two ribs broken in July 1967 in what was officially described as "a struggle" and died of cancer in 1974. Chen Yi, the minister of foreign affairs, was sent to the countryside in 1969 but persuaded the authorities to allow him to return in time to be present at the deathbed of Lin Biao before himself dying shortly afterward. The most dramatic case was that of the minister of security, Luo Ruiqing, who was removed in a purge in November 1965 to clear the way for Kang Sheng, was imprisoned the following year, and subsequently suffered a serious foot injury while attempting to throw himself out a window. His foot was amputated in 1969, and the difficult operation was long delayed to get him to make a full confession. Nevertheless he went on to outlive Chairman Mao. Prison conditions for the leaders were humiliating and painful, but they were much less severe than anything experienced by the millions of prisoners whom they themselves had sent to the *laogai,* and they at least had a minimum of medical care.[173]

Red Guard tactics were sadly similar all over the country, in every city and university. Everything began on 1 June 1966, after the reading out on the radio of a *dazibao* (a notice in large characters) by Nie Yuanzi, who was a philosophy teacher at Beida University in Beijing, the most prestigious university in the country. The notice called for a "struggle" and demonized the enemy: "Break the evil influence of revisionists, and do it resolutely, radically, totally, and completely! Destroy these monsters, these Khrushchev-like reformers!"[174] Millions of students began to organize into committees, and soon they identified their professors, their teachers, and the municipal and provincial authorities who had tried to defend them as the "monsters and devils" to be hunted down. With a certain amount of imagination, they termed them "evil geniuses," "bovine ghosts," or "reptilian spirits." Qi Benyu, an extremist from the Cultural Revolution Group, said of Peng on 18 July 1967: "The poisonous snake is no longer moving, but he is not dead yet. The paper tiger Peng Dehuai can kill without blinking. He is a master of death. Don't be fooled by his pose, he's an immobile lizard, he's simply feigning death, that's his instinct. Even insects and the lowest animals have an instinct for survival; with carnivores like him it's even worse. Kick him to the floor, and stamp on him."[175] These images must be taken very seriously, for their purpose was to suppress pity by making it impossible to identify with the victim. Such name-calling promoted the "struggle" and often the death of the person in question. The call to "kill all the monsters," which launched the university movement in Beijing, was not an idle threat. "Class enemies" had notices stuck on their backs, were dressed up in ridiculous clothes and hats (particularly women), and forced into grotesque and painful positions. Their faces were smeared with ink, they were forced to bark like dogs on all fours so that they would be deprived of human dignity. One professor named Ma, which means "horse," was forced to eat grass. Another professor, one of whose colleagues was beaten to death by his students, said: "I can almost understand how it happened. The landlords were enemies then. They were not people really. You could use violence against them. It was acceptable."[176] In August 1967 the Beijing press declared that anti–Maoists were "rats that ran through the streets" and should all be killed.[177] This process of dehumanization had been seen before, in the period of the agrarian reform in 1949. In one example, a landowner was tied to a plow and whipped while being forced to plow the field, while the peasants shouted: "You treated us like beasts. Now you can be our animal!"[178] And millions of other "animals" were exterminated in similar fashion. Some were even eaten: at least 137 in Guangxi, mostly teachers and college principals, and this with the help of cadres from the local branch of the Communist Party. Some Red Guards asked to be served human flesh in the canteen, and apparently this did actually happen in some places. Harry Wu remembers one man who was executed in a *laogai* in 1970 and whose brain was then eaten by a member of the security forces. His crime had been to scribble "Down with Chairman Mao" on a wall.[179]

It is unclear what the main motivation of the Red Guards was in these early days of violence. They seemed to oscillate between a real desire to transform society and a sense of participation in a large-scale "happening" that was perhaps a reflection of the long hot summer. These feelings were combined with a traditional conformist desire to avoid trouble, at a time when doing nothing meant one risked being treated as a revisionist. All these factors led naturally to further revolt. Contradictions were apparent from the very outset: the simplistic slogan "One is always right to revolt," which Mao had announced on 18 August, was heard everywhere. Somehow this slogan was assumed to sum up the "thousand tenets" of Marxism. At the same time a real personality cult began to take root around the president and his works, such as the famous Little Red Book. Above all it was the government that seemed to decide who had the right to revolt and when revolt should take place. The result was ferocious competition among Red Guard organizations to qualify for the precious label "left." The claim was that all organizations were under attack, but the army, under the control of Lin Biao, protected the Red Guards, who were given free transport and top priority throughout China in the autumn of 1966. The "experience exchanges" that were used to justify this often became little more than dizzying tourist excursions for young people who had never left their villages, with the five-star attraction of a chance of meeting Chairman Mao himself. Such meetings featured obligatory displays of fervor and tears from the girls. Sometimes people were crushed to death in the rush.[180]

On 18 August Mao decreed: "We don't want gentleness; we want war," and the Red Guard Song Binbin (whose name meant "Gentle Song") swiftly changed her name to Song Yaowu ("Song Wants War").[181] The new minister of security, Xie Fuzhi, who was one of Jiang Qing's circle, told an audience of police cadres in late August:

> We can't act like everyone else and follow normal police procedure. If you arrest people because they have beaten others, you are mistaken: should Red Guards who kill be punished? My opinion is that if people have died, well, they're dead; there's nothing we can do about that, and it isn't our problem. I am not happy with the idea that the masses are killing people, but if the masses hate bad people so much that we can't stop them, then let's not bother trying to stop them. The people's police has to be behind the Red Guards. We must sympathize with them and pass information to them, particularly where the Five [black] Categories are concerned.[182]

Thus initially conflict was relatively risk free: faced with a Party buffeted by contradictory currents, stunned by Mao's audacity, and afraid to condemn what they saw, intellectuals and everything associated with them—books, paintings, porcelain, libraries, museums, and monuments—were easy targets on which all the factions could easily agree.

The Chinese Communist Party had a long tradition of anti-intellectualism, and Mao was a particularly noteworthy example. Red Guards everywhere repeated his slogan: "The capitalist class is the skin; the intellectuals are the hairs that grow on the skin. When the skin dies, there will be no hair."[183] Officials became incapable of pronouncing the word "intellectual" without adding the adjective "stinking." Jean Pasqualini, when he was once cleaning his sandal after emerging from a pigsty, was told by a guard: "Your brain is dirtier than that, and it smells worse too! Stop that immediately. That is a bourgeois habit. Clean your head instead!"[184] At the beginning of the Cultural Revolution, all schoolchildren and students were given a little volume by Mao about teaching, in which he condemned all teachers who could not distinguish the five different types of grain, and who "become stupider the more they learn." He favored shorter periods of study and the abolition of selective entry by an exam system: universities were for training Reds, not experts, and they should be open to anyone who was born a Red.[185]

Having for the most part already been through several self-criticisms, the intellectuals had little will to resist. Older writers, often wearing ridiculous outfits, were paraded through the streets for hours until they dropped from exhaustion, while the young hurled insults and blows. A number of them died that way. Others killed themselves, including the great Lao She in August, and Fu Lei, the translator of Balzac and Mallarmé, in September. Teng To was killed; Wu Han, Chao Shu-li, and Liu Ching died in prison; and Pa Kin spent years under house arrest. Ding Ling had ten years' work confiscated and destroyed.[186] The sadism and fanaticism of these rebellious killers was overwhelming; at the University of Xiamen (Fujian), "Some teachers could no longer stand the constant attacks and criticism and fell ill and died more or less in our presence. I felt no pity for them, no more than I did for the handful who killed themselves by throwing themselves out of windows or for the one who threw himself into our hot spring and boiled to death."[187] About one in ten of all teachers were removed, and many more suffered serious intimidation.

Cities waited for the arrival of the Red Guards in the way that one waits for a storm to hit, particularly during the campaign against "the Four Old-Fashioned Things"—old ideas, old culture, old customs, and old habits—which was launched by Lin Biao on 18 August. Temples were barricaded (although a great number were badly damaged or destroyed all the same, often in public *autos-da-fé*), treasures were hidden, frescoes were whitewashed for protection, and books were hidden. All the sets and costumes at the Beijing Opera were burned to make way for the revolutionary operas with contemporary themes that were demanded by Mao's wife and that for a decade were to be the only authorized form of cultural expression. The Great Wall itself was partially destroyed as bricks were removed from it to build pigsties. Zhou had the Imperial Palace in Beijing partially walled up and protected by his troops.[188] Various religious groups were affected: the monks were expelled from the famous Buddhist monastery on Wutai Mountain, its ancient manuscripts were burned, and several of its sixty temples were partially destroyed; the Korans of the Uighurs in Xinjiang were burned; and celebrations of the Chinese New Year were banned. Xenophobia, which had a long history in China, was taken to an extreme. "Imperialist" tombs in some cemeteries were looted,[189] all Christian practices were more or less banned, and all English or French inscriptions on the Bund in Shanghai were chiseled away. Nien Cheng, who was the widow of an Englishman and who had offered a Red Guard a cup of coffee while he was on requisition duty, found herself being asked: "Why do you have to drink a foreign beverage? Why do you have to eat foreign food? Why do you have so many foreign books? Why are you so foreign altogether?"[190] The Red Guards, who took themselves extremely seriously, thought it was a good idea to ban "wastes of revolutionary energy" such as cats, birds, and flowers. The prime minister himself was forced to intervene to prevent legislation that would have made a red traffic light mean "go." In big cities such as Shanghai, teams shaved the head of anyone caught in the streets with long or lacquered hair, tore up trousers that were too tight, ripped high heels off shoes, slit open pointed shoes, and forced shops to change their names; the presence of hundreds of shops called "East Is Red," all filled with identical portraits of the leader, caused the inhabitants to lose their bearings.[191] Anyone who failed to comply received a picture of Mao that it was considered a sacrilege to destroy. Red Guards stopped passersby and forced them to recite their favorite quotation from Mao.[192] Many people were afraid to leave their houses.

The hardest times for millions of "Black" families were the cycles of Red Guard requisitioning. Searching for proof of imaginary crimes, looking for silver and gold for the local authorities, their organization, or themselves, and carrying out acts of wanton vandalism, the Guards looted and destroyed many houses. Humiliation, insults, and blows were all part of the process. Anyone who tried to resist was punished severely. The slightest expression of disdain or mockery, or any refusal to reveal the location of "treasures," led to a rain of blows often ending in death, and at the very least to wholesale destruction of the property.[193] There were also a few deaths among the Guards. People were often "visited" several times, by different units, and so as not to lose face, the last to arrive would often carry off the tiny amount of belongings that remained, which had been left by the others to enable the family to survive. In such conditions most deaths undoubtedly came about as a result of suicide, but it is impossible to put a number on these deaths; many murders were also made to look like suicides.

Some figures are available, however. The Red Terror in Beijing caused approximately 1,700 deaths, 33,600 houses were raided, and 84,000 "blacks" were chased out of the city.[194] In Shanghai, 150,000 lodgings were taken over, and 32 tons of gold was seized. In the great industrial city of Wuhan, in Hubei

Province, 21,000 properties were raided, 32 people were beaten to death, and there were 62 suicides.[195] Sometimes genuine atrocities were committed. In the Daxing district, south of the capital, 325 "blacks" and their families were murdered in the space of five days—the eldest was eighty and the youngest was thirty-eight days old. One doctor was executed for "assassinating a Red"—his patient had died of an allergic reaction to penicillin.[196] The "investigations" inside the government administration, carried out by policemen dressed as Red Guards, were massive and sometimes murderous: there were 1,200 executions in the purge of the Ministry for Security; 22,000 people were interrogated and many imprisoned during the investigation into Liu Shaoqi; 60 percent of the members of the Central Committee (which hardly ever met) and 75 percent of all provincial Party secretaries were expelled and usually also arrested. In all, for the whole period of the Cultural Revolution, between 3 million and 4 million of the 18 million cadres were imprisoned, as were 400,000 soldiers, despite the banning of Red Guards in the PLA.[197] Among the intellectuals, 142,000 teachers, 53,000 scientists and technicians, 500 teachers of medicine, and 2,600 artists and writers were persecuted, and many of them were killed or committed suicide.[198] In Shanghai, where intellectuals were especially numerous, it was officially estimated in 1978 that 10,000 people had died violent deaths as a result of the Cultural Revolution.[199]

It is astonishing how easy it was for these young Red Guards, who in 1966 and 1967 had relatively few allies in the other strata of society, to attack and criticize Party leaders in the stadiums of Beijing, or even torture them to death, as was the case for the Party leader in Tianjin and the mayor of Shanghai. The latter was attached to the crane of a street-car breakdown truck and severely beaten while announcing that he would rather die than confess to anything.[200] The only possible explanation was that Chairman Mao, which meant the state apparatus, supported the "revolutionaries" with decisions like the one on 26 July 1966 (subsequently revoked) to close all secondary schools and higher-education establishments for six months to mobilize what was in effect a force of 50 million schoolchildren. With nothing to do, and free to do whatever they liked, even killing (deaths were later described as "accidents"), and endlessly egged on by the official media, what could have stood in the way of these schoolchildren?

One of their first pogroms took place in one of the top secondary schools in Xiamen:

> At twelve o'clock . . . as a few of us were on our way back from a swim in the sea, we heard screams and shouts as we approached the school gate. Some schoolmates ran up to us shouting, "The struggle has begun! The struggle has begun!"

I ran inside. On the athletic field and farther inside, before a new four-story classroom building, I saw rows of teachers, about 40 or 50 in all, with black ink poured over their heads and faces so that they were now in reality a "black gang." Hanging on their necks were placards with words such as "reactionary academic authority so-and-so," "corrupt ringleader so-and-so," "class enemy so-and-so," "capitalist roader so-and-so": all epithets taken from the newspapers. On each placard was a red cross, making the teachers look like condemned prisoners awaiting execution. They all wore dunce caps painted with similar epithets and carried dirty brooms, shoes, and dusters on their backs.

Hanging from their necks were pails filled with rocks. I saw the principal: the pail around his neck was so heavy that the wire had cut deep into his neck and he was staggering. All were barefoot, hitting broken gongs or pots as they walked around the field crying out: "I am black gangster so-and-so." Finally, they all knelt down, burned incense, and begged Mao Zedong to "pardon their crimes."

I was stunned by this scene and I felt myself go pale. A few girls nearly fainted.

Beatings and torture followed. I had never seen such tortures before: eating nightsoil and insects, being subjected to electric shocks, being forced to kneel on broken glass, being hanged "like an airplane" by the arms and legs.

Those who immediately took up the sticks and applied the tortures were the school bullies who, as children of Party cadres and army officers, belonged to the five "red" categories, a group that also included children of workers, poor and lower-middle peasants, and revolutionary martyrs . . . Coarse and cruel, they were accustomed to throwing around their parents' status and brawling with the other students. They did so poorly in school that they were about to be expelled, and presumably resented the teachers because of this.

Greatly emboldened by the instigators, the other students also cried "Beat them!" and jumped on the teachers, swinging their fists and kicking. The stragglers were forced to back them up with loud shouts and clenched fists.

There was nothing strange in this. Young students were ordinarily peaceful and well-behaved, but once the first step was taken, all were bound to follow . . .

The heaviest blow to me that day was the killing of my most respected and beloved teacher, Chen Ku-teh . . .

Teacher Chen, over sixty years old and suffering from high blood pressure, was dragged out at 11:30, exposed to the summer sun for more than two hours, and then paraded about with the others carrying a placard and hitting a gong. Then he was dragged up to the second floor of a classroom building and down again, beaten with fists and broomsticks all along the way. On the second floor some of his attackers ran into a classroom to get some bamboo carrying poles with which to beat him further. I stopped them, pleading, "You don't have to do this. This is too much!"

He passed out several times but was brought back to consciousness each time with cold water splashed on his face. He could hardly move his body. His feet were cut by glass and thorns. But his spirit was unbroken. He shouted, "Why don't you kill me? Kill me!" This lasted for six hours, until he lost control of his excrement. They tried to force a stick into his rectum. He collapsed for the last time. They poured cold water on him again—it was too late. The killers were stunned momentarily, as it was probably the first time they had ever beaten a man to death, and it was the first time most of us had ever witnessed such a scene. People began to run away, one after another . . . They dragged him off the field to a wooden shack where the teachers used to play ping-pong. There they put him on a dirty gym mat and summoned the school doctor.

"Check carefully whether he died of high blood pressure. You are not allowed to defend him."

The doctor examined him and pronounced him dead of torture. Some of those present seized the doctor and began to beat him up, too.

"Why are you breathing air from the same nostril as his? Do you want to be like him?"

Finally, the doctor wrote on the death certificate "Death due to a sudden attack of high blood pressure."[201]

The Revolutionaries and Their Master

For a long time there was a much-cherished legend in the West: that the Red Guards were nothing more than a slightly more fanatical version of the French revolutionaries of 1968.[202] After the fall of the Gang of Four, a legend just as far from the truth arose in China: that the Red Guards were the cryptofascist helpers of a bunch of political opportunists. The reality was very different: the "rebels" thought of themselves as good Maoist Communists, untouched by any democratic or libertarian ideal; and for the most part they were precisely that. In the absence of democratic centralism, the whole experiment effectively ended in less than two years, but during that time they collectively represented a strange alternative Communist Party at a moment when the real "Communist Party" was paralyzed by division at its very heart. They were ready to give up their lives for Mao, and although they also had strong personal and ideological links to Lin Biao and to the Cultural Revolution Group of Jiang Qing, they were only really an alternative insofar as they opposed the municipal and provincial authorities who were opposed to Mao. They were also of course a supplementary force in the struggles for power inside the palace in Beijing. The boundless energy of these tens of millions of young people was almost purely destructive. During the brief periods when they did hold positions of power they achieved absolutely nothing and failed to modify the totalitarian structure that was already in place in any significant way. The Red Guards often pretended that their aim was to model themselves on the French Communards of 1871, but the elections that they organized were never free or open. All decisions were taken by small, self-appointed groups, and any changes were simply the result of struggles within the movement and in the administrative structures that were under their control.[203] From time to time there were small, individual victories, and some of the social demands by workers in factories were met; but these achievements only made the swing back again in 1968 more difficult.[204]

The Red Guards were linked to the Communist movement in many different ways. In June and July 1966 the working parties that were sent into the main educational establishments by Liu Shaoqi's group and the various provincial groups that depended on them established the first "black dens" for professors and provided the impetus for the first Red Guard groups. Although they were officially taken out of service in early August, as part of Mao's task force in the Central Committee they sometimes had a lasting influence in various local organizations.[205] In any case they were a major cause of the systematic recourse to violence against teachers and cadres in the education system, and they opened the way for the movement against the Four Old-Fashioned Things. That movement, though supported by local authorities, was largely the work of the police, who provided all the necessary information, gathered evidence, and confiscated property. In 1978 Nien Cheng was surprised and overjoyed to recover a large amount of her porcelain collection, which had been seized under such violent circumstances twelve years earlier. At that time those who had taken part in previous campaigns, as well as a few middle-ranking cadres, were used as scapegoats to protect the people who had really been directing operations.

The extension of the movement into the factories, along with Mao's growing sense that his goal—the elimination of all political rivals—was slipping out of his grasp, led to ever-greater confrontations between rebels and municipal or provincial authorities. But the local authorities invariably knew very well how to orchestrate mass demonstrations, which were hard to distinguish from demonstrations by rebels closer to the Maoist line. The rebels on the other hand were more independent locally and saw their salvation in alignment with the "super-Central Committee" that the Cultural Revolution Group had become, in which Kang Sheng played a discreet but essential role. Specialized teams maintained close contact with Beijing (in the early days, these teams were often made up of students from the capital), which sent advice and blacklists (including the names of two-thirds of the members of the Central Committee), waited for results and evidence, and rewarded its allies with the precious "good labels" that served as a sort of magic shield against the PLA.[206] The rebels were just as dependent on the state machinery as their adversaries were, but in a different manner. All groups were united on the question of repression, which was one enormous difference from the revolutionary tradition in the West. If the *laogai* camps were ever criticized (something that happened very rarely), it was for their laxity: Nien Cheng, for example, recalls how brutal and inhumane the new Maoist prison guards were. Hua Linsham, who was an ultraleft rebel and openly opposed to the PLA, worked in the part of a prison factory where arms were manufactured; yet "throughout our stay there, the prisoners stayed in their cells and we had almost no contact with them."[207] The Red Guards, who used kidnaping as an essential weapon in their repressive armory, had their own network of penitentiaries in every school, government office, and factory. In these "stables" or "foyers" (the preferred euphemism was "study centers") people were confined, interrogated, and tortured incessantly, with great care and imagination. Ling recalls one informal "psychological study group" in his school: "At group meeting we avoided mentioning the tortures, but we regarded torture as an art . . . We even thought our study inadequate . . . there were many methods we could not test."[208] One "radical" militia in Hangzhou, consisting mostly of "blacks" who had themselves been persecuted, had on average 1,000 people in its three "investigation centers" at any given time. It condemned twenty-three people for slandering its leader, Weng Senhe; and its workers received three days off for every day that they worked, as well as free meals.[209] In all statements made by former Red Guards, descriptions of repressive practices have a central place. There are countless stories of adversaries who were beaten to the floor, paraded around, humiliated, and sometimes killed, seemingly without opposition from any quarter. The period of the Cultural Revolution was also marked by the reimprisonment of former detainees, by the reapplication of previously removed "right" labels, and by the systematic arrest of foreigners or Chinese people who had lived abroad. There were also new infamies, such as a daughter's obligation to serve out the remainder of the sentence of a father who had died.[210] Civil administration suffered considerably, that of the *laogai* much less. Perhaps this generation was a generation of jailers rather than rebels.[211]

From the ideological point of view, even radical rebel groups that were concerned with the elaboration of new theories, such as the Shengwulian group in Hunan, were unable to break from the extremely limited Maoist frame of reference.[212] Mao's thinking was always so vague and his words so contradictory that they could be turned to mean almost anything: both conservatives and rebels had their stock of quotations—sometimes the same quotations, interpreted differently.[213] In the strange place that was China during the Cultural Revolution, a beggar could justify stealing by quoting Mao's words about mutual assistance, and a worker in the underground economy who had stolen bricks could reject all scruples, for "the working class must exercise leadership in everything."[214] But there was always one hard, central idea: the sanctification of violence, the radical nature of class struggle and its political implications.[215] For people who followed the correct line, anything was permitted. Even the rebels could not distance themselves from official propaganda; their texts closely imitated the official language of the Party. They lied outrageously not only to the masses but also to their own comrades.[216]

Perhaps the most dramatic effect of the Cultural Revolution was its reinforcement of the consensus favoring the caste system created in the 1950s. Things could have gone quite differently. To speed things along, the Cultural Revolution Group had opened the doors of its organization to "blacks," who rushed to join. Since 45 percent of the children of all intellectuals in China were enrolled in schools in Canton, a disproportionate number signed up in the south. The children of cadres and of people formally recognized as workers made up 82 percent of conservatives in the great southern metropolis. The rebels, buoyed by the support of workers who had no recognized status, were the natural enemies of political cadres, while the conservatives concentrated their fire on the "blacks." But because the rebels' program included the elimination of sociopolitical divisions (an aspect that promised escape from the stigma of their own inferior status), they launched a campaign of repression against both the conservatives and the "blacks," hoping that the blows would not fall on their own relatives. Worse still, they accepted for themselves the new notion of class heredity that had been put forward by the Beijing Red Guards, most of whom were the children of cadres and soldiers.

This notion was expressed, for example, in a remarkable marching song:

> If the father is brave, the son will be a hero.
> If he's a reactionary, the son will be an asshole.
> If you're a revolutionary, step forward and join us.
> If you're not, get lost!
> . . .
> Get lost!
> We're gonna chase you out of your fucking job!
> Kill! Kill! Kill![217]

One "well-born" person commented: "We were *born Red!* Our Redness comes from the body of our mother. And I tell you quite clearly: You were born

Black! What can you do about that?"[218] The racialization of categories was devastating. Zhai Zhenhua, belt in hand and insults at the ready, forced the "black" half of his class to spend all their time studying Mao: "If they are to save themselves, they must first learn to be ashamed of their horrible family origins, and to hate their parents."[219] Naturally there was no question of their joining the Red Guards. Red Guards patrolled the train station in Beijing, beating up and sending home any Red Guard who had the wrong origins. People were often more tolerant in the provinces, and there "blacks" sometimes did hold positions of responsibility, but the advantage always went to the "wellborn." Thus, in the case of a schoolgirl nicknamed "Piggy," Ling recalls: "Piggy's class background, a major qualification, was very good: she was from a mason's family and often boasted that for three generations her family had never had a roof over their heads."[220] In any verbal confrontation, the class card was always played and always won. Hua Linsham, who was a very militant rebel, was once thrown off a train by some rather conservative Red Guards: "What I still feel today was how much they found my physical presence offensive and dirty . . . I suddenly had the feeling that I was something quite disgusting."[221] In demonstrations, children with parents in the Five Red categories (Party cadres, army officers, workers, poor peasants, and revolutionary martyrs) always played the leading role.[222] Apartheid divided the entire society. At a meeting of a neighborhood committee in 1973, Nien Cheng sat down by mistake with the proletariat. "Almost as if an electric shock had hit them, the two workers closest to me immediately moved their stools away from me so that I sat isolated in the crowded room." She then went over to join a group of women, "members of the denounced capitalist class and intellectuals, the outcasts of the Cultural Revolution."[223] She makes it clear that it was neither the police nor the Party that imposed this segregation.

From Factional Fighting to the Crushing of the Rebels

The second phase of the movement began in early January 1967, when the question of power came to the fore. The Maoist Center knew that the point of no return had been reached in the confrontation with the former Liuist leadership, which was up against the ropes in Beijing but could still count on powerful allies in most of the provinces. To kill it off definitively, the rebels had to seize power. Since the army, the major player in the game, was steadfastly refusing to step in, it was clear that the president's new troops would have all the room to maneuver that they needed. Shanghai gave the first signal in January, and quickly all the municipalities and Party committees were overthrown. Suddenly the rebels could no longer simply criticize from the sidelines, but had to take on the task of governing. And so the disaster began:

tensions began to mount between rival groups of rebels, between students and workers, and between workers on long-term contracts and day laborers.[224] These tensions quickly grew into major confrontations involving entire cities, and then escalated into hand-to-hand fighting with guns and knives. The Maoist leaders, now so close to seizing power, suddenly took fright: industrial production was collapsing (falling 49 percent in Wuhan in January),[225] the government administration was crumbling, and splinter groups were beginning to take power. China was suffering from a cruel lack of competent cadres, and so the rebels had no option but to reinstate most of those who had come under attack. Production at factories had to be restored, and educational establishments could not remain closed indefinitely. So at the end of January the leadership made two decisions: to create a new power structure, composed of the Revolutionary Committees and based on the principle of "three in one," meaning an alliance among the rebels, the former cadres, and the PLA; and to push the Red Guards gently toward the exits (or back to the classrooms), if necessary by making use of Mao's other weapon, the army itself, which had been on alert for six months.

Proximity to the Center was no protection to the rebels then, and the Cultural Revolution still had many surprises to come. In April the return to normalization was going so smoothly that Mao was worried. Everywhere the conservatives and the people who had been pushed out in January were lifting their heads again and in some cases even forming a potentially dangerous alliance with the PLA. Such was the situation in Wuhan, where the rebels were in retreat. The time had therefore come for another swift turn to the left, which was reinforced in July by the arrest of Wuhan's military leaders over a two-day period by CRG representatives. But as occurred whenever the Maoist Red Guards felt that things were going well, the shift unleashed violence and factional fighting verging on anarchy, making the formation of Revolutionary Councils impossible in some places. As a result, in September the PLA was authorized to use its weapons (until then it had been forced to stand by and watch as its arsenals were raided). This move gave a new impetus to the rebels. In some senses 1968 was a repetition of 1967. In March Mao was again worried and made another but more moderate turn to the left. The confrontations became more and more bloody, and the rebels were completely crushed in July.

Thus much depended on Mao's hesitations as he found himself faced with a cruel and inescapable dilemma: chaos on the left or order on the right. All the actors awaited the director's next move, hoping it would be to their advantage. It was a strange situation, with mortal enemies all dependent on the same living god. So, for example, when the powerful conservative Confederation of the Million Heroes in Wuhan learned in July 1967 that things were not to go its way, it declared: "Whether we are convinced or not, we must follow and apply the decisions that come from the Center, without any reservations" and immediately disbanded.[226] Because there was never a definitive interpretation of what Mao said, those who might be imagined to be in a position of authority—the Party committees—were little heeded in practice. Confusion also reigned concerning the real intentions of the Center, as people found it hard to believe that Mao himself could be so indecisive. The swings of the pendulum were so great that soon everyone was demanding some sort of vengeance, and the victors of the moment never practiced magnanimity.

In addition to these external factors, two internal factors played an important role in increasing violence, particularly inside the rebel organizations. The interests of small groups and individual ambitions, which were never arbitrated in a democratic fashion, constantly led to new splits inside the parties, while cynical "political entrepreneurs" tried to improve their positions by associating with the new local powers, especially by cultivating close relations with the regional PLA headquarters. Many ended up having close links with the Gang of Four and effectively became provincial dictators. Little by little the factional struggles lost their political character and became straightforward struggles for power between those who had the top positions and the people who wanted to replace them.[227] And as was the case in the *laogai*, anyone who made accusations was always right, since the accusations came with a barrage of quotations and sacrosanct slogans. As a rule, those who tried to defend themselves always ended up in even deeper trouble. The only effective riposte was a counteraccusation at a higher level. It mattered little whether the accusation had any basis; the important thing was that it be couched in correct political terms. The logic of the debate thus constantly expanded the battlefield and the number of targets.[228] In the final analysis, since everything was political, the tiniest incident could be overinterpreted as proof of the worst criminal intentions. The outcome was arbitration through physical elimination.

These events might be described as civil war rather than massacre, although the one leads almost automatically to the other. It was increasingly a war that involved everyone. In Wuhan, in late December 1966, the rebels imprisoned 3,100 cadres and conservatives.[229] The first death in the confrontations between the rebels and the Million Heroes came about on 27 May 1967. As a result armed positions were taken up at strategic points. The rebel headquarters was seized on 17 June with 25 deaths. Casualties rose to 158 by 30 June. After their defeat, 600 conservatives were killed, and another 66,000 suffered persecution of one sort or another. At the moment of the turn to the left in March 1968, the hunt suddenly intensified. Tens of thousands were held in a stadium, militia groups that were increasingly ruled by the mob sowed panic in the streets, and arms flooded in from neighboring provinces. In May, fighting between rebel factions led to a generalized belief that civil war was under way once more, and on 27 May 80,000 weapons were stolen from the army in a single day. This was a new record. A real black market in arms opened up on a nationwide scale. Factories even began to turn out tanks and explosives for the different rebel factions. By mid-June, 57 people had been killed by stray bullets. Shops were looted, banks were raided, and the population began to flee the city. But like a *deus ex machina,* a single statement from Beijing saved the day, causing the rebels to fold. The PLA intervened on 22 July and took charge without the firing of a single shot, and the factions were forced to disband in September.[230] In areas such as the relatively nonindustrial Fujian region, the split was less one between conservatives and rebels than it was the age-old divide between town and country. When Red Guards from Xiamen arrived in the provincial capital, they were attacked by people shouting: "Fuzhou belongs to the Fuzhou natives! . . . People of Fuzhou, do not forget your ancestors! We shall always be sworn enemies of the people of Xiamen!"[231] In Shanghai, in a slightly less direct manner, the real confrontation was between people from regions to the north and south of Jiangsu Province.[232] Even on the tiny local level of Long Bow, the struggle among revolutionary factions barely disguised the reemergence of the old quarrel between the Lu clan, which dominated the north side of the village, and the Shen clan, which ruled the south side. This was also the moment when old scores were settled, including quarrels that dated back to the Japanese occupation or the bloody beginnings of agrarian reform in 1946.[233] In the highly rural Guangxi region, the conservatives, who had been thrown out of Guilin, progressively encircled the town with peasant militias and ultimately emerged victorious.[234] In Canton in July and August 1967, pitched battles among various factions of the Red Flag and East Wind groups led to 900 deaths.[235] Some of the battles even involved artillery.

How hard conditions really were during this period can be gauged from the following statement by a Red Guard who was then fourteen years old: "We were young. We were fanatical. We thought that Mao was a really great man, that he alone had the truth, that he was the truth. I believed everything that he said. And I believed that there were good reasons for the Cultural Revolution. We thought we were revolutionaries, and because we were the revolutionaries who followed Mao's orders, we thought we could solve everything, solve all the problems of our society."[236] Atrocities became more and more widespread, and were of a more "traditional" nature than they had been the year before. The following events were witnessed near Lanzhou, in Gansu: "There must have been about fifty vehicles . . . each one had a body strapped across the radiator. Some lorries had more than one tied to them. They were all stretched out diagonally, and tied there with rope and wire . . . The crowd surrounded one man and stabbed him with spears and rustic swords, until he fell to the ground and lay there, a bleeding heap of flesh."[237]

In the second half of 1968 the army reasserted control and tightened its grip. The Red Guards were disbanded, and that autumn millions of young people (by 1970 the total was 5.4 million) were sent out into the countryside in the hope that they would remain there.[238] Many stayed for a decade or more. Before Mao's death, between 12 million and 20 million people were forcibly ruralized in this fashion, including 1 million people from Shanghai, representing 18 percent of the city's population.[239] Three million cadres who had been removed from their posts were sent (often for several years) to the 7 May Schools, rehabilitation centers that were prisons in all but name.[240] Without any doubt this was the year of the greatest massacres, as worker parties and soldiers took back various campuses and cities in the southern regions. Wuzhou, in Guangxi, was destroyed with heavy artillery and napalm. Guilin was taken on 19 August by 30,000 soldiers and armed peasants after a real military campaign in which political and military teams managed to fan the country dwellers' indifference toward the Cultural Revolution into active hostility. For six days rebels were executed en masse. In the month after the fighting in Guilin had ended, the terror spread throughout the countryside, this time directed against the "blacks" and the Kuomintang, who were the eternal scapegoats. It was so thorough that at the end some regions could boast that they were "entirely free of any member of any of the five Black categories."[241] It was then that the future chairman of the Communist Party, Hua Guofeng, who was in charge of security for his province, gained the title "the butcher of Hunan." The southern part of the country suffered most: there were perhaps 100,000 deaths in Guangxi, 40,000 in Guangdong, 30,000 in Yunnan.[242] The Red Guards were extremely cruel, but the worst atrocities were carried out by their executioners, the soldiers and militias carrying out the Party's orders.

Former Red Guard Hua Linshan recalls the reprisals in Guilin:

> As soon as day broke, the soldiers started searching the houses and arresting people. At the same time they shouted instructions through megaphones. They had drawn up a list of ten crimes, including the seizure of a prison, raids on a bank, attacks on any military installation, forcible entry into any facility of the security services, raids on trains, and participation in the armed struggle. Anyone who was suspected of any of these crimes was arrested and suffered the justice of the "dictatorship of the proletariat." I did a quick calculation and realized that I was guilty or at least six of those crimes. But I had done all of them "for the good of the revolution." I had not obtained any personal advantage or profit from any of them. If I had not wanted to take part in the

revolution, I would not have carried out any of those criminal acts. Suddenly I was being asked to be responsible for them. It seemed quite unfair, and naturally I was very afraid . . .

I learned later that the soldiers had killed a number of our wounded heroes who were lying in the hospital, and they had cut the supplies of blood and oxygen to those who were undergoing transfusions, killing more of these sorts of people. Those who could still walk had all their medication taken away, and they were taken to temporary prisons.

One wounded man managed to slip away, and the soldiers cordoned off the whole area. They searched all the rooms all over again. Anyone whose name was not written on the local lists was arrested, and that was my fate too . . .

When I was in prison [in School No. 7 in Guilin] I met up with an old classmate from the time I was studying to be a mechanic. He told me that one of the combat heroes from our school had been killed by the soldiers. He had become a hero by holding out on a hilltop against the enemy assault for three days and three nights. The rebel general, in recognition of his courage, had given him the nickname "unique and courageous hero." The soldiers who took over the school and arrested so many people had asked him to come out from the crowd. They tied him up in a sack and hung him from a tree in front of all the students so that he truly resembled a "gall bladder" [in Chinese the term evokes the notion of "unique and courageous hero"]. Then they beat him to death in the sack with their rifle butts.

There were many other stories as horrible as that one going around the prison, but I tried not to listen to them. Executions had gone on for two days all over town, and they had become the major topic of conversation. The killing started to seem almost normal. The people who were carrying them out did not seem much bothered by them, and the people who talked about them had become cold and unfeeling. I listened to these stories as though they were about some other world.

The worst thing in prison was always when one of the prisoners agreed to cooperate with the authorities, and came around to try to single out his previous companions. The guards would suddenly give us an order like "Lift your horrible dog heads!" and a few masked individuals would then enter the room and stare at us for a long time. If they saw someone they knew, the soldiers would point a gun at him and order him to leave with them. Often they were executed immediately.[243]

Thus, in 1968 the state reasserted itself with all its former perquisites. It again assumed a monopoly of institutionalized violence, and did not hesitate to use it. An increase in the number of public executions marked a return to the police tactics used before the Cultural Revolution. In Shanghai, former worker Wang Hongwen, a protégé of Jiang Qing and soon to be vice chairman of the Party, proclaimed a "victory over anarchy." On 27 April several rebel leaders were condemned to death and immediately killed in front of a vast crowd.[244] Zhang Chunqiao, another member of the Gang of Four, said in July: "If a few people are wrongly accused, it does not really matter; but it would be disastrous to allow any of the guilty to escape."[245] China entered a dark era of nonexistent plots and conspiracy theories, during which arrests were carried out on a massive scale, and society returned to dumb silence. Only the death of Lin Biao, in 1971, attenuated the worst period of terror that China had seen since the 1950s.

The first plot was that of the so-called People's Party of Inner Mongolia, which in fact had been dissolved and absorbed by the Communist Party in 1947, but which the authorities claimed had secretly reconstituted itself. More than 346,000 people were investigated in February–May 1968. Three-quarters of the suspects were Mongols, and xenophobia was undoubtedly a major factor in the affair. There were 16,000 deaths from execution, torture, and suicide, and 87,000 people were maimed for life.[246] Similar accusations led to 14,000 executions in Yunnan, another province with a large number of ethnic minorities.[247] Especially sinister was the "conspiracy" of the 16 May Regiment. This was probably a tiny and very ephemeral organization of ultra-left-wing Beijing Red Guards, one of thousands of comparable groups. The group had left a few traces, including statements hostile to Zhou Enlai made in July 1967. For reasons that are still unclear, the Maoist Center decided to portray the organization as a huge network of "black bandits" and counterrevolutionaries. The campaign against them, launched in 1970, ended quite inconclusively and without any major trials in 1976, after years of torture and forced confessions all across the country. Of the 2,000 staff at the Foreign Affairs Ministry, 600 were investigated during the affair. Mao's own personal guard, Unit 8341, distinguished themselves at Beijing University by unmasking 178 "enemies" and killing 10 during their investigations. In a factory in Shaanxi in late 1968, 547 "spies" were unmasked, together with 1,200 accomplices. Yan Fengying, an actress in the Beijing Opera, was accused on thirteen different counts and committed suicide in April 1968. An autopsy was carried out in an attempt to find a radio transmitter that she supposedly had hidden inside her body. Three great table-tennis champions also took their own lives.[248]

Nien Cheng provides an account of one episode of theatricalized terror, a "struggle meeting" in 1969:

> The audience in the room was shouting slogans and waving Little Red Books. After "Long Live Our Great Leader Chairman Mao!" came "Good Health To Our Vice-Supreme Commander Lin, Always Good

Health!" This seemed to me not only a reflection of the elevated position of Lin Biao after the Ninth Party Congress, but also testimony to the fact that those who organized this meeting were his intimates, anxious to promote Lin Biao's personality cult.

Two legs came into my limited field of vision. A man's voice spoke in front of me. He introduced me to the audience by giving an account of my family background and personal life. I had noticed already that each time my life story was recounted by the Revolutionaries I became richer and my way of life became more decadent and luxurious. Now the farce reached fantastic proportions. Since I had promised not to answer back but to remain mute, I was much more relaxed than at the previous struggle meeting in 1966. However, the audience jumped up from their seats when the speaker told them that I was a spy for the imperialists. They expressed their anger and indignation by crowding around me to shout abuse.

To be so maligned was intolerable. Instinctively I raised my head to respond. The women suddenly jerked up my handcuffed hands. Such sharp pain tore at my shoulder joints that I had to bend my body forward with my head well down to ease the agony. They kept me in this position during the rest of the man's denunciation of me. Only when the people were again shouting slogans did they allow my arms to drop back. I was to learn later that I had been subjected to the so-called "jet position" invented by the Revolutionaries to torment their more recalcitrant victims and to force them to bow their heads in servile submission . . .

The people in the audience soon worked themselves into a state of hysteria. Their shouts drowned out the voice of the speaker. Someone pushed me hard from behind. I stumbled and knocked over the microphone. One of the women tried to pick it up, tripped over the wires, and fell, dragging me with her. I fell in an awkward position. My face was pressed against the floor; many others fell on top of us in the confusion. Everybody seemed to be yelling. There was pandemonium. Several minutes passed. Finally I was pulled up again.

Utterly exhausted, I longed for the meeting to end. But the speeches continued. It seemed everyone sitting around the table on the platform wanted to make a contribution. They had ceased to denounce me; instead they were competing with each other to sing the praises of Lin Biao in the most extravagant flattery the rich Chinese language could provide. Their efforts to register their devotion to Lin Biao could be explained, I thought, only by the probable presence of Lin Biao's loyal lieutenants listening in an adjacent room.

Suddenly the door behind me opened. A man's voice shouted, "Zuo-la!" This meant that someone had departed. The two simple words produced an effect that was electrical. The speaker stopped in midsentence. Since the important person or persons listening in the adjoining room had gone, there was no more need to go on with the performance. Some of the audience were already on their feet, while others were collecting their bags and jackets. Hastily the speaker led them to shout slogans. He was largely ignored. Only a few responded while walking out of the room. It seemed the people were no longer angry with me. Though they did not smile, the glances directed at me were indifferent. I was just one of the many victims at whose struggle meeting they had been present. They had done what was required of them. Now it was over. Once when a man brushed against me, someone behind him even stretched out a hand to steady me.

The room cleared in a moment. I could hear members of the departing audience chatting as they left the building. "Getting rather chilly, isn't it?" "Where are you going for supper?" "Not raining, is it?" etc., etc. They sounded no different from an audience departing after a show at a cinema or theater.[249]

All witnesses concur that in 1969 and the years that followed China was a violent place ruled by slogans and political campaigns. The obvious failure of the Cultural Revolution caused most city dwellers to lose all faith in politics. The young were particularly affected because they had invested so much in the process. Their frequent refusal to go to the countryside led to the formation of an underclass that lived a semiclandestine existence. Cynicism, criminality, and selfishness were the norm everywhere. In 1971 the brutal and unexpected elimination of Lin Biao, the man whom Mao himself had named as his successor, opened many people's eyes at last. Mao, "the Great Helmsman," was not infallible after all.[250] The Chinese were tired and fearful, and rightly so: the number of people in the *laogai* had grown by 2 million between 1966 and 1976.[251] The darkness, however, was about to lift. People still pretended to be faithful to their leader. But underneath, civil society was emerging from its torpor, prior to its explosion in the years 1976–1979. This was a movement much more fertile than the Cultural Revolution, which would always be best summed up by the slogan with which Mao had rewarded a good student in August 1966: "It is because I am obedient that I revolt."[252]

The Deng Era: The End of Terror

When Mao finally died in September 1976, he had been a spent force politically for some time. The muted nature of the popular response to his death was sufficient proof of that, as was his obvious incapacity to assure his own succession. The Gang of Four, to whom he was very close ideologically, were all imprisoned within a month of his death. Hua Guofeng, who was supposed to be the guarantor of continuity, relinquished most of his powers in December 1978 to make way for the irrepressible Deng Xiaoping, who was hated by the Maoist camp. The great turning point perhaps had been 5 April 1976, the Chinese Day of the Dead, when, in what was apparently a spontaneous outpouring of grief, the people of Beijing commemorated the death of Prime Minister Zhou, who had died in January. The government was astonished at the unforeseen scale of the demonstrations: it could not be explained away by reference to any faction or to Party manipulation. Some of the poems included with the wreaths contained thinly veiled attacks on Mao. The crowds were dispersed by force (although, unlike in 1989, there was no shooting in Tiananmen Square itself), leaving 8 dead and 200 wounded. There were many demonstrations outside the capital; thousands were imprisoned all over the country. In the aftermath there were at least 500 executions including at least 100 demonstrators who had been arrested. Investigations continued until October, affecting tens of thousands of people.[253] But this was not simply "business as usual." The post-Maoist era had already begun, with politicians in retreat and the Center no longer capable of directing all operations. "Whereas in 1966 Tiananmen Square was filled with intimidated crowds of people tearfully watching the man who had taken away their liberty, ten years later those same people had gathered their strength, and they looked him right in the eye."[254]

The Democracy Wall, lasting from the winter of 1978 to the spring of 1979, symbolized this new state of affairs, but it also showed its limits. With Deng's consent, several former Red Guards posted on the wall their opinions, which were almost unthinkable for people who had been brought up under Maoism. The most articulate of these thinkers, Wei Jingsheng, in a poster titled "The Fifth Modernization: Democracy," actually came out and said that people were being exploited by the ruling classes through a system of feudal socialism.[255] He argued that democracy was the only way forward to lasting change, that it was the natural fifth consequence of the four other modernizations suggested by Deng, and that Marxism, as the source of all totalitarianism, should be discarded in favor of more democratic forms of socialism. In March 1979, when Deng was somewhat more secure in his position, he had Wei and several others arrested. Wei was sentenced to fifteen years in prison for passing information abroad, which was regarded as a counterrevolutionary crime. He never made a confession, and was freed in 1993. But he continued to speak out so forcefully that he was arrested again eight months later and in 1995 sentenced to fourteen years in prison for "drawing up a plan for a campaign to overthrow the government."[256] In November 1997 he was suddenly released from prison and sent into exile in the United States.

Under Deng Xiaoping, however, it was possible to be critical and to survive. This was a great step forward from the Mao era, when a word out of place or a scribble on a wall was enough to have someone shot. The major post-Maoist reforms were economic, but politics were not forgotten among the changes. Everything bore witness to a growing sense of emancipation and a rejection of the government's arbitrary decisions. In the 1980s, the suppression of organizations of poor and middle-rank peasants meant that only about one-tenth of the peasantry was actually represented in the Chinese Communist Party, and the peasantry as a whole returned to traditional family farming on a massive scale.[257] In the cities, the explosion of private enterprise meant that a large section of the workforce was no longer under direct political control. The state machinery became more formal and predictable, providing citizens with a better line of defense against the state. After 1978 the freeing of prisoners (approximately 100,000) became commonplace, and rehabilitations (though often posthumous) became increasingly widespread, particularly as far as artists and writers were concerned. For example, Ding Ling, a victim of the rectification campaign of 1957–58, was finally allowed to return from his rural exile in 1959, ending a long series of persecutions stretching back to Yan'an. This was the beginning of a "literature of scars," and of a still timid return to creative freedom. Two-thirds of the people who had been sent to the countryside during the Cultural Revolution were allowed to return to the cities. The new constitution afforded a basic minimum of legal rights. In 1979 the People's Republic of China produced its first penal code; Mao had never wanted one because he feared that it would unnecessarily restrict the room he needed to maneuver. In this new code, the death penalty was reserved for "abominable crimes," a right to appeal was instituted (so that appeals no longer automatically brought stiffer sentences), and the entire legal mechanism was removed from direct Party control.

An even larger wave of rehabilitations came in 1982, when 242,000 people were rehabilitated in Sichuan alone. In Guangdong, 78 percent of all people who had been labeled "counterrevolutionaries" had that label removed and were given a small indemnity for each year they had spent in prison. Of the new prisoners who were sentenced that year, only 0.5 percent were political prisoners. In 1983 the minister of security's area of responsibility was drastically reduced, and administration of the *laogai* was transferred to the Ministry of Justice. The courts began to reject a number of arrests, a complaints procedure against the police was established, torturers were prosecuted and tried in public, and new inspections of the camps were carried out. Social class was no longer to be taken into account during trials. In 1984 integration of people emerging from prison or camp was made much easier, while inside the prisons professional training began to take the place of ideological study. Innovations such as the reduction of sentences for good behavior, suspended sentences, and parole were introduced, and families were encouraged to maintain their links with prisoners. By 1986 the number of people in prison had fallen to 5 million and has remained steady ever since. This is half the figure for 1976, and represents 0.5 percent of the total population, more or less identical with the proportion in the United States, though lower than the proportion in the U.S.S.R. during its final few years. Despite strenuous efforts, the share of gross domestic product accounted for by the *laogai* remains large, although it is three times lower than it was in the late 1950s.[258]

Progress has continued despite the events of Tiananmen Square. Since 1990 citizens have been allowed to sue the government. Since 1996 all detention without trial has come under strict regulation and has been reduced to a maximum of one month, while the maximum *laojiao* sentence has been reduced to three years. The role and autonomy of lawyers have increased considerably; their number more than doubled between 1990 and 1996. Since 1995 magistrates and judges have been recruited by a process of open competition, although most are still former soldiers or policemen.[259]

Much remains to be done, however, before China becomes a free and open society. People are still not innocent until proved guilty, and the crime of counterrevolution is still on the statute books, although it is now used with much greater restraint. In December 1994 the term *laogai* was replaced with the much more banal "prison," but as the *Legal Gazette* noted, "the function, character, and role of our penal institutions remain unchanged."[260] Most trials still take place *in camera,* and judgment is often passed extremely quickly and without due care. No case is ever prepared for more than three months. Although corruption is enormously widespread among cadres, in 1993–1995 less than 3 percent of prosecutions were for crimes of corruption.[261] In general, while the 4 percent of the population who were members of the Communist Party accounted for 30 percent of all people who were charged with crimes, they made up only 3 percent of people who were executed;[262] clearly, solidarity persists between the political and legal spheres. The arrest in the 1990s of several members of the political administration in Beijing on charges of corruption and embezzlement caused quite a stir, but was a relatively isolated event. Communist officials, who are increasingly involved in business, are still quite invulnerable.

The death penalty continues to be widely used in China. Each year hundreds of people are sentenced to death for crimes ranging from serious cases of smuggling, including the illegal export of art works, to "passing state secrets," which in practice can mean almost anything. Presidential pardons, which technically have been available since 1982, are never used. Thousands of people are executed each year; China accounts for more than half the total annual number of executions worldwide. Furthermore, the number of executions is rising in comparison to the 1970s, as it did in the last centuries of the Chinese empire.[262]

Exercise of the death penalty remains linked to political campaigns and crises. In 1983 the rising crime rate resulted in perhaps 1 million arrests, and there were at least 10,000 executions. Many of these were held in public as a lesson for the people, even though such practices are forbidden by the penal code. All of these were part of a mass campaign reminiscent of the events of the 1950s. As then, there was an attempt to group together all the "criminal" elements. Many intellectuals, priests, and foreigners were intimidated during what was termed the "Campaign against Spiritual Pollution," which was launched amid much publicity. The occupation of Tiananmen Square in the spring of 1989 resulted in significant repression, reflecting the fragility of Deng Xiaoping's position. Unlike the Maoist leaders of 1976, Deng gave the order to open fire. At least 1,000 people were killed and perhaps 10,000 injured in Beijing. Hundreds of additional executions in the provinces were carried out in secret or disguised to look like normal executions for criminal activity. At least 10,000 people were arrested in Beijing, and another 30,000 throughout the country. Thousands of people were given prison sentences, and the leaders of the movement, who refused to repent, received up to thirteen years in prison. Much pressure was brought to bear on the families of the accused (a practice that most people believed had disappeared for good), and the practice of forcing criminals to hang their heads in public was reinstated. The treatment received by prisoners and the length of their sentences were directly related to the amount of contrition they expressed and the number of colleagues they denounced. Although political prisoners are still a small minority of all detainees, there were 100,000 of them in 1991, including at least 1,000 recent dissidents.[264]

Communist China in the late twentieth century is considerably more prosperous and less violent than it was under Mao, and it seems to have definitively rejected utopian goals and permanent civil war. But because the regime has never really disavowed its founder, it is still prepared to return to some of his original methods in difficult moments.

Tibet: Genocide on the Rooftop of the World?

Tibet was the site of some of the worst excesses of the Deng era, and nowhere was the long-term influence of Mao more strongly felt. Although China is a unitary state, the government gives special rights to national minorities, and a certain amount of administrative autonomy to the larger ones. But the 4 million to 6 million Tibetan nationals had made it quite clear that they were not happy being part of the Chinese state and longed for a return to the days when they had been masters of their own country, before their historic region was divided into the Autonomous Region of Tibet, which in fact included only half of the country's former territory, and several Chinese provinces. Qinghai was constituted in the 1950s from the Tibetan region of Amdo. The small Tibetan minorities in Sichuan, Gansu, and Yunnan had very few rights. For the most part they were treated worse than Tibetans who lived in the autonomous region, a fact that led to the rebellion of the nomad Golok warriors of the Amdo, in northern Tibet, in May 1956.[265]

Tibet had been through much since the first arrival of the PLA in 1950. Although the intensity of repression varied from region to region, it was also largely a result of the traditional prejudice among people of the Chinese lowlands against the "backward savages" of the highlands. According to dissidents, 70,000 Tibetans died of hunger in 1959–1963 (as in other isolated regions, pockets of famine persisted longer there than elsewhere).[266] That figure represents 2 to 3 percent of the population, considerably less proportionally than in the rest of China. Jasper Becker's more recent study gives figures that are considerably higher, with a mortality rate of 50 percent in Qinghai, the native district of the Dalai Lama.[267] From 1965 to 1970 Tibetan families were grouped together into people's communes that were run along almost military lines. Famine resulted from the absurd attempt to produce the same "great" cereals that were being grown in mainland China through ill-conceived irrigation and terracing projects, abandonment of the fallow farming system that was vital for agriculture on such poor unfertilized soil, the replacement of barley crops that were well adapted to cold and drought with more fragile wheat crops, and a reduction in the amount of grazing land for yaks. Many yaks died, leaving Tibetans without dairy products (butter is a staple of their diet) and without animal skins to cover their tents in winter; many people died of cold. As elsewhere, government quotas were excessively high. Beginning in 1953, tens of thousands of Chinese colonizers were resettled in eastern Tibet (Sichuan), where they were given a share of the collectivized land. The presence in the autonomous region of some 300,000 Han Chinese, two-thirds of whom were soldiers and all of whom needed feeding, further increased the strain on local agriculture. The 1965 report on rural liberalization measures implemented by Liu Shaoqi in 1962 noted that these measures were symbolized in Tibet by the slogan "One farm, one yak."[268]

Tibet also suffered under the Cultural Revolution. In July 1966 Red Guards, including some Tibetans (despite denials by supporters of the Dalai Lama), began requisitioning private property and replacing Buddhas on altars with pictures of Mao Zedong. They forced the monks to participate in "struggle meetings" that they did not always survive. Above all they attacked the temples, including the most famous ones. Zhou Enlai was forced to protect the Potala (the ancient home of the "living God") in Lhasa with his own troops. The sacking of the Jokhang monastery in Lhasa was followed by similar incidents throughout the region. According to one monk who witnessed the events at Jokhang, "There were several hundred chapels, but only two were spared.

All the others were pillaged or defiled. All the statues, sacred texts, and objects were broken or carried off . . . Only the statue of Çakyamuni at the entrance to Jokhang was spared by the Red Guards because it symbolized the links between China and Tibet. The destruction went on for more than a week. After that the Jokhang was transformed into a barracks for the Chinese soldiers . . . Another part . . . was turned into an abattoir."[269] Given the absolutely central place of religion in traditional Tibetan society, these measures—which were fairly typical for the time—must have been felt more deeply in Tibet than elsewhere. It would also appear that the army, which had fewer links to the local population, provided more assistance to the Red Guards than was the case elsewhere, at least wherever resistance was encountered. Most of the massacres took place in 1968, at the end of the movement, as a result of battles among Maoist factions that had caused hundreds of deaths in Lhasa in January. The casualties were particularly high in the summer, when the army imposed a Revolutionary Committee on the population. As a result of these actions, more Chinese than Tibetans died in Tibet during the Cultural Revolution.[270]

But the worst years by far for Tibet were those that had begun with the arrival of the Chinese troops in 1950 and culminated in forced collectivization in 1959, three years after the rest of the country. The collectivization drive sparked an insurrection, which was put down with brutal repression and led to the flight to India of the Dalai Lama, the spiritual and temporal leader of Tibet, together with 100,000 other refugees, including the majority of the country's tiny cultivated elite. Although the 1950s were also an extremely difficult decade for China proper, exceptionally violent measures were used in Tibet to impose both Communism and Chinese domination on a ferociously independent people who were either seminomadic (about 40 percent) or attached to monasteries. Tensions increased further during collectivization in the middle of the decade. The army responded to an uprising by Khampa guerrillas with atrocities out of all proportion to the rebellion's scale. In 1956, during the Tibetan New Year celebrations, the great Chode Gaden Phendeling monastery in Batang was destroyed by aerial bombardment; at least 2,000 monks and pilgrims were killed.[271]

The litany of atrocities is hair-raising and in many cases unverifiable. But the eyewitness reports concur so precisely that the Dalai Lama's assessment of this period seems beyond challenge: "Tibetans not only were shot, but also were beaten to death, crucified, burned alive, drowned, mutilated, starved, strangled, hanged, boiled alive, buried alive, drawn and quartered, and beheaded."[272] The darkest moment was undoubtedly 1959, in the aftermath of the uprising in Kham, in eastern Tibet, in which the rebels captured Lhasa. Several factors promoted the uprising, including reaction against the people's communes, the Great Leap Forward, several years of Chinese quotas, and the large-scale repatriation by the U.S. Central Intelligence Agency of the Khampa warriors they had trained in guerrilla camps in Colorado and Guam.[273] The civilian population, which was quite sympathetic to the rebels and allowed them to blend into society, suffered massive bombardment by the Chinese army. The wounded were left untended and were often buried alive or devoured by stray dogs—accounting for the high number of suicides on the losing side. Lhasa itself, a bastion of 20,000 Tibetans armed with only muskets and swords, was retaken on 22 March at a cost of between 2,000 and 10,000 lives, with the Ramoche and Potala temples suffering major damage. The Tibetan leader and 100,000 of his followers then set off for India. Another large-scale revolt in Lhasa in 1969 was put down with great bloodshed. The Khampa guerrillas struggled on until 1972. The cycle of revolt and repression began again in Lhasa in October 1987, leading to a declaration of martial law in 1989 after three days of rioting in favor of independence and what were depicted as the beginnings of anti-Chinese pogroms. According to General Zhang Shaosong, there were more than 600 deaths in eighteen months. Despite some atrocities, particularly against nuns, Chinese methods have clearly changed; there have been no more massacres. But by now almost all Tibetans have at least one family member who has suffered under the Chinese.[274]

The worst tragedy in modern Tibet was the internment of hundreds of thousands of people—perhaps as many as one in ten Tibetans—during the 1950s and 1960s. It appears that very few people (perhaps as few as 2 percent) ever returned alive from the 166 known camps, most of which were in Tibet or the neighboring provinces.[275] In 1984 the Dalai Lama's intelligence service estimated that 173,000 people had died during detention. Entire monastic communities were sent to the coal mines. Detention conditions on the whole appear to have been dreadful, with hunger, cold, or extreme heat the daily lot of the prisoners. There are as many tales of execution of prisoners refusing to renounce Tibetan independence as there are tales of cannibalism in prison during the Great Leap Forward.[276] It was as though the entire population of Tibet (one in four of all adult men in Tibet are lamas) were suspects. Nearly one in six was classified as a right-winger, as opposed to one in twenty in China. In the Tibetan prairie region in Sichuan, where Mao had rested and gathered his strength during the Long March, two-thirds of the population were arrested in the 1950s, and not freed until 1964 or 1977. In 1962 the Panchen Lama, the second-highest dignitary in Tibetan Buddhism, protested to Mao against the famine and repressions that were decimating his countrymen. In retaliation, he was thrown into prison and then placed under house arrest until 1977. The verdict by which he had been sentenced was not annulled until 1988.[277]

If there is no definitive proof that the Chinese planned a physical genocide in Tibet, there is no doubt that they carried out a cultural genocide. Immediately after the Cultural Revolution, only 13 of the 6,259 designated places of Buddhist worship were still open. Most of the others were turned into barracks, storerooms, or detention centers. Some of those that survived have subsequently reopened. But many were emptied totally, and their treasures—manuscripts, frescoes, *thanka* paintings, statues, and other objects—were destroyed or stolen, particularly if they contained any precious metals. By 1973, one Beijing foundry had melted down 600 tons of Tibetan sculptures. In 1983 a mission from Lhasa found 32 tons of Tibetan relics in the Chinese capital, including 13,537 statues and statuettes.[278] The attempt to eradicate Buddhism altogether was accompanied by a drive to give Chinese names to all newborn Tibetan babies. Until 1979 all school classes were taught in Mandarin. Finally, as a last reminder of the anti-Manchu revolution of 1911, the Red Guards cut off the pigtails of Tibetans of both sexes and tried to impose Han-style Chinese dress on the whole nation.

Violent deaths were proportionally much greater in Tibet than in China proper. Even so, it is difficult to believe the figures released by the Tibetan government-in-exile in 1984: 1.2 million victims, or approximately one-quarter of all Tibetans. The figure of 432,000 deaths in combat seems even less credible. But one can legitimately speak of genocidal massacres because of the numbers involved, the lack of heed paid to the wishes and rights of civilians and prisoners, and the regularity with which atrocities were committed. According to official Chinese figures, the population of the autonomous region fell from 2.8 million inhabitants in 1953 to 2.5 million in 1964. If one takes into account the number of exiles and the (admittedly uncertain) birth rate, the number of deaths could be as high as 800,000—a scale of population loss comparable to that in Cambodia under the Khmer Rouge.[279] The fact that so many Tibetan women fear that any form of hospitalization may result in abortion or enforced sterilization is an indication of the draconian nature of the region's recently adopted antinatal policies, which are modeled on the practices in force for the Han. Previously, minorities had been excused from these measures. It is said that the secretary general of the Chinese Communist Party, Hu Yaobang, when visiting Lhasa in 1980, cried in shame when confronted with so much misery, discrimination, and segregation between Hans and Tibetans, a situation he described as "colonialism pure and simple." The Tibetans, so long forgotten or unknown in their remote country of snow and gods, have the misfortune to live in a region of enormous strategic importance, in the heart of Asia. Although they seem no longer threatened by physical extermination, their culture remains in jeopardy.

22 Crimes, Terror, and Secrecy in North Korea

Pierre Rigoulot

The People's Democratic Republic of Korea was created on 9 September 1948 in the part of the Korean peninsula north of the 38th parallel. In accordance with an agreement signed with the United States in August 1945, the Soviet Union was provisionally responsible for administering this zone, while the United States was to administer South Korea, below the 38th parallel.

North Korea quickly became the most closed state in the world. The Soviet Union in effect banned access to the North to anyone from the international community, and during the first two years of the Republic's existence, the closure became more formal. The war launched by the North on 25 June 1950 and formally ended by an armistice on 27 July 1953 increased the diet of lies, disinformation, and propaganda fed to its citizens to the point that almost any information was classified as a state secret.

But the war was not the only cause. The North Korean regime is intrinsically inward looking, even to the exclusion of other Communist powers; during the Sino-Soviet conflict it vacillated constantly between one side and the other. In addition, like the Cambodians and the Albanians, the North Korean leaders feared that influence from the outside world might corrupt the "ideological unity of the people and the Party." Together these factors explain why North Korea is sometimes called "the hermit kingdom." This inward-looking tendency has been theorized as the ideology of *juche,* which means self-control, independence, and self-sufficiency. This ideology was officially introduced at the Fifth Congress of the Korean Workers' (Communist) Party in November 1970.

Under these conditions, and because North Korea is unique in lacking an active opposition movement either inside the country or abroad, which could gather and pass on information, it is almost impossible to provide a general picture of the country or details about the realities of repression there. We must therefore content ourselves with official statements, which need to be interpreted and decoded; with statements from people who have managed to escape; and with information from the intelligence services of neighboring countries, especially South Korea. All these sources of information have to be treated with care.

Before the Establishment of the Communist State

Contrary to the claims made in the hagiographies released by the North Korean authorities, Korean Communism was not founded by Kim Il Sung, but dates back considerably earlier. In 1919 there were already two groups that claimed to be Bolshevik in origin. Moscow did not give its immediate support to either faction, and the struggle between them was ferocious. Thus the first victims of Communism in Korea were Communists themselves. The anti-Japanese guerrillas of the Pan-Russian Korean Communist Party, known as the Irkutsk group, fought an armed battle with guerrillas from a group who had founded a Korean Workers' Party in June 1921. The affair resulted in several hundred deaths and forced the Comintern to try to impose unity on the Korean Communist movement.

Korea had been a Japanese colony since 1910. Korean Communists were at the forefront in the struggle for independence, and fierce colonial repression claimed many victims in their ranks. The Communists themselves were to blame for some of these deaths. Many of the cadres had been trained abroad and knew little about the country, and heroic actions often brought disastrous consequences; demonstrating on symbolic days such as 1 May was an invitation to the authorities to take repressive action against them.

After the defeat of Japan, when the country was divided into two zones, more Communists fell in factional fighting. Kim Il Sung, the commander of a small anti-Japanese guerrilla group near Manchuria, was chosen by the Soviet Union to be the Korean leader over several other militant Communists who had been in the country a long time. In September 1945 potential rivals of Kim Il Sung, notably Hyon Chun Hyok, were assassinated in Pyongyang. Whether these assassinations ran to the dozens or the hundreds is still unknown.

Nationalists who had been allowed to stay in Pyongyang in the winter of 1945–46 were then hunted down and arrested. Together with their leader, Cho Man Sik, they had objected to the decision made at the conference of Allied ministers of foreign affairs, held in Moscow in December 1945, to keep Korea under a sort of trusteeship for at least five years. Cho was arrested on 5 January 1946 and executed in October 1950, during the evacuation of Pyongyang that preceded the advance of United Nations troops. Many of his close political allies met the same fate.

Repression was felt by the entire population. In the northern part of the country, the Soviet Union quickly established a state in its own image; agrarian reform opened the way to collectivization, the population was forced into large-scale organizations, and a one-party state was introduced. Political opponents, landowners, opponents of agrarian reform, and suspected collaborators with the Japanese were systematically intimidated. But the purge that followed cannot be blamed entirely on the Communists; it was also prompted by an upsurge in nationalist sentiments. The arrival of the new regime was heralded not by a bloodbath, but by a migration of hundreds of thousands of people to the South. The migrants included not only the categories mentioned above, but anyone who feared for his life or possessions. Although the North was quickly closed to any official organizations from the South, until 1948 it remained reasonably easy to pass from one zone to the other.

Victims of the Armed Struggle

This generalized exodus, during the first three years of the existence of a Communist regime that had not yet declared itself to be an autonomous state, did not put an end to its leaders' interest in the "Communization" of the entire peninsula. On the contrary, they believed that the whole country would soon be unified under their authority. Archives recently opened in Moscow show that Kim Il Sung was impatient to overthrow what he was already calling the American "puppets." The puppets in question had a much smaller army than the North Koreans; furthermore, they were under pressure from strikes and terrorist and guerrilla actions by various Communist groups. Kim Il Sung believed (or said he did) that the people of the South trusted both him and his army. In the spring of 1950 Stalin approved the invasion, which began on 25 June 1950 and took the South by surprise. Over the next three years more than 1 million civilians on both sides died, and millions lost their homes. An additional 400,000 died, and almost the same number were wounded among the Chinese troops who rescued the North Koreans from defeat by General Douglas MacArthur's United Nations forces. There were 200,000 dead among the North Korean soldiers, 50,000 among the South Koreans, and 50,000

American dead. Three hundred French soldiers died in the UN forces, and another 800 were wounded.

Few wars have been so clearly designed to extend the Communist zone of influence. At the time a number of French left-wing intellectuals, including Jean-Paul Sartre, supported the Communists, seeing South Korea as the aggressor against the North. Today, thanks to the archives that are now open, there is no longer any room for doubt. All this suffering, including the suffering of prisoners (6,000 Americans and as many again from other countries, mostly South Koreans, died in detention), and the personal hell of British and French diplomats who had remained in Seoul and of Christian missionaries working in the South who were deported by the advancing North Koreans, was attributable to actions by the Communist regime in North Korea.[1]

The armistice signed in July 1953 established a demilitarized zone between the two countries more or less where the fighting began, on the 38th parallel. This was an armistice but not a peace. Subsequent incursions and attacks by the North on the South, against both civilians and military personnel, have claimed many lives. In one action carried out in 1968 by a squad of thirty-one commandos against the South Korean presidential palace, all but one of the attackers were killed. An assassination attempt against members of the South Korean government in Rangoon, Burma, on 9 October 1983 led to the death of sixteen people, including four Korean government ministers. The midflight explosion of a Korean Air Lines jet on 29 November 1987 killed 115 people.

North Korea is not a mere suspect; it is clearly guilty of these acts. A terrorist who was arrested shortly before the Olympic games in Seoul in 1988 explained that he was working for Pyongyang and that his mission was to demonstrate that the South was not capable of assuring the security of the games, and thus to destroy its international reputation.[2]

Furthermore, North Korea's war against the entire capitalist world led it in the 1960s and 1970s to assist various terrorist groups, including most notably the Japanese Red Army (which carried out actions in Israel), several Palestinian organizations, and guerrillas in the Philippines.

Communist Victims of the North Korean Party-State

As in Stalin's Soviet Union, in North Korea the list of victims of purges within the Party would be extremely long. One human-rights organization has calculated that of the twenty-two members of the first North Korean government, seventeen were assassinated, executed, or purged.[3]

The ink was barely dry on the Panmunjon armistice before a purge struck a number of high-ranking cadres at the heart of the North Korean Party. On

3 August 1953 there was a major trial of Communists accused of spying for the Americans and plotting to overthrow the regime. Tibor Meray, a Hungarian journalist and writer, witnessed the events. He knew one of the accused, Sol Jang Sik, who had served as an interpreter for the North Korean delegation in the Kaeshong negotiations in July and August 1951. Sol Jang Sik was also a poet and a translator of Shakespeare.

> All the prisoners had a large number sewn onto the back of their jackets. The main suspect was number 1, and the others were classified in decreasing order of importance, through number 14.
>
> Number 14 was Sol Jang Sik.
>
> I hardly recognized him. His once handsome, impassioned face was now a picture of misery, fatigue, and resignation. No spark was left in his eyes at all. He moved like a robot. I learned years later that the accused were all fed very well in the weeks leading up to their first public meeting, so that their appearance would improve after all the torture and stress they had been through. When trials took place in public, the authorities tried to show the audience, and particularly any representatives from the international press who might be there, that the prisoners were in good health, were well fed, and were generally in good shape both physically and mentally. Foreign correspondents from the West were never present in North Korea, but there were always journalists from the Soviet Union and other Communist states. The clear aims of the trial were to demonstrate the defendants' guilt and thereby humiliate people who had once been major figures in society but were now just prisoners sitting in the dock.
>
> Apart from that, the trial was exactly the same as political trials in Czechoslovakia, Hungary, or Bulgaria. I was so surprised by Sol's condition, and the translation was so cursory, that I can hardly remember what the charges were. My only hope was that Sol could see me, but I do not think that he could because the room was so full. As far as I can remember, the main issue was some story about a plot against the Korean People's Republic, and an assassination attempt against Kim Il Sung, the leader they all loved so much. The idea was that the accused had been trying to turn the country back into a feudal state and to hand North Korea over to Syngman Rhee, and that they had been spying for the American imperialists and passing information to their agents, etc.[4]

Among the accused were a number of high-ranking officials, including Lu Sung Yop, one of the secretaries of the Party's Central Committee; Paik Hyung Bok, the minister of internal affairs; and Cho Il Myung, assistant minister of culture and propaganda. Sol was a small fish in this group. Some of the others came from South Korea.

Pak Hon Yong, the minister of foreign affairs, a Communist who had fought for the country for many years, was sentenced to death on 15 December 1955 and executed three days later as an American secret agent. Others followed in 1956, including Mu Chong, a member of the so-called Yenan group, who had been a general in the Eighth Chinese army, a commander in the North Korean artillery forces, and then chief of staff of the combined Sino–North Korean forces in the war against the South. A separate purge affected all cadres who had links to the Soviet Union, including Ho Kai; cadres linked to the Yenan faction who were close to the Chinese, including Kim Du Bong in March 1958; and cadres who had voiced approval of the Khrushchev reforms in the Soviet Union. Various other purges took place in 1960, 1967 (when Kim Kwang Hyup, a secretary in the Party's Secretariat, was sent to the camps), and 1969, when the best-known victim was Hu Hak-bong, who was in charge of secret operations against the South. The disappearance of eighty students from the Revolutionary Institute for Foreign Languages in Pyongyang was also presumably connected with the purge. In 1972 Pak Kum Chul, a former deputy prime minister and member of the Politburo, was sent to a camp. In 1977 Li Yong Mu, another former Politburo member, was sent to a prison camp, and more students disappeared. Most of the latter were the children of cadres who were under investigation. Other purges occurred in 1978 and 1980.

These purges were sufficiently common that they seem to have been structural in nature, rather than contingent on events. The latest purge occurred in September 1997. One of the secretaries of the Party Central Committee, So Hwan Hi, who was in charge of agriculture, was executed in public together with seventeen other cadres as a scapegoat for the severe food shortages currently afflicting the country. According to statements made by refugees, whenever tension rises in the country because of material difficulties such as shortages, Communist cadres are held responsible, and a number are sent to prison camps or executed.

Executions

There is no way of knowing exactly how many executions have taken place in North Korea, but an indication can be gained from the penal code. At least forty-seven crimes are punishable by the death penalty. These can be broken down into crimes against the sovereignty of the state, crimes against the state administration or against state property, crimes against individuals, crimes against property, and military crimes.

Kang Koo Chin, one of the great specialists on the North Korean legal system, has estimated that in 1958–1960, a period of particularly brutal repression, at least 9,000 people were ejected from the Party, tried, and sentenced to death. Extrapolating from this estimate to include the other nine purges of a similar scale, one arrives at a figure of 90,000 executions. For now, this figure must be merely an estimate of the size of the problem; perhaps one day the Pyongyang archives will reveal the full story.

People who have escaped from the country have attested to the routine execution of civilians for crimes such as prostitution, treason, murder, rape, and sedition. The crowd is invited to participate, and sentencing is accompanied by cries of hatred, insults, and stone-throwing. Sometimes the prisoner is kicked and beaten to death while the crowd chants slogans. Class origin is very important in determining punishment. Two witnesses told Asia Watch that rape was punishable by death only for members of the lower social classes.

The North Korean justice system exists solely to promote the interests of the regime. All judges and almost all lawyers act on the orders of the Party and are explicitly instructed to work along strict Marxist-Leninist lines. Trials often cover only some of the accusations, leaving the rest to be handled extrajudicially. Much more drastic measures are often taken independently of the trial.

Prisons and Camps

Mrs. Li Sun Ok was a member of the Workers' Party and in charge of a supply center reserved for cadres. She fell victim to one of the purges and was arrested together with some of her comrades. She was tortured for a long time with water and electricity, was beaten and deprived of sleep, and ended up confessing to anything she was asked, including specifically the misappropriation of state goods. She was then given a thirteen-year prison sentence. It was indeed a prison sentence, although that was not the official term used. In her penitentiary, some 6,000 people, including 2,000 women, worked as slave labor from 5:30 A.M. until midnight, manufacturing slippers, holsters, bags, belts, detonators, and artificial flowers. Any detainees who became pregnant were brutally forced to have abortions. Any child who was born in the prison was smothered or had its throat cut.[5]

The harshness of prison conditions is well known from earlier testimony. One exceptional account of life in the prisons of North Korea in the 1960s and 1970s comes from Ali Lameda, a Venezuelan Communist poet who was well disposed toward the regime and went to Pyongyang to work as a translator of official propaganda. In 1967, after expressing reservations about the effectiveness of some of the propaganda, he was arrested and imprisoned.[6] In a brochure published by Amnesty International, Lameda described his farcical trial, which ended with a sentence to twenty years of hard labor for "attempted sabotage, espionage, and trying to help foreign agents infiltrate North Korea." Although he himself was never tortured during the year he was in prison, he heard the cries of many who were. During his six-year detention he lost about 45 pounds and developed abscesses and sores all over his body.

Other witness statements mention the pervasive use of hunger as a weapon to break prisoners' resistance. Not only was the amount of food inadequate, but everything possible was done to spoil whatever was distributed. Many prisoners succumbed to diarrhea, skin complaints, pneumonia, hepatitis, and even scurvy.

Prisons and camps are part of a vast ensemble of repressive institutions. Among them are:

- "Help posts," which are essentially transit camps where people await trial for minor political crimes and nonpolitical crimes.
- "Work regeneration centers," which house between 100 and 200 people who have been labeled antisocial, ineffective, or simply lazy. Most major towns have one of these centers. People stay for between one month and a year, often without ever having been to trial or even having been charged with a specific offense.
- Hard-labor camps. At least twelve of these exist in the country, each holding between 500 and 2,000 people. Most inmates there are common criminals accused of theft, attempted murder, rape, or similar crimes. Children of political prisoners, people who have been caught attempting to flee the country, and other minor political prisoners are also incarcerated in these camps.
- Deportation zones, where "untrustworthy elements" such as former landowners or people with family members who have escaped to the South are kept. Tens of thousands of such people are placed under house arrest in distant regions.
- Special dictatorship zones. These are full-fledged concentration camps for political prisoners. Approximately a dozen such camps exist, containing a total of 150,000–200,000 people. This figure is approximately 1 percent of the population of the country, a much lower share than that in the Soviet gulags in the 1940s. The figure should not be interpreted as a sign that the Koreans are particularly lenient, but as a sign of how cowed the population has become.

Most of the special dictatorship zones are in the northern part of the country, in inaccessible mountainous regions. The Yodok zone is the biggest and holds approximately 50,000 prisoners. It includes the Yongpyang and Pyonjon camps, which are extremely isolated and contain some two-thirds of all prisoners in the region, as well as the Kou-oup, Ibsok, and Daesuk camps, where, among other groups, the families of people who have lived in Japan are incarcerated. Other special dictatorship zones are located in Kaeshong, Hwasong, Hoiryong, and Chongjin.

These camps were established in the late 1950s to house political criminals and Kim Il Sung's opponents within the Party. Their population grew considerably in 1980 as a result of a particularly large purge after the opponents of the institutionalization of dynastic Communism were defeated at the Sixth Congress of the Workers' Party. Some of these camps, especially Camp 15 in the Yodok zone, are divided into a "revolutionization" sector, where prisoners who hope to be set free are kept, and a high-security sector, which no one has any hope of ever leaving. The "revolutionization" section is filled mainly with prisoners from the political elite and people repatriated from Japan who have links with Japanese organizations known to be favorably disposed toward North Korea.

The few eyewitness descriptions of these camps mention total isolation—high barbed-wire fences, German shepherd dogs, armed guards, surrounding minefields—poor and insufficient food, and extremely hard work, involving the excavation of mines, quarries, and irrigation canals, as well as wood-cutting operations. Prisoners work twelve hours a day, followed by two hours of "political training." Hunger is perhaps the worst torture; detainees try to eat anything from frogs and toads to rats and earthworms. Prisoners not only suffer progressive physical decay; they also are used for special tasks such as the digging of secret tunnels or work at dangerous nuclear projects. Some have been used as moving targets during shooting practice by guards and troops. Torture and sexual violence are common.

As part of the regime's affirmation of familial responsibility, entire families have been sent to camps because one member has received a sentence. At the time of the first great purge of Kim Il Sung's opponents, in 1958, this form of punishment was often extended to include three generations. One young man who managed to escape to the South, Kang Chul Hwan, had been sent to a prison camp in 1977 at the age of nine along with his father, one of his brothers, and two of his grandparents. The grandfather, who had once been in charge of a Korean association in Kyoto, Japan, had been arrested for making remarks about life in a capitalist country that were judged to be too complimentary. Until he was fifteen, Kang Chul Hwan followed the schedule laid down for children in the camp: school in the mornings, where most of the teaching involved studying the life of Kim Il Sung, and work such as weeding and picking up stones in the afternoon.[7]

A number of French diplomats who were taken prisoner by the North Koreans in July 1950, when the war first broke out, later spoke about their experiences. Other statements have come from Americans on the *Pueblo,* a U.S. surveillance ship captured off the Korean coast in 1968. Both sources attest to the brutality of the interrogations, the indifference shown toward human life, and the systematically bad conditions of detention.[8]

In 1992 two refugees brought more information about life in Yodok, one of the biggest camps in North Korea. They noted that detention conditions were so bad that about fifteen people would try to escape each year, despite electrified fences, watchtowers, and the guarantee that failure would result in trial and execution in front of all the other prisoners. So far, no one had ever managed to escape.

Another exceptional testimony that is now available is that of a camp guard in the Hoiryong zone, near the China border. Thanks to this man, who fled first to China and then to Seoul in 1994, we now have considerably more knowledge about the world of the concentration camps in Korea.[9] According to this witness, whose name is An Myung Chul, "bad subjects" are singled out to be executed: "rebels, ringleaders, murderers, pregnant women (all prisoners are forbidden to have sexual relations), and people who have killed cattle and livestock or sabotaged material used in production. In the tiny cell, a big lump of wood is tied to their folded legs and buttocks, and they stay like that on their knees. In the end the damage to the circulation is enormous, and even if they are set free, they are no longer able to walk; they die after a few months."

This particular guard had been assigned to the execution center, where since 1984 all executions have been carried out in secret. At this camp, executions were no longer carried out in public because killing was so common that it no longer inspired fear and terror but became an incentive to rebel.

> Who carried out the executions? The choice was left to the discretion of security agents, who shot when they did not want to dirty their hands or killed slowly if they wished to prolong the agony. I learned that people could be beaten to death, stoned, or killed with blows from a shovel. Sometimes the executions were turned into a game, with prisoners being shot at as though they were targets in a shooting competition at a fairground. Sometimes prisoners were forced to fight each other to the death and tear each other up with their bare hands . . . With my own eyes I saw several atrocious deaths. Women rarely died peacefully. I saw breasts slashed with knives, genitals smashed in with shovel handles, necks broken with hammers . . . In the camps, death is very banal. And political criminals do whatever they have to do to survive. They do anything to get a fraction more corn or pig fat. Even so, every day four or five people would die in this camp, of hunger, by accident, or through execution.
>
> Escape from the camps is almost unthinkable. A guard who catches anyone trying to escape can aspire to join the [Korean Workers' Party] and then maybe go to university. To get these rewards, some guards

force prisoners to climb the fence and then shoot them or pretend to have arrested them.

In addition to the guards, attack dogs watch the political prisoners. These terrifying animals are basically killing machines. In July 1988 two prisoners in Camp 13 were assailed by dogs. Nothing was left but their bones. In 1991, two boys of fifteen were devoured by these dogs.

An Myung Chul reports a conversation between the chief of the guards and two other personnel of Camp No. 13 that alluded to practices reminiscent of Nazi death camps. The second in command of the squad addressed his chief: "Comrade, I saw a lot of smoke coming out of the chimneys in the Third Bureau yesterday.[10] Is it true that the bodies are being pressed to extract the fat?"

The chief said that he had once gone into one of the tunnels of the Third Bureau, near a hill. "I could smell blood, and I saw a lot of hair stuck to the walls. I couldn't sleep that night. The smoke you saw would have come from the cremation of the bones of those criminals. But don't talk about it or you'll regret it. Who knows when you'll get a black bean [a bullet] in the head?"

Other guards described experiments carried out in the camp, including deliberate efforts to starve prisoners to death so that their resistance could be studied. According to An,

> The people who carry out these executions and these experiments all drink before they do it. But they are real experts now; sometimes they hit prisoners with a hammer, on the back of the head. The poor prisoners then lose their memory, and they use them as zombies for target practice. When the Third Bureau is running out of subjects, a black van known as "the crow" turns up and picks out a few more prisoners, sowing panic among the rest. The crow comes about once a month and takes forty or fifty people off to an unknown destination.

Arrest is always discreet, with no legal procedures, so that relatives and neighbors know nothing about it. When they realize that someone has disappeared, they avoid asking questions to keep out of trouble themselves.

Despite appalling working conditions, insufficient food, armed guards, and tiny prison cells for anyone who fails to observe North Korean ways, the North Korean logging camps, which have been located in Siberia since 1967, pale by comparison with such horrors. Thanks to the testimony of workers who have escaped from the camps and of Sergei Kovalev, the former human-rights commissioner of the Russian Federation, the working conditions of these rather special immigrants have improved enormously since the breakup of the U.S.S.R., and they are no longer solely under North Korean control.

As in the case of Party purges, no extensive investigation is necessary to reveal the scale of the problem. By extrapolating from the estimate of an eyewitness, who reported that 5 of every 10,000 prisoners in Camp 22 were dying every day, we can see that of the total camp population of about 200,000, 100 people died every day and 36,500 died every year.[11] If we multiply this number by the forty-six years of the regime's existence, we find Korean Communism directly responsible for the death of more than 1.5 million people.

Control of the Population

Even outside the camps, individual freedom of choice is almost nonexistent in North Korea. According to a radio commentator on 3 January 1996, "The whole of society should be welded together into one solid political force, which breathes, moves, and thinks as one, under the leadership of a single man." A contemporary slogan in the country says: "Think, talk, and act like Kim Il Sung and Kim Jong Il."

From the top to the bottom of the social ladder, the state and the Party, with their large organizations and police forces, control the citizens of the country in the name of "the Party's ten principles in the drive toward unity." That text, not the constitution, controls the everyday life of the citizens of North Korea. Article 7 is a good indication of its nature: "We must impose the absolute authority of our leader."

In 1945 a Social Security Bureau was established to monitor and control the population. The Ministry of National Political Protection, set up by the secret police in 1973 and now renamed the National Security Agency, is subdivided into bureaus, including the Second Bureau, for foreigners; the Third Bureau, for border security; and the Seventh Bureau, for the camps. The official establishment of a National Censorship Committee in 1975 institutionalized a practice that had existed from the regime's inception. The Legal Committee for Socialist Life was created in 1977.[12]

Once a week every North Korean attends an obligatory indoctrination meeting and a criticism and self-criticism meeting. The latter is known in North Korea as a "balance sheet of life." Everyone must accuse himself of at least one political fault and must reproach his neighbor for at least two faults.

North Korean cadres receive a number of privileges and material benefits, but they are also under extremely tight control. They are forced to live in a special area, all their telephone conversations are closely monitored, and any audio or video cassettes in their possession are regularly examined. Because of the systematic jamming of foreign broadcasts, all radios and televisions in North Korea can pick up only state channels. To make any journey, special permission is required from the relevant local authority and the necessary work unit. In Pyongyang, the capital and hence a showplace for the country, all housing is tightly controlled by the government.

Repression and terror affect the mind and spirit as well as the body. The effects of deliberate total isolation on the inhabitants of the country, together with the permanent ideological barrage to which they are subjected on a scale unknown elsewhere, must also be counted among the crimes of Communism. The reports of the few who have managed to slip through the net and leave the country are a remarkable testimony to the resilience of the human spirit.

There are two main forms of propaganda in North Korea. One is the classic Marxist-Leninist axis, which claims that the socialist and revolutionary state offers the best of all possible worlds to its citizens. People are to be constantly alert, on the lookout for the imperialist enemy, all the more so today since so many erstwhile friends on the outside have now "surrendered." The second type of propaganda is peculiarly national and almost mystical. Instead of relying on the arguments of dialectical materialism, the government has created a whole mythology around the idea that the Kim dynasty represents the will of both heaven and earth. A few examples from among the thousands that could be cited may clarify this type of propaganda. On 24 November 1996 in Panmunjon—the village where the armistice was negotiated, and the only place where the armies of North and South Korea and the United States are in immediate contact—during an inspection of the North Korean army by Kim Jong Il, a thick fog suddenly covered the area. The leader could thus come and go in the mist, examining the positions while remaining more or less hidden. Equally mysteriously, the fog lifted at the moment he was to be photographed with a group of soldiers ... A similar thing happened on an island in the Yellow Sea. He came to an observation post and began to study a map of the operations. The wind and rain suddenly stopped, the clouds cleared, and the sun came out and shone radiantly. Dispatches from the same official agency also mention "a series of mysterious phenomena that have been noted all over Korea as the third anniversary of the death of the Great Leader [Kim Il Sung] approaches ... The dark sky was suddenly filled with light in the Kumchon canton ... Three groups of red clouds were seen to be heading toward Pyongyang ... At 8:10 P.M. on 4 July the rain that had been falling since early morning suddenly stopped, and a double rainbow unfolded over the statue of the President ... then a bright star shone in the sky right above the statue."[13]

A Strict Hierarchy

In a state claiming to base itself on socialism, the population is not only carefully monitored and controlled; it is also subject to disparate treatment depending on social origin, geographic origin (that is, whether the family originates in North or South Korea), political affiliation, and recent signs of loyalty toward the regime. In the 1950s the whole society was carefully subdivided into fifty-one social categories that powerfully determined people's social, political, and material future. This extremely cumbersome system was streamlined in the 1980s; now there are only three social categories. Even so, the system of classification remains very complex. In addition to these three basic classes, the secret services are particularly vigilant in regard to certain categories within the classes, particularly people who have come from abroad, who have traveled overseas, or who have received visitors.

The country is divided into a "central" class, which forms the core of society, an "undecided" class, and a "hostile" class, which includes approximately one-quarter of the North Korean population. The North Korean Communist system uses these divisions to create what is in effect a sort of apartheid: a young man of "good origin," who might have relatives who fought against the Japanese, cannot marry a girl of "bad origin," such as a family that originated in the South. One former North Korean diplomat, Koh Young Hwan, notes that "North Korea has what is in effect an extremely inflexible caste system."[14]

Although this system in its early days may have had some basis in Marxist-Leninist theory, biological discrimination is much harder to justify. Yet the facts are there: anyone who is handicapped in North Korea suffers terrible social exclusion. The handicapped are not allowed to live in Pyongyang. Until recently they were all kept in special locations in the suburbs so that family members could visit them. Today they are exiled to remote mountainous regions or to islands in the Yellow Sea. Two such locations have been identified with certainty: Boujun and Euijo, in the north of the country, close to the Chinese border. This policy of discrimination has recently spread beyond Pyongyang to Nampo, Kaesong, and Chongjin.

Similar treatment applies to anyone out of the ordinary. Dwarves, for instance, are now arrested and sent to camps; they are not only forced to live in isolation but also prevented from having children. Kim Jong Il himself has said that "the race of dwarves must disappear."[15]

Escape

Despite heavily guarded borders, some North Koreans have managed to escape. Since the war, some 700 have crossed to the South, and it is estimated that several thousand have gone to China. The number arriving in the South has quintupled since 1993 and continues to grow; about 100 arrived there in 1997. Most of them either are fleeing some sort of punishment or already have some experience of the outside world. Thus a number of diplomats and high-ranking Party officials are among the escapees. In February 1997, Hwang Jang Yop, one of the Party's chief ideologists, fled to the South Korean embassy in Beijing and then to Seoul. The ambassador to Egypt, who defected to the United States in August 1997, had been afraid for his political future; his son had "disappeared" a year previously. Koh Young Hwan, the North Korean diplomat mentioned above, feared that he would be arrested because of an imprudent remark, after a televised broadcast of the Ceauşescu trial, that he "hoped nothing similar would happen in [his] own country"; the statement was taken to be flagrant evidence of a lack of trust in the leaders of his country. He fled when he heard that agents from the state security bureau would be coming to the embassy a few days later. According to his statement, failure to escape would have meant at best automatic arrest and a camp sentence. At worst, as he had seen in Amman, Jordan, an attempt by a diplomat to flee could end in "neutralization," being totally encased in plaster and returned to Pyongyang. Once at the airport, the story would probably have been that he had been in an auto accident.

Ordinary people who failed in their attempts to flee fared little better. According to a 1997 report in the French press, "Statements taken from people all along the [Yalu] river are in agreement: the police who picked up fugitives held them together by putting a wire through the cheeks or noses of these traitors to the nation who had dared to try to leave the fatherland. As soon as they reached their destination they were executed, and their families were sent to labor camps."[16]

Activities Abroad

Not content with crushing attempts to flee the country, the North Korean authorities send agents abroad to attack enemies of the regime. In September 1996, for example, the cultural attaché at the South Korean consulate in Vladivostok was assassinated. Japan also suspects the North Koreans of kidnapping about twenty Japanese women and forcing them to train spies and terrorists. Another bone of contention between Japan and North Korea is the situation of the hundreds of Japanese women who went to North Korea in 1959 with their Korean husbands. Despite promises made at the time by the North Korean government, none of them has ever been allowed to return home, even temporarily. According to statements made by the very few Koreans who have managed to escape after being in a camp, several of these women were subsequently detained, and the death rate among them has been extremely high. Of the fourteen Japanese women who were incarcerated in the Yodok camp in the late 1970s, only two were still alive fifteen years later. The North Korean government has consistently used these women as a bargaining chip in negotiations, often promising their imminent departure in exchange for Japanese food aid. It is not known exactly how the North Korean authorities make their calculations, or how much rice would have to be provided for one Japanese woman to be set free. Amnesty International and other international human rights organizations have examined these cases several times.

The North Koreans also kidnap South Koreans. According to the South Korean government, more than 400 fishermen were abducted between 1955 and 1995. Those still missing include the passengers and crew members of an airliner hijacked in 1969, a South Korean diplomat captured in Norway in April 1979, and a priest, Father Ahn Sung Un, who was kidnapped in China and taken to North Korea in July 1995. All these people are examples of the many South Korean citizens who have been victims of North Korean violence on foreign soil.

Shortages and Famine

Another grave charge against the North Korean government involves the food supply for the population. The situation has long been poor, but over the last few years it has grown so bad that the North Korean authorities, disregarding their sacrosanct principle of self-sufficiency, have launched an appeal for international aid. In 1996 the grain harvest was 3.7 million tons, almost 3 million tons less than at the beginning of the decade. The poor harvests of 1997 and 1998 made the situation worse. When asked by the UN World Food Program, the United States, and the European Union about the situation, the North Koreans have blamed it on a series of natural disasters, including flooding in 1994 and 1995 and drought and tidal waves in 1997. The real causes of this breakdown in the food supply are linked to the structural difficulties invariably experienced by centrally planned socialist economies. Large-scale errors, including the deforestation of entire areas and the hasty construction of badly planned terraces on orders from the very top of the Party, contributed to the seriousness of the flooding. In addition, the collapse of the Soviet Union and the political reorganization in China have curtailed aid from these two countries; both now seek to trade in accordance with the normal laws of the international market. Because the North Korean government is extremely short of hard currency, the acquisition of agricultural machinery, fertilizer, and fuel is increasingly difficult.

It is impossible to know how grave the food situation really is. World Vision has forecast a possible 2 million victims; the German Red Cross claims that 10,000 children are dying of starvation every month.[17] There is no doubt that the situation is serious, and the rumors that circulate among the inhabitants on the Chinese border have been confirmed by reports from experts at the United Nations. Shortages exist in many places, and in some places there is famine. But the exploitation of well-meaning individuals on goodwill visits, who claim that millions of deaths will inevitably result if aid is not increased, and the dissemination abroad of photographs of undernourished children and videos of television programs, which apparently teach the population how to eat grass instead of food, are perhaps signs of a highly organized campaign to blacken a picture that, though far from ideal, is perhaps not as catastrophic as suggested. While North Korea is trying to convince the world that it is facing a grave crisis and that any interruption in aid would have catastrophic consequences for political stability in the peninsula and peace in the Far East, the North Korean army is extremely well fed and is building bigger and better missiles.

Almost the only figures available for the number of victims of the food crisis come from data released by the North Koreans themselves, which show a not negligible number of children suffering from the effects of malnutrition. Nutrition experts from the World Food Program made a study of a population sample, provided by the government, of 4,200 children, which revealed that 17 percent were suffering from malnutrition.[18] This figure seems to confirm the existence of widespread shortages and probably regional and local pockets of famine. The shortages and famine, which are closely linked to political decisions made by the North Korean regime, have been held in check to some extent by the efforts of the "imperialist" outside world, which has provided millions of tons of grain in aid. Deprived of such aid, the population of North Korea would face a real famine with catastrophic consequences.

Final Figures

In North Korea, perhaps more than anywhere else, the effects of Communism are difficult to translate into numbers. Some of the reasons are insufficient statistical data, the impossibility of carrying out any field research, and the inaccessibility of all the relevant archives. But there are also other reasons. How can one calculate the soul-destroying effects of constant, mindless propaganda? How can one put a figure on the absence of freedom of expression, freedom of association, and freedom of movement; on the ways in which a child's life is destroyed simply because his grandfather received a prison sentence; on the consequences for a woman who is forced to have an abortion in atrocious conditions? How could statistics show what life is really like when people are obsessed by the possibility of starvation, by lack of heating, and by other acute shortages and privations? How can one compare the admittedly imperfect democracy in the South with the nightmarish situation in North Korea?

Some have argued that North Korean Communism is a caricature, a throwback to Stalinism. But this museum of Communism, the Asian Madame Tussaud's, is all too alive.

To the 100,000 who have died in Party purges and the 1.5 million deaths in concentration camps must be added at least 1.3 million deaths stemming from the war, which was organized and instigated by the Communists, a war that continues in small but murderous actions, including commando attacks on the South and acts of terrorism; and the uncertain but growing number of direct and indirect victims of malnutrition. Even if we content ourselves with a figure of 500,000 victims of the primary or even secondary effects of malnutrition (including the usual, unverifiable rumors of cannibalism), we end up with an overall figure of more than 3 million victims in a country of 23 million inhabitants that has lived under Communism for fifty years.

23 Vietnam and Laos: The Impasse of War Communism

Jean-Louis Margolin

We must transform our prisons into schools.
Le Duan, secretary general of the Vietnamese Communist Party

Admitting the damage caused by Communism in Vietnam is today still anathema to many Westerners, who took a stand against French colonialism and American "imperialism" in the area and found themselves in the same camp as the Vietnamese Communist Party. At the time it seemed quite logical to assume that the Party was an expression of the hopes and aspirations of the people to build a fraternal and egalitarian society. Its appeal was enhanced by the charisma of Ho Chi Minh, who founded the Party and led it until 1969, as well as the extraordinary tenacity of its members and its clever manipulation of propaganda abroad, where it presented itself as a peace-loving, democratic organization. At the very time when it was becoming increasingly difficult to feel sympathy for Kim Il Sung and his odious regime, it seemed ever more logical to prefer the smiling austerity of the Hanoi mandarins to the rotten and corrupt regime of Nguyen Van Thieu that ruled in Saigon from 1965 to 1975. People genuinely wanted to believe that the Vietnamese Communist Party was not just another Stalinist regime, but instead was above all a nationalist regime that used a Communist label in order to receive aid from China and the Soviet Union.

It would be ridiculous to question the sincerity of the Vietnamese Communists' nationalist aspirations, given the unparalleled determination with which they fought against the French, the Americans, the Chinese, and the

Japanese. For them the accusation of "treachery" or "collaboration" had the same force that the label "counterrevolutionary" did in China. But Communism was never incompatible with nationalism or even xenophobia, particularly in Asia. Unfortunately, beneath the surface of this apparently amiable and unanimously accepted nationalism there lurked a Stalinist form of Maoism that followed its prototypes extremely closely.

The Indochinese Communist Party (ICP) got off to a bad start.[1] Soon after its founding in 1930, several Party activists were involved in a spectacular trial for actions taken in Saigon in 1928. Influenced by traditions of the local secret societies and by nationalist terrorism, Party members had judged and executed one of their comrades and then burned his corpse. His crime had been to seduce a female member of the Party.[2] In 1931 the Party threw itself into the creation of rural "soviets" in Nge Tinh and started liquidating local landowners by the hundreds. In creating the soviets, the ICP followed the Jiangxi model, despite Vietnam's comparatively minuscule size. The flight of many of the inhabitants facilitated the rapid return of colonial troops. When the Indochinese Communist Party, which hid behind the "united front" of the League for the Independence of Vietnam (Viet Minh), finally dared to launch a full-scale armed struggle in the spring of 1945, it seemed more hostile to "traitors" and "reactionaries" (who sometimes included its own functionaries) than to the better-armed occupying Japanese forces. One of the Party's leaders proposed an assassination campaign to "speed up the advance of the movement." Landowners and local mandarins were targets of choice, and popular tribunals were established to sentence them and confiscate their goods. The terror was also aimed at political opponents of the comparatively weak ICP, which at the time had only 5,000 members. The Party wanted to produce a power vacuum as soon as possible so that it could assume leadership of the nationalist movement. The Dai Viet, a nationalist party allied with the Japanese, was savagely persecuted, and the Viet Minh units under Son Tay asked Hanoi to send an electricity generator and a specialist so that they could torture "traitors" on a larger scale.[3]

The August revolution that catapulted Ho Chi Minh to power in the wake of the Japanese surrender made the ICP the central element in the new state. In the several weeks preceding the arrival of Allied troops (French and British from the south, Chinese from the north), the ICP redoubled its campaign to liquidate all competition. The victims of this terror included leaders of most of the major opposition forces in Vietnam, including the emblematic moderate constitutionalist Bui Quang Chieu, the great intellectual and right-wing politician Pham Quynh, and Huynh Phu So, the founder of the political religious sect Hoa Hao, who had himself ordered numerous assassinations. But it was the Trotskyites, who though relatively thin on the ground were still active in the Saigon region, who were the objects of systematic extermination. Their main leader, Ta Tu Thau, was arrested and killed in September 1945 in Quang Ngai, an area that suffered particularly badly in the cleansing.[4] These actions were supported by the Communist leader in Saigon, Tran Van Giau, who had spent time in Moscow, though he was later to deny any involvement in the assassinations. He declared on 2 September: "A number of traitors to the fatherland are swelling their ranks to betray their country and serve the enemy . . . we must punish the groups who are creating trouble in the Democratic Republic of Vietnam and facilitating an invasion by the enemy."[5] An article in the Viet Minh press in Hanoi on 29 August recommended that the people set up "traitor elimination committees" in every neighborhood and village.[6] Dozens, perhaps hundreds, of Trotskyites were captured and killed. Others, who in October had helped defend Saigon against British and French forces, were deprived of munitions and food, and most were killed.[7] On 25 August a state security organization was established in Saigon on the Soviet model, and the prisons that had just been emptied began to fill again. The Viet Minh formed an Assault Assassination Committee, which marched through the streets. Most of its members were recruited from the local underworld, and it was at the head of the anti-French pogrom of 25 September that left dozens of mutilated corpses in its wake.[8] Vietnamese women who had married Frenchmen were also systematically slaughtered, although these actions were blamed on people who were not really members of the Viet Minh. In August and September alone the Viet Minh carried out thousands of assassinations and tens of thousands of kidnappings. These were often local initiatives, but there is no doubt that the central authorities were encouraging such actions on a huge scale, and the ICP later declared publicly that it regretted not having wiped out more of its enemies at that time.[9] In the north, which was the only part of the country really under ICP control before the outbreak of the Indochina war in 1946, secret police and detention camps were already in place. In practice, the Democratic Republic of Vietnam (DRV) was already a one-party state; the radical nationalists of the Vietnam Quoc Dan Dang (VNQDD, the Vietnamese National Party, founded in 1927), who had been engaged in a bloody struggle with the Viet Minh, had been eliminated as a political force in July 1945 as a result of the combined efforts of the ICP and the colonial powers. The latter had come down hard on the VNQDD ever since the party had organized the Yenbai mutiny in 1930.

After World War II the repressive violence of the Communists was redeployed as armed resistance against the French colonial powers. Numerous eyewitness accounts are available about the prison camps in which soldiers of the French Expeditionary Force were held.[10] Many suffered and died there; out of 20,000, only 9,000 were still alive to be liberated when the Geneva peace accord was signed in 1954.[11] The terrible diseases endemic to the mountains of Indochina decimated the prisoners, who received woefully inadequate medical care, lived in extremely unhygienic conditions, and were often deliberately starved. Beatings and torture were also common, but French soldiers could be useful to their captors. The ICP considered them "war criminals" and forced them to repent and take on the values of their captors so that they could be used in propaganda against their own camp. This Chinese-style reeducation was assisted by many advisers sent by Mao after 1950. These propaganda sessions forced all "students" to participate actively and divided all participants into "reactionaries" and "progressives." They made extensive promises, including the possibility of liberation, and met with some impressive successes, mainly because of the physical and psychological exhaustion of the prisoners, but also because, later on, the French prisoners were treated less badly than the Vietnamese themselves were in South Vietnam.

In December 1953, when victory seemed imminent, the Viet Minh launched agrarian reforms in the liberated zones. By the end of 1954 this measure had been extended to all the land north of the 17th parallel, which had been given to the Communists in the Geneva peace accord. The reforms were completed in 1956. The aims and pace of the land reforms were similar to those of the Chinese agrarian reforms of 1946–1952, and they strengthened the links between the Party, which had officially reappeared in 1951, and the poor and middle-range peasantry. By eliminating potential centers of resistance to Communism, the land reform became an important stepping-stone on the way to complete state control of the economy. And yet, even more so than in China, the traditional elite in the countryside maintained strong support for the Viet Minh because of the Party's strongly nationalist stance. The Viet Minh's ferocious and murderous methods were identical with those of their neighbors to the north. In every village, activists, occasionally enlisting the help of theatrical troupes, tried to incite the poorer peasants (this was often extremely difficult) and encourage them to put their victims on public trial. The victims were chosen in a fairly arbitrary manner, frequently according to a quota of 4–5 percent, recalling again the sacred 5 percent of Maoism.[12] These victims were often killed, or at the very least imprisoned, and their goods confiscated. As in China, the entire family was forced to suffer. By not taking political merit into consideration, these fanatics showed not only their unpitying dogmatism, but also the will toward a totalitarian classification of society that was a driving force inside the Vietnamese Communist Party. One woman who was a rich landowner and a successful entrepreneur was singled out for the attention of the peasants even though she was a benefactor of the revolution and the proud mother of two Viet Minh soldiers. When the peasants refused to react, "a group who had been well trained in China were called in, and they managed to turn the situation around . . . Mme. Long was accused of having killed three sharecroppers before 1945, of having slept with a Frenchman, and of having collaborated with the French and spied for them. Exhausted by the treatment she received, she ended up admitting everything and was sentenced to death. One of her sons, who was in China at the time, was brought home, deprived of his rank, stripped of his medals, and sentenced to twenty years in prison." As in Beijing, people were found guilty simply because they had been accused by the Party, which never made mistakes. Therefore, the best response was often to do what was expected of you: "It was better to have killed your father and mother and admitted it than to say nothing and to have done nothing wrong at all."[13]

The scale of violence was extraordinary. The theme of hatred of the adversary was hammered home again and again. According to Le Duc Tho, who was later to share the Nobel Peace Prize with Henry Kissinger, "If one wishes to convince the peasants to take up arms, first of all you have to fill them with hatred for the enemy." In January 1956, in an article in *Nhan da* (The people), the official organ of the Communist Party, one could read that "the landowning classes will never be quiet until they have been eliminated." The motto was similar to those found in China: "Better ten innocent deaths than one enemy survivor." Torture was practiced routinely, to an extent that began to worry Ho Chi Minh by the end of 1954: "A number of cadres have once again made the mistake of using torture. This is a savage method that is used by the imperialists, capitalists, and feudal landlords to hold the masses and the revolution in check . . . Throughout this phase, the recourse to torture is once again strictly banned."[14]

There was one major difference from the Chinese model. Whereas in China reform of the Party came after the experiment in social engineering that was agricultural reform, in Vietnam the two were carried out simultaneously. The reason was undoubtedly the relative sizes of the privileged classes in the two countries. In Vietnam, as in China, 5 percent of the population was suspected of being infiltrators from the VNQDD, a party that was compared to the Chinese Kuomintang. In a distant echo of the Jiangxi purges, the Vietnamese authorities engaged in witch-hunts for phantom "anti-Bolshevik counterrevolutionary elements." Paranoia swept the country, and even heroes of the Indochina war were assassinated or sent to camps. In the discourse of the Vietnamese Communists, the memory of 1956 (the *chinh huan* reached its high point early in that year) still evokes horror in all the participants: "One Communist Party secretary who fell before a firing squad died shouting 'Long live the Indochinese Communist Party!' Unable to understand what was happening, he died convinced that he was being shot by the fascists."[15] The exact number of losses is hard to gauge, but they were certainly catastrophic. There were probably some 50,000 executions in the countryside (excluding combat deaths), that is, 0.3–0.4 percent of the population (a figure very similar to the fraction of the population that died in the Chinese agrarian reforms).[16] Between 50,000 and 100,000 people were imprisoned; 86 percent of the members of Party cells in the countryside were purged, as were 95 percent of the cadres in the anti-French resistance. In the words of the leader of the purge, who in 1956 admitted that mistakes had been made, "the leadership [of the rectification committee] made some rather tendentious judgments about the Party organization. It was decided that the rural cells, particularly those in zones that had been newly liberated, were without exception controlled by the enemy or had been infiltrated by them, and that all the district or provincial leadership committees were being controlled by the landowners or by counterrevolutionaries."[17] These purges foreshadowed the mass condemnations of entire classes by the Khmer Rouge (see Chapter 24).

The army was the first to organize a *chinh huan*, which was more ideological than repressive, within its ranks in 1951. From 1952 to 1956 "rectification" was a constant. Tension was so high in some reeducation camps that razors and knives had to be confiscated, and the lights kept on all night to prevent suicides among the inmates.[18] And yet it was the army that finished its purge first. Persecutions hit its own cadres so hard that many deserted to the South.[19] This trend seriously worried the authorities, whose aim after all was to reunify the country. By contrast with China, the weight of military necessity brought a certain realism to the whole business, and the relatively small size of the country meant that those who were unhappy found it easier to flee. These factors led to a certain attenuation of the violence. This is also evident from the fate of Catholics in the North, who at 1.5 million people made up 10 percent of the population. Initially persecuted, they were well enough organized to take advantage of the mass exodus to the South, leaving under the protection of the last French troops. At least 600,000 of them reached South Vietnam.

The effects of the Twentieth Congress of the Soviet Communist Party were also beginning to be felt, and Vietnam experienced a timid Hundred Flowers movement in April 1956. September marked the appearance of the review *Nhan van* (Humanism), symbolizing the aspirations of a number of intellectuals for freedom. The daring writers mocked the prose of the official censor To Huu, the author of the following poem:

> Long live Ho Chi Minh
> The guiding light of the proletariat!
> Long live Stalin
> The great eternal tree!
> Peace grows in his shadow!
> Kill, kill again, let your hands never stop
> Let fields and paddyfields produce rice in abundance

So that taxes can be paid at once.
Let us march together with the same heart
So that the Party may last for ever
Let us adore Chairman Mao
And build an eternal cult to Stalin.[20]

The intellectuals were punished for their audacity. Literary reviews that criticized the regime were soon banned, and a campaign similar to the one in China against Hu Feng and freedom of artistic expression began, with the personal support of Ho Chi Minh.[21] The plan was to ensure a united front among all intellectuals in Hanoi who were members of the Party or close to it and many of whom had previously fought in the resistance. Early in 1958, 476 "ideological saboteurs" were forced to make public acts of self-criticism and were sent either to work camps or to the Vietnamese equivalent of the Chinese *laojiao*.[22] As in the People's Republic of China, the temptation to enact Khrushchev-style reforms was quickly rejected in favor of strengthening the orthodox line. The factor that both limited repression and kept it going was the war in the South, which flared up again in 1957 in response to the ferocious anti-Communist policies of the U.S.-supported Ngo Dinh Diem regime. In May 1959 the Vietnamese Communist Party made a secret decision to try to spread the war and to support it by sending troops and arms, despite the immense cost to the people of North Vietnam. This did not prevent the government from also attempting a Chinese-style Great Leap Forward in agriculture, initiated with a series of enthusiastic articles by Ho Chi Minh himself in October 1958.[23] The combination of massive irrigation projects and a long period of drought led, as it did in China, to a fall in production, followed by a serious famine with an unknown number of victims.[24] The war effort was not enough to prevent the purging of numerous pro-Soviet cadres inside the Party in 1964–65 and again in 1967, including the former personal secretary of "Uncle Ho." Such events were enough to show that the leaders of the Vietnamese Communist Party shared the antirevisionist tendencies of their Chinese counterparts. Some victims of the purges remained in prison for more than a decade, without ever being brought to trial.[25]

The so-called American war, which ended only with the final withdrawal of U.S. troops following the signing of the Paris peace treaty in January 1973 and the subsequent fall of the South Vietnamese regime on 30 April 1975, was not in fact followed by the bloodbath that so many feared and that did take place in neighboring Cambodia. But the Vietnamese prisoners of the Communist forces—including "traitors" from their own ranks—were severely abused and often simply liquidated rather than moved.[26] It is clear that the civil war and struggle for freedom were accompanied by many atrocities on both sides.

Atrocities were also committed against civilians who had elected to support one side or the other. As a result, it is extremely difficult to calculate the numbers involved or even to describe the methods used. But the Communists did carry out at least one large-scale massacre. During the few weeks when the Viet Cong controlled the ancient imperial capital, Hue, during the Tet offensive in February 1968, at least 3,000 people were massacred, including Vietnamese priests, French religious workers, German doctors, and a number of officials and government workers.[27] The number of deaths was far higher than in the massacres carried out by Americans. Some of the victims were buried alive; others were taken away to "study sessions" from which they never returned.[28] It is difficult to understand such crimes, which have never been officially recognized and which were clearly an adumbration of what was to come from the Khmer Rouge. Would the Communists have acted in the same manner if they had taken Saigon in 1968?

In any case, they did not act in such fashion when they captured it in 1975. For a few brief weeks, the approximately 1 million officials and soldiers in the Saigon regime could even believe that the much-vaunted "policy of clemency" of President Ho was more than simple political rhetoric. As a result, these officials began to cooperate and register with the new authorities. Then, in early June, people were suddenly called in for reeducation, which officially lasted three days for simple footsoldiers and an entire month for officers and civil servants.[29] In fact three days often became three years, and the month became seven or eight years. The last survivors of the reeducation programs did not return home until 1986.[30] Pham Van Dong, the prime minister at the time, admitted in 1980 that 200,000 had been reeducated in the South. Serious estimates range from 500,000 to 1 million out of a population of 20 million. The victims included a large number of students, intellectuals, monks (both Buddhist and Catholic), and political militants (including Communists). Many of these people had been in sympathy with the National Liberation Front of South Vietnam, which revealed itself to be no more than a cover for Northern Communists and which almost immediately broke all its promises to respect the wishes of the people of the South. As in 1954–1956, onetime comrades-in-arms were soon suffering in the rectification campaigns. To the number of prisoners who were trapped in special camps must be added an indeterminate but large number of "minor" reeducation cases who were locked up for several weeks in their place of work or study. By comparison, during the worst periods of the anti-Communist regime in the South, enemies on the left claimed that some 200,000 people were locked up in camps.[31]

Conditions of detention under Communist rule varied considerably. Some camps near towns did not even have barbed-wire fences, and the regime there was more one of constraint than of actual punishment. The more difficult cases were sent farther north, to the more unhealthy, distant areas, to camps originally built for French prisoners. Isolation was total, and there was almost no medical care. Survival in these camps often depended on parcels sent by the families of prisoners. Undernourishment was as bad as it was in the prisons; detainees were fed only 200 grams of poor-quality rice filled with stones per day. As elsewhere, hunger was often used as a weapon by the authorities against those awaiting trial. Doan Van Toai has left a gripping account of life in one such prison, which shows that this universe shared many of the characteristics of the Chinese prison camps, but was somewhat worse in terms of overcrowding, sanitary conditions, the prevalence of violent and often fatal punishments such as whipping, and long delays before trial. There were sometimes seventy to eighty prisoners in a cell built for twenty, and walks were often impossible because of construction inside the prison yard. The cells of the colonial period were seen as havens of peace and tranquillity in comparison. The tropical climate and the lack of air made breathing very difficult. All day long, people took turns standing by the one small airhole. The smells were unbearable, and skin complaints were rife. Even water was severely rationed. The hardest punishment was undoubtedly solitary confinement, sometimes for years on end, with no contact allowed with family. Torture was hidden but ever-present, as were executions. In prison, the tiniest infringement of regulations was punished harshly, and rations were so small that death often came within weeks.[32]

One testament about prison conditions, "signed" orally by forty-eight courageous prisoners, was memorized and circulated through the prisons of Ho Chi Minh City:

We,
    workers, peasants, and proletarians,
    believers, artists, writers, and patriotic intellectuals interned in different prisons across Vietnam,
    wish first of all to express our debt of gratitude to:
    progressive movements throughout the world,
    workers' and intellectual struggle movements,
    everyone who over the last ten years has supported the fight for human rights in Vietnam and supported the struggle for democracy and the freedom of oppressed and exploited Vietnamese citizens . . .

The prison system of the old regime (which was itself widely condemned by international opinion) was quickly replaced by a more subtly planned system that is far harsher and crueler. All contact between prisoners and their families is forbidden, even by mail. The families of prisoners are kept in the dark about the fate of those in prison, which adds to the suffering and anguish. In the face of these humiliating, discriminatory procedures prisoners keep quiet, fearing that any objections they raise might result in further punishment for their relatives, who could be killed at any moment without their knowledge . . .

Conditions inside the prisons are unimaginably bad. In the Chi Hoa prison, the official Saigon prison, 8,000 people under the old regime were kept in conditions that were universally condemned. Today there are more than 40,000 people in the same prison. Prisoners often die from hunger, lack of air, or torture, or by their own hand . . .

There are two sorts of prison in Vietnam: the official prisons and the concentration camps. The latter are far out in the jungle, and the prisoner is sentenced to a lifetime of forced labor. There are no trials, and hence no possibility of using a legal mechanism in their defense . . .

If it really is the case that humanity at present is recoiling from the spread of Communism, and rejecting at last the claims of the North Vietnamese Communists that their defeat of American imperialism is proof of their invincibility, then we, the prisoners of Vietnam, ask the International Red Cross, humanitarian organizations throughout the world, and all men of goodwill to send us cyanide capsules as soon as possible so that we can put an end to our suffering ourselves. We want to die now! Help us to carry out this act, and help us kill ourselves as soon as possible. We would be eternally in your debt.

Vietnam, August 1975—October 1977[33]

To this strange tableau of "liberation" should be added the spectacle of hundreds of thousands of boat people who fled misery and repression, many of whom drowned or were killed by pirates. The first real sign of relaxation in repression came only in 1986, when the new secretary general of the Vietnamese Communist Party, Nguyen Van Linh, freed a large number of political prisoners and closed the killing camps of the northern region. A new penal code is at last going to be promulgated. The process of liberalization has been timid and contradictory, and the 1990s have been marked by an uneasy balance between conservatives and reformers. Repressive urges have dashed the hopes of many, even though arrests are now much more carefully targeted and carried out on a relatively small scale. Many intellectuals and religious figures are still persecuted and imprisoned, and rural discontent in the north has sparked riots that have been put down with extreme violence. The best chance for a relaxation of the situation in the longer term is probably the hope that private enterprise will inevitably bring change, as it has in China, enabling an ever-growing number of inhabitants to escape the direct control of the state and the

Party. At the same time, there is a growing business mafia that is extremely corrupt and that itself constitutes a new, more ordinary form of oppression of a population that is even poorer than the population of China.

Laos: A Population in Flight

Everyone has heard about the drama of the Vietnamese boat people, but Laos, which became Communist in the aftermath of the events of 1975 in Vietnam, has seen a proportionally larger section of the population take flight. Admittedly, all that Laotians have to do to flee is to cross the Mekong River into Thailand. Since most of the population of Laos lives in the river valley or nearby, and since repressions are relatively limited, departure is quite easy. Around 300,000 people (10 percent of the population) have fled the country, including well over 30 percent of the Hmong minority in the mountains (around 100,000 people) and about 90 percent of all intellectuals, technicians, and officials. In Communist Asia, only North Korea in 1950–1953 saw a larger share of its population flee the country.

Since 1945 the fate of Laos has depended on that of Vietnam. The French and subsequently the Americans lent their support, including military support, to what was basically a right-wing monarchy. The Vietnamese Communists backed the Pathet Lao, which was dominated by a few local Communists who invariably had personal links to Vietnam. The movement was totally dependent on Vietnam for military support. The sparsely populated eastern part of the country was directly involved in the American phase of the Vietnamese conflict. Ho Chi Minh's supply lines passed through the area, and as a result it was bombed relentlessly by the Americans. The U.S. Central Intelligence Agency established a powerful, armed anti-Communist movement among the local Hmong. No significant atrocities occurred in the ensuing military campaign, which in general was desultory and intermittent. By 1975 the Communists controlled the greater part of the eastern region but only one-third of the country's population. The rest, including some 600,000 interned refugees (20 percent of the inhabitants), were along the Mekong, to the west.

The seizure of power, in the new Indochinese political configuration, was quite peaceful, a sort of Asiatic "velvet revolution." The neutral former prime minister, Souvanna Phouma, became a special adviser to the new regime headed by Prince Souphanouvong, a relative of the deposed king. The new "people's democratic republic" followed the Vietnamese example. Almost all officials of the old regime (around 30,000 people) were sent to reeducation camps in distant northern and eastern provinces along the Vietnamese border, where the climate is inhospitable. Many remained there for as long as five years. Around 3,000 "hardened criminals"—mainly police and army officers—were interned in camps with particularly harsh regimes on the Nam Ngum Islands. The royal family itself was arrested in 1977, and the last prince died in detention. Such events are probably enough to explain most of the departures, which were often quite dramatic. It was not unusual for people fleeing the country to be fired upon.

The main difference from the pattern of events in Vietnam was the presence of an anti-Communist guerrilla force that was several thousand strong, consisting primarily of Hmong. In 1977 the guerrilla resistance was a sufficient cause of concern in Vientiane that the government ordered aerial bombardment of the region. Unconfirmed statements claim that there was a "yellow rain" of chemical or biological weapons. What is certain is that after their mobilization during the war, the Hmong guerrilla forces took part in the large-scale departures from the country. In 1975 huge columns of Hmong civilians set off for Thailand, leading to at least one serious incident with the Communist army. Refugees' accounts claim that at least 45,000 victims either were killed or died of starvation during the journey. In 1991 there were still 55,000 people from Laos, including 45,000 Hmong people from the mountain regions, in camps in Thailand, waiting for a final destination. Some later managed to find sanctuary in French Guyana.

There have been several purges of state and Party leaders, but these have not been bloody. One took place in 1979 as part of a rupture with China; another occurred in 1990, when some people advocated a course similar to the one being pursued in Eastern Europe. The departure of some 50,000 Vietnamese soldiers in 1988, a series of liberal economic reforms, and the reopening of the border with Thailand have also lightened the atmosphere. Today there are few political prisoners, and Communist propaganda is quite attenuated. But only a few thousand refugees have returned to the "country of a million elephants." Laos remains extremely poor and backward, and its future depends on increasing ties with the hundreds of thousands of wealthy and educated people who left at the height of the Communist regime.[34]

24 Cambodia: The Country of Disconcerting Crimes

Jean-Louis Margolin

We must give a pure and perfect depiction of the history of the Party.
Pol Pot

The lineage from Mao Zedong to Pol Pot is obvious. This is one of the paradoxes that make the Khmer Rouge revolution so difficult to analyze and understand. The Cambodian tyrant was incontestably mediocre and a pale copy of the imaginative and cultivated Beijing autocrat who with no outside help established a regime that continues to thrive in the world's most populous country. Yet despite Pol Pot's limitations, it is the Cultural Revolution and the Great Leap Forward that look like mere trial runs or preparatory sketches for what was perhaps the most radical social transformation of all: the attempt to implement total Communism in one fell swoop, without the long transitional period that seemed to be one of the tenets of Marxist-Leninist orthodoxy. Money was abolished in a week; total collectivization was achieved in less than two years; social distinctions were suppressed by the elimination of entire classes of property owners, intellectuals, and businessmen; and the ancient antagonism between urban and rural areas was solved by emptying the cities in a single week. It seemed that the only thing needed was sufficient willpower, and heaven would be found on Earth. Pol Pot believed that he would be enthroned higher than his glorious ancestors—Marx, Lenin, Stalin, Mao Zedong—and that the revolution of the twenty-first century would be conducted in Khmer, just as the revolutions of the twentieth century had been in Russian and then Chinese.

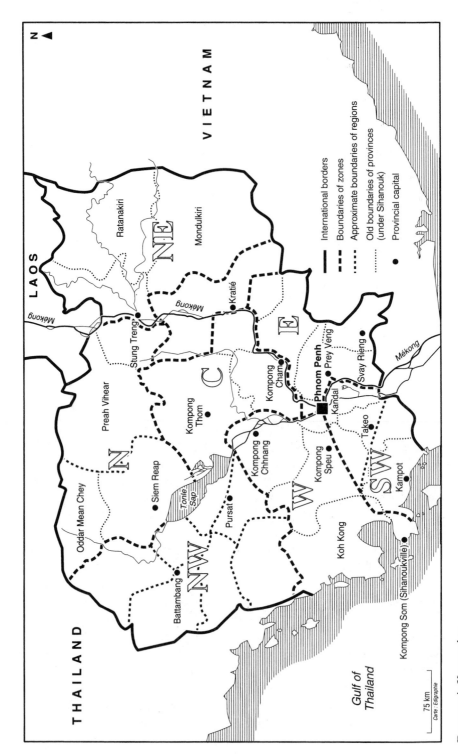

THAILAND

LAOS

VIETNAM

N

Mekong

Mekong

Mekong

Ratanakiri

Mondulkiri

N.E

Kratié

Stung Treng

Preah Vihear

Kompong Thom

Kompong Cham

Phnom Penh

Prey Vêng

Kandal

Svay Riêng

C

E

N

Siem Reap

Tonle Sap

Kompong Chhnang

Kompong Speu

Takeo

SW

Oddar Mean Chey

Pursat

W

Kampot

N.W

Battambang

Koh Kong

Kompong Som (Sihanoukville)

Gulf of
Thailand

75 km

Carte : Édigraphie

International borders

Boundaries of zones

Approximate boundaries of regions

Old boundaries of provinces
(under Sihanouk)

Provincial capital

Democratic Kampuchea

In reality, the Khmer Rouge's mark in history will always be written in blood.[1] There is now an abundant bibliography to ensure that this is the case. All eyewitness statements and analyses by researchers highlight the theme of inhuman repression. The only real questions are why and how such horror could have come about. In the scope of repression, Cambodian Communism surpasses and differs radically from all other forms of Communism.[2] Depending on how one phrases these questions, one can see it as an extreme and aberrant case, pointing to its brevity—it lasted only three years and eight months—or as a grotesque but revealing caricature of certain fundamental traits of the Communist phenomenon. The debate is far from over, not least because we still know very little about the leaders of the Khmer Rouge themselves—they hardly ever spoke in public and they published almost nothing—but also because Chinese and Vietnamese archives, which might be of help, are still inaccessible.

Still, we do have an abundance of information at our disposal. Although Cambodia was one of the last countries in the world to become a Communist state, it was also Communist for only a brief period, and by 1979 it had dissociated itself altogether from the more extreme forms of Communism. The strange "people's democracy" that accompanied the decade of Vietnamese military occupation seemed to base its ideology entirely on condemnation of the "Pol Pot–Ieng Sary genocidal clique," judging all forms of socialism to be too traumatic after the events of those years.[3] Victims, for the most part refugees who had managed to escape abroad, were encouraged to speak about their experiences and were often very eager to do so. Researchers were also welcomed into the country. A pluralist political regime was established under the watchful eye of the United Nations in 1992.[4] (At the same time, a sizable research grant was given by the U.S. Congress to the Cambodian Genocide Program run by Yale University, which made material conditions in the country considerably easier.) For some, however, these stabilization measures have gone too far. For them, the reintegration of the last surviving Khmer Rouge officials into the political sphere seems to indicate a worrying form of amnesia inside the country. The Museum of Genocide has also been closed, and many of the killing fields are buried once again.

Nevertheless, we do know more or less what happened in Cambodia from 1975 to 1979, although there is still much work to be done in determining the exact number of those who died, the extent of local variations in policy, the exact chronology of events, and the manner in which decisions were made inside the Communist Party of Kampuchea (CPK). We certainly know enough to prove that the early claims of François Ponchaud were justified.[5] Like Simon Leys before him, he shook up the conformism among leftist intellectuals, who at first refused to accept his message.[6] Because these claims slowly came to be recognized as the truth, in part thanks to the efforts of the Vietnamese Communists, stories of life under the terror of the Khmer Rouge played an important role in the crisis faced by Communism and Marxism in the West. Like the Jews who gave their last ounce of strength so that the world would know about the realities of the Holocaust, bearing witness was sometimes the last despairing goal of a number of Cambodians who braved all sorts of dangers to escape abroad. Their tenacity often bore fruit. All of mankind should take up their flame today, remembering cases like that of Pin Yathay, who wandered alone and starving through the jungle for a month "to bring news of the genocide in Cambodia, to describe what we have been through, to tell how several million men, women, and children were all coldly programmed for death . . . how the country was razed to the ground and plunged back into a prehistoric era, and how its inhabitants were tortured so relentlessly . . . I wanted to live so that I could beg the world to come to the aid of the survivors and try to prevent total extermination."[7]

The Spiral of Horror

Despite a rather prickly nationalism, rational Cambodians recognize that their country was really a victim of a purely domestic tragedy—a small group of idealists turned toward evil—and that the traditional elites were tragically incapable of reacting to save the country or themselves. The combination is far from exceptional in Asia or elsewhere, but only rarely does it lead to revolutions. Other factors were also to blame, including the unique geographic situation of the country, especially its long border with Laos and Vietnam, and the historical moment. The full-scale war that had been raging in Vietnam since 1964 was undoubtedly a decisive factor in these events.

Civil War (1970–1975)

The Khmer kingdom, which had been a French protectorate since 1863, escaped the Indochinese war of 1946–1954 more or less unharmed.[8] At the moment when resistance groups linked to the Viet Minh began to form in 1953, Prince Sihanouk began a peaceful "crusade for independence." Facilitated by excellent diplomatic relations between Sihanouk and Paris, this "crusade" met with considerable success and undercut his adversaries on the left. But in the face of the ensuing confrontation between the Vietnamese Communists and the United States, the subtle balancing act by which he attempted to preserve Cambodian neutrality earned him only the mistrust of all parties and growing incomprehension inside the country.

In March 1970 the prince was ousted by his own government and by the

Assembly, with the blessing (but apparently not the active participation) of the U.S. Central Intelligence Agency. The country was thrown into disarray, and terrible pogroms against the Vietnamese minority began. Of the roughly 450,000 Vietnamese in the country, two-thirds were forced to flee to South Vietnam. Communist Vietnamese embassy buildings were burned down, and an ultimatum was issued for all foreign troops to leave the country immediately. The ultimatum was of course ignored. Hanoi, which found itself with no ally except the Khmer Rouge inside the country, decided to back them to the hilt, supplying arms and military advisers and providing access to training camps inside Vietnam. Vietnam eventually occupied the greater part of the country in the name of the Khmer Rouge, or rather in the name of Sihanouk, who was so furious at his earlier humiliation that he joined with the local Communists, until then his worst enemies. On the advice of Beijing and Hanoi, the Communists rolled out the red carpet for him but gave him no actual political power. Thus the internal conflict became one of royalist Communists versus the Khmer Republic, with the latter led by General (soon Marshal) Lon Nol. The forces of the Khmer Republic were considerably weaker than those of the North Vietnamese and seemed unable to capitalize on Sihanouk's unpopularity among intellectuals and the middle classes in the cities and towns. They were soon forced to ask for American aid in the form of bombing raids, arms, and military advisers; they also accepted a futile intervention from the South Vietnamese.

After the catastrophic failure of operation Chenla-II in early 1972, when the best republican troops were decimated, the war became a long agony as the Khmer Rouge tightened the screws around the main urban areas, which eventually could be supplied only by air. But this rearguard action was murderously destructive, and it destabilized the population, who, unlike the Vietnamese, had never experienced anything like it. American bombing raids were massive: more than 540,000 tons of explosives were dropped on the combat zones, mostly in the six months before the U.S. Congress cut off funding for such raids in August 1973. The bombing slowed the progress of the Khmer Rouge, but it also ensured that there would never be a shortage of recruits in a countryside now filled with hatred for the Americans. It also further destabilized the republic by causing a tremendous influx of refugees into the cities, probably one-third of a total population of 8 million.[9] This buildup of refugees facilitated the evacuation of urban areas after the Khmer Rouge's victory and enabled the Khmers to claim repeatedly in their propaganda: "We have defeated the world's greatest superpower and will therefore triumph over all opposition—nature, the Vietnamese, and all others."[10]

The fall of Phnom Penh and the last republican cities on 17 April 1975 had been expected for so long that it came as something of a relief, even to the losers. Nothing, it was assumed, could be worse than such a cruel and futile civil war. Yet the signs had always been there: the Khmer Rouge had not waited for victory to demonstrate their disconcerting aptitude for violence and extreme measures. Tens of thousands of people were massacred after the capture of the ancient royal capital, Oudong, in 1974.[11]

As "liberation" swept the country, "reeducation centers" were established and became harder and harder to distinguish from the "detention centers" that, in theory, were reserved for hardened criminals. Initially the reeducation centers were modeled on the Viet Minh prison camps of the 1950s and reserved chiefly for prisoners from Lon Nol's army. There was never any question of applying the Geneva Convention here, since all republicans were considered traitors rather than prisoners of war. In Vietnam there had been no deliberate massacres of prisoners, whether French or native. In Cambodia, by contrast, the strictest possible regime became the norm, and it seems to have been decided early on that the normal fate of a prisoner was to be death. One large camp, which contained more than 1,000 detainees, was studied by Henri Locard.[12] Established in 1971 or 1972, it confined enemy soldiers and their real or supposed families, including children, together with Buddhist monks, suspect travelers, and others. As a result of harsh treatment, a starvation diet, and widespread disease, most of the prisoners and all the children died very quickly. Executions were also very common, with as many as thirty killed in a single evening.[13]

Massive deportations of civilians began in 1973. Some 40,000 were transferred from Takeo Province to the border zones near Vietnam, and many fled toward Phnom Penh. After an abortive attempt to take the town of Kompong Cham, thousands of citizens were forced to accompany the Khmer Rouge in their retreat.[14] Kratie, the first city of any size to be taken, was entirely emptied of its population. The year 1973 also marked a decisive break with North Vietnam. Offended by the Kampuchean Communist Party's refusal to join the negotiations in Paris in January 1973 concerning the U.S. withdrawal, the North Vietnamese drastically reduced assistance, and thus their ability to influence the Khmer Rouge. Pol Pot's team[15] took advantage of this turn of events to begin eliminating approximately 1,000 "Viet Minh Khmers" who had returned to Cambodia. These former anti-French resistance fighters had left for Hanoi after the Geneva peace accord of 1954.[16] Because of their experience and their links with the Vietnamese Communist Party, they represented a real alternative to the Khmer Rouge leaders, most of whom had come to Communism only after the Indochinese war or while studying in France. A number of the latter had begun their political training as militants in the French Communist Party.[17] After the break with Vietnam, the Khmer Rouge began to rewrite history, imposing the dogma that the Kampuchean Communist Party had been founded in 1960, not, as was really the case, in 1951 as part of Ho Chi Minh's Indochinese Communist Party, which was centered in Vietnam. This tactic removed all historical legitimacy from the "'51s," who were then persecuted. It also paved the way for an artificial break with the Vietnamese Communist Party. The first serious clashes between Vietnamese troops and the Khmer Rouge date from this period.[18]

Deportation and Segregation of the Population (1975–1979)

The total evacuation of Phnom Penh following the Khmer Rouge victory came as a great shock both to the city's inhabitants and to the rest of the world,[19] which began to realize for the first time that exceptional events were unfolding in Cambodia. The city's inhabitants themselves seemed to accept the explanation given by their new masters, who claimed that the evacuation was a safety measure to ensure protection from possible American bombing raids and that people would be better fed elsewhere. The evacuation of the cities, for which the regime will undoubtedly always be remembered, was a spectacular event but cost relatively few lives. At the time people were still well fed and healthy, and they were allowed to take some belongings and articles of exchange value, such as gold, jewelry, and even dollars.[20] There was little systematic brutality, although an example was made of people who resisted, and there was certainly no shortage of executions of enemy prisoners. Most deportees were neither robbed nor searched. Direct or indirect victims of the evacuation—hospital patients, the old, the sick, and the infirm, as well as people (sometimes whole families) who committed suicide—numbered perhaps 10,000, out of a total city population of 2 million to 3 million. Several hundred thousand were also moved out of other cities, so that 46–54 percent of the population of the country found themselves on the road.[21] Despite the lack of brutality, the evacuation of the cities was a traumatic event that remains indelibly etched on the memory of all survivors. They had twenty-four hours to leave their homes. Though somewhat reassured by the lie that they would be allowed to return after three days,[22] they found themselves caught up in a human maelstrom in which it was easy to lose their closest relatives, perhaps forever. Unsmiling soldiers *(yothea)* dragged them away to a departure point whose destination depended on the neighborhood from which they left; thus families who were separated before reaching the departure point stood little chance of meeting again. Scenes of death and despair abounded, and no one received any food or medical assistance from the Khmer Rouge during the journey to the destination, which often lasted several weeks.

The first classification of city dwellers took place during this first deportation, at the roadside in the country. It was quite rudimentary and depended more or less on what people said about themselves. The aim was to find as many army officers and middle- and high-ranking officials as possible, in theory so that Sihanouk, who was nominally head of state until 1976, could form a new government in the capital. In practice, most of them were immediately massacred or died shortly afterward in prison. Inexplicably from the point of view of police control, the Khmer Rouge had ordered that all identity papers be destroyed;[23] as a result, many government employees and former soldiers were able to pass themselves off as peasants and, with a bit of luck, survive.[24]

Controlling such a huge exodus was well beyond the organizational capacity of the Khmer Rouge, who in 1975 numbered only 120,000 activists and sympathizers; most of these had joined recently, and only half were soldiers. Evacuees were thus allowed to establish their new homes wherever they wanted (or wherever they could), provided the village chief agreed. Cambodia is neither big nor densely populated, and almost all city dwellers had relatives somewhere in the country. Many simply went to join them, and thus vastly increased their chances of survival, provided they were not deported again. On the whole, things were not too difficult. Sometimes the villagers even killed a cow in honor of the evacuees, and often they helped the evacuees set up new homes.[25] More generally, from this moment until the fall of the regime, all witness statements concur that people tended to help one another and did not engage in much physical violence or carry out spontaneous murders.[26] Relations seem to have been particularly amicable with the Khmer Loeu (an ethnic minority in a remote region).[27] The fact that this last group, among whom the Khmer Rouge had established their first base, was particularly favored by the regime until at least 1977 allows us to conclude that tensions between the peasants and the new arrivals, which were increasing elsewhere, usually resulted from the generalized poverty that caused a mouthful for one to mean hunger for another. Such situations are rarely conducive to acts of great altruism.[28]

The influx of city dwellers to the villages caused a tremendous upheaval in rural life, particularly in the balance between resources and consumption. In the fertile rice plains of Region 5, in the northwest, the 170,000 inhabitants were joined by 210,000 new arrivals.[29] The CPK did all it could to drive a wedge between the *prasheashon shah*, the country people, also known as the "'70s," most of whom had been under the control of the Khmer Rouge since the war had broken out; and the *prasheashon thmei*, the "New People," also known as the "'75s" or the "17 Aprils." It tried to incite class hatred among the "patriotic proletariat" for these "lackeys of the capitalist imperialists." A two-tier legal system was introduced; in effect only the rural people, who were in a small majority, had any rights. In the early days they were allowed to cultivate a small amount of private property to eat in the obligatory canteen before the others. Their food was marginally better, and occasionally they were also allowed to vote in elections in which only a single candidate appeared on the ballot. An apartheid system was quickly achieved. The two groups lived in separate areas of the village and, in principle, were not allowed even to talk to each other, let alone intermarry.[30]

These two population groups were soon subdivided. As part of total collectivization, the peasants were divided into "poor peasants," "landed peasants," "rich peasants," and former traders. Among the New People, nonofficials and those who lacked an education were soon separated from former civil servants and intellectuals. The fate of these last two groups was generally dire: they were purged little by little, with each successive purge reaching a little further down the hierarchy, until both groups completely disappeared. After 1978 the purges also included women and children.

But ruralizing the entire population was not enough for the leaders of the CPK. After only a few months, many of the New People were ordered to new deportation centers, and this time they had no voice in their fate. For example, in September 1975 alone, several hundred thousand people left the eastern and southeastern regions for the northwest.[31] It was not uncommon for an individual to be deported three or four times. In addition there were "work brigades," which would take all young people and parents with no young children far from their assigned village for several months. The intention of the regime was fourfold. First, to preclude any potential political threat, the regime sought to forestall the formation of any lasting links between the peasants and the New People.[32] Second, the regime sought to "proletarianize" the New People ever more thoroughly by preventing them from taking their possessions with them and from having the time to reap what they had sown.[33] Third, the Khmer Rouge sought to maintain total control of population movements through the initiation of large-scale agricultural projects, such as cultivating the relatively poor land in the mountains and the sparsely populated jungle regions in the outlying areas of the country. Finally, the regime undoubtedly sought to rid itself of a maximum of "useless mouths." Each successive evacuation— whether on foot, in carts, or in slow, badly overcrowded trains that sometimes took as long as a week to reach their destination—was an extremely demanding experience for severely undernourished people. In light of the severe shortage of medical facilities, losses were high.

"Voluntary" transfers were a slightly different matter. New People were often given the chance to "return to their native village" or to work in a cooperative where conditions were easier, with better health care and better food. Invariably the volunteers, who were often quite numerous, would then find themselves in places where conditions were even worse. Pin Yathay, the victim of one such transfer, learned to see through these promises: "This was really nothing more than a ploy to weed out people with individualist tendencies . . . Anyone who fell into the trap showed that he had not yet got rid of his old-fashioned tendencies and needed to go through a more severe regime of retraining in a village where conditions were even worse. By coming forward as volunteers, people in effect denounced themselves. Using this infallible criterion, the Khmer Rouge rooted out the more unstable among us, those who were least satisfied with their fate."[34]

The Time of Purges and Massacres (1976–1979)

The mania for classification and elimination of different elements of society slowly reached to the very top of the political hierarchy. As noted above, genuine supporters of the Vietnamese such as Hou Youn were wiped out quite early on. Diplomats from the "royal government," not all of whom were Communists, were recalled in December 1975. All but two were tortured and executed.[35] But because the CPK never seemed to have any regular pattern of behavior and because the different geographic zones had varying degrees of autonomy, there was a constant air of mutual suspicion. The army was not unified until after 17 April. Things were made still more difficult by the disintegration of the economy and by increasingly successful Vietnamese counteroffensives in 1978.

With the arrest of Keo Meas, "Number 6" in the CPK hierarchy, in September 1976, it became apparent that the Party was being devoured from within at an ever-increasing rate. There were never any trials or clear charges brought, and everyone who was imprisoned was tortured in a barbaric fashion before being killed. Only the victims' "confessions" provide an idea of what "charges" might have been brought against them, but divergences from the Pol Pot line were never very clear. Undoubtedly the aim was to crush anyone who showed exceptional qualities or the slightest sign of a spirit of independence, not to mention any past association with the Vietnamese Communist Party (or, like Hu Nim, with the Chinese Gang of Four). Any quality that might threaten the preeminence of Pol Pot led to repression.[36] The paranoia among the leadership was like a caricature of the worst excesses of Stalinism. During one study session for Communist Party cadres, immediately following a debate about the purge, the top leaders in the "Center" concluded proceedings by talking about "a fierce and uncompromising fight to the death with the class enemy . . . especially in our revolutionary ranks."[37] In July 1978 the Party monthly, *Tung padevat* (Revolutionary flags), announced: "There are enemies everywhere within our ranks, in the center, at headquarters, in the zones, and out in the villages."[38] By that point, five of the thirteen highest-ranking officials of October 1975 had been executed, along with most regional secretaries.[39] Two of the seven new leaders who took office in 1978 were executed before January 1979. The purge fueled itself; all that was required for an arrest was a total of three denunciations as a "CIA agent." The interrogators zealously extorted successive confessions by any means possible in order to please their bosses. Imaginary conspiracies abounded, and more networks were constantly being uncovered. The blind hatred of Vietnam caused people to lose all sense of reality. One doctor was accused of being a member of the "Vietnamese CIA"; he had allegedly been recruited in Hanoi in 1956 by an American agent disguised as a tourist.[40] Liquidations were also carried out at the grass-roots level; according to one estimate, 40,000 of the 70,000 inhabitants in one district were killed as "traitors collaborating with the CIA."[41]

But the really massive genocide took place in the eastern zone. Hostile Vietnam was nearby, and Sao Phim, the military and political chief of the region, had built up a solid local power base. It was here that the only full-fledged rebellion against the central regime ever occurred, in a short-lived civil war in May and June 1978. In April, after 409 cadres from the east had been locked up in the central prison in Tuol Sleng and it was clear that all was lost, Sao Phim killed himself, and his wife and children were murdered while attending his funeral. A few fragments of the armed forces in the region tried to foment a rebellion, then crossed into Vietnam, where they established the embryonic Front for National Salvation, which later accompanied the Vietnamese army from Hanoi to Phnom Penh. When the central authorities regained control in the east, they condemned to death all the people living in the region, labeling them "Vietnamese in Khmer bodies." From May to December 1978 between 100,000 and 250,000 people out of a population of 1.7 million were massacred, starting with militants and young people. In Sao Phim's village all 120 families (700 people) were killed. In another village, there were 7 survivors out of 15 families, 12 of which were totally wiped out.[42] After July any survivors were taken away in trucks, trains, and boats to other zones, where they were progressively exterminated. Thousands more died in transit. They were forced to wear blue clothes specially imported from China; everyone else under Pol Pot's rule wore black. Gradually, with little fanfare, and generally out of sight of the other villagers, the people dressed in blue disappeared. In one cooperative in the northwest, when the Vietnamese army finally arrived, only about 100 easterners of the original 3,000 remained.[43] These atrocities took a horrific new turn just before the fall of the regime. Women, children, and old people were massacred together with the young men, and the original peasants were killed together with the New People. Because the task was so overwhelmingly large, the Khmer Rouge forced the ordinary population, including even the "'75s," to help them carry out the massacres. The revolution was out of control and was threatening to engulf every last Cambodian.

The scale of despair created by the Khmer Rouge is attested by the number who fled abroad. Excluding those who arrived in April 1975, more than 23,000 refugees had fled to Thailand by November 1976.[44] By October 1977, there were 60,000 Cambodians in Vietnam.[45] All these refugees braved terrible dangers when they fled: capture meant certain death, and escape entailed wandering for days or weeks through hostile jungle.[46] People were invariably in a state of exhaustion before setting out, and such dangers were enough to deter most. Of those who did try, only a small fraction succeeded. Pin Yathay's group planned their escape quite meticulously, but out of the original twelve only four survived.

After twenty months of sporadic border clashes, the Vietnamese invaded in January 1979. The vast majority of Cambodians perceived their arrival as a moment of tremendous liberation, and it is still remembered as such today. In one typical incident, the villagers in Samlaut (heroes of the 1967 revolt) massacred their Khmer Rouge tormentors.[47] The Khmer Rouge also carried out a number of atrocities at the last minute; in several prisons, including Tuol Sleng, the liberators found almost no one to set free.[48] Although many Cambodians became disenchanted with their liberators in the following months, and although the intentions of the Hanoi regime were by no means humanitarian, a central fact remains: given the increasing murderousness of the Khmer Rouge, especially in 1978, the Vietnamese incursion saved an incalculable number of lives. Since then the country has been gradually nursing itself back to life; the inhabitants are slowly recovering their rights, cultivating their crops, pursuing their religion and education, and reintegrating their country into the rest of the world.

The Various Forms of Martyrdom

Horror is not always a matter of numbers. The account above gives a good idea of the real nature of the Kampuchean Communist Party. But numbers do help us to understand. If no section of the population was spared, which section suffered most, and when? How does the tragedy of Cambodia relate to the other tragedies of the century and to its own larger history? A combination of methods (demography, quantitative microstudies, eyewitness reports), none sufficient in itself, can advance us inch by inch toward the truth.

Two Million Dead?

Inevitably we must begin with an overall figure; yet even here we find enormous disparity among the claims. This fact in itself can be taken as an indication of the scale of events: the bigger a massacre is, the harder it is to come to terms with it, to reduce it to exact numbers. Everyone has an interest in stretching the figure in one direction or another—the Khmer Rouge to deny their responsibility, the Vietnamese and their allies to justify their intervention. Pol Pot, in the last interview he ever gave to a newspaper as leader of the CPK, claimed in December 1979 that "only a few thousand Cambodians have died as a result of the application of our policy of bringing abundance to the people."[49] Khieu Samphan, in an official pamphlet in 1987, was a little more precise: 3,000 died "by mistake," 11,000 "Vietnamese agents" were killed, and 30,000 people were killed by "Vietnamese agents who had infiltrated the country." The document adds that the invading Vietnamese killed approximately 1.5 million Cambodians in 1979 and 1980. This last figure is enormously exaggerated, and can reasonably be taken as an involuntary admission that close to that number died after 1975, mostly as a result of the activities of the Khmer Rouge.[50] The manipulation of figures is even more flagrant in the claims about the number who died before 17 April, during the civil war. In June 1975 Pol Pot cited the grossly inflated figure of 600,000; by 1978 he was talking about "more than 1.4 million."[51] As for the victims of the Khmer Rouge, President Lon Nol cited 2.5 million; Pen Sovan, the former secretary general of the People's Revolutionary Party of Kampuchea (PRPK), which took power in 1979, cited 3.1 million, the figure used in Vietnamese propaganda and by the PRPK.

The first two studies that can be taken seriously—although they, too, acknowledge uncertainties—are those of Ben Kiernan, who calculates 1.5 million dead, and Michael Vickery, who arrives at a figure half that size.[52] Stephen Heder, using Kiernan's figures, asserts that the dead were evenly divided between peasants and New People (a claim that is hard to accept) and also evenly divided between victims of famine and victims of assassinations.[53] David Chandler, a renowned specialist in the field, but who has not himself carried out an analytical evaluation, estimates a minimum of 800,000 to 1 million dead.[54] A CIA study based on approximate data estimates the total demographic deficit (including the fall in the birth rate as a result of the situation) at 3.8 million for the years 1970–1979, including war losses for the years 1970–1975, with a resulting population of 5.2 million in 1979.[55] Another study based on a comparative analysis of the extent of cultivated rice fields in 1970 and 1983 comes up with a figure of 1.2 million victims.[56] Marek Sliwinski, in a recent innovative study using demographic techniques (rendered less reliable by the lack of any census from the late 1960s to 1993), speaks of a little more than 2 million dead, or 26 percent of the population, not including deaths from natural causes, which he estimates at 7 percent. Sliwinski's is the only study that tries to break down the 1975–1979 figures by age and gender. He concludes that 33.9 percent of men and 15.7 percent of women died. A difference of that size is strong evidence that most of the deaths were from assassinations. The death rate is horrendous for all ages, but especially high for young males (34 percent of men aged twenty to thirty, 40 percent of men aged thirty to forty, and 54 percent of people of both sexes over age sixty). As during the great famines and epidemics that occurred under the *ancien régime,* the birth rate plummeted to nearly zero: in 1970 it was 3 percent; in 1978 it was 1.1 percent. No other country in the world seems to have suffered so much since 1945. In 1990 the total population had still not returned to the level of 1970. And the population is still unbalanced, with 1.3 women for every man. In 1989, 38 percent of adult women were widows, whereas only 10 percent of adult men were widowers.[57] Close to 64 percent of the adult population was female, and 35 percent of heads of families were women; these proportions are the same among Cambodian refugees in the United States.[58]

This level of losses—at the very least one in seven, and more likely one in five or four—is enough to obliterate the oft-heard argument that the violence of the Khmer Rouge, however terrible it was, was only the reaction of a people driven mad by the original sin of American bombing.[59] Many other peoples— including the British, the Germans, the Japanese, and the Vietnamese—have suffered badly in bombing raids in this century, and no extremist fervor took root in their populations as a result; in fact the contrary was often the case. However bad the ravages of war were, they were not comparable to what the Kampuchean Communist Party achieved in times of peace, even if one excludes the last year and the border conflict with Vietnam. Pol Pot himself, who had no interest in minimizing the figures, stated that the civil war claimed 600,000 lives. Although he never explained how this figure was determined, it was often taken up by other specialists. Chandler talks rather lightly about "half a million victims" and cities various studies claiming that the American bombing raids cost anywhere from 30,000 to 250,000 victims.[60] Sliwinski reckons 240,000 victims to be a reasonable figure, to which perhaps 70,000 Vietnamese civilians should be added, most of whom died in the pogroms of 1970. By his calculations 40,000 died in the bombing, a quarter of whom were military personnel. He also notes that the areas worst affected by the bombing were relatively unpopulated, and in 1970 probably contained no more than a million inhabitants, many of whom fled to the cities. By contrast, assassinations carried out by the Khmer Rouge during the war period probably totaled around 75,000.[61] There is no doubt that the war weakened society's resistance and destroyed or demoralized the elite and educated sections of the population. At the same time, the power of the Khmer Rouge was increased tremendously thanks to Hanoi's strategic choices and Sihanouk's irresponsible decisions. Accordingly, the people behind the 1970 coup attempt have much to answer for. But none of that affects the responsibility of the CPK for its actions after 1975; there was nothing spontaneous about the violence of those years.

The serious quantitative studies also furnish some estimates of the number of victims of different modes of mass murder. The forced ruralization of city dwellers (including deaths in transit, exhaustion at work, and the like) led to 400,000 deaths at most, and quite possibly fewer. Executions are the hardest to calculate; the average hovers around 500,000. Henri Locard, by a process of extrapolation, calculates that between 400,000 and 600,000 died in prison. That figure excludes executions carried out on the spot, which were also extremely numerous.[62] Sliwinski arrives at a total of 1 million executions. Hunger and disease were undoubtedly the biggest killers, accounting for at least 700,000 deaths.[63] Sliwinski mentions 900,000 in that context, including lives lost as a direct result of ruralization.[64]

Targets and Suspects

Trying to arrive at overall figures from local studies is difficult because circumstances varied tremendously across the country. The "'70s" suffered considerably less than the "'75s," especially from hunger, even if one takes into account the distortions arising from the fact that most published eyewitness statements come from New People rather than the peasants. The death rate was extremely high among the people who had come from the cities; today it is almost impossible to find a family that did not lose one or several of its members. City dwellers made up half the population. Out of the 200 families that settled in a village in the northern zone, only 50 survived until January 1979, and only one family had lost "only" its grandparents.[65] Certain categories were even more severely affected. We have already seen how former officials and high-ranking soldiers from the Lon Nol administration were persecuted; successive purges struck even lower in the hierarchy.[66] Only railway employees, who were judged to be impossible to replace, were unaffected. The wiser among the station chiefs declared that they occupied a post more lowly than the one they actually held.[67] Monks, who had traditionally played an important role in society, were considered to represent too much competition, and those who did not defrock were systematically eliminated. In 1979, out of a group of 28 monks who had been evacuated to a village in Kandal Province, there was only 1 survivor.[68] Nationwide, their number fell from approximately 60,000 to 1,000.[69] Almost all press photographers disappeared.[70] The fate of the "intellectuals" varied considerably:[71] sometimes they were persecuted simply for being who they were; more often, though, they apparently were allowed to survive if they renounced all pretense to expertise in any field and abandoned attributes such as books and spectacles.

The peasants were treated considerably better, particularly when it came to food supplies. Within certain limits they could consume fruit, sugar, and a little meat. Their rations were larger, and they could eat hard rice rather than the universal clear rice soup, which came to be a symbol of famine for so many inhabitants of the country. The Khmer soldiers were always the first to eat, despite their pretensions of frugality. The "'70s" sometimes had access to pharmacists and real medicines from China. But such advantages were only relative. Although the villagers had not been deported, they were still forced to carry out duties far from their homes and villages, and they worked extremely long hours. The tiny working class, which lived in the military–camp atmosphere of Phnom Penh, was also subjected to extremely harsh discipline. Gradually, poor peasants, who were considered more reliable than workers, replaced workers who had been in Phnom Penh before 1975.[72]

In 1978 there were some signs that the barriers between the peasants and the New People were to be abolished. By that time some New People had even begun to take up low-ranking position of local authority. The positive interpretation here would be that such people had adapted to the demands of the new regime. A more sinister interpretation would be that unification of the population was being attempted in the face of the brewing conflict with Vietnam, similar to Stalin's unification of the Soviet population against the Germans in 1941. Or, given the generalized scale of the purges, there may simply have been so many holes in the state apparatus that there was no other option. Whatever the reason, the general increase in repression in the last year of the regime seems to have been a downward leveling movement; it was during this period that a major change took place, as a majority of the "'70s" began silently opposing the Khmer Rouge.

The fate of the twenty or so ethnic minorities who in 1970 made up 15 percent of the population was often quite different. An initial distinction should be drawn between essentially urban minorities, such as the Chinese and the Vietnamese, and the rural minorities, such as the Cham Muslims in the lake and river regions and the Khmer Loeu, a generic term covering various groups that were spread thinly through the mountains and jungles. The urban groups did not suffer specific reprisals until 1977. Some 150,000 Vietnamese were repatriated on a voluntary basis between May and September 1975 (half as many as in 1970, under Lon Nol). This action reduced the community to a few tens of thousands, most of whom had intermarried with Khmers. But escaping from the Khmer Rouge was important enough for many Khmers to try to pass themselves off as Vietnamese, an action that did not seem to be particularly dangerous. In the regions where deportees ended up, there seems to have been little discrimination between urban minorities and other former city dwellers. Their new common test seemed to provide an important social bond: "Cambodians from the towns, Chinese, and Vietnamese were gathered together indiscriminately, all under the invidious label 'New People.' We were all brothers. We forgot ancient nationalist rivalries and grudges . . . The Cambodians were probably the most depressed. They were sickened by the actions of the

Khmer Rouge, who were their compatriots and their executioners . . . All of us were revolted by the idea that our torturers were of the same nationality as we."[73]

How then did it come about that some minorities were entirely wiped out by the Khmer Rouge regime? It has been suggested that 50 percent of the 400,000 Chinese died,[74] as did an even higher proportion of Vietnamese who stayed after 1975; Sliwinski calculates a 37.5 percent death rate for the Vietnamese and 38.4 percent for the Chinese. The answer must lie in the comparison with other groups of victims: according to Sliwinski, 82.6 percent of officers in the republican army, 51.5 percent of all "intellectuals," and, most important, 41.9 percent of all residents of Phnom Penh perished.[75] This last figure is very close to the one generally quoted for minorities, many of whom were pursued as "ultra city dwellers" (according to the 1962 census, 18 percent of the residents of Phnom Penh were Chinese, and 14 percent Vietnamese) or as merchants and traders, many of whom were unable to disguise their recent past.[76] Many of these were better off than the Khmers, which was both a blessing and a curse: it meant that they could survive longer by using the black market, but it also turned them into easy targets for their new masters.[77] However, as good Communists, the Khmer Rouge believed that the class struggle was much more important than struggles between different peoples or races.

This is not to say that the Khmer Rouge were not above using and abusing nationalism and xenophobia. In 1978 Pol Pot stated that Cambodia was building socialism on its own model. His 1977 speech in Beijing in homage to Mao Zedong was not reported at home. Hatred for Vietnam, which had "stolen" Kampuchea Krom in the eighteenth century and integrated it into Cochin China, became a central theme in Khmer propaganda and seems to be the only raison d'être for the few Khmer Rouge who are still politically active today. After mid-1976 the Vietnamese who had stayed in the country found themselves forbidden to leave. A few killings took place on a local level. They became more widespread after a directive from the Center on 1 April 1977 required that all Vietnamese be arrested and handed over to the central security forces. By this stage their numbers were already considerably reduced. For good measure, their friends were to be arrested as well, as was anyone else who spoke Vietnamese. In Kratie Province, which shared a border with Vietnam, having a Vietnamese ancestor was enough to make people liable to arrest, and the authorities classified all Yuon as "historical enemies."[78] In this atmosphere, accusing all the inhabitants of the eastern zone of being "Vietnamese in Khmer bodies" was tantamount to condemning them to death.

According to Sliwinski, Cambodian Catholics were the group that met the worst fate; at least 48.6 percent of them disappeared.[79] Many factors conspired against them: they came mostly from the cities, were primarily Vietnamese in origin, and inevitably were associated with colonial imperialism. The cathedral in Phnom Penh was one of the few buildings razed to the ground. Ethnic minorities saw their separate identity denied. According to one decree, "in Kampuchea there is only one nation and one tongue, the Khmer. Henceforth there are no more different nationalities inside Kampuchea."[80] People from the mountains, such as the Khmer Loeu and small groups of forest hunters received reasonably preferential treatment in the early days because the CPK had had its first bases there and had recruited a large number of troops from these groups. But after 1976, to satisfy the official obsession with rice production, the Khmer Rouge destroyed highland villages and forced their inhabitants to settle in the valleys, totally disrupting their traditional way of life.[81] Even Pol Pot's guards, who belonged to the Jarai ethnic group, were arrested and liquidated in February 1977.

The Cham, who were the largest indigenous minority—numbering 250,000 in 1970—and who were for the most part farmers and fishermen, had a unique fate because of their Muslim faith.[82] Because they were reputed to be excellent warriors, they were courted by the Khmer Rouge in the early stages of the "war of liberation." At that time they were generally integrated into the peasant group, although they were often reprimanded for being overly involved in commerce. They were the main suppliers of fish for most of Cambodia. But beginning in 1974, on secret orders from Pol Pot, their tiny villages were destroyed. In 1976 all cadres with Cham origins were removed from their posts. A Khmer Rouge text in 1975 demanded that the Cham take new names that would more closely resemble Khmer names. "The Cham mentality is abolished forthwith. Anyone who does not conform to these orders will be punished accordingly."[83] In the northwestern zone, people were sometimes killed merely for speaking Cham. Women were also forbidden to wear the sarong and were forced to cut off their hair.

The attempt to eradicate Islam provoked some extremely serious incidents. In 1973, mosques were destroyed and prayers banned in the liberated zones. Such measures became more widespread after May 1975. Korans were collected and burned, and mosques were either transformed into other buildings or razed. Thirteen Muslim dignitaries were executed in June, some for having gone to pray rather than attending a political rally, others for having campaigned for the right to religious wedding ceremonies. Often Muslims were forced to make a choice between raising pigs and eating pork or being put to death—an ironic demand, given that meat all but disappeared from the Cambodian diet during these years. Some Cham were forced to eat pork twice a month (a number of them of course then vomited up the meal). The more fervent were all but wiped out: of the 1,000 who had made the pilgrimage to Mecca, only 30 survived these years. Unlike other Cambodians, the Cham frequently rebelled, and large numbers of them died in the massacres and reprisals that followed these uprisings. After mid-1978 the Khmer Rouge began systematically exterminating a number of Cham communities, including women and children, even though they had agreed to eat pork.[84] Ben Kiernan calculates that the overall mortality rate among the Cham was 50 percent; Sliwinski's figure is 40.6 percent.[85]

Geographic and Temporal Variations

There were large regional differences in the mortality rates. The place of origin of the victims was a major factor. According to Sliwinski, 58.1 percent of the population of Phnom Penh was still alive in 1979 (that is, 1 million died, accounting for approximately half the total number of dead), whereas 71.2 percent of the inhabitants of Kompong Cham (another densely populated region) survived, as did 90.5 percent of the people of Oddar Mean Chhey, in the north. In this last region there was only a 2.1 percent increase in the death rate.[86] Not surprisingly, the zones that were conquered last, which were more densely populated and were closer to the capital (the evacuation of the suburbs was less dramatic than the evacuation of the capital itself), were the zones that suffered most. In Democratic Kampuchea, survival depended most of all on the destination to which one was deported. Being sent to a wooded or mountainous zone or to a region where the main crop was jute was a sentence to almost certain death, since there was very little interregional communication, and supplies rarely arrived.[87] The regime demanded identical production quotas from all regions and never supplied any form of assistance. Because people had to begin by clearing the land and building cabins to live in, when they were already exhausted from working on starvation rations and were also exposed to dysentery and malaria, the loss of human life was appallingly high. According to Pin Yathay, one-third of the population of his camp died in the space of four months in 1975. In the village of Don Ey, famine was widespread, there were no births at all, and as many as 80 percent of the inhabitants died.[88] If by contrast one ended up in a prosperous agricultural region, the odds of surviving were relatively good, particularly if there were not too many New People to upset the equilibrium of the local economy. But such villages did suffer in other ways. The population was more closely controlled, and there were more purges. Chances of survival were also quite good in remote regions, where cadres were more tolerant, the Khmer Loeu locals were quite welcoming, and the main danger was most often disease.

At the village level the behavior of local cadres was decisive, since they controlled how the peasants were treated. The weakness and mediocrity of the Khmer bureaucratic apparatus meant that for better or for worse, local leaders had considerable autonomy.[89] There were sadistic brutes (many of them young women),[90] neophytes with something to prove, or the usual failures who tried to stand out by being more repressive or more demanding than the rest when it came to fulfilling work quotas. Two types of cadres improved chances of survival: humane ones, such as the village chief who in 1975 made sure that refugees worked no more than four hours a day, or those who allowed the sick or exhausted to rest, permitted husbands to see their wives, and turned a blind eye to people's efforts to feed themselves, a practice that was forbidden yet vital to survival; and the corrupt, notably the officials who accepted bribes of watches or gold jewelry to issue permits allowing people to switch residences or work teams, or even to drop out of the work teams altogether for a while.[91] Over time, as the regime became more centralized, such tolerance was increasingly rare. Furthermore, under the regime's infernal logic, cadres suspected of weakness or corruption were inevitably replaced in purges by leaders who were younger, more zealous, and crueler.

The mortality rate also varied considerably over time. The regime's short duration and the geographic variation in its policies make clear distinctions among periods difficult. Hunger and terror were constant and widespread. Their intensity varied, and chances of survival depended on that intensity. Nevertheless, eyewitness statements make a chronology possible. The first months of the regime were marked by mass killings of carefully targeted social groups; these slaughters were facilitated by the initial naïveté of the "'75s" about their new masters. Hunger was not a major factor until at least the autumn, and it was not until then that the collective canteens forbade families from eating together.[92] On several occasions between the end of May and October the Center ordered massacres to cease, either as a result of the residual influence of the more moderate leaders or in an attempt to rein in zones that were perceived to be out of control. The murders continued, but at a reduced rate. According to Komphot, a banker who escaped to the northern zone, "people were killed one by one—there were no mass killings. The first to go were a dozen New People, people who were suspected of having been soldiers, and so forth. During the first two years about a tenth of them were killed, one by one, together with their children. I don't know how many died in all."[93]

The year 1976 appears to have been marked by terrible famines. The Center was involved in large-scale projects at the expense of agriculture. Although the main harvest, in December and January, staved off famine in the first half of the year, the total harvest was probably only half that normally produced in the 1960s.[94] According to some accounts, 1977 was the worst year, marked by both widespread famine and massive purges.[95] These purges differed from those of 1975: they were more political (often the result of the increasingly bitter in-fighting within the regime), more ethnically biased, more systematically targeted against groups that had previously escaped the attentions of the authorities (such as schoolteachers and wealthy and middle-income peasants), and more ferocious. Although the instructions in 1975 had forbidden the execution of women and children of officers of the former regime, in 1977 the wives of men who had already been executed (sometimes considerably earlier) were themselves arrested and killed. Whole families were slaughtered, and sometimes entire villages, such as that of former president Lon Nol, where 350 families were wiped out on 17 April 1977 to celebrate the anniversary of the "liberation."[96] There are contradictory accounts regarding 1978: Sliwinski believes that the famine abated because of a better harvest and better management of the economy; in Charles Twining's version, which is backed up by several witnesses, drought and war combined to make the situation worse than ever before.[97] What is certain is that the killings became more and more widespread among the peasants, particularly in the eastern zone, and reached an all-time high.

Daily Death under Pol Pot

In Democratic Kampuchea, there were no prisons, no courts, no universities, no schools, no money, no jobs, no books, no sports, and no pastimes . . . There was no spare moment in the twenty-four-hour day. Daily life was divided up as follows: twelve hours for physical labor, two hours for eating, three hours for rest and education, and seven hours for sleep. We all lived in an enormous concentration camp. There was no justice. The Angkar [Angkar Padevat, or Revolutionary Organization, the semisecret cover for the CPK] regulated every moment of our lives . . . The Khmer Rouge often used parables to justify their contradictory actions. They would compare people to cattle: "Watch this ox as it pulls the plow. It eats when it is ordered to eat. If you let it graze in the field it will eat anything. If you put it into another field where there isn't enough grass, it will still graze uncomplainingly. It is not free, and it is constantly being watched. And when you tell it to pull the plow, it pulls. It never thinks about its wife or children . . ."[98]

For all the survivors, the memory of Democratic Kampuchea is extremely strange. It was a place with no values or stable points of reference. It really was the nightmare world on the other side of the mirror. To survive there, everyone had to adapt to a completely new set of rules. The first article of faith was a radical dismissal of the idea that human life had any value. "Losing you is not a loss, and keeping you is no specific gain" went one terrifying official slogan that recurs time and again in statements by witnesses.[99] What the Cambodians experienced was a descent into the underworld, which for some began as early as 1973. From that time on the "liberated" zone in the southwest experienced the suppression of Buddhism, the forced separation of young people from their families, a uniform dress code, and the militarization of all cooperatives. What must now be told are the myriad ways in which one could perish.

Slavery, Famine, and the Radiant Future

The first thing that people had to do was accept their new condition. For the "'75s" this was halfway between being a beast of burden and a war slave (in accordance with the Angkor tradition).[100] It was a lot easier to gain access to a peasant village if one looked strong and healthy and was not accompanied by too many "useless mouths."[101] People were progressively stripped of their possessions: during the evacuation, by the Khmer Rouge soldiers; in the countryside, by the cadres and peasants; and finally through the black market, where a 250-gram box of rice sometimes sold for as much as 100 dollars.[102] All education, all freedom of movement and trade, all medicine worthy of the name, all religion, and all writing disappeared. Strict dress codes were imposed: people had to wear black, long-sleeved shirts buttoned up to the neck. There were also strict codes of behavior: all public displays of affection were banned, as were arguments, insults, complaints, and tears. All figures of authority were to be blindly obeyed. People were forced to attend interminable meetings and while there to look alert, shout disapproval or approbation on command, and to voice public criticism of others or themselves. The 1976 constitution of Democratic Kampuchea specified that the first right of all citizens was the right to work; many of the New People never received any other rights. Not surprisingly, the early days of the regime were marked by a huge increase in suicides, particularly among those who were separated from their loved ones, among the old who felt that they were a burden on their family, and among those who had been accustomed to a comfortable life style.

It was often very hard for the "'75s" to adapt to the terrible conditions at their destination. Many were sent to unhealthy regions, particularly in the autumn of 1975. They had only the most rudimentary tools and were invariably given insufficient rations. They never had any technical assistance or practical training and were punished severely for failures of any sort, regardless of the reason. People with handicaps were simply treated as shirkers and executed. Unless one had particularly strong family ties, location was always provisional; constant transfers of production teams and repeated deportations to new areas reinforced the impression of arbitrary power. Thus even the strongest were often tempted to flee to some place still governed by reason and humanity. Too often, flight itself was only suicide of a different kind, since it was usually carried out without maps or compasses, in the rainy season to avoid pursuit and to cover one's traces more easily, and with little food.[103] People were exhausted before they set out, and many must have died before even meeting a Khmer Rouge patrol. Nevertheless, escape attempts were numerous, and facilitated by the relatively lax surveillance, since the number of Khmer soldiers and cadres was never very high.[104]

As though it was not already difficult enough to adjust to a new way of life, the system gave people no time to rest and recover. The leaders seemed convinced that the radiant future was just around the corner, at the end of the Four-Year Plan presented by Pol Pot in August 1976. His objective was to increase production massively by increasing capital through the export of agricultural products, which were the country's only obvious resource. The Khmer Rouge believed that the way forward would come through the industrialization of agriculture and the development of diversified light industry, followed later by the construction of heavy industry.[105] Strangely, this modernist mystique was based on the old mythology about the state of Angkor: "Because we are the race that built Angkor, we can do anything," said Pol Pot in a long speech on 27 September 1977, in which he also announced that the Angkar was really the Communist Party of Kampuchea.[106] His other justification for his belief in the Khmer Rouge was the "glorious 17 April," which had demonstrated the superiority of the poor peasants of Cambodia over the world's greatest imperial power.

These were days of tremendous futility. The population was asked to increase production to three tons of paddy per hectare,[107] despite the fact that production levels had remained stable at around one ton since 1970. Equally pointless was the attempt to triple the surface area of the rice fields in the rich northwest, which would involve clearing huge amounts of land and developing enormous irrigation projects—previously unimportant in this country with a small population, abundant rainfall, and an annual flood. The goal was to pass quickly to two, and eventually to three, harvests a year. The planting of all other crops was suspended. No calculations were made regarding the size of the "work army" of New People that would be necessary to implement this project.[108] The effort quickly drained off the strongest: since the fittest were worked the hardest, they often died first. Ordinarily the working day was eleven hours long; but sometimes, during competitions among villages, launched by the cadres, workers were obliged to rise at four in the morning and to work until ten or eleven at night. In some places rest days were abolished entirely; elsewhere one was allowed every ten days, but was filled with obligatory and interminable political meetings. Usually the pace at which people were expected to work was no higher than that of the Cambodian peasant. The differences lay in the absence of rest periods and work breaks and in the chronic undernourishment.[109]

The future might have been radiant, but the present was disastrous. In

November 1976 the American embassy in Bangkok calculated, on the basis of refugee reports, that the surface area being farmed in Cambodia had fallen by 50 percent from its pre-1975 level.[110] People who traveled through Kampuchea described the countryside as being almost deserted, with existing fields abandoned as a result of the massive population movements to newly cleared land and the major development projects. Laurence Picq's testimony is typical:

> On both sides of the road abandoned rice fields stretched to the horizon.
> I looked in vain for planting teams. There were none; only a team of a few young girls every ten kilometers or so.
> Where were the hundreds of young mobile brigades that were mentioned on the radio every day?
> Here and there groups of men and women wandered around, their possessions wrapped up in a handkerchief and a vacant look in their eyes. From their clothes, old rags that had once been brightly colored, you could see that they were New People, city dwellers who had been driven out of the towns. .
> I learned that new population transfers were planned for the middle of the year, to offset the effects of the absurd policies of a "gang of traitors."
> In the early days these city dwellers had been sent to the desolate regions of the southwest, where in total deprivation they had been forced to create "a new concept of the world." During all that time, the fertile regions had been left untended. People were dying of hunger all over the country, and only one-fifth of the fields were actually being tended!
> What had happened to the peasant workforce that traditionally worked the land? Many such questions remained unanswered.
> The much-vaunted mobile brigades lived in very difficult conditions too. Meals were brought to them in the fields: bindweed in boiled water, with a few spoonfuls of rice, about half of what we used to eat in Phnom Penh. With rations like that it was impossible to make a real effort to produce anything . . .
> I stared hard. The spectacle was frightening: indescribable human misery, total disorganization, and appalling waste.
> As the car moved quickly on, an old man came toward us gesturing with his arms. At the roadside there lay a young woman, obviously ill. The driver just swerved around him, and the old man remained in the middle of the road, his arms raised to heaven.[111]

The economic project of the CPK caused intolerable tensions. These were made even worse by the high-handed incompetence of the cadres who were supposed to oversee the work. Irrigation was the cornerstone of the plan, and huge efforts were made to develop it, sacrificing the present for the future. But the poor planning and execution of the projects rendered the sacrifice largely futile. Although some dikes, canals, and dams were well planned and continue in use today, many were carried away by the first flood. On occasion hundreds of villagers and workers were drowned in the process. Other projects caused the water to flow in the wrong direction or created ponds that silted up in a matter of months. Hydraulic engineers in the workforce were powerless to stop such events. Any sort of criticism was viewed as an act of hostility toward the Angkar, which inevitably brought consequences that can be imagined all too easily. "To build dams, all you need is political education," the slaves were told.[112] For the illiterate peasants who were often in charge of operations, the solution was always more manpower, more man-hours, and more earth.

This rejection of technology and technicians was often accompanied by a rejection of the most elementary common sense. It was perhaps the sons of the soil who controlled operations on the ground, but their real masters were urban intellectuals who were in love with rationality and uniformity and convinced of their own omniscience. They ordered that all dikes dividing the rice fields be abolished so that all fields would measure exactly one hectare.[113] The agricultural calendar for the whole region was regulated from the Center, regardless of local ecological conditions.[114] Rice production was the only criterion of success. Some cadres decided that all trees, including fruit trees, should be cut down in the agricultural regions to destroy the habitat of a few small birds, thus destroying a vital source of food for the starving population.[115] While nature was steamrollered, the workforce was divided into absurdly specialized groups, with each age category— seven- to fourteen-year-olds, people of marriageable age, old people, and so forth—"mobilized" separately.[116] Special teams dedicated to one particular task became more and more common. The cadres, by contrast, remained distant figures, caught up in their own importance and power, seldom working alongside their teams, giving out unchallengeable orders.

The hunger that crushed so many Cambodians over the years was used deliberately by the regime in the service of its interests. The hungrier people were, the less food their bodies could store, and the less likely they were to run away. If people were permanently obsessed with food, all individual thought, all capacity to argue, even people's sex drive, would disappear. The games that were played with the food supply made forced evacuations easier, promoted acceptance of the collective canteens, and also weakened interpersonal relationships, including those between parents and their children. Everyone, by contrast, would kiss the hand that fed them, regardless of how bloody it was.[117]

It was a sad irony that a regime that wished to sacrifice everything to an almost mystical belief in rice (in the same way that Russia had a belief in the power of steel, and Cuba in sugar) managed to turn this once-plentiful product into something almost unobtainable. Since the 1920s Cambodia had regularly exported hundreds of thousands of tons of rice each year while feeding its own population frugally but adequately. After collective canteens became the norm in early 1976, the majority of Cambodians were reduced to a daily diet of thin rice soup, containing on average four teaspoons of rice per person.[118] Harvests varied from the miserable to the catastrophic. Daily rations fell constantly, to extraordinarily low levels. It has been calculated that before 1975, an adult in the Battambang region would have consumed on average 400 grams of rice per day, the minimum quantity required in a normal diet. Under the Khmer Rouge, a box of rice for one person was an almost unheard-of feast. Rations varied considerably, but it was not unusual for five, six, or even eight people to share a single box.[119]

For that reason the black market became essential to people's survival; there they could obtain rice, particularly from cadres who kept the rations of peasants whose deaths had not been reported. Foraging for food was officially prohibited on the ground that because the Angkar acted for the good of the people, the rations it provided should suffice. Nevertheless, foraging was tolerated, officially or unofficially, unless the food was considered to be stolen.[120] Nothing was safe from these starving people: not the communal goods such as the paddy fields before or during the harvest, not the tiny strips of land that people cultivated for themselves, or the chicken coops and domestic animals of the peasants, or even the crabs, frogs, snails, lizards, and snakes so common in the rice fields, or the red ants and large spiders that were eaten raw, or the shoots, mushrooms, and forest roots that, when badly chosen or undercooked, were the cause of many deaths. New depths were reached, even for a poor country. People would steal food from pigs and feast on rats that they caught in the fields.[121] Individual searching for food was always one of the main pretexts for punishment. Such punishments ranged from a simple warning to outright execution, if it was felt that the harvest was being threatened.[122]

Chronic undernourishment and malnutrition promoted the spread of diseases such as dysentery and made people sicker than they would have been otherwise. There were also diseases and complaints specific to hunger; the commonest of these was edema, which was brought on chiefly by the high salt content in people's daily soup. Edema led to a relatively peaceful death—people grew weaker until they fell into unconsciousness—an outcome that many, especially the old, came to see as desirable.[123]

This universe of death and decay—sometimes the sick and dying formed the majority of a community[124]—seemed to have no effect on the Khmer Rouge authorities. Anyone who fell ill was guilty of damaging the Angkar workforce.[125] Sick people were always suspected of malingering and were allowed to stop work only if they actually went to the hospital or the infirmary, where food rations were only half the normal size and the risk of epidemics was even higher. According to Henri Locard, "the purpose of the hospitals was more to eliminate the population than to cure to it."[126] Pin Yathay lost several members of his family within a few weeks in one hospital. There a group of fifteen young people suffering from chicken pox were kept at work with no medical attention and were obliged to sleep on the floor despite their sores. Only one survived.

The Destruction of All Values

Hunger dehumanizes, causing one person to turn on another and to forget everything except his own survival. How else can one explain cannibalism? It was perhaps less widespread than in China during the Great Leap Forward, and it seems to have been limited to the eating of people who were already dead. Pin Yathay reports two examples: a former teacher who ate her sister, and the inmates of a hospital ward who ate a young man. In both cases, punishment for the "ogres" (a particularly bloodthirsty spirit in the Khmer tradition) was death; the teacher was beaten to death in front of the assembled village and her own daughter.[127] As in China, cannibalism also existed as an act of revenge: Ly Heng tells of a Khmer Rouge deserter who was forced to eat his own ears before being killed.[128] There are also many stories about the eating of human livers. This act was not confined to the Khmer Rouge: republican soldiers ate the livers of their enemies during the 1970–1975 civil war. Similar traditions can be found all across Southeast Asia.[129] Haing Ngor describes how in one prison the fetus, liver, and breasts of a pregnant woman who had been executed were treated; the child was simply thrown away (others had already been hung from the ceiling to dry), and the rest was carried away with cries of "That's enough meat for tonight!" Ken Khun tells of a cook in a cooperative who prepared an eye remedy from human gall bladders (which he shared out quite liberally to his bosses) and who praised the tastiness of human liver.[131] These instances of cannibalism reflect the loss of all moral and cultural values, and particularly the disappearance of the central Buddhist value of compassion. Such was one of the paradoxes of the Khmer Rouge regime: it claimed that its intention was to create an egalitarian society in which justice, fraternity, and altruism would be the key values, yet like other Communist regimes it produced a tidal wave of selfishness, inequality, and irrationality. To survive, people were forced to cheat, lie, steal, and turn their hearts to stone.

The loss of all human compassion and decency had long been the norm at the highest level of power. After Pol Pot disappeared into the jungle in 1963 he did nothing to get back in touch with his family, even after 17 April 1975. His two brothers and his sister-in-law were deported along with everyone else.

One of them died very quickly. Only much later did the two survivors realize, thanks to an official portrait, who Pol Pot really was, and (probably quite rightly) they never let on that they even knew him.[132] The regime did all it could to break family ties, which it saw as a threat to the totalitarian project of making each individual totally dependent on the Angkar. Work teams had their own houses, which were often simply barracks or collections of hammocks or mats for sleeping located near the village. It was very difficult to get permission to leave these compounds, and husbands and wives were often separated for weeks or longer. Children were kept from their extended families, and adolescents sometimes went six months without seeing their parents. Mothers were encouraged to spend as little time as possible with their children. Because the postal service had stopped altogether, it was sometimes months before people learned of the death of a relative.[133] Here again the example came from above, as many of the leaders lived apart from their wives or husbands.[134]

The power of husbands over their wives and of parents over their children was shattered. Men could be executed for striking their wives, denounced by their children for hitting them, and forced to make a humiliating public confession before the assembled village for any insult or injury. This policy can be seen as an attempt by the state to ensure that it had a monopoly on violence, and to destroy any relationship of authority in which it was not directly involved. Kinship bonds were given the lowest possible priority: people were separated, often permanently, simply because they had been unable to board the same truck, or because the two handcarts they were pulling were ordered to go in separate directions at a crossroads. The cadres cared little for old people or children who found themselves alone: "Don't worry: the Angkar will take care of them. Have you no faith in the Angkar?" was the typical response received by those who begged for clemency and reunion with their loved ones.[135]

The switch from cremation of the dead to simple burial (there were exceptions to the rule, but people had to fight extremely hard for such exceptions, and these depended on the humanity of the cadres) was yet another assault on traditional family values. For a Khmer, to leave a loved one in the cold and the mud without going through the traditional rites was to show an atrocious lack of respect, to compromise the possibility of reincarnation, and perhaps even to condemn the loved one to existence only as a ghost. By contrast, possessing a few ashes was valued extremely highly, particularly because evacuation was so common. This was one of the main battlegrounds in the systematic attack on traditional Buddhist or pre-Buddhist values in Cambodia, and no more respect was paid to the "primitive" ceremonies specific to the Khmer Loeu than to the old traditions that had come down from the Angkor empire, regardless of whether these were popular traditions such as courtship rituals and jokes, or high art such as courtly dances, temple painting, and sculpture. The 1976 plan, doubtless in imitation of the Chinese Cultural Revolution, allowed for no forms of expression other than revolutionary songs and poems.[136]

This denial of all status to the dead was the natural consequence of the denial of the humanity of the living. "I am not a human being, I am an animal," one can read at the end of the confession by the former leader and minister Hu Nim.[137] The implication was that a human life quite literally had no more value than that of a beast. People were killed for losing cattle and tortured to death for having struck a cow.[138] Men were tied to plows and whipped mercilessly to be shown unworthy of the cow they were supposed to be looking after.[139] Human life was worthless. "You have individualist tendencies . . . You must . . . shed these illusions," Pin Yathay was told by one Khmer Rouge soldier when he attempted to keep his wounded son by his side. Several days after his son's death, Pin Yathay had to beg for permission from the authorities to go and see his body. He was made to swear that even though he was ill this visit would not waste his energy, which belonged to the Angkar. Neither did he have the right to visit his sick wife in the hospital; he was simply told that "the Angkar is looking after her." When he came to the assistance of a neighbor with two children who was seriously ill, he was told by a Khmer Rouge soldier: "You don't have a duty to help these people. On the contrary, that proves you still have pity and feelings of friendship. You must renounce such sentiments and wipe all such individualism from your mind. Go home."[140]

This systematic denial of the humanity of the country's citizens did occasionally backfire on the leaders. It meant that their victims no longer had any scruples about lying, shirking, or stealing whenever the guards or informers turned their backs. It was a question of life and death, given how small the rations supplied by the Angkar were. Everyone, from children to old men, stole. But the term "stealing" came to have little meaning, since absolutely everything belonged to the state, and even picking a little wild fruit constituted a theft. Everyone was caught in the trap. Those who didn't cheat and steal, died. This lesson has had serious consequences in contemporary Cambodia, creating a cynical and selfish generation and seriously compromising the country's chances of development.

The Triumph of Brutality

There was another strange contradiction inherent in the regime: whereas in theory the lives and thoughts of the people were supposed to be absolutely transparent and public, almost nothing was known about the people in power. Uniquely in the history of Communism, the existence of the Communist Party

of Kampuchea was kept hidden for thirty months after the regime came
to power; it was officially declared only on 27 September 1977. The personality
of Pol Pot himself was also a closely guarded secret. He appeared in public
for the first time during the "elections" of March 1976, described as "a worker
from the Hevea plantations." In fact he had never worked there, any more
than he had on his parents' farm, as was claimed in an official biography
circulated during a visit to North Korea in October 1977. Western secret
services were the first to realize that Pol Pot and Saloth Sar, the militant
Communist who had fled Phnom Penh in 1963 and who, according to certain
CPK cadres, had died in the jungle, were one and the same person. Pol Pot's
desire to remain in the shadows, the better to exercise his omnipotence, was
such that there were never any official portraits, official statues, or even an
official biography. His photograph appeared only rarely, and there was never
an official collection of his thoughts for publication. No trace of a personality
cult ever existed, and it was only after January 1979 that many Cambodians
finally learned who their prime minister had been over the preceding years.[141]
Pol Pot and the Angkar were one and the same. Everything happened as
though he were the supreme anonymous deity of the organization, at once
absent and present in every village, inspiring everyone who held the smallest
position of authority. Ignorance is the mother of terror, and no one ever felt
secure.

The slaves of the system had no control over their own lives. Each moment
was carefully planned and was part of a timetable that never gave a moment's
respite, in which food was all-important and self-criticism meetings were crucial, since the tiniest error could bring about one's downfall. Each person's past
was also carefully monitored.[142] The slightest doubt about the veracity of one's
statements was followed by arrest and torture, through which the authorities
sought to extract a declaration about whatever the person might be hiding.
Everyone ran the risk of a denunciation following a chance encounter with an
old friend, colleague, or student; the future was always hanging by a thread,
dependent on the whim of those who pulled the strings. Nothing escaped the
vigilant eyes of the authorities, who according to one slogan had "as many eyes
as a pineapple." Everything was taken to have a political meaning, and the
smallest infringement of the regulations became an act of opposition and a
"counterrevolutionary crime." Even an involuntary slip brought disaster: in the
paranoid logic of the Khmer Rouge, accidents never happened, and one could
never blame chance or clumsiness; there was only treachery. Breaking a glass,
failing to control an ox, or plowing a crooked furrow was enough for people to
be brought before the court, which consisted of members of the cooperative,
often including friends and relatives. Someone would always be present to make
an accusation. People were forbidden to speak about the dead, who were either

traitors who had been rightly punished or cowards who had robbed the Angkar of the manpower it needed. Even words like "death" became taboo, leading people to use circumlocutions and euphemisms such as *bat kluon*, "a body that has disappeared."

Legal procedures were entirely absent. There were never any real trials, and no police force worthy of the name existed. The army took over this role, for which it was extremely badly prepared. The inefficiency of the repressive machinery accounts for the relative ease of smuggling and stealing and of talking freely in private. It also goes some way toward explaining the widespread use of children and young adolescents as police auxiliaries. A number of them, integrated into the Khmer Rouge and known as *chhlop*, were basically spies, hiding under houses to listen in on private conversations and to hunt out forbidden stores of food. Others, often the youngest members, would be given the task of tracking the political views of their parents and relatives to denounce them "for their own good" if they ever showed evidence of deviant thoughts. For most Cambodians, anything that was not explicitly allowed was forbidden or could be considered as such. Because prison, in practice, was a waiting room for imminent death, minor crimes that were not repeated, and that were immediately admitted and followed with a sufficiently humble, spontaneous act of self-criticism, were either pardoned, punished with a job change (for instance, as in China, being sent to work in a pigsty), or disciplined by a beating administered in full view of the assembled village. There were many such crimes. Families were forced to accept that they would not meet for months on end even though their work teams might be only a few kilometers apart. Little mistakes were common at work, since workers seldom had experience in performing the tasks to which they had been assigned, and tools were usually insufficient or old and worn. Few people could resist the temptation to hoard a little food, when "hoarding" could mean simply hiding a banana.

Any of these "crimes" could bring imprisonment or death.[143] Everyone committed such crimes; hence the most common received milder sanctions. But everything was relative: whipping was a minor punishment for the young, but for adults it sometimes resulted in death. Although the torturers were often Khmer Rouge military personnel, it was most common to be beaten by one's work colleagues, "'75s," who would compete to be the most zealous in the execution of the punishment, while knowing very well that they could be next. As always, the key was to appear to be totally submissive. Any complaint or protest would be interpreted as opposition to the punishment and hence to the regime. The aim was to punish, but also to terrorize; hence there were also occasional mock executions.[144]

Murder as a Means of Government

"All we need to build our country is a million good revolutionaries. No more than that. And we would rather kill ten friends than allow one enemy to live." Such statements by the Khmer Rouge were commonplace at cooperative meetings,[145] and indeed they put this genocidal logic into practice. Under Pol Pot, death by violent means was far more common than death through disease or old age. What is known elsewhere as "the supreme punishment" became banal here because of its frequency and because of the trivial reasons for which it was invoked. By a strange inversion, in the cases considered most serious people received only prison sentences, even though in practice that merely meant a stay of execution, for it was in prison that they were expected to confess the details of their plot and the names of their accomplices. Although the reality of the prison system was carefully hidden—and this was a mystery that made it more frightening still—some deportees had a reasonable idea of how the system worked: "Perhaps, I thought, there were two parallel systems of punishment: first, a prison system that was part of a bureaucracy that needed to be fed to justify its existence; and second, an informal system that gave the leader of the cooperative freedom to hand out punishments, although the effect of each on the prisoner was ultimately the same."[146] This description is backed up by Henri Locard.[147] There was also a third way of putting people to death, which was very common in the last year of the regime: the military purge, similar in form to the events in the Vendée in France in 1793–1795. Teams of disgraced local cadres, whole villages of "suspects," and even entire populations of areas as large as the eastern zone were slaughtered en masse by government troops. In these cases no charges were ever brought, no one was allowed to defend himself, and the news of people's deaths was never passed on to relatives or colleagues: "The Angkar kills but never explains." So went one of the new proverbs that appeared during these years.[148]

It is difficult to draw up a list of specific crimes that were punishable by death. The problem is not that information is lacking, but that it is extremely hard to find any crime that was clearly not punishable by capital punishment; Khmer Rouge cadres were encouraged to interpret all deviant actions in the most paranoid manner. What follows, then, is just a recapitulation of the main reasons for which the death sentence was invoked, beginning with the most common. Theft of food was without doubt at the top of the list. Given the importance of rice in the local diet and the mystical significance that it had for the regime, the death sentence was widely applied to anyone caught pilfering in the fields or foraging supplies from kitchens or storage areas. People out marauding were often beaten to death on the spot with pick-ax handles, then left to rot where they died, to serve as an example.[149] People who stole vegetables or fruit had a greater chance of escaping with just a beating. But there were exceptions: Khun relates an instance of the theft of a few bananas by a woman who was nursing a starving child, and who was killed as a result.[150] In another instance, a group of adolescents who had stolen some fruit from an orchard were judged by their comrades (who had no option but to cooperate), condemned to death, and immediately shot in the back of the head. "We were shaking. They said it should serve as a lesson to us." It was rarer for animals to be killed in secret; poultry and pets quickly disappeared or were watched very closely, and it was extremely difficult to dispose of a large carcass in secret because of the cramped living conditions. But in some cases whole families were killed for having shared out a cow.[151]

Secret visits, even short ones, to family members were treated as desertions and were thus extremely dangerous. If one repeated the offense, one's life was clearly at risk, since one had thereby committed the cardinal crime of missing work. Being overly close to one's family was also frowned upon, as was arguing with them, or with anyone else for that matter, and one could pay for such crime with one's life (though in this case, too, death was rarely meted out for a first offense). The atmosphere was extremely puritan; men and women talking to each other were expected to stand at least three meters apart unless they were close relatives. Any sexual relations outside marriage were systematically punished with death. Life was extremely difficult for young lovers, as it was for lascivious cadres, many of whom were punished for crimes of the flesh.[152] The consumption of alcoholic beverages, which generally consisted of fermented palm juice, was another capital crime.[153] However, usually only cadres and peasants were convicted of these offenses; New People had a hard enough time just finding enough to eat. Religious practices were frowned upon but were more or less tolerated, provided they were carried out discreetly and on an individual basis (something that is possible in Buddhism but extremely difficult in Islam). Any trance ceremonies, however, were punishable by death.[154] Insubordination meant immediate death. The few who in the early days took advantage of the supposed freedom of speech that they were given at meetings to criticize the insufficiency of the food they were given or the poor quality of the clothes they were expected to wear "disappeared" very quickly, as did one courageous group of teachers who, in November 1975, organized a demonstration against the tiny food rations. Although their protest was not actually stopped, all were deported soon afterward.[155] Defeatist remarks, calling for the end of the regime or victory by the Vietnamese—which many Cambodians desired by 1978—or even admitting that one was hungry could have fatal consequences. The task of the *chhlop* was to record, and even trap people into making, such incriminating remarks.

Failure to complete the task one was assigned, for whatever reason, was an extremely serious matter. No one was safe from accidents, mishaps, or minor errors, but all of these were potentially fatal, and it was mainly on grounds of failure that many handicapped and mentally ill people were killed. Anyone who failed to carry out his or her task was a saboteur, and even more useless than the mass of New People. Anyone from the republican army who had been wounded in the war or had lost a limb also disappeared. Especially at risk were people who were unable to understand or carry out the instructions they were given. A madman picking a manioc shoot (a root crop) or expressing his discontent even in incoherent terms would usually be shot.[156] The Khmer Communists were in effect practicing a de facto eugenics program.

The general level of violence in Democratic Kampuchea was staggering. But for the majority of Cambodians, what was most terrifying was the mysterious and seemingly random nature of the disappearances, rather than the spectacle of death. Death was usually discreet and hidden away. In that respect, it accorded with the approach almost invariably taken by soldiers and CPK cadres: "Their words were quite cordial and polite, even at the worst of times. They could often go as far as murder without abandoning that tone. They administered death with kind words . . . They could promise anything that we wanted to hear to lull us into a false sense of security. But I knew that their soft words followed or preceded terrible crimes. The Khmer Rouge were polite in every possible case, even while they were slaughtering us like cattle."[157] The first explanation for this behavior is inevitably a tactical one, as Yathay suggests, to ensure that they always had surprise on their side and to discourage revolts. A cultural explanation can also be made, based on the high prestige of self-discipline in Buddhism, and the accompanying loss of face for anyone who gives in to emotion. Finally, there is the political explanation. As in the heyday of Chinese Communism before the Cultural Revolution, lack of emotion served to display the implacable rationality of the Party, in which nothing was ever a matter of chance or the result of a momentary whim. The Party was shown to be all-powerful under all circumstances. This discretion in executions might be considered evidence that they were coordinated from the Center. Primitive and spontaneous violence such as that of the pogroms had no qualms in showing itself for what it really was. One afternoon, or one night, the soldiers simply turned up and took you away for interrogation, study, or woodcutting detail. Your arms were tied behind your back, and that was it. Sometimes they would find your body later, left unburied in the woods, to instill fear in others; but just as frequently the bodies were unidentifiable. In each of the provinces that have been investigated, more than 1,000 burial grounds have been found; and there are twenty provinces.[158] On occasion the Khmer Rouge really did put into practice their constantly repeated threat to use human bodies as fertilizer for the rice fields.[159] "Men and women were often killed to make fertilizer. They were buried in the mass graves located near the crop fields, particularly where manioc was being grown. Often when you pulled out the manioc roots you would pull up a human bone that the roots had grown down into."[160] It was almost as though the country's leaders were convinced that there was no better fertilizer for crops than human remains;[161] but what can also be discerned here is the logical endpoint, together with the cannibalism practiced by the cadres, of the denial of the humanity of anyone judged to be a class enemy.

The extreme savagery of the system would reappear at the moment of execution. To save bullets, and also to satisfy the sadistic instincts of the executioners, shooting was not the most common means of execution.[162] According to Sliwinski's research, only 29 percent of victims died that way.[163] Some 53 percent of victims died from blows to the head, inflicted with iron bars, pick-ax handles, or agricultural implements; 6 percent were hanged or asphyxiated with plastic bags; and 5 percent had their throats slit. All witness statements agree that only 2 percent of all executions took place in public. Most of these were intended to set an example, and involved cadres who had fallen from favor. They were usually killed by particularly barbaric means that in one way or another involved fire. Often these disgraced cadres were buried up to their chest in a ditch filled with firebrands, or their heads were doused with gasoline and set alight.[164]

The Prison Archipelago

In principle, Democratic Kampuchea had no prisons. According to Pol Pot, speaking in August 1978, "We don't have prisons, and we don't even use the word 'prison.' Bad elements in our society are simply given productive tasks to do."[165] The Khmer Rouge were extremely proud of this, emphasizing the double rupture with the political past and religious tradition, whereby punishment was deferred and detention supplanted by Buddhist *karma*, in which sins are paid for only in the next life. Under the Khmer Rouge, punishments were to be carried out immediately.[166] There were, however, "reeducation centers" *(munty operum)*, sometimes called "district police headquarters." The old colonial prisons were deserted just like all the other buildings in the towns, and were reoccupied only in a few small provincial towns, where as many as thirty detainees would be crammed into a cell designed for two or three. The buildings that served as prisons under the new regime were often old school buildings, which were now useless, or temples.[167]

There is no doubt that these were quite different from traditional prisons, even from prisons with an extremely harsh regime. The least one can say is that nothing was done to make the life of the prisoners any easier, or even to help them survive. Food rations were minuscule—sometimes a single box of rice for forty prisoners.[168] There were no medical facilities, and overcrowding was endemic. Prisoners were constantly kept in chains: one ankle for women and the lighter categories of male prisoner, two for normal male prisoners, sometimes with elbows tied behind the back as well, and all chains tied to an iron bar fixed to the floor *(khnoh)*. There were no toilets and no possibility of washing. Average life expectancy under these conditions was three months; very few people survived.[169] One of the rare exceptions described his luck in prison in the western zone: "They killed only about half of the prisoners or fewer."[170] He was lucky enough to have been locked up in late 1975, when freeing prisoners was still conceivable, as it was until 17 April. Until 1976, between 20 percent and 30 percent of prisoners were set free, perhaps because at that time people still took quite seriously the idea of reeducation through exhausting physical work, which was central to the Sino-Vietnamese prison system. Officials and even soldiers from the old regime had a real chance of escaping alive provided they behaved themselves and worked hard. This was still true even during the early days of the evacuation.[171] Thereafter the old terminology was preserved but emptied of all meaning. Imprisonment was often described as an invitation to a "study session," the Khmer term being borrowed from the Chinese *xuexi*. The disappearance of all pedagogical intention (with the possible exception of the Bung Tra Beck camp, for Cambodians who returned from abroad, most of whom were students, as described by Y Phandara) is tacitly acknowledged in a note from one local headquarters stipulating that all children should not be locked up with their mothers, regardless of their age, "to get rid of them all at a stroke."[172] This was the implementation of the slogan "When you pull up a weed, you have to dig up the roots too," which was a radical formulation of the notion of "class heredity" among Maoist extremists.[173] The fate of these children, left alone, not tied up but with no one to look after them, was particularly poignant. Worse still was that of the young delinquents, for whom there was no minimum age limit for confinement. According to one former official,

> What moved us most was the fate of twenty young children, most of whom belonged to people who had been evacuated after 17 April 1975. These children stole because they were too hungry. They had been arrested not so that they could be punished, but so that they could be put to death in an extremely savage manner:
>
> · Prison guards hit them or kicked them to death.
> · They made living toys out of them, tying up their feet, hanging them from the roof, swinging them, then steadying them with kicks.
> · Near the prison there was a pond; the executioners threw the

children into it and held them down by their feet, and when they started to thrash about they would let their heads up, and then start the process all over again.

We, the other prisoners and myself, cried in secret about the fate of these children, who were leaving this world in such an atrocious manner. There were eight executioners and guards. Bun, the chief, and Lan (these are the only two names I remember) were the worst, but they all took part, competing to see who could make their compatriots suffer most cruelly.[174]

The main division between the inmates was between those who had been condemned to die slowly and those who were to be executed immediately. That depended above all on the reason for which they had been locked up: whether they had broken a law, had impure social origins, had openly shown dissatisfaction with the regime, or had taken part in some sort of conspiracy. In the last three cases, people were generally interrogated so that they would either admit to previous employment in one of the proscribed categories or confess their guilt and name their accomplices. If they put up any hint of resistance, torture was used, and it was more widespread than in any other Communist regime. The Khmer Rouge were particularly morbid and sadistically inventive in this area.[175] One of the most common methods was partial asphyxiation by use of a plastic bag. Many prisoners, already quite weak, failed to survive these torture sessions; women above all suffered terribly. The executioner's excuse was that the worst tortures brought the best results. One report stated that the prisoner "was first questioned politely, without any violence at all. It was thus impossible to know whether he was telling the truth or not." In the worst cases, when admissions were particularly promising in regard to future convictions, detainees were moved up to the next circle in the prison hell. One could thus go from the local jail to the district facility, then to the main zone prison, and end up in the central prison at Tuol Sleng. Regardless of the level attained, the outcome was usually the same. Once the prisoner had no more information to convey, having been pressed to the end by his torturers (and this could take weeks or even months), he was simply executed. This was often done with a knife or, as in Tramkak, with an iron bar. Loudspeakers would blare out revolutionary music to disguise the death throes of prisoners who died in such fashion.

One could also be imprisoned for some of the same offenses that could lead to trouble or death in the cooperative, especially if these offenses were of larger dimensions. The prisons housed many thieves who had organized large-scale operations, often with accomplices. But there were also many people who had had sexual relations outside marriage, and many more who had made "subversive" remarks: complaints about inadequate food or about Cambodia's submission to China, statements about being fed up with an agricultural context presented as a form of military operation, jokes about the hymn to the revolution, the spreading of rumors about anti-Communist guerrillas, or references to Buddhist predictions about an atheist topsy-turvy world that was destined to be destroyed. One woman (who was a "'70'") was imprisoned for having broken a spoon in a canteen after becoming enraged that, having already lost four children to the famine, she was still not granted permission to stay with her last one, who was dying in hospital.

In 1996 Kassie Neou, the director of the Cambodian Institute for Human Rights, reported:

> For the crime of speaking English, I was arrested by the Khmer Rouge and dragged with a rope around my neck, hobbling and swaying, to the Kach Roteh prison, near Battambang. This was only the beginning. I was chained up with the other prisoners in irons that cut into my skin. I still have the scars on my ankles. I was tortured repeatedly for months. My only respite came when I passed out.
>
> Every night the guards would come into the cell and call out the names of one, two, or three prisoners. They would be led away, and we would never see them again. They were assassinated on orders from the Khmer Rouge. As far as I know, I'm one of a very small number of prisoners to have survived from Kach Roteh, which was really a torture and extermination camp. I survived only because I'm good at telling Aesop's fables and the classic animal stories from Khmer mythology, and I could thus entertain the adolescents and children who were our guards.[176]

As well as these political cases, there were a good number of social cases: people who had lied about their previous profession or concealed compromising episodes in their past history such as a lengthy stay abroad in the West. There were also a significant number of peasants in the prisons (although they were very much in the minority), and even soldiers and Khmer Rouge officials. In the Tramkak prison these accounted for 10 percent of all prisoners, or 46 out of 477. They had shown signs of laziness or had "deserted," which in most cases meant having tried to visit their loved ones. Middle- or higher-ranking cadres were generally sent directly to a central prison such as Tuol Sleng.

To visit this old school building, which in the CPK era was known in code simply as S-21, is to feel that one is plumbing the depths of horror. And yet this is just one detention center among hundreds of others, and although it claimed 20,000 victims, this was not an extraordinarily high number. Living conditions were appalling, but were equally bad elsewhere. Only 2 percent of all the people who died and perhaps 5 percent of all prisoners came through

Tuol Sleng; thus there is no comparison with the central role of an Auschwitz in the Nazi concentration-camp system. Nor was there a specific mode of torture, other than the widespread use of electricity. Its only specific features were that it was in a sense the "Central Committee" prison to which disgraced cadres and fallen leaders were sent, and that it was a particularly powerful "black hole" from which there was almost no chance of emerging alive; only six or seven detainees survived. It is also unique in that it kept a complete list of all inmates admitted to the prison between 1975 and mid-1978 (14,000 names), as well as a huge archive of confessions and interrogation reports, including some concerning high-ranking figures in the regime.[177]

Around four-fifths of the prisoners were themselves Khmer Rouge members. Others were workers and technicians, many of Chinese origin, who had been sent there in 1978. There were also a few foreigners (mostly sailors) who had been unlucky enough to fall into the hands of the regime.[178] At any given time there were between 1,000 and 1,500 detainees, but the turnover was truly massive; the constantly growing entrance figures are about equivalent to the annual number of victims. In 1975 there were barely 200, by 1976 there were 2,250, more than 6,330 in 1977, and 5,765 for the first quarter of 1978 alone. Interrogators faced a dilemma: according to one notebook, "torture is considered absolutely necessary"; but the problem was that prisoners died too quickly, before having confessed enough, which was a sort of defeat for the Party. Hence there was a minimal amount of medical care available in the one place where all the prisoners were certain to die.[179] Some detainees were easier cases than others; the wives and children of prisoners (who often had been executed already) were disposed of swiftly at prearranged times. Thus on 1 July 1977, 114 women (90 of whom were the wives of prisoners) were hanged; the next day, 31 boys and 43 girls were killed, all of them the children of prisoners. Fifteen had been moved there from a special children's home. Soon after the proclamation of the CPK's existence the daily number of executions reached its peak; on 15 October 1977, 418 were killed.[180] It is estimated that 1,200 children died at S-21.[181]

Reasons for the Madness

As with the other mass crimes of the century, there is a temptation to seek an ultimate explanation in the madness of one man or in the dazed enthrallment of an entire people. But although there is no way to minimize the responsibility of Pol Pot, neither should the national history of Cambodia, the impact of the international Communist movement, and the influence of other countries (principally of course China) be ignored. The Khmer Rouge dictatorship, though anchored in a specific geographic and temporal context, can be seen as a distillation of the worst possible factors from each of these categories.

A Khmer Exception?

"The Khmer revolution has no predecessors. What we are trying to bring about has never been accomplished at any time in history." As soon as the Khmer Rouge freed themselves from their Vietnamese protectors, they were at pains to underscore the unique nature of their experiment. Their official statements hardly ever made reference to the outside world, except in extremely negative ways; and they hardly ever quoted the founding fathers of Marxism-Leninism or even Mao Zedong. To a large extent, their brand of nationalism had the same stamp as that of their predecessors Sihanouk and Lon Nol—the same mixture of self-pity and delusions of grandeur. Kampuchea, in this depiction, was a victim, constantly oppressed by untrustworthy, cruel neighbors who were determined to destroy the country to ensure their own survival. Vietnam was first among these oppressors. At the same time the country was portrayed as a sort of arcadia, beloved of the gods, with an impressive history and a population like no other, whose mission it was to lead the way into a new order for the entire planet.[182] Their triumphalism sometimes knew no bounds: "We are making a unique revolution. Is there any other country that would dare abolish money and markets the way we have? We are much better than the Chinese, who look up to us. They are trying to imitate us, but they haven't managed it yet. We are a good model for the whole world"—so went one speech by an intellectual cadre who had been abroad.[183] Even after Pol Pot was ousted, he continued to believe that 17 April 1975 was the greatest date in the history of all revolutions, "with the exception of the Paris Commune in 1871."[184]

The sad reality was that Cambodia was a provincial country that had looked inward for too long, where (thanks to the French protectorate) some curious conservative traditions remained in place, where several clans who were constantly fighting for control invariably accepted any foreign offers of intervention in their favor, and where the question of economic development had never really been posed seriously. There was little business or industry, a tiny middle class, few technicians, and a massive dependence on subsistence agriculture. The country was the "sick man" par excellence of Southeast Asia.[185] The extent to which the country was out of step with reality undoubtedly encouraged extreme solutions. The deadly combination of an almost paranoid mistrust of its neighbors and a megalomaniacal exaggeration of its own capacities magnified its isolation and autarkic approach, while the weakness of the economy, combined with the poverty of most inhabitants, increased the appeal of those who appeared to be the new heralds of progress. Cambodia was thus a weak link, both economically and politically. The international context, and above all the war in Vietnam, did the rest. The savagery of the Khmer Rouge owes its origins in part to the contradiction between the huge ambitions of its leaders and the tremendous obstacles they faced.

Some scholars also believe that a number of characteristics peculiar to the Cambodian nation played a part in facilitating the murderous actions of the Khmer Rouge. Buddhism, for example, played an ambiguous role: its indifference to social contrasts and to the present in general, together with the idea that retribution will come only in a future incarnation, abetted the implementation of the revolutionary ideal. Its anti-individualism was also answered in a bizarre fashion by the Khmer Rouge's suppression of the individual personality. The idea that one particular existence is of limited value in the great wheel of reincarnations led to fatalism in the face of what was perceived as inevitable destiny and thus diminished resistance among Buddhists to the events surrounding them.[186]

When Haing Ngor (who had told his captors that his name was Samnang) emerged from prison, sick and suffering, one old woman voiced to him what was in fact the opinion of many:

> "Samnang," she said, "maybe you did something bad in a previous life. Perhaps you are being punished for it today."
> "Yes," I said. "I think my *kama* is not so good!"[187]

Although Buddhists suffered violent repression, their religion did not inspire any resistance comparable to that inspired by the Islam of the Cham.

Contemporary events often cause us to reconsider the past—not to alter the facts, in the manner of the North Koreans, but to change priorities and to reinterpret events. For a long time Cambodia was seen as the peaceful country of Sihanouk, an island of neutrality during the wars in Indochina, typified by the "Khmer smile" of Apsara goddesses on the Angkor reliefs and by the happy faces of an urbane monarch and his peaceful peasant people who contentedly tended their rice crops and palm canes. But the events of the last three decades have brought out the darker side of the Khmer past. Angkor is one of the marvels of the world, but most of its miles of low-relief sculptures represent warlike scenes.[188] And such huge constructions, with even bigger water reservoirs *(baray)*, would have required massive deportations and enslavements.

There are very few written records about the Angkor period, which lasted from the eighth to the fourteenth century; but all the other Hindu and Buddhist monarchies of the Southeast Asian peninsula (in Thailand, Laos, and Burma) were constituted along the same lines. Their rather violent history resembles that of Cambodia: throughout the region repudiated concubines were trampled to death by elephants, new dynasties began with the massacre of the previous monarch's family, and conquered populations were deported to desert zones. Absolute power was the norm in all these societies, and disobedience was tantamount to sacrilege. The more enlightened despots did not abuse their power, but administrative structures were invariably extremely weak and fragile, and the situation was often volatile as a result. Everywhere the populations seemed to have a tremendous capacity simply to accept things; unlike in China, revolts against monarchic power were rare. Instead, people tended to flee to other states, which were never far away, or simply to more remote regions.[189]

Sihanouk's reign (from 1941, although the French protectorate lasted until 1953) appears almost idyllic in comparison to the events that followed his dethroning in March 1970. But he himself never hesitated to resort to violence, particularly against his leftist opponents. There is a good deal of evidence that in 1959 and 1960, when he was concerned with the growth in popularity of the Communist left—which was highly critical of corruption within the regime— he had the editor of the newspaper *Prasheashun* (The people) assassinated, and had Khieu Samphan, the editor of the best-selling paper in the country, the biweekly French language paper *L'observateur*, beaten up in the street. In August 1960 eighteen people were thrown into prison, and all the main left-wing papers were banned. In 1962, in conditions that are still unclear today, Tou Samouth, the secretary general of the underground Communist Party of Kampuchea, was assassinated, most likely by the secret police, an event that facilitated Saloth Sar's ascension to the top of the hierarchy. In 1967 the Samlauth revolt and the influence of the Cultural Revolution in some Chinese schools brought the worst episodes of repression of Sihanouk's reign, leading to numerous deaths, including those of the last Communists who were still out in the open. One side effect of this was that about 100 intellectuals who were sympathetic to the leftist cause then enlisted in the Khmer Rouge resistance movement.[190] In Henri Locard's view "Polpotist violence grew out of the brutality of the repression of the Sihanoukists."[191] From a strictly chronological point of view, he is undoubtedly correct. Both the regal autocrat and the marshal silenced anyone who was remotely critical of their inept regimes. In so doing, they left the CPK as the only opposition with any credibility. But it is harder to agree with Locard from the point of view of genealogy: the ideological foundations and the political ends of the Khmer Rouge were never a reaction to Sihanouk, but were instead part of the great tradition of Leninism found in the successive figures of Stalin, Mao Zedong, and Ho Chi Minh. Cambodia's calamitous evolution after independence and its participation in the war facilitated the seizure of power by CPK extremists and lent some legitimacy to their unparalleled recourse to violence, but the radicalism itself cannot be explained away by external circumstances.

1975: A Radical Break

It was much easier for the revolution in Cambodia to define what it opposed than actually to announce a positive program. For the most part, the Khmer Rouge sought revenge, and it was through this intention that they found most of their popular support, which then gained new impetus through radical collectivization. The revolution was also the revenge of the countryside against the towns. In no time at all the peasants had taken everything from the New People, either through the black market or by quite simply going through their baggage.[192] In the villages, the poorest peasants took revenge on the local "capitalists," who were identified as anyone who had anything to sell or who employed someone. But revenge was often personal, too, as old professional and familial hierarchies were overturned. Eyewitness statements often emphasize the surprising promotion of previously marginal characters, such as alcoholics, to new positions of authority in the villages: "Often these people were rehabilitated by the Angkar and given positions of authority because they could kill their compatriots without showing any scruples or remorse."[193] Haing Ngor saw in this action the political sanctification of what he considered to be the lowest part of the Khmer soul, known as *kum*, a murderous thirst for revenge that time is powerless to assuage. Many suffered as a result: Ngor's aunt, for instance, stayed behind in her native village, lost without the help of her parents in the city. Ngor also met a nurse who had been promoted to the position of doctor and who tried to have him killed even though he was a newcomer. The nurse was then promoted to the position of ward leader, radically overturning the hierarchy he had helped support.[194] What exploded in Cambodian society was thus a complex of tensions, only some of which could be termed social in the strictest sense of the word.

Values were turned on their heads. Jobs that had been extremely low status, such as chef or canteen cleaner, became the most sought after, as they offered ready opportunities to steal food on the job. Degrees and qualifications became useless bits of paper and a real liability if one ever attempted to use them. Humility became the cardinal virtue: among cadres who came back to the countryside, "strangely enough, the job they wanted most was toilet cleaner . . . getting over one's repugnance for such things was proof of ideological transformation."[195] The Angkar wanted a monopoly on familial relations, and sought to be addressed by people in public as "mother-father." This typical feature of Asiatic Communism caused considerable confusion between the Party-state and the adult population. The whole of the post-1975 revolutionary period was known as *samay pouk-me,* "the era of fathers and mothers," and military chiefs were known as "grandfathers."[196] Hatred and fear of the cities were extreme: as a cosmopolitan city centered around consumerism and pleasure, Phnom Penh was known to the Khmer Rouge as "the great prostitute on the Mekong."[197] One of the reasons put forward for the evacuation of the capital was that "a secret political military plan by the American CIA and the Lon Nol regime" was aimed in particular at "corrupting our soldiers and softening their combat spirit with women, alcohol, and money" after the "liberation."[198]

Even more than the Chinese revolutionaries, Cambodians took seriously Mao's famous adage: "It is on a blank page that the most beautiful poems are written."[199] The aim was to get rid of everything that would not normally be found in the house of a poor peasant. Cambodians returning to the country had to get rid of almost all their baggage, including their books. Anything in "imperialist writing"—that is, French or English—as well as anything in Khmer ("relics of feudal culture") was destined for destruction; Haing Ngor was told by ten-year-old Khmer Rouge soldiers: "No more capitalistic books now! Capitalistic books are Lon Nol style, and Lon Nol betrayed the country! Why do you have foreign books? Are you CIA? No more foreign books under the Angkar."[200] It was a good idea to burn any certificates and even photo albums along with one's identity papers, since revolution meant beginning from zero.[201] Quite logically, it was people with no past who were most favored: "Only the newborn baby is spotless," said one slogan.[202] Education was reduced to a bare minimum: either there was no school at all, or there were a few classes for reading, writing, and revolutionary songs for children aged five to nine, lasting no more than an hour a day and taught by teachers who themselves were often barely literate. Practical knowledge was all-important. In contrast to useless bookish culture, "our children in the rural zones have always had very useful knowledge. They know a calm cow from a nervous one. They can stand both ways on a buffalo. They are the masters of the herd. They are practically masters of nature too. They know all the different varieties of rice like the back of their hands . . . they know and they really understand . . . the sort of things that correspond to the realities facing the nation today."[203]

In Pol Pot's day it really was the children who were in charge. All witnesses agree that the majority of soldiers were extraordinarily young. They were signed up when they were twelve years old or less. Sihanouk had pre-adolescents among his guards, who often amused themselves by torturing cats.[204] Ly Heng remembers the last recruitment campaign immediately before the arrival of the Vietnamese, which was extended to include the New People and was aimed at boys and girls from thirteen to eighteen. Because there were by then so few volunteers, the mobile brigades of young people were forced to move from work into the army.[205] New recruits immediately lost touch with their family and usually also with their village. Living in camps and relatively isolated from a population that feared them, yet well treated by the government, they knew that they were all-powerful and much less at the mercy of purges than the cadres. Beyond the revolutionary verbiage, the motivation of many, sometimes on their own admission, was that they "didn't have to work and could kill people."[206] Those under fifteen were the most feared: "They were taken very young, and the only thing they were taught was discipline. They learned to obey orders, without asking for any justification. They didn't have any belief in religion or in tradition, only in the orders of the Khmer Rouge. That's why they killed their own people, including babies, the way you kill a mosquito."[207]

Until 1978, only "'70s" were allowed to be soldiers. The children of "'75s," on the other hand, were often enlisted at the age of eight or nine as spies; but the regime inspired so little faith that a tacit sort of complicity was often established with the people they spied upon to discreetly make them aware of the presence of the spies.[208] Following the massive purge of local cadres, children scarcely any older than that were sometimes enrolled as "militia children," helping the new cooperative chiefs in their daily business by searching out and beating people who were feeding themselves.[209] The experience of Laurence Picq at headquarters shows there was a clear intention of eventually extending the "dictatorship of infants" to include a civic role. She describes the accelerated training of one group of children from the countryside.

> It was explained to them that the first generation of cadres had betrayed the country and that the second generation had not been much better. So they would have to take over quite quickly . . .
>
> It was with this new generation that the child doctors appeared. They were six girls aged between nine and thirteen. They could hardly read, but the Party had given each of them a big box of syringes. It was their job to give injections.
>
> "Our children doctors," it was said, "are from peasant stock. They are ready to serve their class. They are remarkably intelligent. If you tell them that 'the red box contains vitamins,' they remember! Show them how to sterilize a syringe, and they will remember that too!"
>
> Of course the children were pure and innocent, but knowing how to give an injection rather went to their heads. In no time at all they were insolent and arrogant beyond belief.[210]

Haing Ngor reports the tirade of a Khmer Rouge cadre at Tonle Bati in the summer of 1975:

> "In Democratic Kampuchea, under the glorious rule of Angkar," he said, "we need to think about the future. We don't need to think about

the past. You New People must forget about the pre-revolutionary times. Forget about cognac, forget about fashionable clothes and hairstyles. Forget about Mercedes. Those things are useless now. What can you do with a Mercedes now? You cannot barter for anything with it! You cannot keep rice in a Mercedes, but you can keep rice in a box you make yourself out of a palm leaf!"

"We don't need the technology of the capitalists," he went on. "We don't need any of it at all. Under our new system we don't need to send our children to school. Our school is the farm. We will write by plowing. We don't need to give examinations or award certificates. Knowing how to farm and how to dig canals—those are our certificates.

"We don't need doctors any more. They are not necessary. If someone needs to have their intestines removed I will do it." He made a cutting motion with an imaginary knife against his stomach. "It is easy. There is no need to learn how to do it by going to school.

"We don't need any of the capitalist professions! We don't need doctors or engineers! We don't need professors telling us what to do. They were all corrupted. We just need people to work hard on the farm!

"And yet, comrades," he said, looking around at our faces, "there are some naysayers and troublemakers who do not show the proper willingness to work hard and sacrifice! Such people do not have the proper revolutionary mentality! Such people are our enemies! And, comrades, some of them are right here in our midst!"

There was an uneasy shifting in the audience. Each of us hoped that the speaker was talking about someone else.

"These people cling to capitalist ways of thinking," he said. "They cling to the old capitalist fashions! We have some people among us who still wear eyeglasses. And why do they use eyeglasses? Can't they see me? If I move to slap your face"—he swung his open hand—"and you flinch, then you can see well enough. People wear them to be handsome in the capitalist style. They wear them because they are vain. We don't need people like that any more. People who think they are handsome are lazy! They are leeches sucking energy from others!"

I took off my glasses and put them in my pocket. Around me, others with glasses did the same . . .

[A number of dances followed] At the end of the last dance all the costumed cadres, male and female, formed a single line and shouted "BLOOD AVENGES BLOOD!" at the top of their lungs. Both times when they said the word "blood," they pounded their chests with their clenched fists, and when they shouted "avenges" they brought their arms out straight like a Nazi salute, except with a closed fist instead of an open hand.

"BLOOD AVENGES BLOOD! BLOOD AVENGES BLOOD! BLOOD AVENGES BLOOD!" the cadres repeated with fierce, determined faces, thumping their fists on their hearts and raising their fists. They shouted other revolutionary slogans and gave the salutes and finally ended with "Long live the Cambodian revolution!"[211]

The breakdown in social relations had much to do with the suppression of religion and with the extremes of moralizing that went on in every domain of life. Because there was no longer any place for anything outside the norm, people with chronic diseases, mentally ill people, and the handicapped all suffered. However, the system wound up operating against the official goal of building a powerful and large population: the constraints imposed on sexuality and marriage, together with chronic malnutrition, often killed off desire altogether, causing the birth rate to plummet from 30 per 1,000 in 1970 to around 11 per 1,000 in 1978.[212]

The revolution's objective was to obliterate anything that could act even involuntarily against the will of the CPK. An air of infallibility surrounded even the least important of its decisions. As in China, the fact that one had been arrested was proof enough that one was guilty. Later confessions would only confirm what the Angkar already knew to be the truth. A case in point is that of one man who was imprisoned in 1972. After surviving two years of interrogation, he managed to clear himself of the accusation that he had been an officer in the republican army; he was set free after a propaganda meeting at which the Angkar boasted about its beneficence in allowing an honest and sincere man to go free "even though he had been an officer in the army of Lon Nol."[213] And that was even before the massive increase in repression that followed the events of 17 April. Everything was arbitrary. The Party had no obligation to justify its political choices, its choice of cadres, or its changes in policy and personnel. Woe betide anyone who had failed to understand in time that the Vietnamese were enemies, or that a certain leader had in fact been an agent of the CIA. Pol Pot and his henchmen invariably imagined that the economic and military disasters that increasingly dogged the regime were acts of treachery or sabotage by the exploiting classes and their allies, a belief that added ever more fuel to their campaigns of terror.[214]

The system thus never progressed beyond its warlike origins, and hatred always formed a crucial part of its ideology. This was often translated into a morbid obsession with blood. The beginning of the national anthem, "The Glorious Victory of 17 April," is revealing:

Bright red blood that covers towns and plains
Of Kampuchea, our motherland,
Sublime blood of workers and peasants,
Sublime blood of revolutionary men and women fighters!
The blood, changing into unrelenting hatred

And resolute struggle
On 17 April, under the flag of revolution,
Frees us from slavery!

Long live, long live, Glorious 17 April,
Glorious victory, with greater significance
than the age of Angkor Wat![215]

Pol Pot once commented: "As you know, our national anthem was not written by a poet. Its essence is the blood of our whole people, of everyone who fell in the course of the past few centuries. It is the appeal of this blood that has been incorporated into our national anthem."[216]

There was even a lullaby that ended with the words: "You should never forget the class struggle."[217]

The Marxist-Leninist Culmination

The exceptionally bloody nature of the Khmer Rouge experience inevitably arouses a temptation to insist on its uniqueness as a phenomenon, similar to the argument for the uniqueness of the Holocaust. Other Communist regimes and the people who defend them have led the way here, claiming that the Pol Pot regime was an ultra-left-wing phenomenon or some sort of red fascism that was thinly disguised as Communism. But two decades later it is clear that the CPK was indeed a member of the family: it had its own peculiarities, but so did Poland and Albania. And in the final analysis, Cambodian Communism was closer to Chinese Communism than Chinese Communism was to the Russian version.

Several possible influences on the Khmer Rouge have been singled out. There has long been a theory that there was a considerable French influence, since almost all the Khmer Rouge leaders were at some point students in France, and most of them—including Pol Pot himself—were members of the French Communist Party.[218] A number of the historical references they used can be explained on that basis. As Suong Sikoeun, Ieng Sary's second-in-command, explained: "I was very influenced by the French Revolution, and in particular by Robespierre. It was only a step from there to becoming a Communist. Robespierre is my hero. Robespierre and Pol Pot: both of them share the qualities of determination and integrity."[219] It is difficult to go beyond this ideal of intransigence and find anything more substantial in the discourse or practice of the CPK that might be described as clearly coming from France or from French Communism. Khmer Rouge leaders were far more practical than they were theoretical: what was genuinely of interest to them was carrying out an experiment in "real socialism."

In fact Vietnamese Communism had the greatest influence, particularly in the founding days of the movement, although it also played an intimate role in the movement's development right up to 1973. Initially the CPK was merely one part of the Indochinese Communist Party, which was totally controlled by the Vietnamese and was broken into three national branches (without actually disappearing) by Ho Chi Minh and his comrades in 1951. Until the civil war broke out, the CPK never showed any autonomy in relation to the Vietnamese Communist Party in terms of its programs, its strategy (the armed actions of Cambodian Communists were above all a means of putting pressure on Sihanouk during the war in Vietnam), or its tactics concerning armaments, political alignment, or logistics.[220] Even after the coup, it was the Vietnamese who took over the administration of the "liberated zones" filled with new Cambodian recruits. Only after the Paris agreement in 1973 did the gaps begin to be filled. Hanoi's strategy brought the CPK to the negotiating table, but the Khmer Rouge opposed a negotiated settlement because it might have resulted in a central role for Sihanouk and revealed the organizational weaknesses of the Khmer Rouge. For the first time they refused to take a subservient role, because at last they had sufficient means to resist.

It is difficult to sum up the influence of Vietnamese Communism on the CPK in simple terms. Many of the CPK's methods were actually Chinese. Even from Phnom Penh it was sometimes hard to see what had come directly from Beijing and what had passed through Hanoi. Certain aspects of the Khmer Rouge's behavior are strongly reminiscent of Vietnam, including the obsession with secrecy and dissimulation: Ho Chi Minh himself first appeared in public in 1945 without making any reference to his rich past as a cadre in the Communist International, where he had worked under the name Nguyen Ai Quoc; several stages of his career became known only with the opening of the Soviet archives.[221] The ICP declared its dissolution in November 1945 in order to make way for the Viet Minh, then resurfaced in 1951 as the Workers' Party of Vietnam, and took up the Communist label again only in 1976. In South Vietnam, the People's Revolutionary Party was only one part of the National Liberation Front. Yet all these organizations were in fact directed by the same tiny group of Communist veterans. The same patterns can be discerned in Pol Pot's life (including the reports of his retirement and death after the defeat of 1979), in the opacity of his leadership, and in the unclear relations between the Angkar and the CPK, all of which have no equivalent in Communist history outside Indochina.

A second trait in common, complementary to the first, is the exceptionally widespread use of the united front. In 1945 the former emperor, Bao Dai, was for a while an adviser to Ho Chi Minh, who also managed to gain support from the Americans and in fact based his declaration of independence on that of the United States. Similarly, in 1970 the Khmer Rouge were officially part of the royal government of national union, and they revived this strategy after their fall. The Viet Minh, like the Angkar, never made any official reference to Marxism-Leninism and made a great show of being a fiercely nationalist party, so much so that this became one of the main tenets of the official ideology. Finally, in these forms of "war Communism," which seem able to prosper only in situations of armed conflict (consider, for example, the problems in Vietnam after 1975), there is inevitably a strong military component.[222] In such cases, the army often forms the backbone and perhaps even the raison d'être of the regime while also providing a model for the mobilization of its citizens, particularly in the economy.

North Korea was also an influence in some measure. The typically Korean image of the flying horse *(chollima)* was often used to illustrate the idea of economic progress.[223] Pyongyang was one of the two foreign capitals most often visited by Pol Pot as head of the government, and a number of North Korean technicians were brought in to restart Cambodian industry.[224] From the particular philosophy of Kim Il Sung, Pol Pot adopted above all the constant purges and the widespread use of secret police and spies, while the discourse about class struggle was shelved in favor of talk of a dialectic between the people and a handful of traitors. In practice this meant that the entire society suffered repression and that no social group could take over from the Party-state. All these aspects were quite distant from Maoism, and much closer in fact to Stalinism.

After breaking with Vietnam in 1973, the CPK decided to change its "Big Brother." The obvious substitute was Mao Zedong's China, not only because of its affirmed radicalism but also because of its capacity to pressure Vietnam along their common border. The Cambodian dictator was triumphantly acclaimed in Beijing during his first official trip abroad in September 1977, and the friendship between the two countries was officially described as "indestructible"; thus Cambodia was put on a par with Albania in the terminology used to describe relationships with China. The first Chinese technicians arrived in Phnom Penh in May 1975, and before long at least 4,000 (Kiernan's figure is 15,000) were stationed in Cambodia. At the same time, the Chinese government promised a billion dollars in various kinds of aid.[225]

The experience of the Chinese was most useful in the enormous campaign to collectivize the whole country. The Chinese popular commune, a vast structure with diverse fields of activity and a relatively autonomous structure that was used to control and mobilize the workforce in a military fashion, was quite clearly the prototype for the Cambodian cooperative. Even in tiny details, a number of Chinese innovations made in 1958 were to be found in the cooperative, including obligatory collective canteens, communal childcare programs, huge hydraulic engineering projects that absorbed so much of the workforce, the collectivization of all useful tools and implements, an almost exclusive concentration on one or two types of production (quite at odds with the rest of the project), totally unrealistic production targets, an insistence that everything be done at great speed, and a belief in the limitless possibilities of well-organized manpower. Mao had once said: "With grain and steel, anything is possible"; the Khmer Rouge echoed: "If we have plenty of rice, we have plenty of everything."[226] The absence of steel in the Cambodian version is striking. Their lack of contact with reality did not go so far as inventing imaginary reserves of iron or coal, neither of which exists in Cambodia. On the other hand, no one seems to have told Pol Pot how the Chinese Great Leap Forward ended;[227] or perhaps he felt that it simply was not his problem. The idea was central in a number of Khmer Rouge speeches, and the national anthem ended with the words: "Let us build our fatherland so that it may take a Great Leap Forward! An immense, glorious, prodigious Great Leap Forward!"[228]

Democratic Kampuchea was faithful to the Chinese Great Leap Forward beyond all hope and reason: and, as in China, it was rewarded with a huge, murderous famine.

The Cultural Revolution, by contrast, had few echoes in Cambodia. Like other Communist powers, the government in Phnom Penh had learned that mobilizing the masses against a certain clan or section of the Party, regardless of how clearly different from one another the targeted sections of the population were, was always a risky business. And in any case the Cultural Revolution had been a fundamentally urban movement, coming largely out of the teaching establishments, and was therefore not transposable to the Cambodian peasant revolution. Cambodia did of course share the anti-intellectual currents of mid-1960s China, including the negation of culture symbolized by the "revolutionary operas" of Jiang Qing (which appear to have been copied under Pol Pot).[229] It might even be claimed that the emptying of the towns was perhaps inspired by the ruralization of millions of former Red Guards.

It looked as though the Khmer Rouge had been inspired more by the theory or the slogans of the Maoists than by the actual practice of the Chinese Communist Party. The Chinese countryside was a hotbed of revolution, and it was there that a huge number of urban intellectuals were exiled, particularly in the aftermath of the Cultural Revolution. Even today the regime still uses quite draconian measures to limit rural migration to the cities. Still, the big cities always had a major role to play both before and after 1949, and it was often the urban workers who were the most favored sons of the revolution. The Chinese Communist Party never thought for a moment of emptying the towns and deporting the populations of entire regions, abolishing money, destroying the education system, or wiping out a whole class such as the intellectuals.

Although Mao never passed up an opportunity to show his disdain for them, in the final analysis he knew he could not do without such people. Many of the Red Guards themselves came from the elite universities. Khieu Samphan was using clearly Maoist rhetoric when he welcomed back to Cambodia intellectuals who had returned from abroad to demonstrate their loyalty to the regime: "I can tell you quite clearly, we don't need you: what we need is people who can work the land, and that's all . . . Anyone who is politically aware and has understood our regime can do anything at all, because technique comes afterward . . . we don't need engineers to grow rice, plant corn, or raise pigs."[230] Despite the rhetoric, denial of the value of expertise in such fashion was never government policy in China. In any case, by a process of inertia over time, each movement toward utopian extremism and each wave of repression soon ended in a return to more traditional and normal methods, with the impetus for the return generally originating inside the Communist Party itself. This was clearly one reason for the stability of the Chinese regime. By contrast, the CPK came close to liquidating itself.

Similar contradictions are discernible in the types of repression used. The main influence here was clearly Chinese (or Sino-Vietnamese), with its obligatory and interminable processes of criticism and self-criticism, all in a vaguely educational or reeducational perspective. There were also the same obsessions with biography and confessional accounts of the past, which were to be rewritten constantly without changes. One's position in the social hierarchy by birth and employment determined one's place in the political hierarchy, which in turn defined one's place in the legal system. Familial origins were always extremely important. And as elsewhere in Asia, the demand that everyone participate in politics in an extremely intense and committed fashion eroded the boundary between society and the Party-state in an obviously totalitarian fashion.

There are of course many features peculiar to the Cambodian experience, but most of these are a sort of exaggeration or intensification of the original model. The main difference, at least until the 1960s, was that Chinese and Vietnamese Communists took reeducation quite seriously and went to great lengths to demonstrate to prisoners, for example, that the state was right to have imprisoned them.[231] As a result prisoners were often well treated, and torture was banned or used rarely. In Cambodia, by contrast, torture was systematic. The other consequence was the lack of even a hypothetical possibility that good behavior could bring freedom and rehabilitation or at least a shortened sentence. Hardly anyone ever left a Cambodian prison; in fact people died there with incredible rapidity. In China and Vietnam massive repressions came in waves and were followed by long periods of calm. Particular groups were targeted, but they accounted for only a small segment of the population.

In Cambodia, at the very least, all the "'75s" were suspects, and there was never a moment's respite. When it came to putting repression into practice, the other Communist Parties in Southeast Asia maintained a facade of organization, efficiency, relative coherence, and a certain perverse intelligence. In Cambodia, by contrast, simple brutality and arbitrariness predominated; the repressions were invariably carried out according to local orders, although the general principles clearly came from on high. Nowhere else in Asia were so many murders and massacres carried out on the spot, except perhaps during periods of agricultural reform (when the victims—the landowners and their associates—were clearly identified and restricted in number) and in the heyday of the Cultural Revolution, though even then in a much more restricted and limited fashion. In short, the Maoists on the Mekong were in many respects far closer to a degenerate version of Stalinism than to Chinese Communism.

An Exemplary Tyrant

The personal imprint of Stalin and Mao was such that their deaths brought considerable changes, particularly in the scale and scope of repression. What of Pol Pot? The man born as Saloth Sar is present in the history of Communism in Cambodia from the beginning to the end, and it is impossible to speak of Communism without him. There is also no doubt that traits discernible in his personality correlate with the bloodiest excesses of his regime. His distant past was highly complex and bore little resemblance to the revolutionary legend he attempted to erect in its place. He had a sister and cousin who were dancers and concubines for King Monivong and a brother who was a palace official until 1975, and he himself had spent part of his childhood in the inner circle of that archaic monarchy. One can easily imagine the guilty conscience that resulted and the consequent desire to destroy the old world. Pol Pot seems to have sunk ever deeper into an alternative reality, perhaps through an inability to come to terms with his own story. An *apparatchik*, ambitious from an early age, more at home in a small group than when faced with a crowd, he set out in 1963 to live cut off from the world in jungle camps or in secret hideouts in the deserted Phnom Penh, about which even today little is known. He seems to have become increasingly paranoid with the passing of time. Even when he was all-powerful, everyone who came to listen to him was searched. He constantly moved from residence to residence, suspected his cooks of trying to poison him, and once executed the electricians who were "guilty" of causing a power outage.[232]

His obsessions are clear in a conversation he had with a journalist from Swedish television in August 1978:

"Could His Excellency explain to the viewers what he considers to be the greatest achievement of Democratic Kampuchea over the last three and a half years?"

"Our greatest achievement . . . is having defeated all the plots and conspiracies, the sabotage, the attempted coups, and all the other acts of aggression carried out by enemies of all types hostile to the regime."[233]

This must surely be taken as a tremendous involuntary admission of the failure of the regime.

There were undoubtedly two sides to Pol Pot. From the 1950s until the 1980s he was often described as a sensitive, timid man who loved reading French poetry, was widely loved by his students, and was a warmhearted and enthusiastic propagator of the revolution. But as a politician he had a number of his old comrades-in-arms arrested, including several people who had believed that they were his close friends. He never answered their begging letters, authorized the use of the worst possible tortures on them, and eventually then had them killed.[234] His "expiatory" speech after his defeat, at a seminar for cadres in 1981, was a model of hypocrisy:

> He said he knows that many people in the country hate him and believe he is responsible for the killings. He said he knows that many people died. When he said this he nearly broke down and cried. He said he must accept responsibility because his policies were too far to the left, and because he did not keep proper track of what was going on. He said he was like the master in a house who did not know what the kids were up to, and that he trusted people too much . . . They would tell him things that were not true, that everything was fine, but that this or that person was a traitor. In the end they were the real traitors. The major problem had been cadres formed by the Vietnamese.[235]

Another thought-provoking testimony is provided by one of his oldest companions, his brother-in-law Ieng Sary, who later accused him of megalomania: "Pol Pot thought he was an incomparable genius in military and economic affairs, in hygiene, in song-writing, in music and dance, in cookery, in fashion, and in everything else, even in the art of lying. Pol Pot thought that he was above everyone else on the whole planet. He was a god on Earth."[236] This portrait bears a remarkable similarity to certain portraits of Stalin. Could this be simply a coincidence?

The Weight of Reality

Besides the nation's uneasy history and the influence of world Communism, the violence of the Khmer Rouge was brought about by the specific spatial and temporal context of the regime. In some ways the regime was almost the accidental product of a war that took place beyond the borders of Cambodia. Once the war ended, the regime found itself weak and isolated in its country of origin. Vietnam's hostility and China's stifling embrace did the rest.

The seventeenth of April came too late for a world that had already passed it by. Perhaps the greatest weakness of the Khmer Rouge was that they were a historical anomaly. They created "late Communism" in the sense in which one speaks of "late antiquity"—that is, a state of affairs that persists while the rest of the world has moved on. When Pol Pot came to power, Stalin was long dead (1953), Ho Chi Minh was dead (1969), and Mao Zedong was very ill (he died in September 1976). Only Kim Il Sung remained, but North Korea was both small and far away. The great Chinese model was falling to pieces before the eyes of the new dictator. The Gang of Four tried to relaunch the Cultural Revolution in 1975, but without success. After Mao's death, the revolution was swept away like a house of cards. The Khmer Rouge sought support among those who refused to give up on Maoism, but the latter became too caught up in a battle with Deng Xiaoping and his partisan reformers. Maoism officially ended a year later, and the country entered the new era symbolized by the Democracy Wall, whereas in Cambodia the killing was just beginning. In China, the Great Leap Forward was over, and "revisionism" set in instead. The rest of Asia, seen from Phnom Penh, was even more depressing: after the momentary stimulus brought by the victory of the revolutionary forces in Indochina, the Maoist guerrillas everywhere else—in Thailand, Malaysia, and Burma—went into decline. Perhaps worst of all, the new Asian mercantile powers emerging alongside Japan (Singapore, Taiwan, South Korea, and Hong Kong) were "little dragons" whose economic prosperity was matched only by their hostility to Communist ideas, and they were managing to find their way without the help of the West. Finally, the Khmer Rouge were bound to feel a little confused, with Marxism seemingly on a steep decline. Was the march of history in fact being reversed?

There were two possible responses to these changes: they could go along with them and revise their doctrines, at the risk of losing their identity and raison d'être; or they could reaffirm their identity and follow the North Korean way by becoming ever more radical in their goals and actions. Eurocommunism, which was then in its heyday, or the Marxist terrorism of the Red Brigades (Aldo Moro was assassinated in 1978)—such was the choice. As we now know, both paths were dead ends, but one was considerably bloodier than the other. It was as though this 1950s generation, which had studied in France, had understood that unless they created their utopia immediately, at any price, they would inevitably be forced into a long series of compromises. Their only possibility, unless they wanted to be swept away, was to impose "year zero" on a population that would not be allowed to have any choice. China's Great Leap

Forward had failed; so had the Cultural Revolution. The reason, in the Khmer Rouge's view, must be that the Chinese had stopped at half-measures; they had failed to sweep away every counterrevolutionary obstacle: the corrupt and uncontrollable towns, intellectuals who were proud of their knowledge and presumed to think for themselves, money and all financial transactions, the last traces of capitalism, and "traitors who had infiltrated the heart of the Party." This desire to create a new society filled with New Men was bound to fail under the weight of reality despite (or because of) the docility of the Cambodians. Unwilling to abandon its plans, the regime slid ever deeper into an ocean of blood that was shed so that it could remain in power. The CPK wished to be the glorious successor to Lenin and Mao, but instead it was the precursor to other groups that have made a travesty of Marxism and used it as a license to commit intolerable acts of violence, such as the Peruvian Sendero Luminoso (Shining Path), the Tamil Tigers in Sri Lanka, and the Kurdistan Workers' Party.

The Khmer Rouge constantly struggled against their own weakness. This was long hidden behind a facade of triumphalist verbiage. In fact there had been two reasons for the events of 17 April: the considerable military support offered by North Vietnam, and the ineptitude of the Lon Nol regime, which had been made worse by inconsistencies in U.S. foreign policy. Lenin, Mao, and even Ho Chi Minh owed little to anyone for their military victories, and their adversaries had been far from mediocre. Their parties and, for the last two, their armed forces had been put together slowly and patiently and had been quite considerable even before they finally came to power. The situation in Cambodia was different. Until the middle of the civil war, the Khmer Rouge were totally dependent on forces from Hanoi. In 1975 there were only about 60,000 Khmer Rouge soldiers (less than 1 percent of the population), who were able to overcome about 200,000 demoralized republican soldiers.

If the army was weak, so was the Party. No sources are wholly reliable, but the figures we do have show a Party membership of 4,000 members in 1970 and 14,000 in 1975: growth from a large group into a small party.[237] These figures also imply a dearth of experienced cadres until the very end of the regime, which made the purges all the more dramatic. The consequences are clearly visible in the tales of the deportees: for every responsible and intelligent cadre, there were dozens who were cruel, stupid, pretentious, and stubborn. "All the peasants who had been promoted to positions as cadres were quite ignorant. They constantly misunderstood and misapplied the principles of the revolution. The madness of the Khmer Rouge regime was intensified by their incompetence."[238] It was as though the real weakness of the regime, which went quite unrecognized, and the consequent feeling of insecurity that it engendered could be compensated only by an increase in violence. This brought disaffection, leading to another increase in terror, and so the cycle continued. The result was an atmosphere in which insecurity, generalized mistrust, and fear for the future were the norm, traumatizing everyone who lived through it. It was also a reflection of the isolation of the leaders, who believed that traitors were lurking everywhere. The result was the blind repression implicit in Khmer Rouge slogans such as "One can always make a mistake and arrest the wrong person, but one should never let the wrong person go."[239] Pin Yathay acutely analyzes the infernal circle that was at work: "In practice, what the Khmer Rouge feared was the anger that might surface in their new people if they eased up on repression. Because they were haunted by the possibility of revolt, they decided to reproach us for our impassivity and to make us pay for it. Hence their constant reign of terror. We were afraid of persecution; they were afraid of insurrection. They were also afraid of the ideological and political maneuvering of their comrades-in-arms."[240] Were they justified in fearing popular insurrection? There are few traces of any such movements, and all were speedily suppressed with tremendous violence.[241] But whenever the opportunity did present itself—for instance, whenever a local administration was wiped out by a purge—the anger of the slaves became quite apparent, even if it brought a commensurate increase in terror.

There were revolts born out of desperation, and others that began because of senseless rumors. At the most modest level of resistance were the insults that would float up through the darkness at a dam construction site to a Khmer Rouge soldier sitting on a wall.[242] On the whole, statements from survivors show that New People working together could take considerable liberties when addressing one another. There was much complicity when it came to petty theft or secret breaks at work; relatively few people were denounced for such things, and spies and informants met with little success on the whole. Hence the division into "'75s" and cadres. The preferred solution of the cadres was to maintain a warlike atmosphere, and even the war itself, since this was a tried and tested method. Some slogans attested the approach clearly: "One hand holds the hoe, the other strikes the enemy," or "With water we grow rice, with rice we make war."[243] The Khmer Rouge were more correct than they realized. They never had enough rice, and they lost the war.

A Genocide?

The crimes of the Khmer Rouge should be judged rigorously and objectively so that the Cambodian experience can be compared to the other great horrors of the century, and its proper weight assigned in the history of Communism. There are also very strong legal reasons for such an approach, since a great number of CPK leaders are still alive and even active in official capacities. Should they be allowed to move around freely? If not, what charges should be laid against them?[244]

It is unquestionable that Pol Pot and his cohorts are guilty of war crimes. Prisoners from the republican army were systematically maltreated; many were executed. Those who surrendered in 1975 were later persecuted without mercy. It is equally clear that the Khmer Rouge also committed crimes against humanity. Entire social groups were found unworthy of living and were largely exterminated. Any political opposition, real or supposed, was punished by death. The chief difficulty involves determining the crime of genocide. If one uses the literal definition, the discussion risks falling into absurdity: genocide refers only to the systematic extermination of national, ethnic, racial, and religious groups. Because the Khmers as a whole were not targeted for extermination, attention would then have to turn to ethnic minorities and eventually to the Buddhist monks. But even taken as a whole they would represent only a small proportion of the victims; and it is not easy to say that the Khmer Rouge did specifically repress minorities—with the exception of the Vietnamese after 1977, when relatively few remained in the country. The Cham on the other hand were targeted because of their Muslim faith, which was a serious cause for resistance. Some authors have tried to resolve the problem by bringing in the notion of *politicide*,[245] which, broadly speaking, means genocide on a political basis (one might also speak of *sociocide*, meaning genocide on a social basis). But this fails to get to the heart of the matter. The real question is, should such crimes be treated as seriously as genocide or not? And if the answer is yes, as these authors seem to believe, why should the issue be clouded by the use of a new term? It is perhaps worth recalling that during the discussions leading to the adoption of the United Nations Convention on Genocide, it was the Soviet Union that—for all too obvious reasons—opposed the inclusion of the word "political" in the definition of the term. But it is above all the word "racial" (which covers neither ethnicity nor nationality) that should provide an answer here. "Race," a phantasm that recedes ever further as human knowledge increases, exists only in the eyes of the beholder; in reality there is no more a Jewish race than there is a bourgeois race. But for the Khmer Rouge, as for the Chinese Communists, some social groups were criminal by nature, and this criminality was seen as transmittable from husband to wife, as well as an inherited trait. Here the ghost of Trofim Lysenko looms large. We can speak of the *racialization* of social groups, and the crime of genocide therefore can be applied to their physical elimination. This elimination, as we have seen, was pushed to its limits in Cambodia and was undoubtedly carried out deliberately. Y Phandara was told by a Khmer Rouge worker that the "17 Aprils" were "the city dwellers who supported the regime of the traitor Lon Nol . . . There are a lot of traitors among them. The Communist Party quite cleverly eliminated a good number of them. The ones who are still alive are now working out in the countryside. Now they're too weak to rise up against us."[246]

For millions of Cambodians today, the era of Pol Pot has left indelible scars. In 1979, 42 percent of the country's children had lost at least one parent. They were three times more likely to have lost their father than their mother. Seven percent had lost both parents. In 1992 the isolation of adolescents was the most dramatic: 64 percent had lost at least one parent.[247] An array of social evils besets Cambodian society today, at rates that are exceptionally high for a Southeast Asian country. Crime is widespread and often very violent since firearms are easily obtained; corruption is everywhere; and most people show little respect for one another and little sense of social solidarity. No one seems to have a sense of the common good at any level. Hundreds of thousands of refugees abroad (there are 150,000 in the United States alone) still feel terrorized because of what they lived through, with recurrent nightmares and the highest rate of depression of any Indochinese national group. Many of the female refugees came alone, and in general there are many more women than men because so many men of that generation fell victim to assassinations.[248] Still, Cambodian society did not break down entirely. When the last vestiges of collectivization were abandoned in 1985, increased production brought an almost immediate end to food shortages.[249]

It is easy to understand Cambodians' overwhelming desire to return to normal life. But they should not be left to face the former leaders of the Khmer Rouge dictatorship alone. The form of Communism that they faced was perhaps the worst of all, and the liquidation of such a terrible past is an almost intolerable burden. The rest of the world, which for so long showed such complacency toward their executioners, should also make the drama of Cambodia its own.

Conclusion

East Asia is nearly the only place on earth where Communists still rule. But is there a specifically Asian brand of Communism, in the same way that one can legitimately speak about a unique East European form of Communism? The answer to this question is not easy. In Europe, with the exception of Albania and the former Yugoslavia, Communism had the same father, and all the Communist governments there (even in Yugoslavia and Albania) finally fell at more or less the same time, when it suddenly became clear that the system was no longer functioning in its birthplace, the Soviet Union. In Asia, a similar relationship is discernible only between Vietnam and Laos, whose destinies are still organically linked. What is remarkable elsewhere in Asia is the distinct nature of the process of conquest and consolidation of power in each country, despite the strong resemblance that North Korea initially bore to the "people's democracies" established by Stalin in Eastern Europe, and despite the great impetus that the Viet Minh received when the Chinese army arrived on the borders of Tonkin. There is not now and never really was a Communist bloc in Asia, except in the minds of the leaders in Beijing. Economic cooperation was lacking, high-ranking cadres seldom visited other countries, no one was ever trained abroad, and the secret police and the military only rarely pooled their information. The occasional attempts to do such things occurred on only a limited scale, and these efforts rarely lasted long except between Laos and its "big brother," Vietnam. China and North Korea were close for a year after the Korean conflict, and China and Vietnam were reasonably close during the 1950s. China was also quite close to Pol Pot's Cambodia, while Cambodia and Vietnam were tightly linked in the 1980s. But Communism in Asia has in general been a national affair, with national defense always the top priority (except in Laos), even though at times Chinese or Soviet aid proved essential. Asia after all has seen intense wars between Communist states, at the end of the 1970s between Vietnam and Cambodia, and then between Vietnam and China. Where education, propaganda, and historiography are concerned, it is hard to find more chauvinistic countries anywhere else, perhaps partly because all these countries came into being as the result of a struggle against foreign imperialism. That experience at least gives them something in common. The problem is that the resulting nationalism has often been turned against their neighbors.

On the other hand, similarities in the details of policies (particularly policies of repression) are readily apparent, and many of them have been adumbrated in the preceding chapters. Before reiterating them, we might pause to consider the comparative chronology of the regimes studied here. In Europe, the broad outlines of the history of each country are quite similar, with the exception of Albania and to some extent Romania and Yugoslavia. In East Asia, the points of origin are disparate, stretching from 1945 to 1975, as are the inception of agrarian reform and collectivization, especially in divided Vietnam. But in all cases the two stages tend to succeed each other quite soon after the seizure of power (the maximum interval in the process is seven years, in China). On the political plane, the Communist Party never acted openly during the taking of power, and the appearance of some sort of united front was maintained for some time after victory (eight years in China), even if it meant not revealing the existence of the Party, as was the case in Cambodia before 1977. However, if many were deluded beforehand by the promise of a pluralist democracy (and this often contributed to the success of the Communists, particularly in Vietnam), the spell was usually broken soon afterward. In one Vietnamese camp for southerners, prisoners until 30 April 1975 were on the whole quite well fed and well dressed, and were not forced to work. But the moment the South was "liberated," rations were cut ruthlessly, discipline was intensified, and forced labor was introduced. The camp chiefs justified their actions as follows: "Until now, you have been treated as prisoners of war . . . Now the whole country is free; we are the winners and you are the losers. You should be happy you are still alive. After the 1917 revolution in Russia, all the losers were exterminated!"[1] Social classes that had been treated very well in the days of the united front, such as intellectuals and national capitalists, suddenly found themselves ostracized and subject to repression when Party dictatorship took over.

A close examination reveals important differences within the chronological similarities. North Korea developed at its own pace in the 1940s and 1950s, and not long after that became quite isolated, a sort of living museum of Stalinism. The Chinese Cultural Revolution had no imitators. Pol Pot triumphed just as Jiang Qing fell, and his dream of a Great Leap Forward came fourteen years too late. But wherever Communist parties were in power, the Stalinist era was marked by purges and by tightened security. Although the shock wave from the Twentieth Soviet Party Congress led to a burst of liberalization throughout Asia, this was generally short-lived and was followed by extremist measures of one sort or another, such as the Great Leap Forward in China, its Vietnamese incarnation, and the Korean *Chollima*. Everywhere but in North Korea, the 1980s and 1990s were marked by a liberalization of the economy. In Laos and South Vietnam this came hard on the heels of collectivization, which was never fully achieved. More quickly than is often acknowledged, economic reform leads to a normalization of society and a disappearance of repressive practices, even if the process is uneven, contradictory, and incomplete. Except in Pyongyang, mass terror and totalitarian attempts at controlling consciousness are now only a memory, and political prisoners are a rarity. In Laos, for example, according to figures from Amnesty International, the number of political prisoners fell from between 6,000 and 7,000 in 1985 to a mere 33 by March 1991. Vietnam has experienced a comparable drop, and China somewhat less so. Clearly, the compulsion to mass murder is no more irresistible in Asian Communism than it was in the European version. It seems possible to conclude that terror has finally outlived its purpose. Even though the terror went on for a long time (at least until 1980) and everywhere, invariably, led to horrendous crimes, it has been replaced today by selective, dissuasive repression, and because of the increasingly widespread reeducation programs it is seen more and more often for what it really was.

The key factor in many of these chronological similarities, which at the end of the day are greater than the differences (at least after 1956), is more often Beijing than Moscow. This focus on China is one of the lasting effects of the Twentieth Soviet Party Congress, which came as a shock to Asian Communists and was considered to be a serious threat by Mao Zedong, Ho Chi Minh, and Kim Il Sung (as well as Maurice Thorez). The fact of the surprise alone demonstrates the bravery of Khrushchev's initiative. Since the days of Yan'an, the Chinese government has played the role of a second Mecca for Communists in Asia. However, the prestige of Stalin and the U.S.S.R. was still immense, and Soviet economic and military might did the rest. The Chinese intervention in Korea and then the size of its aid to the Viet Minh caused the first disturbances in the Sino-Soviet relationship, but it was 1956 that made Mao the leader of the "antirevisionist" camp that quickly came to include every Communist country in Asia. The disaster of the Cultural Revolution did some damage to Chinese hegemony, and Vietnam's military needs in the 1960s pushed it closer to the Soviet camp. But this chronology on the whole is quite trustworthy: initiatives regularly came from China, and were usually followed with great dedication. There is an unmistakable similarity among all Communist regimes, but in East Asia the similarity sometimes seems to border on cloning; the Vietnamese agrarian reform, for example, was almost a carbon copy of the earlier Chinese version.

The "goulash Communism" so dear to Khrushchev found few proponents in Asia until the 1980s, in part because the continent was still involved in so many revolutionary wars, but also because ideology had such a major role to play in these countries. In the Confucian tradition of "the rectification of names" (and all these countries, with the exception of Cambodia, had a strong tradition of Confucianism), it is reality that must adapt itself to language. In the prison system, this meant that what mattered was not the act that had been committed, but the verdict that had been passed and the label that had been applied, both of which depended on many factors independent of the act itself. Peace of mind came not from good deeds, but from saying the right word in the right place. Accordingly, two major factors influenced Communism in Asia: an overextension of ideology, and an overreliance on willpower. The first functioned as a mania for classification and reorganization based on the combination of Confucianism with a revolutionary vision through which the entire society was to be remade. The second sought the transformation of the whole world through reliance on the idea that the mind of every individual in society can be completely filled with new, better ideas, and that the actions of these individuals will thereafter be based on that new knowledge. Mention was made above of the verbal jousts in which victory came to the person who made the best use of quotations from Mao Zedong. In that sense, the Great Leap Forward was a feast of words. But even the Asians could not escape reality forever, and when it intruded too far into language, this phenomenon did not escape them. After the failure of so many words and the innumerable catastrophes that such language had brought, all anyone wanted to hear was the profoundly anti-ideological language of Deng Xiaoping: "Who cares if a cat is black or gray, provided that he catches mice."

The great originality of East Asian Communism resided in the manner in which it managed to transfer this ideology and belief in the will from the Party to society as a whole. This happened in a more attenuated fashion in Stalin's Russia, where it relied on different traditions. In Chinese Asia (and thus in

Vietnam and Korea too) the Western divide between high and popular culture has never existed, and Confucianism in particular was a way of life for all classes, from the leaders in the center to the peasants in the most far-flung regions. The same could be said of many other traditions and barbaric practices, such as the binding of feet. Moreover, the state was never an institution set apart from society, founded on complex laws. Contrary to the image that they tried to present, Chinese monarchs, and leaders elsewhere who modeled themselves upon them, had almost none of the formal means of intervention that most Western kings possessed by the end of the Middle Ages.[2] They could survive and govern only with the consent of their subjects, consent obtained not by any form of democratic consultation, or by institutionalized arbitration between conflicting interests, but by the widespread acceptance of certain social civic norms, founded on a complex familial and interpersonal system of morality, which Mao termed "the mass line." The moral (or ideological) state has a long and rich history in eastern Asia. In itself, such a state is poor and weak, but if it succeeds in persuading each group, family, and individual of the value of its norms and ideals, its power is limitless. Its only bounds are those of nature itself, which was the cause of Mao's undoing during the Great Leap Forward. Asian Communism thus attempted—and for a short while it succeeded in its objectives—to create profoundly holistic societies. Hence one comes across cases such as that of the Vietnamese cell chief who was a prisoner himself but felt obliged to shout at a recalcitrant detainee: "You are resisting the head of cell nominated by the revolution—so you are resisting the revolution itself!"[3] Hence also the extraordinarily patient and relentless drive to make every prisoner, even French officers who had passed through Saint Cyr,[4] a bearer of the Party's good news. Whereas the Russian Revolution never succeeded in destroying the "us and them" mentality, the Cultural Revolution convinced the entire population for a while that they were a part of the state and the Party. In some cases, Red Guards who were not themselves Party members seemed somehow to have the right to decide who was to be excluded from it. Communism in the West also had criticism and self-criticism, endless discussion meetings, and its own selection of canonical texts. But such things were in general reserved for Party members. In Asia, they became the norm for all people.

There were two main consequences for the form of repression. The most obvious, which we have noted so often above, was the absence of even cursory references to the mechanisms of law and justice: everything was political. In each country, the introduction of a penal code generally marked the end of the period of terror, as in China in 1979 or in Vietnam in 1986. The other consequence was the nature of the waves of repression, which were more notable for their wide sweep than for their intrinsically bloody nature. They focused on society as a whole or on extremely large groups such as peasants, city dwellers, and intellectuals. Deng Xiaoping's regime stated that the Cultural Revolution had persecuted 100 million people, a figure that is unverifiable. At the same time, it is unlikely that there were more than 1 million deaths. The ratio was quite different in the Stalinist purges. But what use was killing, when the leaders could terrorize so effectively? This form of repression also explains the high number of suicides: the intensity of campaigns, backed up by friends, colleagues, neighbors, and one's own family, brought tension that for many individuals became intolerable, as there was literally nowhere to turn.

The exception that proves the rule is Cambodia (and, to a lesser extent, Laos). Cambodia was never affected by Confucianism. In fact its political tradition was much more Indian than Chinese. This fact may be one of the main reasons that violence there was so widespread and bloody. It is possible that what happened there was the effect of applying Sino-Vietnamese ideas to a population that was fundamentally opposed to them. Much more work remains to be done in this area to get a precise idea of the reasons for such a terrible aberration.

This analysis of the specific nature of Communism in East Asia (at least in Chinese Asia) affords a basis for comparisons with the entire history of Communism, and in particular with the Soviet model. Many of the phenomena, such as the obsession with notions of a tabula rasa and a fresh start, the cult of youth, and the constant manipulation of the young, are clearly to be found elsewhere. But the differences, too, are noteworthy; and the survival of Communism in Asia, even after its collapse in Europe, requires serious analysis.

Select Bibliography for Asia

Cambodia

Becker, Elizabeth. *When the War Was Over: The Voices of Cambodia's Revolution and Its People.* New York: Simon and Schuster, 1986.

Chandler, David P. *Brother Number One: A Political Biography of Pol Pot.* Boulder: Westview Press, 1992.

———— *The Tragedy of Cambodian History: Politics, War, and Revolution since 1945.* New Haven: Yale University Press, 1991.

Haing S. Ngor with Roger Warner. *Surviving the Killing Fields: The Cambodian Odyssey of Haing S. Ngor.* London: Chatto and Windus, 1988.

Jackson, Karl D., ed. *Cambodia 1975–1978: Rendezvous with Death.* Princeton: Princeton University Press, 1989.

Kiernan, Ben. *The Pol Pot Regime: Race, Power, and Genocide in Cambodia under the Khmer Rouge, 1975–1979.* New Haven: Yale University Press, 1996.

Locard, Henri. *Le petit livre rouge de Pol Pot.* Paris: L'Harmattan, 1996.

Martin, Marie-Alexandre. *Cambodia: A Shattered Society,* trans. Mark W. McLeod. Berkeley: University of California Press, 1994.

Picq, Laurence. *Beyond the Horizon: Five Years with the Khmer Rouge,* trans. Patricia Norland. New York: St. Martin's Press, 1989.

Pin Yathay. *Stay Alive, My Son.* London: Bloomsbury, 1987.

Sliwinski, Marek. *Le génocide Khmer rouge: Une analyse démographique.* Paris: L'Harmattan, 1995.

China (including Tibet)

Becker, Jasper. *Hungry Ghosts: China's Secret Famine.* London: John Murray, 1996.

Bergère, Marie-Claude. *La République populaire de Chine de 1949 à nos jours.* Paris: Armand Colin, 1987.

Bergère, Marie-Claude, Lucien Bianco, and Jürgen Domes, eds. *La Chine au XXe siècle.* Vol. 1: *D'une révolution à l'autre 1895–1949;* vol 2: *De 1949 à aujourd'hui.* Paris: Fayard, 1989 and 1990.

Cheng Nien. *Life and Death in Shanghai.* London: Macdonald, 1986.

Chevrier, Yves. *Mao et la révolution chinoise.* Florence: Casterman/Giunti, 1993.

Domenach, Jean-Luc. *Chine: L'archipel oublié.* Paris: Fayard, 1992.

Donnet, Pierre-Antoine. *Tibet: Survival in Question.* London: Zed Books, 1994.

Fairbank, John K., and Albert Feuerwerker, eds. *The Cambridge History of China.* Vol. 13, Part 2: *Republican China, 1912–1949.* Cambridge: Cambridge University Press, 1986.

Hinton, William. *Fanshen: A Documentary of Revolution in a Chinese Village.* Berkeley: University of California Press, 1966.

Hua Linshan. *Les années rouges.* Paris: Seuil, 1987.

Ling, Ken, Miriam London, and Ta-ling Lee. *Red Guard: From Schoolboy to "Little General" in Mao's China.* London: Macdonald, 1972.

MacFarquhar, Roderick, and John K. Fairbank, eds. *The Cambridge History of China.* Vol. 14: *The People's Republic, Part 1 (1949–1965); Vol 15, Part 2: Revolutions within the Chinese Revolution, 1966–1982.* Cambridge: Cambridge University Press, 1987 and 1991.

Pasqualini, Jean, with Rudolf Chelminski. *Prisoner of Mao.* London: André Deutsch, 1973.

Roux, Alain. *La Chine populaire,* Vol. 1: *1949–1966; Vol. 2: 1966–1984.* Paris: Editions Sociales, 1983 and 1984.

Wei Jingsheng. *The Courage to Stand Alone: Letters from Prison and other Writings,* trans. Kristina M. Torgeson. London: Penguin, 1998.

Wu, Harry. *Laogai: The Chinese Gulag.* Boulder: Westview Press, 1992.

Yan Jiaqi and Gao Gao. *Turbulent Decade: A History of the Cultural Revolution,* trans. and ed. D. W. Y. Kwok. Honolulu: University of Hawaii Press, 1996 (first published in Chinese, 1986).

Laos

Stuart-Fox, Martin, and Mary Koogman. *Historical Dictionary of Laos.* Metuchen and London: Scarecrow Press, 1992.

Vietnam

Boudarel, Georges. *Cent fleurs écloses dans la nuit du Vietnam: Communisme et dissidence 1945–1956.* Paris: Jacques Bertoin, 1991.

Boudarel, Georges, et al. *La bureaucratie au Vietnam.* Vietnam-Asie-Débat no. 1. Paris: L'Harmattan, 1983.

Dalloz, Jacques. *The War in Indo-China, 1945–1954,* trans. Josephine Bacon. Savage, Md.: Barnes and Noble Books, 1990.

Doan Van Toai. *The Vietnamese Gulag,* trans. Sylvie Romanowski and Françoise Simon-Miller. New York: Simon and Schuster, 1986.

Hémery, Daniel. *Révolutionnaires vietnamiens et pouvoir colonial en Indochine, 1932–37.* Paris: Maspero, 1975.

Karnow, Stanley. *Vietnam: A History.* Harmondsworth: Penguin Books, 1984.

Marr, David G. *Vietnam 1945: The Quest for Power.* Berkeley: University of California Press, 1995.

Ngo Van. *Revolutionaries They Could Not Break: The Fight for the Fourth International in Indochina, 1930–1945.* London: Index Books, 1995.

V The Third World

Pascal Fontaine, Yves Santamaria, and Sylvain Boulouque

25 Communism in Latin America

Pascal Fontaine

Cuba: Interminable Totalitarianism in the Tropics

Since the beginning of the century, the biggest island in the Caribbean has had a turbulent political history. In 1931–1933 an army clerk named Fulgencio Batista took part in a revolt against the dictator Gerardo Machado. In 1933 Batista led a military coup against Cuba's provisional president, Carlos Céspedes. Thereafter, as head of the army, Batista was the major powerbroker for a succession of provisional and de facto governments. Throughout this period and afterward, he remained fiercely opposed to the United States. In 1940, after Batista was elected president, he enacted a liberal constitution. In 1952 he returned to power through a military coup, disrupting the prospects of democratization symbolized by the elections scheduled for the following year. Batista continued to govern with the support of various political parties, including the local Communist Party, which at that time was called the People's Socialist Party (PSP).

The Cuban economy began to grow rapidly under Batista, but wealth remained unevenly distributed, with a particularly marked contrast between the countryside and the cities, with their impressive infrastructure.[1] The cities also benefited from money brought in by the Italian-American mafia. In 1958 there were 11,500 prostitutes in Havana alone. The Batista era was notable for corruption and an obsession with short-term gain, and the middle classes gradually distanced themselves from the regime.[2]

On 26 July 1953 a group of students attacked the Moncada barracks in Santiago de Cuba. Several of them were killed, and one of the leaders, Fidel Castro, was arrested. Though initially sentenced to fifteen years in prison, he was soon freed and fled to Mexico, where he set up a guerrilla group called the 26 July Movement (M-26), made up for the most part of young liberals. In 1957 this group entered Cuba and began a twenty-five-month armed conflict with Batista's forces in the Sierra Maestra. At the same time, urban students led by José Antonio Echevarria formed the Student Revolutionary Directorate, whose armed wing attacked the presidential palace in March of that year. The operation was a total failure: Echevarria was killed, leaving the student movement without impetus and Castro's group as the only viable opposition to Batista. During the ensuing conflict, violent repression by the regime claimed thousands of victims.[3] The urban guerrilla network was especially heavily affected, losing 80 percent of its members; the rural guerrilla groups in the Sierra lost only 20 percent.

On 7 November 1958, at the head of a column of guerrillas, Ernesto Guevara began a march on Havana. On 1 January 1959, Batista and the other leading figures in the dictatorship fled. Rolando Masferrer, the head of the sinister police apparatus known as "the Tigers," and Esteban Ventura, chief of the secret police, both of whom had a penchant for torture, fled to Miami. The leader of the Confederation of Cuban Workers (CTC), Eusebio Mujal, who had signed a number of agreements with Batista, took refuge in the Argentine embassy. The guerrillas' easy victory overshadowed the role played by other movements in Batista's downfall. In fact the guerrillas were involved in only a few minor actions, and Batista was defeated mainly because he had lost control of Havana to urban terrorism. The current U.S. arms embargo also worked against him.

On 8 January 1959 Castro, Guevara, and their forces made a triumphant entry into the capital. As soon as they had seized power, they began to conduct mass executions inside the two main prisons, La Cabaña and Santa Clara. According to reports in the foreign press, 600 of Batista's supporters were summarily executed during a five-month period. Extraordinary courts were established for the sole purpose of sentencing these opponents of the new regime. In the words of Jeannine Verdès-Laroux, "The form of the trials, and the procedures by which they were conducted, were highly significant. The totalitarian nature of the regime was inscribed there from the very beginning."[4] These travesties took place in a carnival-like atmosphere; a crowd of 18,000 people gathered at the Palace of Sports to "judge" the Batistan commandant

Jesús Sosa Blanco, who was accused of carrying out assassinations, by giving him the thumbs-down sign. As Sosa Blanco remarked before he was shot, the scenes were "worthy of ancient Rome."

In 1957, while still in the Sierra, Castro gave an interview to Herbert Matthews, a journalist from the *New York Times*, in which he declared: "Power does not interest me. After victory I want to go back to my village and just be a lawyer again." This statement was immediately contradicted by his policies. After seizing power, the new revolutionary government immediately fell victim to serious in-fighting, leading to the resignation of Prime Minister José Miró Cardona on 15 February 1959. Castro, who was already commander in chief of the army, replaced him. Although he initially promised to hold free elections within eighteen months, by June he had decided to postpone the elections indefinitely. Castro justified his decision in an address to the inhabitants of Havana, saying: "Elections? What for?" thus renouncing one of the fundamental points of the anti-Batista guerrilla program. In effect, he took over the position vacated by the fallen dictator. He also suspended the 1940 constitution and its guarantees of fundamental rights, governing by decree until 1976, when he imposed a constitution modeled on that of the U.S.S.R. The new laws 53 and 54 (relating to freedom of association) were particularly important in abrogating civil liberties by limiting the rights of citizens to meet in groups.

In the spring of 1959 Castro, who until then had collaborated closely with his associates, changed course and began removing democrats from the government. He relied increasingly on his brother Raúl (who was a member of the People's Socialist Party) and on Guevara, who was a convinced supporter of the Soviet Union. Agricultural reform was launched on 17 May 1959; by June the opposition between liberals and radicals had begun to crystalize. The initial plan, proposed by Agriculture Minister Humberto Sori Marin, had aimed at establishing a program to reallocate land that belonged to bourgeois landowners. Castro, however, was supportive of the radical policies proposed by the Instituto Nacional de Reforma Agraria (National Institute for Agricultural Reform), or INRA, which he had placed under the control of a group of orthodox Marxists, and of which he was the head. With a stroke of the pen he annulled the agriculture minister's program. In June 1959 Castro sought to radicalize the agrarian reform by ordering the army to take control of 100 estates in Camagüey Province.

The gathering storm finally broke in July 1959 when President Manuel Urrutia, a former magistrate who had courageously defended the rebels in 1956, resigned. Soon the minister of foreign affairs, Roberto Agramonte, was replaced by Raúl Roa, a staunch Castro supporter. Shortly afterward the minister of social affairs also resigned to protest a verdict against several pilots accused of crimes against civilians.[5] This pattern continued throughout 1960. Rupo Lopez Fresquet, the finance minister since January 1959, broke with Castro in March, joined the opposition, and then went into exile; Anres Suarez, another member of the government, also left the country that year. The last independent newspapers disappeared, and the rest were muzzled. On 20 January 1960 Jorge Zayas, who had been the editor of an anti-Batista newspaper called *Avance,* also went into exile; Miguel Angel Quevedo, the editor of *Bohemia,* the weekly that in 1959 had published Castro's testimony from his 1953 trial for the attack on the Moncada barracks, left in July. The only newspapers left were the Communist *Granma* (Grandma, named after a ship) and *Hoy* (Today). In the fall of 1960 the last remaining political and military opposition leaders, including William Morgan and Humberto Sori Marin, were arrested. Morgan, a guerrilla leader in the Sierra, was shot the following year.

Soon thereafter the last democrats, including Manolo Ray, the minister for public works, and Enrique Oltusky, the communications minister, were removed from the government.[6] The first great wave of departures now began. Nearly 50,000 people from the middle classes, many of whom had originally supported the revolution, all took the road to exile. This exodus of doctors, teachers, and lawyers did irreparable harm to Cuban society.

The workers were the next group to suffer repression. The labor unions had resisted the new regime from its earliest days. One of the principal leaders was the head of the Sugar Union, David Salvador. As a man of the left, he had broken with the PSP over its refusal to take a stand against Batista. He had organized strikes at the big sugar plants in 1955, had been arrested and tortured, and had supported the April 1958 strike, which was masterminded by Castro's 26 July Movement. After being democratically elected as secretary general of the CTC in 1959, Salvador was made to work with two assistants who were orthodox Communists appointed without a democratic mandate. He tried to resist their influence and to put a brake on their activities, but after the spring of 1960 he became increasingly marginalized. In June Salvador went into hiding, but in August 1962 he was arrested and spent the next twelve years in prison. Thus Castro forced off the stage another major figure in the anti-Batista movement. As a final blow against the workers, Castro forbade their sole remaining union, the CTC, to stage strikes. As a Party spokesman noted: "The union must not be used for the wrong purposes."

After being arrested in 1953, Castro had been saved mainly through the intervention of the archbishop of Santiago de Cuba, Monsignor Perez Serantes. The clergy were happy to see Batista's departure; several priests had even participated in the guerrilla organizations in the Sierra. Nevertheless, the church protested the overhasty condemnation of Batista's supporters in the same way that it had protested the actions of Masferrer's Tigers. In 1959 the church denounced Communist infiltration of parishes. Castro used the 1961 Bay of Pigs affair as a pretext to ban the periodical *La quincena*.[7] In May all religious colleges were closed and their buildings confiscated by the government, including the Bethlehem Jesuit College, where Castro himself had been educated. In full military dress, the "Lider Maximo" (Supreme Chief) declared: "Let the Falangist priests start packing their bags!" This warning was serious; on 17 September 131 priests were forced to leave the country. To survive, the church had to scale back its operations considerably. The regime continued to marginalize religious institutions and believers; though claiming that it would allow all Cubans to profess their faith freely, it subjected those who did to repressive measures, such as forbidding them access to university education or to jobs in the civil service.

Repression was also felt in the world of the arts. In 1961 Castro had stated that the position of the artist was at the very center of society. But a slogan perfectly encapsulated his real views: "The revolution is all; everything else is nothing." Heberto Padilla, a distinguished poet, finally left Cuba in 1980 after many years of persecution. Similarly, Reinaldo Arenas, after ten years of ostracism, left the country in the Mariel exodus.

Like other Communist leaders, Fidel Castro loves comparisons to the French Revolution; and just as Jacobin Paris had Louis Antoine de Saint-Just, revolutionary Havana had Che Guevara, a Latin American version of Nechaev, the nineteenth-century nihilist terrorist who inspired Dostoevsky's *The Devils*.

Ernesto Guevara was born into a well-off family in Buenos Aires in 1928, and as a young man he traveled throughout South America. Because of chronic asthma, his health was always fragile, but this did not prevent him from riding a motorbike all the way from the pampas to the jungles of Central America after finishing his medical studies. He came to hate the United States in the early 1950s, when he encountered the misery that ensued in Guatemala after the leftist regime of Jacobo Arbenz had been overthrown in a coup supported by the Americans. As Guevara wrote to a friend in 1957: "My ideological training means that I am one of those people who believe that the solution to the world's problems is to be found behind the Iron Curtain." One night in 1955 in Mexico he met a young Cuban lawyer in exile named Fidel Castro, who was preparing to return to Cuba. Guevara decided to accompany Castro, and they landed on the island in December 1956. In the resistance, Guevara soon became commander of a detachment, quickly gaining a reputation for ruthlessness; a child in his guerrilla unit who had stolen a little food was immediately shot without trial. Régis Debray, who was his companion in Bolivia, described him as "an authoritarian through and through" who wanted to impose a revolution of total Communism and sometimes found himself opposed to more democratic Cuban guerrilla commanders.[8]

In the autumn of 1958 Guevara opened a second front on the plains in Las Villas Province, in the center of the island. He carried out a highly successful action in Santa Clara, attacking a train of reinforcements sent there by Batista. The soldiers fled, refusing to fight. After the rebel victory, Guevara was assigned the post of state prosecutor, which gave him authority over pardons. He worked in La Cabaña prison, where a great number of people were executed, including some of his former comrades-in-arms who refused to abandon their democratic beliefs. "I can't be the friend of anyone who doesn't share my ideas," he once said.

As minister of industry and head of the Central Bank, Guevara found occasion to apply his own political beliefs, imposing the "Soviet model" on Cuba. He was an avid disciple of Lenin, in whose honor he named his son Vladimir. Though claiming to despise money, he lived in one of the rich, private areas of Havana. Despite later serving as minister of the economy, he had no notion of the most basic ideas of economics and ended up ruining the Central Bank. Social issues were more his forte, and he introduced "voluntary work Sundays" in emulation of the U.S.S.R. and China. He was a great admirer of the Cultural Revolution. According to Régis Debray, "It was he and not Fidel who in 1960 invented Cuba's first 'corrective work camp' (we would say 'forced labor camp')."[9]

In his will, this graduate of the school of terror praised the "extremely useful hatred that turns men into effective, violent, merciless, and cold killing machines."[10] He was dogmatic, cold, and intolerant, and there was almost nothing in him of the traditionally open and warm Cuban temperament. He was the architect of the militarization of Cuban youth, sacrificing them to the cult of the New Man.

His strongest desire was to spread the Cuban experiment far and wide. In 1963 he was in Algeria, and then in Dar es Salaam, then in the Congo, where he crossed paths with the Marxist Laurent Kabila, who is now the president of the Democratic Republic of Congo and who never hesitated to massacre civilians. Filled with passionate hatred for the United States, in 1966 he took his guerrilla forces on a crusade through South America, with a slogan encouraging the creation of "two, three, many Vietnams!"

Castro used Guevara for tactical purposes. Once their rupture was complete, Guevara went to Bolivia. There he tried to apply his theory of the guerrilla *foco* (cell), taking no notice of the policies of the Bolivian Communist Party. Not a single peasant joined his group there. Increasingly isolated and hunted by government forces, he was captured on 8 October 1967 and executed the following day.

Castro even modified his rebel army. In July 1959 one of Castro's closest advisers, the air force commander Diaz Lanz, resigned and fled to the United States. The following month, a wave of arrests was organized on the pretext that a coup was being planned.

Since 1956, Hubert Matos had helped the rebels in the Sierra, getting support from Costa Rica, supplying them with arms and munitions in a private plane, and liberating Santiago de Cuba, the country's second-largest city, at the head of the 9th detachment, named after Antonio Guiteras. Soon after being made governor of Camagüey Province, he found himself in profound disagreement with the "Communization" of the regime and resigned from his post. Castro believed that he was part of a conspiracy and had him arrested by Camilo Cienfuegos, another guerrilla hero, on the grounds that he had displayed "anti-Communist" tendencies. With scant regard for Matos' previous exemplary conduct as a freedom fighter, Castro subjected him to a Moscow-style show-trial in Havana and intervened personally against his former ally. Castro stood up in court and brought tremendous pressure to bear on the judges, saying: "I'm telling you that you must choose: it's Matos or me!" He also prevented witnesses for the defense from testifying. Matos received a twenty-year sentence, which he served to the last day. Several people close to him were also sent to prison.

Deprived of the means of expressing themselves, many of Castro's opponents went into hiding, where they were joined by people who had fought in the anti-Batista urban guerrilla groups. In the early 1960s this underground movement grew into a revolt based in the Escambray Mountains, the movement rejected forced collectivization and dictatorship. Raúl Castro sent in all the military forces at his disposal, including armored vehicles, artillery, and hundreds of infantry militia, to put down the rebellion. The families of rebel peasants were moved out of the area to eliminate popular support. Hundreds of people were forcibly moved to the tobacco plantations in Pinar del Río Province, hundreds of kilometers away in the west of the island. This was the only occasion when Castro actually deported parts of the population.

Despite these measures, the fighting continued for five years. Over time, however, as the rebels became increasingly isolated, they began to be captured. Justice was harsh for them. Guevara took the opportunity to liquidate Jesús Carreras, one of the leaders of the anti-Batista rebellion as a young man, who had opposed Guevara's policies since 1958. Wounded in combat, Carreras was dragged before a firing squad, where Guevara refused to grant him a stay of execution. Some 381 "bandits" were judged in similar fashion in the Santa Clara prison. In La Loma de los Coches prison more than 1,000 "counterrevolutionaries" were shot in the years between the triumph of 1959 and the final liquidation of the Escambray protest movement.

After resigning from the Ministry of Agriculture, Humberto Sori Marin tried to establish a *foco* in Cuba. He was soon arrested, court-martialed, and sentenced to death. His mother begged Castro for mercy, reminding him that he and Sori Marin had known each other since the 1950s. Castro promised that his life would be spared, but Sori Marin was shot a few days later.

The revolt in the Escambray Mountains was folowed by periodic attempts to land armed commando groups on Cuban soil. Many belonged to the Liberación group, headed by Tony Cuesta, and to the Alpha 66 group, both formed in the early 1960s. Most of these efforts, modeled on Castro's own return, resulted in failure.

In 1960, in a move typical of all dictatorships, the judiciary was forced to surrender its independence and was placed under the control of the central government.

The universities were also affected. Pedro Luis Boitel was a young student in civil engineering who put himself forward as a candidate for the presidency of the Federation of University Students. He had previously opposed Batista but was also a determined opponent of Fidel Castro. Another student named Rolando Cubella was the prefered candidate of the regime, and it was he who was elected with the help of the Castro brothers. Boitel was arrested soon afterward and sentenced to ten years in Boniato, a particularly harsh prison. Boitel went on hunger strike several times to protest the inhuman conditions there. On 3 April 1972, as he began yet another, he said to one of the prison governors: "I'm going on strike for the same rights as other political prisoners—rights that you are happy to demand for prisoners in other South American dictatorships, but that you won't allow here!" Nothing came of his protests, however. Boitel received no medical assistance and suffered terribly. After forty-five days his condition became critical; after forty-nine he slipped into a coma. The authorities continued to refuse to intervene. At three in the morning on 23 May 1972, 53 days after beginning his hunger strike, Boitel died. The authorities refused to allow his mother to see the body.

Soon after taking power, Castro began to organize an extensive security and intelligence service. As minister of defense, Raúl Castro reinstituted military tribunals, and soon the firing squad again became a judicial weapon. The first formal security organization was called the Dirección General de Contra-Inteligencia (State Security Department; DGCI). Popularly known as the Red Gestapo, the DGCI began to evolve in 1959–1962, when its task was to infiltrate and destroy the various groups opposed to Castro. The DGCI violently liquidated the Escambray guerrilla movement and oversaw the creation of forced-labor camps. It was also the department that ran the prison system.

Inspired by the Soviet model, the DGCI was initially directed by Ramiro Valdés, who had been one of Castro's closest advisers since their days in the Sierra. As the years passed, the department played an ever-larger role and gained a certain amount of autonomy. Information on its organizational structure comes from air force general Rafael Del Pino, who defected to Miami in 1987. In theory the DGCI is accountable to the Ministry of Internal Affairs (Minit) and is divided into various sections. Certain sections are charged with surveillance of officials in all other government departments. The Third Section observes everyone who works in culture, sports, and artistic fields, including writers and film directors. The Fourth Section oversees everyone who works in economic organizations and the ministries of transport and communication. The Sixth Section, which has more than 1,000 agents, is in charge of telephone wiretaps. The Eighth Section oversees the postal service; that is, it screens mail. Other sections watch over the diplomatic corps and keep tabs on visiting foreigners. The DGCI promotes the Castro regime's survival economically by using thousands of detainees as forced labor. Thus the department constitutes a world of privilege, whose staff have almost unlimited powers and a broad range of perquisites.

To control the population, the Dirección Special del Ministerio del Interior (DSMI) recruits *chivatos* (informers) by the thousand. The DSMI works in three different fields: one section keeps a file on every Cuban citizen; another keeps track of public opinion; the third, in charge of the "ideological line," keeps an eye on the church and its various congregations through infiltration.

Since 1967, Minit has had its own means of intervention, the Fuerzas Especiales, which in 1995 consisted of 50,000 soldiers. These special shock troops work quite closely with Dirección 5 and the Dirección de Seguridad Personal (DSP), Castro's praetorian guard. The DSP is made up of three escort units of approximately 100 men each, as well as a naval detachment consisting of sailors and frogmen. According to a 1995 estimate, the DSP numbers several thousand men. Its experts are constantly studying possible assassination scenarios; food tasters test Castro's food before he eats it, and a special medical team is on alert around the clock.

Dirección 5 specializes in the elimination of opponents. Two famous opponents of Batista who subsequently clashed with Castro fell victim to this section: Elias de la Torriente was killed in Miami, and Aldo Vera, one of the chiefs of the urban guerrilla group that fought against Batista, was killed in Puerto Rico. Hubert Matos, who now lives in exile in Miami, is forced to protect himself with armed bodyguards. Dirección 5 carries out its detentions and interrogations at a detention center in Villa Marista in Havana, a building that previously belonged to a congregation of Marist monks. Far from prying eyes and in conditions of extreme isolation, prisoners there are often subjected to psychological and physical torture.

Another component of the secret police is the Dirección General de la Inteligencia, which is in many ways a typical state intelligence-gathering service. It works above all in espionage, counterespionage, and the infiltration of foreign governments and organizations of Cuban exiles.

During the repressions of the 1960s, between 7,000 and 10,000 people were killed and 30,000 people imprisoned for political reasons. Thus the Castro government quickly faced the problem of what to do with a large number of prisoners, especially those from the Escambray rebellion and the failed Bay of Pigs invasion.

The Military Unit of Production Assistance (MUPA), which existed from 1964 to 1967, was the first attempt to use prisoners as a labor force. Beginning in November 1965, the MUPA organized concentration camps in which everyone who was considered a "potential danger to society," including religious prisoners (Catholics, notably Monsignor Jaime Ortega, the bishop of Havana; Protestants; and Jehovah's Witnesses), pimps, and homosexuals, was incarcerated. The prisoners were forced to build their own shelters, particularly in camps located in the Camagüey region. "Socially deviant people" were subjected to military discipline, which quickly degenerated into poor treatment, undernourishment, and isolation. Many detainees mutilated themselves to escape this hell; others emerged psychologically destroyed by their experiences. One of the MUPA's functions was the "reeducation" of homosexuals. Even before these camps were established, many homosexuals, and especially those employed in the cultural sphere, had lost their jobs. The University of Havana was the subject of antihomosexual purges, and it was common practice to "judge" homosexuals in public at their place of work. They were forced to admit their "vice," and had to vow to give it up or face dismissal and imprisonment. Two years after their establishment, the MUPA camps were closed as a result of widespread international protest. Nevertheless many sorts of harsh treatment continue to be reserved for homosexuals. Sometimes they are kept in a particular section of the prison, as is the case in East Havana's Nueva Carceral.

After the MUPA was dissolved, the regime forcibly conscripted prisoners into the military. First organized in 1967, the Centenary Youth Column (commemorating the 1868 revolt against the Spanish) became El Ejército Juvenil de Trabajo (the Young People's Work Army) in 1973. In this a paramilitary organization young people did agricultural and construction work, often under terrible conditions with hours that were almost intolerable, for a derisory wage of 7 pesos, equivalent to 30 cents in 1997 dollars.

In 1964 a forced labor program known as the Camilo-Cienfuegos plan was established on the Isle of Pines. The penal population was organized into brigades divided into groups of forty, known as *cuadrillas*. Each group was commanded by a sergeant or lieutenant and was assigned to agricultural and mining work. Working conditions were extremely harsh, and prisoners worked almost naked, wearing little more than undergarments. As a punishment, "troublemakers" were forced to cut grass with their teeth or to sit in latrine trenches for hours at a time.

The violence of the prison regime affected both political prisoners and common criminals. Violence began with the interrogations conducted by the Departamento Técnico de Investigaciones (DTI). The DTI used solitary confinement and played on the phobias of the detainees: one woman who was afraid of insects was locked in a cell infested with cockroaches. The DTI also used physical violence. Prisoners were forced to climb a staircase wearing shoes filled with lead and were then thrown back down the stairs. Psychological torture was also used, often observed by a medical team. The guards used sodium pentathol and other drugs to keep prisoners awake. In the Mazzora hospital, electric shock treatment was routinely used as a punishment without any form of medical observation. The guards also used attack dogs and mock executions; disciplinary cells had neither water nor electricity; and some detainees were kept in total isolation.

Because responsibility in Cuba was generally considered to be collective, punishment was also frequently collective. The regime exerted pressure on its opponents by forcing their relatives to pay a social cost; the children of detainees were banned from higher education, and spouses were often fired from their jobs.

Sentences are often lengthened by the prison authorities. Anyone who rebels has another stretch added. Similar penalties apply to prisoners who refuse to wear the uniform of common criminals, who refuse to take part in "rehabilitation plans," or who take part in a hunger strike. The courts view such actions as attacks on the state and add another one or two years of incarceration in a labor camp. Prisoners commonly serve an additional third or half of their original sentence. Boitel, who was initially sentenced to ten years in prison, ultimately served forty-two.

A distinction should be made between "normal" prisons and the high-security prisons of the G-2, the secret police. Prison Kilo 5.5 is a high-security prison situated 3.5 miles from the Pinar del Río freeway. For a time, under the authority of Captain Jorge González, known as "El Nato," common criminals and political prisoners were routinely kept together. Cells originally intended for two often contained as many as seven or eight prisoners, most of whom were thus forced to sleep on the floor. The disciplinary cells were dubbed *tostadoras* (toasters), because of their terrible heat in both winter and summer. A separate section exists for women. Pinar del Río, another high-security prison, contains underground cells and interrogation rooms. Over the last few years, psychological torture has largely replaced physical torture; sleep deprivation, adopted from the U.S.S.R., is a particularly common technique. Once the sleep pattern is broken, the notion of time is lost. Prisoners are also told that their families are under threat and that they will no longer be allowed family visits. The Kilo 7 prison, in Camagüey, is especially violent. In 1974, forty prisoners died in a rebellion there.

The G-2 center in Santiago de Cuba, built in 1980, possesses cells with extreme temperatures (both high and low). Prisoners are awakened every twenty or thirty minutes. This sort of treatment may continue several months. Kept naked and totally cut off from the outside world, many of the prisoners who have undergone the terrible psychological tortures here emerge with irreparably damaged psyches.

For many years La Cabaña was the most infamous prison in Cuba, known as the place where Sori Marin and Carreras were executed. As late as 1982, nearly 100 prisoners were shot there. La Cabaña specialized in holding its prisoners in tiny cells known as *ratoneras*, or rat holes. It was finally closed in 1985. Elsewhere, however, executions have continued, including at Boniato, a high-security prison known for extreme violence. Some political prisoners held at Boniato have been known to smear themselves with excrement to avoid being raped by other prisoners. Boniato houses all prisoners sentenced to death, regardless of the category of their crime. It is known for its grillwork cells or *tapiadas*. Several writers—including the poets Jorge Valls, who was there for 7,340 days, and Ernesto Diaz Rodriguez, as well as a commanding officer, Eloy Guttierrez Menoyo—have described the terrible conditions there. The food is contaminated, and infectious diseases such as typhus and leptospirosis are common. As a result, hundreds of prisoners have died from hunger and lack of medical care. In August 1995 a hunger strike was launched jointly by the political and common prisoners seeking to draw attention to the deplorable conditions. The strike continued for almost a month but achieved no improvement.

Iron cages are still used in some prisons. In the late 1960s the Tres Macios del Oriente prison used cages originally intended for common criminals for political prisoners as well. The cages were 1 meter wide, 1.8 meters high, and about 10 meters long. Such closed quarters are extremely hard to bear, especially with no water or sanitation; yet prisoners of both types were kept here for weeks or even months at a time.

The 1960s also saw the invention of *requisas* (requisitionings) as a form of repression. In the middle of the night, detainees would be awakened and violently removed from their cells. They were then beaten, often while naked, and forced to wait until the end of the inspection before being allowed to return to their cells. *Requisas* might be carried out several times a month.

Visits by relatives provide another opportunity to humiliate prisoners. In La Cabaña prisoners were made to appear naked before their family, and imprisoned husbands were forced to watch intimate body searches carried out on their wives.

Female inmates in Cuban prisons are especially vulnerable to acts of sadism by guards. More than 1,100 women have been sentenced as political prisoners since 1959. In 1963 they were housed in the Guanajay prison. Numerous eyewitness statements attest to beatings and other humiliations. For instance, before showering, detainees were forced to undress in full view of the guards, who then beat them. Havana's Nuevo Amanecer (New Dawn) prison is the largest in the country. Dr. Martha Frayde, a long-standing friend of Castro, who was the Cuban representative at UNESCO in the 1960s, described this prison and its exceptionally harsh conditions:

> My cell was six meters by five. There were twenty-two of us sleeping there in bunk beds of two or three layers. Sometimes there were as many as forty-two of us. Sanitation was dreadful. The basins we had to wash in were filthy, and it became impossible to wash at all . . . We were often short of water. It became impossible to empty the toilets, which filled up and overflowed. A layer of excrement formed, invading our cells. Like an irresistible wave it reached the corridor, then flowed down the stairs and into the garden . . . The political prisoners . . . made such a fuss that the prison authorities brought in a water truck . . . We managed to sweep away some of the excrement with the pressure hoses, but there still wasn't enough water, and we had to live with this vile layer for another few days."[11]

One of Cuba's largest concentration camps, El Manbu, in the Camagüey region, contained more than 3,000 people in the 1980s. At the camp at Siboney, where living conditions and food are execrable, German shepherd dogs are used to track escaped prisoners. Those who are caught are judged by a popular tribunal inside the camp and sent on to a forced-labor camp, where a "severe regime" operates. At these camps, *consejos de trabajo de les pressos* (prisoner work councils) judge and punish their own companions.

In 1986 some 3,000 women were incarcerated in the Potosí camp, in Victoria de las Tunas, mostly for juvenile delinquency, prostitution, and political crimes. There are also special camps for children and adolescents. Situated near Santiago de las Vegas, the Arco Iris (Rainbow) camp was designed to hold 1,500 adolescents. The Nueva Vida (New Life) camp is in the southwestern region. In the Palos zone is the Capitiolo, a special internment camp for children up to age ten. The adolescents cut cane or make simple objects by hand, which can then be sold by the government.

Although prisoners have no rights, they are subject to a rehabilitation program, which is intended to prepare them for reintegration into the socialist society. The program has three stages: the first, called the "period of maximal security," takes place in prison; the second, called "medium security," takes place on a *granja* (farm); the third, called "minimal security," is considered an "open regime."

Detainees who are included in the program wear the blue uniform *(azul)* of common criminals, as part of the regime's effort to blur the distinction between the two types of prisoner. For a while, anyone who refused to follow the program was forced to wear the yellow uniform *(amarillo)* of Batista's army—a harsh punishment for those prisoners who had previously belonged to guerrilla groups that fought against Batista. Prisoners who refused to wear either uniform were forced by the authorities to wear nothing but their underwear for years on end and were banned from receiving visits. Hubert Matos was one such prisoner. He later reported: "I lived for several months with no uniform and no visits. I was cut off from the outside world simply because I had refused to conform to the whims of the authorities . . . I preferred being naked, among other naked prisoners, even in those badly overcrowded conditions."

The transition from one stage of the program to the next depended upon the decision of a "reeducation officer." On the whole, the officer's intention was to impose acceptance through physical and mental exhaustion. Carlos Franqui, a former official in the regime, described the spirit of the system: "The opponent of the regime is a patient, and the guard is a doctor. The prisoners will be set free when the guard decides that the cure has been effective. Time is of no account until the patient is cured."

The longest sentences were served out in the prisons. In 1974 La Cabaña had a special section (zone 2) reserved for civilian offenders and another for military prisoners (zone 1). More than 1,000 men were housed in zone 2 in galleries thirty meters long and six meters wide. Other prisons are run by the G-2, the secret police.

People who receive relatively light sentences, between three and seven years, are sent to *granjas,* an invention of the Castro era very similar to the Soviet corrective labor camps. These "farms" consist of barracks surrounded by rows of barbed-wire fences and several observation towers, manned by guards from the Ministry of Internal Affairs, who are allowed to open fire on anyone they believe is attempting to escape.[12] Each camp generally contains between 500 and 700 prisoners, who are required to work for twelve to fifteen hours a day. The guards are permitted to use any tactics, including clubbing prisoners with their guns, to make them work faster.

The "open regime" is generally a construction site where prisoners live, usually under the control of the military. The number of prisoners at each site ranges from 50 to 200, depending on the size of the project. Detainees on the *granjas* make the prefabricated elements that are assembled at the open-regime sites. Here detainees are granted three-day furloughs at the end of each month. Evidently, the food is not as bad at these sites as it is in the camps. Each site is maintained as an independent entity; this strategy makes it easier to manage the detainees, ensuring that not too many are ever together at the same time to present united resistance. Some of the open-regime sites are in urban settings; there were six operating in Havana during the late 1980s.

This type of system affords a clear economic benefit.[13] For example, all detainees are mobilized to harvest the sugar crop, the *zafra*. The head of the prisons in Oriente Province, Papito Struch, declared in 1974: "Detainees are the island's main workforce." In 1974 the work they carried out was worth 348 million dollars. Many government departments make use of the prisoners. About 60 percent of the labor force of the Department for Development of Social and Agricultural Works is made up of detainees. The prisoners work on dozens of farms in the Picadura valleys, which constitute the main showplace for the work reeducation program. Among the many heads of state who have been given tours of these sites are Leonid Brezhnev, Houari Boumediene, and François Mitterrand.

All the provincial secondary schools were built by political prisoners with minimal input from civilian society, usually consisting of no more than a handful of civil engineers. In Oriente and Camagüey, detainees have built more than twenty polytechnic schools. They have also built numerous sugar stores throughout the island. A list in *Bohemia* of other projects built by penal labor included dairies and livestock centers in Havana Province; carpentry workshops and secondary schools in Pinar del Río; a sty, dairy, and woodworking center in Matanzas; and two secondary schools and ten dairies in Las Villas. The work plans become more complex every year, requiring an ever larger prison workforce.

In September 1960 Castro formed the Committees for Defense of the Revolution (CDRs), small neighborhood committees based around the *cuadra* (block). The leader is charged with surveillance of "counterrevolutionary" activities. The resulting social control is extremely tight. Members of the committees attend all CDR meetings and patrol constantly to root out "enemy infiltration." The surveillance and denunciation system is so rigorous that family intimacy is almost nonexistent.

The purpose of the CDRs became all too apparent in March 1961 when, at the instigation of Ramiro Valdés, the chief of the security forces, a huge raid was organized and carried out in the space of a single weekend. On the basis of lists drawn up by the CDRs, more than 100,000 people were questioned, and several thousand were taken away to detention centers scattered across the country.

The CDRs are responsible for organizing *actos de repudio* (acts of repudiation) designed to marginalize and break the resistance of opponents—labeled *gusanos* (worms)—and their families. A crowd gathers in front of the opponent's house to throw stones and attack the inhabitants. Castroist slogans and insults are written on the walls. The police intervene only when they decide that the "mass revolutionary action" is becoming physically dangerous for the victims. This quasi-lynching is designed to encourage reciprocal hatred between inhabitants of the small island. *Actos de repudio* destroy the links between neighbors and damage the fabric of society to bolster the omnipotence of the socialist state. The victim has no means of defending himself. Ricardo Bofill, the president of the Cuban Human Rights Committee, was forced to undergo one such act of repudiation in 1988. The liberation theologian Oswaldo Payas Sardinas underwent the same treatment in 1991. But because Cubans by the end of the 1980s were beginning to tire of this avalanche of social hatred, in both of these cases the authorities were forced to bring in assailants from elsewhere.

According to Article 16 of Cuba's constitution, the state "organizes, directs, and controls all economic activity in accordance with the directives of the single plan for social and economic development." This collectivist phraseology hides a simple truth: inside their own country, Cubans are not free to work where they want or to spend their money as they wish. In 1980 the country experienced a wave of discontent and unrest, with factories and warehouses being attacked and burned. The DGCI arrested 500 opponents of the regime during a seventy-two-hour period. The security services then intervened in the provinces to close the free peasant markets. Finally, a major campaign was launched against the black market across the whole country.

Law 32, against absenteeism in the workplace, was passed in March 1971. In 1978 a law was adopted to prevent criminality before it actually happened. What this meant in practice was that any Cuban could be arrested on any pretext if the authorities believed that he presented a danger to state security, even if he had not committed any illegal act. In effect the law criminalized any thought that did not accord with the ideas of the regime, turning every Cuban into a potential suspect.

In the 1960s Cubans began to "vote with their oars." The first large group to leave were the fishermen, in 1961. The *balseros* were the Cuban equivalent of the Southeast Asian boat people and were as much a part of the human landscape of the island as the cane cutters. Exile was subtly used by Castro as a means of regulating internal tensions. The phenomenon dates from the earliest days of the regime and was used constantly until the mid 1970s. Many of the exiled fled to Florida or the American base at Guantánamo.

The phenomenon first came to the world's attention in April 1980 with the Mariel crisis. Thousands of Cubans mobbed the Peruvian embassy in Havana, demanding exit visas to escape from an intolerable daily life. After several weeks the authorities allowed 125,000—out of a population of 10 million—to leave the country from the port of Mariel. Castro also took this opportunity to get rid of a number of criminals and people who were mentally ill. The massive exodus was a demonstration of the regime's failure, for many of the *Marielitos* came from the poorest segments of society, for whom the regime had always claimed to care above all others. People of every race and age were fleeing Cuban socialism. After the Mariel episode numerous other Cubans registered on lists of people seeking permission to leave the country. Nearly twenty years later, most of them are still waiting.

In the summer of 1994, violent riots occurred in Havana for the first time since 1959. A number of people who wanted to leave the country on the makeshift rafts called *balsas* were prevented from doing so by the police. They reacted by sacking and looting the Colombo quarter on the Malecón seafront. By the time calm was restored, dozens of people had been arrested, and Castro was again forced to authorize the departure of 25,000 people. Departures have been constant ever since, and the American bases at Guantánamo and in Panama are full of voluntary exiles. Castro has tried to prevent people from leaving by sending helicopters to drop sandbags onto the *balsas* when they are at sea. In the summer of 1994, 7,000 people lost their lives while attempting to flee. It is estimated that approximately one-third of all *balseros* have died while at sea. Over thirty years, approximately 100,000 have attempted the journey. The result of this exodus is that out of 11 million inhabitants, 2 million now live in exile. Exile has scattered many families among Havana, Miami, Spain, and Puerto Rico.

From 1975 to 1989 Cuba was the major supporter of the Marxist-Leninist regime of the Popular Movement for the Liberation of Angola (MPLA; see

Chapter 26), which was engaged in a civil war with UNITA forces led by Jonas Savimbi. In addition to sending innumerable "cooperators" and dozens of technical advisers, Cuba sent an expeditionary force of 50,000 men.[14] The Cuban army behaved in Africa as though it was a conquered territory, engaging in systematic corruption and smuggling (of silver, ivory, and diamonds). When an agreement signed in 1989 put an end to the conflict, the Cuban troops, most of whom were black, were repatriated. Cuban fatalities in the war were estimated at between 7,000 and 11,000.

This experience shook the convictions of many officers. General Arnaldo Ochoa, the head of the expeditionary force in Angola and a member of the Central Committee of the Communist Party, organized a plot to overthrow Castro. He was arrested and brought before a military court on corruption charges, together with a number of other high-ranking officers from the army and the security services, including the de la Guardia brothers, António and Patricio. The de la Guardias had also been smuggling drugs for the MC (Moneda Convertible) service, popularly known as the "marijuana and cocaine" service. Ochoa's involvement in smuggling was in fact quite limited; he had returned from Angola with only a little ivory and a few diamonds. But Castro used corruption as an excuse to rid himself of a potential rival, who, by virtue of his prestige and high political office, could easily have channeled disaffection into an anti-Castro movement. Ochoa's sentencing and execution were followed by a purge in the army, causing further destabilization and trauma. Conscious of the strong resentment that many officers felt toward the regime, Castro appointed a trusted general minister of internal affairs. Henceforth the regime could count on only the special forces for certain blind devotion.

In 1978 there were between 15,000 and 20,000 prisoners of conscience in Cuba. Many came from M-26 or the student anti-Batista movements, or were still in prison from the days of the Escambray resistance and the Bay of Pigs.[15] In 1986 some 12,000–15,000 political prisoners were kept in fifty regional prisons throughout the island. Others were still at the many open-regime sites, with their brigades of 50, 100, or 200 prisoners. Today the government admits to holding between 400 and 500 political prisoners. In the spring of 1997 there was another wave of arrests. According to Cuban human rights representatives, many of whom are themselves former detainees, physical torture no longer occurs in Cuban prisons. These sources, together with Amnesty International, put the number of political prisoners in Cuba in 1997 at between 980 and 2,500 (including men, women, and children).

From 1959 through the late 1990s more than 100,000 Cubans experienced life in one of the camps, prisons, or open-regime sites. Between 15,000 and 17,000 people were shot. "No bread without freedom, no freedom without bread," said the young lawyer Fidel Castro in 1959. But as one dissident said before the start of the "special regime," when Soviet aid had come to an end: "A prison where you eat well is still a prison."

Like a tyrant from a different age, faced with the failures of his regime and the difficulties plaguing Cuba, Castro announced in 1994 that he "would rather die than abandon the revolution." What price must the Cuban people pay to satisfy his pride?

Nicaragua: The Failure of a Totalitarian Project

Nicaragua is a small country in Central America, sandwiched between Honduras and Costa Rica, with a tradition of bloody upheavals. Starting in the 1930s, it was dominated by the Somoza family, whose most recent head, General Anastasio Somoza Debayle, was "elected" president in February 1967. Little by little, thanks to a formidable National Guard, the Somoza family took control of 25 percent of all arable land and most of the tobacco, sugar, rice, and coffee plantations, as well as a large number of the country's factories.

This situation led to the formation of several armed opposition movements. Following the Cuban model, Carlos Fonseca Amador and Tomás Borge founded the Frente Sandinista de Liberación Nacional (FSLN) in 1961. The group was named after Augusto César Sandino, a leftist army general who had led a guerrilla war from the 1920s until his assassination by the Somoza government in 1934. Despite several catastrophic failures, the FSLN survived with some assistance from Cuba and North Korea. In 1967 riots broke out in Managua and were put down by the National Guard; the death of at least 200 people in the streets of the capital helped to stimulate popular support for the FSLN. After the assassination in 1978 of Pedro Joaquín Chamorro, the owner of the liberal newspaper *La prensa* and one of the leaders of the anti-Somoza opposition, the Sandinistas resumed their guerrilla activities. A genuine civil war then began between the FSLN and Somoza's National Guard. On 21 February 1978 the town of Masaya rose up. In August a guerrilla leader named Edén Pastora captured the Somoza presidential palace in Managua, taking 1,200 hostages; the government freed several FSLN leaders in exchange for them. In September the National Guard, in an effort to retake Estelí after a Sandinista assault, bombed the town with napalm and massacred a number of civilians in violent street fighting. More than 160,000 people fled Nicaragua for neighboring Costa Rica. In April 1979 the towns of Estelí and León rose up again, as did the city of Granada. The rebels were better organized than they had been the previous year, and they were further aided by the rapidly growing popular revulsion toward the Somocistas. Throughout June the Sandinistas took over more and more of the countryside, gradually approaching the outskirts of Managua. On 17 July 1979 the dictator, who had lost all international support, was obliged to leave the country. Between 25,000 and 30,000 people died in the civil war and the repression, although the Sandinistas claimed that the figure was 50,000. Whatever the total losses were, the population of 3 million had paid an extremely high price.

The Revolutionary Careers of Ortega and Pastora

As young men, both Edén Pastora and Daniel Ortega had experience of the prisons of the Somoza regime. Pastora was from a landed middle-class family and was about twenty at the time of Castro's triumph in Cuba. Ortega, born in 1945 into a more modest family, was already taking part in the anti-Somoza youth organizations in the early 1960s.

The Frente Sandinista de Liberación Nacional, created by Fonseca and Borge, brought together people of various political tendencies. The two founders themselves had different political views: Fonseca was an admirer of Castro, Borge of Mao Zedong. Over the years, three currents became discernible in the group. The "prolonged people's war" faction was a Maoist group that assigned the highest priority to the struggle in the countryside. The Marxist-Leninist or "proletarian" faction, led by Fonseca and Jaime Wheelock, sought support from the embryonic proletariat. The *tercerista* (third-way) faction, led by Marxist dissidents and democrats, sought to foment mass insurrection by creating an urban guerrilla network through alliances with non-Marxists. Pastora belonged to this group, as did Ortega initially, although he soon switched to the Marxist-Leninist proletarians. Ortega joined the revolution out of a sense of political commitment; for Pastora the revolution was an opportunity to avenge his father, who had been a democratic opponent of the regime and had been killed by the Somocistas. After the violent strikes that followed the rigged presidential elections of 1967, Pastora was arrested and tortured (first bled, then forced to drink his own blood). After his release he launched a punitive campaign against his torturers. The two guerrillas who accompanied him were Daniel and Humberto Ortega. Later Daniel Ortega fell into the hands of Somoza's police, who kept him in prison until 1974. Meanwhile Pastora continued to build the guerrilla movement; he was received by Fidel Castro, reiterated his allegiance to parliamentary democracy, and established links with other Central American democrats such as José Maria Fuguérés in Costa Rica and Omar Torrijos in Panama. Ortega was freed in 1974 in exchange for a Somocista dignitary who had been taken hostage; he soon flew to Havana. Pastora remained with the guerrillas.

In October 1977 an uprising was organized in several Nicaraguan cities. Harried by the National Guard and pounded by the Somoza air force, Pastora and Ortega took refuge in the jungle. In January 1978 the revolt spread throughout the country. Pastora assaulted the Chamber of Deputies in the National Palace and liberated Tomás Borge and all other political prisoners. While Ortega was dividing his time between Havana and the northern front in Nicaragua, one of his brothers, Camilo, died during an attack on Masaya. Supported by Cuban military advisers, the uprising continued to gain ground. FSLN cadres who had been in hiding in Cuba returned to Nicaragua, while Pastora and his guerrillas fought hard against the elite units of the National Guard in southern Nicaragua.

When the Sandinistas triumphed in July 1979, Pastora became deputy minister of internal affairs; Ortega was elected president. Ortega openly aligned himself with Cuba, allowing military advisers and Cuban "internationalists" to flock to Managua. Pastora, commited to parliamentary democracy, became increasingly isolated. In June 1981 he resigned and began to organize armed resistance in the south of the country.

Following their victory, the Sandinistas immediately formed a Junta de Reconstrucción Nacional, which included socialists, Communists, democrats, and moderates. The Junta proposed a fifteen-point program that envisaged a democratic regime based on universal suffrage and the freedom to establish multiple political parties. In the meantime, executive power was to remain in the hands of the Junta, which the Sandinistas soon controlled.

The Junta acknowledged special ties to Cuba but did not exclude the possibility of Western participation in the reconstruction of Nicaragua;[16] the civil war had caused about 800 million dollars' worth of damage to property and infrastructure. However, the democrats were quickly marginalized. In April 1980 both Alfonso Robelo and Violeta Chamorro, the widow of Pedro Joaquín Chamorro, resigned from the Junta. Among the reasons they gave for their resignation was their disapproval of the way in which the FSLN had taken control of the State Council.

During this early period of political crisis, the Junta, which was now firmly under the control of the Sandinistas, established a secret police force. The Sandinistas transformed the 6,000 guerrillas of 1979 into an army, which over the next decade expanded to 75,000 troops. After 1980 military service became obligatory; all men aged seventeen to thirty-five were mobilized and obliged to report to military tribunals that had been created in December 1980. Students could pursue their education only after undergoing military training. The Sandinistas sought to use the army to help guerrilla groups throughout Central America, beginning with El Salvador. In January 1981 the Salvadoran authorities publicly announced that Sandinista patrols were encroaching on their territory.

In line with the Sandinistas' leftist views, the regime enacted a centrally planned economy and pursued rapid nationalization; the state soon controlled more than 50 percent of all the means of production. The whole country was forced to accept the social model imposed by the FSLN. Following the Cuban model, the Sandinista government covered the country with mass organizations. Each neighborhood had a Comité de Defensa Sandinista (Sandinista Defense Committee), or CDS, with the same role as that of the Cuban CDRs: to divide up the country and watch over its inhabitants. Children, who had much more access to schooling than they had under the Somoza regime, belonged to scouting and pioneer organizations known as Camilitos, after Camilo Ortega. Women, workers, and peasants were drafted into associations and brigades that were closely controlled by the FSLN. Political parties had no real freedom. The press was quickly gagged, and journalists worked under pervasive censorship. Gilles Bataillon correctly characterized these conditions when he wrote that the Sandinistas wanted "to occupy the whole social and political space of the country."[17]

The Sandinistas and the Indians

Roughly 150,000 Indians live on the Atlantic coast of Nicaragua: the Miskito, Sumo, and Rama tribal groups, as well as creoles and Ladinos (those of mixed Spanish and Mayan ethnic background). Under previous regimes these groups had enjoyed a certain degree of autonomy and were excused from paying taxes and from military service. Soon after coming to power, the Sandinistas began to attack the Indian communities, which were determined to hold onto their land and their language. Lyster Athders, the leader of the Alliance for Progress of the Miskitos and Sumo (Alpromisu), was arrested in August 1979 and killed two months later. Early in 1981 the national leaders of the Misurasata, a political organization that united several tribes, were arrested. On 21 February 1981 the armed forces killed seven Miskito Indians and wounded seventeen others. On 23 December 1981 in Leimus, the Sandinista army massacred seventy-five miners who had demanded payment of back wages. Another thirty-five miners suffered the same fate the next day.

The Sandinistas also carried out forcible displacements of native populations on the pretext of protecting them against "armed incursions of Somocista guards" operating out of Honduras. In 1982 the Sandinista army forcibly moved nearly 10,000 Indians inland. Hunger became a formidable weapon: the Indians in the interior received a plentiful supply of food from the government, while those who remained on the coast were allowed to suffer. During these operations the army committed a number of atrocities. Thousands of Indians (estimates at the time ranged from 7,000 to 15,000) took refuge in Honduras; thousands more (perhaps as many as 14,000) were imprisoned in Nicaragua.

The Sandinistas regularly opened fire on people attempting to flee across the Coco River. These three factors—massacres, displacements of the population, and exile abroad—led the anthropologist Gilles Bataillon to speak of "a politics of ethnocide" in Nicaragua.

The Indians turned against the Managua administration and formed two guerrilla groups, the Misura and Misurasata, which contained people from the Sumo, Rama, and Miskito tribes. Although these tribes had very different life styles, they were united in their opposition to the government's assimilationist policies.

Scandalized by the repressive policies, Edén Pastora exclaimed in the Council of Ministers that "even that tyrant Somoza left them alone! He might have exploited them a bit, but you want to turn them into proletarians by force!" Tomás Borge, the Maoist minister of the interior, replied that "the revolution could tolerate no exceptions."

The government had made its decision, and the Sandinistas opted for forced assimilation. A state of siege, declared in March 1982, lasted until 1987. The first years of Sandinista power were thus characterized on the Atlantic coast by abuses of power, flagrant violations of human rights, and the systematic destruction of Indian villages.

From north to south, the country quickly rose up against the dictatorial regime in Managua and its totalitarian tendencies. A new civil war began, affecting numerous zones in the regions of Jinotega, Estelí, and Nueva Segovia in the north, Matagalpa and Boaco in the center, and Zelaya and Río San Juan in the south. On 9 July 1981 Pastora broke publicly with the FSLN and left Nicaragua. Resistance against the Sandinistas—wrongly labeled "Contra," that is, "counterrevolutionary" by the outside world—became more organized. Operating in the north was the Fuerza Democrática Nicaragüense (Nicaraguan Democratic Force; FDN), which was made up of both former Somoza supporters and genuine freedom fighters. In southern Nicaragua, resistance was organized by former Sandinistas and reinforced by peasants who rejected collectivization of the land and Indians who had fled to Honduras or Costa Rica. Together, these groups formed the Alianza Revolucionaria Democrática (ARDE), with Alfonso Robelo as political leader and Edén Pastora as military leader.

The new civil war spread quickly. The most violent confrontations took place in the northern and southern parts of the country between 1982 and 1987, with atrocities committed by both sides. The Nicaraguan conflict turned into a confrontation between East and West. Fidel Castro played the role of mentor to the new regime. Cubans were present in all units of the Sandinista army and advised the Council of Ministers in Managua. While Edén Pastora was still in the government, during a visit to Havana he saw the entire Sandinista cabinet assembled in Castro's office to receive his advice on how to manage agriculture, defense, internal affairs, and other branches of government. For a while the Cuban military advisers were led by General Arnaldo Ochoa. The population transfers of the Indian population were assisted by Bulgarian, East German, and even Palestinian advisers.

In 1984 the government attempted to restore its credibility by presenting a democratic façade through organized presidential elections. A May 1984 speech by Bayardo Arce, one of the nine members of the leadership council of the FSLN, is particularly revealing of the Sandinistas' intentions: "We believe that these elections should be used to vote for Sandinism, because it has been called into question and stigmatized by imperialism. It should allow us to demonstrate that whatever happens, the people of Nicaragua support totalitarianism and Marxism-Leninism . . . We should now agree to do away with pluralism and the existence of a Socialist Party, a Communist Party, a Christian Democratic Party, and a Social Democratic Party. All of that has been useful up to now, but it has had its day, and we should do away with it." Arce then invited his listeners (who were members of the pro-Soviet Nicaraguan Socialist Party) to establish a single party for all.[18]

The conservative candidate Arturo Cruz withdrew from the campaign because of the violence caused by the *turbas,* the thugs of the Sandinista party. It thus came as no surprise when Daniel Ortega won, although this outcome failed to curb the tension and unrest in the country. In 1984 and 1985 the government organized several major offensives against the anti-Sandinista resistance. In 1985 and 1986, troops from Managua attacked opposition forces along the Costa Rican border. Despite continuing popular support, Edén Pastora gave up the fight in 1986 and withdrew with his troops into Costa Rica. Outmaneuvered by Sandinista commandos, the Miskito Indians offered only sporadic resistance to the government after 1985. The Contra forces and the anti-Sandinista resistance also suffered but continued fighting.

The government used the Contra attacks to justify the suspension of numerous individual and political freedoms and to excuse the country's poor economic performance. Nearly 50 percent of the budget was devoted to military spending. The economy was further devastated by the trade embargo imposed by the United States on 1 May 1985 with the support of most Western European countries. The coffee plantations, one of the main sources of export income, were ravaged by the war. The country's external debt soared and inflation peaked at 36,000 percent in 1989. At that point the government introduced rationing, but acute shortages of milk and meat persisted.

The Sandinista government frequently used repressive measures to deal with its opponents. Soon after coming to power, it established special courts to try political opponents. Decree No. 185, dated 5 December 1979, created special tribunals to pass judgment on former members of the National Guard and civilian Somoza supporters, in much the same way that the Castro regime had judged Batista's supporters. Although detainees were judged according to the penal code in place at the time the offenses were committed, the appeals process had to go through these same extraordinary courts. This strategy allowed the Sandinistas to establish a special legal mechanism outside the normal justice system. Trials were marked by many procedural irregularities. Sometimes crimes were considered to have been proved even when no concrete evidence had been produced. Judges operated without the presumption of innocence, and sentences often rested on notions of collective responsibility rather than on any proof of individual guilt.

On 15 March 1982 the Junta declared a state of siege, which allowed it to close independent radio stations, suspend the right of association, and limit the freedom of trade unions, which had been hostile to the Sandinistas and had resisted attempts to transform them into extensions of the central government. There were also campaigns against religious groups, including the Moravians and Jehovah's Witnesses. In June 1982 Amnesty International estimated that more than 4,000 former Somoza national guardsmen were imprisoned by the Junta, as well as several hundred prisoners of conscience. One year later, the number of political prisoners had soared to 20,000. At the end of 1982 the United Nations Human Rights Commission drew attention to two even more worrying phenomena, the number of "disappeared" among people who had been arrested as counterrevolutionaries and the number of people who had died "while attempting to escape."

To combat the opposition groups, the Sandinistas in April 1983 established Tribunales Populares Anti-Somocista (Popular Anti-Somoza Tribunals; TPAs) to pass judgment on anyone who belonged to a Contra group or participated in other military activity. Any act of rebellion or sabotage meant an appearance before the TPA. Members of the TPA were nominated by the government and came from organizations closely associated with the FSLN. Lawyers, some of whom had not even completed their training, carried out the legal formalities. The TPAs often accepted any extrajudicial admission of guilt as proof, regardless of its provenance. The TPAs were finally dissolved in 1988.

Waves of arrests began in rural zones in 1984. Carlos Nueves Tellos, an FSLN delegate, defended the prolonged periods of preventive detention, arguing that they were "a necessity imposed by the difficulties inherent in having to carry out hundreds of interrogations in the rural zones." Members of opposition parties—liberals, Social Democrats, and Christian Democrats—and unionists were arrested for "activities favorable to the enemy." There was no possible means of appeal. The secret police force, which had a reputation for extreme violence, could detain any suspect indefinitely without bringing charges. The police could also use whatever sort of detention they deemed necessary and were authorized to keep prisoners from making contact with their lawyers or families. Some detainees never managed to contact their lawyers at all.

The Sandinistas quickly created an effective mechanism of repression. The country was put under the control of 15,000 special troops from the Ministry of Internal Affairs. One service in particular, the Dirección General de Seguridad del Estado (DGSE), was responsible for surveillance and special operations. Trained by Cuban agents from the G-2, the DGSE answered directly to the Ministry of Internal Affairs. The DGSE was in charge of the arrest and interrogation of political prisoners and practiced what is known as "clean torture," adopted from Cuban and East German experts. Most interrogations took place in the El Chipote detention center in the German-Pomarés military complex on the slopes of the Loma de Tiscapa volcano, just behind the Managua Intercontinental Hotel. Two members of the Christian Socialist Party, José Rodriguez and Juana Blandon, confirm that when they were interrogated there, they were deprived of sleep and their families were threatened. The security forces also used much more degrading methods. Detainees were kept in dark cubicles with a surface area of less than one square meter, known as *chiquitas* (little ones). It was impossible to sit in them; they were totally dark and had little ventilation and no sanitation. Prisoners were sometimes kept there for more than a week. Interrogations were carried out at any time of day or night, sometimes at gunpoint and amid death threats and simulated executions. Some prisoners were deprived of food and water. After being detained for a few days, physically exhausted, many of them agreed to sign self-incriminating false confessions. In distant rural regions, units from the regular army often arrested and detained suspect civilians for several days in military camps before handing them over to the DGSE.

Some of the DGSE prisons were notorious for their harsh conditions. At Las Tejas, for example, prisoners were forced to stand without bending their arms or legs. All prisons were constructed on the same model: the minuscule cells had beds set into the concrete walls. There was no electicity or sanitation. Nor were there windows; the only illumination came from a tiny ray of light that slipped through the ventilation grill situated above the steel door. In times of crisis, prisoners were kept in such cells for several months. After a campaign by human-rights organizations, the *chiquitas* were abolished in 1989.

According to Amnesty International, only a few people actually died in the DGSE centers. Danilo Rosales and Salomon Tellevia officially died of "heart attacks." In 1985 José Angel Vilchis Tijerino, who himself had been beaten with a rifle butt, saw one of his companions die from the ill treatment he received. Amnesty International and other nongovernmental organizations denounced similar abuses in rural zones. One detainee from the Río Blanco prison in Matagalpa stated that he was locked up with twenty other prisoners in a cell so small that they all had to sleep standing up. Another was deprived of food and water for five days and had to drink his own urine to survive. The use of electric batons was common.

The penitentiary system was closely modeled on that of Cuba. The clemency law of 2 November 1981, based on Cuban texts, allowed the prisoner's attitude and behavior to be taken into account in decisions on eventual liberation. The limitations of the law quickly became apparent. Although hundreds of prisoners sentenced by the exceptional courts were pardoned, no systematic revision of those sentences was ever undertaken.

People were arrested for "Somocista crimes," a notion that signified nothing concrete. In 1989 only 39 of the 1,640 people arrested for "counterrevolutionary crimes" had actually been members of Somoza's entourage. Members of Somoza's guards never accounted for more than 20 percent of the Contras, yet the threat of rebellion by Somoza's supporters was the key argument used by the Sandinistas to lock up their opponents. More than 600 were imprisoned for this reason in the Carcel Modelo. The early years of the Sandinista regime were characterized above all by the falsification of evidence and by the invention of spurious charges against opponents.

By 1987 there were more than 3,700 political prisoners in Nicaraguan prisons. On 19 August 1987 in El Chipote, about a dozen detainees were beaten by their guards. Prisoners also reported the use of electric batons by their guards. In February 1989, as a protest against the harshness of the conditions they faced, 90 prisoners in the Carcel Modelo, twenty kilometers outside Managua, began a hunger strike. Thirty of the strikers were transferred to El Chipote, where as punishment they were all kept naked in one cell for two days. In other prisons as well, detainees were kept naked, handcuffed, and deprived of water.

In 1989 there were 630 prisoners in the Carcel Modelo. Thirty-eight former Somoza guardsmen were also serving their sentences there, in a separate block. Political prisoners were kept in the regional prisons in Estelí, La Granja, and Granada. For ideological reasons, a number of prisoners, particularly in the Carcel Modelo, refused to do the work they were assigned; they suffered violent reprisals. Amnesty International also reported ill treatment of prisoners after protests and hunger strikes.

Some prisoners were eligible for a program of reeducation through work. There were five categories of imprisonment. Those declared unfit for the work program for reasons of security were kept in a high security compound. They saw their families only every forty-five days and could leave their cells for only six hours a week. Prisoners who were integrated into the readaptation programs were allowed to carry out paid work. They were permitted one conjugal visit per month and a visit by another close relative every two weeks. People who satisfied the demands of the work program had the right to request transfer to a work farm, where a "semi-open" regime was in operation, and they could eventually pass to an open regime.

The offensives and counteroffensives of the two sides in the civil war make the calculation of losses difficult, but there is no doubt that hundreds of opponents were executed in the rural zones, where the fighting was particularly violent. The massacres appear to have been carried out by army combat units and by special troops from the Ministry of Internal Affairs, which were accountable to Tomás Borge, the minister. These troops were the Nicaraguan equivalent of the Cuban Minit special forces.

Executions of villagers were reported in the Zelaya region, although no precise figures on casualties are available. Bodies were often mutilated and men emasculated. The massacred peasants were suspected of having either assisted or belonged to the Contra movement. The suspects' houses were destroyed, and survivors were forcibly deported. These actions were carried out by troops from the regular army. The intention of the government was to impose its policies by terror and through this terror to deprive the enemy of its bases. Unable to catch the resistance fighters, the army took revenge on their relatives. In February 1989 Amnesty International reported dozens of extrajudicial executions, particularly in the provinces of Matagalpa and Jinotega. The mutilated bodies of the victims were found by their families near their homes. Throughout the war there were numerous reports of "disappearances" carried out by groups from the DGSE. Furthermore, the minister of internal affairs rarely hesitated to shoot political prisoners in Managua. The total human cost of the war was between 45,000 and 50,000 people, most of them civilians. At least 400,000 Nicaraguans fled to Costa Rica, Honduras, or the United States, particularly to Miami and California.

The treaties signed in Esquipulas, Guatemala, in August 1987 relaunched the peace process, and in September 1987 the opposition daily *La prensa* was authorized to reappear. On 7 October a unilateral cease-fire was signed for the provinces of Segovia, Jinotega, and Zelaya. More than 2,000 political prisoners were freed, although another 1,200 remained in prison as of February 1990. In March 1988 direct negotiations began between the government and the opposition in Sapoa, Costa Rica. In June 1989, eight months before the presidential elections, most of the 12,000 anti-Sandinista guerrillas returned to their bases in Honduras.

Unable to impose their ideology by force, under attack by both internal and foreign forces, bereft of support from their erstwhile Eastern-bloc patrons, and weakened by internal quarrels, the Sandinistas took the country to the polls again. On 25 February 1990 the democrat Violeta Chamorro was elected president, winning 54.7 percent of the vote. For the first time in 160 years of independence, a peaceful transfer of political power took place in the country. The desire for peace seems to have triumphed over the permanent state of war. For whatever reason—perhaps they finally understood the need for democracy or perhaps they simply bowed to the inevitable as their support ebbed away— the Sandinistas did not resort to the extremes of terror used by Communists elsewhere in attempts to cling to power. But in their attempt to impose their point of view and apply their policies without regard to the political realities facing the country, they led a genuine revolution astray, provoked a second civil war that delayed the coming of democracy to Nicaragua, and caused the loss of many lives.

Peru: The Long Bloody March of the Sendero Luminoso

On 17 May 1980, the day of presidential elections, Peru witnessed the first armed action by a Maoist guerrilla group calling itself the Sendero Luminoso (Shining Path). To announce the start of a "people's war," young militants seized and set fire to voting booths in Chuschi. Nobody took much notice. A few weeks later, the inhabitants of the capital, Lima, found dogs hanging from lampposts with signs around their necks bearing the name Deng Xiaoping. The "revisionist" Chinese leader was accused of betraying the Cultural Revolution. Who had resorted to such macabre practices?

The late 1970s were a particularly turbulent time for Peru. Six general strikes took place in 1977–1979, all preceded by large demonstrations in the main provincial towns of Arequipa, Ayacucho, Cuzco, Huancayo, and Pucallpa. They were accompanied by the emergence of massive "defense fronts" structured around the demands of the protestors. These fronts became the backbone of the Sendero Luminoso. In Ayacucho the defense front had already been in existence for some time. In Quechua, Ayacucho means "the dead area," and in truth it was long one of the most deprived areas in the country. Here less than 5 percent of the land could be cultivated, the average annual per-capita income was less than 100 U.S. dollars, and life expectancy was only about forty-five years. Infant mortality was approximately 20 percent, whereas the national average was 11 percent. It was in this region, plagued by social problems, that the Sendero Luminoso first came into being.

Ayacucho has also had an active university center since 1959, which specialized in pediatrics, applied anthropology, and rural engineering. A revolutionary student front developed there and played an important role at the university. Initially, orthodox Communists, supporters of Che Guevara, and Maoists all vied for control, but beginning in the early 1960s a young Maoist and philosophy teacher named Abimaël Guzmán assumed a dominant role.

Born in Lima on 6 December 1934, Guzmán started out a taciturn young man and a brilliant student. In 1958 he had joined the Communist Party, where he soon gained notice through his rhetorical talent, developed after his student days. In 1965 he helped found the Communist group Bandera Roja (Red Flag), which was a product of a schism inside the Peruvian Communist Party following the Sino-Soviet split. According to some accounts, Guzmán visited China.[19] In 1966 the government closed the university in the wake of insurrectionist riots. At this time the Maoists of the Bandera Roja, led by Guzmán, set up the Front for Defense of the Population of Ayacucho, beginning their armed struggle the following year. In June 1969 Guzman took part in the kidnapping of the assistant prefect Octavio Cabrera Rocha in Huerta, in the north of Ayacucho Province. He was imprisoned in 1970 for attacking state security, but was freed a few months later. At the Fourth Conference of the Bandera Roja, in 1971, another schism resulted in the formation of a new Communist group calling itself the Sendero Luminoso. The name is taken from José Carlos Mariátegui's claim that "Marxism-Leninism will open the shining path toward the revolution."[20] The hero of the militants, Guzmán is known as the "fourth sword of Marxism" (after Marx, Lenin, and Mao). The novelist Mario Vargas Llosa analyzed Guzmán's revolutionary project as follows: "In his eyes, the Peru that Mariátegui described in the 1920s is essentially identical with the reality of China as described by Mao at that time—'a semifeudal, semicolonial society' that can be liberated by following a strategy identical with that of the Chinese revolution: a prolonged people's war waged on the towns and based in the countryside . . . The socialist model he claims to follow is that of the Russia of Stalin, the Cultural Revolution of the Gang of Four, and the Pol Pot regime of Cambodia."[21]

From 1972 to 1979 the Sendero seemed to content itself with taking control of student organizations. It received the support of students in the Technical University of San Martín de Torres in Lima and also infiltrated the union of primary school teachers. Many of Sendero's rural guerrilla networks were headed by teachers. In late 1977 Guzmán went into hiding and began preparing the organization to embark on armed struggle, a course that was formally ratified by party members on 17 March 1980. Sendero troops were reinforced by Trotskyites led by Carlos Mezzich and by Maoist dissidents from the Pukallacta group. The hour of the armed struggle had come, and the Chuschi operation, followed on 23 December 1980 by the assassination of a landowner called Benigno Medina, was the first case of "popular justice." Although the Sendero in these early days had no more than 200 to 300 men at its disposal, it quickly began methodically eliminating the middle and upper classes and members of the country's security forces.

In 1981 the police stations in Totos, San José de Secce, and Quinca were attacked. In August 1982 the Senderistas stormed the police headquarters in Viecahuaman, killing six antiguerrilla policemen (*sinchis*, the Quechua word for "brave" or "courageous"); fifteen others either took flight or were taken prisoner. Because the guerrillas had no outside assistance, they took arms from police stocks and explosives from the mines, not hesitating to attack the miners if they put up any resistance. The stick of dynamite thrown as a *maraka*, a traditional act of resistance, quickly became the Sendero's favorite weapon. In addition to these attacks, the guerrillas carried out a multitude of assaults on public buildings, power lines, and bridges.[22] With a firm foothold in Ayacucho, the commandos invaded the city in March 1982, freeing 297 political prisoners and common criminals. The careful planning of the attack, the infiltration of the town, and the simultaneous actions against several different police targets all revealed a long and careful apprenticeship in subversion.

To establish a countrywide network of "people's communes," the Sendero Luminoso set about destroying all government installations and infrastructure. In August 1982 a Sendero commando group destroyed the Center for Agricultural Research and Experimentation in Allpahaca, slaughtering animals and setting fire to machinery. A year later, the Institute for Technical Research on Camelidae (llamas, guanacos, and alpacas) went up in smoke. Engineers and technicians, who were considered to be vectors of capitalist corruption, were also massacred. Tino Alansaya, the head of the project, was murdered and his body dynamited. In justifying this act, the Senderistas claimed that he was "an agent of the feudal and bureaucratic state." Over the next eight years, sixty engineers were killed in rural areas. Nongovernmental operatives were not spared either: in 1988 an American citizen working for the U.S. Agency for International Development, Constantin Gregory, was killed by the Sendero; two French aid workers were killed on 4 December of the same year.

Guzmán had predicted that "the triumph of the revolution will cost a million lives"—at a time when the population of Peru was only 19 million. Following that principle, the Sendero Luminoso set about eliminating all symbols of the hated political and social order. In January 1982 they executed two teachers in front of their students. A few months later, sixty-seven "traitors" were killed in public, ostensibly on the basis of a "people's verdict." In the early days, the peasants had not been too concerned by the murder of a few landowners and state officials, in part because taxes were high and borrowing rates extortionate. But the targeting of traders and members of the middle class deprived peasants of some key benefits, including loans at affordable rates, work, and aid of various kinds. As part of a "revolutionary purity" campaign and an effort to consolidate the Sendero's hold, the guerrillas also attacked the groups of *abigeos* (cattle thieves) who lived on the high plains. This campaign against delinquency was purely tactical, since from 1983 onward the Sendero collaborated with the drug smugglers in Huánuco.

In regions plagued by ethnic conflicts, the Senderistas did all they could to stir up hatred of the central government in Lima, which, in the words of "President Gonzalo" (Abimaël Guzmán's *nom de guerre*), was an outdated colonial relic. Sendero claimed to defend the Indians in the same manner that Pol Pot had sought to reclaim the Khmer purity of the Angkor dynasty period. As a result, the guerrillas initially received the backing of a number of Indian tribes. Before long, however, almost all the Indian and peasant leaders grew disaffected with the Sendero's graphic violence and coercive tactics. In 1989 in Upper Amazonia, the Ashaninkas were forced to enlist in the Sendero or face reprisals. Nearly 25,000 of them lived in the jungle before being placed under the protection of the army.

By the late 1980s the Ayacucho region was entirely under the control of the Sendero Luminoso, which attempted to set up a new social order in the province. Prostitutes had their heads shaved, unfaithful and drunken husbands were whipped, and anyone who showed any sign of resistance had a hammer and sickle shaved into his hair. Any celebration judged to be "unhealthy" was banned. Communities were controlled by "people's committees," each run by five "political commissars," in a pyramidal structure that echoed the political and military organization of the Sendero itself. Committees were organized into small cells that reported to the main "column" for the area, which typically had seven to eleven members. Attached to the political commissars were assistants whose task was to promote rural organization and production and who were in charge of collective work in the "liberated zones." Insubordination or a refusal to cooperate was immediately punished by death. Because the Sendero wanted the rural village zones to be autarkic and isolated, the guerrillas began blowing up bridges, a policy that sparked strong opposition from the peasants. The Sendero frequently enlisted children by force to maintain its control of the population.

The government's initial response to the terrorism was to send in special commando groups *(sinchis)* and marines, but this effort met with little success. In 1983 and 1984, the "people's war" was intensified. In April 1983, fifty Sendero guerrillas took control in Luconamanca, using axes and knives to massacre thirty-two "traitors" and a number of other people who were caught fleeing. Sixty-seven people died, including four children. This massacre was intended to show the authorities that the Sendero was without mercy. In 1984 and 1985 the group expanded its offensive to members of the government, a policy that had begun in November 1983 with the assassination of the mayor in the mining center Cerro de Pesco. Sensing that the authorities had abandoned them, several mayors and deputy mayors resigned; priests also fled.

In 1982 the war cost 200 lives. Ten times that number died the following year. In 1984 alone the terrorists carried out more than 2,600 actions, and more than 400 soldiers and policemen died in these operations. The army launched reprisals. When militants mutinied in three prisons in Lima in June 1986, government repressions were ferocious, resulting in more than 200 deaths. The Senderistas failed to gain any significant footholds in the well-structured mining unions and in the barrios, where a strong social support network already existed. To maintain credibility, they concentrated their efforts on the majority party in power, the Alianza Popular Revolucionaria Americana (American Revolutionary Popular Alliance; APRA).[23] In 1985 seven Aprists were killed and mutilated in the manner reserved for police informers, with their ears, tongues, and eyes cut out. The Sendero also opened a new front in Puno that year. Several zones in La Libertad and the provinces of Huánuco, La Mar, and Upper Amazonia were also affected by guerrilla action. Plastic explosive attacks were carried out on the electricity generating centers in Cuzco and Arequipa. In June 1984 the guerrillas derailed a train carrying concentrated lead, and shortly afterward they did the same to a train carrying copper.

The army responded with ever-greater repression. In 1984 a state of emergency was declared in 10 of Peru's 146 provinces. The army announced that mass killings were justified if three people out of every sixty killed turned out to be guerrillas; there were widespread massacres of peasants in Ayacucho. Not surprisingly, undecided peasants began to look more favorably upon the Sendero Luminoso. But in the early 1990s the government changed its strategy, declaring that it would consider the peasants partners instead of enemies. The military hierarchy was reorganized, and better methods of recruitment resulted in closer collaboration with the peasants. The Sendero also began to change its tactics, splitting into separate units at its third conference. Autonomous units were put in charge of guerrilla warfare, sabotage, terrorism, and psychological warfare.

To punish anyone who betrayed the "forces of the people," the Sendero set up labor camps in Amazonia. Since 1983, enslaved peasants had been trying to leave the zones controlled by the guerrillas, who had forced them to work the land and the coca fields to meet the Sendero's own needs. Many children born on the high plains died there, and anyone who was caught attempting to escape was executed immediately. Trapped in the camps and forced to attend study sessions where they read the works of President Gonzalo, the prisoners suffered greatly from hunger and deprivation. This was the case for the 500 detainees in the camp in the Convención region. In December 1987, 300 starving men, women, and children managed to escape from the "Peruvian gulag" and arrived in Belém, on the edge of the jungle.

Revolted by the cruelty of the Sendero, which had proved itself incapable of improving the lot of the lower classes, the vast majority of peasants gradually abandoned the Guzmán revolution. The Sendero also found itself in competition with other political groups. The United Left, strongly supported by the unions, had successfully resisted infiltration by the Sendero, which had shown itself to be more at home carrying out bloody repressions than organizing community projects. In 1988 and 1989 the Sendero targeted Lima and Cuzco, especially the surrounding shantytowns, which were hotbeds of revolutionary culture. The Sendero began to set up cells there, and resistance was quickly eliminated. Militants also infiltrated several charities, including Peruvian Popular Aid. The Senderistas systematically attempted to eliminate all the classic Marxist organizations and to take control of the unions, but this latter effort again met with failure. The Sendero also clashed with the Movimiento Revolucionario Tupac Amaru (MRTA) terrorist group, resulting in significant casualties on both sides and among civilians. In 1990, for example, 1,584 civilians and 1,542 rebels died. Outmaneuvred by the MRTA and harried by the army, the Sendero began to decline. The process had been hastened by brief internal dissidence in the late 1980s, followed by executions of some key figures as "traitors following the bourgeois line."

In September 1983 the Peruvian police achieved their first major victory against the rebels by arresting Carlos Mezzich, one of Guzmán's closest associates. Nearly a decade passed, however, before the government made further progress in eliminating the leadership of the Shining Path. On 12 and 13 September 1992, Guzmán and his companion Elena Iparraguire were arrested. A few weeks later the organization's third in command, Oscar Albert Ramirez, fell into the hands of the police. On 2 March 1993 the Sendero's military leader, Margot Dominguez (code name Edith), was also arrested. Finally, in March 1995 a group of thirty guerrillas with Margie Clavo Peralta at its head was uncovered by the security forces. Despite this progress in eliminating the group's leadership, a downturn in Peru's economy led to an increase in popular support: in the middle and late 1990s the Sendero Luminoso still had about 25,000 members, including between 3,000 and 5,000 regulars.

The cost of the conflict in Peru has been estimated at 20 billion dollars. According to some sources, the Shining Path has been responsible for between 25,000 and 30,000 deaths. Children in the countryside have paid a particularly heavy toll in the Sendero's violent campaign; between 1980 and 1991 more than 1,000 died in terrorist actions, and another 3,000 were seriously wounded. The breakup of families in war zones has also left some 50,000 children abandoned or orphaned.

Select Bibliography

General

Lowy, Michael, ed. *Marxism in Latin America from 1909 to the Present: An Anthology*, trans. Michael Pearlman. Atlantic Highlands, N.J.: Humanities Press, 1992.

Mercier-Vega, Louis. *Guerrillas in Latin America: The Technique of Counter-State*, trans. Daniel Weissbort. New York: Praeger, 1969.

—— *La révolution par l'état: Une nouvelle classe dirigeante en Amérique latine*. Paris: Payot, 1978.

—— *Roads to Power in Latin America*, trans. Robert Rowland. New York: Praeger, 1969.

Publications of La Documentation Française, Amérique Latine series.

Cuba

Clark, Juan. *Cuba, mito y realidad: Testimonios de un pueblo*. Miami: Saeta Ediciones, 1992.

Franqui, Carlos. *Diary of the Cuban Revolution*. New York: Viking Press, 1980.

Valladares, Armando. *Against All Hope: The Prison Memoirs*. New York: Alfred A. Knopf, 1986.

Valls, Jorge. *Mon ennemi, mon frère*. Paris: Gallimard, L'Arpenteur, 1989.

Verdès-Leroux, Jeannine. *La lune et le caudillo: Le rêve des intellectuels et le regime cubain (1959–1971)*. Paris: Gallimard, L'Arpenteur, 1989.

Nicaragua

Bataillon, Gilles. "Communistes et sociodémocrates dans la révolution." *Communisme*, no. 13, 1987.

—— "Nicaragua: De la tyrannie à la dictature totalitaire." *Esprit*, October 1983, special issue: "Amériques latines à la une."

—— "Nicaragua: Des élections à l'état d'urgence." *Esprit*, January 1986.

—— "Le Nicaragua et les indiens de la côte atlantique." *Esprit*, July 1983.

—— "Le Nicaragua et les indiens Miskito." *Esprit*, July–August 1982.

—— "L'opposition nicaraguayenne à la recherche d'une stratégie." *Esprit*, June 1987.

—— "Paysage après la bataille (Nicaragua)." *Esprit*, January 1986.

Berreby, Geneviève, and Elie-Georges Berreby. *Commandant Zéro*. Paris: Robert Laffont, 1987.

Caroit, J. M., and V. Soulé. *Le Nicaragua, le modèle sandiniste*. Paris: Le Sycomore, 1981.

Dumont, René. *Finis les lendemains qui chantent*. Paris: Seuil, 1982.

——— *Nicaragua: Colonialisme et révolution*. Paris: Inti, 1982.

Peru

Hertoghe, Alain, and Alain Labrousse. *Le sentier lumineux: Un nouvel intégrisme dans le Tiers-Monde*. Paris: La Découverte, 1989.

26 Afrocommunism: Ethiopia, Angola, and Mozambique

Yves Santamaria

Even before the Cold War was fully under way, France sought to establish a linkage between the international Communist movement and anti-colonial struggles. Under pressure from the United States to relinquish over-seas colonies, the French Fourth Republic tried to make Washington believe that any surrender to nationalist movements in the colonies was automatically an invitation for Moscow to take over. Time and again, Lenin's old adage was trotted out in support of this view: from the East, he had said, the road to Paris passed through Algeria. This strange mixture of the exotic and the familiar, of Africa and Communism, did not really coalesce until a vacuum emerged after the American defeat in Vietnam, when pro-Soviet regimes took hold in what had been the Portuguese part of Africa and in Ethiopia. For the first time it seemed that these countries were not merely pawns in a geopolitical game. Although the constant threat of socialist control over sectors judged vital by the West still existed, what seemed even more worrying was Communism's apparent success in offering the Third World an illusory remedy for under-development. On top of all the suffering that these countries had already experienced, their leaders seemed to believe that the force of history was to make them the final inheritors of the glorious October Revolution.

Communism African Style

In 1989, not long after the fall of the Berlin Wall, the Tutsis of the Rwandan Patriotic Front found themselves labeled the "black Khmers" for their suspected sympathies with Pol Pot. At the same time, their U.S.-educated leader, Paul Kagame, was labeled "American" by the French, who have always been wary of possible Anglo–Saxon interventions in Francophone Africa.[1] Politics in the Great Lakes region are extremely complex, and the region is a good indicator of the difficulties faced by observers of the African political scene. The West has always projected its political fantasies onto the "Dark Continent." Therefore, one might think it would be difficult to talk about "African Communism" without falling into ethnocentricity. But in reality, debates about the authenticity of African states' role in the Communist universe take exactly the same form as debates about other forms of Communism throughout the world. Even the president of Mozambique, Joaquim Chissano, readily admitted, as Communism began to crumble in Eastern Europe, that "the history of Marxism was beginning to pose serious problems for us."[2] General Charles de Gaulle always perceived the U.S.S.R. as first and foremost a Russian state, so why should the Popular Movement for the Liberation of Angola (MPLA) not be viewed as the Marxist-Leninist expression of the country's creole, Indian. and Mbundu ethnic patchwork? People have often denied Mengistu Haile Mariam the label "Communist" in the same way it was denied to Stalin himself by the extreme Marxist left and by the Trotskyites in particular.

Nevertheless these African movements made serious reference to Marx, Bolshevism, and the U.S.S.R. throughout the period 1974–1991, and these references were taken seriously by the protagonists and their supporters in the Soviet Union and the Communist International. Actual membership in Communist Party organizations was certainly limited to a minority: Soviet estimates of the number of Communist Party members in the whole of Africa were only around 5,000 in 1939, increasing to 60,000 by the early 1970s.[3] But numerous examples of Communist states, especially in Europe, demonstrate that in Leninist logic, societal power relations and the vanguard party's ideological adherence to Marxism are much more important than the impregnation of society with a Communist ethos. As soon as the new leaders were in power, they symbolically divided up the landscape, carefully making a significant break with the "African socialism" of the first independence movements in the 1950s and 1960s. The lessons to be learned from the first wave of failures were quite clear. If the policy of communal agriculture (ujamaa) carried out in Tanzania by Julius Nyerere had not brought the desired results, this was because, as noted by Frelimo—the Mozambique National Liberation Front—and by Ethiopian experts, the Tanganyika African National Union/Afro Shirazi Party had not been sufficiently Marxist-Leninist. The adoption of a "scientific socialist" framework enabled the new elites to avoid the dangers of tribalism, which they considered to be the major risk facing their countries and which would naturally have resulted from traditional bonds of solidarity among the peasants. It was accepted in advance that the role of the state was to build the nation, just as it had been in Europe in earlier times. The new Marxist leaders hoped that as a result of this state-building process they would be accepted into the international community. No one who landed at the airport in Maputo, the capital of Mozambique, could ignore the placard announcing that he was entering one of "the free zones of humanity."[4]

Rather than an invitation to ignore human rights, the slogan illuminating the airport facade was an illustration of two different aspects of the Communist project: anti-imperialism, in opposition to racist South Africa; and enrollment in the Communist world order, alongside the other socialist states. Like Mozambique, Angola and Ethiopia joined the ranks of countries with a "socialist orientation." Soviet analysts had refined their terminology since the days of Khrushchev, and the emergence of new progressive states required the invention of a new vocabulary to describe countries that had broken with capitalism but that (unlike Cuba or Vietnam) could not really be labeled "socialist."[5] The socialist label was a guarantee of economic aid from the Soviet Union, but this was not always forthcoming in the case of African states. Most of those with a socialist orientation had to rely on their own resources and on financial aid from the West for their development. On the other hand, the military aspect of cooperation was part of the long tradition of "Red imperialism" that had existed since the earliest days of the Communist International, establishing an absolute duty to aid the international proletariat.[6] Although Soviet weaponry was supplied to many parts of Africa, the three states discussed here were the main recipients of Soviet military aid. These states benefited from a whole galaxy of resources provided by the worldwide Communist network. In addition to the 8,850 Soviet advisers to be found all across the African continent, there were 53,900 Cubans and a large contingent of East German specialists in many African countries in the middle and late 1980s. The East Germans and Cubans specialized in assisting the local security services.[7]

It is certainly possible to find, in the adoption of Marxist-Leninist rhetoric by the MPLA in Angola, by the Frelimo in Mozambique, and by the Dergue/Ethiopian Workers' Party in Ethiopia, the process known to historians of antiquity as "interpretation," through which, for example, the pagan gods of Gaul long survived in Roman form. This "instrumentalization" was not a one-way process, as is evident from the way the imperial Ethiopian bureaucracy used the real centralizing potential of the Communist model to consolidate its own control. Nonetheless, however powerful that explanatory model might be, several common and distinct features of African Communist policy can be identified. Taken individually, many of them, including the rejection of pluralism and the idea that only the party in power represents the real vanguard, can also be found in other African states. But Moscow gave the label of a "vanguard party relying on revolutionary theory" only to the MPLA Workers' Party in Angola, the Frelimo in Mozambique, the Congo Workers' Party, and, after its founding in 1984, the Ethiopian Workers' Party. Another feature found elsewhere in Africa was the Mafia-like "politics of hunger," an arrangement that arose because the absence of a middle class meant that individuals could get rich only through the state.[8] State control of all appointments was, of course, a practice not unique to Africa. Still, the chief underlying aim of these three regimes, identical in form and rhetorical presentation, can be defined very simply: to create a "new man," authorizing the Ministry of Truth to decide what should be retained or eradicated from ancestral folklore.

One might still wonder why, in the ideological bazaar of the twentieth century, these African states decided to follow Marxism-Leninism rather than some other theory.[9] One element of the debate here might be the fascination exerted by the vertiginous use of violence by previous proponents of the doctrine. Just as it is becoming apparent to researchers in the West that there is a link between totalitarianism and the "war culture" that prevailed in Europe from 1914 to 1945, it might well be that the Communist era in the history of Africa is related to the continent's long history of violence. However, the study of this matter is only just beginning to emerge from its focus on three Manichean oppositions: precolonial harmony versus barbarism, colonial order versus oppression, and the chaos that followed independence versus the excesses of neocolonialism.[10] Communist Africa was by no means the only center of violence on the continent: both the Biafran civil war in Nigeria and the Hutu genocide in Rwanda gave the people in those countries ample reason to despair. But quarrels about numbers aside, the violent actions in Ethiopia, Angola, and Mozambique still have a unique criminal specificity, if only in the state's attempts to remodel the fabric of society through enforced "villagization" of the traditional countryside and in the use of hunger as an instrument of government policy. Such tactics are familiar to historians of Communism who have no special knowledge of Africa. Equally familiar are the Party purges and the liquidation of all rivals, whether leftist groups or nationalist, partisan, religious, or ethnic opposition forces.

Although mass murder is more difficult to conceal than it was in the past, several large-scale atrocities have been carried out in Africa. For commentators not burdened with the need to observe events with impartiality, these initiatives by Marxist-Leninist states appear to be merely a measured reply to counter-revolutionary forces. This quarrel over the legitimacy of state-sponsored violence first appeared during the Terror of the French Revolution, and was revived by the Bolshevik Revolution. Other commentators, attempting impartiality, often invoke the "tyranny of circumstances." In that respect the polemic in the West about these three countries—which includes no comparison with other African countries with socialist tendencies—justifies their being singled out for special attention here.[11] In Ethiopia, Mozambique, and Angola, aside from the traditional twin evils of the legacy of the past and imperialist interventionism, Communist officials have often emphasized that there are other natural forces at work, particularly the endless danger of drought. But besides variations in rainfall and ethnic factors, there has always been the temptation simply to blame some sort of African soul. Such societies are of course as much a product of their time as they are of their heritage, and it is for that reason that totalitarian bloodletting was perhaps inevitable.

The Red Empire: Ethiopia

The Revolution and the Rise of Mengistu Haile Mariam

When the empire ruled by Haile Selassie I, then aged eighty-two, suddenly crumbled on 12 September 1974, the reasons seemed quite obvious. Made fragile by the uncertainty surrounding his successor, the worldwide oil crisis of the previous year, border wars, food shortages, and the discontent of a middle class that was growing fast as a result of social modernization, the regime disappeared without putting up much resistance. The army, which had been created to achieve the geopolitical ambitions of the exiled sovereign during Italy's colonization of the country in 1936–1941, and which had distinguished itself fighting alongside the Americans in Korea in 1950, decided to take over. The new government, called the Provisional Military Administrative Committee or Dergue, was made up of 108 officers. Initially, ideological disagreements within the Dergue seemed inconsequential as the entire group rallied around the slogan *"Ethiopia tikdem"*—"Ethiopia first." But this honeymoon was short-lived, and General Aman Andom, of Eritrean origin and a hero of the war against Somalia who had been made the head of state, came into conflict with the Dergue and was killed trying to resist arrest during the night of 22–23 November 1974. A few hours later, 59 others were also executed. As is so often the case, liberal politicians met the same fate as traditionalists with links to the previous regime. The fate of the Dergue was henceforth linked to that of Mengistu Haile Mariam, who had been elected its first deputy chairman in July and who on 21 December 1974 made the public announcement that the country would henceforth be a socialist regime.

The definitive biography of Mengistu has yet to be written.[12] He enjoyed playing the role of a pariah, making the most of his dark skin and his short stature (although he often wore platform soles to disguise this) to pose as a *bariah,* or slave, opposed to the Amhara ethnic group, which had been at the heart of the imperial regime. Despite this underdog role, Mengistu had links to the circles of privilege through his mother, who was a genuine aristocrat. He was born out of wedlock (his father was an illiterate corporal), and he benefited from the protection of an uncle who, as a minister in the Selassie regime, set him on the fast track in his military career. Mengistu's education was very limited, and it was with no qualifications at all that he entered the military school in Holetta, which was reserved for people from disadvantaged backgrounds. As the commander of a mechanized brigade, his leadership qualities twice earned him a place in a training program at Fort Leavenworth, Kansas. He had no ideological baggage, but he did have a strong appetite for power. After the revolution, it took him three years to displace his rivals. The first step was the elimination of Major Jamor Sisay Habte, for right-wing tendencies in July 1976. After growing conflict between Mengistu and the more moderate faction led by General Teferi Bante, Mengistu ordered members of his security force to open fire with machine guns at a Dergue meeting on 3 February 1977, killing Bante and seven of his supporters. He then set out to eliminate his civilian political rivals.

The "Ethiopian way" proposed in December 1974 by the provisional committee took shape in January 1975, when the Dergue nationalized banks and insurance companies together with most of the manufacturing sector. Above all, the abolition of land ownership in March 1975 and the introduction of a one-per-family limit on property ownership demonstrated the radical nature of the regime. To expedite land reform in rural areas, the government dispatched over 50,000 high school and university students to set up peasant associations and assist in rural reform in what became known as the *zemacha* (cooperation) campaign. Because of the Dergue's opposition to student efforts to create Maoist peasant communes, most students quickly became hostile to the military government and sought to mobilize the peasants against it.

When the students returned, they formed two rival Marxist-Leninist organizations called the Ethiopian People's Revolutionary Party (EPRP) and the All-Ethiopian Socialist Movement, or Meison. The population in general was unimpressed, and the rivalry between the two movements was largely a result of their ethnic makeup: the EPRP consisted predominantly of Amhara, whereas the Meison, was largely Oromo. Although they were extremely close in ideology and on most policy questions, the Meison initially was allied with the Dergue while the EPRP opposed the military government from the start. The two organizations also differed on the question of Eritrea, with the EPRP accepting secession, whereas the Meison wanted to crush the secessionist movement. Playing up the armed confrontations between the two organizations, and decrying the "white terror" (the terror committed by the EPRP), Mengistu successively destroyed both movements. He first launched a campaign of "red terror" against the EPRP and its sympathizers in the autumn of 1976. The terror reached its peak in the spring of 1977, after Mengistu, in a public speech on 17 April, called on the people to attack the "enemies of the revolution." Backing up his words with dramatic actions, he broke open three flasks of what was supposed to be blood, which represented imperialism, feudalism, and bureaucratic capitalism. Much of the terror campaign was carried out by 293 *kebele,* urban militia groups established by the Dergue on the model of the Parisian "sections" of the French Revolution;[13] the army had provided these groups with training and equipment. The Meison supported this operation, which resulted in the destruction of the EPRP in Addis Ababa. Next the Dergue turned on the Meison and its allies in the Political Bureau, blaming them for the excesses of the red terror. After the execution on 11 November of their principal supporter in the Dergue, Lt. Colonel Atnafu Abate (who had been especially fierce in the repression of the EPRP), the noose began to tighten around the Meison, and that organization, too, fell victim to the death squads of the security forces, who were instantly recognizable in their infamous white Peugeot 504s.[14]

The new supreme leader of Ethiopia took up residence in the Great Palace, built by Menelik II after the founding of Addis Ababa in 1886.[15] His implacable style of leadership, publicized by an extremely elaborate system of communications, failed to surprise a nation that had grown accustomed to the previous "king of kings." Mengistu's legitimacy was uncontested in socialist countries, which saw in him a stable long-term partner. The coup in February 1977 had been preceded by Mengistu's visit to Moscow the previous December. In April 1977 Ethiopia broke off military relations with the United States. The Cubans and the Soviet Union stepped in with massive aid, including both personnel and equipment, which proved decisive in defeating the Eritrean independence movement and the Somalian offensive of July 1977 in Ogaden.[16] Soviet leaders appreciated the new regime's attempts at Sovietization, sometimes in imitation of the process that was taking place in Somalia, which was another Soviet ally at the time.

Moscow pushed all the harder for the creation of what it considered to be the only instrument that would enable a society to cross a decisive threshold: a full-fledged Communist Party. Not until 1979, however, was a Commission for the Organization of the Ethiopian Workers' Party set up. The results of its second congress in January 1983 were judged sufficiently fruitful by the Soviet Union for the Ethiopian Workers' Party (EWP) to be created in 1984 in celebration of the tenth anniversary of the revolution. Calling itself the heir of the "great October Revolution," the EWP was accorded complete integration into the system of world Communism through inter-Party agreements. The only cloud on this success was the Soviet refusal to grant Ethiopia the status of a "people's democracy" because of the country's multiethnic fragmentation and its continued economic dependence on the West.[17]

The speed with which the Party grew resulted in an "improper" sociological composition. Despite initial all-out efforts to show that anyone could join the Party, workers stayed away in droves, making up less than one-fourth of the membership. Over three-fourths of the members consisted of soldiers and civil servants, representing the reality of social relations inside the country. Although peasants were 87 percent of the total population, they accounted for a mere 3 percent of Party members.[18] The vast majority of leaders were from the army. Most of the EWP Politburo was made up of former Dergue members. The intelligentsia constituted only a small proportion of the Party, since many of their organizations had been broken up.

The Consequences of the Terror

At present there is no way to know exactly how many people fell victim to the terror. For the period February 1977–June 1978 the figure of 10,000 political assassinations in the capital alone was cited during trials in Addis Ababa in May 1995.[19] It is perhaps rather out of place to try to divide the victims into categories (pro-Chinese, Jewish Falashas massacred in 1979, and so on). As Karel Bartošek remarked about Czechoslovakia, the days when we looked for a satanic figure hovering in the background, devouring his own children, are gone.[20] The Dergue killed and buried everyone indiscriminately, as Stalin did, attaching a perfunctory label such as "reactionary," "counterrevolutionary," or "antipeople subversive anarchists from the EPRP" only after the fact. As is the case in the former Soviet Union, mass graves are still being discovered, graves in which many of the "disappeared" recorded by Amnesty International are to be found. As was the case in China, families were even asked to pay the state for the cost of the execution. The nylon rope, or "Mengistu bowtie," was one of the most widely used and distinctive methods, practiced in particular by Colonel Teka Tulu, who was known as "the Hyena" and was one of the most hated chiefs of the state security forces. It was also the method used one night in August 1975 on the fallen emperor (though it was claimed officially that he had died during a surgical operation) and on his granddaughter, Princess Ijegayehu Asfa.

Assistance from the East German state security forces, the Stasi, and from the Soviet KGB was provided through many channels. In several cases the

Soviet security forces handed over Ethiopian students in Moscow to Ethiopian security personnel. In Addis Ababa, Sergeant Legesse Asfaw acted as an intermediary between Eastern European and Soviet specialists and their Ethiopian counterparts. It was common practice to expose the victims of torture on the pavements of the capital. On 17 May 1977 the Swedish general secretary of the Save the Children Fund lamented that "1,000 children have been killed, and their bodies are left in the streets and are being eaten by wild hyenas . . . You can see the heaped-up bodies of murdered children, most of them aged eleven to thirteen, lying in the gutter, as you drive out of Addis Ababa."[21]

Most of the 1,823 cases that went to trial after 1991 under the justice system of the new president, Meles Zenawi, concerned well-known figures in the cities;[22] but the terror extended throughout the 1.22 million square kilometers of the country and affected the whole population of over 30 million. Welo, where the EPRP had a relatively firm foothold, suffered badly. In May 1997, Colonel Fantaye Yhdego, Lieutenant Haile Gebeyahu, and Colonel Alemu Ambachew were brought before the criminal bench of the High Court in Addis Ababa to answer for their actions, which included the gassing of twenty-four members of the EPRP in February 1977 in Dese and Kombalcha.[23] Outside the central province of Shewa, the best-known situation is that of Eritrea, where the nationalist opposition, which was extremely well organized and had solid support among other Third World Marxist groups, succeeded in gathering and spreading information to discredit the Addis Ababa regime in the eyes of the international community.[24] On 20 December 1974 the regime had reaffirmed the indivisibility of the nation, pointing out that any secession by the former Italian colony and British protectorate would cut the country off from its Red Sea coast.[25]

In the southeast, near the Indian Ocean, conflict was provoked by Somalia's demands for Ogaden, a region of Ethiopia inhabited mainly by Somalis. From 1969 on, the Somali leader Mohammed Siad Barre had officially embraced Marxism-Leninism, and relations between Moscow and Mogadishu had grown ever closer after the signing of a friendship treaty in 1974. The Soviet Union was forced to make a choice between two clients, and after vainly trying to convince Ethiopia, Somalia, and South Yemen to form a federation, Moscow chose the Addis Ababa regime. Thereafter Mengistu could draw on the firepower and the naval and aerial logistical support of the Soviet army, as well as the Cuban expeditionary force, to repulse the guerrilla offensives of the (also Marxist-Leninist) Popular Front for the Liberation of Eritrea and incursions by the Somalian army from June 1977 to January 1978.

Mengistu's actions were so effective that at the thirty-ninth meeting of the Worldwide Unionist Federation Bureau, held in Addis Ababa on 28–30 March 1988, the organization presented him with a gold medal "for his contribution to the struggle for peace and the security of nations, and for their national and economic independence." In June 1988, shortly after the meeting ended, some 2,500 inhabitants of Hawzen, in Tigre Province, died in a bombing raid. As in Guernica during the Spanish civil war, it had been market day when the attack occurred. Whether during a colonial war or during antinationalist repression, the peripheral areas of the old empire (Eritrea, Tigre, Oromo, Ogaden, Welega, Welo) were often shaken by revolts led by "popular fronts," whose cadres used the same Marxist-Leninist rhetoric as their adversaries.[26] Various military resources were deployed to deal with these situations, and certain far-left and pro-Chinese factions were at pains to point out that some of the atrocities perpetrated during the revolts had the backing of the United States, the Soviet Union, and Israel.[27]

A "Permanent Tribunal of the International League for the Rights and Liberation of Peoples," which modeled itself on the movement against American intervention in Vietnam, went into session in Milan in May 1980 and focused on atrocities committed in Eritrea. Its report was published in 1981 by the Belgian Committee for Aid to Eritrea, and its opinions largely reflected those of the Eritrean Popular Liberation Front.[28] Some of the information it gathered (backed up by Amnesty International reports) bears comparison with atrocities committed by the Nazis; the French observer at the session drew a comparison with Oradour-sur-Glane, where groups of people had been herded into churches that were then burned down. The brochure published by the "Permanent Tribunal" cites the example of the village of Wokiduba, where, in the summer of 1975, 110 people were massacred inside the Orthodox church. Instead of the white Peugeots of Addis Ababa, the death squads in Wokiduba drove brown Volkswagen vans, which whisked bodies away to dump them in mass graves. There was also a concentration camp in Adi Qualla, near Mendefera.

It is still unclear how many died in the "total war" that Mengistu declared in August 1977 on the Eritrean secessionists. An estimate of 80,000 civilians and military personnel for 1978–1980 includes victims of the massive air raids that were used as reprisals, but does not include those who must have died as a result of the government's subsequent systematic disruption of the traditional way of life.[29] Whereas the urban centers had a reasonable supply network and benefited from the presence of salaried military personnel who ensured a reasonably stable economy, agricultural areas suffered badly from destruction of livestock—often by air force personnel, who especially enjoyed bombing camels—minefields, deforestation, and the disrupting effects of authoritarian control. Women, who had traditionally played a major role in agriculture, were subjected to systematic rape by soldiers, whose presence also led to a permanent climate of insecurity that did little to encourage trade and commerce with other regions.[30]

It is perhaps going too far to say that the main reason for the massive displacement of the population during the famines of 1982–1985 was an intention to cut the guerrillas off from their civilian bases, but there were significant local demographic movements. Although Eritrea was barely altered, Welo was sharply affected. Of the 525,000 people moved between November 1984 and August 1985, 310,000 (8.5 percent of the population of the province) came from Welo.[31] Some border regions such as Godar were emptied of a significant proportion of their population (30–40 percent), many of whom took refuge in camps controlled by opposition groups in Sudan.[32] Despite the vast publicity that the famine received in the West, it was not a countrywide or unprecedented phenomenon. Although the famine was extremely serious, it was no more than a regional crisis affecting 25 percent of the population, and was one of a series of famines stretching back centuries. (The most recent famine, in 1972–73, had been a major factor in the downfall of the previous regime.) The effects of the famine were made worse by the impoverishment of millions of peasants who had been forced to give up their food reserves to meet the delivery quotas demanded by the state. The peasants were already taxed very heavily and had to buy grain at extremely inflated prices on the black market, only to be forced to sell it back to the state at a fixed price. Many of them were also forced to dispose of their livestock, and were thus acutely short of food at the worst moment. When the famine began in 1982, it was the result of a genuine drought, but the crisis was made considerably worse by the virtual cessation of trade, stemming partly from the rigid persecution of traders and partly from a widespread feeling of insecurity.

By controlling aid and displacing the population, the hunger weapon was used by the authorities to help realize their objectives, which naturally included the silencing of dissidents and the improved "scientific" use of space by the Party-state.[33] The ban on intervention by nongovernmental organizations in regions other than Welo and the diversion of aid intended for Tigre forced the rural population to flee from areas that were under guerrilla control and to flock to the zones held by Mengistu's forces. These forced transfers, often facilitated by an announcement that food was on the way, were presented as the demographic redeployment of people from the dry north to the more humid and fertile south. For the most part, the transfers affected not the victims of the famine, but sections of the population that were under military control, regardless of their situation regarding food and their geographic location. Inhabitants of regions in which conflict was raging between the Dergue forces and the Tigre Liberation Front were a case in point. Although in theory people had the option of staying, in practice the size of the exodus meant there was little point in remaining. This accommodating despotism was what the authorities called *bego teseno*, "well-meaning coercion" or "coercion for the good of others." The policy was introduced in 1980, before the famine, to find "volunteers" in the big cities to work on the state farms, where living conditions were so bad that they attracted the attention of Anglo-American antislavery organizations.[34]

The "villagization" policy, aimed at nomadic populations, met with stiff and sometimes bloody resistance from the tribes in question, and in many ways was typical of the peasant wars under Communist regimes. As was the case in Mozambique, the intention was to group rural communities into associations that could more easily be controlled by the Party, encouraging the peasants to "change their way of thinking and their way of life, and open a new chapter in the creation of a new modern society in rural zones, and thus help build socialism."[35] As with the population transfer program, the aim was both the extension of the state farm sector and the creation of "new men." As the geographer Michel Foucher pointed out, "the effects of the famine went far beyond the areas affected by the drought and the climatic crisis inasmuch as it was used as a pretext for a significant spatial reorganization of the country."[36] Although some operations were a considerable success, the human cost of these operations is extremely difficult to calculate. The 14 percent death rate in certain transit camps, such as Ambassel and Welo, was even higher than that recorded in the pockets of famine.[37] The 200,000 to 300,000 victims of this incompetence were supplemented by an equivalent number of people sacrificed during the accelerated passage from "feudalism" to "socialism," who were deliberately deprived of international aid, killed in raids or while trying to escape, suffocated or frozen in the depressurized holds of Antonov airplanes taking them to the promised Eden, or simply abandoned with insufficient reserves of food to the whims of the (sometimes murderous) first group to find them.

The famine generally brought mixed results for the regime. Mengistu at first tried to hide the scale of the problem, but then counterattacked, using to his own advantage the shocking pictures of starving victims that appeared in the West in the autumn of 1984. On 16 November 1984, when emotion was running at its highest, he announced his decision to transfer 2.5 million people and, despite the hostility of the Reagan administration to the idea, managed to enlist the support of the international community in the enterprise. Reactions were somewhat muted in France, where familiarity with the culture of Communism among French intellectuals was perhaps one reason behind the decision of Medecins sans Frontières to protest the forced resettlement. As a result of this decision, members of the organization were declared persona non grata by the Mengistu regime on 2 December 1985. On a wider level, the exemplary management of images and support from United Nations experts enabled the regime to build up food stocks—most of which went to the military—and to reap the benefits of an unprecedented wave of human solidarity created by a variety of rock stars who sang the anthem "We Are the World." This song may well be the only trace left by the Ethiopian drama on the consciousness of millions of people who were adolescents in the early 1980s.

Mengistu's declining fortunes after 1988 coincided in part with the fate of Communism in the Soviet Union. The departure of Soviet military advisers from the combat zones was announced in March 1990. By this time, the balance of power was already beginning to swing to the other side. On all fronts the army was in retreat from the Popular Fronts for the Liberation of Eritrea and Tigre, and the regime was giving out distress signals to the international community. The halting of the resettlement policy and the ostentatious announcement of measures to liberalize the economy coincided with a final purge of the army following an abortive coup attempt on 16 May 1989. The plotters had been infiltrated by the secret services, and reprisals were extremely bloody. On 21 June 1990 Mengistu decreed a general mobilization, which in theory applied to people age eighteen and over but in practice included fourteen- to sixteen-year-olds who were picked up in football stadiums or at schools. In 1991 higher-education establishments were closed, and all students were ordered to take part in the war effort. When the vise continued to tighten on Addis Ababa, Mengistu on 19 April 1991 announced his intention of forming a conscript army as large as Iraq's, with more than 1 million soldiers. At that moment his army already numbered 450,000 (compared to 50,000 in 1974) and was the largest in the sub-Saharan region by a considerable margin. As the Ethiopian army continued to suffer major defeats, Mengistu began to lose control. On 21 May 1991 he fled via Kenya to Harare, Zimbabwe, where he was granted sanctuary by Robert Mugabe, the hero of the struggle against the white Rhodesian colonizers. In the autumn of 1994, when Mengistu was summoned to appear for trial in Addis Ababa to take responsibility for the Ethiopian tragedy, Zimbabwe refused to extradite the man whom East German reporters had once quoted in the *Ethiopian Herald* as saying: "We will liquidate the satanic heritage of the past and place nature itself under our control!"[38]

Lusophone Violence: Angola and Mozambique

Portugal had maintained a presence on the African coast since the fifteenth century, but it was a latecomer in colonizing a vast empire (twenty-five times its own size), which it had been granted when the European powers divided up Africa at the Berlin Conference in 1884–85. This belated and superficial colonization prevented a feeling of unity from developing among the various colonized peoples. As a result, the groups that launched armed struggles in the early 1960s were forced to rely on anticolonial sentiments, which were considerably more powerful than any putative nationalist aspirations.[39] Conscious of the obstacles to their extremist viewpoint, after independence the nationalist groups focused on the *inimigo interno,* the "enemy within," by which they meant traditional chiefs, people who had collaborated with the colonizers, and political dissidents, all of whom were accused of endangering the country. Such were the characteristic traits of a political culture torn between Stalin and the Portuguese dictator António Salazar, which had few incentives to build representative democracies despite the hasty departure of the Portuguese colonial power.

The People's Republic of Angola

At the very moment when, to the fury of the white colonial population, the officers who took power in Lisbon in 1974 pronounced themselves to be in favor of independence for the colonies, the Portuguese army was still firmly in charge of Angola. The swift withdrawal of the army after July 1974 opened the way for a coalition government, consisting of the three organizations that had fought for independence since the 1960s: the Movimento Popular de Libertação de Angola (Popular Movement for the Liberation of Angola; MPLA), the Frente Nacional de Libertação de Angola (National Front for the Liberation of Angola; FNLA), and the Uniao Nacional para a Independência Total de Angola (National Union for the Total Independence of Angola; UNITA). On 15 January 1975, when the independence treaty was signed in Alvor, the new Portuguese republic recognized these organizations as "the only legitimate representatives of the people of Angola." The timetable looked promising: elections were to be held for a Constituent Assembly within nine months, and full independence was to be proclaimed on 11 November 1975. But after the departure of 400,000 Portuguese in February–June 1975 and the emergence of tensions among the three groups, the coalition government (in which the MPLA had charge of the information, justice, and finance ministries) rapidly ceased to be viable. Bloody incidents became more and more common, and the Nakuru cease-fire of 14 June was simply used as a truce by all sides to strengthen their reserves and prepare for intervention by their foreign allies.

From October 1974 onward the Soviet Union significantly increased its financial and military assistance to the MPLA, which also received support from the left wing of the Portuguese army, the so-called Armed Forces Movement, and from the "Red admiral" António Rosa Coutinho, who was based in Luanda and had been charged by the Portuguese government with overseeing the Angolan transition to independence. In March 1975 the first Cuban and Soviet advisers landed in the country. Fidel Castro later described this decision in the following terms: "Africa is today a weak link in the imperialist chain. It is there that the best hopes exist of passing from tribalism to socialism without passing through the different stages that other parts of the world have been obliged to experience."[40] After the collapse of the coalition government on 14 August 1975, the *Vietnam Heroico* docked in Luanda, with several hundred (mostly black) Cuban soldiers on board. By the time South Africa intervened on the side of UNITA on 23 October, the Soviet and Cuban advisers numbered 7,000. UNITA was not taken very seriously by the MPLA and its patrons; *Pravda* described it as "a farcical army, filled with mercenaries from China and the CIA and aided by racist South Africans and Rhodesians."[41] There was some truth in this description. Originally a Maoist organization, UNITA was forever signing pacts with the devil. Its heterogeneous organization and allies reflected the bitter realism of the Leninist and Stalinist approach, and the fact that Jonas Savimbi sat at the same table as Pik Botha should not surprise those who remember Stalin's pact with Hitler.

Soviet and Cuban air support proved decisive for the survival of the regime. On 11 November 1975 the MPLA and UNITA declared the country's independence separately,[42] while maps of what had been the jewel among Portugal's colonies were redrawn. The MPLA held the coastline, including not only the ports but also the oil reserves and the diamonds, while its rivals (among whom UNITA was soon the most important) held the north and the central plains.

After the interventions by South Africa and the Communist bloc, it became easier for the Western powers and for other leaders in southern Africa to sort out the different groups. For the Mozambican leader Samora Machel, the relentless nature of the struggle was clear from the alignment of the forces: "In Angola, two parties are facing each other: imperialism, with its allies and puppets, and the progressive forces which support the MPLA. It is that simple."[43] The uncontested leader of the MPLA, Agostinho Neto, was an assimilated black who came from a line of Protestant pastors and had been a member of the pro-Soviet Portuguese Communist Party since the 1950s. The MPLA had been founded in 1956, and many of its cadres, such as J. Mateus Paulo and A. Domingos–Van Dunem, had been trained in the U.S.S.R. in the 1960s and were well versed in the prevailing Marxist-Leninist theories. In addition to this training in scientific socialism, some of them, like J. Njamba Yemina, had also received military training while abroad, either in the Soviet Union or in the guerrilla schools of Cuba.

After taking power, the MPLA decided at the Congress of Luanda (on 4–11 December 1977) that it was time to move from a popular-front type of movement to a vanguard party structured along Bolshevik lines. Only such a party, MPLA leaders realized, would be allowed to join the international Communist movement. The new MPLA Workers' Party was immediately recognized by Raúl Castro, who was present at the congress, as the only possible means by which "the interests of working people could be correctly expressed."

The idea of the state as "the only instrument capable of applying the decisions made by the single Party" implied extreme vigilance against rival parties, which presumably were masking their counterrevolutionary nature behind left-wing phraseology. Not surprisingly a number of the "antideviationist" practices that until then had been the preserve of Communist regimes in the Northern Hemisphere began to emerge in Angola. Even before Bolshevism was officially installed as the new faith in Angola, Neto had gained considerable experience in that area. When in February 1975 (with the help of Portuguese troops) he attacked the "Eastern Revolt" faction, led by the Ovimbundu cadre Daniel Chipenda, Chipenda claimed that the episode was only the latest in a series of liquidations of MPLA dissidents since 1967. Bearing that in mind, we can understand more clearly the MPLA communiqué, issued in February 1974, that claimed to have "uncovered and neutralized" an internal counterrevolutionary plot aimed at "the physical elimination of the president and several his cadres."[44]

Nito Alvès, the minister of internal affairs and one of Neto's main rivals, had been present in Luanda during the events of 25 April 1974, which had sounded the death knell of the colonial regime. In the absence of the other leaders, he managed to win over a sizable proportion of the urban black population by denying Angolan nationality to whites unless they could prove significant anticolonial behavior. Alvès had the support of a network of neighborhood committees thanks to what he termed *poder popular* (popular power), which he had gained by not hesitating to use what were quite clearly Stalinist practices. These practices were not surprising to the victims, most of whom had been brought up in the Maoist tradition.[45] Trusting in the promises of support he had received from the Soviet Union, the Cubans, and the Portuguese Communists, he attempted a coup on 27 May 1977 to prevent a purge of his partisans that had just been getting under way. When it became clear that the operation failed (partly because of the hesitancy of Alvès' foreign advisers), Neto said in a radio broadcast: "I am sure that the people will understand why we will be forced to act somewhat harshly toward the people involved in these events." Accused of "racism, tribalism, and regionalism," the conspirators suffered a radical purge. The membership of the Central Committee and of the major offices of state was entirely changed,[46] there were bloody confrontations in the capital, and the repression reached deep into the provinces. In Ngunza (South Kuanza) 204 deviationists were killed during the night of 6–7 August;[47] this figure lends credibility to those put forward after 1991 by survivors, who reported that the MPLA was definitively purged of several thousand members on that occasion. Many of the political commissars in the armed forces were liquidated in Luena (Moxico) by Aníbal Sapilinia, a member of the MPLA Central Committee.[48]

Before the attempted coup, Nito Alvès was popular because of his columns in the newspaper *Diario de Luanda* and his commentaries on two radio programs, "Kudibanguela" and "Povo em armas," which constantly denounced the country's poor living conditions. These items confirmed the existence of severe food shortages (his supporters went so far as to speak of famine) in certain regions. They also highlighted the exhaustion of urban salaried workers who were forced to work for the regime. A law introduced in November 1975 and a decree in March 1976 tightened discipline in the manufacturing sector through the criminalization of "extra-union" (that is, anti-Party) strikes and the creation of a political climate filled with slogans such as "Produce and resist." New forms of protest, which went beyond the usual denunciations of the war and of the chaos after white rule, began to appear. The Angolan economy had prospered in the 1960s, but it crumbled in 1975, and despite state control of the system, the government found it harder and harder to deny that the economy was gradually being dollarized. A governing class largely indifferent to the living conditions of ordinary people began to emerge, partly as a result of the MPLA's monopoly on power and partly because of the difficulty of procuring foreign currency, which changed hands on the black market at fifty times its official price. For more than a decade it was impossible to get even a reasonable idea of what conditions inside the country were really like. The government succeeded in separating the urban market—supported by oil exports—from local producers, and the state more or less abandoned the war-torn countryside to its fate. Forced conscription was practiced in rural areas by both sides in the conflict. The term "famine" was carefully avoided in official circles, but was used in a warning in 1985 by the World Food Organization. With the advent of *perestroika* in the Soviet Union, the Angolan government began publicly to admit the gravity of the situation, leading to an announcement by UNICEF in early 1987 that tens of thousands of children had died of famine in Angola over the previous year.

Despite the wealth created in the oil-producing region of Cabinda, the state's administrative and military resources were quite limited, and the regime made few attempts at collectivization and rural reorganization.[49] Nevertheless, there was considerable resentment toward the government in the countryside. Problems in tax collection, a lack of investment in infrastructure, barriers to commerce, and the disappearance of the urban market meant that the country-side often was left to fend for itself. Thirteen years after independence, the Angolan state published an official report based on the findings of the agrono-mist René Dumont, who sharply criticized the trading conditions in Angola because they failed to recognize the true worth of the peasants' contribution.[50] The situation led to increasing hostility toward the coastline, which was domi-nated by the Marxist culture of the creole or mixed-race *assimilados,* many of whom held positions in the MPLA.

It was among the rural population, many of whom also hated foreigners, that Jonas Savimbi's UNITA Party found a growing number of supporters outside the Ovimbundu territories where it had its origins. UNITA's support grew even though Savimbi made the same demands on the population that the government did. The ensuing conflict, rather than a Stalinist war led by the MPLA against the peasantry, was in effect a war in which the peasants were often in conflict with one another. Supported by the Reagan administration, but taking most of their ideas from Maoism, UNITA leaders were always eager to play up the conflict between town and country; they often denounced the creole aristocracy of the MPLA in the name of the "African people."[51] None-theless, it is difficult to gauge the extent to which the peasantry rallied to Savimbi's cause before upheavals engulfed the Soviet bloc. When the South Africans and Cubans finally withdrew after peace accords were signed in New York on 22 December 1988, the MPLA's conversion to Western ideas produced the expected results. In July 1990 the MPLA leadership accepted the necessity of a market economy and political pluralism, a change that proved to be the undoing of UNITA, which suffered a heavy defeat in the elections of 1992.

The undeniable changes undergone by the MPLA during fifteen years of independence were essentially the result of a massive popular rejection of the idea of an MPLA Party-state and of the traumatic experience of fifteen years of economic instability, forced conscription, and massive population move-ments.

The transitional period in the evolution toward a multiparty democracy was clearly not the time to begin the search for those in charge of the secret police or responsible for the violation of human rights. As in the Soviet Union, many of those responsible were members of ethnic minorities and have never been forced to answer for their previous activities, not least because of the essential continuity inside the government. With the exception of a few small groups of people who survived the purges, none of the major parties has asked for an investigation into the disappearance of the tens of thousands of victims whose fate, as the carefully worded Amnesty International reports put it, did not "conform to internationally recognized standards of equity."

Mozambique

On 25 December 1974, when Portuguese army officers established a multiparty democracy in Lisbon, they entrusted the destiny of Mozambique to one party, the Frente de Libertação do Moçambique (Mozambique National Liberation Front), or Frelimo.[52] The Front, founded in June 1962 under the leadership of Eduardo Chivambo Mondlane, a doctor of anthropology, managed to win the sympathy of the international community and had the military support of both China and the Soviet Union. Unlike in Angola, Frelimo managed on the eve of the Portuguese revolution of 25 April 1974 to cause serious problems for the colonial troops, most of whom were African in origin.[53] Because Frelimo had already won over a significant proportion of the nationalist intellectual elite, the Front mirrored the different ideological tendencies among intellectuals. By 1974, however, it was clear that Marxism-Leninism predominated among Frelimo's leadership. After Frelimo's second congress in 1968, the significance of the anti-imperialist struggle, as formulated by Samora Machel in accordance with the Chinese notion of "liberated zones," gradually took the shape proposed by Mondlane shortly before his death in 1969: "I conclude today that Frelimo is more socialist, revolutionary, and progressive than ever, and that our line is now firmly oriented toward Marxist-Leninist Socialism." To explain this evolution, he added: "With living conditions the way they are in Mozambique, our enemy leaves us no choice."

In the immediate aftermath of independence, this "enemy" seemed to give some respite to the new rulers of the country. The white, mixed-race, and Indian *assimilado* elements who played a dominant role in the new system launched a major reorganization of the country. In the belief that the essentially rural Mozambique could take shape only as a party-state, they sought to control the country though a process called "villagization."[54] This policy was first implemented in the early 1970s in the "liberated zones," where it had met with varying degrees of success. Frelimo decided to extend it systematically throughout the territory. All peasants (80 percent of the population) were expected to abandon their traditional homes and to regroup in new villages. In the initial enthusiasm of independence, the population responded quite favorably to the government's requests, creating collective farms and sometimes cooperating in the construction of communal buildings, although they generally refused to inhabit them and soon abandoned the communal fields. On paper it appeared that the country was under the careful control of a hierarchical administration though a network of Communist cells.

In 1977 the Frelimo leaders had openly proclaimed their allegiance to the Bolshevik ideal, calling for extended collectivization and closer links with the international Communist movement. Various treaties were signed with the countries of the Soviet bloc, which provided arms and military instructors in exchange for close support of the Rhodesian nationalists of the Zimbabwe African National Union (ZANU).

While Mozambique was busy signing accords with the Eastern bloc (which soon came to dominate the country), white Rhodesians led by Ian Smith sought to retaliate by supporting the resistance movement that was beginning to emerge in the countryside. Under the leadership of Alfonso Dhlakama, the Resistencia Nacional Moçambicana (National Resistance of Mozambique), or Renamo, benefited from the support of the Rhodesian special services until Zimbabwe achieved independence in 1980. At that point the South African government took over responsibility for providing logistical support to Renamo. To the surprise of numerous observers, the population of the villages rallied to the resistance movement despite the barbarism of Renamo's methods, which had frightened even the Rhodesians. Some of Renamo's supporters were people who had escaped from the "reeducation camps" of the Serviço Nacional de Segurança Popular (National Service for the Security of the People), or SNASP, which had become ubiquitous after 1975.[55] The SNASP had assumed that even if most people could not be won over, they could at least be kept under control. Control of the population was of vital consequence for both parties. The few studies carried out on the ground confirm the the scale and seriousness of the violence committed by both sides against the civilian population.[56] The actions of Renamo, on the whole, were considerably less systematic than the state violence perpetrated by Frelimo, and the support that Renamo received demonstrated just how hated the regime had become. Frelimo justified its actions in terms of a struggle against tribalism, against antiquated and outdated religious practices, and against the deep-seated belief in lineage and ancestral fiefdom, which the Front had rejected at independence, disparaging it as "feudalism."[57]

The prerogatives of the SNASP had been considerably expanded even before the authorities in Maputo realized the extent of the danger presented by Renamo. Established in 1975, the SNASP was responsible for arresting or detaining anyone suspected of being a threat to state security on either political or economic grounds. The SNASP was supposed to follow normal judicial procedure and did its own prosecuting, but it also had the right to send people directly to "reeducation camps." This practice was facilitated by Article 115 of the penal code, which eliminated the right of detainees to habeas corpus (although the extent to which it had ever existed under the Salazar regime was quite limited). The first large-scale attack by the resistance was on the reeducation camp at Sacuze in 1977. The *ofensivas pela legalidade* (offensives for legality) that were periodically championed by Samora Machel did not remove the SNASP's prerogatives. Instead, these campaigns were aimed at bringing the law into line with the de facto situation. This was the logic behind Law No. 2/79 of 28 February 1979, regarding crimes against national security of the people and the people's state. This law also reintroduced the death penalty, which had been abolished in both Portugal and its colonies in 1867. The death penalty, however, was not systematically used, except in the elimination of Frelimo dissidents. Such was the fate, for instance, of Lazaro Nkavandame, Joana Simaiao, and Uria Simango, who were liquidated while in detention in 1983, and whose deaths were kept secret until the formal ending of the Party's Marxist-Leninist period.[58] In 1983 the Eduardo Mondlane law faculty at the University of Maputo was closed. This was perhaps no great loss; according to government legal reports, the function of the institution was not to prepare lawyers to defend the interests of the people, but to train those who exploited them.[59]

The intelligentsia rapidly became disenchanted with the movement, although they did show considerable sympathy with an organization that in theory protected their interests, the Associaçao dos Escritores Moçambicanos (Association of Mozambican Writers). They also forged secret links with organizations such as the CIA, the KGB, and the SNASP itself.[60] Rather rarer were those who, like the poet Jorge Viegas, paid for their dissidence with enforced stays in psychiatric hospitals and exile.

A hardening of the political line, following the logic of the early years of the Soviet system, went hand in hand with an opening of the economy. Investment had always come in from abroad, and continued to do so under Frelimo, as befitted a country that the U.S.S.R. had barred from entering the Council for Mutual Economic Assistance (COMECON).[61] After Frelimo's Fourth Party Congress in 1983, the organization turned its attention to the rural population, putting a halt to the policy of collectivization that had had such disastrous consequences. In a typical condemnation, Samora Machel did not mince his words: "We tend to forget that our country is made up mostly of peasants. We keep on talking about the working classes and relegating the vast majority of the country to the background."[62] Every time the government militia had burned another haystack to try to ensure the villagization quota, it had increased Renamo's support. The severe damage done to traditional systems of agriculture, together with the wildly erratic exchange rates for consumer goods versus foodstuffs, had led to severe problems with the food supply.

Neither the government nor Renamo appears to have used the weapon of hunger in a systematic fashion. But control of the food supply was a vital tool for Frelimo when moving populations from areas that were in dispute between the two sides. Separating farmers from their land was also a disastrous policy that contributed in no small measure to the food shortages in the country.

According to Human Rights Watch, in the period 1975–1985 food shortages caused more deaths than did armed violence.[63] This view is shared by UNICEF, which calculated that 600,000 died of hunger during this period, a loss of life comparable to that caused by famine in Ethiopia. International aid was a major factor in helping the affected population to survive. In January 1987 the U.S. ambassador in Maputo reported to the State Department that as many as 3.5 million Mozambicans were at risk from hunger,[64] prompting an immediate response from Washington and several international organizations. Despite this effort, the most exposed regions fell victim to a terrible famine whose scale has never been fully appreciated. In the Memba region alone, humanitarian organizations report that 8,000 died of hunger in the spring of 1989.[65] Market forces soon took over in the regions that received support from abroad. Such was one of the lessons drawn in a European Community report in 1991, which revealed that only 25 percent of food aid was sold at the agreed rate, while the other 75 percent remained in the hands of the authorities, who, after the usual pilfering, sold it on the black market.[66] The Mozambican "new man" whom Samora Machel and his associates had been so zealous to foster revealed himself to be "the deeply pathological product of compromises inside each individual, which take the form of dishonor, deception, and schizophrenic madness. The individual wants to live, but he must split in two to do it, and live a double life, a hidden, true life and a false public life, the second protecting the first, and he must constantly lie to have a tiny parcel of truth for himself."[67]

The sudden collapse of the Communist states in Eastern Europe led people to realize how fragile these regimes were and how resistant civil society could be. Even if, during the fifteen years covered here, the public characterization of African Communism as "modern political legitimation" might have had painful consequences for a university lecturer from the region, that perception does have a certain explanatory power.[68] The brief nature of the African experiment with Communism, together with the dominant perception of Africa as doomed to violence by its very nature, risks blurring the contours of the project as it was outlined at the outset. To resist this temptation, we should perhaps invert the perspective. Although it may be difficult to see the specific nature of violence in these Marxist-Leninist states themselves, as Achille Mbembe suggests, it is likely the case that the famines and massacres of civilians occurred because the African countries, "having been colonized and led into independence by the Western powers, chose to take the Soviet-style regimes as their model." This pattern ensured that efforts to promote democratization would do little to change the deeply Leninist nature of most African states.

27 Communism in Afghanistan

Sylvain Boulouque

$\mathbf{A}$fghanistan has a surface area of 640,000 square kilometers and is thus slightly bigger than France.[1] Until 1991 the country was neatly tucked amid four other states: the Soviet Union to the north, Iran to the west, Pakistan to the east and south, and, for a few dozen kilometers, China to the east. More than one-third of the country is mountainous, with several peaks exceeding 22,900 feet. In 1979 the population of 15 million was divided among a variety of ethnic groups. The dominant group, numbering more than 6 million and living mainly in the south, are the mostly Sunni Pushtuns, who speak their own language. The more than 4 million Tajiks, who live primarily in the eastern part of the country, are also Sunni Muslims but speak the Dari dialect of Persian. Approximately 1.5 million Uzbeks, who are also Sunni and speak a Turkic language, live in the north. The 1.5 million Hazaras are mostly Shiite and live in the center of the country. Other ethnic groups, including Turkmens, Kirgiz, Baluchis, Aymaqs, Kohistanis, and Nuristans, are scattered through the territory and account for the remaining 10 percent of the population of Afghanistan.

Traditionally, Afghanistan has been held together primarily by its Muslim faith. Ninety-nine percent of the population is Muslim; 80 percent are Sunnis, and the rest are Shiite. There are also Sikh and Hindu minorities and a tiny Jewish community. The Afghan version of Islam was traditionally quite moderate in both urban and rural areas. It was closely integrated into the traditional tribal structure, in which village chiefs served as the community leaders. Most of the population lived in rural areas; in 1979 the only large city was the capital, Kabul, situated in the east and home to 500,000 people. Smaller cities included Herāt in the west, Kandahār in the south, and Mazār-i-Sharīf and Kundūz in the north, each with a population of less than 200,000. The Afghans had a long tradition of resisting invasions, especially those by the Mongols and the Russians. Afghanistan was under the protection of the British from the mid nineteenth century until just after World War I, in 1919. While England and Russia (later the Soviet Union) were engaged in a series of conflicts with the people of Central Asia, the Afghan monarchy always succeeded in maintaining independence by playing off the two great powers against each other. When King Zahir Shah came to power in 1963, he accelerated the drive toward cultural, economic, and political modernization. After 1959 women were no longer obliged to wear veils and were granted access to schools and universities. Once the king had decided in 1965 that something akin to democracy was the way forward, the country began to develop a parliamentary system with full-fledged political parties and free elections. The Communist coup in April 1978 and the subsequent Soviet intervention destroyed the political equilibrium in the country and undid the process of modernization that by then was well under way.

Afghanistan and the U.S.S.R. from 1917 to 1973

Links between Afghanistan and the Soviet Union went back a long way. In April 1919, Khan Amanullah established diplomatic relations with the new government in Moscow, allowing the Bolsheviks to open five consulates in the country. On 28 February 1921 a treaty of peace and economic cooperation was signed. As a result of this treaty, the Soviet Union assisted in the construction of a new telegraph line and agreed to pay the king 500,000 dollars annually. This was partly an attempt by the Soviet government to show its goodwill and to counterbalance the still-dominant British influence in the country,[2] but it was also an attempt to spread the revolution to countries that were still under colonial influence. At the Congress of Eastern Peoples, held in Baku in September 1920, the heads of the Communist International concluded that anti-colonialist and anti-imperialist slogans might attract nations under European colonial influence to the Communist camp. The Comintern soon issued a number of proclamations in which the term "class struggle" was replaced by the term *jihad* (holy war). It appears that three Afghans were present at the congress: Agazade, of the Afghan Communists; Azim, who represented people with no particular party attachment; and Kara Tadjiev, another representative of those with no clear party alignment.[3] In a similar vein, the resolutions of the

Fourth Congress of the Communist International, which opened on 7 November 1922, sought to weaken the imperialist powers by creating and organizing "unified anti-imperialist fronts."

In September 1920, just before these events, Soviet troops led by Mikhail Frunze, one of the leaders of the Red Army who had also taken part in the repression of Nestor Makhno's Ukrainian anarchist movement, annexed the Bukhara Khanate, which for a time had been part of the Afghan kingdom. Several reprisal operations were carried out against the peasants and *basmachis*, the resistance fighters labeled "brigands" by Soviet officials. The *basmachis* fought against Russian and later Soviet domination of the region. The methods used by Soviet army personnel in Afghanistan were analogous to those used against rebellious peasants in Russia. The region was definitively annexed in 1924, although some fighting continued into the 1930s, and more than a million *basmachis* took refuge in Afghanistan. *Basmachi* resistance was not definitively crushed by the Soviet Red Army until 1933. The Communists soon began to exert influence on the leadership in Afghanistan, and a number of Afghan officers left for training in the U.S.S.R. At the same time, Soviet diplomats carried out a variety of underground activities, causing one attaché and several engineers to be expelled from the country for espionage.[4] There is also evidence that GPU agents were present in the country, most notably Georgy Agabekov, who had been a member of the Cheka since 1920 and was a member of its foreign section. Agabekov was in charge of the Afghan operation while living illegally first in Kabul and then in Istanbul, before he finally broke with the GPU in 1930.[5]

In 1929 Khan Amanullah introduced a policy of agricultural reform but simultaneously began an antireligious campaign. The new antireligious laws were modeled on the Turkish reforms of Kemal Ataturk and provoked a peasant uprising led by Bacha-i Saqqao ("Son of the Water Carrier"), who succeeded in overthrowing the regime.[6] Initially this uprising was interpreted by the Communist International as anticapitalist, but Soviet officials later changed their mind and sought to help the troops of the old regime under the command of Gulam-Nabi Khan, the Afghan ambassador in Moscow, to return to Afghanistan. Soviet troops (the best units from Tashkent, with the assistance of the Soviet air force) penetrated Afghanistan while disguised in Afghan uniforms. Five thousand Afghans fighting for the government were killed. Any villagers whom the Red Army encountered were immediately executed.[7] Despite some battlefield successes, Gulam-Nabi's forces retreated north after receiving word that Amanullah had abdicated and fled abroad. At this point Soviet support for the anti-Saqqao forces ceased. The fight was taken up by Nadir Shah, a noble with close ties to Great Britain who returned from his exile in France and took over the leadership of the Afghan army. He was quickly proclaimed king by the nobility and tribal leaders. Bacha-i Saqqao found himself without a disciplined army and on the verge of defeat, but soon after he went into hiding he was arrested and executed. Nadir Shah tried to come to an arrangement with both the British and the Soviet Union. He was recognized and accepted in Moscow on condition that he withdraw Afghan support for the *basmachis*. After Nadir Shah agreed to this condition, the leader of the *basmachis*, Ibrahim Bek, was forced by the Afghan army to retreat into Soviet territory, where he was arrested and executed.[8] A new treaty of nonaggression with the Soviet Union was signed on 24 June 1931. Nadir Shah was assassinated by a student in 1933, and his son, Zahir Shah, became king in his place, although actual power remained in the hands of the king's uncles and cousins.

After 1945 there were several more waves of modernization, which were particularly notable in the capital, where five- and seven-year development plans were enacted. Further treaties of friendship and cooperation were signed with the Soviet Union, including a 1955 treaty providing for noninterference in internal affairs. A number of Soviet advisers were welcomed into the country, mainly to help modernize the Afghan army.

From 1953 to 1963 Prince Mohammed Daoud, a cousin of the king, served as prime minister and was responsible for governing the country. Despite Daoud's role in helping to create the nonaligned movement, Soviet influence in the country became more and more pronounced as time passed, and Soviet officials were gradually assigned to key positions in the Afghan army and civil service. Economic accords were almost invariably slanted in favor of the Soviet Union, despite efforts by Prince Daoud to move closer to the United States. In 1963 Daoud was sidelined by Zahir Shah, who over the next ten years attempted to transform Afghanistan into a constitutional monarchy. Political parties were legalized, and the first free elections took place in 1965. A second round of elections followed in 1969. On both occasions the results favored the local nobility and groups supporting the government. Afghanistan was slowly becoming westernized and more modern, although the country was not yet close to a true democracy. As Michael Barry noted, "The regime was far from perfect: it was high-handed, privileged, and often corrupt. But it was a long way from being the barbarous regime that the Afghan Communists claimed it had been. The royal family had outlawed torture back in 1905, and even the corporal punishments normal under Koranic law had fallen into disuse. In that respect, the Communist regime represented a serious step backward."[9]

The Afghan Communists

Zahir Shah's democratization allowed the Afghan Communist Party, which had long been an underground organization, finally to come into the open. The

Communists took part in elections in the 1960s under the name of the Democratic Party of the People of Afghanistan (DPPA). The DPPA held a congress in early 1965 at which the Soviet-backed candidate, Nur-Mohammed Taraki, was elected secretary general. However, serious tribal divisions and personal rivalries swirled behind the facade of Party unity. One DPPA founder, Babrak Karmal, was an aristocrat from the royal family: "Karmal" was a pseudonym meaning "friend of the workers"; his real name was Mohammed Hussein Khan. According to a KGB defector, Karmal was for many years a KGB informer.[10] Nur-Mohammed Taraki, the other founder of the Party, was the son of a wealthy peasant from a village in the province of Ghazni. He was a Pushtun who had gained high government office thanks to his knowledge of English. Hafizullah Amin was also a Pushtun, but born in the suburbs of Kabul into a family of civil servants.[11] In the 1965 election Babrak Karmal and two other Communists won seats in the parliament. In 1969 Karmal was reelected and was joined in parliament by Amin.

The DPPA was made up of two factions, the Khalq (the People) and the Parcham (the Flag), each of which was named after its respective newspaper. Khalq was the paper of the Pushtuns from the southeast, while Parcham was read primarily by middle-class Persian speakers, whose project was to put into practice the theory of the united front. Both groups were orthodox Communists and hewed very closely to Soviet policy, although the Parcham were perhaps slightly closer to the Soviet line. The schism between the two groups lasted from 1966 to 1976, with both sides claiming the right to be known as the Afghan Communist Party and to act on behalf of the entire DPPA. In 1976 they reunited at Moscow's behest. The Party never had more than 4,000–6,000 members.[12] In addition to these factions of the DPPA, there were several groups whose ideologies were oriented toward Marxism. The Shola-i-Javaid (Eternal Flame) was a Maoist group founded in the early 1970s, which recruited most of its members among Shiites and students. It later divided into several factions, all of which joined the anti-Soviet resistance.

From 1965 to 1973 all Afghan Communist groups systematically denigrated the government and the monarchy. Demonstrations became more and more common, as did disruptions in parliament. The DPPA also began to recruit more widely, particularly among the political elite.

The Coup of Mohammed Daoud

Daoud, who had been sidelined by Zahir in 1963, carried out a coup in 1973 with the help of a number of Communist army officers. Outside observers have offered various interpretations of these events. Some are convinced that the strings were being pulled by Moscow;[13] others believe that Daoud was manipulating the Communists. Wherever the truth may lie, seven members of the

Parcham faction entered the Daoud government as ministers. After the coup, constitutional liberties were suspended, and, at the instigation of the Communists, the government unleashed a wave of repression. As one analyst noted, "The nationalist leader Hashim Maiwandwal (who had been a liberal prime minister of the country in 1965–1967) was arrested along with about forty others for conspiring to overthrow the government; four of them were executed. The official version was that Maiwandal 'committed suicide' in prison. The widely held belief was that Daoud had him assassinated because he was one of the few non-Communist opponents who presented the country with any real alternative."[14] Torture and terror became commonplace, and the sinister Pol-e-Charki prison was opened in 1974.

In 1975, however, Daoud got rid of the Communists and signed new commercial agreements not only with Eastern-bloc countries, but also with Iran and India. Relations with the U.S.S.R. deteriorated, and during an official visit to the U.S.S.R., Daoud quarreled with Brezhnev and began openly promoting the economic independence of his country. Thereafter his days were numbered, and he was toppled in a coup on 27 April 1978. Barry describes the situation in the country on the eve of the coup as follows: "Pre-1978 Afghanistan was a secular state, with little time for Muslim extremism, officially neutral, accommodating toward the Soviet Union, and not questioning either its borders or its relations with other Muslim states . . . To say that the U.S.S.R. acted to block the rise of Muslim extremism is simply not true: by overthrowing Daoud, the U.S.S.R. instead aided the rise of Muslim extremists, whose strength it had perhaps rather underestimated. Quite clearly the Soviets aided the Communist coup d'état to ensure that Afghanistan did not escape their clutches at the last minute."[15]

The April 1978 Coup, or "Saour Revolution"

The incident that provoked the Communist coup d'état was the assassination of Mir-Akbar Khaybar, one of the founders of the DPPA, on 17 April 1978 in circumstances that remain mysterious. One theory put forward after the Parcham had seized power is that he was eliminated by agents from the Khalq led by Hafizullah Amin. Another theory is that it was the work of Mohammed Najibullah, the future leader of the Afghan secret service, with help from the Soviet secret services.[16] The immediate result of the assassination was the staging of a large Communist demonstration, followed by the overthrow of Daoud's government. The seizure of power does appear to have been premeditated. Amin, head of the Khalqs, who were particularly well represented in the military, was planning a coup that was to take place in April 1980.[17] The spread of Communism in Afghanistan had been brought about through the methods developed in Spain and then used in other "people's democracies." First, Party members sought high-ranking positions in industry, the army, and the civil service. This infiltration was followed by the actual seizure of power in the "Saour [Bull] Revolution" of April 1978. Daoud's attempts to outmaneuver the Communists, together with the assassination of Mir-Akbar Khaybar, merely accelerated the process. Shortly after the assassination, Communist demonstrations became more and more widespread. Daoud ordered the main Communist leaders to be arrested or kept under close watch. Amin was also placed under house arrest, but he was secretly aided by the policemen sent to guard him, who apparently were members of the DPPA. As a result, he was able to organize the whole coup from his home.[18]

The presidential palace was attacked with tanks and planes on 27 April 1978. Daoud, his family, and the presidential guard refused to surrender. The president and seventeen members of his family were killed the following day. The first purge of non-Communist members of the military took place on 29 April. In the coup's aftermath, repressions of the old regime's supporters led to the death of about 10,000 people and the imprisonment of between 14,000 and 20,000 for political reasons.[19]

The new government was proclaimed on 30 April. Nur-Mohammed Taraki, a Khalq, was named president of the Democratic Republic of Afghanistan; Babrak Karmal, of the Parcham faction, was named vice president and deputy prime minister; and Hafizullah Amin, a Khalq, was named second vice president and foreign minister. The Soviet Union was the first state to recognize the new government,[20] and a treaty of cooperation and mutual assistance was quickly signed. Taraki proposed a series of reforms that, according to observers, broke with the traditional ways of Afghan society. Rural debt and mortgages on land were abolished, school attendance became obligatory for all children, and antireligious propaganda began to appear. Taraki was proclaimed the "guide and father of the April Revolution." The spate of reforms led to widespread discontent, and by July 1978 the first revolts had broken out in Asmar, in the southeast. Political violence became widespread. On 14 February 1979 the U.S., ambassador Adolph Dubs, was kidnapped by the Maoist Group Setem-i-Milli (Oppression of the Nation), which demanded the release of one of their leaders, Barrudem Bâhes. Bâhes, however, had already been executed by the KHAD, the Afghan security service, which was under the control of the Soviet KGB. Officers from the KHAD tried to intervene, but ended up killing both the ambassador and his kidnappers.[21] According to Etienne Gille, "Some say that this operation was carried out in secret to compromise the diplomatic situation of the Khalq regime."[22] In any case, no witnesses of the events survived.

Shortly afterward the government began an antireligious crusade. The

Koran was burned in public, and imams and other religious leaders were arrested and killed. On the night of 6 January 1979 all 130 men in the Mo-jaddedi clan, a leading Shiite group, were massacred.[23] All religious practices were banned, even for the tiny 5,000-strong Jewish community living in Kabul and Herāt, who responded by fleeing to Israel.

The rebellion began to grow, although it lacked any real structure. It spread fastest in the cities and from there into the country. According to Eric Bachelier, "In every tribe and every ethnic group with its own traditions, networks of resistance began to spring up. The resistance was the result of a multitude of groups in permanent contact with the population, and the common link was invariably Islam."[24] Faced with this widespread resistance, the Afghan Communists and their Soviet advisers began to practice terror on a large scale. Michael Barry describes one such incident:

> In March 1979 the village of Kerala became the Oradour-sur-Glane of Afghanistan; 1,700 adults and children, the entire male population of the village, were all assembled in the town square and machine-gunned at point-blank range. The dead and dying were thrown into three mass graves and buried with a bulldozer. For a while afterward the women could still see the earth move slightly as the wounded struggled to escape, but soon all movement stopped. All the women fled to Pakistan. They were labeled "feudal counterrevolutionaries who had sold them-selves to American and Chinese interests" by the Afghan leaders, and they told these stories crying with anguish in the refugee shelters.[25]

The Afghan Communists were constantly asking for more assistance from the U.S.S.R. In March 1979, several MiG fighters based in Soviet territory bombed the small city of Herāt, which had just fallen into the hands of anti-Communist rebels. The army then entered the city to mop up the remain-ing resistance. The ensuing bombardment, together with the repression that followed the town's recapture, claimed between 5,000 and 25,000 lives out of a total population of 200,000. There is not currently, and may never be, any way to tell exactly how many died in the repression.[26] After this action, the rebellion spread throughout the country, forcing the Communists once again to ask the Soviet Union for aid. In this instance, the dissident Vladimir Bu-kovsky reports, Soviet assistance included "special supplies, for 53 million rubles, of 140 artillery pieces, 90 armored vehicles (including 50 ambulances), 48,000 guns and rifles, nearly 1,000 grenade launchers, and 680 aerial bombs . . . As an immediate response [the Soviet Union] sent 100 stocks of incendiary gas and 150 cases of bombs, but were unable to meet the Afghan request for chemical weapons and bombs filled with poisonous gas. They were also unable to send pilots for the helicopter teams."[27] At the same time, terror reigned in Kabul. The Pol-e-Charki prison, on the eastern outskirts of the city, became a concentration camp.[27] As Sayyed Abdullah, the director of the prison, explained to the prisoners: "You're here to be turned into a heap of rubbish." Torture was common; the worst form entailed live burial in the latrines. Hundreds of prisoners were killed every night, and the dead and dying were buried by bulldozers. Stalin's method of punishing entire ethnic groups for the actions of some of its members was adopted, leading to the arrest on 15 August 1979 of 300 people from the Hazaras ethnic group who were suspected of supporting the resistance. "One hundred fifty of them were buried alive by the bulldozers, and the rest were doused with gasoline and burned alive." In September 1979 the prison authorities admitted that 12,000 prisoners had been eliminated. The director of Pol-e-Charki told anyone who would listen: "We'll leave only 1 million Afghans alive—that's all we need to build socialism."[28]

While the country was being transformed into a giant prison, the struggles between the Khalq and the Parcham continued inside the DPPA, with the Khalq gradually gaining the upper hand. As Parcham leaders were steadily removed from positions of power, they were sent as ambassadors to countries behind the Iron Curtain. Babrak Karmal was sent to Czechoslovakia at the express request of the Soviet Union. Conflicts occurred within the ruling Khalq as well. On 10 September 1979, Amin overthrew Taraki, becoming prime minister and secretary general of the DPPA. He quickly eliminated his opponents within the Khalq and had Taraki assassinated, although the official newspapers stated that Taraki had died as the result of a long illness. Foreign observers noted the presence of 5,000 Soviet advisers in Afghanistan at the time, as well as a special visit by General Ivan Grigorievich Pavlovsky, the commander in chief of Soviet ground forces.[29]

One year after the Communist coup, the situation in the country was terrifying. As Shah Bazgar explains:

> Babrak Karmal claimed that 15,000 people had died in the purges carried out by his two predecessors, Taraki and Amin. The real number was at least 40,000. Among them, alas, were two of my maternal cousins, who died in Pol-e-Charki. One of them, Selab Safay, was a well-known man of letters, whose poems used to be read on the radio and television. I was extremely fond of him. My other cousin, his brother, was a teacher. The whole elite of the country was purged. The few who survived all told of terrible Communist atrocities. The doors of the cells would be opened, and, lists in hand, soldiers would call out the names of the detainees. They would slowly get up. A few minutes later muffled machine-gun fire would be heard."[30]

These casualty figures include only Kabul and the other cities. Executions in the countryside, where the Communists sought to wipe out the resistance through a genuine reign of terror, including a bombing campaign, led to the death of approximately 100,000 additional people. The number of Afghan refugees who fled these massacres en masse has been estimated at more than 500,000.[31]

The Soviet Intervention

Afghanistan by the fall of 1979 was deep into civil war. Despite the repressions, the Communists were unable to enforce their authority in the country and were compelled once more to seek assistance from the Soviet Union. This assistance proved to be greater than Amin's government had expected. Amin had been starting to shy away from Moscow, increasing contacts with countries not directly under Soviet influence and even with the Americans (as a young man he had studied in the United States). Soviet leaders decided to intervene to reassert control. The decision was approved by the Soviet Politburo on 12 December 1979. On 25 December Operation Storm 333 was launched, and Soviet troops crossed the borders into Afghanistan. Ostensibly they were honoring the treaty of friendship and cooperation and were offering "fraternal" assistance to the authorities in Kabul. According to a former KGB officer, "A commando assault team from the KGB led by Colonel [Grigory] Boyarinov . . . attacked the palace, assassinating Amin and any witnesses who could have reported on the events."[32] Before his death, Amin was given the opportunity to retire and accept a generous pension. When he refused, he was killed and replaced by Babrak Karmal. The new government was proclaimed in a radio broadcast from the Soviet Union before Amin was executed.[33]

There are numerous hypotheses concerning the Soviet intervention. Some commentators view it as an attempt by Moscow to expand to the south. Others see it as part of a project to bring stability to a region in which the expansion of radical Islam posed a clear threat. The intervention might also be seen simply as a case of Soviet imperialism, a further expression of the messianic character of Marxist regimes desiring all peoples to be Communist. Another possibility is that the Soviet government felt a genuine desire to defend another Communist state that was under attack from "agents of imperialism."[34]

The first Soviet troops arrived in Afghanistan on 27 December 1979; by early 1980 there were nearly 100,000 on the ground. The war fell into four distinct phases. In the first phase, in 1979–1982, Soviet troops occupied the country. The second, most difficult phase was the "total war" of 1982–1986. Soviet retreat in 1987–1989 marked the third phase. The final phase, lasting until 1992, began after the Soviet Army's withdrawal on 15 February 1989, when Mohammed Najibullah became the head of state and initiated an effort to create national unity and reform in a manner akin to Gorbachev. In 1989 the Soviet government sent aid in the form of military technology worth 2.5 billion rubles. Another 1.4 billion rubles' worth of weaponry was provided the following year. The Najibullah government fell when military assistance ceased in 1992 after the Soviet Union's collapse.[35]

Throughout this time the country was caught between two different modes of terror: the Soviet Army practiced a form of total war and a scorched-earth policy, while in areas not under direct Soviet attack Afghans experienced traditional methods of terror at the hands of the Communist regime. The systematic elimination of real or imaginary opponents took place in the special prisons of the AGSA (Organization for the Protection of Afghan Interests). The AGSA quickly went through various incarnations, becoming the KHAD (State Information Service) and then the WAD (Ministry of State Security). By 1986 the secret police organs were directly dependent on the KGB for both finances and advisers. This method of government by terror theoretically lasted until 1989, when the Soviet troops left the country. In practice, however, it lasted until the fall of Mohammed Najibullah's government in 1992.

Throughout the nine years of the war, the Soviet Army and the Afghan Communists never fully controlled more than 20 percent of the country. They contented themselves with the main centers of power, such as the cities, the grain-producing areas, and the areas with gas and oil reserves—which were of course inevitably destined for the U.S.S.R. "The extraction of resources and the development of Afghanistan were carried out in a typically colonial fashion. The colony produced the primary resources and provided a market for the industrial products of the metropolis, keeping its industry going . . . In line with the well-established Russian technique, the occupying forces made the country itself pay for the cost of the war. The armies, tanks, and bombing of villages were invoiced and paid for with gas, cotton, and, later, copper and electricity."[36] During these years the Soviet Union, with the aid of the Afghan army, carried out what was in practice a total war. Meanwhile the Afghan army suffered massive losses from desertions, falling in strength from 80,000 in 1989 to barely 30,000 two years later. In 1982 all reserves were called up, and in March of the following year general mobilization was decreed for all men aged eighteen and over. Children were also forcibly conscripted at age fifteen.

Aside from elite units of special operations (Spetsnaz) forces, the Soviet soldiers sent to Afghanistan were primarily from the western peripheral republics, including Ukraine, Latvia, Estonia, and Lithuania. They replaced the contingents of troops based in Central Asia, whom the Soviet government may have seen as potentially susceptible to a radical form of Islam. More than 600,000 troops were sent to the country, and 14,751 of them died in the war.[37] Their bodies were rarely returned to their families, and many were not even brought back to the U.S.S.R. The sealed, lead-lined coffins that were sent to the families usually held nothing but sand or sometimes the bodies of unidentified soldiers.[38] Demoralized by this war that had no name, countless soldiers fell prey to alcoholism and drug abuse involving hashish, opium, and heroin. Some of these drugs were supplied by the KGB. Profits from drug production in Afghanistan were even greater than those of Southeast Asia's Golden Triangle. To be sent home, many soldiers mutilated themselves. Upon their return they were generally abandoned to their fate, and some were sent to psychiatric hospitals.[39] Many others drifted into a life of crime. The war also gave birth to a number of right-wing nationalist groups, most notably the ultra right-wing and antisemitic Pamyat group, to which the KGB turned a blind eye.[40]

The Afghan resistance gathered strength in the face of the Soviet invasion, growing to between 60,000 and 200,000 fighters. With support from a majority of the population, the Afghan resistance consisted of seven Sunni parties, whose headquarters were in Pakistan, and eight Shiite groups, with bases in Iran.[41] All claimed some basis in radical or moderate Islam. The resistance also had the support of the U.S. government, which supplied the guerrillas with arms, including surface-to-air Stinger missiles, which deterred low-level aerial attacks by Soviet bombers, thus foiling one of the key elements in the Soviet war effort. Other than aerial bombardment, the Soviet Army's main strategy had been simply one of terror. Any person or village suspected of assisting the resistance in the smallest degree suffered immediate reprisals. Repression was constant and omnipresent.

The atrocities committed were those to be found in all large-scale wars, and the violence born of total war and constant attrition spread throughout the country.[42] The Afghan resistance also carried out atrocities, likewise barbaric and inexcusable. Unlike other conflicts, notably the war in Vietnam, to which Afghanistan was often compared, the war received very little attention from the world press, and very few pictures of the conflict were ever released. The Afghan resistance was in fact waging a general insurrection in response to both the Communist coup d'état and the invasion from abroad. The powers who supported the resistance fighters paid scant attention to the extent of their respect for human rights and on occasion supported some extremely unsavory groups. But on the whole, responsibility for the origins of the conflict must rest with the Communists and their Soviet allies. Government by mass terror and the system of coercion established by the Communists in Afghanistan were constants in the history of the Communist movement.

The Scale of Repression

The Refugee Problem

The number of refugees grew constantly. At the end of 1980, it was estimated that more than 1 million refugees had fled Afghanistan. Eighty percent of the intellectuals had left by mid-1982. Early in 1983 there were more than 3 million refugees out of a total prewar population of 15.5 million. In 1984 the number passed 4 million,[43] and it reached 5 million in the early 1990s. In addition to those who had left the country, there were 2 million internal refugees who were forced to leave their villages to escape the war and repression. According to Amnesty International, the refugees who left Afghanistan were "the largest refugee group in the world."[44] More than two-thirds of all refugees fled to Pakistan; most of the rest went to Iran; a tiny number reached Western Europe or the United States. Michael Barry recalled that "in the autumn of 1985, during a secret mission on horseback in four provinces in eastern and central Afghanistan on behalf of the International Federation for the Rights of Man, the Swedish doctor Johann Lagerfelt and I made a survey of twenty-three villages and found that 56.3 percent of the population had been displaced."[45] Over the whole territory, more than half the population was forced to move as a direct consequence of the politics of terror deployed by the Soviet Army and its Afghan assistants.

War Crimes and the Destruction of Villages

From the outset, Soviet attacks were concentrated in four areas: along the border; in the Panjshir valley; in the Kandahār region, in the south of the country; and in Herāt, in the east; the last two zones were occupied in February 1982. The total-war strategy pursued by the Soviet army received swift condemnation in 1981 from the Permanent Peoples' Tribunal in Stockholm and London, heir to the "Russell Tribunals" (the International War Crimes Tribunals) that had been "inspired directly by the Nuremberg tribunals, of which they are a legal offshoot."[46] The Permanent Peoples' Tribunal began an investigation into one case of mass killing. It was entrusted to Michael Barry, a specialist in Afghan affairs; to a legal expert, Ricardo Fraile; and to a photographer, Michel Baret. The investigation confirmed that on 13 September 1982 in Padkhwab-e Shana (south of Kabul, in Logar Province), 105 villagers who were hiding in an underground irrigation canal were burned alive by Soviet troops. The investigators determined that the Soviet troops had killed the Afghans with a combination of gasoline, pentrite, and dinitrotoluene (a highly combustible substance) from pipes plugged into tankers that they had brought in. This crime received official condemnation at a session of the Peoples' Tribunal held at the Sorbonne on 20 December 1982. The representative of the Afghan government in Paris claimed that the tribunal was an instrument of imperialism and denied the crime, arguing that "the ceilings inside the Afghan *kârêz* [water pipes] are only a few centimeters high, and it would be impossible for humans to fit inside."[47]

    In the village of Khasham Kala, also in Logar Province, 100 civilians, who had put up no resistance at all, died in the same manner.[48] Whenever the Soviet troops entered a village, they brought terror with them, as one observer described: "The convoy stops within sight of a village. After an artillery barrage, all the exits are blocked; then the soldiers enter the village in armored vehicles looking for 'enemies.' All too often, and there are innumerable reports of this, the searching of villages is accompanied by acts of blind barbarism, with women and old men killed if they show any sign of fear. Soldiers, Afghans as well as Soviets, steal radios and carpets, and tear jewelry off the women." War crimes and acts of savagery recurred with monotonous regularity: "Soviet soldiers poured kerosene over the arms of one boy and set fire to him in front of his parents to punish them for refusing to hand over any information. Villagers were forced to stand barefoot in the snow in freezing temperatures to force them to talk." One soldier explained: "We never took prisoners of war, not a single one. We just killed the prisoners wherever we found them . . . If we were on a punitive expedition, we didn't shoot the women and children with bullets. We just locked them in a room and threw in a few grenades."[49]

The intention was to sow terror, to cow the population into submission, and to prevent Afghan civilians from helping the resistance. Reprisal operations were always carried out in the same spirit. Women were thrown naked from helicopters, and entire villages were destroyed to avenge the death of one Soviet soldier. Observers recalled that "after an attack on a convoy near the village of Muchkizai in the region of Kandahār, the population of the villages of Kolchabad, Muchkizai, and Timur Qalacha was massacred on 13 October 1983 in a reprisal operation. There were 126 dead in total: 40 in Timur Qalacha (i.e., the entire village), 51 in Kolchabad, and 35 in Muchkizai. Most of the victims were women and children—50 women aged twenty to thirty-two, and 26 children. All the young men had left the villages as soon as the convoys arrived, to avoid conscription."[50] Villages were also systematically bombed to prevent the resistance forces from launching any sort of counterattack. On 17 April 1985, for instance, Soviet troops destroyed villages to wipe out resistance bases in Laghmān Province, killing nearly 1,000 people. On 28 May 1985, having "cleansed" the villages, the Soviet Army left the Laghmān-Kounar zone.[51]

International conventions were systematically violated. All evidence suggests that poison gases of various types were used regularly against the civilian population. There are numerous reports of the use of toxic gases, tear gas, and asphyxiants. Napalm and phosphor gas were used intensively during the bombardment of the Afghan countryside by the Soviet air force.[52] On 1 December 1982 neurotoxic gases were allegedly used against the Afghan resistance, resulting in an unknown number of victims.[53] In 1982 the U.S. State Department reported the use of mycotoxin, a biological weapon. The periodical *La nouvelles d'Afghanistan* noted in December 1986 that "the Soviets this summer have used a chemical weapon in Kandahār," and *Le point* on 6 October 1986 noted that deadly chemical weapons had been used in Paghman. In addition, the Soviet army was known to have poisoned water supplies, causing the deaths of both people and cattle.[54] The Soviet high command ordered the bombing of villages known to shelter deserters to discourage the Afghans from showing them any hospitality.[55] The Soviet army also used Afghan soldiers as front-line troops in mine-clearing operations, and sent them out to test the ground ahead of Soviet troops. In late 1988, Soviet forces used Scud and Hurricane missiles to clear the main routes for their withdrawal. In 1989 Soviet troops retraced the route taken ten years earlier, making sure they controlled all the access roads to prevent attacks from the resistance.

Before withdrawing, the Soviet Union had begun a new strategy of killing refugees. Amnesty International remarked that

> groups of men, women, and children fleeing their villages have been subjected by the Soviets to intense bombardments as reprisals for guerrilla attacks. Among the cases cited is one group of 100 families from the village of Sherkhudo, in Faryab Province, in the extreme northwest of the country, who were attacked twice during their 500-kilometer flight toward the border with Pakistan. In the first attack, in October 1987, government forces encircled them, killing nineteen people, including seven children under six years of age. Two weeks later, helicopters again opened fire on the group, killing five men.[56]

Several times, refugee villages in Pakistan that were suspected of harboring resistance bases were relentlessly bombed, including the Matasangar camp on 27 February 1987.[57]

Observers also noted the extensive use of antipersonnel mines. Some 20 million mines were laid, mainly around security zones. These mines were used to protect Soviet troops and the industrial complexes that supplied products to the Soviet Union. Mines were also dropped from helicopters into agricultural areas to render the land useless. Antipersonnel mines have so far maimed at least 700,000 people and are still a major hazard today. During the height of the war, Soviet troops also deliberately targeted children, dropping booby-trapped toys from airplanes.[58] Shah Bazgar described the systematic destruction of villages: "The Soviets attacked every single house, looting and raping the women. The barbarism was worse than instinctive, and appeared to have been planned. They knew that in carrying out such acts they were destroying the very foundation of our society."[59]

The scorched-earth and total-war policies were accompanied by the systematic destruction of Afghanistan's cultural heritage. Kabul had been a cosmopolitan city in which "the Kabuli spirit was alive, with good humor verging on the risqué, and a generally relaxed air toward morals and social mores far removed from the norm in the countryside."[60] These cultural characteristics disappeared as a result of the war and the Soviet occupation. The small city of Herāt suffered terribly from repeated Soviet bombardments and reprisals for the general uprising that had taken place in the west of the country in March 1979. All the monuments in the town, including a twelfth-century mosque, and the old town, which dated back to the sixteenth century, were seriously damaged. Their reconstruction was stymied by the continuing Soviet presence.[61]

Political Terror

The war not only was directed against the civil population, but was accompanied by political terror in the zones controlled by the Afghan Communists, with the support of the Soviet forces. Soviet-occupied Afghanistan was effectively transformed into a giant concentration camp. Prison and torture were systematically applied against anyone who opposed the regime.

Political terror was the province of the KHAD, the Afghan secret police, which was the equivalent of the KGB. The KHAD controlled all detention centers and practiced torture and murder on a grand scale. Although the secret police were officially controlled by Mohammed Najibullah, "Vatanshah, a Soviet Tajik aged around forty . . . took charge of the torture and interrogation service in the KHAD headquarters after Soviet troops moved into the country."[62] The Pol-e-Charki prison had been emptied after the amnesty declared by Babrak Karmal upon coming to power. It did not stay empty for long. In February 1980, after Karmal imposed martial law, the prisons quickly filled once more. Bernard Dupaigne described Poi-e-Charki:

> The prison is made up of eight wings laid out like the spokes of a wheel . . . Block 1 is reserved for people whose interrogation is completed but who have not yet been judged. Block 2 holds the most important prisoners, particularly survivors of the group of Communist officials from the faction that has lost favor . . . Block 4 holds prisoners of great importance . . . Block 3 is feared most because it is between the others and receives no direct sunlight. It is here that the most obstreperous prisoners are kept. Its cells are so small that the prisoners can neither stand nor stretch out. Overcrowding is common . . . The size of the prison was increased in the spring of 1982 by the creation of underground cells. These are probably what prisoners are referring to when they speak with such fear of "the tunnels" . . . Between 12,000 and 15,000 people are imprisoned in Pol-e-Charki. To that number we should add at least 5,000 political prisoners in the eight other detention centers and in the other prisons in Kabul."[63]

In early 1985 a United Nations report on the human-rights situation in Afghanistan accused the KHAD of being an immense torture machine. The report indicated that the KHAD controlled seven detention centers in Kabul: "(1) Bureau 5 of the KHAD, known as Khad-i-Panj; (2) the KHAD headquarters in the Shasharak district; (3) the Ministry of Internal Affairs building; (4) the Central Interrogation Bureau, known as the Sedarat; (5) the offices of the military branch of the KHAD, known as the Khad-i-Nezami, with two private houses near the Sedarat building; (6) the Ahmad Shah Khan house; and (7) the Wasir Akbar Khan house, the KHAD offices in the Howzai Bankat district."[64] The KHAD had also requisitioned 200 individual houses around the capital, in addition to its prisons and military outposts in the major towns.[65]

The UN report continued:

> With regard to the nature of the tortures practiced [by the Afghan government], the reporter's attention has been drawn to a wide range of techniques. In his statement, a former security police officer listed eight different types of torture: electric shocks applied to the genitals of men and the breasts of women; tearing out fingernails, combined with electric shock; removing all toilet facilities from the prisoners' cells, so that after a certain time they are obliged to perform such functions in full view of their cellmates; the introduction of wooden objects into the anus, a practice used in particular with aged or respected prisoners; pulling out the beards of prisoners, particularly if they are old or religious figures; strangulation of prisoners to force open their mouths, which are then urinated into; the use of police dogs against prisoners; hanging by the feet for an indefinite period; the rape of women, with their hands and feet tied, and the introduction of a variety of objects into the vagina.[66]

To these physical tortures should be added an array of psychological tortures, including mock executions, the rape of a member of the prisoner's family in his presence, and the pretense that the prisoner was to be freed.[67] Soviet advisers took part in interrogations and assisted the executioners.[68]

Christopher Andrew and Oleg Gordievsky maintain that "the KGB reenacted some of the horrors of the Stalinist period on Afghan territory."[69] The KHAD employed 70,000 Afghans, including 30,000 civilians, and was controlled by 1,500 KGB officers.[70]

Despite the politics of terror that immediately followed the Communist coup, resistance groups proliferated, and bombs rained down on Communist centers. Demonstrations also took place. Students went on strike on 27 April 1980 to celebrate the coup d'état in their own fashion. Their initial demonstration was repressed, and sixty students, including six young girls, were killed.[71] The strike lasted for one month, ending in the imprisonment of numerous students both male and female, many of whom were subsequently tortured. "The lucky ones were merely expelled from their schools, on a temporary or permanent basis."[72] Non-Communists found many opportunities barred to them, and repression of students and teachers became ever more severe. "To frighten the schoolgirls, the executioners would take them to visit the chamber of horrors where resistance fighters were tortured: Farida Ahmadi saw severed limbs scattered around one room in the KHAD building . . . These selected victims from the student milieu were then released back into the community to spread panic among their comrades, so that their experiences might serve as a lesson to the others."[73]

In the autumn of 1983 Amnesty International published a report and launched an appeal to obtain the release of a number of prisoners. Professor Hassan Kakar, who was the head of a history department specializing in the history of Afghanistan, and who had earlier taught at Harvard, was arrested for having helped members of the Parcham faction (even though he was not a member of the DPPA) and for having given shelter to several others. His trial took place *in camera,* with no lawyer permitted to defend him. He was accused of counterrevolutionary activities and sentenced to eight years in prison. Two of his colleagues, who were also professors, were sentenced to eight and ten years in prison, respectively. Mohammed Yunis Akbari, the only nuclear physicist of any renown in Afghanistan, was relieved of his duties in 1983 and simultaneously arrested and detained without charge. Having already been arrested on two previous occasions, in 1981 and 1983, he was sentenced to death in 1984 and finally executed in 1990.[74] Intellectuals who belonged to research and discussion groups whose aim was to find an end to the conflict were systematically imprisoned. A similar fate was in store for anyone who was deemed to present any sort of threat to the regime.

Information was strictly controlled throughout the Communist era. Foreigners not accredited by the government were considered personae non gratae, as were journalists and medical personnel. When arrested, they were taken to the central prison and interrogated. They were not physically tortured because humanitarian organizations were invariably aware of their presence in the country and would immediately demand their release. But when they were tried and it became clear that the prosecution's case was based on falsified evidence, they were often forced to admit that they had been spying for foreign governments and had taken part in resistance forces, despite their presence there in a purely humanitarian capacity.[75]

Although foreigners were a nuisance, they were neither tortured nor killed.[76] By contrast, Afghan suspects who were arrested were often tortured and killed. Militants from Afghan Mellat, for instance, the social democratic Pushtun party founded in 1966, were arrested on 18 May 1983 despite lack of proof that they had supported resistance activity. Amnesty International published a list—to which more names were added later—of eighteen members of Afghan Mellat who had been arrested for allegedly making public statements in support of the rebels. Officially, between 8 June 1980 and 22 April 1982, the government announced more than fifty death sentences for counterrevolutionary activity. Another seventy-seven were announced in 1984, and forty more in 1985.[77]

In the summer of 1986 Shah Bazgar put together a list of more than 52,000 prisoners in Kabul and 13,000 in Jelalabad. According to his figures, there were more than 100,000 prisoners in all.[78] On 19 April 1992 the Pol-e-Charki prison was captured by the resistance, which freed 4,000 prisoners. In May 1992 a mass grave was discovered nearby, containing the remains of 12,000 people.[79]

When Babrak Karmal was dismissed in 1986, he was replaced by Mohammed Najibullah, a president who closely resembled Gorbachev and who usually called himself "Comrade Najib" to avoid all reference to Allah. After assuming power, he restored his last name in the interests of national unity. Najibullah was a member of the Parcham and a retired physician who had been a diplomat in Iran and was extremely close to Moscow. He had been the head of the KHAD from 1980 to 1986 and had been praised for his work there by Yuri Andropov, the longtime head of the Soviet KGB who went on to become general secretary of the Soviet Communist Party. Najibullah was called "the ox" by his brother Seddiqullah Rahi, who once compared him to Lavrenti Beria, and claimed that he had signed execution orders for 90,000 people in the space of six years.[80] In addition to being the head of the secret services, Najibullah was responsible for personally torturing countless people. One of the rare survivors had the following to say: "Because I had denied the accusations several times, Najibullah approached me and dealt me several blows to the stomach and the face. I fell to the ground. On the ground, half-conscious, I remember receiving more kicks in the face and in the back. Blood was pouring out of my mouth and my nose. I did not regain consciousness until a few hours later, when I was back in my cell."

Frequently blind chance had a major role to play in the repressions. One merchant, who had been a deputy in parliament during Zahir's reign, was arrested by mistake, tortured, and subsequently released.

My arrest took place at about 9:30 in the evening . . . I was put into a cell with two other prisoners, a builder from Kalahan, to the north of Kabul, and an official from Nangarhār Province who worked in the Ministry of Agriculture. It was clear that the builder had been very badly beaten already. His clothes were covered in blood, and his arms were badly bruised . . . I was taken away for interrogation. I was told that in the last few weeks I had visited Mazār-i-Sharif and Kandahār, and that the purpose of my visit had been to sow discontent with the government among the populace there . . . In reality, I hadn't left Kabul for more than six months. I protested my innocence, but as soon as I did that the blows started to rain down . . . An old-fashioned telephone was connected to my toes, and they used it to give me electric shocks . . . I wasn't interrogated any more after that. Two days later one of the KHAD men who had taken part in the interrogation came into my cell and told me I was to be released. He said that the KHAD was satisfied that my arrest had been a mistake.[81]

Terror was also used on Afghan children. They were picked up and sent to the Soviet Union, where they were trained as child spies to be sent to infiltrate the resistance. Children were drugged in order to limit their independence, and the older ones were offered the services of prostitutes. One boy, Naim, told Shah Bazgar:

I come from Herāt. When I was eight, I was taken out of school and placed in the Sazman [the Afghan Communist Youth organization] and then sent to the U.S.S.R. for nine months. My father was a Communist, and he was in favor of this. My mother had died by then, and my father had remarried. At home, apart from one brother and one sister, everyone was a Khalq. My father sold me to the Soviets. For several months he got money like that . . . Our task was to be spies.

When Bazgar asked Naim whether he had ever seen a child die, the boy answered: "Several times. Once by electricity. The child's body sprang about a meter up into the air and then fell to the ground. The child had refused to work as a spy. On another occasion a child was brought before us. He was accused of not having told on one of his comrades who had apparently placed a bomb underneath a Russian armored car. We watched as they strung him up from a tree. They shouted out: 'This is what happens if you don't do what you're told!'"[82] More than 30,000 children between the ages of six and fourteen were sent to the Soviet Union. If the parents dared to protest, they were labeled resistance fighters and thrown into prison.

The terror touched the whole population. Every age group fell victim to this total war and the government's repressive policies. The Soviet occupying forces tried to stamp out the resistance by every possible means, including the use of indiscriminate terror, the bombing of civilians, massacres of entire villages, and the sending of countless people into exile. Hand in hand with the civil terror came the political terror. All the large towns had special prisons where detainees were tortured and then usually killed.

The Consequences of the Intervention

The Communist coup d'état and the subsequent intervention by the Soviet army had tragic consequences for Afghanistan. In the 1960s the country was on the road to prosperity, modernization, and democracy; Daoud's coup, which was supported by the Communists, ended economic development and plunged Afghanistan deep into civil war. The country was forced to make do with a war economy, which was oriented heavily in favor of the Soviet Union. Smuggling (of drugs, guns, and other goods) became common, and the economy rapidly fell into ruins. The scale of the disaster is still hard to measure today. Out of a population of approximately 15.5 million, more than 5 million inhabitants have left for Pakistan and Iran, where they now live in miserable conditions. The number of dead is extremely hard to determine, but most observers agree that the war took between 1.5 million and 2 million lives, 90 percent of whom were civilians. Between 2 million and 4 million were wounded. The direct and indirect role played by Communism in the growth of extremist Islamic movements, and in the reawakening of tension between different ethnic groups, is undeniable, although it may be hard to quantify. Afghanistan was once on the path to modernity, but it has become a country in which war and violence seem to have become the central reference points in society.

Conclusion: Why?

Stéphane Courtois

The blue eyes of the revolution burn with cruel necessity.
Louis Aragon, *Le front rouge*

This book has attempted to look beyond blind spots, partisan passions, and voluntary amnesia to paint a true picture of all the criminal aspects of the Communist world, from individual assassinations to mass murder. It is part of a more general process of reflection on the phenomenon of Communism in the twentieth century, and it is only one stage, but it comes at a key moment, with the internal collapse of the system in Moscow in 1991 and the consequent availability of rich new sources of information that until recently had been inaccessible. Better knowledge of the events is indispensable, but no matter how sophisticated our knowledge may become, it will never on its own satisfy either our intellectual curiosity or our conscience. The fundamental question remains: Why? Why did modern Communism, when it appeared in 1917, almost immediately turn into a system of bloody dictatorship and into a criminal regime? Was it really the case that its aims could be attained only through such extreme violence? How can one explain how these crimes came to be thought of as part of normal procedure and remained such for so many decades?

Soviet Russia was the first Communist regime. It became the heart and engine of a worldwide system that at first established itself slowly, and then expanded rapidly after 1945. The Leninist and Stalinist U.S.S.R. was the cradle of all modern Communism. The fact that it became a criminal regime so quickly is extremely surprising, particularly given the manner in which the socialist movement had developed until then.

Throughout the nineteenth century, theories about revolutionary violence were dominated by the founding experience of the French Revolution. In 1793–94 the French Revolution went through a period of extreme violence that took three distinct forms. The most savage were the "September massacres," during which 1,000 people were spontaneously killed by rioters in Paris, with no intervention by the government, and no instructions from any party. The best-known form of violence was carried out by revolutionary tribunals, surveillance committees, and the guillotine, accounting for the death of 2,625 people in Paris and 16,600 in the provinces. Long hidden was the terror practiced by the "infernal columns" of the Republic, whose task was to put down the insurrection in the Vendée, and who killed tens of thousands of innocent and unarmed people in that region. But these months of terror, bloody though they were, were only one episode in the long history of the country's revolution, which ultimately resulted in the creation of a democratic republic with a constitution, an elected assembly, and genuine political debate. As soon as the Convention regained its courage, Robespierre was deposed and the terror ceased.

François Furet has demonstrated how a particular idea of revolution was then born. This concept was inseparable from extreme actions: "The Terror was government by fear, which Robespierre theorized as government by virtue. Invented to destroy the aristocracy, it soon became the means to dispose of the wicked and to combat crime. It became an integral part of revolution and appeared to be the only means of forming the future citizens of the republic . . . If the republic of free citizens was not yet a possibility, it must be because certain individuals, corrupted by their past history, were not yet pure enough. Terror became the means by which revolution, the history yet to be created, would forge the new human beings of the future."[1]

In several respects, the Terror prefigured a number of Bolshevik practices. The Jacobin faction's clever manipulation of social tensions, and its political and ideological extremism, were later echoed by the Bolsheviks. Also, for the first time an attempt was made in France to eliminate a particular section of the peasantry. Robespierre laid the first stones on the road that spurred Lenin to terror. As the French revolutionary declared to the Convention during the vote on the Prairial Laws: "To punish the enemies of the fatherland, we must find out who they are: but we do not want to punish them; we want to destroy them."[2]

Yet this founding moment of terror did not inspire any other followers among the main revolutionary thinkers of the nineteenth century. Marx himself accorded it relatively little attention. Admittedly, he emphasized and defended the "role of violence in history," but he saw it more as a general proposition than as a systematic program of violence against particular people. There were of course ambiguities in Marx's writings that were seized on by a number of believers in terror to justify the violent resolution of social conflict. At the same time, Marx was extremely critical of the disastrous experience of the Paris Commune and the resulting bloody repressions, in which more than 20,000 workers died. During the early debates in the First International, which saw Marx opposed to the Russian anarchist Mikhail Bakunin, it was clear that Marx came out on top. Hence on the eve of World War I, debate within the socialist and workers' movements about terrorist violence seemed nearly closed.

In parallel to these events, the rapid development of parliamentary democracy in Europe and the United States represented a new and fundamental factor for socialist strategists. Parliamentary practice enabled socialists to become a genuine force within the political system. In the elections of 1910, the French Section of the Workers' International obtained 74 seats. An additional 30 independent socialists were also elected, including their leader, Etienne Millerand, who had entered a "bourgeois" government for the first time in 1899. Jean Jaurès was another figure who managed to combine revolutionary rhetoric and reforming democratic action in everyday matters. The best-organized and most powerful socialists were undoubtedly the Germans. On the eve of World War I they had more than 1 million members, 110 deputies, 220 provincial Landtag representatives, 12,000 municipal councillors, and 89 other delegates. The British Labour movement was also numerous and well-organized, with strong support from powerful unions. The Social Democratic Party rapidly gained strength in Scandinavia, where it was highly active, influential in reforms, and well represented in parliament. In general, socialists hoped that they would soon have an absolute parliamentary majority in many different countries, which would allow them to implement fundamental social reforms peacefully in the near future.

This evolution found its theorist in Eduard Bernstein, one of the most influential Marxist thinkers of the late nineteenth century, who, together with Karl Kautsky, was one of the great interpreters of Marx. He argued that capitalism was not showing the signs of collapse that Marx had predicted, and that what was required was a progressive and peaceful move toward socialism, with the working classes slowly learning the processes of democracy and liberty. In 1872 Marx had expressed hope that the revolution could take a peaceful form in America, England, and Holland. This view was developed further by his friend and disciple Friedrich Engels in the preface to the second edition of Marx's *Class Struggles in France*, published in 1895.

Socialists often had an ambivalent attitude toward democracy. When the

Dreyfus affair erupted in France at the turn of the century, they took some contradictory positions: Jaurès came out in favor of Dreyfus, whereas Jules Guesde, who was the central figure in French Marxism at the time, declared with disdain that the proletariat would do well to keep out of the internal squabbles of the French bourgeoisie. The left in Europe was far from united, and some currents within it—particularly anarchists, syndicalists, and supporters of Louis Auguste Blanqui—were still strongly inclined to reject all aspects of the parliamentary process, often through violent means. Nonetheless, on the eve of the 1914 war, the Second International, which was officially Marxist, endorsed a series of peaceful solutions, relying on mobilization of the masses and universal suffrage.

The extremist wing of the International, which had coalesced around the turn of the century, included the most hard-line Russian socialists—Lenin's Bolsheviks. Although the Bolsheviks were clearly descended from the European Marxist tradition, they also had strong roots in the revolutionary Russian land movement. Throughout the nineteenth century one section of this revolutionary movement was linked to violent activity. The most radical proponent of violence within the movement was Sergei Nechaev, whom Dostoevsky used as a model for the revolutionary protagonist of *The Devils.* In 1869 Nechaev published a *Revolutionary Catechism* in which he defined a revolutionary as

> a man who is already lost. He has no particular interest, no private business, no feelings, no personal attachments, and no property; he does not even have a name. Everything in him is absorbed by one interest to the exclusion of all others, by a single thought, a single passion . . . revolution. In the depths of his being, not simply in words but in his actions as well, he has broken all links with society and the world of civilization, with its laws and conventions, with its social etiquette and its moral code. The revolutionary is an implacable enemy, and he carries on living only so that he can ensure the destruction of society.[3]

Nechaev then set out his objectives: "The revolutionary never enters the political or social world, the so-called educated world, and he lives with faith only in its swift and total destruction. No one who feels pity for anything can truly be called a revolutionary." His plan of action argued that "this whole sick society must be divided into several categories. In the first category are the people who are to be killed immediately . . . The second should include individuals who are to be allowed to continue living for a while, so that by their monstrous acts they merely accelerate the inevitable uprising of the people."[4]

Nechaev had several imitators. On 1 March 1887 an attempt was made on the life of Tsar Aleksandr III; it failed, but the perpetrators were arrested. Among them was Aleksandr Ilich Ulyanov, Lenin's older brother, who was hanged together with his four accomplices. Lenin's hatred for the regime was thus deep-seated, leading him personally to decide and to organize the massacre of the imperial Romanov family in 1918 without the knowledge of the rest of the Politburo.

For Martin Malia, this violent action by one faction of the intelligentsia represented "a fantasy reenactment of the French revolution [that] was the beginning of political terrorism (as opposed to isolated acts of assassination) as a systematic tactic in the modern world. Thus, the populist strategy of mass insurrection from below, in conjunction with that of elite terror from above, combined in Russia to lend further legitimacy to political violence over and above the initial legitimation provided by the Western revolutionary tradition from 1789 to 1871."[5]

This political violence on the margins of society was fueled by the violence that for centuries had been a common feature of life in Russia, as Hélène Carrière d'Encausse emphasizes in her study *The Russian Syndrome*: "This country, in its unparalleled misfortune, remains an enigma for students of its history. In trying to shed light on the underlying causes of this age-old tragedy, a specific—and always damaging—link has emerged between the seizure or maintenance of power and the practice of political murder, be it individual or mass, real or symbolic . . . This long tradition of murder has doubtless created a collective consciousness that has little hope for a pacified political world."[6]

Tsar Ivan IV, known to posterity as Ivan the Terrible, was only thirteen when in 1543 he had his prime minister, Prince Chuisky, devoured by dogs. In 1560 his wife's death threw him into a murderous rage, leading him to suspect everyone of being a potential traitor and to exterminate his real or imagined enemies in ever-widening circles. He created a new guard with sweeping powers, called the Oprichnina, which set about sowing terror among the populace. In 1572 he liquidated the members of the Oprichnina and then killed his own son and heir. Peter the Great was scarcely more compassionate toward Russia's enemies, the aristocracy, or the people, and he also killed his own son with his own hands.

From Ivan to Peter, a solid tradition arose that linked progress under absolute power to the enslavement of the people and the elite to the dictatorial and terrorist state. As Vasily Grossman noted regarding the end of serfdom in 1861: "This act, as the following century showed, was more genuinely revolutionary than the October Revolution. Emancipation shook the millennial foundations of Russian life, as neither Peter nor Lenin could shake them: the subjection of progress to slavery."[7] And as always, the slavery had been held in place for centuries through a high level of permanent violence.

Tomáš Masaryk, a great statesman and the founder in 1918 of Czecho-slovakia, who visited Russia frequently during the revolution and consequently knew the country well, was quick to draw a link between tsarist and Bolshevik violence. He wrote in 1924:

> The Russians, including the Bolsheviks, are all sons of tsarism: this has been their culture and their education for centuries. They got rid of the tsar, but they cannot get rid of tsarism overnight. They still wear the uniform of tsarism, even if it is back-to-front . . . The Bolsheviks were not ready for a positive, administrative revolution. What they wanted was a negative revolution whose doctrinal fanaticism, meanness of spirit, and general lack of culture they could use as a pretext for any number of acts of destruction. One thing I hold against them above all is the pleasure they took in murder, just like the tsars before them.[8]

The culture of violence was not uniquely the preserve of the powerful. When the peasant masses began to revolt, they engaged in massacres of the nobility and truly savage terror of their own. Two such revolts that left a deep imprint on the Russian consciousness were the Stenka Razin revolt of 1667–1670 and the Pugachev rebellion of 1773–1775, which spread quickly and posed a serious threat to the reign of Catherine the Great, leaving a long and bloody scar all across the Volga region. After his capture, Emelyan Pugachev was executed in an atrocious manner—quartered, cut into pieces, and fed to dogs.

Maksim Gorky was a great interpreter of pre-1917 Russian culture, and if he is to be believed, the violence emanated from society itself. He disapproved of the Bolsheviks' methods, and in 1922 he wrote a long, almost visionary text:

> Cruelty has stupefied and tormented me all my life. What are the roots of human cruelty? I have thought much about this and I still do not understand it in the slightest . . . But now, after the terrible madness of the European war and the bloody events of the revolution . . . I am forced to remark that Russian cruelty appears not to have evolved at all; its forms have remained the same. A chronicler from the turn of the seventeenth century recorded that in his day the following tortures were practiced: "The mouth was filled with gunpowder, and then set alight; others have their nether regions filled with powder. Holes were made in women's breasts and ropes passed through the wounds, and the women were suspended by the ropes." In 1918 and 1919 the same practices were used in the Don and the Urals; men had dynamite placed in their rear and blown up. I think the Russians have a unique sense of particular cruelty in the same way that the English have a unique sense of humor: a cold sort of cruelty that seeks to explore the limits of human resistance to suffering and to study the persistence and stability of life. One can

sense a diabolical refinement in Russian cruelty; there is something quite subtle and refined about it. This quality cannot fully be explained by words like "psychosis" or "sadism," words that in essence explain nothing at all . . . If such acts of cruelty were the expression of the perverse psychology of a few individuals, they would not concern us here; they would be material for the psychiatrist rather than for the moralist. But I am concerned here with human suffering as a collective entertainment . . . Who are the more cruel, the Whites or the Reds? They are probably equal, as they are both Russians. In any case, history answers quite clearly—the most cruel is the most active.[9]

Despite this tradition of violence, Russia by the mid-nineteenth century seemed to have adopted a more moderate, Western, and democratic course. In 1861 Tsar Aleksandr III abolished serfdom and established *zemstvos,* which were local centers of power. In 1864 he approved judicial independence as the first step toward the rule of law. The universities, the arts, and the press all flourished. A civilizing current flowed through society, and violence decreased everywhere. Even the failed revolution of 1905 had the result of stirring up the democratic fervor of society. Paradoxically, it was precisely at the moment when reform seemed to have conquered violence, obscurantism, and old-fashioned ways that the process was interrupted by the outbreak of the worst mass violence ever seen in Europe, on 1 August 1914.

As Martin Malia has written, "The burden of Aeschylus' *Oresteia* is that crime begets crime, and violence violence, until the first crime in the chain, the original sin of the genus, is expiated through accumulated suffering. In similar fashion, it was the blood of August 1914, acting like some curse of the Atreidae on the house of modern Europe, that generated the chain of international and social violence that has dominated the modern age. For the violence and carnage of the war were incommensurate with any conceivable gain, and for any party. The war itself produced the Russian Revolution and the Bolshevik seizure of power."[10] Lenin would not have rejected this analysis. From 1914 on he constantly called for the transformation of "the imperialist war into civil war," prophesying that the socialist revolution would emerge from the capitalist war.

The violence of the world war was extreme and went on for four years, a continuous massacre that seemed totally insoluble, leading to the death of 8.5 million soldiers. It was a new type of war, which General Ludendorff labeled "total war," bringing death not only to soldiers but also to civilians. Yet the violence, which reached a level never before seen in the history of the world, remained constrained by a whole series of laws and international conventions.

The daily slaughter, often under terrible conditions—gas, men buried alive under earth thrown up by explosions, the long agony between the lines—

weighed heavily on the consciousness of everyone concerned and weakened the psychological defenses of the men who faced death every day. Many people were completely desensitized by these events. Karl Kautsky, the main leader and theorist of German socialism, returned to that theme in 1920:

> The real cause of the change . . . into a development toward brutality is attributable to the world war . . . When, therefore, the war broke out and dragged in its train for four years practically the whole of the healthy male population, the coarsening tendencies of militarism sank to the very depths of brutality, and to a lack of human feeling and sentiment. Even the proletariat could no longer escape its influence. They were to a very high degree infected by militarism and, when they returned home again, were in every way brutalized. Habituated to war, the man who had come back from the front was only too often in a state of mind and feeling that made him ready, even in peacetime and among his own people, to enforce his claims and interests by deeds of violence and bloodshed. That became, as it were, an element of the civil war.[11]

None of the Bolshevik leaders actually took part in the war, either because, like Lenin, Trotsky, and Zinoviev, they were in exile or because they had been sent to Siberia, as was the case with Stalin and Kamenev. Most of them were inclined to work in the bureaucracy or to make speeches at mass rallies. Most had no military experience, and they had never really seen combat or the deaths that it involved. Until they took power, all they knew was the ideological and political war of words. Theirs was a purely abstract vision of death, massacre, and human catastrophe.

This personal ignorance of the horrors of war was perhaps a factor that itself engendered more brutality. The Bolsheviks developed a largely theoretical analysis of class, which ignored the profoundly national, not to say nationalistic, aspects of the conflict. They made capitalism the scapegoat and sanctioned revolutionary violence against it in advance. By hastening the end of capitalism, the revolution would put an end to massacres, even if it meant disposing of a certain number of the capitalist leaders. This was a macabre gamble, based on the theory that evil should be fought with evil. But in the 1920s, a certain degree of pacifism arising from revulsion toward the war was often strongly influential in converting people to Communism.

It is still the case, however, as François Furet emphasizes in *The Passing of an Illusion*, that

> war is waged by regimented civilian masses, who have gone from the autonomy of citizenship to military obedience for a time of unknown duration, and who are plunged into a raging inferno where staying alive rather than being intelligent or courageous is the main objective, and

where even victory is a distant abstraction. Military service can rarely have seemed less noble than it did to the millions of men plucked from civilian life and trapped in the trenches . . . War is the political state furthest removed from normal civilian life . . . It is a purely instinctive business totally removed from other interests and intellectual pursuits . . . An army at war is a social order in which individuals no longer exist, and whose inhumanity creates a sort of inertia that is almost impossible to break.[12]

The war gave a new legitimacy to violence and cheapened the value of human life; it weakened the previously burgeoning democratic culture and gave new life to the culture of servitude.

In the early years of the twentieth century the Russian economy entered a period of vigorous growth, and society gradually became more autonomous. But the exceptional constraints imposed on people and on the means of production by the war suddenly highlighted the limitations of a political regime that clearly lacked the energy and foresight required to save the situation. The revolution of February 1917 was a response to a catastrophic situation and put society on a classic course: a "bourgeois" democratic revolution with the election of a constituent assembly, combined with a social revolution among workers and peasants. Everything changed with the Bolshevik coup of 7 November 1917, which was followed by a considerably more violent phase. The question that remains is why, of all the countries in Europe, did the cataclysm take place in Russia?

The world war and the tradition of violence in Russia are undoubtedly factors that allow some understanding of the context in which the Bolsheviks seized power; but they do not explain the Bolsheviks' propensity for extreme violence. This violence was apparent from the outset, all the more so in comparison with the largely peaceful and democratic February revolution. This violence was imposed on the Party by Lenin himself as soon as it seized power.

Lenin established a dictatorship that quickly revealed itself to be both bloody and terrorist in nature. Revolutionary violence no longer appeared to be a reactive defense mechanism against tsarist forces, since the latter had disappeared months before, but an active process that reawakened the old Russian culture of brutality and cruelty, sparking the latent violence of social revolution. Although the Red Terror was not officially inaugurated until 2 September 1918, it existed in practice from November 1917. Lenin employed it despite the absence of any genuine manifestation of overt opposition from other parties and social movements. For example, on 4 January 1918 he broke up the first Constituent Assembly, which had been elected by universal suffrage, and opened fire on anyone who protested in the streets.

The first phase of the terror was immediately and forcefully denounced by a leading Russian socialist, Yuri Martov, the head of the Mensheviks, who wrote in August 1918:

> From the first day of their coming into power, having proclaimed the abolition of the death penalty, the Bolsheviks began to kill. They killed prisoners captured in the battles of the civil war. They killed enemies who surrendered on the condition that their lives would be spared . . . These wholesale murders, organized at the instigation of the Bolsheviks, were followed by murders at the direct behest of the Bolshevik government . . . Having assassinated tens of thousands of men without trial, the Bolsheviks started their executions by verdicts of the courts. They established a supreme revolutionary tribunal to convict enemies of the Soviet regime.[13]

Martov had a dark premonition:

> The beast has licked hot human blood. The man-killing machine is brought into motion. Messrs. Medvedev, Bruno, Peterson, Veselovsky, and Karelin [the judges of the Supreme Revolutionary Tribunal] have turned up their sleeves and set to work as butchers . . . But blood breeds blood. The reign of terror established by the Bolsheviks since October 1917 has filled the air of Russian fields with vapors of human blood. We witness the growth of the bitterness of the civil war, the growing bestiality of men engaged in it. The great principles of true humanity that formed the basis of socialist teachings have sunk into oblivion.

Martov then went on to attack Karl Radek and Christian Rakovsky, two socialists who had joined the Bolsheviks, one of whom was a Polish Jew, the other a mixture of Romanian and Bulgarian: "You came to us to cultivate our ancestral barbarism, long nurtured by the tsars, and to place offerings on the antique Russian altar to murder, to elevate disdain for the life of others to a degree the like of which has never been seen; you came to bring the rule of the executioners throughout the country . . . The executioner is now again the chief figure in Russia!"

Unlike the terror of the French Revolution, which with the exception of the Vendée touched only a small section of the population, terror under Lenin was directed at all political parties and at all the layers of society: nobles, the bourgeoisie, soldiers, policemen, Constitutional Democrats, Mensheviks, Socialist Revolutionaries, and the entire mass of the population, including peasants and workers. Intellectuals were treated especially badly. On 6 September 1919, after the arrest of several dozen members of the intelligentsia, Gorky sent a furious letter to Lenin: "For me, the richness of a country, the power of a people is to be measured by the quantity and quality of its intellectual development. Revolution is a useful enterprise only if it favors such development. Scholars should be treated with care and respect. But in trying to save our own skins, we are decapitating the people, destroying our own brain."[14]

The brutality of Lenin's response matched the lucidity of Gorky's letter: "We would be wrong to equate the 'intellectual strength of the people' with the strength of the bourgeois intelligentsia . . . The intellectual strength of workers and peasants grows in the struggle to overturn the bourgeoisie and their acolytes, those second-rate intellectuals and lackeys of capitalism who think they are the brain of the nation. They are not the brain of the nation. They're shit." This response on the subject of intellectuals is one of the first indicators of the profound disdain that Lenin felt for his contemporaries, even the most eminent among them. And he quickly passed from disdain to murder.

Lenin's primary objective was to maintain his hold on power for as long as possible. After ten weeks, he had ruled longer than the Paris Commune, and he began to dream about never letting go of the reins. The course of history was beginning to change, and the Russian Revolution, under the direction of the Bolsheviks, was to take humanity down a previously untraveled path.

Why should maintaining power have been so important that it justified all means and led to the abandonment of the most elementary moral principles? The answer must be that it was the only way for Lenin to put his ideas into practice and "build socialism." The real motivation for the terror thus becomes apparent: it stemmed from Leninist ideology and the utopian will to apply to society a doctrine totally out of step with reality.

In that respect one may well ask exactly how much pre-1914 Marxism there was to be found in pre-1914 or post-1917 Leninism. Lenin of course used a number of Marxist axioms as the basis for his theories, including the class struggle, the necessity of violence in history, and the importance of the proletariat as the class that brought meaning to history. But in 1902, in his famous address *What Is to Be Done?* he proposed a new conception of a revolutionary party made up of professionals linked in an underground structure of almost military discipline. For this purpose, he adopted and further developed Nechaev's model, which was quite different from the great socialist organizations in Germany, England, and France.

In 1914 Lenin made a definitive break with the Second International. At the moment when almost all socialist parties, brutally confronted with the power of nationalist sentiments, rallied around their respective governments, Lenin set off on an almost purely theoretical path, prophesying the "transformation of the imperialist war into civil war." Cold reason led him to conclude that the socialist movement was not yet powerful enough to counter nationalism, and that after the inevitable war he would be called on to regroup his forces to prevent a return to warfare. This belief was an act of faith, a gamble that raised the stakes of the game to all or nothing. For two years his prophecy seemed sterile and empty, until suddenly it came true and Russia entered a revolutionary phase. Lenin was sure that the events of this period were the confirmation of all his beliefs. Nechaev's voluntarism seemed to have prevailed over Marxist determinism.

If the prediction that power was there to be seized was correct, the idea that Russia was ready to plunge into socialism, making progress at lightning speed, was radically wrong. And this was one of the most profound causes of the terror, the gap between a Russia that wanted more than anything to be free and Lenin's desire for absolute power to apply an experimental doctrine.

In 1920 Trotsky predicted the turn that events were to take: "It is quite clear that if our problem is the abolition of private property in the means of production, the only road to its solution lies through the concentration of state power in its entirety in the hands of the proletariat, and the setting up for the transitional period of an extraordinary regime . . . Dictatorship is necessary because this is a case not of partial changes, but of the very existence of the bourgeoisie. No agreement is possible on this basis. Only force can be the deciding factor . . . Whoever aims at the end cannot reject the means."[15]

Caught between the will to apply his doctrine and the necessity of retaining his grip on power, Lenin created the myth of a worldwide Bolshevik revolution. In November 1917 he wanted to believe that the revolutionary fire was going to engulf all countries involved in the war, and Germany above all others. But a worldwide revolution did not come about, and after Germany's defeat in November 1918, a new European order emerged that seemed to care little for the abortive revolutions in Hungary, Bavaria, and Berlin. This was already obvious when the Red Army was defeated in Warsaw in 1920, but it was not admitted until 1923, after the failure of the German October. The failure of the Leninist theory of European and worldwide revolution left the Bolsheviks quite isolated and in a head-to-head conflict with an increasingly anarchic Russia. In a desperate attempt to hold onto power, the Bolsheviks made terror an everyday part of their policies, seeking to remodel society in the image of their theory, and to silence those who, either through their actions or by their very social, economic, or intellectual existence, pointed to the gaping holes in the theory. Once in power, the Bolsheviks made Utopia an extremely bloody business.

This double gap—a gap both between Marxism and Leninism and between Leninist theory and reality—led to one of the first fundamental debates about the meaning of the Russian and Bolshevik revolution. Kautsky was quite clear about it in August 1918: "In no case need we anticipate that in Western Europe the course of the great French Revolution will be repeated. If present-day Russia exhibits so much likeness to the France of 1793, this shows only how near it stands to the stage of middle-class revolution."[16] Kautsky saw 1917 not as the first socialist revolution, but as the last bourgeois revolution.

Following the Bolshevik seizure of power, the status of ideology within the socialist movement changed radically. Before 1917 Lenin had already demonstrated his adamant conviction that he was the only one who truly understood the doctrine of socialism and who could decode the "true meaning of history." The outbreak of the Russian Revolution and the Bolshevik seizure of power appeared to Lenin as portents from above and as an incontestable confirmation that his ideology and his analyses were infallibly correct.[17] After 1917 his policies and the theoretical elaboration that accompanied them became gospel. Ideology was transformed into dogma and absolute, universal truth. This conversion of ideology into sacred writ had immediate consequences, which were noted by Cornelius Castoriadis: "If there is one true theory in history, if there is a rationality at work in things, then it is clear that its development should be entrusted to specialists in that theory and technicians of that particular rationale. The absolute power of the Party . . . has a philosophical status; its foundation is a function of the materialist conception of history . . . If that concept is true, power should be absolute, and democracy is a concession to the human fallibility of the leaders, or a pedagogical procedure that they alone can measure out in the correct dosages."[18]

This transformation of ideology and politics into absolute, "scientific" truth is the basis of the totalitarian dimension of Communism. The Party answered only to science. Science also justified the terror by requiring that all aspects of social and individual life be transformed.

Lenin affirmed the verity of his ideology when proclaiming himself to be the representative of the numerically weak Russian proletariat, a social group he never refrained from crushing whenever it revolted. This appropriation of the symbol of the proletariat was one of the great deceptions of Leninism, and in 1922 it provoked the following outburst from Aleksandr Shlyapnikov, one of the few Bolshevik leaders who really did have proletarian origins. At the Eleventh Party Congress he addressed Lenin directly: "Vladimir Ilich affirmed yesterday that the proletariat as a class in the Marxist sense does not exist in Russia. Allow me to congratulate you for managing to exercise dictatorship on behalf of a class that does not actually exist!" This manipulation of the symbol of the proletariat was common to all Communist regimes in Europe and the Third World, as well as in China and Cuba.

The manipulation of language was one of the most salient characteristics of Leninism, particularly in the decoupling of words from the reality they were supposed to represent, as part of an abstract vision of society in which people lost their real weight and presence and were treated as no more than pieces in a social and historical erector set. This process of abstraction, closely linked to ideology, is another key factor in the birth of the terror. It was not human beings who were being killed, but "the bourgeoisie," "capitalists," or "enemies of the people." It was not Nicholas II and his family who were killed, but "the representatives of feudalism," "bloodsuckers," "parasites," or "lice."

This transformation of ideology gained considerable weight thanks to the Bolsheviks' swift seizure of power, which immediately brought legitimacy, prestige, and the necessary means for taking action. In the name of Marxist ideology, the Bolsheviks passed from symbolic violence to real violence while establishing a system of absolute and arbitrary power that they called "the dictatorship of the proletariat," reusing an expression Marx had once used in a somewhat offhanded manner in his correspondence. They also began a formidable process of proselytism, which brought new hope and seemed to purify their revolutionary message. That message of hope quickly resonated among those driven by a desire for revenge at the end of the war, and among those who dreamed of a reactivation of the revolutionary myth. Bolshevism quickly acquired a universal relevance and attracted imitators throughout the world. Socialism had come to a crossroads: democracy or dictatorship.

In his book *The Dictatorship of the Proletariat,* written during the summer of 1918, Kautsky turned the knife in the wound. Although the Bolsheviks had been in power for only six months and there had been only a few hints of the dreadful massacres that were to follow, Kautsky already saw what was at stake:

> The antagonism of the two socialist movements . . . is the clashing of two fundamentally distinct methods: that of democracy and that of dictatorship. Both movements have the same end in view: to free the proletariat, and with it humanity, through socialism. But the view taken by one is held by the other to be erroneous and likely to lead to destruction . . . We place ourselves, of course, by asking for the fullest discussion, firmly on the side of democracy. Dictatorship does not ask for the refutation of contrary views, but the forcible suppression of their utterance. Thus, the two methods of democracy and dictatorship are already irreconcilably opposed before the discussion has started. The one demands, the other forbids it.[19]

Putting democracy at the center of his argument, Kautsky continued:

> A minority dictatorship always finds its most powerful support in an obedient army, but the more it substitutes this for majority support, the more it drives the opposition to seek a remedy by an appeal to the bayonet, instead of an appeal to the vote that is denied them. Civil war becomes a method of adjusting political and social antagonisms. Where complete political and social apathy or dejection does not prevail, the

minority dictatorship is always threatened by armed attack or constant guerrilla warfare . . . The dictatorship is then involved in civil war, and lives in constant danger of being overthrown. There is no greater obstacle to the building of a socialist society than internal war . . . In a civil war, each party fights for its existence, and the vanquished are threatened with complete destruction. The consciousness of this fact is why civil wars are so terrible.[20]

This prophetic analysis demanded a response, and Lenin wrote an angry rejoinder that became famous in its own right, *The Proletarian Revolution and the Renegade Kautsky.* The title was a fair indication of the tone of the discussion therein, or, as Kautsky argued, the refusal to conduct a discussion. Citing Engels, Lenin made clear what was at the center of his thought and his actions: "In reality the state is nothing but a machine for the suppression of one class by another." This reductive concept of the function of the state was accompanied by an analysis of the essence of dictatorship: "Dictatorship is rule based directly on force and unrestricted by any laws. The revolutionary dictatorship of the proletariat is rule won and maintained through the use of violence by the proletariat against the bourgeoisie, rule that is unrestricted by any laws."[21]

Faced with the central question of democracy, Lenin evaded it with an intellectual pirouette: "Proletarian democracy, of which Soviet government is one of the forms, has brought a development and expansion of democracy hitherto unprecedented in the world, precisely for the vast majority of the population, for the exploited and toiling people."[22] The expression "proletarian democracy," it should be remembered, was used for decades afterward to cover up a large number of terrible crimes.

The quarrel between Kautsky and Lenin highlights exactly what was at stake in the Bolshevik revolution. The quarrel was between Marxism, which claimed to be the codification of "the inevitable laws of history," and an activist subjectivism that was willing to use anything to promote revolutionary action. The underlying tension in Marx's writings between the messianic rhetoric of the *Communist Manifesto* of 1848 and the clinical analysis of social movements to be found in *Das Kapital* was transformed by the triple influence of the world war, the February revolution, and the October Revolution into a profound and irreparable split between socialists and Communists that brought them into conflict throughout the twentieth century. The choices underlying the quarrel were no less important: democracy or dictatorship, humanity or terror.

Completely in thrall to revolutionary fervor and confronted by a whirlwind of events, Lenin and Trotsky, the two main actors in this first phase of the Bolshevik Revolution, theorized their actions extensively. Or, rather, they transformed conjecture into ideological conclusions. They invented the idea of a "permanent revolution," which they based on the Russian case, in which the bourgeois February revolution supposedly led straight into the proletarian October Revolution. They dressed up this situation in ideological terms as the transformation of a "permanent revolution" into "permanent civil war."

The importance of the war can be gauged by the impact it had on the revolutionaries. As Trotsky wrote, "Kautsky sees one of the reasons for the extremely bloody character of the revolution in the war and in its hardening influence on manners." But Trotsky and Kautsky did not come to the same conclusion: The German socialist, faced with the weight of militarism, was ever more open to the question of democracy and the defense of the rights of the individual. For Trotsky, "the development of bourgeois society itself, out of which contemporary democracy grew, in no way represents the process of gradual democratization that figured before the war in the dreams of the greatest socialist illusionist of democracy—Jean Jaurès—and now in those of the most learned of pedants, Karl Kautsky."[23]

Generalizing from this, Trotsky went on to speak about the "unpitying civil war that is unfolding the world over." He believed that the world was entering an era in which "political struggle is rapidly turning into civil war" between "two forces: the revolutionary proletariat under the leadership of the Communists, and counterrevolutionary democracy headed by generals and admirals." There was a double error of perspective at work here. On the one hand, subsequent events demonstrated that the desire for representative democracy and its realization was a worldwide phenomenon, reaching even the U.S.S.R. in 1991. On the other hand, Trotsky, like Lenin, had a strong tendency to develop general conclusions based on the Russian experience, which in any case was often exaggerated in his interpretation. The Bolsheviks were convinced that once the civil war had begun in Russia—largely because of their own efforts—it would spread to Europe and the rest of the world. These two major errors would serve as the justification for Soviet terror for decades to come.

Trotsky drew definitive conclusions from these premises:

> It could, and must, be explained that in the civil war we destroyed White Guards so that they would not destroy the workers. Consequently, our problem is not the destruction of human life, but its preservation . . . The enemy must be made harmless, and in wartime this means that he must be destroyed. The problem of revolution, as of war, lies in breaking the will of the foe, forcing him to capitulate and to accept the conditions of the conqueror . . . The question about who will rule the country—that is, about the life or death of the bourgeoisie—will be decided on either side not by reference to the paragraphs of the constitution, but by the employment of all forms of violence.[24]

Trotsky's rhetoric uses many of the same expressions that are found in Ludendorff's explanation of the concept of total war. The Bolsheviks, who believed themselves to be such great innovators, were in fact very much a product of their time and of the highly militarized atmosphere that surrounded them.

Trotsky's remarks about freedom of the press demonstrate the pervasiveness of a war mentality:

> During war all institutions and organs of the state and of public opinion become, directly or indirectly, weapons of war. This is particularly true of the press. No government waging a serious war will allow publications to exist on its territory that, openly or indirectly, support the enemy. Still more so in a civil war. The nature of the latter is such that each of the struggling sides has in the rear of its armies considerable circles of the population who support the enemy. In war, where both success and failure are repaid by death, hostile agents who penetrate into the rear are subject to execution. This is inhumane, but no one ever considered war—or, all the more, civil war—to be a school of humanity.[25]

The Bolsheviks were not the only group implicated in the civil war that broke out in Russia in the spring and summer of 1918, beginning a four-year-long orgy of killing by all sides, with people crucified, impaled, cut into pieces, and burned alive. But they were the only group to theorize civil war, and to seek it openly. Under the joint influence of their doctrine and the new modes of behavior created by the world war, *civil war became for them a permanent form of political struggle.* The civil war between Whites and Reds hid a different war of far greater significance: the war of the Reds against the majority of the working population and a large part of the peasantry, who after the summer of 1918 began to rebel against the Bolshevik yoke. The war was not a traditional confrontation between two opposing political groups, but a conflict between the government and the majority of the population. Under Stalin, the war put the Party-state in opposition to society as a whole. This was a new phenomenon, which could exist only because of the ability of the totalitarian system, backed by mass terror, to control all spheres of activity in society.

Recent studies based on the newly opened archives show that the "dirty war" (the expression is taken from Nicolas Werth) of 1918–1921 was the founding moment of the Soviet regime, the crucible in which the people who would develop and continue the revolution were formed. It was an infernal caldron in which the mentality peculiar to Leninism and Stalinism originated, with its unique mélange of idealist exaltation, cynicism, and inhuman cruelty. The Bolsheviks hoped that the civil war would spread across the country and throughout the world and would last as long as it took for socialism to conquer the planet. The war installed cruelty as the normal means by which people were to relate to one another. It broke down traditional barriers of restraint, replacing them with absolute, fundamental violence.

From the earliest days of the Bolshevik Revolution, the issues raised by Kautsky were a thorn in the side of the revolutionaries. Isaac Steinberg, a left Socialist Revolutionary allied to the Bolsheviks, who was the people's commissar for justice from December 1917 to May 1918, spoke in 1923 about a "methodical system of state terror" used by the Bolsheviks. He posed the central question about the limits of violence in the revolution:

> The overturning of the old world, and its replacement by a new life in which the same old evils are kept in place, a life that is contaminated by the same old principles, means that socialism is forced to make a crucial choice during the decisive struggle about whether to use the old-fashioned violence of the tsars and the bourgeoisie, or to resort instead to revolutionary violence . . . Old-fashioned violence is merely a protection against slavery, while the new violence is the painful path toward emancipation . . . That is what should be decisive in our choice: We should take violence into our own hands to be sure that we bring about the end of violence. For there is no other means of fighting against it. Such is the gaping moral wound of the revolution. Therein lies the central paradox, the contradiction that will be the inevitable source of much conflict and suffering.

He added: "Like terror, violence (considered both as a means of constraint and as deception) will always contaminate the soul of the conquered first, before affecting the victor and the rest of society."[26]

Steinberg was well aware that this experiment represented a huge risk for "universal morals" and "natural law." Gorky clearly felt the same way when he wrote to the French novelist Romain Rolland on 21 April 1923: "I have not the slightest desire to return to Russia. I would not be able to write a thing if I had to spend the whole time returning to the theme of 'Thou shalt not kill' time and again."[27] The scruples of non-Bolshevik revolutionaries and the last concerns of the Bolsheviks themselves were all swept away by Lenin's and Stalin's enthusiasm. On 2 November 1930 Gorky, who had just aligned himself with the "genius leader" himself, again wrote to Romain Rolland:

> It seems to me, Rolland, that you would judge events inside the Soviet Union more evenhandedly if you admitted one simple fact: that the Soviet regime, together with the avant-garde of the workers, is locked in a civil war, which takes the form of a class war. The enemies they fight—and must fight—are the intelligentsia, who are desperately attempting to bring back the bourgeois regime, and the rich peasants, who are desperate to look after their own interests in the traditional capitalist

manner and are preventing the advance of collectivization. They are also using terror, killing collectivists, burning collective goods, and the like. War is all about killing.[28]

Russia then entered a third revolutionary phase, which until 1953 was incarnated in Stalin. It was characterized by widespread terror, which found its strongest expression in the Great Purge of 1937 and 1938. Thereafter Stalin found ever more groups to eliminate, targeting not only society as a whole, but also the state and Party apparatus. This terror had no need of the exceptional circumstances of a war to start it rolling; it came about in a time of peace.

Hitler rarely played a personal role in repression, leaving these ignoble tasks to trusted subordinates such as Himmler. By contrast, Stalin always took a strong personal interest in such matters and played a central role in the process. He personally signed lists of thousands of names of people to be shot and forced other members of the Politburo to do the same. During the Great Terror, in fourteen months of 1937 and 1938, 1.8 million people were arrested in forty-two huge, minutely prepared operations. Nearly 690,000 of them were killed. The climate of civil war varied considerably, but it remained a fixture of everyday life. The expression "class war," often used in place of "class struggle," had nothing metaphorical about it. The political enemy was not a named opponent or even an enemy class: it was society as a whole.

It was inevitable that the terror, whose aim was the destruction of society, would ultimately, in a process of contagion, reach the countersociety formed by the Party itself. Although it is true that under Lenin, beginning in 1921, anyone who deviated from the Party line suffered punishment, the main enemies had always been people who were not actually Party members. Under Stalin, Party members themselves became potential enemies. The Kirov assassination provided Stalin with the excuse he needed to begin applying capital punishment inside the Party. In doing so he moved closer to Nechaev, whom Bakunin had addressed at the time of their break with the following warning: "The basis of our activity should be simple ideals like truth, honesty, and trust among revolutionary brothers. Lying, cheating, mystification, and—of necessity—violence should be employed only against the enemy . . . Whereas you, my friend—and this is where you are most gravely mistaken—you have fallen under the spell of the systems of Loyola and Machiavelli . . . You are enamored of police tactics and jesuitical methods, and you are using such ideas to run your organization . . . so you end up treating your own friends as though they were enemies."[29]

Under Stalin, the executioners eventually became victims. Bukharin, after the execution of his old Party comrades Zinoviev and Kamenev, publicly declared: "I am so happy that they have been shot like dogs."[33] Less than two years later, Bukharin himself was shot like a dog. This characteristic of Stalinism was to become widespread in Communist states throughout the world.

Before exterminating his enemies, Stalin had them displayed in public in a show-trial. Lenin had introduced this strategy in 1922, with the show-trial of the Socialist Revolutionaries. Stalin merely improved on the formula and made it a permanent feature of his apparatus of repression, applying it widely in Eastern Europe after 1948.

Annie Kriegel has shown how these trials served as a terrible mechanism of social cleansing and how, in an atheist state, the trials came to replace the hell that religion had traditionally promised.[31] They also served to reinforce class hatred and publicly to stigmatize the enemy. Asian Communism took this procedure to its logical extreme, going so far as to organize "hate days."

Stalin added mystery to the pedagogy of hatred: total secrecy shrouded the arrests, sentences, and fates of the victims. Mystery and secrecy, closely linked to terror, brought terrible anguish to the entire population.

Considering themselves to be at war, the Bolsheviks installed a vocabulary of "the enemy" such as "enemy agents" and "populations lending support to the enemy." In accordance with the war model, politics reverted to simplistic terms. The binary "friend/foe" opposition was applied across the board as part of a relentless "us versus them" mentality[32] and the military term "camp" turned up repeatedly: the revolutionary camp was opposed to the counterrevolutionary camp. Everyone was forced to choose his camp, on pain of death. The Bolsheviks thus returned to an archaic form of politics, destroying fifty years of democracy and bourgeois individualism.

How was the enemy to be defined? Politics was reduced to a civil war in which two opposing forces, the proletariat and the bourgeoisie, were in conflict, and the former had to exterminate the latter by any means necessary. The enemy was no longer the *ancien régime*, the aristocrats, the bourgeoisie, and the military officers, but anyone opposed to Bolshevik policy. Those who expressed opposition were immediately designated "bourgeois" and treated accordingly. To the Bolshevik mind, an "enemy" was anyone, regardless of social category, who presented an obstacle to the Bolsheviks' absolute power. This phenomenon appeared immediately, even earlier than terror, in the electoral assemblies of the Soviets. Kautsky foresaw this development when he wrote in 1918 that the only people allowed to elect deputies to the Soviets were to be those

> "who procure their sustenance by useful or productive work." What is "useful and productive work"? This is a very elastic term. No less elastic is the definition of those who are excluded from the franchise. They

include any who employ wage laborers for profit . . . One sees how little it takes, according to the Constitution of the Soviet Republic, to be labeled a capitalist, and to lose the vote. The elasticity of the definition of the franchise, which opens the door to the greatest arbitrariness, is due to the subject of this definition, and not to its framers. A juridical definition of the proletariat that is distinct and precise is impossible to formulate.[33]

The word "proletarian" played the same role here that the term "patriot" had for Robespierre. "Enemy" was also a totally elastic category that expanded or contracted to meet the political needs of the moment, becoming a key element in Communist thought and practice. As Tzvetan Todorov put it,

The enemy is the great justification for terror, and the totalitarian state needs enemies to survive. If it lacks them, it invents them. Once they have been identified, they are treated without mercy . . . Being an enemy is a hereditary stain that cannot be removed . . . As has often been pointed out, Jews are persecuted not for what they have done but for what they are, and Communism is no different. It demands the repression (or in moments of crisis, the elimination) of the bourgeoisie as a class. Belonging to the class is enough: there is no need actually to have done anything at all."[37]

One essential question remains: Why should the enemy be exterminated? The traditional role of repression, in Foucault's terminology, is to "discipline and punish." Was the time of discipline and punishment over? Had class enemies become "unredeemable"? Solzhenitsyn provides one response by showing that in the Gulag common criminals were systematically treated better than political prisoners. This was the case not solely for practical reasons—that they helped run the camps—but also for theoretical reasons. One of the aims of the Soviet regime was to build new men, and doing this implied the reeducation of the most hardened criminals. It was also a key propaganda issue in the Soviet Union under Stalin, as well as in China under Mao and in Cuba under Castro.

But why should the enemy be killed? The identification of enemies has always played an important role in politics. Even the gospel says: "He who is not with me is against me." What was new was Lenin's insistence not only that those not with him were against him, but also that those who were against him were to die. Furthermore, he extended this principle outside the domain of politics into the wider sphere of society as a whole.

Terror involves a double mutation. The adversary is first labeled an enemy, and then declared a criminal, which leads to his exclusion from society. Exclusion very quickly turns into extermination. The friend/foe dialectic no longer suffices to solve the fundamental problem of totalitarianism: the search for a reunified humanity that is purified and no longer antagonistic, conducted through the messianic dimension of the Marxist project to reunify humanity via the proletariat. That ideal is used to prop up a forcible unification—of the Party, of society, of the entire empire—and to weed out anyone who fails to fit into the new world. After a relatively short period, society passes from the logic of political struggle to the process of exclusion, then to the ideology of elimination, and finally to the extermination of impure elements. At the end of the line, there are crimes against humanity.

The attitude of Communists in Asia—in China and Vietnam—was sometimes a little different. Because of the Confucian tradition, greater allowance was made for the possibility of reeducation. The Chinese *laogai* was run on the expectation that prisoners—described as "students" or "pupils"—would reform their thinking under the instruction of their guard-teachers. But in the final analysis such thinking was even more hypocritical than straightforward assassination. Forcing one's enemies to change their ways and submit to the discourse of their executioners might well be worse than simply killing them. The Khmer Rouge, on the other hand, from the outset adopted a radical policy. Believing that the reeducation of an entire section of the population was an impossible task (since these enemies were already too corrupt), they sought to change the people. To this end, they carried out a massive extermination of intellectuals and the urban population, seeking to destroy their enemies psychologically by breaking up their personalities and by imposing on them a constant process of self-criticism, which forced them to suffer acute dishonor while still in all likelihood being subject to the supreme punishment.

The leaders of totalitarian regimes saw themselves as the moral guardians of society and were proud of their right to send anyone they chose to his death. The fundamental justification was always the same: necessity with a scientific basis. Tzvetan Todorov, reflecting on the origins of totalitarianism, writes: "It was scientism and not humanism that helped establish the ideological bases of totalitarianism . . . The relation between scientism and totalitarianism is not limited to the justification of acts through so-called scientific necessity (biological or historical): one must already be a practitioner of scientism, even if it is 'wild' scientism, to believe in the perfect transparency of society and thus in the possibility of transforming society by revolutionary means to conform with an ideal."[35]

Trotsky provided a clear illustration of this "scientific" approach in 1919. In his *Defense of Terrorism* he claimed: "The violent revolution has become a necessity precisely because the imminent requirements of history are unable to find a road through the apparatus of parliamentary democracy." In support of this claim he advanced "proofs":

> The proletariat is the historically rising class . . . The bourgeoisie [by contrast] today is a falling class. It no longer plays an essential part in production and by its imperialist methods of appropriation is destroying the economic structure of the world and human culture generally. Nevertheless, the historical tenacity of the bourgeoisie is colossal. It holds to power, and does not wish to abandon it. It thereby threatens to drag after it into the abyss the whole of society. We are forced to tear off this class and chop it away. The Red Terror is a weapon used against a class that, despite being doomed to destruction, does not wish to perish.[36]

Trotsky thereby made history into a divine force to which everything must be sacrificed, and he displayed the incurable naïveté of a revolutionary who imagines that a more just and humane society will emerge out of a dialectical process, despite the criminal nature of the methods employed. Twelve years later, Gorky was considerably more brutal: "Against us is a whole outmoded society that has had its day, and that should allow us to think of ourselves as still being in a civil war. So quite naturally we can conclude that if the enemies do not surrender, it is up to us to exterminate them."[37] That same year found Aragon writing lines of poetry such as "The blue eyes of the Revolution burn with cruel necessity."

Unlike these writers, Kautsky in 1918 faced the issue squarely, with courage and honesty. Refusing to be taken in by the revolutionary rhetoric, he wrote: "To be exact, however, our goal is not socialism as such, which is the abolition of every kind of exploitation and oppression, be it directed against a class, a party, a sex, or a race . . . Should it be proved to us that . . . somehow the emancipation of the proletariat and of humanity could be achieved solely on the basis of private property, we would discard socialism without in any way giving up our objective. On the contrary, this would be conducive to our objective."[38] Kautsky, though one of the most eminent advocates of Marxism, put his humanism before his Marxist belief in science.

Putting people to death required a certain amount of study. Relatively few people actively desire the death of their fellow human beings, so a method of facilitating this had to be found. The most effective means was the denial of the victim's humanity through a process of dehumanization. As Alain Brossat notes: "The barbarian ritual of the purge, and the idea of the extermination machine in top gear are closely linked in the discourse and practice of persecution to the animalization of the Other, to the reduction of real or imaginary enemies to a zoological state."[39]

There were many examples of this process. During the great trials in Moscow, the procurator Andrei Vyshinsky, who was an intellectual with a traditional classical training, threw himself into a veritable frenzy of animalization:

Shoot these rabid dogs! Death to this gang who hide their ferocious
teeth, their eagle claws, from the people! Down with that vulture Trotsky, from whose mouth a bloody venom drips, putrefying the great
ideals of Marxism! Let's put these liars out of harm's way, these miserable pygmies who dance around rotting carcasses! Down with these
abject animals! Let's put an end once and for all to these miserable
hybrids of foxes and pigs, these stinking corpses! Let their horrible
squeals finally come to an end! Let's exterminate the mad dogs of
capitalism, who want to tear to pieces the flower of our new Soviet
nation! Let's push the bestial hatred they bear our leaders back down
their own throats!

Jean-Paul Sartre also crudely remarked in 1952 that "any anti-Communist is a
dog!" This demonizing animal rhetoric seems to support Annie Kriegel's remarks about the public instructive function of the rigged show-trials. As in
medieval mystery plays, everything was arranged so that the good people were
in no doubt about the real identity of the bad Trotskyite heretics or "cosmopolitan Zionists": they represented the devil incarnate.

Alain Brossat recalls that European shivarees and carnivals had begun a
long tradition of the animalization of the other, which resurfaced in the political
caricatures of the eighteenth century. This metaphoric rite allowed all sorts of
hidden crises and latent conflicts to be expressed. In Moscow in the 1930s, there
were no metaphors at all. The animalized adversary really was treated like a
prey to be hunted, before being shot in the head. Stalin systematized these
methods and was the first to use them on a large scale, and they were adopted
by his heirs in Cambodia, China, and elsewhere. But Stalin himself did not
invent these methods. The blame should probably rest on Lenin's shoulders.
After he took power, he often described his enemies as "harmful insects," "lice,"
"scorpions," and "bloodsuckers."

During the rigged spectacle known as the "Industrial Party trial," the
League for the Rights of Man sent a protest petition signed by, among others,
Albert Einstein and Thomas Mann. Gorky responded with an open letter: "In
my opinion the execution was entirely legitimate. It is quite natural that a
worker-and-peasant regime should stamp out its enemies like lice."[40]

Brossat draws the following conclusions about this process of animalization:

As always, the poets and butchers of totalitarianism reveal themselves
first of all by the vocabulary they use. The "liquidation" of the Musco-
vite executioners, a close relative of the "treatment" carried out by the
Nazi assassins, is a linguistic microcosm of an irreparable mental and
cultural catastrophe that was in full view on the Soviet stage. The value
of human life collapsed, and thinking in categories ("enemies of the

people," "traitors," "untrustworthy elements," etc.) replaced ethical thought . . . In the discourse and practice of the Nazi exterminators, the animalization of the Other, which could not be dissociated from the obsession with cleanliness and contagion, was closely linked to the ideology of race. It was conceived in the implacably hierarchical racial terms of "subhumans" and "supermen" . . . but in Moscow in 1937, the discourse about race and the totalitarian measures associated with it were quite different. What mattered instead was the total animalization of the Other, so that a policy under which absolutely anything was possible could come into practice.[41]

Some, however, did not hesitate to cross the ideological barrier and move from social to racial concerns. In a 1932 letter, Gorky (who it should be remembered was a personal friend of Genrikh Yagoda, the head of the GPU, an organization for which his son also worked) wrote: "Class hatred should be cultivated by an organic revulsion as far as the enemy is concerned. Enemies must be seen as inferior. I believe quite profoundly that the enemy is our inferior, and is a degenerate not only on the physical plane but also in the moral sense."[42]

Taking these ideas to their logical extreme, he favored the creation of the U.S.S.R. Institute of Experimental Medicine. Early in 1933, he wrote that

the time is nearing when science will imperiously address normal people and say, would you like all diseases, handicaps, imperfections, senility, and premature death of the organism to be studied minutely and precisely? Such study cannot be carried out solely with experiments on dogs, rabbits, and guinea pigs. Experiments on human beings are indispensable, for what must be studied are the human mechanisms of the functioning of the organism, intracellular processes, hematopoiesis, neurochemistry, and all the processes that go on inside the organism. Hundreds of human guinea pigs are required. This will be a true service to humanity, which will be far more important and useful than the extermination of tens of millions of healthy beings for the comfort of a miserable, physically, psychologically, and morally degenerate class of predators and parasites.[43]

The worst aspects of sociohistorical scientism thus rejoined those of biological scientism.

This biological or zoological strain of thinking enables us to understand better why so many of the crimes of Communism were crimes against humanity, and how Marxist-Leninist ideology managed to justify these crimes to its followers. Considering legal decisions about recent discoveries in biology, Bruno Gravier writes: "Legal texts about bioethics . . . act as signposts about some of the more insidious threats linked to the progress of science, whose role in the birth of ideologies linked to terror (J. Asher's 'law of the movement') has yet to be fully recognized. The fundamentally eugenic thrust of work by well-known doctors such as [Charles] Richet and [Alexis] Carrel clearly paved the way for Nazi extermination and the wayward actions of Nazi doctors."[44]

In Communism there exists a sociopolitical eugenics, a form of social Darwinism. In the words of Dominic Colas, "As master of the knowledge of the evolution of social species, Lenin decided who should disappear by virtue of having been condemned to the dustbin of history."[45] From the moment that a decision had been made on a "scientific" basis (that is, based in political and historical ideology, as well as in Marxism-Leninism) that the bourgeoisie represented a stage of humanity that had been surpassed, its liquidation as a class and the liquidation of the individuals who actually or supposedly belonged to it could be justified.

Marcel Colin, speaking of Nazism, refers to "classifications, segregation, exclusions, and purely biological criteria that are brought in by this criminal ideology. We are thinking of scientific ideas (heredity, hybridization, racial purity) and the fantastic, millenarian, or apocalyptic aspects that are clearly also the product of a particular historical moment."[46] The application of scientific presuppositions to history and society—such as the idea that the proletariat is the bearer of the meaning of history—is easily traceable to a millenarian cosmological phantasmagoria, and is omnipresent in the Communist experience. It is these presuppositions that lie behind so much of the criminal ideology in which purely ideological categories determine arbitrary separations, like the division of humanity into bourgeoisie and proletariat, and into classifications such as petit- and grand-bourgeois or rich or poor peasant. By reifying these categories, as though they had long existed and were utterly immutable, Marxism-Leninism deified the system itself, so that categories and abstractions were far more important than any human reality. Individuals and groups were seen as the archetypes of some sort of primary, disembodied sociology. This made crime much easier: The informer, the torturer, and the NKVD executioner did not denounce, cause suffering, or kill people; they merely eliminated some sort of abstraction that was not beneficial to the common good.

The doctrine became a criminal ideology by the simple act of denying a fundamental fact: the unity of what Robert Antelme calls the "human species," or what the preamble to the Universal Declaration of Human Rights described in 1948 as "the human family." The roots of Marxist-Leninism are perhaps not to be found in Marx at all, but in a deviant version of Darwinism, applied to social questions with the same catastrophic results that occur when such ideas are applied to racial issues. One thing is certain: Crimes against humanity are the product of an ideology that reduces people not to a universal but to a particular condition, be it biological, racial, or sociohistorical. By means of propaganda, the Communists succeeded in making people believe that their conduct had universal implications, relevant to humanity as a whole. Critics have often tried to make a distinction between Nazism and Communism by arguing that the Nazi project had a particular aim, which was nationalist and racist in the extreme, whereas Lenin's project was universal. This is entirely wrong. In both theory and practice, Lenin and his successors excluded from humanity all capitalists, the bourgeoisie, counterrevolutionaries, and others, turning them into absolute enemies in their sociological and political discourse. Kautsky noted as early as 1918 that these terms were entirely elastic, allowing those in power to exclude whomever they wanted from humanity whenever they so wished. These were the terms that led directly to crimes against humanity.

In discussing biologists such as Henri Atlan, who "recognize that the notion of humanity extends beyond the biological approach, and that biology 'has little to say about the human person,'" Mireille Delmas-Marty concedes: "It is true that it is perfectly possible to consider the human species an animal species like any other, a species that man is learning to make himself, as he already makes other animal and vegetable species."[47] But is this not in fact what Communism tried to do? Is the idea of a "new man" not at the heart of the Communist project? Did Communism not have a series of megalomaniacs such as Trofim Lysenko who tried to create not merely new species of tomato or corn but also a new human species?

The scientific mentality of the late nineteenth century, which emerged at the time of the triumph of medicine, inspired the following remarks by Vasily Grossman concerning the Bolshevik leaders: "This sort of person behaves among other people as a surgeon does in the wards of a hospital . . . His soul is really in his knife. And the essence of these people lies in their fanatical faith in the surgeon's knife. The surgeon's knife—that is the great theoretician, the archphilosopher of the twentieth century."[48] The idea was taken to its furthest extreme by Pol Pot, who with a terrifying stroke of the knife excised the gangrenous part of the social body—the "New People"—while retaining the "healthy" peasant part. As insane as this idea was, it was not exactly new. Already in the 1870s, Pyotr Tkachev, a Russian revolutionary and worthy heir of Nechaev, proposed the extermination of all Russians over twenty-five years old, whom he considered incapable of carrying out his revolutionary ideal. In a letter to Nechaev, Bakunin objected to this insane idea: "Our people are not a blank sheet of paper on which any secret society can write whatever it wants, like your Communist program, for instance."[49] The International demanded that the slate of the past be wiped clean, and Mao famously compared himself to a poetic genius writing on a blank sheet of paper, as though he genuinely believed that thousands of years of history could simply be ignored.

Most of the mechanisms of terror discussed above originated in the U.S.S.R. under Lenin and Stalin, but some of their features are to be found, with differing degrees of intensity, in all regimes claiming to be Marxist in origin. Every Communist country or Party has its own specific history and its own particular regional and local variations, but a linkage can always be traced to the pattern elaborated in Moscow in November 1917. This linkage forms a sort of genetic code of Communism.

How can we possibly understand the people who took part in this terrifying system? Did they have specific psychological features? Every totalitarian regime seems to find a segment of the population that has a special calling for such behavior, and it actively seeks them out and promotes them within its ranks. Stalin's own case is representative. In terms of strategy, he was a worthy heir of Lenin, capable of expediting business with ease on either a local or a global scale. To the eyes of history he might well appear as one of the great men of the century, transforming the weak Soviet Union of 1922 into one of the two world superpowers, and for decades causing Communism to appear to be the only real alternative to capitalism.

But he was also one of the greatest criminals in a century in which great criminals have been all too easy to find. As far back as 1953 Boris Suvarin and Boris Nikolaevsky labeled Stalin the century's Caligula, and Trotsky always believed that he was a paranoid maniac. But more than that, Stalin was an extraordinary fanatic with a particular talent for politics, and a man with no belief in democracy. Stalin was the logical result of the movement begun by Lenin and dreamed of by Nechaev: a man using extremist means to implement extremist policies.

The fact that Stalin so deliberately engaged in crimes against humanity as a means of governance returns us to the specifically Russian aspects of his personality. A native of the Caucasus, he was surrounded during his childhood and adolescence by tales of brigands with hearts of gold, and of *abreks*, mountain dwellers who had been expelled from their clan or who had solemnly sworn bloody vengeance—stories, in short, of men filled with despairing courage. He used the pseudonym Koba, which was the name of one such mythical brigand prince, a local Robin Hood figure who came to the assistance of widows and orphans. Bakunin, in his letter disavowing Nechaev, wrote:

> Do you remember how angry with me you became when I called you an *abrek*, and described your beliefs as a sort of *abreki* catechism? You said that all men should be made so, and that the abandonment of the self and the renunciation of personal needs and desires, all feelings, attach-

ments, and links should be a normal state, the everyday condition of all humanity. Out of that cruel renunciation and extreme fanaticism you now want to make a general principle applicable to the whole community. You want crazy things, impossible things, the total negation of nature, man, and society![50]

Despite his total commitment to the ideal, as early as 1870 Bakunin had understood that even revolutionary action had to submit itself to a number of fundamental moral constraints.

Communist terror has often been compared to the great Catholic Inquisition. Here novelists are probably of more use than historians. In his magnificent novel *La tunique d'infamie*, Michel del Castillo remarks: "The purpose is not to torture or to burn the victim: the aim is to ask the right question. No terror without truth, which is its foundation. Without truth, how can error be recognized? . . . If one is certain that one possesses the truth, how can one leave one's neighbor in error?"[51]

The Church promised the remission of original sin, and salvation or eternal damnation in another world. Marx had a redemptive belief in the Promethean destiny of mankind. This was the messianic dream of the Great Evening. But for Leszek Kolakowski, "the idea that the world we see is so totally corrupt that it is beyond improvement, and that accordingly the world that will follow will bring plenitude, perfection, and ultimate liberation is one of the most monstrous aberrations of the human spirit . . . Of course this aberration is not an invention of our own time, but we should recognize that religious thought, which opposes all temporal values to the force of supernatural grace, is much less abominable than doctrines that tell us we can assure our salvation by jumping from the edge of the abyss to the glorious heights of the heavens."[52]

Ernest Renan was probably quite correct when he claimed in his *Philosophical Dialogues* that the sure way to guarantee oneself absolute power in an atheist society was not to threaten people with some mythological inferno, but to institute a real hell—a concentration camp to punish insurgents and to frighten all others, with a special police force made up of beings devoid of conscience and entirely devoted to the government in power—"obedient machines, unencumbered by moral scruples and prepared for every sort of cruelty."[53]

After the liberation of most of the prisoners in the Gulag in 1953, and even after the Twentieth Congress of the Soviet Communist Party, when some forms of terror seemed to have disappeared, the principle of terror retained its function and continued to be extremely effective. The memory of the terror lived on and paralyzed people's wills, as Aino Kuusinen recalled: "The memory of the terror weighed on people's minds; no one could believe that Stalin had really gone for good. There was scarcely a family in Moscow that had not suffered in some way from persecution, yet no one ever talked about it. I, for instance, would never talk about my experiences in the camps in front of my friends. And they never asked about it. The fear was too deep-rooted in everyone's minds."[54] If the victims carried their memories of the terror wherever they went, their executioners were just as dependent on those memories. In the middle of the Brezhnev period, the Soviet Union brought out a postage stamp to commemorate the fiftieth anniversary of the Cheka, and published a book in homage to its memory.[55]

In conclusion, the last word should go to Gorky and his homage to Lenin in 1924:

> One of my old friends, a worker from Sormov, a kind-hearted man, complained that it was hard to work for the Cheka. I answered him: "It seems to me that it's not for you. It's just not in your character." He agreed, sadly. "No, not at all." But after thinking for a moment, he added, "But when I think about it, I'm sure Ilich often also has to hold his soul back by its wings and that makes me ashamed of my weakness" . . . Did Lenin really have to "hold his soul back by its wings"? He paid so little attention to himself that he never talked about himself with others; he was better than anyone at never revealing the storms that blew inside his mind. But he told me once as he was stroking some children, "Their lives will be better than ours: they'll be spared many of the things we have been forced to live through. Their lives will be less cruel." He stared off into the distance, and added dreamily: "Mind you, I don't envy them. Our generation will have carried out a task of tremendous historical importance. The cruelty of our lives, imposed by circumstances, will be understood and pardoned. Everything will be understood, everything!"[56]

We are beginning to understand it, but not quite in the manner that Lenin imagined. What remains today of this "task of tremendous historical importance"? Not the illusory "building of socialism," but an immense tragedy that still weighs on the lives of hundreds of millions of people, and that will mark the entry into the third millennium. Vasily Grossman, the war correspondent from Stalingrad, the writer who saw the manuscript of his magnum opus confiscated by the KGB and who died a broken man as a result, still drew an optimistic lesson from his experiences that is well worth repeating:

> Our century is the century of the greatest violence ever committed against human beings by the state. But it is precisely here that the strength and hope of humanity lie. It is the twentieth century that has at last shaken the Hegelian concept of the historical process whereby

"everything real is rational." It was this concept, violently debated for decades, that Russian thinkers of the past century finally accepted. But now, at the height of the state's triumph over individual freedom, Russian thinkers wearing padded camp jackets have dethroned and cast down the old Hegelian law and proclaimed their new, supreme, guiding principle of world history: "Everything inhuman is senseless and worthless" . . . Amid the total triumph of inhumanity, it has become self-evident that everything effected by violence is senseless and worthless, and that it has no future and will disappear without a trace.[57]

Notes

Foreword

An earlier version of the Foreword appeared in the *Times Literary Supplement*, 27 March 1998.

1. For the development of American historical writing on Russia and the Soviet Union see Martin Malia, "Clio in Tauris: American Historiography on Russia," in *Contemporary Historiography in America*, ed. Gordon Wood and Anthony Mohlo (Princeton: Princeton University Press, 1998). For recent American scholarship on Soviet history see Stephen Kotkin, "1991 and the Russian Revolution: Sources, Conceptual Categories, Analytical Frameworks," *Journal of Modern History*, 70, no. 2 (June 1998).

2. Stephen F. Cohen, *Bukharin and the Bolshevik Revolution: A Political Biography, 1888–1938* (New York: Alfred A. Knopf, 1973); and Moshe Lewin, *The Political Undercurrents of Soviet Economic Debates: From Bukharin to the Modern Reformers* (Princeton: Princeton Univeristy Press, 1974).

3. Sheila Fitzpatrick, ed., *Cultural Revolution in Russia, 1928–1931* (Bloomington: Indiana University Press, 1988), especially the editor's introduction, and her *Russian Revolution 1917–1932*, rev. ed. (New York: Oxford University Press, 1994).

4. Maurice Merleau-Ponty, *Humanism and Terror*, trans. John O'Neil (Boston: Beacon Press, 1969).

5. Raymond Aron, *Democracy and Totalitarianism*, trans. Valence Ionescu (London: Weidenfeld & Nicolson, 1968); and François Furet, *The Passing of an Illusion: The Idea of Communism in the Twentieth Century* (Chicago: University of Chicago Press, 1999).

6. For example, Aleksander Wat, *My Century: The Odyssey of a Polish Intellectual*, ed. and trans. Richard Lourie, with a foreword by Czesław Miłosz (Berkeley: University of California Press, 1988); and Vasily Grossman, *Life and Fate*, trans. Robert Chandler (New York: Harper and Row, 1985).

7. Alain Besançon, *Le malheur du siècle: Sur le communisme, le nazisme, et l'unicité de la Shoah* (Paris: Fayard, 1998).

8. Sheila Fitzpatrick and Robert Gellately, eds., *Accusatory Practices: Denunciation in Modern European History, 1789–1989* (Chicago: University of Chicago Press, 1997).

9. For the ideological delusions of the time see Tony Judt, *Past Imperfect: French Intellectuals, 1944–1956* (Berkeley: University of California Press, 1992); and Oliver Todd, *Albert Camus: A Life*, trans. Benjamin Ivry (New York: Alfred A. Knopf, 1997). The great classic of political philosophy to emerge from this debate is Raymond Aron, *The Opium of the Intellectuals*, trans. Terence Kilmartin (Garden City, N.Y.: Doubleday, 1957, first published in French, 1995).

Introduction

1. Raymond Queneau, *Une histoire modèle* (Paris: Gallimard, 1979), p. 9.

2. Quoted in Kostas Papaionannou, *Marx et les marxistes*, rev. ed. (Paris: Flammarion, 1972).

3. Andre Frossard, *Le crime contre l'humanité* (Paris: Robert Laffont, 1987).

4. Vasily Grossman, *Forever Flowing*, trans. Thomas P. Whitney (New York: Harper & Row, 1972), p. 247.

5. Quoted in Jacques Baynac, *La terreur sous Lénine* (Paris: Le Sagittaire, 1975), p. 75.

6. Gracchus Babeuf, *La guerre de Vendée et le système de dépopulation* (Paris: Tallandier, 1987).

7. Jean-Pierre Azema, "Auschwitz," in J.-P. Azema and F. Bédarida, *Dictionnaire des années de tourmente* (Paris: Flammarion, 1995), p. 777.

8. Pierre Vidal-Naquet, *Réflexions sur le génocide* (Paris: La Découverte, 1995), p. 268. Moreover, Vidal-Naquet wrote, "There has been discussion of Katyń and the massacre in 1940 of Polish officers who were held as prisoners by the Soviets. Katyń dovetails perfectly with the definition of Nuremberg."

9. Denis Szabo and Alain Joffé, "La répression des crimes contre l'humanité et des crimes de guerre au Canada," in Marcel Colin, *Le crime contre l'humanité* (Paris: Erès, 1996), p. 655.

10. See the analysis by Jean-Noël Darde, *Le ministère de la vérité: Histoire d'un génocide dans le journal* (Paris: L'Humanité, Le Seuil, 1984).

11. Robert Conquest, *The Great Terror: Stalin's Purge of the Thirties*, rev. ed. (New York: Oxford University Press, 1990).

12. Louis Aragon, *Prélude au temps des cerises* (Paris: Minuit, 1944).

13. Quoted in Joseph Berger, *Shipwreck of a Generation: The Memoirs of Joseph Berger* (London: Harvill Press, 1971), p. 247.

14. Ibid.

15. Martin Malia, *The Soviet Tragedy: A History of Socialism in Russia, 1917–1991* (New York: Free Press, 1994), p. 4.

16. Tzvetan Todorov, *L'homme dépaysé* (Paris: Le Seuil, 1996), p. 36.

17. Rudolf Hess, *Commandant of Auschwitz: The Autobiography of Rudolf Hess*, trans. Constantine FitzGibbon (Cleveland: World Publishing, 1959), p. 180.

18. Grossman, *Forever Flowing*, pp. 142, 144, and 155.

19. Raul Hilberg, *The Destruction of the European Jews*, rev. ed. (Chicago: Quadrangle Books, 1967).

20. Nikita Khrushchev, *Khrushchev Remembers*, trans. and ed. Strobe Talbott (Boston: Little, Brown, 1970), pp. 345–348.

21. Grossman, *Forever Flowing*.

22. Simone Weil, *The Need for Roots: Prelude to a Declaration of Duties toward Mankind*, trans. Arthur Wills (Boston: Beacon Press, 1952), p. 125.

23. Tzvetan Todorov, "La morale de l'historien," paper presented at the colloquium "L'homme, la langue, les camps," Paris IV–Sorbonne, May 1997, p. 13.

24. See Pierre Nora, "Gaullistes et Communistes," in *Les lieux de mémoire*, vol. 2 (Paris: Gallimard, 1997).

25. Witold Gombrowicz, *Testament: Entretiens avec Dominique de Roux* (Paris: Folio, 1996), p. 109.

26. See Piotr Pigorov, *J'ai quitté ma patrie* (Paris: La Jeune Parque, 1952); or Michel Koryakoff, *Je me mets hors la loi* (Paris: Editions du Monde Nouveau, 1947).

27. Khrushchev, *Khrushchev Remembers*, pp. 347–349.

28. François Furet, *The Passing of an Illusion: The Idea of Communism in the Twentieth Century* (Chicago: University of Chicago Press, 1999), p. 501.

29. See Pierre Rigolout, *Les Français au goulag* (Paris: Fayard, 1984); and esp. Jacques Rossi, *Le Goulag de A à Z* (Paris: Le Cherche Midi, 1997).

30. Varlam Shalamov, *Kolyma Tales*, trans. John Glad (New York: W. W. Norton, 1980); Pin Yathay with John Man, *Stay Alive, My Son* (London: Bloomsbury, 1987).

31. Paul Barton (pseud.), *L'institution concentrationnaire en Russie, 1930–1957* (Paris: Plon, 1959).

32. Bernard Chapuis, *Le monde*, 3 July 1975.

33. See, e.g., Ludo Martens, *Un autre regard sur Staline* (Paris: EPO, 1994); and, in a less fawning style, Lilly Marcou, *Staline, vie privée* (Paris: Calmann-Lévy, 1996).

34. François-René Chateaubriand, *Memoirs of Chateaubriand*, trans. and ed. Robert Baldick (New York: Alfred A. Knopf, 1961), p. 218.

2. The Iron Fist of the Dictatorship of the Proletariat

1. Until 1 February 1918 Russia used the Julian calendar, which was thirteen days behind the Gregorian system. Thus what for Russia was 25 October 1917 was 7 November 1917 in the rest of Europe.

2. A. Z. Okorokov, *Oktyabr' i krakh russkoi burzhuaznoi pressy* (October and the destruction of the Russian bourgeois press) (Moscow: Mysl', 1971); Vladimir N.

Brovkin, *The Mensheviks after October: Socialist Opposition and the Rise of the Bolshevik Dictatorship* (Ithaca: Cornell University Press, 1987).

3. G. A. Belov, *Iz istorii Vserossiiskoi Chrezvychainoi Komissii, 1917–1921: Sbornik dokumentov* (From the history of the All-Russian Extraordinary Commission, 1917–1921: A collection of documents) (Moscow: Gos. izd-vo polit. lit-ry, 1958), p. 66; George Leggett, *The Cheka: Lenin's Political Police* (New York: Oxford University Press, 1981), pp. 13–15.

4. Belov, *Iz istorii VChK*, pp. 54–55.

5. Ibid., p. 67.

6. D. I. Kurskii, *Izbrannye stat'i i rechi* (Selected articles and speeches) (Moscow: Gos. izd-vo iurid. lit-ry, 1958), p. 67.

7. E. A. Finn, "Antisovetskaya pechat' na skam'e podsudimykh" (Anti-Soviet press in the dock of the accused), *Sovetskoe gosudarstvo i pravo*, no. 2 (1967), 71–72.

8. S. A. Pavlyuchenkov, *Krestyanskii Brest* (The peasants' Brest) (Moscow: Russkoe knigoizd. tov., 1996), pp. 25–26.

9. Leggett, *The Cheka*, p. 7.

10. V. D. Bonch-Bruevich, *Na boevykh postakh fevralskoi i oktyabrskoi revolyutsii* (At combat posts in the February and October Revolutions) (Moscow: "Federatsiia," 1930), p. 191.

11. Ibid., p. 197.

12. Leggett, *The Cheka*, p. 16.

13. *Lenin i VChK: Sbornik dokumentov 1917–1922* (Lenin and the Cheka: A collection of documents, 1917–1922) (Moscow: Politizlat, 1975), pp. 36–7; full text in the State Archives of the Russian Federation, Moscow (hereafter GARF), 130/2/134/26–27.

14. *Delo naroda*, 3 December 1917.

15. V. I. Lenin, *Polnoe sobranie sochinenii* (Complete collected works) (Moscow: Gos. izd-vo polit. lit-ry, 1958–1966), 35: 311.

16. GARF, "Prague Archives," files 1–195. For the period in question see files 1, 2, and 27.

17. Quoted in Orlando Figes, *A People's Tragedy: The Russian Revolution, 1891–1924* (London: Jonathan Cape, 1996), p. 379.

18. "Polozhenie o ChK na mestakh" (The state of the Cheka in localities), 11 June 1918, B. I. Nikolaevsky Archives, Hoover Institution, Stanford, Calif.

19. Leggett, *The Cheka*, p. 29–40.

20. M. I. Latsis, *Dva goda borby na vnutrennom fronte* (Two years of struggle on the internal front) (Moscow: Gos. izd-vo, 1920), p. 6.

21. Isaac Steinberg, *In the Workshop of the Revolution* (New York: Rinehart, 1953), p. 155.

22. Leonard Schapiro, *The Origin of the Communist Autocracy: Political Opposition in the Soviet State, First Phase, 1917–1922* (London: London School of Economics and Political Science, 1955), pp. 84–86; Brovkin, *The Mensheviks after October*, pp. 46–47 and 59–63.

23. E. Berard, "Pourquoi les bolcheviks ont-ils quitté Petrograd?" *Cahiers du monde russe et soviétique,* 34 (October–December 1993), 507–528.

24. Lenin, *Polnoe sobranie sochinenii,* 35: 311.

25. Russian Center for the Conservation and Study of Historic Documents, Moscow (henceforth RTsKhIDNI), 158\1\1\10; Pavlyuchenkov, *Krestyanskii Brest,* p. 29.

26. *Dekrety sovetskoi vlasti* (Decrees of the Soviet regime) (Moscow: Gos izd-vo polit. lit-ry, 1957–), 1: 490–491.

27. P. G. Sofinov, *Ocherki Istorii vserossiiskoi chrezvychainoi komissii* (Outline of the history of the All-Russian Extraordinary Commission) (Moscow: Gos. izd-vo polit. lit-ry, 1960), pp. 43–44; Leggett, *The Cheka,* p. 35.

28. Belov, *Iz istorii VChK,* pp. 112–113.

29. Brovkin, *The Mensheviks after October,* p. 159.

30. Lenin, *Polnoe sobranie sochinenii,* 36: 265.

31. *Protokoly zasedanii VSIK 4-sozyva, Stenograficheskii otchet* (Protocols of the sessions of the CEC in the fourth phase: Stenographic account) (Moscow, 1918), pp. 250, 389.

32. Karl Radek, "Puti russkoi revoyiutsii" (The paths of the Russian Revolution), *Krasnaya,* no. 4 (November 1921), 188.

33. Andrea Graziosi, *The Great Soviet Peasant War: Bolsheviks and Peasants, 1917–1933* (Cambridge, Mass.: Harvard University, Ukrainian Research Institute, 1996), p. 18.

34. Brovkin, *The Mensheviks after October,* pp. 220–225.

35. RTsKhIDNI, 17\6\384\97–98.

36. *Novaya zhizn',* 1 June 1918, p. 4.

37. N. Bernstam, *Ural i Prikamie, noyabr' 1917–yanvar' 1919* (The Ural and Kama regions, November 1917–January 1919) (Paris: YMCA Press, 1982).

38. "Instruktsii-Chrezvychainym Komissiyam" (Instructions to local Chekas), 1 December 1918, Nikolaevsky Archives, Hoover Institution, quoted in Leggett, *The Cheka,* pp. 39–40.

39. L. Trotsky, *O Lenine* (On Lenin) (Moscow: 1924), p. 101.

40. *Novaya zhizn',* 16, 26, 27, 28 June 1918; Brovkin, *The Mensheviks after October,* pp. 243–249; S. Rosenberg, "Russian Labor and Bolshevik Power," *Slavic Review* 44 (Summer 1985), 233 ff.

41. Lenin, *Polnoe sobranie sochinenii,* 50: 106.

3. The Red Terror

1. L. M. Spirin, *Klassy i Partii v grazhdanskoy voine v Rossii* (Classes and parties in the civil war in Russia) (Moscow: Mysl', 1968), pp. 180 ff.

2. V. I. Lenin, *Polnoe sobranie sochinenii* (Complete collected works) (Moscow: Gos. izd-vo polit. lit-ry, 1958–1966), 50: 142.

3. RTsKhIDNI, 2/1/6/898.

4. GARF, 130/2/98a/26–32.

5. RTsKhIDNI, 76/3/22.

6. *Leninsky sbornik* (A Lenin collection), vol. 18 (1931), pp. 145–146, quoted in Dmitry Volkogonov, *Lenin, politicheskii portret: v dvukh knigakh* (Lenin, a political portrait) (Moscow: Novosti, 1994), p. 248.

7. Lenin, *Polnoe sobranie sochinenii,* 50: 143.

8. RTsKhIDNI, 76/3/22/3.

9. *Izvestiya,* 23 August 1918; George Leggett, *The Cheka: Lenin's Political Police* (New York: Oxford University Press, 1981), p. 104.

10. S. Lyandres, "The 1918 Attempt on the Life of Lenin: A New Look at the Evidence," *Slavic Review* 48 (1989), 432–448.

11. *Izvestiya,* 4 September 1918.

12. Raphael Abramovich, *The Soviet Revolution, 1917–1939* (London: Allen & Unwin, 1962), p. 312.

13. *Severnaya Kommuna,* no. 109 (19 September 1918), 2, quoted in Leggett, *The Cheka,* p. 114.

14. *Izvestiya,* 10 September 1918.

15. G. A. Belov, *Iz istorii Vserossiiskoi Chrezvchainoi Komissii, 1917–1921: Sbornik dokumentov* (From the history of the All-Russian Extraordinary Commission, 1917–1921: A collection of documents) (Moscow: Gos. izd-vo polit. lit-ry, 1958), pp. 197–198.

16. Leggett, *The Cheka,* p. 111.

17. *Utro Moskvy,* no. 21, 4 November 1918.

18. *Ezhenedelnik VChK,* 22 September–27 October 1918.

19. M. I. Latsis, *Dva goda borby na vnut rennom fronte* (Two years of struggle on the internal front) (Moscow: Gos. izd-vo, 1920), p. 25.

20. Yu. Martov to A. Stein, 25 October 1918, quoted in V. I. Brovkin, *Behind the Front Lines of the Civil War* (Princeton: Princeton University Press, 1994), p. 283.

21. N. Bernstam, *Ural i Prikamie, noyabr' 1917–yanuar' 1919* (The Ural and Kama regions, November 1917–January 1919) (Paris: YMCA Press, 1982), p. 129.

22. M. N. Gernet, *Protiv smertnoi kazni* (Against the death penalty) (Moscow: Tip. I. D. Sufina, 1907), pp. 385–423; N. S. Tagantsev, *Smertnaya kazn* (The death penalty) (St. Petersburg: Gos. tip., 1913). Similar figures are arrived at by K. Liebnecht (5,735 condemned to death, 3,741 executed between 1906 and 1910; 625 condemned to death and 191 executed between 1825 and 1905), in Marc Ferro, *The Russian Revolution of February 1917* (Englewood Cliffs, N.J.: Prentice-Hall, 1972), p. 483.

23. RTsKhIDNI, 5/1/2558.

24. *Lenin i VChK: Sbornik dokumentov 1917–1922* (Lenin and the Cheka: A collection of documents, 1917–1922) (Moscow: Politizlat, 1975), p. 122.

25. Leggett, *The Cheka,* pp. 204–237.

26. GARF, 393/89/10a.

27. *Vlast' Sovetov,* nos. 1–2 (1922), 41; L. D. Gerson, *The Secret Police in Lenin's Russia* (Philadelphia: Temple University Press, 1976), pp. 149 ff.; Leggett, *The Cheka,* p. 178; GARF, 393/89/182; 393/89/295.

28. GARF, 393/89/182; 393/89/231; 393/89/295.

4. The Dirty War

1. L. G. Gorelik, ed., *Goneniya na anarkhism v Sovietskoi Rossii* (The persecution of anarchism in Soviet Russia) (Berlin, 1922), pp. 27–63.

2. *Izvestiya*, 18 March 1919; L. D. Gerson, *The Secret Police in Lenin's Russia* (Philadelphia: Tample University Press, 1976), pp. 151–152; G. Leggett, *The Cheka: Lenin's Political Police* (New York: Oxford University Press, 1981), pp. 311–316.

3. V. I. Brovkin, *Behind the Front Lines of the Civil War: Political Parties and Social Movements in Russia, 1918–1922* (Princeton: Princeton University Press, 1994), p. 54.

4. G. A. Belov, *Iz istorii Vserossiiskoi Chrezvchainoi Komissii, 1917–1921: Sbornik dokumentov* (From the history of the All-Russian Extraordinary Commission, 1917–1921: A collection of documents) (Moscow: Gos. izd-vo polit. lit-ry, 1958), p. 354; CRCEDHC 5/1/2615.

5. Brovkin, *Behind the Front Lines*, pp. 252–257.

6. *Tsirkulyarnoe pis'mo VChK* (Cheka circular), pp. 267–268, B. I. Nikolaevsky Archives, Hoover Institution, Stanford, Calif.

7. RTsKhIDNI, 17/84/43/2–4.

8. Brovkin, *Behind the Front Lines*, p. 69; RTsKhIDNI, 17/84/43.

9. Leggett, *The Cheka*, p. 313; Brovkin, *Behind the Front Lines*, p. 71; *Petrogradskaya pravda*, 13 April 1919, p. 3.

10. RTsKhIDNI, 17/66/68/2–5; 17/6/351.

11. Ibid., 17/6/197/105; 17/66/68.

12. Ibid., 17/6/351; *Izvestiya TsKa RKP(b)* (News from the Central Committee of the Russian Communist Party), no. 3 (4 July 1919); RTsKhIDNI, 2/1/24095; GARF, 130/3/363.

13. Brovkin, *Behind the Front Lines*, pp. 82–85; S. P. Melgunov, *The Red Terror in Russia* (London: Dent, 1925), pp. 58–60; P. Silin, "Astrakhanskie rasstrely" (The shootings in Astrakhan), in *Cheka: Materialy po deyatelnosti Chrezvichainoi Komissii* (Cheka: Materials on the activities of the Extraordinary Commission), ed. V. Chernov (Berlin: Izd. TSentr. biuro Partii sotsialistov-revoliutsionerov, 1922), pp. 248–255.

14. RTsKhIDNI, 2/1/11957.

15. *The Trotsky Papers, 1917–1922*, ed. Jan M. Meijer (The Hague: Mouton, 1964–1971), 2: 22.

16. Brovkin, *Behind the Front Lines*, p. 289.

17. *Trotsky Papers*, 2: 20.

18. Brovkin, *Behind the Front Lines*, pp. 297 ff.

19. Ibid., pp. 292–296.

20. Andrea Graziosi, *The Great Soviet Peasant War: Bolsheviks and Peasants, 1917–1933* (Cambridge, Mass.: Harvard University, Ukrainian Research Institute, 1996).

21. S. A. Pavlyuchenkov, *Krestyanskii Brest* (The peasants' Brest Treaty) (Moscow: Russkoe knigoizd. tov., 1996), pp. 188–240.

22. Orlando Figes, "The Red Army and Mass Mobilization during the Russian Civil War, 1918–1920," *Past and Present*, no. 129 (November 1990), 199–200.

23. *Dekrety sovietskoi vlasti* (Decrees of the Soviet regime) (Moscow: Gos. izd-vo polit. lit-ry, 1957–), 4: 167.

24. Brovkin, *Behind the Front Lines*, p. 318.

25. Russian State Military Archives, Moscow, 33987/3/32.

26. A collection of these reports, assembled by a team of Russian, French, and Italian historians, under the direction of V. P. Danilov, appeared in Russian at the end of 1997.

27. M. S. Frenkin, *Tragedia krestyanskikh vosstaniy v Rossii, 1918–1921* (Tragedy of peasant uprisings in Russia, 1918–1921) (Jerusalem: Leksikon, 1987); Orlando Figes, *Peasant Russia, Civil War: The Volga Countryside in the Revolution* (New York: Oxford University Press, 1989); Brovkin, *Behind the Front Lines.*

28. Taros Hunczak, ed., *The Ukraine, 1917–1921: A Study in Revolution* (Cambridge, Mass.: Harvard Ukrainian Research Institute and Harvard University Press, 1977).

29. Volin (V. M. Eikhenbaum), *The Unknown Revolution, 1917–1921,* trans. Holley Cantine (New York: Free Life Editions, 1974), pp. 509–626; Alexandre Skirda, *Les Cossaques de la liberté* (Paris: J. C. Lattes, 1985); Richard Pipes, *Russia under the Bolshevik Regime, 1919–1924* (London: HarperCollins, 1994), pp. 106–108.

30. Pipes, *Russia under the Bolshevik Regime,* pp. 105–131.

31. Figes, *Peasant Russia, Civil War,* pp. 333 ff.; Brovkin, *Behind the Front Lines,* pp. 323–325.

32. RTsKhIDNI, 76/3/109.

33. V. L. Genis, "Raskazachivanie v Sovietskoi Rossii" (The de-Cossackization in Soviet Russia), *Voprosy istorii* (Problems of history), no. 1 (1994), 42–55.

34. *Izvestiya TsKPSS,* no. 6 (1989), 177–178.

35. RTsKhIDNI, 5/2/106/7.

36. Genis, "Raskazachivanie v Sovietskoi Rossii," pp. 42–55.

37. RTsKhIDNI, 17/6/83.

38. Genis, "Raskazachivanie v Sovietskoi Rossii," p. 50; RTsKhIDNI, 17/84/75.

39. Melgunov, *The Red Terror in Russia,* p. 77; Brovkin, *Behind the Front Lines,* p. 346.

40. RTsKhIDNI, 17/84/75/28.

41. Ibid., 17/84/75/59.

42. Quoted in Brovkin, *Behind the Front Lines,* p. 353.

43. RTsKhIDNI, 85/11/131/11.

44. Ibid., 85/11/123/15.

45. *Krasnyi mech* (Red sword), no. 1 (18 August 1919), 1.

46. RTsKhIDNI, 5/1/2159/35–38.

47. Ibid., 76/3/70/20.

48. Ibid., 17/6/384/62.

49. Ibid., 17/66/66.

50. *Izvestiya Odesskogo Sovieta rabochikh deputatov,* no. 36, p. 1, quoted in Brovkin, *Behind the Front Lines,* p. 121.

51. Melgunov, *The Red Terror in Russia,* pp. 61–77; Leggett, *The Cheka,* pp. 199–

200; Brovkin, *Behind the Front Lines*, pp. 122–125; GARF, Denikin Commission files, nos. 134 (Kharkiv), 157 (Odessa), 194, 195 (Kyiv).

52. Chernov, *Cheka: Materialy.*

53. Estimates based on Melgunov, *The Red Terror in Russia*, p. 77; and on Socialist Revolutionary sources from Kharkiv in May 1921.

54. V. I. Lenin, *Polnoe sobranie sochinenii* (Complete collected works) (Moscow: Gos. izd-vo polit. lit-ry, 1958–1966), 42: 74.

55. Melgunov, *The Red Terror in Russia*, p. 81.

5. From Tambov to the Great Famine

1. V. Danilov and T. Shanin, *Krestyanskoe vosstanie v Tambovskoi gubernii v 1919–1921* (The peasant revolt in Tambov Province, 1919–1921) (Tambov: Intertsentr: Arkhivnyi otdel administratsii Tambovskoi obl., 1994), pp. 38–40.

2. RTsKhIDNI, 17/86/103/4; S. Singleton, "The Tambov Revolt," *Slavic Review* 26 (1966), 498–512; Oliver Radkey, *The Unknown Civil War in Russia: A Study of the Green Movement in the Tambov Region* (Stanford, Calif.: Hoover Institution Press, Stanford University, 1976); Orlando Figes, *Peasant Russia, Civil War: The Volga Countryside in the Revolution* (New York: Oxford University Press, 1989).

3. Danilov and Shanin, *Krestyanskoe vosstanie*, pp. 63–64; Radkey, *The Unknown Civil War*, pp. 122–126.

4. V. I. Lenin, *Polnoe sobranie sochinenii* (Complete collected works) (Moscow: Gos. izd-vo polit. lit-ry, 1958–1966), 51: 310.

5. M. Bogdanov, *Razgrom zapadno-sibirskogo kulachko-eserovskogo myatezha* (Destruction of the west Siberian kulak-SR rebellion) (Tyumen: Polit Tyum, 1961).

6. RTsKhIDNI, 76/3/208/12.

7. Ibid., 76/3/166/3.

8. V. I. Brovkin, *Behind the Front Lines of the Civil War: Political Parties and Social Movements in Russia, 1918–1922* (Princeton: Princeton University Press, 1994), p. 392.

9. RTsKhIDNI, 76/3/167/23.

10. P. Avrich, *Kronstadt, 1921* (Princeton: Princeton University Press, 1970), pp. 153–183.

11. RTsKhIDNI, 76/3/167.

12. "Kronstadt, 1921," in *Dokumenty* (Moscow, 1997), p. 15.

13. George Leggett, *The Cheka: Lenin's Political Police* (New York: Oxford University Press, 1981), p. 328.

14. S. A. Malsagov, *An Island Hell: A Soviet Prison in the Far North*, trans. F. H. Lyon (London: A. M. Philpot, 1926), pp. 45–46.

15. "Kronstadt, 1921," p. 367.

16. Brovkin, *Behind the Front Lines*, p. 400.

17. Andrea Graziosi, "At the Roots of Soviet Industrial Relations and Practices—Piatokov's Donbass in 1921," *Cahiers du monde russe* 36 (1995), 95–138.

18. Danilov and Shanin, *Krestyanskoe vosstanie*, pp. 179–180.

19. Ibid., pp. 178–179.

20. Ibid., pp. 226–227.

21. Ibid., p. 218.

22. GARF, 393/89/182; 393/89/295.

23. RTsKhIDNI, 5/2/244/1.

24. Ibid., 17/87/164; 76/3/237.

25. Ibid., 17/87/296/35–36.

26. *Pravda*, 21 July 1921; Mikhail Heller, "Premier avertissement: Un coup de fouet. L'histoire de l'expulsion des personnalités culturelles hors de l'Union soviétique en 1922," *Cahiers du monde russe et soviétique*, 20 (April–June 1979), 131–172.

27. GARF, 1064/1/1/33.

28. RTsKhIDNI, 2/1/26847.

29. Heller, "Premier avertissement," p. 141.

30. Ibid., p. 143.

31. Ibid., pp. 148–149.

32. Ibid., p. 151.

33. S. Adamets, "Catastrophes démographiques en Russie soviétique en 1918–1923" (Doctoral thesis, EHESS, December 1995), p. 191.

34. A. Beliakov, *Yunost vozhdya* (The adolescence of the leader) (Moscow: Molodaya gvardiia, 1958), pp. 80–82, quoted in Heller, "Premier avertissement," p. 134.

35. RTsKhIDNI, 2/1/22947/1–4.

36. *Russkaya Pravoslavnaya tserkva i kommunisticheskoe gosudarstvo, 1917–1941* (The Russian Orthodox Church and the Communist state, 1917–1941) (Moscow: Terra, 1996), p. 69.

37. Dmitry Volkogonov, *Lenin: politicheskii portret: v dvukh knigakh* (Lenin: A political portrait) (Moscow: Novosti, 1994), p. 346.

38. Ibid.

39. Hélène Carrère d'Encausse, *The Russian Syndrome: One Thousand Years of Political Murder* (New York: Holmes & Meier, 1992), p. 400.

40. Lenin, *Polnoe sobranie sochinenii*, 54: 189.

41. Ibid., p. 198.

42. Ibid., pp. 265–266.

43. RTsKhIDNI, 76/3/303.

44. Ibid., 2/2/1338.

6. From the Truce to the Great Turning Point

1. A. Livshin, "'Lettres de l'intérieur' à l'époque de la NEP: Les campagnes russes et l'autorité locale," *Communisme*, nos. 42–44 (1995), 45–56; V. Izmozik, "Voices from the Twenties: Private Correspondence Intercepted by the OGPU," *Russian Review* 55 (April 1996), 287–308.

2. Nicolas Werth and Gael Moullec, *Rapports secrets soviétiques, 1921–1991: La société russe dans les documents confidentiels* (Paris: Gallimard, 1994), p. 36.

3. Ibid., p. 105.

4. RTsKhIDNI, 76/3/307/4–15.

5. *Voprosy istorii KPSS*, no. 11 (1988), 42–43.

6. RTsKhIDNI, 76/3/362/1–6.

7. Ibid., 76/3/306. In a letter to Mekhlis, Dzerzhinsky noted the execution of 650 people by his services in 1924 for the republic of Russia alone (ibid., 76/3/362/7–11).

8. *Istoriya sovetskogo gosudarstva i prava* (History of the Soviet state and law) (Moscow, 1968), 2: 580–590.

9. RTsKhIDNI, 76/3/390/3–4.

10. Aleksandr Solzhenitsyn, *The Gulag Archipelago,* trans. Thomas P. Whitney (New York: Harper and Row, 1974); Varlam Shalamov, *Grani,* no. 77 (1972), 42–44; A. Melnik et al., "Materialy k istoriko-geografic heskomu atlasu Solokov" (Documents for a historical-political atlas of the Solovetski), *Zvenya* 1 (1991), 301–330.

11. Alexandre Bennigsen and Chantal Lermercier-Quelquejay, *Les Musulmans oubliés. L'Islam en Union soviétique* (Paris: Maspéro, 1981), pp. 55–59.

12. Ibid., pp. 53–54.

13. Markus Wehner, "Le soulèvement géorgien de 1924 et la réaction des Bolsheviks," *Communisme,* nos. 42–44 (1995), 155–170.

14. "Dokumenty o sobytiakh v Chechnye, 1925" (Documents concerning the events in Chechnya, 1925), *Istochnik,* no. 1 (1995), 140–151.

15. Andrea Graziosi, *The Great Soviet Peasant War: Bolsheviks and Peasants, 1917–1933* (Cambridge, Mass.: Harvard University, Ukrainian Research Institute, 1996), p. 44.

16. Ibid., pp. 44–45.

17. Moshe Lewin, *Russian Peasants and Soviet Power: A Study of Collectivization,* trans. Irene Nove (Evanston: Northwestern University Press, 1968); E. H. Carr and R. W. Davies, *Foundations of a Planned Economy* (London: Pelican, 1974), 1: 71–112.

18. Carr and Davies, *Foundations of a Planned Economy,* pp. 610–642.

19. *Sovetskaya yustitsia,* nos. 24–25 (1930), 2.

20. Werth and Moullec, *Rapports secrets soviétiques,* p. 355.

21. O. Khlevnyuk, *Politbyuro: Mekhanizmy politicheskoi vlasti v 1930-e gody* (The Politburo: Mechanisms of political power in the 1930s) (Moscow: ROSSPEN, 1996), pp. 38–40.

7. Forced Collectivization and Dekulakization

1. N. A. Ivnitskii, *Kollektivizatsiya i raskulachivanie* (Collectivization and dekulakization) (Moscow: Izd-vo Magistr, 1996), pp. 32–49.

2. Ibid., pp. 49–69.

3. Andrea Graziosi, "At the Roots of Soviet Industrial Relations and Practices—Piatokov's Donbass in 1921," *Cahiers du monde russe* 36 (1995), 449.

4. M. Fainsod, *Smolensk under Soviet Rule* (Boston: Unwin Hyman, 1989), pp. 271–277; R. W. Davies, *The Socialist Offensive: The Collectivization of Soviet Agriculture* (Cambridge, Mass.: Harvard University Press, 1980), pp. 243–251.

5. V. P. Danilov and Alexis Berelovich, "Les documents de la VCK—OGPU—NKVD sur la campagne soviétique, 1918–1937," *Cahiers du monde russe* 35 (1994), 671–676.

6. Ibid., p. 674; Andrea Graziosi, "Collectivisation, révoltes paysannes, et politiques gouvernmentales à travers les rapports du GPU d'Ukraine de février–mars 1930," *Cahiers du monde russe* 35 (1994), 437–632.

7. Danilov and Berelovich, "Les documents," pp. 674–676.

8. L. Viola, "Babii bunty" (Peasant women riots), *Russian Review* 45 (1986), 23–42.

9. Graziosi, "Soviet Industrial Relations."

10. Ibid., p. 462; V. P. Popov, "Gosudarstvennyi terror v Sovetskoi Rossii, 1923–1953" (State terror in Soviet Russia, 1923–1953), *Otechestvennye arkhivy*, no. 2 (1992), 28.

11. Ivnitskii, *Kollektivizatsiya i raskulachivanie*, p. 106.

12. Danilov and Berelovich, "Les documents," pp. 665–666.

13. Oleg Khlevnyuk, *Politbyuro: Mekhanizmy politicheskoi vlasti v 1930-e gody* (The Politburo: Mechanisms of political power in the 1930s) (Moscow: ROSSPEN, 1996), p. 37.

14. V. N. Zemskov, "Kulatskaya ssylka v 30-ye gody" (The deportation of the kulaks in the 1930s), *Sotsiologicheskie issledovania*, no.10 (1991), 3–20.

15. Nicolas Werth, "'Déplacés spéciaux' et 'colons du travail' dans la société stalinienne," *XXe siècle*, no. 54 (April–June 1997), 34–50.

16. Ivnitskii, *Kollektivizatsiya i raskulachivanie*, p. 124.

17. Nicolas Werth and Gael Moullec, *Rapports secrets soviétiques, 1921–1991: La société russe dans les documents confidentiels* (Paris: Gallimard, 1994), p. 140.

18. V. P. Danilov and S. A. Krasilnikov, *Spetspereselentsy v Zapadnoi Sibiri* (Special deportees in western Siberia), 3 vols. (Novosibirsk: "EKOR," 1993, 1994), 1: 57–58.

19. Ibid., p. 167.

20. Ibid., 3: 89–99.

21. Zemskov, "Kulatskaya ssylka," pp. 4–5.

22. GARF, 9414/1/1943/56–61, in Werth and Moullec, *Rapports secrets soviétiques*, pp. 142–145.

23. Danilov and Krasilnikov, *Spetspereselentsy v Zapadnoi Sibiri*, 2: 81–83; GARF, 9479/1/7/5–12; Werth and Moullec, *Rapports secrets soviétiques*, pp. 363–374.

24. GARF, 9414/1/1943/52.

25. GARF, 1235/2/776/83–86.

26. Danilov and Krasilnikov, *Spetspereselentsy v Zapadnoi Sibiri*, 3: 244–245.

27. GARF, 374/28s/4055/1–12.

8. The Great Famine

1. A. Blum, *Naître, vivre et mourir en URSS 1917–1991* (Paris: Plon, 1994), p. 99.

2. Quoted in F. Kupferman, *Au pays des Soviets: Le voyage français en Union soviétique 1917–1939* (Paris: Gallimard, 1979), p. 88.

3. Andrea Graziosi, "Lettres de Kharkov: La famine en Ukraine et dans le Caucase du Nord à travers les rapports des diplomates italiens, 1932–1934," *Cahiers du monde russe et soviétique* 30 (1989), 5–106.

4. Moshe Lewin, *The Making of the Soviet System* (London: Methuen, 1985), pp. 206–237.

5. GARF, 1235/2/1521/71–78; Nicolas Werth and Gael Moullec, *Rapports secrets soviétiques, 1921–1991: La société russe dans les documents confidentiels* (Paris: Gallimard, 1994), pp. 152–155.

6. GARF, 3316/2/1254/4–7.

7. N. A. Ivnitskii, *Kollektivizatsiya i raskulachivanie* (Collectivization and dekulalization) (Mosco: Izd-vo Magistr, 1996), pp. 192–193.

8. Ibid., pp. 198–206.

9. V. N. Zemskov, "Kulatskaya ssylka v 30-ye gody" (The deportation of kulaks in the 1930s), *Sotsiologicheskie issledovaniya*, no. 10 (1991), 4–5.

10. Graziosi, "Lettres de Kharkov," p. 51.

11. Ivnitskii, *Kollecktivizatsia i raskulachivanie*, pp. 198–199.

12. Ibid., p. 204.

13. Graziosi, "Lettres de Kharkov," pp. 59–60.

14. Ibid., p. 79. Robert Conquest, *Harvest of Sorrow* (New York: Oxford University Press, 1987), pp. 267–296.

15. Presidential Archives of the Russian Federation, Moscow, 45/1/827/7–22.

16. Ibid., 3/61/549/194.

17. N. Aralovets, "Poteri naseleniya v 30-ye gody" (Demographic losses in the 1930s), *Otechestvennaya istoriya*, no. 1 (1995), 135–145; N. Osokina, "Zhertvy goloda 1933—Skolko ikh?" (The victims of the famine of 1933—How many were there?), *Otechestvennaya Istoria*, no. 5 (1995), 18–26; V. Tsaplin, "Statistika zhertv stalinizma" (Statistics of the victims of Stalinism), *Voprosy istorii*, no. 4 (1989), 175–181.

18. S. Merl, "Golod 1932–1933—Genotsid Ukraintsev dlya osushchestvleniya politiki russifikatsii?" (The famine of 1932–1933: Genocide of the Ukrainians for the realization of the policy of Russification?), *Otechestvennaya istoriya*, no. 1 (1995), 49–61.

9. Socially Foreign Elements and Cycles of Repression

1. Moshe Lewin, *The Making of the Soviet System* (London: Methuen, 1995), pp. 330–334.

2. Oleg Khlevnyuk, *Politbyuro: Mekhanizmy politicheskoi vlasti v 1930-e gody* (The Politburo: Mechanisms of political power in the 1930s) (Moscow: ROSSPEN, 1996), pp. 40–50.

3. Ibid., p. 49.

4. *Pisma I. V. Stalina V. M. Molotovu* (Letter from J. Stalin to V. Molotov) (Moscow: "Rossiia molodaia," 1995), pp. 193–194.

5. S. Ikonnikov, *Sozdanie i deyatelnost obëdinennykh organov TsKK-RKI v 1923–1934* (The creation and the activity of the bureaus of the CCC Worker and Peasant Inspectorate, 1923–1934) (Moscow: Nauka, 1971), pp. 212–214.

6. Sheila Fitzpatrick, *Education and Social Mobility in the Soviet Union, 1921–1934* (New York: Cambridge University Press, 1979), pp. 213–217.

7. N. Timasheff, *Religion in Soviet Russia* (New York: Sheed & Ward, 1942), p. 64.

8. Nicolas Werth, "Le pouvoir soviétique et l'Eglise orthodoxe de la collectivisation à la Constitution de 1936," *Revue d'études comparatives Est-Ouest* nos. 3–4 (1993), 41–49.

9. GARF, 374/28/145/13–26.

10. W. C. Fletcher, *The Russian Orthodox Church Underground, 1917–1970* (New York: Oxford University Press, 1971).

11. Nicolas Werth and Gael Moullec, *Rapports secrets soviétiques 1921–1991: La société russe dans les documents confidentiels* (Paris: Gallimard, 1994), pp. 291–304.

12. A. I. Dobkin, "Lishentsy, 1918–1936" (Those deprived of their civil rights), *Zvenya*, 2 (1992), 600–620.

13. Lewin, *Making of the Soviet System*, pp. 311–317.

14. GARF, 1235/2/1650/27–54.

15. Ibid.

16. GARF, 9479/1/19/7; Werth and Moullec, *Rapports secrets soviétiques*, pp. 43–44.

17. GARF, 9479/1/19/19.

18. V. Danilov and S. A. Krasilnikov, *Spetspereselentsy v Zapadnoi Sibiri*, vol. 3: *1933–1938* (Novosibirsk: "EKOR," 1993), pp. 96–99.

19. RTsKhIDNI, 17/120/94/133–136.

20. Khlevnyuk, *Politbyuro: Mekhanizmy*, pp. 154–156.

21. GARF, 1235/2/2032/15–29.

22. J. A. Getty, G. T. Rittersporn, and V. N. Zemskov, "Les victimes de la répression pénale dans l'URSS d'avant-guerre," *Revue des études slaves* 65 (1993), 641.

23. Andrea Graziosi, "Lettres de Kharkov: La famine en Ukraine et dans le Caucase du Nord à travers les rapports des diplomates italiens, 1932–1934," *Cahiers du monde russe et soviétique* 30 (1989), 77.

24. RTsKhIDNI, 17/3/922/56–58.

25. V. P. Popov, "Gosudarstvenniy terror v Sovetskoi Rossii, 1923–1953" (State terror in Soviet Russia, 1923–1953), *Otechestvennye arkhivy*, no. 2 (1992), 28.

26. Alla Kirilina, *L'assassinat de Kirilov. Destin d'un stalinien 1888–1934* (Paris: Seuil, 1995).

27. Robert Conquest, *The Great Terror: Stalin's Purge of the Thirties*, rev. ed. (New York: Oxford University Press, 1990), pp. 429–430.

28. Khlevnyuk, *Politbyuro: Mekhanizmy*, pp. 150–154.

29. Ibid., p. 158.

30. Ibid., pp. 156–159. On this campaign see also J. A. Getty, *Origins of the Great Purges: The Soviet Communist Party Reconsidered, 1933–1938* (New York: Cambridge University Press, 1985); RTsKhIDNI, 17/120/240.

31. RTsKhIDNI, 17/162/17; Khlevnyuk, *Politbyuro: Mekhanizmy*, p. 154; Werth and Moullec, *Rapports secrets soviétiques*, pp. 376–377.

10. The Great Terror (1936–1938)

1. Quoted in Nicolas Werth, *Les procès de Moscou 1936–1938* (Brussels: Complexe, 1987), p. 61.

2. Robert Conquest, *The Great Terror: Stalin's Purge of the Thirties*, rev. ed. (New York: Oxford University Press, 1990).

3. J. A. Getty, *Origins of the Great Purges: The Soviet Communist Party Reconsid-*

ered, 1933–1938 (New York: Cambridge University Press, 1985); G. Rittersporn, *Stalinist Simplifications and Soviet Complications: Social Tensions and Political Conflicts in the USSR, 1933–1953* (New York: Harwood Academic, 1991); J. A. Getty and R. T. Manning, eds., *Stalinist Terror: New Perspectives* (New York: Cambridge University Press, 1993).

4. *Stalinskoe Politburo v 30-ye gody* (The Stalinist Politburo in the 1930s), a collection of documents assembled by O. V. Khlevnyuk, A. V. Kvashonkin, L. P. Kosheleva, and L. A. Rogovaya (Moscow: AIRD, 1995); O. V. Khlevnyuk, L. P. Kosheleva, J. Howlett, and L. Rogovaya, "Les sources archivistiques des organes dirigeants du PC(b)R," *Communisme*, nos. 42–44 (1995), 15–34.

5. *Trud*, 4 June 1992.

6. GARF, 9479/1/978/32.

7. *Trud*, 4 June 1992.

8. Oleg Khlevnyuk, *Politbyuro: Mekhanizmy politicheskoi vlasti v 1930-e gody* (The Politburo: Mechanisms of political power in the 1930s) (Moscow: ROSSPEN, 1996), pp. 208–210.

9. Ibid., p. 212.

10. *Reabilitatsiya. Politicheskie protsessy 30–50 godov* (Rehabilitation: The political trials of the years 1930–1950) (Moscow: Navka, 1991), p. 39; *Istochnik*, no. 1 (1995), 117–130.

11. *Izvestiya*, 10 June 1992, p. 2.

12. Stalin's work diary and the list of his visitors at the Kremlin for 1936 and 1937 were published in *Istoricheskii arkhiv*, no. 4 (1995), 15–73.

13. *Istochnik*, no. 1 (1995), 117–132; V. P. Popov, "Gosudarstvenniy terror v Sovetskoi Rossii, 1923–1953" (State terror in Soviet Russia, 1923–1953), *Otechestvennye arkhivy*, no. 2 (1992), 20–31.

14. J. A. Getty, G. T. Rittersporn, and V. N. Zemskov, "Les victimes de la répression pénale dans l'URSS d'avant-guerre," *Revue des études slaves* 65 (1993), 631–663.

15. Ibid., p. 655.

16. V. N. Zemskov, "Gulag," *Sotsialogicheskie issledovaniya*, no. 6 (1991), 14–15.

17. *Leningradsky martirolog 1937–1938* (List of Leningrad martyrs, 1937–1938) (St. Petersburg: Akademiya, 1995). For statistics on executions see pp. 3–50.

18. RTsKhIDNI, 17/120/285/24–37.

19. Conquest, *The Great Terror*, pp. 918–921.

20. Ibid., pp. 886–912.

21. *Volia*, nos. 2–3 (1994), 45–46.

22. A. Cristiani and V. Mikhaleva, eds., *Le repressioni degli anni trenta nell'Armata rossa*, a collection of documents (Naples: Istituto universitario orientale, 1996).

23. Ibid., pp. 20 ff.

24. Conquest, *The Great Terror*, pp. 749–772; Vitalii Shentalinskii, *The KGB's Literary Archive* (London: Harvill Press, 1995).

25. M. I. Odinsov, *Na puti k svobode sovesti* (On the path to freedom of conscience) (Moscow: Progress, 1989), pp. 53–54.

26. GARF, 3316/2/1615/116–149.

11. The Empire of the Camps

1. J. A. Getty, G. T. Rittersporn, and V. N. Zemskov, "Les victimes de la répression pénale dans l'URSS d'avant-guerre," *Revue des études slaves* 65 (1993), 631–663; Nicolas Werth, "Goulag, les vrais chiffres"; Alec Nove, "Victims of Stalinism, How Many?" in *Stalinist Terror: New Perspectives,* ed. J. A. Getty and R. T. Manning (New York: Cambridge University Press, 1993).

2. See V. P. Popov, "Gosudarstvenniy terror v Sovetkoi Rossii, 1923–1953" (State terror in Soviet Russia, 1923–1953), *Otechestvennye arkhivy,* no. 2 (1992), 20–31.

3. V. N. Zemskov, "Gulag," *Sotsiologicheskie issledovaniya,* no. 6 (1991), 11.

4. Oleg Khlevnyuk, "Prinuditelniy trud v ekonomike SSSR, 1929–1941" (Forced labor in the U.S.S.R. economy), *Svobodnaia mysl,* no. 13 (1992), 78–92.

5. Nicolas Werth and Gael Moullec, *Rapports secrets soviétiques, 1921–1991: La société russe dans les documents confidentiels* (Paris: Gallimard, 1994), pp. 345–379.

6. Zemskov, "Gulag," pp. 11–15.

7. Khlevnyuk, "Prinuditelniy trud," pp. 88–89.

8. Getty, Rittersporn, and Zemskov, "Les victimes de la répression," pp. 650–657.

9. These calculations are based principally on the works quoted above, notably Getty, Rittersporn, and Zemskov, "Les victimes de la répression"; Zemskov, "Gulag"; Werth, "Goulag, les vrais chiffres"; Popov, "Gosudarstvenniy terror"; Khlevnyuk, "Prinuditelniy trud," *Istochnik,* no. 1 (1995), 117–130; A. Blum, *Naître, vivre, et mourir en URSS 1917–1991* (Paris: Plon, 1994).

10. Keith Sword, *Deportation and Exile: Poles in the Soviet Union, 1939–1948* (Basingstoke: Macmillan Press in association with School of Slavonic and East European Studies, University of London; New York: St. Martin's Press, 1994), p. 7.

11. V. N. Zemskov, "Massivnoe osvobozhdenie spetzposelentsev i ssylnykh" (The large-scale freeing of special dispaced and exiled people), *Sotsiologicheskie issledovaniya,* no. 1 (1991), 5.

12. Z. S. Siemaszko, *W sowieckim osaczeniu* (In Soviet surroundings) (London: Polska Fundacja Kulturalna, 1991); Władysław Wielhorski, *Los Polaków w Niewoli Sowieckiej* (The fate of Poles in Soviet captivity) (London, 1956).

13. Sword, *Deportation and Exile,* pp. 15–23.

14. GARF, 9401/1/4475.

15. Zemskov, "Gulag," p. 19.

16. GARF, 9492/2/42/125.

17. GARF, 9492/2/42.

18. Werth and Moullec, *Rapports secrets soviétiques,* p. 229.

19. *Istochnik,* no. 3 (1994), 107–112.

20. *Moskva voennaya: Memuary i arkhivnye dokumenty* (Moscow at war: Memoirs and archive documents) (Moscow: Izdatel'stvo ob'edineniya Mosgorarkhiv, 1995).

21. RTsKhIDNI, 17/88/45.

12. The Other Side of Victory

1. N. F. Bugai, *L. Beria–I. Stalinu, "Soglasno vashemu ukazaniu"* (L. Beria to

J. Stalin, "In accordance with your instructions") (Moscow: AIRO XX, 1995), pp. 27–55; idem, *40-ye gody: "Avtonomiu Nemtsev Povolzhe likvidirovat"* (The 1940s: "Liquidate the Autonomous Territory of Volga Germans"), *Istoriya SSSR*, no. 2 (1991), 172–182; J.-J. Marie, *Les peuples déportés d'Union soviétique* (Brussels: Complexe, 1995), pp. 35–56.

2. Bugai, *L. Beria–I. Stalinu*, pp. 56–220; V. N. Zemskov, "Gulag," *Sotsiologicheskie issledovaniya*, no. 6 (1991), 8–17; M. Guboglo and A. Kuznetsov, eds., *Deportatsii narodov SSSR 1930ye–1950ye gody* (The deportation of the peoples of the U.S.S.R., 1930s–1950s) (Moscow: Rossiya molodaya, 1992); Marie, *Les peuples déportés*, pp. 57–128.

3. Bugai, *L. Beria–I. Stalinu*, p. 153.

4. Marie, *Les peuples déportés*, pp. 81–82.

5. Ibid., p. 103.

6. Ibid., p. 66.

7. Ibid., pp. 64–65.

8. Zemskov, "Gulag," p. 9.

9. Quoted in Bugai, *L. Beria–I. Stalinu*, pp. 153–156.

10. Marie, *Les peuples déportés*, pp. 107–108.

11. Zemskov, "Gulag," p. 9.

12. V. N. Zemskov, "Kulatskaya ssylka nakanune i v gody Velikoi Otechestvennoi voiny" (The kulak deportations on the eve of and during the Great Patriotic War), *Sotsiologicheskie issledovaniya*, no. 2 (1992), 3–26.

13. GARF, 9414/1/330/56–62.

14. Nicolas Werth and Gael Moullec, *Rapports secrets soviétiques, 1921–1991: La société russe dans les documents confidentiels* (Paris: Gallimard, 1994), pp. 379–391; Edwin Bacon, *The Gulag at War: Stalin's Forced Labor System in the Light of the Archives* (Basingstoke: Macmillan in association with the Centre for Russian and East European Studies, University of Birmingham, 1994).

15. Zemskov, "Gulag," pp. 14–15.

16. The passage is underlined in pencil, and in the margin is written: "Why were they also brought to the destination?"

17. Section 10 of Article 58, which punished all "counterrevolutionary crimes," referred to "propaganda or incitement calling for destruction or the weakening of the Soviet regime." In cases of "group propaganda," which were extremely common, punishments ranged from three years' imprisonment to the death sentence.

18. Another passage underlined in pencil, with a note in the margin: "These people must be tried again, or sent before the OS" (the NKVD Special Board, an extrajudicial body whose task was to deal with "counterrevolutionary crimes").

19. Bacon, *The Gulag at War*.

20. J. Rossi, *Spravochnik po Gulag* (The Gulag handbook) (Moscow: "Prosvet," 1991); see the articles on special camps and convict prisons.

21. GARF, 9414\1\68\1–61, quoted in *Istoricheskii arkhiv*, no. 3 (1994), 61–86.

22. GARF, 9414\1\330\56–62.

23. Zemskov, "Gulag," p. 4.

24. *Sotsiologicheskie issledovaniya*, no. 7 (1991), 4–5.

25. Guboglo and Kuznetsov, *Deportatsii narodov*, p. 162.

13. Apogee and Crisis in the Gulag System

1. Elena Zubkova, *Obshchestvo i reformy, 1945–1964* (Society and reforms, 1945–1964) (Moscow: Rossiya molodaya, 1993), pp. 16–44.

2. V. F. Zima, "Poslevoennoe obshchestvo: Prestupnost i golod, 1946–1947" (Postwar society: Crime and famine, 1946–1947), *Otechestvennaya istoriya*, no. 5 (1995), 45–58.

3. V. P. Popov, "Golod i gosudarstvennaya politika, 1946–1947" (Famine and state policy, 1946–1947), *Otechestvennye arkhivy*, no.6 (1992), 36–60; Nicolas Werth and Gael Moullec, *Rapports secrets soviétiques, 1921–1991: La société russe dans les documents confidentiels* (Paris: Gallimard. 1994), pp. 162–165.

4. V. P. Popov, "Gosudarstvennyi terror v Sovetskoi Rossii, 1923–1953" (State terror in Soviet Russia, 1923–1953), *Otechestvennye arkhivy*, no. 2 (1992), 27.

5. V. N. Zemskov, "Gulag," *Sotsialogicheskie issledovania*, no. 6 (1991), 10–11.

6. Popov, "Gosudarstvennyi terror," p. 27.

7. Zemskov, "Gulag," p. 11.

8. Zima, "Poslevoennoe obshchestvo," pp. 45–58; Zubkova, *Obshchestvo i reformy*, pp. 63–69.

9. J.-J. Marie, *Les peuples déportés d'Union soviétique* (Brussels: Complexe, 1995), p. 124.

10. Ibid., pp. 122–126.

11. N. F. Bugai, *L. Beria–J. Stalinu*, "Soglasno vashemu ukazaniu" (L. Beria to J. Stalin, "In accordance with your instructions") (Moscow: AIRO XX, 1995), p. 232.

12. V. I. Tsaranov, "O likvidatsii kulachestva v Moldavii letom 1949" (On the liquidation of kulaks in Moldavia in the summer of 1949), *Otechestvennaya istoriya*, no. 2 (1996), 71–79; Marie, *Les peuples déportés*, pp. 127–128.

13. Yaroslav Bilinsky, *The Second Soviet Republic: The Ukraine after World War II* (New Brunswick, N.J.: Rutgers University Press, 1960), pp. 132–135.

14. O. L. Milova et al., eds., *Deportatsii narodov SSSR 1930ye–1950ye gody* (The deportation of the peoples of the U.S.S.R., 1930s–1950s) (Moscow: Rossiya molodaya, 1992), p. 160.

15. GARF, 9414/1s/1391–1392.

16. M. Craveri and N. Formozov, "La résistance au Goulag. Grèves, révoltes, évasions dans les camps de travail soviétiques de 1920 à 1956," *Communisme*, nos. 42–44 (1995), 197–209.

17. GARF, 9414/1s/513/185.

18. GARF, 9414/1s/642/60–91; Nicolas Werth, "L'ensemble concentrationnaire de Norilsk en 1951," *XXe siècle*, no. 47 (July–September 1994), 88–100.

19. M. Craveri and O. Khlevnyuk, "Krizis ekonomiki MVD" (The economic crisis of the MVD), *Cahiers du monde russe* 36 (1995), 179–190.

14. The Last Conspiracy

1. Gennadii Kostyrchenko and Shimon Redlikh, *Evreiskii Antifashistskii Komitet v SSSR: Sbornik dokumentov* (The Jewish Anti-Fascist Committee in the U.S.S.R.: A

collection of documents) (Moscow: Mezhdunarodnye otnosheniya, 1996); Gennadii Kostyrchenko, *V plenu u krasnogo faraona* (Inside the prisons of the Red pharaohs) (Moscow, 1994); Amy Knight, *Beria, Stalin's First Lieutenant* (Princeton: Princeton University Press, 1993); J.-J. Marie, *Les derniers complots de Staline: L'affaire des Blouses blanches* (Brussels: Complexe, 1993).

2. Kostyrchenko, *V plenu u krasnogo faraona*, pp. 45–47.

3. Ibid.

4. *Izvestiya KPSS*, 12 (1989), 37.

5. Kostyrchenko and Redlikh, *Evreiskii Antifashistkii Komitet*, pp. 326–384.

6. Marie, *Les derniers complots de Staline*, pp. 60–61.

7. Kostyrchenko, *V plenu u krasnogo faraona*, pp. 136–137.

8. V. I. Demidov and V. A. Kutuzov, *Leningradskoie Delo* (The Leningrad Affair) (Leningrad, 1990), pp. 38–90.

9. Ibid., pp. 139–151; Marie, *Les derniers complots de Staline*, pp. 77–99.

10. Marie, *Les derniers complots de Staline*, pp. 90–91.

11. Knight, *Beria*, pp. 239–247.

12. Pavel Sudoplatov and Anatoly Sudoplatov, *Special Tasks: The Memoirs of an Unwanted Witness, A Soviet Spymaster* (Boston: Little, Brown, 1994) pp. 385–434; Kostyrchenko, *V plenu u krasnogo faraona*, pp. 289–314.

13. V. P. Naumov, ed., *Nepravednyi sud. Stenogramma sudebnogo protsessa nad chlenami Evreiskogo Antifashistskogo Komiteta: Posledni stalinskii—rasstrel* (Court of Injustice: The final Stalinist execution—stenogram of the trial of members of the Jewish Anti-Fascist Committee) (Moscow: "Nauka," 1994).

14. Marie, *Les derniers complots de Staline*, p. 159; Sudoplatov and Sudoplatov, *Special Tasks*, pp. 424–426.

15. Yakov Rapoport, *Souvenirs du procès des Blouses blanches* (Paris: Alinéa, 1989), pp. 140–141.

15. The Exit from Stalinism

1. *Istochnik*, no. 1 (1994), 106–111; *Izvestiya TsK*, no. 1 (1991), 139–214; no. 2 (1991), 141–208.

2. Amy Knight, *Beria, Stalin's First Lieutenant* (Princeton: Princeton University Press, 1993), p. 276.

3. M. Craveri and N. Formozov, "La résistance au Goulag," *Communisme*, nos. 42–44 (1995), 197–209.

4. V. N. Zemskov, "Massivnoe osvobozhdenie spetzposelentsev i ssylnykh" (The mass release of specially displaced and exiled people), *Sotsiologicheskie issledovaniya*, no. 1 (1991), 5–26.

5. J.-J. Marie, *Les derniers complots de Staline: L'affaire des Blouses blanches* (Brussels: Complexe, 1993), pp. 120 ff.

6. Zemskov, "Massivnoe osvobozhdenie," p. 14.

7. Nicolas Werth and Gael Moullec, *Rapports secrets soviétiques, 1921–1991: La société russe dans les documents confidentiels* (Paris: Gallilmard, 1994), pp. 501–503.

8. Liudmila Alexeeva, *Soviet Dissent: Contemporary Movements for National, Relig-*

ious, and Human Rights (Middletown, Conn.: Wesleyan University Press, 1985). This is the most complete synthesis of dissident movements, and the source of most of the data provided here.

16. The Comintern in Action

1. In his last article in *Die Rote Fahne* (The Red flag) Liebknecht gave full vent to his lyrical revolutionary fervor: "To the thunder of the economic collapse that is coming, the still sleeping army of the proletariat will awake as though in answer to the trumpets of the Last Judgment, and the bodies of the fallen will arise again . . ."

2. Arthur Koestler saw in this one of the main reasons for the success of the Hungarian Commune, which according to him "was the direct consequence of the policies pursued by the West, when the great democracies turned their backs on their liberal allies"; *La corde raide* (Paris: Robert Laffont, 1994), p. 78.

3. Ibid.

4. Miklós Molnar, *From Béla Kun to János Kádár: Seventy Years of Hungarian Communism* (New York: St. Martin's Press, 1990); Arpád Szepal, *Les 133 jours de Béla Kun* (Paris: Fayard, 1959).

5. Jan Valtin, *Sans patrie ni frontières* (Paris: Self, 1947). See also Eric Wollenberg, *Der Apparat. Stalins fünfte Kolonne* (Bonn: Bundesministerium für Gesamtdeutsche Fragen, 1951).

6. Quoted in Henri de Chambon, *La République d'Estonie* (Paris: Editions de la Revue Parlementaire, 1936).

7. Joseph Berger, *Shipwreck of a Generation: The Memoirs of Joseph Berger* (London: Harvill Press, 1971).

8. Viktor Serge, *Memoirs of a Revolutionary, 1901–1941*, trans. Peter Sedgewick (New York: Oxford University Press, 1967); Arkadi Vaksberg, *Hôtel Lux* (Paris: Fayard, 1993).

9. Margaret Buber-Neumann, *La révolution mondiale* (Paris: Casterman, 1971), chap. 17, "La soulèvement de Canton."

10. Chao-Iuy, *La Commune de Canton* (Moscow: Politizdat, 1929).

11. On this see Valtin, *Sans patrie* (heavily abridged by Babel in 1996), esp. chap. 17.

12. In the book the Tallinn insurrection was analyzed by General Josif Unshlikht, the Hamburg uprisings by Hans Kippenberger, the Canton and Shanghai uprisings by General Vasily Blücher and Ho Chi Minh, who also wrote about peasant uprisings. There were also two chapters on military theory by Marshal Tukhachevsky.

13. Roger Faligot and Rémi Kauffer, *The Chinese Secret Service,* trans. Christine Donougher (London: Headline, 1989).

14. See *Le contrat social,* no. 4 (July–August 1966), 253.

15. Roger Faligot and Rémi Kauffer, *Histoire mondiale du renseignement,* vol. 1: *1870–1939* (Paris: Robert Laffont, 1993).

16. *Un crime soviétique devant la cour d'assises de la Seine (5–14 décembre 1938): L'enlèvement du général Miller par le général Sklobline. Le procès de la Plevitzkaïa. Plaidoirie de Me Maurice Ribet* (Paris: Imprimerie du Palais, 1939); Marina Grey, *Le général meurt à minuit* (Paris: Plon, 1981); Marina Gorboff, *La Russie fantôme: L'émigration*

russe de 1920 à 1950 (Paris: L'Age d'Homme, 1995); Pavel Sudoplatov and Anatoly Sudoplatov, *Special Tasks: The Memoirs of an Unwanted Witness, a Soviet Spymaster* (Boston: Little, Brown, 1994).

17. V. I. Lenin, *Polnoe sobranie sochinenii* (Complete collected works) (Moscow: Politizdat, 1957), 17: 137–138.

18. Aino Kuusinen, *The Rings of Destiny: Inside Soviet Russia from Lenin to Brezhnev*, trans. Paul Stevenson (New York: Morrow, 1974).

19. Leonard Schapiro, *The Origin of the Communist Autocracy: Political Opposition in the Soviet State* (Cambridge, Mass.: Harvard University Press, 1955); and Pierre Broué, *Le Parti bolchevique* (Paris: Editions de Minuit, 1977).

20. See Ante Ciliga, *Dix ans au pays du mensonge déconcertant* (Paris: Champ Libre, 1977); Philippe Bourrinet, *Ante Ciliga 1898–1992. Nazionalisme e communismo in Jugoslavia* (Genoa: Graphos, 1996).

21. Ante Ciliga, *The Russian Enigma* (London: Routledge and Sons, 1940), pp. 167, 168.

22. José Bullejos, *La Comintern en España* (Mexico: Impresiones Modernas, 1972), p. 206.

23. Quoted in Jean Malaquais, *Le nommé Aragon ou le patriote professionel*, supplement to *Masses*, February 1947.

24. Guillaume Bourgeois, "Comment Stalin dirigeait le PC," *Le nouvel observateur*, 5–11 August 1993; Vaksberg, *Hôtel Lux*, pp. 62–64; Annie Kriegel and Stéphane Courtois, *Eugen Fried. Le grand secret du PCF* (Paris: Seuil, 1997), chap. 13.

25. Elizaveta Poretskaya, *Les nôtres*, 2d ed. (Paris: Denoël, 1995).

26. Inventory no. 1 of blacklists 1–8, n.d.

27. Quoted in Vaksberg, *Hôtel Lux*, p. 32. In a letter to the Russian Opposition in November 1927 Boris Suvarin had tried to draw attention to this phenomenon and its consequences. See Boris Souvarine, *A contre-courant: Ecrits, 1925–1939* (Paris: Denoël, 1984), pp. 138–147.

28. Kriegel and Courtois, *Eugen Fried*, p. 293.

29. Quoted in Vaksberg, *Hôtel Lux*, pp. 46–47.

30. Alla Kirilina, *L'assassinat de Kirov: Destin d'un stalinien, 1888–1934* (Paris: Seuil, 1995).

31. Berger, *Shipwreck*, pp. 97–98.

32. *Cahiers Léon Trotski*, no. 53 (April 1994).

33. *Le contrat social*, no. 6 (November–December 1965).

34. Alfred Burmeister, *Dissolution and Aftermath of the Comintern: Experiences and Observations, 1937–1947* (New York: NYU Press, 1995), pp. 4–8.

35. Mikhail Panteleev, "La terreur stalinienne au Komintern en 1937–1938: Les chiffres et les causes," *Communisme*, nos. 40–41 (1995).

36. François Fejtö, "Comment Staline liquida Béla Kun," *France observateur*, 9 April 1959. Fejtö bases this account on the memoirs of Arvo Tuominen, *The Bells of the Kremlin: An Experience in Communism* (Hanover, N.H.: University Press of New England, 1983).

37. Panteleev, "La terreur stalinienne," p. 48.

38. *La correspondance internationale*, no. 15 (12 March 1938).

39. *In der fangen des NKWD. Deutscher Opfer des stalinistchen Terrors in des UdSSR* (Berlin: Dietz Verlag, 1991).

40. Margaret Buber-Neumann, *Under Two Dictators*, trans. Edward Fitzgerald (New York: Dodd, Mead, 1950).

41. Alexander Weissberg, *The Accused*, trans. Edward Fitzgerald (New York: Simon and Schuster, 1951).

42. Margaret Buber-Neumann, "Déposition au procès Kravchenko contre *Les lettres françaises* 14e audience, 23 fevrier 1949. Compte rendu sténographique," *La jeune parque*, 1949.

43. Mario Kessler, "Der Stalinische Terror gegen jüdische Kommunisten," in *Kommunisten verfolgen Kommunisten: Stalinischer Terror und "Säuberungen" in den kommunistischen Parteien Europas seit des dreissiger Jahren* (Berlin: Akademie Verlag, 1993), pp. 87–102. For the full history of Birobidzhan, see Henri Slovès, *L'état juif de l'Union soviétique* (Paris: Les Presses d'Aujourd'hui, 1982).

44. On the Reiss affair, see the memoirs of his wife, Elizaveta Poretskaya, *Les nôtres*; and Peter Hubr and Daniel Kunzi, "L'assassinat d'Ignaz Reiss," *Communisme*, nos. 26–27 (1990).

45. Jan Van Heijenoort, *De Prinkipo à Coyoacan: Sept ans auprès de L. Trotski* (Paris: Maurice Nadeau, 1978), p. 172.

46. See Pierre Broué, *Léon Sedov, fils de Trotski, victime de Staline* (Paris: Les Editions Ouvrières, 1993); and Sudoplatov and Sudoplatov, *Special Tasks*, pp. 115–116.

47. Sudoplatov and Sudoplatov, *Special Tasks*, pp. 99–100.

48. Leon Trotsky, *Oeuvres complètes*, vol. 24 (Paris: Institut Léon-Trotski, 1987), pp. 79–82.

49. Leon Trotsky, "L'attentat du 24 mai et le Parti communiste mexicain, le Komintern et le GPU," ibid., pp. 310–361.

50. For the details of the operation, see Sudoplatov and Sudoplatov, *Special Tasks*, pp. 97–120.

51. Julian Gorkin and General Sanchez Salazar, *Ainsi fut assassiné Trotski* (Paris: Self, 1948).

52. René Dazy, *Fusillez les chiens enragés! Le génocide collectif des trotskistes* (Paris: Olivier Orban, 1981), p. 248.

53. Recently Pierre Broué and Raymond Vacheron, *Meurtres au maquis* (Paris: Grasset, 1997), put forward the somewhat dubious idea that Demazière's involuntary escape was the main reason for the execution of his companions, thus excusing the behavior of the French Communists who were behind the killings.

54. Dazy, *Fusillez les chiens enragés!* pp. 238–244.

55. Rodolphe Prager, "Les trotskistes de Buchenwald," *Critique communiste*, no. 25 (November 1978).

56. Dazy, *Fusillez les chiens enragés!* pp. 266–274.

57. Panagiotis Noutsos, "'Säuberugen' innerhalb der griechischer KP (1931 bis 1956)," in *Kommunisten verfolgen Kommunisten*, pp. 487–494.

58. Ho Chi Minh, letter of 10 May 1939, *Cahiers Léon Trotski*, no. 46 (July 1991).

59. *Action*, 19–25 June 1950.

60. Kuusinen, *Rings of Destiny*, pp. 94–97.

61. Tuominen, *The Bells of the Kremlin*, quoted in B. Lazich, "Le martyrologe du Komintern," *Le contrat social*, no. 6 (November–December 1965).

62. Armand Maloumian, *Les fils du Goulag* (Paris: Presses de la Cité, 1976).

63. Vasily Grossman, *Life and Fate* (London: Collins Harvill, 1985), p. 301.

64. Romolo Caccavale, *Communisti italiani in Unione sovietica: Proscritti da Mussolini soppressi da Stalin* (Rome: Mursia, 1995).

65. Charles Jacquier, "L'affaire Francesco Ghezzi: La vie et la mort d'un anarcho-syndicaliste italien en URSS," *La nouvelle alternative*, no. 34 (June 1994). See also Emilio Guaraschelli, *Une petite pierre. L'exil, la déportation et la mort d'un ouvrier communiste italien in URSS 1933–1939* (Maspéro, 1979); Etienne Manach, *Emilio: Récit à voix basse* (Paris: Plon, 1990).

66. Hans Schafranek, *Zwischen NKVD und Gestapo: Die Auslieferung deutscher und österreichischer Antifaschisten aus der Sowjetunion an Nazideutschland 1937–1941* (Frankfurt am Main: ISP Verlag, 1990).

67. *Les syndicats de l'Union soviétique* (Paris: Editions du Secours Ouvrier International, 1935).

68. Schafranek, *Zwischen NKVD und Gestapo*.

69. Karlo Štajner, *7,000 jours en Sibérie* (Paris: Gallimard, 1983).

70. Wolfgang Leonhard, *Child of the Revolution*, trans. C. M. Woodhouse (Chicago: H. Regnery, 1958).

71. Božidar Maslarić, *Moskva–Madrid–Moskva* (Zagreb: Tidens, 1952).

72. Gustaw Herling, *Un monde à part* (Paris: Denoël, 1985).

73. Sylvestre Mora and Pierre Zwierniak, *La justice soviétique* (Rome: Magi-Spinetti, 1945), pp. 161–162.

74. Israel Joshua Singer, *Camrade Nachman* (Paris: Stock, 1985).

75. Jules Margoline, *La condition inhumaine: Cinq ans dans les camps de concentration soviétiques* (Paris: Calmann-Levy, 1949), pp. 42–43.

76. Ibid., pp. 149–150.

77. Lukasz Hirszowicz, "NKVD Documents Shed New Light on Fate of Erlich and Alter," *East European Jewish Affairs*, no. 2 (Winter 1992).

78. Jacques Pat, *Jewish Daily Forward*, 30 June and 7 July 1946.

79. Quoted in Georges Coudry, *Les camps soviétiques en France: Les "Russes" livrés à Staline en 1945* (Paris: Albin Michel, 1997).

80. "Nous réclamons le droit d'asile pour les émigrés soviétiques," *Masses*, nos. 9–10 (June–July 1947).

81. Nicholas Bethell, *The Last Secret: The Delivery to Stalin of Over Two Million Russians by Britain and the United States* (New York: Basic Books, 1974); Nikolai Tolstoy, *Victims of Yalta* (London: Hodder and Stoughton, 1977).

82. Pierre Rigoulet, *La tragédie de Malgré-nous: Tambov le camp des Français* (Paris: Denoël, 1990).

83. Vladimir Dedijer, *Tito* (New York: Simon and Schuster, 1953).

84. Milovan Djilas, *Wartime*, trans. Michael Petrovich (New York: Harcourt Brace Jovanovich, 1977), p. 168.

85. Paul Garde, *Vie et mort de la Yougoslavie* (Paris: Fayard, 1992).

86. Djilas, *Wartime*, pp. 452–453.

87. Dobrica Ćosić's huge novel, *Le temps du mal,* 2 vols. (Paris: L'Age d'Homme, 1990), gives a good idea of the extraordinary complexity of the situation in Yugoslavia.

88. Christophe Chiclet, *Les Communistes grecs dans la guerre. Histoire du Parti communiste de Grèce de 1941 à 1949* (Paris: L'Harmattan, 1987).

89. The ELAS falsely accused the EDES of having signed an agreement with the Germans.

90. Quoted in Evangelos Averoff Tossizza, *By Fire and Axe: The Communist Party and the Civil War in Greece, 1944–1949,* trans. Sarah Arnold Rigos (New Rochelle, N.Y.: Caratzas Brothers, 1978). The author seems to have known the leader well, from his student days to his time as a lawyer in Athens.

91. In April the Democratic Army numbered 16,000 freedom fighters.

92. Irène Lagani, "Les Communistes des Balkans et la guerre civile grecque," *Communisme,* no. 9 (1986).

93. Nikos Marantzidis, "La deuxième mort de Nikos Zachariadis: L'itinéraire d'un chef communiste," *Communisme,* nos. 29–31, (1992).

94. UN Special Commission on the Balkans, *The Greek Question at the UN General Assembly* (New York: United Nations, 1950).

95. Philippe Buton, "L'entretien entre Maurice Thorez et Joseph Staline du 19 novembre 1994: Méthodologie et historiographie de la stratégie communiste à la Libération," *Communisme,* nos. 45–46 (1996).

96. Torgrim Titlestad, *I Stalins skygge: Om korleis ein politisk leiar byggjer og taper makt—Peder Furubotn, NKP og SVKP, 1945–1948* (Bergen: Fagbokforlaget, 1997).

97. Federigo Argentieri, "Quando il PCI comdamno a morte Nagy," *Micromega,* no. 4 (1992).

17. The Shadow of the NKVD in Spain

1. These statistics, from the General Directorate of the Security Services, were given to the Spanish parliament by Miguel Maura, the former minister of internal affairs, in the autumn of 1934; see Joaquin Maurin, *Révolution et contre-révolution en Espagne* (Paris: Editions Rieder, 1937). For the relative strengths of the parties, see Gerald Brenan, *Le labyrinthe espagnol. Origines sociales et politiques de la guerre civile* (Paris: Champ Libre, 1984).

2. Léon Blum signed this pact much against his will, under pressure from Britain and from French radicals who feared war with Germany. Blum almost resigned over the affair but was dissuaded from doing so by the Spanish ambassador.

3. M. Ercoli (Palmiro Togliatti), *The Spanish Revolution* (New York: Workers' Library, 1936).

4. Dolores Ibarruri, *Speeches and Articles, 1936–1938* (London: Lawrence & Wishart, 1938).

5. Jef Last, *Lettres d'Espagne* (Paris: Gallimard, 1939).

6. Julian Gorkin, *España, primer ensayo de democracía popular* (Buenos Aires, 1961).

7. Antonio Elorza, "Le Front populaire espagnol à travers les archives du Komin-

tern," in *Une histoire en révolution? Du bon usage des archives, de Moscou et d'ailleurs* (Dijon: Editions Universitaires de Dijon, 1996), pp. 253–278.

8. His son, a historian, declared on Catalan television that "most of the people who were posted to Spain—soldiers, generals, advisers, pilots, and others—were NKVD agents." See the 1992 film by Llibert Ferri and Dolorès Genovès, *Opération Nikolaï.*

9. "Spain was a sort of children's playground, where we perfected many of our later espionage techniques"; Pavel Sudoplatov and Anatoly Sudoplatov, *Special Tasks: The Memoirs of an Unwanted Witness, a Soviet Spymaster* (Boston: Little, Brown, 1994), p. 59.

10. Patrik von zur Mühlen, *Spanien war ihre Hoffnung. Die deutsche Linke im spanischen Bürgerkrieg, 1936 bis 1939* (Bonn: Verlag Neue Gesellschaft, 1983).

11. Julian Gorkin, *Les Communistes contre la révolution espagnole* (Paris: Belfond, 1978), pp. 18–19, 81–82.

12. Elorza, "Le Front populaire," p. 265.

13. See especially *L'humanité*, 24 January 1937.

14. Elorza, "Le Front populaire," p. 266.

15. Gorkin, *Les Communistes*, p. 96.

16. See also the film by Llibert Ferri and Dolorès Genovès, *Opération Nikolaï.*

17. Quoted in Gorkin, *Les Communistes*, p. 181.

18. *Los antros del terror stalinista*, a clandestine brochure put out by the POUM, quoted in Gorkin, *Les Communistes.*

19. Gorkin, *Les Communistes*, p. 205.

20. Katia Landau, *Le Stalinisme bourreau de la révolution espagnole* (Paris: Spartacus, 1938), p. 8.

21. Burnett Bolloten, *The Spanish Revolution: The Left and the Struggle for Power during the Civil War* (Chapel Hill: University of North Carolina Press, 1979), p. 506.

22. Cézar M. Lorenzo, *Les anarchistes espagnols et le pouvoir, 1869–1969* (Paris: Seuil, 1969). Lorenzo indicates that the freedom fighters were also assassinated by the hundreds at the front.

23. Pierre Broué, *Le Parti bolchevique* (Paris: Editions de Minuit, 1977), p. 178.

24. Landau, *Le Stalinisme*. When confronted by militants whose sincerity he could not contest, von Ranke was suddenly filled with doubts, broke with the Servicio Alfredo Hertz, and fled to France, where he lived in secret to escape his previous colleagues. He fought in the resistance during World War II.

25. Indalecio Prieto, *Comment et pourquoi je suis sorti du ministère de la défense* (Paris: Imprimerie Nouvelle [Association Ouvrière], 1939). Ramon Rufat, in *Espions de la République* (Paris: Allia, 1990), summarizes the role of the SIM: "Contrary to the initial intention, its mission had nothing to do with work within the rebel zone. Its real purpose was surveillance and counterespionage in the Republican zone, behind the lines."

26. Gorkin, *Les Communistes*, p. 170.

27. Peter Huber, "Die Ermordung des Ignaz Reiss in der Schweiz (1937) und die Verhastung dissidenter Schweizer Spanienkämpfer durch den Geheimapparat der Komintern," in *Kommunisten verfolgen Kommunisten: Stalinischer Terror und 'Säuberungen' in den Kommunistischen Parteien Europas seit des dreissiger Jahren* (Berlin: Akademie Verlag, 1993), pp. 68–86.

28. Letter from Karl Bräuning, quoted in von zur Mühlen, *Spanien war ihre Hoffnung.*

29. Quoted in "La Terreur communiste en Espagne," *La révolution prolétarienne*, no. 263 (25 January 1938).

30. On 8 February 1938 in *L'humanité*, Marcel Cachin reported on the opening of the trial of Bukharin and his colleagues: "And if the crime is proved, and admitted, let no one be surprised by the severity of the judges . . . The idea instead should be to imitate the vigilance of Soviet judges against saboteurs and traitors to the fatherland. No doubt our Spanish friends understand the implications here."

31. In February 1938 Jef Last wrote: "The place where the Communist Party was strongest of all was in the International Brigades, where almost all officers and political commissars were Communists"; *Lettres d'Espagne*, p. 39. Recent studies by other historians have confirmed this view.

32. Huber, "Die Ermordung des Ignaz Reiss."

33. El Campesino, *Jusqu'à la mort: Mémoires* (Paris: Albin Michel, 1978).

34. Gustav Regler, *Le glaive et le fourreau* (Paris: Plon, 1960).

35. RTsKhIDNI, 545/6/1034, quoted in R. Skoutelsky, "André Marty et les Brigades internationales," *Cahiers d'histoire*, 2d trimestre, 1997.

36. Ute Bönnen and Gerald Endres, *Internationale Brigaden: Freiwillige im spanischen Bürgerkrieg*, SDR/Arte, Vienna, 1996).

37. Gorkin, *Les Communistes*, p. 82.

38. *La révolution prolétarienne*, 25 October 1937.

39. Rolf Reventlow, *Spanien in diesem Jarhundert* (Vienna: Europa-Verlag, 1969).

40. Broué, *Le Parti bolchevique*, pp. 180, 185; and Gorkin, *Les Communistes*, p. 175.

41. General "El Campesino," *La vie et la mort en URSS (1939–1949)* (Paris: Les Iles d'Or, 1950).

42. David W. Pike notes that some 6,000 Spaniards came to Russia, including 2,000 children and 102 teachers; "Les républicains espagnols incarcérés en URSS dans les années quarante," *Matériaux pour l'histoire de notre temps*, nos. 4–5 (1985).

43. According to El Campesino, Lister, while drunk, raped five young girls.

44. Jesús Hernández, *La grande trahison* (Paris: Fasquelle, 1953).

45. Gorkin, *Les Communistes*, p. 192; René Dazy, *Fusillez ces chiens enragés!* (Paris: O. Orban, 1981), pp. 247–249. *1944, Les Dossiers noirs d'une certaine résistance . . . Trajectoire du fascisme rouge* (Perpignan: Edition du CES, 1984), describes the Communists' liquidation of the National Spanish Union of Anti-Fascists, which had taken refuge in France.

18. Communism and Terrorism

1. Pierre Marion, *Mission impossible* (Paris: Calmann-Lévy, 1991).

2. This text, extracts of which have been made public by Paul Quinn-Judge of the *Boston Globe*, was published in its entirety in French in *Les nouvelles de Moscou*, no. 25 (23 June 1992).

3. Pierre Péan, *L'extrémiste* (Paris: Fayard, 1996).

4. John Barron, *KGB: The Secret Work of Soviet Secret Agents* (New York: Reader's Digest Press, 1974), with a foreword by Robert Conquest.

19. Poland, the "Enemy Nation"

1. Quoted by N. Petrov, "L'Opération polonaise du NKVD," *Karta*, no. 11 (1993), 27.

2. Stanisław Swianiewicz, *W cieniu Katynia* (In the Shadow of Katyń) (Paris: Instytut Literaki, 1976), pp. 110–111.

3. See K. Popinski, A. Kokurin, and A. Gurjanov, *Routes de la mort. L'évacuation des prisons soviétiques des "confins" de l'Est de la IIe République en juin et juillet 1941* (Warsaw, 1995), pp. 96 ff.

4. Quoted in Marian Papiński, *Tryptyk Kazachstanski: Wspomienia y Zeslania* (The Kazakhstan tryptych: Memoirs in exile) (Warsaw: Wydaw. Adam Marszalek, 1992).

5. *Volksdeutsche* were Polish citizens who declared themselves to be of German origin and consequently members of the German nation.

6. This term was used to refer to Poles in the territories annexed by the Third Reich who were forced to register as being "close to German culture" and who served in the Wehrmacht.

7. Central MSW Archives, Warsaw, sygn. 17/IX/36, vol. 2.

8. Kazimierz Moczarski, *Conversations with an Executioner* (Englewood Cliffs, N.J.: Prentice-Hall, 1981).

9. *Cahiers historiques*, no. 53 (1980).

10. Several theories have been put forward to explain this, including the ideas that Bolesław Bierut, Gomułka's successor, adroitly opposed the directives from Moscow, or that Stalin himself opposed the proposals he received from Warsaw. There is as yet no proof to back up either of these theories.

11. From Danuta Suchorowska, *Wielka edukacja: Wspomienia wieznów politycznych PRL, 1945–1956* (A great education: Memoirs of political prisoners in the People's Republic of Poland, 1945–1956) (Warsaw: Agencja Omnipress, 1990).

12. Before the war, Włodzimierz Lechowicz had been a civilian employee of the military counterespionage organization and a GRU collaborator. During the German occupation he worked inside the Polish government-in-exile in London while still belonging to the Communist Party counterespionage network. His boss was Marian Spychalski.

13. Central MSW Archives, sygn. 17/IX/268, vol. 7.

14. The KGB had had offices in Poland since 1956. After 1986 the Stasi also established offices in Bulgaria, Czechoslovakia, and Hungary, but it had fewer agents there than in Poland.

20. Central and Southeastern Europe

1. See Tamás Stark, "Hungarian Prisoners in the Soviet Union (1941–1955),"

1945: Consequences and Sequels of the Second World War (bulletin of the Comité International d'Histoire de la Deuxième Guerre Mondiale, Paris), nos. 27–28 (1995), 203–213.

2. See Frédy Foscolo, "Epurations: passé et présent," *La nouvelle alternative*, special issue, "Poids et enjeux des épurations," no. 21 (1991), 8–9.

3. Quoted in Tzvetan Todorov, *Au nom du peuple* (Paris: L'Aube, 1992), pp. 52–53.

4. Cristina Boico, "Les hommes qui ont porté Ceauşescu au pouvoir," *Sources—Travaux historiques*, no. 20 (1990).

5. Quoted in François Fejtö, *History of the People's Democracies: Eastern Europe since Stalin*, trans. Daniel Weissbort (London: Pall Mall Press, 1971), p. 99.

6. Miklós Molnar, *From Béla Kun to János Kádár: Seventy Years of Hungarian Communism* (New York: St. Martin's Press, 1990), p. 164.

7. Paul Wergent and Jean Bernard-Derosne, *L'Affaire Petkov* (Paris: Self, 1948), pp. 188–192.

8. Klement Gottwald, *Vybrané spisy* (Selected works), vol. 1 (Prague: SNPL, 1954), p. 139.

9. Claude Roy, *Nous* (Paris: Gallimard, 1980), pp. 389–390.

10. Lubomir Sochor, "Peut-on parler de la 'société civile' dans les pays du bloc soviétique?" *Communisme*, no. 8 (1985), 84.

11. "Ich habe den Tod verdient: Schauprocesse und politische Verfolgung in Mittel- und Osteuropa, 1945–1956," in *Archiv 1991. Jahrbuch des Vereins für Geschichte der Arbeiterbewegung*, ed. Wolfgang Maderthaner, Hans Schafranek, and Berthold Unfried (Berlin: Akademie, 1991).

12. These represented 65 percent of all primary schools, 50 percent of secondary schools for boys, and 78 percent of secondary schools for girls.

13. František Miklosko, *Nebudete ich mocí rozvratit* (You will never have the power to destroy them) (Bratislava: Archa, 1991), pp. 272–273.

14. Catherine Durandin, *Histoire des Roumains* (Paris: Fayard, 1995), pp. 72–73.

15. Bulgarian Commission for Aid to Anti-Fascists, *Les Bulgares parlent au monde* (Paris: BCAA, 1949).

16. Quoted in Jacques Rupnik, *The Other Europe* (New York: Pantheon, 1989), p. 139.

17. For a detailed analysis of these laws and of the regime that operated in these camps, see Paul Barton and Albert Weil, *Salariat et contrainte en Tchécoslovaquie* (Paris: Librairie Marcel Rivière, 1956).

18. Virgil Ierunca, *Piteşti, laboratoire concentrationnaire (1949–1952)* (Paris: Michalon, 1996), p. 59

19. Ibid., p. 152.

20. Ibid., pp. 59–61.

21. Todorov, *Au nom du peuple*, p. 38.

22. At the request of the Hungarians, backed up by Soviet advisers, Noel Field was arrested in Prague. He was never tried and was set free in October 1954 with his wife, Herta (who was arrested in Czechoslovakia and set free on 28 August 1949 in Budapest), and his brother Hermann (who was arrested in August 1949 by a collaborative effort of the Czechoslovak and Polish security services).

23. AÚV KSČ, Barnabitky Commission, letter to T. Balaz, in Karel Kaplan, *Zpráva*

o zavrazdení generalního tajemnika (Report on the assassination of the General Secretary) (Prague: Mladá Fronta, 1992), p. 68.

24. Jindřich Madrý, "La période de l'armement et réarmement," *Soudobé dějiny* (Contemporary history), nos. 4–5 (1994).

25. Kaplan, *Zpráva o zavrazdení.*

26. Molnar, *From Béla Kun to János Kádár,* p. 187.

27. Kaplan, *Zpráva o zavrazdení.*

28. See Mikhail Agurski, "La bataille au sein de la Sécurité d'état," *Le monde,* 2–3 October 1983.

29. Kaplan, *Zpráva o zavrazdení,* p. 141.

30. On the activity of the Cominform and the formation of the Soviet bloc, see the work of Leonid J. Gibianskii, e.g., "Problemy mezhdunarodno-politicheskogo strukturirovaniya Vostochnoi Europy v period formirovaniya sovetskogo bloka 1940-e gody," *Kholodnaya voïna: Novye podkhody, novye dokumenty* (The Cold War: New approaches, new documents), ed. I. V. Gaidak et al. (Moscow: Otvet, 1995), pp. 99–126. For a revised version in English, see "The Soviet-Yugoslav Split and the Cominform," in *The Establishment of Communist regimes in Eastern Europe, 1944–1949,* ed. Norman M. Naimark and Leonid Gibianskii (Boulder: Westview Press, 1997), pp. 231–312. Gibianskii draws on Russian, Polish, Czech, and Yugoslav archives.

31. Dieter Staritz, *Geschichte der DDR* (Frankfurt am Main: Suhrkampf, 1996).

32. Details here come from the study published by researchers at the Institute for the History of the Hungarian Revolution in 1956 in Budapest, Csába Bekes, János M. Rainer, and Pál Germuska, in *Soudobé dějiny,* no. 4 (1997).

33. *Comminisme,* nos. 26–27 (1990).

34. For the events surrounding the first anniversary of the occupation of Czechoslovakia, see a collection of documents edited by Oldřich Tuma, *Srpen '68* (August 1968) (Prague: ÚSD-Maxdorf, 1996).

35. Raïna Foscolo and Alfredo Foscolo, "Prisonniers à Sofia," *La nouvelle alternative* no. 47 (September 1997).

36. *La nouvelle alternative,* no. 7 (September 1987).

37. György Dalos, "Liberté sans paroles," *Le monde-liber,* no. 6 (December 1990).

38. Maria Ferretti, *La memoria mutilata: La Russia ricorda* (Mutilated memory: Russia remembers) (Milan: Corbaccio, 1993).

39. *La nouvelle alternative,* no. 46 (June 1997). The Czech legal system, like many others, distinguishes between crimes with statutory limitation—those that must be prosecuted within a certain period after the offense is committed—and those without stautory limitation.

40. *Dziennik ustaw Rzeczypospolitej polskiej* (Law Digest of the Polish Republic), no. 45 (Warsaw, 29 May 1991).

Introduction to Part IV

1. *American editor's note:* This is an inaccurate description of the archival situation in Moscow. At least three archives in Moscow that have been open since 1992—the

Russian Center for the Storage and Study of Documents from Recent History (RTsKhIDNI), the Center for Storage of Contemporary Documentation (TsKhSD), and the Foreign Ministry archive—contain large holdings about Soviet relations with the East Asian countries after World War II. Although access to documents in these archives (especially TsKhSD) is often problematic, a good deal of valuable material is available. It is true that several key archives in Moscow, such as the Presidential Archive and the foreign intelligence archive, have never been opened, but their inaccessibility should not cause researchers to overlook declassified items that are available in some of the open (or partly open) repositories.

21. China

1. Mao Zedong, "Report to the Second Plenary Session of the Central Committee of the Seventh Congress of the Chinese Communist Party, 5 March 1949," in *Selected Works*, vol. 4 (Beijing: Foreign Language Editions, 1962). A fragment is reprinted in the Little Red Book, in the chapter "Class and Class Struggle." During the Cultural Revolution, this quotation was often read out to prisoners before interrogation began.

2. In these pages, Chinese characters are transcribed in accordance with the *pinyin* style imposed by China, which is now almost universally accepted. Thus, Mao Tse-tung is written as Mao Zedong. The only exceptions are names from before 1949.

3. See Roger Faligot and Rémi Kauffer, *The Chinese Secret Service (1927–1987)*, trans. Christine Donougher (London: Headline, 1989).

4. Kim Il Sung, *Works*, vol. 30, p. 498, quoted in Oh Il-whan, "La propagande et le contrôle de pensée: Les facteurs de résistance du système communiste nord-coréen" (thesis, University of Paris X, 1994), p. 209.

5. Hoang Van Hoan, *Une goutte d'eau dans le grand océan—Souvenirs révolution-naires* (Paris: Dentu, 1989).

6. The daily *Nhan Dan*, 7 May 1964, quoted in "Révolutionnaires d'Indochine," *Cahiers Léon Trotski*, no. 40 (December 1989), 119–120.

7. Ibid., p. 119.

8. Georges Boudarel, "L'idéocratie importée au Vietnam avec le Maoïsme," in *La bureaucratie au Vietnam—Vietnam-Asie-Débat no.1* (Paris: L'Harmattan, 1983), pp. 31–106.

9. Li Zhisui, *The Private Life of Chairman Mao: The Memoirs of Mao's Personal Physician* (New York: Random House, 1994).

10. This idea and the discussion that follows owe much to Richard Shek, "Sectarian Eschatology and Violence," in *Violence in China: Essays in Culture and Counterculture*, ed. Jonathan N. Lipman and Stevan Harrell (New York: State University of New York Press, 1990), pp. 87–109.

11. Ibid., p. 101.

12. Ibid.,p p. 105, 106.

13. Quoted in Sun Tzu, *The Art of War*, trans. Thomas Cleary (Boston: Shambhala, 1988), p. 38.

14. Ibid., pp. 103, 108, 105.

15. Danielle Elisseeff and Vadime Elisseeff, *La civilisation de la Chine classique* (Paris: Arthaud, 1981), p. 296.

16. John K. Fairbank, *The Great Chinese Revolution, 1800–1985* (London: Chatto and Windus, 1987).

17. Jen Yu-wen, *The Taiping Revolutionary Movement* (New Haven: Yale University Press, 1973).

18. Marie-Claire Bergère, Lucien Bianco, and Jürgen Domes, eds., *La Chine au XXe siècle*, 2 vols. (Paris: Fayard, 1989, 1990), 1: 125.

19. Roderick MacFarquhar and John K. Fairbank, eds., *The Cambridge History of China*, vol. 14: *The People's Republic, Part 1 (1949–1965)* (Cambridge: Cambridge University Press, 1987), p. 371.

20. John K. Fairbank and Albert Feuerwerker, eds., *The Cambridge History of China*, vol. 13: *Republican China, 1912–1949*, part 2 (Cambridge: Cambridge University Press, 1986), pp. 605–606.

21. Ibid., p. 292.

22. Ibid., pp. 291 and 293.

23. Ibid., pp. 294–297 and 312–314.

24. Legal treatise *Souei-chou*, quoted in Elisseeff and Elisseeff, *Chine classique*, p. 264.

25. Fairbank and Feuerwerker, *Republican China*, pp. 307–322.

26. Roland Lew, *1949: Mao prend le pouvoir* (Brussels: Complexe, 1980).

27. Jean-Luc Domenach, *Chine: L'archipel oublié* (Paris: Fayard, 1992), p. 47.

28. Gregor Benton, "Under Arms and Umbrellas: Perspectives on Chinese Communism in Defeat," in *New Perspectives on the Chinese Communist Revolution*, ed. Tony Saich and Hans Van de Ven (Armonk: M. E. Sharpe, 1995), pp. 131–133.

29. Chen Yung-fa, "The Blooming Poppy under the Red Sun: The Yan'an Way and the Opium Trade," ibid., pp. 263–298.

30. Quoted in Yves Chevrier, *Mao et la révolution chinoise* (Florence: Casterman/ Giuntim, 1993), p. 65.

31. François Godemont, "La tourmente du vent communiste (1955–1965)," in Bergère, Bianco, and Domes, *La Chine au XXe siècle*, 2: 58.

32. This vague term is used to designate whoever in the Party was exercising power. It corresponds in part to official practice, as decision-making practices were often quite fluid, and certain members could easily find themselves in a marginal position. The converse was also true; thus it was possible for someone who had technically retired, such as Deng Xiaoping, to remain the de facto leader for more than a decade.

33. Benton, "Under Arms and Umbrellas"; and Lucien Bianco, "Peasant Responses to CCP Mobilization Policies, 1937–1945," in Saich and Van de Ven, *New Perspectives*, pp. 175–187.

34. Stephen C. Averill, "The Origins of the Futian Incident," ibid., pp. 218–219.

35. David Apter, "Discourse as Power: Yan'an and the Chinese Revolution," ibid., pp. 218–219.

36. Vladimirov (Comintern representative in Yan'an), in Boudarel, "L'idéocratie importée," pp. 55–56.

37. Idem in ibid., p. 56.

38. Frederick C. Teiwes and Warren Sun, "From a Leninist to a Charismatic Party: The CCP's Changing Leadership, 1937–1945," in Saich and Van de Ven, *New Perspectives*, p. 372.

39. Ibid., p. 373.

40. Ibid., pp. 370–375; Apter, "Discourse as Power"; Faligot and Kauffer, *Chinese Secret Service*, pp. 153–170.

41. During three months in 1940 in a small part of Hebei, more than 3,600 were killed; Domenach, *Chine*, p. 48.

42. Ye Fei, interview in 1983, in Benton, "Under Arms and Umbrellas," p. 138.

43. Domenach, *Chine*, pp. 44–52.

44. Ibid., pp. 52–55.

45. Despite many indications to the contrary in his work, this was, for example, the thesis of Jack Belden in one of the earliest reports on the Chinese Revolution, *China Shakes the World* (1949; reprint, Harmondsworth: Pelican, 1973).

46. William Hinton, *Fanshen: A Documentary of Revolution in a Chinese Village* (1967; reprint, Berkeley: University of California Press, 1997).

47. Alan Roux, *La Chine populaire*, 2 vols. (Paris: Editions Sociales, 1983, 1984), 1: 81.

48. Bianco, "Peasant Responses."

49. Hinton, *Fanshen*, pp. 581–583.

50. Lynn T. White III, *Policies of Chaos: The Organizational Causes of Violence in China's Cultural Revolution* (Princeton: Princeton University Press, 1989), p. 82.

51. A. Doak Barnett and Ezra Vogel, *Cadres, Bureaucracy, and Political Power in Communist China* (New York: Columbia University Press, 1967), p. 228; Domenach, *Chine*, p. 71; Claude Aubert, "Economie et société rurales," in Bergère, Bianco, and Domes, *La Chine au XXe siècle*, 2: 150.

52. Domenach, *Chine*, pp. 70–72.

53. Hinton, *Fanshen*, p. 285. Hinton, though on the whole very favorably disposed toward Chinese Communism, is a remarkable witness and a farmer himself (in the United States).

54. He Liyi with Claire Anne Chik, *Mr. China's Son—A Villager's Life* (Boulder: Westview Press, 1993), pp. 52–54.

55. Richard Masden, "The Politics of Revenge in Rural China during the Cultural Revolution," in Lipman and Harrell, *Violence in China*, p. 186.

56. Werner Meissner, "La voie orthodoxe (1949–1955)," in Bergère, Bianco, and Domes, *La Chine au XXe siècle*, 2: 19.

57. In "Comments on the Repression and Liquidation of Counterrevolutionary Elements," quoted in MacFarquhar and Fairbank, *Cambridge History of China*, 14: 89.

58. Roux, *La Chine populaire*, p. 164.

59. Domenach, *Chine*, pp. 67 and 80.

60. Meissner, "La voie orthodoxe," p. 25.

61. White, *Policies of Chaos*, pp. 93–101.

62. Roux, *La Chine populaire*, p. 170.

63. Domenach, *Chine*, pp. 77–79.

64. "Quinze ans de persécution contre les catholiques en Chine communiste" *Est et ouest*, 16–30 September 1966, pp. 4–9; Domenach, *Chine*, p. 504.

65. Domenach, *Chine*, pp. 80–81.

66. Quoted in MacFarquhar and Fairbank, *Cambridge History of China*, 14: 88.

67. White, *Policies of Chaos*, pp. 104–124.

68. Jacques Andrieu, "Le mouvement des idées" in Bergère, Bianco, and Domes, *La Chine au XXe siècle*, 2: 268–269.

69. Domenach, *Chine*, p. 118.

70. Some rectification movements even occurred inside prisons. See Jean Pasqualini with Rudolf Chelminski, *Prisoner of Mao* (London: André Deutsch, 1973).

71. Domenach, *Chine*, pp. 121–126.

72. Jean-Luc Domenach, *The Origins of the Great Leap Forward: The Case of One Chinese Province* (Boulder: Westview Press, 1995), p. 154.

73. Ten years later these children would become Red Guards. The verb "to fight" in Chinese, when employed transitively as here, meant to denounce collectively, to extract an act of contrition, or, lacking one, to call for condemnation. It was a very special kind of "fight," since it was impossible for victims to defend themselves even in words. In principle it was known in advance whether there would simply be shouting or whether there would also be blows, and, if the latter, whether the blows might eventually lead to death. Death was quite common during the agrarian reforms and the Cultural Revolution, but quite rare between them.

74. He, *Mr. China's Son*, pp. 3–8.

75. The figure 5 percent seemed to have an almost mystical value, so often was it mentioned during the campaigns. But it meant the bare minimum. It also recurred frequently in the speeches of Pol Pot.

76. MacFarquhar and Fairbank, *Cambridge History of China*, 14: 257.

77. Hinton, *Fanshen*, p. 484.

78. Justin Yifu Lin, "Collectivization and China's Agricultural Crisis in 1959–1961," *Journal of Political Economy* 98 (1990), 1228–50.

79. Domenach, *Chine*, p. 152.

80. William Hinton, *Shenfan* (New York: Random House, 1983).

81. Domenach, *Origins of Great Leap Forward*, p. 152.

82. Mao, a secret speech, in *The Secret Speeches of Chairman Mao*, ed. Roderick MacFarquhar, Timothy Cheek, and Eugene Wu (Cambridge, Mass.: Council on East Asian Studies, Harvard University, 1989).

83. MacFarquhar and Fairbank, *Cambridge History of China*, 14: 380.

84. Ibid., p. 369.

85. Domenach, *Origins of Great Leap Forward*, p. 160.

86. Much of this information is taken from Jasper Becker, *Hungry Ghosts: China's Secret Famine* (London: John Murray, 1996). This is the only book we know of that gives a good overall picture of the famine that followed the Great Leap Forward.

87. Ibid., p. 133.

88. Roux, *La Chine populaire,* pp. 295–296.

89. Becker, *Hungry Ghosts,* p. 283.

90. MacFarquhar and Fairbank, *Cambridge History of China,* 14: 370 and 383.

91. Ibid., pp. 376–377.

92. Becker, *Hungry Ghosts,* p. 113.

93. Ibid., p. 146.

94. Ibid., p. 139.

95. Domenach, *Origins of Great Leap Forward,* p. 157.

96. Becker, *Hungry Ghosts,* pp. 112–149.

97. Wei Jingsheng, "Mon évolution intellectuelle entre seize et vingt-neuf ans," in *La Cinquième Modernisation et autres écrits du 'Printemps de Pékin,'* trans. and ed. Huang San and Angel Pino (Paris: Christian Bourgois–Bibliothèque Asiatique, 1997), pp. 244–246.

98. A celebrated formula used to describe Mao Zedong by Lin Biao in a speech on 18 September 1966.

99. Roux, *La Chine populaire,* pp. 296–297.

100. Ibid., pp. 213–216.

101. Pasqualini, *Prisoner of Mao,* pp. 248, 238–239.

102. Lin, "Collectivization"; Becker, *Hungry Ghosts,* pp. 270–273.

103. MacFarquhar and Fairbank, *Cambridge History of China,* 14: 370–372.

104. Ibid., pp. 372–386, for these and most other figures regarding the Great Leap Forward.

105. Ibid., p. 381.

106. Becker, *Hungry Ghosts,* pp. 235–254.

107. Domenach, *Chine,* p. 154.

108. Lin, "Collectivization"; Aubert, "Economie et société rurales," pp. 166–168.

109. Hua Linshan, *Les années rouges* (Paris: Seuil, 1987), p. 202.

110. Becker, *Hungry Ghosts,* p. 243.

111. Harry Wu, *Laogai: The Chinese Gulag,* trans. Ted Slingerland (Boulder: Westview Press, 1994), pp. 117, 178.

112. Yan Jiaqi and Gao Gao, *Turbulent Decade: A History of the Cultural Revolution* (Honolulu: University of Hawaii Press, 1996), p. 164.

113. Pasqualini, *Prisoner of Mao,* p. 172.

114. Ibid., p. 248.

115. Wu, *Laogai,* p. 38.

116. Domenach, *Chine,* p. 242; Pasqualini, *Prisoner of Mao,* p. 318.

117. Domenach, *Chine,* pp. 318, 512.

118. On this subject see Wu, *Laogai,* pp. 23–39; Domenach, *Chine,* pp. 139–226.

119. Pasqualini, *Prisoner of Mao,* p. 97.

120. Domenach, *Chine,* p. 541.

121. Wu, *Laogai,* p. 30.

122. Wu prefers "retraining."

123. Ibid., pp. 142–143.

124. Pasqualini, *Prisoner of Mao*, p. 266.

125. Domenach, *Chine*, p. 162.

126. Wu, *Laogai*, pp. 49 and 55.

127. Pasqualini, *Prisoner of Mao*, p. 196.

128. Wu, *Laogai*, p. 50.

129. Pasqualini, *Prisoner of Mao*, pp. 32, 48.

130. Ibid., p. 50.

131. Ibid., pp. 253–254.

132. Ibid., pp. 51–56, 110–115, 249.

133. Ibid., pp. 45–46.

134. Ibid., pp. 36, 73.

135. Ibid., p. 298.

136. Ibid., p. 147.

137. Ibid., p. 81.

138. Albert Stihlé, *Le prêtre et le commissaire* (Paris: Grasset, 1971).

139. Domenach, *Chine*, p. 170.

140. Pasqualini, *Prisoner of Mao*, pp. 219, 231.

141. Ibid., p. 32.

142. Domenach, *Chine*, p. 168.

143. Pasqualini, *Prisoner of Mao*, p. 42

144. Nien Cheng, *Life and Death in Shanghai* (London: Macdonald, 1986), pp. 224–226.

145. Ibid., pp. 298–299.

146. Pasqualini, *Prisoner of Mao*, p. 72.

147. Nien, *Life and Death*, part 3.

148. Domenach, *Chine*, pp. 170 and 185.

149. Nien, *Life and Death*, p. 318.

150. Pasqualini, *Prisoner of Mao*, pp. 39–40.

151. Domenach, *Chine*, p. 211.

152. Ibid., p. 213.

153. Pasqualini, *Prisoner of Mao*, pp. 178–181.

154. Ibid., p. 187.

155. See, e.g., Fairbank, *Great Chinese Revolution*, p. 449; Anne F. Thurston, "Urban Violence during the Cultural Revolution: Who Is to Blame?" in Lipman and Harrell, *Violence in China*, p. 149; Domenach, *Chine*, p. 211.

156. This committee was formed at an extraordinary Politburo meeting on 16 May 1966 and answered only to its permanent committee—that is, to Mao. It removed control of the Cultural Revolution's direction from Peng Zhen and from the Secretariat of the Central Committee, led by Liu Shaoqi and Deng Xiaoping. The CRG was dominated by Maoist extremists such as Jiang Qing ("Madam Mao"), Chen Boda, and Zhang Chunqiao; Kang Sheng was its leading adviser. It worked very closely with Mao and, after 1968, replaced both the Central Committee and the Politburo as the fundamental decision-making body.

157. Harry Harding, "The Chinese State in Crisis," in *The Cambridge History of*

China, ed. Roderick MacFarquhar and John K. Fairbank, vol. 15, Part 2: *Revolutions within the Chinese Revolution, 1966–1982* (Cambridge: Cambridge University Press, 1991), p. 209.

158. Domenach, *Chine,* p. 259.

159. Yves Chevrier, "L'empire distendu, esquisse du politique en Chine dès Qing à Deng Xiaoping," in *La greffe de l'etat—Trajectoires du politique 2,* ed. Jean-François Bayart (Paris: Karthala, 1996), pp. 383 and 375.

160. Wei, "Mon évolution," p. 227.

161. See Frederick C. Tiewes and Warren Sun, *The Tragedy of Lin Biao: Riding the Tiger during the Cultural Revolution, 1966–1971* (Honolulu: University of Hawaii Press, 1966).

162. Hua, *Années rouges,* p. 251.

163. See in particular the fascinating memoirs of Ni Yuxian, who was a student in the naval academy in Shanghai, collected in Anne F. Thurston, *A Chinese Odyssey: The Life and Times of a Chinese Dissident* (New York: Charles Scribner's Sons, 1991).

164. White, *Policies of Chaos,* p. 203.

165. In contrast, the Red Guards' discovery, on goodwill visits and exchanges or during the forced ruralization of 1968, of the widespread misery in the countryside accelerated their distancing from the regime, as described by Wei Jingsheng.

166. Mao Zedong, *Little Red Book;* song quoted in Zhai Zhenhua, *Red Flower of China* (New York: Soho, 1992), p. 81.

167. Pasqualini, *Prisoner of Mao,* p. 294.

168. Harding, "The Chinese State in Crisis," p. 150. Anyone who had been in prison, however, was forbidden to take part in political activity; Hinton, *Shenfan,* p. 529.

169. White, *Policies of Chaos,* pp. 245–247.

170. This led to some spectacular reversals of fortune. For example, the moderate Henan chief Pan Fusheng, who had been sacked at the instigation of the ultra-Maoist Wu Zhipu just before the Great Leap Forward, took up office again in 1966 as part of the ultraleft clan of Chen Boda. Meanwhile, Wu was arrested and probably killed in 1967 by the Red Guards in Canton. See Domenach, *Origins of Great Leap Forward,* p. 167.

171. See on this point the fascinating picture drawn by one former Red Guard who became a university lecturer in the United States: Wang Shaoguang, *Failure of Charisma: The Cultural Revolution in Wuhan* (Hong Kong: Oxford University Press, 1995), pp. 95–111, and 161–209.

172. Roux, *La Chine populaire,* 2: 45–46.

173. Yan and Gao, *Turbulent Decade,* pp. 152–166 and 197–228.

174. Ibid., p. 28.

175. Ibid., p. 210.

176. Quoted in Thurston, "Urban Violence."

177. Quoted in Marie-Claude Bergère, *La République populaire de Chine de 1949 à nos jours* (Paris: Armand Colin, 1987), p. 133.

178. Belden, *China Shakes the World*, p. 228.

179. Becker, *Hungry Ghosts*, p. 218; Wu, *Laogai*, p. 46.

180. Ling, *Red Guard*, pp. 174–183; Zhai, *Red Flower*, pp. 84–90. Seeing Mao close up was often a disappointment: "He was older than I thought, and more than half of his hair was white. His face was that of an old man, and it really didn't shine like it should have. His movements were slow. He was like a senile old man"; Zhai, p. 87.

181. Thurston, "Urban Violence," p. 149.

182. Yan and Gao, *Turbulent Decade*, p. 76.

183. Nien, *Life and Death*, p. 69.

184. Pasqualini, *Prisoner of Mao*, p. 184.

185. Zhai, *Red Flower*, p. 62.

186. Douwe Fokkema, "Creativity and Politics," in MacFarquhar and Fairbank, *Cambridge History of China*, 15: 600; Yan and Gao, *Turbulent Decade*, p. 79.

187. Statement by a Red Guard, in Roux, *La Chine populaire*, 2: 37.

188. Yan and Gao, *Turbulent Decade*, p. 70.

189. Ling, *Red Guard*, p. 49; Yan and Gao, *Turbulent Decade*, p. 71.

190. Nien, *Life and Death*, p. 76.

191. Ibid., p. 56.

192. Some chose "Comrade Norman Bethune is a member of the Canadian Communist Party." Were they joking?

193. See, for example, Zhai, *Red Flower*, pp. 92–100.

194. Ibid., p. 100.

195. Wang, *Failure of Charisma*, p. 72.

196. Yan and Gao, *Turbulent Decade*, p. 77.

197. Domenach, *Chine*, pp. 273–274 and 284–285.

198. Yan and Gao, *Turbulent Decade*, p. 212; these figures, which are not entirely reliable, are those used in the trial of the Gang of Four in 1981.

199. Nien, *Life and Death*, p. 443.

200. Roux, *La Chine populaire*, 2: 50.

201. Ken Ling, Miriam London, and Lee Ta-ling, *Red Guard: From Schoolboy to "Little General" in Mao's China* (London: Macdonald, 1972), pp. 18–21.

202. For an exception see the pioneering works of Simon Leys, which are still valuable both for their chronological precision and for their ideological decoding of the Cultural Revolution: *The Chairman's New Clothes: Mao and the Cultural Revolution* (New York: Alison and Busby, 1981) and *Chinese Shadows* (New York: Penguin, 1981).

203. Five such changes occurred in the space of five months at the top of General Workers' Headquarters in Wuhan; Wang, *Failure of Charisma*, p. 89.

204. Ling, *Red Guard*, pp. 260–262.

205. See in particular Ling, *Red Guard*.

206. Harding, "The Chinese State in Crisis," p. 168.

207. Hua, *Années rouges*, p. 311.

208. Ling, *Red Guard*, p. 31.

209. Keith Forster, "Spontaneous and Institutional Rebellion in the Cultural Revolution: the Extraordinary Case of Weng Senhe," *Australian Journal of Chinese Affairs*, no. 27 (1992), 38–75.

210. Domenach, *Chine*, pp. 278–286.

211. "The students used to say: 'Once we control the Central Bureau for Public Security, we can arrest whomever we like'"; Ling, *Red Guard*, p. 252.

212. See the essential texts in Hector Mandarès et al., *Revo cul dans la Chine pop: Anthologie de la presse des Gardes rouges (mai 1966–janvier 1968)* (Paris: Bibliothèque Asiatique, 1974), pp. 353–427.

213. Mao did nothing to explain his thinking, for that would have meant taking sides in the struggle; he never made a single speech about the Cultural Revolution.

214. Ling, *Red Guard*, p. 115; Nien, *Life and Death*, p. 370.

215. "What the two of us had in common was our belief that violence should solve our problems: force replaced propaganda"; Ling, *Red Guard*, p. 193.

216. See, for example, Hua, *Années rouges*, p. 328.

217. Zhai, *Red Flower*, p. 81.

218. Ibid.

219. Ibid., p. 105.

220. Ling, *Red Guard*, p. 42.

221. Hua, *Années rouges*, p. 106.

222. Ibid., p. 108.

223. Nien, *Life and Death*, p. 363.

224. There was a basic difference between the students and the workers: the students wanted power, while the workers wanted money; Ling, *Red Guard*, p. 243.

225. Wang, *Failure of Charisma*, p. 118.

226. Ibid., p. 158.

227. Hinton, *Shenfan*, p. 521.

228. Wang, *Failure of Charisma*, p. 66.

229. Ibid., p. 94.

230. Ibid., pp. 143–208.

231. Ling, *Red Guard*, p. 83.

232. White, *Policies of Chaos*, p. 325.

233. Hinton, *Shenfan*, pp. 519 and 527–528.

234. See esp. Hua, *Années rouges*.

235. Bergère, *La République*, p. 133.

236. Thurston, "Urban Violence," pp. 158–159.

237. Roux, *La Chine populaire*, 2: 54–55.

238. Thurston gives the figure 12 million, Fairbank 14 million, and Bergère (*La République*) 20 million.

239. White, *Policies of Chaos*, p. 294.

240. Harding, "The Chinese State in Crisis," p. 212.

241. Hua, *Années rouges*, pp. 345–346.

242. Domenach, *Origins of Great Leap Forward*, p. 284.

243. Hua, *Années rouges*, pp. 338 and 341–342.

244. White, *Policies of Chaos,* p. 260.

245. Ibid., p. 277.

246. Yan and Gao, *Turbulent Decade,* pp. 266–267.

247. Faligot and Kauffer, *Chinese Secret Service,* p. 407; Harding, "The Chinese State in Crisis," p. 214.

248. Yan and Gao, *Turbulent Decade,* pp. 252–265.

249. Nien, *Life and Death,* pp. 274–276.

250. Hua, *Années rouges,* p. 365.

251. Domenach, *Chine,* p. 279.

252. Quoted in Mandarès et al., *Revo cul dans le Chine pop,* p. 50.

253. Sebastian Hellmann, "The Suppression of the April 5th Movement and the Persecution of 'Counter-Revolutionaries' in 1976," *Issues and Studies* 30 (January 1994), 37–64.

254. Wei, "Mon évolution," p. 226.

255. For the complete text (with various other relevant texts), see Wei, *La Cinquième Modernisation.*

256. Angel Pino, "Postface," ibid., pp. 261–347. In the wake of Jiang Zemin's visit to the United States in November 1997, Wei Jingsheng was released from prison and forced to leave the country.

257. Jürgen Domes, "La société politique," in Bergère, Bianco, and Domes, *La Chine au XXe siècle,* p. 251.

258. Domenach, *Chine,* pp. 335–345, 415, 491.

259. Jean-Pierre Cabestan, "Chine: Un état de lois sans état de droit," *Revue Tiers Monde* 37 (July–September 1996), 649–668.

260. Quoted in Wu, *Laogai,* p. 186.

261. Cabestan, "Chine," pp. 662–663.

262. Andrew Scobell, "The Death Penalty in Post-Mao China," *China Quarterly,* no. 123 (September 1990), 503–520.

263. Ibid.

264. Domenach, *Chine,* pp. 365–378.

265. Becker, *Hungry Ghosts,* p. 171.

266. Vania Kewley, *Tibet: Behind the Ice Curtain* (London: Grafton Books, 1990), p. 251.

267. Becker, *Hungry Ghosts,* p. 166.

268. Ibid., p. 171.

269. Pierre-Antoine Donnet, *Tibet—Survival in Question* (London: Zed Books, 1994), pp. 41–42.

270. Ibid., pp. 128–129.

271. Kewley, *Tibet,* pp. 269–270.

272. Quoted in Donnet, *Tibet,* p. 63.

273. Kewley, *Tibet,* p. 165.

274. Donnet, *Tibet,* pp. 54–60, 127.

275. Kewley, *Tibet,* p. 255.

276. Ibid., pp. 122–124, 291, and 314–318.

277. Becker, *Hungry Ghosts,* pp. 173–176.

278. Donnet, *Tibet*, pp. 126–127.
279. Becker, *Hungry Ghosts*, p. 181.

22. Crimes, Terror, and Secrecy in North Korea

1. V. Charles Martel and Georges Perruche, "Prisonniers français en Corée," *Les cahiers d'histoire sociale*, no. 3 (October 1994).

2. Kim Hyun Hee, *The Tears of My Soul* (New York: William Morrow, 1993); and an interview with the author in February 1997.

3. Asia Watch, *Human Rights in the Democratic People's Republic of Korea* (Washington, 1988).

4. Tibor Meray, "Wilfred Burchett en Corée," *Les cahiers d'histoire sociale*, no. 7 (Fall–Winter 1996), 87.

5. Interview with the author, Seoul, February 1997.

6. Another foreigner, a Frenchman named Jacques Sédillot, was arrested at the same time. He had also come to work in the Department of Foreign-Language Publications in Pyongyang. Like Lameda he received a twenty-year sentence, but as "an agent of French imperialism." He was set free in 1975 in a state of such physical deterioration that he died a few months later, without ever being able to return to France.

7. Interview with the author, Seoul, February 1977.

8. See Martel and Perruche, "Prisonniers français," for the statements made by the diplomats; Asia Watch, *Human Rights*, for the American sailors.

9. Long extracts from this testimony were published in *Coreana*, the bulletin of the Société d'Etudes Coréennes, no. 1 (March 1995).

10. The Third Bureau is the subsection of the National Security Agency in charge of border security.

11. Estimates of the total camp population vary from 150,000 to 400,000.

12. Jean-Pierre Brulé, *La Corée du Nord de Kim Il Sung* (Paris: Editions Barré-Dayez, 1992).

13. *La lettre de Corée*, nos. 4 and 5, June and August 1997.

14. *Le Figaro magazine*, 8 March 1997.

15. Ibid.

16. Marc Epstein, *L'express*, 14 August 1997.

17. *Le monde*, 10 October 1997.

18. Interview with Catherine Bertini, *La croix*, 8 October 1997. By way of comparison, a study by the World Bank in the early 1990s showed that 43 percent of children in India showed some traces of malnutrition.

23. Vietnam and Laos

Epigraph: quoted in Doan Van Toai, *The Vietnamese Gulag*, trans. Sylvie Romanowski and Françoise Simon-Miller (New York: Simon And Schuster, 1986), p. 17. Le Duan visited the prison on the island of Con Son after the "liberation" of South Vietnam in 1975.

1. Although most of its members were Vietnamese, who totally controlled the Party, the ICP aimed at extending the revolution throughout French Indochina, including Laos and Cambodia. It formally dissolved itself as an organization in 1945 but continued to function until 1951, when it spawned three closely linked parties that no longer had official Communist status (see Chapter 24).

2. Ngo Van, *Vietnam 1920–1945: Révolution et contre-révolution sous la domination coloniale* (Paris: L'Insomniaque, 1996), pp. 128–129.

3. David G. Marr, *Vietnam 1945: The Quest for Power* (Berkeley: University of California Press, 1995), pp. 234–237, 403, 409, 415–416.

4. Ibid., pp. 434–435.

5. Ngo, *Vietnam*, p. 341.

6. Marr, *Vietnam 1945*, p. 518.

7. Ngo, *Vietnam*, pp. 352 and 358–361.

8. Ibid., pp. 338, 341, and 350.

9. Marr, *Vietnam 1945*, pp. 517 and 519–520.

10. See, e.g., Albert Stihlé, *Le prêtre et le commissaire* (Paris: Grasset, 1971).

11. *L'histoire*, no. 149 (May 1991). According to estimates by the French Army in 1954, 15,500 out of 36,900 prisoners (including Vietnamese allies of France) were set free either before or after the cessation of hostilities. Both studies agree that the proportion of losses was around 60 percent. Cf. Colonel Robert Bonnafous, "Les prisonniers français des camps Viet-minh" (Thesis, Centre d'Histoire Militaire et d'Etudes de Défense Nationale, Université Paul-Valéry Montpellier, 1985), p. 217. By way of comparison, it should be noted that according to a letter dated March 1955 from General Beaufort, who was head of the French mission at the International Commission established to oversee the implementation of the Geneva peace accord, 9,000 of the 63,000 Viet Minh prisoners of war died in captivity.

12. Georges Boudarel, *Cent fleurs écloses dans la nuit du Vietnam: Communisme et dissidence 1954–1956* (Paris: Jacques Bertoin, 1991), p. 177.

13. Ibid., pp. 174–175, 176.

14. Ibid., pp. 171, 191, 170, 177–178.

15. Ibid., p. 190.

16. Ngo, *Vietnam*, p. 375.

17. Quoted in Boudarel, *Cent fleurs*, p. 200; see also pp. 199–202.

18. Georges Boudarel, "L'idéocratie importée au Vietnam avec le maoisme," in *La bureaucratie au Vietnam—Vietnam-Asie-Débat no. 1* (Paris: L'Harmattan, 1983), pp. 61, 63.

19. Boudarel, *Cent fleurs*, pp. 183–184.

20. Quoted in Ngo, *Vietnam*, p. 404.

21. Georges Boudarel, "1954: Les dilemmes de l'indépendance," in *Hanoi 1936–1996: Du drapeau rouge au billet vert*, ed. Georges Boudarel and Nguyen Van Ky (Paris: Autrement, 1997), p. 141.

22. Ngo, *Vietnam*, p. 404.

23. Boudarel, *Cent fleurs*, p. 150.

24. Gérard Tongas, *J'ai vécu dans l'enfer communiste au Nord Vietnam* (Paris: Nouvelles Editions Debresse, 1960), pp. 231–232.

25. Daniel Hémery, interview, Paris, October 1997; Georges Boudarel, "1965–1975: Guerre ou paix?" in Boudarel and Nguyen, *Hanoi 1936–1996*, p. 154.

26. Doan, *The Vietnamese Gulag*, pp. 199–200.

27. The term "Viet Cong," which originated in the South, means "Communist Vietnamese."

28. Stanley Karnow, *Vietnam: A History* (Harmondsworth: Penguin Books, 1984), pp. 530–531.

29. Doan, *The Vietnamese Galag*, pp. 170-171.

30. Interview with a former Communist leader, Ho Chi Minh City, 1996.

31. See, e.g., Communauté Vietnamienne, *Les prisonniers politiques* (Paris: Sudestasie, 1974).

32. Doan, *The Vietnamese Gulag*.

33. Quoted in ibid.

34. Most of this information comes from Martin Stuart-Fox, *Contemporary Laos: Studies in the Politics and the Society of the Lao People's Democratic Republic* (St. Lucia: University of Queensland Press, 1982); Martin Stuart-Fox and Mary Koogman, *Historical Dictionary of Laos* (London: Scarecrow Press, 1992); and an interview with Christian Culas, whom I thank most warmly.

24. Cambodia

Epigraph: quoted in Michael Vickery, *Cambodia 1975–1982* (Boston: South End, 1984), p. 148.

1. The name Khmer Rouge which they always rejected, was bestowed by Sihanouk, who used it to describe the first guerrilla groups in the late 1960s. We prefer this term to the name "Polpotists," which is more common in Cambodia but which overpersonalizes a movement that was not led by Pol Pot alone. Use of this latter term has also allowed leaders such as Ieng Sary and Khieu Samphan to dissociate themselves from previous events. The fact that they escaped the purges of 1975–1979 implies that they must have gone along with and abetted some monstrous crimes.

2. The term "Cambodian" is used here to refer to anything connected with Cambodia, and "Khmer" is used to describe the major ethnic group in a country in which other minorities made up 15 percent of the population until 1970. Influenced by ethnic nationalism, recent governments in Phnom Penh have tended to substitute "Khmer" for "Cambodian." "Kampuchea," which was the official name of the country from 1975 to 1991, was simply the Khmer pronunciation of the French name for the country, "Cambodge." The word originates in Sanskrit.

3. Curiously, it was thus the Communists themselves who first began to talk about genocide within a Communist regime, before commentators in the West latched onto the term.

4. More recent events, however, such as the July 1997 coup d'état by the second

prime minister, Hun Sen, against Prince Ranariddh, who won the 1993 elections, have brought renewed instability.

5. François Ponchaud, *Cambodia, Year Zero* (New York: Penguin, 1978).

6. There were also counterattacks, reassuring and filled with lies. See, e.g., Jérôme Steinbach and Jocelyne Steinbach, *Cambodge, l'autre sourire* (Paris: Editions Sociales, 1976).

7. Pin Yathay with John Man, *Stay Alive My Son* (London: Bloomsbury, 1987), p. 384.

8. The best recent history of Democratic Kampuchea (the official name of the Khmer Rouge state) is David P. Chandler, *The Tragedy of Cambodian History: Politics, War, and Revolution since 1945* (New Haven: Yale University Press, 1991); see also Marie-Alexandrine Martin, *Cambodia, a Shattered Society* (Berkeley: University of California Press, 1994).

9. David P. Chandler, *Brother Number One: A Political Biography of Pol Pot* (Boulder: Westview Press, 1992); and Ben Kiernan, *The Pol Pot Regime: Race, Power, and Genocide in Cambodia under the Khmer Rouge, 1975–1979* (New Haven: Yale University Press, 1996), pp. 20–25.

10. See, e.g., Haing S. Ngor and Roger Warner, *Surviving the Killing Fields: The Cambodian Odyssey of Haing S. Ngor* (London: Chatto and Windus, 1988), p. 71.

11. Chandler, *Brother Number One*, p. 308, n. 28; Kiernan, *Pol Pot Regime*, p. 108.

12. Henri Locard, "Tramkâk District in the Grip of the Khmer Rouge," paper presented at the conference "Cambodia: Power, Myth, and Memory," Monash University, December 1996, pp. 26–33.

13. Because of their obsession with secrecy, the Khmer Rouge always carried out executions at night.

14. Kiernan, *Pol Pot Regime*, p. 167.

15. The other leaders were Hou Youn, Hu Nim, and Khieu Samphan, all of whom were the legal front of the Communist Party in Phnom Penh until 1967 and were former government ministers. Others, intermittently fighting as rebels since 1963, included Nuon Chea, Sao Phim, Son Sen, Vorn Vet, Ieng Sary and his wife, the wife of Saloth Sar (aka Pol Pot), Ieng Thirith, and Khieu Ponnary. The last two were sisters. All of this group belonged to the same generation, having been born in the late 1920s.

16. Kiernan, *Pol Pot Regime*, p. 108.

17. Chandler, *Brother Number One*, pp. 63–64.

18. Serge Thion, "Chronology of Khmer Communism, 1940–1982," in *Revolution and Its Aftermath in Kampuchea: Eight Essays*, ed. David P. Chandler and Ben Kiernan (New Haven: Yale University Southeast Asia Studies, 1983), pp. 301–302.

19. The measure apparently was decided in January 1975, at the same time as the abolition of money directly after the printing of a new currency. The only leader to oppose the move, the influential Hou Youn, a former minister in the Sihanouk regime and a founding member of the KCP, disappeared in the following months in the first of a series of high-level purges.

20. The Khmer Rouge immediately abolished the Khmer currency. One unforeseen consequence was that the dollar immediately became the (illegal) means of exchange.

21. Marek Sliwinski, *Le génocide Khmer rouge: Une analyze démographique* (Paris: L'Harmattan, 1995), p. 30.

22. This would explain why some people left with very few belongings, and in particular without any articles that could be exchanged on the black market, which proved to be the key means of survival over the following months and years.

23. The only explanation for this is the dogmatic hostility to anything written down that was not revolutionary by nature. Books were destroyed and abandoned, as at the National Library, or they were transformed into cigarette paper.

24. See Pin Yathay, *Stay Alive, My Son,* pp. 62, 68; Haing Ngor, *Surviving the Killing Fields,* p. 130.

25. Statement by Channo, *Phnom Penh Post* (hereafter *PPP*), 7 April 1995, p. 5.

26. See, e.g., Pin Yathay, *Stay Alive, My Son,* pp. 59, 97, 221–223.

27. Usha Welaratna, *Beyond the Killing Fields: Voices of Nine Cambodian Survivors in America* (Stanford: Stanford University Press, 1993), p. 78.

28. See the general discussion about relations between the peasants and the New People in Kiernan, *Pol Pot Regime,* pp. 210–215.

29. Ibid., p. 219.

30. Pin Yathay, *Stay Alive, My Son,* p. 93.

31. Kiernan, *Pol Pot Regime,* pp. 97.

32. Pin Yathay cites several instances of planned flights or revolts that were foiled by sudden forced movements of the population.

33. People often ended up possessing nothing more than a bowl and a spoon. See Charles H. Twining, "The Economy," in *Cambodia 1975–1978: Rendezvous with Death,* ed. Karl D. Jackson, (Princeton: Princeton University Press, 1989), p. 121.

34. Pin Yathay, *Stay Alive, My Son,* p. 124.

35. According to Julio Jeldres, one of Sihanouk's advisers, in *PPP,* 20 September 1996.

36. Chandler, *Brother Number One,* pp. 205–209.

37. Kiernan, *Pol Pot Regime,* p. 333.

38. Chandler, *Tragedy of Cambodian History,* p. 298.

39. Each zone was composed of several such departments.

40. Chandler, *Brother Number One,* pp. 207, 209; idem, *Tragedy of Cambodian History,* p. 295.

41. Kiernan, *Pol Pot Regime,* p. 418.

42. Ben Kiernan, "Wild Chickens, Farm Chickens, and Cormorants: Kampuchea's Eastern Zone under Pol Pot," in Chandler and Kiernan, *Revolution and Its Aftermath,* pp. 191–197.

43. Chandler, *Tragedy of Cambodian History,* pp. 296–297; Kiernan, *Pol Pot Regime,* pp. 392–411.

44. Kiernan, *Pol Pot Regime,* p. 144.

45. Several reports agree (see esp. Chandler, *Tragedy of Cambodian History,* p. 276) that a number of people were sent back to Cambodia, sometimes in exchange for cattle, even after the fighting had begun. It is probable that such people were being sent back to certain death.

46. See, e.g., Pin Yathay, *Stay Alive, My Son,* pp. 368–413.

47. Y Phandara, *Retour à Phnom Penh: Le Cambodge du génocide à la colonisation* (Paris: A. M. Métailié, 1982), p. 228.

48. Quoted in Henri Locard, *Le goulag Khmer rouge* (University of Lyon II, Department of Languages, 1995), p. 17, reprinted in *Communisme,* nos. 47–48 (1996), 127–161.

49. Quoted in Chandler, *Brother Number One,* p. 265.

50. Ibid., p. 322.

51. Quoted in Locard, *Le goulag Khmer rouge,* pp. 8–9.

52. Kiernan, *Pol Pot Regime*; Vickery, *Cambodia, 1975–1982.* Vickery seriously underestimates the original size of the population. Kiernan's figure is an extrapolation from several microstudies of different sectors of the population: 25 percent losses in the families of refugees; 35 percent, 41 percent, and 53 percent losses in three villages; 42 percent in one neighborhood in Phnom Penh (of whom only 25 percent died of hunger or disease); and 36 percent losses, almost all by assassination, in a group of 350 inhabitants in the eastern zone.

53. Kiernan, *Pol Pot Regime,* pp. 456–460; Stephen R. Heder, *Kampuchean Occupation and Resistance* (Bankok: Institute of Asian Studies, 1980).

54. Chandler, *Brother Number One,* p. 261.

55. Craig Etcheson, *The Rise and Demise of Democratic Kampuchea* (Boulder: Westview, 1984), p. 148.

56. Leo Mong Hai, president of the Khmer Institute for Democracy, interview with the author, December 1996.

57. Sliwinski, *Le génocide,* pp. 49–67.

58. Welaratna, *Beyond the Killing Fields,* pp. xix and 2.

59. An idea that underlies the otherwise informative and important study by William Shawcross, *Sideshow: Nixon, Kissinger, and the Destruction of Cambodia* (London: Deutsch, 1979); see also Kiernan, *Pol Pot Regime,* pp. 20 and 24.

60. Chandler, *Brother Number One,* pp. 13 and 163.

61. Sliwinksi, *Le génocide,* pp. 42–48.

62. Locard, *Le goulag Khmer rouge,* p. 10.

63. Etcheson, *Rise and Demise,* p. 148.

64. Sliwinski, *Le génocide,* p. 82.

65. Munthit, *PPP,* 7 April 1995, p. 6.

66. See, e.g., Kenneth M. Quinn, "The Pattern and Scope of Violence," in Jackson, *Cambodia 1975–1978,* p. 190.

67. Interview with the author, December 1996.

68. *PPP,* 7 April 1995, p. 7.

69. David Hawk, "The Photographic Record," in Jackson, *Cambodia 1975–1978,* p. 212.

70. *PPP,* 7 April 1995, p. 6.

71. It was enough to have gone to secondary school, or sometimes even simply to be literate, to be classified as an intellectual.

72. Charles H. Twining, "The Economy," in Jackson, *Cambodia 1975–1978,* p. 134.

73. Pin Yathay, *Stay Alive, My Son*, p. 178.

74. Kiernan, *Pol Pot Regime*, p. 295, who quotes Stephen Heder's in-depth study, *Kampuchean Occupation and Resistance.*

75. Sliwinski, *Le génocide*, pp. 76, 77.

76. François Ponchaud, "Social Change in the Vortex of Revolution," in Jackson, *Cambodia 1975–1978*, p. 153.

77. Pin Yathay mentions a number of Chinese who died of hunger after having to exchange their gold savings for a few boxes of rice; *Stay Alive, My Son*, p. 243.

78. Kiernan, *Pol Pot Regime*, p. 297.

79. Sliwinski, *Le génocide*, p. 76.

80. Quoted in Elizabeth Becker, *When the War Was Over: Voices of Cambodia's Revolution and Its People* (New York: Simon and Schuster, 1986), p. 240.

81. See the statement by Niseth, who was moved to a Pnong village, in Welaratna, *Beyond the Killing Fields*, p. 180.

82. Most of the information here concerning the Cham is drawn from Kiernan, *Pol Pot Regime*, pp. 252–288.

83. Becker, *When the War Was Over*, p. 246.

84. Kiernan, *Pol Pot Regime*, pp. 428–431.

85. Sliwinski, *Le génocide*, p. 76.

86. Ibid., p. 57.

87. See Michael Vickery, "Democratic Kampuchea: Themes and Variations" in Chandler and Kiernan, *Revolution and Its Aftermath*, pp. 99–135.

88. Pin Yathay, *Stay Alive, My Son*, pp. 217, 264.

89. Unlike the leaders of other Communist countries, Khmer Rouge leaders rarely traveled around the country, perhaps because of their paranoia. No eyewitness statements mention visits from the leaders.

90. See, e.g., Ly Heng and Françoise Demeure, *Cambodge: Le sourire bâillonné*, (Xonrupt-Longemer: Anako, 1994), pp. 105, 150–151, and 172–173.

91. Pin Yathay, *Stay Alive, My Son*, pp. 90, 292–293, 341–343.

92. The picture was immediately much darker for people deported to mountainous or jungle zones where the land was to be cleared.

93. Quoted in Becker, *When the War Was Over*, p. 271.

94. Twining, "The Economy," p. 143.

95. *PPP*, 7 April 1995, p. 5; Sliwinski, *Le génocide*, p. 65, backs up this version of events.

96. Quinn, "Pattern and Scope of Violence," pp. 201–202.

97. Sliwinski, *Le génocide*, pp. 64–65; Twining, "The Economy," pp. 143–145.

98. Pin Yathay, *Stay Alive, My Son*, p. 317.

99. See, e.g., Chandler, *Brother Number One*, p. 195; Heng and Demeure, *Cambodge*, p. 100.

100. Haing Ngor was in a Khmer Rouge pharmacy one day when he overheard one nurse ask another whether she had "fed the war slaves yet"; *Surviving the Killing Fields*, p. 202.

101. Pin Yathay, *Stay Alive, My Son*, p. 67.

102. Ibid., p. 263.

103. Pin Yathay paid a huge price for a tiny map.

104. Pin Yathay, *Stay Alive, My Son*, p. 159.

105. Chandler, *Brother Number One*, pp. 191–193 and 197–198. The section of the plan devoted to heavy industry is the longest.

106. Ibid., p. 223.

107. This was the same figure announced by the deputy prime minister of China, Hua Guofeng, at the National Conference on the Example of Dazhai, in 1975.

108. Chandler, *Brother Number One*, pp. 193–194; Karl D. Jackson, "The Ideology of Total Revolution" in Jackson, *Cambodia 1975–1978*, p. 60.

109. Pin Yathay, *Stay Alive, My Son*, pp. 111, 152, 160; Twining, "The Economy," p. 130.

110. Kiernan, *Pol Pot Regime*, p. 235.

111. Laurence Picq, *Beyond the Horizon: Five Years with the Khmer Rouge*, trans. Patricia Norland (New York: St. Martin's Press, 1989), pp. 147–148.

112. Pin Yathay, *Stay Alive, My Son*, pp. 178–179.

113. Ibid., p. 210.

114. Twining, "The Economy," p. 122.

115. Pin Yathay, *Stay Alive, My Son*, p. 302.

116. This sort of military vocabulary was a constant feature of the regime.

117. Picq, *Beyond the Horizon;* Pin Yathay, *Stay Alive, My Son*, pp. 175, 197, 208.

118. *PPP*, 7 April 1995, p. 5.

119. See esp. Twining, "The Economy," pp. 149–150; Kiernan, *Pol Pot Regime*, p. 240; Pin Yathay, *Stay Alive, My Son*, p. 147.

120. Pin Yathay, *Stay Alive*, p. 240; Haing Ngor, *Surviving the Killing Fields*, p. 325.

121. Heng and Demeure, *Cambodge*, pp. 139–140; *PPP*, 7 April 1995, p. 7.

122. Haing Ngor relates the story of a child who took four days to die, tied to a pole in front of his parents; *Surviving the Killing Fields*, p. 272.

123. Ibid., pp. 135–136; Pin Yathay, *Stay Alive, My Son*, p. 278.

124. See, e.g., Haing Ngor, *Surviving the Killing Fields*, p. 145.

125. Pin Yathay, *Stay Alive, My Son*, p. 184.

126. Locard, *Le goulag khmer rouge*, p. 6.

127. Pin Yathay, *Stay Alive, My Son*, pp. 221–239.

128. Heng and Demeure, *Cambodge*, pp. 172–173.

129. Ponchaud, "Social Change," p. 160.

130. Haing Ngor, *Surviving the Killing Fields*, pp. 174 and 193–194.

131. Ken Khun, *De la dictature des Khmers rouges à l'occupation vietnamienne: Cambodge, 1975–1979* (Paris: L'Harmattan, 1994), p. 94. The gall-bladder remedy was common among the Khmer Loeu; see Ponchaud, "Social Change," p. 160.

132. Chandler, *Brother Number One*, pp. 174–175.

133. Interview with author, Cambodia, December 1996.

134. Picq, *Beyond the Horizon*.

135. Pin Yathay, *Stay Alive, My Son*, pp. 101, 140.

136. Chandler, *Brother Number One*, p. 202; Henri Locard, "Les chants révolutionnaires khmers rouges et la tradition culturelle cambodgienne, ou la révolution triom-

phante," paper presented at a conference on the Khmer Rouge, Phnom Penh, August 1996.

137. Françoise Corrèze and Alain Forest, *Le Cambodge à deux voix* (Paris: Editions L'Harmattan, 1984).

138. Heng and Demeure, *Cambodge*, p. 132.

139. Haing Ngor, *Surviving the Killing Fields*, p. 166.

140. Pin Yathay, *Stay Alive, My Son*, pp. 242-247, 336; similar episodes abound in all the statements made by people who survived and escaped.

141. *PPP,* 7 April 1995, p. 7; Chandler, *Brother Number One*, pp. 185–186, 227, 245, and 265.

142. In some cases people were required to write an autobiography every month, and if there was ever the slightest variation among versions, the punishment was death; Welaratna, *Beyond the Killing Fields*, p. 125.

143. Seng Kimseang tells of a young adolescent who was beaten unconscious for stealing rice, and who later disappeared at the hands of the Angkar; *PPP,* 7 April 1995, p. 7.

144. Heng and Demeure, *Cambodge*, p. 185.

145. Pin Yathay, *Stay Alive, My Son*, p. 248.

146. Haing Ngor, *Surviving the Killing Fields*, p. 228–229.

147. Locard, *Le goulag Khmer rouge.*

148. Chandler, *Tragedy of Cambodian History*, p. 260.

149. Pin Yathay, *Stay Alive, My Son*, p. 300.

150. Ken Khun, *De la dictature des Khmers rouges*, p. 96; in that case the woman was also raped by the soldiers before being killed; the cadre responsible died shortly afterwards in a purge.

151. *PPP,* 7 April 1995, pp. 6, 7.

152. Pin Yathay, *Stay Alive, My Son*, p. 337; Heng and Demeure, *Cambodge*, p. 107.

153. By contrast, everyone smoked tobacco, even the youngest Khmer Rouge soldiers. Drug-taking, though less widespread, was not specifically prohibited.

154. Ponchaud, "Social Change," p. 169; *PPP,* 7 April 1995, p. 7.

155. Pin Yathay, *Stay Alive, My Son*, pp. 172–175, 201–202.

156. Haing Ngor, *Surviving the Killing Fields*, p. 236; Welaratna, *Beyond the Killing Fields*, p. 53.

157. Pin Yathay, *Stay Alive, My Son*, pp. 174, 402.

158. *Le monde*, 18 June 1997, p. 16.

159. Pin Yathay, *Stay Alive, My Son*, p. 319.

160. Statement by a medical student, quoted in Ken Khun, *De la dictature des Khmers rouges*, p. 123. Manioc is one of the staples of the Cambodian diet.

161. Locard, *Le goulag Khmer rouge*, pp. 12–13.

162. See, e.g., Haing Ngor, *Surviving the Killing Fields*, p. 230.

163. Sliwinski, *Le génocide*, p. 78; I am rounding up his numbers, since they have only a notional value.

164. Haing Ngor, *Surviving the Killing Fields*, p. 338; Heng and Demeure, *Cambodge*, p. 109. This recalls the perhaps apocryphal torture that was inflicted on Khmers during

the Vietnamese occupation in the first half of the nineteenth century, when tea kettles were brought to a boil on their burning heads.

165. Locard, *Le goulag Khmer rouge,* p. 18.

166. See Pin Yathay, *Stay Alive, My Son,* p. 321.

167. Information about the prisons comes from the two excellent studies by Locard, *Le goulag khmer rouge,* and "Tramkâk District in the Grip of the Khmer Rouge."

168. Pin Yathay, *Stay Alive, My Son,* p. 245.

169. For example, of the eighty prisoners in one prison described by Pin Yathay (*Stay Alive, My Son,* p. 240), there were three survivors.

170. Kiernan, *Pol Pot Regime,* p. 345, n. 169.

171. *PPP,* 7 April 1995, p. 5.

172. Locard, *Le goulag Khmer rouge,* p. 6.

173. Ibid., p. 11.

174. Quoted in Ken Khun, *De la dictature des Khmers rouges,* p. 131.

175. See, e.g., Haing Ngor, *Surviving the Killing Fields,* pp. 220–222, 239–250, 302–308; Heng and Demeure, *Cambodge,* pp. 144–149.

176. *PPP,* 20 September 1996, p. 8.

177. Chandler, *Tragedy of Cambodian History,* pp. 285–302.

178. Quinn, "Pattern and Scope of Violence," p. 198; Kiernan, *Pol Pot Regime,* pp. 432–433.

179. Chandler, *Tragedy of Cambodian History,* p. 374, n. 27; Quinn, "Pattern and Scope of Violence," p. 210.

180. Kiernan, *Pol Pot Regime,* pp. 353–354.

181. Quinn, "Pattern and Scope of Violence," p. 198.

182. For more on this unhappy mix, see Jean-Claude Pomonti, "Angoisses khmères," *Le monde,* 10 March 1995.

183. Phandara, *Retour à Phnom Penh,* p. 88.

184. This view reflected the influence of the Chinese Cultural Revolution; the "Shanghai Commune" of 1967 was modeled on the Paris revolution.

185. Two other countries are in a similar position today: Laos and Burma. But the first has existed as a unified political entity only since 1945, and the second, which was remarkably prosperous as a British colony, is not quite as weak in relation to its neighbors.

186. Ponchaud, "Social Change," pp. 170–175.

187. Haing Ngor, *Surviving the Killing Fields,* p. 227. *Kama* is the Cambodian version of karma.

188. Unlike, for example, the temples of Java, such as Borobudur, which date from more or less the same period.

189. Several ethnographers have shown that in Cambodia there is a very weak link to the land and to ancestors, unusual for this part of the world.

190. Chandler, *Brother Number One,* pp. 101, 105–106, and 135; Raoul Marc Jennar, *Cambodge: Une presse sous pression* (Paris: Reporters Sans Frontières, 1997), p. 23.

191. Locard, *Le goulag Khmer rouge,* p. 15.

192. Haing Ngor, *Surviving the Killing Fields,* p. 208.

193. Pin Yathay, *Stay Alive, My Son*, pp. 101–103. Similar tactics were used by the Chinese Communist Party when they were seizing power.

194. Haing Ngor, *Surviving the Killing Fields*, pp. 143, 161, and 298–300.

195. Picq, *Beyond the Horizon*, p. 22.

196. Pin Yathay, *Stay Alive, My Son*, p. 284; Ponchaud, "Social Change," p. 164.

197. Chandler, *Tragedy of Cambodian History*, p. 247.

198. Ieng Sary, in *Newsweek*, 4 September 1975.

199. *Red Flag* (Beijing), 1 June 1958.

200. Pin Yathay, *Stay Alive*, p. 68; Haing Ngor, *Surviving the Killing Fields*, p. 130.

201. Picq, *Beyond the Horion*, p. 21; Phandara, *Retour à Phnom Penh*, p. 91.

202. Locard, *PPP*, 20 May 1994, p. 16.

203. Radio Phnom Penh, 18 April 1977, quoted in Jackson, *Cambodia 1975–1978*, p. 74.

204. Norodom Sihanouk, *Prisonnier des Khmers rouges* (Paris: Hachette, 1986).

205. Heng and Demeure, *Cambodge*, pp. 189–190.

206. Chandler, *Tragedy of Cambodian History*, p. 243.

207. Dith Pran (on whom the film *The Killing Fields* was based), quoted in Sidney Schanberg, "The Death and Life of Dith Pran," *New York Times Magazine*, 20 January 1980.

208. Heng and Demeure, *Cambodge*, p. 112.

209. Khun, *De la dictature des Khmers rouges*, pp. 97–98.

210. Picq, *Beyond the Horizon*.

211. Haing Ngor, *Surviving the Killing Fields*, pp. 139–140.

212. Sliwinski, *Le génocide*, p. 67.

213. Locard, *Le goulag Khmer rouge*, p. 28.

214. See, e.g., Chandler, *Brother Number One*, p. 214.

215. Haing Ngor, *Surviving the Killing Fields*, p. 203.

216. Speech on 27 September 1977, quoted in Jackson, *Cambodia 1975–1978*, p. 73.

217. Pin Yathay, *Stay Alive, My Son*, p. 193.

218. Chandler, *Brother Number One*, pp. 63 and 72–73.

219. An interview after the partisans had rallied to Ieng Sary, *PPP*, 15 November 1996, p. 6. For other ideas about links between Jacobinism and Communism see François Furet, *The Passing of an Illusion: The Idea of Communism in the Twentieth Century* (Chicago: University of Chicago Press, 1999).

220. Even the Samlaut uprising in 1967, which was officially the beginning of the armed resistance, was a reaction to Lon Nol's decision to reduce the amount of Cambodian rice given to the North Vietnamese army.

221. Sophia Quinn-Judge, "Ho Chi Minh: New Perspectives from the Comintern Files," in *Viet Nam: Sources et approches*, ed. Philippe Le Failler and Jean-Marie Mancini (Aix-en-Provence: Publications de l'Université de Provence, 1996), pp. 171–186.

222. Discernible in China during the short reign of Marshal Lin Biao (1967–1971).

223. Chandler, *Tragedy of Cambodian History*, p. 276.

224. Twining, "The Economy," p. 132.

225. Chandler, *Brother Number One*, pp. 176, 225–226; Kiernan, *Pol Pot Regime*, p. 379.

226. Radio Phnom Penh, 25 July 1975, in Jackson, "Ideology," p. 60.

227. Sihanouk claims that Zhou Enlai warned the Cambodian leadership in 1975 that they should not follow the Chinese example.

228. Locard, *Le goulag Khmer rouge*, p. 17.

229. See Pin Yathay, *Stay Alive, My Son*, p. 335.

230. Quoted in Martin, *Le mal cambodgien*, p. 193.

231. After 1960 there was a considerable drop in the prison population, particularly in the number of political prisoners, especially in China.

232. Chandler, *Brother Number One*, pp. 216–217.

233. Locard, *Le goulag Khmer rouge*, p. 19.

234. Chandler, *Brother Number One*, pp. 210–211.

235. From an account by a participant, ibid., pp. 171–172.

236. *PPP*, 20 September 1996, p. 7. Sihanouk claims that it was Pol Pot who composed the Angkar anthem.

237. Timothy Carney, "The Organization of Power," in Jackson, *Cambodia 1975–1978*, p. 95.

238. Pin Yathay, *Stay Alive, My Son*, p. 320.

239. Locard, *Le goulag Khmer rouge*, p. 19.

240. Pin Yathay, *Stay Alive, My Son*, p. 299.

241. The best summary of these is found in Kiernan, *Pol Pot Regime*.

242. Haing Ngor, *Surviving the Killing Fields*, p. 286.

243. Locard, *Le goulag Khmer rouge*, p. 19; Kiernan, *Pol Pot Regime*, p. 247.

244. Many of the following arguments are taken from Craig Etcheson, "Genocide: By the Laws, Not by Emotion," *PPP*, 11 August 1995, p. 20.

245. Barbara Harff and Ted Robert Gurr, "Towards an Empirical Definition of Genocides and Politicides," *International Studies Quarterly*, no. 32 (1988).

246. Phandara, *Retour à Phnom Penh*, pp. 72–73.

247. Sliwinski, *Le génocide*, p. 128.

248. Welaratna, *Beyond the Killing Fields*, p. 128.

249. Sliwinski, *Le génocide*, p. 153.

Part IV Conclusion

1. Doan Van Toai, *The Vietnamese Gulag*, trans. Sylvie Romanowski and Françoise Simon-Miller (New York: Simon and Schuster, 1986).

2. See Yves Chevrier, "L'empire distendu: Esquisse du politique en Chine des Qing à Deng Xiaoping," in *La greffe de l'état—trajectoires du politique 2*, ed. Jean-François Bayart (Paris: Karthala, 1996).

3. Doan, *The Vietnamese Gulag*, p. 100.

4. The French equivalent of West Point.

25. Communism in Latin America

1. In 1952 Cuba was ranked third among the twenty Latin American countries in terms of per-capita gross domestic product. Thirty years later, after more than twenty years of Castroism, Cuba had dropped to fifteenth, ahead of Nicaragua, Guatemala, El Salvador, Bolivia, and Haiti. See Jeannine Verdès-Leroux, *La lune et la caudillo* (Paris: Gallimard, 1998), p. 16.

2. Although there are many reasons to be critical of the Batista regime, the new Castro regime significantly exaggerated the country's poverty to increase Castro's credibility and to gain sympathy from Western intellectuals. For instance, Castro stated that 50 percent of the population was illiterate, while the actual figure in 1958 was 22 percent, at a time when the world average was about 44 percent.

3. Jeannine Verdès-Leroux has concluded that the figure of 20,000 dead, the number cited by the Castro regime and repeated by left-wing intellectuals in the West, was in fact false. After close analysis of the sources, she proposes a figure of 2,000.

4. Verdès-Laroux, *La lune et la caudillo,* pp. 179–189.

5. During the pilots' trial, in February 1959, the defense minister acted as prosecutor. After the pilots were acquitted, Castro intervened to have them condemned in a second trial in March, showing that the law was at the service of the dictator.

6. Manolo Ray launched a new armed movement, the People's Revolutionary Movement, which was very active in 1960 and 1961.

7. The Bay of Pigs operation, an unsuccessful attempt to land anti-Castro guerrillas in Cuba, was organized by the CIA during the Eisenhower administration and carried out under Kennedy.

8. Régis Debray, *Loués soient nos seigneurs* (Paris: Gallimard, 1996), p. 186.

9. Ibid., p. 185.

10. Ibid., p. 186.

11. Martha Frayde, *Ecoute Fidel* (Paris: Denoël, 1987).

12. Alfredo Carrion was shot at point-blank range by a guard known as "Jaguey Grande" for attempting to escape from the Melena 2 Farm.

13. The government weekly *Bohemia* acknowledged the value of this labor force in April 1973, when it spoke of "the use of counterrevolutionary prisoners for tasks in the public interest."

14. Castro consistently supported revolution abroad until the late 1980s. In 1979 and 1980 he sent 600 military advisers to Grenada to prop up the pro-Soviet regime of Maurice Bishop. When U.S. forces invaded in 1983, they took prisoner 750 Cubans.

15. At the same time, an additional 35,000 young people were enrolled in the Patriotic Military Service, where they were forcibly engaged in heavy work as a penal or disciplinary measure.

16. The links to Cuba were attested by the presence of 500 Nicaraguan military personnel among the Cuban forces in Angola. The Sandinistas' political alignment was also made clear by their opposition to the United Nations resolution condemning Soviet intervention in Afghanistan.

17. Gilles Bataillon, "Nicaragua: De la tyrannie à la dictature totalitaire," *Esprit,* October 1983.

18. Bayardo Arce, "De la stratégie révolutionnaire et de la construction du social-isme," *Esprit,* January 1986.

19. Cf. Mario Vargas Llosa, "Bréviare d'un massacre," *Esprit,* October 1983: "Un-like the case of other leaders of the Sendero Luminoso, we don't know whether he ever visited China, or whether in fact he has ever left Peru."

20. José Carlos Mariátegui (1895–1930) was the author of the famous *Seven Essays on the Reality of Peru.* His politics were halfway between Marxism and populism, allowing both the Communists and the Aprists to claim him as their predecessor.

21. Vargas Llosa, "Bréviare d'un massacre."

22. In August 1982 the Sendero claimed to have carried out 2,900 such actions.

23. APRA was established by the Peruvian Victor Raúl Haya de la Torre in 1924. Although it initially had ambitions for the whole continent, it had gradually limited itself to Peru.

26. Afrocommunism

1. Eric Fottorino, "Dans le piège rwandais," *Le monde,* 25 July 1997.

2. Interview, Lisbon *Expresso,* 12 May 1990, quoted in M. Cahen, "Le socialisme, c'est les Soviets plus l'ethnicité," *Politique africaine,* June 1991.

3. Marina and David Ottway, *Afrocommunism* (New York: Holmes and Meier, 1986), pp. 30–35. The word "Afrocommunism" used in the title of this chapter is borrowed from these authors. This borrowing is purely lexical and is not intended to have connotations similar to those of the term "Eurocommunism" as used in the 1970s. Eurocommunism implied the relationships among the Communist parties of Italy, France, and Spain and the hopes on the left for "socialism with a human face" that avoided mistakes made by the Soviet Union.

4. Christian Geffray, "Fragments d'un discours du pouvoir (1975–1985): Du bon usage d'une méconnaissance scientifique," *Politique africaine,* no. 29 (March 1988).

5. Marie Mendras, "La stratégie oblique en Afrique subsaharienne," in Group for Research and Study of Soviet Strategy, "L'URSS et le tiers-monde: Une stratégie oblique," *Cahiers de la Fondation pour les études de défense nationale,* no. 32 (1984).

6. Bukharin made explicit statements on this point at the Fourth Comintern Con-gress on 18 November 1922; see the supplement to *La correspondance internationale,* 4 January 1923.

7. Gareth M. Winrow, *The Foreign Policy of the GDR in Africa* (New York: Cam-bridge University Press, 1990).

8. Jean-François Bayart, "L'état," in Christian Coulon and Denis-Constant Mar-tin, *Les Afriques politiques* (Paris: La Découverte, 1991), p. 219.

9. This question must be addressed if one is take African adherence to Commu-nism seriously, as is pointed out by Michael Walter in his editorial in *Journal of Communist Studies,* nos. 3–4 (September–December 1985), a special issue on Marxist military regimes in Africa.

10. See esp. René Lemarchand, "La violence politique," in Coulon and Martin, *Les Afriques politiques,* which also contains a sizable bibliography on the question.

11. In 1985, just before the start of the Gorbachev era, in addition to these three

countries the Soviet Union regarded Algeria, Benin, Cape Verde, the Congo, Guinea, Guinea-Bissau, Madagascar, São Tomé and Príncipe, and Tanzania as allies.

12. See the portrait by Jacques de Barrin in *Le monde*, 23 May 1991.

13. Haile Fida, one of the leaders of MEISON and a member of the Dergue's Political Bureau, had acquired his Marxist-Leninist tendencies while studying in France. He was arrested in August 1977 and disappeared after being detained for several months.

14. Patrice Piquard, "L'Ethiopie juge Mengistu, le boucher rouge," *L'evénement du Jeudi*, 22–28 December 1994.

15. See Paul B. Henze, "Communism and Ethiopia," *Problems of Communism*, May–June 1981.

16. American sources estimate that 15,000 Cuban personnel were stationed there.

17. Christopher Clapham, "The Workers' Party of Ethiopia," *Journal of Communist Studies*, no. 1 (March 1985).

18. Ogla Kapeliouk, "Quand le paysan est tenu à l'écart des décisions politiques," *Le monde diplomatique*, April 1984.

19. Bertrand Le Gendre, "Ethiopie: Le procès de la Terreur rouge," *Le monde*, 13 May 1995. In 1997 the secretary general of the Federation of Ethiopian Teachers suggested a figure of 30,000 political murders since 1974; Amnesty International, *Human Rights Violations in Ethiopia* (London, 1978), p. 16.

20. Karel Bartošek, *Les aveux des archives, Prague—Paris—Prague, 1948–1956* (Paris: Seuil, 1996).

21. See Amnesty International, *Human Rights Violations in Ethiopia*, pp. 9–11, 14–15.

22. Zenawi became president immediately after Mengistu fled. The trial of the leaders of the Mengistu regime, who were accused of genocide and crimes against humanity, was adjourned in December 1994 and resumed on 13 May 1995 with further pretrial proceedings. The prosecution's case began in early 1996, and the trials of 71 former senior officials (including 25 being tried *in absentsia*) continued slowly over the next few years. The most recent indictment came in January 1998, when Major Melaku Tefera, the former head of the Dergue's powerful Revolutionary Campaign Coordinating Committee, was charged with the killings of 1,100 people.

23. *Ethiopian Herald*, 13 May 1997.

24. Eritrea was by no means united in the face of an oppressor. The region has many ethnic minorities, and bloodshed among the various groups was common.

25. Eritrea had been occupied by Italy in 1882 and was annexed by Haile Selassie in 1962.

26. There were also a number of more heterogeneous armed groups that existed on a regional level: the Ethiopian Democratic Union included monarchists, people who had lost their land in the 1974 revolution, and others who had suffered under the Dergue. This group fought alongside Beni Amaer and Afar groups in specific actions and generally added to the climate of insecurity in the country.

27. When Gorbachev began to withdraw support from Africa there was an immediate rapprochement between Addis Ababa and Tel Aviv, which was worried by the prospect of the weakening of an anti-Islamic power in the region.

28. The Eritrean Popular Liberation Front was basically a Marxist organization that recruited among the Christian population. The EPLF emerged from a schism with the more conservative Eritrean Liberation Front, which thereafter remained a largely Muslim organization. See Alain Fenet, "Le programme du FPLE, nation et révolution," in *La Corne de l'Afrique. Questions nationales et politique internationale* (Paris: L'Harmattan, 1986).

29. Africa Watch, *Evil Days: Thirty Years of War and Famine in Ethiopia* (New York, 1991), p. 117.

30. Ibid., p. 127.

31. Georges Lecomte, "Utopisme politique et transfert de population en Ethiopie," *Esprit*, June 1986.

32. Jean Gallais, "Sécheresse, famine, état en Ethiopie," *Hérodote*, no. 39 (October–December 1985).

33. Michel Foucher, "L'Ethiopie: A qui sert la famine?" *Hérodote*, no. 39 (October–December 1985).

34. Anti-Slavery Society, *Forced Labour in Humera: Intervention on behalf of the Anti-Slavery Society*, a report presented to UNESCO's Human Rights Commission, Working Party on Slavery (Geneva, August 1981). See Africa Watch, *Evil Days*, p. 167.

35. Report from President Haile Mariam Mengistu to the Central Committee of the Ethiopian Workers' Party, 14 April 1986.

36. Foucher, "L'Ethiopie," p. 112.

37. Cultural Survival, *Ethiopia: More Light on Resettlement* (London: Survival International, 1991).

38. Quoted in Le Gendre, "Ethiopie."

39. On this point, see the work of Michel Cahen, especially his disagreements with Elisto M. Macamo in *Lusotopie*, 1996, pp. 365–378.

40. Interview, *Afrique Asie*, 16 May 1977, quoted in *Angola, bilan d'un socialisme de guerre*, ed. Pierre Beaudet (Paris: L'Harmattan, 1992).

41. *Pravda*, 5 November 1975, quoted in Branko Lazitch and Pierre Rigoulot, "Angola 1974–1988: Un échec du communisme en Afrique," supplement to *Est et ouest*, no. 54 (May 1988).

42. To the name People's Republic of Angola, the only one recognized by Portugal in February 1976, UNITA and the FNLA added the adjective "democratic."

43. Quoted in Lazitch and Rigoulot, "Angola 1974–1988," p. 33.

44. *Libération-Afrique*, no. 9 (March 1974).

45. See an informed Trotskyite point of view in Claude Gabriel, *Angola, le tournant africain?* (Paris: La Brèche, 1978).

46. Of thirty members of the Central Committee, five were shot (including Nito Alvès), three disappeared in mysterious circumstances, and two were expelled; Lazitch and Rigoulot, "Angola 1974–1988," p. 21.

47. The Portuguese Trotskyite review *Acçao comunista*, quoted in Gabriel, *Angola*, p. 329.

48. Ibid.

49. Cabinda was annexed to Angola in 1956 by the Portuguese, but it is separated

from the rest of the country by the mouth of the Congo River. Its Bacongo people have long dreamed of independence, which would allow them to keep the profits from their oil reserves for themselves. Since 1975 the presence of 10,000 Angolan troops and 2,000 Cubans has prevented this.

50. Républica Popular de Angola, *Sintese do plano de recuperaçao economica a nivel global para o bieno 1989–90,* (Luanda, 1988).

51. Christine Messiant, "Angola, les vois de l'ethnisation et de la décomposition," *Lusotopie,* 1994.

52. Frelimo was basically the result of a merger of various nationalist organizations made up of émigré Mozambicans in Tanganyka, Rhodesia, and Nyassaland. See Luis de Brito, "Une relecture nécessaire: La genèse du parti-Etat Frelimo," *Politique africaine,* no. 29 (March 1988).

53. On the weaknesses of Mozambican nationalism, see Claude Cahen, "Sur quelques mythes et quelques réalités de la colonisation et de la décolonisation portugaises," paper presented at the conference "Décolonisations comparées," Aix-en-Provence, 30 September–3 October 1993.

54. Christian Geffray, *La cause des armes au Mozambique. Anthropologie d'une guerre civile* (Paris: Karthala, 1990), p. 27.

55. One of the biggest camps, at Milange, near the frontier with Malawi, contained 10,000 Jehovah's Witnesses.

56. Human Rights Watch, *Conspicuous Destruction: War, Famine, and the Reform Process in Mozambique* (New York, 1992).

57. Michel Cahen, "Check on Socialism in Mozambique: What Check? What Socialism?" *Review of African Political Economy,* no. 57 (1993), 54.

58. At the Fifth Frelimo Congress, July 1989.

59. Amnesty International, *Mozambique: Independence and Human Rights* (London, 1990), p. 24.

60. Michel Laban, "Ecrivains et pouvoir politique au Mozambique après l'indépendance," *Lusotopie,* 1995.

61. See Michel Cahen, *Mozambique, la révolution implosée,* (Paris: L'Harmattan, 1987), pp. 152–154.

62. Speech by President Samora Machel at the December 1985 session of the Popular Assembly, quoted in M. Cahen, *Mozambique,* p. 163.

63. Human Rights Watch, *Conspicuous Destruction,* p. 4. UNICEF calculated that 600,000 people died from starvation over that ten-year period; the same number died of hunger in Ethiopia in 1984–85.

64. Jean-François Revel, "Au Mozambique aussi, le marxisme-léninisme engendre la famine," *Est et ouest,* no. 40 (March 1987).

65. Geffray, *La cause des armes,* p. 209.

66. H. Gebaver, "The Subsidized Food Distribution System in Mozambique and Its Socio-Economic Impact," Technical Assistance, EC Food Security Department, Maputo, 1991, quoted in Human Rights Watch, *Conspicuous Destruction,* p. 120.

67. Alain Besançon, "La normalité du communisme selon Zinoviev," *Pouvoirs,* no. 21 (1982).

68. The term is that of Jean Leca, quoted in M. Cahen, *Mozambique,* p. 161.

27. Communism in Afghanistan

1. For the history of Afghanistan, see Mike Barry, *La résistance afghane du Grand Moghol à l'invasion soviétique* (Paris: Flammarion, 1989) (an earlier version appeared in 1984 under the title *Le royaume de l'insolence*); Olivier Roy, *Islam and Resistance in Afghanistan* (New York: Cambridge University Press, 1996); Assem Akram, *Histoire de la guerre d'Afghanistan* (Paris: Balland, 1996); Pierre Centlivres and Michèle Centlivres, eds., *Afghanistan, la colonisation impossible* (Paris: Le Cerf, 1984); Jacques Lévesque, *L'URSS en Afghanistan* (Brussels: Complexe, 1990); Eric Bachelier, *L'Afghanistan en guerre. La fin du grand jeu soviétique* (Lyon: Presses Universitaires de Lyon, 1992); and André Brigot and Olivier Roy, *The War in Afghanistan: An Account and Analysis of the Country, Its People, Soviet Intervention, and the Resistance,* trans. Mary Bottomore and Tom Bottomore (New York: Harvester Wheatsheaf, 1988). See also *Les nouvelles d'Afghanistan,* which since 1980 has provided regular information of extremely high quality. For ease of reading, proper names are transcribed according to European conventions.

2. See Louis Fisher, *The Soviets in World Affairs: A History of the Relations between the Soviet Union and the Rest of the World, 1917–1929* (Princeton: Princeton University Press, 1951), esp. chaps. 13 and 29.

3. Nicholas Tandler, "'Désinformation' à propos de l'Afghanistan," *Est et ouest,* no. 616 (1–15 June 1978), 19–20.

4. Ibid., p. 20.

5. Georgi Agabekov, *OGPU: The Russian Secret Terror* (New York: Brentano's, 1931).

6. Ludwig Adamec, "Le fils du porteur d'eau," *Les nouvelles d'Afghanistan,* no. 48 (July 1990), 16–17.

7. Marc Lazarévitch, "L'intervention soviétique en Afghanistan de 1929," *Les cahiers d'histoire sociale,* no. 1 (1993), 158. For more on this uprising see Roy, *Islam and Resistance,* pp. 83–84.

8. Barry, *La résistance afghane,* p. 241.

9. Ibid., p. 253.

10. Christopher Andrew and Oleg Gordievsky, *KGB: The Inside Story of Its Foreign Operations from Lenin to Gorbachev* (New York: HarperCollins, 1990), p. 569.

11. For more details on these leaders, see Barry, *La résistance afghane,* pp. 294–297.

12. Etienne Gille, "L'accession au pouvoir des communistes prosoviétiques" in Centlivres and Centlivres, *Afghanistan,* p. 184; Lévesque, *L'URSS en Afghanistan,* p. 35.

13. Olivier Roy, "De l'instauration de la République à l'invasion soviétique," in Brigot and Roy, *The War in Afghanistan,* pp. 29–30.

14. Ibid., p. 30.

15. Barry, *La résistance afghane,* p. 252.

16. Ibid., p. 301; and Akram, *Histoire de la guerre d'Afghanistan,* p. 93–95. Akram produces testimony by Mohammed Najibullah as evidence for this theory.

17. Barry, *La résistance afghane,* p. 300.

18. Ibid., p. 302.

19. Amnesty International, *Annual Report, 1979,* covering the year 1978 (London, 1979), p. 101.

20. Barry, *La résistance afghane*, p. 304.

21. Rémi Kauffer and Roger Faligot, *Les maîtres espions. Histoire mondiale du renseignement*, vol. 2: *De la guerre froide à nos jours* (Paris: Robert Laffont, 1994), p. 391. See also Patrice Franceschi, *Ils ont choisi la liberté* (Grenoble: Arthaud, 1981), pp. 41–42; and Gille, "L'accession au pouvoir," pp. 199–200.

22. Gille, "L'accession au pouvoir," p. 199.

23. Akram, *Histoire de la guerre d'Afghanistan*, p. 516; and Marie Broxup and Chantal Lemercier-Quelquejay, "Les expériences soviétiques de guerres musulmanes" in Brigot and Roy, *The War in Afghanistan*, p. 41.

24. Bachelier, *L'Afghanistan*, p. 50.

25. Barry, *La résistance afghane*, p. 314. For the Kerala widows see also *Les nouvelles d'Afghanistan*, nos. 35–36 (December 1987), 33. Barry also points out that five Soviet officers were in charge of the operation.

26. Lévesque, *L'URSS en Afghanistan*, p. 48; Gille, "L'accession au pouvoir," p. 200. See also Amnesty International, "Violations of Human Rights and Fundamental Liberties in the Democratic Republic of Afghanistan," 11 April 1979. This report, which draws only on official cases, mentions cases of children in detention.

27. Vladimir Bukovsky, *Reckoning with Moscow: A Dissident in the Kremlin's Archives* (London: John Murray, 1998), pp. 380–382. The author reproduces excerpts from discussions between Aleksei Kosygin and Nur-Mohammed Taraki, who was asking for aid from the Soviet Union. The initial response from Moscow was not particularly favorable. An English translation of the full transcript was published in the *Cold War International History Project Bulletin*, nos. 8–9 (Winter 1996–97), 146–150.

28. Barry, *La résistance afghane*, pp. 306–307.

29. Kauffer and Faligot, *Les maîtres espions*, p. 390.

30. Shah Bazgar, *Afghanistan, la résistance au coeur* (Paris: Denoël, 1987), pp. 65–66. Shah Bazgar died on 23 November 1989 in an ambush while researching a report on irrigation systems. The only weapon he had was a camera. See Gilles Rossignol and Etienne Gille, "Un témoin: Shah Bazgar," *Les nouvelles d'Afghanistan*, no. 45 (December 1989), 6.

31. Roy, *Islam and Resistance*, p. 125; Gille, "L'accession au pouvoir," p. 199.

32. Andrew and Gordievsky, *KGB*, pp. 570–571. The authors note that Boyarinov was killed by his own men when he was mistaken for an Afghan.

33. Politburo archives, quoted in Akram, *Histoire de la guerre d'Afghanistan*, pp. 149–150; and Bukovsky, *Reckoning with Moscow*, pp. 385–386.

34. Akram, *Histoire de la guerre d'Afghanistan*, pp. 150–154, explores the various possibilities concerning Soviet expansionism.

35. Bukovsky, *Reckoning with Moscow*, pp. 493–494. Christophe de Ponfilly and Frédéric Laffont report in *Poussières de guerre* (Paris: Robert Laffont, 1990), p. 91: "The Russians used the most modern weapons they had at their disposal, and planes like the Su-25 dropped their bombs from more than 32,000 feet."

36. *Les nouvelles d'Afghanistan*, no. 7 (November 1981), 9. A survey titled "Intérêts économiques soviétiques en Afghanistan," detailing the extent to which the Soviet Union pillaged the natural resources of the country, can be found in the same issue.

37. G. F. Krivosheev, *Grif sekretnosti sniat: Poteri Vooruzhennykh sil v voinakh, bo-evykh deistviyakh, i voennykh konfliktakh* (The stamp of secrecy lifted: Losses of the armed forces in wars, combat operations, and military conflicts) (Moscow: Voenizdat, 1983), p. 407.

38. S. Jenis, "Un bonjour d'Afghanistan," *L'alternative,* no. 19 (November–December 1982), 43. See also Svetlana Aleksievitch, *Les cercueils de zinc* (Paris: Christian Bourgois, 1991).

39. De Ponfilly and Laffont, *Poussières de guerre,* p. 175.

40. See Bukovsky, *Reckoning with Moscow,* pp. 263, 460; and Françoise Thom, "Le KGB et les Juifs," *Pardès,* nos. 19–20 (1994), 7–24.

41. Bachelier, *L'Afghanistan,* p. 52. On the various resistance groups, see also Roy, *Islam;* and Akram, *Histoire de la guerre d'Afghanistan,* chap. 8.

42. On the pattern of mass suffering under total war and the way that civilization seems to disappear, see Annette Becker and Stéphane Audoin-Rouzeau, "Violence et consentement: La culture de guerre du Premier conflit mondial," in *Pour une histoire culturelle,* ed. Jean-Pierre Rioux and Jean-François Sirinelli (Paris: Le Seuil, 1997), pp. 251–271; and François Furet, *The Passing of an Illusion: The Idea of Communism in the Twentieth Century* (Chicago: University of Chicago Press, 1999), chaps. 2 and 3.

43. Olivier Roy, "Les limites de la pacification soviétique en Afghanistan," *L'alternative,* no. 31 (January–February 1985), 14.

44. Amnesty International, *Annual Report, 1989,* covering the year 1988 (London, 1989), p. 172. See also "Les réfugiés afghans," *Les nouvelles d'Afghanistan,* nos. 35–36 (December 1987).

45. Barry, *La résistance afghane,* p. 18.

46. Marina Isenburg, "Les origines du Tribunal permanent des peuples," *Bulletin d'information et de liaison du Bureau international afghanistan. La Lettre du BIA,* special issue, "Afghanistan, Tribunal des peuples. Stockholm: 1981—Paris: 1982, compte rendu des travaux," p. 3.

47. Quoted in Barry, *La résistance afghane,* p. 80. On the massacre in the village of Padkhwab-e Shana, see *Bulletin d'information* and Barry, chap. 1.

48. Amnesty International, *Annual Report, 1983,* covering the year 1982 (London, 1983), p. 227; and Bernard Dupaigne, "L'armée soviétique en Afghanistan," *L'alternative,* no. 31 (January–February 1985), 8–9.

49. Dupaigne, "L'armée soviétique en Afghanistan," pp. 8–9.

50. Quoted in Roy, "Les limites de la pacification soviétique," p. 13. Amnesty International, *Annual Report, 1984,* p. 240, also noted the murder of twenty-three civilians in the village of Raudza, in Ghazni Province. Similar reports of villages destroyed were published in every Amnesty report for the period in question.

51. Akram, *Histoire de la guerre d'Afghanistan,* p. 523; Amnesty International, *Annual Report, 1986,* p. 222.

52. *Bulletin d'information,* p. 15.

53. Pierre Gentelle, "Chronologie 1747–1984," *Problèmes politiques et sociaux,* 15 December 1984, p. 14.

54. Akram, *Histoire de la guerre d'Afghanistan,* p. 523. Gennadii Bocharov reports a

similar practice; cattle were then systematically slaughtered; *La roulette russe* (Paris: Denoël, 1990), p. 30.

55. Bukovsky, *Reckoning with Moscow*, p. 534.

56. "Afghanistan, assassinats et réfugiés," *La chronique d'Amnesty International*, no. 19 bis (June 1988), 10. Amnesty repeated the claim in a press communiqué dated 4 May 1988, Amnesty International Archives, London, Afghanistan file for 1988.

57. *Les nouvelles d'Afghanistan*, nos. 35–36 (December 1987), 17.

58. Akram, *Histoire de la guerre d'Afghanistan*, pp. 178–179; and Anne Guérin, "Une sanglante lassitude," *La chronique d'Amnesty International*, no. 2 (December 1986), 9.

59. Bazgar, *Afghanistan, la résistance au coeur*, pp. 101–102.

60. Olivier Roy, "Kabul, la sinistrée," in *Villes en guerre*, ed. Eric Sarner (Paris: Autrement, 1986), p. 74.

61. *Les nouvelles d'Afghanistan* published a special issue on the town, "Hérat ou l'art meurtri," nos. 41–42 (March 1989), 40.

62. Barry, *La résistance afghane*, p. 308.

63. Bernard Dupaigne, "Les droits de l'homme en Afghanistan," *Les nouvelles d'Afghanistan*, nos. 24–25 (October 1985), 8–9.

64. Report by Felix Ermacora, a special rapporteur for the United Nations, in application of Resolution 1985/88 of the UN Human Rights Commission, *Report on the Situation of Human Rights in Afghanistan*, UN Document No. E/CN.4/1985/21 (New York, 19 February 1985). Ermacora prepared updates on this report (under the same title) twice a year over the next four years.

65. Amnesty International, press communiqué, 2 November 1983, Amnesty International Archives, Afghanistan file for 1983.

66. Ermacora, *Report on the Situation*, p. 11, quoted in Bazgar, *Afghanistan, la résistance au coeur*, p. 132.

67. Amnesty International, *Afghanistan: Torture of Political Prisoners* (London, 1986), pp. 19–26; and Cristina L'Homme, "Les soviétiques interrogent, les Afghans torturent," *La chronique d'Amnesty International*, no. 2 (December 1986), 6–8.

68. Statement by Tajwar Kakar, quoted in Doris Lessing, *The Wind Blows Away Our Words and Other Documents Relating to the Afghan Resistance* (New York: Vintage, 1987), pp. 193–204.

69. Andrew and Gordievsky, *KGB*, p. 572.

70. Kauffer and Faligot, *Les maîtres espions*, p. 392.

71. Amnesty International, *Annual Report, 1981*, p. 225; and *Les nouvelles d'Afghanistan*, "Les manifestations étudiantes d'avril 1980," no. 48 (July 1990), 18–20.

72. Akram, *Histoire de la guerre d'Afghanistan*, p. 169.

73. Barry, *La résistance afghane*, p. 308.

74. Amnesty International, "Afghanistan," External Document, SF/83/E/162—ASA 11/13/83, 11 October 1983, pp. 6–7; idem, *Afghanistan: Torture;* idem, annual reports for 1983–1991. The exact date of the execution is uncertain, according to the 1991 report, p. 20.

75. See esp. Alain Guillo, *Un grain dans la machine* (Paris: Robert Laffont, 1989);

Philippe Augoyard, *La prison pour délit d'espoir. Médecin en Afghanistan* (Paris: Flammarion, 1985); and Jacques Abouchar, *Dans la cage de l'Ours* (Paris: Balland, 1985).

76. François Missen, *La nuit afghane* (Paris: Ramsay, 1990), reports that he was arrested together with his cameraman, Antoine Darnaud, and his guide, Osman Barai. The latter was never released.

77. Amnesty International, "Afghanistan," p. 8; for Afghan Mellat see the 1989 annual report, for the release of twenty-three of the thirty imprisoned party activists.

78. Bazgar, *Afghanistan, la résistance au coeur,* pp. 227–229.

79. Bachelier, *L'Afghanistan,* p. 62; and Akram, *Histoire de la guerre d'Afghanistan,* pp. 207–208.

80. Seddiqoullah Rahi, *Connaissez-vous Najiboullah?* quoted in Akram, *Histoire de la guerre d'Afghanistan,* p. 210.

81. Amnesty International, "Afghanistan," p. 13. For obvious reasons, the witness statements quoted are usually anonymous.

82. Statement by Naim, age ten, in Bazgar, *Afghanistan, la résistance au coeur,* pp. 25–28.

Conclusion

1. François Furet, "Terror," in *Dictionary of the French Revolution,* ed. F. Furet and Mona Ozouf (Cambridge, Mass.: The Belknap Press of Harvard University Press, 1989).

2. Quoted in Jacques Baynac, *La terreur sous Lénine* (Paris: Sagittaire, 1975), p. 75.

3. Quoted in Michael Confino, *Violence dans la violence. Le débat Bakounine–Netchaïev* (Paris: Maspéro, 1973).

4. Ibid., p. 102.

5. Martin Malia, *The Soviet Tragedy* (New York: Free Press, 1994), pp. 63–64.

6. Hélène Carrière d'Encausse, *The Russian Syndrome: One Thousand Years of Political Murder* (New York: Holmes and Meier, 1992), pp. xvii, 6.

7. Vasily Grossman, *Forever Flowing* (New York: Harper & Row, 1972), p. 214.

8. Tomáš G. Masaryk, *The Making of a State: Memories and Observations, 1914–1918* (New York: Frederick A. Stokes, 1927), p. 201.

9. Maksim Gorky, *O Russkom Krestyanstve* (On the Russian peasantry) (Berlin: Izdatelstvo Ladyzhnikova, 1922), pp. 16–19.

10. Malia, *Soviet Tragedy,* p. 3.

11. Karl Kautsky, *Terrorism and Communism: A Contribution to the Natural History of Revolution,* trans. W. H. Kerridge (London: Allen and Unwin, 1920), pp. 149, 152.

12. François Furet, *The Passing of an Illusion: The Idea of Communism in the Twentieth Century* (Chicago: University of Chicago Press, 1999), pp. 67–68.

13. Yuli Martov, *Down with Executions,* pamphlet from 1918 reprinted in *The Opposition: At Home and Abroad,* vol. 1 (Nendeln: Kraus Reprint, 1975), p. 5.

14. Quoted in Arkadi Vaksberg, *Le mystère Gorki* (Paris: Albin Michel, 1997), p. 111.

15. Leon Trotsky, *The Defence of Terrorism,* trans. H. N. Brailsford (London: Allen and Unwin, 1921), pp. 21–22.

16. Karl Kautsky, *The Dictatorship of the Proletariat*, trans. H. J. Stenning (Ann Arbor: University of Michigan Press, 1964), p. 55.

17. See the portrait by Nicolas Valentinov in *Mes recontres avec Lénine* (Paris: Plon, 1964).

18. Cornelius Castoriadis, *The Imaginary Institution of Society* (Cambridge, Mass.: MIT Press, 1998).

19. Kautsky, *Dictatorship of the Proletariat*, pp. 1–3.

20. Ibid, pp. 51–53.

21. V. I. Lenin, *The Proletarian Revolution and the Renegade Kautsky* (Moscow: Foreign Languages Publishing House, 1952), pp. 32–33, 20.

22. Ibid., p. 37.

23. Trotsky, *Defence of Terrorism*, p. 83, 86.

24. Ibid., pp. 51–52.

25. Ibid., p. 56.

26. Isaac Steinberg, *L'aspect éthique de la révolution* (Berlin: Skify, 1923), quoted in Baynac, *La terreur,* p. 370.

27. Quoted in Vaksberg, *Le mystère Gorki,* p. 183.

28. Ibid., p. 264.

29. Confino, *Violence,* p. 137.

30. Quoted in Alain Brossat, *Un Communisme insupportable* (Paris: L'Harmattan, 1997), p. 266.

31. Annie Kriegel, *Les grands procès dans les systèmes communistes* (Paris: Gallimard, 1972).

32. Carl Schmitt, *The Concept of the Political* (Chicago: University of Chicago Press, 1996).

33. Kautsky, *Dictatorship of the Proletariat*, pp. 81–82.

34. Tzvetan Todorov, *L'homme dépaysé* (Paris: Le Seuil, 1995), p. 33.

35. Idem, *On Human Diversity* (Cambridge, Mass.: Harvard University Press, 1993), p. 170.

36. Trotsky, *Defence of terrorism*, pp. 35, 60.

37. Vaksberg, *Le mystère Gorki.*

38. Kautsky, *Dictatorship of the Proletariat*, pp. 4–5.

39. Brossat, *Un Communisme insupportable,* p. 265.

40. Vaksberg, *Le mystère Gorki,* p. 262.

41. Brossat, *Un Communisme insupportable,* p. 268.

42. Vaksberg, *Le mystère Gorki,* pp. 286–287.

43. Ibid., p. 312.

44. Bruno Gravier, "Une actualité toujours plus cruciale," in *La crime contre l'humanité,* ed. Marcel Colin (Ramon-Ville Saint-Agen: Eres, 1996), p. 10.

45. Dominique Colas, *Lénine et le léninisme* (Paris: Presses Universitaires Françaises, 1987), p. 101. See also his doctoral dissertation, *Le léninisme* (Paris: Presses Universitaires Françaises, 1982).

46. Colin, *La crime contre l'humanité,* p. 14.

47. Mireille Delmas-Marty, "L'interdit et le respect: Comment définir le crime contre l'humanité?" in Colin, *La crime contre l'humanité,* p. 26.

48. Grossman, *Forever Flowing*, p. 200.

49. Confino, *Violence*, p. 120.

50. Quoted in ibid., p. 112.

51. Michel del Castillo, *La tunique d'infamie* (Paris: Fayard, 1997), p. 25.

52. Leszek Kolakowski, *L'esprit révolutionnaire* (Paris: Editions Complexe, 1978), p. 22.

53. Todorov, *On Human Diversity*, p. 165.

54. Aïno Kuusinen, *The Rings of Destiny: Inside Soviet Russia from Lenin to Brezhnev* (New York: William Morrow, 1974), p. 227.

55. The text has been analyzed by Michel Heller in "Lénine et la Vetcheka," *Libre*, no. 2 (1971), 19.

56. Maksim Gorky, *Lenin: A Biographical Essay* (London: Morrison & Gibb, 1967), pp. 29–32.

57. Grossman, *Forever Flowing*, pp. 239–240.

Index

About the Authors

STÉPHANE COURTOIS is a director of research at the Centre National de la Recherche Scientifique (CNRS) and editor of the review *Communisme*. His publications include *Le PCF dans la guerre* (1980); *Qui savait quoi? L'extermination des Juifs, 1941–1945* (1987); *Le Communisme* (1987, with M. Lazar); *Le sang de l'étranger. Les immigrés de la MOI dans la Résistance* (1989); *Cinquante ans d'une passion française. De Gaulle et les communistes* (1991, with M. Lazar); *Rigueur et passion. Hommage à Annie Kriegel* (1994, with A. Wievorka); *Histoire du Parti communiste français* (1995, with M. Lazar); and *Eugen Fried. Le grand secret du PCF* (1997, with A. Kriegel).

NICOLAS WERTH is a researcher at the Institut d'Histoire du Temps Présent, specializing in the history of the Soviet Union. He is the author of *Etre communiste en URSS sous Staline* (1981); *La vie quotidienne des paysans russes de la Révolution à la collectivisation, 1917–1939* (1984); *Histoire de l'Union soviétique, de l'Empire russe à la CEI* (1992); *Rapports secrets soviétiques. La société russe dans ses rapports confidentiels, 1921–1991* (1995, with Gaël Moullec).

JEAN-LOUIS PANNÉ is a specialist on the international Communist movement and the author of *L'Enterprise sociale, le pari autogestionnaire de Solidarnosc* (1987) and *Boris Souvarine, le premier désenchanté du communisme* (1993). He also collaborated on the *Dictionnaire biographique du mouvement ouvrier français* (1914–1939).

ANDRZEJ PACZKOWSKI is the deputy director of the Institute for Political Studies of the Polish Academy of Sciences and a member of the archival commission for the Polish Ministry of Internal Affairs. He is the author of *Stanisław Mikołajczyk (czyli klęska realisty: Zarys biografij politycznej* (1991); *Aparat bezpieczéntwa w latach, 1944–1956* (1994, 1996); and *Pół wieku dziejów Polski, 1939–1989* (1995), which won the Clio prize in 1996 for the best history book.

KAREL BARTOŠEK is a historian from the Czech Republic and the editor of *La nouvelle alternative.* He is the author of *The Prague Uprising* (1965) and *Les aveux des archives, Prague–Paris–Prague, 1948–1968* (1996).

JEAN-LOUIS MARGOLIN is a lecturer at the University of Provence and a researcher at the Research Institute on Southeast Asia, CNRS. He is the author of *Singapour, 1959–1987. Genèse d'un nouveau pays industriel* (1989).

SYLVAIN BOULOUQUE is a research associate at GEODE, Université Paris X.

PASCAL FONTAINE is a journalist with special knowledge of Latin America.

RÉMI KAUFFER is a specialist in the history of intelligence, terrorism, and clandestine operations. He is the coauthor with Roger Faligot of *Service B* (1985), *KGB objectif Pretoria* (1986), and *The Chinese Secret Service (1927–1987)* (1987; English edition 1989).

PIERRE RIGOULET is a researcher at the Institut d'Histoire Sociale and editor-in-chief of *Cahiers d'histoire sociale.* His books include *Des Français au Goulag* (1984), *La tragédie des Malgre-nous* (1990), and *Les paupières lourdes, Les Français face au Goulag* (1991).

YVES SANTAMARIA is a historian and the coauthor (with Brigitte Waché) of *Du printemps des peuples à la société des nations* (1996).